BY

AUGUST MEIER AND ELLIOTT RUDWICK

The Making of Black America (editors)   1969
*From Plantation to Ghetto: An Interpretive History of
American Negroes*   1966

BY

AUGUST MEIER

Negro Protest Thought in the Twentieth Century
(editor, with Francis Broderick)   1966
Negro Thought in America, 1880–1915   1963

BY

ELLIOTT RUDWICK

Race Riot at East St. Louis, July 2, 1917   1964
W. E. B. *Du Bois: A Study in Minority Group Leadership*   1960

THE
MAKING OF
BLACK AMERICA

VOLUME I

The Origins of Black Americans

THE
MAKING OF
BLACK AMERICA

Essays in Negro Life & History

EDITED BY

AUGUST MEIER &
ELLIOTT RUDWICK

VOLUME I

The Origins of Black Americans

STUDIES IN AMERICAN NEGRO LIFE
August Meier, General Editor

Atheneum NEW YORK

1969

For Paul and Sey

FOREWORD

Slightly over a half century ago, in 1915, the late Carter G. Woodson organized the Association for the Study of Negro Life and History. A year later he founded the *Journal of Negro History*. Due to his efforts, the study of the American Negroes' past was placed on modern scholarly foundations. Later, in the 1930's and early 1940's, appeared a number of notable sociological monographs dealing with the Negro community and race relations.

In choosing essays for *The Making of Black America*, we have included a substantial selection of materials from the behavioral sciences, particularly sociology and political science, as well as history. We have for the most part limited ourselves to the periodical literature, and only in unusual cases have we excerpted passages from books. Nearly all of the selections from learned journals are reprinted in their entirety. Space limitations, however, necessitated excisions in a few instances.

Unfortunately the periodical literature is uneven in its coverage of the many and varied aspects of American Negro life, and we have been unable to include materials on several subjects, such as the history of Negro colleges and Negro business since the Civil War. Conversely we have found that certain areas, such as Negro political participation, have received a relatively large amount of attention from scholars. Our selection reflects the weaknesses and strengths of the scholarly literature. Moreover, because of our inclusion of articles from sociology and political science, the twentieth century is naturally heavily represented in this book.

For the most part we have chosen articles that concern themselves entirely or in large part with what Negroes were doing, rather than with what white Americans were doing about Negroes. Inevitably we have been compelled to omit many excellent studies. Nevertheless, we believe that the ones included in this book illustrate most of the major themes in the making of black America.

We have made the headnotes brief, preferring to let the selections speak for themselves.

August Meier
Elliott Rudwick

ACKNOWLEDGMENTS

WE ARE grateful for leaves of absence provided by Roosevelt and Southern Illinois Universities, which greatly facilitated the preparation of these volumes. We also wish to acknowledge with appreciation the splendid cooperation given by the Princeton University Library and particularly by the Newark, New Jersey Public Library and the Dana Library of Rutgers University (Newark).

CONTENTS

III THE ANTE-BELLUM FREE PEOPLE OF COLOR

IV CIVIL WAR AND RECONSTRUCTION

VOLUME II:

The Black Community in Modern America

V THE FOUNDATIONS OF THE
TWENTIETH-CENTURY BLACK COMMUNITY

VI   THE MAKING OF THE BLACK GHETTO

VII THE NEW MILITANCY AND THE
ENDURING GHETTO

PART ONE

FROM AFRICA
TO AMERICA

Joseph Greenberg

THE NEGRO KINGDOMS OF THE SUDAN

The overwhelming majority of Africans brought in slave ships to the New World came from West Africa—from a belt of land stretching from the Senegal River to modern Angola, and extending inland from the coast for about two or three hundred miles. This territory encompassed parts of the African tropical rain forest and, in its northern section, of the vast grasslands known as the Sudan.

In political structure the ancestral societies of New World Negroes ranged from tribal organizations, through city-states in the Niger Delta area, to large and complex kingdoms. The earliest West African monarchies, located in the Sudan and going back at least to the fourth century A.D., were the prototypes for the kingdoms of the Guinea and southern Sudan—such as Dahomey, Ashanti, Yoruba and Benin—with whom the Europeans traded during the height of the transatlantic slave traffic between the sixteenth and eighteenth centuries.

For many years it was generally held that the political organization of the West African kingdoms was based upon Caucasoid models. In his seminal article on "The Negro Kingdoms of the Sudan," Joseph Greenberg not only summarized existing knowledge about the development of kingdoms in the western Sudan, but demonstrated conclusively that the institution of African kingship was of indigenous African origin.

Mᴏɴᴀʀᴄʜɪᴄᴀʟ patterns are widespread in Negro Africa and have been reported from peoples as distant from each other as the Shilluk of the Upper Nile Valley, the Zulus of South Africa and the Wolofs of Senegal on the Atlantic Coast. Among African kingdoms, those of the Sudan, particularly in its western portions, have been conspicuous for their size, in which they are without rival in Negro Africa. Their early date of historical attestation is only

Joseph Greenberg, "The Negro Kingdoms of the Sudan," reprinted with permission from *Transactions of the New York Academy of Sciences*, Ser. II, Vol. II, February, 1949, pp. 126–134. Copyright 1949 by The New York Academy of Sciences.

surpassed by Ethiopia and by the kingdoms of the Nile Valley known from Egyptian records. Moreover, the cultural contributions of these Sudanese kingdoms, under the aegis of Islam, are unique in African history. What follows is a brief attempt to consider some of the factors operative in the rise of these empires and to evaluate those theories, found frequently in this literature, which assign a predominant part in their foundation and expansion to Caucasian influences of one kind or another.

The Sudan is the term applied to that vast portion of the African continent which stretches between the Sahara Desert on the North and the tropical rain forests of the Guinea Coast and the Belgian Congo on the south. In keeping with its transitional nature, it is predominantly steppe in its northern portions and savannah towards the south. Rainfall is generally adequate and both agricultural and pastoral populations are found. A conspicuous trait of the area is the relative ease of west-east movement over its open terrain, a facility intensified by the use of the horse as a riding animal, which is at least as old as the introduction of Islam in this region and perhaps older. At the exit of the last century, Rabeh, an adventurer who had been a lieutenant of Zubeir Pasha, active in a rebellion in the Anglo-Egyptian Sudan, fled across the entire eastern and central Sudan and carved out an empire for himself in the shores of Lake Chad. What has occurred so recently in the full light of history may have happened many times in the past also. Certainly, in this ease of communication in the open lands of the Sudan, we have an encouraging factor for the formation of large territorial units.

The great importance of the Sudan in the commercial history of Africa is its position as an entrepôt for goods crossing the Sahara, and for their exchange with the products of the Sudan itself and of the frost area farther south. The Sudan first enters written history, in this guise, with the activities of Mohammedan merchants from the cities of North Africa. Whether this trade first began after Islam had made its conquest of North Africa in the seventh century, or whether it existed even earlier, has been the subject of some speculation. The Romans, to whom is usually assigned the introduction of the camel into North Africa, without which this trade would have been seriously handicapped, if possible at all, are not likely to have bothered to assure themselves of the control of the oases of the Fezzan in southwestern Libya, had not some trade existed. There is no evidence concerning the Carthaginians before them, though some have thought that Carthage maintained such trans-Saharan routes.

It is clear, at any rate, that the large size of the Negro empires of the western Sudan, their stability over centuries, and the security of travel which they provided, were powerful factors in the development of this trade, while the prosperity which it engendered was, in turn, the *raison-d'être* for their expansion and wealth. The mere need for such a route is, however, not adequate as an over-all explanation of the existences of these kingdoms. In the seventeenth century, the old organization of the Niger areas in the western Sudan collapsed under the impact of the Moroccan conquest and was never re-established, in spite of the continued operation of the geographical and economic factors which tended to favor this portion of the Sudan. It was the shortness of the route from Morocco, the great bend of the Niger in western Sudan, which led to its early prominence. Islam spread into the interior of Africa along this western path of penetration, trade and religion proselytization going hand-in-hand. The eastern route via the Nile Valley was far less prominent, not only because of its greater length, but because of the persistence of Christian kingdoms in Nubia, which throughout the Middle Ages blocked the southward expansion of Islamic trade and religious conversions.

Our knowledge of the great empires of the western Sudan rests first upon accounts furnished by Arab travelers and by geographers who utilized the reports of Islamic merchants who traded in these regions. Arab materials commence with the tenth century and continue through the Middle Ages. They are sparse in ethnographic detail, but they at least furnish the main outlines of political history. A second source is the Negroes themselves, who borrowed writing and the exercise of historiography, along with other branches of literature from Islam. The records range from mere lists of kings, with the length of their reigns, to such lively and detailed accounts as the *Tarikh-es-Sudan* of *es-Sa'di*, a native of Timbuctoo. They are an invaluable supplement to the information furnished by Modern European explorers and ethnographers, beginning with the exploration of Mungo Park at the end of the eighteenth century.

The first large kingdom which these sources disclose is that of Ghana, whose existence is attested as early as the tenth century by Ibn-Haukal and is described by El-Bekri, in the eleventh century. The exact location of Ghana is disputed, but it is generally agreed that it was west and north of the great bend in the Niger River, so that it stood as a kind of outpost in the desert for the transmission to the Sudan of goods from the south Moroccan city of Sijilmassa. The rulers of Ghana were pagan throughout its history, although Moslems were welcomed as traders and held important official posts. The capital was divided into two distinct parts, a Moslem city and a pagan city. From El-Bekri's account, it is clear that Islam had spread to the ruling class of other kingdoms of the western Sudan as far west as the Senegal Basin, and eastward to the region of Kukia or Kaokao on the lower Niger, the center of the later Songhoi empire. Ghana became engaged in a struggle with the Almoravids in the eleventh century. These Almoravids were a Berber group from north of the Senegal who, moved by the familiar combination of religious reforming zeal and desire for plunder, finally advanced into Spain, for a time controlling a vast empire, stretching from the Sudan almost to the Pyrenees. They captured Ghana, which subsequently lost most of its commercial as well as political importance although it was not abandoned until the fourteenth century.

With the decline of Ghana, empire and trade both moved to the east and the hegemony which it had enjoyed passed to the Mandingo empire of Mali. Its racially Negroid rulers spoke a Mandingo dialect, affiliated with the western Sudanese linguistic stock. Its capital, whose exact location is disputed, was certainly somewhere on the Niger, southwest of the great bend. The great commercial center, however, was now Timbuctoo, which, located on the Niger bend, was beginning to establish the reputation for learning and commerical prosperity that made it eventually a name to be conjured with in Europe. The height of its prosperity was attained in the fourteenth century, to which period belongs the celebrated pilgrimage of Mansa Musa to Mecca, recorded by contemporary Arab writers, and the visit of the great Moslem traveler, Ibn Batutah, to Timbuctoo and to the Mandingo capital.

The Mandingo empire, in its turn, entered a period of decline and its position of leadership fell to the Songhoi, formerly a vassal state. In 1468, the Songhoi ruler, Sonni Ali, entered Timbuctoo and under his successor, Askia-El-Hajj, the Songhoi empire became the largest in the history of Negro Africa, extending from the Atlantic almost to Lake Chad and controlling the important oases of the western Sahara. Timbuctoo, also, attained its greatest intellectual importance during the sixteenth century, especially the university associated with Dyingerey Bey, the great Mosque.

In 1590, a trans-Saharan expedition, launched by the Sultan of Morocco, put an end to the Songhoi empire and with it to the prosperity of Timbuctoo and the pre-eminent position enjoyed for so long by Negro political units in the Niger area. The Moroccan pashas' power soon declined until it was limited to the city of Timbuctoo. The distant ties with Morocco were dissolved and the activities of the Moroccan soldiery, which deposed and set up pashas at will, prevented the re-establishment of public security and the remarkable safety of travel in these regions noted by such earlier travelers as Ibn Batutah.

As a consequence of this situation, the main lines of trade moved more eastward to the Hausa States, a series of city units bound together by language and traditions of common origin for the ruling class, but without any wider political organization. Native records, if their chronology is to be trusted, put the founding of these States in the eleventh century. Subsequently, the rulers of most of them became at least nominally Moslem. For a time, the western Hausa States were under the rule of the Songhoi Empire, when it was at the zenith of its power under Askia-el-Hajj early in the sixteenth century. The great period of prosperity for the Hausa States dates from the Moroccan conquest of Songhoi, after which the route from the great Hausa cities of Kano and Katsina to Tripoli became the chief avenue of trans-Saharan commerce.

The last important political events in the western Sudan before the advent of the European colonial powers involve the people known variously in the literature as Ful, Fula, Peul, Fulani, and Fellata. An essentially pastoral people, they spread, in historic times, eastward from the Senegal basin in scattered groups, often of considerable size, as far east as Waldai, almost half the distance across the entire African continent. All through these regions they lived as politically impotent, often oppressed groups. Some, at least, became enthusiastic and learned Moslems, while others stayed in the bush as pagans or near-pagans. At the beginning of the nineteenth century under the leadership of Osman-dan-Fodio, and a decade later in the Niger basin under Ahmadu, they proclaimed a holy war against the existing political rulers of the Sudan, whom they called pagans. This crusade was, in general, successful and two great confederations were organized, one, in the east, embracing the Hausa States in a loose confederation with its capital at Sakato, and the other at Hamdallahi in the upper basin of the Niger. These political aggregates were in the process of dissolution when the European colonial powers appeared upon the scene. There were other important political units in the western Sudan in the period under consideration: for example, the cluster of kingdoms with related rulers, the most important of which was Mossi, in the basin of the Volta River south of the Songhoi Empire. The Mossi remain stubbornly resistant to Islam up to the present day and have formed a bulwark against the spread southward to the frost belt of the Guinea Coast. Another notable kingdom is that of Kanem, later Bornu, on the shores of Lake Chad. It has existed with many vicissitudes from the eleventh century, according to native records. Its ruler was converted to Islam in the twelfth century. At times, this kingdom has been of enormous extent and at one time it controlled a portion of the Hausa States. It successfully resisted the Fulani onrush in the nineteenth century, but finally succumbed to Zubeir Pasha's lieutenant, Rabeh, just before the arrival of the French. In the central Sudan, we find the kingdom of Bagirmi, southeast of Lake Chad, Wadai, east of the same lake, and further east still, Darfur, within the boundaries of the Anglo-Egyptian Sudan. All these kingdoms are authenticated by native records from a more recent period than those of the western Sudan, approximately from the sixteenth century onward, but it is probable that at least small material states existed in this area previously. There are local traditions to this effect almost everywhere.

There are a number of theories in regard to the great empires of the Sudan whose history we have just traced in general outline, attributing their origin or their main features to Caucasian influence.

One intepretation in regard to these kingdoms is that they owe their existence to the application of Mohammedan political patterns by racially Caucasoid groups. An early and explicit statement is that of Leo Africanus, the well-known sixteenth century scholar and traveller, who attributes the introduction of political organization in the Sudan to the Berber Moslem Almoravids. In a statement which forcibly reminds us of the pre-Rousseau conception of the primitive we read:

> Our ancient chroniclers of Africa, to wit, Bishri and Meshudi, knew nothing of the land of the Negroes but only the region of Guechet and Cano, for in their times all other places of the land of the Negroes were undiscovered. But in the year of the Hegira 380, by means of a certain Mohumetan which came into Barbary, the residue of the said land was found out, being as then inhabited by great numbers of people which lived a brutish and savage life, without any king, governour, commonwealth or knowledge of husbandry.

Clad they were in skins of beasts; neither had they any peculiar wives
... using hairy skins for beds and each man choosing the leman he
had any fancy unto ... These Negroes were first subject to Joseph, the
founder of Morocco, and afterwards under the five nations of Libya.[1]

Elsewhere we find less baldly stated the suspicion that these kingdoms
are essentially the result of Moslem influence. Thus Delafosse, a standard
authority, tells us that there are legitimate doubts concerning the purely
Negro character of the great Sudanese kingdoms, by way of contrast with
Mossi, which, in his opinion, is purely Negro. The writer in the *Enciclopedia
Italiana* mentions "the very interesting hypothesis of the purely Negro origin of
these monarchical institutions." P. C. Meyer in his historical survey of the
Sudan distinguishes four periods. The first is that of the numerous small
heathen kingdoms, which last into the eleventh century, to be followed by the
large empires coincidental with the spread of Islam in the Middle Niger. He
thus attributes the growth of large states, even if not of political institutions in
general in this area, to the influence of Islam.

All these views attributing, in whole or in part, the organization of the
large, west Sudanese kingdoms to direct Moslem influences are easily refuted
by reference to the known facts about these kingdoms, some of which have
already been adduced. On grounds of simple chronological priority, it can
be pointed out that each one of them had centuries of stable political organization and wide territorial expansion before the introduction of Islam among
the ruling group. For the first of these, Ghana, the evidence is indisputable,
inasmuch as its rulers were never converted and it remained pagan throughout
its history. So also for Mali, Songhoi, and Bornu the evidence is clear that
there was a period of pagan political rule before the introduction of Islam and
that the continuity of political institutions was not seriously interrupted by
the conversion. The Negro character of Mossi, which was never converted, was,
we have seen, emphasized by Delafosse, who is willing to entertain theories of
Islamic origin regarding the other states. Indeed, the changes wrought by Islam
in the domain of political institutions in this area is very small, and it is
striking, that, despite the sparseness of the sources at our disposal, the
essentially African nature of Sudanese kingship stands out clearly.

Thus, in the brief account of Ghana by el-Bekri, we find the throwing of
dust on the head in greeting the king, the use of royal "interpreters" to repeat
everything the king says, the beating of drums to summon a royal audience,
the sacrifice of the king's attendants at his death, and sacrifices to the royal
ancestors. All of these are clearly African traits and none of them are found
in the Islamic kingdoms of North Africa and the Near East. In the Mandingo
Empire of Mali, we have likewise the throwing of dust on the head in
saluting the king, which struck Ibn Batutah as a characteristic Negro custom,
the use of royal "interpreters," and the important position accorded to the

---

[1] By Joseph is meant Yusuf ibn Tashfin, the Almoravid leader. The five nations of
Libya are the Berbers. In this division, Leo follows Ibn-Khaldun.

king's wife. Similarly in the Songhoi State we find the throwing of dust on the head as a mode of salutation and the office of royal interpreter. We hear on one occasion that a prince regards as a deadly insult the threat on the part of a rival to destroy his drum. This points clearly to the widespread African connection between royal position and the possession of specific drums. In the Songhoi Empire there is present, at least since the time of Askia-el-Hajj, fixed territorial division, each with an associated title and specific privilege and duties, another usual feature of African Monarchial organization absent in the Moslem areas of the Near East. In Bornu, we have, in addition to most of the features already mentioned, the institution of the queen-mother and the queen-sister, each with her own court and officials, which finds its exact parallel in the Uganda kingdom of East Africa.

If the evidence for the essentially Negro character of these kingdoms is so clear, one may well ask why there has been so much hesitation or opposition to this view. Outside of the general tendency to deprecate the Negro which permeates the literature on Africa, there are certain superficial data which lend credibility to a theory of direct Moslem origin. For example, the use of the term "Sultan" and "Vizier" in the literature gives the impression that we are dealing with Moslem political institutions of the Near Eastern type. Our suspicions should be aroused regarding the validity of such deduction when we read that "in Dar-Fur the use of the term Sultan is connected with the possession of certain drums." Sometimes Sultan, Emir and Vizier have been borrowed into a language of the Sudan from Arabic, most frequently as an alternative to an already existing native word. More frequently, when we find such expressions in secondary sources, they have been drawn from Arab accounts in which Sultan would designate any ruler and Vizier any minister. It no more indicates Moslem origin or influence than the title "king of the Zulus" found in an English account would indicate the British origin of Zulu kingship. Occasionally an Arabic term is borrowed and a new office created, but even in this instance, the institutions remain African. Typical in this respect is the Hausa adoption of the word *waziri,* "*vizier,*" to designate an additional position of nobility. It is but one of a large number of varied titles without any special pre-eminence. The *waziri,* just as other Hausa noblemen, has his territorial fief and fixed prerogatives. The addition of this office has not produced any significant alteration in the existing political system. The only important Moslem influences on political life of which I am aware is the Fulani establishment of an Amiru l-Mu'minina, "Commander of the Faithful," on the model of the caliphate, and the office of the Alcali or judge (from the Arabic *gadi*), who judges in accordance with Moslem law in many Sudanese states.

That it is through Islamic influence that writing was introduced into this region and with it a certain development of intellectual life is indisputable. Impressed with the contributions of Negro intellectuals, particularly those of Timbuctoo and Jenne during the Songhoi period, there is a tendency to attribute all developed institutions, whether intellectual, economic, or political, to Moslem influence. However, as the data already adduced indicate, political organization was Negro in structure before Islam and remained so after its diffusion through the Sudan. It is not legitimate to argue from the undoubted Moslem influence on intellectual life to a Moslem origin for political. So, in early Medieval England, intellectual life was Latin and Christian, but political organization was based on Germanic tradition.

Perhaps more than any other factor, the native African traditions regarding the origin and migration of ruling groups have lent credibility to theories of Moslem origin. These reports have not usually been treated with the scepticism they deserve. In spite of Mohammed's admonition that 'the noblest among you is the most pious," the view has always had some currency in Islam that nobility depends upon nearness of kinship to the Prophet. Hence, the constant attempt in the Islamic world to demonstrate descent from the Prophet or at least from a well-known Arab tribe or ruling family. For this reason, the accounts of migrations from Arabia and of Arabian descent found among practically all Moslem Negro ruling groups are to be discounted. Thus, the founder of the old Sefawa dynasty of Bornu is said to be the celebrated Saif ibn Dhu Yazan, a pre-Islamic ruler of Yemen in southwestern Arabia. The first ruling house of the Songhoi attribute their origin to the same area. The pre-Fulani rulers of the Hausa states trace their descent from Abu-Yazid of Baghdad. Many other examples could be cited of this general tendency. It is amusing to note what short shrift the Arabist, Basset, gives to some of the most cherished views of Africanists on the subject, in his reply to the African student, Carbou's queries regarding the credibility of these accounts. Whenever the specific individuals mentioned in native tradition as ancestors are known from Arabic literary documents, the evidence is clear that they died in the Near East without ever having migrated to Sudan. Were all African native accounts of this nature true, Near Eastern history would be filled with the exodus of eminent men to the Sudan. But not a trace of these movements is authenticated from Arab sources.

The vogue of these stories in the Sudan is so great that they have on occasion been adopted by non-Moslem Negro groups. The royal house of the pagan, Mossi, tell the same story as their Moslem Songhoi neighbors concerning their origin from Za-Alyamen, a migrant from Yemen in Arabia. It is a corollary of this view of migration from Arabia that in at least two instances, Ghana and Songhoi, we hear of an early dynasty of "white kings." Both of these accounts lack all historic authentication and so must be accepted or rejected along with the accounts of migration from Arab with which they are connected.

Since writing did not exist in this area until the introduction of Islam, all our written accounts come from those areas which are already Islamic and "they try to forget... their predecessors, because they are ashamed of the pagan period." Our narratives are all written by members of the learned class, who are the most enthusiastic Moslems among the population and anxious to develop the theme of the connection with the land and kin of the Prophet.

An allied but distinct point of view does not specifically stress Moslem influence but attributes the establishment of these kingdoms to Negroes with a large Caucasoid racial admixture which supplies the leaven for cultural achievement. This view is clearly stated by A. H. Keane. "Standing out in marked contrast to all these primitive peoples are the relatively civilized Hamito-Negro or Semito-Negro nations, such as the Mandingo, Songhois, and Fulahs in the west; the Hausas, Kanuri, Baghirmi, and Mabas of the Wadai in the centre; and the Furs and Nubians in the east. . . . From these striking contrasts between the pure Negro and the mixed Negroid peoples, the inference has been drawn that the Negro, left to himself, remains a Negro in every sense of the term, and without miscegenation is incapable of making any advances beyond a low social and intellectual level." Another statement of similar import is that of Meyer that "all these data point to the impulse for the building of States originating from Hamito-Semites who influenced the Negroid elements by mixing with them." Seligman, in his standard work "Races of Africa," describes this process in the following terms: "The mechanism of the origin of Negro-Hamitic peoples will be understood when it is realized that the incoming Hamites were pastoral Caucasians—arriving wave after wave—better armed as well as quicker witted than the dark agricultural Negroes." In the same work, we find the common view that the Bantu languages are the result of a linguistic mixture between a Hamite stratum and a Negroid stratum similar to the Sudanic languages of West Africa, while the Masai and similar pastoral peoples of East Africa are called half-Hamites and stated to reflect an even greater Hamitic linguistic, cultural, and racial preponderance.

It will be observed in these statements that there are both a physical anthropological and a linguistic side to the question. Negroes are declared to be incapable of founding advanced political structures except through physical mixture with racially Caucasoid groups. Such groups are identified with those Negroids or half-Negroids who speak either Hamitic or Semitic languages, presumably imposed on them by Caucasoid speakers of these languages.

With considerable diffidence, inasmuch as I am not a physical anthropologist, I should like to enter a demurrer to the views which dominate the literature on the physical anthropology of the Negro. We are told that only the "forest Negro of the forest zone of the West African Guinea Coast is the true Negro," since it is only here that the dark-skinned, fuzzy haired, broad-nosed and dolichocephalic type is found in his pure form. All other Negroid types are the result of intermixture with Caucasoid peoples, producing such varieties as the Nilote, the Nilo-Hamite, and the Bantu-speaking groups which dominate the southern part of the continent. It would seem just as logical to assert that only the Nordic show the full Caucasoid characteristics of blond hair, blue eyes and tall stature. We could then attribute classical and oriental civilization to Negroid intermixture and state that the leaders of western European civilization—England, France, and Germany—were only so by virtue of admixture with Negroid types producing the Alpine and Mediterranean types found in large or dominant numbers in England, France and Germany.

Even were we to restrict the term Negro to those of the West African tropical forests, we would find such important Negro political structures as the kingdoms of Dahomey, Ashanti, Benin, and the Yoruba states as evidence of the political abilities of the "pure Negro."

The linguistic side of this doctrine is notable chiefly for its reliance on an extension of the term Hamitic, particularly by Meinhof, to many languages beyond the established Hamitic groups of ancient Egyptian, Berber, and Cushite langauges of Ethiopia, without adequate and convincing proof of linguistic relationship. A conspicuous case is Fulani. The political successes of this people have perhaps been the point of departure, whether consciously or not, for declaring them to be Hamitic. The linguistic evidence, which would take us too far afield to discuss here, clearly points to Fulani being simply another of the vast group of West-Sudanese languages, all spoken by Negroes. It shows special points of resemblance to the Serer language of Gambia and the Biafada of Portuguese Guinea. Again, the view espoused by Meinhof, that the Bantu languages are a result of intimate fusion of Hamitic with languages of the Sudanese "Negro," is in a relation of mutual support to the doctrine that the Bantu physical type is the result of admixture between Negroes and Hamitic speaking Caucasoids. Here again the technical linguistic problems cannot be treated adequately at this point. However, languages do not "mix" after this fashion, or at least such views are looked upon with extreme suspicion by linguists as unusual and requiring real proof, which has not been offered in this case. The clear fact seems to be that the Bantu languages are related to those of the Western Sudan and that the "Hamitic" features are illusory.[2] Likewise, the Masai and other so-called half Hamitic languages are not Hamitic at all, but clearly related to the Nilotic languages of the Shilluk and other tribes of the White Nile as well as the Nuba farther north.[3]

The independence of language and physical type is a fundamental theoretical achievement of contemporary anthropology and there is no wish to sacrifice it here. It is interesting to see, however, that if we grant the premise that Hamitic and Semitic speech are evidence of Caucasoid racial descent, we can then ask what has been accomplished by peoples of the Sudan who speak indisputable Hamitic and Semitic languages. If infusion of the precious Hamitic and Semitic 'blood' has such civilizing effects on the Negro, it should be most manifest in those groups which speak languages of the Semitic and Hamitic group. Actually, the record is most uninspiring. The Tuareg, a Berber Hamitic group, has been present in the Niger bend region since the Middle Ages in large numbers without overcoming surrounding Negroid groups, or founding any political structure of note. The Moroccans, Semitic-speaking

[2] This relationship has been noted particularly by D. Westermann without affecting standard doctrine regarding African linguistic relationship. Proof of this extremely obvious connection will soon be published by the writer.

[3] This was clearly demonstrated by G. W. Murray (1920) in a common-sense demonstration.

Caucasoids, as we saw, conquered the Songhoi Empire, but brought in its stead chaos. The Tunjur Arabs, found throughout the central Sudan, were apparently either pagan or very loosely Moslem Arabs, and yielded political sovereignty to the Mohammedanized Negro people of the Fur in Dar-Fur and of the Negro Maba of Wadai. Other Arabs of the Sudan, for example, the Shuwa of Lake Chad, have been politically impotent and contributed scarcely anything to Islamic culture. All this is not meant to prove that Hamitic and Semitic speaking peoples in Africa are incapable of political organization, but to demonstrate the *reductio-ad-absurdum* of the coventional arguments.

Our conclusion, then, is that the great empires of the Sudan were instances of a widespread Negro pattern of political structure and that, stimulated by the trans-Saharan trade and taking advantage of the open terrain afforded by the Sudan, territorial organization on a wide scale and of considerable stability became possible.

Finally, the remarkable degree to which Negro institutions survived under a Moslem exterior may be documented from the example of Dar-Fur. Although under Moslem rulers since approximately 1600, all of the characteristic features of Negro kingship already enumerated were found in a flourishing condition by Nachtigal in the middle of the nineteenth century, although the country was then raided by the Mohammedan governor of the Sudan. There was a keeper of the sacred stool, as in the West African kingdom of Ashanti. The Queen Mother had her own troops and courtiers. An aboriginal compilation of customary law was in alternative use in place of the Moslem Maliki law. The great annual festival was the feast of the drums in the Mohammedan month of Rajab. On this occasion, the slaves devoted to each of the past kings sacrificed animals to the royal souls. For those kings who were Mohammedans, learned men read chapters of the Koran, while, for the ancient pagan line, all proceeded to a pre-Islamic sacred place at Jebel Kora where animals were sacrificed to the pagan royal ancestors.

The skins of the slain animals were employed to cover anew the royal drums for the succeeding year. These are just a few of the observances which convince us that the institution of Darfur resemble those of Ashanti, Dahomey, Uganda, and other Negro kingdoms in a thoroughgoing fashion.

There are indications that the traits of Negro political structure also continued with great persistency under a Christian façade in Ethiopia and under Egyptian influence in ancient Cush and Meroe.[4]

[4] See, for example, the account of king-killing Diadorus's account of the Nubian Kingdom of Napata (iii, 6). King-killing, a widespread African trait, is unlikely to have been borrowed from Egypt in this instance, since it was already abolished in the early dynastic period, more than two thousand years earlier, and is postulated by Egyptologists from such survivals as the Sed-festival.

K. O. Dike

TRADE AND POLITICS IN THE NIGER DELTA

In Trade and Politics in the Niger Delta, 1830–1885, *the African scholar K. O. Dike produced a tour de force based upon years of work in English colonial archives and a thorough mastery of local African oral tradition. In the passages reprinted here, K. O. Dike examines the political and social structure of the city states of the Niger Delta, and describes the mechanics of the slave trade in this part of the Guinea Coast.*

FROM Lagos to the Cameroons lies the low country of the Nigerian coastal plain. The Niger Delta occupies the greater part of this lowland belt and may be described as the region bounded by the Benin river on the west and the Cross river in the east, including the coastal area where the Cameroon mountains dip into the sea. It covers an area of some 270 miles along the Atlantic coast and is 120 miles in depth. The two mouths of the Niger are the Forcados and the Nun, but the rivers Benin, Brass, Bonny, Kwa-Ibo, the Cross, and other separate streams are linked to these by a labyrinth of creeks and lagoons. "I believe," wrote Mary Kingsley, "the great swamp region of the Bight of Biafra [Niger Delta] is the greatest in the world, and that in its immensity and gloom, it has a grandeur equal to that of the Himalayas." [1] There remains, however, the intriguing paradox that this area, notorious among nineteenth-century travellers for its unhealthiness, with a soil too poor "to produce a ton of oil" as Macgregor Laird put it in 1832, and practically uninhabited by the tribes of the Nigerian interior before the Portuguese adventure to the Guinea coasts began had become by 1830 the greatest single trading area in West Africa.

It was as navigable waterways that the rivers of the Niger Delta became so important in the economic history of modern Nigeria. A canoe could be taken from Badagry on the west coast of Nigeria to Rio del Rey in the east without going into the open sea. This "Venice of West Africa," as Winwood Reade

From K. O. Dike, *Trade and Politics in the Niger Delta, 1830–1885* (London: Oxford University Press, 1956), pp. 19–21, 30–41. Reprinted with permission of the Clarendon Press, Oxford.

[1] *Travels in West Africa* (1897). Cf. A. C. C. Hastings, *The Voyage of the Day Spring* (London, 1857), pp. 73–74.

described it in 1867, linked together not only places in the Delta but towns and villages along the 2,600 miles of the Niger valley. "The Oil Rivers are chiefly remarkable among our West African possessions," wrote Sir Harry Johnston in 1888, "for the exceptional facilities which they offer for penetrating the interior by means of large and navigable streams and by a wonderful system of natural canalization which connects all the branches of the lower Niger by means of deep creeks. There are hardly any roads existing in the Delta; the most trivial distance that a native requires to go, he generally achieves in a canoe." This water system links the Delta with "the markets and sources of production far inland." [2]

Geographically the Delta divides easily into two sections. The northern section is comparatively drier and higher than the area of swampland to the south. Even in the lowland belt the dank and humid surroundings are interspersed with vast stretches of dry land, a maze of islands intersected by creeks and rivers, and on these settlements have been built. Some of these southern colonies, being placed on points of control for internal and external commerce, quickly grew in importance and became the trading centres on the Atlantic seaboard. Just as the growing volume of Atlantic commerce drew Europe irresistibly to the lands of Guinea, so the natives of tribal areas, impelled by the urge "to traffic and exchange," flocked to the coast to do trade. From now on the coastland became the frontier of opportunity. As in medieval West Africa trade with the Arabs by way of the Sahara caravans led to an outcrop of commercial cities on the Niger bend such as Jenne, Timbuktu, Gao, and others, so the rise of Lagos, Accra, Dahomey, and the Delta states must be attributed to the development of maritime commerce. The seaboard trading communities which emerged with this commerce transcended tribal boundaries; their history belongs both to Atlantic and to tribal history.

Every item of the export trade in the ports of Biafra was a product of the tribal interior, and the carrying-trade on which the prosperity and greatness of the Delta states rested linked their fortunes decisively with those of the producers in the tribal locations. The coastal communities united in their blood and institutions elements of the Atlantic and tribal societies which fashioned them. Each of the adventurous groups that pioneered these settlements was different in language and culture and in political and social organization. The Jekris of Warri (on the Benin river) could not understand the Ijaws on the Brass river. These migrants represented many Nigerian tribes in movement— Ibos, Binis, semi-Bantus from the Cameroons Highlands, Ijaws, Efiks, Ibibios, to name only a few and the most important. This fact must be noted. It helps to explain the haphazard way in which the Delta communities grew. Down to the nineteenth century this movement of populations continued. Opobo, the main centre of trade and politics in the eighties, was founded in 1870. . . .

In the peopling of the Delta the points occupied by the migrants were widely separated from each other. Usually they were islands like Bonny

[2] F.O.84/1882, Memorandum by Consul H. H. Johnston on the British Protectorate of the Oil Rivers, Part II.

dominating the mouth of a river which linked the hinterland to the sea. In time each community developed the independence and individualism so typical of island dwellers. Every river mouth, every centre of trade, and, in some areas, every town had its overlord. Each city-state had all the apparatus of rule which enabled it to maintain law and order, administer justice, make war and peace, organize and prosecute peaceful commerce for four centuries. The term "city-state" as applied to the Delta communities embraces not only the settlements on the coast but also their extensions (by way of trading posts) in the interior. This is in line with the Greek idea of city which means a community of people rather than an area of territory; for although the Delta trading colonies were all outside her political boundaries, they were indissolubly bound by strong economic ties. Moreover "city-state" is a more appropriate designation than "tribal-state," since the period of migrations disorganized the tribal entities and the slave trade further accentuated the mingling of peoples. In the nineteenth century, therefore, the Delta states were grouped not by considerations of kinship but by contiguity, and in the period under survey citizenship came increasingly to depend not on descent but on residence.

The city-states divide broadly into two political groupings—the monarchies and the republics. The former include Bonny (Ibani), New Calabar (Kalabari), and Warri, not to mention petty monarchies such as those of Bell Town and Aqua Town in the Cameroons. The republics were in reality single trading units with divided political authority as in Old Calabar, Brass, and the Cameroons. Bonny and Old Calabar best illustrate these two types of political systems.

Bonny was the economic and political centre of the Niger Delta during the greater part of the nineteenth century, and even its successor from the 1870's, Opobo, was an offshoot of the older kingdom. The former has always been a monarchy as far as can be ascertained; a list of her kings from the foundation of the monarchy to the end of the nineteenth century was recorded by A. G. Leonard in 1906.[3] A more detailed list and a fuller account of their

[3] Leonard, op. cit., p. 47.

Kings of Bonny

1. Alagbariye.	6. Edimini.
2. Opkraindole.	7. Kamalu.
3. Opuamakubu.	8. Dappa (Great or Opu).
4. Okpara-Ashimini.	9. Amakiri.
5. Ashimini.	10. Appinya.

11. Warri

King Holliday Owsa ⎫
                (Igbani.   ⎧ Short quartumvirate—
                (Bupor.   ⎨ all princes of the blood.
12. Perekule, (Ipor.   ⎩
       afterwards King Pepple.

13. Foubra (Agbaa).	16. Bereibibo.
14. Foubra ⎫ Sons of	17. Dappa (William).
15. Opobo ⎭ Perekule.	18. George.

reigns, corroborating Leonard, is preserved by the descendants of the Pepples at Bonny.[4] If, as is generally supposed, the monarchy was founded around the mid-fifteenth century, in 1830 that institution was almost 400 years old.

The reigning king in that year was Opubu (of the House of Pepple). The first king of this House was Pelekule or Perekule (anglicized Pepple) and although Opubu was the third of the Pepples he was the fourteenth king (Ama-nya-na-bo) in an unbroken line of succession. The monarchy was therefore a deep-rooted institution at Bonny. Moreover, the Royal House of Pepple which reigned from the eighteenth to the nineteenth centuries had a knack of producing remarkable men. In the Pepples Bonny found, New Calabar excepted, a focal point for unity and strength unknown to the other Delta communities.

Impressed by the might of the Pepple monarchs European observers have tended to credit them with autocratic powers; indeed, Adams's statement in 1790 that the power of the king of Bonny "is absolute" and that "the surounding country, for a considerable distance, is subject to his dominion" represents the general contemporary opinion.[5] Nor was this view altogether unfounded. The Pepples sought by alliance and conquest to gain ascendancy over the entire Delta and the markets of the interior. In this they well nigh succeeded but for the stubborn opposition of the kingdom of the Kalabaris (New Calabar) which refused to accept subjection. The recurrent wars between the two kingdoms not infrequently ended in the defeat of New Calabar, yet that state's powers of recuperation were demonstrated time and again.

In 1790 it was reported that the king of Bonny had "destroyed the town of New Calabar twice," had compelled its "inhabitants ... to take their merchandise to Bonny for sale," and had not permitted them "to have any communication whatsoever with the shipping." [6] In 1826 Captain Owen noted that one of the titles of the reigning Pepple was "Conqueror of the Callabar," a title "he derived from his grandfather, who subdued that country, but which has long since been independent, although the present king threatens again to reduce it to his dominion." [7] Notwithstanding this threat New Calabar was a thriving independent state in 1830.

Even in home affairs the powers of a Bonny king were limited by the country's constitution. This did not altogether escape the attention of contemporary European observers and one of them made this significant comment: "The Kings of Bonny, although in many respects they appear to exercise absolute power unrestrained by any fixed principles, may be properly termed heads of an aristocratic government. This is evinced by having a grand palaver house, in which they themselves presided, but the members of which composed

4 In 1949 I was permitted to study several well-preserved documents and other relics relating to the Bonny monarchy in the possession of the present Head of the Royal House.
5 Talbot, *Peoples of Southern Nigeria*, i. 250–1.
6 Ibid., p. 250.
7 Owen, op. cit., p. 345.

of the great chiefs or great men, were convened and consulted on all matters of state urgency." [8] The king was nothing if not king in council, and as the analysis of the social organization will reveal the king's powers were everywhere limited by the peculiar political system of the city-states.

In contrast to the hereditary monarchies of the Pepples at Bonny and of the Amakiris at New Calabar there was the divided authority of the Efik community on the mouth of the Cross river. At Old Calabar, from the eighteenth century onwards, there were four trading towns—Creek Town, Henshaw Town, Duke Town, and Obutong, each—except on questions of common interest—under separate and independent rulers. As an eyewitness put it in 1847, "The towns of Calabar, are, in fact, a number of small republics, each with its own chief and council, united only by the Egbo confraternity." [9] The Egbo Society was a sort of freemasonry, a secret cult, uniting the ruling classes in all four towns; membership was open to freemen only. This "confraternity" came into being because the nobility felt the need for "a bond of union," a "supreme authority" for "enforcing peace and order among equals and rivals," and for safeguarding the interests and privileges of the nobility. "It seemed especially designed to keep" women, slaves, and the masses of the population in subjection.[10]

For all practical purposes the Egbo Order was the supreme political power in Old Calabar; it exercised not only executive and legislative functions but was the highest court of appeal in the land. Its President became the first citizen of the community. Hutchinson reported that at Duke Town (the seat of Egbo power) there was in 1856 a "Palaver-House, a species of senatorial forum, where all matters public or private, are discussed and settled by the Egbos." [11] Similar organizations existed in communities of divided authority, such as the Cameroons, primarily to protect the privileges of the nobility against the insurrection of the lower orders.

The pivot of Delta social organization was the "House System" or "House Rule." This peculiar constitution is common to all the trading states and was the direct result of the trade with the Europeans. As used in the Delta it is a European term and a descriptive one at that. The mixture of peoples often meant that African law and custom vanished and a new law and order was evolved based partly on African precedent and experience and partly on the lessons of the contact with Europe. In its full development the House became at once a co-operative trading unit and a local government institution. As a rule every trader of any importance owned so many slaves bought from various tribes. These, along with the trader's family, formed the nucleus of a "House." Even in the hey-day of the slave traffic the Delta middlemen retained the best slaves in their personal service, some of whom manned the fleet of canoes

[8] H. Crow, op. cit., pp. 215–16.
[9] Waddell, op. cit., p. 314.
[10] Ibid., pp. 313–15.
[11] T. J. Hutchinson, *Impressions of Western Africa* (London, 1853), p. 119.

indispensable for the trade with the interior or engaged in agricultural work on the farms. The smaller Houses numbered anything from 300–1,000 members; others, such as the royal Houses, numbered many thousands. In 1847 King Eyo of Creek Town, Old Calabar, "had in his House many thousand slaves, and four hundred canoes with a captain and crew for every one. Besides his extensive trade, which amounted to several puncheons annually, he employed his people reclaiming waste land, founding towns, and planting farms in well-selected positions which gave him command of the rivers and channels of trade." [12] Along with the king's House there would be scores of smaller Houses, each presided over by a wealthy merchant.

The House system, which grew out of the needs of Delta society, followed, in a measure, the pattern of social organization of the interior tribes. Among the Ibos and Ibibios each town or village is composed of a group or of several groups, at the head of which is the eldest member of the group. Such a group among the Ibos is called "Umunna" and among the Ibibios "Ekpuk," i.e., an extended family. In each group all the members are related by blood. It is significant that with the emergence of the "House" the words "Umunna" and "Ekpuk" disappeared from the vocabulary of the extribal Ibibio and Ibo-speaking peoples in the Delta; in their place we have "Ulo" and "Ufok"— House, expressing the new coast relationship based not on kinship but on common interests and economic necessities. Master and servant, the bond and the free, all became members of one House, a veritable hierarchy, with numerous gradations, each rank with its duties and responsibilities, its privileges and rewards.

But, unlike the "Umunna" and the "Ekpuk" the House system did not make for "excess of democracy"; the House Head, unlike the Elder of the interior, was not just a mere figurehead, registering the people's will. He was in theory absolute, with powers of life and death over his subordinates. How far this power was exercised is another matter. It cannot be denied, however, that the element of autocracy in House rule was very strong: it had to be, particularly if the discordant and often rebellious elements composing a House in the semi-military society of Delta were to be welded into a coherent whole.

Estimates of the House system vary considerably. There are some, like Dr. Jeffreys, who would declare that "the authority of the Head of a House" was based on the principle that "might is right." He spoke of the "iniquitous reign of the Houses" and from his account one would derive the impression that the system was all darkness and no light.[13] It cannot be denied that an element of cruelty and even brutality was ever present. A cruel master could, on occasion, take the life of his slave for very trifling offences. de Cardi enumerated punishments that could be inflicted on the domestic slaves:

> ear cutting in its various stages, from clipping to total dismemberment; crucifixion round a large cask; extraction of teeth; suspension

[12] Waddell, op. cit., p. 320.
[13] Jeffreys, op. cit., pp. 55–62.

by the thumbs; Chilli peppers pounded and stuffed up the nostrils, and forced into the eyes and ears; fastening the victim to a post driven into the beach at low water and leaving him there to be drowned with the rising tide, or to be eaten by the sharks or crocodiles piecemeal; heavily ironed and chained to a post in their master's compound ...and reduced to living skeletons; impaling on stakes; forcing a long steel ramrod through the body until it appeared through the top of the skull.[14]

These speak plainly of the dark side of the system.

Yet, as he himself emphasized, these extremities were resorted to only in exceptional circumstances, and he admitted that the chances of a slave "improving his condition are manifold." While allowing, therefore, that the life of a slave before he "gets his foot on the first rung of the ladder of advancement" could be terrible, once he had graduated beyond the domestic hierarchy progress was usually rapid. In the nineteenth century, European observers, who were by no means uncritical of some aspects of House rule, did not overlook its merits. This peculiar system defies definition and does not lend itself to generalization. It cannot be assessed apart from the context of the society which produced it. Delta society in the nineteenth century rested on a foundation of slavery; terror and despotism were normal features of a system that had to keep the masses in subjection. Yet if House rule may be judged from its practical results, on the whole it met the needs of the day. "Absolute authority on the one part, and entire subjection on the other, is the theory; but in practice both the authority and subjection are checked and limited in many ways...the harsh terms master and mistress are not in the Calabar language. The sweet and precious names, father and mother, alone are used to express the relation. The children of both classes (slave and free) grow up together as playmates, and equally regard the Head of the House as their father. In our schools they sat side by side, read in the same classes, and were treated as they deserved, without reference to their relation." [15] Another observer declared that "it is remarkable how clannish the slaves belonging to the same house become. Each one considers that he partakes of the honour of the house, and is zealous in maintaining it. Any slight upon his master or father [the one word 'ete' signifying both] is resented as a personal offence." [16]

The British Consul to the Bight of Biafra, T. J. Hutchinson, declared in 1861 that "in many of the palm oil trading rivers slavery is purely mythical. In Bonny, the men who rule the roost in political debate, as well as on the palm oil change, are of the slave class." [17] "The best thing in it" [the House system], said another, "is that it gives to the poorest boy who paddles an oil canoe a chance of becoming a king." [18] That many slave boys rose to the rank of the

[14] M. H. Kingsley, *West African Studies* (London, 1899), p. 535.
[15] Waddell, op. cit., p. 315.
[16] Goldie, op. cit., pp. 19–20.
[17] *Ten Years Wandering Among the Ethiopians* (London, 1861), pp. 2–6.
[18] M. H. Kingsley, op. cit., p. 427.

nobility in the city-states is writ large in Delta history of the nineteenth century. Forceful and energetic Ibo slaves such as JaJa and OkoJumbo took advantage of the peculiar constitution of the House system and became the Heads of the Houses to which they were attached.

It was in the interest of every House Head to foster and increase the trade of his people: as trade cannot flourish under conditions of terror, the Heads must have used their absolute power with great discretion and restraint. Discipline might have been severe and brutal in certain cases,[19] but as a general rule, loyalty from the slaves and confidence from the master (father) was the prevalent mood. For the difference between the plantation slavery of the New World and the domestic slavery as practised in the Niger Delta lies in this: whereas in the former the slaves performed, on the whole, an indirect and impersonal service and were regarded as some form of capital goods, in the latter the wealth produced by a slave eventually set him free, for the master knew his slave intimately and the value of his work and rewarded him accordingly. It was this incentive, ever present in the House system, that made it in the nineteenth century an institution full of vitality, flexible, and in a large measure beneficial to all.

The "House" was primarily the unit of local government in the Delta, and as each occupied a separate quarter in the community the Head of the House was responsible for law and order in his section. It followed then that in a place like Bonny the king, who was as a rule the leading merchant in the state, had no direct power over the Houses of his chiefs. He could intervene to resolve a conflict between one house and another, to confirm the election of new House Heads and to determine the rank a chief might occupy in the state. But although he was in direct control of foreign relations, war and peace, and was the initiator of commercial policies, he always acted within his authority as king in council.

The trading organization of the hinterland was closely linked with the Delta states. No tribe in eastern Nigeria achieved a highly centralized political organization in the nineteenth century; and the clans, local government units, recognized few authorities higher than themselves. Although this "excess of democracy" was the characteristic feature of the political organization, it must not be imagined that there were no threads of unity in the commercial and cultural spheres nor that the fragmentation of authority necessarily impeded the flow of trade.

Two types of trading organization operated in the hinterland. The first, centered upon the Aros, obtained mainly in the period of the slave trade. Their influence was based on the Aro Chuku Oracle which was universally respected and feared throughout Iboland, and in fact by every tribe in eastern Nigeria. This Oracle was supposed to reside in the territory of the Aros, a section of the Ibo tribe. In 1854 Baikie wrote of the "noted City of Aro where there is the

[19] M. H. Kingsley, op. cit., pp. 533–8.

celebrated shrine of Tshuku [God], to which pilgrimages are made, not only from all parts of Igbo proper, but from Old Calabar, and from the tribes along the coast, and from Oru and Nembe. The town is always mentioned with great respect, almost, at times, with a degree of veneration, and the people say 'Tshuku ab yama,' or 'God lives there.' " [20] Aro people (whom the Ibos call "Umu-Chukwu"—the Children of God) exploited this belief in their Oracle in many ways, principally in order to dominate the life of the region economically, and they made themselves the sole middlemen of the hinterland trade. This they did by establishing Aro colonies along the trade routes of the interior [21]—like the Greeks, the course of whose colonizing expeditions was largely directed by the priests of the Delphic Oracle. In its wake they organized a trading system which had its ramifications throughout practically the whole of the country between the Niger and the eastern side of the Cross river. Every quarter of Aro Town had its "sphere of influence" in matters of trade. "For instance, the country between AroChuku and Awka belonged to the quarters of Utari, Amove and Ndizioggu." [22] Acting as mediators between God and the clans and assuming themselves to be the spokesmen of the Almighty, they held a privileged position throughout the land, erecting what amounted to a theocratic state over eastern Nigeria. Aro colonies became the divinely ordained trade centers in the interior; Aro middlemen the economic dictators of the hinterland. During the time of the slave trade and in the period of legitimate commerce they acquired immense wealth through a monopoly all believed to be divinely appointed, and with wealth came great political influence. [23]

The numerous political units represented by the clans, admirable as organs of local government, proved inadequate for handling matters of common interest such as commerce and justice. A central organization was needed to facilitate inter-tribal trade, and provide a "pax" without which commerce could not flourish. [24] It was this vacuum existing at the centre of the tribal organization that the Aros, working through the medium of their Oracle, filled. The trading settlements they established at the crossing of rivers and at the intersection of the main routes became the "free cities" to which all who

[20] Baikie, op. cit., pp. 310–11.

[21] See K. Umo, *The Aro Settlements* (Lagos, 1945). The author traced more than twenty-five of these settlements.

[22] Talbot, *Peoples of Southern Nigeria*, i. 182–3.

[23] The predominant position held by the Aros during the slave-trade period is acknowledged by all sections of Ibo country. Today sites of Aro colonies exist, and although no longer trade routes, are still inhabited by descendants of the Aros. The great Oracle, known to Europeans as "Long Ju Ju," was destroyed by the British in 1900.

[24] In *The Ibo People* S. R. Smith describes the conditions requisite for the establishment and development of oracles. These are (1) A quiet place remote from main routes. (2) Some natural features which inspire the sense of dread, such as rocks, caves, steep valleys with water, groves, or dense bush. (3) A system by which travelling agents get to know local disputes and encourage reference for settlement to their own oracles. (4) An easy and secret method for the disposal of the victims of the oracles. As an example a victim sold in slavery would be announced as having been "eaten" by the Oracle.

wished to "traffic and exchange" safely repaired, international courts where individuals and clans in conflict sought justice from the undisputed authority of the Oracle.[25] "From most parts of the Niger Delta and the Cross River litigants proceed to invoke the aid of the oracle in the settlement of their claims and disputes," wrote Sir Harry Johnston in 1888. That the astute Aros abused the use of this Oracle and diverted it to their own ends must not obscure the need which called it into being.

The position of power the Aros occupied was of course dependent on the universal belief in their Oracle as the supreme deity. This belief they sought by every means at their disposal to sustain. They hired the services of the famous professional warriors of Iboland—"the Abam, Abiriba, Awhawfia, and Edda" (or Ada)—whenever there was fighting to be done—arming these mercenaries with "the guns obtained from the white traders" and "conquered all the people who resisted their influence or killed their agents." [26] Thus to the supernatural powers of the Oracle was added the military might of its adherents. This explains the contemporary fear and dread of the Aro name. Even in the Niger Delta the fear for this hinterland deity was great. "The terror inspired by the threat that if a slave gave trouble to his master he would be sent to Chukwu [the Oracle] was sufficient to enable the numerically inferior people of the Delta to hold thousands of slaves in subjection, and herein probably lies one of the reasons for the establishment and maintenance of the Oracle at Aro-Chukwu." [27]

The intimate link between the interior trade organization and that of the Delta led many writers to suggest that the Aros might have emigrated originally from the Delta itself and founded the towns of Aro-Chukwu "primarily for the supply and forwarding of slaves to the coast," and that the Oracle was a device in the name of religion for attracting people from the surrounding country, and so kept up a steady flow of human beings whose lot was represented as being "eaten by Chukwu." [28] The theories of Aro origin are legion. Their close economic ties with the Delta have never been disputed. There is no doubt that "they sold most of the slaves at Bonny" [29] and that the Obi-Nkita quarter (the leading Aro town) monopolized the trade with that city-state. Thus it was that Bonny became a leading slave market in West Africa.

The system of obtaining slaves by use of oracular devices was fairly widespread in the Ibo country and, apart from the Chukwu at Aro-Chukwu, there were other oracles such as the Agballa at Awka, the Igwe at Umunora in the Owerri district, the Onyili-ora near Nri, and Ogba, a cave in the Nkisi

[25] F.O.84/1882, Memorandum of Sir Harry Johnston on Oil Rivers.

[26] Talbot, *Peoples of Southern Nigeria*, i. 184. Cf. Smith, op. cit., pp. 135–45.

[27] Smith, op. cit., p. 136, where he also states that the Aro Oracle "was some 80 miles from Bonny, 60 miles from Kalabar [New Calabar], and 70 from the mainstream of the Niger above Abo, it was sufficiently remote for its purpose, while at the same time it was in close touch with the dense populations of the Ibo people, and the neighbouring tribes, the Ibibio, Ijo, Isokos, Jekiri, Usobos, and the Benis of the Niger Delta."

[28] Ibid., p. 136.

[29] Talbot, op. cit., pp. 184–5.

stream at Ogbunike in the Onitsha district,[30] all of which merely supplemented the work of the all-powerful Aro Oracle, undoubtedly the dominating power in the country.

The belief that the bulk of the slaves handled in the Atlantic trade were captives from tribal wars or that kidnapping and raids were the normal methods of obtaining the human victims is now seen to be but a half truth when applied to the tribes east of the Niger. The Oracle, directed by the Aros, was the medium through which the slaves exported from Delta ports were largely recruited. As the highest court of appeal, this deity was supposed to levy fines on convicted individuals and groups. These fines had to be paid in slaves who were believed to be "eaten" by Chukwu (the Oracle), although in fact they were sold to the coast middlemen. This recruiting campaign, carefully staged under conditions of awe and reverence, was rarely attended by violence. Only when the injunctions of the Oracle were defied did the Aros, in his name, turn their fierce mercenaries on the offending party. Then the process of terrorizing the victims began and with their superior arms and immense wealth they invariably emerged victorious. But the dominant power of the Oracle was widely understood and rarely opposed, so that the slaves obtained by violence and kidnapping could not have greatly exceeded, and may even have been fewer than, those who surrendered to the dictates of the Oracle. Nevertheless, both methods of recruitment—whether by violence or the invocation of super-stitious fears—led to unsettlement and terror, and exposed the interior tribes to exploitation by the middlemen.[31]

[30] Smith, op. cit., p. 135.
[31] In *Tribes of the Niger Delta*, p. 289, Talbot confirmed the statements already quoted and declared that the greatest source of Aro wealth was the slave trade.

Richard R. Wright

NEGRO COMPANIONS OF THE
SPANISH EXPLORERS

Europeans first engaged in the slave trade with sub-Saharan Africa during the latter part of the fifteenth century. Both then and later many Africans were held as slaves in Spain and Portugal. It was not unnatural, therefore, that black bondsmen were to be found in the expeditions that explored the Americas. Richard R. Wright, in his early article, was the first scholar to inform the public of the role of Negroes in the exploration of the New World. Even two generations later his research, except for minor details, has not been superseded.

THE fact seems to be well established that Negroes were introduced into the New World with the first discoverers and explorers. Indeed, there is evidence which leads to the surmise that some of the pre-Columbians may have been Negroes. Peter Martyr, a learned historian and an acquaintance of Columbus, mentions "a region, not two days' journey from Quarequa's territory, in the Darien district of South America, where Balboa, the illustrious discoverer of the Pacific ocean, found a race of black men, who were conjectured to have come from Africa and to have been shipwrecked on this coast.[1] In connection with this statement may be noted a report by the Bureau of Ethnology which describes "early American pottery with physiognomies of decided African lineaments."[2] The late Justin Winsor stated in a letter to the writer that "there is a possible chance that at some early time the ocean currents may have swept across from the Canaries and the African coasts canoes with Guanches and other African tribes from which some considerable strains of Negro blood may have mixed with the pre-Columbian peoples of tropical

Richard R. Wright, "Negro Companions of the Spanish Explorers," reproduced by permission of the American Anthropological Association from *American Anthropologist*, IV, No. 2 (1902), pp. 217–228.

[1] Helps, *Spanish Conquest in America*, I, p. 360.

[2] *Fourth Annual Report*, Bureau of Ethnology, p. 407.

America. The skulls found in caves in the Bahamas seem to be very like those in the early burial places of the Canaries."

The good Bartolomé de las Casas, the "Protector of the Indians," is often charged with the introduction of Negro slavery into this continent.[3] It is claimed that he introduced Negro slaves to relieve the hard-worked natives, and it is charged that "at one inauspicious moment of his life he advised a course which has ever since been the one blot upon his well-earned fame, and too often has this advice been the only thing which has occurred to men's minds respecting him, when his name has been mentioned. He certainly did advise that Negroes should be brought to the New World." "I think, however," wrote Sir Arthur Helps, "I have amply shown in the *Spanish Conquest* that he [Las Casas] was not the first to give this advice and that it had long before been largely acted upon."[4] It is said again that Las Casas, as early as 1498, with his father, accompanied Columbus and was therefore familiar with the companions of the latter and especially with Ovando, the successor to the Discoverer in the government of the Indies. It was during the year 1501 that Columbus was deposed from the government of the Indies, and he may probably himself have been cognizant of the fact that Negro slaves had been introduced into the new Spanish possessions. But there seems to be no positive evidence either way as to the great admiral's attitude toward the introduction of African slavery into the New World. There is a letter of Columbus in which he refers to Negroes in Guinea, and it is known that he gave an Indian slave to Las Casas' father, but all beyond this seems to be mere surmise.[5]

The year 1501 is the date of the earliest reference in American history to Negroes coming from Spain to America.[6] Sir Arthur Helps, in his *Spanish Conquest in America*, states that, in the year mentioned, instructions were given to the authorities that while Jews, Moors, or new converts were not to be permitted to go to the Indies or to remain there, "Negroes born in the power of Christians were to be allowed to pass to the Indies, and the officers of the royal revenue were to receive the money to be paid for these permits.[7]

From this time forward Negroes were more or less familiar personages in the West Indies.[8] On September 15, 1505, King Ferdinand of Spain wrote to Ovando, then governor of Hispaniola, a letter of the following tenor: "I will send more Negro slaves as you request; I think there may be a hundred. At each time a trustworthy person will go with them who may share in the gold they may collect and may promise them ease if they work well.[9] Some time prior to this, soon after he had become governor, Ovando had objected to the importation of Negro slaves into Hispaniola on the ground that "they fled

[3] Helps, *Spanish Conquest in America*, III, p. 210.
[4] Helps, *Life of Las Casas*, preface.
[5] Ellis in Winsor's *Narrative and Critical History*, II, p. 304.
[6] Helps, *Spanish Conquest*, I, p. 180. Irving, *History of Columbus*, III, p. 162.
[7] Helps, ibid.
[8] Helps. Navarrete, *Coleccion*, I, p. 233. Herrera, *Historia de las Indias*, dec. I, lib. 5. Irving, *History of Columbus*, III, p. 162.
[9] Helps, *Spanish Conquest*, I, p. 219 (Coleccion de Muñoz, MS., tomo 90).

among the Indians and taught them bad customs and never would be captured." [10]

In 1510, according to Antonio de Herrera, the royal historiographer to
Philip II, King Ferdinand informed Admiral Don Diego Columbus that he
had given orders to the officials at Seville that they should send fifty Negroes
to work in the mines of Hispaniola.[11] The next year, 1511, the king complained
in language like this: "I do not understand how so many Negroes have died;
take much care of them." [12]

Again, on September 27, 1514, King Ferdinand, in response to a request
of the Bishop of La Concepcion, in Hispaniola, that more Negroes should be
imported, said that there were already many Negroes and it might occasion
inconvenience if more males of the race should be introduced into the island.[13]
There seems, therefore, to have been no cessation, but rather a yearly increase
in the number of Negroes sent to the New World. On his accession to the
Spanish throne, Charles V granted "license for the introduction of Negroes
to the number of four hundred." [14] From this time onward the importation of Negroes into the West Indies became a considerable industry, and
the monopoly was greedily sought by Cortés and more eagerly bestowed by
King Charles in 1523.[15] There were sent to Hispaniola, 1500 (half of these
males); to Cuba, 300; to Jamaica, 300, and 500 to the province of Costilla del
Oro on the mainland.[16] By 1528 there were in the New World, according to
Herrera's account of the Indies, nearly 10,000 Negroes. It is said that the
treatment of the Negroes was injudiciously lenient; they had four months'
holiday.[17]

In Honduras, in 1539, Francisco de Montejo sent a Negro of his, who
knew the Indian language, to burn a native village.[18] In 1554, in Peru, 30
Negroes accompanied a military force of 70 Spaniards, under Francisco Her-
nandez.[19] In 1541, in Tolanite, a settlement in New Galicia, Mexico, the
Indians killed a Negro, "de Bovadilla," perhaps the name of the owner, and
robbed him of his cattle and hacienda—his establishment—and everything he
had.[20] On April 14, 1559, the *cabildo* or town council of Santiago de Chile,
voted to grant a petition of one Tomé Vasquez, a free or enfranchised Negro,
by allowing him possession of a lot of land in the town, provided this was
found to be vacant and unclaimed.[21] The wording of the record seems to

[10] Herrera, *Historia de las Indias*, dec. I, lib. 5, cap. 12.
[11] Ibid., *Hist. West Indies*, Stevens' trans., I, p. 374.
[12] Helps, *Spanish Conquest*, I, p. 245 (Coleccion de Muñoz, MS., tomo 90).
[13] Ibid., I, p. 491.
[14] Ibid., I, p. 505.
[15] Helps, *Spanish Conquest*, III, p. 210 (Coleccion de Muñoz, MS., tomo 90).
[16] Ibid.
[17] Ibid., tomo 81.
[18] Pacheco-Cardenas, *Coleccion de Documentos de las Indias*, II, 216.
[19] Ibid., III, p. 319.
[20] Ibid., III, p. 37.
[21] *Coleccion de Historiadores de Chile*, Santiago, 1898, XVII, p. 66.

show that Vasquez received precisely the same treatment as the white applicants for permission to settle in the town.

On St. Luke's day, October 18, 1526, Lucas Vasquez de Ayllon died.
According to Navarrete he was among the first to bring Negroes to the present
confines of the United States.[22] He explored our eastern coast and attempted
to found a colony at San Miguel de Gualdape, since known as Jamestown,
Virginia.[23] In this colony, under his successor, a Porto Rican, the Negroes
were so grievously oppressed that they arose in insurrection against their oppressors and fired their houses.[24] The settlement was broken up and the Negroes and their Spanish companions returned to Hayti, whence they had come.
This ended the first introduction and the first insurrection of Negroes on our
eastern shores. Thus Hayti, the place where Negro slaves were first introduced
into the New World, was strangely enough the first to manifest an awful retribution against human slavery. It would be interesting to know what part
Ayllon's fugitive Negroes, in the persons of their descendants, took in the
dreadful revolution which swept over that island nearly three centuries later
under the lead of Toussaint L'Overture, Dessalines, and their associates. A
singular incident connected with Ayllon's expedition along this coast is the
fact that he, with the assistance of his Negro slaves, built the first ships constructed on our coast. This fact is made more interesting when it is known
that Vasco Balboa had with him some thirty Negroes who in 1513 assisted
in building the first ships on the Pacific coast of America.

The introduction of Negroes into the western portion of the United
States was about as early as the coming of the Spaniards. George Bancroft
thinks that there was no part of the United States into which the Spanish
explorers did not land Negroes. Cortés had with him three hundred Negro
slaves in 1522.[25] Under date of July 19, 1537, the governor of Mexico wrote:
"I have written to Spain for black slaves because I consider them indispensable
for the cultivation of the land and the increase of the royal revenue." [26] Also
Gustav Adolf Bergenroth, the collector of Spanish papers, has shown that
Negroes at an early date were considered and called the "strength and sinew
of the western world." [27] The Great Antilles especially had already been
crowded with Negroes on the plea that they were sent thither with a view of
facilitating the christianization, and to relieve the toil and suffering of the
unfortunate natives; [28] but their advent into the western portion of America

[22] Shea in Winsor's *Narrative and Critical History*, II, 241.

[23] Ibid. [For a discussion of the location of the settlement of San Miguel, see
Lowery, *Spanish Settlements within the Present Limits of the United States*, pp. 448–
452.—EDITOR.]

[24] Ibid.

[25] Prescott, *Conquest of Mexico*, III, p. 350.

[26] Pascual de Gayangos, *Calendar of Spanish State Papers*, Col. V. p. 441.

[27] State Papers of Spain in British Museum, collected by Gustav Adolf Bergenroth.
Revetus Enys to Secretary Sir Henry Burnet. Paper Col. Entry Bk., vol. XI, p. 82.

[28] Winsor, Letter to author, July 9, 1894.

was fraught with a good deal of concern. Before 1530 there were enough Negroes in Mexico to warrant an attempt at self-liberation from the Spanish yoke.[29] Their plan was to massacre the Indians friendly to the Spanish, form an alliance with the others, elect a ruler, and set up a government for themselves in the City of Mexico. H. H. Bancroft, speaking of this event, says that "the Negroes neither gave nor accepted quarter." [30] Their enterprise, however, failed, the ringleaders being betrayed, captured, and executed. In this connection there is another interesting story of the followers of a certain Bayano, a Negro insurgent captured and sent back to Spain, whose followers in 1570 founded the town of Santiago del Principe.

There is, however, some reason for the belief that many of the Negroes imported by the Spaniards were not savages nor ignorant; that many of them were nominally Mohammedans or Spanish Catholics. One writer mentions his Mandingo servant who could write the Arabic language with great beauty and exactness.[31] The Guinea or Gold-coast Negroes were bold, brave, and liberty-loving, as the history of the Pacific states will attest.

Bandelier says that the most interesting period in the history of the discoveries on the American continent was during that part of the sixteenth century when the efforts of the Spaniards were directed from the already settled coasts and isthmuses into the interior of both North America and South America. It was during this interesting period that certain Negroes connected with the Spanish explorers rendered conspicuous service on various expeditions.[32] Mr. George Parker Winship mentions, in his *Coronado Expedition*,[33] a Negro slave of Hernando de Alarcon who, in the expedition of 1540, was the only one in the party who would undertake to carry a message from the Rio Colorado across the country to the Zuñis in New Mexico when Alarcon wished to open communication with Coronado.

In 1527, some time prior to Coronado's expedition to New Mexico and the buffalo plains, we are introduced to another Negro who was, perhaps, the most conspicuous of those who took part with the Spaniards in the early expeditions and discoveries on this continent. Reference is here made to him who was one of the four survivors of the ill-fated expedition to the New World made by Pamfilo de Narvaez who sailed from Spain, June 17, 1527, having received from King Ferdinand a commission as governor of Florida, Rio de las Palmas, and Espiritu Santo. This is the best authenticated case at hand, however, of a Negro participating in exploring this continent. Estevanico, or Estevanillo, the Negro here referred to, was most likely not the only Negro who accompanied Narvaez from Spain in 1527, but he was the only one whose identity has been made known. That he was the discoverer of the Zuñi Indians and of New Mexico is, I think, a fact now well known. It has often been

[29] H. H. Bancroft, *History of the Pacific States*, III, p. 384.
[30] Ibid., II, p. 385.
[31] Bryan Edwards, *History of the British West Indies*, II, p. 72.
[32] Bandelier, Letter of February 4, 1900.
[33] Bureau of Ethnology, *Fourteenth Annual Report*, p. 406.

claimed that Alvar Nuñez Cabeza de Vaca, the treasurer of the ill-starred expedition of Narvaez, was the discoverer of that country; but Bandelier has shown quite conclusively that Cabeza de Vaca never saw New Mexico, and that he was absent from the country at the time of the exploration of the New Mexican territory in 1539.[34] The evidence which this authority adduces to show that the Zuñi Indians and New Mexico were not discovered by Cabeza de Vaca is, in the opinion of the writer, equally conclusive against the claim of discovery by any other man than the Negro Estevanillo. Bandelier's historical researches show beyond doubt that only one of two men can possibly be credited with the discovery—Fray Marcos de Niza or his Negro guide and interpreter, Estevanillo, or Estevanico; for a careful reading of his own narrative does not reveal any evidence upon which the discovery can be attributed to Cabeza de Vaca.

The only claimant worthy of consideration against Estevanillo is the friar Marcos de Niza. Bandelier ably supports Fray Marcos' claim to the honor of the discovery, but this claim can certainly have no foundation except as it is based upon the fact of the guidance and information which Niza received from the Negro Estevanillo. While it is true, therefore, that Estevanillo disobeyed Niza's order to "stop and send messages," it is likewise a fact, supported by all authorities, that Estevanillo saw the territory of New Mexico some days before the arrival of the friar. According to the information, Fray Marcos followed days in the rear of his ambitious guide.

Later historians, in writing of this discovery, have not only ignored any right which Estevanillo, or Estevanico, had to the discovery, but have charged him with undue ambition and avarice. In writing of Fray Marcos, Cortés called the monk "a common impostor" and declared that he claimed to discover countries that he never saw. While it may not be proper to accept this wholesale charge, it is safe to say that Fray Marcos was too far in the rear of his Negro guide to lay claim to the discovery of New Mexico.

Fiske, in his *Discovery of America*, writes rather slightingly, in our opinion, of this interesting episode of American history, laying particular stress on the "illo" or "ico" in Estevanillo's, or Estevanico's, name.[35] Although it would perhaps be improper to charge so distinguished a historian with flippancy in his reference to "poor silly little Steve," [36] it would not, perhaps, be pretentious to suggest that the termination alluded to in Estevan's name does not warrant such a reflection on the man. Indeed, it seems clear that a fair interpretation of the facts related in Dr. Fiske's work (II, pp. 500–508) would warrant the conclusion that a "man [Estevanillo] who visited and sent back reports of a country," is more entitled to the honor of its actual discovery than one who, according to Dr. Fiske's own statement, "from a hill only got a Pisgah's sight of the glories of the country, and then returned with all possible

[34] Bandelier, *Contributions to the History of the Southwestern Portion of the United States*, chap. IV.

[35] Fiske, *Discovery of America*, chap. IV, p. 500.

[36] Fiske, *Discovery of America*, chap. IV, p. 505.

haste"—without having set foot actually within the Cibolan settlements of New Mexico.

Dr. Henry W. Haynes treats Estevanico with greater justice. He says: "The Negro was ordered to advance in a northerly direction fifty or sixty leagues, and to send back [to Fray Marcos] a report of what he should *discover*." [37] This the Negro did; he sent back information that he had *discovered* "a country, the finest in the world." It was Cibola, one of the long-sought-for "Seven Cities." [38] Now, instead of giving credit to his guide, who had been killed in prosecuting his discoveries,[39] Fray Marcos claimed all the honor for himself, and subsequent historians, if they have not sustained the friar have not placed the honor where it belongs.

It is a pity that we have no connected narrative of this important Negro discoverer. An account of his connection with the ill-fated expedition of Narvaez in 1527, and of his association with Marcos de Niza in 1539, may be found in the various writings bearing on this period. But aside from these little is known of his early history. Estevan was born in Azamor,[40] one of the principal cities of Morocco, Africa, and may be supposed to have been about twenty-eight or thirty years of age when he joined the expedition of Narvaez, which sailed from San Lucas de Barrameda, Spain, June 17, 1527. With the first fleet were 506 persons. After landing on the coast of Florida they wandered through the country, harassed by the Indians until they had lost all but 240 of their number; then, about September 22, they set sail, in a number of boats, in the Gulf of Mexico. Narvaez, as usual, proved a poor leader; misfortune befell him and his men. At the end of the year only four survived [41] —three whites and the Negro Estevanico. These four men discovered and landed upon the coast of Texas. They strove to keep together so that they might render mutual aid, but found this to be impossible. For eight years [42] they wandered among the savages, and it is evident that the Negro manifested fully as much tact and ability as the white men for self-maintenance among the savages and for exploration. Each of these unfortunate Spanish wanderers labored as a slave, and all finally became "medicine-men" of distinction among the natives. They are reported to have become so expert in healing the sick that the savages came from great distances to be cured, and crowds followed them from place to place.[43]

[37] Winsor, *Narrative and Critical History*, VII, p. 477.

[38] It was called "Cibola" by mistake, this being the name of the seven Zuñi settlements collectively. The pueblo of Hawikuh, now in ruins near the Zuñi summer village of Ojo Caliente, is the pueblo meant.—EDITOR.

[39] For the Zuñi account of the killing, see Lowery, *Spanish Settlements*, pp. 280, 281.

[40] Buckingham Smith, *Narrative of Alvar Nuñez Cabeza de Vaca*, chap. XXXVIII, p. 123.

[41] Ibid., chaps. XVII and XXXVIII. Bryant and Gay, *Popular History of the United States*, vol. I. Bancroft, *History of the United States*, I, p. 20.

[42] Herrera, op. cit., Stevens' trans., V, p. 105.

[43] Smith, *Narrative of Cabeza de Vaca*, op. cit., chap. XXII, p. 74.

The black explorer was as successful as his white brothers; he became familiar with the Indian dialects and characteristics, and the experience gained in these eight years of wandering afterward proved valuable to him. At the conclusion of their marvelous journey Estevan's three white companions left for Spain,[44] but Estevan remained in Mexico, where he was held in esteem by those who were interested in extending the Spanish dominion.

Accordingly it was not long before Estevan was selected as guide for an expedition into the northern country, a selection which gave him the opportunity of his life. He evidently had a strong ambition to become an explorer and a discoverer, as is shown by the fact that he risked disobedience to instructions in order that he might be the first to find Cibola. The story of the search for this supposed El Dorado is most interesting, but it is sufficient here to say that though he lost his life, the Negro succeeded in discovering the famous "Seven Cities" of the Zuñi Indians of New Mexico.

The importance of the discovery of Estevan to his time, and its influence on the early progress of Spanish America, may be judged from the fact that various expeditions had been planned for this discovery, but had failed. Cortés had vainly spent nearly twelve years in trying to push an expedition into the northern country, and following Estevan's discovery there was a wild desire on the part of explorers to find the now famous Seven Cities of Cibola. Coronado longed to be the discoverer, and he did visit the country the year following the discovery made by Estevan and which resulted in the latter's death. Bandelier, who gives all the credit of the discovery to Niza, asserts that this journey, which he acknowledges to have been led by Estevan, was of the greatest value to Christendom, and to Spain in particular. The value of the discovery was such that we can only rightfully accord to Estevan an important place among the early explorers of America.

It is not inappropriate to add testimony from Sir Clements R. Markham, the noted historian, who writes: "Owing to information brought to Mexico by Cabeza de Vaca in 1528 [1536], the viceroy, Don Antonio Mendoza, determined to send an expedition to search for the powerful towns reported to exist in the north of Mexico. A friar named Marcos de Niza was sent in search of these towns. A Negro named Estevan, who had previously served in the expedition of Cabeza de Vaca, accompanied Niza; and they set out from Culiacan, on the Gulf of California, in March, 1539. Niza and his Negro companion met with a good reception everywhere. They crossed deserts and came to Indians who had never heard of the Spaniards. Here they received tidings that in an extensive plain some days' journey to the north there were several large towns. Niza sent his faithful Negro companion *alone*, and *waited* for his return with news. Estevan sent back word to Niza that he had found the way to the great city called Cibola. Niza then followed; but after a few days he received news from an Indian that Estevan had reached Cibola, but had been killed by the natives. Niza fled back to Mexico. This," concludes the English

---

[44] Herrera, op. cit., Stevens' trans., V, p. 105.

historian, "is one instance of a Negro having taken an important part in the exploration of the continent. Estevan was the discoverer of Cibola," the territory of New Mexico.

It may be asked, Why is it that this Negro's name has remained practically in obscurity for more than three and a half centuries? The answer is not difficult. Until recently historians were not careful to note with any degree of accuracy and with due credit the useful and noble deeds of the Negro companions of Spanish conquerors, because Negroes were slaves, the property of masters who were supposed to be entitled to the credit for whatever the latter accomplished. The object of this paper is to direct attention to this apparent injustice, and if some one more competent will undertake a thorough investigation of the subject, the purpose of the writer will have been accomplished.

William R. Bascom

ACCULTURATION AMONG THE

GULLAH NEGROES

In 1941 Melville J. Herskovits published his path-breaking volume,
The Myth of the Negro Past. He maintained that, contrary to gen-
eral scholarly opinion, substantial survivals of African culture existed
in the culture of the black population of the United States (and
that, indeed, some of these Africanisms had diffused into the culture
of white Americans). Herskovits based his conclusions on substantial
ethnographic work in Africa, the Caribbean, and Brazil, as well as
drawing upon empirical data from the sub-culture of Negroes in the
United States. While it was agreed that the evidence for African
survivals in the Latin-American societies was incontrovertible, con-
troversy raged over his assertions about Negro life in the United
States. Certainly African survivals to the extent that they persist in
this country are greatly attenuated. The strongest evidence for them
exists among the Negroes who live on the Sea Islands along the coast
of South Carolina and Georgia. William R. Bascom, who was a close
associate of Herskovits, has described the cultural traits from Africa
which were retained by these Gullah Negroes. His article should be
supplemented with Lorenzo J. Turner's definitive work, Africanisms
in the Gullah Dialect (1949).

Tʜᴇ analysis of the accommodation of African and European customs in
the New World presents a particularly difficult problem in the United States
because the processes of acculturation have gone much farther here than in
other regions. In dealing with the Negro cultures in South America and the
West Indies, the African traits that have been retained are specific enough

William R. Bascom, "Acculturation Among the Gullah Negroes," reprinted by
permission of American Anthropological Association from *American Anthropologist*,
XLIII, No. 1 (1941), pp. 43–50.

and numerous enough to make possible the identification of the tribes whose cultures have been involved. But even among the Gullah in the coastal regions of South Carolina and Georgia,[1] where the Negroes have been as isolated as anywhere in the United States, resemblances to specific African tribes are very rare. For the most part the similarities are to those elements which are common to West Africa as a whole—to the common denominators of West African culture—and not to those aspects of culture which are distinctive of the tribes within that area. It is therefore extremely difficult to determine what particular West African cultures have contributed to the present situation.

It is now recognized that the differences in the general pattern of the cultures of Africa and Europe were not great; in fact their fundamental similarity justifies the concept of an Old World Area which includes both Europe and Africa. There were a number of institutions common to both regions, including a complex economic system based on money, markets, and middlemen, as well as a large number of crafts among which iron-making was important; a well developed system of government based on kings, and courts of law in which cases were tried by specialists (lawyers) and in which ordeals were employed to decide certain cases; a religious system with a complex hierarchy of priests and deities; a common stock of folklore and a common emphasis on moralizing elements and proverbs. Aside from writing, the wheel, the plow, and Christianity, most of the distinctive traits of Western civilization seem to have followed the industrial revolution.

This similarity between the fundamental patterns of Europe and Africa has further complicated the problem of assessing the relative influences of these areas in the culture of the Gullahs. Since most African traits of a specific nature have disappeared, what is to be found is, for the most part, a series of institutions which differ from the European forms only in their African flavor. To a person who is not familiar with West African cultures, it might seem possible to explain Gullah customs entirely in terms of European influence. The resemblances that are to be found might well be rejected as too general and too indefinite to prove diffusion from Africa to the Sea Islands, if taken by themselves. But we have the historical record of contact with Africa through the importation of African slaves into this region, so that the problem becomes not one of proving that there has been contact, but of assessing the importance of a known factor.

The result of the contact of the Negroes with the whites, both in slavery and in the period of freedom, seems to have been that in those cases where there was a difference or a conflict between African and European customs, the African customs have for the most part disappeared. But those institutions which were present in similar forms in both Africa and Europe, while manifesting a great many specifically European details, have retained an African

[1] Field work in Georgia and South Carolina during the summer of 1939 was made possible by a grant-in-aid from the Social Science Research Council of Northwestern University.

stamp and have had a place in Gullah life the importance of which cannot be explained in terms of European forms alone. In these cases the two streams of tradition have reinforced one another.

An excellent example of the operation of this process is to be found in the institution of cooperative work among the Gullahs. In West Africa, cooperative work is a widespread and important institution, which among the Yoruba,[2] for example, takes two forms. There is first of all the *aro* which is a simple labor exchange between two or three farmers who have small families and are too poor to own slaves or "pawns." Such men work a certain amount of time on the farm of one, and then the same amount on the farms of the second and third. The other form of cooperative work is the more spectacular social event, *owe*, in which a man calls upon his friends, relatives, or society members to help him with the work he is required to do for his father-in-law: hoe the fields, thatch the house, build its mud walls, or whatever may be required. On such occasions a large number of men work together while the host directs the activities. Meanwhile the wife, who has called her friends and society together to help her, prepares a large feast for the men with palmwine or gin, if her husband can afford it. In this case there is no attempt to keep track of the amount of work accomplished or time spent, as is done for *aro*.

In Dahomey,[3] besides the cooperative work done by members of the same guild, there is the *dokpwe* which is the equivalent of the Yoruba *owe* or working bee. The *dokpwe* is apparently even more closely associated with the society, however, and it differs in that the host hires a drummer to set the pace for the men working in the field, so that all the workers keep step and finish their rows at the same time. The Yoruba work in a line, so that each man hoes his own row, but they do not work in unison to music, although they are familiar with this procedure from contact with the Hausa. This Dahomean form of cooperative work, complete with hoeing in unison to a drummer, is a pattern which has been retained among other New World Negro cultures. It has been observed by Herskovits in Haiti,[4] by J. C. Trevor in the Virgin Islands,[5] and by Miss Katherine Dunham in Jamaica.[5]

Cooperative work, on the other hand, is not foreign to the European pattern. Certainly it played an important part in American colonial life in the form of house-raisings, quilting bees, log-rollings, husking bees, and the general pattern of neighborliness. According to informants, the white masters frequently loaned their slaves to one another for occasions of this sort, so that the Gullah had first hand contact with the European forms. Memories of the house-raisings, log-rollings, quilting bees, and even the associated candy pulls which the Negroes held on their own accord after freedom are still vivid

---

[2] Discussion of Yoruba material is based on field work in Nigeria, carried on during 1937–38 under terms of a fellowship grant from the Social Science Research Council of New York City.

[3] M. J. Herskovits, *Dahomey* (Augustin, New York, 1938), Vol. I, pp. 63–77.

[4] M. J. Herskovits, *Life in a Haitian Valley* (Knopf, New York, 1937), pp. 70–76.

[5] From unpublished field notes.

in the minds of the older individuals. But at the same time certain forms of cooperative work show a closer correspondence to the West African pattern, especially with regard to hoeing side by side, hoeing in unison to music, and the association between cooperative work and the societies.

On Sapeloe Island in Georgia informants remember large groups, apparently of between 30 and 50 persons, hoeing side by side in the fields. This in itself is significant, since, during the period of slavery, work was assigned by the task in this region so that each slave worked out a separate area by himself. Furthermore, after freedom when a man got behind in his work, he would call on his neighbors or his society for help; and even today, on Sapeloe, people will still "jump right into the field and help you out." In the old days the man would give a big dinner on a long table under a tree, but nowadays people are invited into the house. In hoeing each person takes his own row, and while the host did not hire a drum for use in the fields, the people frequently sang church songs and worked in unison, finishing their rows at the same time. When they worked without singing, couples talked and fell behind so that they did not all finish together. As in Africa, working together is said to make the work more pleasant and to make it go faster; as one informant put it, "You're really cuttin' grass then."

Similarly, if a man needed help, he might call upon a neighbor, and this favor would be returned when requested. This resembles the Yoruba *aro* except that no strict account was kept of the amount of work done. The person called upon might be a relative, or a good friend, or just a neighbor. Significantly, these arrangements were more or less permanent, so that a man would always call upon the same person to help him out. Usually the host gave the helper a meal; but if he were alone and ill, this was omitted.

On the island of Hilton Head, South Carolina, cooperative work has disappeared, but shortly after slavery it existed in two forms. In the first place neighbors might help each other even when they were not ill, working first in the fields of one family and then in the fields of the other. In the second place, the societies such as Mutual Friendly Aid would come without being asked to help a member who fell behind in his work. In this case they did not take note of the amount of work done, but just went in and "hoed him out," while the host provided a dinner for his helpers, serving whatever he could afford. When several people hoed the fields together, each took his own row, and when they sang their hoeing was in unison and was said to go faster and with less effort. In recent times the Hilton Head societies have been primarily "policy clubs" of the type so common in the South, and the function of working in the fields has been abandoned.

African elements are not so evident in other parts of the coastal regions as they are in Hilton Head and Sapeloe. On St. Simons Island, Georgia, neither neighbors nor societies helped in the fields; and while several members of the same family might hoe side by side, each taking his own row, even when they did sing they did not work in unison. On St. Helena, South Carolina, it is said that neighbors never worked each other's fields, but on this island the society called Knights of Wise helped members who were not well and fined those who did not show up to work. Members of the Sisters of Zion were likewise expected, but not forced, to turn out to work the fields of a sick member; if the man proved to be lazy instead of ill, he was given a mock whipping. There was no singing while farming on St. Helena, where they say they had to "sing with the hoe." About Darien and on Harris Neck, on the Georgia mainland, the pattern of cooperative work was once strong, but the forms it took were mainly European, with log-rollings, quiltings, and the like. People would come to hoe the fields of a neighbor who was not well, but the work was not done in unison to music, and while societies were important shortly after slavery, they did not help their members with their work.

It is difficult to explain these local variations in terms of the information at hand, but explanations are probably to be sought in differentials in isolation, the rules laid down by individual slave owners, and perhaps the African sources of the slaves and the dates at which slaves were last imported directly from Africa. While cooperative work persisted in these localities for a long time, it has disappeared in all of them except Sapeloe Island. In all these places except St. Simons, informants respond with conviction to the suggestion that people were more neighborly in the old days than they are now.

Friendship is another institution which is common to both the European and African tradition, but in West Africa it takes a slightly different form and is considerably more formalized than it is in our society. Among the Yoruba there is a distinct emphasis on the best friend (*korikosun*) with whom every contemplated undertaking is discussed, and whose advice in financial matters, or affairs with women, or any matter whatsoever is very seldom disregarded. The best friend is told how a man wants his property to be divided and is called in by the family to see that these wishes are carried out when his partner dies. There are folktales which show that a man's best friend is more to be trusted than his own mother; and the best friend is told things which a man does not confide to his wife. A man's wife or members of his family would attempt—supposedly always without success—to find out a man's plans by "pumping" his best friend.

The affection between best friends is legendary. A man speaks of loving his best friend "like a woman," and there are stories of men dying of grief at the passing of their friends. The Yoruba belief is that women's mouths are "too big" to keep a secret; they do not remain faithful to any friend, but go through life with a series of them. In Dahomey [6] the same general pattern holds but the institution is itself more elaborate in form. Each man has a first best friend in whom he confides everything; a second best friend to whom he tells slightly less; and a third best friend who receives only a part of his confidence.

In the Sea Islands the European practice of writing wills has been accepted completely so that an important and distinctively African function of

[6] M. J. Herskovits, *Dahomey* (Augustin, New York, 1938), Vol. I, pp. 239–242.

friendship has disappeared. At most a man asks his friend's advice about the way his property should be divided. A few informants in their discussion of friendship, did, however, give an emphasis to the institution which seems characteristically African.

On Hilton Head men used to have one or two "sworn friends" upon whom they could depend and to whom they told all their secrets. These friends interpreted each other's dreams, gave advice on financial ventures, and criticized each other's behavior, for instance, in such matters as having "affairs" with women. A man's wife or even his parents might go to his sworn friend in an attempt to find out what plans he had in mind, and in some cases a wife's persistence in this led to a gradual breaking up of the friendship, since the man would stay away from the house rather than be forced to betray his confidence.

Such friendship had a special importance in the time of slavery when slaves banded together against the master. They continued for a time after slavery, but in succeeding generations people came to confide in too many individuals—having too many sworn friends—so that secrets soon spread. The inability of women to keep a secret was blamed in part for the disappearance of the institution, for "as soon as you tell a girl, your secret is gone."

An African influence can be seen in the present form of a number of other institutions which will simply be enumerated. It is apparent in the functions of the local clubs or societies such as the Mutual Friendly Aid, the Jolly Boys, the Golden Link, the Seaside Branch, and the Union Gospel Travellers on Hilton Head. In most other regions these local societies were followed by the well-known, national, chartered lodges, which in turn have almost disappeared. In the structure of the Gullah family there seems to be a certain matrilineal emphasis for which there are counterparts in West Africa. For example, there is the feeling that an individual is somehow more closely related to his mother than to his father. There are several rationalizations for this, but one is the same as that offered in Africa, namely that a person is fed on his mother's milk.

The emphsis on special circumstances of birth is characteristically African. Parsons [7] has already pointed out how children born with a caul, children born "foot fo'mos'," twins, and the seventh child are all believed to have special qualities or abilities. The Gullah, like the West Africans, bury the naval cord in the yard, and frequently nursed their children for one, two, or three years in the old days. One woman was said to have nursed her child after it was old enough to help her in the fields. And people today remember women who carried their children on their backs, in some cases when working the fields. Certain Gullah beliefs are obviously comparable to the taboos of the West Africans; for example, the idea that a nursing mother should not eat beans, green corn, crabs, prawns, or net fish (channel fish caught with hook and line are all right), because it is not good for the baby's stomach.

[7] E. C. Parsons, *Folk-Lore of the Sea Islands, South Carolina* (Memoirs of the American Folk-Lore Society, Vol. XVI, Cambridge and New York, 1923), pp. 197–198.

The interpretation of dreams in order to predict the future is important in West African as well as in European tradition and it is wide-spread in the Sea Islands. Magic likewise is not foreign to the European tradition, but certain details of the practice are specifically African; the importance of "graveyard dirt," of "foot track dust," and of hair and nails in working conjure; and the importance of "frizzled chickens" as a means of detecting charms buried in the earth.[8]

The belief in multiple souls, the very vivid belief in ghosts, the special burial rites for persons who die by drowning, lightning, small-pox, and suicide, all resemble African beliefs more closely than they do European. A baby that is taken to a funeral must be passed across the coffin so that its soul will not accompany that of the deceased.[9] When a mother starts home after a visit she takes her baby in her arms, and then calls its name so that its soul will not be left behind.[10] As in Africa, a distinction is made between ghosts and witches, who take off their skins and can be caught either by sprinkling pepper and salt about the room in good African tradition,[11] or by the distinctly European method of putting a Bible under the pillow.

Turning once more to agriculture, we find that a specifically West African form of motor behavior has been retained widely in this region. In the planting of several crops, and especially of rice in the old days, the hole into which the seed was dropped was first made with the heel and then covered over with the foot. Moving pictures taken in West Africa and in Haiti by Herskovits [12] show very plainly this West African procedure which, as far as can be ascertained, was entirely foreign to European tradition.

Gullah speech, which has long been recognized as distinctive among Negro dialects in the United States, has a number of African idioms and grammatical peculiarities. A detailed analysis may show African influences in the phonetic system as well. Dr. Turner of Fisk University has listed several thousand words which he believes to be of West African origin.[13] These are mainly in the form of nicknames and words for plants and animals, and are used only within the family circle so that they would not be noticed unless someone set out to look for them. Lastly there are the very specific correspondences between the animal tales of the Gullah and those of West Africa, the first aspects of Gullah culture to be recognized as having an African origin.

In conclusion then, while it is impossible in the case of the Sea Island Negroes to assign African influences to particular tribes, and while we are

[8] Cf. *Drums and Shadows* by the Savannah Unit of the Georgia Writers' Project (University of Georgia Press, Athens, 1940).

[9] Cf. E. C. Parsons, *op. cit.*, p. 213; G. B. Johnson, *Folk Cuture on St. Helena Island, South Carolina* (Chapel Hill, The University of North Carolina Press, 1930), p. 172.

[10] Cf. E. C. Parsons, *op. cit.*, p. 199; G. B. Johnson, *op. cit.*, p. 172.

[11] Cf. J. Peterkin, *Black April* (Grosset & Dunlap, 1927), p. 100.

[12] See M. J. Herskovits, *Life in a Haitian Valley* (Knopf, New York, 1937), illustrations facing p. 100.

[13] By personal communication.

dealing with the problem of the relative influence of European and African culture on institutions common to both traditions, rather than with African origins of non-European institutions, these influences can be recognized in many aspects of present-day Gullah life. It would thus seem historically incorrect as well as methodologically unsound to explain Gullah customs by reference only to European culture. It is quite true that, as elsewhere in the United States, the European elements outnumber by far the African elements which have been retained, yet that Africanisms can be traced indicates the importance of the study of this society as an aid in the analysis of acculturation.

Hollis R. Lynch

PAN-NEGRO NATIONALISM IN THE
NEW WORLD, BEFORE 1862

Throughout their history most American Negroes have felt some de-
gree of identification with Africa. As early as the end of the eight-
eenth century, a few had advocated migration to that continent. Not
until the middle of the nineteenth century, however, did this interest
become a major theme in Negro thinking. At that time the status
of the ante-bellum free Negroes was declining in most parts of the
Union. In the North, the passage of the Fugitive Slave Act of 1850
and economic competition from the rising tide of Irish immigrants
were prominent factors causing Negroes to become more despairing
for their safety and their rights. In the South, increasingly re-
strictive legislation made life ever more difficult. Under these con-
ditions, colonization—i.e., emigration to Africa, to Haiti, or to some
part of Central America—became increasingly attractive to many
free Negroes.

Hollis Lynch's essay describes these early efforts and the rising
nationalism that flourished among articulate Negroes in the years
before the Civil War.

P AN-AFRICANISM and pan-Negro nationalism are historically related phenomena with similar origins.[1] Both grew out of resentment at the treatment of
black-skinned peoples, whether as slaves in the West Indies and in the American South, as "free persons of color," or, later, as subjects of new European

Hollis R. Lynch, "Pan-Negro Nationalism in the New World, Before 1862," reprinted by permission of the publishers from *Boston University Papers on Africa*, Volume
II, *African History*, pp. 149–179, Boston, Massachusetts: Boston University Press. Copyright © 1966 by the Trustees of Boston University.

[1] This article on Pan-Africanism and pan-Negro nationalism is based on a paper
given at the University of Massachusetts on December 13, 1962. I am grateful to
Professor Gwendolen Carter for her assistance. Research was made possible by a travel
grant from the Central Research Fund of the University of London, and by the British
Commonwealth Scholarship Commission; to both of these bodies I am grateful.

empires in Africa. Pan-Africanism as an organized movement, concerned with the grievances of all black-skinned peoples, and particularly involving an attack on colonialism in Africa, is a twentieth-century phenomenon: the term came into use in 1900 when Henry Sylvester Williams, a West Indian barrister from Trinidad, organized a Pan-African conference in London, attended by delegates from the West Indies and the United States.[2]

Five other conferences were held, largely through the efforts of the American Negro scholar, W. E. B. Du Bois, at which delegates met to articulate their grievances and to devise means of removing them.[3] These delegates were almost entirely from the New World; indeed, it was only at the last of the extra-African conferences—at Manchester in 1945—that Africans were adequately represented.[4] No meetings had been held on African soil, though African issues were discussed at every conference. After Ghana gained its independence in 1957, the Pan-African movement began to take on a more African character, largely because it had the support of the first of the new African states created after World War II. Though New World Negroes had played, and continued to play, a part on the African continent, the movement passed finally into the hands of African leaders.[5]

This specifically named and organized Pan-Africanism was not the first Negro movement with "African" and "all-African" aspirations. There were at least two earlier such manifestations of thought and feeling, the most recent—Marcus Garvey's "Back to Africa" movement in the nineteen-twenties—being the best known.[6] But early in the nineteenth century there developed among Negroes in the West Indies and in the United States a movement preoccupied with the promotion of emigration and the creation of new states, most of them in Africa. As in the case of Garvey's movement, these early pan-Negro nationalists were concerned with the plight of Negroes in the New World. They failed, however, to produce a charismatic leader or a mass movement. Nevertheless, in their statements and actions these pan-Negro leaders anticipated many of their twentieth-century successors,[7] particularly in their interest in Africa, their belief in a great African past, and their dilemma of

[2] The Times, July 24, 25, 26, 1900; also the account by an American delegate, Bishop Alexander Walters, My Life and Work (New York, 1917), xx.

[3] See W. E. B. Du Bois, The World and Africa (New York, 1947), 7–12, 236–242; George Padmore, Pan-Africanism or Communism? (London, 1956), 137–151; American Society of African Culture, ed., Pan-Africanism Reconsidered (Los Angeles, 1962), 37–52; and Vernon McKay, Africa in World Politics (New York, 1963), 93–108.

[4] For a list of the delegates of the 1945 Pan-African conference, see George Padmore, ed., History of the Pan-African Congress (Manchester, n.d.), 71–73.

[5] For Pan-Africanism since 1958, see Colin Legum, Pan-Africanism (London, 1962); also McKay, Africa, 109–133.

[6] See Edmund David Cronon, Black Moses (Madison, 1955).

[7] See George Shepperson, "Notes on American Negro Influences on the Emergence of African Nationalism," Journal of African History, 1.2:299–312 (1960); Nnamdi Azikiwe, "The Future of Pan-Africanism," Présence africaine, 12:11 (1962).

choice between reform of the New World and "regeneration" of their ancestral home.

I

Haiti had a chance to be the first state to provide a base for a pan-Negro program. The slaves of Haiti revolted in 1804 and gained their independence from the greatest military power in Europe, to become the second modern sovereign state in the Americas. The rulers of the Negro "empire" were aware of a responsibility to the Negro race when they invited Negroes to cooperate in building a model state as the final, convincing answer to assertions of Negro inferiority.[8] However, because of internal division, Haiti failed to fulfil its promise.[9] Even so, its continued existence remained for many Negroes proof of Negro ability, and a source of hope for a better future for the race.

Of course, many New World and British Negroes had maintained a sentimental attachment to, and interests in, Africa. It is noteworthy that practically all Negro organizations formed in the United States up to about the third decade of the nineteenth century had the word "African" in their titles.[10] And among the Negroes in Britain, set free by Lord Mansfield's judicial decision in 1772, there were a few who advocated what was essentially the point of view of British evangelicals and humanitarians, namely, that Britain should exert itself to stop the slave trade, replace it by legitimate commerce, and help to christianize and civilize Africa.[11] These Negroes of Britain also played a part in inducing British humanitarian groups to found the colony of Sierra Leone in 1787. The Negroes themselves formed the great majority of the emigrants who embarked from Britain.[12] Less than two years after the first emigrants landed, the Free African Society of Newport, Rhode Island, showed an interest in the colony and in 1795 sent out a delegate to prospect.[13] Sierra Leone also attracted Negroes from Nova Scotia, where they had been settled after fighting on the side of the British in the American revolution. Anxious to leave behind an uncongenial climate and society, 1,131 of them—

[8] James Redpath, ed., A Guide to Hayti (Boston, 1861), see preface and 104.
[9] See James G. Leyburn, The Haitian People (New Haven, 1941), passim.
[10] Some examples are: Prince Hall's African Lodge No. 1, the Free African Societies of Philadelphia and Newport, the African Institutions of New York and Philadelphia, various independent African Baptist churches, and the African Methodist Church. From about the third decade on, when American Negroes became convinced that the American Colonization Society (founded in 1817) wished forcibly to deport them to Africa, the title "African" became less popular among them and was replaced by "Colored."
[11] See Ignatius Sancho, Letters (London, 1782); Ottobah Cugoano, Thoughts and Sentiments on the Evil of Slavery (London, 1787); and Gustavus Vassa, The Interesting Narrative of the Life of Olaudah Equiano, or Gustavus Vassa, the African (London, 1789).
[12] R. R. Kuczynski, Demographic Survey of the British Colonial Empire (London, 1948), 40–43; also Christopher Fyfe, History of Sierra Leone (London, 1962), 13–19.
[13] Ibid., 112.

led by Thomas Peters, a millwright, who had negotiated with the directors of the Sierra Leone Company, and David George, a zealous Baptist preacher—emigrated to the "Colony of Freedom" in 1792. Both Peters and George can be regarded as prototypes of those Negro leaders who sought to lead Negroes out of "bondage" and back to the "fatherland" in Africa.

Moreover, the arrival of the Nova Scotians saved the colony from complete dissolution. Further reinforcements came in 1800 in the form of 532 Maroons who had taken part in a revolt in Jamaica, had been transported to Nova Scotia, and had then elected to emigrate to Sierra Leone. In 1807, the British government outlawed the slave trade and on January 1, 1808, assumed from the Sierra Leone Company direct control of the colony, which was to be used as a center for the suppression of the slave trade in West Africa as well as for settling and civilizing liberated Africans. In 1804, the Church Missionary Society began work in the colony, and Sierra Leone became the center of British humanitarian activities in West Africa. By 1808, Sierra Leone had a population of nearly two thousand westernized Negroes and had become an obvious focus for further Negro emigration to Africa. Sierra Leone might do what Haiti was failing to do.

In the early years of the nineteenth century, there were already signs that the freed American Negro might have to seek a home outside the United States. Those years marked a sharp decline in his fortune. The invention and use of the cotton gin in the last years of the eighteenth century, and the subsequent remarkable spread of the cotton kingdom to the south and southwest, had served to revive the waning institution of slavery. Manumission of slaves, which had been frequent in the years following the American revolution, had come to a virtual end in the South by the turn of the century. The relatively large free Negro population that had grown up was regarded by many white Southerners as an anomaly and a threat to its society.[14] In the North, Negroes fared no better: although by 1804, all slavery there had been abolished, Negroes were not accepted as an integral part of American society.[15] And as the Southern states began taking measures intended to return free Negroes to slavery or to drive them out, the North, fearful of an influx, seemed to vie with the South in making their lives difficult.

Despite the growing discrimination against them, however, many American Negroes continued to assert their rights as American citizens. Many, for instance, began to look upon the efforts of the American Colonization Society,[16] founded in 1817 as a barely disguised attempt on the part of slaveholders, who

[14] In 1800, there were 108,435 free Negroes in the United States. By 1830, this had risen, mainly by natural increase, to 319,599, and to 488,070 by 1860. The free Negro population remained at roughly one tenth of the entire Negro population. See *Negro Population of the United States*, Bureau of Census (Washington, 1918), 57.

[15] For an elaboration of this thesis, see Leon F. Litwack, *North of Slavery: The Negro in the Free States, 1790–1862* (Chicago, 1962).

[16] For the history of the society, see Earle Lee Fox, *The American Colonization Society, 1817–1840* (Baltimore, 1919); and P. J. Stadenraus, *The African Colonization Movement, 1816–1865* (New York, 1961).

were prominently associated with the organization, to rid the United States of a potentially troublesome element and thus make secure the Southern system of slavery.[17] From 1830 on, Negroes met in national conventions to denounce slaveholders and the American Colonization Society, and to declare their determination to fight for their civil rights.[18]

II

While many Negroes in the United States sought to achieve complete integration within American society, others became pan-Negro nationalists. Despairing of becoming first-class citizens in their own country, they became advocates of Negro emigration to Africa and elsewhere, and held visions of new states on a continent regenerated by their efforts. Prominent among them were Paul Cuffee, Daniel Coker, Lott Cary, and John Russwurm.[19] All but Cuffee died in the newly established Negro settlements in West Africa.

Cuffee was a devout Quaker from Massachusetts, a prosperous trader and shipowner who, as a young man, had fought for the rights of Negroes in his native state.[20] When this met with little success, he turned to Africa, and particularly to Sierra Leone, to work for the "improvement and civilization of the blacks" of Africa, to provide selective emigration to Sierra Leone, and to seek the suppression of the slave trade and its replacement by legitimate commerce. His trader's mind was excited by the possibility of extensive commerce between Negro America and West Africa, to raise the wealth and prestige of the race. In 1808, he obtained the support of the African Institution, a British humanitarian organization comprised mainly of former directors of the Sierra Leone Company and still influential in directing the affairs of the colony. Three years later he visited Sierra Leone, where he showed considerable care in making plans for emigration. Finally, he founded the Friendly Society of Sierra Leone "to open a channel of intercourse" between Negro America and Sierra Leone; as an earnest of his good faith, he bought a house in Freetown.[21]

Long interested in Negro education in America, Cuffee also showed interest in promoting education in Sierra Leone: "Africa calls for men of character

[17] See Louis B. Mehlinger, "The Attitude of the Free Negro Toward Colonization," *Journal of Negro History*, I (July 1916).

[18] See John W. Cromwell, "The Early Negro Convention Movement," *Occasional Papers* [of the American Negro Academy], IX (Washington, 1940); August Meier, "The Emergence of Negro Nationalism," *Midwest Journal*, IV (Winter 1951–52), 96–104; and Howard H. Bell, "A Survey of the Negro Convention Movement, 1830–1861" (unpublished dissertation, Northwestern University, 1953).

[19] This is not, of course, meant to be an exhaustive list: these were chosen because they were articulate or outstanding men of action. For a discussion of American Negro procolonization views in this period, see Mehlinger, "Attitude." For an example of a project for colonization outside Africa, see the discussion of Delany and Holly below.

[20] For Cuffee's biography, see Henry Noble Sherwood, "Paul Cuffee," *Journal of Negro History*, VIII (April 1923), 153–229.

[21] *Ibid.*, 176.

to fill stations in the Legislature," he wrote.[22] On his return to America, he sought personally to persuade Negroes in such centers as Baltimore, Philadelphia, New York, Boston, and his own town of Westport to support colonization in Africa. In 1815 Cuffee made his second trip to Sierra Leone, taking, largely at his own expense, thirty-eight Negroes in family groups. In letters to America these emigrants urged other Negroes to follow their example.[23] When Cuffee returned, he made his experience available to the founders of the American Colonization Society. Indeed, he was chosen to lead emigrants to be sent out by the society, but he died before the first expedition left for West Africa. However, shortly before this he expressed the widespread feeling Negroes shared against the society by cautioning against too eager an acceptance of its scheme.[24]

Despite Cuffee's warning, the society won the support of his friend Daniel Coker. A runaway slave who as a boy had acquired a rudimentary education, Coker had become schoolmaster and religious leader in the free Negro community of Baltimore. As a young man, he had angrily denounced the institution of slavery and asserted that, despite its handicap, "the African Race ... had given proof of talents." [25] Coker had played a leading role in the break with the Methodist Episcopal Church, which resulted in the formation of the African Methodist Episcopal Church.[26] Elected its first bishop, he had declined the honor. Intent on emigrating to West Africa, he was among the first eighty-eight emigrants sent out by the Colonization Society. Although the expedition was led by three white officials, it seems that in the eyes of the emigrants Coker was the leader.[27] His journal shows him as keenly conscious of the possibilities of the enterprise and of some responsibility for its success. In the two years of hardship and uncertainty that followed before the emigrants finally settled at Cape Mesurado—the first beginnings of Liberia—the leadership devolved mainly on him. He later settled in Sierra Leone.

Lott Cary, who was among the second group of emigrants, played a versatile role as clergyman, doctor, militiaman, builder, and pioneer in agriculture.[28] He regarded himself as primarily a missionary to the native Africans, and from the start he was concerned that the colonists should have friendly relations with the tribes and so exert a civilizing influence. He was born a slave, and,

[22] Ibid., 206.

[23] Ibid., 218.

[24] Ibid., 213–221; also Henry N. Sherwood, "Paul Cuffee and his Contribution to the American Colonization Society," Proceedings of the Mississippi Valley Historical Association, VI (1913), 370–402.

[25] A Dialogue Between A Virginian and an African Minister, Written by Daniel Coker, a Descendant of Africa, Minister of the African Methodist Episcopal Church in Baltimore (Baltimore, 1810), 10.

[26] Daniel A. Payne, History of the African Methodist Episcopal Church (Nashville, 1891), 89.

[27] The Journal of Daniel Coker, A Descendant of Africa ... in the Ship Elizabeth, on a Voyage for Sherbro in Africa ... (Baltimore, 1820), 15–16.

[28] Harry Johnston, Liberia (London, 1906), I, 135; R. R. Gurley, Life of Jehudi Ashmun (Washington, 1835), 147–160; Alexander, History, 241–254.

though ignorant at twenty-seven, he acquired considerable learning and became a well-to-do Baptist preacher in Richmond, Virginia, by the age of thirty-three. Yet he gave up this relatively comfortable position to go to Liberia. He wrote: "I am an African; and in this country, however meritorious my conduct and respectable my character, I cannot receive the credit due to either. I wish to go to a country where I shall be estimated by my merits not by my complexion, and I feel bound to labour for my suffering race." [29] Cary died, in an accident, on November 10, 1828.

John B. Russwurm was born in Jamaica, and became one of the first two Negro graduates from an American college.[30] In March 1827, he founded and became the editor of the first American Negro newspaper, *Freedom's Journal*. He abandoned his opposition to the American Colonization Society, and in 1829 announced his conversion to the view that the free Negro could help himself and his race best by giving strong support to Liberia.[31] He soon left for Liberia and in 1830 founded the *Liberia Herald*. He also held the positions of superintendent of education and colonial secretary; from 1836 until his death in 1851, he was governor of Maryland, a colony adjacent to Liberia to the south, which was founded by the Maryland Colonization Society in 1834.[32] As the first Negro governor in West Africa, Russwurm felt that the conduct of his office was a test of the ability of the Negro: he seems to have ruled, with substantial justice to colonists, Africans, and missionaries alike.[33]

These four leaders in the early phase of the Pan-African movement had much in common. All were men of substance, in nearly every case through their own talent and industry. All of them, including Russwurm the Jamaican, were protesting against discrimination in the United States. Indeed, Coker had taken part in the setting up of an "African" church, an early example of the use of historical origins as the basis of a protest. Although Russwurm and Cuffee showed an understandable suspicion of the white-dominated American Colonization Society, they gave Liberia their support, perhaps on the good practical ground that, whatever the motive of the society's leaders and supporters, the society was creating a Negro state in Africa.

Between 1830 and about 1850, there seems to have been something of a falling off of activity among American Negroes. No new and effective leader appeared to take up the pan-Negro cause, although there is evidence that sentiment in favor of emigration continued to grow.[34] In the West Indies,

[29] Quoted in *ibid.*, 243.

[30] See William M. Brewer, "John B. Russwurm," *Journal of Negro History*, XIII (Oct. 1928), 413–422.

[31] See his editorials in *Freedom's Journal*, II (Feb. 14, 1829 et seq.).

[32] For a history of the founding of the colony, see *Journal of the Maryland Historical Society*, V (Feb. 1850), 129–152.

[33] Russwurm's letters and reports as governor, not used in Brewer's "Russwurm," are in the archives of the Maryland Historical Society.

[34] Carter G. Woodson, *The Mind of the Negro as Reflected in Letters Written during the Crisis, 1800–1860* (Washington, 1926), *passim*.

particularly in Jamaica and Barbados, there was widespread interest both in leaving the place of former bondage and continued discrimination and in taking Christianity to "benighted brothers" in Africa.[35] In Barbados, in the three decades after the abolition of slavery, at least three organizations were formed for promoting emigration to Liberia: the Barbados Colonization Society, the Fatherland Union Society, and the Barbados Company for Liberia.[36] But because of the lack of adequate financial resources among Negroes or external aid, the opposition of the still powerful West Indian sugar planters, and perhaps the absence of any oppressive discrimination, little emigration was organized.[37]

It is, however, interesting that groups in the West Indies should have looked to Liberia. After the emancipation of the slaves, there was less pressure on them in the form of discrimination than on the American Negro to seek a home elsewhere. It is significant that the three important West Indian advocates of pan-Negro nationalism discussed here—Russwurm, Edward W. Blyden,[38] and Robert Campell [39]—had all experienced and resented the discrimination against Negroes in the United States.

The desire of West Indian Negroes who wanted to emigrate for other reasons had important consequences for West Africa. It was these people who urged the start of missionary work in West Africa by both the British Baptist and the United Scottish Presbyterian societies. West Indians played an important role in their work, as well as in that of the Basel and Wesleyan missions. They accounted also for the formation of the West Indian Church Association, whose missionaries worked in the Rio Pongo area in West Africa. The association was an autonomous body which, unlike the other missionary societies, derived its support in money and men mainly from West Indian Negroes.[40] The West Indian missionaries and teachers worked, so they felt, for the regeneration of Africa and on behalf of the Negro race.[41] Men like Joseph Fuller,

[35] See A. E. Payne, Freedom in Jamaica (London, 1946), 73–74; C. P. Groves, Planting of Christianity in Africa (London, 1954), II, 54; A General Account of the West Indian Church Association for the Furtherance of the Gospel in West Africa (London, 1855), 5–7.

[36] Maryland Colonization Journal, IV (1848), 213; also American Colonization Society, Forty-Ninth Annual Report (Washington, 1866), 7.

[37] There is one exception to this. In 1865, 365 Negroes from Barbados emigrated to Liberia in an expedition sponsored by the Liberian government but financed mainly by the American Colonization Society. See American Colonization Society, Fifty-Second Annual Report (Washington, 1869), 53; and chap. 3 my book on Blyden cited below.

[38] See discussion of Blyden below; also Hollis R. Lynch, Edward W. Blyden (1832–1912), Pan-Negro Patriot (London, 1966).

[39] See discussion of Campell below; also Robert Campell, A Pilgrimage to My Motherland (New York, 1861), 11.

[40] A. Barrow, Fifty Years in Western Africa: Being a Record of the West Indian Church on the Banks of the Rio Pongo (London, 1900), passim.

[41] In addition, many West Indian artisans and professionals were attracted to West Africa, particularly to Sierra Leone, but primarily because of the better economic opportunities there. See Abioseh Nicol, "West Indians in West Africa," Sierre Leone Studies, N.S., no. 13 (June 1960), 14–23. Also from about 1840, Brazilian and Cuban

Henry Wharton, and John Duport respectively spent forty, twenty-eight, and eighteen years in Africa.[42]

In the eighteen-fifties, however, there was a rapid revival of interest among American Negroes, as the conflict over slavery became more intense. Negroes were, of course, deeply involved and, as events appeared to be set on a course against them, more wanted to emigrate. In 1850, the Fugitive Slave Bill was passed giving federal commissioners virtually unlimited power for the apprehension and return of alleged fugitives. This was only the first shock in a decade of "sorrowful and unmixed gloom." [43] There followed the Kansas-Nebraska Act, the Dred Scott decision, the failure of John Brown's raid, and an apparent blow from the Republican Party when Abraham Lincoln, a compromise candidate, assumed the presidency. It would be useful to study the period between 1850 and 1862 in detail because not until Garvey's "Back to Africa" movement of the 1920s did pan-Negro nationalism seem again to possess real vigor.

The independence of Liberia in 1847 could hardly have come at a more opportune time for the cause of emigration from the New World. Congratulations to the new republic came from all major Negro groups, and many hoped with John B. Hepburn of Port-au-Prince that Liberia's course was now "onward to empire and to fame." [44] In 1848, the American Colonization Society sent out delegates to report on Liberia's possibilities as a future home.[45] West Indian Negroes, too, showed interest: the Barbados Colonization Society "for assisting in the suppression of the Slave Trade, and the introduction of civilization into Africa" received the news of Liberia's independence with "inexpressible joy" and regarded it "as another demonstration to the world, that the descendants of Africa, when placed in a fair position, are not inferior in civilization, religion, and morality, to those nations amongst whom it was their lot to be cast for a given time." [46] The new interest in Liberia reflected itself in a substantial increase in the annual number of American emigrants, which rose from 51 in 1847 to 441 in 1848. This increase in emigration was maintained throughout the next decade.[47]

Negroes trickled back to Lagos and its hinterland where, as artisans, agriculturists, and traders, they formed an important section of the community.

[42] For biographical details on these three missionaries, see Robert Glennie, *Joseph Jackson Fuller* (London, 1925); G. G. Findlay and W. W. Holdsworth, *The History of the Wesleyan Methodist Society* (London, 1922), 164; and Barrow, *Fifty Years*, *passim*.

[43] The phrase is that of the American Negro leader, James McCune Smith. See his introduction to a *Memorial Discourse by Rev. Henry Highland Garnet, Delivered in the Hall of the House of Representatives* ... (Washington, 1865), 56.

[44] *Maryland Colonization Journal*, IV (1848), 213.

[45] The American Colonization Society, *Thirty-Second Annual Report* (Washington, 1849), 8.

[46] *African Repository*, XXIV (Aug. 1848), 24.

[47] American Colonization Society, *Fifty-Second Annual Report* (Washington, 1869), 53.

III

The new Liberian republic, of which so much was hoped, had a disappointing beginning. In 1850, three years after independence, it was a country of roughly 13,000 square miles, with a coastline of approximately 300 miles. Its emigrant population, depleted by a high mortality rate, was about 6,000. Since 1827 the majority of those sent out by the Colonization Society had been slaves who were emancipated expressly for that purpose,[48] and many were unfit for pioneering.[49]

It is not surprising, then, that the sense of mission and destiny which inspired the early emigrants was largely missing among the later ones. Between its founding and 1850, Liberia seems to have produced only one outstanding champion of the pan-Negro ideology, the "poet and philosopher," Hilary Teage, son of Colin Teage, who had come from Lott Cary's congregation in Richmond, Virginia. He succeeded Russwurm as editor of the *Liberia Herald* in 1835, and for the next fourteen years used it to express his pan-Negro sentiments. He was certainly the first poet of pan-Negro nationalism: his poetry is concerned with the themes of the past achievements of his race and of a mission to fulfill.[50] He was also an accomplished orator. He said to a group of Liberians in 1846: "Upon you, rely upon it, depends, in a measure you can hardly conceive, the future destiny of the race. You are to give the answer whether the African race is doomed to interminable degradation—a hideous blot on the fair face of creation, a libel upon the dignity of human nature; or whether they are capable to take an honourable rank amongst the great family of nations." [51] In 1847 he was a representative at Liberia's constitutional conference.

On the whole, however, Liberians did not demonstrate much unity of purpose or public spirit. They were berated by their white governors and their progressive leaders for their "want of self-respect" and their easy dependence on foreign philanthropy.[52] Socially there had quickly developed in Liberia an American pattern of stratifications based on color, the mulattoes considering themselves superior to the black emigrants while the colonists, generally speaking, held the natives in contempt.[53] The Liberians exploited native labor on their plantations, but, on the whole, agriculture was neglected for trading,

---

[48] Up to 1850, 6,116 emigrants were sent out by the Society: 2,315 were born free, 165 purchased their freedom, and 3,636 were emancipated for emigration.

[49] Edward W. Blyden, A *Voice from Bleeding Africa* (Monrovia, 1856), 26.

[50] For quotations from his poems extolling the Negro past and urging Liberia to "press towards the prize in glory's race," see Edward W. Blyden, *From West Africa to Palestine* (Freetown, Manchester, London, 1873), 104; also Frederick Alexander Durham, *The Lone-Star of Liberia* (London, 1892), 1.

[51] Quoted in Wilson Armistead, A *Tribute to the Negro* (Manchester and New York, 1848), 532; also J. A. B. Horton, *West African Countries and Peoples* (London, 1868), 273.

[52] Johnston, *Liberia*, 149, 182–184.

[53] Abayomi Karrnga, *History of Liberia* (Liverpool, 1926), 45.

which brought quick profits without developing the productive capacity of the country.

Until its independence, the supreme authority in the colony was the American Colonization Society. Independence came from the demand by Liberians for, among other things, the sovereign power to deal with recalcitrant European traders scornful of the developing Negro nation.[54] And so on July 26, 1847, Liberia became a sovereign nation with a constitution modeled on that of the United States.[55] Unfortunately, the constitution contained a provision which was later to keep the young nation in a chaotic political condition: the president, the House of Representatives, and half of the senators were to be elected every two years. Moreover, the franchise was confined mainly to American colonists.

With renewed support from New World Negroes, however, the new nation could have retrieved itself. Such was the view of Edward Wilmot Blyden, probably the most articulate advocate of pan-Negro nationalism in the nineteenth century.[56] Born free [57] on the Danish West Indian island of St. Thomas in 1832, and educated at the local primary school and by private tuition from his American pastor, the Reverend John Knox, and his own mother, Blyden early decided on the ministry as a career. In May 1850, Knox took him to the United States and attempted to enroll him in Rutgers' Theological College, Knox's alma mater. Blyden was refused admission because of his race, and, aware of the operation of the Fugitive Slave Law, he accepted an offer from the New York Colonization Society to emigrate to Liberia.

Even before he left the United States, Blyden expressed pride in the newly independent Negro republic: Liberia, he thought, could "include within its limits the dark regions of Ashantee and Dahomey and bring those barbarous tribes under civilized and enlightened influence." [58] In his first letter to the United States he described his pleasure at being on African soil: "You can easily imagine the delight with which I gazed upon the land of Tertullian, ancient father in the Christian Church; of Hannibal and Henry Diaz, renowned generals; yes, and the land of *my* forefathers . . . The land here is teeming with everything necessary for subsistence of man." The skeptics, he wrote, should come and see for themselves.[59] He continued his studies at Alexander High School, a Presbyterian school in Monrovia. In 1858 he was ordained a minister and became principal of the high school. From the beginning of his time in Liberia, Blyden was active in public life, both as a correspondent for the *Liberia Herald* and as editor during 1855–56. Moreover,

[54] Johnston, *Liberia*, 187–195.

[55] The basic document was drafted by Simon Greenleaf, Professor of Law at Harvard University, but was somewhat revised at Liberia's constitutional convention; Liberians wrote the preamble.

[56] See Lynch, *Edward W. Blyden*.

[57] Slavery was not abolished in the Danish West Indies until 1848, but here, too, there was a small group of free Negroes before general emancipation.

[58] *New York Colonization Journal*, I (Dec. 1850).

[59] *African Repository*, XXVII (Sept. 1851), 266.

he remained an active propagandist for Liberia and the cause of emigration, writing often for the *African Repository* (the journal of the American Colonization Society) and for the journals of the New York and Maryland Colonization societies.

Blyden was an articulate and critical defender of his new home, and from an early stage he was concerned about diverting the expected flow of emigration from the United States to Africa, particularly to Liberia. It is probable that his first pamphlet, *A Voice from Bleeding Africa*, published in Monrovia in 1856, appeared just before the emigration conference of 1856 was scheduled to meet in Cleveland,[60] though there is no evidence that it was discussed there. In the pamphlet he appealed to "colored men of every rank and station, in every clime and country" to support the colonization movement. Moreover, he urged Negroes to take the name of the new state seriously: the object of the creation of Liberia was "the redemption of Africa and the disenthralment and elevation of the African race, objects worthy of every colored man." At the same time, he attacked Liberians for a lack of dedication to the cause:

> How painful is the reflection that there are but few of the young men of Liberia who seem to give the future of their country a moment's thought ... ! O young men and women of Liberia, arise from your lethargy, shake off your puerile notions and practices! It is high time to bestir yourselves to be men and women. Let the brave achievements and noble deeds of your fathers arouse you to effort. Let the future glory that awaits your country kindle within you an honorable ambition and urge you onwards.[61]

He wanted to see "the young men of Liberia, like the youth among the ancient Spartans, exercise themselves vigorously in all things which pertain to the country's welfare." [62]

An opportunity for him to act as a defender of Liberia came in 1852. Gerrit Smith, a veteran abolitionist and member of Congress from New York, in opposing a scheme to send Negroes to Liberia, dubbed the American Colonization Society "the deadliest enemy of the Negro race," and Liberia "a frightful graveyard." [63] Blyden attacked Senator Smith for "doing ... considerable harm ... by blinding the minds of colored men to their true interests." Colonization in Africa, he contended, was "the only means of delivering the colored man from oppression and of raising him up to respectability." He would not accept the advice of Smith and other abolitionists that, if necessary, free Negroes should retire to Canada to await the outcome of the issue of

---

60 The conference is discussed below. See also Martin R. Delany, *Official Report of the Niger Valley Exploring Party* (New York, 1861), for a discussion of the conference.

61 *New York Colonization Journal*, IV (Aug. 1854).

62 *African Repository*, XXXI (April 1855), 18.

63 Howard H. Bell, "The Negro Emigration Movement, 1849–54: A Phase of Negro Nationalism," *Phylon*, XX (Nov. 1959), 136.

slavery. Admitting that the mortality rate in Liberia was high, Blyden claimed that this was a temporary condition, common to all pioneer communities.[64]

While Blyden was rebuking Senator Smith, Martin R. Delany, a Negro doctor trained at Harvard and a former newspaper editor and abolitionist, was devising a scheme based on a Negro empire in the Caribbean and South and Central America. After the passage of the Fugitive Slave Bill, he despaired of American Negroes ever enjoying the full rights of citizenship in the United States. He had grown impatient even with the white abolitionists when he realized that Negroes were "occupying the very same position, in relation to our anti-slavery friends, as we do in relation to the pro-slavery part of the community—a mere secondary, underling position, in all our relations to them, and anything more than this comes by mere sufferance." He dismissed with "contemptuous indignation the absurd idea of the natural inferiority of the African," warned Negroes not to carry their religion to the point of hoping for a divine intervention on their behalf, and urged them to support him in constructive action.[65]

His projected empire was to be formed by American Negroes emigrating to South America, an area for which he made two doubtful claims: first, that it was predominantly Negroid and, second, that there had "never existed there an inequality on account of color or race." [66] His advocacy of a Negro empire in the Americas was partly for strategic reasons: by its proximity it would, either by moral or physical force, bring about the collapse of slavery in the United States. But he also believed that Negroes, as developers of the economic base of the New World, were entitled to their full share of its fruits. Still he did not overlook Africa, which he hoped would be "civilized and enlightened," with Liberia in a "high and elevated position . . . among the nations of the earth." Yet he continued to regard the American Colonization Society as working to promote the interest of slaveholders and was, therefore, severely critical of Liberia's dependence on it.[67]

It is hardly surprising that Blyden and Delany came into conflict. Blyden defended the American Colonization Society and Liberia with some spirit. Delany's plan was a diversion, he wrote, and doomed to failure in any case. Only in Africa could the Negro race rise to distinguished achievement.[68]

Before Delany could act on his scheme, the largest Negro national conference up to that time was convened in Rochester, New York, in 1853, and

[64] *Liberia Herald*, n.s., III (July 7, 1852); also *Maryland Colonization Society*, VI (Nov. 1852), 277–280.

[65] See Martin R. Delany, *The Condition, Elevation and Destiny of the Colored People of the United States, Politically Considered* (Philadelphia, 1852).

[66] *Ibid.*, 27. Although Delany's statement was not strictly true, it is true that in Latin American countries Negroes were on the whole better treated than in Anglo-Saxon America. For a comparative study of the treatment of Negroes in the Americas, see Frank Tannenbaum, *Slave and Citizen* (New York, 1947); also Stanley M. Elkins, *Slavery* (Chicago, 1959).

[67] *Ibid.*, 169, 170.

[68] *Liberia Herald*, n.s. III (Oct. 6, 1852).

the persistent division between emigrationists and anti-emigrationists was forced into the open. The anti-emigrationists, led by the Negro leader Frederick Douglass, persuaded the conference to go on record as opposing emigration.[69] But as soon as the conference was over, the emigrationists, led by Delany, James M. Whitfield, a popular poet, and James T. Holly, an accomplished Episcopalian clergyman, called a conference for August 1854, from which anti-emigrationists were to be excluded. Douglass described this action as "narrow and illiberal," and he sparked the first public debate among American Negro leaders on the subject of emigration.[70]

The conference on emigration met in Cleveland as planned. It was, according to Delany, the most widely representative one ever convened by Negroes.[71] Shortly before it met, the passage of the Kansas-Nebraska Act had provided another triumph for the supporters of slavery. Understandably, the mood of the conference was militant. Delany repeated his call for the creation of a Negro empire in the New World, where "the inherent traits, attributes ... and native characteristics peculiar to our race could be cultivated and developed." [72] He warned that "submission does not gain for us an increase of friends nor respectability, as the white race will only respect those who oppose their usurpation, and acknowledge as equals those who will not submit to their rule." They were to take concerted action: "We must make an issue, create an event and establish for ourselves a position. This is essentially necessary for our effective elevation as a people, in shaping our national development, directing our destiny and redeeming ourselves as a race." A Negro empire was further necessary to put "a check to European presumption and insufferable Yankee intrusion and impudence." [73]

Although the conference adopted Delany's report, there were distinct territorial preferences among those who thought in terms of the Western hemisphere. Whitfield favored colonization in Central America, while Holly opted for Haiti. No public announcement about Africa emerged from the conference, but that too had been discussed. According to Delany: "The Convention ... in its Secret Session made Africa, with its inexhaustible productions and the great facilities for checking the abominable Slave Trade, its most important point of dependence; though our first gun was levelled, and the first shell thrown at the American continent driving the slave-holding faction into despair ... Africa was held in reserve." [74] As a result of the conference, the National Emigration Board was set up. Delany began negotiations with "several states of Central and South America as well as Jamaica and Cuba." [75] Holly left for

[69] Cromwell, "Early Negro Convention," 16.

[70] *Frederick Douglass' Paper*, VI (Oct. 6, 1853 *et seq.*).

[71] Delany, *Official Report*, 6.

[72] Martin R. Delany, "Political Destiny of the Colored Race of the American Continent," appendix no. 3, in *Report of the Select Committee on Emancipation and Colonization* (Washington, 1862), 37–59.

[73] *Ibid.*, 43.

[74] Delany, *Official Report*, 8–9.

[75] *Ibid.*, 10.

Haiti to conduct negotiations there, which, although inconclusive, were encouraging enough to cause him on his return to begin agitating for Negro emigration to that territory.[76] In August 1856, the biennial meeting of the National Emigration Conference convened again in Cleveland; delegates supported emigration again and decided to organize a publishing company for propaganda purposes.

I V

As the conflict between Delany and Blyden shows, it was not merely a dispute between emigrationists and their opponents that was preventing a rapid flow of Negroes back to Africa. The emigrationists were quarreling among themselves. Fortunately for those who wished emigration to Africa, Delany abandoned his scheme for an empire in the Americas, soon after the National Emigration Conference in Cleveland. Whitfield died in California on his way to Central America, and Delany began to develop a positive enthusiasm for Africa, stimulated by the publication in 1857 of works by Thomas Bowen and David Livingstone.[77] In particular, it was Bowen's "intelligent and interesting account of Yorubaland" which spurred him to explore the Niger Valley in search of a base for a Negro nation.[78] Even when he turned to Africa, Delany persisted in looking beyond Liberia. His enthusiasm for an expedition to Yorubaland was matched by that of his assistant, Robert Campell, a young Jamaica-born chemist. When the third National Emigration Conference met in Chatham, Ontario, in August 1858, Delany had his plans ready. The conference endorsed the expedition to the Niger Valley as well as Holly's Haitian scheme.

Those interested in West Africa received further help in 1858 when the African Civilization Society was formed, with Henry Highland Garnet as president, to support emigration to that region. Garnet was one of the most aggressive of the American Negro leaders. As early as 1843, he had called on slaves "to rise in their might and strike a blow for their lives and liberties," a counsel which, although it won the endorsement of John Brown, failed to win the general support of Negroes.[79] He left the United States in 1850 for England, where he lectured as an abolitionist for three years. On his return to the United States in 1855, he became a strong supporter of emigration. He had no sym-

[76] James T. Holly, A Vindication of the Capacity of the Negro Race for Self-Government, and Civilized Progress, as Demonstrated by Historical Events of the Haitian Revolution; and the Subsequent Act of the People since their National Independence (New Haven, 1857), preface.

[77] These were Thomas J. Bowen, Central Africa: Adventures and Missionary Labors in the Interior of Africa, from 1849–1856 (Charleston, 1857), and Dr. Livingstone's Seventeen Years' Explorations and Adventures in the Wilds of Africa, John Hartley Coomb, ed. (Philadelphia, 1857).

[78] Delany, Official Report, 10.

[79] John W. Cromwell, The Negro in American History (Washington, 1916), 126; also William Wells Brown, The Black Man: His Antecedents, His Genius, and His Achievements (Boston, 1863), 149–152.

pathy for those Negro leaders who opposed free emigration to Africa simply because slaveholders promoted it, and he castigated Frederick Douglass and his associates as "humbugs who oppose everything they do not originate."[80] The main object of Garnet's society was "to establish a grand center of Negro nationality from which shall flow the streams of commercial, intellectual, and political power which shall make colored people respected everywhere." [81] Though he preferred such a center to be founded in West Africa through select American Negro emigration, he was not averse to the building of a Negro state in the Americas. Furthermore, by 1858, a few Liberian trading vessels were plying regularly between the Negro republic and eastern American ports. Garnet was impressed by this; the establishment of a vast commercial network between West Africa and Negro America, he wrote, "would do more for the overthrowing of slavery, in creating a respect for ourselves, than fifty thousand lectures of the most eloquent men of this land." [82]

In turning to West Africa as the geographical center for their pan-Negro program, the Delany-Garnet groups were not overlooking one of their major objectives: the overthrow of slavery in the United States. The new plan, in theory, represented a more effective strategy: it would bring about the collapse of American slavery as well as annihilate the slave trade at its source. The first object was to be attained by the planting of cotton in the selected sites, with the object of underselling in world markets the cotton produced in the Southern states.[83] American Negroes, with their special knowledge of the cotton culture, so it was reasoned, were peculiarly well fitted to succeed in this.

Campell, Delany's assistant, reached West Africa before his leader. On June 24, 1859, he sailed from Liverpool aboard the "splendid ship, Ethiopia," in the company of an American Negro from New York, John Bennet, who had invested $125 in two cotton gins and was on his way to Lagos to start an independent venture in cotton growing.[84] Campell landed at Freetown, Sierra Leone, on July 12, and here met "several natives . . . of respectability and . . . education." [85] He made short stops at Cape Palmas and Cape Coast before arriving at Lagos on July 21. Through the acting British consul of Lagos, Lieutenant Lodder, Campell met Okukenu, the Alake of Abeokuta, and found him favorable to the idea of select Negro emigration into his territory. Already in the Alake's domains were several hundred emigrants—"semi-civilized" liberated Africans from Sierra Leone who had returned to their homeland or had been repatriated from Brazil and Cuba.[86] In Campell's view, these emigrants "had inaugurated a mighty work, which . . . must be continued in a higher

[80] *Weekly Anglo-African,* I (Sept. 3, 1859).
[81] *Ibid.*
[82] *Ibid.*
[83] *Ibid.*; also Delany, *Official Report,* 14.
[84] *Weekly Anglo-African,* I (Sept. 3, 1859).
[85] Campell, *Pilgrimage,* 11.
[86] *Ibid.,* 18. For the fullest treatment of this, see Jean F. Herskovitts, "Liberated Africans and the History of Lagos Colony to 1886" (unpublished dissertation, Oxford, 1960).

form by the more civilized of the race." He advocated that emigrants should organize on "municipal" lines. But his goal was that of a "national government" which would require the cooperation and support of native Africans. He therefore advised prospective emigrants to "remember that the existing rulers must be respected, for they alone are the *bona fide* rulers of the place. The effort should be to fit them up to the proper standard, and not to supersede or crush them." [87]

Delany, leader of the Niger Valley exploring party, sailed from New York aboard the Liberian vessel, *Mendi*, on May 24, 1859, and arrived in Monrovia early in July. Also aboard the *Mendi* as an emigrant to Liberia was William C. Monroe, an Episcopalian clergyman from Detroit, a former missionary to Haiti, and former president of the National Emigration Conference, who had come to believe that Liberia was "the chief instrument in determining the future destiny of the Negro race." [88] In Monrovia Delany received a hero's welcome as he reported to a large public meeting of Liberians, who had come "from all parts of the country," that "the desire of African nationality has brought me to these shores." [89] At Grand Bassa, a council of "the most eminent Liberians" approved Delany's mission and policy. This meeting gave Delany "one of the most happy hours of his life" and produced in him "an unforgettable and profound sensation." [90] On July 26, he participated in Liberia's twelfth annual Independence Day celebration, which "came off with grand effect." [91] On August 1, Delany and Blyden, now much closer together in policy, were speakers at the twenty-fifth anniversary of the emancipation of British West Indian Negroes, celebrated "with great spirit by the leading citizens of Liberia." [92]

Delany left Monrovia on August 4, 1859, for Cape Palmas, where he stayed six weeks. During his two and a half months' stay in Liberia, Delany moved even further toward Blyden's views: his opposition to the Negro republic had been transformed into support. He was especially impressed with the area up St. Paul's River—its beautiful location, its thriving sugar and coffee plantations, its "livestock of all kinds," and its neat brick houses.[93] Although still wishing to see the Negro republic more self-reliant, he was now able to recommend it to the "intelligent of the race." [94] Blyden had also been prominent in welcoming Delany. He hailed him as "the far-famed champion of the elevation of colored men," as the "Moses" who would "lead the exodus of his people from the house of bondage." [95]

Delany reached Lagos on September 20, spending five weeks there and

[87] Campell, *Pilgrimage*, 137.
[88] *Weekly Anglo-African*, I (Oct. 1, 1859). Holly's *Vindication* was dedicated to Monroe.
[89] *Weekly Anglo-African*, I (Oct. 1, 1859).
[90] Delany, *Official Report*, 23.
[91] *Weekly Anglo-African*, I (Sept. 24, 1859).
[92] *Ibid.*, I (Oct. 15, 1859).
[93] *Ibid.*, I (Sept. 24, 1859).
[94] *New York Colonization Journal*, IX (Oct. 1859).
[95] *Ibid.*

winning the confidence of Docemo, king of Lagos. Delany wrote to Garnet from Lagos:

> Lagos is a fine, and will be a great, commercial city. It is destined to be the great metropolis of this part of the world. Entirely under a black government, it only wants a few of the right stamp of black men to make it one of the most desirable cities in the world. They bid us come, and to that end the authorities have presented me with two acres of land in the heart of the city plot on which to build my residence . . .
>
> There will be for you and also Mr. J. T. Holly, after our return to Africa, a fine prospect in this rich city of Lagos, where Christians . . . desire to have black instead of white preachers.[96]

From Lagos he went to Abeokuta, where he joined his fellow commissioner, Robert Campell, and together they spent six weeks touring the principal cities of Yorubaland. On their return to Abeokuta, they held talks with the obas and chiefs and, on December 27, signed a treaty that assigned to them as "Commissioners on behalf of the African race in America the right and privilege of settling in common with the Egba people, on any part of the territory belonging to Abeokuta, not otherwise occupied." [97] The signing of the treaty was witnessed by the famous African missionary, Samuel Crowther, and his son, Samuel, Jr. Delany had taken the first step, he felt, in "the grandest prospect for regeneration of a people that ever presented itself in the history of the world." [98]

The expedition had aroused great curiosity and interest in both humanitarian and commercial circles in England; men were deeply divided on the issues of the coming American civil war, and attention was turning to sources of supply of cotton in areas outside the United States.[99] On their way back to the United States, Delany and Campell arrived in London on May 17, 1860, and on the next day were invited to a meeting "of a number of noblemen and gentlemen interested in Africa's Regeneration," held in the parlor of Dr. Thomas Hodgkin. A series of meetings was subsequently called, from which grew the African Aid Society, founded to assist by "loans or otherwise" the emigration of Negroes from North America to Africa for the purpose of cultivating tropical products, including cotton, and of promoting "the Christian Civilization of the African Races and the annihilation of the slave trade." Though extremely cautious of any alliance with white men, Delany agreed to cooperate with the society after he had impressed upon its members that the relations between the two groups were to involve strictly business, and that Negro emigrants were to be completely free in managing their own affairs. "Our policy," Delany emphasized, "must be . . . Africa for the African race and black men to rule them." [100]

V

Although Delany had abandoned his idea of an empire in Central America and Whitfield had died, James T. Holly was still active in promoting his scheme for emigration to Haiti. The scheme began to gain support even before Delany and Campell left for West Africa. The emigrationist position was generally strengthened by the Dred Scott decision of 1857,[101] which led directly to the founding of the *Weekly Anglo-African* and the *Anglo-African Magazine* by Robert Hamilton, who in 1859 urged Negroes to "set themselves zealously to work to create a position of their own—an empire which shall challenge the admiration of the world, rivalling the glory of their historic ancestors." [102] Meanwhile Holly was leading his campaign and in 1857 wrote of Haiti's revolution: "This revolution is one of the noblest, grandest and most justifiable outbursts against oppression that is recorded in the pages of history ... [it] is also the grandest political event in this or any other age ... it surpasses the American revolution in an incomparable degree." [103] "Never before," he continued, "in all the annals of the world's history did a nation of abject and chattel slaves arise in the terrific might of their resuscitated manhood, and regenerate, redeem and disenthral themselves: by taking their station at one gigantic bound, as an independent nation among the sovereignties of the world."

His object in recounting this phase of Haitian history was to arouse Negroes of the United States "to a full consciousness of their own inherent dignity." They were to help in building up Haiti "until its glory and renown overspread and cover the whole earth, and redeem and regenerate by its influence in the future, the benighted Fatherland of the race of Africa." As a tactical measure, Holly was against immediate American Negro emigration to Africa: for a start, efforts should be concentrated on building a "Negro Nationality in the New World." Such a successful state would then "shed its ... beams upon the Fatherland of the race." [104]

The Haitian emigration movement received a further fillip when the Haitian government gave it official sanction. The Haitian "Call for Emigration" was issued on August 22, 1859, by R. E. DuBois, Secretary of State for Justice and Public Worship.[105] Haiti's doors were now open to all Negroes who wished to emigrate. Fabre Geffrard, the new president who seemed bent on reforming Haitian society, joined in the appeal, inviting Negroes to bring "their arms and minds." He predicted: "Haiti will soon regain her ancient splendor ... and ... will be a formal denial, most eloquent and peremptory, against the detractors of our race who contest our ability to attain a high degree of civilization." [106] And F. J. Joseph, Secretary of State for Agriculture, who was directly responsible for settling emigrants, said that "welcoming men of

[101] John Hope Franklin, *From Slavery to Freedom* (New York, 1956), 264.
[102] *Weekly Anglo-African*, I (July 23, 1859).
[103] Holly, *Vindication*, 7.
[104] *Ibid.*, 8.
[105] *New York Colonization Journal*, X (July 1860); Redpath, *Guide*, 97–99.
[106] *Ibid.*, preface.

our blood, the victims of these outrageous persecutions, is to continue the work of rehabilitation undertaken by the Founders of the Republic, and to remain faithful to the National Traditions." [107] Among the agents of the Haitian emigration bureau were Holly and Garnet, the latter showing his willingness to support emigration both within the New World and to Africa.

Events in the United States were continuing to give impetus to the emigration movement: the failure of John Brown's raid, the split in the Democratic Party, and the founding of the avowedly anti-slavery Republican Party had both exacerbated feelings against Negroes and increased the interest in emigration. By January 1861, the Haitian emigration campaign seemed to be succeeding. After five weeks in Philadelphia, Holly reported that "the choicest spirits among our people...are thoroughly awake to the importance of the present movement and ready to give it their contribution." [108] Garnet also rejoiced "to see that there are more of the colored people...in favor of this movement than they are of any other of the present age." [109] Indeed, by 1861 almost all American Negro leaders had given some expression of support to Negro emigration. Even the formidable Frederick Douglass gave in and accepted an invitation by the Haitian government to visit that country.[110]

Thus, when Delany and Campell returned to the United States in late December 1860, they found that the feeling for emigration was stronger than ever. But Delany did not become involved in a conflict with the Haiti group. He soon let it be known that he was preparing for "a hasty return to Africa where my duty calls me." He called for the cooperation in his venture "of intelligent persons...of various occupations, among whom mechanics and cotton cultivators are acceptable." Select emigration was essential, he felt, to ensure the success of his plan; for "Africa is our fatherland, we, its legitimate descendants, and we will never agree or consent to see this...step that has been taken for her regeneration by her own descendants blasted." [111]

Liberians, too, were encouraged by the steady, if moderate, flow of emigrants. In the 1850s, Liberia had settled a total of 5,029—almost as many as had been settled in the previous thirty years. The Negro republic's incorporation of Maryland in 1857 and purchase of territory in the area of the Mano and Gallinas Rivers had given it a coastline of 500 miles. Late in 1860, the Reverend James Payne wrote a series of articles in the *Liberia Herald* entitled "A Plea for Liberia," with a view to arresting the attention of American Negroes and directing their attention to the land of their fathers. And the vice-president, D. B. Warner, a close friend of Blyden's, wrote that he was gratified "that Liberia had begun to make a favourable impression abroad among whites and colored." He hoped American Negroes would "reestablish themselves in this our fatherland." [112]

---

[107] *Ibid.*, 104.   [108] *Weekly Anglo-African*, II (Feb. 16, 1861).
[109] *Ibid.*, II (Jan. 26, 1861).
[110] Howard H. Bell, "Negro Nationalism: A Factor in Emigration Projects, 1858–61," *Journal of Negro History*, XLVIII (Jan. 1962), 43.
[111] *Weekly Anglo-African*, I (Jan. 26, 1861).
[112] *African Repository*, XXXVI (Jan. 1861), 87.

There is one more Negro leader who should be mentioned here, Alexander Crummell. He left the United States in 1847 at the age of thirty-six; after graduating from Queens College, Cambridge, he went to Liberia in 1853. As in the case of Blyden, he sought to bring about reform in Liberian society and to impress upon his countrymen their high responsibility.[113] He wanted Liberia to extend its influence and jurisdiction over the inland peoples, and he took a leading part in organizing schemes for exploring and opening up the interior. In September 1860 he published an open letter to win the support of all the American Negro leaders, both emigrationists and anti-emigrationists, for Africa.[114]

To appease the anti-emigrationists, he rejected the idea that America could never be the home of the Negro, but he maintained that the task of civilizing Africa was peculiarly that of westernized Negroes: "without doubt God designs great things for Africa and ... black men themselves are without doubt to be the chief instruments." The civilizing process could be accomplished by voluntary emigration, by the pooling of economic resources and inauguration of trade between America and Africa, and by support of the missionary activities of American Negro churches. "From the port of Lagos in almost direct line through a crowded population, and passing by cities containing tens of thousands of people, a highway is now open reaching to Rabba on the banks of the Niger. All through this country the coloured churches of America can send their missionaries, build up Christian churches, and lay the foundation of Christian colleges and universities." [115] By utilizing this combination of commerce and Christianity, not only would Africa be civilized, but American Negroes would gain in wealth and respect:

> At an early date whole fleets of vessels, manned and officered from the United States and Liberia, would outrival all the other agencies which are now being used for grasping West African commerce. Large and important houses will spring into existence among you, all through the States. Wealth will flow into your coffers, and affluence would soon exhibit itself amid all your associations.
>
> The kings and tradesmen of Africa, having the demonstration of Negro capacity before them, would hail the presence of their black kinsmen from America and would be stimulated by a generous emulation ... To the farthest interior, leagues and combinations would be formed with men of commerce, and thus civilization, enlightenment and Christianity would be carried to every state and town, and village of interior Africa.[116]

[113] See, for example, Alexander Crummell, *The Duty of a Rising Christian State, Annual Oration Before the Common Council and Citizens of Monrovia, Liberia, July 26, 1855.* (London, 1856).

[114] Alexander Crummell, *The Relation and Duties of the Free Colored Men in America to Africa* (Hartford, 1861), 55.

[115] *Ibid.,* 45.   [116] *Ibid.,* 25.

Crummell, like Blyden and Delany, had strongly supported the founding of Liberia College, on which construction had begun by 1860. The college was to be the first modern, secular English-speaking institution of higher education in tropical Africa. Crummell and other Negro patriots hoped that the college would attract Negro scholars and students from all parts of the world.

Crummell and Blyden left Liberia in February 1861 for England and America, to win financial support for the college and to study institutions of higher learning. In England, Blyden met W. E. Gladstone, Chancellor of the Exchequer, with whom he had been in correspondence, and Lord Brougham, the great humanitarian, both of whom he sought to interest in the "little Republic" that was destined to "revolutionize for good that whole portion of Africa." [117]

When Blyden and Crummell arrived in the United States in June 1861, war had already begun between the Union and the Confederacy. But this seemed to make no difference to the plans of the emigrationists. By May, Delany and Campell had joined forces with Garnet's African Civilization Society in an attempt to raise funds to promote colonization in the Niger Valley.[118] Campell, "appearing in native costumes," lectured regularly on West Africa and vowed that "my home shall be in Africa though I be the only person from America." [119] Delany and Campell had each published a book describing the expedition to the Niger Valley and propagandizing for the cause of colonization.[120] In November the African Civilization Society increased its strength by gaining the support of men who held high offices in the African Methodist Episcopal Church.[121]

Blyden and Crummell joined with the other emigrationists. Blyden himself welcomed the civil war as the "purifier of a demoralised American conscience," [122] and no doubt as a means of bringing slavery to an end. However, he warned Negroes that they were deceiving themselves if they thought they could earn proper respect in the United States. He urged them to be makers and witnesses of history: "It need not imply any pretensions to prophetic insight for us to declare that we live in the shadows of remarkable events in the history of Africa."[123] Crummell asserted that "the free black man of this country . . . is superior to the Russian, the Polander, the Italian" and was now "in a state of preparedness for a new world's history, for a mission of civilization." He saw the decline of Anglo-Saxon civilizations in "the moral and political convulsion" within the United States. But "now the Negro is

[117] Blyden to Gladstone, May 3, 1861, British Museum Add. Mss. 44396/63; Blyden to Lord Brougham, May 24, 1861, Brougham Papers, University College, London.

[118] Constitution of the African Civilization Society (New Haven, 1861), 1.

[119] Weekly Anglo-African, II (March 16, 1861).

[120] Delany, Official Report, and Campell, Pilgrimage.

[121] Constitution of the African Civilization Society, 4.

[122] Blyden to Gladstone, June 16, 1862, British Museum Add. Mss. 44398/183.

[123] Edward W. Blyden, Hope for Africa, A Discourse . . . (tract no. 8 from the Colonization Journal, 1861), 16.

rising and will rise ... God has destined a great future for the Negro race ...
On the continent of Africa, a civilization of a new type and more noble and
generous ... than has ever existed, is on the eve of starting a new life." [124]

When Blyden and Crummell returned to Liberia in the fall of 1861, they
reported the support of American Negroes for emigration. The Liberian government decided to act: legislation was passed by which Blyden and Crummell
were appointed commissioners "to protect the cause of Liberia to the descendants of Africa in that country, and to lay before them the claims that
Africa had upon their sympathies, and the paramount advantages that would
accrue to them, their children and their race by their return to the fatherland." [125]

The action of the Liberian government had little effect. The outbreak
of the civil war was the turning point after which there was a fairly sharp
decline in pan-Negro nationalism. At the start of the war, Douglass canceled
his trip to Haiti and urged American Negroes to stay and help to decide the
outcome of the struggle, advice that apparently found quick response. The
emigrationists, who had at first regarded the war as irrelevant to their plans,
were unable to act because of lack of funds. The war apart, emigration to Haiti
had by December 1861 virtually come to an end because of reports of the
high mortality rate among the emigrants and unattractive living conditions.[126]
There was a correspondingly swift decline in emigration to Liberia. By early
1862, Negro leaders were again united to work for the victory of the North.
Indeed, when in the summer of 1862 Lincoln decided to put into effect his
scheme for gradual Negro emancipation with colonization, he received no
support from American Negro leaders.[127] Thus when Blyden and Crummell
returned to the United States as official commissioners in the summer of 1862,
to urge American Negroes to "return to the fatherland," they found "an
indolent and unmeaning sympathy—sympathy which put forth no effort, made
no sacrifices, endured no self-denial, braved no obloquy for the sake of advancing African interests." [128] Further, Lincoln's proclamation of January 1,
1863, ending slavery, and the use later in that year of Negro troops in the
Union army, made American Negroes feel sure that a new day had dawned
for them.

In this they were wrong, of course. Although Negroes were awarded
political and civil rights during the period of Reconstruction (1867–1877),
their hopes of full integration within American society were largely frustrated.
This disappointment, continuing throughout the nineteenth century and into
the twentieth, again resulted in a desire to leave for other parts of the Americas or for Africa. Many Negro leaders once more urged emigration to Africa:

[124] *African Repository*, XXXVII (Sept. 1861), 279.
[125] Cited in the American Colonization Society, *Forty-Sixth Annual Report*
(Washington, 1863), 6.
[126] Benjamin Quarles, *Lincoln and the Negro* (New York, 1962), 120.
[127] Benjamin Quarles, *The Negro in the Civil War* (Boston, 1953), 147–149.
[128] Blyden, *Liberia's Offering*, 69.

Henry M. Turner, bishop in the African Methodist Episcopal Church; Pap Singleton; R. H. Cain, like Turner an AME bishop; J. McCants Stewart, a lawyer; and J. Albert Thorne, a doctor from Barbados. Their activities are, however, beyond the scope of this article.[129]

VII

Pan-Negro nationalists before 1862 did not succeed in creating and sustaining either a return to Africa on a large scale or any significant and persistent contact with African communities. The movement did not come to an end in 1862 and, in spite of the difficulties of the years following the American civil war, it is hardly likely that everyone at the first Pan-African conference of 1900 had forgotten the personalities and events of fifty years earlier. The twentieth-century Pan-Africanists were concerned that Negroes should mobilize to defend and extend their rights wherever they lived. They held their first congress in London, the most imperial of capital cities, in the middle of the South African War, and increasingly they identified themselves with the larger movement against imperialism.

Nineteenth-century pan-Negro nationalism and Garveyism had much in common. They both owed their existence almost entirely to discrimination against Negroes in the New World, particularly in the United States. They shared a preoccupation with emigration, with a great African past, and with an equally great future, and both relied heavily on leaders from the West Indies, particularly those who had lived in the United States. Nineteenth-century pan-Negro nationalism produced no leader to match Marcus Garvey in the emotional quality of his oratory, the scale of organization and mobilization of resources he achieved, or, indeed, the bitter disillusionment that followed his failure. Though the nineteenth-century movement did achieve a sustained, if limited, emigration, both movements failed to achieve a massive emigration to Africa or its "regeneration."

In their frequent references to the need for action to save Africa, and to prove by deeds the fundamental equality of Africans with other peoples, these Negroes from the New World showed their indebtedness to the societies from which they came. References to the effects of "commerce and Christianity," "the mission of civilization," the great resources of Africa, and the racial bases of society are found as much in the writings of the pan-Negro nationalists as in the writings of missionary groups and subsequently among some believers in imperial rule. It is, however, in reference to "regeneration," with its implication of a great African past, and to the frontal attack on notions of white superiority that the pan-Negro nationalists of the nineteenth century were pioneers.

[129] See August Meier, *Negro Thought in America, 1880–1915* (Ann Arbor, 1963).

St. Clair Drake

"HIDE MY FACE?"
ON PAN-AFRICANISM AND NEGRITUDE

I ran to the rocks to hide my face;
The rocks cried out, No hiding place,
There's no hiding place down here.

A SPIRITUAL

As the selection by Hollis Lynch indicates, identification with
Africa has been a persistent theme in American Negro thinking,
muted in some periods, heightened in others. This concern—often
laden, it is true, with considerable ambivalence toward the ancestral
continent—has ranged from an interest in the African past and
African culture to the advocacy of colonization as a solution for the
problems facing black men in America. In "Hide My Face?" St.
Clair Drake has explored with great sensitivity and subtlety the
attitudes of American Negroes toward Africa in the twentieth cen-
tury. Although written in 1965, before the current emphasis upon
"black consciousness," the essay perceptively predicted the swelling
sense of race pride and identification with Africa which exists today.

THE end of the Second World War marked the beginning of the liberation of Africa and of racial integration in the United States. Although there is no direct causal connection between the two momentous developments, they are interrelated and they influence each other. That they occurred at approximately the same time has profound implications for Negro Americans, all of whom are aware that they are "of African descent." In America, this "African descent" is considered to be the only really socially relevant fact about Negroes, and some states actually define a Negro as "anyone with an ascertainable trace of Negro blood." Whether those who are defined as "American Negroes" like it or not, history and the peculiar evaluations of American society have linked them

St. Clair Drake, "Hide My Face?" in Herbert Hill, ed., *Soon, One Morning* (New York: Alfred A. Knopf, 1963), pp. 78–105. Reprinted with permission of St. Clair Drake.

with the fate of Africa and its peoples. This is a reality to which Negroes in the United States have always had to adjust.

In 1925, the distinguished American Negro literary critic Alain Locke presented an anthology to the public which bore the title *The New Negro*. The poets, essayists, and writers of fiction whose works appeared in the volume were participants in what came to be called the "Negro Renaissance," that remarkable outburst of literary creativity which followed the First World War. The dominant theme in the work of all these writers was "the Negro experience." The intellectual vanguard of ten million Negro Americans were expressing the moods and wishes, the aspirations and frustrations, the joy as well as the anger, of their ethnic group. They were also revealing their own sensitive reactions to reality, and laying bare the distinctive configurations of ideas and emotions which each had elaborated in order to cope with reality. For some of them, Africa was a part of this reality.

Alain Locke in his own essay, "The Negro's Americanism," dissociated himself from those who saw extensive evidence of African cultural survivals in the United States, insisting that "what there is today in Harlem distinct from the white culture that surrounds it is, as far as I am able to see, merely a remnant from the peasant days in the South. Of the African culture not a trace." But he did not mean by this that he was unconcerned with Africa or African culture. African art was one of his consuming interests.

The two most talented of the "New Negro" poets, Langston Hughes and Countee Cullen, felt impelled to speak of a sense of "kinship" with Africa. Langston Hughes's confrontation of the African reality was composed of bewilderment tinged with nostalgia, as these lines from "Afro-American Fragment" suggest:

> So long,
> So far away
> Is Africa....
> Through some vast mist of race
> There comes the song
> I do not understand...

Apparently Langston Hughes could not bring himself to accept the kind of "understanding" which his fellow troubadour, a white man, Vachel Lindsay, had achieved. He too had heard the song "Boomlay, boomlay, boomlay, BOOM." Lindsay was so sure *he* understood that he gave his poem "The Congo" a subtitle, "A Study of the Negro Race." The poetic "study" was divided into three parts: "Their Basic Savagery," "Their Irresponsible High Spirits," and "The Hope of Their Religion." Vachel Lindsay had no doubts about the origin of the gusto which expressed itself in drunken table pounding by

> Fat black bucks in a wine-barrel room,
> Barrel house kings with feet unstable.

They had inherited the wild emotions of "tatooed cannibals." He could plainly see "the Congo creeping through the black," and this "insight" also explained to him why

> Wild crap shooters with a whoop and a call
> Danced the juba in their gambling hall. . . .
> Guyed the policemen and laughed them down . . .

These American Negroes were simply blood kinsmen of "cake walk princes . . . fat as shotes" cavorting in the jungle, and putting "the skull-faced lean witch doctors" to rout with their exhuberant dancing. Both Africans and American Negroes such as these were under the spell of "Mumbo Jumbo, God of the Congo," the god who will "hoodoo you."

But Vachel Lindsay also saw a vision of hope for Negroes, in Africa and America:

> A good old Negro in the slums of the town
> Preached at a sister for her velvet gown,
> Howled at a brother for his low down ways. . . .
> And the people all repented a thousand strong
> From their stupor and savagery and sin and wrong.

So Mumbo Jumbo died in the jungle, and "pioneer angels cleared the way for a Congo paradise . . . a singing wind swept the Negro nation . . . and redeemed were the forests, the beasts, and the men . . ."

Such eschatological anthropology was widely shared by Americans during the early years of the century, offensive as it may sound to modern ears. Both the image of African savagery and the implications of inherited African traits repelled many American Negroes, while others accepted the image, believed in the myths, and worked for the specific variety of "redemption" about which Vachel Lindsay wrote. The "New Negro" had to come to terms with the image and the popular Negro reaction to it.

Langston Hughes did not reject identification with Africa because he saw it as a derogation. He sought, rather, for the deeper understanding that comes from knowledge and empathy.

Countee Cullen, too, chose to grapple with the African reality and America's distortion of it. In his long, rich, image-laden poem "Heritage," Africa emerges as a romantic land of "wild, barbaric birds, Goading massive jungle herds," a land of supple cats and slithering snakes." Mumbo Jumbo was present too, for Cullen found "Quaint, outlandish heathen gods, Black men fashion out of rods." Africa was, to him, the setting for a D. H. Lawrence paradise where "Young forest lovers lie, Plighting troth beneath the sky."

Vachel Lindsay's evangelical Puritanism led him to reject Africa until it should have been "redeemed." Cullen not only accepts it as it is, but also rejects the vision of "redemption." He even expresses regret that he and other American Negroes have been subjected to such "redemption," for he sees them as having been symbolically castrated in the process:

> *My conversion came high-priced,*
> *I belong to Jesus Christ....*
> *Lamb of God although I speak*
> *With my mouth thus, in my heart*
> *Do I play a double part....*
> *Wishing he I served were black ...?*
> *Not yet has my heart or head*
> *In the least way realized*
> *They and I are civilized.*

Cullen bemoans the fact that Christianity has forced him to "Quench my pride and cool my blood." This romantic, neo-pagan response to Africa was probably as shocking to most middle-class Negroes as Vachel Lindsay's was repulsive. The significant thing is that Countee Cullen felt he *had* to respond to Africa.

Langston Hughes heard "the song" through "some vast mist of race," and said frankly, "I do not understand." Countee Cullen, however, reported that he too felt "the Congo creeping through the black," or, as he phrased it, "The unremitten beat Of cruel padded feet Walking through my body's street." And like the feet in Thompson's "Hound of Heaven," they beat with "majestic instancy," and made him cry out, "Ever must I twist and squirm, Writhing like a baited worm." Cullen, in this mood, felt that American culture was stifling what the African poet Senghor would call his *negritude*. Cullen began his poem with a query:

> *What is Africa to me*
> *Copper sun or scarlet sea,*
> *Jungle star or jungle track,*
> *Strong bronzed men, or regal black,*
> *Women from whose loins I sprang*
> *When the birds of Eden sang?*
> *One three centuries removed*
> *From the scenes his fathers loved,*
> *Spicy grove, cinnamon tree,*
> *What is Africa to me?*

In 1951, Akinsola Akiwowo, a Nigerian student studying in the United States, wrote "Song in a Strange Land," which appeared in *Phylon*, a quarterly published by Atlanta University. His artistry is not so polished as that of either Langston Hughes or Countee Cullen, but the sentiments are significant:

> *Shall I sing your song, Africa,*
> *In this strange land of hate and love?*
> *Shall I sing to them whose forebears*
> *Were torn away from you long ago?*
> *For they know you not, but believe*

All the strange and gory stories
They oft have read and seen in films:
Apes, thick jungles, and men with spears,
And nude women with pancake lips.
They have not seen how, what, you are;
That long estrangement shuts their eyes . . .
Some say you are a thing of shame!

.   .   .

But fill our hearts, Africa's sons,
With holy untiring zest to work,
And ask no rest till She is free
And great with true greatness from Thee.
Then make them see again, dear Lord;
Open their ears, unleash their tongues
And make them see, hear, proclaim
What they now refuse to apprehend!

Since "Song in a Strange Land" was sung, "holy untiring zest" has brought results. In 1961 African states were sitting in the United Nations. A new image of Africa was in the making.

The struggle for independence and for national development is something all American Negroes can understand, and it is a phenomenon with which they can all identify.

The wheel has come full circle, for when the Governor General of Nigeria was inaugurated, Langston Hughes was among the honored guests. (He had been a schoolmate of Governor Azikiwe at Lincoln University.) The governor ended his address by quoting Hughes's poem of optimism, "Dawn." Meanwhile, Langston Hughes had been hearing songs from Africa which he could understand. He had never abandoned the effort to understand. So he compiled an anthology, *An African Treasury: Articles, Essays, Stories, Poems by Black Africans.* Having understood, he was now taking it upon himself to interpret, and in the introduction to this volume he wrote:

When I first began to gather this material, the term *negritude*—currently popular with African writers, especially poets influenced by Senghor—had not come into common use. But there was in most of the writing that reached me an accent of Africanness—blackness, if you will—not unlike the racial consciousness found in the work of American Negro writers a quarter of a century ago. The Harlem writers of that period, however, had to search for their folk roots. The African writer has these roots right at hand. . . . Evident in most African writing, of course, is a pride in country, which underlies everything that is thought and spoken south of the Sahara today. It is an African pride with a character all its own, which owes allegiance neither to West nor East but to its newly emerging self. . . . Perhaps the phrase that best sums up this swelling pride and fierce insistence on individual identity is *African Personality*. . . . While it is a personality necessarily—and happily—as varied as the people of Africa, it is founded on a common bond, a common yearning . . . 'Come back, Africa!'

CULTURAL PAN-AFRICANISM

The term "negritude" was first used by the Haitian poet Aimé Césaire and by the Senegalese scholar-poet Léopold Senghor. The American Negro scholar Samuel Allen has pointed out in his essay "Tendencies in African Poetry":

The term is not amenable to easy definition. . . . It represents in one sense the Negro African poet's endeavor to recover for his race a normal self-pride, a lost confidence in himself, a world in which he again has a sense of identity and a significant role.

But, in another dimension, the term denotes the assumption that there are impulses, traits, and conceptions of the world which are characteristic of Negroes everywhere. To Senghor, these include "softness" and a non-mechanical approach to men and things, "spirituality," and a direct but symbol-laden approach to sexuality. Senghor sees negritude as that quality of life in Harlem which "softens" the hardness of New York. And he recognizes it in the American soldiers on the streets of Paris, to whom he speaks as follows:

> Behind your strong face, I did not recognize you.
> Yet I had only to touch the warmth of your dark hand—
> my name is Africa!
> And I discovered lost laughter again, and heard old
> voices, and the roaring rapids of the Congo.
>
>   .   .   .
>
> Oh black brothers, warriors whose mouths are
> singing flowers—
> Delight of living when winter is over—
> You I salute as messengers of peace!

Allen points out that many American Negro intellectuals are

inclined to feel that to affirm the rights and dignity of the Negro as a man among men is one, and a valid, thing but to acclaim a specific quality or a complex of traits or attitudes as peculiarly Negro . . . is distinctly another matter and smacks of the racism American social scientists have patiently been attempting to erase.

However, he notes that, in fact, negritude has a dialectical dimension, that it involves what Jean-Paul Sartre calls in his *Black Orpheus* anti-racist racism;

it accentuates differentness in order to win respect and abolish differences. Those who assert their negritude most vigorously have never isolated themselves from the main stream of French intellectual and political life and are "deeply aware that man, ultimately, is man and that his race is an attribute, only, of his more basic membership in the human community." One suspects that, had he lived to know them, Countee Cullen would have felt very much at home with "the poets of negritude." Langston Hughes, on the other hand, displays a depth of understanding but does not seem to have been caught up in the mystique of either negritude or the "African Personality."

Whatever one may think of the concept of negritude in its relation to modern social science, or as it applies to American Negroes, it is important to realize that it serves the function of reinforcing the self-esteem of an emergent Africa, and of investing the struggle for African liberation with meanings that transcend the continent—a struggle believed to benefit people of African descent everywhere. And it is significant, too, that those who developed the concept of negritude have been profoundly influenced by the "Negro experience" in America. The Haitian intellectuals of the early 1920's were influenced by the Negro Renaissance in the United States, and a most distinguished member of their ranks, Dr. Jean Price Mars, influenced Senghor, who in his essay "Que Sais-Je?" has written:

> Studying at the Sorbonne, I began to reflect upon the problem of a
> cultural renaissance in Black Africa, and I was searching—all of us
> were searching for a "sponsorship" which could guarantee the success
> of the enterprise. At the end of my quest it was inevitable that I
> would find Alain Locke and Jean Price Mars.

In 1947 an African intellectual from Senegal, Alioune Diop, established the magazine Présence Africaine in Paris, under the sponsorship of such patrons as Sartre, Camus, and Paul Rivet, as a medium for self-expression by Negroes everywhere. Richard Wright, the American Negro novelist, was a member of the sponsoring group. In 1956 the Society of African Culture, which had arisen to give organized expression to the objectives of Présence Africaine, convened the First International Congress of Negro Writers and Artists in Paris. A number of American Negroes accepted an invitation to attend, and as a result, an American Society of African Culture came into being.

When the poet-philosopher of negritude, Léopold Senghor, visited the United States in 1962 in his role as President of Senegal, the American President arranged a literary luncheon in his honor at the White House. In his introduction, President Kennedy referred to the 16,000,000 American Negroes as a bridge between the United States and Africa. Senghor, in turn, payed tribute to the poets of the American Negro Renaissance of the twenties as an early source of inspiration for him and his fellow intellectuals in Paris. Both men seemed to assume that something other than the color of the skin forms an enduring—and desirable—bond between Africans and Negroes in the United States. So long as white Americans and Africans act upon such an assumption, Negro American intellectuals will be forced to participate in what their Continental counterparts refer to as a "dialogue," an effort to discover what the "something" is. "What is Africa to me?" becomes an inescapable question.

The French-speaking "poets of negritude" feel that the bond between New World Negroes and Africans lies in the persistence of certain African behavior patterns and approaches to life which have survived in the New World. Senghor is very explicit about this when he speaks of *the sense of communion, the gift of myth-making, the gift of rhythm*" as "the essential elements of negritude which you will find indelibly stamped on all the works and activities of the black man..." To him there is a Negro *élan*, the "active abandon of the African Negro toward the object" which is not only very real but is also a much-to-be-desired trait. He is convinced, furthermore, that Negroes differ fundamentally from white men in that "European reason is analytic through utilization; Negro reason is intuitive through participation." He even insists that "emotion is Negroid," and complains that he has been "wrongly reproached" for saying so, adding, "I do not see how one can account otherwise for our characteristics, for this negritude, which is the 'ensemble of cultural values of the black world' including the Americas, and which Sartre defines as 'a certain emotional attitude in respect to the world.'" As Sartre and Senghor see it, this Negro ethos expresses itself in various forms of art and ritual as well as in customs and institutions. It finds its purest expression, of course, in Negro-African cultures, but it is also evident in various aspects of Afro-Cuban, Afro-Brazilian, Afro-Haitian, and Afro-American cultural and social life. According to this view, where Negroes from Africa have been subjected to the influences of other cultures, they have borrowed and blended, rephrased and reinterpreted, but the end product always bears the stamp of negritude. (Senghor would probably cite the "swinging" of Anglo-Saxon hymn tunes in American Negro churches or the embroidering of Bible stories as vivid examples.) When groups or individuals try to suppress their negritude—and they can do so—they become "inauthentic Negroes, carbon copies of white men. They also thereby deprive the World Culture of the fructifying stimulus of 'Negro emotion.'"

In a paper prepared for the Second Congress of Negro writers and Artists, which met in Rome in 1959, Senghor presented an erudite and eloquent defense of his belief that the African tropical environment has, through the centuries, produced a human being with a special type of nervous and glandular system, "a being with open senses, permeable to all solicitations, even to the very waves of nature, without intermediary filtrants—I do not say without gaps —between subject and object. A thinking man to be sure, but first of all a man sensitive to forms and colors and especially to odors, sounds and rhythms." Such men are not confined to Africa. He writes:

> What strikes me concerning Negroes in America is the permanence
> of non-physical but psychic traits of the African Negro, despite the

mixture and despite the new environment. Some may try to explain this by segregation. To be sure, segregation explains partially the permanence of psychic traits, particularly the gift of emotion, but it does not explain all, especially not with Negroes of Latin America, where segregation is less real.

Certain of the reality of negritude and convinced that the African environment has produced it, Senghor falls back upon heredity for an explanation of both its tenacious persistence and the manner in which it changes. Speaking to a group of students at Oxford in 1962, he made an attempt to explain why negritude becomes diluted and attenuated when Negroes come in contact with other cultures, and revealed a Lamarckian view of inheritance in his comment that "as certain biologists point out, the psychological mutations brought about by education are incorporated in our genes and are transmitted by heredity." Thus, the negritude of New World Negroes has been changed through contact with a dominant culture (and by miscegenation), while the existence of negritude in Africa has been, and is, threatened by political and cultural imperialism.

It is not clear to what degree the so-called "apostles of negritude" agree with Senghor in detail, but all of them feel that the primary task of Negro intellectuals everywhere is to express negritude, proudly and without shame or apology, and to protect their cultures and literary and artistic traditions from being denigrated and disintegrated by bearers of "Western" culture (whether capitalist or communist). They feel that negritude should be cherished and cultivated and that enrichment from contact with other cultures should be carefully controlled. Negro Americans are summoned to participate along with Africans and West Indians in this historic task.

Most American Negro intellectuals have declined the invitation, although they have not broken off the dialogue. They feel that they have heard all of this before from the lips of enemies and patronizing white friends, and from Negro romantic primitivists of the twenties, such as Countee Cullen, as well as from less sophisticated members of their own group. It is disquieting to hear it now from a cultivated French-African savant. The concept of negritude elaborated by Senghor conjures up the ghost of Vachel Lindsay. It evokes unpleasant memories of Southern orators warning against the powerfulness of Negro blood that "always tells." It is a reminder of all the preachers—black and white (including Arnold Toynbee)—who espouse a peculiar kind of black messianism in which Negroes are said to have a mission to teach white men how to abjure materialistic goals and to demonstrate that patience and long-suffering are higher virtues than the iniquitous struggle for power. It presents an image of a kind of man they do not want to be, for they have no desire for "intuitive reason" in the place of "analytical reason." It rejects those values of the Western world which they have learned to prize—critical rationality, success in controlling the natural environment, Aristotle's Law of Measure, and, above all, individuality. It confuses race and culture, cause and effect, in a fashion they have learned to avoid. Senghor's voice seems to resound with echoes of Marcus Garvey, Mr. Mohammed, and Senator Bilbo. But above all, most Negro intellectuals reject this concept of negritude not only because they consider it undesirable but because they feel that it substitutes mysticism for science and ignores reality as they see it.

Yet, of the essential ingredients of negritude—a sense of communion, the gift of myth-making, and the gift of rhythm—they cannot deny their prevalence in the character structure and institutional expressions of thousands of American Negroes. Church services and political rallies, dancing and drama, as well as the songs and sagas of work and play and worship, are suffused with these characteristics. But modern social science has shown us that the presence of such traits has nothing to do with the inheritance of a special kind of nervous system or with inborn emotionality. In fact, there is nothing uniquely African about this particular combination of traits. They are to be found among peasant and tribal peoples everywhere. They are characteristic of what anthropologists call "folk societies." And until recently, most American Negroes were folk—rural and unsophisticated. Admittedly, the specific cultural forms through which these traits manifested themselves were, in the beginning, African; and African survivals are today perhaps more prevalent than many American Negroes wish to admit (although less widespread than some enthusiastic anthropologists would have us believe). No one denies that Negro American life has developed a "flavor" all its own. But it is Negro American not African. Even those who emphasize the presence of African survivals in American Negro life, such as Melville J. Herskovits in his *Myth of the Negro Past*, are careful to stress the fact that the culture of Negroes in the United States is Afro-*American* and not African, and that heredity has nothing to do with the retention of Africanisms.

Such African survivals as do exist, as well as a folk "sense of communion" and tendencies toward "myth-making," are rapidly disappearing as Negroes become predominantly urban and as participation in America's mass culture obliterates the ethos of the folk. Prosaic disenchantment and routine decorum are important earmarks of the constantly growing Negro middle-class, which has, moreover, set complete integration into American society as its goal. A "sense of communion" and the habit of "myth-making" still persist in lower-class churches in America, but as Senghor himself states, these are really characteristics of peasant societies. They will exist for decades to come in Africa and the West Indies, but in America, where Negroes are a numerical minority and share the values of the larger society, the processes of mobility and secularization are inexorable and irreversible. Negritude as Senghor defines it could not continue to persist in the United States even if all of the intellectuals desired it to do so.

One folk trait—"the gift of rhythm"—does persist, however, though not for the reasons Senghor would adduce. Rhythm is a salable commodity. It is marketed by members of jazz bands as well as by athletes of the Harlem Globetrotters variety. But it is a "gift" that has been acquired in large measure

by the white Benny Goodmans in competition with the black Louis Arm-
strongs. It is probable that this aspect of negritude, expressed through music
and dance, will persist in urban areas as well as rural, among white people as
well as black. And insofar as it is not tied up with beliefs that "that's why
darkies were born," it will be approved and treasured. But Langston Hughes's
note of warning always sounds in the background:

> Because my mouth is wide with laughter
> And my feet are gay with song
> You do not know I suffer
> I've held my pain too long.

Although African cultural survivals and the folk character of American
Negro life will become more and more attenuated, it is likely that an appreciation for African cultures and cultural products on the part of American
Negroes will increase. Growing numbers of American Negroes, of all social
levels, are learning to look at African art without laughing at the techniques
of distortion or being puzzled by its stylization. They are beginning to face
the bare bosoms and wild leaps of African concert artists without embarrassment and shame. They feel less threatened personally by the sight of sweating
black bodies gyrating in magic rituals on screen and stage. They are beginning
to feel that African cultural phenomena are not a "reflection upon the Negro
race." Such transformations in attitude are taking place, in part, because of a
growing awareness that white people of importance and influence think of
African cultural products as important, beautiful, and acceptable. Negro American intellectuals can, perhaps, help to provide a more meaningful basis for
acceptance.

But however much Negro Americans come to appreciate African cultures
for what they are, it is likely that they will continue to think of the African
folk and their products as different, non-Western, exotic, strange—as *African*.
Some will come to understand what negritude means to the African intellectual, but they will not feel that it has any reference to them. They will identify
but not emulate and will admire and appreciate without any desire to imitate.
(And very, very few will feel the call to "return 'home.' ") A few artists and
intellectuals will "cash in" on the growing interest in Africa, but most will
have more immediate American concerns to engage their time and attention.
As familiarity with and appreciation of the poets of negritude grow among
Negro Americans, they will feel a real sense of identity with the French-Guianese
poet, Damas, who sings:

> The white man killed my father
> My father was proud—
> The white man seduced my mother
> My mother was beautiful—
> The white man burnt my brother
> Beneath the noonday sun—

> *My brother was strong*
> *His hands red with black blood—*
> *The white man turned to me*
> *And in a conqueror's voice said,*
> *"Hey boy, a chair, a napkin, a drink."*

Every American Negro will know what this poet is talking about. Some will also understand what makes Damas write:

> *Give me back my black dolls*
> *To disperse the image of pallid wenches, vendors of love*
> *going and coming*
> *on the boulevard of my boredom*

But such words will have no personal significance except for those who have known a type of interracial sexual experience that is still rare in America. Most will even understand the psychology of rejection which appears in Aimé Césaire's poem which exalts black people as

> *... those who have never invented anything*
> *They abandon themselves possessed to the essence of all things*
> *Ignoring surfaces but possessed by the movement of all things.*

But here American Negroes will begin to pull back emotionally. They are not prepared to glorify "those who have never invented anything"; they will be inclined to dismiss such sentiments as a "sour-grapes mechanism" which American Negroes no longer feel that mature sophisticated people should use. And they are likely to comment cynically that "Africans will sing another tune as soon as they have the sense of power that comes from independence and factories and dams." The mysticism and surrealism of Césaire is likely to leave them cold except for the enjoyment of words superbly handled:

> *My negritude is not a rock, its deafness*
> *hurled against the clamor of the day*
>
> .   .   .
>
> *It plunges into the red flesh of the earth*
> *It plunges into the burning flesh of the sky*
> *It pierces the opaque prostration by its upright patience*

Lovers of *avant-garde* poetry will enjoy Césaire and perhaps allow themselves to wish for a moment that they too had been born in a setting that could produce such an impassioned affirmation of identity.

In a sense the African writer stands today where the American Negro writer stood in the twenties. Now Sartre's *Black Orpheus* has overtones that echo what Carl Van Vechten used to say. This is nothing for Africans to be ashamed of or apologetic about, for the black man of letters has to go through this experience in a white man's world. But American Negroes have already passed through it. As Africans shake off colonial controls and confront the white world as political equals, as Negro poetry and fiction become more abundant, the concept of negritude itself will change. For instance, we already find Senghor in his Oxford address saying:

> Today our negritude no longer expresses itself in opposition to European values, but as a complement to them. Henceforth its militants will be concerned, as I have often said, not to be assimilated but to assimilate. They will use European values to arouse the slumbering values of negritude which they will bring as their contribution to the Civilization of the Universal.

As Senghor begins to think in these terms he is led to emphasize a dimension of negritude quite different from discussions of nervous systems and genes and the inheritance of acquired characteristics—negritude viewed as *myth*.

In defending his concept he reminded his English audience that all men live by myths. "For what are Free Enterprise, Democracy, Communism, but myths around which hundreds of millions of men and women organize their lives? Negritude itself is a myth (I am not using the word in any pejorative sense), but a living dynamic one, which evolves with its circumstances into a form of humanism... it welcomes the complementary values of Europe and the white man, and indeed of all other races and continents. But it welcomes them in order to fertilize and reinvigorate its own values, which it then offers for the construction of a civilization which shall embrace all mankind." He himself has been working all along to weave Marxism and Catholicism into the fabric of negritude in order to produce an ideology of "African Socialism." Presumably negritude as myth can stand on its own feet without the prop of belief in the inheritance of acquired characteristics—as a body of belief about the nature of African society and its worth, including the cultural products of African society which have survived here and there in the New World.

Intellectuals are continuously involved in the process of making and remaking myths to replace those elaborated by the folk. American Negro intellectuals do not reject the dialogue with their African and West Indian counterparts as the process of remaking the myth goes on. They have the obligation, however, to submit the myth of negritude to ruthless critical analysis as a part of their contribution to the process. There is some evidence, for instance, that Senghor misunderstands some of the findings of modern science as well as the nature of race relations in the United States. For instance he writes:

> The Negro is quite different. American psychotechnicians have already confirmed that his reflexes are more natural, better adapted. That explains his utilization in industry and in the technical services of the armed forces in a higher percentage than that which he represents in the population of the United States of America.

What American Negroes know to be pseudo science in the service of those who are looking for rationalizations for segregation and discrimination is interpreted by Senghor as welcome fact! And he explains the consequences of a caste system in industry and in the armed services as a recognition of the Negro's anatomical uniqueness! This lack of familiarity with the natural and social sciences is prevalent to a surprising extent among British and Continental men of letters, but for African and West Indian writers to emulate them and to perpetuate their errors is a disservice to "the race" which they so passionately profess to defend and to advance.

Yet, if purged of its antiquated notions of biology and instinctual psychology, the concept of negritude has value in focusing our attention upon the cultural survivals and subtle African orientations which may still exist among us. It encourages serious consideration of African cultures and frees us from prejudices and distortions to which we have all been subjected. It opens up whole new vistas of appreciation for the great contributions which Africa has made to the stream of world culture. The myth of negritude—the belief that black men have developed cultures of worth, and that although these cultures may be different from those of the West they have values which all can appreciate and share—has important morale-building functions. It can give confidence to the masses in the West Indies and America, as well as in Africa, who smart under the stigma of their blackness and of being of African descent, although the intellectuals hardly need such a crutch.

Equally important is a recognition that *American* Negroes are involved in a struggle to become fully integrated into the nation and culture of their birth. This fight for equal rights does not mean that they deny their African heritage. It does, however, pose problems quite different from those faced in the West Indies and Africa, where dignity and equality are to be sought in a creative nationalism which leads toward sovereign states and federations of states. There is no danger that American Negroes will forget that they are Negroes, for no matter how much one may wish to be a Negro *American*, society forces him to see himself as an American *Negro*.

French-speaking African and West Indian writers have developed the concept of negritude as an ideology and a program to give meaning to their literary efforts. In its emphasis upon mystique, it is peculiarly French. Perhaps it is more than language which draws American Negro intellectuals closer to English-speaking writers and artists in Africa and the West Indies. They have no "program," no mystique, no ideology. They simply write and dance and sing and argue to express what they loosely and half-jokingly refer to as the African Personality.

In this era of African liberation, the myth of negritude should be, and probably will be subordinated to the broader myth of "Pan-African solidarity," viewed as the attempt to unite all Africans irrespective of race, creed, and color into some kind of functioning cohesive political unit. But negritude will live as an important subsidiary myth in the Pan-African movement, emphasizing that black Africans, West Indians, and Negro Americans *are* one people because they all suffer from the world's low estimation of Negroidness, blackness, African origins. They are bound together by memories of past suffering and by the hope of future triumphs. The success of one fragment of the dispersed peoples of African descent reflects credit upon all; the failure of one injures the reputations of all the rest. It is this common fate, not genes, which binds them together and reinforces the struggle against racism. It was the Negro folk in America who produced the spiritual "Walk Together, Children, Don't Ya Get Weary, There's a Great Camp Meeting in the Promised Land."

POLITICAL PAN-AFRICANISM

While preparations were being made in 1921 for the Second Pan-African Congress in London, a new and colorful leader burst upon the Harlem scene— the Honorable Marcus Aurelius Garvey, D.C.L., as he styled himself, a self-educated, eloquent, and fanatically zealous Jamaican who had come to the United States in 1915 to study Booker T. Washington's program and leadership. He had remained to organize his own Universal Negro Improvement Association with a doctrine of "Africa for the Africans," Black Zionism for picked cadres of New World Negroes, and racial solidarity for the rest so that they could carry on mutually beneficial trade with Africa through an African Communities League and the Black Star Line.

Garvey began to build up a following as the war ended, and on August 1, 1920, the First International Convention of the U.N.I.A. met in Harlem with evangelical fervor. A motto was proclaimed: "One God! One Aim! One Destiny." The U.N.I.A. welcomed everyone who desired "to work for the general uplift of the Negro peoples of the world." As the movement grew Garvey became the "Provisional President of Africa." The African Orthodox Church was organized with a black hierarchy and gave its blessings to the idea of a black God, a black Jesus, a black Madonna, and black angels. (Garvey gave Countee Cullen the black God he yearned for, but the poet could not accept Him on U.N.I.A. terms.)

The Universal African Legion rode on horseback in Harlem parades, the forerunners of the shock troops who would someday, at Garvey's call, hurl the white men into the sea, as "400,000,000 black men" rose under the banner of the red, black, and green. The Black Eagle Flying Corps marched in their uniforms, awaiting the day when the movement would supply them with planes to scourge those who had ravished "the Motherland." The Universal Black Cross Nurses studied first aid so they could give succor to black bodies everywhere. Pioneers were selected to begin what Garvey called Africa's "redemption." The uniforms, the parades, the speeches, the promises, and the hopes drew hundreds of thousands of urban Negroes to the Garvey movement in the immediate postwar years. How many actually dreamed of emigrating we shall never know.

There was a tone of superiority and condescension in the New World Negroes' U.N.I.A. manifesto, but the "Beloved and Scattered Millions," schooled as they were in church and lodge, knew no other idiom in which to speak:

To establish a universal confraternity among the race; to promote the spirit of love and pride; to reclaim the fallen; to administer to and assist the needy; to assist in civilizing the backward tribes of Africa; to assist in the development of independent Negro nations and communities; to establish a central nation for the race; to establish commissaries or agencies in the principal countries of the world for the representation of all Negroes; to promote a conscientious spiritual worship among the native tribes of Africa; to establish universities, colleges, academies, schools for the racial education and culture of the people; to work for better conditions among Negroes everywhere.

Garvey's collected speeches appeared in the *Philosophy and Opinions of Marcus Garvey.* Passionate in their espousal of black nationalism, they made such an impact upon Nkrumah when he was a student in America that he cites them as one of the primary sources of his "inspiration" as a developing nationalist leader.

The American Communist Party was founded the same year that Garvey called his first convention, and the Negro members of the Party received orders to bore from within and try to capture both the Garvey movement and the National Association for the Advancement of Colored People, which was founded in 1909. The N.A.A.C.P., the Pan-African movement, and the Communist Party were alike in one respect. They were all led by intellectuals whose problem was how to make contact with the masses. Garvey had no such problem, and while his movement grew apace in American cities and in the West Indies, another type of popular leader was emerging in Africa.

Just before the Second Pan-African Congress met in Brussels to chide the Belgians, a half-educated carpenter in the Congo, Simon Kimbangu, announced that he was "touched by the grace of God on the 18th March, 1921." His followers announced that the world would end in October, and fire from heaven would wipe out all white men. Some Kimbanguist preachers, however, declared that American Negroes would soon be coming to deliver their Congo brothers from white oppression. Kimbangu was immediately jailed, but the movement spread. (In 1958 eighteen years after Kimbangu's death, Belgian authorities in the Congo arrested over 3,000 Kimbanguists.) Similar "prophet movements" arose in the twenties in Kenya, the Rhodesias, and South Africa.

During 1923 the Garvey movement grew rapidly. Negotiations were proceeding for land in Liberia for the establishment of a colony. Steamships were being purchased for the Black Star Line. The ingathering of the exiles seemed about to begin. All the while, Du Bois and other Negro leaders were denouncing Garvey as a menace and a fraud and warning the Negro public against supporting him. But in 1924 a mission left for Liberia to complete arrangements for the settlement. Then, under pressure from Britain and France and fearful of Garvey's pretensions, Liberia suddenly broke off all negotiations. The Black Star Line ran into financial difficulties. The U.N.I.A. was facing the beginning of the end.

Although the Garvey movement was heading for disaster in the United States, its influence was spreading in Africa. In 1920, the President of the newly organized Congress of British West Africa said in his inaugural address that he had heard of the U.N.I.A. and charged his members to draw inspiration from it, and to be ready to welcome their "brothers" from overseas to share in the wealth of the country and to help in developing it. Nigerians slept on the beaches at Calabar with bonfires burning to light the ships of "Moses Garvey" in for the landfall. And Kadalie, leading the most powerful social movement South Africa had ever seen, said he had been profoundly influenced by Garveyism. George Padmore, a West Indian ex-Communist, in *Pan Africanism or Communism?* has called attention to the fact that

> In certain places the punishment for being seen with a *Negro World* [the U.N.I.A. paper] was five years at hard labor, and in French Dahomey it was life imprisonment. It was suppressed in such places as Trinidad, British Guiana, Barbados, etc., in the West Indies and all French, Italian, Portuguese, Belgian, and some of the British colonies in Africa.

Thomas Hodgkin, in his *Nationalism in Colonial Africa*, notes that "the impact of Garveyism can be traced in British and French West Africa as well as in South Africa, particularly during the period of unrest and revolt immediately following the First World War"; referring to the growth of African independent churches, he writes:

> Probably the most important single outside stimulus was the American-born Garvey movement, in which the strands of Ethiopianism and Pan Africanism were closely interwoven. Marcus Garvey . . . was successful in spreading the idea of Independent African churches as an instrument of African liberation.

About 1935 the African separatist churches among the Kikuyu in Kenya brought in one of Garvey's bishops to train and ordain preachers. It was this group of churches and their affiliated schools that formed part of the seedbed from which the Mau Mau eventually grew.

But in 1925, the year of the publication of *The New Negro*, the Garvey bubble burst. The Provisional President of Africa was sent to a federal prison, convicted of using the mails to defraud. As the gates closed upon him, he promised that if he died he would return in the wind and the rain to trouble the white man and lead the black man to victory. Garvey was an embarrassment to Negro intellectuals. (It is significant that none has ever chosen to write a biography of him.) But all of them concede that black folks were given a sense of pride and worth as a result of his efforts.

Du Bois convened his Fourth (and last) Pan-African Congress in 1927, in New York. Most of the 220 delegates represented American Negro women's organizations, but representatives of ten foreign countries were also present, including Chief Amoah II from the Gold Coast. It was in this year, too, that President Harding pardoned Garvey and deported him to Jamaica.

Garvey blamed the leaders of the N.A.A.C.P., the Communists, and the Jews for his downfall rather than his own business ineptitude and overweening arrogance. His charges were, of course, absurd. The Communists, on the other hand, after their failure to infiltrate the Garvey movement, denounced it. The Sixth Congress of the Communist International in 1928 made a slashing attack upon the movement in a formal ideological statement:

> Garveyism, which formerly was the ideology of the masses, like Gandhism, has become a hindrance to the revolutionization of the Negro masses. Originally advocating social equality for Negroes, Garveyism subsequently developed into a peculiar form of Negro "Zionism" which instead of fighting American imperialism advanced the slogan: "Back to Africa!" This dangerous ideology, which bears not a single genuine democratic trait, and which toys with the aristocratic attributes of a non-existent "Negro kingdom," must be strongly resisted, for it is not a help but a hindrance to the mass Negro struggle for liberation against American imperialism.

George Padmore, writing in *Pan Africanism or Communism?* in 1955, claims that

> Had the Communists succeeded in capturing the Garvey movement and in gaining control of other black nationalist groups, specially selected Negro militants were to have been recruited and trained in Moscow as cadres for colonial work in Africa.

Padmore was himself a leader in the colonial section of the Communist International during the period of which he writes. In 1935 he broke with the Communists, and went to London, where he organized the International African Service Bureau and the Pan-African Federation.

By the time the Second World War erupted, Padmore had developed a distinctive Pan-African theory, namely, that only Africans could liberate Africa, and that only "Pan-African Socialism" could prevent an eventual Communist takeover there. Kwame Nkrumah joined the small group of nationalists around Padmore in 1943, and the two of them, together with Jomo Kenyatta, did the preparatory political work for the Fifth Pan-African Congress.

When the Sixth Pan-African Congress (the All African Peoples Conference organized by Padmore and Nkrumah) met in Ghana in 1958, Nkrumah began his speech to the final session with these words:

> We are happy to see so many of our brothers and sisters from the New World here today. Before many of us were conscious of our own degredation, it was the New World Negroes who raised the banner of African liberation. Two names I must mention, Marcus Garvey and W. E. B. Du Bois.

NEW IMAGES IN THE MAKING

Both Countee Cullen and the church-oriented segment of the American Negro population shared Vachel Lindsay's widely accepted image of Africa. But whereas the Negro poet made a virtue of African "primitivism," the Christians deplored it. Negro Christians differed from white Christians, however, in their appraisal of what were, to them, the undesirable aspects of contemporary African reality. They saw Africa in a larger time perspective. They visualized a Golden Age in the remote past, before the present state of affairs had come to pass, as well as an Africa to be "redeemed" in the future. Du Bois, Garvey, and the Communists, too, were convinced that Africa would be "redeemed," but not in a religious sense. The Communists looked forward to the classless society that would emerge from a revolution led by New World Negroes. Garvey had an apocalyptic vision of a united Africa functioning as a powerful equal in the comity of nations. In his view, too, Negroes would play a messianic role. Some kind of African Socialism lay in the future, as Du Bois and Padmore conceived it, but African leaders would make their own revolution, with New World Negroes operating only as catalytic agents. Some Africans were influenced by all the varieties of "redemption" which emanated from the New World, but history did not assign a decisive role to any of them.

The African leaders who breached the bastions of colonialism in the 1950's and 1960's elaborated their own ideas of Pan-Africanism, negritude, and the "African Personality," ideas which reflect the influences of Marxism and Western democratic thought, but also acknowledge some intellectual indebtedness to New World Negro intellectuals and leaders. But the product is their own, based upon a fierce and passionate conviction that Africans alone must determine the goals and the strategies of their own liberation and development. It is this African "pride" that Hughes came eventually to understand. Du Bois understands it, too, but feels that the Communist world is more likely to respect it than is the West. The relation of New World Negroes to contemporary Africa is now in the process of redefinition.

For a very small group of American Negroes, the New Africa will offer a refuge from the race prejudice of the present or the integration of the future, but latter-day Garveyism is likely to have a very limited appeal. The African states will probably welcome the few exiles who want to be gathered in so long as they become peaceful and industrious citizens. There will not be, however, any campaigns urging them to "come home."

For a somewhat larger group, Africa will offer a focus for meaningful social action. It has served this function in the past for members of missionary societies. It does so today for a growing number of American Negroes who are interested in cementing intercultural ties or doing research. A "cult of Africa" has always existed within the Negro community. It will probably grow in size, and will include a mutually incompatible group of devotees ranging from Harlem's fanatical black nationalists who heckle at United Nations meetings, through middle-class families that specialize in entertaining African dignitaries, to members of the American Society for African Culture. Varied groups of Africans are beginning to cherish their relationships with these segments of the Afro-American world. Thoughtful American Negroes are aware of some of the dangers inherent in this type of close identification with Africa. Tendencies to gloss over, and even to suppress, the less favorable aspects of African life will appear. Temptations to claim a monopoly of understanding Africa will manifest themselves. There may even be sharp conflicts of loyalty if some African states veer away sharply from the West. There is also the risk of isolation from white friends and colleagues, although this has not happened to French-African intellectuals who emphasize their negritude. Despite the dangers, some American Negroes will continue to feel that the rewards of a close identification with Africa are worth the risks.

Increasing numbers of American Negroes, too, are likely to find careers in Africa with American church, government, or business institutions. African attitudes toward them, will, no doubt, always be a mixture of pride at seeing successful Negroes occupying high places and some measure of apprehension, wariness, and resentfulness over Negroes allowing themselves to be "used" by the white man in his contact with Africans. But insofar as Negroes are not involved in the exploitation of Africans or in attempts to frustrate their national aspirations, Pan-African sentiments of friendliness are likely to override antagonism. The fortunes of Negroes who represent the American government abroad, however, can be expected to vary with the twists and turns of both African and American foreign policy. As for missionaries, the "African Personality" is certain to reject any among them, whether they be black or white, who stand in the way of the development of Africa's own brand of Christianity or try to control Africa's churches.

For most American Negroes, however, Africa is likely to remain the far-off but inescapable fact that it has always been. It will become less and less a source of embarrassment, however, as the image of successful nations replaces that of "savages." Leaders cut in the heroic mold of Kenyatta and Lumumba will continue to stir the imagination and provide symbols of protest and courage with which American Negroes can identify, but there will be no ever-present sense of involvement with Africa. Feelings of shame and rejection, however, are likely to give way to pride over specific persons and events. At the same time, any attempts to suggest that they are Africans and not Americans will certainly be resisted. They will be interested in Africa, but not especially "concerned," and the idea that American Negroes have any mission to "redeem" Africa, in either a religious or a secular sense, will disappear.

When the executive secretary of the N.A.A.C.P., in welcoming Nkrumah to America, spoke of the "blood tie," everyone knew that he was using the term in symbolic and metaphorical sense, that he was talking about historical experiences and sentiments which bind American Negroes to the peoples of Africa. "Blood" will continue to function as a most inadequate verbal symbol for something else, and American Negro intellectuals must accept it as one of their never-ending duties to explain to less highly trained Americans, as well as to many of their European and African counterparts, that insofar as they accept the idea of negritude (as either a present reality or a convenient myth), they speak of qualities which have survived by virtue of the toughness of a culture, not through immutability of genes.

As the processes of integration in the United States proceed at an accelerated pace, many Negroes may find themselves wishing to cling to certain aspects of Negro life in America which seem to them rich, familiar, and warm, despite the fact that they will, at the same time, demand all of their civil rights. This is in no way inconsistent with the pluralistic conception of American society which is gaining popularity in some quarters. But, in any event, full integration into American life is a long way off, and amalgamation is even further away. There will be Negro Americans and a "Negro community" in America for many, many years to come. Their white fellow Americans are not going to let Negro Americans forget that they are of African descent even if they want to. Negro Americans will continue to confront the question: "What is Africa to me?" Seeing integration opening up before them, many will be inclined to answer: "Nothing!" Others will give Langston Hughes's answer of the 1920's—"So long, so far away"—and for them the song will be, forever, the song they cannot understand.

For others, however, because of the African friends they have made, or because they wish to be identified with the process of "poetic justice" now working itself out, or because of sentiments which became deeply imbedded in their youth, or because they smart under the continued impact of deprecatory definitions placed upon their own physical Negroidness, Africa will function as a "spiritual homeland." They will share the feelings which made a Nigerian who had studied in America, Mboni Ojike, write a book entitled *I Have Two Countries*. There is nothing "un-American" about this, for such identification has its parallel among the Poles and the Irish, the Jews and the Swedes, and numerous other groups who keep alive both memories and contacts with an "ancestral homeland."

Perhaps the most significant impact which the New Africa and America's changing image of it will have may be the reassurance it will give in regard to the capacity and worth of "blackness." Seeing successful and forceful Africans winning the respect of white Americans—people like Senghor and Azikiwe—will bolster the self-esteem of many American Negroes. For darker and more Negroid individuals whose self-esteem is frequently threatened by the derogatory appraisals which American aesthetic standards place upon their physical traits, the New Africa will have the same tonic effect that the Garvey moment had—an acceptance of their own physical image. There will be no need, however, for fantasy symbols such as black angels and Madonnas, for attractive black airline hostesses and African beauty queens competing in international contests, as well as the artists and the diplomats, will exist in reality.

Many American Negroes will feel no need for the psychological support that comes from identification with the New Africa. For those Negroes who do feel the need for "roots," however, the New Africa will, no doubt, excite emotions similar to those which stirred Jean Toomer, the American Negro poet of the "Renaissance," when he came to terms with his Southern background, and sang:

> Oh land and soil, red soil and sweet gum tree,
> So scant of grass, so profligate of pines
> Now just before an epoch's sun declines,
> Thy son, in time, I have returned to thee,
> Thy son in time I have returned to thee....

PART TWO

AMERICAN NEGROES
AND THE
SYSTEM OF SLAVERY

Carl N. Degler

SLAVERY AND THE GENESIS OF AMERICAN
RACE PREJUDICE

Historians have long recognized that the first Negroes brought to Virginia in 1619 did not become slaves, but were assimilated into the existing system of indentured servitude. Carl Degler has written what is probably the definitive account of how, in the New England and Chesapeake colonies during the seventeenth century, Negro slavery evolved from indentured servitude.

Degler also concerns himself with another major theme: the relationship between slavery and race prejudice. As he points out, in a different cultural context enslavement of one racial group by another does not necessarily involve hostility and prejudice. Observers have noted that the character of slavery and race relations in Latin American countries stands in striking contrast to the situation in the United States. Degler, in a sharply revisionist interpretation, proposes the provocative thesis that in the United States, rather than slavery causing race prejudice, it was race prejudice that led to slavery. Going a step beyond Degler, we wish to suggest that the process was circular: as the majority of Negroes became assigned to a state of perpetual servitude, the fact that they were identified with a lowly status reinforced the prejudice existing among the whites.

O VER a century ago, Tocqueville named slavery as the source of the American prejudice against the Negro. Contrary to the situation in antiquity, he remarked: "Among the moderns the abstract and transient fact of slavery is fatally united with the physical and permanent fact of color." Furthermore, he wrote, though "slavery recedes" in some portions of the United States, "the prejudice to which it has given birth is immovable." [1] More modern observers of

Carl N. Degler, "Slavery and the Genesis of American Race Prejudice," *Comparative Studies in History and Society,* II (October, 1959), pp. 49–66. Copyright © 1959 by The Editorial Committee of the Comparative Studies in History and Society. Reprinted with the permission of the author and publisher.

[1] *Democracy in America* (New York, 1948), I, 358–60.

the American past have also stressed this causal connection between the institution of slavery and the color prejudice of Americans.[2] Moreover, it is patent to anyone conversant with the nature of American slavery, particularly as it functioned in the nineteenth century, that the impress of bondage upon the character and future of the Negro in the United States has been both deep and enduring.

But if one examines other societies which the Negro entered as a slave, it is apparent that the consequences of slavery have not always been those attributed to the American form. Ten years ago, for example, Frank Tannenbaum demonstrated that in the Spanish and Portuguese colonies in South America, slavery did not leave upon the freed Negro anything like the prejudicial mark which it did in the United States.[3] He and others [4] have shown that once the status of slavery was left behind, the Negro in the lands south of the Rio Grande was accorded a remarkable degree of social equality with the whites. In the light of such differing consequences, the role of slavery in the development of the American prejudice against the Negro needs to be reexamined, with particular attention paid to the historical details of origins.

Tannenbaum showed that in the Portuguese and Spanish colonies there were at least three historical forces or traditions which tended to prevent the attribution of inferiority to the Negro aside from the legal one of slavery. One was the continuance of the Roman law of slavery in the Iberian countries, another was the influence of the Roman Catholic Church, and the third was the long history—by Anglo-American standards—of contacts with darker-skinned peoples in the course of the Reconquest and the African explorations of the fifteenth and sixteenth centuries. Roman law, at least in its later forms, viewed slavery as a mere accident, of which anyone could be the victim. As such it tended to forestall the identification of the black man with slavery, thus permitting the Negro to escape from the stigma of his degraded status once he ceased to be a slave. The same end, Tannenbaum showed, was served by the Roman Church's insistence upon the equality of all Christians and by the long familiarity of the Iberians with Negroes and Moors.

In North America, of course, none of these forces was operative—a fact which partly explains the differing type of slavery and status for Negroes in the two places. But this cannot be the whole explanation since it is only negative. We know, in effect, what were the forces which permitted the slave and the Negro in South America to be treated as a human being, but other than the negative fact that these forces did not obtain in the North American colonies, we know little as to why the Negro as slave or freedman, occupied a degraded position compared with that of any white man. A more positive explanation is

[2] Most recently, Oscar and Mary Handlin, "The Origins of the Southern Labor System," *William and Mary Quarterly*, 3rd Series, VII (April, 1950), 199–222.

[3] *Slave and Citizen; The Negro in the Americas* (New York, 1947).

[4] Gilberto Freyre, *Brazil: An Interpretation* (New York, 1945), pp. 96–101; Donald Pierson, *Negroes in Brazil* (Chicago, 1942), pp. 330–6.

to be found in an examination of the early history of the Negro in North America.

It has long been recognized that the appearance of legal slavery in the laws of the English colonies was remarkably slow. The first mention does not occur until after 1660—some forty years after the arrival of the first Negroes. Lest we think that slavery existed in fact before it did in law, two historians have assured us recently that such was not the case. "The status of Negroes was that of servants," Oscar and Mary Handlin have written, "and so they were identified and treated down to the 1660's." [5] This late, or at least, slow development of slavery [6] complicates our problem. For if there was no slavery in the beginning, then we must account for its coming into being some forty years after the introduction of the Negro. There was no such problem in the history of slavery in the Iberian colonies, where the legal institution of slavery came in the ships with the first settlers.

The Handlins' attempt to answer the question as to why slavery was slow in appearing in the statutes is, to me, not convincing. Essentially their explanation is that by the 1660's, for a number of reasons which do not have to be discussed here, the position of the white servant was improving, while that of the Negroes was sinking to slavery. In this manner, the Handlins contend, Negro and white servants, heretofore treated alike, attained different status. There are at least two major objections to this argument. First of all, their explanation, by depending upon the improving position of white servants as it does, cannot apply to New England, where servants were of minor importance. Yet the New England colonies, like the Southern, developed a system of slavery for the Negro that fixed him in a position of permanent inferiority. The greatest weakness of the Handlins' case is the difficulty in showing that the white servant's position was improving during and immediately after the 1660's.

Without attempting to go into any great detail on the matter, several acts of the Maryland and Virginia legislatures during the 1660's and 1670's can be cited to indicate that an improving status for white servants was at best doubtful. In 1662, Maryland restricted a servant's travel without a pass to two miles beyond his master's house; [7] in 1671 the same colony lengthened the time of servants who arrived without indenture from four to five years.[8] Virginia in 1668 provided that a runaway could be corporally punished and also have additional time exacted from him.[9] If, as these instances suggest, the white

[5] Handlin, "Origins of Southern Labor," p. 203.

[6] Virtually all historians of the institution agree on this. See U. B. Phillips, *American Negro Slavery* (New York, 1933), pp. 74–77; J. C. Ballagh, *History of Slavery in Virginia* (Baltimore, 1902), pp. 28–35. More recently, however, Susie Ames, *Studies of the Virginia Eastern Shore in the Seventeenth Century* (Richmond, 1940), pp. 101–10 and W. F. Craven, *Southern Colonies in the Seventeenth Century, 1607–1689* (Baton Rouge, 1949), pp. 217–19 have more than suggested that it is possible that slavery existed in Virginia almost from the very beginning of the Negro's history in America.

[7] *Maryland Archives*, I, 451.

[8] *Ibid*, II, 335.

[9] W. W. Hening, *Statutes at Large; being a Collection of all the Laws of Virginia* ... (Richmond, 1809), II, 266.

servant's status was not improving, then we are left without an explanation for the differing status accorded white and Negro servants after 1660.

Actually, by asking why slavery developed late in the English colonies we are setting ourselves a problem which obscures rather than clarifies the primary question of why slavery in North America seemed to leave a different mark on the Negro than it did in South America. To ask why slavery in the English colonies produced discrimination against Negroes after 1660 is to make the tacit assumption that prior to the establishment of slavery there was none. If, instead, the question is put, "Which appeared first, slavery or discrimination?" then no prejudgment is made. Indeed, it now opens a possibility for answering the question as to why the slavery in the English colonies, unlike that in the Spanish and Portuguese, led to a caste position for Negroes, whether free or slave. In short, the recent work of the Handlins and the fact that slavery first appeared in the statutes of the English colonies forty years after the Negro's arrival, have tended to obscure the real possibility that the Negro was actually *never* treated as an equal of the white man, servant or free.

It is true that when Negroes were first imported into the English colonies there was no law of slavery and therefore whatever status they were to have would be the work of the future. This absence of a status for black men, which, it will be remembered was not true for the Spanish and Portuguese colonies, made it possible for almost any kind of status to be worked out. It was conceivable that they would be accorded the same status as white servants, as the Handlins have argued; it was also possible that they would not. It all depended upon the reactions of the people who received the Negroes.

It is the argument of this paper that the status of the Negro in the English colonies was worked out within a framework of discrimination; that from the outset, as far as the available evidence tells us, the Negro was treated as an inferior to the white man, servant or free. If this be true, then it would follow that as slavery evolved as a legal status, it reflected and included as a part of its essence, this same discrimination which white men had practiced against the Negro all along and before any statutes decreed it. It was in its evolution, then, that American colonial slavery differed from Iberian, since in the colonies of Spain and Portugal, the legal status of the slave was fixed before the Negro came to the Americas. Moreover, in South America there were at least three major traditional safeguards which tended to protect the free Negro against being treated as an inferior. In summary, the peculiar character of slavery in the English colonies as compared with that in the Iberian, was the result of two circumstances. One, that there was no law of slavery at all in the beginning, and two, that discrimination against the Negro antedated the legal status of slavery. As a result, slavery, when it developed in the English colonies, could not help but be infused with the social attitude which had prevailed from the beginning, namely, that Negroes were inferior.

It is indeed true as the Handlins in their article have emphasized that before the seventeenth century the Negro was rarely called a slave. But this fact should not overshadow the historical evidence which points to the institution without employing the name. Because no discriminatory title is placed upon the Negro we must not think that he was being treated like a white servant; for there is too much evidence to the contrary. Although the growth of a fully developed slave law was slow, unsteady and often unarticulated in surviving records, this is what one would expect when an institution is first being worked out.[10] It is not the same, however, as saying that no slavery or discrimination against the Negro existed in the first decades of the Negro's history in America.

As will appear from the evidence which follows, the kinds of discrimination visited upon Negroes varied immensely. In the early 1640's it sometimes stopped short of lifetime servitude or inheritable status—the two attributes of true slavery—in other instances it included both. But regardless of the form of discrimination, the important point is that from the 1630's up until slavery clearly appeared in the statutes in the 1660's, the Negroes were being set apart and discriminated against as compared with the treatment accorded Englishmen, whether servants or free.

The colonists of the early seventeenth century were well aware of a distinction between indentured servitude and slavery.[11] This is quite clear from the evidence in the very early years of the century. The most obvious means the English colonists had for learning of a different treatment for Negroes from that for white servants was the slave trade [12] and the slave systems of the Spanish and Portuguese colonies. As early as 1623, a voyager's book published in London indicated that Englishmen knew of the Negro as a slave in the South American

[10] John C. Hurd, *Law of Freedom and Bondage in the United States* (Boston, 1858–61), I, 163, points out that the trade "in negroes as merchandise was . . . recognized as legitimate by European governments, without any direct sanction from positive legislation, but rested on the general customs among nations, known both in municipal and international private law." Furthermore, he reported that none of the colonies ever found it necessary to pass laws legalizing slavery. He quotes from the Connecticut Code of 1821: "Slavery was never directly established by statute; but has been indirectly sanctioned by various statutes and frequently recognized by courts, so that it may be said to have been established by law." I, 212 n.

[11] The Handlins, "Origins of Southern Labor," pp. 203–4, have argued that in the early years slavery meant nothing more than a low form of labor and that it had no basis in law. This is true insofar as statute law is concerned, but, as will appear later, in practice quite a different situation obtained.

[12] The Handlins, "Origins of Southern Labor," pp. 203–4, argue that the continental colonies could not have learned about a different status for Negroes from that of white servants from the slave trade because, they say, "the company of Royal Adventurers referred to their cargo as 'Negers,' 'Negro-servants,' 'Servants . . . from Africa,' or 'Negro Persons' but rarely as slaves." They overlook, however, abundant references to Negro slaves in the correspondence of the contemporary Royal African Company. Thus in 1663 a warrant for that company refers to "negro slaves" as a part of its monopoly. *Calendar of State Papers, Colonial*, V, 121; see also p. 204. In that same year the Privy Council wrote that the Spanish were "seeking to trade with our island of Barbada for a supply of Negro Slaves. . . ." And then the letter referred to a "supply of Negro Servants," and later still "for every Negro Person a Slave" and then "all such Negro Slaves." E. Donnan, *Documents Illustrative of the History of the Slave Trade* (Washington, 1930), I, 161–2.

colonies of Spain. The book told of the trade in "blacke people" who were "sold unto the Spaniard for him to carry into the West Indies, to remaine as slaves, either in their Mines or in any other servile uses, they in those countries put them to." [13] In the phrase "remaine as slaves" is the element of unlimited service.

The Englishmen's treatment of another dark-skinned, non-Christian people —the Indians—further supports the argument that a special and inferior status was accorded the Negro virtually from the first arrival. Indian slavery was practiced in all of the English settlements almost from the beginning [14] and, though it received its impetus from the perennial wars between the races, the fact that an inferior and onerous service was established for the Indian makes it plausible to suppose that a similar status would be reserved for the equally different and pagan Negro.

The continental English could also draw upon other models of a differentiated status for Negroes. The earliest English colony to experiment with large numbers of Negroes in its midst was the shortlived settlement of Providence island, situated in the western Caribbean, just off the Mosquito Coast. By 1637, long before Barbados and the other British sugar islands utilized great numbers of Negroes, almost half of the population of this Puritan venture was black. Such a disproportion of races caused great alarm among the directors of the Company in London and repeated efforts were made to restrict the influx of blacks.[15] Partly because of its large numbers of Negroes, Old Providence became well known to the mainland colonies of Virginia and New England.[16] A. P. Newton has said that Old Providence

> forms the connecting link between almost every English colonising enterprise in the first half of the seventeenth century from Virginia and Bermuda to New England and Jamaica and thus it is of much greater importance than its actual accomplishments would justify.[17]

Under such circumstances, it was to be expected that knowledge of the status accorded Negroes by these Englishmen would be transmitted to those on the mainland with whom they had such close and frequent contact.

Though the word "slave" is never applied to the Negroes on Providence, and only rarely the word "servant," "Negroes," which was the term used, were obviously *sui generis*; they were people apart from the English. The Company, for example, distrusted them. "Association [Tortuga island] was deserted thro' their mutinous conduct," the Company told the Governor of Old Providence in 1637. "Further trade for them prohibited, with exceptions, until Providence be

[13] Quoted in Donnan, *Slave Trade*, I, 125.
[14] See particularly, Almon Lauber, *Indian Slavery in Colonial Times Within the Present Limits of the United States* (New York, 1913), Chap. IV.
[15] A. P. Newton, *The Colonising Activities of the English Puritans* (New Haven, 1914), p. 258.
[16] *Ibid.*, p. 260.
[17] A. P. Newton, *The European Nations in the West Indies, 1493–1688* (London, 1933), pp. 173-4.

furnished with English." [18] In another communication the Company again alluded to the dangers of "too great a number" of Negroes on the island and promised to send 200 English servants over to be exchanged for as many Negroes.[19] A clearer suggestion of the difference in status between an English servant and a Negro is contained in the Company's letter announcing the forwarding of the 200 servants. As a further precaution against being overwhelmed by Negroes, it was ordered that a "family of fourteen"—which would include servants—was not to have more than six Negroes. "The surplusage may be sold to the poor men who have served their apprenticeship." [20] But the Negroes, apparently, were serving for life.

Other British island colonies in the seventeenth century also provide evidence which is suggestive of this same development of a differing status for Negroes, even though the word "slave" was not always employed. Though apparently the first Negroes were only brought to Bermuda in 1617,[21] as early as 1623 the Assembly passed an "Act to restrayne the insolencies of Negroes." The blacks were accused of stealing and of carrying "secretly cudgels, and other weapons and working tools." Such weapons, it was said, were "very dangerous and not meete to be suffered to be carried by such Vassals...." Already, in other words, Negroes were treated as a class apart. To reinforce this, Negroes were forbidden to "weare any weapon in the daytyme" and they were not to be outside or off their master's land during "any undue hours in the night tyme...." [22]

During the 1630's there were other indications that Negroes were treated as inferiors. As early as 1630 some Negroes' servitude was already slavery in that it was for life and inheritable. One Lew Forde possessed a Negro man, while the Company owned his wife; the couple had two children. Forde desired "to know which of the said children properly belong to himself and which to the Company." The Council gave him the older child and the Company received the other.[23] A letter of Roger Wood in 1634 suggests that Negroes were already serving for life, for he asked to have a Negro, named Sambo, given to him, so that through the Negro "I or myne may *ever* be able" to carry on an old feud with an enemy who owned Sambo's wife.[24]

There is further evidence of discrimination against Negroes in later years. A grand jury in 1652 cited one Henry Gaunt as being "suspected of being unnecessarily conversant with negro women"—he had been giving them pres-

---

[18] *Calendar of State Papers, Colonial*, I, 249.

[19] *Ibid.*, pp. 277–8.

[20] *Ibid.*, pp. 278–9.

[21] J. H. Lefroy, *Memorials of the Discovery and Early Settlement of the Bermudas or Somers Islands, 1515–1685* (London, 1877), I, 127.

[22] *Ibid.*, I, 308–9.

[23] *Ibid.*, I, 505. Cases in 1676 and 1685 indicate that this practice of dividing the children became the standard practice under slavery in a colony where the parcels of slaves were so small that few masters could have a spouse on their plantations for each of his adult Negroes. *Ibid.*, II, 427, 547–8.

[24] *Ibid.*, I, 539. Emphasis added.

ents. The presentment added that "if he hath not left his familiarity with such creatures, it is desired that such abominations be inquired into, least the land mourne for them." [25] The discrimination reached a high point in 1656 when the Governor proclaimed that "any Englishman" who discovered a Negro walking about at night without a pass, was empowered to "kill him then and theire without mercye." The proclamation further ordered that all free Negroes "shall be banished from these Islands, never to return eyther by purchase of any man, or otherwise...." [26] When some Negroes asked the Governor for their freedom in 1669, he denied they had such claim, saying that they had been "purchased by" their masters "without condition or limitation. It being likewise soe practised in these American plantations and other parts of the world." [27]

In Barbados Negroes were already slaves when Richard Ligon lived there in 1647–50. "The Iland," he later wrote, "is divided into three sorts of men, viz: Masters, servants, and slaves. The slaves and their posterity, being subject to their masters for ever," in contrast to the servants who are owned "but for five years...." [28] On that island as at Bermuda it was reported that Negroes were not permitted "to touch or handle any weapons." [29]

On Jamaica, as on the other two islands, a clear distinction was made between the status of the Negro and that of the English servant. In 1656 one resident of the island wrote the Protector in England urging the importation of African Negroes because then, he said, "the planters would have to pay for them" and therefore "they would have an interest in preserving their lives, which was wanting in the case of bond servants...." [30]

It is apparent, then, that the colonists on the mainland had ample opportunity before 1660 to learn of a different status for black men from that for Englishmen, whether servants or free.

From the evidence available it would seem that the Englishmen in Virginia and Maryland learned their lesson well. This is true even though the sources available on the Negro's position in these colonies in the early years are not as abundant as we would like. It seems quite evident that the black man was set apart from the white on the continent just as he was being set apart in the island colonies. For example, in Virginia in 1630, one Hugh Davis was "soundly

[25] *Ibid.*, II, 30.

[26] *Ibid.*, II, 95–6.

[27] *Ibid.*, II, 293. As late as 1662 the perpetual character of slavery for Negroes was being obscured by their serving for ninety-nine years. See *Ibid.*, II, 166, 184.

[28] Richard Ligon, *A True and Exact History of the Island of Barbados* (London, 1657), p. 43.

[29] *Ibid.*, p. 46.

[30] Quoted in Richard B. Morris, *Government and Labor in Early America* (New York, 1946), p. 499. As early as 1633, on the island of Tortuga, the separation of whites, servants or no, from Negroes was in evidence. At a time of anarchy on the island, "The eighty-odd Englishmen in the island had formed a council among themselves for the government of the colony and to keep in subjection the one hundred and fifty negroes, twenty-seven of whom were the company's property." Newton, *Colonizing Activities*, p. 214.

whipped before an Assembly of Negroes and others for abusing himself to the dishonor of God and the shame of Christians, by defiling his body in lying with a negro." [31] The unChristian-like character of such behavior was emphasized ten years later when Robert Sweet was ordered to do penance in Church for "getting a negro woman with child." [32] An act passed in the Maryland legislature in 1639 indicated that at that early date the word "slave" was being applied to non-Englishmen. The act was an enumeration of the rights of "all Christian inhabitants (slaves excepted)." [33] The slaves referred to could have been only Indians or Negroes,[34] since all white servants were Christians. It is also significant of the differing treatment of the two races that though Maryland and Virginia very early in their history enacted laws fixing limits to the terms for servants who entered without written contracts, Negroes were never included in such protective provisions.[35] The first of such laws were placed upon the books in 1639 in Maryland and 1643 in Virginia; in the Maryland statute, it was explicitly stated: "Slaves excepted." [36]

In yet another way, Negroes and slaves were singled out for special status in the years before 1650. A Virginia law of 1640 provided that "all masters" should try to furnish arms to themselves and "all those of their families which shall be capable of arms"—which would include servants—"(excepting negros)." [37] Not until 1648 did Maryland get around to such a prohibition, when it was provided that no guns should be given to "any Pagan for killing meate or to any other use," upon pain of a heavy fine.[38] At no time were white servants denied the right to bear arms; indeed, as these statutes inform us, they were enjoined to possess weapons.[39]

[31] Hening, *Statutes*, I, 146.

[32] *Ibid.*, I, 552.

[33] *Maryland Archives*, I, 80.

[34] It is not known whether there were any Negroes in Maryland at that date. J. R. Brackett, *The Negro in Maryland* (Baltimore, 1889), p. 26 found no evidence of Negroes before 1642.

[35] Handlin, "Origins of Southern Labor," p. 210; Hening, *Statutes*, I, 411, 539. This is not to say that some Negroes were not indentured servants, for there is evidence to show that limited service was enjoyed in the statutes. In October, 1673, for instance, the Council and General Court of Virginia ordered that "Andrew Moore A Servant Negro," who asserted he was to serve only five years, and who had the support of several "oathes," was declared free. Moreover, his erstwhile master was compelled to "pay him Corne and Clothes According to the custome of the country" and 400 pounds of tobacco and cask for the Negro's service since his time expired and to "pay costs." *Minutes of the Council and General Court of Colonial Virginia*, edited by H. R. McIlwaine (Richmond, 1924), p. 354.

[36] Hening, *Statutes*, I, 257; *Maryland Archives*, I, 80.

[37] *William and Mary Quarterly*, Second Series, IV (July, 1924), 147.

[38] *Maryland Archives*, I, 233.

[39] Handlin, "Origins of Southern Labor," p. 209, implies that these early restrictions were later repealed. "Until the 1660's," the Handlins write, "the statutes on the Negroes were not at all unique. Nor did they add up to a decided trend." In substantiation of this point they instance the "fluctuations" in the Negro's right to bear arms. Their cited evidence, however, does not sustain this generalization. Four references to the statutes of Virginia are made; of these four, only two deal with arms bearing. The first one, that

One other class of discriminatory acts against Negroes in Virginia and Maryland before 1660 also deserves to be noticed. Three different times before 1660—in 1643, 1644 and 1658—the Virginia Assembly (and in 1654, the Maryland legislature) included Negro and Indian women among the "tithables." But white servant women were never placed in such a category,[40] inasmuch as they were not expected to work in the fields. From the beginning, it would seem, Negro women, whether free or bond, were treated by the law differently from white women servants.[41]

It is not until the 1640's that evidence of a status for Negroes akin to slavery, and, therefore, something more than mere discrimination begins to appear in the sources. Two cases of punishment for runaway servants in 1640 throw some light on the working out of a differentiated status for Negroes. The first case concerned three runaways, of whom two were white men and the third a Negro. All three were given thirty lashes, with the white men having the terms owed their masters extended a year, at the completion of which they were to work for the colony for three more years. The other, "being a Negro named John Punch shall serve his said master or his assigns for the time of his natural Life here or elsewhere." [42] Not only was the Negro's punishment the most severe, and for no apparent reason, but he was, in effect, reduced to slavery. It is also clear, however, that up until the issuing of the sentence, he must have had the status of a servant.

The second case, also in 1640, suggests that by that date some Negroes were already slaves. Six white men and a Negro were implicated in a plot to run away. The punishments meted out varied, but Christopher Miller "a dutchman" (a prime agent in the business) "was given the harshest treatment of all: thirty stripes, burning with an "R" on the cheek, a shackle placed on his leg for a year "and longer if said master shall see cause" and seven years of service for the colony upon completion of his time due his master. The only other one of the seven plotters to receive the stripes, the shackle and the "R" was the Negro Emanuel, but, significantly, he did not receive any sentence of work for

referred to in the text above, indicates that Negroes were not to be armed. The other reference is at best an ambiguous statement about who is taxable and which of the taxables are to serve in the militia. It in no wise constitutes either a repeal or even a contradiction of the earlier statute, which, therefore, must be presumed to be controlling. Their evidence for "fluctuations" in the right of Indians to bear arms suffers from the same weakness of sources. The two statutes they cite merely confirm the right of certain Indians to possess guns and deny them to other Indians. No "fluctuation" in rights is involved.

[40] Hening, *Statutes*, I, 242, 292, 455; *Maryland Archives*, I, 342. The statement in Handlin, "Origins of Southern Labor," p. 217 n, that the "first sign of discrimination was in 1668 when white but not Negro women were exempt," is therefore erroneous.

[41] In his well-known emigrant pamphlet, *Leah and Rachel* (London, 1656), p. 12, John Hammond casts some interesting light on contemporary opinion regarding women who worked in the fields in Virginia. "The Women are not (as is reported) put into the ground to work, but occupie such domestique imployments and housewifery as in England . . . yet some wenches that are nasty, beastly and not fit to be so imployed are put into the ground . . ."

[42] *Minutes of the Council*, p. 466.

the colony. Presumably he was already serving his master for a life-time—*i.e.*, he was a slave.[43] About this time in Maryland it does not seem to have been unusual to speak of Negroes as slaves, for in 1642 one "John Skinner mariner" agreed "to deliver unto . . . Leonard Calvert, fourteen negro-men-slaves and three women-slaves." [44]

From a proceeding before the House of Burgesses in 1666 it appears that as early as 1644 that body was being called upon to determine who was a slave. The Journal of the House for 1666 reports that in 1644 a certain "mulata" bought "as a slave for Ever" was adjudged by the Assembly "no slave and but to serve as other Christian servants do and was freed in September 1665." [45] Though no reason was given for the verdict, from the words "other Christian servants" it is possible that he was a Christian, for it was believed in the early years of the English colonies that baptism rendered a slave free. In any case, the Assembly uttered no prohibition of slavery as such and the owner was sufficiently surprised and aggrieved by the decision to appeal for recompense from the Assembly, even though the Negro's service was twenty-one years, an unheard of term for a "Christian servant." [46]

In early seventeenth century inventories of estates, there are two distinctions which appear in the reckoning of the value of servants and Negroes. Uniformly, the Negroes were more valuable, even as children, than any white servant. Secondly, the naming of a servant is usually followed by the number of years yet remaining to his service; for the Negroes no such notation appears. Thus in an inventory in Virginia in 1643, a 22-year old white servant, with eight years still to serve, was valued at 1,000 pounds of tobacco, while a "negro boy" was rated at 3,000 pounds and a white boy with seven years to serve was listed as worth 700 pounds. An eight-year old Negro girl was calculated to be worth 2,000 pounds. On another inventory in 1655, two good men servants with four years to serve were rated at 1,300 pounds of tobacco, and a woman servant with only two years to go was valued at 800 pounds. Two Negro boys, however, who had no limit set to their terms, were evaluated at 4,100 pounds apiece, and a Negro girl was said to be worth 5,500 pounds.[47]

These great differences in valuation of Negro and white "servants" strongly

---

[43] *Ibid.*, p. 467.

[44] Catterall, *Judicial Cases*, I, 57 n. Mrs. Catterall does not think any Negroes came under this agreement, but the language itself testifies to an accepted special status for Negroes at that time.

[45] *Journals of the House of Burgesses of Virginia*, edited by H. R. McIlwaine (Richmond, 1914), II, 34.

[46] *Ibid.*, II, 34–5. His plea, however, was turned down, the Assembly not knowing "any Reason why the Publick should be answerable for the inadvertency of the Buyer. . . ."

[47] John H. Russell, *The Free Negro in Virginia, 1619–1865* (Baltimore, 1913), p. 36. Russell concludes from his survey of inventories of estates for this early period that Negroes were valued from 20 to 30 pounds sterling, "while white servants of the longest term . . . receive a valuation of not more than £15 sterling." *Ibid.*, p. 35. Catterall, *Judicial Cases*, I, 58 n, upon concluding her investigation of inventories of estates, picked 1644 as the date at which " 'servant' standing alone, had generally become synonomous with 'white servant' and 'negro' with 'negro slave,' . . ."

suggest, as does the failure to indicate term of service for the Negroes, that the latter were slaves at least in regard to life-time service. Beyond a question, there was some service which these blacks were rendering which enhanced their value—a service, moreover, which was not or could not be exacted from the whites. Furthermore, a Maryland deed of 1649 adumbrated slave status not only of life-time term, but of inheritance of status. Three Negroes "and all their issue both male and female" were deeded.[48]

Russell and Ames culled from the Virginia court records of the 1640's and 1650's several instances of Negroes held in a status that can be called true slavery. For example, in 1646 a Negro woman and a Negro boy were sold to Stephen Charlton to be of use to him and his "heyers etc. for ever." A Negro girl was sold in 1652 "with her Issue and produce . . . and their services forever." Two years later a Negro girl was sold to one Armsteadinger "and his heyers . . . forever with all her increase both male and female." [49] For March 12, 1655 the minutes of the Council and General Court of Virginia contain the entry, "Mulatto held to be a slave and appeal taken." [50] Yet this is five years before Negro slavery is even implied in the statutes and fifteen before it is declared. An early case of what appears to be true slavery was found by Miss Ames on the Virginia eastern shore. In 1635 two Negroes were brought to the area; over twenty years later, in 1656, the widow of the master was bequeathing the child of one of the original Negroes and the other Negro and her children.[51] This was much more than mere servitude—the term was longer than twenty years and apparently the status was inheritable.

Wesley Frank Craven, in his study of the seventeenth-century Southern colonies, has concluded that in the treatment of the Negro "the trend from the first was toward a sharp distinction between him and the white servant." [52] In view of the evidence presented here, this seems a reasonable conclusion.

Concurrently with these examples of onerous service or actual slavery of Negroes, there were of course other members of the race who did gain their freedom.[53] But the presence of Negroes rising out of servitude to freedom [54]

[48] Catterall, *Judicial Cases*, IV, 9.

[49] Russell, *Free Negro in Virginia*, pp. 34–5. He also reports the instance of a Negro by the name of John Casor who was claimed, in 1655, as a "Negro for his life," but he was rescued from such a status by two witnesses testifying that he had an indenture. *Ibid.*, pp. 32–3.

[50] *Minutes of the Council*, p. 504. Handlin, "Origins of Southern Labor," p. 216, in arguing the late development of a different status for Negroes as compared with whites in Virginia, says: "As late as the 1660's the law had not even a word to describe the children of mixed marriages. But two decades later, the term mulatto is used. . . ." Such a statement is obviously misleading, for though the Handlins presumably mean statute law, the decisions of the General Court were also "law." The *Oxford English Dictionary* cites references for the word "mulatto" for 1595, 1613 and 1657.

[51] Ames, *Eastern Shore*, p. 105.

[52] Craven, *Southern Colonies*, p. 219.

[53] See especially Russell, *Free Negro in Virginia*, pp. 36–9. See also Brackett, *Negro in Maryland*, p. 37.

[54] An indication that even freedom for the Negro carried certain disabilities is afforded by an instance reported by Ames, *Eastern Shore*, p. 107 from the Northampton County

does not destroy the evidence that others were sinking into slavery; it merely underscores the unsteady evolution of a slave status. The supposition that the practice of slavery long antedated the law is strengthened by the tangential manner in which recognition of Negro slavery first appeared in the Virginia statutes.[55] It occurred in 1660 in a law dealing with punishments for runaway servants, where casual reference was made to those "negroes who are incapable of making satisfaction by addition of time," [56] since they were already serving for life.

Soon thereafter, as various legal questions regarding the status of Negroes came to the fore, the institution was further defined by statute law. In 1662 Virginia provided that the status of the offspring of a white man and a Negro would follow that of the mother—an interesting and unexplained departure from the common law and a reversion to Roman law. The same law stated that "any christian" fornicating "with a negro man or woman . . . shall pay double the fines imposed by the former act." Two years later Maryland prescribed service for Negroes "durante vita" and provided for hereditary status to descend through the father. Any free white woman who married a slave was to serve her husband's master for the duration of the slave's life, and her children would serve the master until they were thirty years of age. Presumably, no penalty was to be exacted of a free white man who married a Negro slave.[57]

As early as 1669 the Virginia law virtually washed its hands of protecting the Negro held as a slave. It allowed punishment of refractory slaves up to and including accidental death, relieving the master, explicitly, of any fear of prosecution, on the assumption that no man would "destroy his owne estate." [58]

court records of 1654. For contempt of authority and abuse of certain persons, Anthony Longoe, a Negro, was ordered, almost twenty years after his release from service, to receive "thirty lashes now applied, and tomorrow morning thirty lashes more."

[55] A year earlier, 1659/60, a statute dealing with trade with the Dutch promised remission of a ten shilling tax if "the said Dutch or other forreiners shall import any negro slaves. . . ." This is the first reference in the Virginia statutes to Negroes as slaves. Hening, *Statutes*, I, 540.

[56] Hening, *Statutes*, II, 26. The equivalent Maryland statute (1663) referred to "Negroes and other Slaves, who are incapeable of makeing Stisfaction [*sic*] by Addition of Tyme . . ." *Maryland Archives*, I, 489.

[57] Hening, *Statutes*, II, 170: *Maryland Archives*, I, 533–4. Handlin, "Origins of Southern Labor," p. 215 sees the genesis of these prohibitions in concern over status rather than in objection to racial intermarriage. This seems to be true for Maryland. But in speaking of the Virginia circumstances they write: "It was to guard against the complications of status that the laws after 1691 forbade 'spurious' or illegitimate mixed marriages of the slave and the free . . ." Actually, however, the Virginia statue of 1691 (Hening, *Statutes*, III, 87) clearly aimed at the prevention of "abominable mixture and spurious issue" by forbidding marriage of "English or other white man or woman being free" with "a negro, mulatto or Indian man or woman *bond or free*." (Emphasis added.)

[58] Hening, *Statutes*, II, 270. The working out of the exact legal status of slave property, however, was a slow one. A Virginia law of 1705 (Hening, *Statutes*, III, 333–4), declared "Negro, Mulatto and Indian Slaves . . . to be real estate," but there were a number of exceptions which suggest the later chattel nature of property in slaves. In South Carolina slaves were decreed to be real estate in 1690 and not until 1740 were they said to be legally chattels. Hurd, *Law of Freedom*, I, 297, 303.

In fact by 1680 the law of Virginia had erected a high wall around the Negro. One discerns in the phrase "any negro or other slave" how the word "negro" had taken on the meaning of slave. Moreover, in the act of 1680 one begins to see the lineaments of the later slave codes. No Negro may carry any weapon of any kind, nor leave his master's grounds without a pass, nor shall "any negroe or other slave... presume to lift his hand in opposition against any christian," and if a Negro runs away and resist recapture it "shall be lawful for such person or persons to kill said negroe or slave...." [59]

Yet it would be a quarter of a century before Negroes would comprise even a fifth of the population of Virginia. Thus long before slavery or black labor became an important part of the Southern economy, a special and inferior status had been worked out for the Negroes who came to the English colonies. Unquestionably it was a demand for labor which dragged the Negro to American shores, but the status which he acquired here cannot be explained by reference to that economic motive. Long before black labor was as economically important as unfree white labor, the Negro had been consigned to a special discriminatory status which mirrored the social discrimination Englishmen practiced against him. [60]

In the course of the seventeenth century New Englanders, like Southerners, developed a system of slavery which seemed permanently to fasten its stigma upon the Negro race. But because of the small number of Negroes in the northern provinces, the development of a form of slavery, which left a caste in its wake, cannot be attributed to pressure from increasing numbers of blacks, or even from an insistent demand for cheap labor. Rather it seems clearly to be the consequence of the general social discrimination against the Negro. For in the northern region, as in the southern, discrimination against the Negro preceded the evolution of a slave status and by that fact helped to shape the form that institution would assume.

References to the status of the Negroes in New England in this period are scattered, but, as was true of the Southern provinces, those references which are available suggest that from the earliest years a lowly, differential status, if not slavery itself, was reserved and recognized for the Negro—and the Indian, it might be added. The earliest date asserted in the sources for the existence of Negro slavery in Massachusetts is that of 1639. John Josselyn tells of a Negro woman held on Noddles Island in Boston harbor. Her master sought to mate her with another Negro, Josselyn says, but she kicked her prospective lover out

[59] Hening, *Statutes*, II, 481–2.

[60] Like Virginia, Maryland developed its slave law and status long before the Negroes had become an important aspect of the labor force. As late as 1712, Negroes made up only slightly more than 20 per cent of the population. Brackett, *Negro in Maryland*, pp. 38–9. If Virginia was slow in bringing her slave practices out into the open air of the statute books, the same could not be said of Carolina. In the Fundamental Constitutions, drawn up in 1669, it is stated in article CX that "Every freeman of Carolina shall have absolute power and authority over his negro slaves, of what opinion or religion so ever."

of the bed, saying that such behavior was "beyond her slavery. . . ." [61] Though the first legal code of Massachusetts, the Body of Liberties of 1641, prohibited "bond-slavery" for the inhabitants, it clearly permitted enslavement of those who are "sold to us," [62] which would include Negroes brought in by the international slave trade.[63]

Such use of Negroes was neither unknown nor undesirable to the Puritans. Emanuel Downing wrote to John Winthrop in 1645 about the desirability of a war against the Indians so that captives might be taken who, in turn, could be exchanged

> for Moores, which wilbe more gayneful pilladge for us then [sic] wee conceive, for I doe not see how wee can thrive untill wee gett into a stock of slaves sufficient to do all our busines, for our children's children will hardly see this great Continent filled with people, soe that our servants will still desire freedome for themselves, and not stay but for verie great wages. And I suppose you know verie well how we shall maynteyne 20 Moores cheaper than one English servant.[64]

The following year the Commissioners of the United Colonies recommended that in order to spare the colonies the cost of imprisoning contumacious Indians they should be given over to the Englishmen whom they had damaged or "be shipped out and exchanged for Negroes as the cause will justly serve." [65] Negroes were here being equated with Indians who were being bound out as prisoners: this was treatment decidedly a cut lower than that visited upon white

[61] Massachusetts Historical Society, *Collections*, Third Series, III, 231. There is no doubt that there were Negroes at this time in Massachusetts, for in 1638 Winthrop reported that Capt. Peirce brought back from Old Providence "some cotton, and tobacco and Negroes. . . ." John Winthrop, *History of New England*, James Savage, ed. (Boston, 1853), I, 305.

[62] Some events of 1645 indicate that those few words were of crucial importance to the Puritans. That year some Negroes were brought to Massachusetts by a Captain Smith and they were ordered by the General Court to be returned to Africa on the ground that their importation constituted "the hainous and crying sinn of man-stealing." But this was man-stealing only because Smith and his men had captured the Negroes in a raid, instead of buying them from traders. *Records of Massachusetts*, III, 48, 58, 84.

[63] Very early in New England history the concept of perpetual servitude—one of the distinguishing marks of slavery—appears in the records. In 1637 Roger Williams, in pleading for the lives of the captured Indians during the Pequot War, alludes to "perpetuall slaverie" as an alternative to their execution. Massachusetts Historical Society, *Collections*, Fourth Series, VI, 214. The will of John Winthrop, written in 1639, deeded to his son Adam "my island" and "also my Indians there and my boat and such household as is there" Robert C. Winthrop, *Life and Letters of John Winthrop* (Boston, 1869), II, 252. Though at least three white men were sentenced to "slavery" in Massachusetts in the early years, in at least two cases this did not, in fact, amount to perpetuity, for they appear to have been released in a short time. The use of the word as a special form of service, however, is most interesting. *Records of Massachusetts*, I, 246, 310, 269.

[64] Massachusetts Historical Society, *Collections*, Fourth Series, VI, 65.

[65] *Records of the Colony of Plymouth* (Boston, 1859), IX, 71.

servants.[66] That enslavement of Negroes was well known in New England by the middle of the century at the latest is revealed by the preamble to an act of Warwick and Providence colonies in 1652. It was said that it "is a common course practised amongst Englishmen to buy negers, to that end they may have them for service or slaves forever...." [67]

By mid-century, Negroes were appearing in the inventories of estates and, significantly, the valuation placed upon them was very close to that found in Virginia inventories of the same period. Their worth is always much more than that of a white servant. Thus in 1650 "a neager Maide" was valued at £25; in 1657 the well-known merchant, Robert Keayne left "2 negros and a negro child" estimated to be worth £30. "A negro boy servant" was set at £20 in an estate of 1661.[68] A further indication of the property character of Negroes was the attachment by the constable of Salem in 1670 of a Negro boy "Seasar" as the "proper goods of the said Powell." [69]

Despite the small numbers of Negroes in New England in this early period, the colonies of that region followed the example of the Southern and insular provinces in denying arms to the blacks in their midst—a discrimination which was never visited upon the English servant. In 1652 Massachusetts provided that Indians and Negroes could train in the militia the same as whites, but this apparently caused friction. The law was countermanded in 1656 by the statement "henceforth no negroes or Indians, altho servants of the English, shalbe armed or permitted to trayne." [70] Although as late as 1680 it was officially reported to London that there were no more than thirty "slaves" in Connecticut, that colony in 1660 excluded Indians and "negar servants" from the militia and "Watch and Ward." [71]

Edward Randolph in 1676 reported that there were a few indentured servants in Massachusetts "and not above two hundred slaves," by which he meant Negroes, for he said "they were brought from Guinea and Madagascar." [72] But it was not until 1698 that the phrase "Negro slave" actually appeared in the Massachusetts statutes.[73] The practice of slavery was preceding the law in

[66] John Cotton in 1651 clearly distinguished between slavery and servitude. He wrote Cromwell in that year in regard to the Scottish prisoners sent to New England, that "we have been desirous ... to make their yoke easy.... They have not been sold for slaves to perpetuall servitude, but for 6, or 7 or 8 yeares, as we do our owne." Quoted in George H. Moore, *Notes on the History of Slavery in Massachusetts* (New York, 1866), p. 17 n.

[67] *Records of the Colony of Rhode Island* ... (Providence, 1856), I, 243.

[68] Quoted in William B. Weeden, *Economic and Social History of New England* (Boston, 1891), p. 149 n. It was officially reported in 1680 by Connecticut colony that three or four "Blacks" were imported each year from the Barbados, and that they usually sold for £22 apiece. This was much more than the going price for servants. *Public Records of the Colony of Connecticut* (Hartford, 1850–90), III, 298.

[69] Quoted in Lorenzo Greene, *The Negro in Colonial New England, 1620–1776* (New York, 1942), p. 172.

[70] *Records of Massachusetts*, III, 268, 397.

[71] *Records of Connecticut*, III, 298, I, 349.

[72] Quoted in Palfrey, *History of New England*, III, 298.

[73] Hurd, *Law of Freedom*, I, 262. Greene, *Negro in New England*, pp. 65–6, says that in 1670 slavery in Massachusetts became legally inheritable, for in that year the word

Massachusetts precisely as it had in the South. Though an official report to London in 1680 distinguished between Negro slaves and servants in Connecticut,[74] the law of that colony did not bother to define the institution of slavery. Indeed, as late as 1704, the Governor gave it as his opinion that all children born of "negro bond-women are themselves in like condition, i.e., born in servitude," though he admitted that there was no statute which said so. His contention was, however, that such legislation was "needless, because of the constant practice by which they are held as such. . . ." [75]

During the last years of the seventeenth century, laws of Connecticut and Massachusetts continued to speak of Negroes as "servants," but it was very clear that the Negro's status was not being equated with that of the white servant. The General Court of Connecticut observed in 1690 that "many persons of this Colony doe . . . purchase negroe servants" and, since these servants run away, precautions have to be taken against such eventualities. It was therefore laid down that all "negroe or negroes shall" be required to have a pass in order to be outside the town bounds. Any inhabitant could stop a Negroe, free or slave, and have him brought before a magistrate if the black man were found to be without such a pass. Moreover, all ferrymen, upon pain of fine, were to deny access to their ferries to all Negroes who could not produce a pass.[76] Massachusetts in 1698 forbade trade with "any Indian, or negro servant or slave, or other known dissolute, lewd, and disorderly person, of whom there is just cause of suspicion." [77]

By the early years of the eighteenth century, the laws of Connecticut and Massachusetts had pretty well defined the Negro's subordinate position in society. Massachusetts acted to restrict the manumission of slaves by providing in 1703 that "molatto or negro slaves" could be freed only if security was given that they would not be chargeable upon the community. Another law set a curfew upon Indians, mulattoes and Negroes for nine o'clock each night. In 1705 Massachusetts became the only New England province to prohibit sexual relations between Negroes and mulattoes and Englishmen or those of "any other Christian nation." [78] Moreover, "any negro or mulatto" presuming to "smite or strike" an English person or any of another Christian nation would be "severely whipped." [79] In 1717 Negroes were barred from holding land in Connecticut.[80]

"strangers" was dropped from the Body of Liberties as a description of those who might be enslaved.

[74] *Records of Connecticut*, III, 298.

[75] Quoted in Bernard C. Steiner, *History of Slavery in Connecticut* (Baltimore, 1893), p. 18.

[76] *Records of Connecticut*, IV, 40.

[77] Hurd, *Law of Freedom*, I, 262–3.

[78] *Ibid.*, I, 263, Massachusetts had prohibited marriages between whites and Negroes, mulattoes and Indians in 1692. Lauber, *Indian Slavery*, p. 253.

[79] Hurd, *Law of Freedom*, I, 263. Rhode Island, too, in 1728, provided that before a Negro or mulatto could be manumitted, security had to given that he would not become a public charge. Hurd, *Law of Freedom*, I, 276.

[80] Greene, *Negro in New England*, p. 312.

Thus, like the colonists to the South, the New Englanders enacted into law, in the absence of any prior English law of slavery, their recognition of the Negroes as different and inferior. This was the way of the seventeenth century; only with a later conception of the brotherhood of all men would such legal discrimination begin to recede; but by then, generations of close association between the degraded status of slavery and black color would leave the same prejudice against the Negro in the North that it did in the South.

It would seem, then, that instead of slavery being the root of the discrimination visited upon the Negro in America, slavery was itself molded by the early colonists' discrimination against the outlander. In the absence of any law of slavery or commandments of the Church to the contrary—as was true of Brazil and Spanish-America—the institution of slavery into which the African was placed in the English colonies inevitably mirrored that discrimination and, in so doing, perpetuated it.

Once the English embodied their discrimination against the Negro in slave law, the logic of the law took over. Through the early eighteenth century, judges and legislatures in all the colonies elaborated the law along the discriminatory lines laid down in the amorphous beginnings. In doing so, of course, especially in the South, they had the added incentive of perpetuating and securing a labor system which by then had become indispensable to the economy. The cleavage between the races was in that manner deepened and hardened into the shape which became quite familiar by the nineteenth century. In due time, particularly in the South, the correspondence between the black man and slavery would appear so perfect that it would be difficult to believe that the Negro was fitted for anything other than the degraded status in which he was almost always found. It would also be forgotten that the discrimination had begun long before slavery had come upon the scene.

Robert C. Twombley and Robert H. Moore

BLACK PURITAN: THE NEGRO IN
SEVENTEENTH-CENTURY MASSACHUSETTS

The institution of slavery actually appeared in New England before it had fully evolved in Virginia. Yet the character of New England slavery, both in law and in fact, was never as severe as bondage in the South. The description by Robert C. Twombley and Robert H. Moore of Negroes in seventeenth-century Massachusetts provides a case study that is representative of colonial New England as a whole.

Historians have assumed that seventeenth-century Massachusetts was no different from other American colonies in its treatment of Negroes.[1] It has

Robert C. Twombley and Robert H. Moore, "Black Puritan: The Negro in Seventeenth-Century Massachusetts," *The William and Mary Quarterly*, XXIV (April, 1967), pp. 224–42. Reprinted with permission of *The William and Mary Quarterly*.

[1] Recent scholarship on early American slavery has ignored Massachusetts or assumed similarity with the South: Oscar and Mary Handlin, "Origins of the Southern Labor System," *The William and Mary Quarterly*, 3d Ser., VII (1950), 199–222, and Oscar Handlin, "The Origins of Negro Slavery," *Race and Nationality in American Life* (New York, 1957), 3–29, argue that discrimination developed because of the institutionalization of slavery. Carl N. Degler, "Slavery and the Genesis of American Race Prejudice," *Comparative Studies in Society and History*, II (1959), 49–66, reverses the Handlin thesis, attributing slavery to innate white discriminatory attitudes. Winthrop D. Jordan, "Modern Tensions and the Origin of American Slavery," *Journal of Southern History*, XXVIII (1962), 18–30, sees both slavery and discrimination as part of a worldwide debasement of the Negro. Other relevant works are: Jordan, "The Influence of the West Indies on the Origins of New England Slavery," *Wm. and Mary Qtly.* 3d Ser., XVIII (1961), 243–250; Lawrence W. Towner, "'A Fondness for Freedom': Servant Protest in Puritan Society," *ibid.*, XIX (1962), 201–219; Towner, "The Sewall-Saffin Dialogue on Slavery," *ibid.*, XXI (1964), 40–52; Jules Zanger, "Crime and Punishment in Early Massachusetts," *ibid.*, XXII (1965), 471–477; Emory Washburn, "Slavery as It Once Prevailed in Massachusetts," in *Early History of Massachusetts: Lectures Delivered ... Before the Lowell Institute, in Boston* (Boston, 1869), 199–225; and Lorenzo J. Greene, *The Negro in Colonial New England, 1620–1776* (New York, 1942).

been easy to overlook a colony where, as late as 1715, there were only 2,000 Negroes in a population of 96,000, and where whites seemed to hold racial views similar to those of other settlers. But an analysis of Negro life in the Puritan Commonwealth reveals the inaccuracy of this view.

Most authorities agree that Negroes first came to Massachusetts in 1638, but it seems clear to us that at least one Negro had arrived as early as 1633. Contemporaries estimated that there were between 100 and 200 in 1680 and 550 by 1708.[2] Although Negroes were numerous enough to be familiar in the everyday affairs of many communities by the 1660's, most Puritans regarded blacks as strange and exotic creatures. Despite the inconsistent terminology used to refer to Negroes,[3] Massachusetts whites held certain derogatory attitudes.

John Josselyn noted that some New Englanders thought Negro blackness resulted from the African climate, while others believed it came from Ham's curse. Blackness was commonly associated with evil. During the witchcraft hysteria many people claimed to have seen the Devil in the form of a "Blackman"; white women accused of having evil spirits were sometimes called "black witches." Blackness connoted ugliness as well as evil. "Sea-Devils," a fish found off the Maine coast, were popularly called "Negroes" because they were a very "ugly," "hideous" species, "having a black scale." [4]

[2] William Wood's 1634 New-England's Prospect . . . (1764 ed.), in Publications of the Prince Society, III (Boston, 1865), 86; and Deloraine P. Corey, The History of Malden, Mass., 1633–1785 (Malden, Mass., 1899), 415, refer to a Negro living in Plymouth at least as early as 1633. Population estimates are taken from Simon Bradstreet to the Committee of Trade and Plantations, May 18, 1680, in Elizabeth Donnan, ed., Documents Illustrative of the History of the Slave Trade to America (Washington, D.C., 1930–35), III, 14–15; Edward Randolph's Report to the Lords of the Committee of the Colonies, Aug., 1681, in Samuel G. Drake, The History and Antiquities of Boston . . . (Boston, 1856), 441; Joseph Dudley to the Council of Trade and Plantations, Oct. 1, 1708, in Cecil Headlam, ed., Calendar of State Papers, Colonial Series, America and West Indies, June, 1708–1709 (London, 1922), 110; and Evarts B. Greene and Virginia D. Harrington, American Population Before the Federal Census of 1790 (New York, 1932), 14.

[3] "Slave" was not precisely defined in seventeenth-century Massachusetts; its flexible usage permitted several meanings. The conventional definition was "one who is the property of, and entirely subject to, another person, whether by capture, purchase, or birth; a servant completely divested of freedom and personal rights." See W. A. Cragie, ed., A New English Dictionary on Historical Principles (Oxford, 1919), X, 182–184. The burden of this article is to demonstrate that Massachusetts never forced Negroes into this status. Puritans also used "slavery" to describe prisoners of war and criminals, and the term functioned as a rhetorical device to indicate dissatisfaction with government or authority. "Slave" and "servant" were used interchangeably in reference to Negroes: John Noble and John F. Cronin, eds. Records of the Court of Assistants of . . . Massachusetts . . . (Boston, 1901–28), I, 74 and John Josselyn, An Account of Two Voyages to New-England, Made during the Years 1638, 1663 (Boston, 1865), 139–140.

[4] The long history of black men in the European experience and the development of white racial opinion has been admirably treated in Winthrop D. Jordan, "White Over Black: the attitudes of the American colonists toward the Negro, to 1784" (unpubl. Ph.D. diss., Brown University, 1960), Ch. I. Puritan racial attitudes are illustrated in Josselyn, Two Voyages, 143; George L. Burr, ed., Narratives of the Witch-

If some derogatory attitudes found expression in metaphor, others appeared in social relations. Whites were insulted when compared closely with a Negro. "A Lieutenant of a Man of War," the perturbed Cotton Mather wrote, "whom I am a stranger to, designing to putt an Indignity upon me, has called his *Negro-Slave* by the Name of COTTON-MATHER." Samuel Sewall recorded in his diary that "Mr. Cotton Mather came to Mr. Wilkins's shop, and there talked very sharply against me as if I used his father worse than a Neger; spake so loud that the people in the street might hear him." Such opinions sometimes led to bizarre actions. Josselyn wrote that fish did not respond to herring as quickly as they did for a "waggish lad at Cape-porpus [Maine], who baited his hooks with the drown'd Negro's buttocks." Puritan racial attitudes do not seem appreciably different from those held by other contemporary white men.[5]

One might expect the Puritans to have treated Negroes with an indignity matching their attitudes. But the real test of the colony's race relations must be based not on what whites thought and said but on what they did. How the Negro fared in day to day activity is the best indication of the nature of Negro life in the Puritan Commonwealth.

II

Central to the maintenance of order and stability in any society is the administration of justice. This was particularly true in Massachusetts where respect for the law was primary in the colonists' conception of a vigorous, stable, and godly society. A profound commitment to the law and the judicial process overpowered antipathetical racial views and assured fair and equal treatment, guaranteeing the basic legal rights of Englishmen to free, servant, and slave Negroes. These rights—including police protection, legal counsel, trial by jury, fair and considered hearings, and impartial justice—are very much expected in the twentieth century. In the seventeenth they were incipient concepts in much of the western world. But Massachusetts guarded these liberties jealously, applying them without regard for skin color. The Puritans did not hold advanced racial views but they did place a high priority on the universality of justice. Throughout the century Negroes and whites received essentially equal treatment before the law.

Important principles were observed even in minor offenses. In 1680, for example, Goodman Wolland accused Daniel King's Negro boy of insulting him

craft Cases, 1648–1706 (New York, 1914), 309–310, 312, 425; and William S. Southgate, "History of Scarborough, from 1693 to 1783," Maine Historical Society, *Collections*, III (1853), 92.

[5] Dec. 10, 1721, in Worthington C. Ford, ed., *Diary of Cotton Mather* (New York, 1957), II, 663; Barrett Wendell, *Cotton Mather: The Puritan Priest* (New York, [1891]), 153, quoting Samuel Sewall, Oct. 20, 1701; Josselyn, *Two Voyages*, 159; Jordan, "White Over Black," Ch. I.

on a Boston street. When the boy denied the allegation, Wolland brought him to court where the case was thrown out for lack of witnesses. That the case went to court at all indicates a predilection to seek legal redress rather than to initiate private action. When, in 1653, "a contravercy" developed between John Smith of Plymouth and John Barnes's "neager maide servant," the Plymouth court listened to "whatsoever could bee saide on either side." Both were cleared of any misdemeanor, but they were admonished for public quarreling.[6]

Like whites, Negroes received police protection and were shielded from extralegal punitive action. When three Indians broke into the home of Angola, a free Negro, in 1672, he prosecuted. All three were given twenty stripes and ordered to remain in prison until they paid court costs. In another case Pelatiah Glover brought suit against Betty Negro for insulting his son and mother. Richard White and Tom, a Negro, testified against her. She was found guilty of slander and given ten stripes but by being taken to court Betty at least found a measure of protection. The principle of using judicial means rather than resorting to personal retribution extended to the colony's Maine jurisdiction where in 1686 George Norton prosecuted his own Negro for stealing his wool. Due process and a willingness to use the courts minimized expeditious extralegal punishment. Even masters recognized this principle.[7]

Other incidents establish that Negro testimony was admissible as evidence against whites. In 1673 a defendant challenged a witness's legal right to testify, but the plaintiff replied "that the negro was of such carriage and knowledge that her testimony had been accepted several times before this." Later, in 1679, Wonn Negro testified against Bridget Oliver, who was suspected

[6] George F. Dow, ed., *Records and Files of the Quarterly Courts of Essex County* (Salem, 1911–21), VII, 425; Nathaniel B. Shurtleff, ed., *Records of the Colony of New Plymouth in New England* (Boston, 1855–61), III, 39. To demonstrate racial equality before the law we shall compare the several kinds of criminal and civil offenses committed by Negroes to similar cases involving whites. We have appraised all the published records (falling between 1650 and 1690) in which Negroes appear; those presented here are not atypical. We believe these cases accurately reflect the temper of the Negro's participation in the legal process.

[7] The Angola case is in Samuel Eliot Morison, ed., *Records of the Suffolk County Court, 1671–1680*, 2 vols., in *Publications of the Colonial Society of Massachusetts, Collections,* XXIX–XXX (Boston, 1933), I, 119. The Glover incident is listed in Joseph H. Smith, ed., *Colonial Justice in Western Massachusetts (1639–1702): The Pynchon Court Record* . . . (Cambridge, Mass., 1961), 375. A comparable case involving a white woman brought a penalty of twenty stripes and the order to wear a paper "pinned upon her forehead with this inscription in capital letters: 'A SLANDERER OF MR. ZEROBABELL ENDICOTT,'" in Dow, ed., *Essex Court Recs.,* I, 380. Norton and Peter appear in Robert E. Moody, ed., *Province and Court Records of Maine* (Portland, 1928–64), III, 226. Carl Degler, on the Southern administration of justice to Negroes, says: "As early as 1669 the Virginia law virtually washed its hands of protecting the Negro held as a slave. It allowed punishment of refractory slaves up to and including accidental death, relieving the master, explicitly, of any fear of prosecution . . . ," in "Slavery and the Genesis of American Race Prejudice," 61. Compare this situation also with the 1694–95 Nathaniel Cane murder case cited in Moody, ed., *Maine Recs.,* IV, 34–35.

of witchcraft. In 1680 Mingo the Negro was a witness in a suit involving warehouse arson. Instances of Negro testimony for and against both races are numerous.[8]

It is also evident from the records that Negroes had access to legal counsel. In 1679 Hannah, a Negro servant, was convicted for stealing a box of "Chyrurgions Jnstruments." From prison she persuaded three white men to post forty pounds bond for her release and petitioned the Suffolk County court for dismissal of her fines. Her appeal, a sophisticated legal argument, cited page and section numbers of the laws governing burglary. Although the jury dismissed it, Zachariah Chaffee, Jr., commenting on Hannah's appeal, noted the "refined distinctions" that could only have been "written by men accustomed to legal problems." [9]

An additional example of the many elements of justice accorded Negroes stemmed from the Salem witch controversy. In 1692 a warrant was issued for the arrest of Mary Black, a Negro owned by Lieutenant Nathaniel Putnam of Salem Village. Although maintaining her innocence, Mary was tried, convicted, and imprisoned for witchcraft. The next year, however, cooler heads had apparently prevailed, and Mary was not forgotten. Upon petition she was released from prison by proclamation of the Governor.[10]

These cases introduce important principles illustrating Negro legal rights. A Negro's word was admissible as evidence and his testimony could be as acceptable as that of whites. Charges against Negroes had to be documented and they received the thoughtful consideration of juries and magistrates. Negroes had police protection and were shielded from extralegal practices that would have denied them due process of law. They could appeal, use legal counsel, and receive gubernatorial pardons.

The principles operative in the cases described above were applicable when more abhorrent crimes were committed. Negroes were given the same judicial treatment as whites in all aspects of the case from indictment to punishment. Some crimes, like burglary, are impossible to analyze, for penalties were distributed on the basis of the kinds and amounts of items stolen; we were unable to find cases in which Negroes and whites appropriated exactly the same things. For this reason we have not attempted comparisons of thefts, but have analyzed arson, murder, manslaughter, and sexual offenses—the four main areas in which comparison between the races is possible.

Of the sexual crimes committed in Massachusetts, fornication, bastardy, and rape were most prevalent. According to the 1675 Laws and Ordinances of War—a compilation of previous statutes—rape, ravishment, and unnatural abuses were punishable by death. Fornication and other "dissolute lascivious-

---

[8] See Dow, ed., *Essex Court Recs.*, V, 179; VI, 255; VII, 329–330, 373, 410. For white testimony on behalf of Negroes see Noble and Cronin, eds., *Assistants Recs.*, III, 194.

[9] Morison, ed., *Suffolk Court Recs.*, II, 1153–1157. Chaffee's remarks are in the Intro., I, xxv.

[10] Charles W. Upham, *Salem Witchcraft* ... (Boston, 1867), II, 128, 136–137.

ness" were penalized at the judge's discretion, taking into account the severity and circumstances of the case. Fornication, by both Negro and white, was a considerable problem in early Massachusetts, and the many recorded cases provide ample opportunity for comparative analysis.[11]

Essex County punished its Negro fornicators by whipping or fine, the choice sometimes being left to the offender. In 1660, Captain White's Negro Jugg was whipped; Grace and Juniper, convicted in 1674, were "to be fined or whipped." In 1678, two "neager" servants, David and Judith, chose to pay a fine rather than feel the lash ten and five times respectively. The whites in Essex County received similar treatment. Mary Dane, an indentured servant, was whipped. The same year, 1654, Elizabeth Osgood was given thirty stripes and her mate twenty-five. Most infringers, regardless of race, received from ten to twenty stripes or were ordered to pay from forty to fifty shillings.[12]

Representative of Suffolk County's treatment of fornicators was the case of Mary Plumb, a white, who was punished with fifteen stripes and court and prison fees for "Lascivious carriage by being seene in bed with a man." For the same offense, Phoebe Lovell received ten stripes or a forty shilling fine plus court costs. Negroes in Suffolk County got the same penalties. Joan and her partner, Jasper Indian, were given their choice of fifteen stripes or a forty shilling fine plus court costs. In a significant case Robert Corbet, a white, and George, a Negro, both servants of Stephen French, received identical sentences for committing fornication with the Negro Maria: twenty stripes and court costs. Fornication between the races was not punished any more stringently than that between members of the same race. In Suffolk, as in Essex County, the most common penalty ranged from ten to twenty lashes or a forty to fifty shilling fine plus fees of court.[13]

Although there is no evidence that it was practiced, racial intermarriage was not illegal until 1705. Before then most miscegenation was illicit. If it led to bastardy, penalties for both races were generally the same as for simple

[11] The 1675 statutes are in Nathaniel B. Shurtleff, ed., *Records of the Governor and Company of the Massachusetts Bay in New England* (Boston, 1854), V, 49–50, Sections 13 and 14. Also see Jordan, "White Over Black," 119. Fornication and adultery were usually treated as one crime in the seventeenth century. Married men, engaging in sexual activity with women other than their wives, were often tried for fornication.

[12] For Essex County Negro fornication cases see Dow, ed., *Essex Court Recs.*, II, 247; V, 411; VI, 73, 135; VII, 141, 411; for whites see I, 71, 80, 82, 337, 347, 404, 414, 420; III, 17, 61, 198–199; VII, 377–378, 398, 406, 410; VIII, 375, 377, 424. This list is by no means exhaustive.

[13] Because the published records are incomplete, the only Suffolk County cases are from the 1670's. For Negro offenders see Morison, ed., *Suffolk Court Recs.*, I, 233; II, 991; for whites see, for example, I, 22, 80, 90–91, 114, 119, 185, 233–234; II, 885, 1012–1014, 1097–1099, 1102, 1153. The Courts sometimes required a couple fornicating before marriage to make public confession before the church. See I, 80, 90–91. In Maine fornicators usually received seven or more stripes or a fine ranging from fifteen to fifty shillings. See Moody, ed., *Maine Recs.*, IV, 268–269, 293, 340, 344–345, 358, 360, and 371 for examples.

fornication. In most cases the court sought to determine paternity in order to provide the child's support, and this led to additional costs for the father. Usually the woman was whipped from ten to twenty stripes or ordered to pay a forty to fifty shilling fine. The man was given a similar number of stripes and then bound to pay weekly support or a lump sum to be administered over the years. In 1682, for example, Richard Prior gave thirty pounds surety to save Ipswich from maintaining his illegitimate child. The same year John Tucker was fined six pounds and ordered to pay an undisclosed amount for birth and support. In 1679 the court ordered John Hunkins to give his partner's father one shilling per week. When the races mixed the penalties were about the same: William Rane, father of a child by the Indian servant Ann, paid three shillings a week. For "haveing a bastard," the white Hannah Bonny was "well whipt"; her mate, Nimrod Negro, was also whipped and made to turn over eighteen pence weekly for his offspring. Illegitimate Negro children were generally awarded financial support in amounts similar to those paid to white and mixed offspring. In 1673 the Negro Silvanus provided two shillings six pence per week for his son's upbringing.

A humorous episode took place in Maine in 1695. Alice Metherill, for being pregnant, was given a choice of ten stripes and fifteen shillings or five pounds and court costs; her alleged partner was ordered to pay eleven shillings six pence bond and two shillings six pence maintenance per week payable monthly. When the child was born, however, it was quite black. The "father," already punished by the court, quickly prosecuted Alice for falsely associating him with her "black bastard." Alice, by now known as a "whore" and a "witch," finally admitted that Black Will, a Negro slave, was her real consort. The province did not hold Black Will's past against him, however, for several years later when he was accused of fathering the baby of Elizabeth Brooks, a single white woman, he was acquitted.[14]

Rape, a more serious offense, could be punished by death. The two Negro cases in the published records reveal the severity dealt offenders. Basto Negro was convicted in 1676 of raping the three year old daughter of Robert Cox, his master. When Cox appealed Basto's death sentence, the jury substituted thirty-nine lashes and ordered him "allwayes to weare a roape about his neck, to hang doune two foot." If ever he was found without his rope Basto would feel an additional twenty lashes. Shortly thereafter John Negro confessed to "pulling Sarah Phillips of Salem off her horse and attempting to ravish her."

---

[14] As with fornication interracial bastardy was not punished more severely than bastardy between two members of the same race. For examples of penalties accorded illegitimate white births see Morison, ed., *Suffolk Court Recs.*, II, 1097–1099; Dow, ed., *Essex Court Recs.*, VII, 97, 187; VIII, 12–13, 279; Shurtleff, ed., *Plymouth Recs.*, I, 127. For illegitimate Negro births see Morison, ed., *Suffolk Court Recs.*, I, 113, 259; II, 809, 841, 1164; Dow, ed., *Essex Court Recs.*, I, 196, 323; VI, 137. Interracial bastardy cases are: Dow, ed., *Essex Court Recs.*, V, 409; VI, 23; VII, 410; Morison, ed., *Suffolk Court Recs.*, I, 185, 232; II, 809; Shurtleff, ed., *Plymouth Recs.*, VI, 177. Alice Metherill and Black Will are in Moody, ed., *Maine Recs.*, IV, 47–49, 64–66; V, 126, 169–171, 199–201; *York Deeds* (Portland, 1887–1910), VI, fol. 88.

John's penalty for attempted rape was a five pound payment to Miss Phillips, prosecution and court costs, and banishment from the colony.[15]

Whites also received stiff penalties. John Man, perhaps the Marquis de Sade of his time, for "wanton and lascivious carriages ... and cruell beating" of his indentured servant, gave two hundred pounds sureties until the next court, paid prosecution costs and court fees, and terminated his girl's contract. John Kempe attempted rape on "3 young girles [and] was censured to bee whiped both heare [Boston], at Roxbury and at Salem very severely and was Comitted for a slave to Lieft Davenport." Two other white rapists, William Cheny and Samuel Guile, were hanged until dead.[16]

Two rapes involving Indians demonstrate important aspects of Massachusetts jurisprudence. In 1674, Tom, indicted for raping another Indian, pleaded not guilty before a "Jury of twelve men six English and six Indians against none of which he Objected." Although he was found guilty, Tom held the right to challenge a jury containing six members of his own race. The second case, from Plymouth in 1682, dealing with "Sam, the Indian," reveals a paternalistic strain in legal approaches to nonwhites. Sam was proven guilty: "although in an ordinary consideration hee deserved death, yett considering hee was but an Indian, and therefore in an incapasity [unable] to know the horibleness ... of his abominable act ... he was centanced ... to be severely whipt att the post and sent out of the country." In spite of this decision, leniency for Indians and Negroes, who ordinarily met the same penalties as whites, does not appear the rule. Indeed, judges followed the argument presented by a defendant in a 1660 Essex County case, although his suggestion about Negroes was not considered valid: "the law is undeniable that the indian may have the same distribusion of Justice with our selves." John Hawthorne had argued. But "ther is as I humbly consieve not the same argument as amongst the negroes for the light of the gospell is [not] a begineing to appeare amongst them...." The application of the law to Negroes followed the pattern of Tom's case and Hawthorne's suggestion for Indians—due process and equality in punishment. The courts did not consider Christianity a prerequisite for equality before the law; nor did they apply Plymouth's leniency for Sam Indian or Hawthorne's views on Negroes to the blacks in their midst.[17]

Equitable treatment for Negroes extended to other capital offenses. According to the law, murder was to be "expiated with the death of the murderer." A measure of Massachusetts's concern for justice was the care with which she appraised murder cases, often meting out punishment for manslaughter instead. Thoughtful scrutiny reflected a recognition of extenuating circumstances. And this attitude did not exclude Negro assailants of whites.

---

[15] Basto's case is in Noble and Cronin, eds., *Assistants Recs.*, I, 74, and Shurtleff, ed., *Mass. Rec.*, V, 117–118. John Negro is in Morison, ed., *Suffolk Court Recs.*, II, 1067.

[16] *Ibid.*, II, 807; Noble and Cronin, eds., *Assistants Recs.*, I, 50, 199; II, 86; innocent whites are *ibid.*, I, 73, 158.

[17] *Ibid.*, I, 21–22; *Plymouth Recs.*, VI, 98; Hawthorne's argument is in Dow, ed., *Essex Court Recs.*, II, 240.

The average penalty for manslaughter was a twenty pound fine and the costs of prosecution, court, and detention. Depending on the circumstances, part of the fine went to the colony and part to the deceased's relatives.[18] Both instances of Negro manslaughter, originally indictments for murder against whites, were handled equitably. A 1684 defendant, "Robert Trayes, negro," wounded the "legg of Daniell Standlake . . ., of which wound, and cutting the legg occationed thereby, died. . . ." Since he had meant to fire at Standlake's door, the jury decided that Trayes was "an instrument of the death of Daniell Standlake by misadventure," and sentenced the defendant to pay the deceased's father five pounds or be whipped. The second case, in which the servant Robin was accused, is of particular note, not only for its dealing with manslaughter but also for its clear statement of Negro legal rights.[19]

Robin was guilty of giving John Cheeny of Cambridge "a mortall wound on the head with a stick" in 1689. His punishment was light: charges of prosecution, fees of court, and costs of prison where he was to remain until he paid. Robin had pled not guilty, but what extenuating circumstances had brought about the easy sentence are not recorded. More important, however, is that after the jury had been selected Robin was allowed to "make . . . challange against any of them." In addition, one juror, feeling as Hawthorne had in 1660, that Negroes did not deserve "the same distribution of Justice with our selves," refused to appear. In reply the court fined him five shillings. Through this concrete act the court clearly stated that shirking jury duty was inexcusable and that due process extended to blacks as well as whites.

The only recorded case in which a white killed a Negro took place in Maine in 1694 when a master's continual mistreatment of his servant led to her death. In the South well before this time, as Carl Degler points out, masters were without "any fear of prosecution" if they killed slaves; the law "allowed punishment for refractory slaves up to and including accidental death. . . ." But the Puritans showed more restraint. Indicted by a grand jury on suspicion of murder, Nathaniel Cane was convicted of manslaughter for "Cruelty to his Negro woman by Cruell Beating and hard usage." His fine—ten pounds ten shillings—was light. Nonetheless, a master could not mistreat, abuse, or murder his Negro without threat of legal action.[20]

Arson, an infrequent but serious offense, brought harsh penalties. Severity was demonstrated early in the colony's history when in 1640 Henry Stevens fired his master's barn and had his indenture extended by twenty-one years.

---

[18] Shurtleff, ed., *Mass. Recs.*, V, 50, lists penalties for manslaughter and murder. White manslaughter cases are cited in Noble and Cronin, eds., *Assistants Recs.*, I, 54, 114, 188, 358–359.

[19] The Trayes case is in Shurtleff, ed., *Plymouth Recs.*, VI, 141–142; Robin's in Noble and Cronin, eds., *Assistants Recs.*, I, 304–305, 321.

[20] Moody, ed., *Maine Recs.*, IV, 34–35. We saw no published court records convicting Negroes of murder. But note the equality of sentence in this extract from Samuel Sewall's diary, June 8, 1693: "Elisabeth Emerson of Havarill and a Negro Woman were executed after Lecture, for murdering their Infant Children." Massachusetts Historical Society, *Collections*, 5th Ser., V (1878), 379.

Throughout the century the penalties were stiff: Jack, a Negro arsonist, was hanged in 1681. Two Negroes implicated in the Maria arson case the same year were banished and Maria was burned alive, the only punishment of its kind in Massachusetts history.[21] Maria's fire had caused the death of a baby girl. She had deliberately destroyed her master's house and had not intended murder. But since she had caused a death by burning she in turn was burned. Her severe sentence may have been prompted by uneasiness over a rash of fires in the Boston vicinity. Social pressure may have induced the court to be unduly harsh in this affair but it was not stampeded. The strict sentence was a response to a specific situation and did not become a precedent for future dealings with either arsonists, murderers, or Negroes. But the case stands as an ugly blot on Puritan history.[22]

This review of legal cases indicates that throughout the seventeenth century the Negro received due process and only in isolated incidents, like the Maria case, was he given unusual treatment. But even on that occasion it is questionable to what extent skin color dictated severity. In general, the Negro held the rights of Englishmen before the courts. The legal apparatus did not undergo subtle shifts when Negroes came before it.

III

If the Negro's legal status was not circumscribed by pigmentation neither were his economic opportunities. Several black men, servant and free, accumulated real and other property; the color of their skin did not by definition render them ineligible for economic gain. Although most Negroes were members of the servant class and therefore at the bottom of the economic ladder, some were able to carve out an enviable niche in the white business world.

The story of Angola illustrates the possibilities. In 1653 he was owned by Captain Robert Keayne, who in his will in 1656 left Angola a two pound legacy. Then the free Negro Bostian Ken purchased Angola and set him free

---

[21] The Stevens case is in Noble and Cronin, eds., *Assistants Recs.*, II, 100. The documents relating to Maria, her accomplices, and Jack have been brought together by John Noble. See *Publication of the Colonial Society at Massachusetts, Transactions, 1899, 1900*, VIII (Boston, 1904), 323–336.

[22] Noble, *ibid.*, argues that Maria was hanged before burning, dismissing both Cotton and Increase Mather's assertions that she was burned alive. But Noble overlooked evidence that substantiates the Mathers' contentions: a Milton minister who had witnessed Jack's and Maria's execution noted in his diary on Sept. 22, 1681: ". . . two negroes burnt, one of them was first hanged." "Rev. Peter Thacher's Journal" in Albert K. Teele, ed., *The History of Milton, Mass. 1640 to 1887* (Boston, 1887), 646. Increase Mather wrote: Maria was "burned to death,—the first that has suffered such a death in New England." Mass. Hist. Soc., *Proceedings*, III (1859), 320. Edgar Buckingham's allegation that in 1675 Phillis, a Negro slave, was burned alive in Cambridge, in "Morality, Learning, and Religion, in Massachusetts in Olden Times," *History and Proceedings of the Pocumtuck Valley Memorial Association, 1880–1889* (Deerfield, Mass., 1898), II, 20, seems unsupported.

by bonding his property to Mrs. Keayne. In 1670 Governor Richard Bellingham sold a piece of land bordered "Upon the North East with the land of Angola, the Negro." Bellingham had given him this fifty-foot square piece in the late 1660's when Angola, paddling in a river, had rescued the Governor from his sinking boat. When he died in 1675 Angola's will confirmed his house, land, and other possessions upon his widow Elizabeth, her children, and her heirs forever. In the twenty years before his death Angola had paid his eighteen pound obligation to Ken and had moved from a servant with a two pound legacy to a free Negro of means.[23]

Bostian Ken, Angola's benefactor, was another prosperous Negro. In order to purchase his friend's freedom in 1656 Ken bonded his house and land in Dorchester plus four and one half acres of wheat. In 1662 he sold his one-third share of the fourteen-ton ship *Hopewell* to his "loving Friend Francis Vernon" along with "one barrell of liquor one barr of Sugar one Barr mackerell and one Barr Codfish." From 1656 to 1662 Ken dealt in considerable amounts of property.[24]

Most of the other seventeenth-century Negro landowners received their holdings from their masters. In 1677 Increase Mather bought land bordered on the "Northwest by the land of Jethro the Negro." If Governor Bellingham and the Reverend Mr. Mather owned choice land, the bordering Negro holdings may have also been desirable.[25] Other Negroes held land, houses, and small businesses. When Thomas, owner of a chair-making establishment, married Katherine in 1678, he drew up a lengthy document granting her his estate in case of his death and bound himself for one hundred pounds surety. Zippora Potter, daughter of one of Robert Keayne's Negroes, bought a twenty-eight by sixty-foot "parcell of land with a dwelling house thereupon" in 1670 for "forty Six pounds currant Mony of New England in hand paid." Although the number of successful Negroes was small, they came from a total Negro population in the colony that was at most only two hundred at this time.[26]

A few Negroes were property owners, but the majority were house servants living with white families. Many resided in Boston but those in the outlying areas and the Boston blacks who traveled about broadened interracial contact. Most Negroes lived in their masters' homes, were often left alone, and could

[23] *Suffolk Deeds* (Boston, 1880–1906), II, 297; III, 78; VII, 22, 144; VIII, 298–299; Morison, ed., *Suffolk Court Recs.*, II, 598; *Report of the Record Commissioners of the City of Boston Containing Miscellaneous Papers* (Boston, 1876–1909), X, 25.

[24] Bostian Ken (Kine, Kajne), also known as Sebastian and Bus Bus, probably took his surname from the Keayne family. It was common for a Negro, if he had a last name, to use his master's or former master's. *Suffolk Deeds*, II, 297; IV, 111, 113.

[25] Angola's land fronted on the main road between Boston and Roxbury and at least one man, James Pennyman, envied it. *Ibid.*, VIII, 298.

[26] Property owning Negroes and master's gifts are *ibid.*, VII, 43; X, 278, 295; Dow, ed., *Essex Court Recs.*, II, 183; VIII, 434; *York Deeds*, IV, fol. 52; Ford, ed., *Diary of Cotton Mather*, I, 278; Henry A. Hazen, *History of Billerica, Mass.* (Boston, 1883), 170–171. Charles Taussig noted a Rhode Island Negro couple that had accumulated a 300 pound fortune and in 1735 sailed back to Guinea where they were independently wealthy; see *Rum, Romance and Rebellion* (New York, 1928), 33.

come and go as they pleased when not working. They were not restricted to the towns in which they lived and in many cases moved freely about the countryside.[27]

Freedom of movement opened up certain options. One option, running away, may have been a product of working class discontent; but running away was also encouraged by alternatives that lack of repression offered.[28] Freedom of movement permitted a certain amount of fraternization between races in the lower classes; the derogatory views of most whites did not preclude informal relations. Occasionally mutual activities were forms of antisocial behavior. In 1673, for example, "John Burrington, Edward Fish, Richard Hollingworths Negro Tom, Thomas [,] Clark Cliffords Servt," and a fifth man, stole saddles and bridles and "complotted to run away." About the same time "Gregory, Nath. Emerson, Arthur Abbot and a Negro" broke into a house, took wine, and improvised a drinking party. But not all interracial mingling was mischievous. For five years in the 1690's one of Boston's four chimney sweepers was "Jeremiah the Negro"; for one year, 1693, he was joined by "Negro Will," who along with Jeremiah brought token integration to Boston's public employ. During the smallpox epidemic in the 1680's Mary Heall, a seventy-four year old widow living alone, took the Negro Zanckey into her home to watch over his recovery. On another occasion, Jack, a runaway Negro, came to Anthony Dorchester's home. Jack was a stranger but Dorchester invited him in and made him welcome:

> . . . after asking for a Pipe of Tobacco which I told him there was some on the Table he tooke my knife and Cut some and then put it in his Pocket, and after that tooke downe a Cutlass and offered to draw it but it Coming out stiff I closed in upon him. . . .

Jack was overpowered and taken to prison, but Dorchester's initial hospitality is noteworthy.[29]

[27] Horizontal mobility and freedom of movement are illustrated by the Maria case, discussed above; Dow, ed., *Essex Court Recs.*, VI, 255; VIII, 297–298; *Suffolk Deeds*, IV, x–xi; Ford, ed., *Diary of Cotton Mather*, II, 139; *Diary of Samuel Sewall*, Mass. Hist. Soc., *Coll.*, 5th Ser., VI (1879), 5; the travel account of an unknown Frenchman, *ca.* 1687, in Nathaniel B. Shurtleff, *A Topographical and Historical Description of Boston* (Boston, 1871), 48; James R. Trumbull, *History of Northampton* (Northampton, 1898), I, 376–377. Exemplifying freedom from masters' supervision is the case of a servant who persisted in wooing a young lady although repeatedly warned by *her* master to keep away. Both were later convicted for fornication. Dow, ed., *Essex Court Recs.*, VII, 141.

[28] Revolts were never a problem in Massachusetts but runaways were frequent. Closest to a slave revolt was an unsuccessful 1690 attempt by a New Jerseyite with abolitionist tendencies to induce Negroes, Indians, and Frenchmen to attack several Bay Colony towns. See Joshua Coffin, *A Sketch of the History of Newbury* . . . (Boston, 1845), 153–154, and Sidney Perley, "Essex County in the Abolition of Slavery," *Essex-County Historical and Genealogical Register*, I (1894), 2.

[29] On informal relations see Dow, ed., *Essex Court Recs.*, I, 287; V, 141; VII, 394–395; VIII, 297; Morison, ed., *Suffolk Court Recs.*, I, 249; II, 648–649; Robert F. Seybolt, *The Town Officials of Colonial Boston, 1634–1775* (Cambridge, Mass., 1939),

The colony's mechanisms of social control which permitted easy interracial contact did not make Negroes full fledged citizens or the social equals of whites, but neither were the blacks shunted to another realm of existence. The absence of rigid barriers in Massachusetts did not create a Negro utopia. But neither were Bay Colony blacks forced into a separate and demeaning world of their own. The Negro hovered on the fringes of full participation in social and economic life.

I V

Overcoming the obstacles of nature was of immediate importance to the first generation of Puritans; in their attempt to construct a "city upon a hill" their first concerns were the problems of building communities, of keeping their children from barbarism, and of reproducing essential and familiar institutions. But as the generations passed, as trade increased, as the frontier receded, and as the complexities of a growing colony burgeoned, the Commonwealth's problems shifted. Social order and stability had been of major importance from the beginning but during the last two decades of the seventeenth century serious social introspection increased. Ministers warned that God was angry with the people; family structure, education, the churches, and other social institutions came under closer scrutiny. It was in this context that the colony passed her first laws to regulate the Negro's behavior.

Except for militia policy, no laws were passed applying only to Negroes until the 1680's.[30] Old and New England had fitted the black man into the social system without legally recognizing slavery or a slave caste. Within the broad guidelines of the Common Law and Puritan religious views Massachusetts had extended century-old rights of Englishmen to Negroes. But in the 1680's the colony began to place restrictions upon them. The new Negro policies were responses to three social concerns: a widespread anathema for the slave trade, a pervasive uneasiness about the colony's economic future, and a growing anxiety about the Negro's behavior.

In spite of the unpopularity of slaving, several Massachusetts merchants were active traders in the 1680's, selling Negroes in Virginia for three to five thousand pounds of tobacco per head. Public pressure could not prohibit businessmen from dealing with Southerners but it could discourage the practice at home. Fear of public reprisal forced John Saffin, John Usher, James Wetcomb, and Andrew Belcher to import Negroes secretly in 1681. Fearing

---

77, 79, 83, 85, 87; Joseph Dudley to Gabriel Bernon, May 20, 1707, in George F. Daniels, *History of the Town of Oxford Massachusetts* (Oxford, 1892), 26–27. The quotation is from Smith, ed., *Colonial Justice in Western Massachusetts*, 298–299.

[30] Massachusetts never formally denied Negroes the right to bear personal arms and specifically included them in the militia in 1652. But in 1656, without explanation, she reversed her policy, excluding Indians and Negroes from training. Shurtleff, ed., *Mass. Records*, IV, Pt. i, 86, 257.

seizure, these merchants rerouted their Guinea trader from Swansea, Rhode Island, to Nantasket, Massachusetts, where, they wrote, "before you come in there take in such negroes ... of ours and come up in the night with them, giveing us notice thereof wth what privacy you can. ..." "Keepe your men Ignorant of your designe," the traders told their agent, and do nothing "prejudiciall to our mayne designe." [31]

Analyses of the economy seemed to demonstrate little benefit in the Negro's presence. In 1702 the General Court decided to promote "the bringing of White Servants and to put a period to Negroes being slaves." Beneath this admirable statement were more complex and mundane considerations. In 1708 Governor Joseph Dudley remarked that Negroes were costly to maintain during the winter months because they did little work and demanded great amounts of clothing. Negroes "are usually the worst servants," he noted. "The planters here do so much prefer white" laborers. The most complete statement of the economic disadvantages of Negroes appeared in an anonymous 1716 pamphlet. "Slaves ... are a great hinderance to the Peopling and Improving the Country," the author began. If Negroes were excluded it "would greatly Encourage [white] Servants to come," and thereby aid the colony's growth. Since the land was "generally taken up," white servants could not acquire property and frequently became runaways and thieves. To avoid unruly indentured labor, a master could buy Negroes, and because of the tax structure, come off "cheaper than his poorer Neighbour that has an Apprentice." Apprentices cost more than slaves to maintain, were subject to regular militia training, and went to war. Slaves discouraged economic growth by draining their owners of wealth and by displacing laborers, apprentices, and craftsmen who used indenture as a stepping stone to greater things. To the author, the Negro posed a serious threat to indenture which, he felt, was the key to economic growth.[32]

The first regulations on Negroes were clauses inserted into general laws prohibiting Negroes, mulattos, Indians, servants, and apprentices from buying or being served alcoholic beverages. Later in the 1680's the same groups were warned about stealing or giving away stolen goods and whites who induced thefts or received stolen merchandise were similarly promised punishment.[33]

---

[31] William Fitzhugh, King George County Virginia, to Mr. Jackson of Piscataway, in New England, Feb. 11, 1683, in R. A. Brock, "New England and the Slave Trade," *Wm. and Mary Qtly.*, II (1894), 176–177; Saffin, Usher, Wetcomb, and Belcher to Welstead, June 12, 1681, in *New-England Historical and Genealogical Register*, XXXI (1877), 75–76.

[32] Drake, *History and Antiquities*, 525, quotes the General Court, June, 1702; Dudley to Council, Oct. 1, 1708, in Headlam, ed., *Cal. State Papers, Col. Ser., June, 1708–09*, 110; "Some Considerations Upon the several sorts of Banks Proposed as a Medium of Trade: And Some Improvements that might be made in this Province, hinted at" (Boston, 1716), in Andrew McFarland Davis, ed., *Colonial Currency Reprints, 1682–1751* (Boston, 1910–11), I, 343, 346.

[33] Acts regulating alcoholic consumption are in the Records of the Council of Massachusetts under the Administration of President Joseph Dudley, "Dudley Records," *Mass. Hist. Soc., Proceedings*, 2d Ser., XIII (Boston, 1899, 1900), 252; Ellis Ames

No further legislation appeared until after the turn of the century. In 1703 Indian, Negro, and mulatto servants and slaves could be on the streets after nine in the evening only with masters' consent. After 1703 no Negro or mulatto could be manumitted unless his master gave fifty pounds surety for the servant's welfare. The first law was directed toward night-time unrest, and the second prevented masters from throwing elderly, unemployable servants on the town charge. Both were concerned with specific and observable social problems.

The most stringent new measure, "An Act for the Better Preventing of a Spurious and Mixt Issue" of 1705, drove a deep wedge between the races. Sexual intercourse and racial intermarriage were now specifically prohibited. Fixed penalties were imposed on both races. Fornication was no longer left to judicial decision; Negro offenders were banished and the white consort, male or female, assumed responsibility for the offspring. The law reemphasized the desirability of Negro marriages, presumably as part of an effort to minimize mulatto births.

The 1705 law also placed a four pound duty on Negroes imported into the colony, and set heavy penalties on violators. The new duty aimed to discourage the slave trade. Some Puritans wished to rid the colony of Negroes or prevent any more from coming but restrictions on importation did not rest on this basis alone. Seven years later, in 1712, the General Court prohibited the trade in Indians. Revulsion for the slave trade and suspicion of outsiders worked to prevent nonwhites from coming to the Puritan Commonwealth.

A five-part law in 1707 prevented free Negroes from harboring or entertaining nonwhite servants in their homes without masters' approval and ordered them to repair highways, clean streets, or perform other tasks equal in time and amount to military duty. Since free Negroes had "a share in the benefit" of common defense, they would also go to the parade ground "in case of alarm" and "perform such tasks as the first commission of the company shall direct. . . ." The several laws were supplemented by town ordinances which, throughout the eighteenth century, further limited Negro freedom of movement.[34]

---

and Abner C. Goodell, eds., *Acts and Resolves of the Province of Massachusetts Bay, 1692–1714* (Boston, 1869–1922), I, 154; Moody, ed., *Maine Recs.*, IV, 51; Edward W. Baker, "The 'Old Worcester Turnpike,' " *Proceedings of the Brookline Historical Society* (Jan. 23, 1907), 29. Laws governing stolen goods are in Ames and Goodell, eds., *Acts and Resolves*, I, 156, 325; see also Greene, *The Negro in Colonial New England*, 130. The only other seventeenth-century statute aimed at Negroes was passed in 1680: that no ship of more than 12 tons should entertain any passenger, servant or Negro, without permit from the governor. *The Colonial Laws of Massachusetts. Reprinted from the Edition of 1672, With the Supplements through 1686* (Boston, 1887), 281.

[34] The laws discussed in these paragraphs are in Ames and Goodell, eds., *Acts and Resolves*, I, 535, 578–579, 606–607; John B. Dillon, ed., *Oddities of Colonial Legislation in America . . .* (Indianapolis, 1879), 206–207, 211–212; *Report of the Record Commissioners of the City of Boston*, VIII, 173–177.

V

The new Massachusetts statutes dealing with Negroes were responses to specific and observable colonial problems. The measures arose from what the Puritans thought were manifestations of social disorder. The legislation was not a premeditated program to debase the Negro, for the Puritans believed that their regulations were in the Negro's best interest. Some colonial leaders like Samuel Sewall and Cotton Mather wanted to incorporate Negroes more intimately into the colony's social and religious institutions; but men of narrower vision passed laws which overruled better intentions. The Bay Colony reluctantly accepted the black man's presence but believed by the 1700's that it precipitated social disorder. Legal restrictions on Massachusetts's Negroes neither followed from nor led to slavery. In the Bay Colony these restrictions were part of a hasty problem-solving endeavor that prevalent attitudes and predispositions made possible. The Negro felt the brunt of discriminatory laws but he was not without due process and never totally removed from participation in the white social and economic orbit. These advantages reflected an attitude that later enabled the Bay Colony to lead the way in constitutional prohibitions of slavery.

Benjamin Quarles

LORD DUNMORE AS LIBERATOR

*The era of the American Revolution, with its ideological com-
mitment to equalitarianism and natural rights, was one of temporary improvement in the status of American Negroes. Antislavery
societies flourished, and the northern states either outlawed slavery
outright or took steps looking toward the gradual emancipation
of the slaves. Though at first the Revolutionary leaders decided to
exclude Negroes from the Continental Army, military exigencies led
to a reversal of this policy. Except for Georgia and South Carolina,
even the southern states made provisions for manumitting those
slaves who fought in the Revolutionary armies.*

*Historians have probably exaggerated and overdramatized the
improvement of the Negroes' status in this period. One example of
this overdramatization has been the traditional view of the impact of the proclamation issued by Virginia's royal governor, Lord
Dunmore, who offered to liberate those slaves joining the British
forces. Not only did a number of slaves achieve their freedom in this
way, but, according to most accounts, it was Dunmore's action which
caused Washington and his advisors to withdraw their prohibition
on Negro enlistments. In a careful study of the subject, Benjamin
Quarles found no evidence that Dunmore's proclamation influenced
the Revolutionary generals. Quarles concludes that most of the
slaves who joined the British performed valuable services but ultimately found death rather than freedom.*

Iɴ American patriotic tradition the first full-fledged villain to step from the
wings as the Revolutionary War unfolded was John Murray, Earl of Dunmore.
Like other royal governors in office as the crisis reached its pitch, the Crown's

Benjamin Quarles, "Lord Dunmore as Liberator," *The William and Mary Quarterly*
XV (October 1958), pp. 494–507. Reprinted with the permission of the publisher and
the author.

* Mr. Quarles is a member of the Department of History at Morgan State College,
Baltimore, Md.

representative in Virginia would have been a marked man no matter how circumspect his behavior. Dunmore, lacking in diplomatic skills, was destined to furnish the colonists with a convenient hate-symbol. The one act that most thoroughly defamed his name was a deed which in Negro circles cast its author in the role of liberator. This was Dunmore's proclamation inviting slaves to leave their masters and join the royal forces.

Issued as of November 7, 1775, on board the *William* in the harbor at Norfolk, the proclamation announced that in order to defeat "treasonable purposes" the governor was establishing martial law. Colonists who refused "to resort to his Majesty's standard" were to be adjudged traitors. Then came the words which were destined to be quoted far and wide: "and I do hereby further declare all indented servants, Negroes, or others, (appertaining to Rebels,) free, that are able and willing to bear arms, they joining His Majesty's Troops, as soon as may be, for the more speedily reducing the Colony to a proper sense of their duty, to His Majesty's crown and dignity." [1]

Dunmore's proclamation had its expected effect. "The colonists," wrote a contemporary, "were struck with horror," [2] the "Poet of the American Revolution" implored the heavens to deliver the colonies from the "valiant" Dunmore and "his crew of banditti" ("who plunder Virginians at Williamsburg city").[3] Taking alarm, the Continental Congress lost no time in bestirring itself. On December 2, 1775, the delegates instructed the "Committee for fitting our armed vessels" to engage ships of war for the taking or destroying of the governor's fleet,[4] and the presiding officer urged the commander in chief of the Continental Army to take such measures against his lordship as would "effectually Repel his violences and secure the peace and safety of that Colony." [5]

---

[1] Original broadside, 11 by 17 inches, in University of Virginia library. For a facsimile which Patrick Henry circulated, and which differs a little in punctuation from the original, see Francis L. Berkeley, Jr., *Dunmore's Proclamation of Emancipation* (Charlottesville, 1941), frontispiece. See also *American Archives*, comp. Peter Force, 4th Ser. (Washington, 1837–46), III, 1385.

[2] David Ramsay, *History of the American Revolution* (Philadelphia, 1789), I, 234.

[3] *The Poems of Philip Freneau*, ed. Fred Lewis Pattee (Princeton, 1902–07), I, 140. "Hell itself could not have vomitted anything more black than his design of emancipating our slaves," wrote a Philadelphia correspondent to a friend abroad. *Morning Chronicle and London Advertiser*, Jan. 20, 1776, quoted in *Letters on the American Revolution, 1774–1776*, ed. Margaret W. Willard (Boston, 1925), p. 233. It was the judgment of Edward Rutledge that the proclamation tended "more effectually to work an eternal separation between Great Britain and the Colonies,—than any other expedient, which could possibly have been thought of." Rutledge to Ralph Izard, Dec. 8, 1775, in *Correspondence of Mr. Ralph Izard* (New York, 1844), I, 165.

[4] *Journal of the Continental Congress, 1774–1789*, ed. Worthington C. Ford and others (Washington, 1904–37), III, 395.

[5] John Hancock to George Washington, Dec. 2, 1775, in *Letters of Members of the Continental Congress*, ed. Edmund C. Burnett (Washington, 1921–36), I, 267. The army commander shared the apprehension of Congress. "If," he wrote to a Virginia delegate, "that man is not crushed before spring, he will become the most formidable enemy America has; his strength will increase as a snow ball by rolling: and faster, if some expedient cannot be hit upon, to convince the slaves and servants of the impotency of his

Two days later the Congress recommended to Virginia that she resist Dunmore "to the utmost. . . ." [6]

The apprehension over Dunmore's proclamation was grounded primarily in the fear of its unsettling effect on the slaves, if not in the fear of a servile insurrection—that nightmarish dread in communities where the whites were outnumbered. A policy that would strike off their shackles would obviously have a marked appeal to the inhabitants of slave row. Moreover, there had been recent evidence that the Virginian bondmen were responsive to the offer of freedom.

Dunmore himself had furnished such evidence. For at least eight months prior to the formal proclamation, the governor had seriously considered the idea of enlisting the slaves. His reasons were plain. Rebellious planters who contemplated a resort to arms would be deprived of their workers and would be compelled to return to their homes to protect their families and their property. Moreover, the slaves would help fill the ranks of military laborers for His Majesty's forces, and such human *potential de guerre* was badly needed. And Dunmore could expect little help from British headquarters in Boston.[7] Obviously, too, the Crown supporters and their sympathizers counted on the disaffection of the Negroes in the South.[8]

Needing supporters to hold the rebellion-bent Virginians in check, Dunmore let it be known late in April 1775 that he might be driven to set up the royal standard, adding that if he did he believed that he could count on "all the Slaves on the side of Government." [9] On May 1 the governor wrote to the Earl of Dartmouth expressing confidence that, once supplied with arms and

designs." George Washington to Richard Henry Lee, Dec. 26, 1775, in R. H. Lee, *Memoir of the Life of Richard Henry Lee* (Philadelphia, 1825), II, 9. Compare Washington to Joseph Reed, Dec. 15, 1775. In *The Writings of George Washington from the Original Manuscript Sources, 1745–1799*, ed. John C. Fitzpatrick (Washington, 1931–44), IV, 167.

[6] *Journals of the Continental Congress*, III, 403.

[7] General Thomas Gage wrote to Dunmore on Sept. 10, 1775: "I can neither assist you with Men, arms or ammunition, for I have them not to spare; should you draw upon me I have not the Cash to pay your Bills." Clinton Papers, William L. Clements Library, University of Michigan. For England's continuing great difficulty in getting man power see Edward E. Curtis, *The Organization of the British Army in the American Revolution* (New Haven, 1926), pp. 51–80.

[8] "Although Virginia and Maryland are both populous," wrote Governor Josiah Martin of North Carolina to Dartmouth on June 30, 1775, "the Whites are greatly outnumbered by the Negroes, at least in the former; a circumstance that would facilitate exceedingly the Reduction of those Colonies who are very sensible of their Weakness arising from it." Clinton Papers. This idea of Negro support was a persistent one: "The Negroes may be all deemed so many Intestine Enemies, being all slaves and desirous of Freedom." Joseph Galloway to Dartmouth, Jan. 23, 1778, *Facsimiles of Manuscripts in European Archives Relating to America, 1773–1783*, ed. Benjamin F. Stevens (London, 1889–98), XXIV, no. 2079. For a similar expression from another loyalist, see "Moses Kirkland to His Majesty's Commissioners, Oct. 21, 1778," Clinton Papers.

[9] "Deposition of Dr. William Pasteur. In Regard to the Removal of Powder from the Williamsburg Magazine," in "Virginia Legislative Papers (from Originals in Virginia State Archives)," *Virginia Magazine of History and Biography*, XIII (July 1905), 49.

ammunition, he would be able "to collect from among the *Indians*,[10] negroes and other persons" a force sufficient to hold his own.[11] Two weeks later, Gage in a letter to Dartmouth touched on Dunmore's proposal: "We hear," wrote the British commander, "that a Declaration his Lordship has made, of proclaiming all the Negroes free, who should join him, has Startled the Insurgents."[12]

In late April a group of slaves, scenting freedom in the air, went to the governor's house and volunteered their services, but Dunmore had them dismissed.[13] He was then not quite ready for the open break, but it could not be long delayed. On June 8, 1775, the governor took the decisive step of quitting Williamsburg and taking asylum aboard the man-of-war *Fowey* at Yorktown, a move he had been turning over in his mind since May 15.[14] "I have thought it best for his Majesty's Service," he wrote, "to retire from amidst such hostile appearances around me." [15] The House of Burgesses, taking note of the governor's flight, assured him that his personal safety was in no danger, but pointedly noted its displeasure that "a Scheme, the most diabolical, had been meditated, and generally recommended, by a Person of great Influence, to offer Freedom to our Slaves, and turn them against their Masters." [16]

Realizing that there was no turning back, Dunmore initiated a policy of unofficial slave solicitation to augment his tiny force of three hundred white soldiers, seamen, and loyalist recruits. In early August the "Officers of the Volunteer Companies" in Williamsburg informed the Convention that the "Governour's Cutter had carried off a number of Slaves belonging to private gentlemen...." [17] Small sloops, which were employed primarily to intercept intracolonial shipments of powder, invited slaves aboard. "Lord Dunmore sails up and down the river," wrote a Norfolk correspondent on October 28, 1775, to a friend in England, "and where he finds a defenceless place, he lands, plunders the plantation and carries off the negroes." [18]

---

[10] Later that year Dunmore concocted a plan to raise the tribes, as Gage phrased it, "on the back Parts of the Province of Virginia, to be Joined by such Inhabitants and Indians as may be at, and about Detroit." Gage to Guy Carleton, Sept. 11, 1775, Gage MSS. (American Series), Clements Library. This so-called "Connolly Plot" is briefly described in Isaac S. Harrell, *Loyalism in Virginia* (Philadelphia, 1926), pp. 35–37.

[11] Dartmouth to Dunmore, Aug. 2, 1775, *Amer. Arch.*, 4th Ser., III, 6. In this passage Dartmouth repeats the contents of a letter from Dunmore dated May 1.

[12] Gage to Dartmouth, May 15, 1775, Gage MSS. (English Series), Clements Library.

[13] "Deposition of John Randolph in Regard to the Removal of the Powder," in "Virginia Legislative Papers," *Va. Mag. of His. and Biog.*, XV (Oct. 1907), 150.

[14] Dunmore to Gage, May 15, 1775, Gage MSS. (American Series).

[15] *Ibid.*, June 17, 1775.

[16] *Journals of the House of Burgesses of Virginia, 1773–1776*, ed. John Pendelton Kennedy (Richmond, 1905), p. 256.

[17] "Proceedings of the Virginia Convention, August 3, 1775," *Amer. Arch.*, 4th Ser., III, 373.

[18] *Morning Chronicle and London Advertiser*, Dec. 22, 1775, in Willard, *Letters on the American Revolution*, pp. 271–272. The number of slaves reaching Dunmore during the preproclamation is indeterminate; "some accounts make them about 100;

Now ready to come out into the open, Dunmore was concerned only with his timing. An apparently auspicious moment came in mid-November 1775 when a skirmish took place at Kemp's Landing on the Elizabeth River. In this action the colonial militia was routed and its two commanding colonels were captured. Entering the village in triumph, Dunmore, on November 14, ordered the publication of the proclamation he had drafted a week earlier on board the *William*. The final break had come—the governor had set up his standard and had officially called upon the slaves to join him.

Tidewater Virginia took alarm as rumors spread that the slaves were stampeding to the British.[19] But there were strong deterring factors. Foremost among these was the military alertness of the Virginians themselves. Before any substantial slave migration to Dunmore could get under way, the governor suffered a decisive defeat at arms. This occurred on December 9 at Great Bridge, a fortified span across the Elizabeth River some ten miles below Norfolk which dominated the land approach thereto. Dunmore had believed that an attack was impending and had rashly decided to take the offensive. His force of six hundred was severely repulsed, suffering sixty-one casualties, including three dead officers. Forced to retreat after twenty-five minutes of combat, Dunmore's troops hurried back to Norfolk. Feeling that he could no longer hold the city and fearing a retaliatory attack, the governor spiked his twenty pieces of cannon and ordered his followers aboard the vessels in the harbor. He was never to regain a foothold on the Virginia mainland.

The military preparation of the colonists was matched by their promptness in adopting "home front" measures to prevent slaves from joining the governor. Newspapers lost no time in publishing the proclamation in full, as information and as a warning. To deter runaways local patrol groups were doubled, highways were carefully watched, and owners of small craft were required to exercise vigilance. Since Dunmore's action had come as no surprise, the Virginians had had time to put the colony in a "tolerable state of defense." [20] Adjacent Maryland, through its Council of Safety, ordered the military to station itself in St. Mary's County "and guard the shores from thence to the river Powtowmack, to prevent any servants, negroes, or others from going on board the Fowey ship of war." [21]

To vigilance the colonists added psychological warfare. In Alexander Purdie's *Virginia Gazette* was published a letter from a subscriber urging that Negroes be cautioned against joining Dunmore. Slaves should be told that the English ministry, in refusing to stop the slave trade, had proved a far greater

others less." Edmund Pendleton and others to Virginia delegates in Congress, Nov. 11, 1775, Lee Family MSS., U. Va. library.

[19] "Letters mention that slaves flock to him in abundance, but I hope it is magnified." Edmund Pendleton to Richard Henry Lee, Nov. 27, 1775, *Amer. Arch.*, 4th Ser., IV, 202.

[20] Ramsay, *American Revolution*, I, 234.

[21] *Journal and Correspondence of the Maryland Council of Safety, Aug. 29, 1775–July 6, 1776*, ed. William H. Browne and others, *Archives of Maryland* (Baltimore, 1883—in progress), XI, 511–512.

enemy to Negroes than their American masters, and that if the colonists were defeated, their slaves would be sold to the West Indies. They should be told, too, continued Mr. Purdie's correspondent, that Dunmore was cruel to his own black servitors. And, finally, they should be urged to place their expectation on "a better condition in the next world." If this information had been spread widely, "not one slave would have joined our enemies." [22]

A week later the *Gazette* carried another letter in similar vein. Colonists were advised to inform slaves that Dunmore proposed to free only those who would bear arms for him, leaving the aged and infirm, the women and children, to bear the brunt of the shorn master's anger. Moreover, under the English flag the slaves would be much worse off than under Virginia masters, "who pity their condition, who wish in general to make it as easy and comfortable as possible, and who would willingly, were it in their power, or were they permitted, not only prevent any more negroes from losing their freedom, but restore it to such as have already unhappily lost it." Contrast this with the British, ran the *Gazette's* warning, who would sell the runaways to the sugar islands. "Be not then, ye negroes, tempted by this proclamation to ruin your selves." [23]

Official action was not long in coming. The Virginia Convention on December 8 appointed a committee to prepare an answer to Dunmore's proclamation. Five days later, when the committee made its report, it was directed to draw up a declaration stating that runaways to the British would be pardoned if they returned in ten days; otherwise they would "be liable to such punishment as shall be directed by the Convention." The following day, with the committee's report at hand, the delegates issued a declaration of policy. Beginning with a reminder that the time-honored penalty for a slave insurrection was death without benefit of clergy, the document stated that Negroes who had been "seduced" to take up arms were liable to punishment. But in order that they might return in safety to their duties, they would be pardoned if they laid down their arms forthwith. The proclamation concluded with a request to "all humane and benevolent persons in the colony" to convey to the slaves this "offer of mercy." [24] To insure a wide circulation, the proclamation was published as a broadside.[25]

The Virginians supplemented techniques of persuasion and sweet reasonableness with alternatives more forthright and punitive. In early December the Convention decreed that slaves taken in arms were to be sold to the foreign West Indies, with the sale money, minus expenses, to go to their masters.[26] Somewhat less severe was the fate of captured runaways who had failed in their

[22] Purdie's *Virginia Gazette*, Williamsburg, Nov. 17, 1775. Hereafter cited as *Va. Gaz.*

[23] *Ibid.*, Nov. 24, 1775.

[24] *Proceedings of the Convention of the Delegates in the Colony of Virginia* (Richmond, 1816), p. 62.

[25] Virginia Broadsides (V. 54), U. Va. library.

[26] William Waller Hening, *The Statutes at Large; Being a Collection of All the Laws of Virginia* ... (Richmond, 1809-23), IX, 106.

attempts to reach the King's forces. Such slaves, if their masters were patriots, were returned to their home plantations, often after first serving a term of imprisonment. An owner of a captured runaway might be ordered to "convey him to some interior part of the Country as soon as may be. . . ." [27] Slaves of British sympathizers were put to work in the lead mines,[28] a practice which became customary in Virginia for the duration of the war. Distrusting all Negroes who had joined the governor, the Convention recommended that military officers "seize and secure" even those who came bearing flags of truce.[29]

The death penalty was used sparingly. In Northampton County the court passed such a sentence on a group of thirteen slaves who had seized a schooner at Hungers Creek and sailed into the bay, their destination the James. Overtaken by a whale boat,[30] their execution was set for April 2, 1776. But the Northampton Committee of Safety sent word to Williamsburg inquiring whether the punishment should not be mitigated since the seizing of the boat was more "intended to effect an escape to Dunmore than any other Design of committing a felony." [31] Whenever the death sentence was passed, as in the case of two runaways who mistook an armed vessel of the Virginia navy for a British man-of-war, it was used mainly "as an example to others." [32]

Despite preventive efforts, whether an appeal to common sense or a resort to legal reprisals, many slaves made their way to the British, spurred in part by loyalist propaganda of the governor's good treatment.[33] Some two hundred "immediately joined him," [34] and within a week after the proclamation the number had reached three hundred.[35] "Numbers of Negros and

[27] Such was the language used by the Virginia Council to William Kirby (July 12, 1776) concerning his slave Frank. *Journals of the Council of State of Virginia,* ed. H. R. McIlwaine and Wilmer L. Hall (Richmond, 1931–32, 1952), I, 67.

[28] On Dec. 14, 1775, the Convention ordered the Committee of Safety to employ captive slaves "in working the Lead Mine in the County of *Fincastle,* for the use of this Colony." *Amer. Arch.,* 4th Ser., IV, 85. Shortly afterward four would-be followers of Dunmore who were captured at Accomac were ordered "sent up the country and employed in some publick works." *Ibid.,* VI, 1553.

[29] *Ibid.,* VI, 1524.

[30] James Kent and William Henry to Maryland Council of Safety, Feb. 28, 1776, *Arch. of Md.,* XI, 191.

[31] Northampton Committee of Safety to General Committee of Safety, Apr. 23, 1776, "Va. Leg. Papers," *Va. Mag. of Hist. and Biog.,* XV (Apr. 1908), 407.

[32] *Va. Gaz.,* Apr. 13, 1776.

[33] Northampton Committee of Safety to General Committee of Safety, Apr. 23, 1776, "Va. Leg. Papers," *Va. Mag. of Hist. and Biog.,* XV, 407. Dunmore would have every reason to welcome runaways, but perhaps his reception of them fell short of the report, circulated in the *Virginia Gazette,* that on the evening the governor's forces landed on Gwynn's Island, they amused themselves "with a promiscuous ball, which opened, we hear, by a certain spruce little gentleman, with one of the black ladies." *Vir. Gaz.,* May 31, 1776.

[34] Northampton Committee of Safety to Continental Congress, Nov. 25, 1775, "Va. Leg. Papers," *Va. Mag. of Hist. and Biog.,* XIV (Jan. 1907), 251.

[35] Andrew Sprowel to Peter Paterson, Nov. 19, 1775, *ibid.,* XIV (Apr. 1907), 387.

Cowardly Scoundrels flock to his Standard," wrote a member of the provincial Committee of Safety.[36]

Since Dunmore had no base on the mainland after mid-December 1775, the Negroes who sought his sanctuary were water-borne. Two weeks after the proclamation a group of slaves came down the James in a thirty-foot vessel, bound for the fleet off Norfolk, but they were captured near Surry.[37] Shortly afterward seven Negroes broke out of a Northampton jail and "went off in a pettinger," bound for the British ships.[38] Colonel Landon Carter of the Sabine Hall plantation made a diary notation of the break for the open water executed by ten of his retainers:

> 26 Wednesday, June, 1776. Last night after going to bed, Moses, my son's man, Joe, Billy, Postillion, John, Mullatto Peter, Tom, Panti-cove, Manuel & Lancaster Sam, ran away, to be sure, to Ld. Dunmore, for they got privately into Beale's room before dark & took out my son's gun & one I had there, took out of his drawer in my passage all his ammunition furniture, Landon's bag of bullets and all the Powder, and went off in my Petty Anger [pettiauger] new trimmed, and it is supposed that Mr. Robinson's People are gone with them, for a skow they came down in is, it seems, at my Landing. These accursed villians have stolen Landon's silver buckles, George's shirts, Tom Parker's new waistcoat & breeches.[39]

The Negroes who reached the British were generally able-bodied men who could be put to many uses.[40] It was as soldiers, however, that Dunmore envisioned them, and he enlisted them from the beginning. By early December he was arming them "as fast as they came in." [41] He made use of Negro privates at the rout of the colonials at Kemp's Landing; indeed, slaves had captured one of the two commanding colonels.[42] In the skirmishes preceding the action at Great Bridge, two runaways who were taken prisoner testified that the garrison was manned by thirty whites and ninety Negroes, and that "all the blacks who are sent to the fort at the great Bridge, are supplied with

[36] John Page to Thomas Jefferson, Nov. 24, 1775, *The Papers of Thomas Jefferson*, ed. Julian P. Boyd (Princeton, 1950—in progress), I, 265.

[37] *Va. Gaz.*, Jan. 10, 1776.

[38] *Maryland Gazette*, Annapolis, Feb. 22, 1776. "Pettinger" and "pettiauger" (below) are corruptions of the Spanish *piragua*, "a dugout," "a two-masted, flat-bottomed boat."

[39] "Diary of Col. Landon Carter," *William and Mary Quarterly*, 1st Ser., XX (Jan. 1912), 178–179.

[40] Two women, however, were among a party of nine slaves who were seized in mid-December after putting out to sea in an open boat in an attempt to reach Norfolk. *Pennsylvania Gazette*, Philadelphia, Dec. 20, 1775.

[41] Dunmore to Sec. of State for the Colonies, Dec. 6, 1775, Peter Force-George Bancroft Transcripts, "Virginia: Official Correspondence," Library of Congress.

[42] Edmund Pendleton to R. H. Lee, Nov. 27, 1775, *Amer. Arch.*, 4th Ser., IV, 202.

muskets, Cartridges &c strictly ordered to use them defensively & offensively." [43] By the first of December the British had nearly three hundred slaves outfitted in military garb, with the inscription, "Liberty to Slaves," emblazoned across the breast of each.[44] The governor officially designated them "Lord Dunmore's Ethiopian Regiment." [45]

The first and only major military action in which Dunmore's forces were engaged was the battle of Great Bridge.[46] Of the governor's troops of some six hundred men, nearly half were Negroes. Of the eighteen wounded prisoners taken by the Virginians in this rout, two were former slaves. James Anderson was wounded "in the Forearm—Bones shattered and flesh much torn," and Casar was hit "in the Thigh, by a Ball, and 5 shot—one lodged." [47] After the fiasco at Great Bridge, the governor was forced to operate from his ships. Taking aboard the hardiest of his Negro followers and placing them under officers who exercised them at small arms, he sanguinely awaited recruits.

Dunmore's use of Negroes also embraced sailoring services. On the six tenders sent by the governor to cannonade Hampton in late October 1775, there were colored crewman. Two of them were captured when the Virginians seized the pilot boat *Hawk Tender*.[48] To man the small craft that scurried in and out of the river settlements, harassing the plantations, the British depended largely on ex-slaves. Particularly were they needed as pilots. Joseph Harris, a runaway, served as pilot of the *Otter*, having come to Captain

[43] William Woodford to Edmund Pendleton, Dec. 5, 1775, "The Woodford, Howe, and Lee Letters," *Richmond College Historical Papers*, I (June 1915), 113. Added Woodford, "The bearer brings you one of the Balls taken out of the cartirages found upon the negro Prisoners, as they were extremely well made." *Ibid.*, p. 112.

[44] *Md. Gaz.*, Dec. 14, 1775.

[45] Dunmore to Sec. of State for Colonies, Dec. 6, 1775, Force-Bancroft Transcripts.

[46] Eyewitness accounts of the action at Great Bridge include: ". . . a Midshipman on board his Majesty's ship *Otter*, commanded by Captain Squires, Dec. 9," in Willard, *Letters on the American Revolution*, pp. 234–235; ". . . a Gentleman, dated ship *William*, off Norfolk, Virginia, Dec. 25, 1775," *ibid.*, pp. 244–245; "Thomas McKnight to Rev. Dr. McKnight, on board the King's Fisher, Dec. 26, 1775," Miscellaneous Collection, Clements Library; "Contemporary English Accounts of the Destruction of Norfolk in 1776," comp. H. S. Parsons, *Wm. & Mary Quart.*, 2d Ser., XIII (Oct. 1933), 219–224; Richard Kidder Meade to Theodorick Bland, Jr., Norfolk Town Camp, Dec. 18, 1775, in *The Bland Papers*, ed. Charles Campbell (Petersburg, 1840–43), I, 38; "The Woodford, Howe, and Lee Letters," *Richmond College Hist. Papers*, I, 96–163, passim; William Woodford to Edmund Pendleton, Dec. 10, 1775, in *Md. Gaz.*, Dec. 21, 1775, and Jan. 4, 1776. For Dunmore's account see Dunmore to Secretary of State for the Colonies, Dec. 13, 1775, Force-Bancroft Transcripts. For the story, relished by Virginians, that a well-coached slave had been sent into Dunmore's lines with instructions to misrepresent the strength of the colonial militia, see John Burk, *The History of Virginia* (Petersburg, 1805–16), IV, 85.

[47] Woodford to Pendelton, Dec. 10, 1775, "The Woodford, Howe, and Lee Letters," *Richmond College Hist. Papers*, I, 118.

[48] John Page to Thomas Jefferson, Nov. 11, 1775, *Papers of Thomas Jefferson*, ed. Boyd, I, 257.

Matthew Squire with the highest recommendation from a fellow naval officer. "I think him too useful to His Majesty's service to take away," wrote the latter, because of "his being well acquainted with many creeks in the *Eastern* Shore, at *York, James* River, and *Nansemond*, and many others, . . ." and "accustomed to pilot. . . ." [49] Two citizens on the Isle of Wight advised the chairman of the Virginia Committee of Safety to go slow on discharging "a Negro fello, named Caesar," who was not only "a very great Scoundrel" but was also "a fello' they can't do well without being an Excellent pilot." [50]

Another service performed by Dunmore's black followers was foraging. The governor's supply of provisions, particularly fresh foods, needed constant replenishing, and the Virginia leaders understandably would not permit the British to send men ashore to make purchases. "Black settlers" who might have been willing to supply his lordship with provisions had "no means of conveying them," [51] and Dunmore was driven to a dependence upon the foraging abilities of his Negro recruits. Marauding parties of predominantly ex-slave composition preyed on the countryside, making a night descent upon a plantation and making off with the choice livestock. One foraging party, captured while on its way to the Eastern Shore, was made up of "one white and sixteen blacks." [52]

Allegedly one of the services of Negroes to Dunmore was germ spreading. That the charge of germ warfare was propaganda-laden did not make it less potent in arousing indignation. The accusation was that Dunmore had inoculated two Negroes and sent them ashore at Norfolk to spread the smallpox.[53] The charge was ironic in view of the fate of the Negroes who fled to the British. The majority of them were disease fatalities. Late in March the governor informed his superior in England that the recruiting of the black regiment "would have been in great forwardness had not a fever crept in amongst them, which carried off a great many very fine fellows." He added that on advice of "medical people here," he had concluded that the trouble came from the overcrowded condition on the ships and the lack of clothing, both of which "we have now provided against." [54]

But the plague persisted, killing off the Negroes and the hope of the governor alike. Writing to Germain in June, Dunmore confessed defeat. The fever, he explained, was malignant, and had "carried off an incredible number of our people, especially blacks." Had this not happened he would have en-

[49] George Montague to Matthew Squire, July 20, 1775, *Amer. Arch.*, 4th Ser., II, 1692.

[50] Thomas Pierce and Thomas Smith to Edmund Pendleton, Dec. 17, 1775, "Miscellaneous Colonial Documents," *Va. Mag. of Hist. and Biog.*, XIX (July 1911), 267.

[51] "Extract of a letter to a gentleman in Scotland, dated Norfolk, Virginia, February 17, 1776," *Amer. Arch.*, 4th Ser., IV, 1166.

[52] Archibald Cary to R. H. Lee, Dec. 24, 1775, in Robert K. Brock, *Archibald Cary of Ampthill* (Richmond, 1937), p. 161.

[53] *Va. Gaz.*, June 15, 1776.

[54] Dunmore to George Germain, Mar. 30, 1776, *Amer. Arch.*, 5th Ser. (Washington, 1848–53), II, 159–160.

listed two thousand Negro followers. He was, ran his letter, separating the sick from the well and would try to keep the two groups from intermingling.[55] The governor's efforts were unavailing; by early June 1776 there were not more than "150 effective Negro men," although each day the black corps was augmented by from six to eight arrivals.[56]

The failure to arrest the smallpox, and the harassment by the Virginia and Maryland militia, finally brought an end to his lordship's stay in Chesapeake waters. In May 1776, faced with the likelihood "of a great reduction of our force" due to disease,[57] the fleet moved from their exposed quarters at Tucker's Mills near Portsmouth and took shelter on Gwynn's Island near the mouth of the Rappahannock. Nowhere were Dunmore and his "floating Town"[58] allowed peace; "we no sooner appear off the land, than signals are made from it," wrote Dunmore to Whitehall, "and if we come to anchor within cannonshot of either shore, guns are immediately brought to bear upon us. . . ."[59]

Early in July the British, after suffering an attack on their shipping, took refuge on St. George's Island in the Potomac. By the end of the month the disease-ridden corps, lacking suitable drinking water, and despairing of re-enforcements, prepared to make their exit. Dismantling, burning, or running aground sixty-three out of their 103 vessels, they sailed out of the Potomac on August 6, seven of the ships bound for Sandy Hook and the others setting a southward course for St. Augustine and the Bermudas.[60] With the departing fleet went some three hundred Negroes, the healthiest going northward, destined for further military service, and Dunmore's schemes came to an inglorious end.[61]

---

[55] Dunmore to Germain, Mar. 30, 1776, Amer. Arch., 5th Ser., II, 162. Dunmore's policy of isolation appears to have prevented the smallpox from decimating the white troops. The monthly return of the 14th Regiment of Infantry, signed by Capt. Sam Leslie, lists a total of 128 men (with breakdowns as to rank) for Mar. 1, 1776, a total of 126 men for Apr. 1, 1776, and a total of 122 for May 1, 1776. "Monthly Return of a Detachment of His Majesty's 14th Regiment of Infantry, off Norfolk, Virginia, 1 March 1776," Clinton Papers; ibid., for Apr. 1, 1776, and for May 1, 1776. In addition to the factor of isolation, the mortality of the Negro soldiers may have been due to their performing most of the garrison and fatigue duties; at Gwynn's Island the entrenchments were guarded "chiefly by the black regiment." Va. Gaz., June 1, 1776.

[56] Entry of June 10, 1776, A. S. Hamond Diaries, 1775–77, U. Va. library. Andrew Snape Hamond, captain of the Roebuck, was the commanding officer in Virginia waters.

[57] Ibid., May 19, 1776.

[58] The descriptive phrase is Hamond's. Letter to Hans Stanley, Aug. 5, 1776, ibid.

[59] Dunmore to George Germain, July 31, 1776, Amer. Arch., 5th Ser., II, 166.

[60] Hamond Diaries, Aug. 6, 1776. Dunmore himself went to New York, arriving on Aug. 14. Journals of Lieut.-Col. Stephen Kemble, New-York Historical Society, Collections (1883–84), I, 84.

[61] Dunmore remained convinced of the soundness of his plan to arm Negroes in large numbers, reviving it even after Yorktown. See Percy Burdelle Caley, "Dunmore: Colonial Governor of New York and Virginia, 1770–1782," unpubl. diss., University of Pittsburgh, 1939, pp. 887–893.

Perhaps not more than a total of eight hundred slaves had succeeded in reaching the British,[62] and perhaps one eighth of these had been brought by loyalist masters. But Dunmore's proclamation undoubtedly had an indirect effect on thousands of additional slaves, quickening their hopes for freedom. Perhaps the imagination of colonial editors was behind such stories as that of a colored mother in New York naming her child after his lordship,[63] and that of a Negro in Philadelphia jostling whites on the streets and telling them to wait until "lord Dunmore and his black regiment come, and then we will see who is to take the wall." [64] But whether fact or fabrication, such reports reflect the attitude of expectation that Dunmore engendered among persons of color along the Chesapeake. It made no difference that he had offered freedom to the bondmen of his enemies only,[65] and that as governor he had withheld his signature from a bill against the slave trade; to those who whispered his name in slave quarters he was in truth the "African Hero" he was derisively dubbed by a Virginia patriot.[66]

If Dunmore was viewed by one group as a tyrant and by another as a liberator, this was but another paradox in a war that abounded in paradox, and another illustration of the war as a social revolution. The Negro who fled to the governor was actuated by the same love of freedom for which the colonists avowedly broke with the mother country. Dunmore's invitation to the slaves was to prefigure the thousands of runaways below the Mason-Dixon line who served as military laborers to His Majesty's forces during the Revolution and who, when peace came, sailed with them from Savannah, Charleston, and New York.

[62] Dunmore's Negro followers were computed in general terms; e.g., "... came in a great number of Black men from the Rebels." Logs of *Roebuck* and *Fowey*, in Greenwich Museum, England, entry of June 27, 1776. Photostat in A. S. Hamond MSS., U. Va. library.

[63] Taking due note, the *New York Journal* carried an occasional poem, copied in the *Va. Gaz.*, May 25, 1776:

> Hail! doughty Ethiopian Chief!
> Though ignominious Negro Thief!
> This BLACK shall prop thy sinking name,
> And damn thee to perpetual fame.

[64] *Va. Gaz.*, Supplement, Dec. 29, 1775.

[65] John King, runaway slave of a loyalist, was ordered discharged from the *King's Fisher*. Logs of *Roebuck* and *Fowey*, Feb. 23, 1776.

[66] R. H. Lee to Thomas Jefferson, July 21, 1776, in *The Letters of Richard Henry Lee*, ed. James C. Ballagh (New York, 1912–14), I, 210.

S. Sydney Bradford

THE NEGRO IRONWORKER IN ANTE BELLUM VIRGINIA

The vast majority of slaves cultivated staple crops—tobacco, rice, hemp, sugar cane and, most important, cotton. Yet surprising numbers were artisans and unskilled industrial laborers, engaged in small-scale manufacturing on the farms and in the towns. This study by S. Sydney Bradford offers a richly detailed description of slavery in an industrial setting. For another type of industrial slavery, mining in the western territories and states, the student should consult W. Sherman Savage, "The Negro on the Mining Frontier," Journal of Negro History, XXX (January, 1945), pp. 30–46.

PECULIAR conditions inherent in the use of hired slave labor in industry are well illustrated in the history of colonial and ante bellum Virginia. In that state many Negroes were taken from plantations and placed in various industries to help construct canals and railroads, operate tobacco factories, and run iron furnaces and forges.[1] Slaves probably helped construct Virginia's first iron furnace, Falling Creek furnace. After this was destroyed by the Indians in 1622 the colony had no successful ironworks until 1716, when Colonel Alexander Spotswood erected the first of the several furnaces built by him. In operating his furnace at Germanna the Colonel used Negro laborers and thought them to be fairly good workers.[2]

Between 1716 and 1775 many furnaces and forges were built in Virginia,

S. Sydney Bradford, "The Negro Ironworker in Ante Bellum Virginia," *Journal of Southern History*, XXV (May, 1959), pp. 194–206. Copyright © 1959 by the Southern Historical Association. Reprinted by permission of the Managing Editor.

[1] Kathleen Bruce's *Virginia Iron Manufacture in the Slave Era* (New York, 1930) treats the Tredegar Works in particular; this paper deals with Virginia's ironworks in general.

[2] Robert Beverly, *The History and Present State of Virginia* (Chapel Hill, 1947), 49, 54–55, 126; J. M. Swank, *History of the Manufacture of Iron in All Ages* (Philadelphia, 1892), 113; Lester J. Cappon (ed.), *Iron Works at Tuball: Terms and Conditions for Their Lease ... by Alexander Spotswood ...* (Charlottesville, Va., 1945), 12.

and by the latter year iron was even being produced in the Shenandoah Valley. Throughout this period and during the war for independence, slaves were used both by private individuals and by the state government at ironworks all over the state, and after the war the industry continued to grow, particularly in the Valley.[3] By 1800 the iron industry had appeared in the westernmost part of Virginia, near present-day Wheeling, though the use of slaves at these works was rare since there were few Negroes in that area and those for hire in the eastern part of the state were not sent west of the Alleghenies.[4] However, slaves supplied the bulk of Virginia ironworks laborers east of the mountains.

The Revolution marked a change in practice with regard to slave labor in ironworks, for prior to that time most of such laborers were owned by the ironmaster, but the practice of hiring slaves for the furnaces began during the war and thereafter the great majority of Negroes used at ironworks in the Old Dominion were hired hands.[5] The source of the hired slaves might be either neighboring plantations or slave hiring marts; the hiring might be initiated by the ironmaster or his partner or agent or by the plantation owner. Agents received a small commission for slaves hired, and perhaps to avoid this cost plantation owners often wrote directly to the ironmasters. The usual hiring period was toward the end of the year, so ironmasters between the Blue Ridge and Allegheny Mountains travelled into the piedmont around Christmastime in order to obtain Negro workers. The hiring took about a month to complete at markets in Pittsylvania, Louisa, Spotsylvania, Orange, Albemarle, Amherst, Nelson, and Fauquier Counties.[6]

[3] J. P. Lesley, *The Iron Manufacturer's Guide to the Furnaces, Forges, and Rolling Mills of the United States* (New York, 1866), 64 and *passim*; Swank, *History*, 170 and *passim*; J. B. Pearse, *A Concise History of the Iron Manufacture of the American Colonies* (Philadelphia, 1876), 9 and *passim*; "Abstract of a Deed," *William and Mary Quarterly*, 1st series, XXII (1913), 70; Williamsburg *Virginia Gazette*, September 7, 1776, February 14, 1777; Memorandum of Negroes employed at Westham Foundry for 1781 (Virginia State Library, Richmond).

[4] Some slaves were used in the iron industry west of the Allegheny Mountains, as at G. F. Hupp's furnace in Hardy County—see deed of trust, February 6, 1852, in Deed Book Number 22 (Hardy County Clerk's Office, Moorefield, W. Va.)—but there is no evidence that Negroes were widely used. Bruce holds that no Southern ironmaster could have succeeded without using slaves (*Virginia Iron Manufacture*, 237), but her conclusion is not valid for trans-Allegheny Virginia.

[5] Swank, *History*, 264; *Virginia Gazette*, January 31, February 14, 1777; Memorandum of Negroes employed at Westham Foundry. This was unlike the situation elsewhere in the South, where the slaves were the property of the owners of the works. E. M. Lander, Jr., "The Iron Industry in Ante-Bellum South Carolina," *Journal of Southern History*, XX (August 1954), 350; Ethel Armes, *The Story of Coal and Iron in Alabama* (Birmingham, 1910), 74, 96.

[6] Deposition of G. Long in Samuel F. Jordan v. William Cash, hereafter cited as Jordan v. Cash; of William Weaver in John Doyle v. William Weaver, hereafter cited as Doyle v. Weaver; and of D. J. Willson in William Weaver v. Jordan, Davis, and Company, hereafter cited as Weaver v. Davis; bonds for Negro hire in Matthew Bryan's Administrator v. Matthew Bryan's Heirs, hereafter cited as Bryan v. Bryan, and in Enos Hord v. S. J. and W. H. Jordan, hereafter cited as Hord v. Jordan. All of the cited cases are in Case Papers of the Rockbridge County Superior Court of Chancery

The same factors determined hiring prices as sale prices of slaves. Thus, the age of a hand was a very important matter, for Negroes in their prime always brought more than boys and old men.[7] Likewise slaves with particular skills were more valuable; in the late 1830's ironmasters paid from $25 to $40 more to hire skilled Negroes than ordinary hands. Negro blacksmiths were constantly sought by furnace and forge owners, and they always commanded premium prices.[8] Competition among those who desired Negroes also influenced Negro hire. In 1830 and 1831 agents complained that the demand for slaves by the builders of canals and turnpikes had increased rates. Over twenty years later a similar objection arose because the hiring of slaves by railroads and tobacco factories had brought about a general rise in cost.[9] In addition, there was a general increase after 1800 in the amounts paid for Negroes, as the following table shows: [10]

Year	Prices Paid for Hired Negroes
1805–1807	$55–$66.98
1836	$110–$120
1840	$85–$90
1854–1855	$113.66–$134.50
1856	$150

Ironmasters usually hired slaves for the period from January 1 until the following Christmas, and shortly after the agreements had been concluded the slaves were sent to their respective ironworks. Severe winter weather oc-

(Superior Clerk's Office, Lexington, Va.). See also bonds for Negro hire in the McCormick Collection (Wisconsin State Historical Society, Madison); J. F. Tanner (for J. R. Anderson) to Col. L. Partlow, December 15, 1848, in Letter Book, Tredegar Company (Virginia State Library); D. G. Garland to William Weaver, May 23, 1828, in Weaver-Brady Collection (Duke University Library, Durham, N.C.); S. McD. Moore, to W. W. Davis, January 16, 1850, and J. L. Dickinson to Davis, February 24, 1852, in McCormick Collection.

[7] In 1838 and 1839 able-bodied Negroes were hired for $93 apiece, while old men and boys went for $63 or $64 each. Deposition of William Lusk in John Alexander v. Sidney S. Baxter, administrator of John Irvine and others, hereafter cited as Alexander v. Irvine's administrator, in Case Papers of Rockbridge County Superior Court of Chancery.

[8] Deposition of Ira F. Jordan in Weaver v. Davis. In 1808 a furnace paid $119.88 for a blacksmith and $83.25 for the next most expensive Negro, and in 1853 a forge paid $150 for a blacksmith and an average of $101.50 for unskilled workers. Ledger, Ridwell Furnace, 1805–1809 (University of North Carolina Library, Chapel Hill); bonds for Negro hire in McCormick Collection.

[9] T. Wyat to Jordans and Irvine, January 6, 1830; P. Boxley to Jordans and Irvine, January 13, 1831; Greenlee Davidson to J. D. Davidson, January 9, 1859, all in McCormick Collection.

[10] Ledger, Ridwell Furnace, 1805–1809; deposition of Matthew Bryan and report of Commissioner Chapin in Alexander v. Irvine's administrator; bonds for Negro hire in Jordan v. Cash and Bryan v. Bryan and those owned by Miss Mabel Jordan (Buena Vista, Va.); C. W. Newkirk to William Weaver, January 4, 1815, and James Coleman to William Weaver, February 19, 1856, both in Weaver-Brady Collection (Duke).

casionally delayed their departure for as much as several weeks, but this might prevent sickness arising from travel in bad weather. For example, one group of hands that crossed the Blue Ridge Mountains in stormy weather fell ill after reaching their ironworks, which upset the ironmaster since more lost time was added to the thirty days the slaves had already spent in travel. If additional workers were needed during the year they were hired for whatever time was necessary.

Unhappy incidents concerned with the hiring of Negroes often occurred. When a slave owner in 1829 allowed an ironmaster who had hired one of his Negroes for $50 to set the price for a second slave, the ironmaster named $20 as a fair price. Such an amount brought an angry protest from the slave's master, concluding with "This letter...will close (I hope forever) my correspondence with you." On the other hand, competition for the slaves appears to have been keen, and an agent for one ironmaster failed to hire a desired Negro because an unknown individual had bribed the slave's owner to obtain him. In this case even the Negro was given a bribe to go elsewhere. The manager of another ironworks found that a slave master from whom he had hired certain Negroes for several years had increased the amount he wanted for the hands and would not lower it because, the manager believed, of a competitor's bidding. Another representative of an ironworks complained in 1855 that "You have no idea of the trouble there is in hiring hands...there is all sorts of trickery and management." [11]

Ironmasters used Negroes for any task that needed to be done at their establishments. At the furnaces and forges slaves tended fires, worked the metal, and in fact did everything but manage the establishments, which was always the job of a white man. Elsewhere on an ironworks plantation Negroes planted and harvested crops, cut and charcoaled wood, mined iron ore, drove wagons and manned boats, made shoes, ground flour, and worked as carpenters and blacksmiths. The elite among them were the refiners, molders, and blacksmiths, and because a skilled slave was as valuable as two ordinary hands, many ironmasters owned a few skilled workers.[12] There was nothing rigid in the use of Negroes at ironworks, however, as skilled slaves were frequently used for unskilled tasks. Bob, a forge helper at Buffalo forge, for

[11] James C. Dickinson to William Weaver, January 21, 1833, in Weaver-Brady Collection (Duke); unsigned letter to W. W. Davis, January 5, 1856, in McCormick Collection; Henry A. McCormick to William Weaver, December 29, 1855, in Weaver-Brady Collection (Alderman Library, University of Virginia, Charlottesville).

[12] The following contain numerous references to work done by Negroes: deposition of Ira F. Jordan in Weaver v. Davis and of Matthew Bryan in Alexander v. Irvine's administrator; Journals, Pine Forge, 1804–1833 (University of North Carolina Library); William W. Davis Papers and Graham Ledgers and Negro Books, 1830–1840, in Weaver-Brady Collection (Virginia). With respect to skilled workers, one forge owner owned six Negro forgemen, one of whom he had purchased to prevent a competitor's buying him. J. Doyle to William Weaver, October 17, 1827, and Weaver to Doyle, October 17, 1827, in Doyle v. Weaver. The following sources also point out that ironmasters owned skilled workers: Journal, Pine Forge, 1804–1808; Negro Book, Graham Ledgers; deposition of Ira F. Jordan, in Weaver v. Davis.

example, was transferred to a chopping gang in February 1836 and stayed with that group, except for a stint at planting oats, until May 30, when he was sent back to the forge. He remained there until August 4 and was then sent back to the woodchoppers, with whom he stayed until August 22, when he returned to the forge for five days.[13]

Of all the jobs assigned to Negroes at ironworks, the two most important were mining and woodchopping. A furnace's ore banks were usually worked by slaves surpervised by a white master miner, the number of hands used in this way varying from furnace to furnace. Lucy Selina furnace used four Negroes and a white master miner in the 1830's, while Vesuvius furnace employed five or six hands, and Jane furnace worked nine or ten slaves in its pits.[14] Shafts had to be dug at some ore banks, and one furnace had holes seventy-two feet deep at its pits. In order to supply another furnace with seven to seventeen cartloads of ore a day, eight hands worked in pits that were twenty to twenty-five feet deep. The ore in the holes was first loosened by powder and then hauled to the surface in buckets. Work in such places was very often difficult because of the presence of water, and occasionally a pump was used to keep the pits as dry as possible.[15]

Vast quantities of charcoal were needed to smelt the ore brought to furnaces. Cotopaxi furnace, before it was abandoned in 1854, made 600 tons of pig iron a year, each ton of which required the burning of 200 bushels of charcoal; and a forge burned fifteen or sixteen cords of wood to make a ton of bar iron.[16] Over the years chopping gangs, usually under the supervision of a white man, denuded many wooded areas for wood to be charcoaled, for both Negro and white hands apparently had a quota to fill of nine cords a week. After the wood had been cut, about thirty cords of it would be slowly burned in a large pile; at the end of six days of smoldering approximately forty bushels of charcoal remained from each cord burned. Colliers supervised this important work, and Negro colliers were so highly valued that in the 1850's an iron-master paid $1,000 for one.[17]

Slaveowners occasionally restricted the use of hands hired to ironmasters. Thus, some Negroes could not work at furnaces and ore mines, nor labor in

[13] Time Book, Buffalo Forge, 1830–1840, in Weaver-Brady Collection (Virginia); Patrick Brady, Home Journal, II, in McCormick Collection.

[14] Deposition of A. Campbell and of L. Shaw in Alexander v. Irvine's administrator; deposition of A. W. Templine in Weaver v. Davis.

[15] Ledger, Ridwell Furnace, 1805–1809; deposition of J. B. Johnson in Weaver v. Davis.

[16] Lesley, Iron Manufacturer's Guide, 70; deposition of Ira F. Jordan in Weaver v. Davis.

[17] Deposition of J. W. Schoolfield and of James Brawley in Weaver v. Maybury; Time Book, Buffalo Forge, 1830–1840, in Weaver-Brady Collection (Virginia); deposition of A. D. Rhodes in Hord v. Jordan; agreement between John Doyle and D. Holmes, 1843, in McCormick Collection; G. P. Grimsley, Iron Ores, Salt and Sandstones (West Virginia Geological Survey, IV, Morgantown, W. Va., 1909), ix, 36; William L. Alexander to Col. Sam McD. Reid, August 23, 1858, in Reid-White Papers (Washington and Lee University Library, Lexington, Va.).

bad weather. One woman would not permit her slave to be worked in a mine because he had already been injured in blasting. Most Negroes, however, were sent to their hirers without any attempt being made to safeguard their welfare.[18]

It was common practice on plantations to allow slaves to do extra work for wages, and this was also permitted at ironworks, where Negroes did such labor as driving wagons, chopping wood, and making baskets, tar, spikes, and rails. Extra work could also be done at night, on Sundays, and over the Christmas holidays. This labor was credited to a slave's account, and at one works slaves earned $2.93 for threshing an extra forty-seven bushels of rye, thirty-three cents for putting a bottom in a chair and making a floor mat, and $9.70 for drawing iron on Easter Monday. Those who did additional skilled labor apparently earned the largest sums, such as $12.75, $22.02, and $25.80 for handling iron at a forge.[19] The Negroes usually spent their money at ironworks' stores, where they bought articles of all kinds, especially clothing. Sugar and coffee were also very popular purchases; one slave at a forge bought twenty-seven pounds of coffee and sixteen pounds of sugar between March 6, 1834, and January 8, 1835. Tobacco was another item very frequently purchased. The accounts of the Negroes were usually settled at the end of a year, when they received cash for the remainder of their credits. Typical payments were those of a forge in Rockbridge County, where the Negroes received from $1 to $14.83 in the years between 1834 and 1839.[20]

Although slaves were widely used in the Virginia iron industry, ironmasters did not believe they could equal the output of white laborers. No matter what type of labor they performed, Negroes were always required to work under white supervision, for it was thought that they could not be taught to do skilled work independently. This view, held by Governor Spotswood in colonial Virginia, was also expressed by a nineteenth century ironmaster: "They are not as good workmen and do not take as good care or as much pains as good white workmen." [21] Another ironmaster believed that even

[18] R. Brooks to Jordans and Irvine, January 2, 1829; [   ] to I. Y. Grevey, 1846; Nancy Matthews to Col. John Jordan, 1831, all in McCormick Collection; bond for Negro hire in Bryan v. Bryan. Only three out of fifty-two slaves hired by one furnace were prohibited from working in ore pits. Bonds for Negro hire in Bryan v. Bryan.

[19] C. S. Sydnor, *Slavery in Mississippi* (New York, 1933), 96; J. B. Sellers, *Slavery in Alabama* (Birmingham, 1950), 91; R. B. Flanders, *Plantation Slavery in Georgia* (Chapel Hill, 1933), 146; Journals, Pine Forge, 1804–1834; Graham Ledgers; Journal, Beauregard Furnace, 1861–1865 (William and Mary College Library, Williamsburg, Va.); F. T. Anderson Papers and Ledger, Union Forge, 1825–1826 (Duke University Library); Negro Books, 1830–1840, and 1844–1849, Buffalo Forge; Ledger, Union Forge, 1825–1826, all in Weaver-Brady Collection (Virginia).

[20] All records of ironworks are full of notations of such purchases. See, for example, Journals, Pine Forge, 1804–1834, and Doyle v. Kirkpatrick papers in McCormick Collection; William W. Davis Papers and Negro Book, 1830–1840, Buffalo Forge, in Weaver-Brady Collection (Virginia).

[21] Cappon (ed.), *Iron Works at Tuball*, 18; deposition of William Norcross in Alexander v. Irvine's administrator.

though Negroes could be taught to work at a forge, it was more costly to refine a ton of bar iron with slave than with white labor because slaves wasted iron ore and charcoal. Just to train Negroes took a long time. When an iron-master was asked in 1836, "Cannot any Negro man of ordinarily good capacity be used as an underhand in a forge?" he replied, "Not with advantage without a servitude of two or three years." After one Negro had worked for five years at a forge it was still said that although he was a "first-rate" underhand for a slave, he was not an excellent worker.[22]

Perhaps naturally, the hirers of Negro ironworkers appear to have been less attentive to slaves' clothing needs than their owners would have been. The bonds for the hired Negroes stated that ironmasters were responsible for feeding and clothing the slaves concerned, and in some instances the bonds definitely prescribed what clothes were to be provided, for example two summer suits, a winter suit, a pair of shoes and socks, and a hat and blanket per man. More often, however, the bonds simply stated that the slaves would be clothed in the "usual manner," a phrase most ironmasters interpreted as they saw fit. An estimate of the clothing furnished at a forge in 1832 states that the hands received two shirts, three pairs of trousers, a coat, four pairs of shoes, a blanket, and a hat; however, they really received only a summer and winter suit, three pairs of shoes, and a hat and blanket, which was less than the amount of clothing recommended for plantation slaves.[23] Despite the rough labor at ironworks, all of the laborers at one establishment were without shoes in August 1828, and no leather had been available for five weeks. In February 1859 and June and September 1860, many slaves at another furnace were barefooted when even the manager admitted that the ore bank was so damp and rough that the workers really needed shoes. Perhaps it was this scarcity of shoes that caused the slaves to break into a building at that ironworks in March 1861 and steal clothing. As a matter of fact the manager was afraid to leave the works because he believed they would steal more.[24] The extensive purchases of clothing by slaves who did extra work also indicates that they were inadequately clothed by ironmasters.

In carrying out their responsibility for feeding the Negroes, ironmasters provided the usual basic foods, four or five pounds of bacon and a peck and half of cornmeal a week. Coffee, sugar, and molasses were not part of the

[22] Deposition of John Doyle in Weaver v. Davis; of Edwin Jordan in John Jordan's Executors v. John Jordan's Heirs, hereafter cited as Jordan v. Jordan, in Case Papers of Rockbridge County Superior Court of Chancery; and of William Norcross in Alexander v. Irvine's administrator.

[23] See, for example, bonds for Negro hire in Alexander v. Irvine's administrator, McCormick Collection, and Bryan v. Bryan; an estimate of the expense of conducting Clifton Forge for the year 1832 and deposition of Ira F. Jordan in Alexander v. Irvine's administrator. See also R. Collins, "Management of Slaves," *DeBow's Review*, XVII (1854), 424; Agricola, "Management of Negroes," *ibid.*, XIX (1855), 359.

[24] John Doyle to William Weaver, August 11, 1828, in Doyle v. Weaver; W. W. Rex to D. C. E. Brady, February 25, 1859, in Weaver-Brady Collection (Virginia); Rex to Brady, June 29, September 21, 1860, March 15, 1861, in Weaver-Brady Collection (Duke).

regular ration; indeed, they were among the most popular items purchased by those who did extra work. At some ironworks individual food allotments would be distributed and the slaves would cook for themselves. At other works the food would be prepared and the Negroes would be fed as a group, a method preferable in the eyes of one ironmaster as it enabled him to keep the slaves under better supervision.[25] Negroes complained about the food situation, for furnaces and forges often were short of food, or handed out bad supplies. The records of one ironworks show that bad flour was distributed early in December 1828, that no flour was on hand by the end of that month, that roughly half a year later bacon was needed, and that between October and the end of December 1829 there was again no flour. At a second ironworks such poor beef was issued that the manager was afraid the white hands would leave. Subsequently, the bacon supply there failed, bad meat was distributed again, and at about the same time the supply of flour was exhausted.[26]

Ledgers of ironworks point to a high rate of sickness among hired Negroes. The causes of illnesses were many, but a random selection from the records of one ironworks shows that "Jack" cut his leg, "Charles" burned his leg, "Billy" was incapacitated for two weeks because of frostbite, "Tom" was visited nine times by a doctor (at $5 a visit) because of his legs and head, and three slaves received treatment for gonorrhea. At another furnace some Negroes who had gone without shoes in the fall were sick for two weeks. In at least two instances ironworks had to be closed because all the personnel had been stricken by some disease.[27] Any sickness among the hired hands was an inconvenience and expense to the ironmaster, especially as a Virginia court had ruled in 1806 that the full contract price of a hired slave who became ill had to be paid.[28] Despite that, many ironmasters adopted the practice of deducting from the hire of a sick slave the cost of medical treatment and the value of time lost. Thus, at one forge over $50 was subtracted from the hire of three slaves because of the time they had lost while sick. In order to combat

[25] Deposition of James Shank and report of Commissioner Chapin in Alexander v. Irvine's administrator. See also Ledger, Union Forge, 1825–1826, and Negro Book, 1830–1840, Buffalo Forge, in Weaver-Brady Collection (Virginia); depositions in Doyle v. Weaver and in Matthews v. McCormick in the McCormick Collection; deposition of John Doyle in Weaver v. Mayburry; and Jordan, Davis and Company to William Weaver, September 8, 1832, in Weaver-Brady Collection (Virginia).

[26] John Doyle to Abraham W. Davis, December 1, 31, 1828; Charles [Gorgas] to William Weaver, March 29, April 6, 1859, and to D. C. E. Brady, August 11, 1859, and Rex to Brady, July 26, 1859, all in Weaver-Brady Collection (Virginia); and Doyle to Davis, August 25, 1829; W. W. Davis to William Weaver, December 4, 1829; and Elizabeth Matthews to Weaver, March 29, 1830; L. K. Gorgas to Brady, April 2, 1860; and W. W. Rex to Brady, May 28, 1860, all in Weaver-Brady Collection (Duke).

[27] Graham Ledgers and Miscellaneous Graham Papers and Rex to Brady, September 21, 1860, in Weaver-Brady Collection (Duke); Stephen McCormick to William Weaver, September 29, 1828, in McCormick Collection; William Viand to Joseph Marston, June 9, 1859, in Bush and Lobdell Collection (Alderman Library, University of Virginia).

[28] George v. Elliott in Helen T. Caterall's Judicial Cases Concerning American Slavery and the Negro (Washington, 1926), I, 113.

that practice some slave owners by the 1840's insisted that the hire bonds absolve them from responsibility for medical charges, and in 1854 the bonds for twenty-seven out of fifty-two hired Negroes said the slaves were to be free of medical costs.[29]

It is difficult to generalize about the discipline enforced at ironworks, but in many instances it was severe. In Rockbridge County a Negro is said to have hurled himself into a furnace rather than face a whipping. For numerous ironmasters and their managers, as well as for plantation managers, the whip was an effective "insignia of office." Although only seven slaves at the Tredegar Works were whipped within a decade, for years after the "great cat o'nine tails which hung somewhere in the yard" was still remembered. Negroes were whipped for various offenses, for example when a slave became involved in a fight over a card game and when two Negroes made a dirk.[30] It is apparent too that whipping was intended not only as a punishment for a culprit, but also as a warning to potential offenders. This was clearly the case at Buena Vista furnace in Rockbridge County when ten Negroes fled in the spring of 1855 because of whipping and generally poor treatment. After an unsuccessful attempt to take them back, their owners sent them elsewhere. This angered the furnace owners, who wanted the Negroes returned and punished before the rest of the slaves.[31] Whipping was not the only form of chastisement, however. At one furnace a slave was struck so severely on the arm that he was laid up for six days, and when another slave resisted handling by an ironworks' manager the latter simply picked up a rock and hit the Negro in the head.[32]

Despite the fear of punishment, Negroes at ironworks were perpetually running away for the same reasons that plantation hands did: to avoid hard work, to see their families, and to win freedom. Running away was a dangerous venture, for the odds against escaping were great and punishment for such boldness was severe, yet many Negroes repeatedly attempted to escape. Twelve members of a gang working on an ironworks' road attempted to run away;

[29] Bond for Negro hire in Jordan v. Jordan; Journal, Pine Forge, 1831–1834; J. R. Anderson to H. Loving, January 24, 1850, in Letter Book, Tredegar Company; and bonds for Negro hire in McCormick Collection, in Doyle v. Kirkpatrick, and in Bryan v. Bryan.

[30] John D. Capron, president, Glamorgan Pipe and Foundry Co., Lynchburg, Va., to author, July 29, 1953; Sydnor, *Slavery in Mississippi*, 71. Kenneth M. Stampp, *The Peculiar Institution* (New York, 1956), 174, says the whip was "the emblem of the master's authority. Nearly every slaveholder used it, and few grown slaves escaped it entirely." Bruce, *Virginia Iron Manufacture*, 255. See also Furnace Account Book, 1829–1832, in Graham Ledgers; R. A. Glasgow to [F. T. Anderson], February 16, 1858, in F. A. Anderson Collection. For another account of discipline by whipping, see W. W. Rex to D. C. E. Brady, October 26, 1860, in Weaver-Brady Collection (Duke).

[31] J. F. Jordan to Enos Hord, March 6, 1855; Hord to S. F. and W. H. Jordan, March 12, 1855; Hord and Tulless to S. F. and W. H. Jordan, March 21, 1855; S. F. and W. H. Jordan to Hord and Tulless, March 26, 1855, all in Hord v. Jordan. The Jordans refused to pay Hord for the Negroes for January and February, but the court in Hord v. Jordan awarded Hord $294.77 for those months.

[32] Negro Time Book, 1833–1839, in Graham Papers; John Watkins to William Weaver, July 28, 1854, in Weaver-Brady Collection (Duke).

four were successful, and of those brought back three eventually escaped after repeated attempts. Coping with this problem was both troublesome and expensive to ironmasters. In one case $37.10 was paid in costs and jail fees to retrieve a slave; in another instance it cost $110.05 to bring back four Negroes.[33]

The extensive use of Negroes by Virginia ironmasters did not prevent the industry from suffering from the competition of British and Northern iron after 1836. This was probably because with slave labor available, furnace and forge owners failed to adopt improved manufacturing methods. This conservative policy meant that the cost of making a ton of pig iron remained the same, about $15, between 1825 and 1855.[34] But English ironmasters followed the opposite path, and in 1841 a number of disturbed iron manufacturers met in Lexington, Virginia, to discuss the threat of imported iron and agreed that a new tariff was indispensable if they were to prosper. The tariff passed in the following year gave them a little help, but in 1846 duties on iron were lowered, and in 1849 a Botetourt County ironmaster declared that only his "peculiar situation" with regard to labor had kept him in business and that if a new tariff was not passed he would stop operating in 1850. The same view was expressed at a meeting of trans-Blue Ridge Mountain ironmasters in September 1849 who felt that if something was not done to relieve their distress their works would all be closed within twelve months. During the same year at least six ironmasters from Virginia attended a national iron convention that demanded added protection for the industry.[35] Another cause for despondency in these years was the fact that Pennsylvania iron undersold slave-made iron in Virginia. In 1841, 1843, and 1845 the owner of the Tredegar Works declared that he could buy Northern iron for less than or equal to what it cost to purchase locally produced iron. This was corroborated by the ironmaster who said that Northern iron at Richmond always undersold iron made in western Virginia.[36]

It is clear that Negroes supplied the bulk of the labor used at charcoal furnaces and forges in Virginia even though ironmasters criticized their ability. Most of the slaves were hired and their life was onerous, as they were worked

[33] Report of Commissioner Chapin in Alexander v. Irvine's administrator; Ledger, Ridwell Furnace, 1805–1809; receipt of jailer of Augusta County, July 27, 1831, in Alexander v. Irvine's administrator; J. Irvine's Cash Book and bond for Negro hire, both in McCormick Collection.

[34] Between 1848 and 1858, for example, apparently only three Virginia furnaces used coke. Swank, History, 371. See also deposition of John Donihoo in Weaver v. MaybURRY; deposition of M. Bryan in Matthews v. McCormick; Joseph R. Anderson to F. T. Anderson, October 28, 1851, in F. T. Anderson Collection; William Mark to [   ], January 18, 1855, in McCormick Collection.

[35] Bruce, Virginia Iron Manufacture, 213, 264–65; Wheeling, W. Va., Daily Gazette, August 23, September 17, 1849; Proceedings of the Iron Convention, Held at Pittsburgh, November 21st, 22d and 23d, 1849 (Pittsburgh, 1849), 13.

[36] Letters of J. R. Anderson to Davis H. Forrer, November 10, 1841, to Col. J. Jordan, December 9, 1843, and to William Weaver, April 19, 1845, all in Letter Books, Tredegar Company; William Weaver to Wm. S. Triplett, August 25, 1862, in Weaver-Brady Collection (Virginia).

hard, were poorly fed and clothed, and were separated from their families. Contrary to Bruce, "the 'kindly relation of protector and protected, of strong and weak,' so well known to have existed on the plantation" did not exist for them, and life at an ironworks was not "a sunny rather than a dreary" thing.[87] The iron industry's continued reliance upon Negroes in the 1840's and 1850's probably contributed to the failure of ironmasters to adopt improved methods of production, and thus put them at an increasing disadvantage with regard to Northern and British iron in those decades. In general, slave labor brought neither satisfaction nor progress to Virginia's ironworkers and their industry.

[87] Bruce, *Virginia Iron Manufacture*, 249, 255–56.

E. Ophelia Settle

SOCIAL ATTITUDES DURING THE SLAVE REGIME: HOUSEHOLD SERVANTS VERSUS FIELD HANDS

Scholarly descriptions of the institution of slavery have generally centered on the activities of the white slaveowners and, even where discussing the Negroes' role and viewpoint, have almost invariably depended on primary sources written by white people. In part this is due to the nature of the source materials available. Yet the narratives of fugitive slaves, and the records of interviews conducted many years later with individuals freed by the Civil War, can, if exploited critically, afford much useful information.

Based on interviews with ex-slaves, the article that follows describes the way in which the system of social stratification among slaves on southern plantations—that is, the distinction between field hands and house servants—shaped their social outlook and their views about slavery.

T HE method of using the person's own story as the sole document in a sociological study has been questioned by social scientists all over the country. It may seem presumptuous, therefore, to offer to a group of sociologists a paper on social attitudes based on an analysis of 100 ex-slave documents. These were collected intermittently over a period of four years, from 34 men and 66 women who had been exposed to slavery for from eight to forty-five years each, and who at the time of the interview were living in middle and west Tennessee. These interviews were taken down by a stenographer who remained in the background while the interviewer attempted to put the subject at ease and allow him to tell his experiences without interruption.

E. Ophelia Settle, "Social Attitudes During the Slave Regime: Household Servants Versus Field Hands," *Racial Contacts and Social Research*, Publications of the American Sociological Society, XXVIII (December, 1933), pp. 95–98. Reprinted with the permission of the author and publisher.

Because the differences between the house and field slaves have been so often emphasized by writers dealing with the period of slavery, it was interesting to note these differences as presented in the attitudes shown by people who had been slaves themselves. This paper is merely an attempt to point out certain attitudes shown in documents and to indicate some possible underlying factors in the genesis of these attitudes. The latter term is here used to mean "the individual tendency to react, either positively or negatively, to a given social value." [1]

Among the group of ex-slaves interviewed, 44 were classified as house servants and 31 as field hands; 6 did both house and field work; 9 were too young to be gainfully employed; and in 10 cases the information secured did not warrant occupational classification. This division is made because the fundamental group of attitudes appear to have had their basis in occupational differences. The house slaves were thrown in close contact with their masters and mistresses and were thus exposed to the cultural influences of that group. They were usually taught to consider themselves superior to the field hands and to hold themselves apart as a group. Their dress was superior because their occupation required it; their food was often identical with that of the master; their cottages were whitewashed and built near the master's residence; their work itself was elevated above that of the toilers of the field. Add to these differences the fact that the house servants were often mulattoes, and it is easy to understand their position as a middle group in the slave régime. Above them were the masters with their families; but below them were the field hands—to whom they often felt less closely akin than to their masters.

While it is not contended that *all* house slaves held a particular set of attitudes in contradistinction to those of field hands, the contrast in these two groups is outlined sharply in the following situations:

1. Situations in which attitudes of superiority on the part of the house servant are manifested.

2. Situations in which attitudes toward runaway or unruly slaves are shown.

3. Situations in which attitudes toward the régime of slavery are presented.

An illustration of the first group of attitudes is found in the statement made by one of the Nashville house slaves who said:

> "We house slaves thought we wuz better'n the others what worked in the field; we really wuz raised a little different; fact is, I kinda think I'm better'n most folks now. Yes'm we wuz raised; they (that is, the field hands) wuzn't."

That the masters often encouraged their house slaves in their feeling of superiority to their fellow-slaves is shown by their treatment of the "play chillen"—the slave companions of the children in the master's family.

> "They wouldn't let us play with the niggers, and they wouldn't cut our hair," said one of these children, "we sat at the table and et

[1] Taken from Reuter's *Introduction to Sociology*, p. 99. Acknowledgment is made to Thomas and Znaniecki, *The Polish Peasant in Europe and America*, pp. 21–24.

after they et. We jest played with white chillen and cullud folks wuz afraid of us."

"I don't know much about the hardships of slavery because I belonged to a wealthy family and my grandmother and great grandmother lived just like the white people," declared a more cultured member of this group. "None of us were ever sold, I suppose the little cabin children had hard times; they never got to go to the big house, but I was raised right in the house."

Nowhere in the documents is the contrast between the attitudes of house and field slaves shown so well as in their statements regarding the runaway or unruly slaves who were found on every large plantation. Of course some house slaves ran away, and some field hands were more sympathetic with the master than with the runaway, but this situation is not the general rule.

A cabin child, who was 8 years old at the time of the incident narrated, said in reference to runaway slaves:

"Yes, I've seen 'em. I've stole bread out of the house and give it to 'em. I remember uncle Stephen Partee had been gone about a year in the woods, and one evenin' I went out to the barn to get some eggs, and he was hiding under the shucks; it liked to skeered me to death. He said 'Don't holler, Honey; just go back to the house and tell your mammy to send me something to eat.' I went back and got it myself and I didn't say a word, 'cause I knowed if Ole Partee (his master) caught him, he would whup him to death."

Another child of about the same age declared:

"I have carried them food and they would say 'God bless you chile,' and ask me to thank the people for them. My folks would come in the cabin and say 'there's a runaway slave' and Aunt Nancy would let me take some milk to him, and he would say 'God help you' and I would keep on taking it to him to hear him say that."

The house child, on the other hand, was usually less sympathetic and had little understanding of the conditions of these people who sought his help. One house girl, on seeing a runaway slave, was so frightened that she ran all the way to the house to tell "the white folks" what she had seen. Another joined her white "play chillen" in throwing stones at a runaway who had been caught and chained near a store. She gleefully joined in tormenting him in every possible way, and declared that she regarded him as a person entirely outside her own group.

The differences in the attitudes of these groups toward the slave régime in general is shown best in their behavior during the [civil] war. The house slave usually remained with his mistress and guarded the plantation while the cabin slave was more likely to run away to the "Yankees" if the opportunity was presented.

A typical attitude of the house servant is shown in the following document:

"I remember one that mamma always likes to tell. She said her old master was sitting on the porch with his legs crossed smoking his pipe and his old nag was tied to a post down in the yard. She looked up and saw the yankees coming with swords and guns, and everything, and she threw up her hands and shouted 'Run, Marster, the yankees are coming!' and old master got up and ran down to where the nag was tied, jumped on him and ran away. The yankees had seen him sitting there, and had seen mamma throw up her hands but they didn't see which way he went. When they got there mamma said one of them raised his gun and said 'I'm a great mind to blow your brains out,' but he didn't and she didn't care nohow because she had saved her master's life then."

One girl, when asked if the slaves on her plantation ran away, replied: "Some of 'em run away"; but added quickly "Them that lived in the quarters run away, but them that worked in the house didn't."

The maid to the wife of a "Yankee" army officer did not even know that she was a slave until her mistress told her she planned to set her free.

However, the field slave children early realized their condition and became adept at keeping secrets from the people in "the big house." They were the slaves who most frequently ran away to the "Yankees" and who, according to one slave woman, would "get out and shout" whenever the "Yankees" won a victory. Some of them ran away in families and, even if caught and returned to their masters, stayed only until they were able to arrange another escape.

Below is an example of the cleverness of these children as well as an illustration of their attitude toward the whole situation:

"I was a little gal, but I remember how the rebels would come by and ask me where the niggers was, and I would tell them I didn't know. They would keep after me and sometimes I would tell them that they went away; then they would ask where did they go and I would tell them that they went away and that was all I knowed. They used to tell me if I would tell them what they wanted to know they would give me some candy, and of course I, like other children, liked candy very much but after I got it, I would only tell them that they went away and I did not know where they went. Sometimes they would ask me 'Where is your mammy, little nigger? Ain't you got no mammy? If you will tell me I'll give you some candy.' I used to say 'Will you sho nuff?' And they would say 'Yes,' and they would give me the candy and then I would tell them that she had gone to keep the yankees from getting her. . . . They would ask me 'Little nigger, do you want to go to the yankees?' And I would say 'No,' because I knowed they might kill me if I said 'Yes.' "

In contrast to the field hands, then, one finds the house slaves usually a separate group, sometimes living in cabins especially built for them and their families but often living in the "big house," responsible for all household duties and taught to hold themselves superior to their brethren of the field, and to be on familiar terms with the "white folks"; always observing, however, a certain social distance in their relationship to both masters and slaves. Under these conditions it is not at all strange that with reference to most social questions the attitudes of these two groups tended to be in contradistinction to each other.

Walter Fisher

PHYSICIANS AND SLAVERY IN THE ANTEBELLUM SOUTHERN MEDICAL JOURNAL

An important aspect of slave life that has received little systematic attention has been the health and medical care of bondsmen. Walter Fisher's article on the treatment of slaves by southern physicians provides an illuminating glimpse into this largely neglected subject.

Today, even as it was generations ago, American Negro slavery is many different things to many different people, both to historians and to lay persons. These variations in views about slavery are partly reflections of what historians have written about it, and reflections, in turn, of the historians' sources. Typically, these sources have included plantation records, letters and diaries, travel accounts, newspapers and other periodicals. Traditionally, however, historians have paid little attention to medical sources, to the writings of physicians in general and, more specifically, to what they have written about slaves and slavery in antebellum medical journals. As Richard H. Shryock declared in a paper read at the meeting of the History of Science Society in 1934, while southern planters and English or northern travelers saw and described the southern scene obscurely through their respective biased glasses, the "relatively reliable professional testimony" of physicians has been neglected.[1]

Of all critics, the Southern physician was perhaps in the best position to report on the physical and moral treatment of the slaves. When he stated, as he sometimes did, that Negroes were overworked and underfed, he can hardly be suspected of antislavery bias since he was the

Walter Fisher, "Physicians and Slavery in the Antebellum Southern Medical Journal," *Journal of the History of Medicine and Allied Sciences*, XXIII (1968), pp. 36–49. Reprinted with permission of *Journal of the History of Medicine and Allied Sciences* and Walter Fisher.

[1] R. H. Shryock, "Medical sources and the social historian," *Am. hist. Rev.*, 1936, 41, 465.

friend of the planter who employed him. As a matter of fact, he usually approved of the institution. Coming into frequent contact with human bondage under the most intimate circumstances, he was in a position to understand it as few travelers could hope to do. On the other hand, his vested interest in the institution was rarely so direct or so great as was that of the planters.[2]

This paper offers a kind of demonstration-by-way-of-suggestion that the southern physicians who wrote in the medical journals published in the American South in the three decades before the Civil War are reporters and witnesses whose testimony concerning slavery should be heard, analyzed, and incorporated into the history of "the peculiar institution." [3] Their writings additionally reveal much concerning the status of medicine as science and art a century and a half ago. Within this frame of reference, the major foci of this paper will be the motives and profits involved in the medical care of slaves; and the antebellum medical practitioners—irregular, regular, and heroic.

I

The vast economic investment represented by the southern slave population was the primary reason why they were provided with medical care. Richard D. Arnold, a leading physician of Savannah, observed that slavery "as it exists with us is the only institution in which Interests and Humanity go hand in hand together." So great, he wrote, was the loss in capital by the death of a slave that a planter understood that "to save his capital was to save his negroes." [4] In correspondence between Dr. George C. Smith, of Oxford, Georgia, and Joseph A. Eve, an Augusta physician, about "a case of probable extra-uterine pregnancy," the slave patient is described as "a valuable servant" whose owners "feel great solicitude on her account, not knowing what may be the final result." [5] The feelings of a Louisiana planter who owned a slave suffering from a vesico-vaginal fistula were described by the attending physician, Dr. Samuel Cartwright of New Orleans:

> He authorized me to call in consulting physicians, and to procure for her all the comforts and conveniences necessary in the treatment of her case. He said that the patient had been pronounced incurable by

[2] Ibid.

[3] The first medical journal published south of the border states was the *Southern Journal of Medicine and Surgery*, begun at Augusta in 1836. In addition to those cited in this paper, other antebellum medical journals of this region were the *Charleston Medical Journal and Review*; the *Medical Journal of North Carolina*, published at Edenton and Raleigh; the *Southern Medical Reformer*, published at Petersburg, Virginia; and the *Virginia Medical and Surgical Journal*, of Richmond.

[4] R. H. Shryock, Ed., *Letters of Richard D. Arnold, M.D., 1806–1876. Papers of the Trinity College Historical Society, Double Series 18–19*. Durham, 1929, pp. 33–34.

[5] *Sth. med. surg. J.*, 1845, n.s. 1, 574.

a number of physicians, but if impossible to effect a cure, he hoped that it was in the power of science to afford some relief to her intolerable sufferings.[6]

Comparable concern is revealed in the following conversation between Jim, an 18-year-old slave, "a likely and quite athletic figure," and Dr. D. Warren Brickell, of New Orleans, during a typhoid epidemic:

> "What is the matter with you, Jim?" "Nothing, sir." "Well, why have you come here?" "The order of the overseer, sir, is to come to the hospital the moment we feel the least unwell: I felt a little tired just now, and thought I ought to obey orders." [7]

These incidents, and many others like them reported in the journals, also attest to the significance of their care of slaves as a source of income for southern physicians. As Dr. Arnold put it, the demand for professional attention for slaves "is the true reason why Physicians get into practice more readily at the South than at the North—and that here he stands some chance of making his bread while he has teeth to chew it." [8]

Other indications of the importance of medical care of slaves in the practice of the southern physician are to be found in the "fee bills" established by southern medical societies. Special rates for the treatment of slaves suggest that the volume of such cases may have compensated for the price differential involved. In 1851 the medical profession of Richmond, Virginia, established a table of rates in which a vaccination for a white person was charged at three dollars, or at two for five dollars, with each subsequent injection in the same family being set at one dollar. By the same schedule the vaccination of a single slave was set at two dollars; each additional vaccination on the same plantation or farm, or in the same family, cost one dollar.[9] In Nottoway County, Virginia, rates for infirmary patients were set in 1853 at seven dollars per week for whites and at five dollars for Negroes.[10]

But the profession was by no means of one mind with respect to such arrangements. The practice of attending families by the year was noticed editorially and condemned in the *New Orleans Medical and Surgical Journal* in 1852. In language matching that of an organized medical profession of a later day, the editors contended that

> yearly practice aims at a species of miserable, petty monopoly, which is at war with the objects ... of a liberal and enlightened profession. You may bargain with your grocer, your butcher, your laundress, and no harm comes of or by it; but for an honorable, an educated physician to hire himself by the year, like a slave; to pledge his talents and his

[6] *New Orl. med. surg. J.*, 1859, 16, 513.
[7] *New Orl. med. News Hosp. Gaz.* 1856, 2, 532.
[8] Shryock, *Letters of Richard D. Arnold,* p. 34.
[9] *Stethoscope Va. med. Gaz.* 1851, 1, 178.
[10] *Ibid.,* 3, 236.

services, for a stipulated sum, is in direct violation of the ethics of the profession.[11]

A similar criticism was voiced by a physician who signed himself "Celsus" in a Richmond, Virginia, medical journal in 1853:

> When an individual asks me to do his practice by the year, I am often inclined to return an answer a young friend of mine did on such an occasion—he indignantly replied, "whenever I am become black and am to be hired, I will let you know." [12]

The physicians of Nashville, following a similar course, agreed in 1858 not to attend either individuals or families by the year at any stipulated price nor to consult with any physician who transgressed the rule.[13]

Underlying the objections of medical practitioners to such contracts was the view, sometimes specifically stated and sometimes intimated, that annual compensation usually involved a "bargain rate." [14] Occasionally, however, another consideration entered the picture. The risks involved in collecting annual fees were greater. Moreover, the hazards involved in collecting fees for services rendered to individuals were great enough to deter the practitioner from entering into long-term group-practice agreements. For example, difficulties encountered in being paid for services furnished to slaves under mortgage or in the hands of trustees and agents led the physicians of Alabama, in a state medical convention in 1847, to recommend that practitioners seek liens on slaves so attended or furnished, "in the same manner and under the same regulations as the lien laws for the security of mechanics and laborers in relation to steamboats." [15] Unfortunately, the medical journals do not report on the implementation of this recommendation. However, the action of the Alabama group is instructive in that it points to the willingness of physicians—in their essential role as business men—to receive payment in the form of the chattels themselves.

Physicians also played an important part in the "warranty" activities associated with the sale and purchase of slaves. Juriah Harris, a professor of physiology at the Savannah Medical College, reported in 1858 that southern physicians were "daily called upon" by prospective purchasers to pronounce upon the soundness of slaves. The frequency of such requests, together with demands that physicians present medical evidence in court "in cases of prosecution for the sale of an unsound negro," led Dr. Harris to the conclusion that it was the duty of southern medical men to establish uniform rules in such practice.[16]

Harris then proceeded to outline what amounted to a code for the direction of physicians and slave-buyers. He regarded diseases of a chronic or con-

[11] New Orl. med. surg. J., 1852, 8, 543.
[12] Stethoscope Va. med. Gaz., 1853, 2, 238.
[13] Nashville J. Med. Surg., 1860, 18, 411.
[14] Stethoscope Va. med. Gaz., 1853, 2, 238.
[15] New Orl. med. surg. J., 1848, 4, 678.
[16] Savannah J. Med., 1858, 1, 146.

stitutional character which incapacitated the Negro "for the performance of the usual duties of his calling, viz: hard labor," as the basis for declaring the slave "unsound." Specific disqualifying diseases and ailments included the loss of arms or legs; injuries to muscles, tendons, and tissue which might prevent the dexterous handling of implements of labor; constant or recurring ulcers on the leg; malignant tumors, cancer, and scrofula; asthma; and some forms of rheumatism. Hemorrhoids, which Dr. Harris said were rare in the Negro— there were, as he put it, ten cases among whites to one in the Negro—should also be considered evidence of unsoundness. Keloid tumors, though benign, were also held to be disqualifying, Harris describing them as having the unfortunate quality of being incurable "either by the knife or medication, and having a strong tendency to scrofulous ulceration." [17]

Gonorrhea, Dr. Harris advised, was never a cause of permanent unsoundness. On syphilis, however, he suggested that the

> soundness of a negro who may be or have been affected with an infecting chancre should be looked upon with suspicion [for]... no one can tell when the constitutional effects may be developed.... It is true that in this country, blessed by Providence with good air and the negro supplied with good food and clothing by his owner, that this rarely results when the chancre has been properly treated.[18]

Secondary syphilis, he continued, was "most unquestionably" a cause of unsoundness—even should the apparent symptoms be relieved by a well-directed treatment, no one could tell at what time it might reappear.[19]

Concurrence in Dr. Harris's views of the disqualifying effect of syphilis is found in the experience of other doctors. Paul F. Eve, of Augusta, reported that he was requested, in 1843, by the prospective purchaser of one Philip to give an opinion on the slave's health. "He was pronounced unsound, and to be then laboring under the tertiary effects of the venereal disease." Notwithstanding, the purchase was made. A year later Philip was "in a very desperate condition" and undergoing treatment by Dr. Eve.[20]

That determination of the soundness or unsoundness of a slave on sale was a matter requiring close attention is further revealed in the experience of "Dr. R. T. L.," of Wilkinson County, Mississippi, who was described as "a practitioner of experience" by Dr. C. S. Magoun, who reported the incident to the *New Orleans Medical Journal*. Dr. L. purchased, in 1844, an 18-year-old pregnant woman who was suffering with a cough. Her soundness, however, was guaranteed by the vendor, an opinion in which the physician-purchaser concurred. Three days later the slave was dead, ostensibly as a result of puerperal fever—the three-day interval between her purchase and her death being marked, however, by her giving birth to a child "of full size, healthy and vigorous."

---

[17] *Ibid.*, 147, 148, 217, 218, 219, 220, 223, 292, 293.
[18] *Ibid.*, 2, 10–11.
[19] *Ibid.*
[20] *Sth. med. surg. J.*, 1845, *n.s.* 1, 682–83.

Moreover, a post-mortem examination disclosed that the slave had a tumor in the thorax, a condition which impelled Dr. Magoun, the reporter, to assert that the "woman was evidently unwell at the time of sale, and must have been so for weeks, if not months." "Under the circumstances," he asked, "ought the seller or buyer to be the loser?" [21]

But while .the Mississippi practitioner was apparently "taking a flyer" in the slave marketplace, his brother practitioners elsewhere augmented their income by "soundness practice," asking fees of wide range. In Virginia in the 1850's charges for "an opinion of health or disease" ranged from two to ten dollars, while "an opinion involving a question of law" might cost from ten to fifty dollars.[22] And in the late fifties, post-mortem examinations in cases of legal investigation were set, in Nashville, at $25.[23]

But establishing fee schedules was one thing, collecting fees was another. Non-payment or postponement of the payment of doctors' bills was a chronic socio-economic habit of the period, whose results were felt by both the younger southern physicians and the more mature. One of the latter, Richard D. Arnold, complained that "it runs me almost crazy to think that with hundreds upon hundreds due me professionally I find the greatest difficulty in raising a simple fifty dollars." [24] And, almost wistfully, Richmond physicians were urged to seek to collect their bills at least once a year, "whenever this can be done without serious inconvenience to the patient." [25]

II

Medical care has never been the monopoly of the professional medical man. The doctor, be he wizard or scientist, has always shared his art and craft with the layman. That medical care of the slave in the antebellum South is no exception to this generalization is amply attested by a variety of data published in southern medical journals of the antebellum period. Comments of the profession on slave care by non-professionals fall into two main categories. Essentially jealous of their professional relationships to health and disease, physician-writers loudly complained of bungling by amateurs. Mistresses and overseers, and particularly midwives, were targets of professional criticism. But in his less warmly critical moments, the antebellum doctor became something of a consulting health engineer, offering in his journal articles practical suggestions for the more efficient health management of slaves.

Dr. D. Warren Brickell, a New Orleans medical editor and professor of obstetrics at the New Orleans School of Medicine, best captured the spirit of physicians who protested the "competition" by owners, overseers, and mis-

[21] *New Orl. med. J.*, 1844, 1, 434–35.
[22] *Stethoscope Va. med. Gaz.*, 1851, 1, 178.
[23] *Nashville J. Med. Surg.*, 1860, 18, 409.
[24] Shryock, Ed. (n. 4), 164.
[25] *Stethoscope Va. med. Gaz.*, 1851, 1, 180.

tresses. The physician derived no pleasure or advantage, he asserted, from treating cases which had been badly nursed. Nor had the planter "fulfilled his duty, either in point of humanity or self-interest" in allowing his slaves to be treated by amateurs. But, most of all, Brickell condemned "the almost universal practice, on the part of owners and overseers, of tampering with their sick negroes ... before applying for medical aid." A physician called to treat a slave patient "thus quacked" was compared to a man called on to stay an already rapidly falling wall. So frequently, Brickell wrote, did physicians encounter such situations that they had relapsed into a limited routine system of medication. The planter, he complained,

> has no confidence in himself or his overseer in ... putting a new spoke in a cart wheel and sends for a mechanic at once. But of the intricate mechanism of man ... their knowledge is sufficient, in their own estimation, to warrant such efforts for the restoration of the sick man as they would not ... have exerted on the comparatively worthless cart wheel.[26]

In criticism of a similar practice, Thomas S. Powell, a physician of Sparta, Georgia, lamented the treatment accorded one Mary, a slave who suffered from a chronic pain in the knee. In this case the slave's mistress, supposing the ailment to be a simple sprain, "applied vinegar and clay from the back of the chimney for several nights." More reprehensible in the eyes of this "regular" practitioner was the calling of "Dr. _____, a celebrated Thomsonian," who proceeded to vomit the patient. Notwithstanding the effects on Mary of her mistress' poultice and of the vegetable compounds which typified Thomsonian practice, Dr. Powell was able quickly to restore to health the slave whose "services were much needed in the field." [27]

Dr. H. V. Wooten, of Lowndesboro, Alabama, was called to prescribe for the slave Betty, whose owner had been treating her for what he took to be diarrhea. Wooten determined that the slave had a prolapsed uterus accompanied by profuse leucorrhoea. Subsequently an operation was performed, and the slave recovered.[28]

Still another complaint made by professional physicians had to do with the common remedies prescribed by lay practitioners. Thomas Affleck, an affluent Mississippi planter, reported to Dr. Erasmus Fenner, editor of the *Southern Medical Reports*, that overseers too often dosed "after a routine— an emetic followed by calomel and oil." [29] L. A. Dugas, professor of anatomy at the Medical College of Georgia, in treating the infant child of "Mr. L. P. D.'s negro woman Pat," for purulent ophthalmia, substituted a chloride of soda wash for the breast-milk lotion treatment which the owner had prescribed and administered.[30]

Of greater seriousness, however, were the untoward results of obstetrical

---

[26] *New Orl. med. News Hosp. Gaz.*, 1856, 2, 545–46.
[27] *Atlanta med. surg. J.*, 1856, 1, 516–18.   [29] *Sth. med. Rep.*, 1849–50, 1, 436.
[28] *Sth. med. surg. J.*, 1845, *n.s.* 1, 845.   [30] *Sth. med. surg. J.*, 1836, 1, 82–83.

practice by midwives. Dr. R. H. Whitfield, of Gainesville, Alabama, in 1855 attacked the "almost universal" employment of "negresses" as midwives. "To their bad management," he contended, "is to be attributed most of the diseases to which our females fall victim." [31] A New Orleans practitioner, alarmed by the frequency of child-birth accidents, declared that there was "probably no city of equal population in Christendom" where the male professional was less employed in obstetrical cases than in the Crescent City.

> none in which the female practitioners are less educated, being chiefly negresses or mulattresses, or foreigners without anatomical, physiological and obstetrical education.... That such uneducated persons should be generally successful is owing to the fact that in a great majority of cases no scientific skill is required, and thus a lucky negress becomes the rival of the most learned obstetrician.[32]

Luck was frequently not on the side of the midwife. A woman thought to be in labor, and so described by a midwife, was found by Dr. Richard D. Arnold to be suffering instead from an extraordinary case of rupture of the rectum and expulsion externally of the intestines.[33] Called hastily to take over where a midwife's art had failed, Dr. J. C. C. Blackburn, of Pike County, Alabama, found his slave patient suffering additionally from a prolapsed uterus.[34] Another physician complained that he owned "a valuable negress who has been made useless by the forcible extraction of the placenta immediately after the birth of her child," the act being that of "an ignorant midwife." [35] And, reporting on the diseases of Lowndesboro, Alabama, and its vicinity, Dr. H. W. Wooten observed that, although obstetrics was beginning, around 1848, to form a very important branch of practice in the region, with "very near all the white women, and many negroes calling for professional assistance in the labors," many cases involving slaves "were rendered complicated and difficult by neglect or bad management on the part of the midwives in whose hands" he found them.[36]

Loud and frequent though they may have been, physicians' complaints about midwives did not include the demand that lay accoucheurs be banned from such practice. Rather, the theme reiterated in their articles is that educational requirements and control measures be instituted for these women. The position taken by Dr. R. H. Day, of Pattersonville, Louisiana, was typical:

> If such cases must be put in the charge of women—to which I yield in hearty assent—let public opinion and the laws of our State require of all such a proper study and due qualification for their important and responsible avocation. Let not old age be their only qualification.[37]

Difficult confinement cases sometimes involved extensive treatment by

[31] New Orl. med. surg. J., 1855, 12, 196–99.
[32] Ibid., 1854, 11, 20–21.
[33] Sth. med. surg. J., 1838, 2, 79–80.
[34] Ga. Blister and Critic, 1854, 1, 133.
[35] New Orl. med. surg. J., 1855, 12, 196.
[36] Sth. med. Rep., 1851, 2, 342, 345.
[37] New Orl. med. surg. J., 1847, 4, 227.

teams of physicians. Dr. John G. Westmoreland, an Atlanta physician, was called to see one Jane, a slave, in labor. Arriving at about eight in the morning, he discovered that Jane's was a case of arm presentation. During the course of the day, until seven in the evening when a dead child was delivered, Dr. Westmoreland called three other physicians into consultation.[38] A similar case was that of Joseph P. Manly's Jane, who was described by the midwife Aunt Winney as having "the usual labor pains." Over a two-day period Jane required the services of two physicians. In Spaulding County, Georgia, Dr. E. F. Knott discovered his slave patient to be suffering from a ruptured uterus. The owner, after consultation, "immediately called my friend Dr. John R. Clark who lived within one mile . . . [and remained] until late in the afternoon." Dr. Knott meanwhile was present throughout the day, and again in the evening called for Dr. Clark. Finding that his associate had left his home to attend another patient, Knott sent for Clark's instruments and with them delivered Jane of a healthy child.[39]

III

During the 1830's James Silk Buckingham, an Englishman, traveled throughout America. In his report on his travels, published in 1841, he presented the transcript of an item appearing in a New York newspaper under the heading "More Pork for the South":

> Yesterday morning it was discovered that a barrell, which had been put into the office of the Charleston packet line .., for the purpose of being shipped to Charleston, contained the bodies of two dead negroes. The cask and its contents were sent up to the police office and placed in the dead house for the coroner.[40]

In discussing this incident, Buckingham relates that it had lately become a common practice in New York to ship off bodies of dead Negroes "for various ports, but especially the South," to medical schools for dissection; that, to elude suspicion, these bodies were put up in salt and brine and packed in the same casks as those in which salted provisions were exported; and that the discovery reported was the third or fourth of the kind in a single month. An inquest was held and a declaration made that the Negroes had died of disease; "no further inquiry," Buckingham commented, "appears to have been made into the matter, as if it were altogether beneath the notice of white men to trace out these traders in the dead bodies of the blacks." [41]

[38] *Sth. med. surg. J.,* 1838, 2, 335.
[39] *Atlanta med. surg. J.,* 1855, 1, 11–13. See also *ibid.,* 591–94, and *New Orl. med. surg. J.,* 1845, 2, 315–16.
[40] J. S. Buckingham, *America, historical, statistic and descriptive.* London, 1841, 1, 159.
[41] *Ibid.,* 159–60.

The propaganda value of Buckingham's disclosure to the then growing American anti-slavery movement is self-evident. But the episode had a more practical significance. It connects directly with problems of medical education, medical care, and even medical experimentation. The free Negro class of the North might occasionally furnish laboratory anatomical specimens, as their persisting fear of "body-snatchers" and "night doctors" indicates. Shipping the cadavers southward, however, is another matter. No data have been uncovered to substantiate the particular Buckingham disclosures; not so, however, with regard to the general problem to which his story is related. An abundance of materials in the southern medical journals reveals that slaves had a fairly significant role in medical education and in experimental and radical medical and surgical practice of the antebellum South.

Four out of eight main articles in the August 1836 number of the *Southern Medical and Surgical Journal* deal in whole or in part with treatment furnished to slaves.[42] Four out of five operations on the eye by Professor Dugas of the Medical College of Georgia, and reported in the June 1838 number of the same journal, were performed on slaves.[43] Three of the six surgical cases reported by Professor Paul F. Eve, of the same school, involved Negroes and were performed in the presence of students in the college's anatomical theater.[44] The Louisiana Medical College, in New Orleans, advertised that among its "admirable advantages for the instruction of medical students—particularly those destined for southern practice," was "the great facility of obtaining subjects for dissection" from the New Orleans Charity Hospital, a large installation treating local patients of both races as well as a considerable transient clientele.[45]

In an editorial extolling the virtues of "Southern Institutions," the editors of the *Savannah Journal of Medicine* called particular attention to the "abundant clinical opportunities for the study of disease" in the large Negro patient population at the Savannah Medical College.[46] Students of the Atlanta Medical College examined during several weeks a slave who constituted "an interesting case" of an abscessed liver. This man was "lectured upon and prescribed for in the presence of the class." [47] And in an operation performed at the Medical College of Georgia, "assisted by the faculty" and viewed by students, Dr. Eve successfully amputated nearly one half of the lower jaw bone (four and three-quarters inches, including one of its angles) of one Dinah, who, after complaining of an aching jaw for years, was discovered to be suffering from sarcoma of the jaw.[48]

Even more dramatic is the scene described by J. Marion Sims in one of his many heroic operations. Even considering the surgical practices of the time

[42] *Sth. med. surg. J.*, 1838, 2, 335.
[43] *Ibid.*, 647–51.
[44] *Ibid.*, 643–47.
[45] *New Orl. med. surg. J.*, 1844, 1, 643–47.
[46] *Savannah J. Med.*, 1860, 2, 354.
[47] *Atlanta med. surg. J.*, 1856, 1, 329.
[48] *Sth. med. surg. J.*, 1838, 2, 120–21.

(1845), the operation was a remarkable affair. For some years Sam, a slave, had suffered from what his owner thought was a gum boil, resulting from the medicine given the slave for syphilis. Subsequently the true nature of the ailment was determined: osteo-sarcoma of the lower jaw. But Sam refused to let "one of the most distinguished surgeons of the whole region ... operate," the slave's objection being that "it would hurt too bad." Eventually Sam was sent to Montgomery to Dr. Sims, who decided that an operation was the only means of saving the life of the patient. "Determined not to be foiled in the attempt," Dr. Sims contrived an ingenious method of securing the patient. Sam was persuaded to sit in a barber's chair, to which some planks had been added at the top and bottom. He was quickly tied down by straps around thighs, knees, ankles, abdomen, thorax, shoulders, wrists, elbows, and head. Sam, Dr. Sims relates, "appeared to be very much alarmed"! Two months after the forty-minute operation Sam left Montgomery. "His mouth," the surgeon reported, "is almost always on a broad grin." [49]

Five physicians assisted Dr. Sims in this operation, while some ten medical students and fifteen other practitioners watched. The editors of the *New Orleans Medical and Surgical Journal,* in which the operation was reported, found "pleasure to record this highly creditable achievement of a Southern surgeon" and related that it had been incorporated into Mott and Velpeau's great work on operative surgery. As for Dr. Sims, among the six points which he considered significant in connection with this surgery was that it had proved its "practicability ... whether the patient is willing or not." [50]

Considered in a larger context, the Sims operation has much to say concerning the relation of the slave to the medical profession and to the problem of medical care of slaves. Sam must have been a burden to his master, having required, at the outset, treatment for venereal disease as well as for "an aching jaw." He was sent from rural Alabama into Montgomery, which suggests the owner's desperation over the constant expenditure for the care of an infirm chattel. Dr. Sims's careful preparations for the operation, the assistance that he was given, the audience which assembled to view the surgery, and the careful record he made of the operation and its results, all attest to the significance attached to the event. Sam, his owner, Dr. Sims, the surgical assistants, the practitioners, the students, and medical science generally were all benefactors—and beneficiaries—in this enterprise.

As remarkable and dramatic as the foregoing operation may be, it is not in connection with such surgery that Sims's name has become famous in modern medicine. Rather, it was as a specialist in women's diseases that he became renowned, particularly in connection with the surgical cure of vesico-vaginal fistula. This ailment, consisting of an abnormal communication between the bladder and the vagina—allowing, among other things, an involuntary discharge of urine—had long been considered incurable. Many surgeons had attempted its cure but had achieved inconclusive results.

[49] *New Orl. med. surg. J.,* 1846, 3, 126–29.
[50] *Ibid.*

In 1845, while examining a slave suffering from the ailment, Sims became convinced that an operation was practicable and perfectible. He ransacked the country for cases; found six or seven among slave women; enlarged his hospital; assumed the costs of providing for these women during their months-long stays; and then trained them to serve as his surgical assistants, for he undertook to perform the operations with only the assistance of the patients themselves. After five years and in his thirtieth operation, on the slave Anarcha in 1849, Sims perfected the surgical procedure which brought him his greatest fame. Ironically, the surgery which came to be so much acclaimed in the South and which utilized so many slaves so prominently in its perfection, was first reported not in a southern medical journal, but rather, in 1852, in the older and more prestigious *American Journal of Medical Sciences,* of Philadelphia.[51]

Another Montgomery surgeon, Dr. N. Bozeman, achieved some fame in connection with the surgical treatment of the same ailment, substituting a "button suture" for Sims's "clamp suture." Bozeman's initial operations were performed on "a young colored girl," "Kitty, a colored girl," "Dinah, a colored woman," and "a mulatto girl." [52]

The surgical cure for vesico-vaginal fistula would have been worked out in time; that it was done in 1849 is in large part a result of a medical use of "the peculiar institution" of the South, for it would have been most improbable that Sims and Bozeman could have established so remarkable a surgical schedule without the slave system which provided the experimental subjects.[53]

This relationship between surgical advance and slavery attests what Richard Shryock has called the "direct and intimate ... interplay between medical science and its social environment." [54] This interaction between society and medicine also had a corollary effect in the unintended, but nevertheless significant, role of southern physicians as sources of social history. Their professional testimony concerning the medical care of slaves, as recorded in the antebellum medical journal, provides insights and revelations important to a balanced picture of slavery and suggests, as Professor Shryock has so often urged, the efficacy and relevance of such sources for understanding other aspects of the American past.

---

[51] See J. Marion Sims, *The story of my life.* New York, 1884, pp. 233–46.

[52] *Louisville R.,* 1856, 1, 83–89.

[53] An additional example of the relationship between slavery and medical development is to be found in the history of caesarian sections in the United States. In 1794 a Virginia physician performed such an operation on his wife. A quarter of a century later, Dr. François Marie Prévost, of Donaldsville, Louisiana, performed the second such operation. Regarded as the outstanding American pioneer in this specialty, Dr. Prévost completed this surgery four times between 1822 and 1831, each time upon a slave woman. *New Orl. med. surg. J.,* June, October 1879, April 1880; *Am. J. med. Sci.,* August 1835.

[54] R. H. Shryock, "The significance of medicine in American history," *Am. hist. R.,* 1956, 62, 82.

Marion D. de B. Kilson

TOWARDS FREEDOM: AN ANALYSIS OF
SLAVE REVOLTS IN THE UNITED STATES

Settle's discussion focuses largely on the accommodative aspects of the Negroes' adjustment to slavery, especially on the part of the house servant class. Other scholars have emphasized resistance to the slave regime. An important early comprehensive survey of the major slave insurrections which the interested student should consult is Harvey Wish, "American Slave Insurrections before 1861," Journal of Negro History, *XXII (July, 1937).*

The number of slave revolts in the United States varied from period to period, and from region to region. Marion Kilson's analysis attempts to explain the factors accounting for these variations.

T HROUGHOUT the history of slavery in the United States there occurred a variety of more or less subtle expressions of opposition to the slave system by the enslaved. Opposition took many forms, ranging from individual attempts to thwart the system through negligence in work to mass endeavors to overthrow the system. One class of opposition to the status of servitude is represented by slave revolts, which may be defined minimally as attempts to achieve freedom by groups of slaves. Although the data on slave revolts are fragmentary, three types may be distinguished on the basis of sixty-five cases meeting this minimal definition. These are Systematic or Rational Revolts, Unsystematic or Vandalistic Revolts, and Situational or Opportunistic Revolts. The analysis of the characteristics of each of these types of revolt, of their distribution in time and space, of their leadership, and of their repercussions is the concern of this paper.

The three types of slave revolt differ in form, purpose, salient attributes, territorial extent, and participants. Variable aspects of these categories are expressed in Tables 1, 2, and 3. While each table summarizes the available evi-

Marion D. de B. Kilson, "Towards Freedom: An Analysis of Slave Revolts in the United States," *Phylon*, XXV (2nd Quarter, 1964), pp. 175–187. Reprinted with the permission of the publisher.

TABLE 1

TYPE I REVOLTS *

Revolt Form	Aim:			Systematic Characteristics:				Area	Participants:	
				Plan:						
	Establish Negro State	Take City	Months Preparation	For Retreat	To Spare Groups	To Allocate Tasks			Leader	Insurgents
Md. 1739	C	x		several	x			1 co		200
N.Y. 1712	R			3			x	1 ci		25–30
Va. 1663	C			several				1 co		WI, S
Va. 1722	C	x						3 co	3S	
Va. 1792	C		x	several			x	4 co		600+
Va. 1793	C			4				1 ci		
Va. 1800 †	C	x	x	6		x	x	4 co	1S	c. 7,000
Va. 1816	C		x					3 co	1W	
S.C. 1720	C		x							"large"
S.C. 1816	C		x	8				1 ci		
S.C. 1822 ‡	C	x	x	7			x	80 mi	1F	c. 7,000
Ga. 1810	C			1			x	2 co		
Ga. 1819	C							1 ci	S	
Ga. 1841	C		x							S, W
La. 1837	C		x			x	x	1 co		F, S
La. 1840	C							7 co		400+S / 4 W
La. 1853	C							1 ci	1S / 1W	2,500 S / 100W

KEY:
C: conspiracy   ci: city   S: slave
R: actual revolt   co: county   W: white
x: variable present   mi: miles   WI: indentured white
    F: Free Negro

* Unless otherwise noted, the data contained in this and subsequent tables are based upon material derived from Herbert Aptheker, *American Negro Slave Revolts* (New York, 1943).

† Gabriel Prosser's Revolt.   ‡ Denmark Vesey's Revolt.

TABLE 2
TYPE II REVOLTS

Revolt	Form	Aim: Destruction Property and/or Slave Holders	Unsystematic Characteristics: Lack Preparation	Gathering Recruits	Area	Participants: Leader	Insurgents
N.Y. 1708	R	x			1 to		"small"
Va. 1687	C	x			1 co		
Va. 1691	R	x			1 co	S	
Va. 1792	R	x		x	1 co		900
Va. 1831 *	R	x	x	x	1 co	S	70
N.C. 1776	C	x			3 co	1 S 1 W	
S.C. 1711	R	x				S	"several"
S.C. 1730	C		x		1 ci		
S.C. 1740	R		x	x			150–200
Ga. 1774	R	x	x		1 co		10 †
La. 1730	C	x			1 ci		
La. 1795	C	x	x		1 co		
La. 1811	R	x		x	2 co	F	400–500
Miss. 1835	C	x			1 co	W	

KEY:
C: conspiracy   ci: city   F: Free Negro
R: actual revolt   co: county   S: slave
x: variable present   to: town   W: white

* Turner's Revolt.
† Carroll, *op. cit.*, p. 38.

TABLE 3
TYPE III REVOLTS

Revolt	Form	Aim: Escape:				Armed	Participants:	
		To Free State	From Sale South	Outside U.S.A.	To Indians		Leader	Insurgents
Penn. 1734 *	C				x			
Md. 1845	R	x				x		75
Ky. 1829	R		x					90
Ky. 1848	R	x				x	1 W	75
Mo. 1836	C			x				
Mo. 1850	R	x				x	1 S	30
Va. 1799	R		x					
S.C. 1826	R				x			
Ga. 1849	C			x				300
Ga.-Md. 1826	R	x						29
La. 1840	C			x			1 S	
Texas 1851	R			x				

KEY:
C: conspiracy
R: actual revolt

x: variable present
S: slave
W: white

* Joshua Coffin, *An Account of Some of the Principal Slave Insurrections* (New York, 1860), p. 14.

dence on revolts of a particular type, further elaboration of the content and implications of these categories is necessary.

The Type I or Systematic Revolt, of which the prototypes are the conspiracies of Gabriel Prosser and Denmark Vesey, is oriented towards overthrowing the slave system itself and establishing a Negro state. It is characterized, therefore, by careful planning and organization which necessitate a considerable period of preparation. Careful planning is evidenced by the means decided upon to realize the establishment of the Negro state. Both Prosser and Vesey planned initially to gain control of a city and thereafter to extend their operations into the surrounding area. Such a plan involves the systematic allocation of tasks to various groups and individuals and the calculation of the numbers of insurgents upon whom reliance could be placed. Further evidence of the rational conception of these uprisings is found in the facts that Gabriel Prosser intended to spare certain sympathetic groups of whites and hoped for aid from poor whites and Indians, and that Vesey hoped to have external aid from the West Indies and Africa to maintain his state after its establishment.[1] One corollary of such systematic planning is a long period of preparation which, in turn, increases the likelihood of discovery by the slavocracy; it is not surprising, therefore, that of the seventeen Type I Revolts [2] which have been distinguished, only one went beyond the planning phase. A second corollary of such rational planning is that it is likely to involve the recruitment of a large number of insurgents from a number of counties.

Two aspects of Type I Revolts merit further comment: the urban factor and armed conflict with the slavocracy. The urban factor is significant in 71 percent of the Type I Revolts, five of them occurring within an urban complex and seven others initially oriented towards gaining control of a city. The urban factor appears to have been significant as a source both of more cosmopolitan ideas and of greater role differentiation for Negroes. This does not imply that Type I Revolts are necessarily urban inspired. While Vesey was a resident of Charleston, South Carolina, Prosser lived six miles outside of Richmond, Virginia. Moreover, 29 percent of the Type I Revolts were not urban oriented. Thus the urban factor seems to facilitate rather than to determine the development of Type I Revolts. The second noteworthy aspect of Type I Revolts is that while the achievement of their ultimate goals necessitates armed conflict with members of the slavocracy potentially leading to bloodshed and property destruction, this is a secondary phenomenon rather than a primary goal.

By contrast, the Type II or Vandalistic Revolt, of which the prototype is Nat Turner's insurrection, represents a haphazard expression of opposition to the slave system aimed at the destruction of slave holders and their property. It lacks systematic preparation but may be either of lengthy or of virtually spontaneous conception. Its unsystematic character and potential spontaneity imply both that it has a greater likelihood of reaching the activist stage [3] than Type I Revolts and that reliance upon the gathering of recruits as the revolt gains momentum is of more importance than in the Type I Revolt. For example,

[1] Herbert Aptheker, *American Negro Slave Revolts* (New York, 1943), pp. 101–02, 220, 225; 272, 98, 269. Joseph Cephas Carroll, *Slave Insurrections in the United States 1800–1865* (Boston, 1938), p. 50.

[2] Table 1 summarizes the evidence for Type I Revolts.

[3] Of the fourteen Type II Revolts, 59 percent succeeded in achieving this stage.

deciding one Sunday afternoon to begin his long contemplated revolt that night, Turner set out with a handful of fellow insurgents whose numbers swelled to seventy during the course of the rising.[4] A further implication of the unsystematic nature of the Type II Revolt is that it tends to be localized within a single county and to be a rural rather than an urban-oriented phenomenon.[5] Moreover, lacking any well-defined goals beyond the immediate destruction of the life and property of the slaveholder, the Type II Revolt implies the insurgents' unconscious acceptance of ultimate capitulation to the power of the slavocracy.[6]

The Type III or Opportunistic Revolt aims at escape from servitude. It is characterized by a group of slaves attempting to escape either to a non-slave area or from removal to areas of more oppressive servitude. It tends, therefore, to be situationally determined. Given the realistic opportunity to escape to a free area by land or sea, the group attempts to realize this objective. Thus like the Type I Revolt it is rationally conceived, and like the Type II Revolt it may be virtually spontaneous.[7] Significantly, the only successful slave revolt of which there is evidence falls into the Type III category.[8]

Slave revolts of all three types occurred throughout the slave period and in all the slave regions of the United States. The distribution of types of slave revolts in time and space is summarized in Table 4. If the slave period is divided into Pre-1776 or Colonial, 1776–1800 or Revolutionary, 1801–1829 or Old South Slave, and 1830–1860 or Deep South Slave periods, a number of broad trends are observable. In the Colonial period, slave revolts occurred in Northern colonies as well as in Southern colonies; in the Southern colonies they developed primarily in Virginia and South Carolina. In the Revolutionary period with the disappearance of the slave system from the North and its extension in the South, slave revolts necessarily originated only in Southern states, primarily in Virginia, South Carolina, and Louisiana. During the predominance of slavery in the Old South, slave revolts mainly occurred there and in border states. As the New South pattern was entrenched in the final period of slavery, slave revolts took place there as well as in other parts of the slave region.[9]

---

[4] Aptheker, *op. cit.*, pp. 297–98.

[5] Table 2 summarizes the data on Type II Revolts.

[6] The characterization of Type I and Type II Revolts has been based primarily on an analysis of their prototypes. Despite necessarily fragmentary evidence, it was decided to classify 28 other revolts as Type I or Type II. There are, however, 22 other conspiracies on which data are insufficient to classify as either Type I or Type II, but on which there is some useful information; they have been placed in a residual category: "?." The following conspiracies fall into Type "?": Ark.-La. 1856; D.C. 1838; Ky. 1810, 1838; La. 1812, 1835, 1856; N.C. 1825, 1835; S.C. 1713, 1829, 1835; Ga. 1835; Md. 1805; N.J. 1772; Tenn. 1856; Texas 1856; Va. 1709, 1710, 1723, 1730, 1810.

[7] Table 3 summarizes the data on Type III Revolts.

[8] Texas 1851. Aptheker, *op. cit.*, p. 343.

[9] For relative and absolute shifts in the Negro population of various states see United States Bureau of the Census, *Negro Population 1790–1915* (Washington, 1918), pp. 51, 57.

A noteworthy aspect of the distribution of slave revolts is the concentration of types of slave revolts in time. Type I Revolts occur fairly consistently throughout the slave period with slight peaks in the Colonial and Old South periods. Type II Revolts are a predominantly Colonial phenomenon (56 percent), while Type III are concentrated in the New South Period (58 percent). The predominance of Type II Revolts in the last period of slavery may be attributed to the increasingly oppressive character of slavery during this time, particularly in the New South, which made any other type of revolt virtually impracticable.

Finally, it should be mentioned that slave revolts were not evenly distributed spatially over the slave region. They were concentrated within three main areas: Virginia (25 percent), Louisiana (15 percent), and South Carolina (15.5 percent). Further, despite variations in time, within these states revolts clustered in a few counties. In Virginia revolts tended to recur in the coastal tobacco counties; Gabriel Prosser's revolt, however, encompassed the inland counties of Henrico, Louisa, Hanover, Chesterfield, and Caroline,[10] some of which were involved in another Type I Revolt in 1816. The following tabulation summarizes the agricultural situation in the eighteen insurrection counties of Virginia in 1860:

Eighteen Revolt Counties (12 percent) of Virginia—1860 [11]
percent of State total

Crop: tobacco	14	Slaves	24
Slave holders	25	Holdings (acres)	
(300–499	0	1,000+	15
200–299	50	3–9	13
1–3	24)		

The slave revolt counties of Virginia were primarily tobacco plantation counties. In tobacco culture "the great properties were usually divided ... into several plantations for more convenient operation." [12] Thus slavery under this system was less oppressive than in the Mississippi Delta region of the New South period.

With one exception the slave revolts of South Carolina was restricted to Charleston County. The principal plantation crop was rice, which involved larger plantation units and a greater number of slaves than tobacco, a task system of production, and frequently absentee landlordism.[13] The following tabulation summarizes the agricultural picture in the two insurrection counties of South Carolina in 1860:

[10] Aptheker, op. cit., p. 226.
[11] United States Census Office, Agriculture of the United States in 1860 (Washington, 1864), pp. 155, 159, 163, 218–19, 243–45.
[12] Ulrich Bonnell Phillips, American Negro Slavery (New York, 1952), p. 84.
[13] Ibid., pp. 89, 228, 250, 258.

TABLE 4
DISTRIBUTION OF SLAVE REVOLTS

Type	Pre-1776	1776–1800	1801–1829	1830–1860	Total
I	*Percent*	*Percent*	*Percent*	*Percent*	*Percent*
N.Y.	1.5	0.0	0.0	0.0	
Md.	1.5	0.0	0.0	0.0	
Va.	3.0	4.5	1.5	0.0	
S.C.	1.5	0.0	3.0	0.0	
Ga.	0.0	0.0	3.0	1.5	
La.	0.0	0.0	0.0	4.5	
	8.0	4.5	8.0	6.0	26.5
II	*Percent*	*Percent*	*Percent*	*Percent*	*Percent*
N.Y.	1.5	0.0	0.0	0.0	
Va.	3.0	1.5	0.0	1.5	
N.C.	0.0	1.5	0.0	0.0	
S.C.	4.5	0.0	0.0	0.0	
Ga.	1.5	0.0	0.0	0.0	
La.	1.5	1.5	1.5	0.0	
Miss.	0.0	0.0	0.0	1.5	
	12.0	4.5	1.5	3.0	21.5
"?"	*Percent*	*Percent*	*Percent*	*Percent*	*Percent*
N.J.	1.5	0.0	0.0	0.0	
Md.	0.0	0.0	1.5	0.0	
D.C.	0.0	0.0	0.0	1.5	
Ky.	0.0	0.0	1.5	1.5	
Tenn.	0.0	0.0	0.0	1.5	
N.C.	0.0	0.0	1.5	1.5	
S.C.	1.5	0.0	1.5	1.5	
Ga.	0.0	0.0	0.0	1.5	
La.	0.0	0.0	1.5	4.5	
Texas	0.0	0.0	0.0	1.5	
Va.	6.0	0.0	1.5	0.0	33.0
	9.0	0.0	9.0	15.0	
III	*Percent*	*Percent*	*Percent*	*Percent*	*Percent*
Penn.	1.5	0.0	0.0	0.0	
Md.	0.0	0.0	0.0	1.5	
Ky.	0.0	0.0	1.5	1.5	
Mo.	0.0	0.0	0.0	3.0	
Va.	0.0	1.5	0.0	0.0	
S.C.	1.5	0.0	0.0	0.0	
La.	0.0	0.0	0.0	1.5	
Ga.	0.0	0.0	0.0	1.5	
Ga.-Md.	0.0	0.0	1.5	0.0	
Texas	0.0	0.0	0.0	1.5	
	3.0	2.0	3.0	11.0	19.0
TOTAL	32.0%	11.0%	22.0%	35.0%	100.0%

Two Revolt Counties (7 percent) of South Carolina—1860 [14]
percent of State total

Crop: rice	63
Slave holders	11
(1,000+	100
500–999	43
1–3	19)
Slaves	14
Holdings (acres)	
1,000+	8
3–9	17

Considering the patently oppressive nature of the slave system associated with rice culture, it does not seem accidental that slave insurrections should have taken place predominantly in Charleston County with its major urban complex.

Although a few slave revolts in Louisiana occurred in the vicinity of New Orleans, most of the revolts recurred in counties bordering the Mississippi River north and west of Baton Rouge. Although there was considerable agricultural diversification in these counties, they were primarily sugar producers. Like rice, sugar production involved large numbers of robust adult slaves.[15] The general agricultural set-up in the insurrection counties of Louisiana in 1860 is summarized in the following tabulation:

Ten Revolt Counties (21 percent) of Louisiana—1860 [16]
percent of State total

Crops: rice	15
cotton	16
cane sugar	41
Slave holders	38
(500–999	25
300–499	35
1–3	23)
Slaves	30
Holdings (acres)	
1,000+	25
3–9	33

Among the factors which may have facilitated the development of these up-river revolts are proximity to a great communication network, agricultural diversification, and a fairly high proportion of small holdings.

Thus the pattern of a real clustering of slave revolts irrespective of temporal variations suggests that aside from the immediate catalysts which might induce a particular slave revolt, certain socio-economic variables facilitated

[14] United States Census Office, *op. cit.*, pp. 129, 214, 237.
[15] Phillips, *op. cit.*, pp. 164–67, 245.
[16] United States Census Office, *op. cit.*, pp. 67, 69, 202, 230.

their occurrence and recurrence in certain areas. Fundamentally, these socio-economic factors imply an alleviation of the condition of slavery due either to the type of plantation system itself or to access to external sources of communication as inherent in propinquity to an urban center or a transportation network. These constitute a few of the factors which are considered necessary preconditions for slave revolts.

Other more immediate factors also seem to constitute preconditions for slave revolts. These may include rapid population fluctuations often leading to a significantly higher proportion of Negroes in an area [17] and revolutionary ideas current in the wider society of the time.[18] In my view, none of these possible preconditions constitute sufficient cause for the development of a slave revolt. Rather there must be a catalyst in the form of an individual or individuals.

This catalyst may arise from within or without the slave system. The leaders of slave revolts have been drawn from the social categories of free Negro, slave, and white. The type of revolt does not appear to be determined by the social type of the catalyst. Vesey (Type I) was a free Negro, Prosser (Type I) and Turner (Type II) were slaves, Boxley (Type I) and Doyle (Type III) were whites.[19] Nevertheless, Boxley is probably exceptional, as the ultimate aim of a Type I Revolt would be unlikely to appeal to many whites.

Although very little data on Negro leaders of slave revolts are available, the three leaders of the most famous revolts furnish suggestions of relevant social and personality variables. Each of these men had had opportunities which the ordinary field hand would never have experienced. Vesey had traveled extensively as a slave; as a freedman he was an urban artisan; he was literate and aware of the Haitiian success and the Missouri debate.[20] Both Prosser and Turner were slaves. Gabriel Prosser was a blacksmith and probably literate.[21] Turner was literate, had been a slave overseer, enjoyed making inventive experiments, and may have been a Baptist preacher.[22] Thus all three leaders had had opportunities to play more than one social role and had had access to a variety of ideas.

The personality of Negro leaders also appears to be a significant variable. The three major leaders were clearly charismatic individuals. They were imbued with a sense of personal destiny and considered themselves to be divinely inspired and sanctioned in their endeavors.[23] It seems likely that such charisma

[17] E.g., Turner's revolt and Mississippi Revolt of 1835; Aptheker, op. cit., pp. 293, 325.

[18] E.g., the influence of the Missouri debate on Vesey: Aptheker, op. cit., p. 270; the importance of David Walker's Appeal for Turner: Carroll, op. cit., p. 121.

[19] Aptheker, op. cit., pp. 255–56, 338. See Tables 1, 2 and 3.

[20] Carroll, op. cit., pp. 83, 85; Aptheker, op. cit., p. 270.

[21] Cf. Carroll, op. cit., p. 48 and T. W. Higginson, "Gabriel's Defeat," Atlantic Monthly X (1862), 338. Aptheker, op. cit., p. 220.

[22] William Sidney Drewry, The Southampton Insurrection (Washington, 1900), p. 28; Carroll, op. cit., p. 131. Cf. ibid., p. 130 and John W. Cromwell, "The Aftermath of Nat Turner's Insurrection," Journal of Negro History V (1920), 209.

[23] E.g., Turner: Carroll, op. cit., pp. 130–31; Gabriel: ibid., p. 149; Vesey: ibid., p. 87.

and egotism would be essential for any Negro leader to dare to challenge the power of the slavocracy. There is, however, an important personality difference between these leaders which appears to be linked to the type of revolt inspired by them. Neither Vesey nor Prosser was so self-absorbed that he could not formulate a rational plan and assign specific duties to assistants. The techniques which Vesey employed for binding the masses to his endeavor are particularly fascinating: among his lieutenants were a "sorcerer" whose charms were considered to make their wearers inviolable and a blind preacher who was believed to possess second-sight.[24] Vesey clearly understood the importance of psychological as well as technological preparation for the success of his scheme. Turner, on the other hand, seems to have been so self-absorbed that it is unlikely that he could have formulated and executed a consistent plan. Thus, there appears to be two personality types represented by these three leaders; the one in which rationality has precedence over egotistical emotionalism, and its converse. This distinction is borne out by the conduct of the men following their capture: Vesey and Prosser revealed very little about their intentions and maintained themselves stoically until their deaths; Turner met his fate no less courageously but after a lengthy and effusive confession. How many Vesey-Prosser and how many Turner personality types led slave revolts is unknown. It is hypothesized that only a Vesey-Prosser type could lead a Type I Revolt, though Types II and III might have been led by either personality type.[25]

The final aspect of slave revolts to be discussed is their repercussions both within the area of the revolt and in other areas. As shown in Table 5, throughout the slavery period the slavocracy reacted in a similar way to slave revolts. In its reactions it distinguished between Type III Revolts and the other types of revolt, but not between Type I and Type II Revolts.[26] Thus Type III Revolts always resulted in reprisals only against the immediate offenders. This is understandable as the situational and limited nature of this type of revolt was clear. Consequently, it was a phenomenon with which the slavocracy could deal in a relatively rational manner.

The reaction of the slavocracy to the Type I and Type II Revolts followed a different but consistent pattern.[27] A slave revolt resulted in a three-step syndrome within the area of revolt. There was an initial period of panic in which vengeance was wrought not only upon known insurgents but often upon innocent Negroes. During this period of mob panic and activity, aggression might also be vented upon white moderates within the area and upon outsiders who were disliked but not directly involved with the revolt. This period was followed

[24] *Ibid.*, pp. 91–93.
[25] Evidence from two Type I Revolts supports this hypothesis: Georgia 1819, Maryland 1739: Aptheker, *op. cit.*, pp. 191, 263.
[26] See Table 5 for summary of data.
[27] This analysis is based on the four reactions for which we have sufficient data: the revolts of Turner, Prosser and Vesey and the Mississippi Revolt of 1835. See Aptheker, *op. cit.*, pp. 226, 228, 271, 275, 300, 305; Carroll, *op. cit.*, pp. 57–60, 107–09, 138–39, 166, 176; Cromwell *op. cit.*, pp. 212, 214–15, 221, 225, 231; Drewry, *op. cit.*, p. 85; E. Franklin Frazier, *The Negro in the United States* (New York, 1957), p. 87; Higginson, *op. cit.*, pp. 341–44; Edwin A. Miles, "The Mississippi Slave Insurrection Scare of 1835," *Journal of Negro History*, XLII (1957), 49, 52–55.

TABLE 5

REPERCUSSIONS OF SLAVE REVOLTS WITHIN THE AREA AND IN OTHER AREAS

Revolt	Within the Area:										In Other Areas:				
	Panic and Vengeance against:				Repressive Measures:			Ameliorative Measures			Revolt Rumors	Slave Unrest	Repressive Measures:		Ameliorative Measures:
	Insurgents	Other Negroes	White Moderates	Outsiders	Increased Armed Oppressions	Legislation Against: Slaves	Free Negro	Increased Emancipation Sentiment	Improved Conditions	Colonization Schemes			Legislation Against: Slaves	Free Negro	Anti-Slavery Sentiment
TYPE I															
Pre-1776															
Va. 1663	x														
N.Y. 1712	x	x				x									
Md. 1739	x														
1776–1800															
Va. 1792	x	x				x									
Va. 1800 *	x	x			x	x	x			x	S.C.	Va.	x	x	
1801–1829															
Va. 1816	x	?													
Ga. 1819	x														
S.C. 1822 *	x	x			x	x	x					no			North
1830–1860															
La. 1837	x	?			x										
Ga. 1841	x														
TYPE II															
Pre-1776															
Va. 1687	x														

	A	B	C	D	E	F	North
N.Y. 1708	x			x			
La. 1730	x						
S.C. 1740	x			x			
1776–1800							
N.C. 1776	x						
Va. 1792	x						
La. 1795	x	?					
1801–1829							
La. 1811		?			x	x	x
1830–1860							
Va. 1831*	x	x	x	x	x		x
Miss. 1835*	x	x	x				
TYPE "?"							
Pre-1776							
Va. 1723	x		x	x			
Va. 1730	x						
1801–1829							
S.C. 1829	x		x	x			
1830–1860							
Ga. 1835	x						
N.C. 1835	x						
La. 1840	x	x					
La. 1856	x	x					
TYPE III							
1801–1829							
Ky. 1829	x						
1830–1860							
Mo. 1836	x				x		
Md. 1845	x						
Ky. 1848	x			x			
Mo. 1850	x						x

* See footnote 27.

by one in which increased armed oppression was used to enforce the threatened slave system. This second period was followed by one in which legislative measures were taken to prevent similar outbreaks. During the legislative debates ameliorative measures such as colonization schemes and proposals to reduce the oppressive character of the slave system were frequently discussed but rarely enacted. The upshot of the legislative period was invariably the harshening of repressive laws against both slaves and free Negroes.

Another aspect of the reaction of the slavocracy to a major slave revolt was the spread of the three-step syndrome, either partially or completely, to other slave areas not affected by the revolt. In part these measures may have been justified, for there is evidence that occasionally slaves in other areas were stimulated to emulate the attempts of the initial insurgents.

Nevertheless, both within the initial area of revolt and in other areas, the actual threat to the slavocracy was never great enough to invoke the exaggerated penalties which it evoked.[28] Yet indubitably the psychological threat makes this pattern comprehensible: a slave revolt whatever its form expresses the realization of the worst fears of the slavocracy and assaults its security at its most vulnerable point. These fears must be suppressed at all costs although the repressive measures taken were perceived by the slavocracy to lead to even greater threats to the system, for the members of the slavocracy assumed that an ill-treated slave was more likely to revolt than a well-treated one.

The data presented in this analysis support a rather different conclusion from that of the slavocracy as to the effect of their measures. This conclusion has been vividly expressed by Frederick Douglass and has been stated more systematically recently by Davies and Elkins.[29] In *My Bondage* Douglass wrote: " 'Beat and cuff your slave, keep him hungry and spiritless, and he will follow the chain of his master like a dog; but feed and clothe him well,—work him moderately—surround him with physical comfort,—and dreams of freedom intrude.' " [30] As has been noted in the preceding analysis, slave revolts tended to cluster in less oppressive slave areas and the catalyst for a revolt was an individual who had had opportunities to play multiple roles.[31] On the other hand, given the high rate of betrayal of conspiracies by oppressed individuals who identified themselves more closely with the master than the slave, the adverse impact upon most slaves of the repressive measures of the slavocracy, and the absolute power of the slavocracy, one can but conclude that slave revolts in the United States were doomed to failure.

[28] This fact was recognized by some contemporary observers. For example, less than ten days after Turner's bloody revolt, General Epps wrote the Governor of Virginia that local fear was exaggerated and that at no time were more than twenty men needed to put down the rebellion. Quoted in Drewry, *op. cit.*, p. 88.

[29] James C. Davies, "Toward a Theory of Revolution," *American Sociological Review*, XXVII (1962), 6; Stanley M. Elkins, *Slavery* (Chicago, 1959).

[30] Quoted in Kenneth M. Stampp, *The Peculiar Institution* (New York, 1956), p. 89.

[31] For the implications of multiple role-playing see Elkins, *op. cit.*, pp. 112 ff, 137–38.

Vincent Harding

RELIGION AND RESISTANCE AMONG ANTEBELLUM NEGROES, 1800–1860

Christianity began as a religion that appealed principally to the slaves and underprivileged freedmen of the Roman Empire. To use Friedrich Nietzsche's phrase, Christian ethics functioned as a "slave morality," sanctifying meekness and nonresistance toward the oppressor while glorifying the weak, the poor, and the humble as the "salt of the earth." For the masses of American Negroes, the Christian religion has likewise functioned principally as a compensatory escape from the harsh realities of daily life. Yet the recent prominence of Reverend Martin Luther King symbolizes the fact that religion has had a dual role. While it has served basically as a mechanism of accommodation to the American social order, it has also provided an important wellspring of Negro protest. Vincent Harding's paper is a fresh and suggestive examination of the religious motivation that often underlay resistance to bondage.

IN these days of ecumenism among the academic disciplines, it would likely be both fair and appropriate to describe the state of our historical understanding of Negro religion in America as a variety of cultural lag. This is clearly the case when we try to assess the role of black religion in the antebellum period of American history, and especially when an attempt is made to understand its relationship to acts of protest and resistance.

Stated in simplest terms, the situation may be described in this way: Thanks to the crucial work of Aptheker, the Bauers, Stampp and others we have moved beyond a naive and often distorted view of happy or indifferent Negro slaves whose docility was a sight to behold.[1] Indeed the movement to-

Printed with the permission of Vincent Harding.
[1] See especially Herbert Aptheker, *American Negro Slave Revolts*, Paperback edition

wards the new theme of slave rebellion and resistance has often been so strong that the inevitable reconsiderations and revisions have already set in.[2] But it would appear unlikely that even such fascinating and worthy caveats as those raised by Elkins, Wade and Genovese will drive us back to the old dominions— if for no other reason than the uneasiness our increasingly black-oriented age feels with such interpretations. So the new slaves seem to be a permanent fixture. On the other hand, we have not yet been released from the traditional views of black religion which supported the older generalizations concerning submissive and humble slaves. Here precisely is the lag.

Much of current historical opinion about the role of religion among antebellum southern Negroes still follows the classic lines set out in Benjamin Mays' *The Negro's God*, which claimed that the Negroes' idea of God "kept them submissive, humble and obedient." [3] Repeatedly Mays referred to this religion as "otherworldly" and "compensatory," inclining its votaries "to do little or nothing to improve their status here..." [4] Even so shrewd and perceptive a scholar as E. Franklin Frazier later adumbrated the theme in his important work on *The Negro Church*. [5] There the antebellum Negroes—especially in the South—were identified with a religion that "turned their minds from the sufferings and privations of this world to a world after death where the weary would find rest and the victims of injustice would be compensated." [6]

The views of Mays and Frazier are representative of most discussions of the black religion that developed before the Civil War. In many ways these men helped to set the theme. Their views, of course, represented an American adaptation of the classic statement by Karl Marx:

> Religion is the sign of the oppressed creature, the heart of the heartless world...the spirit of a spiritless situation. It is the *opium* of the people.[7]

In this essay what we question is not the applicability of such an understanding of religion to a majority of antebellum Negroes. Indeed, the tradi-

---

(New York: International Publishers, 1963); Raymond A. Bauer and Alice H. Bauer, "Day to Day Resistance to Slavery," *Journal of Negro History*, xxvii, 4 (October, 1942), 388–419; Kenneth M. Stampp, *The Peculiar Institution*, Paperback edition (New York: Vintage Books, 1956), particularly Chap. III.

[2] Some of the most persuasive concerns are raised in Stanley M. Elkins, *Slavery*, Paperback edition (New York: Grosset and Dunlap, 1963); Richard C. Wade, *Slavery in the Cities* (New York: Oxford University, 1964); also Wade's "The Vesey Plot: A Reconsideration," *Journal of Negro History*, xxx, 2 (May, 1964), 143–161; Eugene D. Genovese, "The Legacy of Slavery and the Roots of Black Nationalism," *Studies on the Left*, vi, 6 (November–December, 1966), 3–26.

[3] Benjamin E. Mays, *The Negro's God as Reflected in His Literature* (Boston: Chapman and Grimes, 1938), 26.

[4] *Ibid.*, 24.

[5] *The Negro Church in America* (New York: Schocken Books, 1964).

[6] *Ibid.*, 45

[7] Karl Marx and Friedrich Engels, *On Religion* (New York: Schocken Books, 1964), 42; quoted from the "Introduction to Marx's Contribution to the Critique of Hegel's Philosophy of Right."

tional view often has much support in the records. For instance, it was not accidental that a slaveholder said in the 1830's, "The deeper the piety of the slave, the more valuable he is in every respect." [8] This was a widespread opinion. Nor was that eloquent refugee from slavery, William Wells Brown, wrong when in 1850 he claimed that religious instruction for his fellow-bondsmen consisted "in teaching the slave that he must never strike a white man; that God made him a slave; and that when whipped he must find no fault . . ." [9]

That was likely an accurate description of most instruction, and many slaves seemed to live by it. (Generally, of course, they had no other choice than to give at least an impression that they did.) However the present dispute does not center there. Rather this paper seeks to raise the issue of the ambiguity, the doubleness, of black religious experience, indeed of all religious experience. It seeks not to deny the opiate quality of much slave religion but to offer the suggestion that there were significant, identifiable black responses to religion which often stormed beyond submissiveness to defiance.

Perhaps Frederick Douglass best sets the scene for an understanding of this ambiguous and two-edged Negro reaction to religious teaching. In one of his autobiographical writings, this most famous of fugitive slaves, recorded words which scarcely covered his underlying scorn. He said,

> I have met, at the south, many good, religious colored people who
> were under the delusion that God required them to submit to slavery
> and to wear their chains with meekness and humility.

Then he added, "I could entertain no such nonsense as this . . ." [10] For Douglass, as for countless others, the requirements of God pointed in other directions, and black religion led them away from slavery. Often it led to protest, resistance and death.

Recently a teacher of religion has tried to articulate this theme of the protest role of Negro faith. In his *Black Religion*, Joseph Washington wrote, "the religion of the Negro folk was chosen to bear roles of both protest and relief." [11] Indeed Washington went on to suggest that "the uniqueness of black religion" since the days of slavery was to be found in its constant and often risky search for "the elusive but ultimate goal of freedom and equality by means of protest and action." [12] Like so much of Washington's work, those last phrases may be overstatement, but they help to balance the scales set by Frazier, Mays and Marx.

Perhaps, then, this paper can be thought of as an attempt to suggest pathways towards an historical documentation of Joseph Washington's intuitive thesis, at least that part of it which seeks to appreciate the proper re-

[8] Quoted in Haven P. Perkins, "Religion for Slaves: Difficulties and Methods," *Church History*, x, 3 (September, 1941), 228–245.
[9] *Narrative of the Life of William Wells Brown* (London: Charles Gilpin, 1850), 82–83.
[10] *Life and Times*, Paperbook edition (New York: Crowell-Collier, 1962), 85.
[11] (Boston: Beacon Press, 1964), 33.
[12] *Ibid*

lationship of black religion to Negro protest and resistance. Without such an attempt we shall be in danger of fruitlessly trying to apply the religion of Ulrich Phillips' Negroes to the defiant men and women who often leap out of the pages of Aptheker and Stampp. To quote Douglass slightly out of context, "we can entertain no such nonsense as this . . ." (Even Marxists came to realize that religious commitment might produce revolutionary action.[13] Those who claim to be unhindered by the fetters of ideology can do no less.)

II

It has seemed wise for the present to confine this statement to the period 1800–1860, and to focus on Negroes in the South. Therefore it may be significant to note that it was in 1800 that South Carolina's legislature indicated a keen awareness of the possible connections between black rebellion and black religion, an awareness that was apparently the property of many southern white persons. In that year the legislature passed one of the first of those countless 19th century laws restricting black religious services. This one forbade Negroes

> even in company with white persons to meet together and assemble
> for the purpose of . . . religious worship, either before the rising of the
> sun or after the going down of the same.[14]

Magistrates were given the power to break up all such gatherings. Behind the legislation was obviously a fear that these religious meetings might lead to trouble, especially if they were held at hours when they could not easily be monitored.

If the fear needed substantiation it was soon available. In Virginia's Henrico county Tom Prosser's slave, Gabriel, and Gabriel's brother, Martin, were then gathering slaves and free Negroes at strange hours and making strange uses of "religious services." Gabriel was plotting insurrection, and building a force that had evidently mounted into the thousands by 1800. At their religious services it was said that both Martin and Gabriel—what fitting names!—regularly set forth

> an impassioned exposition of Scripture . . . The Israelites were glow-
> ingly portrayed as a type of successful resistance to tyranny; and it
> was argued, that now, as then, God would stretch forth his arm to
> save, and would strengthen a hundred to overthrow a thousand.[15]

[13] See Engels on "The Peasant War in Germany," in Marx and Engels, On Religion, 97–118; also Eduard Bernstein, Cromwell and Communism (New York: Schocken Books, 1963).

[14] Quoted in W. E. B. DuBois (ed.), The Negro Church (Atlanta: The Atlanta University Press, 1903), 22.

[15] Harvey Wish, "American Slave Insurrections Before 1861," Journal of Negro History, xxii, 3 (July, 1937), 311; Thomas Wentworth Higginson, Travellers and Outlaws (Boston: Lee and Shepard, 1889), 1899; Aptheker, Slave Revolts, 220–224.

The black men of Henrico county were the new Israelites. Gabriel was their Moses. Would they follow?

It is not known how deeply this appeal from the Old Testament moved the persons who gathered in those secret meetings, nor which of them joined the attempted rebellion in response to it. But the analogy to the Israelites was a traditional one in the black community, and it continued to have great force among the slaves. Therefore it would not be too much to expect that some of the men who set themselves on the path of rebellion in those Virginia meetings were responding to a profoundly religious call, as well as to the news from Santo Domingo, or to the stirring cries of "Death or Liberty." Haiti was a good example, and the political motto was a moving cry, but it surely helped to believe as well that the God of Israel would "stretch forth his arm" to intervene on behalf of the blacks.[16]

When the insurrection was foiled by the sudden downpour of torrential rains, the white residents of Virginia would, of course, have been justified in thinking that divine intervention was indeed present—on their side.[17] But they were likely caused to be suspicious about other religious matters as the trials of the rebels revealed that Methodists and Quakers—as well as Frenchmen—were to be spared the vengeful swords of Gabriel's band.[18] What could that mean?

Religion and its relationship to black rebellion continued to be a matter for concern and for questions in Virginia, even before the coming of Nat Turner. For instance, one Richard Byrd of that state wrote to his Governor in May, 1810, to express his conviction that "slave preachers used their religious meetings as veils for revolutionary schemes," and he cited a "General Peter" from Isle of Wight as an example of the danger.[19]

Six years later this kind of fear was given solid ground in the Old Dominion again, but it was a white preacher who now seemed to be using black religion for seditious purposes. George Boxley, proprietor of a county store, was a regular participant in the religious meetings held by the Negroes of Spottsylvania and Louisa counties. Soon he began telling them "that a little white bird had brought him a holy message to deliver his fellowmen from bondage . . ."[20] Again the promise of divinely aided deliverance found active response, and Phillips says that Boxley "enlisted many blacks in his project" for messianic insurrection. Unfortunately for the black believers, as was so often the case, the plot was betrayed. Some Negro followers were hanged, others were sold out of the state, but Boxley escaped from jail.[21] Perhaps the message of deliverance had been meant only for him. After all, it was a white bird.

[16] *Ibid.*, 220.

[17] See citations in note 15.

[18] Aptheker, *Slave Revolts*, 224.

[19] *Ibid.*, 246.

[20] Ulrich B. Phillips, *American Negro Slavery*, Paperback edition (Baton Rouge: Louisiana State University, 1966), 476.

[21] *Ibid.*

The pattern of religious connections to rebellious movements continued consistently into South Carolina in the same year—1816. There, in Camden, a plot had evidently been maturing, and when the almost inevitable betrayal and arrests finally came, a local newspaper offered its own version of the relationship between religion and resistance:

> It is a melancholy fact [the editor said] that those who were most active in the conspiracy occupied a respectable stand in one of the churches, several were professors [i.e., avowed Christians], and one a class leader.[22]

Camden was not the only place in South Carolina where black Christians and class leaders were making life difficult for the keepers of the established order. Charleston was having its difficulties with the darker variety of Methodists, trouble that would eventually lead into deep distress.[23]

The Negroes in the port city's Methodist congregations had long outnumbered their white brethren by ten to one. They had known a sense of significant independence through their own quarterly conference and as a result of the control they exercised over finances and the discipline of their members. In 1815 alleged "abuses" had led to the loss of these privileges as well as much of the independence that went with them. But black church leaders like Denmark Vesey, Peter Poyas and Jack Pritchard (Gullah Jack) had no intentions of accepting such debilitating penalties without offering direct and open response.

They led agitation among the Negro members, rounded up a thousand new members and sent two of their leaders up to Philadelphia to be ordained by the African Methodist Episcopal bishops there. Then in 1818 a dispute over their burial ground provided the occasion for more than 4000 of the 6000 black Methodists to withdraw their membership *en masse* from the white Charleston congregations. With ordained ministers of their own they now moved ahead to build a meeting house and establish an independent congregation called the African Church of Charleston.

It is in this context that we may speak more precisely of rebellion. Here the crucial issue is not the nature of what happened in 1822, not the matter of whether widely organized insurrection was being planned.[24] At this juncture it is of critical importance simply to see that organized rebellion on another level had already been built deeply into the structure of black church life in Charleston. The agitation from 1815 to 1818 and the concerted withdrawal from the white congregations in the latter year took significant courage for the slaves. The raising of an independent house of worship implied not only the gathering of financial resources, but it was clearly an act of defiance for

[22] Aptheker, *Slave Revolts*, 258.

[23] The story of the pre-1822 struggles of the black Methodists of Charleston is developed most fully in Phillips, *American Negro Slavery*, 420–421.

[24] Richard Wade, in his works cited in note 2 above, expresses strong doubts about the extent and significance of the insurrectionary plans.

the world to see. The municipal officials knew this and responded accordingly with harassments, arrests, banishments, and finally with the closing of the church in 1821.[25] It is, then, essential to note that the sense of black solidarity was imbedded in the organization of the Negro church. Attempts to dilute this or break it down met inevitably with resistance, resistance centered in that church's life.

Did the defiance include a wider plan for insurrection? It is not the purpose of this essay to enter into the argument that has been interestingly raised by Mr. Wade. However, my own examination of available evidence leads me to suspect that the plot was "more than loose talk by aggrieved and embittered men."[26] These men had already given evidence of impressive skill in organizing black discontent for action. They had followers in their defiance, and their leadership was evidently trusted. There was no reason for them to be content with "loose talk" by 1822.

Whatever the extent of the new action being planned, it seems clear that some continuing organizing was going on, that it was centered in the membership of the African Church and that the charismatic Denmark Vesey was at the heart of the affair.[27] Now, for our purposes it is necessary only to continue to deal with the role of religion as it participated in a movement that went beyond the defense of church-oriented prerogatives to new and likely bolder concerns. If, as seems probable, an insurrection was being planned, Vesey surely knew how to continue to use themes that had led the blacks to organize for independent church status.

His focus was regularly on religion. One witness testified that this leader's "general conversation . . . was about religion, which he would apply to slavery." Indeed, "all his religious remarks were mingled with slavery," according to the testimony.[28] Was this surprising? For the most part these were church members who were being addressed, and they were also slaves. What other focus was more natural? These were also persons whose extant religious records indicate that they were profoundly attracted to the analogy between their condition and the condition of the Hebrews in Egypt. As a class leader, Vesey surely knew all this very well. So one of the alleged conspirators was probably quite accurate when he said that Denmark Vesey "read to us from the Bible, how the *children of Israel were delivered out of Egypt from bondage* . . ."[29] Nor did the persuasive exhorter stop there. It is said that he made it clear to

[25] Phillips, *loc. cit.*

[26] Wade, "The Vesey Plot," 160.

[27] See Aptheker, *Slave Revolts*, 268–276; Higginson, 215–275; John W. Lofton, Jr., "Denmark Vesey's Call to Arms," *Journal of Negro History*, xxxiii, 4 (October, 1948), 395–417; Sterling Stuckey, "Remembering Denmark Vesey," *Negro Digest*, xv, 4 (February, 1966), 28–41—a direct response to Wade's questions; Marion L. Starkey, *Striving to Make It My Home* (New York: W. W. Norton and Company, 1964), 152–210; Corporation of Charleston, *An Account of the Late Intended Insurrection* (Charleston: n.p. 1822.)

[28] Higginson, 228.

[29] Corporation of Charleston, 34 [italics in original].

the bondsmen that it was imperative to their faith that slaves "attempt their emancipation, 'however shocking and bloody might be the consequences.' " And on the strength of his magnificent authority as a class leader—and as a man—he declared that such efforts would be "pleasing to the Almighty," and that their success was thereby guaranteed.[30]

If, as we are suggesting, religion did play a critical role in the motivating of his followers, then Vesey chose wisely (or was fortunate, if he did not make the choice himself) when he gained an accomplice like Jack Pritchard, better known as Gullah Jack. This black man of Angolan background provided an excellent counterpoint to Vesey's Old Testament theme. For he was not only a member of the African Church but a conjurer, a medicine man in the African tradition. Therefore Vesey had the best of both religious worlds, and we are told that Gullah Jack exerted tremendous influence over the other members of his ancestral group.[31]

This, of course, does not mean that Vesey did not seek to rally his forces through the use of other issues as well. The tradition of Santo Domingo, the debate over Missouri, the general mistreatment of the Negroes by the city authorities and by some of their masters—these were all part of the strategy.[32] But it would be derelict to fail to note how crucial was the religious issue, especially in the light of the post-1814 church experiences. Was this not the significance of the note found in Peter Poyas' trunk after he was arrested: "Fear not, the Lord God that delivered Daniel is able to deliver us."[33]

Then in the summer of 1822, when deliverance appeared to have been aborted and the gallows were heavy with black bodies, it was fitting that the city should demolish the First African Church[34] This was not only a rehearsal of more modern southern church treatment, but it was a testimony to the significant role the people of that congregation had played in carrying the contagion of rebellion. Nor was it surprising that an Episcopalian minister boasted that such things could never happen among black Episcopalians because their Negroes "were not allowed to exhort or expound scriptures in words of their own . . . and to utter . . . whatever nonsense might happen into their minds."[35]

Regardless of how we see such matters now, it was evidently clear to most Charlestonians of the time that "religious enthusiasm" had been one of the motivating forces in Vesey's action. So all preachers of the gospel to slaves —white and black—were suspect.[36] And a Charleston editor condemned the white Christian missionaries who

[30] Higginson, 404.
[31] On Gullah Jack see especially Starkey and Corporation of Charleston, as cited in note 27.
[32] Corporation of Charleston, 39.
[33] Wish, 410.
[34] Phillips, 421.
[35] Quoted in Perkins, "Religion for Slaves," 232.
[36] Donald G. Mathews, *Slavery and Methodism* (Princeton: Princeton University Press, 1965), 41.

with the Sacred Volume of God in one hand scattered with the other
the firebrands of discord and destruction; and *secretly* dispensed among
our Negro Population, the seeds of discontent and sedition.[37]

Though he saw much, the editor did not see that the firebrands and the seeds
were often in the same hand as "the Sacred Volume," but he surely must have
known that the hands were often black.

At least this was the case with Nat Turner, who carried his own Volume,
fire and seeds. Whatever doubts we may entertain about the authenticity of
Vesey's rebellion, Turner leaves us with no choice. Even more important for
our present concerns is the central theme of Turner's *Confession*—the theme
of a black, avenging Messiah, urged into action by nothing less than the repeated calling of God.[38] Here was religion and resistance that would not be
separated.

Based primarily on the *Confession*, the story develops. As a child he
became convinced that he was "intended for some great purpose." Evidently
he nurtured the search for his destiny through arduous prayer and fasting and
the development of an austere personal life. Turner claimed to be directed
many times by "the Spirit" as it spoke to him in his lonely vigils or as he
worked in the fields. A major theme of that direction was "Seek ye the kingdom
of Heaven and all things shall be added unto you." When asked later about this
"Spirit," the 31-year-old prisoner made it clear that he stood self-consciously in
the prophetic tradition, for he said that he had been visited by "The Spirit that
spoke to the Prophets in former days."

Eventually the young mystic became fully confirmed in his sense of
ordination to some "great purpose in the hands of the Almighty," and he
went through his own Wilderness experience—thirty days in the forests of
Virginia as a runaway slave. Then the Spirit drove him back for his great encounter with the future. In 1825 Turner saw his first major vision suggestively
describing his ultimate calling. White and black spirits were battling in the
air. Thunder rang out, the sun was darkened, and he watched in awe as blood
flowed through the land. The same Spirit promised him the wisdom and
strength needed for the task.

After a fascinating variety of other visions, the critical revelation came
in May, 1828. According to Nat,

I heard a loud noise in the heavens and the Spirit instantly appeared
to me and said the Serpent was loosened, and Christ had laid down
the Yoke he had borne for the sins of men, and that I should take it

[37] *Ibid.*, 42.
[38] Turner's *Confession, Trial and Execution* was originally published in 1881 by
T. R. Gray in Petersburg, Virginia. However it is most accessible in Herbert Aptheker,
Nat Turner's Slave Rebellion (New York: Humanities Press, 1966). I have used the
same text as it appeared in "The Confession, Trial and Execution of Nat Turner,"
Negro Digest, xiv, 9 (July, 1965), 28–48. The source will not be cited again until it
seems appropriate in the development of Turner's story.

on and fight against the Serpent, for the time was fast approaching when the first should be last and the last should be first.

The Spirit also revealed to him that there would be adequate signs in nature to let him know when he should begin the messianic work for which he was ordained, when to "arise and prepare myself to slay my enemies with their own weapons." In an eclipse of the sun—that most ancient of signs— Nat Turner found his signal to begin. He ate a last supper with some of his followers and went forth to carry out his own version of the work of Christ, using the weapons of the Old Testament, drenching the ground with blood, for "neither age nor sex was to be spared." And when he was asked if he thought himself mistaken as he faced execution at the end, Turner's response came fittingly enough: "Was not Christ crucified?" To the charge of dastardly crime, his plea, of course, was "Not Guilty."

Obviously Nat Turner was one of those religious charismatics who arise in a variety of settings, from the walls of Münster to the fields of Southampton County.[39] He was not a "preacher" in any formal sense of the word, and evidently belonged to no structured church group. But he was an "exhorter," and he clearly convinced his fellow slaves by the power of his message and the strange sense of his presence that he was the anointed one of God for their deliverance—a deliverance for which slaves never ceased to yearn.

No other explanation will open the intricacies of Nat Turner. Thus when they were wounded and waiting to die, it was said of his companions that some of them "in the aggonies [sic] of Death declared that they was going happy fore that God had a hand in what they had been doing . . ."[40] They still believed that "Prophet Nat" was sent from God.

When all the dyings were over, after the fierce retaliations had taken place, the conviction and the legend lived on. Black people believed and remembered, and some acted. The religion of Nat Turner, the religion of black rebellion became part of their tradition.[41] Whites, on the other hand, believed variations of the black themes and acted in their own ways. Their response was well summed up by a writer in the Richmond *Enquirer* who said then:

> The case of Nat Turner warns us. No black man ought to be permitted to turn a preacher through the country. The law must be enforced—or the tragedy of Southampton appeals to us in vain.[42]

In the minds of blacks and whites alike religion and rebellion had been welded into one terrifying—or exalting—reality through the black body of Nat Turner.

[39] For the story of the Münsterites see George H. Williams, *The Radical Reformation* (London: Weidenfeld and Nicolson, 1962), 362–386.

[40] Aptheker, *Nat Turner's Slave Rebellion*, 38.

[41] From the lives of Frederick Douglass and Harriet Tubman to "The Ballad of Nat Turner" in a recently published book of poems by Robert Hayden, *Selected Poems* (New York: October House, 1966), the tradition has been carefully and faithfully maintained.

[42] Quoted in George Washington Williams, *History of the Negro Race in America*, 2 vols. (New York: G. P. Putnam's Sons, 1883), II, 90.

So the laws set off by fear swept through the states, forbidding Negroes to preach, in many places interdicting all meetings, attempting as it were to exorcise so troubling a religious spirit.[43] The Mississippi law of 1831 provided a good example when it ruled that "It is 'unlawful for any slave, free Negro, or mulatto to preach the gospel' under pain of receiving thirty-nine lashes upon the naked back of the . . . preacher."[44]

The laws did not stop the strange gospel of freedom from infiltrating into the ranks of the slaves—partly because it was already there. So an insurrectionary attempt came to light in Duplin County, North Carolina, in the fall of 1831, even before Turner had been captured. In the course of its account a newspaper article revealed that "a very intelligent negro preacher named David, was put on his trial . . . and clearly convicted . . ." as one of the ringleaders.[45] Elsewhere in that same year another newspaper correspondent says, "It is much to be regretted that [the apparent wave of insurrectionary attempts] are instigated by fierce, ignorant fanatics, assuming to be preachers." His comment closed with this prophecy: "I forsee that this land must one day or other, become a field of blood."[46] Thus in the mind of at least one man, black preachers of religion might well lead a people to bloody revolution. Strange opium.

In 1833 when Frederick Douglass, still a slave, tried to organize a Sabbath School class among the black young people of the Eastern Shore of Maryland, he found out that this white co-religionists had not yet disassociated themselves from earlier memories and convictions. Two Methodist class leaders led the mob that stormed Douglass' Sabbath School and Douglass said he was told by one Methodist that "I wanted to be another Nat Turner, and that, if I did not look out, I should get as many balls in me as Nat did into him."[47]

Two years later, during the slave insurrection scare in Mississippi, it was again said that "suspicion centered around the 'itinerant preachers'" and other troublemakers in the neighborhood.[48] In New Orleans the newspapers were complaining in 1839 about a Negro church which was "the greatest of all public nuisances and den for hatching plots against [the] masters."[49] Seven years later the same problem existed in the city as the police arrested twelve Negroes in "a makeshift church" and charged them with "the habit of repairing to this place for . . . singing hymns and cantiques which was followed by sermons the subject of which was the most inflammatory character."[50] Firebrands and sermons were continually being combined by black men whose re-

[43] DuBois (ed.), The Negro Church, 25.
[44] Ibid.
[45] Narrative of the Tragical Scene . . . in Southampton County (n.p., Werner and West, 1831), 23.
[46] Ibid., 20.
[47] Douglass, 111.
[48] Quoted in Edwin A. Miles, "The Mississippi Slave Insurrection Scare of 1835," Journal of Negro History, xlii, 1 (January, 1957), 51.
[49] Quoted in Wade, Slavery in the Cities, 83.
[50] Ibid., 83–84.

ligion had not yet made them "otherworldly" enough to suit the authorities.

It may be that the ambiguous nature of American religion, as it related to antebellum blacks, was best seen by a visitor to this land, one who had become a heroic figure among abolitionists by 1841. This was Joseph Cinquez, the African who had led a rebellion aboard the vessel, *Amistad*, as it carried a load of slaves along the coast of Cuba in 1839.[51] In the course of the revolt the captain and the cook had been killed by the rebels, the ship was steered to American shores and Cinquez had been brought to New England with his fellow slaves. There they were exposed to American Christianity with all of its contradictory potentials.

Then, in 1841, just before leaving for his native continent Cinquez was given the rare opportunity to apply this nation's religion to his rebellion—after the fact. One of his fellow rebels said to a group of Christians, "We owe everything to God; he keeps us alive and makes us free." Filled with enthusiasm, another went on to claim that he would now pray for the Captain and cook rather than kill them if the rebellion were to be done over again. We are told that "Cinquez, hearing this, smiled and shook his head. When asked if we would not pray for them, he said: 'Yes I would pray for 'em, an' kill 'em too.' "[52]

III

While the religion of some slaves could lead them to pray and kill, and though the Jesus of Southampton beckoned black men through streams of the masters' blood, there were other bondsmen who were evidently no less religiously motivated but who were led to seek different alternatives in their struggle. The Bauers have reminded us of the many levels of resistance to slavery that existed in the South, and they have indicated that some slaves who shed blood as an act of protest were known to draw their own or to take the lives of their children.[53] Death and self-mutilation were preferred to slavery, and one of the accounts of such death may offer some hint concerning the religious motivation involved here.

In Kentucky it was reported that "a father and mother, shut up in a slave baracoon and doomed to the southern market ... did by mutual agreement send the souls of their children to Heaven rather than have them descend to the hell of slavery, and then both parents committed suicide." [54] No one may be sure that the theology of the contemporary writer was shared by the parents he described, but is it impossible to conceive that a religion which

[51] A brief account of the *Amistad* story is most conveniently found in Louis Filler, *The Crusade Against Slavery 1830–1860* (New York: Harper and Row, 1963), 167–168.

[52] Quoted in Williams, *History*, II, 96.

[53] See reference to the Bauer's work in note 1 above, especially pp. 415–418.

[54] *Ibid.*, 417.

stressed the reality of heaven after death might strengthen slaves to leave their bondage for the freedom they had heard was ahead? If the "other world" was really so good, why allow children to suffer the agonies that parents had known?

In spite of the possible force of such reasoning, especially in extreme situations, it is certain that the action of the Kentucky parents was not typical. Perhaps a more common religious response to slavery was simply the act of refusing to believe the Christian teachings that justified the system of exploitation. A most striking instance of this alternative was found in Georgia shortly before 1830. In Liberty County a group of slaves were listening to a white minister hold forth on a staple topic—the escaped slave, Onesimus, and his return to his master. According to the report from Georgia, half of the Negro group walked out when the point of the sermon became clear, and "the other half stayed mostly for the purpose of telling [the preacher] that they were sure there was no such passage in the Bible."[55]

Because action could often be more costly than thoughts it is likely that many more slaves were involved in the kind of resistance to such religion that was identified by a former slave who said that Negroes simply refused to believe "a pro-slavery doctrine."[56] But Henry Bibb went on to point to what might have been an even more significant kind of defiance when he said that "This kind of preaching has driven thousands into infidelity."[57] Bibb's observations were supported by a southern Presbyterian minister who noted that many white ministers had assumed that Negroes "are an unsophisticated race" only to discover among them "deism, universalism, skepticism, and all the strong objections against the truth of God ... which he may perhaps have considered peculiar only to the cultivated minds ... of critics and philosophers."[58]

May we not suggest that the turn to "deism, universalism" and other unapproved forms of southern faith on the part of the slaves was in itself a profoundly religious act of protest against a system that seemed to be supported by all the correct lines of doctrine? Thus one may possibly speak of both protest and accommodation, if the accommodation were carried out under the new religiously protestant ground rules, rules that needed perforce to remain largely interior, but nonetheless real for that.

We are, however, concerning ourselves here with the more exterior, reportable, forms of resistance, and it is clear that one of the most obvious of these was the act of running away from slavery. It was not an act lightly taken up nor easily accomplished, and a sampling of fugitive slave narratives readily reveals the level of inner conviction and strength that was most often necessary for a slave to strike out for freedom. The difficulty of the path and the dis-

[55] Perkins, 236.

[56] Henry Bibb, *Narrative of the Life and Adventures of* (New York: the author, 1850), 24.

[57] *Ibid.*

[58] Quoted in Perkins, 237.

obedience of the act provided good testing grounds for the nature of religious faith.

Frederick Douglass recalled his own struggle with the issue of escape as an older man continued to speak to him of the great things that he thought Douglass was meant to do in the world. Young Frederick responded: "I am a slave, and a slave for life, how can I do anything?" To this "Uncle Lawson" replied:

> The Lord can make you free, my dear; all things are possible with him
> ...If you want liberty, ask the Lord for it in faith, and he will give
> it to you.[59]

From that point on Douglass began asking—in his own unorthodox way—and planning, until he felt he had freedom grasped securely in his hands. This was why the religion of chains and submission seemed like "nonsense" to him.

Samuel Ringgold Ward, another fugitive who became a brilliant abolitionist lecturer, lived the struggle through his mother. When he was a child this matriarch had to decide whether she would remain in Maryland and likely be sold further south or whether she would encourage her husband to lead them all to freedom. The will of God was discussed at that point, and the strong, single-minded black woman decided that they should leave. As Ward later described it,

> Submission to the will of God was one thing, she was prepared for
> that, but submission to the machinations of Satan was quite another
> thing; neither her womanhood nor her theology could be reconciled
> to the latter.[60]

In one of the most famous of the antebellum slave narratives William Wells Brown spoke of the same issue—the relationship of his mother's God to freedom. He told of how he confided in her his own plans for escape from slavery in St. Louis just as she was being sold into the deep South. Without any hesitation she urged him to go, and her last word may have expressed her theology of slave rebellion: "God be with you."[61]

There is only one woman whose journey from Southern slavery to freedom is readily available, and that story—half legend by now—is a religious pilgrimage in itself.[62] Harriet Tubman grew up on the stories of the Hebrew

[59] Douglass, 91.

[60] Samuel Ringgold Ward, *Autobiography of a Fugitive Negro* (London: John Snow, 1855), 19. The family ran away in 1820.

[61] Brown, *Narrative*, 79.

[62] Three of Harriet Tubman's most widely read biographers tend to encourage the legendary aspects: Henrietta Buckmaster, *Let My People Go* (Boston. Beacon Press, 1959); Earl Conrad, *Harriet Tubman* (Washington, D.C.: Associated Publishers, 1943); and Dorothy Sterling, *Freedom Train: The Story of Harriet Tubman* (New York: Doubleday and Company, 1954). In a recent study of the Underground Railroad, Larry Gara attempts to suggest Harriett's real life size. See his *The Liberty Line* (Lexington, University of Kentucky Press, 1961).

children, heard the whispered descriptions of Nat Turner, and sang the songs of impossible hope. Like Turner she saw visions and dreamed dreams of struggle and conflict and searching for freedom. Like him she prayed and talked with God and became fully convinced that her God willed freedom. Indeed, one of her more radical biographers said that by the time she escaped from her native Maryland in 1849 "she was ready to kill for freedom, if that was necessary, and defend the act as her religious right."[63]

The year after Harriet's arrival in the North her fellow black runaways were cast in a new light as a result of the Compromise of 1850 and its Fugitive Slave law. Therefore, while Douglass and Harriet Tubman gained most lasting fame as fugitives, it was a slave who arrived north in 1854—Anthony Burns— whose case became the *cause célèbre* of his time.[64] As a result of the notoriety resulting from the Boston abolitionist furor, Burns received a letter of rebuke and excommunication from the white Baptist church he had joined as a slave in Virginia. In his response we have one of the best statements of the religious apologia for resistance through flight.

Burns wrote,

> You charge me that, in escaping, I disobeyed God's law. No, indeed! That law which God wrote upon the table of my heart, inspiring the love of freedom, and impelling me to seek it at every hazard, I obeyed, and by the good hand of my God upon me, I walked out of the house of bondage.

Then, in response to the inevitable citation of Paul and Onesimus which had been in the church's letter, Burns said he would be glad to return if he had any reason to believe that he too would be received in the brotherly spirit that Paul had requested for Onesimus. But Burns said that he did not believe in such a possibility, and was staying North. Finally he stated his basic defense and comfort in the terms of his faith: "You have thrust me out of your church fellowship. So be it. You cannot exclude me from heaven . . ." [65]

Such was the religion of the runaways. They were obviously a self-selective group, but an important and impressive one too. None of them was willing to wait for Frazier's "world after death" to find their rest or to gain compensation for their condition, and they had thousands of brothers in their impatience. (Even heaven-oriented Anthony Burns wanted to try out Boston before confirming his reservation in heavenly places.)

Indeed, persons like Brown, Ward, Douglass and Harriet Tubman (to say nothing of their Northern-born counterparts) seemed unwilling to accept rest anywhere. Their religion was a restless one while slavery existed in the South and segregation shamed the North. The extreme form of this eternally protesting religion was expressed, of course, by Harriet Tubman shortly after

[63] Conrad, 35.

[64] See Buckmaster for an account of Burns' situation, especially 230–236.

[65] Herbert Aptheker (ed.), A *Documentary History of the Negro People in the United States*, 2 vols. (New York: Citadel Press, 1965), I, 372.

her arrival in Philadelphia. There, upon being asked to settle in the city, she was quoted as having said,

> There are three million of my people on the plantations of the south.
> I must go down, like Moses into Egypt, to lead them out.[66]

Such a spirit breeds legends and makes history difficult to write, but Harriet Tubman did return and she delivered some small, but important fragment of the waiting people. She returned often enough to end up with rewards amounting to 40,000 dollars being offered for her. Just as her own escape from slavery was the Lord's doing in her mind, so too did a sense of divine obsession now drive Harriet Tubman to continue this strange and courageous work of deliverance.[67] She too knew how to exhort, sing spirituals and carry a gun.

If the sparse evidence available is any guide, Harriet Tubman's efforts were child's play compared to a plan that was already at work in the South when she was escaping. It was a plan that revived memories of Gabriel and Vesey and Prophet Nat, expanding them beyond imagination. According to the Reverend Moses Dickson, the founder of a post-Civil War Negro benevolent society, in 1846 he had been instrumental in forming a group of twelve young men who called themselves the twelve Knights of Tabor.[68] They vowed in that year to spend the next decade organizing an army of liberation throughout the South, and were preparing to strike for the freedom of the slaves sometime after 1856. The Old Testament name was self-consciously chosen, Dickson said, for it "gave the members courage."[69]

According to his story, they were encouraged because they knew that

> God was with Israel, and gave the victory to the bondsmen, though they were opposed by twenty times their number. Our cause was just, and we believed in the justice of the God of Israel and the rights of man. Under the name of Tabor we resolved to make full preparation to strike the blow for liberty.[70]

With this sense of divine calling the members supposedly organized within ten years more than forty thousand recruits who were "well drilled, with ample arms and ammunition." They were located in all the slave states except Texas and Missouri. The larger group was dubbed Knights of Liberty.[71]

In 1857 they were prepared, by Dickson's account, to gather more followers and converge on Atlanta with 150,000 troops. They were to spare women and children, but "march, fight, and conquer was the command, or leave their

---

[66] Sterling, 81.

[67] See references in note 62 above.

[68] For an account of this fascinating story, see Aptheker, *Documentary History*, I, 378–380 and Moses Dickson, *Manual of the International Order of Twelve* (St. Louis: A. R. Fleming, 1891), 7–17.

[69] *Ibid.*, 15.

[70] *Ibid.*, 16.

[71] Aptheker, *Documentary History*, I, 380.

bodies on the battle field." Their flag was to have a cross made up of twelve stars. Then when all was prepared, just before an unidentified "Chief" was about to give the command to march, Dickson says, "it was plainly demonstrated to [the leader] that a higher power was preparing to take part in the contest between the North and South ..." So the group was told to hold off, and it disbanded when the Civil War came.[72]

If this account is true, America was on the verge of experiencing the work of a Holy Liberation Front. So far it has not proved possible to go beyond one or two documentary sources related to this movement. However it is important to note that if such a movement was indeed on foot, it was self-consciously arrayed in the train of Nat Turner. Event or legend, it testified to the fact that there was a strong tradition of religious rebellion among antebellum blacks.

While the Knights of Liberty failed to march, John Brown did not fail. His religious self-image is well known. Less known is the fact that many Negroes took John Brown's insurrectionary action and fitted it into their understanding of religion without any apparent difficulty.

For instance, Frances Ellen Watkins, a gifted writer who published constantly in the cause of Negro freedom, wrote these words to Brown as he awaited execution:

> The Cross becomes a glorious ensign when Calvary's ... sufferer yields up his life upon it. And, if Universal Freedom is ever to be the dominant power of the land, your bodies may be only her first stepping stones to dominion.[73]

A writer representing "The Colored Women of Brooklyn" became even more explicit in setting the messianic theme as she wrote, "We ... recognize in you a Saviour commissioned to redeem us, the American people, from the great National Sin of Slavery ..."[74]

Harriet Tubman had meant to march with Brown, but became ill and was evidently on her way to meet him when the old man was captured. Out of the religious world in which she moved it was clear that she spoke honest words when she said after his death: "It was not John Brown that died at Charleston ... It was Christ—it was the savior of our people."[75] The black cross had passed from Nat Turner to John Brown. Therefore it was fitting that a traditional Negro tune should be used to carry the words of "John Brown's Body."

IV

Though "John Brown's Body" is not a spiritual, its presence bears a reminder that it is impossible to conclude any discussion of black religion without at least a reference to those songs. They represent the most profound

[72] *Ibid.*
[73] *Ibid.*, 441.

[74] *Ibid.*
[75] Sterling, 129–133.

verbal expression of Afro-American religious experience. As W. E. B. DuBois has said, they are "the siftings of centuries . . ."[76]

In spite of their significance it will not be fitting to attempt any lengthy exposition of them here—neither time nor skill allows that. However, it should be noted that these songs have been subjected to much of the same difficulties that we encountered at the outset of this discussion of black religion. Frazier is found again speaking of them as "essentially religious in sentiment and . . . otherworldly in outlook," thereby suggesting that he had missed the point of much of the greatest religious sentiments of man.[77] (Perhaps he was not blessed to hear Paul Tillich's definition of religion.)

Mays also describes most of the spirituals as expressing "compensatory" and heaven-oriented attitudes, but he faces the texts and is willing to admit that some of them clearly bespeak real protest in the present world. Especially does he cite "Go Down Moses" and "Oh Freedom" in this vein.[78] But the author of one of the most carefully wrought attempts to set the spirituals in a historical context goes much further, and develops a theme concerning the spirituals quite similar to the one being suggested here for all of Negro religion.

Miles Mark Fisher sees black religion so closely allied to protest that he suggests that some of the spirituals were likely the creation of Nat Turner, Denmark Vesey, and Harriet Tubman.[79] Especially provocative is Fisher's suggestion that "Steal Away" emerged directly out of Nat Turner's vision of 1825, when the call of God came to him through convulsions in the elements, as he grew increasingly convinced that his great future task would lead him away from all that he had known before.[80] By this Fisher does not mean to deny that many persons have sung that haunting song with longings for a heavenly place, but he affirms that it may well have originated in a marvelously earthbound experience, an experience of affirmation and rebellion.

This recognition that the spirituals surely bore many possible meanings for many persons is strongly supported by Frederick Douglass, who sang so many of them while they were yet fresh in the air. As he later recalled his youth, Douglass pointed to two examples of the potential for profound ambiguity which rested at the center of the songs. There was one with the words

> O Canaan, Sweet Canaan
> I am bound for the land of Canaan.

In Douglass' experience, as he put it, "The North was our Canaan." There

---

[76] DuBois, *The Souls of Black Folk* (Greenwich, Conn.: Fawcett Publications, 1961), 183. DuBois' justly famous work contains a number of important essays on black religion. See especially chapters X, XII and XIV.

[77] Frazier, 12.

[78] Mays, 28–29.

[79] Miles Mark Fisher, *Negro Slave Songs in the United States*, Paperback edition (New York: Citadel Press, 1963), 66–67, 181–185.

[80] *Ibid.*, 67.

was no doubt about that. He says, too, that a song with the words "I don't expect to stay much longer here" (probably a variant of "Steal Away") was another favorite and had "a double meaning." He explained the duality in this way: "On the lips of some it meant the expectation of a speedy summons to a world of spirits, but on the lips of our company [of young men in Maryland] it simply meant a speedy pilgrimage to a free state, and deliverance from all the evils and dangers of slavery."[81]

It would then appear that even in the midst of so community-oriented an experience as the singing of spirituals, many men may have sung out of many varied visions. For some—perhaps for most—the visions took them beyond this earth entirely, and made the experiences of their surroundings fade in importance. For other black persons the music and the faith it expressed—and engendered—filled them with a sense of God's awesome calling for their present moment, and supplied new determination to struggle, build, and resist here.

This dual function of religion should not be surprising. Speaking of another oppressed people in another time, Reinhold Niebuhr lately reminded us that "The radical sectarians [of the Reformation period] appropriated Messianism to make of it an instrument of social revolt, while the more conservative religious forces used otherworldly hopes to beguile men from injustices in history."[82]

Unless we grasp that common historical truth and apply it to the black experience in America we shall not only be unprepared to meet those Negroes who break out of the pages of Aptheker and Stampp, but we shall certainly fail to understand so recent and lately controversial a phenomenon as Martin Luther King. He stands in a long tradition of black exhorters whose lives and whose religion can neither be spiritualized, captured or denied. They can, however, be understood, and that is our task.[83]

[81] Douglass, 159–160.

[82] Introduction to Marx and Engels, *On Religion*, viii.

[83] After I completed this paper my attention was called to a sociological study which will attempt to relate Negro religion to protest in the modern era: Gary T. Marx, *Protest and Prejudice* (New York: Harper and Row, forthcoming).

PART THREE

THE ANTE-BELLUM
FREE PEOPLE OF COLOR

James H. Brewer

NEGRO PROPERTY OWNERS IN SEVENTEENTH-CENTURY VIRGINIA

Early in the history of American Negroes, a group known as the "Free People of Color" emerged. James H. Brewer discusses the origins of this class of seventeenth-century Virginia, and the ironic fact that the most prosperous individuals among the free Negroes themselves cultivated staple crops with slave labor.

T HREE centuries have passed since there appeared on the Eastern Shore, along the banks of the Pungoteague River, perhaps the first community of Negro property owners in historic Virginia. Within a few years other infant black communities were to be found scattered throughout parts of Tidewater Virginia. The story concerning those forgotten African families, partially revealed by Philip Alexander Bruce nearly sixty years ago, cannot be told in its entirety. However, further light is shed on their economic pursuits in the early colonial period by a somewhat fuller exploitation of the county records of Virginia.

It is highly significant that some of the former Negro servants found the environment of seventeenth-century Virginia conducive to the amassing of property in land or chattel in various ways. For example, a few received land grants ranging from 50 to 500 acres, made possible by the head-rights system. Others acquired their property in chattel; while there were some who came into ownership of land or chattel through grants in the wills of their former masters. Through these various means a class of Negro property owners gradually came into existence. How large this class was, it is not possible to say, but the records seem to indicate that their number was relatively small.

The influx of blacks into the colony during the major part of the seventeenth century was still too meager to affect seriously the social and economic

James H. Brewer, "Negro Property Owners in Seventeenth-Century Virginia," *The William and Mary Quarterly*, XII (October, 1955), pp. 575–80. Reprinted with the permission of the publisher and author.

life of Virginia. For example, in 1625 there were only 23 Negroes in Virginia, and by the middle of the century only 300 blacks were to be found, while the whites numbered 15,000. Between 1670 and 1680 the Negro population had increased from 2,000 to 3,000. During the last two decades of the century the Negro population grew rapidly, and by 1700 there were approximately 6,000 Negroes in Virginia. It was during this period that Virginia became disturbed by the increase of blacks within her borders. Her fears were manifested by the enactment of two statutes which listed types of property the Negroes might not acquire. The first law, passed in 1670, prohibited them from owning white servants, while the second act denied to them the ownership of fire-arms or other weapons.[1]

Even though the rapid increase of the Negro population of Virginia was paralleled by certain limitations placed on their rights of ownership, the Negro never lost his right to own and to alienate his property. This is dis-closed by a study of the head-rights system.[2] Beginning in 1651, a few Negro families took advantage of the head-rights custom and received acreage along the banks of the Pungoteague River on the Eastern Shore. The first of such grants was made in July, 1651, to Anthony Johnson of Northampton County, who received 250 acres of land for the importation of 5 persons into the colony.[3] At this time Anthony Johnson and his wife, Mary, were perhaps the wealthiest Negroes in Virginia.[4] After Anthony, other free blacks whose last name was Johnson procured property under the head-rights system in the forgotten Pungoteague Community. For example, John Johnson received as head-rights for the transporting of 11 persons a tract of 550 acres of land.[5] Likewise, John Johnson, Senior, was allowed his claim of 50 acres.[6] When Johnson attempted to increase his land holdings, he was summoned in 1653 to appear in court to answer proceedings instituted by his neighbor, another

[1] William W. Hening, compiler, *The Statutes at Large . . . of Virginia* (Rich-mond, 1819–1823), II, 280, 481.

[2] This was a law designed to stimulate immigration, which stipulated that the government pledged itself to grant 50 acres of land to any person who would pay the passage of a person to Virginia. The person receiving the grant was required to record with the clerk of his respective county court the names of all persons for whose transportation the claim was made. This statute was one of the means by which the Virginia Negro was able to accumulate land of 50 acres or more. For a more detailed discussion of the head-rights system see Thomas J. Wertenbaker, *The Planters of Colonial Virginia* (Princeton, 1922), 34.

[3] Land Patents of Virginia, 1643–1651, Book No. 2, 326, Virginia State Library. Hereafter cited as Land Patents. See also Court Records of Northampton County, 1651–1654, 226; 1655–1658, 10, Virginia State Library. Hereafter cited as CRNC. The names of the five persons imported are Tho. Bembrose, Peter Bughby, Antho. Cripps, Jno. Gesorroro, and Richard Johnson.

[4] See below, p. 578.

[5] Land Patents, 1652–1655, Book No. 3, 101. The names of those imported are Jno. Edwards, William Routh, Thomas Yowell, Fra. Mayland, William Price, John Owens, Dorthy Riley, Richard Hemstead, Law. Barnes, Row. Rith, and Mary Johnson.

[6] CRNC, 1651–1654, 17.

John Johnson, to recover 450 acres of land.[7] The next member of the African community to acquire land under the head-rights was a carpenter by trade, Richard Johnson. Richard was perhaps among the 5 servants imported in 1651 by Anthony Johnson. Three years later he was assigned 100 acres adjoining the property of John and Anthony Johnson.[8]

Soon after various Johnsons had achieved a status of moderate economic importance in the historic Pungoteague Community, the records disclose that elsewhere in the colony other free Negroes had made progress in land ownership. For example, in December, 1656, Benjamin Doyle was granted a patent for 300 acres of land in Surry County "for the transportation of six persons into the colony." [9] There is also a record of a grant of 50 acres in April 18, 1667, to Emanuel Cambew of James City County.[10] In the adjoining county of York a deed dated October 28, 1668, calling for the transfer of 50 acres of land in New Kent County, was executed by Robert Jones, a white tailor of Queen's Creek, to "John Harris, a negro his heyers, Executrs, admtrs, and assigns forever."[11] On at least one occasion, a Negro leased land on a long-term basis. Philip Morgan and his heirs were "peacefully and quietly [to] enjoy the 200 acres," for 99 years, when the land was to revert to the owner's heirs.[12]

It hardly needs to be said that in sections of Tidewater Virginia there were many free blacks too poor to acquire land. As free persons, however, they inevitably acquired small amounts of personal property in various forms— cattle, household effects, and clothing. Frequently they received such items when they were freed; others, of course, earned them; and, we suspect, others came by them somewhat illegally. Manuscript records dealing with this kind of property are to be found more frequently than those dealing with land. Even the simple sale of cattle, "a black cow and a red calf" to Emanuel Dregis, is recorded.[13] Negroes were also involved in litigation, which not only became a part of the court records but also disclosed their small property holdings. Thus, in 1647 Tony Kongo was compelled by court order to pay a debt of 382 pounds of tobacco due Lewis White. The mulatto Kongo was allowed thirty days to guarantee payment out of "ye next croppe."[14] A judgment for 486 pounds of tobacco against the estate of Edward Jessop, Negro, is recorded in the court records of Northampton County.[15]

[7] Ibid., 200. John Johnson sought relief from the authorities by testifying that John Johnson, Senior, "Most unrightly detayneth a pattent for 450 acres of land." The decision of the court was not revealed.

[8] Land Patents, 1652–1655, Book No. 3, 294; also 101.

[9] Ibid., 1655–1664, Book No. 4, 71f.

[10] Ibid., Book No. 6, 39.

[11] Court Records of York County, 1664–1672, Book No. 4, 327, Virginia State Library. Hereafter cited as CRYC.

[12] Court Records of Accomac County, 1676–1690, 185, Virginia State Library.

[13] CRNC, 1645–1651, 83. See Virginia Magazine of History, XI (1904), 281.

[14] CRNC, 1645–1651, 83.

[15] CRNC, 1683–1689, 258.

The most remarkable record in property holding, however, is that of Anthony Johnson, "the black patriarch" of Pungoteague Community. Within 7 months after acquiring 250 acres in July, 1651, Johnson's holdings were practically wiped out by an unfortunate fire. Johnson then petitioned the court for relief, and the judgment of the court stated, "be it therefore fitt and ordered that... (during their natural lives) the sd Mary Johnson & two daughters of Anthony Johnson be disengaged and freed from payment of taxes and leavyes in Northampton County for public use."[16] Ultimately the enterprising "black patriarch" managed to re-establish himself as a moderate property owner. In 1653 Anthony appeared as a claimant in a suit brought against Robert Parker to recover his Negro servant John Casor. Testimony in the trial discloses that Johnson attempted to show that he was intimidated by Parker to free his black servant because of threats by Parker that the servant would enter suit against Johnson to recover his master's cows as damages. The court ordered that the servant be returned to Johnson.[17] The court records also afford additional evidence as to Johnson's business transactions in an effort to replenish his losses through fire. One record shows that Anthony and his son John sold "two heifers collored black and of three years old... unto John Williams his heirs executors and assigns forever."[18] In August, 1659, Anthony managed to enlarge his land holdings when his son John "do hereby bargain and make sail of all my right title and interest of this within... patent of land to my father Anthony Johnson Negro...."[19] Finally, a chattel mortgage recorded the same year entailed the exchange of more property within the family when John transferred to his father Anthony "two heifers of two year old and four yearling heifers and one calf... and also one black cow...."[20]

The growth of a class of Negro property owners was also facilitated by the emancipation provisions of liberal and appreciative masters. Thus, former Negro servants as well as emancipated slaves did not always go forth empty-handed from their masters' services. Many were furnished either land or chattel or both to embark upon their new life as freemen. This was true of two blacks, Philip and Nicholas, of York County. Each was bequeathed a cow and allotted a certain plot of land to cultivate for the "balance of their natural lives."[21] John, another Negro of York County, was emancipated by one Thomas Whitehead, and included among the several items he was bequeathed were the possession of a house and the use of as much land as he could cultivate.[22]

Elsewhere in Virginia other Negroes were recipients of property through wills in the seventeenth century. Notable is the will of Richard Vaughan of

16 CRNC, 1651–1654, 161.
17 Ibid., 10. See also John H. Russell, The Free Negro in Virginia, 1619–1865 (Baltimore, 1913), 33.
18 CRNC, Deeds, Wills, 1657–1666, 17.
19 Ibid., 9.
20 Ibid., 9.
21 CRYC, Will of Nicholas Martin, 1633–1694, 109.
22 Ibid., 1657–1662, 211, 217.

Northampton County, which left property to each Negro he set free. A portion of Vaughan's will reads:

> ...and for my old Negro woman...and the receive twoe Cowes with calfe (or calves by their side) two suits of clothes and bedd and a Rugge, a chest and a pott with foure Barrells of corn and a younge breedinge Sowe; Likewise my Negro girle Temperance... to bee possessed of two cowes and to have their increase male and female....[23]

Continuing, Vaughan's will stated, "that ye three Negro girls be possessed of the plantacon of John. Walthome, being to this plantacon some 144 acres of land; and he to build them a Home twenty-five feete in length and twenty feete broad, with one chimmey."[24] Under the terms of the will of John Carter, of Lancaster County, a married slave couple were to be set free and "allowed...the use of a convenient house...and as much land as they could cultivate...."[25] Robert Griggs showed equal generosity to a mulatto when he bequeathed him a home and a "certain area of ground for life...."[26] Of greater significance are the terms of the will of John Nicholls, filed in 1697, whereby the two mulatto children of one of his female slaves were to be set free and to have possession of several hundred acres of land. In addition to 310 acres left to the mulatto boy and 200 acres left to his mulatto sister, they were to receive a variety of chattel.[27]

The question concerning the economic activities of the Negro inhabitants of Pungoteague and other Virginia communities is not one of major historical significance. Yet their story in many respects parallels that of other ethnic and cultural groups in seventeenth-century Virginia. For example, some Negroes eventually became financially able to pay for the transportation of indentured servants either from Europe or Africa or both, and in this way they acquired 50 acres for each European or African they imported. Others found it more feasible to purchase their property from native Virginians. However, the bulk of the wealth among the Negro population was in chattel property. Finally, the response by the Negro to the need for economic stability resulted in the now-forgotten communities of Negro property owners in seventeenth-century Virginia.

[23] CRNC, 1654–1655, 102.
[24] Ibid., Will of Richard Vaughan, 103. For a more detailed analysis of seventeenth-century wills see Philip A. Bruce, Economic History of Virginia in the Seventeenth Century (New York, 1896), II, 123f.
[25] Court Records of Lancaster County, original vol., 1690–1709, 3, Virginia State Library.
[26] Ibid., 1674–1687, 91.
[27] Court Records of Lower Norfolk County, original vol., 1695–1703, 96, Virginia State Library. See Bruce, Economic History of Virginia in the Seventeenth Century, II, 125.

E. Horace Fitchett

THE TRADITIONS OF THE FREE NEGRO IN CHARLESTON, SOUTH CAROLINA [1]

If the slave population was overwhelmingly rural, the free Negroes were preeminently an urban group. There were about half a million of them in 1860, distributed roughly equally between the North and the South, and concentrated largely in coastal and river ports like Providence, New York, Cincinnati, Louisville, Baltimore, Charleston, Mobile, and New Orleans.

In the South the free Negroes lived mainly in areas of older settlement along the Atlantic Seaboard and Gulf of Mexico, where the slave system was somewhat more benevolent and paternalistic. There, a significant free population had emerged before the states, during the course of the nineteenth century, imposed practically insuperable barriers to manumission.

One of the most perceptive discussions of the ante-bellum urban free Negroes is found in the work of E. Horace Fitchett. In the article published here, he not only describes the origins, economic attainment, and social organization of the free people of color in Charleston, S.C., but he also analyzes the way they functioned as a buttress to the system of slavery.

THE free Negro in the slave system was an anomaly. The system was designed for free white men and Negro slaves. In a large measure the position of the

E. Horace Fitchett, "The Traditions of the Free Negro in Charleston, South Carolina," *Journal of Negro History*, XXV (April, 1940), pp. 139–152. Reprinted with the permission of the publisher.

[1] Paper read before the 18th Annual Institute of the Society for Social Research, August 19, 1939, at the University of Chicago. This paper was based on an investigation the writer was making of the free Negro in Charleston, S.C. It was made possible by an award from the Julius Rosenwald Fund for the year 1938–39. The writer expressed his appreciation to Professors Robert E. Park, W. Lloyd Warner, and Herbert Blumer for many stimulating and valuable suggestions.

emancipated Negro, prior to the Emancipation Proclamation, was comparable to that of the slave. Some of them preferred slavery to the type of freedom which they received.[2] They were by law deprived of education, of suffrage, and of freedom of movement; they could not testify in court against a white man, and from time to time they were prohibited from assembling in groups of more than seven without the presence of a white man.[3] However, before the slave structure was disrupted by the Civil War there were approximately one half of a million people of this class in the United States.[4] In a few communities, particularly along the seacoast, they developed into a respectable, economically independent, class-conscious group. This is notable in the case of Charleston, South Carolina.

In this discussion I shall answer briefly the following questions: (1) How did this group arise? (2) What was its economic position and how was it attained? (3) What relations did this class of people sustain with out-group members and in its own group? (4) Were there any evidences of deviations from the approved patterns of behavior? If so, what form did they take? And (5) What was the nature of the process of accommodation and social adjustment to the social system?

When the first census was taken in 1790 there were 8,089 white persons, 7,684 slaves, and 586 free Negroes in Charleston, South Carolina. Hence, the latter group constituted 3.58 per cent of the total population.[5] Many of the members of this group had no memory of a slave background or tradition. This was particularly true of the mixed bloods. Dr. Reuter advances the generalization that: "There seems to be no historical exception to the rule that when peoples come into contact and occupy the same area there is a mixture of blood that results, ultimately, in the establishment of a new modified ethnic type."[6] This condition is no less true of Charleston than of other areas. Documentary evidence may be presented to support this generalization. In 1720 one slave master, James Gilbertson, a planter, made the following provisions in his will for a mulatto woman and her children:

> My will is that my mulatto woman Ruth shall be free immediately after my Decease, & also my will is that her three female children Betty, Molly, and Keatty shall be free at the age of one and Twenty years, my will is also that Ruth have the feather bed W:ch the Indians did Cutt up, also a pot and her maintenance upon my plantation during her natural life.[7]

[2] Phillips, U. B., *American Negro Slavery* (New York, 1918), p. 446.
[3] *Ibid.*, p. 448; *A Digest of the Ordinance of Charleston, 1783–1844*, p. 377.
[4] *Negro Population in the United States, 1790–1915*, p. 53.
[5] *Census of Charleston, 1848*, p. 10.
[6] Reuter, E. B. (ed.), *Race and Culture Contacts* (New York, 1934), pp. 7–9.
[7] *Record of Wills of Charleston County*, Vol. 1, 1671–1724, p. 50. Through the courtesy and cooperation of Miss Parmelee Cheves of the Charleston Free Library, and Professor J. H. Easterby of the College of the City of Charleston, I was permitted to examine a large number of verbatim, typewritten copies of old wills of Charleston County.

In 1834, a prominent Charlestonian, a native of France, acknowledged in his will that the children of his housekeeper and slave were his offspring and his executors were instructed to provide for the mother and her children out of the estate. He states:

> I do hereby recognize and declare that the issue of my slave and housekeeper, Celestine, are my children and I will order and direct that my executors herein named, or such person or persons that may qualify on this will, shall and do, as soon after my death as may be convenient, send the said woman Celestine and all her said issue my children, out of this State to some other State, territory or country, where they can severally be made free and their liberty secured to them respectively; and I will, order and direct that said executors or such person or persons that may qualify and act on this will shall defray the expense of transportation or conveyance of the said Celestine and her issue to said State, territory or country as expressed from the funds of my estate.[8]

In 1826 one of the wealthiest and most influential citizens of Charleston made the following stipulation in his will for his mulatto man:

> In consideration of the good conduct and faithful valuable service of my mulatto man Toney by Trade a millwright I have for some years past given him to himself one half of his time say from the middle of May to the middle of November every year. It is my will and desire and I do direct that the same indulgence be given to him for six years from the time of my death during which time he may instruct other servants in his Profession to supply his place and at the expiration of six years from the time of my death I will and direct that his whole time be given up to him . . . . after the expiration of six years he may be emancipated and set free or allowed to depart from this State as (he) may . . . think proper.[9]

These wills are typical of many of those which I examined. They not only provided for the freedom of a slave but also for his economic security. In a very real sense they imply that these persons were not slaves. They were in some instances recognized as the offspring of the upper caste member; they were allowed freedom of action and movement; and they were accorded special privileges. Thus they were not treated as slaves nor did they conceive of themselves as slaves. Indeed, in some of the wills the testator indicated that the servant should not be considered a slave. Such was the desire expressed in the will of Mrs. Bonneau in 1807.[10] Moreover, some of these persons obtained their freedom so early in the history of the country that the conditions of slave status could easily have been lost to their descendants. Their emancipation was indeed coeval with that of many of the white servant class. In the *South*

---

[8] *Record of Wills of Charleston County*, Vol. 40, Book A, 1834–1839, p. 203.
[9] *Record of Wills*, Vol. 37, Book A, 1826–1834, pp. 184–185.
[10] *Record of Wills*, Vol. 33, Book C, 1807–1818, p. 1180–1181.

Carolina Gazette for January, 1738, the following advertisement was made for a white servant girl:

> Runaway the 28th of December last, a white woman servant, about 16 years of age, named Anne Brown, born in London and can talk a little French, belonging to Edw. Townsend of Savannah, Georgia. Whoever brings the said Servant to Charleston shall have £5 in currency reward.[11]

There were also cases in which free Negroes entered Charleston from other states. Such was the case of Richard Holloway, whose citizenship papers were dated January 21, 1794. He is designated in this document as a seaman, a native of Essex County, Maryland, and a mulatto about twenty years of age.[12]

In general it is fair to say that the free Negro arose out of: (1) Children born of free colored parents; (2) Mulatto children born of free colored mothers; (3) Children of free Negro and mixed Indian parentage; (4) Manumitted slaves.[13]

In the latter part of the eighteenth and during the first part of the nineteenth centuries there emerged in Charleston a relatively economically independent group of free Negroes. They were primarily the artisans of the system. Records show, moreover, that they engaged in business transactions which made the system a going concern. In 1819 they were listed in thirty branches of work. Among them were 11 carpenters, 10 tailors, 22 seamstresses, 6 shoemakers and one owner of a hotel.[14] Thirty years later they were listed in fifty different types of work. In 1859 there were among them 50 carpenters, 43 tailors, 9 shoemakers, and 21 butchers. In these trades some of them became wealthy. In the above mentioned year, "353 persons paid taxes on property and one-hundred-and-ninety were slave holders. The property on which they paid taxes was assessed at $724,570 and the amount paid on slaves aggregated $1,170." [15] If we divide this group of taxpayers into three approximately homogeneous classes, we find that there were 192 who paid taxes on property whose assessed value ranged from $1,000 to $5,000; this group owned 105 slaves, or an average of .54 slaves each. In the second division there were 21 persons who paid taxes on property whose assessed value ranged from $5,000 to $10,000, and they owned 68 slaves, or 3¼ slaves each. And in the third bracket, there were 9 persons who paid taxes on property whose value ranged from $10,000 to $40,075. This group owned 54 slaves, an average of 6 slaves each. In this class one individual paid taxes on $23,000 worth of real estate and 14 slaves; another $33,000 worth of real estate and 5 slaves; and a third paid taxes on $40,075 worth of real estate and 14 slaves.[16]

[11] *The South Carolina Gazette*, No. 209, Jan., 1738.
[12] *Citizenship Papers of Richard Holloway.* By the courtesy of Mrs. Mae Holloway-Purcell, a descendant of the family, I was permitted to examine this document.
[13] Russell, John H., *The Free Negro in Virginia, 1619–1865*, pp. 40–41.
[14] Based on a study of the *Directory of Charleston*, 1819, pp. 21–98.
[15] *List of Taxpayers of the City of Charleston for 1860*, pp. 315–334.
[16] *Ibid.*

Moreover, the wills and deeds which they made indicate that they engaged in some of the most important business ventures of the system. In 1815, Jehu Jones bought a hotel at public auction for $13,000.[17] This hotel was located on the most important street in the city and in close proximity to the most fashionable Episcopal Church in the community.[18] It was patronized by the elite of the white society, including the governor of the state.[19]

In 1853 Joseph Dereef, another wealthy person of color, sold a piece of property to the city council for $3,600 for the extension of a street.[20] In 1870 his brother, R. E. Dereef, sold a part of his wharf to the South Carolina Rail Road Company for $17,000.[21] In 1833 Thomas Ingliss made provisions in his will for the support of a relative from the stocks which he held in the Mechanics Bank of the city.[22]

One of the characteristics of the free Negro of Charleston, which attracts the attention of the sociologists, is that it was a class-conscious group; and identified its interest, loyalties, and manners with the upper caste members of the society in so far as that behavior did not offend or disturb the *status quo*. They organized themselves into societies with high eligibility requirements. These associations were ostensibly charitable and benevolent, but in reality they were social and status organizations. In 1790 the Brown Fellowship Society was formed.[23] The preamble of this organization stated that its members were bona fide free brown men of good character. The fee of admission was $50.00 and the membership was restricted to fifty members. The society provided for the education of the children, assistance to the orphans and widows and burial grounds for their dead. They maintained a clubhouse where meetings were held monthly, and on each anniversary provisions were made for special observance. This institution had a continuous existence for more than a hundred years. In fact vestiges of it are still in evidence. There is left the cemetery, with large imposing tombstones and vaults; so is the foundation of the hall in which they met. It still has a secretary and a president. In spite of the fact that other Negro organizations, including a church, were abolished during crises periods in this slave community, the Brown Fellowship Society kept alive. The members and their organizations were careful and cautious in their conduct. We only need to remember the conflicting philosophies and the revolutionary movements of the underprivileged groups of this period to appreciate how delicate and precarious the position of this group was. At their meetings they prohibited any discussion of local or national problems. Rule XVIII of the by-laws states: "All debates on controverted points of divinity or matters of the nation, governments, states or churches, shall be excluded from the conversation of this society, and whoever shall persist in such shall be fined...."[24] The secretary

[17] *Register of the Mesne Conveyance Office*, Book M8, pp. 399–402.
[18] *Register of Mesne Conference Office*, pp. 21–98.
[19] Adams, F. C., *Manuel Periera* (Washington, D.C., 1853), pp. 88–89.
[20] *Conveyance Deed Book*, H13, p. 237.
[21] *Ibid., Deed Book*, P15, p. 81.
[22] *Record of Wills*, Vol. 40, Book A, 1834–1839, pp. 289–290.
[23] *Rules and Regulations of the Brown Fellowship Society*. (1st November, 1790.)
[24] *Rules and Regulations of the Brown Fellowship Society*, p. 12.

of the organization kept very careful minutes of the proceedings of the meetings, and on one occasion when the mayor of the city asked to inspect them, because of a recently enacted law to prohibit more than seven Negroes to assemble at a time, the group was praised highly for its records and avowed objectives. So they were informed that the law was not intended for them.[25] Among other things the minutes showed that a member had been expelled from the society on April 17, 1817, for violating its rules.[26]

Now the question may be asked, what were the attitudes of this class to other groups in the community? As I envisage it, their behavior was a replica of that class in the white society which they aspired to be like. Their attitudes towards their slaves ranged from exploitation to humanitarianism. Again the wills which they left give us some indication of their position. In 1825 William Pinceel made the following stipulation in his will:

> I give and bequeath unto my Son Emanuel forever my Negro boy slave named Joe. I also give and bequeath unto Said Son for life my Negro boy slave named Tom and immediately after the death of my said Son, should the said Negro boy have conducted himself towards my Said Son as a faithful servant, then I direct that he be emancipated, but should he not have conducted himself then I give the said Negro boy to such person as my Said Son nominate and appoint in his last will and writing.[27]

The following will was made by a school teacher in 1831. He taught in Charleston between 1815 and 1830, and was one of the most active members of the Brown Fellowship Society:

> I desire that soon after my decease instruction shall be given to have all my stock and other things appertaining to my plantation in the country together with the plantation itself sold and the money arising from the same shall go to defray all expenses, taxes & provided however the said plantation cannot be sold at a fair price and it can be worked by the hands now there viz. Scipio, Abram and Peggy so as to pay expenses taxes and so forth in such case the same shall not be sold but retained for the benefit of the family if at all event, the Negroes on said plantation whose names are above mentioned be disposed of there shall be an exception of Scipio whom it is my wish shall be retained together with my slaves in town viz.: Fanny and Mary to be subservient to the wishes of my beloved wife Jennet Bonneau and children.[28]

Some of these masters also left their slaves or former slaves provided for

[25] Jervey, T. D., *Robert Y. Haynes and His Times*, pp. 63–69. Jervey quotes here a letter which he obtained from the minutes of the Society.

[26] *Ibid.*

[27] *Record of Wills*, Vol. 36, Book C, 1818–1826, p. 1125.

[28] *Ibid.*, Vol. 39, Book C, 1826–1834, p. 905.

economically. In 1859 John L. Francis left $1,000 to one servant and $200 to another, together with his wardrobe.[29]

The emphasis which the free Negro of this class placed upon mixed blood, free ancestry, economic position, and a devotion to the tenets of the slave system set them apart from and above other classes in the community. Moreover, their in-group tendencies were so strong that the free black people of the city were constrained to organize themselves into a society of free blacks. The first rule of this society says that it will "... consist of a number of respectable Free Dark men, as a majority may determine: not less than seven or more than thirty-five which number of seven shall be considered a quorum to transact business at any time...." [30]

It is fair to say that the upper caste free Negro served as a custodian of the system. He interrupted plans which the detached, discontented, underprivileged Negroes designed to overthrow or to offend the mores of the system. In 1822 the Intended Denmark Vesey Insurrection [31] was circumvented by a member of this class who instructed an informed slave to go and tell his master. The insurrection had been in the process of development for four years and was considered one of the most intricate ever undertaken in this country. It had as its model the uprising of the blacks in San Domingo. Its leader had travelled through the Islands as the slave of a slave trader. Upon receiving his freedom he settled in Charleston and assumed the position of the leader of the slaves. It is estimated that from 6,000 to 9,000 slaves were identified with this movement. Only about thirty of the leaders were executed for the plot.[32] On the other hand the slave who divulged the plans was emancipated by the State of South Carolina and paid an annual stipend for the rest of his life.[33] Meantime the free Negro received $1,000 and exemption from taxation for the rest of his life.[34]

There are other evidences of unrest, but I shall take time to mention only a few of them. Between 1832 and 1853 approximately 400 free Negroes left South Carolina for Liberia, Africa.[35] They were impelled by the claims of the American Colonization Society on the one hand and the insecurity of their positions on the other. In a mass meeting which was held by this group in 1831 in the interest of emigrating to Africa, the theme was that "in Liberia

[29] *Ibid.*, Vol. 51, Book B, 1862–1868, p. 588.

[30] Browning, J. B., "The Beginnings of Insurance Enterprise among Negroes," *Journal of Negro History*, Vol. XXII, No. 4, Oct., 1937, p. 424.

[31] "Denmark Vesey," *The Atlantic Monthly*, Vol. 7, 1861, pp. 728–744.

[32] *Ibid.*, p. 740.

[33] *Statutes at Large of South Carolina*, Vol. 6, p. 194. This volume was the property of Jonathan Jasper Wright, the Negro Associate Justice of the Supreme Court of South Carolina during the Reconstruction era. He is the only Negro ever to hold such a position in the United States. His books were donated to Claflin College, S.C. by the late Dr. William Francis Holmes of Florence, S.C. Dr. Holmes read law under Judge Wright and the degree was conferred upon him at Claflin University.

[34] *Ibid.*, p. 195.

[35] *The African Repository and Colonial Journal*, Vol. III (Washington, D.C., 1833), "Opinions of a Freeman of Colour in Charleston," Oct., 1832, pp. 241–242, pp. 76–77.

you will enjoy moral and political freedom." In December, 1832, one-hundred-forty-six persons of this class departed from Charleston for Liberia.[36] As far as I have been able to ascertain none of them were members of the Brown Fellowship Society.

The relations which the aristocratic free Negro sustained in his own family and among other members of his group deserve study and analysis. They provided for the education of their children; they married inside a restricted class; dowries were apparently provided for the daughters; and great care was taken in the protection and transmission of property and slaves.

In 1794 George Bedon indicated in his will that:

...it is my particular desire and request that my two Sons.... should be brought up in a Christian like manner and kept to school for the benefit of an Education until they arrive at the age of fifteen years then my two sons to be bound out during the term of six years to some handicraft trade under a kind and able master and in like manner my Daughter until she arrives at the age of fourteen years to be bound to a discreet and careful Mantua-maker a person of good character who will be so kind as to take care of an orphans morals as well as to teach her the trade.[37]

In 1861 Jacob Weston, one of the wealthier members of this caste, stipulated in his will that his wife and son should live in England after his death and that the son should be educated there. It was indicated that they be maintained out of the family estate.[38] The same testator designated that the support of his wife should be revoked if she married again.[39]

As was the practice generally, so it was in this group that marriage and courtship relations were expected to have the approval of the parents of the interested parties. The following letter was written in 1832, in reply to one which a young man had sent to the parents of his friend:

Charleston, March 19th, 1832

DEAR SIR:

It affords me the pleasure of giving you the approbation of Mr. Kougley and myself towards the affection you have for my daughter Cecelia. It has met her approbation for your visiting the house on her account, as to your standing in life we are perfectly acquainted with, as to objections we can have none, therefore we must join both hand and heart in wishing you all the prosperity and happiness this world can afford. I hope it is with the approbation of your family that you have addressed my daughter with respect. Dear Sir

We are yours,

Jacob and Mary Kougley [40]

---

[36] *Ibid.*, Vol. XXXIII, May, 1857, No. 5, pp. 152–155.
[37] *Record of Wills*, Vol. 25, Book A, 1793–1800, p. 208.
[38] *Records of Wills*, Vol. 50, Book A, 1860–68, p. 222.
[39] *Ibid.*
[40] *The Holloway Scrap Book.*

The Marriage Book of St. Phillip's Church, founded in 1672, shows that 168 mulattoes were married by the rectors of that institution between 1828 and 1860.[41] There were a considerable number of marriages among the families who were either business partners or who were identified with the same social and fraternal organization; in other words by usage and expectation, selections were made from in-group members. Records show that even the slaves of business partners entered into marriage relations. On November 16, 1837, Mingo, the slave of R. E. Dereef, was married to Hatira, the slave of Robert Howard.[42] These men were partners in the wood business.

The exhibition of a feeling of class-consciousness and the effort to maintain group solidarity were best exemplified in the activities of the Brown Fellowship Society. Through this medium social relations were cultivated, a system of education fostered, provisions for caring for the sick, the orphan and widow were made; and many men of wealth acted in an advisory and legal capacity as executors of the last wills of the members of the group.[43] When the Society was one hundred years old its name was changed to the *Century Fellowship Society*. Early in the twentieth century an auxiliary organization was formed which they named the *Daughters of the Century Fellowship Society*. The object of this branch of the association ". . . the erection of a hall to the memory of the men who won a page in the social history of the eighteenth century." [44] On the 117th anniversary of the organization, the president, in his annual address, epitomized the career of his caste in the following words: "Fortunately there were the classes in society, and as our forefathers allied themselves with them, as a consequence they had their influence and protection and they had to be in accord with them and stood for what they stood for. If they stood for high incentive so did our fathers. *If they stood for slavery so did our fathers to a certain extent but they sympathized with the oppressd,* for they had to endure some of it. . . ." [45]

In conclusion, the free Negro of Charleston answers nicely to the "marginal man" concept.[46] By virtue of his biological characteristics; because of his partial accessibility to two social worlds; as a result of his feeling of superiority to one of these worlds, and his position of inferiority to the other, he was either constrained to become a misfit or to carve out a position which the community accepted and which he respected. Because of the nature of the social system he became a member of a separate caste which incorporated the interests, loyal-

---

[41] By the courtesy of Rev. Merritt Williams, Rector of St. Phillip's Church, the writer was permitted to examine the *Marriage Book* for entries of free Negroes.

[42] *Marriage Book of St. Phillip's Church.*

[43] *Minute Book of the Brown Fellowship Society*, 1869–1911. This material was made accessible through the courtesy of Mr. W. S. Montgomery, the Secretary.

[44] *The Holloway Scrapbook.*

[45] *Ibid.*

[46] Stonequist, Everett V., "The Problem of the Marginal Man," *The American Journal of Sociology*, Vol. XLI, July, 1935, pp. 3–4; and Park, Robert E., "Human Migration and the Marginal Man," *The American Journal of Sociology*, Vol. XXXIII (1928), pp. 881–893.

ties and usages of the upper caste members of the society in so far as this behavior did not offend or disturb the hierarchical arrangements. In this position he was able to circumvent the harsh ordinances which were designed to perpetuate the slave economy and to assuage the circumstances of his existence.

It is fair to say, however, that when the system was disrupted during the Civil War, this group provided the leadership, and the basis of organized, stable life for the Negro community.

This study has shown that (1) intimate human relations, whether between subordinates and superiors or between persons of equal rank, result in irresistible and inevitable *claims* [47] and *obligations* of each upon the other. In this case these relations gave rise to the emergence of a large group of free Negroes in the slave society. (2) City life with its heterogeneous population and its consequent conflict and fusion of cultures, with its competition and division of labor, tends to secularize human relations and institutions, and to facilitate freedom of movement, action and thought. Hence, if the city economy is to move on with efficiency, even the lowest servant in it must have economic value, and this is inevitably interlaced with the process of mobility. The city offered the free Negro his best opportunity for economic success. It is further shown that (3) in a society in which a group's position is not definitely defined by the mores and traditions efforts will be made to copy the patterns of conduct of those groups which have prestige, recognition and security. Lastly, it is shown that (4) the extent to which this class of Negroes in Charleston differed from similar groups in the total slave economy marked the extent to which the modes of life and patterns of conduct in the community as a whole, differed from the rest of the slave communities. The difference, in other words, is one of degree rather than kind.

[47] This idea was received from a lecture by Dr. R. E. Park in a class in collective behavior in the summer of 1935 at the University of Chicago. The course was offered by Dr. Herbert Blumer.

John Hope Franklin

THE FREE NEGRO IN THE ECONOMIC LIFE

OF ANTE-BELLUM NORTH CAROLINA

*Free Negro farmers have received far less attention than their coun-
terparts in the towns. A pioneering student of the agrarian group was
the late Luther P. Jackson, who uncovered detailed evidence about
free Negro farmers through intensive research in the musty records
of Virginia county courthouses. Their ranks included laborers, tenants
and landowners.* In North Carolina, where the urban population was
small, the free Negro farmers were, relatively speaking, an even more
important segment of the population than they were in the neighboring states of Virginia and South Carolina. In the selection that
follows, John Hope Franklin describes the farming operations and
property holdings of the free Negro yeomanry in North Carolina,
which, like the other older southern states, had a substantial free
Negro population that was practically absent from the Deep South,
except in Louisiana.*

I N a state that was as decidedly rural as ante-bellum North Carolina, and
where the majority of the free Negroes lived in the rural areas,[1] it was only
natural that most of them made their living from the soil. The majority of the
free Negro apprentices were bound out to learn the trade of a farmer, and upon
reaching manhood they expected to pursue this occupation.[2] Since, moreover,

John Hope Franklin, "The Free Negro in the Economic Life of Ante-Bellum
North Carolina," Part II, *North Carolina Historical Review*, XIX (October, 1942),
pp. 359–375. Reprinted with the permission of the *North Carolina Historical Review*.
    * Luther P. Jackson, "The Virginia Free Negro Farmer and Property Owner,
1830–1860," *Journal of Negro History*, XXIV (October, 1939).
    [1] Only 3,197, or scarcely ten percent, of the free Negroes lived in towns in 1860.
Census Office, *The Population in 1860*, pp. 350–359.
    [2] See the occupations of free Negro apprentices in the unpublished population
schedules for the census of 1860. (Unless otherwise indicated, all manuscripts cited in
this article are in the archives of the North Carolina Historical Commission, Raleigh.)

it was extremely difficult for free Negroes to secure training in the skilled trades, many who may have had the inclination were forced into other fields. They *had* to make a living. Tradition and their meager training compelled the majority of the free Negroes to seek their living from the soil.

North Carolina was never one of the chief slaveholding states. In numbers, its slaves were fewer than those of her neighbor states of Virginia, South Carolina, and Georgia.[3] As a matter of fact, sixty-seven per cent of the slaveholding families held fewer than ten slaves in 1860, while seventy-two per cent of North Carolina's families held no slaves at all.[4] This suggests that in a state where the plantation system was only fairly well entrenched, the supply of slave labor was definitely limited. The farm labor in North Carolina was done not only by the slave but, in some areas, by the members of the white farming family, by white farm laborers, and by free Negro farm laborers.[5] In finding this work opportunity, the free Negro was extremely fortunate, and his labor was not as frequently rejected as it was in the more skilled occupations. Naturally there were objections to his presence on plantations where there were slaves, but these objections were more likely to be raised to the hiring of free Negroes on the neighbor's plantation than on one's own. Though there may have been fears that the free Negro's presence on a slave plantation might cause insolence among the slaves as well as inspire desires of freedom among them, this did not prevent the white slaveholders from hiring free Negroes to perform some of the tasks from time to time.[6]

There was, moreover, an opportunity for the free Negro to secure seasonal work on the farms of North Carolinians who had no slaves at all. The yeoman frequently harbored violent antipathies for the slave system and would refuse to hire slave labor even when it was available. He was more likely to look for assistance, during rush seasons, among the poor landless whites or among the free Negroes. The large number of free Negro farm laborers in counties where there was little or no slaveholding seems to support this point of view. In Cabarrus County, for example, where the slave population was small, there were fourteen free Negro farm laborers in 1860 and only four free Negro farmers.[7]

Naturally there were more free Negro farm hands in counties where the

---

[3] Census Office, *Population in 1860*, pp. 214, 452, 518.

[4] Guion G. Johnson, *Ante-Bellum North Carolina*, p. 468 ff.

[5] In describing the small farmer (white) in ante-bellum North Carolina, Dr. Guion Johnson refers to this group as the largest single class of whites in the state, and continues, "Their farms were small, and they cultivated their own land with the assistance of their families and an occasional hired hand or slave." Johnson, *Ante-Bellum North Carolina*, p. 65.

[6] See the unpublished population schedules for the census of 1860. Many free Negro farm laborers were listed as living with white families. This is all the more remarkable in view of the fact that, in such instances, the white farmer was responsible for all of the debts and obligations that were incurred by the free Negro.

[7] See the unpublished population schedules for the census of 1860. It is quite likely, moreover, that many of the free Negroes who gave their occupation as "common laborer" found work on the farms and may have been, more properly, "farm hands."

free Negro population was large. These counties, incidentally, also had a large slave population. As field hands, drivers, and all-around laborers, free Negroes found work opportunities on the largest of plantations. It was not unusual for free Negroes to live on slave plantations and to participate in the life there. Some of them had slave wives or husbands, and the benevolent master frequently permitted them to live there together, hiring the services of the free person.[8] Thomas Newton of Craven County secured his freedom from his master, Benjamin Woods, and by continuing to work for him Newton was able to purchase his wife, who had been a slave on the same plantation.[9]

Of course the number of free Negro farm laborers varied from county to county. The number to be found in any particular county depended not only upon the scarcity or abundance of farm labor, slave or free, and the attitude of the whites toward free Negro labor, but also upon the mobility of the landless free Negro population. It was extremely difficult for free Negroes, although without the trappings which usually tie people to a particular location, to move from one place to another. The reluctance of the authorities to grant passes permitting free Negroes to move about [10] and the impecunious state of a majority of the free Negroes made it quite difficult for free Negro farm laborers to migrate even to the adjoining county. It was possible, therefore, for a newly freed Negro to live and die in an area that was least suited for his advancement.

With these facts in mind, it is interesting to observe the location of the bulk of the free Negro farm hands in ante-bellum North Carolina. Of the 1,746 free Negro farm hands in the state in 1860, more than one thousand were located in the seven eastern counties which constituted the stronghold of the slave system.[11] Halifax County alone had 384 free Negro farm hands, while Pasquotank County had 284. Thirty-one counties were without any free Negro farm hands at all, while 700 were scattered among the remaining forty-eight counties.[12]

A more interesting group of free Negroes who made their living from the soil were those who either rented land or owned land and planted their own crops. They may properly be called the free Negro yeomanry. It was possible for a free Negro to obtain permission from a white landowner to live on the

---

[8] See, for example, the unpublished population schedules for the census of 1860 (Wake County). It seems that such a practice was quite inconsistent with the point of view that the presence of free Negroes among slaves "contributes to excite and cherish a spirit of discontent and disorder among the slaves." Petition of the citizens of New Bern to the General Assembly, December, 1831, MS. in the Legislative Papers for 1831–1832.

[9] Minutes of the Court of Pleas and Quarter Sessions for Craven County, March, 1811.

[10] After 1831 free Negroes desiring to go to other countries had to receive a license from the clerk of the Court of Pleas and Quarter Sessions of the county in which they resided. *Laws, 1830–1831*, p. 11.

[11] The seven counties were Granville, Halifax, Hertford, Northampton, Pasquotank, Perquimans, and Sampson.

[12] This information was taken from the unpublished population schedules for the census of 1860. Most of the counties with no free Negro farm hands were located in the western part of the state.

latter's land and to cultivate a portion of it and share in the returns from his labor. This, however, was looked upon with disfavor, and white owners of land were discouraged in the practice. A law of 1827 required each white person to list all free Negroes living on his land and to be responsible for the taxes which might be levied on such free Negroes.[13] Free Negro tenants who showed a disposition to work and to shoulder their responsibilities could still convince landowners that they would not be a burden to them. The tax lists of various counties and the census reports bear witness to the fact that there were free Negro tenants on the lands of white persons down to the end of the period. In the tax list for Beaufort County in 1850, for example, A. Eborn, a free Negro, was listed as the tenant of John Cutter, white. One wealthy white farmer, R. H. Reddick of Lower Broad Creek, had fourteen free Negro tenants on his land and was responsible for $143.93 in taxes for them. In the same list, F. Hackey, a free Negro, was the tenant of Samuel Swan, white.[14] At the end of the period, despite the financial risks on the part of white landowners, many free Negro tenants were still living on the land of white landowners.[15]

That the number of free Negroes who owned their farms was considerable can be seen in the real property columns of the unpublished population schedules of the census returns. Many of these individuals, like John Stanly of New Bern, had started with small holdings, and by thrift and business acumen had accumulated sizable holdings. They usually engaged in tobacco and cotton farming and marketed their crops in much the same way that other farmers in the state marketed theirs. By far the majority of the property owned by free Negroes was in the rural areas and was, of course, in the possession of free Negro farmers.

The free Negro farmer was generally in better circumstances than free Negroes in other areas of economic activity. In 1860 there were 1,047 free Negroes who gave their occupation as farmers. Of this number, approximately fifty per cent possessed some real property. In some cases they did not own an amount sufficient for their purposes, but the figures seem to suggest that the free Negro was becoming a landowner. David Reynolds, a farmer of Halifax County, owned $3,000 worth of real property in 1860. J. A. Collins of Hyde County had $1,000 worth of real property at the same time. The well known Thomas Blacknall of Franklin County owned $6,000 worth of land. Of the fifty-three Negroes with property valued at more than $2,500 each in 1860, thirty-one were farmers.[16]

In North Carolina the free Negroes who made their living from the soil numbered approximately three thousand. Doubtless this number could be augmented considerably when one takes into account the number of minors and

[13] *Laws*, 1827–1828, p. 21.

[14] MS. in the County Records for Beaufort County, 1850 (Beaufort County Courthouse, Washington, N.C.).

[15] See the unpublished population schedules for the census of 1860.

[16] Unpublished population schedules for the census of 1860.

housewives who assisted their fathers, brothers, and husbands in the fields. That they constituted the most important element in the economic life of the free Negro in ante-bellum North Carolina in terms of numbers and holdings is clearly shown by the facts. For the most part they went their way unnoticed. The disproportionate part of the stage occupied by the free Negroes in other pursuits was the result of the focus of light thrown upon them in the more thickly settled communities. Meanwhile the free Negro farmer, living in the inarticulate and relatively sparsely settled countryside, steadily rose in economic independence and, consequently, in the respect—somewhat disquieted, perhaps—of his fellows.

At no time during the period before the Civil War was the free Negro's right to own real property questioned. He enjoyed all the protection in the matter of acquisition, transfer, devise, and descent that other citizens of North Carolina enjoyed. The records of the county courts indicate that free Negroes used them regularly for the purpose of recording changes in ownership of real and personal property. The following record is typical of many that were found in the minutes of the county court: "A deed from Ezra F. Holmes to Southey Kease (free Negro) was proved in open court by the oath of William T. Bryan a witness thereto ordered to be registered." [17]

Having once acquired land, the free Negro could be fairly certain that the courts would protect him during his period of possession. In 1838 Benjamin Curry, a free Negro of Guilford County, was driven off the property which he had owned for twelve years. Of the four white men charged with dispossessing Curry, one claimed that the free Negro had sold him his house, land, and five slave children, and that the transaction had been executed in a deed of trust between the two parties. At the trial the solicitor for the state objected to the deed as evidence, contending that it was a slick piece of extortion and that the free Negro did not intend to give up his land. The lower court convicted the defendants of having "riotously and routously" assembled to disturb the peace of the state and with force of arms trespassed upon the property of the free Negro.

The defendants appealed the case to the Supreme Court. After making a thorough review of the facts in the case and after listening to lengthy arguments from both sides, Judge Gaston, speaking for the Court, said:

> We are of the opinion that there was no error in the conviction of which the defendant complains. In cases where the law gives to the judges a discretion over the quantum of punishment, they may, with propriety, suspend the sentence [In this case, the principal defendant had received a fine of $100.] for the avowed purpose of affording the convicted an opportunity to make restitution to the person peculiarly aggrieved by his offense.
>
> The judgment against the defendant is, therefore, reversed, and

[17] Minutes of the Court of Pleas and Quarter Sessions for Beaufort County, December, 1843 (Beaufort County Courthouse, Washington, N.C.).

this opinion is to be certified to the Superior Court—for the County of Guilford, with directions to award sentence of fine or of fine and imprisonment against the defendant agreeably thereto and to the laws of the state.[18]

The leniency of Judge Gaston was inspired by the defendant's having already restored the property to the free Negro. Though there was a reversal of the conviction, the case remains significant in that the Supreme Court went on record as being vigorously opposed to the abridgment of property rights even in the case of a free Negro.[19]

Free Negroes could sell or transfer their land at will as long as it was for a legal consideration. In 1833, for example, Benjamin Neale of Craven County sold one hundred acres of land, and the following indenture makes known the transaction:

February 4, 1833)
State of N.C.   )
County of Craven)
    Be it known that Benjamin Neale (coloured man) for and in consideration of the sum of fifty dollars to me paid in hand by William B. Masters of the same State and County aforesaid, have bargained sold enfeoffed and confirmed unto the same Wm. B. Masters his heirs and assigns forever a certain parcel of land. . . . [A description of the land is given.] The said Benjamin Neale purchased of Thomas Cooke dec. containing by estimation one hundred acres be the same more or less. To have and to hold the said piece or parcel of land with all the woods ways waters and every other appurtenances thereunto belonging against the lawful claims of all and every other person.
                                                        Benjamin Neale [20]

The right of a free Negro to sell his property was confirmed by the Supreme Court in a decision of 1843. A white man, Pearson, rented a small tract of land for one year to Elijah Powell, a free Negro, who promised to give him one-half of the corn crop. The Justice of the Peace gave Pearson permission to sell Powell's crop. Powell asked that the sale be postponed until after the corn was gathered. When the corn was sold, one Hare objected, saying that he had already bought half of the crop from Powell. Pearson denied that Powell could sell his share, contending that he was only a servant. The Nash Superior Court said that Powell was a tenant and could dispose of his property as he

[18] State v. John H. Bennett, 20 N.C., p. 135 ff.
[19] See also the case of State v. Emory, 51 N.C., p. 142, in which the Supreme Court held that a free Negro could not be forcibly ejected from the possession of a house.
[20] MS. in the James W. Bryan Papers (University of North Carolina Library, Chapel Hill, N.C.). See also the deed from John and Rebecca Hambleton, free Negroes, to Churchill Moore, in the Minutes of the Court of Pleas and Quarter Sessions for Beaufort County, December, 1842 (Beaufort County Courthouse, Washington, N.C.).

pleased. In upholding this view, the Supreme Court, through Judge Daniel, said:

> Even if Powell was a servant, the division had given him a share which all would have to admit. The corn had been placed in the defendant's barn upon the naked bailment for safe-keeping. The sale of it and the demand by the purchaser put an end to the bailment.[21]

It was not at all unusual for free Negroes to direct the disposition of their property through wills. Upon the death of the testator, the will was recorded in the minutes of the county court and an executor was appointed by the court. The minutes of the Beaufort County Court for 1843 give a typical example:

> State of North Carolina)
> Beaufort County   )
> A paper writing purporting to be the last will and testament of John Hambleton deceased (free Negro) was duly proved in open court to be the last will and testament of said John Hambleton and duly executed so as to pass seal on personal estate by the oath of John W. Latham the subscribing witness thereto and ordered to be recorded and Edward Hyman the Executor named therein was qualified as Executor.[22]

An interesting case involving the will of a free Negro woman was that of the aged Mary Green of Wilmington, who left all of her property to a white attorney. She looked to him not only for counsel, the records showed, but also for protection and occasionally small sums of money. In addition to these favors, he also collected rent on the property that had been accumulated by the testator's free Negro husband. The only relative, a niece, had received a house and lot from her aunt before she died. Upon the advice of the free Negro husband, all the property was left to the white attorney. The niece went into court and contended that her aunt had been under "undue influence" and sought to have the will invalidated. Upon losing the case in the New Hanover Superior Court, the niece appealed to the Supreme Court. In upholding the decision of the lower court, Judge Manly said,

> It seems that the legatee [Joshua Wright] and the decedent [Mary Green] stood in relation of client and attorney *patron* and *dependent*, and the court below—informs the jury that persons bearing these relations are to be suspected and scrutinized more closely and carefully

---

[21] Hare v. Pearson, 26 N.C., p. 62.

[22] Minutes of the Court of Pleas and Quarter Sessions of Beaufort County, June, 1843 (Beaufort County Courthouse, Washington, N.C.). Free Negroes were sometimes appointed executors, as in the case of Southey Keis, of Beaufort County, who in March, 1856, appeared in court and qualified as the executor of the estate of Mary Keis. Minutes of the Court of Pleas and Quarter Sessions of Beaufort County, March, 1856 (Beaufort County Courthouse, Washington, N.C.).

than dealings between others. These relations, as facts pertinent to the issue—were submitted to the jury with proper instructions. That was all, we think, the court was authorized to do by the law of the land.

We concur with the court below that undue influence must be fraudulent and controlling and must be shown to the satisfaction of a jury, in a court of law, upon an issue of *devisavit vel nom*.[23]

Free Negroes, as other individuals, sometimes had difficulty in establishing their rightful claim to property left to them in a will. If, however, their freedom could be established and if the circumstances under which the will was made were valid, the free Negro could secure the necessary protection in the courts of the state. In 1851, one Benjamin Dicken of Edgecombe County died. His will directed his executor to free all of his slaves and send them to some free state and divide $12,000 among them. All except one woman, who died soon after, left the state. Her daughter, who had gone to Canada, claimed her mother's share of the estate for her and the other children. The executor claimed that the mother had not complied with the stipulation of the will since she had not left the state and therefore, that her heirs could claim no part of the money intended for her. Judge Pearson, of the Supreme Court, said that the removing of the Negroes was not a condition precedent to emancipation, but a condition subsequent, "by the non-performance of which they may forfeit their newly acquired freedom." The Judge was satisfied that the deceased free Negro woman had good intentions:

1. We are satisfied that Mariah the mother of the plaintiff at the time of her death—was to all intents and purposes, a free woman, and had the capacity to take property and transmit it by succession to her personal representative.

2. We are also satisfied that the children of Mariah were entitled to call upon her administrator to make distribution among them, as her next of kin—and we think it clear that all of her children are to be considered distributees.[24]

In one case several technicalities arose which made it difficult for a free Negro devisee to retain the town property that had been left her by a wealthy white man of Tarboro. In his will he said: "I give and devise to Mary Ann Jones, a free colored woman of the town of Tarboro and to her heirs and assigns forever, the lot of ground and house thereon erected on which she now lives." Since two lots belonging to the testator were adjacent, the executor interpreted the will literally and proceeded to take possession of the lot next to the one on which the devisee's house stood. Before his death, the testator had fenced in both lots together, and the free Negro woman used both lots for a garden and for other purposes. In 1860 Judge Manly of the Supreme Court awarded both lots to the estate of the free Negro woman—by that

[23] Wright *v.* Howe, 20 N.C., 318.
[24] Alvany, a free woman of color, *v.* Powell, 54 N.C., p. 34.

time deceased. He took the point of view that the gift to the free Negro woman "is not confined to the fifty yards square called a lot in the plan of the town, but extends at least to the lands enclosed and used in connection with the house." In the will the testator used the word "lot" to mean "parcel" or "piece." [25]

Perhaps the most interesting case of the period involving the inheritance of property by free Negroes arose in 1857. While a slave, a certain Miles married another slave. Afterward he was freed and subsequently purchased his wife. They had one child; then the wife was set free, and they had several other children. After this wife died, Miles married a free Negro woman by whom he had three children. When he died intestate, in 1857, a contest arose between the two sets of children over the division of the property. The children by the first wife claimed tenancy in common with the children by the second wife. When the case came before the Supreme Court, that body denied that the children by the first wife had any valid claims:

> A slave cannot make a contract. Therefore, he cannot marry legally. Marriage is based upon contract. Consequently, the relation of "man and wife" cannot exist among slaves. Neither the first nor the others of the children by the first wife were legitimate. The parties after being freed ought to have married according to law; it is the misfortune of their children that they neglected or refused to do so, for no court can avert the consequences.[26]

The possession of slaves by free Negroes was the only type of personal property holding that was ever questioned during the ante-bellum period. There may not have been much objection to the ownership of one's own family by a free Negro; but when one undertook to acquire slaves to improve his economic status, there were those who looked upon it as a dangerous trend, the legality of which was seriously questioned. If the free Negro was not a full citizen, could he enjoy the same privileges of ownership and the protection of certain types of property that other citizens enjoyed? Around this question revolved a great deal of discussion at the beginning of the militant period of the antislavery movement.[27]

When a slave was found guilty of concealing a slave on board a vessel, in violation of the act of 1825, it was contended by his owner that the prisoner, a slave, was not a person or mariner within the meaning of the act and that Green, the owner of the concealed slave, was a mulatto and hence not a citizen of the state and could not own slaves. The decision of the Supreme Court, handed down in 1833 by Judge Daniel, established once and for all the rights

[25] Doe on the demise of Mary Ann Jones *v.* Norfleet, 20 N.C., p. 365. A plan of the lots was included in the report of the court.

[26] Doe on the demise of Frances Howard *v.* Sarah Howard, 51 N.C., p. 238.

[27] Since the possession of slaves enhanced one's social position in the community, the whites may well have objected to the ownership of slaves by free Negroes on the grounds that it would tend to upset the social structure—or that by such possession the free Negroes might begin to feel that they had "arrived" socially.

of the free Negro in the matter of the ownership of slaves. He said:

> By the laws of this State, a free man of color may own land and hold lands and personal property including slaves. Without therefore stopping to inquire into the extent of the political rights and privileges of a free man of color, I am very well satisfied from the words of the act of the General Assembly that the Legislature meant to protect the slave property of every person who by the laws of the State are entitled to hold such property. I am, therefore, of the opinion that the owner is a citizen within the meaning of the Act of Assembly, and it appearing he was a mulatto is not a reason to grant a new trial to the person who concealed his slave.[28]

The decision of Judge Daniel in this case remained the accepted point of view until the very end of the period. When the hostility between the sections was developing into open conflict, the free Negro in the South witnessed an almost complete abrogation of his rights. One of the most significant laws passed during the momentous session of the legislature in 1860–1861 was the "Act to prevent free Negroes from having the control of slaves." While it did not affect a large number of free Negroes within the state,[29] it showed the extent to which the North Carolina solons were willing to go in order to combat the forces that were striking at the heart of their long-cherished system. Among other things, the law provided:

> That no free Negro, or free person of color, shall be permitted or allowed to buy, purchase, or hire for any length of time any slave or slaves, or to have any slave or slaves bound as apprentice or apprentices to him, her or them, or in any other wise to have the control, management or services of any slave or slaves, under the penalty of one hundred dollars for each offence, and shall further be guilty of a misdemeanor, and liable to indictment for the same.

Another section of the law provided that free Negroes already in the possession of slave property would not be affected by the enactment.[30]

Despite the innumerable obstacles that stood in the way of the accumulation of property by free Negroes, several amassed a considerable amount of property during their lifetime. The life of Julius Melbourn is about as interesting as one can find in the period. Born a slave in 1790 on a plantation near Raleigh, he was bought, at five years of age, by the wealthy widow of a British army official, who lived in Raleigh. When her only son was slain in a duel—said to have been fought because of some derogatory remarks concerning his mother having reared Melbourn as a gentleman—the slave was emancipated and made the sole heir to the estate of $20,000. By the time Melbourn

---

[28] State v. Edmund, a slave, 15 N.C., p. 278.

[29] The number of free Negroes who owned slaves was steadily decreasing. See below, pp. 372, 373.

[30] Laws, 1860–1861, p. 69.

was twenty-five years old his estate was worth about $30,000. By careful saving and shrewd investment, he was soon worth $50,000. When he decided that he could not live and die in a country "where the laws sustained and justified such disregard to individual rights and tolerated such inhumanity," as was manifested in the treatment of free Negroes, he sailed for England, where he spent the remainder of his life. That he was still wealthy is attested by the fact that he set up his son in a $20,000 mercantile business in London.[31]

Most of the free Negroes who owned property were possessors of small estates worth a few hundred dollars or less. These individuals, moreover, comprised only a small percentage of the total free Negro population. The great majority of free Negroes in North Carolina were, during the entire period, without any property whatsoever. At the end of the period, only 3,659, or slightly more than ten per cent, owned any property. Of this number, only 1,211 owned any real estate. In few counties did more than ten per cent of the free Negroes own property. Craven County, with 1,332 free Negroes in 1860, had only 179 free Negro property owners. Cabarrus County, with 115 free Negroes, had twelve free Negro owners of property. Halifax County, with its 3,452 free Negroes, however, had 463 free Negroes who owned property.[32] In 1860 the following free Negroes had property valued at $2,500 or more: [33] While this table does not represent the average holdings of the free Negro in ante-bellum North Carolina, it suggests that there was a number of individual cases in which free Negroes rose to a position of economic independence, despite obstacles.

In six counties in 1860 free Negroes owned no real estate.[34] While each county listed some personal property held by free Negroes, eight counties listed only one such person each.[35] Perhaps nothing is a more striking commentary on the plight of the free Negro in North Carolina than his inability to acquire property, both real and personal.

A study of the value of the property which free Negroes did possess will shed further light on the economic status of the free Negro in ante-bellum North Carolina. Of course it is difficult for one living in the fifth decade of the twentieth century to appreciate the figures which reveal the value of property owned by free Negroes in, say, 1860. Land values were so much lower at the time that it was quite possible for an individual with one hundred dollars worth of real property to have an adequate amount for farming purposes, and with a few hundred dollars he could erect a house that would be about as modern as the age could provide. There was a likelihood, however, that the land of the free Negro would be the least desirable in a given area.

---

[31] Julius Melbourn, *Life and Opinions of Julius Melbourn, passim.*

[32] Unpublished population schedules for the census of 1860.

[33] These statistics were compiled from the unpublished population schedules for the census of 1860.

[34] They were Alleghany, Davie, Harnett, Haywood, Jackson, and Madison. Interestingly enough, none of these counties was in the eastern part of the state.

[35] They were Catawba, Haywood, Henderson, Hyde, Jackson, Martin, McDowell, and Rutherford.

FREE NEGROES HAVING PROPERTY VALUED AT MORE THAN $2,500

Name	Occupation	Value	Name	Occupation	Value
Alee, M.	Baker	$2,750	Knight, J.	Confection	$5,905
Alston, O.	Farmer	17,644	Lan'ton, D.	Carpenter	2,500
Bell, H.		14,000	Lewis, W.	Farmer	2,750
Bethel, J.	Barber	3,550	Locklier	Farmer	5,200
Blacknall, T.	Farmer	7,300	Mangum, L.	Farmer	20,816
Bryan, C.	Farmer	2,535	Martin, W.	Farmer	2,500
Burchett, J.	Farmer	2,500	Men'hall	Farmer	3,197
Butch, H.	Farm Hand	3,450	Michael, S.	Farmer	5,000
Collins, J.	Farmer	9,000	Miller, E.	Wheelwright	8,150
Corn, D.	Farmer	5,250	Moore, D.	Barber	4,400
Corn, N.	Farmer	2,800	Norris, A.	Carpenter	3,000
Cuff, N.	Farmer	3,475	Ox'dine, J.	Farmer	9,825
Day, T.	Cab. Maker	4,000	Picar, E.		2,500
Dial, G.	Farmer	4,900	Piles, A.	Clerk	5,000
Erwin, J.	Musician	3,100	Reed, W.	Farmer	3,300
Evans, E.	Farmer	11,830	Revel, E.	Farmer	4,826
Evans, W.	Farmer	3,932	Reynolds	Farmer	4,000
Freeman, J.	Farmer	20,300	Sampson, J.	Carpenter	36,000
Graham, J.	Farmer	2,800	Scott, A.	Farmer	3,766
Green, M.	Farmer	2,600	Silvester	Farmer	2,670
Guy, W.	Farmer	2,695	Smith, N.	Farmer	2,500
Hites, E.	Carpenter	4,000	Stanly, C.	Dress Maker	4,000
Howard, J.		2,500	Steward, W.	Farmer	3,000
Jacobs, J.	Farmer	3,712	Taboon, A.	Farm Hand	5,554
Jones, M.	Housekeeper	5,500	Webb, S.	Farmer	2,810
Jones, T.		6,700	Winn, C.	Blacksmith	2,800
Jordan, J.	Farmer	4,700			

Since the majority of free Negroes were small farmers, they faced the same difficulty that other North Carolina yeomen faced: that of trying to obtain satisfactory property in the same market where the more resourceful plantation owner was making his purchases. It is a point of interest, therefore, that some free Negroes, like John C. Stanly of New Bern and James D. Sampson of New Hanover, were able to acquire some of the most desirable land in their respective communities.

On the whole, a larger number of free Negroes possessed some type of personal property, ranging from silver watches to farming tools. Thus, in the larger number of counties, the value of personal property was higher than the value of real property. But the poverty of the free Negro group can be seen clearly through this study of the value of the property of the group. They possessed an aggregate wealth of $1,045,643. (See table below.) When one considers that more than 30,000 people had to share in this wealth of slightly more than one million dollars, the realization of their plight is inescapable. The per capita wealth of the free Negroes of North Carolina was only $34 in 1860. Thousands of these were landless and without any kind of property. Even when one ascertains the per capita wealth of the free Negro property owners, the picture remains gloomy, for they had a per capita wealth of $287.

It must be remembered that fifty-three were worth more than $2,500, while several were worth more than $15,000.[36] The following table shows the value of real and personal property of free Negroes in 1860.[37]

AGGREGATE VALUE OF PROPERTY OWNED BY FREE NEGROES

County	Real	Personal	County	Real	Personal
Alamance	$13,500	$7,415	Jackson		$125
Alexander	500	390	Johnston	$4,060	4,853
Alleghany		600	Jones	1,500	1,875
Anson	3,798	7,660	Lenoir	625	2,250
Ashe	2,200	2,495	Lincoln	100	270
Beaufort	12,410	6,960	Macon	4,050	5,100
Bertie	1,280	3,615	Madison		615
Bladen	6,289	5,112	Martin	5,549	1,200
Brunswick	6,487	6,239	McDowell	4,000	1,000
Buncombe	3,540	3,184	Mecklenburg	8,875	3,720
Burke	200	785	Montgomery	362	1,285
Cabarrus	1,072	2,050	Moore	550	1,975
Caldwell	1,295	1,284	Nash	8,939	10,889
Camden	1,000	768	New Hanover	37,720	35,060
Carteret	3,150	950	Northampton	12,824	15,359
Caswell	4,208	5,530	Onslow	1,735	3,475
Catawba	50	75	Orange	2,800	13,375
Chatham	1,680	2,960	Pasquotank	20,440	22,195
Cherokee	350	515	Perquimans	5,000	8,601
Chowan	3,600	2,793	Person	5,180	3,080
Cleveland	3,150	4,652	Pitt	2,100	5,560
Columbus	9,135	8,990	Polk	700	1,446
Craven	29,865	21,137	Randolph	5,290	8,745
Cumberland	11,500	7,722	Richmond	10,750	20,930
Currituck	1,270	1,745	Robeson	37,555	42,159
Davidson	1,200	1,428	Rockingham	2,750	1,900
Davie		1,040	Rowan	1,300	970
Duplin	3,360	3,777	Rutherford	225	100
Edgecombe	7,100	10,350	Sampson	10,014	4,742
Forsyth	1,530	1,665	Stanly	950	835
Franklin	6,535	6,013	Stokes	325	550
Gaston	2,700	2,300	Surry	925	1,144
Gates	5,125	18,755	Tyrrel	725	1,615
Granville	15,987	13,845	Union	300	975
Greene	2,475	2,920	Wake	22,204	45,362
Guilford	5,425	13,445	Warren	9,931	13,935
Halifax	30,948	42,778	Washington	5,843	5,077
Harnett		375	Watauga	475	595
Haywood		75	Wayne	13,380	9,900
Henderson	150	100	Wilkes	2,710	3,835
Hertford	15,482	16,624	Wilson	4,984	3,999
Hyde	1,000	8,000	Yadkin	840	2,912
Iredell	330	150	Yancey	1,525	1,803

[36] Unpublished population schedules for the census of 1860.

[37] These statistics were compiled from the unpublished population schedules for the census of 1860.

One area in which considerable interest has always been manifested is the ownership of slaves by free Negroes. At no time during the ante-bellum period were free Negroes in North Carolina without some slaves. The motives for such ownership were perhaps varied, as in other groups. Without a doubt there were those who possessed slaves for the purpose of advancing their economic well-being. With such a view in mind, these free Negro slaveholders were more interested in making their farms or carpenter shops "pay" than they were in treating their slaves humanely. The enterprising free Negro owners of slaves can usually be identified because of their extensive holdings of real and personal property and because of their inactivity in the manumission movement. For thirty years Thomas Day, the free Negro cabinet maker of Milton, used slaves to help him in his business. In 1830 he had two; [38] by 1860 he had three.[39] For thirty years Thomas Blacknall of Franklin County kept slaves, though the number fell from seven to three between 1830 and 1860.[40] It seems clear that these enterprising free Negroes were at least as deeply interested in the labor of their slaves as they were in their comfort.

It seems that by far the larger portion of free Negro owners of slaves were possessors of this human chattel for benevolent reasons. There are numerous examples of free Negroes having purchased relatives or friends to ease their lot. Many of them manumitted such slaves,[41] while others held title to slaves who were virtually free. An examination of the slaveholding by free Negroes seems to bear out this point. Slave Richard Gaston ran away from his master and remained in the woods until his free Negro wife had saved the necessary funds for his purchase.[42] Lila Abshur continued to hold title to her father when the legislature acted unfavorably on her petition to emancipate him.[43] While John S. Stanly undoubtedly held some slaves with the view to increasing his wealth,[44] he held others purely out of benevolence.[45]

The fluctuation in the number of free Negro owners of slaves during the period under observation is an interesting development. At the time of the taking of the first census in 1790, twenty-five free Negroes in eleven counties owned seventy-three slaves.[46] In 1830 the number of free Negro slaveholders had increased to 191, distributed in thirty-seven counties, while their human

---

[38] C. G. Woodson, *Free Negro Owners of Slaves in 1830*, p. 24.

[39] Unpublished population schedules for the census of 1860.

[40] Woodson, *Free Negro Owners*, p. 25, and the unpublished population schedules for the census of 1860.

[41] See the Minutes of the Court of Pleas and Quarter Sessions of Craven County, March, 1811. These records show that Thomas Newton, a free Negro, liberated his slave wife.

[42] C. D. Wilson, "Negroes Who Owned Slaves," *Popular Science Monthly*, LXXXI, p. 485.

[43] MS. in the Legislative Papers for 1856.

[44] In 1830 he held eighteen slaves. Woodson, *Free Negro Owners*, p. 24.

[45] In 1815 Stanly emancipated a slave woman and her five children, as well as a slave man. Minutes of the Court of Pleas and Quarter Sessions of Craven County, March, June, 1815.

[46] Census Office, *Heads of Families in the United States in 1790, passim.*

chattel numbered 620.[47] Interestingly enough, by 1860 there were only eight free Negro owners of slaves, the latter numbering only twenty-five.[48]

Several observations can now be made. In the first place, the number of slaves held by free Negroes was usually small. Notable exceptions are the eleven slaves held by Samuel Johnston of Bertie County in 1790;[49] the forty-four slaves each owned by Gooden Bowen of Bladen County and John Walker of New Hanover County in 1830; and the tweny-four slaves owned by John Chrichlon of Martin County in 1830.[50] Free Negroes usually held one, two, or three slaves; and the petitions of free Negroes to manumit relatives suggest that a sizable number of slaves had been acquired as a result of benevolence.

In the second place, the increase in the number of free Negroes with an accompanying increase in economic independence on the part of some caused a larger number of Negro slaves to be acquired by free Negroes. No doubt, moreover, there was some effort to conform to the pattern established by the dominant slaveholding group within the state in the effort to elevate themselves to a position of respect and privilege. Thus by 1830 more than 600 slaves were held by free Negroes. Finally, the remarkable decline both in the number of free Negro slave owners and in the number of slaves held toward the end of the period suggests the increasing economic and political difficulty that the free Negro was encountering. Many of those slaves held in 1830 had been manumitted according to the plans of the free Negro owners. Other slaves had been lost in the maze of the economic setbacks that many free Negroes were experiencing.[51] Perhaps also the fervor to acquire slave relatives and set them free was waning, as the free Negro himself began to doubt the blessings of freedom.[52] Thus even before it became illegal for free Negroes to acquire slaves—in 1861—the group had ceased to make such acquisitions. In this case the enactment made legally impossible that which the free Negro had already ceased to do.

Surrounded on all sides by a legal system which denied them the opportunity to seek a livelihood where they could and by a hostile community that often made them as unwelcome as a contagious disease, the free Negroes tried to find their place in the economic life of ante-bellum North Carolina. If they were "idle, thievish, roguish, and indolent"—a sweeping generalization that can reasonably be doubted—they merely reflected the restraints and

[47] Woodson, *Free Negro Owners*, pp. 24–26, and the unpublished population schedules for the census of 1830.

[48] The list was compiled by the writer from the unpublished population schedules for the census of 1860.

[49] *State Records*, XXVI, 278.

[50] Woodson, *Free Negro Owners*, pp. 24–25.

[51] In such cases the free Negro was losing his slaves in much the same way that the white slaveholder was losing his. By 1860 the rate of increase of slaves in North Carolina was noticeably declining. Taylor, *Slaveholding, passim.*

[52] By 1858 free Negroes had begun to send petitions to the General Assembly asking to be reenslaved. See the MSS. in the Legislative Papers for 1958, 1859, and 1860.

stigma that society had placed upon them, and their reactions were no more than natural. In view of the circumstances, it is not surprising that they were not a more powerful economic force than they were. The amazing thing is that under such adverse circumstances they were able to acquire more than a million dollars worth of property by the end of the period and to have possessed several hundred slaves during the seventy-year period ending in 1860.

Dixon Ryan Fox

THE NEGRO VOTE IN OLD NEW YORK

Though less proscribed than the Free People of Color in the South, northern Negroes also suffered many forms of racism and discrimination, and in most states did not enjoy full citizenship rights. For example, though most of the New England states did accord them the franchise, they were excluded from the ballot box in all the states of the Old Northwest and, after 1837, in Pennsylvania. New York was unique, providing in its constitution of 1821 for universal white manhood suffrage, with a discriminatory property qualification for Negroes.

Dixon Ryan Fox's article describes the political and social forces that produced this partial disfranchisement of the black population. His description is especially timely because it presents early examples both of Negro bloc voting and of a white backlash.

THE attachment of the colored citizen to the Republican party is usually explained by reference to the memory of Lincoln, Stevens, Grant and Sumner; but in New York, at least, the freedman learned to vote against St. Tammany before most of those apostles of his "rights" were born, and the jealous hatred of poor mechanics helps far more than reconstruction policies to account for the attitude of New York Democrats towards Negro suffrage.

The appearance of the Negro in the Hudson River region is no novelty of recent years. The Dutch brought the *swarten* to the colony before Manhattan houses were a decade old; [1] when the English made Fort Amsterdam Fort James, the encouragement of the slave trade with New York became an object of solitude in London.[2] The demand for "negears" was larger and more steady here than in other colonies of the same latitude,[3] yet slaves were not

Dixon Ryan Fox, "The Negro Vote in Old New York," *Political Science Quarterly*, XXXII (June, 1917), pp. 252–75. Reprinted with permission of *Political Science Quarterly*.

[1] Mrs. S. Van Rensselaer, *History of the City of New York in the Seventeenth Century*, N.Y., 1909, vol. i, pp. 191–195.

[2] Instructions to Governors Bellomont, Hunter etc., in *N.Y. Colonial Documents*.

[3] H. R. Stiles, *History of the City of Brooklyn*, Albany, 1869, vol. i, p. 231.

massed in large plantations but scattered by twos and threes as household servants among the well-to-do, chiefly in the houses of the aristocracy.[4] They were treated with a careful kindliness, and in return they developed an affection for the master that no shock of fortune could disturb.[5]

What was the partizan connection of New York slave owners? The Federalist party was the party of the aristocracy, especially in large communities,[6] the party of the wealth won by a century of trade. Since slaves in this colony were a luxury rather than an investment in agriculture, we should expect to find them belonging largely to members of this party; the records show such to have been the case.[7]

A great historian has truly remarked: "That New York is not a slave state like South Carolina is due to climate and not to the superior humanity of the founders." [8] Slavery for them did not pay. The Federalist masters preferred to see their Negroes free, and led the movement in New York state for their betterment. Governor John Jay organized the Society for Promoting the Manumission of Slaves and became its first president in 1785; [9] he was succeeded by Alexander Hamilton.[10] It was Rufus King who had moved "that there shall be neither slavery nor involuntary servitude in any of the states described in the resolve of Congress of 23rd of April, 1784," dealing with the Northwest Ordinance.[11] General Schuyler was found, when the time came, voting for

[4] In the *Documentary History of New York* (edition of 1850), vol. iii, pp. 505–521, is a list of slave-holders in the colony in 1755. Few masters had more than five slaves. The rolls of New York city and Albany have been lost, but we are able to form some estimate of the distribution of slaves in the "Wills on File in the Surrogate's Office," abstracts of which have been printed in the *Collections of the New York Historical Society*, volumes from 1900 to 1906 dealing with the years 1780 to 1800. See also Stiles, *op. cit.*, vol. ii, p. 65, and J. Munsell, *Collections on the History of Albany*, vol. i, p. 60, vol. ii, pp. 49, 382.

[5] C. F. Hoffman, *The Pioneers of New York* (delivered before St. Nicholas Society), N.Y., 1848, pp. 30–33; T. E. V. Smith, *The City of New York in the Year of Washington's Inauguration*, N.Y., 1889, p. 122. For legal status of slaves see E. V. Morgan, "Slavery in New York," *Papers of the American Historical Association*, vol. v, pp. 337–380.

[6] A. C. McLoughlin, *The Confederation and the Constitution*, N.Y., 1905, pp. 290–291. C. A. Beard, *Economic Interpretation of the Jeffersonian Democracy*, N.Y., 1915, *passim*. On the New York aristocracy, see T. Roosevelt, *Gouverneur Morris*, Boston, 1892, pp. 17 *et seq.*

[7] E.g., "Wills" as cited, liber xxxix, p. 127; xli, pp. 48, 128, 141; xlii, p. 191; N.Y. *Doc. Hist.*, vol. iii, pp. 510, 512, 514, 519, for well-known Federalist names.

[8] George Bancroft, *History of the United States* (edition 1883), vol. i, p. 513.

[9] Wm. Jay, *Life of John Jay*, N.Y., 1833, vol. i, pp. 229–235; vol. ii, p. 406. It was Jay's custom to purchase slaves of promise that he might, after due instruction, set them free. G. Pellew, *John Jay*, p. 294. See also *Correspondence of John Jay*, N.Y., 1893, vol. iv, p. 320.

[10] For Hamilton on slavery see "A Full Vindication," in *Works* (edited by J. C. Hamilton), N.Y., 1851, vol. ii, p. 9, and vol. vi, p. 298. See also F. G. Mather, "Slavery in the Colony and State of New York," in *Magazine of American History*, vol. ix, p. 408.

[11] *The Life and Correspondence of Rufus King* (edited by C. R. King), N.Y., 1900, vo. i, pp. 39, 268–292. On King's later stand against slavery see J. Q. Adams, *Memoirs*, Philadelphia, 1877, vol. vi, p. 467.

emancipation of the Negroes of the state.[12] Next to Jay in his importance in the constituent convention at White Plains in 1776 was Gouverneur Morris, who made earnest efforts for some scheme of gradual emancipation.[13] Party editors from Noah Webster [14] to William L. Stone [15] took up the cause with much enthusiasm. Certainly the leaders of the party might lay a claim to the black man's loyalty, and the party followed their leaders on this question. They finally enacted a well-calculated scheme of gradual emancipation which prevented the distress of any sudden readjustment.[16] The measure was opposed by the party of the small tradesman and the mechanic, for reasons of economic jealousy as we shall see. The workman did not like to see the Negro change his butler's coat for cap and jeans, and his salver for pick and shovel. It was a Federalist legislature and a Federalist governor who enacted the law of 1799, by almost a straight party vote of sixty-eight to twenty-three.[17] The Negroes had been reared in Federalist households; their cause had been advocated by distinguished Federalists, and now under the auspices of that party, freedom was provided. When they reached the estate of citizens, their political attachment could be easily foretold.

In numbers they were not to be neglected. New York had been the most important slave state in the North, and continued to have more Negroes than any other state in that section.[18] In New York city the proportion of Negroes to whites at the beginning of the nineteenth century was several times larger than now.[19] As soon as any slave was freed he became a voter, on the same terms as a white man, namely, if he paid taxes to the state, if he owned a freehold of the value of twenty pounds, or if he rented a tenement of the yearly

[12] N.Y. Assembly Journal, 1799, pp. 47, 49, 77.

[13] Jared Sparks, Life of Gouverneur Morris, Boston, 1841, vol. i, p. 125. See also his speeches in the Federal Convention of 1786, The Records of the Federal Convention (edited by Max Farrand), New Haven, 1911, vol. ii, pp. 221, 415, 417, 574. See also A. J. Northrup, "Slavery in New York," in N.Y. State Library Bulletin, History, no. 4, 1900.

[14] See his Effects of Slavery on Morals and Industry (pamphlet), Hartford, 1793; see also Frederick Hudson, Journalism in the United States, N.Y., 1873, p. 192.

[15] W. L. Stone, Jr., Life and Writings of William Leete Stone (bound with W. L. Stone, Life of Red Jacket, 1866), pp. 41–42.

[16] After July 4, 1799, no man or woman was to be born a slave; C. Z. Lincoln, Constitutional History of New York, Rochester, 1906, vol. i, 658; also comment in J. H. Dougherty, Legal and Judicial History of New York, N.Y., 1911, vol. ii, p. 94. Those who set free their slaves had to guarantee that their freedmen would not become public charges.

[17] See on the principle of general emancipation, N.Y. Assembly Journal, 1799, p. 77. Comparing the names of the minority with those who voted for Addison and Haight, the candidates of the opposition for members of the Council of Appointment (cf. J. D. Hammond, History of Political Parties in the State of New York, N.Y., 1842, vol. i, p. 122), we see that of those who objected to the measure all but three were Republicans.

[18] U.S. Census of 1790; Census of 1820, supplement, p. 1.

[19] See table in Mary W. Ovington, Half a Man, N.Y., 1911, p. 10; and Analectic Magazine, vol. xiii (1819), p. 279.

fee of forty shillings.[20] In the eighteenth century manumission had not been uncommon, and it became more general after 1800. The erstwhile slave became in politics a client of his former master. To say that Jay or Hamilton in urging manumission had been largely moved by the hope of adding to the Federalist vote would be not only ungenerous but absurd. Yet it was only natural that in his voting, as well as in his talk and dress, the Negro should follow the example of his former master. In Brooklyn, for example, five of the thirteen Federalist candidates in 1810 were men who had set free their slaves, while there was but one such among their opponents.[21] The credit for the first manumission under the new law in this community goes to John Doughty, who served his generation as town clerk from 1796 to 1830,[22] who registered the birth of every child of slave parents after 1799, and in whose ceremonious presence almost every manumitted slave was given his certificate of liberty.[23] Is it to be expected that the freedmen who came into Albany from Rensselaerwyck where they had been so kindly treated,[24] or those who came from the great house of General Schuyler where so many had been granted freedom,[25] would vote against "the lord"? [26]

On this question the political philosophers of Tammany Hall had entertained but little doubt; they soon saw their forebodings realized. When in 1808 the colored voters in a meeting held in New York city voiced unanimous approval of the "old party." Republicans prepared a campaign song beginning "Federalists with blacks unite." [27] In 1809 a Negro orator drew applause from a large audience when, after picturing the sad conditions under Jefferson, he exclaimed, "How important then, that we, my countrymen, should unite our efforts with those of our Federal friends in endeavoring to bring about this desirable change, so all-important to commerce, to our own best interests, and the prosperity and glory of our country." [28] Republican inspectors at the polls, to minimize the danger of this co-operation, presumed as slaves all

[20] Constitution of 1777, article vii, in U.S. House Documents, vol. xci, part 1, pp. 2630–2631. The New York pound was the equivalent of $2.50.

[21] Compare the ticket printed in the N.Y. Herald, April 7, 1810, with the list of manumissions, 1797 to 1825, as printed in the Corporation Manual of the City of Brooklyn, 1864, pp. 153–165. Jacob Hicks, the Quaker, was the single Republican nominee who had held slaves.

[22] Corporation Manual of the City of Brooklyn, 1864, pp. 167–179.

[23] T. F. DeVoe, in Historical Magazine, Second Series, vol. ii, p. 342. E. A. Doty, "The Doughty Family on Long Island," in the N.Y. Genealogical and Biographical Record, vol. xliii, p. 321; H. R. Stiles, op. cit., vol. ii, p. 65.

[24] M. Van Rensselaer, Annals of the Van Rensselaers, Albany, 1888, p. 170.

[25] G. W. Schuyler, Colonial New York, N.Y., 1885, vol. ii, p. 497.

[26] Had the promising movements toward gradual emancipation by state action in the South in the early part of the nineteenth century succeeded, no doubt the same conditions would have followed there.

[27] From a broadside quoted in T. E. V. Smith, Political Parties and Their Places of Meeting in New York City (pamphlet), N.Y., 1893, p. 10.

[28] Joseph Sydney, An Oration Commemorative of the Abolition of the Slave Trade in the United States (delivered before the Wilberforce Philanthropic Association), N.Y., 1809, a pamphlet in the N.Y. Historical Society Collection.

black men who could not prove their freedom by sufficient evidence. The Federalists denounced this practice,[29] and organized among the Negroes a chapter of their partizan fraternity, the Washington Benevolent Society.[30] In 1811 a Republican legislature drew up a drastic law as to the suffrage of the blacks,[31] which passed in spite of the objections of the Federalist Council of Revision.[32]

The election of 1813 in the midst of "Mr. Madison's war" was closely contested; for some time the returns for members of assembly were in doubt.[33] The result was long remembered. Eight years afterward in the constitutional convention, General Root, speaking for the limitation on the franchise for men of color, recalled that "the votes of three hundred Negroes in the city of New York, in 1813, decided the election in favor of the Federal party, and also decided the political character of the legislature of this state." [34] Not the number of the Negroes who were qualified made them formidable, but the strategic strength of their location. At the next election, however, the Federalist majority was overturned, and it is not surprising to find soon presented before the reformed legislature a more severe measure to limit the political influence of the Negro in New York city. This not only provided for the elaborate registration of every freedman, but obliged him always to bring full copies of such registration to the officers of election.[35] Yet these laws were made effective with much difficulty; in spite of all precautions, "Negro ballots" had to be accepted. When Clinton brought to his standard the majority of Federalists he gained the colored men as well.[36] Therefore in 1821 the Republicans were in no mood to trifle with this question.

[29] N.Y. Commercial Advertiser, April 26, 1809. See resolutions, Federalist meeting, ibid., May 22, also N.Y. Spectator, April 29, 1809. The practice was defended the following year by the Republican N.Y. Advertiser, April 26, 1810.

[30] Analectic Magazine, vol. xiii (1819), p. 287.

[31] J. D. Hammond, Political History, vol. i, p. 296.

[32] See objections stated in N.Y. Spectator, May 8, 1811. The N.Y. Evening Post called in an "Act to prevent people of colour from voting at the next election"; see issues of April 16, 22, 1811. The official caption was "An Act to prevent frauds at election and slaves from voting"; Laws of New York, Revision of 1813, vol. ii, p. 253. See N.Y. Assembly Journal, 1811, pp. 251, 310 etc., and N.Y. Senate Journal, 1811, pp. 143, 163.

[33] Hammond, vol. i, p. 357.

[34] Carter, Stone and Gould, Reports of the Proceedings and Debates of the Convention of 1821 etc., Albany, 1821, p. 212. In 1813 there was a bill providing for a very strict superintendence of the colored voters, which passed the senate only. The six senators who voted against it were Federalists; N.Y. Senate Journal, 1813, p. 120.

[35] See N.Y. Assembly Journal, 1814–1815, pp. 469 et seq., and N.Y. Senate Journal, 1814–1815, p. 326. At a large Negro meeting in New York city thanks were voted to the Federalist Judges Kent and Platt for their spirited opposition in the Council of Revision, the Republicans were berated, and continued support was promised to those "whose opinions appear more consonant to our own." N.Y. Spectator, April 19, 1815. This matter was made an issue in the next campaign and was the subject of the longest of the resolutions of a Federalist meeting; see N.Y. Commercial Advertiser, April 11, 1816.

[36] "Extracts from the minutes of the Electors Of the People of Colour of the 5th Ward at a Meeting to Express Congratulations to his Excellency. Resolve[d] that we

The convention of 1821 has been called with somewhat pompous phrase-ology "a dominant emancipating agent in American democracy." [37] That one of its major purposes was to extend the suffrage to new classes was realized by friend and foe alike. "This is one of the crying evils for which we were sent here to provide a remedy," said Mr. Ross, of the committee to which this subject was referred.[38] Old qualifications of property, the remnant of the English practice of colonial days, were to be swept away, and it was known that the question of Negro suffrage would be an important subject of debate. The members of the convention were chosen on party grounds, and a large majority of them were Democrats.[39] The convention was conducted on party principles; the chairmen of all committees were appointed by the president, ex-Governor Tompkins, from his own supporters. These gentlemen differed sharply with the Federalist minority on the extension of the suffrage to poor white men, and to Negroes also. The committee in charge proposed, not to continue a twenty-pound qualification for the Negro, while giving the indigent white the vote, but actually to take away the privilege that the Negro already had.

At the opening of the debate, Mr. Ross laid down the doctrine of the Democracy: "They are a peculiar people, incapable, in my judgment, of exer-cising that privilege with any sort of discretion, prudence, or independence." Probably the last-named quality gave him most concern, for later he com-plained that the black vote was a controlled vote. A petition in behalf of Negro voters "now on your table, in all probability had been instigated by gentlemen of a different colour who expect to control their votes." [40] For others the test of contribution to the state might be sufficient, but not so for the colored men.[41] There were reasons enough why the franchise should be denied the Negro altogether, said Colonel Young, a leading Democrat from Saratoga County; and if reasons did not prove sufficient, one could easily

the People of Colour present Our humble Congratulations to his Excellency's Venera-tion of Being Reelected By our utmost Endeavors as our Chief Commander and Gov-ernor of the State of New York"; N.Y., June 15, 1820, DeWitt Clinton MSS., Columbia University.

[37] F. N. Thorpe, *Constitutional History of the American People*, Chicago, 1901, vol. ii, p. 354. *Cf.* E. Olbrich, *The Development of Sentiment on Negro Suffrage to 1860*, University of Wisconsin, 1912, p. 38.

[38] Carter, Stone and Gould, *Debates etc.*, pp. 180, 193. The report of the debates on Negro suffrage is quoted extensively in C. Z. Lincoln, *Constitutional History of New York*, vol. i, pp. 661–668, and in the admirable monograph of E. Olbrich, pp. 30–39. But neither of these authors has given his attention to the connection between the arguments and the partizan allegiance of the members. The same is true of Dr. H. L. Young's dissertation on The New York Constitutional Convention of 1821, which may be consulted in manuscript in the library of Yale University.

[39] J. D. Hammond, *Political History*, vol. ii, p. 2. Judge Hammond from this date uses the designation "Democratic" to describe the old Republican party.

[40] *Debates*, pp. 180, 181.

[41] The suffrage was extended by this constitution to all male residents of proper age who paid taxes (or were exempt by law), who did militia duty (or were exempt), or who worked at call upon the highways (or paid an equivalent), except Negroes, for whom, as we shall see, special provision was made.

fall back on prejudice. The Negro should be entirely shut out.[42] Jacob Radcliff, who now represented the Tammany Society, "considered the privilege of exclusion to be derived, not from the distinction of color—but resorted to as a rule of designation between those who understand the worth of the privilege, and those who are degraded, dependent, and unfit to exercise it." [43] Here was a scholastic refinement that would have graced a medieval disputation. As to the Negro voter having by the exercise of the franchise for forty years and more acquired a *vested* right to such exercise, as was maintained by Abraham Van Vechten, a leader of the Albany Federalists, it was answered that the sovereign people in convention could do anything.[44]

Again and again the complaint was heard that the Negro lacked independence, that he was amenable to other influences than argument. The contention, significantly enough, came from one party only.[45] The Democrats had every reason to subscribe to the opinion that the Negroes, born in slavery, and accustomed to take orders, would now vote according to the dictates of their employers.[46] To extend to blacks the same provisions as were contemplated for whites would, as Mr. Radcliff well observed, be attended with most serious results. It would let loose two thousand five hundred Negro voters in the city of New York, and a small part of these might determine the result in such close state elections as, for example, that of 1801.[47] General Root declared himself an abolitionist as to slavery [48]—for now, as later, we find opinion upon slavery and upon the suffrage bearing small relation—but he was aware of the dangerous importance of the Negro vote. He said:

> At present the number of blacks who are voters is so small, that if they were scattered all over the state, there would not be much danger to be apprehended, but if we may judge of the future by the past, I should suppose that there was some cause for alarm, when a few hundred Negroes of the city of New York, following the train of those who ride in their coaches, and whose shoes and boots they had so often blacked, shall go to the polls of the election and change the political condition of the whole state. A change in the representation of that city may cause a change in your assembly, by giving a majority to a particular party, which would vary your council of appointment, who make the highest officers of your government. Thus would the whole

[42] *Debates*, pp. 190–191. Colonel Young criticized the argument for suffrage from natural right when Dr. Clarke quoted the Declaration of Independence. It was a question of expediency. Democratic doctrine was beginning to be modified in statement.

[43] *Debates*, p. 190.

[44] *Ibid.*, p. 193; see Hammond, vol. ii, pp. 3 etc., on Van Vechten's importance in the party.

[45] One Federalist opposed his colleagues—Chief Justice Ambrose Spencer, who, however, classed the improvident mechanic with the Negro. With him it was not a matter of race; *ibid.*, p. 377.

[46] *Ibid.*, p. 185.

[47] *Ibid.*, pp. 198, 199 (Livingston).

[48] D. S. Alexander, *Political History of New York State*, N.Y., 1906, vol. i, p. 229.

state be controlled by a few hundred of this species of population in the city of New York.[49]

The Federalist members did not content themselves with silence. The committee had scarcely presented their report, in which there appeared no provision for any Negro vote, when Peter Augustus Jay, an able father's able son, arose to ask an explanation why, while extending the privilege of the franchise to some men, "they deny it to others who actually possess it." Though he abhorred slavery, he was not, he said, what was called an abolitionist; yet he would not stand by and hear it said that this denial was made "because all who were not white ought to be excluded from political rights, because such persons were incapable of exercising them discretely, and because they were peculiarly liable to be influenced and corrupted." [50] Mr. Van Vechten had not understood that the convention was expected "except by some of the citizens of New York to disfranchise anybody." Why should the Negro voters be attacked? "Have they done anything to forfeit the right of suffrage? This has has not been shown." [51] Dr. Clarke, a Federalist from Delaware County, desired to learn why Negro soldiers should not vote as well as whites; there had been nothing but applause for their service as state troops in the War of 1812. The fact that they were not liable to militia duty had made their volunteering in that crisis all the more occasion for respect and gratitude.[52] General Van Rensselaer thought any man of either race should vote, provided he had property and paid taxes.[53]

Mr. Jay moved that the word "white" be struck out of the committee's proposed amendment. After due debate the matter was referred to a select committee,[54] which finally proposed:

> That no male citizen, other than white, shall be subject to taxation, or entitled to vote at any election, unless in addition to the qualifications of age and residence, last above mentioned, he shall be seised and possessed in his own right of a freehold estate of the value of two hundred and fifty dollars, over and above all debts and incumbrances charged thereon, and shall have been, within the next year preceding the election, assessed, and shall have actually paid a tax to the state or county.[55]

Judge Jonas Platt, who had been the Federalist candidate for governor in 1810, moved to strike out the words, "other than white." The qualification of

[49] *Debates*, pp. 185–186.
[50] *Debates*, p. 180 (Ross), and p. 183 (Jay).
[51] *Ibid.*, pp. 193, 195.
[52] *Ibid.*, p. 187.
[53] *Ibid.*, p. 182.
[54] *Cf.* Olbrich, *op. cit.*, p. 36. Ex-Governor Tompkins, who presided, contrary to parliamentary usage appointed as nine of the thirteen members men who had voted against the Jay motion; *Debates*, p. 298.
[55] *Debates*, p. 329.

two hundred and fifty dollars freehold he thought might be applied to white
and black alike; if poor Negroes were to be excluded, then he would have
the same exclusion for poor white men. He declared:

> I am not disposed, sir, to turn knight-errant in favour of the men of
> color. But the obligations of justice are eternal and indispensable.
> ... The real object is, to exclude the oppressed and degraded sons
> of Africa, and, in my humble judgment, it would better comport with
> the dignity of this Convention to speak out, and to pronounce the sen-
> tence of perpetual degradation on Negroes and their posterity forever,
> than to establish a test, which we know they cannot comply with, and
> which we do not require of others.[56]

No man was more opposed to running after the *ignis fatuus* of universal
suffrage than Chancellor Kent, but he could see no proper reason for discrimination against the Negro.[57] Rufus King believed that "universal suffrage
was perilous to us and to the country" and yet took this same position.[58] But the
majority were not moved by Federalist oratory. The qualification of two
hundred and fifty dollars passed into the fundamental law to remain until
1870.[59]

The difference regarding Negro suffrage between the opposing parties
was not fortuitous; their contemporaries noticed the alignment. The careful
Hammond writes:

> It is somewhat curious that General Root, Colonel Young, Mr. Liv-
> ingston, Mr. Briggs, &c., who were most anxious to abolish the prop-
> erty qualification and extend the right of suffrage to all white men,
> were equally zealous to exclude black citizens from the right to exer-
> cise the elective franchise; while those who most strenuously con-
> tended for retaining the freehold qualification as respected white citi-
> zens, were very solicitous to prevent an exclusion of the blacks from
> an equal participation with the whites. Of this last description of
> members, Chancellor Kent, Mr. Van Rensselaer, Mr. Jay, Mr. Van
> Vechten and Judge Platt were the most prominent.[60]

We have seen that the Negro had been a Federalist.[61] As soon as an
ambitious freedman gained the prescribed amount of property—and we shall

[56] *Ibid.*, pp. 374, 375. Two hundred and fifty dollars had been the sum qualifying
for the vote for governor, lieutenant-governor and senators. It was now extended in
the Negro's case to that for member of assembly.

[57] *Ibid.*, pp. 190, 191, 221, 377.

[58] *Ibid.*, pp. 191, 287. King, though elected with the help of Democratic votes,
was still a Federalist.

[59] The qualification was removed only with the passage of the Fifteenth Amendment to the Constitution of the United States. The New York Democrats protested
bitterly against this amendment.

[60] *Political History*, vol. ii, p. 21.

[61] "The Negroes, with scarcely an exception, adhered to the Federalists. Their
number in the city of New York was very great, and parties in that city were so

see that this group grew—he would now hesitate still less in choosing between the two parties. We are not to understand that the Negro was a lover of strong government in the abstract, or that he admired the British Constitution or suspected Jacobinical innovation; his Federalism was in his feeling. As long as the party lasted under the old designation, he voted faithfully for its candidates; and we have traced, it is hoped sufficiently, the considerations that commanded his allegiance.

The Federalist party as an organization was in 1821 already passing into history, but the feud between Van Buren's "Bucktails" [62] and all others was kept up. When in 1826 the few restrictions on white suffrage which had survived five years before were swept away, it was a Democratic legislature which retained the qualification for the blacks.[63] This fact was probably not lost upon the colored voter; and despite the hope and expectation of the convention of 1821, his tribe increased in thrift,[64] so that his political importance was not lost. In the decade after 1830, in three contests for governor, in New York city, always of such critical importance, the fifth ward— where the Negroes were most largely settled—was carried against Tammany, apparently by Negro influence.[65] The same result was brought about here in at least three municipal elections, and likewise in the eighth ward, next to the fifth in Negro population, in 1834, 1837 and 1838.[66] The sachems had little reason to look with complacency upon the slowly growing Negro influence. In Brooklyn, the fourth, ninth and seventh wards, where the Negroes were most numerous, yield corroborative evidence.[67] In Albany, a little later, it was probably Negroes in the first and tenth wards who swelled the Whig majorities.[68]

When the people of New York voted that a convention for the revision

---

evenly divided, that it was often sufficient to hold the balance between them, at times, too, when the vote of New York, in the legislature, not unfrequently decided the majority of that body"; *Life of Martin Van Buren*, a campaign pamphlet, published in Philadelphia in 1844 (in N.Y. Public Library), p. 6.

[62] The bucktail was the badge of the Tammany Society.

[63] The six senators (out of twenty-eight) who voted for equal suffrage were all anti-Tammany men; N.Y. Senate Journal, 1825, p. 147. For names *cf.* Hammond, vol. i, pp. 235, 237; vol. ii, pp. 139, 175, 193; and Alexander, vol. i, p. 156.

[64] See the testimony of W. E. Shannon, formerly of New York, in the *Report of the Debates in the Convention of California etc.*, 1849, Washington, 1850, p. 143. Much was accomplished in New York city by the Phoenix Societies; see *Minutes and Proceedings of the Third Annual Convention for the Improvement of Free People of Color etc.* (pamphlet), N.Y., 1833, pp. 36–40; F. Bancroft, *Life of Seward*, vol. i, p. 139; C. C. Andrews, *History of the New York African Free Schools etc.*, N.Y., 1830.

[65] E. Williams, New York Annual Register, 1835, p. 52; *ibid.*, 1840, p. 224; N.Y. *Evening Post*, Nov. 26, 1836; Census of N.Y. State, in O. C. Holley, *New York State Register*, p. 109.

[66] Williams, 1834, p. 279; *ibid.*, 1837, p. 348; *ibid.*, 1840, p. 225; Holley, *loc. cit.*

[67] *Cf.* N.Y. *Evening Post*, Nov. 4, 1836; Williams, 1836, p. 95; *ibid.*, 1840, p. 222; Holley, 1843, p. 82; *ibid.*, 1846, p. 107.

[68] *Cf.* J. Munsell, *Annals of Albany*, Albany, 1870, vol. ii, pp. 361–362; Holley, 1846, p. 107; *ibid.*, 1843, p. 69; *ibid.*, 1845, p. 69; N.Y. *Tribune*, Nov. 4, 1846.

of the constitution should be held in 1846, no gift of prophecy was needed to foretell that Negro suffrage would again furnish a theme of bitter controversy. The movement to take away the privilege altogether was begun before the delegates were chosen. A pamphleteer [69] who declared himself "a steady supporter of the principles and regular nominations of the Democratic party" urged the complete exclusion of all men of color from the right to vote. "Some of our people, from false notions of benevolence, or political hypocrisy, deny the natural inferiority of the black race," but as for himself he would maintain that their political proscription was in no way inconsistent with good Democratic doctrine:

> In the country, where there are but few Negroes, the danger of encouraging them to remain in the State, invite others from adjacent States and fugitive slaves to join them, and interfere in our political affairs, through the aid of a fanatical party of whites, is not so apparent as in our great cities where they are already numerous.

This broad distinction founded on geography we shall later put to test. On the other hand, the Whigs, in a mass meeting in New York city, October 28, 1845, presided over by the venerable Federalist, Philip Hone,[70] resolved that one of the first reasons for holding a convention was that "the inestimable Right of Suffrage is not secured equally to all citizens, but is clogged as to a part with a proscriptive and anomalous Property Qualification." [71]

Horace Greeley, publishing an address from colored men who asked the return of equal suffrage, endorsed their claim that manhood alone must be the test for the elective franchise,[72] and later printed this demand at the head of seven reforms that must be struggled for.[73] He bewailed "the Colorphobia which prevails so extensively in the ranks of our modern 'Democracy,' " [74] and declared that the "body of the People are divided into two great parties, one of which is generally favorable, and the other notoriously hostile to the extension of the Right of Suffrage to every peaceable, orderly citizen, without regard to the color of his skin or the amount of his property." He urged the

[69] H. P. Hastings, *An Essay on Constitutional Reform*, N.Y., 1846, in N.Y. Public Library.

[70] To see how important a part Hone played in carrying this measure through, consult report in N.Y. *Evening Post*, Oct. 29, 1845; yet Hone had no sympathy with abolitionism. See *Diary of Philip Hone*, N.Y., 1889, vol. i, p. 79. (The full manuscript is in the N.Y. Historical Society Collections.)

[71] N.Y. *Tribune*, October 30, 1845. It must be said that this was not the unanimous opinion of those attending. Col. Webb, of the *Courier and Enquirer*, who had written very gingerly about the Texas question and was anxious that the party in New York should commit itself to no principle distasteful to the southern Whigs, was able at a subsequent smaller meeting to have all such resolutions stricken out.

[72] N.Y. *Tribune*, January 23, 1846. The address itself is interesting, apparently in the hope of proselyting among Democrats its authors recalled general statements of D. D. Tompkins and Silas Wright about slavery and the rights of man.

[73] *Ibid.*, March 23, 1846.

[74] *Ibid.*, Feb. 12.

Birneyites, the members of the small and struggling group of abolitionists, to name no candidates for the convention, but to vote for Whigs, who, however they might differ with these enthusiasts as to the proper way to deal with slavery, were one with them upon the poorest Negro's right to vote.[75] As to the candidates the colored voters would themselves prefer, he, of course, had little doubt. He knew they would recall that it was the Democrats of 1821 who had excluded them, when "every Federalist in the Convention strenuously opposed the proscription." [76] And the Negro voter seemed to understand. "The Democratic party of this City," wrote one of them, "with the loud profession of the largest liberty, is the first and the only one to announce its determination to go for the curtailment of Human Freedom." [77]

It must not be considered that this was but a passing crotchet of Greeley's. The other most important Whig editor in the state was Thurlow Weed, who attempted to lead no forlorn hopes. For universal suffrage in the abstract he had no approval; [78] that was one thing in which he would if necessary stand alone. He did not care to jeopardize the union of the party and of the nation [79] by stirring up trouble in the South, and he made no secret of his hatred for the fanatical zeal of northern abolitionists.[80] Indeed, in after years Greeley charged him with a "poor white" prejudice against the black.[81] Yet at the very outset of this contest he had written, "Above all, let the class of our fellow-citizens, whose intellectual capacities are measured under our present Constitution by *property*, be relieved from the stigma under which they rest, and be placed on the footing where they belong—that of men." [82] Seward, the other member of that famous firm, likewise favored equal suffrage.[83] And despite the opposition of a few, the majority of Whigs seem to have stood behind the trusted leaders.[84]

There was as little doubt as to the policy of the Democrats. The *Journal of Commerce*, the *Argus* and the *Evening Post* had no word to say for the extension of the franchise. Bryant, who in his vagarious days of Equal Rights had brought upon his own head round condemnation for countenancing

[75] N.Y. *Tribune*, Feb. 17. It seems that the inference as to a connection between these sentiments was unwarranted.

[76] *Ibid.*, March 23.

[77] *Ibid.*, April 28.

[78] *Life of Thurlow Weed* (Autobiography), Boston, 1884, pp. 89–90. For his later revision of opinion, see *ibid.* (Memoir), p. 561.

[79] *Cf.* W. E. Dodd, *Expansion and Conflict*, N.Y., 1915, p. 171.

[80] *Albany Evening Journal*, Nov. 30, 1860; also Autobiography, p. 98.

[81] Horace Greeley, *Recollections of a Busy Life*, N.Y., 1873, p. 313. This reference to Weed's humble origin was no less ungenerous than unfair. See Weed's Memoir, p. 297.

[82] *Albany Evening Journal*, Oct. 30, 1845.

[83] See his "Reply to the Colored Citizens of Albany," *Works*, N.Y., 1853–1854, vol. iii, pp. 437–438.

[84] N.Y. *Evening Post*, Oct. 6, 1845. See Greeley's comment on the Webb faction, "so utterly out of place in our party"; N.Y. *Tribune*, April 1, 1846. After the election the Young Men's General County Committee of the Whigs tried to read Webb out of the party.

abolition, who had pointed out with all Cassandra's certainty the danger which followed in the train of the "domestic institution," and had stood among the staunchest in support of Adams in his fight for freedom of petition, now wrote with care to establish the doctrine that civil freedom and the suffrage presented two quite different questions. The Negro as a voter was the Negro as a peril.[85] Bennett, who in spite of claims of independence was at heart a Tammany man, complained in the *Herald* of "the detestable cry of Negro suffrage raised as a rallying cry for the election of delegates to the Convention"; [86] the *Globe* expressed a similar sentiment; [87] and the *Morning News* attributed all the Whigs' zeal to an appetite for votes.[88] This view is doubtless exaggerated; yet the hope of party gain certainly performed its part.

The election of the delegates to the convention of 1846, as a quarter of a century before, was made a party question, and again the Democrats were represented by the large majority.[89] In the course of time the matter of the franchise was presented and a long debate was begun.[90] There was no doubt as to how the parties stood. The committee report, presented by its chairman, ex-Governor Bouck, recommended suffrage for white men only; [91] if the convention should desire, it might offer unrestricted color suffrage as a separate option. If this report were adopted by the delegates, the proposition of the black man's complete exclusion, as the majority of Democrats in 1821 had wished, would go before the people with the prestige of the approval of the convention. No provision was here made for the continuation of the existing limitation of two hundred and fifty dollars, but the minority report called for equal suffrage. Mr. Bruce, a Whig from Madison County, moved to strike out the word "white," and the contest was begun. J. Leslie Russell, of St. Lawrence, took up the challenge:

> For one, he knew ... that nine-tenths of the people in St. Lawrence county—abolitionists and all—were opposed to the admission of the Negroes to the right of suffrage.... He agreed in this perfectly with his constituents. This was the only issue in St. Lawrence at the Convention election. He was interrogated on this subject, and informed them expressly that he should vote against suffrage to the Negro.[92]

[85] Parke Godwin, A *Biography of William Cullen Bryant*, N.Y., 1883, vol. i, pp. 327–331, and N.Y. *Evening Post*, April 21, 1836.

[86] He "was a recognized member of the Tammany party"; *Memoirs of James Gordon Bennett and His Times*, N.Y., 1855, p. 80. He was not complimentary to the Negro, "on whom education, and every other means of moral enlightenment have been tried in vain"; N.Y. *Herald*, March 17, 1846.

[87] Quoted in N.Y. *Tribune*, Feb. 12, 1846.

[88] March 24, 1846. See Frederic Hudson, *Journalism in the United States*, pp. 576, 667.

[89] Hammond, *op. cit.*, vol. iii, p. 605.

[90] Croswell and Sutton, *Debates and Proceedings in the New York State Convention etc.*, Albany, 1846, pp. 246, 775, 782 etc. See also C. Z. Lincoln, *Constitutional History*, vol. ii, pp. 118–123 and E. Olbrich, *op. cit.*, pp. 72–78.

[91] No. 51 in Documents of the Convention of the State of New York, 1846, vol. i.

[92] *Debates*, p. 777. Mr. Russell, like the majority of the voters of St. Lawrence County, was an ardent Democrat. He was in the complete confidence of his fellow-

He was answered by Mr. Strong, a Whig member from Monroe, who declared himself no abolitionist, but who knew this question would never be finally settled until right should be done all classes of the citizens of the state.[93] Mr. Kirkland from Oneida wanted at least to save the Negro what he had.[94] But Mr. Kennedy, a Democrat from New York city, declared that a holding of real property or any other kind was no fit test for the franchise; in any change only character and manhood should be considered; but

> the females of mature age, of our own race, were entitled to a prefer-
> ence, when we were prepared to make such an extension. [A gentle-
> man had] remarked that delicacy should prevent females from uniting
> in the exercise of political power, but what sort of delicacy was that
> which . . . would squander it upon those whom nature had marked
> as a distinct race; and who were merely an excrescence upon our
> society! . . . Nature revolted at the proposal.

He claimed that the freedmen in New York were more degraded than the like class in the South. He had statistics to prove Negroes far more vicious than whites.[95]

Federal Dana, Mr. Bruce's colleague, said if the Negro were but given decent opportunities in life like the suffrage, he would not be so vicious. Mr. Young, a Wyoming Whig, contended that colored people were as intelligent as immigrants from foreign countries and as much entitled to the elective franchise. He regretted that statistics of the good portion of those other groups had not been furnished also. Mr. Rhoades, of Onondaga, scouted a so-called democracy that would deprive men of rights simply on the ground of a difference in complexion. Mr. Waterbury, of Delaware, reverted to the case of women. "The wives and children of all our white citizens were protected in their rights and privileges by husbands and brothers. Where do you find anyone to stand up for the colored man?—Not one." But Mr. Hunt, from Tammany Hall, would listen to no such talk. "His doctrine and that of his constituents, in relation to the right of suffrage, was briefly this: We want no masters and least of all no Negro masters, to reign over us."

It was Mr. Hunt who introduced a new note in the debate. In 1821 the franchise question had been settled without reference or citation beyond the plain facts of social prudence and the experience of this world. But a new day of religious enthusiasm had come since then, and the simple words of

citizen of Canton, Governor Wright, who had taken a deep interest in his career; R. H. Gillett, *Life and Times of Silas Wright*, N.Y., 1874, vol. ii, p. 1727; J. D. Hammond, *Life of Silas Wright*, Syracuse, 1849, p. 730; and Russell to A. C. Flagg, Flagg MSS., N.Y. Public Library. We may infer that Wright's opinions were similar to Russell's.

[93] *Debates*, p. 777.

[94] *Ibid.*, p. 778. It may be said here that no Democrat spoke for the extension of the franchise, and no Whig against it, except Mr. Kirkland and Mr. Stow, who were content with a restricted suffrage, and Mr. Harrison, who stood with the Tammany men in the desire to shut out the Negro altogether.

[95] *Debates*, pp. 782–786, for this and the speeches in the next paragraph.

scripture were frequently taken as the unfailing guide of life.[96] In the view of most men, "common sense, reason and reflection pronounced a solemn amen to every doctrine taught in that fearful and precious book" and it was held "that all the truth to which reason ever assented had been first taught by revelation." [97]

Mr. Hunt appealed to Leviticus: "The Jews were forbidden to yoke animals of different kinds together; and if it were wrong to unite the cow and the ass in the same yoke, would it be right to unite the Caucasian and the Negro race in the same government?" [98] In some way equal suffrage was considered to imply social equality as well. Mr. Perkins, of St. Lawrence, said he should not enter the controversy further than to say that if there were any verity in scripture, mankind were at Babel divided into separate classes, "that it was the fiat of the Almighty that they should remain separate nations— that he put his mark on these creatures, that it might be known that it was a violation of the law of God to commingle our blood with them in marriage." —"Does the gentleman find that in the Bible?" asked Mr. Dana.—"Yes," was the reply; "not in those words, however." Mr. Waterbury wished to know, "If they were thus separated at Babel, how came they to go through the ark with the rest?" [99] Pausing for a moment's comment on the limitations of the gentleman from Delaware in the field of sacred chronology, the debate went forward. Mr. Dana remembered nothing in the account of Babel that properly could be cited against the right of the colored man to vote. "And before he could be convinced of that, he must have chapter and verse." Mr. Harrison, of Richmond, offered specific reference to Ham and Canaan: "Cursed be Canaan; a servant of servants shall he be to his brethren." [100] Yet Mr. Dana recalled that Noah was at this time intoxicated, and that at any rate this had no bearing upon political rights. Mr. Perkins "laid it down as the economy of Providence that there should be separate races and grades of beings on earth." The great offense that had brought on the flood had been the commingling of races. He maintained his exegesis that the female progeny of Cain, lately damned with a black mark, had as partners to this indiscretion occasioned that calamity.[101] Mr. Simmons, of Essex, on the other hand, attributed the deluge to God's wrath at slavery. "My Bible says so," he exclaimed; but he was interrupted by a voice, "Yours is a Whig Bible." [102]

When the vote was taken on Mr. Bruce's proposition to strike out the word "white," there were thirty-seven for and sixty-three against. Among the

[96] W. Walker, *History of the Congregational Churches in the United States*, N.Y., 1894, p. 320; R. E. Thompson, *History of the Presbyterian Churches in the United States*, N.Y., 1895, pp. 129–149.

[97] David Nelson, *The Cause and Cure of Infidelity*, N.Y., 1841, p. 351. This was one of the most popular and influential of the volumes issued by the American Tract Society.

[98] *Debates*, p. 786.

[99] *Debates*, p. 789.

[100] *Ibid.*, p. 790.

[101] *Ibid.*, p. 796.

[102] *Ibid.*

thirty-seven that favored equal suffrage there were two Democrats; while among the sixty-three opposed there were eight Whigs.[103] But when a member of the latter party proposed that the property qualification for the Negro be lowered from two hundred and fifty to one hundred dollars, seven of these eight were willing to make this reduction.[104] The Democrats were in the majority, however, and the Whigs had to be satisfied with a separate submission to the people of the paragraph on equal suffrage.[105]

The Democrats had won a party victory. But since 1842 at least, there had been internal strife. Because of differences about canal expenditures or the Texas annexation, or from jealousies in office-holding, there had been developing a breach within the Democratic party of the state.[106] The Conservatives, or "Hunkers," abhorred the radical "Barnburners," and were themselves despised in turn. Yet faction made no break in this alignment in the convention. Bouck, the foremost Hunker, was no more against the Negro voter than was Michael Hoffman, the Barnburners' champion.[107] It was as straight a party question as one often finds. The charge that the country districts, ignorant of the true nature of the Negro, would unite in his behalf,[108] could not be sustained. Six counties were divided in their delegation—Albany, Greene, Wayne, Dutchess, Onondaga and Schoharie, and in every one the Whig members voted on the one side and the Democrats, if present, on the other. Acquaintance with the black man seemed to count for little. In St. Lawrence, where there were thirty-seven Negroes,[109] it had been "the only issue" and the delegates had been instructed to exclude them altogether. At the election in the autumn their position was maintained in that county by a vote of nearly two to one. Neighboring Franklin county gave equal suffrage a majority of seven hundred and thirty-two.[110] Essex county had forty Negroes; the adjacent Warren, with a population somewhat less, had thirty-five. Essex went for equality; Warren, by nearly the same majority, against.[111] Livingston, with about the same proportion of colored population as Steuben, next to it in the south, went in favor, and Steuben against.[112] The same was true of Oneida and Herkimer, Cortland and Tioga, and other pairs of counties in the different sections of the state. Yet when one looks at the political complexion of these counties the inference

[103] *Ibid.*, p. 788. The party affiliation of each member of the convention may be learned from the list published in the *N.Y. Tribune*, May 5, 1846.

[104] *Debates*, p. 790.

[105] The proposition was heavily defeated at the polls, especially in New York city.

[106] J. S. Jenkins, *Lives of the Governors of New York State*, Auburn, 1851, p. 705; D. S. Alexander, *op. cit.*, vol. ii, pp. 56–76.

[107] J. S. Hammond, *Political History*, vol. iii, p. 314, 387. In the partial list published in the *N.Y. Herald*, May 1, 1846, the Hunkers and Barnburners among the Democrats are differentiated. No relation to the vote on suffrage is observable.

[108] H. P. Hastings, *loc. cit.*

[109] Census of the State of New York, 1845, in O. L. Holley, *New York State Register*, 1846, p. 115.

[110] Table in *N.Y. Tribune*, Nov. 19, 1846.

[111] Holley, *op. cit.*, pp. 104, 119.

[112] *Ibid.*, pp. 108, 117.

is plain. Whig counties followed the direction of their leaders, and Democratic counties did the same. When Washington gave its vote in favor, Greeley wrote, "This Washington is called a *Federal* county, while the party which has polled ninety-nine hundredths of its vote *against* Equal Rights vaunts itself *Democratic*." [113]

Nor did abolitionism play a considerable part in the opinion on Negro suffrage. St. Lawrence abolitionists, if Mr. Russell is to be credited, were emphatically against all concession in the franchise. Men who did not follow Birney, like Mr. Strong and Dr. Backus,[114] were in favor of equality. It has been said that there was a connection between equal-suffrage sentiment and that which produced the Free-Soil party in 1848.[115] Yet in the convention no man was more steadily opposed to Negro suffrage than Samuel J. Tilden,[116] who became a pillar of that party: [117] and in the test of the ballot box such an hypothesis fails utterly. In 1848 seven counties voted for Van Buren, but only one of these had desired equal suffrage, and the county which by far surpassed all others in affection for Free Soil was none other than St. Lawrence.[118] The ward in New York city most favorable to equal suffrage was the fifteenth, always Whig,[119] which in 1844 had given Birney but twelve votes out of three thousand, and which in 1848 gave Van Buren a lower fraction of its votes than almost any other ward.[120] The sixth, which gave the largest vote against the Negro, was the very citadel of Tammany. Horace Greeley, long afterward at a public meeting, recalled that election: "Twenty-five years ago, I stood at the poll of the nineteenth ward of this city all one rainy, chilly November day, peddling ballots for Equal Suffrage. I got many Whigs to take them, but not one Democrat." [121] In this recollection he no doubt was right. It was a party matter in which personalities or the fortunes of slavery in southern states or in the territories had but little bearing.

The traditional alliance between the well-to-do and the Negroes was maintained. This of itself would pique the fear of Tammany and sharpen its attack, but this was not all. The Democratic party in the cities was the party of the little man, the day worker and the mill-hand. The laborers of the forties certainly prized the luxury of feeling themselves better than the Negro; on his

---

[113] N.Y. *Tribune*, Nov. 14, 1847.

[114] Thurlow Weed, Autobiography, p. 98.

[115] E. Olbrich, *Negro Suffrage before 1860 etc.*, p. 77.

[116] At least as indicated by his votes; *Debates*, pp. 788, 790, 791.

[117] John Bigelow, *The Life of Samuel J. Tilden*, N.Y., 1908, vol. 1, p. 119. Tilden wrote much of the address called "The Corner Stone of the Free Soil Party."

[118] See returns of election of 1846 in N.Y. *Tribune*, Nov. 14, 1846, and those of 1848 in *Whig Almanac*, N.Y., 1849, p. 54.

[119] Table in N.Y. *Evening Post*, Nov. 7, 1846, and election tables in E. Williams, *New York Annual Register*, 1832–1840.

[120] *Whig Almanac, loc. cit.*

[121] In a speech at a meeting of welcome after his southern journey of 1871; *Mr. Greeley's Record on the Question of Amnesty and Reconstruction* (pamphlet), N.Y., 1872, p. 21. As to exactly where he stood, Mr. Greeley's memory must have been at fault, as there was in 1846 no nineteenth ward.

subordination hung their pride. And then there was the economic danger of too much encouragement. In Tammany Hall it had been resolved that suffrage for the Negro was "fraught with incalculable evil and mischief, both in a social and political point of view," [122] but this organization had reasons, based on work and wages, to fear the Negro's rise. It had likewise laid down the doctrine "that the inevitable result of the success of abolitionism would be to create a pinching competition between the labor of the Negro and that of the white man. Thus the aspiration of the blacks for suffrage met with the "steady and determined opposition of Tammany Hall." [123] Reason was supported by race prejudice in the heart of the mechanic. It was in the sixth and fourteenth wards of New York city that the anti-Negro vote was strongest, and here were found the largest number of immigrant citizens.[124] The connection of these facts was plain, and it was accepted as a large factor in the explanation of the outcome.[125]

Though the average Negro did not think of the connection, there was doubtless, now and then, a leader to whom these things were clear. Allied by long tradition to the Federalist Whig party, he accepted its direction with docility. As to the charge that the Whigs were low-hearted opportunists on the slavery issue he made no extensive inquiry. In feeling more concern about his own improvement than about the labor system beyond the Mississippi, he presented no exception to the custom of mankind. The Wilmot Proviso was interesting in its way, but Texas was a long way off. Since the leaders of the Free-Soil party had been Democrats, he felt no strong enthusiasm to march behind their banner. In the abolitionists he no doubt felt an interest, but there was little use in casting votes for them.[126] When the Whigs made their transition to the Republican party he of course followed, but he had no hunger for third parties. "For the last five or six years before I left New York," testified a witness in far-away Iowa, "their votes were deposited sometimes for the third-party candidate, but most generally for the old Whig party." [127] They were Whigs because their fathers had been Federalists. If there had never been a Negro south of the Potomac, still the Negro in New York would never have voted the Democratic ticket.

[122] Report of meeting, N.Y. *Evening Post*, Oct. 31, 1846.

[123] *Ibid.*, Oct. 31, 1845.

[124] Greeley claimed this question brought out extra thousands of Tammany votes; N.Y. *Tribune*, Nov. 7, 1846.

[125] N.Y. *Tribune*, Nov. 8. Yet Greeley was a steady opponent of nativism.

[126] Compare Birney's total vote in New York city in 1844 with the Negroes' voting strength; *Constitutional Debates*, 1846, p. 790, and Holley, *op. cit.*, 1845, p. 85.

[127] Mr. Clarke in the *Debates of the Constitutional Convention of the State of Iowa*, 1857, Davenport, 1857, vol. ii, p. 671. Mr. Clarke had left New York in 1831; *ibid.*, vol. i, p. 4 (biographical table).

Robert Ernst

THE ECONOMIC STATUS OF
NEW YORK CITY NEGROES, 1850–1863

Even in the North the ante-bellum free people of color were, to use John Hope Franklin's words, "quasi-free Negroes." Though conditions were on the whole better in the Northeast than in the old Northwest, in most states Negroes faced disfranchisement, mob violence, economic discrimination, and varying degrees of exclusion and segregation, especially in regard to schools, places of recreation, and transportation. Nevertheless, as in the South, a few achieved a modicum of prosperity. Robert Ernst's article describes the role of Negroes in the economic life of the nation's leading seaport, and the degree of progress which they made in view of the many obstacles facing them.

"THERE is now in session in this City a Convention composed entirely of colored citizens. The object of the Convention is to consider the present condition of the Negro race, and to devise means for its improvement." In an obscure column of Horace Greeley's *Tribune*, March 20, 1851, these words introduced a remarkable Report on the Social Condition of the Colored Race, delivered at the meeting by James McCune Smith, one of the best educated Negroes in the metropolis, a physician and civic leader. Smith weighed the advantages and disadvantages of city life for the Negro and offered a plan whereby, through their own efforts, the free Negroes of the Empire City might improve their lot.

However optimistic Smith may have seemed, he painted a dismal picture of actual conditions. New York offered small comfort to its two thousand colored families. "Our lives are much shortened. Look at the preponderance of widows and children among us. They so far exceed the calamities of mere sickness, that our benevolent societies have been obliged to cut off the widows

Robert Ernst, "The Economic Status of New York City Negroes, 1850–1863," published by the Association for the Study of Negro Life and History in Vol. XII of *Negro History Bulletin*, pp. 131–132, 139–143 (March, 1949). Reprinted by permission of the publisher.

and orphans, in order to help the sick. ... Next, the seductions of the City—policy gambling, porter houses ... create a gang of lazaroni of both sexes ... signs which our foes call the type of our condition."[1]

Of more importance was the reflection in this report of an awakening race consciousness, born of discrimination and segregation, and an emerging class consciousness born of the failure to maintain status in a growing industrial society. "City life shuts us from general mechanical employment; while journeymen in the cities refuse to work with us, and colored bosses have either too little capital, or too little enterprise, to bring up and employ apprentices and journeymen." Only menial jobs were left to the Negro. Relentlessly, the uncontrollable, impersonal forces of industrialism affected the Negro as a wage earner. "The enormous combination of capital, which is slowly invading every calling in the city, from washing and ironing to palace steamers," the report asserted, "must tend more and more to grind the face of the poor in the cities, and render them more and more the slaves of lower wages and higher rents."

Of these restrictions upon the Negro's freedom, discrimination was much the older. Racial prejudice and custom had erected an almost impenetrable barrier between whites and Negroes. If some colored person were found to be ignorant, dirty, or boisterous, shiftless or lacking in ambition, pleasure-loving or an inveterate gambler, his traits were allegedly due to the inferiority of his race. An intelligent Englishman remarked during the Civil War that some whites "would shoot a black man with as little regard to moral consequences as they would a wild hog."[2] Even immigrants, themselves held in contempt by the natives, looked down upon the Negroes. When the colored people tried to better their condition, the German *Staats-Zeitung* called them "apes of the white race" who belonged in Africa and not in the United States; equality of blacks and whites was "unnatural" in a country which belonged to the whites.[3] As early as 1833 an English traveller noted that Negroes could not sit in any public assembly, court or church, except in a special section "generally in the most remote or worst situation."[4] In 1843 the New York Zoological Institute announced that "PEOPLE OF COLOR [were] not permitted to enter, EXCEPT WHEN IN ATTENDANCE UPON CHILDREN AND FAMILIES."[5] During the fifties, Negroes were refused passage on omnibuses and street railroads, and attempts to eject colored persons from the cars sometimes resulted in violence.[6]

[1] New York Daily *Tribune*, March 20, 1851. The report, including its plan of a mutual savings association, is fully presented.

[2] [James D. Burn], *Three Years among the Working Classes in the United States during the War* (London, 1865), p. xiv. For the Negro reaction, cf. Carter G. Woodson (ed.), *The Mind of the Negro as Reflected in Letters written during the Crisis* (Washington, 1926), pp. 276–280.

[3] *New Yorker Staats-Zeitung*, March 29, 1851.

[4] [James Boardman], *America and the Americans* (London, 1833), p. 311.

[5] *Colored American*, March 25, 1843.

[6] *Courrier des Etats-Unis*, April 25, 1856; New York *Tribune*, September 18, 24, December 20, 1855. By 1861 such discrimination had all but disappeared, although one

In employment, as in transportation, discrimination was customary. White artisans in skilled occupations would have little or nothing to do with the Negroes. In the year 1833 a French traveller wrote that in not a single trade in New York City were colored persons allowed to work with whites.[7] Almost thirty years later Henry Ward Beecher averred that there was "not a foundary, a machine shop, a shipyard, a carpenter's shop, a cabinet shop, a blacksmith shop" which a Negro could enter.[8] The refusal of the whites to let Negroes work with them often forced the colored artisans to accept menial occupations, and it precluded any serious organization of skilled Negro craftsmen. When, for example, Negro and white barbers planned to create a mutual protective association with the object of raising the price of shaves to 8c and haircuts and shampoos to 15c each, the white barbers urged separate associations for each race.[9]

Segregation was partly responsible for the "Harlem" of the time, although it must be conceded that many colored people normally and voluntarily lived in their own communities. The Negro section harbored only the poorest white persons, usually foreign-born. Despite the political emancipation of the Negro in New York State in 1827, a large part of the city's colored population had long lived apart from the white—at least since 1800.[10] In 1825 more than one-fifth of Manhattan's Negroes inhabited the unhealthy sixth ward, spreading from the notorious slums of the Five Points north and west to the Hudson River. Individuals and some families, however, were scattered throughout the city, many as servants in white homes.[11] A decade later the fifth and eighth wards near the Hudson had become the center of the colored population; in West Broadway and in Thomas, Leonard, Sullivan, Greene, Mercer, and Mulberry streets the Negro inhabitants remained well beyond the middle of the century.[12]

The Negroes were slow to follow the northward trend of migration on Manhattan. Dispersion was blocked on the north for decades by Greenwich

---

line still posted signs reminding Negroes that riding in its cars was a privilege, not a right. *Anglo-African*, October 19, 1861, July 16, 1864.

[7] E. S. Abdy, *Journal of a Residence and Tour in the United States* (London, 1835), Vol. I, p. 358.

[8] New York Daily *Tribune*, December 1, 1862.

[9] *Anglo-African*, November 28, 1863.

[10] George E. Haynes, *The Negro at Work in New York City* (New York, 1912), pp. 48, 144. I cannot wholly agree with Mary Ovington's statement (*Half a Man*, New York, 1911, p. 26) that "until 1860 the race was infrequently segregated, and black and white were neighbors, not only in their homes but in business."

[11] *New York State Census*, 1825 and 1835. The loss in the sixth ward is accounted for by the fact that the northern part of this ward became in 1827 the fourteenth ward. Although its growth as a Negro area never equalled that of the fifth and eighth wards, the fourteenth continued to attract Negroes.

[12] *Longworth's Directory*, 1832–33; *Staats-Zeitung*, April 7, 1860; New York *Herald*, July 15, 16, 1863; *Anglo-African*, August 22, 1863. On the occasion of the riot of 1834, a note from Joseph Curtis introducing a colored woman to Mayor Lawrence referred to "many families of color" living in the neighborhood of Sullivan Street. This note, dated July 12, is now in the possession of the New York Historical Society.

Village, where an exclusive if somewhat impoverished Knickerbocker element held sway.[13] To a lesser extent the fashionable Washington Square neighborhood also limited Negro expansion. By 1860, however, a large colored settlement had appeared far to the north near the Hudson between Twenty-Sixth and Fortieth streets, and some Negroes had already filtered into the Greenwich and Washington Square strongholds.[14]

If the city's colored inhabitants spread gradually over a wider area on the island, their ranks were thinned by migration elsewhere. While Manhattan's population as a whole rose steadily throughout the period, its Negro population grew only until 1840. Thereafter the colored folk lost ground. The 13,358 of 1840 shrank to 12,574 at the outbreak of the Civil War, owing probably to the higher death rate of the Negro than of the white, the strong hostility toward the blacks aroused by anti-slavery agitation, and the flights of southern fugitive slaves who had settled in the city and were terrified at the passage of the Fugitive Slave Law of 1850.[15]

Living conditions of the Negroes were shaped largely by the growth of the city. During the forties and fifties commercial New York was becoming industrial New York. Warehouses along the crowded South Street wharves and the stores and factories in lower Manhattan obscured the gracious old private homes, and hordes of European immigrants streamed into the Empire City, marking the end of an era. Almost overnight the city felt a housing shortage. Speculators and property owners partitioned old mansions into tenements to accommodate three or more families. The newcomers and the Negroes, including some from the South, poured into these reconstructed buildings, sometimes "swarming from cellar to garret," as unscrupulous owners divided their space into "the smallest proportions capable of containing human life within four walls." [16] Property values soared; rents were raised. Housing failed to meet the demand for shelter at low rentals despite the erection of new buildings designed especially as tenement houses.

The new type of tenement building often contained a narrow hall with access to two suites of rooms on each of three or four floors, all of which had inadequate light, air, and sanitary facilities. Indeed, washing and toilet conveniences were rarely, if at all, available inside these barracks. Frequently another tenement was built in the rear of the same lot, accessible only through a narrow alley. Along such buildings and in the yards were the privies and

[13] Citizens' Association of New York, *Report of the Council of Hygiene and Public Health* (New York, 1865), pp. 120–121.

[14] *Eighth Census of the United States*, 1860, population schedule, p. 337.

[15] Leo H. Hirsch, Jr., "New York and the Negro, from 1783 to 1865," *Journal of Negro History*, Vol. XVI, No. 4, October 1931, p. 415, citing census figures. (In 1850 some 2,120 of the 13,815 New York City Negroes were born in the South. *Ibid.* Haynes, *op. cit.*, pp. 46–47, gives Manhattan's Negro population as 18,600 in 1840 and 15,000 in 1860; however, in less densely settled Brooklyn the Negro population increased from 2,000 in 1840 to 5,000 in 1860. *ibid.*

[16] New York State Assembly, *Report of the Select Committee . . . to Examine into the Condition of Tenant Houses in New York and Brooklyn* (Albany, 1857), p. 22.

flimsy frame sheds and shanties, some inhabited by the overflow of the tenements living amid an accumulation of stinking filth and rubbish.[17] Here it was that most of the Negroes lived—in the poorest houses in the poorest neighborhoods. Rent gouging was common, as agents leased from the owners and collected enough in tenants' rents to purchase the properties in a short time. Many such speculators in human misery were enriched by charging $3 to $13 per month for apartments and 75c to $1.25 per week for single rooms twelve feet square.[18]

The Negro could ill afford high rents, especially when the cost of living rose to unprecedented heights in the middle of the century, since occupations open to Negroes were severely limited and the chances of advancement were poor. The majority of colored workers were unskilled. In 1850 nearly three-quarters of all gainfully employed Negroes (exclusive of seamen) were servants, laborers, and other unskilled or occasional workers.[19] Most of the rest were men of varying skills, including barbers and coachmen. Each of these two occupations alone attracted over a hundred persons. In business and the professions, Negroes were almost unrepresented. A mere sixty colored men were clerks, merchants, druggists, doctors, lawyers, ministers, teachers, and students, or, according to the census analysis, only one in about fifty-five.[20]

Five years later, in 1855, the situation was even worse. Of 3,688 gainfully employed colored persons for whom information is available, fully 3,225, or

[17] *Ibid.*, p. 23; *Reports of the United States Industrial Commission* (Washington, 1901), Vol. XV, p. 453.

[18] New York State Assembly, *Report of the Select Committee . . . [op. cit.]*, pp. 15–19.

[19] Computed from figures in J. D. B. DeBow, *Statistical View of the United States . . . Compendium of the Seventh Census* (Washington, 1854), pp. 80–81. I have not included "mariners" in this computation because they were an unstable floating element of the city's population. Of course, many "mariners" were unskilled seamen. DeBow's statistics are not absolutely accurate; they do not agree precisely with data gleaned from the New York City directory (Cf. Charles H. Wesley, *Negro Labor in the United States*, New York, 1927, p. 39), but they may be regarded as the best available approximations. A total of 3,337 individuals were classified:

1,144 laborers	21 ministers	4 printers
808 servants	21 boarding	3 barkeepers
434 mariners	house keepers	3 druggists
122 barbers	12 carpenters	3 jewelers
107 coachmen	12 sextons	3 merchants
95 cooks	11 hostlers	2 apprentices
44 stewards	9 doctors	2 confectioners
39 carmen	8 teachers	2 hatters
33 butchers	8 cigar makers	2 mechanics
28 boatmen	7 clerks	("generally")
24 farmers	7 gardners	1 blacksmith
24 musicians	5 ink makers	1 gunsmith
23 shoemakers	4 bakers	1 student
23 tailors	4 painters	Also 207 other occupations
		(sweeps, scavengers, etc.)

[20] *Ibid.*, p. 81.

87½ per cent, were engaged in menial or unskilled employment.[21] Of these, one-third were domestic servants, another third were laborers (including "whitewashers"), and about one-tenth were laundresses. The remainder consisted largely of seamstresses and dressmakers, cooks, porters, teamsters, coachmen, hackmen and drivers of other types of vehicles. Among the reasons for the Negroes' depressed status were the tradition of servitude, the continuing stigma of inferiority, the lack of education and opportunity to develop skills, and, as Dr. Smith pointed out to the Negro convention in 1851, the dearth of capital and the small number of colored employers.

The large proportion of Negroes who were servants, waiters, and laundresses, moreover, is partly attributable to their relative docility: they were frequently hired in preference to the Irish and German immigrants who were pouring into the city. Irish "turbulence" was contrasted with Negro "humility." Colored domestics usually were regarded as more tractable and better mannered than the children of Erin, while Negro waiters were "quicker in manipulation" and "less doggedly independent" than whites. Sometimes the favoritism in hiring was clearly reflected in the want ads of the newspapers:

WANTED—A Cook, Washer, and Ironer; one who perfectly understands her business; any color or country except Irish . . .[22]

WOMAN WANTED—To do general housework . . . English, Scotch, Welsh, German, or any country or color will answer except Irish . . .[23]

COACHMAN WANTED—A Man who understands the care of horses and is willing to make himself generally useful, on a small place six miles from the city. A colored man preferred. No Irish need apply . . .[24]

The Negroes could welcome this preference as long as they remained docile. As a perspicacious Englishman later remarked, much of their civility was "forced upon them by the circumstances of their helpless and degraded condition." [25] Meanwhile, immigrants were taking jobs which traditionally had been reserved for the colored folk.

As the Empire City grew wealthy on commerce and industry, much of the necessary labor was supplied by the foreign-born. Some 156,000 of these newcomers lived and worked on Manhattan in 1855; in comparison, the 3,688 gainfully employed Negroes were numerically insignificant.[26] Colored workers gradually were supplanted not only in a few of the better-paid posi-

---

[21] Statements in this paragraph are based upon my analysis of the manuscript schedules of the census marshals for New York City in the New York State Census of 1855. These volumes are now located in the county clerk's office, Hall of Records, New York City. My tabulation was limited, of course, to residents of Manhattan Island. Despite the exclusion of data from small portions of two of the volumes illegible because of their fragile condition, I believe the figures here given are reasonably accurate. In this article all further references to this material appear as: MSS., *New York State Census*, 1855.

[22] New York *Herald*, May 13, 1853.

[23] New York Daily *Sun*, May 11, 1853, as quoted by the *Irish American*, May 28, 1853.

[24] New York Daily *Tribune*, May 14, 1852.

[25] [Burn], *Three Years among the Working Classes, op. cit.*, p. xiii.

[26] MSS., *New York State Census*, 1855.

tions but as menial workers of all sorts, laborers, porters, dock hands, waiters, cooks, and maids.[27]

Even as colored domestics remained in demand, the Irish quickly surpassed them in numbers. Whereas in 1833 a traveller observed that the servants in New York City were "generally blacks," two decades later the city's Irish servants outnumbered by ten to one its entire Negro population.[28] At the same time, about 500 colored laborers and an equal number of colored waiters competed for employment with over 17,000 laborers and about 1,500 waiters born in the Emerald Isle.[29]

Economic rivalry between Negroes and immigrants intensified racial prejudices. The superior training and experience of many whites enabled them to obtain positions in most of the trades, while the black man found himself the eternal laborer. For him it was usually a question of manual labor or no job at all. This explains in part the willingness of Negroes to be hired on occasion as strikebreakers, should white laborers become unruly and demand higher wages. In 1853, for example, when Irish laborers at the Erie Railroad depot struck for $1.25 a day and a working limit of ten hours, Negroes, allegedly armed with revolvers, were hired in their places.[30] Whenever employers used colored men as scabs, mistrust and smouldering fears were fanned into passionate hatred.

The unrest of white workers was further fomented during the Civil War by the Conscription Act of 1863, which permitted the rich to exempt themselves from the draft by money payments. Many workers, including the foreign-born—who constituted half the city's population—believed that when they were drafted employers would replace them with Negroes. Fearing that newly emancipated southern Negroes might join with the colored workers of the North in taking away their jobs, the whites vented their blind rage in assaults upon innocent Negro citizens.[31] Native, German, and French workingmen were aroused by rumors of the importation of colored men to displace them at lower wages, and during a strike on the docks Irish longshoremen assaulted Negro strikebreakers.[32]

[27] Charles H. Wesley, *Negro Labor in the United States* (New York, 1927), p. 76; Arnett G. Lindsay, "The Economic Condition of the Negroes of New York Prior to 1861," *Journal of Negro History*, Vol. VI, No. 2, April 1921, p. 194; J. H. Harmon, Jr., "The Negro as a Local Business Man," *Journal of Negro History*, Vol. XIV, No. 2, April 1929, p. 119.

[28] John Finch, *Travels in the United States of America and Canada* (London, 1833), p. 35; MSS., *New York State Census*, 1865.

[29] MSS., *New York State Census*, 1855.

[30] *Irish American*, July 9, 1853.

[31] *Freeman's Journal*, August 16, 18, 1862; *Courrier des Etats-Unis*, August 16, October 7, 1862, April 14, 1863; *Albion*, November 18, 1863. Cf. Madeleine H. Rice, *American Catholic Opinion in the Slavery Controversy* (New York, 1944), pp. 124, 154; Basil L. Lee, *Discontent in New York City, 1861–1865* (Washington, 1943), chapter IV, *passim*.

[32] *Staats-Zeitung*, April 18, 1863; *Criminal-Zeitung*, April 24, 1863; Andreas Dorpalen, "The German Element and the Issues of the Civil War," *Mississippi Valley*

Racial hatred and class consciousness, inflamed by the Emancipation Proclamation and the enforcement of conscription, burst into flames during the hectic week of July 11, 1863 as the enrollment of conscripts touched off the furious draft riots. For several days the metropolis was thrown into an uproar. Desperate mobs attacked the registry offices, sacked the residence of anti-slavery agitators, intimidated peaceable workingmen, assaulted and lynched Negroes, wrecked their homes and places of business, and burned the Colored Orphan Asylum into a shambles of blackened ruins. After an orgy of pillage and destruction, the police and militia finally restored order.[33]

While these riots were clear evidence of working class discontent, more important though less spectacular instances are afforded by the efforts of workingmen to improve their status by concerted action. During the fifties and sixties workers in nearly every industry struck for higher wages and fewer working hours. Some, like the German tailors, shoemakers, and bakers, tried to by-pass the wage system by organizing co-operative shops, and a number turned to Marxian socialism introduced at New York by the German, Joseph Weydemeyer. No Negroes joined the attacks upon capitalism, and, despite the formation in New York City of an American League of Colored Laborers in 1850, the Negro workers seem to have taken a negligible part in the labor struggles of the time.[34]

Apparently in only one instance did colored and white workers co-operate in the battle for higher wages. It was an exceptional situation, involving the hotel waiters, most of whom were Irish-born. Because the Negroes were fewer in number and more tractable (and hence more desirable from

Historical Review, Vol. XXIX, No. 1, June 1942, p. 68; George E. McNeill, The Labor Movement: The Problem of Today (Boston, 1887), p. 126.

[33] Joel T. Headley, The Great Riots of New York, 1712–1873; Including a Full and Complete Account of the Four Days' Draft Riot of 1863 (New York, 1873), pp. 136–289; Wesley, op. cit., pp. 100–101; Albion, July 18, 1863; Messager Franco-Américain, July 15, 1863. My forthcoming Immigrant Life in New York City shows that the European newcomer took part in the riots not as immigrants but as members of the white working classes. The twentieth annual report of the Association for Improving the Conditions of the Poor (1863, pp. 44–45) refers to Irish rowdies as the instigators of the violence but absolves from blame the immigrants as a group. The confused character of the riots is indicated by the fact that German grocery, liquor store, and beer garden proprietors suffered injury and property losses at the hands of the mob. Persuaded that the Orientals were but a "modification" of the Negro, a crowd of whites launched an attack upon the Chinese. New York Herald, July 16, 1863; Anglo-Africa, July 25, 1863; Lee, op. cit., p. 195; County of New York, Board of Supervisors, Document No. 13, December 27, 1867 (New York, 1868), Vol. I, pp. 90–91, 101, 111, 193, 207, 222–224, 424–425, 465, 507, 550–552, 684–686, 694–696.

[34] The league was a philanthropic and educational enterprise rather than a typical labor union. Headed by S. R. Ward, Lewis Woodson, Frederick Douglass, James McCune Smith, and others, its object was to promote union of skilled colored workmen, to improve their "social and physical condition," and to recommend commercial, mechanical, and agriculture education to Negro youth. It also planned a fund which would assist Negroes to go into business. New York Daily Tribune, July 30, 1850. An industrial fair which it contemplated for 1852 does not seem to have taken place. I have found no further mention of this organization.

the proprietors' viewpoint) they were paid more than the whites. In 1853, when Negro waiters were receiving $16 a month and white waiters only $12, the whites gathered to discuss means of equalizing their wages. A colored delegate to the meeting advised the group to hold out for $18 a month, hoping thereby to aid Negroes in raising their own pay (or perhaps to dupe the whites into making impossible demands!). A strike ensued, but it was a miserable failure. Some employers retained their best white waiters at higher wages but fired the rest, replacing them with women or Negroes.[35]

In skilled occupations Negroes and whites made no common efforts to improve conditions of work. Had Negro cooperation been desired by the whites, it would have been of no material help. There were too few skilled colored workers. Of 3,688 gainfully employed Negroes in 1855, about 200, or only four tenths of one per cent were engaged in the skilled trades.[36] In a traditionally Negro calling, 74 colored barbers and 4 hairdressers were easily outnumbered by Germans, Irishmen, English and French, together with a small but growing number of Italians.[37] Tailors, shoemakers, carpenters, sawyers, tinsmiths, coopers, cabinetmakers and upholsterers, nurses, cigar makers, and jewellers accounted for another 107 Negro working people of varying degrees of skill, while some of the 73 colored boatmen (of whom 56 were stewards) may have been partly skilled.[38]

Not only were the Negro artisans few in number; most of them were geographically isolated from the white artisans. Perhaps the main reason for

[35] New York *Herald*, March 31, 1853, as cited by the *European*, May 2, 1857; New York *Tribune*, April 26, May 3, 1853.

[36] *MSS., New York State Census*, 1855. Cf. *supra*, note 21; *infra*, note 38. In the late 1830's the city's Negro community included 3 carpenters and joiners, 5 boot and shoemakers, 5 tailors, an engraver, a watch and clock maker, a sign painter, and 2 dress and cloak makers. Haynes, *op. cit.*, p. 67.

[37] *MSS., New York State Census*, 1855; *Staats-Zeitung*, April 7, 1860.

[38] From the manuscript schedules of the *New York State Census* of 1855. Excluding professionals, I tabulated occupations of some 204 Negroes who, it seemed to me, possessed some degree of occupational skill. These are listed here (the figures in parentheses show the total number of whites and Negroes in the several occupations, as listed in the printed version of the census):

78 barbers (including 4 hairdressers) (997)
19 tailors (12,609)
13 boot and shoemakers (6,745)
13 nurses (636)
12 carpenters (excluding ship carpenters) (6,901)
10 sawyers (285)
8 cigar makers (1,996 "tobacconists")
6 coopers (1,018)
5 jewelers (1,099)
5 tinsmiths (897)
3 cabinetmakers (2,606)
3 masons, plasterers, bricklayers (3,634)

2 moulders (593)
2 bakers (2,856)
2 clock makers (79)
2 printers (1,901)
2 sail makers (281)
2 upholsterers (711)
1 each of the following: boat builder, blacking maker, blacksmith, confectioner, carver and gilder, cage maker, chandler, "cutter," gold and silversmith, hat and cap maker, iron worker, painter, roofer and slater, ship carpenter, shirt and collar maker, tool maker.

the existence of this class of colored workers was the fact that, with a few exceptions, they served the Negro community almost exclusively. In this respect they resembled the German shoemakers, carpenters, painters, and masons who catered to the needs of the German immigrants and seldom were found outside New York City's "Little Germany." Each Negro craftsman had his own clientele which, if not entirely colored, included immigrants of little means who usually shared the same slum areas.

In some respects the Negro population developed a degree of self-sufficiency. Negro shops and services were available in the community. About 1840, Negroes published a newspaper and operated two first-class restaurants, two dry goods stores, a hairdressing establishment, three tailor shops, four "pleasure gardens," a confectionery, a fruit store, and two coal yards.[39] The restaurants and the richer stores were in the financial district or in the white shopping neighborhoods, but most were in localities where Negroes congregated. The smallest shops which did not advertise were probably in run-down localities inhabited chiefly by the colored people themselves. Among these were numerous second-hand clothing stores and barber shops. Fifteen years later, some 31 Negroes were dealers in foodstuffs, mostly butchers, while 11 were peddlers and traders, 4 were retail shopkeepers, and 18 served as clerks; there were also 5 merchants, agents, or salesmen, a contractor, a distiller or brewer, an express man, a clothier, an undertaker, and a stable keeper.[40] Colored persons were proprietors of 14 hotels and boarding houses and 5 restaurants in 1855.[41] On the whole, however, the small number of Negro businesses reflected a lack of opportunity, while such colored enterprises as existed showed the courage of Negro businessmen who risked their capital in property which might be damaged or ruined by a race riot.

Few Negroes entered the professions. Considering the difficulties in the way of Negro self-improvement, however, it is remarkable that approximately 50 colored professional men were reported by the state census marshals in 1855. Exactly half were teachers and clergymen. Fifteen Negro musicians included, no doubt, dancers and minstrel singers. Five physicians, a dentist, a lawyer, and an artist complete the list.[42]

---

[39] Haynes, *op. cit.*, pp. 96–97.

[40] MSS., *New York State Census,* 1855. Among the more prominent Negro enterprises were Thomas Dowling's restaurant near the corner of Wall and Broad streets, Edward Bidwell's two thriving stores in Broadway, Austin Steward's liquor business, Henry Scott's pickling business, and James McCune Smith's drug store. Lindsay, "The Economic Condition of the Negroes . . . ," *loc. cit.*, pp. 106, 139, 197–198; Harmon, "The Negro as a Local Business Man," *loc. cit.*, p. 120. Cf. Martin R. Delany, *The Condition, Elevation, Emigation, and Destiny of the Colored People* . . . (Philadelphia, 1852), chapter X.

[41] MSS., *New York State Census,* 1855. Others in supervisory occupations were 7 housekeepers and janitors, 2 watchmen and 8 miscellaneous superintendents. In addition there were 7 farmers, 4 gardeners, florists, and nurserymen, and 4 fishermen.

[42] *Ibid.* There were 13 teachers and 12 clergymen; 3 "engineers" and a student were also reported. Cf. Delany, *op. cit.*, chapter XI.

Perhaps more important as an index of the well-being of any community is the degree to which real and personal property is owned. Colored folk sometimes acquired real estate despite their lowly position in society. In 1837, before the famous panic of that year, the *Colored American* asserted that Negro freeholders to the amount of $250 did "not fall far short of 300."[43] Twelve years later such freeholders represented 2.2 per cent of the Negro population; in 1855 this percentage had risen to 8.7, and by 1865 to 10.5.[44] As to the dollar value of real estate, only one estimate seems to be available: in 1859 the taxed real estate owned by Negroes on Manhattan amounted to $1,400,000, while perhaps a like amount was owned in Brooklyn.[45] The value of personal property owned by Negroes is harder to assess. An indication, at least, is afforded by savings bank deposits. In 1837 the *Colored American* claimed that the colored folk had from $50,000 to $80,000 in New York City savings banks, an amount which seems grossly exaggerated when compared with James McCune Smith's estimate in 1851 of "$40,000 or $50,000 belonging to the colored people invested in savings banks in Wall-st."[46] By 1855 the Negro deposits reached $60,000.[47] Apart from savings, colored businessmen and artisans acquired property and equipment necessary for their work, and in 1861 Smith stated that the Negroes of the Empire City had invested in their own businesses some $755,000.[48]

While we may conclude from this evidence that a colored aristocracy had appeared by the middle of the century, the great mass of Negro families saw no improvement of their lot. Wages failed to keep pace with rising rents and the prices of provisions, while in depression years, as in 1857, unemployment swelled the relief rolls. Hard times, the many disabilities of colored workers, heightened prejudice aroused by abolitionist propaganda, and the filling of unskilled and semiskilled occupations by immigrants contributed more than

[43] *Colored American*, July 22, 1837. One of these was probably E. Davis who, during the abolitionist riot of 1834, owned the brick buildings at 121 Broome and 123 Forsyth streets. MS letter from H. and A. Averill to Mayor Lawrence, July 12, 1834, now in the possession of the New York Historical Society.

[44] Hirsch, "New York and the Negro . . . ," *loc. cit.*, p. 434, which cites census figures and yearbooks as sources. By Article II, Section 1, of the State Constitution of 1821, Negro freeholders to the value of $250 were permitted to vote; they also were taxed, while Negroes possessing less than this were exempted from taxation.

[45] Wesley, *op. cit.*, p. 49. In Philadelphia, Negroes owned real estate amounting to $400,000 in 1847 and $800,000 in 1856. Abram L. Harris, *The Negro as Capitalist* (Philadelphia, 1936), p. 6. For mention of Negro-owned houses in New York in 1864 cf. the Citizens Association's *Report of the Council of Hygiene, op. cit.*, p. 240.

[46] *Colored American*, May 22, 1837; New York Daily *Tribune*, March 20, 1851.

[47] Harris, *op. cit.*, p. 23. According to a report published in the *African Repository*, Vol. XXXI, January 1856, p. 8, "free persons of color" had $600,000 deposited in savings fund institutions in New York, a figure which I consider highly dubious. Cf. Arnett G. Lindsay, "The Negro in Banking," *Journal of Negro History*, Vol. XIV, No. 2, April 1929, p. 159.

[48] Wesley, *op. cit.*, pp. 49–50, citing Clark, *The Condition of the Colored People of the United States*, p. 11; cf. Harris, *op. cit.*, p. 6. The Brooklyn figure was $76,200, and in Williamsburg, $4,900.

anything else to the remarkable decline in the Negro population of Manhattan during the 1850's. New York might afford the first step toward the foreigner's fortune, but for the colored man it held out little hope.

SPECIAL STATISTICAL NOTE. The following material, made available for the first time, shows occupations in which ten or more Negroes were engaged in 1855 (derived from the manuscript schedules of the *New York State Census of 1855*):

1,025 domestic servants
536 laborers (including carpet shakers)
499 waiters
366 laundresses
176 porters
151 cooks
129 whitewashers
111 dressmakers, seamstresses
102 drivers, coachmen, hackmen
78 barbers (including 4 hairdressers)
56 stewards
55 cartmen, draymen, teamsters
19 butchers
19 tailors
18 clerks
17 boatmen
16 longshoremen
15 chimney sweeps
15 musicians
14 hotel and boarding house keepers
13 boot and shoemakers
13 nurses
13 teachers
12 clergymen
12 carpenters
12 wine and liquor dealers
11 peddlers, traders
11 farmers, gardeners, florists, nurserymen
10 sawyers

Louis Ruchames

JIM CROW RAILROADS IN MASSACHUSETTS

Segregation, with its diverse manifestations, had its beginnings more in the North than in the South. Especially in the northeastern states, Negroes mounted indignant protests against the practice. They achieved their greatest measure of success in Massachusetts, where white sentiment was more sympathetic to their cause than in any other state. Louis Ruchames' article describes one of these early Negro protests against segregation. As he shows, their tactics were quite similar to those employed by civil rights organizations today.

MASSACHUSETTS is today in the forefront of those states that have sought to achieve equality of status and opportunity for all racial groups. Its fair employment and fair educational practice laws are among the finest in the country and have achieved notable successes in opening up new opportunities for racial and religious groups within the state. Segregation of Negroes and whites, although it still exists to some extent, is a steadily shrinking element in the social structure of Massachusetts.

How different is this situation from what obtained a century or more ago. In the 1830's and 1840's segregation was the dominant pattern in the state. As late as 1843 Negroes were forbidden to marry whites; they were segregated in the churches, where they occupied the "Negro pew"; they were confined to the most menial occupations; they could not attend the same schools as white children—in Boston this situation continued to 1855; they were segregated on stagecoaches, railroads and steam boats. Writing in 1836, Lydia Maria Child, a prominent author and Abolitionist, charged that "our prejudice against colored people is even more inveterate than it is at the South. The planter is often attached to his Negroes, and lavishes caresses and kind words upon them, as he would on a favorite hound: but our cold-hearted, ignoble prejudice admits of no exception—no intermission."[1]

Louis Ruchames, "Jim Crow Railroads in Massachusetts," *American Quarterly*, VIII (Spring, 1956), pp. 61–75. Reprinted with permission of *American Quarterly* and Louis Ruchames.

[1] *An Appeal in Favor of That Class of Americans Called Africans* (New York, 1836), p. 195.

The basic causes of this change are well known. The expansion of industry and the rise of large urban centers seriously weakened the system of caste. The growth of a large middle class whose interests and ideals favored individual freedom and equality before the law was a no less significant factor. Less well known, however, is the day to day activity of a large body of men and women, enrolled in the Abolitionist movement under the leadership of William Lloyd Garrison, whose self-sacrificing efforts on behalf of racial equality in the North, in addition to their efforts against slavery in the South, provided the motive power for the changes that did take place. It was they who exposed segregation and discrimination to the public eye, condemned them unreservedly and organized the campaigns which helped to diminish or eliminate such practices from significant areas of public life.

The first important Abolitionist campaign against segregation began with the appearance of the *Liberator*, edited and published by Garrison, in 1831. In its third issue it called attention to the existing law prohibiting the marriage of Negroes and whites, and demanded its repeal. The movement for repeal reached its peak in the 1840's, and success was finally achieved in 1843. It was in the midst of this campaign that the question of "Jim Crow" cars on certain of the railways of Massachusetts came to the fore.

Railroads had first come into public use in Massachusetts in 1836. Following existing customs on many stagecoaches and passenger vessels, several railroads instituted the practice of segregating Negroes in a separate car. These were the Eastern Railroad, extending at first from Boston to Salem and later reaching the New Hampshire border; the New Bedford and Taunton trunk line; and the Boston and Providence Railroad.

At first, the car for Negroes had no definite name. A letter to the *Massachusetts Spy* of Worcester in 1838, referred to it as a "dirt car." [2] In 1841, however, it came to be referred to quite widely as the "Jim Crow" car. The name was taken from a song and dance routine popularized during the 1830's by Thomas D. Rice, "the father of American Minstrelsy." The routine was called "jumping Jim Crow" and was an imitation, by a white, of a Negro referred to as Jim Crow, doing a song and dance. Reflecting prevailing white prejudices, it caricatured the Negro as an inferior and ignorant creature. Thus, the application of "Jim Crow" to the cars for Negroes on the railroads of Massachusetts was a natural development, and Massachusetts has come to have the dubious distinction of first using the term with reference to a segregated Negro car.

Before 1841 there were occasional references in the press of the Commonwealth to instances of enforced segregation on the railroads. There was no discernible public agitation on the subject, however, until the early part of 1841, when the issue came to a head through a series of incidents involving Negro and white leaders of the Abolitionist movement.

David Ruggles, a Negro Abolitionist of New York, who had played a prominent part in the Underground Railway and had helped more than five

[2] Reprinted in the *Liberator*, VIII (December 14, 1838), 197.

hundred Negro slaves to escape to the North, was ordered by a conductor, while going from New Bedford to Boston on the New Bedford and Taunton branch railroad on July 6, to leave the car in which he was seated and to move to another set aside for Negroes. On refusing, he was dragged out by the railroad superintendent and several others employed by the company, his clothing torn in the process, and thrown off the train. Ruggles brought suit for assault and battery against those who were involved in removing him.

The trial took place in New Bedford before Justice Henry A. Crapo on July 19 and 20. The company based its eviction of Ruggles on a regulation issued by its agent, William A. Crocker, on January 1, 1841, which read: "Passengers who go in the cars of the Taunton and New Bedford branch railroad, will take such seats as may be assigned them by the conductor." The company contended that a copy of the regulation had been pointed out to Ruggles when he had been asked to move to the Negro car. He had refused, and was then ejected. In delivering his opinion, Justice Crapo suggested that two issues were involved: (1) the right of the company to issue the regulation in question; and (2) whether or not undue force had been used to put the regulation into effect. On the first issue, he ruled that the railroad was the private property of the company, which therefore had the right to issue such regulations ensuring the welfare and comfort of its passengers as were not forbidden by the existing law of the state. The regulation in question, he ruled, was not contrary to the law of the state. As to the question of undue force, he ruled that such had not been proven. The charges brought by Ruggles were thereupon dismissed and the defendants adjudged not guilty.[3]

A few weeks later, on September 8, Frederick Douglass, the Negro Abolitionist, and J. A. Collins, the General Agent of the Massachusetts Anti-Slavery Society, a white man, were the center of another violent fracas. They had purchased tickets in Newburyport and were on their way, together, to the annual meeting of the Strafford County Anti-Slavery Society. On taking seats side by side in a car of the Eastern Railroad, they were approached by the conductor, who ordered Douglass to move into the Jim Crow car. Collins and several of the other passengers objected to the conductor's demand. Collins was ordered to leave his seat, the better to enable the conductor to drag or "snake" Douglass out of the car. He refused, remarking, "If you haul him out, it will be over my person, as I do not intend to leave this seat." The conductor left and returned with four or five men who seized Douglass and carried him into the Jim Crow car. In the process, Collins was injured and Douglass had his clothing torn.

About three weeks later, Collins, Douglass, J. M. Buffum, a white Abolitionist, and an unidentified woman were travelling on the Eastern Railroad to Newburyport. Collins and Douglass occupied one seat, with Buffum sitting behind them and the woman in front. In Lynn the conductor approached

[3] For a summary of the proceedings and the ruling see the *New Bedford Mercury*, July 22, 1841; also the *Liberator*, XI (August 6, 1841), 165.

Douglass and ordered him out. The following colloquy, reported in detail in the *Liberator*, then took place:

Buffum: Can't I ride with him, if he goes into the forward car! I want to have some conversation with him, and I fear I shall not have another opportunity so favorable.

The Conductor: No! I'd as soon haul you out of his car, as I'd haul him from this.

Douglass: There are but very few in this car, and why, since no objection has been made, do you order me out?

A Passenger: I've no objection to riding with him—let's take a vote on the question.

Buffum: That's just what I want—let us have a vote on the question.

A second passenger: I've no objection to that step.

The conductor remained adamant.

Douglass: If you will give me any good reason why I should leave this car, I'll go willing; but, without such reason, I do not feel at liberty to leave; though, you can do with me as you please, I shall not resist.

The Conductor: You have asked that question before.

Douglass: I mean to continue asking the question over and over again, as long as you continue to assault me in this manner.

Others took up the cry and called out: "Give him one good reason." Finally, forced to speak, the conductor muttered. "Because you are black."

Finding himself unequal to the task of dragging Douglass out, the conductor secured the help of eight or ten toughs. What happened next is vividly described by Collins:

"Snake out the d----d nigger," cried one. "Out with him," responded another guardian of the "peculiar institution" of the South. The gang of men stood in a leaping posture, with their hands extended and fingers half bent, ready for the going forth of the command of the captain to seize him. The word was given—"Take him out!" Five or six, like so many tigers, laid hold of Douglass, but he happened to be exceedingly heavy, as the laws of gravity were in full force. His attachment to his seat was so great, that these half dozen bullies found it no easy task to snake him out over me. "Damm that Collins," cried out one of them, "out with him, out with him." Whereupon five or six laid violent hands upon me. One gave me a severe blow upon the back part of my head, and another hit me in my face, cutting my lip considerably. Like my friend Douglass, I did not feel inclined to part with my seat at the command of these ruffians, if I may be allowed the use of such an expression; in consequence of which, our seat gave way, and we, with five or six of these villains laying hold of our head, arms and legs, were dragged out head foremost, and deposited upon the ground in no very gentle manner. One of the gang gave me a very severe kick in my back, in consequence of which, I am lame at the present time. I was so badly bruised that my person, in various parts, is now black and blue. Buffum remained behind with Douglass, whose baggage was thrown out after him. I was allowed to pass on in the same train. Soon after the cars started, the conductor approached me, and made use of the most abusive language. I asked him if he was employed by the company to insult passengers; and, :f so, I considered him the most faithful servant I ever met with; and then turned myself around, and began to read. He shook his little fist about my head a few times, and was greatly enraged because I would hold no conversation with him. I was now left to myself until we arrived at Salem.[4]

On arriving in Salem, Collins was accosted by the conductor and other officials of the railroad, including its president, Mr. Neal, and was ordered to leave the train because of his earlier defence of Douglass. After some remonstrance and only when it became clear that he would be dragged out if he failed to leave peacefully, he walked out of the train and took a private conveyance to Newburyport.

In the ensuing months, there occurred numerous other incidents. One morning, at the end of September, Mrs. Mary Newhall Green, the secretary of the Lynn Anti-Slavery Society, a light-complexioned Negro, who had previously without incident used the Eastern Railroad for trips from Lynn to Boston, was dragged out of the white car, with a baby in her arms. In the process, the baby was injured, and Mrs. Green's husband, who had sought to defend her, was badly beaten.

On the evening of that day, some three or four white men, who had boarded the train of the Eastern Railroad in East Boston, were dragged out of their car, together with a Negro whose ejection they had protested.[5] One of the whites, Dr. Daniel Mann, a dentist of Boston, brought charges of assault and battery against George Harrington, the conductor, who had led the assault. The trial took place in the Boston Police Court before a Justice Simmons. The lawyer for the defense was a Mr. Lord of Salem; Dr. Mann's counsel was Samuel E. Sewall, a well-known Abolitionist who was a descendant of Massachusetts Chief Justice Samuel Sewall, an outspoken opponent of Negro slavery in Colonial days.[6]

Lord argued that "all corporations in the Commonwealth have power to make such reasonable and proper by-laws for the management of their business as their own interests and the public good may require; that the established usage and the public sentiment of this community authorise a separation of the

[4] *Liberator*, XI (October 15, 1841), 165.
[5] *Ibid.*, XI (October 15, 1841), 165.
[6] *Ibid.*, XI (November 5, 1841), 180.

blacks from the whites in public places; that the regulation adopted by the Eastern Railroad Corporation was reasonable and proper, and such as they had a perfect right to adopt; that if the rule was unreasonable, neither Dr. Mann nor any other person had power to take the law into their own hands, and to right the wrong; and that he and his friends formed a conspiracy to prevent the execution of this rule; and in this they were trespassers." [7]

On the other hand, Sewall argued that the directors of the railroad did not have the legal right to authorize a conductor to separate passengers on the basis of color; that a rule of that kind was arbitrary and unlawful, as was the attempt to enforce it; that the conductor had no right to evict any person by force without first notifying him of the company's regulation—which had not been done in this case; and that the conductor had no right to evict passengers who had merely expressed their objections to his action.

Justice Simmons decided, however, "that the conductor was justified by the disorderly and unlawful conduct of Dr. Mann and his friends in ejecting them from the cars—and ordered that the defendant be discharged." [8]

Toward the end of the year, there occurred an incident that had a strong impact upon public opinion. It involved Charles Lenox Remond, a Negro Abolitionist who had been chosen one of the American delegates to the World Anti-Slavery Convention held in London in June, 1840. Endowed with an attractive personality and eloquence of speech, Remond had been warmly received by the foremost leaders of English society. He returned to America in December, 1841, carrying with him the signatures of 60,000 Irishmen urging their countrymen in America to oppose slavery. On his arrival in Boston, Remond boarded a train of the Eastern Railroad to visit his parents, who were living in Salem. The conductor ordered him into the "Jim Crow" car. When several white friends, who had just welcomed him in Boston and were eager to hear the story of his visit abroad, moved to the "Jim Crow" car with him, they were ordered by the conductor to leave immediately or be dragged out.

In describing the incident, the Abolitionists were not slow to point out the difference between Remond's insulting reception in his own country and the love and respect accorded him in Europe. "In England, Scotland, and Ireland, Mr. Remond was received into the best circles, and treated with the utmost courtesy and respect. In Exeter Hall, London, with a royal duke in the chair, and succeeding Daniel O'Connell as one of the speakers on that occasion, he was listened to with admiration, and elicited thunders of applause. . . . But, in his own land, as soon as he steps his foot on the shore, he is treated more vilely than a dog, and prohibited from enjoying the society even of those who have crucified their own prejudices, and whose hearts are touched with sympathy for his lot! And America is the land of liberty and equality—the land which cannot tolerate a nobility—the land which scoffs at monarchy!" [9]

[7] Massachusetts Anti-Slavery Society, *Tenth Annual Report*, January 26, 1842.
[8] *Liberator*, XI (November 5, 1841), 180.
[9] Massachusetts Anti-Slavery Society, *Tenth Annual Report*, January 26, 1842.

As these incidents came to their notice, the Abolitionists expressed their indignation and took steps to combat the policy of the railroads.[10] A speech in the state legislature, in March, 1841, by Representative George Bradburn, who had been leading the campaign for repeal of the marriage law, helped bring the problem to public attention.[11] Speaking on a bill to authorize the owners of the Eastern Railroad to extend their wharves, Bradburn surprised the House when he announced that, despite his interest in railroad expansion, he would vote against the bill because of the Eastern Railroad's policy of segregation. It was not until the attack upon David Ruggles, however, that public opinion was really aroused. On July 12, a mass meeting of protest, attended by prominent residents of the city, was held in New Bedford. Ruggles presented his version of the attack upon him and was followed by several other speakers. The meeting adjourned and reconvened the following day to hear the report of an investigating committee appointed to look into the incident. After hearing the report, those assembled resolved "that as citizens of a free and enlightened community, and descendants of those Revolutionary worthies who poured out their hearts' blood in the cause of our civil liberty, we do remonstrate in the most solemn manner against those inhuman proceedings as took place at the railroad depot, in this town on the 6th of the present month, in expelling David Ruggles of New York, from the car, for the unworthy cause of his having a color which the God of Nature was pleased to give him." [12]

The failure of Ruggles' suit against the New Bedford and Taunton Railroad outraged the Abolitionists and stimulated their campaign for further action. Soon after the trial, the *Liberator* printed a letter from Ruggles, dated July 24, giving his version of the proceedings before Justice Crapo. He charged that, "It was hardly to be supposed that his honor could give an equitable decision in this case—himself being a stockholder in said company, and therefore lawfully rendered incapable of occupying the bench of justice under such circumstances. In relation to Justice Crapo's court, I must confess, he rendered it the greatest farce I ever witnessed. In giving his opinion, he declared his

[10] Even before railroads had come into use, Abolitionists had condemned segregation on public conveyances. In 1834, the *Liberator* had characterized the treatment of Negroes on stagecoaches and steamboats as "vulgar and shameful in the extreme." (*Liberator*, IV [June 4, 1834], 91.) In 1836, Lydia Maria Child, the prominent Abolitionist author, had asked in her famous *Appeal*: "Will any candid person tell me why respectable colored people should not be allowed to make use of public conveyances, open to all who are able and willing to pay for the privilege? Those who enter a vessel, or a stagecoach, cannot select their companions. If they can afford to take a carriage or boat for themselves, then, and then only, they have a right to be exclusive." (*An Appeal in Favor of That Class of Americans Called Africans* [New York, 1836], p. 206.) In the ensuing years, the *Liberator*, from time to time, reported instances of segregation, which it condemned in no uncertain terms. See VIII (December 14, 1838), 197; IX (July 19, 1938), 116; IX (October 18, 1839), 167; IX (October 25, 1839), 170; X (June 26, 1840), 101.

[11] The marriage law, first enacted in 1705–6, and revised in 1834, forbade the intermarriage of whites with Negroes, Indians or Mulattoes. It was repealed in 1843 after a long struggle which began in 1831.

[12] *Liberator*, XI (July 24, 1841), 118.

ignorance of the law in the case, and, of course, adhered to the authority of Judge Lynch." Entitling the letter "Lynching in New Bedford, Justice Henry A. Crapo and Lynch Law," the *Liberator* commented: "The conduct of Justice Crapo, in giving his legal sanction to the dastardly assault and battery upon the person of Mr. Ruggles at the New Bedford depot by the conductors of the railroad train, is in our view, unspeakably atrocious." [13]

As the attacks upon Negroes and their white sympathizers in the railroad cars continued, other newspapers besides the *Liberator* condemned them, and public demand for action began to intensify. The Boston *Daily Times*, the Lynn *Record*, the Dover *Morning Star*, the Quincy *Patriot* and the Massachusetts *Spy* printed reports of incidents and letters from readers, and forcefully denounced the conduct of the railroad companies and the courts. The Dover *Morning Star* actually called for a boycott of the Eastern Railroad.[14] The *Liberator* emphasized that Stephen Chase, the superintendent of the Eastern Railroad, was a member in good standing of the Society of Friends, and called upon the Society to "disown" him or "be willing to lie under the imputation of conniving at the sanctioning of high-handed villainy and brutal ruffianism."[15]

The Abolitionists of Massachusetts initiated a concerted campaign against the railroads at a meeting of the Massachusetts Anti-Slavery Society on August 17, 1841. It was decided that in addition to the petitions for repeal of the marriage law, which they were circulating, they would also distribute petitions "for a law declaring equal rights of persons in the use of the means of conveyance furnished under charters from the State." [16] In September, three large public meetings were held in Lynn, with people of all shades of political opinion attending. At one of the meetings, in the First Universalist meeting house, resolutions were unanimously adopted condemning the attack upon Collins and Douglass as "a gross violation of our State constitution as well as of all law and decency," "the substitution of Lynch law and mobocracy for order and decorum," and asserting that those present would "use all the means in their power, consistent with their views of law and christianity, to defend the colored people who may see fit to take their seats in the long cars, in the enjoyment of their rights." [17]

At a meeting on September 30, it was further resolved that the attacks "demand the interference of Legislative authority," and that petitions to that effect be presented to the legislature. In order to secure the widest public support, another resolution affirmed that the Eastern Railroad's practices "be viewed not as a question between Abolitionists and Anti-Abolitionists, but as a matter connected with the freedom of every citizen." [18]

The campaign for legislative action quickly gathered momentum. On

13 *Ibid.*, XI (August 6, 1841), 127.
14 *Ibid.*, XI (October 1, 1841), 157.
15 *Ibid.*, XI (October 8, 1841), 163.
16 *Ibid.*, XI (August 20, 1841), 139.
17 *Ibid.*, XI (October 15, 1841), 166.
18 *Ibid.*, XI (October 15, 1841), 166.

October 15, the *Liberator* printed a copy of a petition that was being circulated by the Board of Managers of the Massachusetts Anti-Slavery Society. The petition requested the legislature "to pass a law declaring and defining the rights of the people of this Commonwealth in the use of the means of conveyance furnished by the Railroad companies therein, in order that the officers of said companies may no longer claim the right of depriving any class of persons of the use of any of their cars, on the sole ground of color, and of insulting, assaulting and ejecting white passengers, merely for claiming the equal means of conveyance for persons of color." [19] Anti-Slavery societies throughout the state quickly swung into action and tied this campaign in with the already powerful one against the marriage law. Thus, the Norfolk County Anti-Slavery Society, at its quarterly meeting, resolved to "recommend to the Abolitionists of the several towns in this county, to interrogate the candidates of the whig and the democratic parties, of their respective towns, for the State Legislature, as to their view for the repeal of the marriage law, and for defining the powers of Rail-Road Corporations." [20] The quarterly meeting of the Worcester North Division Anti-Slavery Society passed a resolution and added the recommendation "to those who may be travelling to New York or Portland, to patronize the Boston and Norwich in preference to the Providence and Stonington Railroad, the Boston and Exeter in preference to the Boston and Newburyport Railroad, inasmuch as colored people are, by these companies respected and treated as equal human beings." [21]

In their public pronouncements, the Abolitionists kept repeating a number of points which proved to be extremely effective in swinging public opinion to their side. They emphasized, for instance, that the railroads which forcefully prevented whites and Negroes from sitting together were most solicitous in permitting Southern slaveholders to keep their Negro slaves by their side when travelling in those very same cars. It was only the free Negro who was segregated, not the slave. Thus, the author of a letter to the *Massachusetts Spy* of Worcester, wrote: "That Corporation [the Eastern Railroad] consider this 'Jim Crow' car good enough for a 'Nigger,' if said 'Nigger' be a *free* man or woman. Let a southern slaveholder, however, get into one of their first class cars, accompanied by his 'chattels personal,' and no matter how black those 'chattels' may be, not a word will be uttered against the arrangement. After all, then, it is *not* color alone which excludes a man from the best car. The colored person to be excluded must also be *free!!* I ask every man or woman who may see these lines, if this be consistent? If it be right? I ask them if they are willing such an insult should be offered to freedom in Massachusetts? Ay, and in sight of Bunker Hill?" [22]

[19] *Ibid.*, XI (October 15, 1841), 166.
[20] *Ibid.*, XI (October 29, 1841), 175.
[21] *Ibid.*, XI (October 29, 1841), 175.
[22] Reprinted in the *Liberator*, XI (November 5, 1841), 177. Similarly, James Buffum, in a letter to the *National Anti-Slavery Standard*, extracts from which were printed in the *Liberator*, XI (November 12, 1841), 184, noted: "Let it be observed that

Another point stressed by the Abolitionists was the repression of freedom of speech by the railroad corporations, whose procedure it was to attack all those who protested the forcible evictions of Negroes from white cars. Dr. Daniel Mann, the white dentist who had been assaulted, emphasized this when he asked, in a letter to the *Liberator:* "But, *reader* are *you* willing to ride in the cars under the cringing sense that a padlock is on your lips, and that a power as despotic as that of the Turk, wielded by hands far less responsible and far more degraded, is ready to insult and trample upon your rights, and can do so with impunity, if by any censure of their abuse, you should provoke their rage?" [23]

A third argument, no less important than the others, concerned the wealth and power of the railroads, which had enabled them to flout public opinion and to secure the sympathetic decisions of those court justices before whom suits had been brought. The spectacle of judges justifying the evictions of Negroes and the attacks upon their white sympathizers strengthened the conviction that only through the power of popular protest, directed into legislative action, could the railroads' arrogance be curbed. As Dr. Daniel Mann emphasized in his letter to the *Liberator*, after Judge Simmons had dismissed his suit against the Eastern Railroad, "Justice was foiled and overcome in her own temple by the power and management of wealth, vested in a corporation which the people have established. The serpent hatched by their kindness has become a boa constrictor, to crush them in its folds. No court can guard the rights of the people against such a power. The people alone who created the power can prescribe its limits, and defend themselves from its encroachments. The need of their action is now demonstrated. . . . It is the contest of the unguarded rights of American citizenship with an overgrown, overbearing and unprincipled monopoly of wealth and power and wrong . . . In short, let all the ready means by which a wealthy corporation can socially violate private rights with impunity, by force of arms, and force of falsehood, purchased by the form of wealth, be guarded against by law; and let every man feel that he is a member of a republic in which an injury offered to the meanest citizen is an insult to the whole community." [24]

The effect of Judge Simmons' decision upon the people and press of Massachusetts is illustrated by the reaction of the Lynn *Record*, which urged that "if the 'Great and General Court of Massachusetts' is not disfranchised, but has yet the power of *making laws* in favor of *the people*, without regard to the color of the skin, the color of the hair, the *breadth of the shoulders,*

---

this murderous prejudice, in reality, exists against *condition* more than against *color*. . . . *Slaves* can travel beside their masters in all our public vehicles without offending northern nerves; why, then, is such a fuss made about colored *freemen?* Our merchants and sea captains can trade with Africans for gold dust and ivory, in exchange for rum and trinkets; they do not shudder at striking heads for such profitable bargains; how is it that they bear such hatred to the colored man in their own country? The plain truth is, it arises from contempt for their *condition.*"

[23] *Liberator*, XI (November 12, 1841), 182.

[24] *Ibid.*, XI (November 12, 1841), 182.

or the quality of the clothes, we trust, in the name of liberty, (if it is yet lawful to speak that word) that the independent voters at the coming election will see to it that men are chosen who will define the powers of corporations somewhat differently from the New Bedford Justice (Judge Crapo) or the Boston Justice." [25]

The movement against the "Jim Crow" car reached its peak at the beginning of 1842. As petitions demanding legislative action poured into the legislature, a joint legislative committee of both houses under the chairmanship of Seth Sprague, Jr., of Boston, was appointed to study the problem and bring in a report. It held a public meeting in February; those who appeared before it were Remond and two of the most prominent white anti-slavery lawyers of Massachusetts, Wendell Phillips and Ellis Gray Loring. The *Bay State Democrat*, reporting that the State House, the scene of the meeting, "was crowded with a large audience, consisting of the members of the two houses, and ladies and gentlemen generally," noted that Remond's speech, "coming as it did from one of the proscribed race, and delivered in a manner at once graceful and pointed, seemed to produce much effect upon the assembly." [26]

Phillips, in his testimony, affirmed the right of the legislature to end segregation on the railroads. The railroad corporations, he argued, were created and protected by the legislature "in the exercise of special privileges and franchises. The legislature creates—of course, it can control them. They are bound to make reports, from time to time, of their proceedings to it. The fact presupposes the right to regulate their proceedings, if need be." The railroad corporations were in duty bound to observe the laws and constitution of the Commonwealth, and to do nothing to contravene "the equal rights of all the people which that Constitution was framed to secure." Declaring that it was "a right, not a privilege to be transported in the cars of the corporations, upon payment of a certain sum," he affirmed that such payment "and conformity to the usual and decent rules of society, *entitle* a man to the use of this conveyance." As a right, therefore, "it surely ought to be an equal right." But forcing a colored man to ride in a "Jim Crow" car constitutes "an injury to his rights, and insult to his person," and should therefore not be permitted by the legislature. Noting that segregation was confined to three roads and that "on the largest and most frequented of the railroads, no such regulation has obtained"—an indication that there was no general public opinion demanding such regulation—he emphasized that "we ask not for the *writing* of law;—we ask the Legislature to say *what is law*." By affirming that the railroads were acting contrary to the constitution and the laws of Massachusetts, the legislature would not only acknowledge the equal rights of all citizens of the Commonwealth but would also end the violence prevailing on those roads. "A most definite action in the case is required," he continued. "If the Legislature be not ready to affirm and defend the rights of all, let them make it law that

[25] Reprinted in *ibid.*, XI (November 12, 1841), 184.
[26] *Ibid.*, XII (February 25, 1842), 32.

color is an important particular in the tenure of rights. Let that be clearly known, and it may be submitted to—till such a demonstration of the sense of the people as no Legislature can mistake, shall procure its repeal. But while uncertainty prevails, there will be continued brawls and breaches of the peace. What the petitioners do claim is action,—on one side or on the other." [27]

Remond argued that complexion could not "be rightfully made the criterion of rights"; he would oppose such a criterion, he said, even if the Negro were in the majority. What he was asking for was justice "and not favor for either complexion"; the regulations in question "do not end with the termination of the route, but, in effect, tend to discourage, disparage and depress this class of citizens"; it means treating all Negroes as though they are one uniform mass. "No distinction is made by the community in which we live. The most vicious is treated as well as the most respectable, both in public and private ... and I submit, whether this unkind and unchristian policy is not well calculated to make every man disregardful of his conduct, and every woman unmindful of her reputation"; the degrading treatment of the Negro in America, "finds a counterpart in no other"; the Negro does not deny to any man the social right of selecting his "society and associates, but he does demand equality of civil rights—such as on the railroads—where one man has not the prerogative to define rights for another. For instance, sir, in public conveyances, for the rich man to usurp the privileges to himself, to the injury of the poor man, would be submitted to in no well regulated society. And such is the position suffered by persons of color." [28]

Loring pointed out, in words that have a contemporary ring as we think of the recent Supreme Court decision in the education cases, that although the accommodations given the Negro were inferior, it was immaterial whether they were or not. "To give inferior accommodations might be an injury; but to make any distinction whatever *is an insult*; one which men of color will suffer more from, than from an injury, if their feelings are what they ought to be. ... Distinctions made between parties that are socially held to be unequal, are always an insult to the reputedly inferior party. If the peer's daughter be forbidden to marry the peasant's son, common sense tells us that the peasant is the insulted party, however plausibly it may be argued that the prohibition touches both alike." As common carriers the railroad corporations "have the right to make any regulations for the management of their business, which are not inconsistent with the public good." The regulations in question, however, are not consistent with the public good. Even if public opinion of the majority of the people of the state approved of the regulations, they would still not have the right to make them. "Are all our rights then at the mercy of a majority? Our Constitution and our laws are framed mainly to protect the rights of the *minority*, and to say to the majority, 'Thus far shalt thou go, and no further.' " [29]

[27] *Ibid.*, XII (February 18, 1842), 26.
[28] *Ibid.*, XII (February 25, 1842), 30.
[29] *Ibid.*, XII (March 4, 1842), 34.

Following the hearing, the joint legislative committee submitted a report which condemned the policy of segregation on the railroads, affirmed the need of remedial action through legislation and the right of the legislature to take such action, and presented a bill which declared that "no rail-road corporation shall ... make or establish any by-law or regulation which shall make any distinction, or give a preference in accommodation to any one or more persons over others on account of descent, sect, or color." Moreover, "Any officer or servant of any rail-road corporation, who shall assault any person for the purpose of depriving him of his right or privilege in any car or other rail-road accommodation, on account of descent, sect, or color, or shall aid or abet any other person in committing such assault, shall be punished by imprisonment in the county jail not less than six days, or by fine not less than ten dollars; and shall also be answerable to the person assaulted, to the full amount of his damage in an action of trespass." [30]

However, notwithstanding strong public sentiment and a unanimous committee recommendation, the bill was defeated in the Senate.[31] Despite this setback, the demands for legislative action continued. Petitions were again circulated and presented to the legislature at the beginning of the next session in January, 1843, and a bill similar to that of the previous year was reintroduced. It passed the Senate but was victimized by a maneuver in the House by Representative Park of Boston. Park moved the deletion of the words "rail-road," so that the bill applied to all corporations—he indicated that he planned to vote against the bill after his amendment was accepted, thus admitting that the purpose of the amendment was to increase opposition to the bill—the amendment was passed by a vote of 164 to 67, and the bill itself indefinitely postponed by a vote of 171 to 61.[32]

The vote was not taken by yeas and nays, which meant that the vote of each legislator was not made public. Apparently, public opinion was too strongly opposed to the policy of the railroads to be openly defied. The *Liberator* was undoubtedly correct in its observation, after characterizing the result as "inexcusable and dastardly," that the legislators "refused to allow the vote to be taken by yeas and nays, in order that they might not be identified." [33]

But the bill's defeat in the legislature actually marked the final stages in the resistance of the railroads to public pressure. During the debate, Representative Adams of Boston, a member of the committee submitting the bill, had observed that he preferred a voluntary abandonment by the railroads of their policy, rather than the passage of legislation. With public pressure rising all about them, and faced with the certainty that the legislation would be enacted the following year if segregation continued, the railroads accepted

[30] *Ibid.*, XII (March 4, 1842), 33.
[31] Henry Wilson, *History of the Rise and Fall of the Slave Power in America* (Boston, 1872), I, 494.
[32] *Liberator*, XIII (February 17, 1843), 21.
[33] *Ibid.*, XIII (February 10, 1843), 23.

Representative Adams' advice and abolished segregation during the ensuing weeks. Although Remond did write, in a letter to the *Liberator* dated April 25, 1843, that on boarding a train in Salem for Boston he had been ordered by the conductor into a separate car, he did admit that for the past three weeks he had had no difficulty at any other point.[34] Thereafter, all discrimination and segregation on the railroads of Massachusetts ended and no further incidents were reported. The *Twelfth Annual Report* of the Massachusetts Anti-Slavery Society observed that "We are happy to have reason to believe that ... no distinctions any longer exist upon any of the Railways of Massachusetts." [35]

One last incident in this drama of the railroads took place in November, 1843. Nathaniel Barney of Nantucket, a member of the Society of Friends, and an Abolitionist, was a stockholder of the New Bedford and Taunton railroad. As long as the company maintained its regulation, Barney refused to accept his dividends. With the regulation abandoned, Barney ordered the company to pay the sum due him—$22.50—"to the order of Francis Jackson for William Lloyd Garrison, in view of his faithful and undeviating advocacy of the rights of humanity." Garrison accepted the sum as a contribution to the *Liberator*, thanked Barney, and noted that "no odious proscription now obtains on that railroad." [36]

[34] *Ibid.*, XIII (April 28, 1843), 67.
[35] Massachusetts Anti-Slavery Society, *Twelfth Annual Report*, January 24, 1844 (Boston, 1844), p. 7.
[36] *Liberator*, XIII (December 1, 1843), 190.

Dorothy Porter

THE ORGANIZED EDUCATIONAL ACTIVITIES

OF NEGRO LITERARY SOCIETIES, 1828-1846

Meeting discrimination in the public school systems and exclusion from many lectures and lyceums, Negroes often organized their own schools and adult literary societies. The selection from Dorothy Porter's study illustrates the character of these efforts.

• • • THE evolution of the early American Negro literary societies, which like the other organizations were expressions of the free Negro's impulses toward organization and improvement, forms an interesting chapter in the cultural and educational history of the American Negro. They began to appear over one hundred years ago when certain Negroes living in Northern cities took definite steps to improve their mental and moral condition through the medium of these societies. These organizations were known not only as literary societies, but also as debating and reading-room societies.

Some of the expressed reasons for the organization of these institutions were the stimulation of reading and the spreading of useful knowledge by providing libraries and reading rooms, the encouragement of expressed literary efforts by providing audiences as critics and channels of publication for their literary productions and the training of future orators and leaders by means of debates. Thus, their activities as a whole were educational. Apart from this, there were certain existing conditions inherent in the race relations of the times which led to the establishment of these societies. The Reverend Theodore S. Wright, a prominent Negro of the day, was thrown out of a white literary meeting of the Alumni of Nassau Hall in New York City.[9] The presence of

From Dorothy Porter, "The Organized Educational Activities of Negro Literary Societies, 1828-1846," *Journal of Negro Education*, V (October, 1936), pp. 556-66, 568-69, 574-76. Reprinted with the permission of *Journal of Negro Education* and Mrs. Dorothy Porter.

[9] American Anti-Slavery Society, *Fourth Annual Report*. New York: William S. Dorr. 1837. p. 110.

Negroes in white literary organizations was not wanted. Even in Massachusetts, often referred to as the "birthplace of freedom," this condition was true. In New Bedford, Massachusetts, Charles Sumner and Ralph Waldo Emerson recalled their engagements to speak at a Lyceum when they learned that colored patrons were not to share the same privileges as the white members.[10] At Lynn, Massachusetts, there was opposition to Charles Lenox Remond, a Negro lecturer, who was to address a white group.[11] New institutions were formed in these places as a result of this discrimination. Thus, Negroes began to form societies of their own, in which they could have fuller and freer discussions and freedom of activity and control. A list of the more important societies which flourished during this period follows:

Negroes Literary Societies Listed by States and Cities
With Dates of Formation

PENNSYLVANIA
Philadelphia
Demosthenian Institute, 1837.
Edgeworth Society. Before 1837.
Female Literary Society, 1831.
Gilbert Lyceum, 1841.
Library Company of Colored Persons, 1833.
Minerva Literary Association, 1934.
Philadelphia Association for Moral and Mental Improvement of the People of Color, 1835.
Reading Room Society, 1828.
Rush Library and Debating Society, 1836.
Pittsburgh
Theban Literary Society, 1831.
Young Men's Literary and Moral Reform Society of Pittsburgh and Vicinity, 1837.
NEW YORK
New York City
Female Literary Society. Before 1836.
Ladies Literary Society, 1834.

New York African Clarkson Society, 1829.
New York Garrison Literary Association, 1834.
New York Philomathean Society, 1830.
Phoenix Society, 1833.
Albany
Literary Societies (two). Before 1843.
Buffalo
Debating Society. Before 1837.
Young Ladies Literary Society. Before 1837.
Poughkeepsie
Literary Society. Before 1837.
Rochester
Debating Society. Before 1843.
Ladies Literary and Dorcas Society, 1833.
Schenectady
Debating Society. Before 1843.
Troy
Debating Society. Before 1837.
Literary Society. Before 1837.
Mental and Moral Improvement Society. Before 1837.

[10] William C. Nell, *The Colored Patriots of the American Revolution.* Boston: R. F. Wallcut. 1855. p. 114.
[11] *Ibid.,* p. 115.

MASSACHUSETTS
Boston
Adelphic Union for the Promotion of Literature and Science, 1836.
Afric-American Female Intelligence Society, 1832.
Boston Philomathean Society, 1836.
Thompson Literary and Debating Society. Before 1835.
Young Men's Literary Society. Before 1845.
New Bedford
Debating Society. Before 1837.
CONNECTICUT
Hartford
Literary and Religious Institution, 1834.
RHODE ISLAND
Providence
Literary Society, 1833.
Debating Society. Before 1837.
NEW JERSEY
Newark
Tyro and Literary Association, 1832.

MARYLAND
Baltimore
Young Men's Mental Improvement Society for the Discussion of Moral and Philosophical Questions of all kinds. Before 1835.
Phoenix Society. Before 1835.
WASHINGTON, D.C.
Debating Society. Before 1837.
Literary Society. Before 1837.
Washington Conventional Society, 1834.
OHIO
Cincinnati
Literary Society. Before 1843.
Columbus
Literary Society. Before 1843.
MICHIGAN
Detroit
Young Men's Lyceum and Debating Society. Before 1846.

THE PHILADELPHIA SOCIETIES

The free Negroes in Philadelphia seem to have taken the lead in the establishment of literary societies among Negroes. On the evening of March 20, 1828, group of free men of color gathered together to organize a society that in some way would have as its purpose "the mental improvement of the people of color in the neighborhood of Philadelphia." [12] William Whipper, one of the most prominent Negroes of the day, was the guiding spirit of the group. In a short address to the men present, he urged them not to sit, "as idle spectators to the movement being carried on by nations to improve themselves," but because of their limited opportunities to "feel bound to open an institution to which they may repair and qualify themselves for future usefulness." A com-

[12] Educational societies were organized much earlier than the literary societies. Their efforts embodied some of those of the literary societies, in that they spread "useful knowledge" and collected books for the use of the members. See the Constitution of the Pittsburgh African Education Society, *Hazard's Register of Pennsylvania*. Philadelphia. V. 9., p. 115.

mittee was formed to draw up a constitution for the society which was to be known as the "Reading Room Society" for young men in Philadelphia. The library was to consist of some books treating on the subject of ancient, modern, and ecclesiastical history, the *Laws of Pennsylvania*, *The Freedom's Journal*, *The Genius of Universal Emancipation*, and other works. For reasons which are not given, all books, "chimerical or visionary," were to be excluded.[13] The public received benefits from this organization, as well as the members. This is evidenced in the appointment of William Whipper, the Secretary, at a meeting held May 2, 1828 to deliver to the public an address on the evening of May 12th, in the African Methodist Episcopal Church, in Lombard Street.[14]

From Whipper's address, we learn that members of the society were required to have certain moral qualifications in order to secure the protection and welfare of the society. Monthly dues and an initiation fee were exacted. All of the money received except that which went for wood, light, and rent was to be expended for the purpose of securing books. These books were to be placed in the care of a librarian who was instructed that "it shall be the duty to deliver to said members alternately such books as they shall demand with strict regard that no member shall keep a book out of the library longer than a week, without paying a fine prescribed in the constitution, unless an apology for sickness, or absence be given—those shall be the only excuses." [15] Meetings were held weekly, at which time members returned and received books. At the meetings they read and expressed among themselves whatever sentiments they may have received from their readings.

Early in the year 1832, William Lloyd Garrison addressed the Female and Literary Society of Philadelphia. He found the group a most interesting and alert one, and writing of it in the *Liberator* said: "If the traducers of the Negro race could be acquainted with the moral worth, just refinement, and large intelligence of this association their mouths would be hereafter dumb." The members of this organization met every Tuesday night for the purpose of "mental improvement in moral and literary pursuits." The majority of the ladies wrote original literary pieces which were placed anonymously in a box and later criticized. The society in 1832 was composed of about twenty members, having been organized in 1831. . . . Scattered through the files of the *Liberator* are found many poems and essays written by members of this society and by members of other female societies organized in other cities. For the most part these writings were signed with just a forename, pseudonym, or simply by "A Lady of Color." This makes the identification of the authors difficult, if not impossible.

There had existed since 1731, a Library Company in Philadelphia, which had its beginning in the "Junto Club" founded by Benjamin Franklin "for literary and scientific discussion, the reading of original essays, poems, etc."

[13] *Freedom's Journal.* New York. 1828. V. 2. p. 98.
[14] *Ibid.*, p. 83.
[15] *Ibid.*, p. 306.

It was called the "club of mutual improvement" and was the forerunner of subscription libraries in the United States. This Library Company is still in existence today.[18] The colored people of Philadelphia, no doubt, attempted to form an organization similar to this one, for on January 1, 1833 the Philadelphia Library Company of Colored Persons was established. Nine members were present at its formation and signed its constitution. The society composed of free colored males grew very rapidly in membership and soon after its establishment applied to the legislature for an act of incorporation, which was granted in 1836.[19]...

The main object of this society was to build up a collection of useful books on every subject for the benefit of its members and to enlighten the group by means of weekly lectures on literary and scientific subjects. The lectures were given by the members of the society and others from the first week in October to the following May of each year.[21] Books were made accessible with comparatively little cost. A systematic order for reading was adopted by those interested. To stimulate reading and research a series of debates was introduced. These debates gave the members practice in the art of public speaking. From time to time the society received books, pamphlets, and maps as gifts. By 1838, the library had 600 volumes and the society had about 150 members who took an active part in the organization.[22] The Right Reverend Bishop White of the Protesant Episcopal Church was a frequent contributor to the collection. There was an admission fee to the society of one dollar and a monthly assessment of twenty-five cents. The meetings were held in the basement of the St. Thomas Episcopal Church.[23]

An editorial appeared in the *Genius of Universal Emancipation* during the year 1833 which summed up the progress of the colored people of Philadelphia and credited them with the establishment of libraries, reading rooms, and debating societies. According to the editorial, a gentleman who was present at the regular meeting of one of the debating clubs included the following information in his report: "Discussions were conducted with a degree of spirit and propriety and displayed a cogency and acuteness of reasoning, and an elevation and elegance of language for which he was little prepared. The subjects of discussion generally relate to their own rights and interests and frequently result in decisions from which the prejudiced mind of the white man would startle and shrink with apprehension." The editorial further states:

> They are numerous [the societies], united and bitterly conscious of the degradation and their power. To this let the pride, the inde-

[18] George M. Abbott, *A Short History of the Library Company of Philadelphia.* Philadelphia: 1913. p. 3.

[19] Joseph Wilson, *Sketches of the Higher Classes of Colored Society in Philadelphia.* (By a Southerner.) Philadelphia: Merrihew and Thompson, 1841. p. 98.

[21] Hazard's *Register of Pennsylvania, op. cit.,* 1833, v. 11, p. 186.

[22] Pennsylvania Society for the Promotion of the Free People of Color of the City of Philadelphia, *op. cit.,* p. 30.

[23] Wilson, *op. cit.,* pp. 99–100.

pendence and ambition which science ever imparts be added, and the consequences though beyond the reach of conjecture would doubtless be such as to involve the character, and condition of the whole country."[24]

The Minerva Literary Association organized in October 1834, with thirty ladies present at its first meeting, was immediately a successful organization and from all indications seems to have been a real "school for the encouragement and promotion of polite literature." The programs consisted of "readings and recitations of original and selected pieces, together with appropriate matters." Many of the essays and other original productions, in both prose and poetry which were written by these ladies, were of sufficient merit to be used in the Poets Corner and other publications of the day. These ladies held their meetings weekly.[25]

On December 16, 1836 the Rush Library and Debating Society was founded in Philadelphia and was incorporated March 1, 1837. Seven men were responsible for its formation and they had in mind the same purposes as those who had formed the Philadelphia Library Company.[26] In 1838 there were forty-one members who belonged to it, and the library contained 132 volumes.[27] By 1841, its library had 200 volumes. The books were all useful although of a miscellaneous character. Regular meetings were held in Salter's Hall.[28]

The Demosthenian Institute, formed at the home of John P. Burr, January 10, 1837, was organized primarily to prepare its members for the public platform. Addresses were made, discussions took place and questions were answered in the presence of the members. The members had planned that the society should be made into a preparatory school until the members had gained sufficient confidence and experience to fit them for public appearances. In 1841 this organization had forty-two members, and the library contained over one hundred scientific and historical works. The *Demosthenian Shield*, a weekly paper, first published on June 29, 1841, was the organ of the society. Its subscription list numbered over one thousand persons before the first issue appeared.[29] According to Wilson, it had a neat typographical appearance and it showed dignity and ability in the editorial department. No information seems available concerning the possible existence of any printed organs for the other literary societies,[30] although a poem "To George Thompson" "By a Lady of Philadelphia" was reprinted in *Human Rights*, which had been taken from

---

[24] *Genius of Universal Emancipation. op. cit.,* v. 3, p. 90.

[25] Wilson, *op. cit.,* p. 108.

[26] *Ibid.,* p. 101.

[27] Pennsylvania Society for the Promotion of the Abolition of Slavery. *Present State and Condition of the People of Color. op. cit.,* p. 3.

[28] Wilson, *op. cit.,* p. 102.

[29] Wilson, *op. cit.,* pp. 105–106.

[30] There is no mention of any other such publications in I. G. Penn. *The Afro-American press and its Editors,* 1891; F. G. Detweiler, *The Negro Press in the United States,* 1922; or in Charles S. Johnson's article "The Rise of the Negro Magazine," *Journal of Negro History,* v. 13, 1928.

The Struggler, "a newspaper edited in Philadelphia by an Association of Colored men."[31] This would seem to indicate that *The Struggler* was an organ of one of the literary societies.

At a meeting of the Council of the Philadelphia Association for the Moral and Mental Improvement of the People of Color, held in Philadelphia June 5th to June 9th, 1837, much attention was given to the "mental state" of the Negro. This association which was incorporated on February 28, 1835, met annually with delegates coming from the various churches, literary and beneficial societies.[32] Among the various resolutions submitted at a meeting held in 1837 was one which called for a survey to be made by a committee of the number of children who were members of their respective churches and who attended daily and weekly schools. Other committees were appointed to ascertain and report on the number and names of moral, literary, and beneficial societies in the City of Philadelphia, in order to have a historical record of the instruments that were being used to elevate the colored people.[33] Other committees were to correspond with similar societies organized in other cities in order to determine the educational progress of the people. Reports were to be made from time to time through the newspapers concerning the progress of the various groups. . . .

The Gilbert Lyceum, which was organized for literary and scientific purposes, seems to have been the first and only society which admitted individuals of both sexes. The society was named after the man who had first suggested its formation. The initial meeting took place on January 31, 1841 under the leadership of Robert Douglass, Jr., a Philadelphia painter of some note. Among the twelve persons present at the first meeting were Joseph Cassey, John C. Bowers, Robert Purvis, Sarah M. Douglass and Harriet Purvis.[37] A series of lectures was delivered before the group, which for the most part was well attended. In 1841, there were forty-one members who belonged to the lyceum. It is stated that these members planned to collect a cabinet of minerals and curiosities for their organization.

The free people of color, as a whole, owe some of their educational progress to the efforts of these societies. A report made in 1836 on the condition of the Negroes who lived in the Districts of Southwark and Northern Liberties, shows that out of 2,560 adults 1,030 could read and 92 could write; and that there were 970 children out of 1,945 who could read. The Negroes supported the following number of churches at this time: 6 Methodist, 2 Presbyterian, 3 Baptist, and 1 Lutheran. In addition to the literary societies, they maintained sixty beneficial societies, two tract societies, two Bible societies, two temperance societies and one moral reform society. Their combined property

---

[31] *Human Rights,* New York. Published for the American Anti-Slavery Society. V. 1, No. 5. Nov., 1835.

[32] *Minutes and Proceedings of the Philadelphia Council of the Philadelphia Association for the Moral and Mental Improvement of the People of Color.* (June 5th–9th, 1837.) Philadelphia: Merrihew and Gunn, 1837, p. 14.

[33] *Ibid.,* p. 6.

[37] Wilson, *op. cit.,* p. 110.

holdings were valued at $200,000.[38] Similar efforts were successful in the organization of societies in the cities of New York, Boston, Hartford, Cincinnati, Washington, D.C., Providence; and in the East and West this movement developed rapidly.

THE NEW YORK SOCIETIES

In New York City, Rochester, and other cities in the State of New York similar endeavors were made to form literary societies and debating clubs for the purpose of self-education. The young women, in particular, in these cities who organized these groups frequently combined the desire to learn with the desire to perform work of an altruistic nature in behalf of those in slavery, as well as for the many destitute Negro children.

In 1829, in New York City, one year after the organization of the first literary society in Philadelphia, the New York African Clarkson Society, composed of the young men of the city, was established. On the evening of April 23, 1834, the society celebrated its fifth anniversary and from the published reports it appears to have been a great occasion. The affair was held in the Abyssinia Baptist Church, with tickets of admission available at six cents. The members of the society arrived on this particular evening in a body and seated themselves together on the rostrum. The program consisted for the most part, of music, furnished by a union band, speech-making and the reading of the constitution. The young men sang *The Clarkson Ode*, which was composed probably when the society was organized and was as follows:

> With joyful hearts join hand in hand,
> And celebrate the Clarkson band.
> This day by legislative aid,
> A corporate body made.
> Prosperity attend our band,
> And gratitude this will demand:
> And let out thankful lays be heard,
> On every April twenty-third.

The church was filled with spectators and it was said that the members who were present were proud of their organization on this occasion.[39]

The leading literary society in New York City was the New York Philomathean Society which was organized in 1830.[40] At a later period in 1843, this society developed into the Odd Fellow's Lodge and became the Philomathean Lodge, No. 646.[41] These facts seem to indicate that the members of the society were all men. The Philomathean Society was "devoted to the improvement of

[38] *The Emancipator.* New York: R. G. Williams. V. 2, Nov. 10, 1836, p. 112.

[39] *Emancipator, op. cit.,* v. 2, May 6, 1834. (Frequently there is no pagination given on the newspapers. It will be given where found.)

[40] *Colored American.* New York: R. Sears. V. 1. No. 27. July 8, 1837.

[41] Charles H. Brooks, *A History and Manual of the Grand United Order of Odd Fellows in America.* Philadelphia: 1893, p. 21.

literature and useful knowledge." In 1837 it had acquired about six hundred volumes for its circulating library. It solicited donations of books and money to be used for the purchase of books and for subscriptions to periodicals. The society asked that books be loaned to the library and it promised that they would be well cared for and returned when wanted.[42] At a meeting held August 18, 1837, the society decided that members of all literary institutions of color would be admitted to all of its meetings, with the exception of the business meeting, and that they would be permitted to take part in the general debates.[43]

There was provided for the members a series of lectures on literary and historical subjects, which took place twice a week. The services of the outstanding men in the fields of science and literature were secured for these lectures. An admission fee was charged. The programs were arranged by a Board of Associates. The chairman of this board was Phillip A. Bell and the secretary was Thomas Jennings, Jr. The society had the following officers: Ransome F. Wake, Prefect; George W. Moore, Scribe; William Garribrance, Treasurer; James Fields, Librarian; Timothy Seamon, Recorder; Henry Williams, Curator.

The society which exerted the widest influence and which had the largest membership was the Phoenix Society, organized in New York City in 1833.[44] The Negroes in New York City had been spiritually and educationally helped by the ministers and by the establishment of Sabbath and day schools; but the Negro population which numbered about 20,000 was excluded from "instruction in its popular and inviting forms." A pamphlet containing the history and describing the animals in the Zoological Institute in New York City was distributed in 1834. This pamphlet included the following statement: "The proprietors wish it to be understood that the people of color are not permitted to enter except when in attendance upon children and families."[45] The colored people felt that until they were able to attend public meetings and places of interest that they should provide a building and appropriate means for self-improvement.

The above type of prejudice toward the Negro was one of the causes for the organization of the Phoenix Society. It was composed chiefly of young colored men, but it had some white members who gave whatever assistance they could. The society was "designed to be the soul of the entire population and their friends in the city." Its primary object was "to promote the improvement of the coloured people in morals, literature, and the mechanical arts." All persons who wished to promote the objects of the society and who were of good "moral character" could become members by paying one dollar joining fee and twenty-five cents quarterly. The applicants had to be accepted, however, by the board of directors. Many prominent men, white and colored, were officers to the society. Some of these persons were also members and officers of the various anti-slavery societies. The constitution and by-laws, published in

[42] *Colored American, op. cit.,* v. 1, No. 27, July 8, 1837.
[43] *Ibid.,* v. 1, No. 31, August 5, 1837.
[44] Arthur Tappan, *The Life of Arthur Tappan.* New York: Hurd and Houghton, 1870, p. 158.
[45] *Emancipator, op. cit.,* v. 1 (new series) March 9, 1837.

1835 listed the officers at that time: Rev. Christopher Rush, President; Rev. Theodore S. Wright, 1st Vice-President; Thomas L. Jennings, 2nd Vice-President; Rev. Peter Williams, Corresponding Secretary; and Arthur Tappan, Treasurer. David Ruggles, William Hamilton, Charles B. Ray, Dr. John Brown and Samuel E. Cornish were on the Board of Directors.

The Phoenix Society attempted large projects which involved many duties for its members. It wished to exploit all possibilities of the situation it had set out to alleviate. One cannot but admire the forthrightness that launched such a program as the following: First of all an attempt to raise $10,000 for the purpose of erecting a public edifice to be appropriated to the use of a library, reading room, museum or exhibition room, hall, etc., where colored youth and others might enjoy the benefit of such courses of lectures and other instruction on morals, literature and the mechanic arts, as are enjoyed by the white community.[46] The Ward Societies were inaugurated whose functions laid a considerable obligation upon every member. Members of the Ward Societies were to visit the various families within the Ward vicinity and make a registry of every colored person, ascertaining his age, sex, occupation and his ability to read or write. They were to induce the old and young to become members of the society. Adults were to be urged to attend school and were to be impressed with the importance of sending their children to school regularly and punctually. Furthermore, each Ward group was organized to maintain a circulating library for the use of the people of color at a moderate fee, to organize lyceums to serve the advantages of public speaking and to promote lectures on science. Finally and characteristically, they were to form moral reform societies and to seek young men of "good moral character" as members whom they could expect to assist ultimately in getting a good liberal education. The Ward Societies served a further general interest by reporting to the board all members who were skilled and capable of conducting trades, by procuring places at trade with respectable farmers for them, and by giving preference in employment to those who could "read and cipher." In addition they encouraged people of color, whenever they could to improve their minds and to abstain from every vicious and demoralizing practice.[47]

The rapid growth of the Phoenix Society made it necessary to abandon the first rented rooms and to hire a hall in which to hold meetings. A course of lectures was given by several clergymen of the city on morals, scientific, and historical subjects. An evening school for adults was started with both white and colored teachers. A high school for colored youth was begun and continued for two years or more."[48]

Samuel E. Cornish, at one time librarian of the society, made strenuous attempts to build up the library....[49] The first annual report of the Board of

[46] *Constitution and By-Laws of the Phoenix Society of New York.* New York: H. R. Piercy, 1835, p. 5.

[47] *Ibid.,* p. 6.

[48] Tappan, *op. cit.,* p. 162.

[49] *Colonizationist and Journal of Freedom.* Boston: George W. Light, February, 1834, p. 307.

Directors of the Phoenix Society shows that the general operations of the Board were confined principally to the "organization of Ward Societies, the institution of historical and scientific lectures, the establishment of reading rooms and libraries and the formation of temperance societies which existed in great numbers." The report indicates that through the organization of the Phoenix Society there was "produced a more intimate and extensive union, and a more anxious concern for the general improvement among the young people of every denomination than had existed at any former period in the city." More public spirit was exhibited and many contributions were made to objects of public utility. The cause of temperance was greatly advanced. Expensive entertainments were less frequent and a desire to acquire useful knowledge was increased. Throughout the year the scientific lectures had brought together four or five hundred persons. In the report much credit was given to Samuel E. Cornish for his services in arranging the lectures, in planning and establishing the library and reading rooms and for promoting the interests of the society generally.[51]

The New York Garrison Literary Association sometimes called the New York Garrison Literary and Benevolent Society seems to be the only institution of its kind, in that it was maintained primarily for the colored youth. Anybody of "good moral character" between the ages of "four and twenty by subscribing to the constitution and by paying 12½ cents admission and 1 cent per week could become a member." The society was formed early in 1834, and its members were primarily interested in religion, virtue, literature, the downfall of prejudice, and slavery and oppression in any form. They desired that the organization would be a means of spreading "useful knowledge." Probably because of the large size of the organization, it had many officers, a board of managers, an executive committee, a visiting committee and other assistants for managing it. These officers were elected annually. John W. Lewis was President; Henry Garnett, Secretary; and Prince Loveridge, Librarian. David Ruggles was a member of the executive committee in the year 1834.[52]

Education and liberty formed the main topics for discussion at their meetings which were devoted to singing, praying, and the reading of original compositions. The meetings were attended by over one hundred and fifty children and were at first held in the public school rooms in Laurens Street. P. Loveridge, a teacher in the public school, stated at one of the early meetings held in April 1834, that one of the trustees of the school objected to the use of the name of Garrison for the society and suggested that it be changed to Finley. The young men insisted, however, on retaining the name of Garrison. At a meeting on the night of April 19, 1834, David Ruggles, who had been appointed to find a new place in which to hold meetings, reported that he had received a letter from Phillip A. Bell, Chairman of the Board of Associates of the Philomathean Society, permitting them to use the Philomathean Hall for

[51] *Ibid.*, v. 2, May 20, 1834.
[52] *Ibid.*, April, 1834.

one year. At this same meeting it was resolved that the anti-slavery hymn book should be adopted for the use of the society and that each member should be supplied with a copy of it.[53]

There existed in New York as in other cities a female literary society. Abigail M. Mathews was one of the founders of the New York Female Literary Society[54] and Henrietta D. Ray, the wife of Charles B. Ray, was the president.[55] The Ladies Literary Society of the City of New York, as it was styled, was started in 1834. At its third anniversary held September 23, 1837, a very lengthy and elaborate program was held. In order to render financial aid to the *Colored American*, a new newspaper, and the New York Vigilance Committee, the society held fairs.[56] Thus its purpose was extended beyond the literary and educational aim to the larger social objectives....

THE DECADENCE OF THE LITERARY SOCIETIES

The efforts of these literary societies deserve recognition and praise for they not only actually helped to disseminate knowledge among a people for the most part poorly educated, but they taught the Negro how to use his leisure time to advantage. The lecturers who addressed these societies chose not only literary topics, but also scientific and educational ones. These lectures were said to be stimulating to the hearers. They prompted many Negroes who could read to read further, and those who were unable to read to learn to read. Many of these addresses were printed and widely circulated throughout several states. Some of them have been preserved and handed down to us as rare items of the book-collecting field. The lecture platform of these societies was the workshop and the preparatory school for many of the Negro anti-slavery lecturers who later won fame in America and England as public speakers.

As a result of the activities of these societies many Negroes started private libraries. In Philadelphia and nearby cities there were 8,333 volumes in private libraries in 1838.[85] David Ruggles, a Negro printer and abolitionist, was probably the earliest Negro book-collector. He maintained a circulating library and made available to many readers anti-slavery and colonization publications. He charged a fee which was less than twenty-five cents a month for the renting of books for the year. He sold books and printed at frequent intervals in the various newspapers lists of books relating to the Negro and to slavery.[86] In this

---

[53] *Ibid.*, May 27, 1834.

[54] *Ibid.*, v. 1, June 9, 1836 (new series), p. 23.

[55] *Ibid.*, v. 1, No. 24, 1936 (new series) p. 119.

[56] *Colored American, op. cit.*, v. 2, No. 1, Jan. 20, 1838, p. 7.

[85] Robert Purvis, *Appeal of Forty Thousand Citizens, Threatened with Disfranchisement, to the People of Pennsylvania.* Philadelphia: Merrihew and Gunn, 1838, p. 11.

[86] See advertisement column of the *Emancipator*, Vol. 4, No. 22, May 31, 1834, p. 87.

same connection, *The Colored American,* a Negro newspaper first published in 1837, maintained a reading room.[87]

With a few exceptions these societies had to struggle to continue their activities. The existence of several societies in one city caused competition for membership. Several of the leaders of the Philadelphia societies felt that the various societies should merge into one large organization which would include men and women of all ages, regardless of their learning. A plan for such an organization was drawn up by Mr. James Needham which proposed "to have lectures by competent persons at stated intervals, to encourage men of color to become professors in particular branches of science, to establish a library, collect a cabinet of minerals and procure philosophical apparatus as soon as its permanent organization might allow of so doing.[88] No evidence has been found to indicate that this society was ever organized.

The various anti-slavery organizations weakened the strength of the literary and debating societies in that they called constantly on the members of the literary societies to furnish audiences for their lectures and some of the leaders in these societies were pressed into service as speakers and workers for the emancipation programs. In many instances members of the literary societies were officers and members of the anti-slavery societies. William Whipper, Samuel E. Cornish, James C. Bowers, Robert and Harriet Purvis, Sarah Douglass and numerous others listed above were members and officers of the literary and also the anti-slavery organizations.[89]

For the most part, these societies were short-lived. Some existed actively for ten or twelve years, others died an early death. As is still true of many organizations, the members became lax in their membership and in the payment of their assessments. Some years later, after the particular societies mentioned in this article had served their purposes and passed out of existence, other organizations with similar purposes were set up, and in turn existed for brief periods. Many of these were influenced by the anti-slavery struggle and were in the main anti-slavery societies until around 1857 when they took on a more definite literary aspect.

These organizations are indications of the activity of self-educative influences in Negro life. They worked from within the group and showed their results not only in organized action but also in trained individuals who joined hands with the white leadership in other religious and philanthropic societies working for the improvement of Negro life. The story of the development of Negro education in its broader implications would be incomplete without some reference to these endeavors of the Negro literary societies. They were frequently the background for the organization of the Negro school. They were the supporters of the educative life among Negroes in a day when there were few formal instruments of education in existence for their use.

[87] *Colored American,* v. 2, No. 5, Feb. 10, 1838, p. 18.
[88] Wilson, *op. cit.,* p. 112.
[89] See the Reports of the American Anti-Slavery Societies 1835–1845.

Ray Allen Billington

JAMES FORTEN: FORGOTTEN ABOLITIONIST

*The fact that many Negroes participated in the abolitionist move-
ment has often been "forgotten." Ray Allen Billington has presented
a portrait of James Forten, one of the most prominent of the
Negro abolitionists. While Billington's article may exaggerate somewhat the extent of Forten's influence upon Garrison, nevertheless
during the early years of the* Liberator *Forten was an important
source of financial and moral support for the noted white leader.
Moreover Forten's career illustrates the antislavery activities of
many free Negroes, most notably their criticism of the American
Colonization Society many years before prominent white antislavery
advocates like Garrison became disillusioned with its program. Billington's article also touches on another phase of Negro protest
activity: the Negro ante-bellum convention movement, which opposed
the southern slavery system and attempted to improve the status of
free Negroes in the North.*

THE most important single incident in the American antislavery crusade
was the conversion of William Lloyd Garrison and Theodore Dwight Weld
to a belief in racial equality. These two men, and the thousands who flocked
to their standards, held that no biological differences distinguished Negroes
from whites. As this was the case, they argued, the slaves should be emancipated
either immediately or gradually, then educated and equipped to share the responsibilities of society with their fellow citizens. Social and political equality
for all Americans was the objective of abolitionists from the day that Garrison
proclaimed his intention to be "as harsh as truth and as uncompromising as
justice" until the last slave was freed.[1]

The Garrisonian doctrine of equality was completely antagonistic to the
generally accepted racial views of both northerners and southerners in the
early nineteenth century. Enlightened men on both sides of the Mason-Dixon
line had, since the Revolution, detested the institution of slavery, yet few

Ray Allen Billington, "James Forten: Forgotten Abolitionist," published by the
Association for the Study of Negro Life and History in Vol. XIII of *Negro History
Bulletin*, pp. 31–36, 45 (Nov., 1949). Reprinted by permission of the publisher.
[1] *The Liberator*, January 1, 1831.

among them were willing to concede that Negroes were physically or intellectually equal to whites. Instead they believed that the blacks were inferior creatures, halfway between animals and humans, who were fit only for the barbarism of Africa or servile life in the United States. The popular attitude was typified in the objectives of the American Colonization Society upon its formation in 1817. Members recognized the evils of slavery but insisted they should be shipped back to the African jungles for which nature had fitted them.

To men who held these views the concepts of Garrisonianism were thoroughly shocking. Between them and the abolitionists there was no compromise. The "colonizers" based their platform on a belief in racial inequality; the "abolitionists" built their program about a belief in racial equality For the next thirty years northerners debated these two beliefs, as abolitionism slowly gained supporters and strength. Southerners, however, moved in the opposite direction. Driven to greater conservatism by the northern attack on white supremacy, they had by the 1850's ceased to apologize for slavery as a necessary evil, viewing the institution instead as a positive good. When a Republican victory in 1860 warned them that the concept of racial equality was to be enshrined in the White House they deserted the Union.

Viewed in this light the doctrines of abolitionism become important in explaining the course of American history. Where did those views originate? Who first suggested that the races were equal, and that Negroes should be accorded the same legal and social status as whites? Doubtless a handful of forward-looking reformers from the days of antiquity onward had preached equality, but their opinions were of little importance; concepts only deserve recognition when they influence man's behavior. Avowals of racial equality, no matter how sincere, had no impact on American life until they fell on the ears of the humanitarians who launched the abolition crusade. Apparently the doctrine, in usable form, was first suggested to Garrison and his followers by a small group of Negro reformers whose contribution has been largely overlooked by historians of antislavery. Of these none was more important than James Forten, a wealthy free Negro of Philadelphia, whose efforts in behalf of the slaves launched pre-Garrisonian abolitionism in the United States.

Born in Philadelphia on September 2, 1766, James Forten was the son of Negro parents whose ancestors had lived in Pennsylvania as freemen for at least two generations.[2] His education was unusually scant even for that day; after a brief introduction to learning in the school of the famed Quaker philanthropist, Anthony Benezet, the death of his father in 1775 forced him to assume his share of the family's financial burdens.[3] For a few years he worked

[2] A close friend of Forten's, Lydia Maria Child, is authority for the statement that so far as he could recollect, no member of his family had been slaves. The Freedmen's Book (Boston, 1865), 100. Another friend, however, later quoted Forten as saying that his great-grandfather had been brought from Africa as a slave, and that his grandfather had obtained his freedom. Samuel J. May, Some Recollections of the Antislavery Conflict (Boston, 1869), 287.

[3] For accounts of Forten's boyhood see Child, Freedmen's Book, 101–102; William C. Nell, Colored Patriots of the American Revolution (Boston, 1855), 166–167; and Robert Purvis, Remarks on the Life and Character of James Forten, Delivered at

in a grocery store, but the outbreak of the Revolution turned his thoughts to a more adventurous career. After repeated pleadings broke down his mother's opposition, the fifteen year old Forten in 1781 enlisted as powder boy aboard the *Royal Louis*, a Pennsylvania privateer commanded by Stephen Decatur, Sr.[4]

The next year was crammed with excitement for the young Philadelphian. The *Royal Louis*, was a formidable vessel, mounting twenty-two guns and carrying a crew of two hundred men, twenty of whom were colored.[5] Its commander, the father of the naval hero of the War of 1812, was already a seasoned privateer, having commanded the *Comet* and the *Fair American* in successful forays against English shipping.[6] Surely with his stout new ship he could surpass the feats of his last voyage when his *Fair American* brought to bay no less than three British merchantmen, four brigs, and a packet.[7] Little wonder that the youthful Forten looked forward to rollicking adventure and handsome profits as Decatur's ship sailed smoothly down the Chesapeake Bay on a warm July day in 1781.

For a time his bright hopes seemed about to come true. Scarcely had the *Royal Louis*, put to sea when a lookout sighted fair game, the English brig-of-war *Active*, which struck its colors after a sharp skirmish.[8] On the next cruise, however, fate was less kind. Once more a sail was sighted; once more Decatur gave chase. This time the expected victim turned out to be a powerful enemy frigate, the *Amphyon*. Undaunted, the crew of the *Royal Louis* prepared to give battle, only to see the sails of two other war vessels, the *Nymph* and the *Pomona*, loom over the horizon. Hopelessly outclassed, Decatur was forced to surrender.[9]

That was a sickening moment for young Forten. Negro prisoners, he knew, were seldom exchanged; instead they were sent in chains to the West Indies to be sold into slavery. That he escaped this grim fate was due to a fortunate

---

Bethel Church, March 30, 1842 (Philadelphia, 1842), 4. A brief sketch of Forten's career is in the *Dictionary of American Biography* (New York, 1928–1937), VI, 536–537.

[4] All contemporary biographers of Forten place the date of his enlistment in 1780 and state that he was fourteen years old. Nell, *Colored Patriots*, 166; Child, *Freedmen's Book*, 101; Purvis, *Remarks on the Life and Character of James Forten*, 4. Actually the *Royal Louis* was not commissioned until July 23, 1781, and sailed from Philadelphia at once. *Naval Records of the American Revolution* (Washington, 1906), 449. Apparently his early biographers based their accounts on Forten's memory, which was faulty. He was also responsible for the statement that the ship mounted twenty-six guns rather than twenty-two. William C. Nell, *Services of Colored Americans in the Wars of 1776 and 1812* (Boston, 1851), 16.

[5] Forten is responsible for the latter statement, as no list of the crew has been located. Nell, *Services of Colored Americans*, 16.

[6] Information about Stephen Decatur will be found in Alexander S. Mackenzie, *Life of Stephen Decatur* (Boston, 1846), 9–10; William Decatur Parsons, *The Decatur Genealogy* (New York, 1921), 10; and the *Dictionary of American Biography*, V, 186–187.

[7] A record of Decatur's previous conquests is in the *Naval Records of the American Revolution*, 445; and more fully in J. Thomas Scharf and Thomas Wescott, *History of Philadelphia* (Philadelphia, 1884), I, 423.

[8] *Pennsylvania Archives, Second Series* (Harrisburg, 1874), I, 373.

[9] Scharf and Wescott, *History of Philadelphia*, 423; Nell, *Colored Patriots*, 168.

circumstance. Aboard the *Amphyon* was the youthful son of its commander, Sir John Beasly, thirsting for the companionship of some one his own age. The two boys, so unlike in background, struck up an immediate friendship. Young Beasly was particularly intrigued by his companion's skill at marbles, and the two spent much time together at the game. According to legend, Sir John was so impressed with Forten's character that he offered to take him to England for an education. This offer, Forten later testified, was haughtily refused. "No, No!" he reported himself as saying. "I am here as a prisoner for the liberties of my country; *I never, never, shall prove a traitor to her interests.*"[10] Thus rebuffed, the British commander transferred the fifteen year old powder boy, with a number of other captives to the prison ship *Jersey*, which was anchored in Wallabout Bay on the lonely shore of Long Island. "Thus," Forten often remarked in later life, "did a game of marbles save me from a life of West Indian servitude."[11]

During the next seven months, however, he probably had occasion to wish that his fingers were less skilled. The *Jersey* was a rotting old hulk, so leaky that pumps ran constantly to keep her afloat and so decayed that snow drifted through the cracks in her hull. A thousand prisoners were crowded into her stinking hold without light, ventilation, or sanitation, there to exist on food condemned as unfit for the English forces; frequently the starving captives had to knock worms from the biscuits or shred mahogany-colored meat that was too hard to cut. Thanks to his youth and stamina, Forten escaped the fate of the ten thousand prisoners who died aboard the ship during the war.[12] So unquenchable was his spirit that on one occasion he even gave up an opportunity to escape in favor of a companion worse off than himself.[13] He was finally released in a general exchange of prisoners, reaching home safely as the Revolution was drawing to a close.[14]

Although still in his teens, Forten was ready to exhibit the freedom-loving spirit that marked his later years. Why, he asked himself, should he stay in a

[10] Child, *Freedmen's Book*, 101–102; Nell, *Colored Patriots*, 168. These two accounts, which agree in substance, were apparently based on Forten's reminiscences.

[11] Nell, *Colored Patriots*, 169.

[12] Descriptions of the *Jersey* are in Gardner W. Allen, *A Naval History of the American Revolution* (Boston, 1913), II, 631–637; Edgar A. Maclay, *A History of the United States Navy* (New York, 1904), I, 138–139; and John R. Spears, *The History of Our Navy* (New York, 1899), I, 223–224. The reminiscences of several prisoners confined to the ship while Forten was aboard fail to mention him, but add colorful details of life aboard. These include Thomas Andros on Board the Old Jersey Prison Ship (Boston, 1833), 1–80; Captain Thomas Dring, *Recollections of the Jersey Prison-Ship* (Providence, 1829); and Ebenezer Fox, *The Revolutionary Adventures of Ebenezer Fox* (Boston, 1839), 93–228.

[13] The youth who escaped was Daniel Brewton who was carried from the ship in a sea chest in which Forten had planned to escape. Later steward of the *Lazaretto* in Philadelphia, Brewton showed both William Nell and Robert Purvis a certificate testifying that he had been aboard the *Jersey* with Forten, and described the rescue. Nell, *Colored Patriots*, 170–172; Purvis, *Remarks on the Life and Character of James Forten*, 7–8.

[14] Forten was released after seven months on the *Jersey*. His mother had given him up for dead when he finally reached Philadelphia.

land that proclaimed all men equal yet condemned those with dark skins to second-class citizenship? Why not escape to England where men were judged by character rather than color? These were the motives that sent him overseas for one of the most important twelve-month periods of his career. The slavery question was just beginning to captivate public interest at that time; the Somerset case[15] had already decreed that any slave touching English soil became free but the slave trade still flourished and the first reformers were lifting their voices against the evil. Forten lent an avid ear to their arguments, particularly to the pleas of Granville Sharp, a humanitarian who led the parliamentary assault on bonded servitude.[16] During the year that he listened young Forten became an avowed abolitionist, ready to dedicate his life to the crusade for freedom.

Back in Philadelphia once more he was apprenticed to Robert Bridges, a sailmaker whose loft was a landmark on the south wharves of the city. With a lack of prejudice all too rare in that day, Bridges in 1786 elevated his twenty-year-old helper to a position as foreman; twelve years later, when the owner died, Forten assumed control of the establishment. For the next forty years he conducted the business successfully, employing as many as forty men at times and amassing a comfortable fortune in the process. According to contemporary accounts many of his profits originated in a device to handle sails which he perfected and patented.[17] The popularity of his invention allowed him to provide a comfortable home for his widowed mother, a sister, a wife, and a growing family of eight children.[18]

The passing years not only assured James Forten economic security but gave him an opportunity to shine as a civic leader among Philadelphia's Negroes. On at least four occasions he rescued persons from drowning near his sail loft, a service that was recognized in 1821 when the managers of the Humane Society presented him with an Honorary Certificate "as a testimony of their approbation of his meritorious conduct." [19] During the War of 1812,

[15] The Somerset case arose in 1771 when a slave, James Somerset, was taken by his master from Virginia to England. Refusing to serve his owner there, he obtained a writ of habeas corpus which allowed him to carry his case before the British courts. They eventually held that slavery was contrary to the laws of England and that Somerset was a free man. John W. Cromwell, *The Negro in American History* (Washington, 1914), 245.

[16] Purvis, *Remarks on the Life and Character of James Forten*, 8–9.

[17] Henry E. Baker, "The Negro in the Field of Invention," *Journal of Negro History*, II (January, 1917), 25. A search of patent lists for the period, however, fails to reveal any patent issued either to Forten or to his employer, Robert Bridges. Apparently the invention was never patented, but was still immensely profitable. See *A Digest of Patents, Issued by the United States from 1790 to January 1, 1839* (Washington, 1840); *A Classified Index of Subjects of Inventions* (Washington, 1872); *A list of Patents Granted by the United States for the Encouragement of Arts and Sciences, alphabetically arranged, from 1790 to 1820; Continued by Supplements to April, 1823* (Washington, 1823); *List of Patents and Inventions and Designs issued by the United States from 1790 to 1847* (Washington, 1847); *Subject-Matter Index of Patents for Inventions issued by the United States Patent Office from 1790 to 1873, Inclusive* (Washington, 1874).

[18] Nell, *Colored Patriots*, 172–174; Child, *Freedmen's Book*, 102–103.

when British troops pressed close on Philadelphia, he enlisted 2,500 colored patriots to improve the city's defenses. Marching with them from the State House yard to Gray's Ferry, Forten directed earthworks construction for two uninterrupted days.[20] Nor did he neglect the spiritual welfare of his race. When the St. Thomas' African Episcopal Church was incorporated in Philadelphia in 1796 he was among the pioneer members, serving on the first vestry. He remained active in the church from that day until his death.[21]

These activities prepared James Forten for a role in the cause that interested him most—abolitionism. His interest in the problem was awakened in 1800 when two of Philadelphia's most prominent Negroes, the Reverend Richard Allen, pastor of the African Methodist Church, and Absalom Jones, a founder of the St. Thomas' African Episcopal Church, circulated a petition among the city's colored citizens, urging Congress to modify the Fugitive Slave Act of 1793 and to adopt "such measures as shall in due course emancipate the whole of their brethren from their present situation."[22] Forten, as a signer, watched the fate of the petition with interest. To his disgust only one congressman sympathized with the petitioners. Representative George Thatcher of Massachusetts[23] supported their request in language faintly prophetic of that used by abolitionists a generation later; the remainder not only refused to listen but resolved that such petitions had a "tendency to create disquiet and jealousy, and ought therefore to receive no encouragement or countenance from this House." When this resolution was adopted by a thumping vote of eighty-five to one (with Thatcher casting the lone ballot in opposition),[24] James Forten wrote a letter of appreciation to the champion of his cause.[25] From that time on he was resolved to change the attitude of his unsympathetic fellow-countrymen.

His next opportunity came in 1813 when the Pennsylvania legislature considered a bill to bar free Negroes from the state. Forten, in a series of five letters published in pamphlet form, led the attack on the measure. "Has the

[19] The certificate, which was dated May 9, 1821, is printed in Nell, *Colored Patriots*, 174–175. Nell states that Forten rescued seven persons during his lifetime; Mrs. Child sets the number at twelve. Child, *Freedmen's Book*, 103.

[20] Scharf and Wescott, *History of Philadelphia*, I, 573–574; Neil, *Colored Patriots*, 191.

[21] William Douglass, *Annals of the First African Church in the United States of America, now styled the African Episcopal Church of St. Thomas* (Philadelphia, 1862), 107. When, in 1804, a school was established by the church, Forten was chosen one of the Board of Trustees. *Ibid.*, 110.

[22] The petition from the "free blacks" of Philadelphia was laid before Congress on January 2, 1800, by Robert Waln, a representative from Pennsylvania. *Annals of Congress*, 6th Cong., 1st Sess., 232.

[23] George Thatcher, a Federalist, represented Massachusetts in Congress between March 4, 1789, and March 3, 1801. *Biographical Directory of the American Congress* (Washington, 1928).

[24] The petition was debated on January 2 and January 3. *Annals of Congress*, 6th Cong., 1st Sess., 239–246.

[25] Nell, *Colored Patriots*, 176. The letter is printed in Purvis, *Remarks on the Life and Character of James Forten*, 12–14.

God who made the white man and the black left any record declaring us a different species?" he asked. "Are we not sustained by the same power, supported by the same food, hurt by the same wounds, wounded by the same wrongs, pleased with the same delights, and propagated by the same means? And should we not then enjoy the same liberty, and be protected by the same laws?" He passionately "hoped that the legislators who have hitherto guarded their fellow creatures, without regard to the colour of their skin, will still stretch forth the wings of protection to that race, whose persons have been the scorn, and whose calamities have been the jest of the world for ages."[26]

The importance of Forten's views on racism cannot be overestimated. Unlike most reformers, even among Negroes, he was convinced that no biological differences distinguished whites and blacks. In this conviction he anticipated the abolitionists of a later day; indeed the basic concept underlying abolitionism was nowhere better expressed before 1820 than in his outspoken letters.

Like most intellectual pioneers, Forten was far ahead of his time. This was demonstrated three years later when the American Colonization Society was formed.[27] This antislavery organization was based on the concept—then generally accepted in North and South alike—that the Negro was fit only for the barbarism of Africa or the servile life of an American slave; its objective was gradual emancipation followed by a wholesale deportation of the freedmen to the land of their ancestors. Despite this, many prominent northerners of both races gave colonization their unqualified support. James Forten, however, refused to be misled. Believing unreservedly in the equality of the races, he hewed to the line later held by William Lloyd Garrison and Theodore Dwight Weld; the slaves, he insisted, should be freed, educated, and fitted to take their rightful place in American society. His views stamp him as one of the first true abolitionists in the United States.

He first made himself heard on the subject in 1817 when supporters of the American Colonization Society, recognizing his influence among the freemen of Philadelphia, asked him to endorse their program. They dangled a tempting bait before him; a man of his prestige, they said, could become the Lord Mansfield of the society's Colony of Liberia if he cast his lot with them. Forten refused to listen. He would, he reputedly told them, "rather remain as James Forten, sailmaker, in Philadelphia, than enjoy the highest offices in the gift of their society."[28]

To a man of such sincere conviction a mere refusal to support colonization was not enough; his fellow countrymen must be warned against a plan that might eventually drive all Negroes from their adopted land. With this in mind Forten sought the support of the Reverend Richard Allen, Absalom Jones, Robert Douglass, and others prominent in Philadelphia's colored population,

[26] James Forten, *Letters from a Man of Colour, on a Late Bill before the Senate of Pennsylvania* (Philadelphia [1813]), 3–4, 7. One of the letters is reprinted in Carter G. Woodson, *Negro Orators and Their Orations* (Washington, 1925), 42–51.
[27] For an account of this organization see Early L. Fox, *The American Colonization Society, 1817–1840* (Baltimore, 1919).
[28] Nell, *Colored Patriots,* 177.

with them arranging a mass meeting of protest at the Bethel Church in January, 1817. The hall was crowded that night when Forten mounted the rostrum to serve as chairman; speeches were heard and then previously prepared resolutions were adopted by a unanimous vote:[29]

> Whereas, our ancestors (not of choice) were the first successful cultivators of the wilds of America, we, their descendants, feel ourselves entitled to participate in the blessing of her luxuriant soil, which their blood and sweat enriched; and that any measure or system of measures, having a tendency to banish us from her bosom, would not only be cruel, but in direct violation of those principles which have been the boast of this republic.
>
> Resolved, That we view with deep abhorrence the unmerited stigma attempted to be cast upon the reputation of the free people of color by the promoters of this measure, "that they are a dangerous and useless part of the community," when, in the state of disfranchisement in which they live, in the hour of danger they ceased to remember their wrongs, and rallied around the standard of their country.
>
> Resolved, That we will never separate ourselves voluntarily from the slave population of this country; they are our brethren by the ties of consanguinity, suffering, and wrong; and we feel there is more virtue in suffering privations with them, than fancied advantages for a season.
>
> Resolved, That without arts, without science, or a proper knowledge of government, to cast into the wilds of Africa the free people of color, seems to us the circuitous route by which they must return to perpetual bondage.
>
> Resolved, That, having the strongest confidence in the justice of God and the philanthropy of the free states, we cheerfully submit our destinies to the guidance of Him who suffers not a sparrow to fall without His special providence.

Persuasive as these resolutions were, they failed to check a mounting interest in colonization among Philadelphia's citizens. By July 23, 1817, the society's leaders felt confident of enough support to call a preliminary meeting to plan a local branch for the city.[30] This stirred Forten into action once more. The protest meeting that he arranged was held on August 10, 1817, in the

[29] A full account of the meeting, together with the text of the resolutions adopted, is in G. B. Stebbins, Facts and Opinions Touching the Real Origin, Character, and Influence of the American Colonization Society (Boston, 1853), 194–196. For briefer accounts of the meeting see: Nell, Colored Patriots, 177–178; William Lloyd Garrison, Thoughts on African Colonization (Boston, 1832), Pt. II, 9–10; Lewis Tappan, Life of Arthur Tappan (New York, 1870), 135–136; Booker T. Washington, The Story of the Negro (New York, 1909), I, 290; Cromwell, Negro in American History, 28; and Louis R. Mehlinger, "The Attitude of the Free Negro toward African Colonization," Journal of Negro History, I (June, 1916), 276–301.

[30] Scharf and Wescott, History of Philadelphia, I, 590.

school house at Green Court with a crowd of almost three thousand present. Again James Forten was in the chair; again enthusiastic speakers denounced colonization before a lengthy "Address to the humane and benevolent inhabitants of the city and county of Philadelphia" was adopted. This able document argued that colonization would doom free Negroes and ex-slaves alike to the hazards of a life for which they had no training, as well as depriving them of the benefits of religious instruction. Liberia, the writers predicted, would soon be the "abode of every vice, and the home of every misery." Furthermore, they believed that wholesale deportations would raise the price of slaves still in bondage, thus tending to perpetuate the institution. "Let not a purpose be assisted which will stay the cause of the entire abolition of slavery in the United States," the Address concluded, "and which may defeat it altogether; which proffers to those who do not ask for them benefits, but which they consider *injuries*, and which must insure to the multitude, whose prayers can only reach through us, *misery, sufferings, and perpetual slavery.*"[31]

Printed copies of this appeal were spread throughout Philadelphia and sent to Joseph Hopkinson, the Federalist representative serving Pennsylvania in Congress.[32] Despite a favorable reaction among Negroes, the Philadelphia Colonization Society was formed on August 12 as an auxiliary of the American Colonization Society.[33]

Undaunted by this defeat, Forten continued the attack with renewed vigor, certain that colonization would collapse when his countrymen learned the true nature of the movement. In November, 1819, he again presided over a large meeting of Philadelphia Negroes which condemned the American Colonization Society's efforts to "perpetuate slavery in the United States:"[34]

> *Resolved,* That the people of color of Philadelphia now enter and proclaim their most solemn protest against the proposition to send their people to Africa, and against every measure which may have a tendency to convey the idea that they give the project a single particle of countenance or encouragement.

A decade later Forten was primarily responsible for a national convention of Negro delegates which assembled at Philadelphia on September 15, 1830, to oppose colonization. Similar conventions were held yearly thereafter, usually in Philadelphia but occasionally in other cities, and in all Forten played a leading role. Due to his influence, as much as any other thing, the free Negroes of the North were arrayed in a solid phalanx against colonizers by the time abolitionism demanded their support.[35]

[31] The meeting is described in Garrison, *Thoughts on African Colonization*, Pt. II, 10–13. The Address is printed in Mehlinger, "Attitude of the Free Negro toward African Colonization," *loc. cit.*, 278–279, and in Woodson, *Negro Orators*, 52–55. See also Herbert Aptheker, *The Negro in the Abolitionist Movement* (New York, 1941), 3–32.

[32] A search of the *Annals of Congress*, 14th Cong., 2nd Sess., and 15th Cong., 1st Sess., failed to reveal any mention of the petition.

[33] Scharf and Wescott, *History of Philadelphia*, I, 591.

[34] *Niles Register*, XVII (November 27, 1819), 201–202.

[35] Carter G. Woodson, *The Negro in Our History* (Washington, 1941 edn.), 271–273.

Nor did the passing years alter his views. In 1833, when nearly sixty years of age, he spoke with all the fire of youth when a companion asked his views on colonization. "My great-grandfather," he said, "was brought to this country a slave from Africa. My grandfather obtained his own freedom. My father never wore the yoke. He rendered valuable service to his country in the war of our Revolution; and I, though then a boy, was a drummer in that war. I was taken prisoner, and was made to suffer not a little on board the Jersey prisonship. I have since lived and labored in a useful employment, have acquired property, and have paid taxes in this city. Here I have dwelt until I am nearly sixty years of age, and have brought up and educated a family, as you see, thus far. Yet some ingenious gentlemen have recently discovered that I am still an African; that a continent, three thousand miles, and more, from the place where I was born is my native country. And I am advised to go home. Well, it may be so. Perhaps if I should only be set on the shore of that distant land, I should recognize all I might see there, and run at once to the old hut where my forefathers lived a hundred years ago."[36]

James Forten's attack on the concept of racial inequality which underlay colonization had important results. In all probability his unwavering belief in the equality of the races helped convince William Lloyd Garrison that colonization was not the answer to the slavery problem, thus laying the basis for the rise of abolitionism.[37] This, in turn, gave Forten the reforming opportunity he had long sought; he threw himself into the Garrisonian crusade with a zeal that belied both his advancing years and his upper class position.

For by the 1830's Forten was a man of substance. His sailmaking shop, where as many as forty white and Negro workmen were employed,[38] had by 1832 rewarded him with a fortune of $100,000, a sizeable sum for that day.[39] This he used "to live in as handsome a style as anyone could wish to live"[40] in a spacious house on Lombard Street in Philadelphia.[41] Under his roof were gathered his ever-growing family: his wife, his eight children and other relatives; at times no less than twenty-two persons gathered about the family board.[42] A man of "commanding mind and well informed," he was highly respected by Negroes and whites alike. Particularly admired were the moral causes to which

[36] May, Some Recollections of the Antislavery Conflict, 287.

[37] Archibald H. Grimké, William Lloyd Garrison (New York, 1891), 144, holds that Garrison's conversations with Forten helped convince him that colonization was an evil, thus laying the basis for the beginnings of abolitionism. This is also the thesis of Clarice A. Richardson, The Anti-Slavery Activities of Negroes in Pennsylvania (unpublished master's thesis, Howard University, 1937), 10–11.

[38] May, Some Recollections of the Antislavery Conflict, 286.

[39] Carter G. Woodson, The Works of Francis J. Grimké (Washington, 1942), IV, 96n.

[40] Some Recollections of the Antislavery Conflict, 286.

[41] Forten occupied a house at 92 Lombard Street through most of his life. Philadelphia Directory for 1813 (Philadelphia, 1813); Philadelphia Directory for 1842 (Philadelphia, 1842), 88.

[42] According to the Census of 1830. Carter G. Woodson, Free Negro Heads of Families in the United States in 1830 (Washington, 1925).

he dedicated his life. He never drank, and was a steadfast supporter of temperance societies. His liberal contributions gave strength to the movements for universal peace and women's rights.[43] Forten was also the guiding spirit behind the American Moral Reform Society, an agency of colored men dedicated to the "promotion of Education, Temperance, Economy, and Universal Liberty."[44] As a founder and perennial president of that organization he directed its efforts toward bettering the standards of Negroes in Philadelphia and the nation.[45]

All this security and comfort James Forten was willing to sacrifice to aid the slaves. Recognizing that abolitionism was the nation's most unpopular cause; knowing that mobs might damage his property or threaten his aging limbs if he persisted in its support, he still showed no hesitation when the banner was unfurled by William Lloyd Garrison. To him the Boston leader was a "chosen instrument, in the Divine hand, to accomplish the great work of the abolition of American slavery,"[46] and must be aided without regard to cost. Even before the first issue of The Liberator appeared, Forten solicited subscriptions among Philadelphia Negroes; on December 31, 1830, he could send Garrison money from twenty-seven subscribers and a pledge of continued support. "I hope your efforts may not be in vain," he wrote "and that 'The Liberator' be the means of exposing more and more the odious system of Slavery, and of raising up friends to the oppressed and degraded People of Colour, throughout the Union. Whilst so much is doing in the world, to ameliorate the condition of mankind, and the spirit of Freedom is marching with rapid strides, and causing tyrants to tremble; may America awake from the apathy in which she has long slumbered. She must sooner or later fall in with the irresistible current. Great efforts are now making in the cause of Liberty; the people are becoming more interested and determined on the subject."[47]

Forten did not relax his efforts after the launching of The Liberator on January 1, 1831. A month later he sent Garrison twenty additional subscriptions; [48] on March 1 he arranged a mass meeting of Philadelphia Negroes where the paper's purposes were explained and unanimously endorsed.[49] From that time on he was a regular contributor to The Liberator and to abolition societies; with the exception of the wealthy New York merchants, Arthur and

[43] Child, Freedmen's Book, 103; Purvis, Remarks on the Life and Character of James Forten, 17.

[44] The objectives of the society are described in its monthly publication, the National Reformer, I (February, 1839), 81.

[45] Nell, Colored Patriots, 181; Cromwell, The Negro in American History, 35.

[46] Nell, Colored Patriots, 178.

[47] James Forten to William Lloyd Garrison, December 31, 1830. Dorothy B. Porter, ed., "Early Manuscript Letters Written by Negroes," Journal of Negro History, XXIV (April, 1939), 199–200.

[48] James Forten to William Lloyd Garrison, February 2, 1831. Ibid., 200–201.

[49] The meeting was held on March 1, 1831. The Liberator, March 12, 1831. See also Herbert Aptheker, "The Negro in the Abolitionist Movement," Science and Society, V (Spring, 1941), 162.

Lewis Tappan, Forten was probably the most generous supporter of the radical antislavery cause.[50] His only reward was the mounting strength of Garrisonianism. "It has," he wrote Garrison jubilantly during the spring of 1831, "roused up a spirit in our Young People, that has been slumbering for years, and we shall produce writers able to vindicate our cause." [51] Garrison, in turn, developed a warm affection for "the greatly esteemed and venerable sail-maker of Philadelphia," as he called Forten.[52] Seldom did he pass through Philadelphia without visiting the spacious house on Lombard Street, to dine with the family, spend the night, or simply engage in an hour's conversation on abolitionism. Such visits, wrote the elderly Forten after one of them, "are cheering, they are as green spots in the journey of life." [53]

His early contacts with Garrison allowed Forten to play a significant role when the American Anti-Slavery Society was formed. Many of the reformers who gathered in Philadelphia for the organizational meeting in December, 1833, made the Forten home their headquarters; about the family table plans were discussed and strategy mapped.[54] Until forced to retire from active labors by advancing age, he served frequently on the society's Board of Managers,[55] as well as collecting subscriptions for *The Liberator* [56] and lending the paper needed financial support.[57] Little wonder that members of the American Anti-Slavery Society, while recognizing the contributions of leading members during the 1840 meeting, lauded Forten with:

> James Forten, right well
> I love to hear tell,
> Of thy aid in our much boasted war;
> And mark with what scorn
> Does thy noble heart spurn
> The friends of Liberia's shore
> James Forten!
> The friends of Liberia's shore.[58]

[50] Woodson, *Works of Francis J. Grimké*, IV, 96n.

[51] James Forten to William Lloyd Garrison, March 21, 1831. Porter, "Early Manuscript Letters Written by Negroes," *loc. cit.*, 201–202.

[52] Washington, *The Story of the Negro*, 290.

[53] James Forten to William Lloyd Garrison, July 28, 1832. "Early Manuscript Letters Written by Negroes," *loc. cit.*, 204–205. For an account of one of Garrison's visits to the Forten home see Anna D. Hallowell, ed., *James and Lucretia Mott. Life and Letters* (Boston, 1884), 119.

[54] May, *Some Recollections of the Antislavery Conflict*, 286. May reported that he and several other convention delegates dined at Forten's home and "were entertained with as much ease and elegance as I could desire to see."

[55] His name appears in the *Second Annual Report of the American Anti-Slavery Society, May 12, 1835* (New York, 1835), 12; *Fifth Annual Report of the Executive Committee of the American Anti-Slavery Society, May, 1839* (New York, 1839), 13.

[56] *The Liberator*, September 17, 1841, contained a letter from Forten stating that he was sending additional subscriptions.

[57] Woodson, *Works of Francis J. Grimké*, IV, 96n.

[58] *The Liberator*, May 22, 1840.

Nor did national acclaim blind Forten to the local aspects of abolitionism during his declining years. In 1832 he circulated a petition among Philadelphia Negroes, praying that the Pennsylvania legislature take steps to prevent the return of escaped slaves.[59] A year later he presided over a large meeting of colored people where resolutions were adopted expressing sympathy for education, antislavery, and anticolonialization.[60] In 1836 he prepared a memorial to the legislature urging the members to condemn slavery and wipe out distinctions against men of color in the state. "Let our motto be," he pleaded, "the Law Knows No Distinction." [61] During the following year he served as one of two delegates from Philadelphia to a convention at Harrisburg which urged the end of slavery and colonization.[62] Undeterred by criticism or advancing age, James Forten gave unstintingly to the day's most unpopular cause. Few men, either white or colored, could boast such an outstanding record.

Only with death could his followers show the full measure of their appreciation. Ill health beset him increasingly in his declining years; by the fall of 1841 he was forced to write Garrison that he could exert himself in the cause of abolition no longer, but that his interest was as firm and ardent as ever.[63] A year later he died at the ripe age of seventy-six. His funeral, held on February 24, 1842, was one of the largest in the history of Philadelphia; several hundred whites and several thousand Negroes marched in the procession that followed his body to the grave.[64] At a public meeting to honor his memory a large group of friends, without distinction of color, paid him tribute in the eulogies common to that day.[65]

James Forten passed from the scene with the cause that he sponsored still in its infancy. Yet even on his deathbed he could take solace in the fact that his children were equipped to carry on the crusade with a zeal matching his own.[66] To them, if not to their father, came the privilege of seeing his fondest dreams fulfilled when Abraham Lincoln's Emancipation Proclamation completed the reform to which he had devoted his life.

[59] *Ibid.*, April 14, 1832.

[60] The meeting was held on April 1, 1833. *Ibid.*, April 13, 1833.

[61] *Human Rights*, II (September 4, 1836).

[62] Forten and Robert Purvis, his son-in-law, were the two delegates from Philadelphia. *Proceedings of the Pennsylvania Convention at Harrisburg* (Philadelphia, 1837).

[63] *The Liberator*, September 17, 1841.

[64] Accounts of the funeral are in *ibid.*, March 18, 1842, and in the *National Anti-Slavery Standard*, March 24, 1842. Briefer descriptions by those who attended are in Child, *Freedmen's Book*, 103; and Hallowell, *James and Lucretia Mott*, 232.

[65] *National Anti-Slavery Standard*, March 24, 1842.

[66] Among Forten's children who were active in abolitionism were Margaretta, who served as secretary of the Philadelphia Female Anti-Slavery Society, James, who spoke and sang in the cause of freedom, Robert, who refused to live in a United States that condoned slavery, Harriet, who was married to the well-known reformer, Robert Purvis, who was one of the organizers of an antislavery convention that met in New York in 1837.

William H. Pease and Jane H. Pease

ANTISLAVERY AMBIVALENCE:
IMMEDIATISM, EXPEDIENCY, RACE *

*If Forten was indeed a "forgotten abolitionist," as Billington refers
to him, the fault lies in part with white historians who have ignored
the role of Negroes in the abolitionist movement. Yet it also lies in
part with the white abolitionists themselves. Generally far in advance
of most of the American public in their racial attitudes, few of them
—even among the most prominent—were fully emancipated from the
prejudices of their age. In recent years a spirited discussion has engaged historians concerning whether or not the white abolitionists,
who practically excluded Negroes from decision-making positions in
antislavery societies, were genuinely racial equalitarians. William and
Jane Pease have explored this subject in a penetrating manner.*

Of constant distress to students of the American antislavery movement has
been its ambivalence, especially its ambivalence over the term Immediatism.
The term had originally defined a means to end British colonial slavery, but it
failed to be similarly applicable to emancipation in the American South. Therefore the antislavery movement strained to give new meaning to emancipation
"instant and universal." Did it not really mean gradual emancipation immediately begun or, perhaps, immediate emancipation gradually achieved? But no
less than over immediatism, antislavery crusaders were beset by a fundamental
ambivalence in their attitude toward the Negro himself. At the simplest level
there was no issue. Slavery was sin; and the crusaders were moved to free the

William H. Pease and Jane H. Pease, "Antislavery Ambivalence: Immediatism,
Expedience, Race." *American Quarterly*, XVII (Winter, 1965), pp. 682–695. Reprinted
with permission of *American Quarterly*, and William H. and Jane H. Pease.
* This article was read, in a slightly modified form, at the annual meetings of the
Mississippi Valley Historical Association, April 1965.

slave by a humanitarianism too genuine to be doubted.[1] Yet, sympathetic as they might appear and believe themselves to be toward the Negro, the abolitionists were, as Leon Litwack and others have shown, in part at least prejudiced against him.[2] And the variety of their response toward him demonstrates the ambivalence so characteristic of the antislavery movement as a whole.

Endemic was the abolitionists' tendency toward abstraction. Frequently they so abstracted both the "Negro" and the "Crusade" that they dealt not with people in a situation but only with intellectualizations in a vacuum. John Thomas has recently noted that William Lloyd Garrison failed "to understand people, black or white" and used them simply "as counters in the grim business of reform." [3] His analysis echoes publisher James Gordon Bennett's conclusion made one hundred years earlier that to Garrison "nothing [was] sacred ... but the ideal intellect of the negro race." [4]

This preoccupation with the ideal is reflected by the American Anti-Slavery Society, which, at its inception in 1833, resolved that to guarantee education to the Negro was more important than to end "corporeal slavery itself, inasmuch as ignorance enslaves the mind and tends to the ruin of the immortal soul." [5] And, on the very eve of Emancipation, Philadelphia anti-slavery leader James Miller McKim, although emphasizing the importance of slave rehabilitation and active in prosecuting it, thought that it was "not the place ... of [the] abolitionists to descend to the details of th[e] work, teaching and the like; let this," he added, "be attended to by the neophytes and others. We are to continue to be what we always have been," he concluded, "a wheel within a wheel; an original motive power." [6] Thus for thirty years abolitionists, to a greater or lesser extent, heeded the kind of exhortation which Henry C. Wright enunciated so forcefully:

[1] The abolitionists were defined and set off from their contemporaries by their opposition to slavery and their concern for the welfare of the slaves, a concern which usually embraced the free Negroes as well. This article is not, however, designed to compare abolitionists as a group with nonabolitionists but rather to explore the variations within the group.

[2] See, for example, Leon Litwack, "The Abolitionist Dilemma: The Antislavery Movement and the Northern Negro," *New England Quarterly*, XXXIV (1961), 50–73; and his *North of Slavery: The Negro in the Free States, 1790–1860* (Chicago, 1961). See also Larry Gara, Louis Filler, Gerda Lerner, Stanley Elkins for considerations of prejudice. For psychological probing see David Donald, Hazel Wolf, Clifford Griffin, Martin Duberman.

[3] John L. Thomas, *The Liberator, William Lloyd Garrison, A Biography* (Boston, 1963), p. 153.

[4] Quoted in Wendell Phillips Garrison and Francis Jackson Garrison, *William Lloyd Garrison, 1805–1879; The Story of His Life as Told by His Children* (4 vols.; New York, 1885–89), III, 283.

[5] American Anti-Slavery Society, *Proceedings of the Anti-Slavery Convention, Assembled at Philadelphia, Decembr 4, 5, and 6, 1833* (New York, 1833), p. 19.

[6] James Miller McKim to Samuel J. May, May 20 [1862], in Samuel J. May Papers, Cornell University.

Watch, Sister, & pray that you enter not into temptation. *Watch, not* ... for Abolition as an Organization, not even for our millions of crushed & bleeding slaves ..., but watch *for* the eternal, immutable Principles of Justice & Right—watch for *Humanity.* ... We are seeking an object that must command the respect of the world—i e *the redemption of man from the dominion of man.* This is Abolition.[7]

The abolitionists did, of course, at least partly understand their own position. They may not have realized just how fully they were depersonalizing the Negroes; but they were quite aware that they had difficulties in matching their protestations to their actions. "We are," said the Connecticut crusader Samuel J. May with a Zolaesque directness, "culpably ignorant of, or shamefully indifferent to the wrongs which are inflicted upon our colored brethren. ... We are prejudiced against the blacks; and our prejudices are indurated ... by the secret, vague consciousness of the wrong we are doing them. Men are apt to dislike those most, whom they have injured most." [8] And despite the teaching of the antislavery periodical, the *Abolitionist,* that the antislavery enthusiast ought "to banish from his own mind the unworthy feelings which would lead him to regard any human being with contempt merely on account of his color," New York abolitionist Lewis Tappan admitted "that when the subject of acting out our profound principles in treating men irrespective of color is discussed heat is always produced." [9]

This much, then, the abolitionists themselves perceived. But for the student of the antislavery movement it is also imperative to recognize that prejudice and abstraction were but the obvious symptoms of an ambivalence which gives to the antislavery crusade in the expediency and temporizing of its actions and in the complexity of its thought an architecture baroque in the richness of its variations.[10]

It was, for example, relatively simple to accept the humanity of the

[7] Henry C. Wright to Maria Weston Chapman, May 2, 1839, in Weston Papers, Antislavery Collection, Boston Public Library.

[8] Samuel J. May, Sermon delivered May 29, 1831, in Boston, as reported in *Liberator,* July 23, 1831.

[9] *Abolitionist,* I (Jan. 1833), as quoted in Merton L. Dillon, "'The Failure of the American Abolitionists," *Journal of Southern History,* XXV (1959), 167. Lewis Tappan, Diary entry [Apr. 1836], as quoted in Litwack, *North of Slavery,* p. 218. See also Garrison's July 4, 1829 oration (*Garrison* I, 133–34); Susan Cabot, *What Have We, as Individuals, to Do with Slavery* (American Anti-Slavery Society, *Anti-Slavery Tract No. 15.* New York, 1855), pp. 3–4; Beriah Green, *American Anti-Slavery Reporter,* I (June 1834), 88; and Birney to William Wright, June 20, 1845, in *Letters of James Gillespie Birney,* 1831–1857, ed. Dwight L. Dumond (2 vols.; New York, 1938), II, 947.

[10] This ideological ambivalence is reflected in the cleavages within the antislavery movement over the appropriate courses of action to be pursued. These cleavages have already been well examined in a variety of studies on antislavery published since 1935. Whether to take political action or to regard it as damaging to the requisite moral fervor, whether to expend time and funds on schools, give aid to fugitives and buy freedom for individual slaves or to work exclusively to propagate the antislavery faith are debates not only about means but also about the basic concepts of antislavery.

Negro; but then how did one account for his patently submerged position vis-à-vis the whites? Abolitionists like Lydia Maria Child of Northampton, Massachusetts, tried to link the two elements by admitting that, while all Negroes were not "Scotts or Miltons," they were "*men*, capable of producing their proportions of Scotts and Miltons, if they could be allowed to live in a state of physical and intellectual freedom." [11] At the other extreme the New York Whig politician, William Henry Seward, defending the mentally deranged William Freeman in 1846, tried to subordinate intellectual lack to simple humanity and to separate it from race. He pleaded with the jury that

> the color of the prisoner's skin, and the form of his features, are not impressed upon the spiritual, immortal mind which works beneath. In spite of human pride, he is still your brother, and mine, in form and color accepted and approved by his Father, and yours, and mine, and bears equally with us the proudest inheritance of our race—the image of our Maker. Hold him then to be a MAN.[12]

In denying, furthermore, that the apparent differences between Negroes and whites were not inherent the abolitionists became environmentalists. John Rankin, ex-slaveholder from Virginia and an ardent abolitionist, asserted with good will but dubious logic that, if racial inferiority were a valid criterion, then all Negroes would be inferior to all whites if but one was. Clearly this was not so. Therefore existing inferiority was explainable only in environmental terms.[13] Slavery it was, asserted German refugee Charles Follen of Boston, that debased and degraded the Negroes and generated among whites an "absurd and cruel prejudice against color." [14] The antislavery solution to prejudice was clear once the cause was thus linked to slavery. Charles Calistus Burleigh of Connecticut optimistically exhorted his fellow whites to "give [the Negro] his liberty, and as strong a motive to exertion as you have;—a prospect of reward as sure and ample; not only wages for his toil, but respect and honor and social standing according to his worth, and see what he can then become." [15]

[11] Lydia Maria Child, *An Appeal in Favor of that Class of Americans Called Africans* (orig. ed. 1833. New York, 1836), p. 171.

[12] William Henry Seward, *Argument in Defense of William Freeman on His Trial for Murder*... (4th ed.; Auburn, N.Y., 1846), pp. 8–9. See also C. T. C. Follen, *Works, with a Memoir of His Life* [by Mrs. E. L. Follen] (5 vols.; Boston, 1841), I, 627–28.

[13] John Rankin, *Letters on American Slavery Addressed to Mr. Thomas Rankin*... (5th ed.; Boston, 1838), pp. 10–11. See also Lewis Tappan, *The Life of Arthur Tappan* (New York, 1870), p. 131; James A. Thome and J. Horace Kimball, *Emancipation in the West Indies. A Six Months Tour in Antigua, Barbadoes, and Jamaica in the Year 1837* (American Anti-Slavery Society, *Anti-Slavery Examiner No. 7*. New York, 1838), p. 75; and Sallie Holley to Gerrit Smith, Nov. 17, 1865, in the Smith Miller Papers, Syracuse University.

[14] Charles Follen, "The Cause of Freedom in Our Country," *Quarterly Anti-Slavery Magazine*, II (Oct. 1836), 65.

[15] Charles Calistus Burleigh, *Slavery and the North* (New York [1855]), p. 4. Rankin essentially held the same view, but thought that it would take a long time to raise the Negro; see *Letters on American Slavery*, pp. 10–11.

Yet, for all their exuberance, for all their belief in equality, for all their efforts to raise the Negro above the debilitating influences of adverse environment, the abolitionists were never wholly convincing. Much of what they said betrayed an implicit and at times explicit belief in racial inferiority. Here again ambivalence emerged. That the abolitionists themselves were usually unconscious of their expression of prejudice and that they denied it when challenged should surprise no one. Nor, indeed, is the thoughtful student surprised to learn that such prejudice did in fact exist. Occasionally crude, more often hidden in underlying assumptions or in appeals to science, prejudice played a more pervasive role than the logic of consistency would admit.

Exasperated by poor printing, inferior paper and numerous misprints, and spurred on by his own literary pride, Edmund Quincy lashed out in a letter to Caroline Weston in 1846 at "Wendell's nigger," whom he held responsible for botching an Antislavery Report. Never, he urged, let the printing out to "*Smart people*"; they get things up so poorly.[16] Here clearly was not only a rather vulgar display of prejudice but also of a value structure in which the typography of a convention's report weighed more heavily than economic opportunity for the free Negro.

The acerbity of these outbursts may be attributed to Quincy alone. The subterranean import, however, was common property among antislavery people. As late as 1860 Theodore Parker, a backer of John Brown, observed that "the Anglo-Saxon with common sense does not like this Africanization of America; he wishes the superior race to multiply rather than the inferior." [17] His neighbor, Samuel Gridley Howe, known for his multiple reform interests, accepted Parker's assumptions but rejected his predictions by observing that, particularly among young Canadian refugee Negroes, many succumbed to "mesenteric and other glandular diseases" and suffered from "phthisical diseases" and a "softening of tubercles." "Many intelligent physicians," he stated, "who have practiced among both [white and Negro] classes, say that the colored people are feebly organized; that the scrofulous temperament prevails among them; that the climate tends to development of tuberculous diseases; that they are unprolific and short-lived." [18]

Whether feebly organized in physique or not, the Negroes were certainly docile in temperament. "It is paying a very poor compliment, indeed, to the courage and superiority of us whites," Richard Hildreth said through the sympathetically portrayed Mr. Mason in *Archy Moore*, "to doubt whether we, superior as well in numbers as in every thing else, could not inspire awe enough to maintain our natural position at the head of the community, and to keep

[16] Edmund Quincy to Caroline Weston, Feb. 1, 1846, in Weston Papers. A year later Quincy complained about Frederick Douglass' independence (what he thought was Douglass' overcharging the *American Anti-Slavery Standard* for copy supplied) by observing that "These niggers, like Kings, are kittle cattle to shoe behind." Quincy to Caroline Weston, July 2, 1847, in Weston Papers.

[17] Theodore Parker, *John Brown's Expedition Reviewed in a Letter from Theodore Parker, at Rome, to Francis Jackson, Boston* (Boston, 1860), p. 14.

[18] Samuel Gridley Howe, *The Refugees from Slavery in Canada West. Report to the Freedmen's Inquiry Commission* (Boston, 1864), pp. 21–22.

these poor people in order without making slaves of them." [19] But, if Hildreth's Mason was fictional, the Lane Rebels were not. They had concluded, in their famous debates on slavery, that *"the blacks are abundantly able to take care of and provide for themselves"*; but had added immediately that they *"would be kind and docile if immediately emancipated."* [20] This emphasis on docility is important, for quite openly it reduced the status of the Negro below that of the white man. J. Miller McKim, for example, negated American standards of self-reliance and manly independence when he praised Negroes for "their susceptibility to control." [21]

Not unreasonably, many Negroes actively resented this abolitionist presumption about their "susceptibility to control." During the 1850s, in fact, this resentment was in large part responsible for the growth and activity of the Negro Convention movement, whose purpose it was to do for the Negroes themselves what they feared the whites, at last, would not accomplish for them. Frederick Douglass and Henry Highland Garnet, two Negro leaders of marked undocility, both took umbrage at Maria Weston Chapman for her paternal concern about their appropriate behavior; and Douglass, disillusioned with radical abolitionism in the face of growing political antislavery activity and ambitious himself to assert his independence from white abolitionist domination, defied the Boston hierarchy by establishing his own newspaper in Rochester, New York. Likewise, Martin Delany, a successful Negro doctor, resented the Negroes' exclusion from antislavery leadership and was highly dubious about the abolitionists' touted support of economic opportunity for free Negroes. Delany's disillusionment led him to abandon America as a viable home for the Negro and in the late 1850s to sponsor projects for African colonization.[22]

Despite concepts of racial inferiority, further borne out by an almost universal preference for the lighter-skinned over the darker-skinned Negro,[23] abo-

[19] Richard Hildreth, *Archy Moore: The White Slave* (1st ed.; 1836. New York, 1856), p. 264.

[20] As reported in Henry B. Stanton to Joshua Leavitt, Mar. 10, 1834, in *American Anti-Slavery Reporter*, I (Apr. 1834), 54.

[21] James Miller McKim, *The Freedmen of South Carolina . . .* (Philadelphia, 1862), p. 9. See also *Letters from Port Royal. Written at the Time of the Civil War*, ed. Elizabeth Ware Pearson (Boston, 1906), pp. 102–03, 315–16; The *Anti-Slavery Record* III (Feb. 1837), 15; *Letters of Theodore Dwight Weld, Angelina Grimké Weld and Sarah Grimké, 1822–1844*, eds. Gilbert H. Barnes and Dwight L. Dumond (2 vols.; New York, 1934), II, 524; and Leon Litwack, *North of Slavery*, p. 223.

[22] In the Weston Papers one may find numerous examples of the patronizing antislavery attitude and of Negro response to it. See also Filler, *Crusade Against Slavery*, p. 143. In particular note Frederick Douglass to Maria Weston Chapman, Mar. 29, 1846, Weston Papers; and Martin Robinson Delany, *The Condition, Elevation, Emigration, and Destiny of the Colored People of the United States Politically Considered* (Philadelphia, 1852), pp. 25–29.

[23] Antislavery literature contains many illustrations of the preference for lighter-skinned Negroes. See Samuel May Jr., *The Fugitive Slave Law and Its Victims* (American Anti-Slavery Society, Anti-Slavery Tract No. 18 [New York, 1855]); George Bourne, *Slavery Illustrated in its Effects Upon Woman and Domestic Society* (Boston, 1837); Hildreth's *Archy Moore*; and William I. Bowditch, *White Slavery in the United States*

litionists in fact did demand just and equitable civil liberties for colored persons. "The oppressive civil disabilities laid upon them in the non-slaveholding States, and the settled opposition to their education and elevation...," said the Andover Theological Seminary antislavery society,

> are but glaring indications of the prevalent spirit of slavery. The same contempt of the black man—the same disposition to trample on his rights and to lord it over his person, follows him, whatever *degree* of emancipation he may have obtained, and in whatever part of the nation he takes his refuge. Though we had in view only the wrongs of the colored people in New-England, we should feel ourselves compelled to take our present stand, and vindicate their rights as brethren, as men, and as Americans.[24]

Abolitionists everywhere asserted that Negroes and whites should be judged and treated according to the same standards in the apportioning not only of civil rights but also of economic and educational opportunities. In its Declaration of Sentiments the American Anti-Slavery Society announced in 1833 that

> all persons of color who possess the qualifications which are demanded of others, ought to be admitted forthwith to the enjoyment of the same privileges, and the exercise of the same prerogatives, as others; and... the paths of preferment, of wealth, and of intelligence, should be opened as widely to them as to persons of a white complexion.[25]

Schools, like Oberlin College and the Noyes Academy in New Hampshire, which admitted Negroes on equal terms with whites,[26] bore out these principles as did Charles Sumner's argument in the Roberts Case in 1849 that separate schools were unequal and threatened cleavages in society.[27] And Samuel J. May, summing up the concept in a statement which avoided many of the pitfalls of prejudice into which his colleagues fell, averred that "all we demand for them is that negroes shall be permitted, encouraged, assisted to become as wise, as virtuous, and as rich as they can, and be acknowledged to be just what they have become, and be treated accordingly." [28]

(American Anti-Slavery Society, *Anti-Slavery Tract No. 2* [New York, 1855]); see also in this connection Theodore Dwight Weld, *American Slavery as it is: Testimony of a Thousand Witnesses* (New York, 1839); and the juvenile [Jonathan Walker], *A Picture of Slavery, for Youth. By the Author of "The Branded Hand" and "Chattelized Humanity"* (Boston, n.d.).

[24] This is a summary given by D. T. Kimball and F. Laine to *Genius of Temperance*, Aug. 22, 1833, as reported in *Liberator*, Sept. 28, 1833. Similar demands for equality of treatment can be found in Child, *Appeal*, pp. 195–208.

[25] American Anti-Slavery Society, *Proceedings of the Anti-Slavery Convention, Assembled at Philadelphia*, contains the Declaration of Sentiments.

[26] See *Liberator*, Oct. 25, 1834, for information about the Noyes Academy.

[27] Charles Sumner, "Equality before the Law: Unconstitutionality of Separate Colored Schools in Massachusetts. Argument before the Supreme Court of Massachusetts, in the Case of Sarah C. Roberts v. The City of Boston...," in *The Works of Charles Sumner* (Boston, 1872), II, 327–76.

[28] Samuel Joseph May, *Some Recollections of Our Anti-Slavery Conflict* (Boston, 1869), p. 29. See also Birney, *Letters*, II, 945; and Garrison, *Garrison*, I, 148.

Yet these appeals to the efficacy of education and economic betterment reveal the middle-class values to which almost all abolitionists subscribed and which both compound and explain much of the ambivalence in the antislavery movement. As middle-class Americans, abolitionists, naturally enough, measured the Negroes against middle-class standards, and to those standards they expected the Negroes to conform—Negroes who were generally ex-slaves from the lowest and most abject class in America. Assuredly the American Anti-Slavery Society was eager to uplift them to "an equality with the whites" but only after carefully disclaiming that it approved any such non-middle-class shenanigans as adopting colored children, encouraging interracial marriages or "exciting the people of color to assume airs." [29]

It was expected, then, that the Negroes should adapt themselves to the values of the white community, should, as one abolitionist advised, submit to prejudice "with the true dignity of meekness" so that their critics might be stilled. Thus was fulfilled the stereotype of the malleable, willing and docile colored man. Still, on limited occasions, the same writer observed, the Negroes should take a positive stand. They should demand admission to the public schools, they should organize or join lyceum groups, they should acquire knowledge and education. And, he said in a condensed version of a middle-class *Poor Richard's*, they should organize uplifting visits to their poor and degraded brethren and teach them "temperance ... cleanliness, neatness, strict honesty, and all that belong to good morality." [30] In addition to these virtues, the American Anti-Slavery Society agents were admonished to instill in the free people of color

> the importance of domestic order, and the performance of relative duties in families; of correct habits; command of temper and courteous manners. Also the duty and advantages of industry and economy; promptness and fidelity in the fulfillment of contrasts or obligations, whether written or verbal; and encourage them in the acquisition of property, especially of real estate in fee simple, particularly dwellings for their own families. Present their duties and privileges as citizens, and encourage them to become voters, and to secure equal privileges with other citizens. ... [31]

Others, varying little from the standard reforming attitudes of the day but less optimistic about raising the Negro to the middle-class, urged him to adopt their own conception of lower-class standards. He should learn a trade and become a mechanic. Since these abolitionists categorized the social strata in

---

[29] Executive Committee of the American Anti-Slavery Society to Mayor Cornelius Lawrence of New York, July 16, 1834, included in the microfilm printing of *Liberator*, between 1833 and 1834, reel 1.

[30] This entire argument appeared in a series of articles, signed "S. T. U.," which appeared in *Liberator*, Feb. 11, 18, 25, and Mar. 3, 1832. The quotations are from the first and last issues, respectively.

[31] Executive Committee of the American Anti-Slavery Society to its agents, n.d. [1834–5?], included in the microfilm printing of *Liberator*, between 1833 and 1834, reel 1.

such a way that the hardy mechanic always fell comfortably below the solid middle class, the Negro was bracketed, at worst, with the Irish hod carrier, and at best only identified with the honest toiler.[32]

Sometimes in the abolitionists' arguments one discovers strong overtones of ordinary self-interest. The *Anti-Slavery Almanac* assured its readers, for example, that emancipated Negroes would not flock to the North. Let no one be perturbed, the *Almanac* urged in unctuous tone. "If the slaves are gradually set free, they must leave the place where they are, (and will be likely to go to the north,) that they may not interfere with the slavery which remains. But if they are all set free at once, they may continue where they are." Putting the argument in other terms, emancipated Negroes would be a great boon to the economy not only in the South but in the North as well.[33] "The southern laborers, when free and paid," C. C. Burleigh had said, "would buy of us many comforts and conveniences not allowed them now . . . which would give new activity to our shops and mills and shipping, and steadier employment, and, most likely, higher wages, to all kinds of labor here." [34a] Thus emancipation would not inconvenience the North with a mass of freed slaves; it would rather prove quite profitable.

Still, there was the thorny issue of defining the social position of the Negro in a predominantly white society. Many of the same abolitionists who demanded so unfalteringly no association with slaveholders found it ticklishly difficult to espouse social intercourse with Negroes and almost impossible to champion holy wedlock with those of black skin. In theory and in conscience, of course, they deplored the bans on interracial marriage; yet in practice they as often betrayed an opposite sentiment.[35] For his own part, Garrison defended the ideal goal but reconciled it with practical reality. "At the present time," he said expediently, "mixed marriages would be in bad taste. . . ." [36] Elizur

[32] See, for example, the *Anti-Slavery Record*, I (June 1835), 68, urging that Negroes be apprenticed at good trades. And see also the commentary reprinted by *Liberator*, Mar. 31, 1837, from the Bangor *Mechanic*, in which it is made quite clear that the laborer is quite aware that the middle class looks down on the working class. See also, for comparisons with the Irish, Hildreth, *Archy Moore*, p. 264; Sarah Grimké to Elizabeth Pease [May 20? 1938], in *Weld-Grimké Letters*, II, 679; William Allen Diary, Nov. 10, 1863, State Historical Society of Wisconsin.

[33] The *Anti-Slavery Almanac* (1837 and 1839). The quotation is from the earlier volume, p. 44. The self-interest showed in other ways as well. Defending what later became Radical Republican doctrine, Maria Weston Chapman wrote to Lizzy (Chapman) Laugel (Sept. 24, 1862) that "black *soldiers* would save our Armies, & black *citizens* our *republican institutions*" (Weston Papers). And Wendell Phillips also unconsciously suggested the same prior self-concern when he spoke at the *Liberator's* 20th anniversary celebration: "My friends, if we never free a slave, we have at least freed ourselves in the effort to emancipate our brother man." (Quoted in Garrison, *Garrison*, III, 320.)

[34] Burleigh, *Slavery and the North*, pp. 8–9.

[35] See Birney, *Letters*, I, 397; Garrison, *Garrison*, II, 356; *Anti-Slavery Record*, I (June 1835), 71; and Gilbert H. Barnes, *The Antislavery Impulse, 1830–1844* (New York, 1933), p. 274, note 20. See also Louis Ruchames, "Race, Marriage and Abolition in Massachusetts," *Journal of Negro History*, XL (1955), 250–73, on the fight for repeal of discriminatory marriage laws.

[36] *Liberator*, Aug. 13, 1831.

Wright, however, scornfully ridiculed such temporizing over prejudice. "Pray, what is the matter? we ask of a generous and enlightened public," he snapped viciously.

> The reply is couched with quaking apprehension, in the appalling interrogatory; *would you have your daughter marry a negro?* And the utter slavery to which this tyrant prejudice has reduced everything that is noble and good in the land, is evinced by nothing more clearly than by the pains taking of even abolitionists to show that colored men *may be* enfranchised and elevated without bringing on the dreaded consequence.[37]

It seemed necessary, in the end, to plaster over the issue and to allay white fears. Mrs. Child, echoing the frequent antislavery assertion that there were scarcely enough abolitionists in the South to account for the evidences of miscegenation there, insisted that to say that abolitionists wished amalgamation was "a false charge, got up by the enemies of the cause, and used as a bugbear to increase the prejudices of the community." In fact, she added, "by universal emancipation we want to *stop* amalgamation." [38] More reassuring to those who hoped that the issues raised by social equality would fail to materialize was Samuel G. Howe's commentary made after a close study of Canadian Negroes. "Upon the whole," he observed,

> ... the experience of the Canadian refugees goes to show that there need be no anxiety upon the score of amalgamation of races in the United States. With freedom, and protection of their legal rights; with an open field for industry, and opportunities for mental and moral culture, colored people will not seek relationship with whites, but will follow their natural affinities, and marry among themselves.[39]

The social distance decreed by class identification provided perhaps the most common and satisfactory framework for abolitionists' contacts with free Negroes. Thus, steeped in middle-class values and having identified the Negroes with the laboring classes, the antislavery band frequently assumed the patronizing air of the uplifter and the saved toward the downtrodden and unwashed. James G. Birney, speaking for a slaveholding background, observed that without question emancipation would, "where the superior intelligence of the master was acknowledged, produce on the part of the beneficiaries, the most entire and cordial reliance on his counsel and friendship." [40] And Sumner, in the Roberts Case, urged that "the vaunted superiority of the white race imposes corresponding duties. The faculties with which they are endowed, and

---

[37] [Elizur Wright Jr.], "Caste in the United States: A Review," *Quarterly Anti-Slavery Magazine*, II (Jan. 1837), 177.

[38] Lydia Maria Child, *Anti-Slavery Catechism* (Newburyport, 1836), pp. 31–32.

[39] Howe, *Refugees from Slavery*, p. 33.

[40] Quoted in *The Legion of Liberty and Force of Truth, Containing the Thoughts, Words, and Deeds, of Some Prominent Apostles, Champions and Martyrs* (New York, 1843), n.p.

the advantages they possess, must be exercised for the good of all. If the colored people are ignorant, degraded, and unhappy," he asserted with a fine sense of noblesse oblige, "then should they be especial objects of care." [41]

Such paternalism was, to be sure, most benign. At times, however, it was most insufferable. "The more I mingle with your people," Angelina Grimké wrote to Sarah Douglass in a display of tactlessness as gargantuan as it was overbearing,

> the more I feel for their oppressions and desire to sympathize in their sorrows. Joshua Leavitt threw out a new and delightful idea on this subject on our way to Bloomfield. He said he believed the Lord had a great work for the colored people to do, and that your long continued afflictions and humiliations was the furnace in which He was purifying you from the dross[,] the tin[,] and the reprobate silver, that you might come out like gold seven times refined. I Hav[e] thought of this and fully believ[e] you will after all get up abov[e] us and be the favored instruments [to?] carry pure and undefiled Religion to the Heathen World. May the Lord lift you from the dung hill and set you among princes....[42]

Helping the Lord hoist the poor Negroes off the dung hill was, as it often turned out, an arduous and dangerous chore, but one which gave the abolitionists a chance many of them coveted to become martyrs in the cause. To defend the Negro in court, to speak on his behalf before hostile audiences, to be harried from town after town by the frenzied mob was the stuff of which martyrdom was made. And the genuine joy in the experience of such martyrdom only enhanced the rewards of protective guardianship, as those who braved the mob when Pennsylvania Hall was burned well knew. Confronting the hostile elements, the stalwart women of the Female Anti-Slavery Convention "maintain[ed] the perilled cause to the last." As they adjourned "the colored members of the convention were protected by their white sisters, and Oh! Shame to say," one of the white sisters wrote, "at both were thrown a shower of stones." [43] And then, Oh! Shame to say, the brand new hall was set ablaze and totally destroyed.

In their enthusiasm to elevate the Negro, the abolitionists frequently carried on their shoulders an early version of the White Man's Burden. They taught their children in heavily freighted moral tales that "negroes, even poor, degraded, despised slaves, are not without reason and understanding. [And that] many of them have a large share of sagacity." Go forth, they directed even the toddlers, instruct the poor and ignorant; become teachers, and help train the Negroes themselves to become missionaries that they may enlighten

[41] Sumner, "Equality before the Law," II, 376.

[42] In Angelina and Sarah Grimké to Sarah Douglass, Feb. 22, 1837, *Weld-Grimké Letters*, I, 364–65. Gerda Lerner contends that the Grimké sisters were almost if not totally above prejudice in "The Grimké Sisters and the Struggle against Race Prejudice," *Journal of Negro History*, XLVIII (1936), 277–91.

[43] Letter from a New York woman, May 18, 1838, in *Liberator*, May 25, 1838.

"their countrymen who are in ignorance and darkness." [44] The adults themselves set the initial example. When Helen Benson, daughter of Rhode Island abolitionist George Benson, was married to Garrison, she refused to allow cake at her wedding or to wear fancy clothes lest she be a poor model for the Negroes to follow.[45] Theodore Weld also cast himself as an exemplar of the good. "I attend Church with our colored friends," he wrote; "but," he honestly admitted, "I do it to cast my lot with them; and," he contentedly concluded, "tho not spiritually edified, I find joy and peace in it." [46]

It was, however, a far more difficult thing for the same abolitionists to follow through, unhesitatingly and courageously, the implications of their theories, to work unfalteringly and without equivocation, straight on to free the slave and obtain equality for the free Negro. Certainly the abolitionists were almost universally too forthright and too dedicated to be faithless to their ideals; certainly they did not knowingly forsake their plighted word. Still it was a constant fact of the antislavery crusade that it was clearly marked by the constant temporizing of its participants.[47] In Ohio, some Lane students objected when one of their number took up residence with Cincinnati Negro families while he was working among them because they thought it would be harmful to their project.[48] Throughout the North antislavery societies debated the questions "Ought abolitionists to encourage colored persons in joining Anti-Slavery Societies?" or "Is it expedient for Abolitionists to encourage social intercourse between white and colored families?" And their composite response was at best an equivocal "perhaps." [49]

This political temporizing was not, of course, without its reasons, particularly in the light of mobs and physical violence provoked by extremists. Some abolitionists, of course, merely thought of public relations and how best to draw support to the cause. Birney, for his part, thought it enough to strive for equal civil rights without, at the same time, trying for social equality. Too much too soon, he argued, would mean a denial of all rights to the Negro.[50] So too the American Anti-Slavery Society, after the serious antiabolitionist riots in New York in 1834, rejected charges that they supported amalgamation or

[44] From a story in the Juvenile Department, signed "H. Sabbath School Treasury," *Liberator*, Jan. 14, 1832. The Juvenile column was a regular feature in the early years of the *Liberator*. Henry C. Wright was designated American Anti-Slavery Society agent to children.

[45] Garrison, *Garrison*, I, 427.

[46] Weld to Sarah and Angelina Grimké, Dec. 15 [1837], in *Weld-Grimké Letters*, I, 496. A similar viewpoint turns up in Unitarian observations quite frequently as a rejection of emotional-evangelical enthusiasms.

[47] In a letter to Lewis Tappan, Weld, for example, wrote concerning a slave case in Connecticut that "not one of the Abolitionists here [in Hartford] was willing to appear *openly* in the matter as the friend of the compla[i]nant. Brother Tyler and myself who are the only persons known publickly in the case as friends of the compla[i]nant, have been and are still plentifully threatened with mob vengeance." June 8, 1837, *Weld-Grimké Letters*, I, 399.

[48] *Liberator*, Jan. 10, 1835.

[49] From Litwack, *North of Slavery*, p. 218.

[50] Birney to Weld, July 26, 1834, *Weld-Grimké Letters*, I, 163.

attacked the Constitution. "We disclaim, and entirely disapprove," they asserted, "the language of a hand-bill recently circulated in this City the tendency of which is thought to be to excite resistance to the Laws. Our principle is, that even hard laws are to be submitted to by all men, until they can by peaceable means be altered." [51]

The abolitionists were painfully aware of their actions, yet in good conscience they believed that their course was the better part of wisdom and thus did not compromise their valor. Arthur Tappan for one was so fearful lest his earlier activities be misconstrued that he assured A. F. Stoddard of Glasgow in 1863 that "if . . . you should know of any one's charging me with any gross assault on the fastidiousness of the age, when I became the avowed friend of the colored man, you may set it down to the score of ignorance or malignant falsehood." [52] But Sarah Forten, member of the actively antislavery Negro family of Philadelphia, understood. "How much of this leaven still lingers in the hearts of our white brethren and sisters is oftentimes made manifest to us," she wrote, referring specifically to an abolitionist who was comfortable with Negroes only under cover of night; "but when we recollect what great sacrifices to public sentiment they are called upon to make," she generously added, "we cannot wholly blame them." [53]

Briefly, then, the antislavery movement was beset, throughout its history, by a fundamental ambivalence. Never could the abolitionists decide collectively, and infrequently individually, whether the Negro was equal or inferior to the white; whether social equality for the Negro should be stressed or whether it should be damped; whether civil and social rights should be granted him at once or only in the indefinite and provisional future; whether, in fact, social and civil rights should be granted or whether only civil rights should be given him. The abolitionists, furthermore, were torn between a genuine concern for the welfare and uplift of the Negro and a paternalism which was too often merely the patronizing of a superior class. And their forthright concern for the Negro was still more qualified by an unhappy degree of temporizing.

These are the hallmarks of a critical and fundamental ambivalence. When such a quandary existed over the position and treatment of the free Negro and over the very nature of the beings to be freed, abolitionist temporizing becomes understandable. When immediate emancipation as a plan of abolition was translated to mean only immediate repentance of the sin of slavery, the needs of the human beings who were slaves were ignored. The abolitionists had sought solace in abstractions about humanity. And their hesitancy and confusion about the question of race illuminate much of the contention and indecision within the antislavery movement—a movement baffled and torn by ambivalence.

[51] *Liberator*, July 19, 1834.
[52] Arthur Tappan to A. F. Stoddard, Aug. 27, 1863, in Tappan, *Tappan*, pp. 201–2.
[53] Sarah Forten to Angelina Grimké, Apr. 15, 1837, *Weld-Grimké Letters*, I, 380.

Howard H. Bell

NATIONAL NEGRO CONVENTIONS OF THE MIDDLE 1840'S: MORAL SUASION VS. POLITICAL ACTION

Between 1830 and 1835 Negro leaders held annual conventions to protest against conditions oppressing the race. Excluded from the inner councils of the antislavery societies, they revived the convention movement during the middle forties. At the same time they were still ideologically involved in the mainstream of abolitionism. When the American Antislavery Society split in 1839–1840 over philosophical and tactical issues, the Negro members were found on both sides. Howard H. Bell analyzes the divergent Negro views on this matter. He also describes the many other proposals for racial advancement—ranging from cultivation of the middle-class virtues to the advocacy of slave insurrection—made at the conventions, and introduces the reader to many of the prominent Negro protest leaders of the ante-bellum generation.

Bᴙ 1840 militant abolitionism was a way of life widely accepted by many people in the North. To that date those championing moral persuasion as the best means of abolishing slavery had been the dominant group. But with the advent of the Liberty Party many turned to political action as more effective in accomplishing that end. By 1843 many Negro leaders, especially in the areas outside of New England, were ardent admirers of the new party since it offered an opportunity for a type of action which had previously been denied them. It was therefore to be expected that national conventions meeting in upstate New York during the middle 'forties would be influenced by Liberty Party ideals.

Howard H. Bell, "National Negro Conventions of the Middle 1840's: Moral Suasion vs. Political Action," *Journal of Negro History*, XLII (October, 1957), pp. 247–60. Reprinted with permission of *Journal of Negro History*.

The annual national conventions which had been carried on for six consecutive years during the early 'thirties had died out when New York and Philadelphia began championing different ways of meeting the problems facing the Negro in the United States. By the end of that decade, however, there was a demand for a revival of the national conventions.[1] In the autumn of 1841 a number of men from Philadelphia set their names to a call for such an assembly. Among the items on the agenda were issues such as temperance, education, economy, agricultural and mechanical trades, and the development of a manual labor school. A new and previously unpopular feature was the consideration of petitioning for a grant of land from Congress for agricultural and other purposes for the use of the Negro.[2] Not content with petitioning for a grant of land, the subject of emigration was also listed for discussion.[3] To say the least the proposed assembly was set to deal with an ambitious schedule and one that might be expected to draw the fire of some abolitionists, especially those opposed to separate Negro organizations and to emigration.

One of the leading abolitionist journals asked God's blessing upon the new enterprise;[4] another was open in its criticism of the proposed convention and carried also in its columns the disapproval of at least two Negro newspapers.[5] As it turned out, both encouragement and criticism were wasted. Shortly before the proposed gathering, a Negro procession celebrating temperance and British West Indian emancipation was broken up by white boys in the streets of Philadelphia, and a protracted riot ensued. Some attempt was made to show that the proposal for the assembly was responsible for the riot,[6] but there were many other factors contributing to the outbreak. Due to the unsettled conditions following this unfortunate but not unusual affair, it was considered ill-advised to hold the convention, and the plans were dropped.[7]

One might speculate endlessly on what turn history would have taken if the convention had been held. Its agenda was broad enough that, if intelligently handled, it could have resulted in much good. And the men who called the convention were not of the same convictions as were those responsible for the revived national convention in 1843. The call for a national convention in 1843[8] was the signal for opposition from certain Boston Negroes, who distrusted the politics of the New Yorkers responsible for the invitation.[9] The Bostonians decided, however, to participate in the convention "as a medium through which we may deliberately devise means to operate and cooperate with

1 The Colored American, September 23, 1837; December 30, 1837; April 12, 1838; April 19, 1838; May 3, 1838.

2 The Liberator, November 5, 1841.

3 The Pennsylvania Freeman, December 8, 1841.

4 The Liberator, November 5, 1841.

5 National Anti-Slavery Standard, July 28, 1842. The Negro newspapers involved were The Northern Star and Freemen's Advocate and the Journal and Messenger, two of those short-lived publications so characteristic of the era.

6 Ibid., August 11, 1842.

7 The Liberator, August 19, 1842.

8 The Liberator, July 28, 1843; National Anti-Slavery Standard, July 27, 1843.

9 The Liberator, July 28, 1843.

our white friends, against TWO of the greatest evils ever inflicted upon an innocent and inoffensive people—slavery and prejudice." [10] Negroes of New Bedford, Massachusetts, were not so tractable; they branded the backers of the convention as deserters of the Garrisonian tradition [which they were] and held that a good dose of real anti-slavery teaching of the old tradition was the only cure for the world's evils.[11]

Despite opposition, the convention assembled on August 15, 1843, at Buffalo, New York. Thirty of the delegates were from the Mohawk River area, five from Michigan, three from the New York metropolitan section, two from Massachusetts, two from Connecticut, and eight from Ohio. In addition, several states were represented by one person each.[12] The tone of the convention was set by a speech from the president *pro tem*, Samuel H. Davis, of Buffalo. He hailed the Constitution of the United States as a document guaranteeing freedom and equality to all citizens.[13] But Davis was not fully supported on this issue,[14] perhaps because those dictating policy were willing to let the constitutional question lie quiescent in the interest of pushing the matter of alignment with the Liberty Party.[15] Nor was Davis himself interested in putting all his faith in the Constitution. Before he had finished, he had hinted at military action by an oppressed people. His speech was aggressive enough to pave the way for any radical action the delegates might choose to take.

Like most of the others of the period the convention was interested in encouragement of accepted patterns of self-improvement—temperance, moral reform, support of mechanical trades and of antislavery.[16] The members spent some time on plans for the establishment of a national Negro press [17] and stressed the development of a frontier agricultural community. But education was neglected "until it was too late for a committee to report upon it, and do the subject justice, as was intended." [18] All of these subjects could be handled with a reasonable degree of unanimity and equanimity, but the more controversial problems were hotly debated.

It was a foregone conclusion that some attempt would be made to pay homage to the new religion of political affiliation (chiefly the Liberty Party);

[10] *Ibid.*, August 4, 1843.

[11] *National Anti-Slavery Standard*, September 7, 1843.

[12] National Negro Convention, 1843, *Minutes of the National Convention of Colored Citizens: Held at Buffalo, on the 15th, 16th, 17th, 18th and 19th of August, 1843, For the Purpose of Considering Their Moral and Political Condition as American Citizens* (New York: Piercy and Reed, printers, 1843), p. 10.

[13] *Ibid.*, p. 4.

[14] *Ibid.*, pp. 16–17, 24.

[15] The Liberty Party was founded in 1840 by abolitionists who believed in political action. Its concentration on antislavery, however, was not conducive to attracting a large following. During the years that the party remained active (1840–1848) it usually played into the hands of its worst enemies, the slave-holders. Nevertheless, it attracted many idealists and was especially appealing to Negroes because of its antislavery ideals.

[16] *National Negro Convention*, 1843, pp. 15–16.

[17] *Ibid.*, pp. 27–30.

[18] *Ibid.*, p. 21, footnote.

but when such a resolution was proposed, Frederick Douglass and Charles L. Remond, both moral suasionists at the time, leaped to spearhead the opposition. Of the two men, Remond had already attained a certain degree of prominence as an antislavery speaker in the Garrisonian tradition, while Douglass, later to become the greatest Negro orator and leader of the antebellum era, was but a few years removed from slavery. Chief supporters of the resolution were listed as Henry H. Garnet, William C. Munro, J. N. Gloucester, Theodore S. Wright, David Lewis, and Charles B. Ray. These men, with the possible exception of Lewis, were ministers, and all lived in the area of the Hudson River or west as far as Ohio and Michigan. They were, therefore, more inclined to the beliefs of western abolitionists than to those of the Garrisonians. Party affiliation, to the Garrisonians, meant affiliation with corruption; they contended, moreover, that it was unwise to tie the abolitionists to any one party. But few at the convention were of like belief, and the Liberty Party received the sanction of the assembly with but seven dissenting votes.[19] Not content with this victory, Liberty Party adherents revived the subject later in the convention and pronounced a second blessing upon the political party which stood for allowing the vote to all free men, regardless of color.[20]

As is evident, a large majority of the delegates at the Buffalo National Convention stood for radical political action, if measured by the Garrisonian standard. The scales, however, were more evenly balanced when it came to the consideration of endorsement of physical violence in the overthrow of slavery. Resort to such means had been much in the minds of the more aggressive Negroes for several years. Samuel E. Cornish had felt called upon in 1838 to criticize an ardent young man who had considered the matter favorably in a public speech.[21] Somewhat later a convention of Maine and New Hampshire Negroes had refused to condemn those who resorted to bloodshed for the sake of freedom.[22] It is not surprising, then, that Samuel H. Davis, when opening the Buffalo National Convention in 1843, should have hinted at using other than peaceful means to obtain rights long overdue, or that Henry Highland Garnet—spectacular, persuasive, and appealing—should have prepared an address to the slaves which he sought to have the convention sanction.

The speech was so effectively presented that he had his audience laughing or crying, almost at will.[23] In fact, one enthusiastic reporter went so far as to contend that Garnet had so swayed the audience that "for one hour of his life his [the reporter's] mind had not been his own, but wholly at the control of the eloquent negro." [24] This address, suppressed by the narrow margin of one

[19] *Ibid.*, pp. 15–16.
[20] *Ibid.*, pp. 21–22.
[21] *The Colored American*, March 3, 1838.
[22] Negro State Convention, Maine and New Hampshire, 1841, *Minutes of the First Colored Convention, Held in the City of Portland, October 6–[9], 1841* (Portland, [Maine]: 1842), p. 7.
[23] *Buffalo Commercial Advertiser*, August 23, 1843. Title varies.
[24] *Emancipator*, October 12, 1843. Title varies, as do the organizations sponsoring the paper.

vote, was not printed until five years later, and then, admittedly, with some modifications, "retaining, however, all of its original doctrine." [25] Much of the address, as printed, is plain antislavery argument. But directed to the slaves as it was, it might have been expected to attract more attention than it otherwise would. Add to this the championship of physical violence in securing freedom,[26] and it is easy to understand why the address could set off such a furor as it did on the convention floor.

Having worked up slowly to the subject of violence, Garnet suggested that the slaves go to their masters and demand their freedom, then refuse to work if that freedom were denied.

> If they then commence the work of death, they and not you, will be responsible for the consequences. You had better all die, *die immediately*, than live slaves, and entail your wretchedness upon your posterity.... However much you and all of us may desire it there is not much hope of Redemption without the shedding of blood. If you must bleed, let it all come at once—rather *die freemen than live to be slaves.*[27]

Although the printed version has some moderating passages at the close, indicating that the speaker did not advocate an insurrection, the slaves were, even there, reminded that they were three million in number, and that resistance should be the motto.[28]

Despite the growing radicalism of the age, the preponderance of Liberty Party sympathizers in the assembly, and the eloquence of the speaker, the convention was not ready to assume the responsibility for such a message. It was turned over to a revision committee consisting of Garnet, Douglass, A. M. Sumner, S. N. [probably S. H.] Davis, and R. Banks.[29] With the exception of Douglass, these men were all from the area west of the Hudson River, and it is probable that not too much revision was made in the text. When the document was once more before the assembly, it was rejected but with the bare majority of one vote.[30] The episode was enlivened by the sardonic remark of Charles L. Remond to Charles B. Ray "not to try to sit on two stools," when Ray asked that his vote be added in support of the address after he had with-

[25] Henry Highland Garnet, *An Address to the Slaves of the United States of America (Rejected by the National Convention of 1843)*, as printed in David Walker's *Walker's Appeal, in Four Articles, Together with a Preamble, to the Colored Citizens of the World, but in Particular, and Very Expressly to Those of the United States of America. Written in Boston, in the State of Massachusetts, Sept[ember] 28, 1829* (2nd ed., with corrections, etc.; [n.p.], 1830), p. 89. In this case Garnet's *Address* was merely added to Walker's *Appeal*, using consecutive pagination, or both articles were printed together in 1848, using the 1830 edition of the *Appeal*.

[26] *Ibid.*, p. 93.

[27] *Ibid.*, p. 94.

[28] *Ibid.*, p. 96.

[29] *National Negro Convention, 1843*, pp. 12–14.

[30] *Ibid.*, pp. 17–19.

held his ballot on the first round.[31] It was not until public opinion had come around to a more aggressive attitude in 1848 that the address received the support of the free Negro community.

The Garrisonian press was bitterly opposed both to the Liberty Party tendencies of the convention and to Garnet's speech. Maria Weston Chapman, ardent Anti-Slavery Society worker, and sometimes relief editor for Garrison on *The Liberator*, was glad to see that the convention had had the good sense to reject the address. She felt that Garnet must have fallen under evil advisers, and she hoped the speech was for effect, rather than in demonstration of Garnet's real attitude. In commenting upon the current tendency to resort to ballots, she held that such action might easily lead to an exchange of bullets.[32] And at least one Negro newspaper was reported to be in accord with Mrs. Chapman's views concerning the Liberty Party.[33] But Garnet showed his readiness to defend himself against all comers when he wrote, "If it has come to this, that I must think and act as you do, because you are an abolitionist, or be exterminated by your thunder, then I do not hesitate to say that your abolitionism is abject slavery." [34] There was little in 1843 which would identify the national convention with those of the early 'thirties. Instead of serious consideration of emigration to Canada, this convention came within a trifle of advocating an insurrection of slaves. Instead of spending extensive time on a plan for a Negro college, it demanded emphatically that Negroes refrain from worshiping in churches where absolute equality was not allowed. Instead of timidly asserting that the Negro should have equality in the suffrage but admitting that there was not much to be done about it, the convention listened respectfully to a proposition for violence if equality were not forthcoming.

Here for the first time the moral suasionists, representing the old order, met in national convention with men who championed the newer confidence in political action as the means by which the salvation of all the people was to be accomplished. Though seriously outnumbered, the moral suasionists were not without modifying influence. The presence of Frederick Douglass and Charles L. Remond, along with a few others, was probably responsible for the rejection of Garnet's address to the slaves. Moreover, the two groups found that they had something in common in hatred of prejudice within the churches. And if Douglass and Remond in 1843 could not stem the tide of the Liberty Party in the West, they could at least hold up the avalanche long enough to make their opponents argue their cause and thus work for the enlightenment of the public.

As the delegates parted to go to their homes, some of them carried with them plans for state conventions which, it was expected, would advance the cause of the Negro. In other cases state conventions had been proposed before

[31] *The Liberator*, September 8, 1843.
[32] *Ibid.*, September 22, 1843.
[33] *Ibid.*, September 29, 1843.
[34] *Ibid.*, December 8, 1843.

the national assembly had gathered. Indiana Negroes issued a call for a state assembly to convene at Indianapolis on September 4, 1843,[35] while to the east in Ohio plans had been set on foot as early as March for such a convention at Columbus.[36] Michigan [37] and New York [38] both held state gatherings shortly after the Buffalo National Convention, and it seems more than probable that Connecticut, and the coalition of Maine and New Hampshire were doing the same.

In 1847 upstate New York leaders once more urged the necessity of a national convention. Scheduled at first for mid-August,[39] the time of meeting was later extended to October. An examination of the list of delegates who gathered at Troy, New York, on October 6, 1847, reveals a surprising number from the state of New York (forty-six of a total of sixty-six). Of the rest, Massachusetts sent fourteen and Connecticut two, while single delegates were present from scattered states.[40] Connecticut was represented by two able ministers, Amos G. Beman, who had encouraged Negro state convention activities in his state for a decade, and J. W. C. Pennington, who had helped in getting the national convention organized in the early 'thirties. Massachusetts sent Frederick Douglass, Leonard Grimes, Boston minister, and William Wells Brown who was soon to attain some prominence as the first Negro novelist and historian. New York City commanded the services of James McCune Smith; Thomas Van Rensselaer, editor of The Ram's Horn, a new Negro newspaper; and Alexander Crummell, known chiefly for his interest in, and affiliation with, Liberia.[41] The brilliant and showy but somewhat erratic Henry Highland Garnet was, as usual, the chief spokesman for the upstate third party men.

The idea of a national press which had been considered favorably in 1843 was revived and debated at length [42] and eventually decided in the affirmative. A separate manual labor college for the Negro was also considered favorably by the majority of those present.[43] But the subject of temperance, assigned to two ministers and an editor for recommendations, was side-stepped by the suggestion from these gentlemen that the matter be turned over to the tem-

[35] The Philanthropist, August 16, 1843. No record of this convention found.
[36] Ibid., March 29, 1843. No record of this convention found.
[37] Negro State Convention, Michigan, 1843, Minutes of the State Convention of the Colored Citizens of the State of Michigan, Held in the City of Detroit, on the 26th & 27th of October, 1843, for the Purpose of Considering Their Moral & Political Condition as Citizens of the State (Detroit: Printed by William Harsha, 1843), p. 4.
[38] National Anti-Slavery Standard, October 17, 1844.
[39] The Liberator, July 23, 1847.
[40] National Negro Convention, 1847, Proceedings of the National Convention of Colored People, and Their Friends, held in Troy, N[ew] Y[ork] on 6th, 7th, 8th, and 9th October, 1847 (Troy, N[ew] Y[ork]: J. C. Kneeland & C[ompany], 1847), p. 3.
[41] Ibid., pp. 8–9.
[42] Ibid., pp. 6–9; The North Star, January 14, 1848. (This paper was founded and edited by Frederick Douglass; the name was later changed to Frederick Douglass' Paper); The Liberator, November 19, 1847.
[43] The North Star, December 3, 1847; National Negro Convention, 1847, pp. 9–11; The Liberator, November 19, 1847.

perance convention to meet at Great Barrington, Massachusetts, almost a year hence.[44]

The committee appointed to express the sentiments of the convention on matters of freedom and slavery was headed by Frederick Douglass. Other members included Thomas Van Rensselaer, John Lyle, R. D. Kenny, and Alexander Crummell. Their report was moral suasionist in tone and incurred the criticism of Garnet who took exception to such terms as "sanctity of religion," when used in the sense of protecting slavery. As a minister, he felt that religion was being blamed too much when it was represented as supporting slavery. It was for this reason that he urged the qualifying phrase, "falsely so called," to identify the brand of religion meant. He also took exception to sole reliance on moral suasion as a means of securing freedom for the slave. He contended that political action should be added as a legitimate means of securing the end in view.

It seems that the attack by Garnet and others was successful, and the report was canceled. Later it was reconsidered and placed in the hands of a new committee, of which Douglass and Garnet were both members.[45] When the report once more appeared, there was no reference to the term "moral suasion"; it was, nevertheless, a decidedly moral suasionist document. It abounded with such declarations as "the best means of abolishing slavery is the proclamation of the truth, and the best means of destroying caste is the mental, moral and industrial improvement of our people." And again,

> Liberty is always sufficient to grapple with tyranny. Free speech— free discussion—peaceful agitation—the foolishness of preaching— these, under God, will subvert this giant crime, and send it reeling to its grave, as if smitten by a voice from the throne of God.[46]

This victory for moral suasionist doctrines at the Troy National Convention—a convention with a strong bent toward radical action—showed Frederick Douglass at his best as a champion of Garrisonian doctrines before he had come under the influence of the western abolitionists of the Gerrit Smith school of thought. Douglass was only then preparing to leave the East and to establish himself at some point in the area of the Great Lakes. It was Douglass who headed the first committee which brought in a report highly moral suasionist in tone. It was Douglass who defended it and when the report had been rejected, Douglass was appointed as one of the members of the new committee. Garnet, as chief spokesman for the opposition group, and thereby a representative of the majority of the delegates attending the convention, was unable to command more than the hollow appearance of victory in the elimination of such specific terms as "moral suasion," and in the softening of the attack on the church—an attack which had become a favorite sport of the Garrisonians.

[44] *National Negro Convention*, 1847, p. 11.
[45] *Ibid.*, pp. 13–15.
[46] *Ibid.*, pp. 31–32.

There remains Garnet's triumph—the renewed address to the slaves, first delivered in 1843 at the Buffalo National Convention, and suppressed by that body. In describing Garnet's speech, William C. Nell, strong and loyal Garrisonian and opponent of physical force, incorporated much into the statement: "To those acquainted with his talent and eloquence, it will be unnecessary to mention that the address produced much sensation." [47] Reaction was not so intense as it had been four years earlier, partly because public opinion had moved rapidly toward accepting a more aggressive attitude in the intervening years. Moreover, Douglass's encouragement of the use of education and propaganda had its influence in softening the effect of Garnet's militancy.[48]

In the field of agriculture, various communal experiments on the American frontier were common, and some were to be found in the older settled communities. Emphasis was placed upon going to the farm as a kind of panacea for the ills of society. It was to be expected, then, that this attitude would be reflected in the Negro conventions of the period. In 1843 an able committee headed by Charles B. Ray presented a convincing address on the merits of an agricultural life. Possession of the soil was represented as giving an independence not easily attainable elsewhere. This committee was well informed. They had a report from a group in Mercer County, Ohio, who had refused to come to the convention but who were happy and reasonably prosperous on the farms which they had taken up only six years earlier.

In keeping with the communal experimentation of the times, it was recommended that agricultural communities be built up by banding together in units of about twenty family groups. These families were to settle on adjacent land, cooperate on matters of common interest such as schools, churches, roads, flour and saw mills, and share in any profits from such ventures —according to the amount of individual investment. A gesture toward erasure of the color line, or at least toward avoiding the accusation of planning a segregated community, was made by the provision that a few carefully selected white families might be accepted in the organization.[49]

When the convention met at Troy four years later the subject of agriculture was handled in much the same manner, except that Gerrit Smith, philanthropist, humanitarian, and dabbler in practically every phase of the reform movement, had meantime made land in New York available for the asking. His generosity had placed 140,000 acres of land at the disposal of some 3,000 Negroes, and in so doing had made many of them eligible for the suffrage for the first time.[50] This was enough to divert the interest of the New Yorkers from such a communal frontier settlement as had been proposed in 1843. The new landholders were anxious to do something to show their appreciation to their benefactor, but Douglass and Garnet agreed that they could best accomplish that end by moving onto the land and improving it.[51]

[47] The North Star, December 3, 1847.
[48] The Liberator, November 19, 1847.
[49] National Negro Convention, 1843, pp. 30–36.
[50] National Negro Convention, 1847, pp. 25–30.
[51] Ibid., p. 13.

The matter of a national press received favorable attention in the middle 'forties. Negroes had long been aware of the urgency for an organ which would be devoted entirely to the uplift of the race. *Freedom's Journal* and *The Rights of All* had attempted in the late 'twenties to fulfill such a need. *The Liberator* had served in that capacity in the early 'thirties. But as Garrison began to embrace other reforms or fads, the Negro once more sought an organ which he could call his own. To this end Philip A. Bell of New York started an ephemeral newspaper called *The Struggler*, to be followed in January, 1837, by *The Weekly Advocate*. This paper, after some reorganization, became *The Colored American*, and for several years was the chief organ of the colored people. With the opening of the decade of the 'forties, however, there were several struggling papers, and not one was receiving adequate support. It needed no prophet to foretell that all were likely to fail and that the cause of the Negro would suffer accordingly. This was one of the problems which faced the Buffalo National Convention in 1843.[52]

A committee appointed to deal with the subject held that a press could be used to build up or to tear down; that it could, if properly used, act as an agency for enlightenment and for getting acquainted; and that it could be utilized as an aid in the building of character. They recommended that a national press be established, either by the creation of a new weekly newspaper or by the support of one already set up.[53] This recommendation was followed by official action in the appointment of able men—Philip A. Bell, Samuel E. Cornish, Charles B. Ray, Amos G. Beman, Theodore S. Wright, and others—to look into the possibilities for establishing such an organ.[54] Most, if not all, of this group were experienced in the editorial field, but if they were successful in organizing a national publication it has not come to light.

Four years later at Troy the subject was again up for discussion. Again there were several Negro publications, and more in the planning stage.[55] Again a committee reported in favor of a national press. This time it was James McCune Smith, once associated with Samuel E. Cornish in editing *The Colored American*, who led the drive for such a publication.[56] Thomas Van Rensselaer had recently set up *The Ram's Horn*, and Frederick Douglass was soon to establish *The North Star*; both men were opposed to the national press. It was Douglass's opinion that such an arrangement would soon result in its being the press of a clique, rather than that of the Negro public.[57]

Opponents of the scheme, including Douglass and Van Rensselaer, came in for some of Garnet's witty sarcasm when that gentleman pointed out that those indisposed were chiefly in the newspaper business, or about to go into it. "Of course," he opined, "there was nothing of selfishness in all this." [58]

[52] *The Liberator*, July 28, 1843; *National Anti-Slavery Standard*, July 27, 1843.
[53] *National Negro Convention*, 1843, pp. 27–30.
[54] *Ibid.*, p. 25.
[55] *National Negro Convention*, 1847, pp. 6–7.
[56] *The North Star*, January 14, 1848.
[57] *National Negro Convention*, 1847, pp. 6–8.
[58] *Ibid.*, p. 6.

But self-interest, it seems, may have colored Garnet's own reaction in favor of the press. Douglass, writing three months later, implied that there had been some thought of appointing a foreign agent to go to England to raise funds for the project.[59] But Garnet, if he was angling for such an appointment from the convention, was unsuccessful. He was awarded the place of home agent.[60]

When the vote was finally taken, less than one-fourth of those casting their ballots were opposed to the press.[61] Of the twenty from New York who voted, sixteen were in favor; of the four opposed, at least one, if not two, was involved in a current newspaper project. The total New York vote, however, was less than half of those recorded as delegates, and among those not voting were such men as William H. Topp, Albany businessman, Charles B. Ray, and Stephen Myers, Albany editor. Nine of the fourteen delegates from Massachusetts voted for the national press. Of the three who refrained from voting, Douglass was about ready to establish his own publication; Nathan Johnson was in the chair; and William Wells Brown was a loyal Garrisonian and therefore opposed to "complexional projects" of any kind. Only two from Massachusetts, William C. Nell and Charles Weeden, voted against the proposition.[62] With the vote of Massachusetts running so favorably for a Negro press, it might appear that the Garrisonian hold was not so strong as it might have been, even in the home state.

When the Cleveland National Convention met in the following year (September 6, 1848) there seem to have been but few present who had been at Troy. In the meantime, Frederick Douglass had established his *The North Star* at Rochester, New York, and it had surged rapidly to front rank among Negro publications. Furthermore, Douglass was present at the convention. And finally, the interest of the assembly was geared to the coming elections. Under these circumstances the press was dealt with effectively but perfunctorily by declaring that Douglass's publication was serving the need of a national press.[63] Thus at last, by official action but without assuming control, the Negro in convention had an official national press.

The conventions of the middle 'forties represent a definite gain for independent Negro leadership. By 1847 the break in the ranks of Negro abolitionists had been partially healed. By that time two national conventions had been held in which Garrisonian moral suasionists and ballot-minded Liberty Party adherents had worked on the problems facing the Negro and had found that they had much in common. Powerful moral suasionists of the Douglass-Nell variety had done business with the strident Garnet and the impatient Charles B. Ray of Liberty Party sympathies. This encounter demonstrated beyond a reasonable doubt that although the greatest of the giants still lived in the house of Garrison, the sheer force of numbers was slowly winning the argument for greater militancy and more dependence upon the ballot. By 1847

[59] *The North Star*, January 14, 1848.
[60] *National Negro Convention*, 1847, p. 9.
[61] *The Liberator*, November 19, 1847.
[62] *National Negro Convention*, 1847, pp. 8–9.
[63] *The North Star*, September 29, 1848.

even the scoffers were forced to admit that the National Negro Convention was once more the most powerful voice in Negro affairs—a voice that had a militant ring which was absent from the deliberations of the 'thirties, a voice commanding the confidence of the Negro masses and the respect of all men of good will.

Larry Gara

WILLIAM STILL AND THE

UNDERGROUND RAILROAD *

One area of antislavery activity in which Negroes took the lead was Underground Railroad work. In a recent revisionist study entitled The Liberty Line (1961), Larry Gara has discounted the traditional emphasis upon the role of white abolitionists. Most of the fugitive slaves, he points out, escaped from the South on their own, without assistance; and once they arrived in the North they were helped chiefly by free Negroes, who in many cities organized vigilance committees to assist the fugitives. One of the most noted of the northern Negro Underground Railroad agents was William Still, secretary of the Philadelphia Vigilance Committee. Gara's account of Still is illustrative of the activities of the northern vigilance committees.

T HE writer of a popular account of the underground railroad in Pennsylvania stated in his preface that "it required the manhood of a man and the unflinching fortitude of a woman, ... to be an abolitionist in those days, and especially an Underground Railroad agent." [1] He was referring to the noble minority who stood firm when the abolitionists were being "reviled and persecuted" in both the North and the South. Other underground railroad books—some of them written by elderly abolitionists—put similar emphasis on the heroic conductors of the mysterious organization. They reflected the history of the underground railroad from the vantage point of the abolitionist con-

Larry Gara, "William Still and the Underground Railroad," *Pennsylvania History,* XXVIII (January, 1961), pp. 33–44. Reprinted with permission of *Pennsylvania History* and Larry Gara.

* A grant from the Penrose Fund of the American Philosophical Society made it possible to complete the research upon which this article is based. A shorter version was read at the annual meeting of the Pennsylvania Historical Association on October 14, 1960.

[1] Robert C. Smedley, *History of the Underground Railroad in Chester and the Neighboring Counties of Pennsylvania* (Lancaster, Pa., 1883), preface, xv.

ductor. They also contributed to the growth of a favorite American legend, which is as much a part of folklore as of history. Two of the forgotten characters in the popular legend are the Negro members of various vigilance committees and the fugitives themselves. If it required strong character to be an abolitionist, it took even more courage to become a hunted fugitive or one of his colored abettors. William Still's work with the Philadelphia vigilance committee called attention to both of these neglected groups.

William Still's parents were both born slaves, and they left slavery at considerable personal sacrifice: his father purchased his freedom, and his mother, after one unsuccessful attempt to escape, finally ran away with two of her four children. They later farmed a forty-acre plot in the New Jersey pines near Medford. William was born there on October 7, 1821, the youngest of eighteen children. With a bare minimum of formal schooling he continued his own education by extensive reading. When he was twenty he left home, and three years later he moved to Philadelphia. He held a number of jobs before joining the staff of the Pennsylvania Society for Promoting the Abolition of Slavery in the fall of 1847.[2]

Still began working with the abolition society as a combination janitor and mail clerk. After several years, both his duties and his salary were increased. He took a special interest in the society's efforts to assist slaves who had run away from the South. They were often boarded at his home before resuming their journey towards Canada. For fourteen years Still served the society. During that time he worked with such well known anti-slavery advocates as Robert Purvis, who was also colored, Lucretia and James Mott, Sarah Pugh, Thomas Garrett, and J. Miller McKim, who was the agent in charge of the Philadelphia office.[3]

In 1838 Philadelphia abolitionists had organized a vigilance committee to assist fugitives coming into the city. There was some underground railroad activity in the area. Thomas Garrett of Wilmington, the more militant anti-slavery Quakers of Philadelphia and the neighboring counties, and the vigilance committee were primarily responsible for the work. Although there was a semblance of organization to these efforts, much of the aid given the fugitive slaves was on a haphazard basis. By 1852 even the vigilance committee had disintegrated. In December of that year a group of abolitionists reported that the old committee "had become disorganized and scattered" and that for several years its duties "had been performed by individuals on their own responsibility, and sometimes in a very irregular manner," causing "much dissatisfaction and complaint." The group decided to organize a new vigilance committee, with an acting committee of four members, which should have the authority to attend "to every case that might require aid," to raise necessary funds, and "to keep a record of all their doings," and especially of their receipts and ex-

---

[2] James P. Boyd, "William Still: His Life and Work to This Time," in William Still, *Still's Underground Rail Road Records* (3rd ed., Phila., 1883), iii–xvii. The title page varied somewhat in each edition of Still's book, but the pagination of the text remained the same.

[3] Boyd, "Still," in Still, *Underground Rail Road*, xviii.

penditures. They appointed William Still chairman of the acting committee.[4]

One of the principal activities of the new Philadelphia vigilance committee was to extend financial aid to fugitives. The committee provided money to board fugitives with families of free Negroes, sometimes for as long as thirteen days but usually for only a few days. As a Negro, William Still easily gained the confidence of the new arrivals and knew where to find them board and lodging among the colored population of Philadelphia. The committee also purchased clothing, medicine, and the fugitives' railroad fares to Canada. It advertised anti-slavery meetings in the newspapers and on one occasion spent twenty dollars for handbills and other expenses of a meeting. Mostly, the committee spent money in small amounts; very few items in its financial reports involved more than five dollars.[5]

At times William Still and other members of the acting vigilance committee were very busy with their labor on behalf of the fugitives. Late in 1857 J. Miller McKim wrote another abolitionist, "Other rail-roads are in a declining condition and have stopped their semi annual dividends, but the Underground has never before done so flourishing a business." He further reported, "Exactly fifty—men, women and children—have passed through the hands of our Vigilance Committee in the last fortnight." [6] It was a dramatic time and a most unusual amount of work for the vigilance committee. According to the committee's journal it assisted approximately 495 fugitives between December, 1852, and February, 1857. In his later published account, covering eight years of vigilance committee activity, Still listed approximately eight hundred fugitives, including sixty children, who had received aid from the committee.[7]

Although a great deal of William Still's work was of such a routine nature as answering correspondence or meeting new arrivals at the railroad station, he had some moments of high adventure too. One arrival from the South, who had purchased his freedom, contacted Still for information about his family. Upon investigation he proved to be Still's own brother, left in slavery forty years earlier when his mother fled to the North. Still also witnessed the arrival of the famous Henry "Box" Brown, who had literally had himself crated and sent north via the Adams' Express Company, and of the clever William and Ellen Craft. The Crafts had traveled all the way from Georgia with the nearly-white Ellen disguised as an ailing planter and William playing the part of the faithful servant. Still observed a number of other unusual and interesting cases, though none got the public attention given to Henry "Box" Brown and the Crafts.[8]

[4] Still, *Underground Rail Road*, 611–12.

[5] Journal of the Philadelphia Vigilance Committee, 1852–1857, in the Historical Society of Pennsylvania.

[6] J. Miller McKim to Mrs. M. W. Chapman, November 19, 1857, in the Weston Papers in the Boston Public Library. McKim's letter was published in the 1858 edition of the *Liberty Bell*.

[7] Journal of the Philadelphia Vigilance Committee; Still, *Underground Rail Road*, passim.

[8] Lucretia Mott to Joseph and Ruth Dugdale, March 28, 1849, in the Lucretia Mott MSS in the Friends Historical Library of Swarthmore College; Still, *Underground Rail Road*, 81–86, 368–377.

One of William Still's duties was to ask the newly arrived slaves their names, the names of their masters and where they had come from, and to question them about their escape experiences and the severity of their servitude. In part the interrogation was meant to protect the vigilance committee from the imposters who not infrequently found the abolitionists easy prey for a handout. Still not only recorded the data but carefully preserved the records. In his book he wrote that he had kept the documents for possible use in helping to reunite relatives and friends.[9] In 1884 he told a meeting of aged abolitionists that he had kept them because they were interesting, and because his family had been connected with the underground railroad.[10] Possibly, too, the records were a protection for him in case any of the Philadelphia abolitionists had requested a detailed accounting of Still's work for the anti-slavery society. To Still the vigilance committee was synonymous with the underground railroad. In 1893 he informed historian Wilbur H. Siebert that his "were the only records that were kept of the U.G.R.R.," and that when he collected them he had never dreamed that they could be published in his lifetime.[11]

Still's voluminous record books were a rich source of indisputable evidence had the government been inclined to invoke the Fugitive Slave Law against him or the vigilance committee. He hid the records after the Harpers Ferry fiasco and for a while they were stored in the loft of the Lebanon Cemetery building.[12] In a number of instances he faced possible prosecution. It was Still and others at the anti-slavery office who had warned the Negroes of Christiana that warrants were out for two slaves hiding there. The slave hunt resulted in a mob scene in which the slaves' master was murdered and his nephew seriously wounded. Several abolitionists and thirty-four Negroes were indicted for treason but none were convicted.[13] Still was not indicted with the Christiana rioters but the government brought charges against him for helping to entice Jane Johnson away from her master, Colonel John H. Wheeler, the American minister to Nicaragua. Still was acquitted, but two of five other Negroes indicted were sentenced to a week in jail on a charge of assault and battery, and Passmore Williamson, a Philadelphia Quaker, spent three months in jail for contempt of court.[14] John Brown had confided his plans to William Still six months before his raid on Harpers Ferry and a memorandum found among the papers of Brown's lieutenant, John Henry Kagi, seemed to implicate Still in the scheme.[15] In all these cases Still avoided punishment, but

[9] Still, *Underground Rail Road*, preface; Boyd, "Still," in Still, *Underground Rail Road*, xxxiv.

[10] *Commemoration of the Fiftieth Anniversary of the Organization of the American Anti-Slavery Society, in Philadelphia* (Philadelphia, 1884), 39–40.

[11] William Still to Wilbur H. Siebert, November 18, 1893, in scrapbook "The Underground Railroad in Pennsylvania, vol. 3," in the Wilbur H. Siebert Papers in the Ohio Historical Society.

[12] Boyd, "Still," in Still, *Underground Rail Road*, xxiii, xxxiv.

[13] Still, *Underground Rail Road*, 348–368.

[14] Still, *Underground Rail Road*, 86–95.

[15] Boyd, "Still," in Still, *Underground Rail Road*, xxii–xxiv.

when a woman sued him for libel in 1860 he was not so fortunate.

The woman, a Mrs. Ellen Wells, who was a former slave from St. Louis, was traveling throughout the country raising money to purchase her mother, her children, and several other relatives from slavery. She stayed at William Still's rooming house in Philadelphia, but he did not encourage her project. When a Boston abolitionist wrote for information about Ellen Wells, Still answered that she was an imposter and a prostitute. The letter fell into Mrs. Wells' hands and she sued Still for scandalous and malicious libel. He pleaded guilty to having written the letter and the court sentenced him to ten days in jail and fined him a hundred dollars. Boston abolitionists supported Still and paid the fine from the treasury of the Massachusetts Anti-Slavery Society.[16]

A year later, with the Civil War in progress, Still resigned his position with the Pennsylvania Anti-Slavery Society.[17] He had already ventured into some real estate transactions, and he then bought and managed first a store and later a very successful retail coal business. In 1872 he published *The Underground Rail Road.* The book was another of William Still's contributions to the progress of his race. His work with the fugitive slaves had impressed upon him the need for Negroes to take the initiative to improve their condition. In August of 1860 he told a Negro audience at Kennett Square celebrating the anniversary of West Indian emancipation, "The hundreds of heroic fugitives who yearly throw off their yokes, ... seem to cry aloud in our ears—'Hereditary bondmen! know ye not who would be free themselves must strike the blow?' " [18]

In 1855 William Still had visited the former slaves who had settled in Canada, and he later wrote a strong defense of their conduct and achievements, answering those who maintained that slaves could not meet the responsibilities of free citizens. In 1859 he initiated a successful eight-year campaign to secure equal service for Negroes in the Philadelphia streetcars. In 1861 he helped organize an association for the purpose of collecting and disseminating accurate information about the American Negro population in order to improve its position.[19] These and many other activities stemmed from Still's determination to help improve the status of the colored people.[20] So did his book. He wanted to make the underground railroad "a monument to the heroism of the bondmen under the yoke." Their "heroism and desperate struggles," said Still, as well as "the terrible oppression that they were under, should be kept green in the memory of this and coming generations." He also believed that books written

[16] J. Miller McKim to R. S. Webb, June 23, 1860, and Samuel May, Jr., to McKim, May 23, 1860, in the Garrison Papers in the Boston Public Library; New York *National Anti-Slavery Standard,* April 28, May 5, 1860.

[17] Boyd, "Still," in Still, *Underground Rail Road,* xxx.

[18] New York *National Anti-Slavery Standard,* August 18, 1860.

[19] Boyd, "Still," in Still, *Underground Rail Road,* xxv–xxviii, li–lvii; Harrod G. Villard, "Wiliam Still," in the *Dictionary of American Biography,* 18:23.

[20] For Still's other activities see Alberta S. Norwood, "Negro Welfare Work in Philadelphia, Especially as Illustrated by the Career of William Still, 1775–1930," unpublished thesis in the Library of the University of Pennsylvania (1931).

by Negroes would prove their mental ability and provide an effective answer
to those who argued that the colored people were inferior. "We very much
need works on various topics from the pens of colored men to represent the
race intellectually," he wrote.[21]

He received added encouragement from the Philadelphia abolitionists. At
a meeting in May, 1871, the Pennsylvania Anti-Slavery Society passed a resolution requesting Still to publish his reminiscences relating to the underground
railroad. That same year there was a seven-months coal strike in Pennsylvania
which made his business very dull but gave him the leisure he needed to prepare his material for publication. Still worked diligently in the preparation of
his book, a task which was made more difficult by the bitter division in the
anti-slavery movement. He corresponded with old acquaintances, put his own
records in order and collected material from others. The Philadelphia abolitionists with whom he had worked were all Garrisonians, but he included the
political abolitionist Lewis Tappan among those whom he asked for information. One of the difficult tasks was to write a sketch of J. Miller McKim, his
superior in the anti-slavery office. When McKim asked Still to outline the
material concerning him, Still tactfully replied that "it would not be just to
confine [McKim] to any special department of the work but to represent [him]
as a general laborer," with many services in the anti-slavery cause.[22] Frederick
Douglass, however, got no mention in Still's book, except in material reprinted
from a British pamphlet. In 1893 Douglass boasted of his long service in the
underground railroad and claimed that Still had omitted him because he had
criticized Still's conduct toward the fugitives.[23]

William Still's book on the underground railroad is unique in that it
emphasized the courage and ingenuity of the fugitives. White conductors are
the heroes in the accounts which the abolitionists recorded for posterity; in
Still's account, the daring fugitives are the heroes. Scattered throughout the
volume are legal documents, letters, and newspaper items, but the focus of the
narrative is always on the slaves themselves. Still placed his sketches of the
abolitionist conductors at the end of the book, after the great bulk of material
on the passengers. The book's numerous illustrations also focus the spotlight
on the absconding slaves and on their heroic struggle for freedom.

In Still's book the vast majority of the fugitive slaves came from the
neighboring border states. Most of them were young men, of more than average intelligence, though there were some women and children too. Although
they were all considered underground railroad passengers, many of them had

---

[21] William Still to Dr. Henry Charles, June 6, 1873, to J. W. Jones, November 4,
1873, and to J. C. Price, June 3, 1873, in the William Still Papers in the Historical
Society of Pennsylvania.

[22] Boyd, "Still," in Still, *Underground Rail Road*, xxxv; William Still to J. Miller
McKim, November 10, 1871, in the J. Miller McKim Papers in the New York Public
Library.

[23] Frederick Douglass to Wilbur H. Siebert, March 27, 1893, in scrapbook, "The
Underground Railroad in New York, vol. 2," in the Siebert Papers in the Ohio Historical
Society.

received little or no assistance before they contacted the vigilance committee. Some passed as white or as free Negroes, some traveled on foot at night, some adopted clever disguises, and more than a few hid or were hidden on steamers running from southern ports. Much of the escape drama was a self-help affair.

Although never a slave himself, William Still hated the South's peculiar institution. Not only did he have the zeal of the abolitionists, but as a Negro he was able to identify himself emotionally with the bondsmen. "The half will never be told of the barbarism of Slavery," he wrote. He described one fugitive as a "decided opponent to the no-pay system, to flogging, and selling likewise." Still said he had taken care "to furnish artless stories, [and] simple facts," and had resorted "to no coloring to make the book seem romantic." He took great care to be factual but his bias was apparent throughout the book. In his preface Still commented that those who sought information regarding "the existence, atrocity, struggles and destruction of Slavery" would have no trouble finding the "hydra-headed monster ruling and tyrannizing over Church and State, North and South, white and black, without let or hindrance for at least several generations." [24]

The fugitives whom Still and the vigilance committee interviewed had confirmed his prejudice against the slave system. Although a few maintained that they had been treated well, the great majority testified to many hardships. Some were probably aware of the committee's preference for cruel and libertine masters. One slave from Maryland said that he had been "treated as bad as a man could be," another had been "allowed no privileges of any kind, Sunday or Monday," and a woman had "endured all outraged nature could endure and survive." The fugitives described their former owners with an abundance of such terms as "always a big devil—ill-grained," an "ill-natured man," and "a notorious frolicker." One described a cruel master who "made a common practice of flogging females when stripped naked." Still and the other committee members were also temperance advocates and duly noted in their records when a master was described as "given to 'intemperance' " and to "gross 'profanity,' " "a gambler and spree'r," and a man "devoted to card playing, rum-drinking and fox-hunting." [25]

Occasionally the committee sharply questioned fugitives whose stories did not seem plausible, but they sometimes took obviously exaggerated statements at face value. After trying to dispute her testimony, the committee gave "the benefit of the doubt" to Amarian, a good-looking girl of twenty-one who said she had always been treated very well. Similarly, they doubted Washington Somlor's description of inhuman treatment at the hands of a master who "believed in selling, flogging, cobbing, paddling, and all other kinds of torture...." Yet they accepted the statements of William Jordon who said that he had lived three months in a cave "surrounded with bears, wild cats, rattle-snakes and the like." Theophilus Collins testified that he was brutally punished for

[24] William Still, *The Underground Rail Road* (Philadelphia, 1872), 144, 290, preface, 3, 5. This preface appears only in the first edition.

[25] Still, *Underground Rail Road*, 185, 260, 307, 383, 388, 416, 480, 519, 533, 754.

attending a Sunday night religious meeting. His master called him in for a whipping and when he refused to remove his shirt, gave him twenty blows on the head with the butt of a cowhide, struck him on the head with fire-tongs, beat him with a parlor shovel until the handle broke, jabbed the shovel blade at his head with all his might, and, when the slave tried to make for the door, stabbed him in the head and stomach with a pocket knife. Nevertheless, Theophilus escaped and ran sixteen miles carrying a part of his entrails in his hands for the whole journey.[26]

William Still believed that a book containing such thrilling tales as the one Theophilus told to the vigilance committee should certainly sell many copies. His previous business experience enabled him to plan and promote the sale of his book to good advantage. He decided to sell it only by subscription and carefully supervised his sales campaign.[27]

Prospective agents for a particular territory had to apply personally to Still. If no suitable person applied, Still preferred to leave the area temporarily unsolicited. He had two editions, one in plain English cloth which sold for five dollars, and a sheepskin edition priced at five-fifty. Still prepared a full set of instructions for his agents and sold each of them a kit with sample copies. He gave them forty or fifty per cent of the purchase price as commission, but they had to adhere strictly to his terms. During the financial panic of 1873 he permitted them to sell on the installment plan, but they were not to deliver the book until the last payment had been made. All of his agents had to submit weekly reports.[28]

Still preferred to hire colored men to sell his book, but he realized that few of his race had the necessary experience. He was confident it would be well received among the Negroes and among the Republicans, if the agents did their part well. "The book only needs to be presented by a man who appreciates and comprehends the value and importance of having our heroes and Martyrs under Slavery well represented in the history of our times—to make the work take exceedingly well," he wrote a representative in Kansas in 1873.[29] And the work took well indeed. A salesman in Pittsburgh cleared about a hundred dollars a week for six weeks. His best agent followed five others who had sold only a few copies in Baltimore, and at the end of six weeks he had more than three hundred subscriptions. In 1873 Still reported, "Agents are doing well with the U.G.R.R. this summer. East, West, North and South, wherever competent persons are presenting it." He first printed ten thousand copies but hoped to sell a hundred thousand before the demand ceased.[30] The

[26] *Ibid.*, 130, 304, 435, 495–496.

[27] Boyd, "Still," in Still, *Underground Rail Road*, xlvi–xlix, lxi–lxii.

[28] Still to T. L. W. Titus, January 7, 1874, to W. D. Teister, June 10, 1873, to Robert Furnas, June 18, 1873, to James E. Thompson, July 9, 1873, and to J. C. Price, June 23, 1873, all in the Still Papers.

[29] Still to Thomas E. Franklin, April 9, 1874, and the Rev. J. C. Embry, October 14, 1873, in the Still Papers.

[30] Still to W. H. Jones, June 3, 1873, the Rev. Jones, November 12, 1873, and to E. Sanborn, June 11, 1873, in the Still Papers.

first edition sold out completely, as did a second edition in 1879. In 1883 Still published a third edition with a new title, *Still's Underground Rail Road Records,* and with a sketch of the author written by James P. Boyd.

William Still's book undoubtedly circulated more widely than any other firsthand account of the underground railroad. In writing and distributing it Still proved that a Negro author could produce a creditable book and sell it on a large scale. He proudly exhibited it at the Philadelphia Centennial Exposition in 1876. It was a fitting tribute to his race. He hoped it would inspire other Negroes to greater efforts until they could exhibit such fruits "of their newly gained privileges" as "well-conducted shops and stores; lands acquired and good farms" well-managed, and "valuable books produced and published on interesting and important subjects." [31] It is not possible to evaluate the book's effect on American Negroes, but in one respect it failed to make its mark. William Still put the courageous fugitive slaves at the center of his stage. His book provided an excellent corrective for the many abolitionist-centered accounts. Yet in the popular mind, the white conductor of the underground railroad remains the leading figure in the drama. Despite Still's financial success, his message has been hidden under a mass of literature written by the abolitionists, their descendants, and admirers.

[31] William Still, *The Underground Rail Road* (Philadelphia and Cincinnati, 1879), preface. This preface appears in the second and third editions.

PART FOUR

CIVIL WAR
AND
RECONSTRUCTION

Benjamin Quarles

THE ABDUCTION OF THE "PLANTER"

The participation of black men in the Civil War, though mostly ignored by the standard histories, has received considerable attention from those scholars who have been interested in the study of the Negroes' past in the United States. In the following selection Benjamin Quarles gives a detailed account of a famous incident in the struggle that resulted in the emancipation of the slaves.

To the confederate capital on a spring afternoon in the second year of the war came a one-sentence dispatch addressed to General R. E. Lee: "I have just learned by telegraph that [the] steamer 'Planter,' with five guns aboard, intended for the harbor, was stolen in Charleston this morning." Dated May 13, 1862, from the Savannah headquarters of the Department of South Carolina and Georgia, the terse report concluded with a "Very respectfully," and bore the name of the commanding officer, J. C. Pemberton.

Pemberton's dispatch referred to the "abduction" by a group of slaves of a Confederate vessel, a dramatic deed which made its instigator, Robert Smalls, "an object of interest in Dupont's fleet," as Admiral David D. Porter phrased it. The spectacular escape of Smalls and his party became one of the war's oft-told stories. Requiring careful planning and brilliant execution, the feat in truth was unparalleled in audacity. "I thought," said Smalls, as he delivered the vessel to the Union Navy, "that the 'Planter' might be of some use to Uncle Abe."

A native South Carolinian, Smalls was born in Beaufort in 1839. When he was twelve his master brought him to Charleston, where, after a succession of occupations, he finally became a rigger and began to learn boating and the twisting coastal waters. When the war came, the stockily built young slave was impressed into the Confederate service, and in March, 1862, he was made a member of the crew of the "Planter."

Formerly a cotton steamer plying the Pee Dee River and capable of

Benjamin Quarles, "The Abduction of the 'Planter,'" *Civil War History*, IV (March 1958), pp. 5–11. Reprinted with the permission of Benjamin Quarles and of *Civil War History*.

carrying 1,400 bales, the "Planter" had been chartered by the war government and converted into a transport running from point to point in the Charleston harbor and the neighboring waters. Built of live oak and red cedar, the boat measured 150 feet in length, had a 30 foot beam, a depth of 7 feet 10 inches, and drew 3 feet 9 inches of water. As a Confederate dispatch boat, she mounted two guns for her own use, a 32-pounder pivot gun and a 24-pounder howitzer. Attached to the engineering department at Charleston, the "Planter" carried a crew of eleven, of whom three were whites—captain, mate, and engineer— and the remainder slaves.

By far the ablest of the slave crew was Smalls. Determined to escape, Smalls hit upon the idea of making off with the "Planter." Wherever the Union Navy extended its blockade along the Southern seacoast, freedom-minded Negroes had sensed a new opportunity. By scow, oyster boat, barge, homemade canoe, or anything that would float, they made their way to the Union men-of-war. But no plan of escape was as imaginative and as daring as Smalls's.

The young wheelsman worked out the details in his mind. The escaping party would number sixteen, of whom half would be women and children, including Smalls's wife and their two young ones. The "Planter" would put out to sea casually, as though making a routine run to reconnoiter. Knowing they could expect little mercy if caught, Smalls bound the party to agree that if they were unable to make good their flight, they would blow up the vessel rather than be taken alive. Smalls's plan embraced one final but essential detail—all three white officers would have to remain ashore for the night. Such an absence would be contrary to standing general orders which stipulated that officers of light draft vessels were to remain "on board day and night" when their boat was docked at the wharf.

Finally came such a night as Smalls waited for—the night of May 12. Coincidentally, on the afternoon of that day, 200 pounds of ammunition and four guns—"a banded rifle 42, one 8-inch columbiad, one 8-inch seacoast howitzer, and one 32-pounder"—had been loaded on the "Planter" for transport to the harbor battery, Fort Ripley.

With the white officers ashore, Smalls began to put his plan into operation. The sixteen slaves got aboard in the crisp early morning, the women and children being led below deck in pin-drop quiet. Smalls broke into Captain C. J. Relyea's cabin and took the captain's hat. At 3:00 a.m. one of the fugitives struck a match and set the kindlings on fire under the boilers; twenty-five minutes later the hawsers which moored the boat to Southern Wharf were cast off. From the pilothouse Smalls sounded the wharf signal. The shore sentinel at his post some fifty yards distant noticed the ship gliding away but sensed nothing afoot; he "did not think it necessary to stop her, presuming that she was but pursuing her usual business," in the language of an official report issued later that day.

Now to run the many fortifications in the harbor. Bristling with sea defenses, the defiant city was ringed with forts and batteries on constant alert.

But for the runaway slaves there was no turning back. Hoisting the ship's two flags, Confederate and Palmetto, Smalls eased into the inner channel. He geared the "Planter" to its customary pace, although not to dash at full speed required the utmost self-control.

The critical minutes of the great deception had arrived. Wearing the captain's hat and mimicking his gait, Smalls stood in the pilothouse with the cord in his hand. As the vessel passed Fort Johnson, he pulled the lanyard on the steam whistle and gave the proper salute. All went well.

Finally the abductors approached the last hurdle, historic Fort Sumter. Thirteen months ago it was here that the opening shots of the war had been fired, and at the identical morning hour. One of the four transport guns on the "Planter" belonged originally, as Smalls well knew, to Fort Sumter, having been struck on the muzzle during the bombardment of that bastion and now having been repaired because of the Confederacy's scarcity of heavy guns.

Abreast of Sumter, Smalls sounded the private signal, three shrill whistles followed by a hissing one. "The sentinel on the parapet called for the corporal of the guard and reported the guard-boat going out," stated the official report of Major Alfred Rhett. In turn, the corporal of the guard relayed the intelligence to the officer of the day, Captain David G. Fleming. The information had been passed along in routine fashion since it was, in Major Rhett's words, "by no means unusual for the guard-boat to run out at that hour." Then came the fateful order to permit the halted vessel to go on her way; by signal Sumter answered, "All right." The "Planter" had been taken for the guard boat and hence allowed to pass!

The slave-manned steamer moved in a southeasterly direction and entered the main ship channel, maintaining her leisurely pace until she had outdistanced the line of fire of the Confederate battery. Then she got up steam, lowered her guns, and ran up a white flag.

Not a minute too soon was the flag of truce hoisted. Off Charleston was a Union blockading fleet of ten warships, and the "Planter" had been spied by the lookout on the inside ship, "Onward." The commander, J. F. Nickels, had ordered his ship swung around so as to train the maximum gunfire on the approaching craft. Just as the "Onward" succeeded in bringing her port guns to bear on the oncoming steamer, Commander Nickels caught sight of the white flag. The gunners relaxed.

Unmolested, the harbor boat drew up alongside the armed sailing vessel. A prize crew boarded the "Planter" and greeted its crew. Down came the white flag, and up went the American ensign. Then and there in the outer harbor the ownership of the captive boat was transferred from the Confederate States of America to the Union Navy.

Later that morning the senior officer commanding the blockading squadron off Charleston, E. G. Parrott, taking advantage of the good weather, ordered the prize crew to take the "Planter" and its captors to Port Royal, and there to report the incident to Flag Officer S. F. Du Pont. No order could have pleased Smalls and his companions more, most of them having originally come from the Sea Island region.

The "Planter" made the sixty-mile trip to Port Royal by way of St. Helena Sound and Broad River, reaching her destination shortly after ten in the evening. Word awaited Smalls that he was to report directly to Du Pont, and the next morning he was ushered aboard the flagship "Wabash." There the elderly admiral, "that stately and courteous potentate, elegant as one's ideal French marquis," listened attentively as the ex-slave told his story.

Later that day, in a lengthy report to the Secretary of the Navy, Du Pont summed up the exploit: "The bringing out of this steamer, under all the circumstances, would have done credit to anyone." The admiral also jotted down another conclusion: "This man, Robert Smalls, is superior to any who have yet come into the lines, intelligent as many of them have been."

Back in Charleston the news was received with consternation not unmingled with disbelief. In a front-page story devoted to the "extraordinary occurrence," the *Courier* reported that "our community was intensely agitated Tuesday morning by the intelligence that the steamer 'Planter' . . . had been taken possession of by her colored crew, steamed up and boldly ran [sic] out to the blockaders." Added the daily, "The news was not at first credited." Another Charleston newspaper, the *Mercury*, concluded its descriptive story of the escape by explaining that "the run to Morris Island goes out a long way past the fort, and then turns. The 'Planter' did not turn."

Voicing the general indignation of Confederate South Carolina over the negligence of the white officers of the boat, the *Columbia Guardian* expressed a fervent wish that the "recreant parties will be brought to speedy justice, and the prompt penalty of the halter rigorously enforced." From army headquarters in Richmond came a dispatch to General Pemberton stating that General Lee had received the papers relative to the "Planter's" escape and that "he very much regrets the circumstances, and hopes that necessary measures will be taken to prevent any repetition of a like misfortune."

News of Smalls's feat quickly spread throughout the North, and public sentiment became strong for awarding prize money to the "Planter's" crew. Congress responded, moving with unusual speed. Two weeks from the day of the seizure, that body passed a bill ordering the Secretary of the Navy to have the vessel appraised and "when the value thereof shall be thus ascertained to cause an equitable apportionment of one-half of such value . . . to be made between Robert Smalls and his associates who assisted in rescuing her from the enemies of the Government." Within another week Lincoln had signed the bill.

Smalls turned out to be right in believing that the "Planter" might be of some use to the North. Admirably suited to the shallow waters of the Sea Island region, she was immediately equipped with musket-proof bulwarks and converted into a navy transport, carrying upwards of seventy men. Exactly one month after the abduction, Admiral Du Pont, in acknowledging two letters from naval officer A. C. Rhind, wrote that he was "glad that the 'Planter' has proved so useful a transport, and that we have again been able so materially to aid the army, especially at a critical time, when its generals were almost helpless for want of transports."

Early in September, 1862, the "Planter" was sold to the army, which could make much better use of a wood-burner than could the sister service. The quartermaster's department welcomed the addition, "as we have comparatively no vessels of light draft." Until she was decommissioned and sold at Baltimore in September, 1866, the "Planter" remained in military service, being used mainly as a troop transport, but seeing occasional service as a supply boat.

During most of its period of use by the armed forces, the "Planter" was piloted or commanded by Smalls. Over the four months the boat remained under navy supervision, the young Negro was employed as pilot. During the year 1863 and for the first two months in 1864, the army employed him in a like capacity, paying him $50 a month until September 30, 1863, then $75 a month from October 1 to November 30, 1863, and thenceforth $150 a month. On March 1, 1864, he was made captain.

The pilot was promoted to master as a reward for bravery under fire (before the war was over, Smalls had fought in seventeen engagements), but the appointment was merited on other grounds. For the fugitive slave brought much with him. His knowledge of the coastline of South Carolina and Georgia was intimate; few men were more familiar with the sinuous windings of those waters, and no hand was more skilled in their navigation. Indeed, "the accession of Smalls is deemed of more importance than the heavy guns of the 'Planter,'" wrote a reporter for the *Philadelphia Inquirer* (May 17, 1862), "as Smalls is thoroughly acquainted with all the intricacies of navigation in that region." Smalls also brought a knowledge of where the torpedoes had been planted to destroy the Union gunboats and where the masked batteries were located.

The intelligence he furnished was so valuable that the Secretary of the Navy, in his annual report to President Lincoln, made it a point to describe them:

> From information derived chiefly from the contraband Pilot, Robert Smalls, who has escaped from Charleston, Flag Officer Du Pont, after proper reconnaissance, directed Commander Marchand to cross the bar with several gun-boats and occupy Stono. The river was occupied as far as Legarville, and examinations extended further to ascertain the position of the enemy's batteries. The seizure of Stono Inlet and river secured an important base for military operations, and was virtually a turning of the forces in the Charleston harbor.

At the war's end Smalls was among the thousands who witnessed the reraising of the American flag at Fort Sumter. This event had been scheduled for April 14, four years to the day after the one on which the Union forces had been forced to haul down the colors. Present at the flag-raising ceremonies was a distinguished roster of reformers and public notables, including William

Lloyd Garrison, Judge Advocate General Joseph Holt, Supreme Court Justice N. H. Swayne, Senator Henry Wilson, and the chief speaker, Henry Ward Beecher. On hand also was Robert Anderson, brought back to Sumter to raise the very shot-pierced flag which the Southerners had forced him to lower four years previously. But perhaps the most symbolic figure present was Captain Robert Smalls, who that morning had left Charleston, Sumter bound, at the helm of the "Planter," profusely decorated with the Stars and Stripes and loaded down with hundreds "of the emancipated race."

After the war Smalls had fifty years to live, many of them spent in the public eye—as a member of the South Carolina legislature, a five-term United States Congressman, and Collector of the Port at Beaufort. But no moment of his eventful life could ever match that memorable dawn when he abducted the "Planter."

Louis R. Harlan

DESEGREGATION IN NEW ORLEANS PUBLIC SCHOOLS DURING RECONSTRUCTION

One of the achievements of the Radical Reconstruction regimes was the inauguration of a system of free public schools in the southern states. Of the state constitutions passed under Radical auspices, only those of Louisiana and South Carolina required legally nonsegregated schools. Yet even in these two states Jim Crow schools were the rule. The only integrated public educational institutions were the University of South Carolina and the public school system of New Orleans. Louis R. Harlan has examined the history of integration in the New Orleans public schools during Reconstruction. His article is of far broader scope than its title indicates, because he also touches upon many aspects of the life of the New Orleans free Negroes.

IT is a fact not generally known even to historians that the New Orleans public schools during the Reconstruction period underwent substantial racial desegregation over a period of six and a half years, an experience shared by no other southern community until after 1954 and by few northern communities at the time. This essay is limited to a summary of the evidence that there was indeed desegregation in New Orleans in the 1870's and to an effort to explain it chiefly in terms of circumstances in New Orleans at the time. It is obvious that New Orleans, as the only real urban center in the overwhelmingly rural South, could not be an example from which any general conclusions can be drawn about Reconstruction in the region or even in Louisiana as a whole. The experience of one southern urban community during Reconstruction, however, may hold interest for students of the rapidly urbanizing contemporary South.

For a generation of historians rather suddenly concerned with past strug-

Louis R. Harlan, "Desegregation in New Orleans Public Schools During Reconstruction," *American Historical Review*, LXVII (April, 1962), pp. 663–75. Reprinted with permission of the author and publisher.

gles over civil rights, the interest of this study lies partly in the new crop that it makes in the much-plowed field of Reconstruction history. The historians both of Louisiana Reconstruction [1] and of southern education [2] have pronounced the desegregation experiment of New Orleans an almost total failure. The conclusions of historians of the Dunning school may be explained by their preoccupation with political themes or their racialistic and sectional blind spots, but perhaps a better explanation is that they read in the partisan press the headlined stories of white walkouts and Negro evictions, but failed to note the undramatic evidence of the return of most of these pupils in the following days and months. Historians of southern education seem to have relied too heavily on a secondary source by the Louisiana educational historian Thomas H. Harris, who in turn depended vaguely on the "testimony of men who lived through the period." Harris declared in 1924: "The schools were never mixed. The law was evaded from the first, and the negroes were about as active in evading it as the whites." [3]

It is with some surprise, therefore, that we read the testimony in 1874 of Thomas W. Conway, the Radical state superintendent and prime mover of New Orleans desegregation:

> I had fully concluded to put the system of mixed schools to a thorough, practical test, and I did. The white pupils all left . . . and the school-house was virtually in the hands of the colored pupils. This was the picture one day. What will you think when I tell you that before I reached my office that day, the children of both races who, on the school question, seemed like deadly enemies, were, many of them, joined in a circle, playing on the green, under the shade of the wide-spreading live oak. In a few days I went back to see how the school was progressing, and, to my surprise, found nearly all the former pupils returned to their places; and that the school, like all the schools in the city, reported at the close of the year a larger attendance than at any time since the close of the war. The children

[1] Alcée Fortier, *Louisiana Studies* (New Orleans, 1894), 267–68; John R. Ficklen, *History of Reconstruction in Louisiana* (Baltimore, 1910), 207–208; Ella Lonn, *Reconstruction in Louisiana after 1868* (New York, 1918), 54–55, 357; John S. Kendall, *History of New Orleans* (3 vols., Chicago, 1922), I, 331, 665; Roger W. Shugg, *Origins of Class Struggle in Louisiana* (University, La., 1939), 226; Garnie W. McGinty, *Louisiana Redeemed* (New Orleans, 1941), 24. George W. Cable, *Strange True Stories of Louisiana* (New York, 1889), 221–32, is more accurate, though limited to a single public school.

[2] Horace M. Bond, *The Education of the Negro in the American Social Order* (New York, 1934), 52; Charles W. Dabney, *Universal Education in the South* (2 vols., Chapel Hill, N.C., 1936), I, 368–71; Harry S. Ashmore, *The Negro and the Schools* (Chapel Hill, N.C., 1954), 7–8; John Hope Franklin, "Jim Crow Goes to School," *South Atlantic Quarterly*, LVIII (Spring 1959), 225–35; Alfred H. Kelly, "The Congressional Controversy over School Segregation, 1867–1875," *American Historical Review*, LXIV (Apr. 1959), 537–63.

[3] Thomas H. Harris, *The Story of Public Education in Louisiana* (New Orleans, 1924), 30; an undocumented work.

were simply kind to each other in the school-room as in the streets and elsewhere! A year ago I visited the same school and saw therein about as many colored children as whites, with not a single indication of any ill-feeling whatever.

All that is wanted in this matter of civil rights is to let the foes of the measure simply understand that we mean it. Do this, and as in the case of the enemies of free schools in Louisiana, they will be quiet.[4]

The whole truth, of course, embraces both the historians' evidence of evasion and strident resistance and Conway's idyl of dancing on the green. Evasion lasted for three years, until the last legal recourse was exhausted, and then desegregation began. As desegregation spread slowly into more and more schools, as Conway said, there was indeed resistance, but it was fruitless, sporadic, separated by long periods of tacit acceptance, and successful in the end only because Reconstruction itself failed.

The forces of evasion were in effect even before the state constitution in 1867 prohibited the establishment of separate schools and required that no public school should deny admission on account of race or color.[5] On the eve of the constitutional convention the city hastily established its first Negro schools to give credibility to its stand for "separate but equal" rather than desegregated schools,[6] and Freedmen's Bureau officials opposed to mixed schools [7] hastily transferred their local schools to the city board.[8] State Superintendent Robert M. Lusher resigned before the end of his term to become the state agent of the Peabody Education Fund, which spent more money in Louisiana than in any other state to aid a system of private white schools.[9]

In New Orleans, where whites outnumbered Negroes nearly three to one, white Republicans in the city government cooperated with the city school board in efforts to thwart Superintendent Conway in his equally determined effort to give desegregation a thorough trial in that city. The city's news-

[4] Conway to the editor of the Washington *National Republican,* in Washington *New National Era,* June 4, 1874.

[5] New Orleans *Tribune,* Oct. 27, 1867 [all New Orleans newspapers hereafter cited without place name].

[6] *Tribune,* July 24, 1867; *Times,* July 31, Sept. 19, Oct. 1, 9, 11, 15, 16, 20, 1867; *Crescent,* Sept. 15, 17, 1867; Minutes of New Orleans City Board of School Directors [hereafter cited as Sch. Bd. Min.] Sept. 16, Oct. 2, 9, 1867 (VII, 203–14, 219–26), MSS volumes in Orleans Parish School Board Office, New Orleans.

[7] L. Jolissaint, Parish of Orleans School Report, Sept. 15, 1868, Tri-Monthly Report Book of Office of Assistant Sub-Assistant Commissioner, Parish of Orleans, Louisiana, Bureau of Refugees, Freedmen, and Abandoned Lands, National Archives; *Crescent,* Sept. 17, 1867; *Picayune,* Dec. 4, 1867.

[8] Sch. Bd. Min., Nov. 6, Dec. 4, 1867 (VII, 235–37, 251–53); *Times,* Dec. 25, 1867.

[9] *Picayune,* Apr. 14, 1868; Peabody Education Fund, *Proceedings of the Trustees* (6 vols., Boston, 1867–1914), I, 91, 262–63, 408–12, 434–39 (July 1868, Feb. 1871, Oct. 1874).

papers meanwhile undertook to create an atmosphere of resistance and fear, advocating desertion of the schools en masse by the whites, establishment of private schools, and refusal to pay school taxes, and predicting the destruction of the public schools and race war.[10] The city school board resorted to a pupil placement system [11] and all of the legal stratagems so familiar today. The loopholes of every school law were sought out, and a bewildering succession of suits and injunctions cluttered the courts. At one time five school cases were simultaneously on the dockets. Finally the sands of delay ran out; a court decision of December 1870 was acknowledged by all parties to be decisive, and desegregation began within a month.[12]

To overcome the forces of delay and evasion, the Radicals found it necessary to centralize and strengthen the school system. The city school board was replaced by another appointed by the state board of education, which in turn was appointed by the governor. The city board was allowed by state law to estimate its annual needs and require the city governments to levy and collect a local tax sufficient to supply the amount. The high salaries that this arrangement made possible, though often tardily paid, attracted good local teachers and created a reasonably good *esprit de corps*.

The extent of desegregation cannot be measured precisely because the official reports made no separate accounting of the races and because the population of New Orleans was so peculiarly mixed, with so many very light colored persons and swarthy white ones, that observers often found it impossible to distinguish between them.[13] Nevertheless, there is considerable evidence of desegregation in official records and in newspapers, particularly in the reports of the annual examinations or closing exercises of the schools. From such sources it is possible to identify by name twenty-one desegregated schools and some others that may have been desegregated, about one-third of the city's public schools.[14] The school authorities at no time initiated desegre-

10 See, e.g., *Picayune*, Oct. 22, 1867, Aug. 13, 1868, Nov. 24, 1870; *Commercial Bulletin*, Feb. 7, 1870; *Times*, May 2, 1868, Feb. 17, Apr. 10, 1870.

11 Sch. Bd. Min., May 21, 27, 1868 (VII, 323, 327–28). According to the *Picayune*, Jan. 12, 1871, "everything worked smoothly, attempts at mixing the schools being frustrated by the plan adopted by Mr. Van Norden, the President of the Board, who issued permits on which alone admission could be gained, to applicants, and taking good care that no negroes were admitted into white schools."

12 *Annual Report of the State Superintendent of Public Education for the Year 1870* [hereafter cited as *Annual Report*] (New Orleans, 1871), 17–28; *Picayune* and *Times* throughout 1869–1870, esp. *Times*, Dec. 20, 1870; *Picayune*, Jan. 12, 1871; *Commercial Bulletin*, Jan. 11, 12, 1871. On earlier desegregation efforts, see *ibid.*, Apr. 27, 30, May 17, 18, June 30, 1870; Sch. Bd. Min., May 21, 27, June 3, 1868 (VII, 322–28, 336–37).

13 *Times*, Oct. 6, 1873; *Louisianian*, Sept. 4, 1875.

14 These were: Barracks, Bayou Bridge, Bayou Road, Beauregard, Bienville, Central Boys' High, Claiborne, Fillmore, Fisk, Franklin, Keller, Lower Girls' High, Madison, Paulding, Pontchartrain (Milneburg), Rampart, Robertson, St. Anne, St. Philip, Spain, Webster schools certainly desegregated, and Cut-off Road, Dunn, Gentilly, McDonoghville vaguely reported to be so. See *Bulletin*, Jan. 11, Feb. 1, 1871, Dec. 11, 18, 19, 1874; *Republican*, Apr. 12, 1873, Dec. 12, 1874; *Picayune*, June 23, 1871, Dec. 11, 12,

gation, but simply required the admission of Negro children to white or mixed schools whenever they applied. Thus by choice or social pressure a majority of the city's school children attended either the separate Negro schools or white schools.[15] A surprising number of colored children, nevertheless, entered mixed schools under this arrangement. In 1877 the number was estimated at three hundred,[16] but that was some six months after the end of Reconstruction. Other evidence indicates that between five hundred and one thousand Negroes and several thousand whites attended mixed schools at the height of desegregation.[17] Light colored children, who could move about more easily in the white world, were usually the first to enter mixed schools and the last to leave them after Reconstruction, but children "as black as ebony" were reported "side by side with the fairest Caucasians" in the same classrooms.[18]

All of the five mixed schools with seventy-five or more Negroes enrolled were in the Second and Third Districts, below Canal Street, where descendants of the original French and Spanish inhabitants and the Irish, German, and Italian immigrants predominated. In this downtown area there was no rigid residential separation, and the houses of prostitution as well as schoolhouses were desegregated, though without causing as much public excitement. Since nearly all of the schools in these districts were desegregated,[19] one might assume that the character of the Latin or immigrant population explained everything. But this is not so. Negro residential areas were dispersed throughout the city, and some of the largest schools in the so-called American districts, the First and Fourth, contained Negro children.[20] One of these, the Fisk School, contained "a considerable number." [21] Below New Orleans proper, in the Fifth and Seventh Districts, the scattered settlements on both sides of the river contained some desegregated primary schools.[22] Of the city's three

19, 1874, Feb. 19, Nov. 10, 1875, Nov. 20, 1876, Dec. 6, 1877; *Times*, Apr. 10, June 7, Oct. 6, Dec. 13, 1873, Dec. 18, 19, 1874, Feb. 19, 1875, Sept. 20, 22, 1876; *L'Abeille*, Dec. 18, 1874; report on Claiborne Boys' School, Mar. 10, 1873, Special Reports of Principals, Louisiana Department of Education Miscellaneous Papers, Department of Archives and Manuscripts, Louisiana State University; *Annual Report*, 1872, 242–43. Contemporaries estimated that between one-third and one-half of the schools were desegregated. *Annual Report*, 1872, 18; *Republican*, July 18, 1873, Sept. 16, 1875; Edward Lawrence, "Color in the New Orleans Schools," *Harper's Weekly*, XIX (Feb. 13, 1875), 147–48; *Louisiana*, Feb. 13, 1875.

[15] *Annual Reports*, 1869, 13, 1871, 308.

[16] City Superintendent William O. Rogers, in *Annual Report*, 1877, 303.

[17] The six leading desegregated schools alone were reported to have more than five hundred Negro pupils. *Picayune*, Dec. 11, 1874; *Times*, June 7, Dec. 13, 1873, Dec. 18, 1874; *Bulletin*, Dec. 19, 1874; *Republican*, Apr. 12, 1873; report on Claiborne Boys' School, Mar. 10, 1873, Education Archives, LSU.

[18] *Bulletin*, Dec. 15, 1874.

[19] *Ibid.*, Oct. 22, 1874; *L'Abeille*, Apr. 16, 1876.

[20] Fisk, Franklin, Madison, Paulding, and Webster Schools in the First District and Keller School in the Fourth District.

[21] *Times*, Dec. 18, 1874.

[22] Pontchartrain, Cut-off Road, Dunn, Gentilly, and McDonoghville.

public high schools, two were desegregated. At the Lower Girls' High School, desegregation proceeded peacefully for years, about one-fifth of the students being colored.[23] At the Central Boys' High several Negro pupils attended after 1875,[24] and a Negro was professor of mathematics there for two years, until after the end of Reconstruction.[25]

Desegregation caused only a temporary decline of enrollment in the schools as a whole and in the mixed schools themselves. Enrollment dropped from 24,892 to 19,091 in the first year of desegregation, but then rose steadily to 26,251 in 1875, which was higher than at any other time in the nineteenth century.[26] The report that 21,000 of these were white and 5,000 colored [27] indicates that there were actually more white pupils in the public schools during desegregation than either before or after.

In the desegregated schools the same trend was evident. The Fillmore Boys' School in the Third District, for example, was desegregated in 1871, when its enrollment was 377, and soon contained 100 colored pupils. In 1873 the conservative New Orleans *Times* reported 700 enrolled, "wonderful" attendance, and good discipline. Fillmore School was the largest in the city, crowded to capacity. In 1874 its enrollment reached 890, and the following year more of its graduates qualified for the high school, through competitive examinations, than those of any other boys' school.[28] Other mixed schools with large Negro enrollments had similar records of increasing enrollment and high academic standing. At the Bienville School, where attendance was cut in half in 1871 by desegregation and a river flood, both enrollment and average attendance by 1874 exceeded the levels prior to desegregation. It sent more of its graduates to high school in 1873 than any two other boys' schools.[29]

Why would desegregated schools be so crowded in a community as race conscious as New Orleans? The explanation seems to be that the quality of instruction was higher in those schools than in most of the others, because of the system of classification of elementary schools. Nearly all the mixed schools

[23] Cable, *Strange True Stories of Louisiana*, 219–32; Dora R. Miller to Cable, May 31, 1889, Feb. 10, May 5, 1890, George W. Cable Papers, Howard-Tilton Memorial Library, Tulane University; *Republican*, Apr. 12, 1873; *Times*, Dec. 17, 18, 1874.

[24] *Ibid.*, Jan. 12, 13, Feb. 4, 1875; *Bulletin*, Jan. 13, 1875; *Picayune*, Feb. 19, 1875; *Republican*, Mar. 3, 1875.

[25] Harris, *Public Education in Louisiana*, 46; Sch. Bd. Min., Sept. 11, 1875, Dec. 6, 1876, Nov. 7, 1877 (VIII, 60, 200, IX, 174, 177).

[26] *Annual Reports*, 1871, 321, 326, 1875, 12, 1877, 289, 1879, 13; Robert M. Lusher, MSS autobiography, June 1890, Robert M. Lusher Papers, LSU. Kendall, *History of New Orleans*, II, 531, reported 23,668 enrolled in 1899.

[27] *Picayune*, Jan. 12, 1875, as reported in *Times-Picayune*, Jan. 25, 1937, clipping in New Orleans Public Schools vertical file, Louisiana Room, LSU; *Times*, Oct. 6, 1873; *Annual Report*, 1877, 303.

[28] *Picayune*, June 23, 1871, Dec. 12, 1874; *Times*, Dec. 13, 1873; *Annual Reports*, 1874, 183, 1875, 208.

[29] *Commercial Bulletin*, Jan. 12, 31, 1871; *Picayune*, June 23, Dec. 11, 1871; *Republican*, June 23, 1871; *Times*, June 7, Oct. 6, Dec. 12, 1873; *Annual Reports*, 1871, 375, 1874, 183, 1875, 208–10.

were classified as Grammar A schools, which had more teachers and a higher salary scale, and sent more graduates to the high schools than the Grammar B schools and Primary schools. Apparently this was why Negro children chose to enter them and why whites also attended them regardless of color, so that their enrollment steadily increased. Most of the Negro schools were Grammar B, and, according to report, "the mixed schools are the best in the city, and the colored schools the poorest—the poorest in quarters, furniture, text-books, and in every way." [30]

Desegregation of the public schools caused enrollment in private and parochial schools to increase, but not enough to damage the public schools. The most ambitious plan of the period, "an elaborate design for the establishment of schools by private enterprise," was presented to a mass meeting of citizens of the Second and Third Districts by former state superintendent Robert M. Lusher.[31] It temporarily evoked much enthusiasm, but Lusher later wrote: "The failure of the Canvassers appointed to raise means for making the plan effectual, to collect a sufficient amount, unfortunately caused the plan to be abandoned." [32] No coordination of private school efforts was ever developed.

Existing Catholic parochial schools, new Presbyterian and Episcopalian parochial schools, and the old and new private schools all expanded. Enrollment in these schools rose from about ten thousand in 1869 to seventeen thousand in 1873, but then declined to fourteen thousand the next year and subsequently even further.[33] "Parochial schools on the pay system are virtually a failure," confessed Father Abram J. Ryan, editor of the local Catholic weekly; the reason he gave was economic: "poor families who have three or four, sometimes eight or ten children . . . cannot possibly send them to the parochial schools at the rate of $2 or even $1 per month, each." [34] This consideration applied with even greater force to the private schools, where tuition was normally twice as high.[35]

Predicted racial violence and tax resistance did not materialize, and after experimenting with walkouts from mixed schools and with private schools, the people of New Orleans learned to live with the change. For three years, from the fall of 1871 until the fall of 1874, the tumult and the shouting

[30] *Republican*, July 18, 1873; *Times*, June 18, 1870.

[31] *Commercial Bulletin*, May 25, June 8, 1870; *Times*, May 25, 1870; *Picayune*, June 8, 1870.

[32] Lusher, autobiographical MSS, May 31, 1889, Lusher Papers; Harris, *Public Education in Louisiana*, 56.

[33] *Annual Reports*, 1869, 27, 76, 1873, 72, 284; *Morning Star and Catholic Messenger*, Jan. 31, 1869, Oct. 18, 1874. The figure for 1869 is a compromise between the state report, which estimated 1,200 in parochial schools, the Catholic press, which estimated 5,000 to 6,000, and the city superintendent, who estimated 15,000. *Reports of the United States Commissioner of Education*, 1873, 547, 1874, 535, 1877, 315 (Washington, D.C., 1874, 1875, 1879), estimate 13,779 enrolled in 1873, 14,235 in 1874, 12,000 in 1877.

[34] *Morning Star and Catholic Messenger*, May 22, 1870, July 4, 1875.

[35] *Picayune*, Sept. 17, 1875.

diminished.[36] At the risk of oversimplification, two explanations may be suggested. First, desegregation was administered with such skill that the opposition was disarmed, but foremost, for reasons largely political, thousands of New Orleans whites and the leading newspapers actually sought to win the Negro's vote on a basis of recognizing his civil rights.

Though statesmanlike qualities are not generally attributed to Reconstruction leaders, and the school officials were certainly not plaster saints, they administered the New Orleans school efficiently and without major scandal. "If an irrational prejudice is exhibited on one side of this question," said Superintendent Conway, "let it not be met by an equally irrational precipitancy on the other side. This great question of education for the people ... should not be imperiled by injudicious action, even in behalf of a principle confessedly just and equitable." [37] Though rewarded with diatribes for their pains,[38] Conway, his Negro successor William G. Brown, and City Superintendent Charles W. Boothby pursued a "firm and yet moderate course" and conducted a school system good enough to win loyalty from the teachers and even occasional compliments from the opposition.[39]

The complex reasons why many New Orleans whites embraced or acquiesced in Negro civil rights between 1871 and 1874 have been treated elsewhere by T. Harry Williams [40] and can only be outlined here. The central fact was that Louisiana Negroes had a majority of the votes and were protected against intimidation by federal troops. As Reconstruction continued in Louisiana after its demise in other states, native whites realized that they had to win a substantial segment of the Negro vote if they hoped to oust the carpetbaggers. The Negroes were ably led, not so much by the white carpetbaggers as by their own well-educated New Orleans persons of color and Negro carpetbaggers. It was to these colored leaders that the white conservatives made overtures when the inevitable conflicts of interest developed between the white and colored wings of the Radical Republicans.

In 1871 and 1872 New Departure Democrats and new parties that abandoned the Democratic label partly because of its unpopularity among Negroes made bids for Negro votes by platform promises of recognition of civil rights and by parading a few Negro speakers at their rallies.[41] The vague commitments

---

[36] There were a few exceptions, such as editorials in *Picayune*, Jan. 4, 1872; *Times*, Apr. 10, 1873. Their news columns, however, reported favorably on desegregated schools. See *Times*, Dec. 13, 1872, June 7, 1873; *Picayune*, Sept. 29, Dec. 11, 1872.

[37] *Annual Reports*, 1869, 12–13, 1871, 47.

[38] *Times*, Nov. 24, 1870; *Bulletin*, Oct. 22, 1874; *L'Abeille*, Feb. 21, 1875.

[39] The moderation was owing partly to opposition and occasional insubordination. M. C. Cole to Thomas W. Conway, Sept. 9, 1871, William G. Brown to City Board of School Directors, June 1873, Department of Education Archives, LSU; Conway to Henry C. Warmoth, Nov. 18, 1871, Henry C. Warmoth Papers, Southern Historical Collection, University of North Carolina; *Republican*, Oct. 7, 1870; *Commercial Bulletin*, Apr. 27, 1870; *Times*, May 6, 1870, July 3, 1873.

[40] T. Harry Williams, "The Louisiana Unification Movement of 1873," *Journal of Southern History*, XI (Aug. 1945), 349–69.

[41] E. John Ellis to Thomas C. W. Ellis, Feb. 29, 1872, E. John and Thomas C. W. Ellis Papers, LSU.

were insufficient to win the Negro vote in the election of 1872, and this failure led to the specific commitments of the unification movement of 1873. Simply stated, the unification movement proposed a fusion of the native white and Negro voters in which the Negroes would promise to assist in ousting the carpetbaggers and cutting the taxes and the whites would guarantee the Negroes full civil rights: suffrage, office holding, desegregated transportation and places of public resort, and mixed schools. Confederate General P. G. T. Beauregard, the merchant Isaac N. Marks, and a thousand other New Orleans citizens of both races signed a unification manifesto endorsing desegregated schools in unmistakable terms and presented it for endorsement to cheering crowds. In this atmosphere it is understandable that the press and pulpits ceased to thunder against desegregation. After Marks had read the school clause of the manifesto to a mass meeting and a voice interrupted to ask, "Will you send your children to the public schools?" that is, to desegregated schools, the question was greeted with "hisses and other demonstrations" and an invitation to leave the hall.[42] The unification movement failed to achieve the interracial political alliance it sought, because of the reluctance of many whites, particularly in the rural areas, to concede so much to the Negroes, and because of Negro suspicion that the white unificationists would be unwilling or unable to make good their commitments. The movement did give desegregation a breathing spell, however, and its spirit continued to animate some New Orleans whites. Marks, stating his freedom of racial bias, took a seat on the city school board and helped to administer school desegregation.[43] In 1875 George W. Cable sent carefully reasoned arguments for mixed schools to a New Orleans paper,[44] and in the same year David F. Boyd, president of the state university, tried to publish a proposal to desegregate his school.[45]

To most New Orleans whites, however, the failure of unification was the signal for a change in policy and leadership. If Negroes could not be persuaded to vote with the whites, then enough Negroes had to be kept from the polls to ensure a white majority. The White League arose in 1874, spread quickly from the rural parishes to New Orleans, staged a three-day *coup d'état* in September until the arrival of federal troops, and installed a Conservative city government in December. In the same period the position of mixed schools was weakened by the removal from the congressional civil rights bill of the school desegregation clause.[46] The stage was set for the well-known school riots of December 1874, which reflected the momentary political climate of that period as clearly as the acquiescent mood of the previous three years reflected an opposite policy.

[42] *Times*, July 16, 1873; *Picayune*, July 16, 1873.

[43] Sch. Bd. Min., Jan. 12, 1876 (VIII, 125).

[44] These are in George W. Cable, *The Negro Question*, ed. Arlin Turner (Garden City, N.Y., 1958), 26–36.

[45] David F. Boyd, "Some Ideas on Education: The True Solution of the Question of 'Color' in Our Schools, Colleges & Universities, &c, &c," [Dec. 12 or 13] 1875, Walter L. Fleming Collection, LSU.

[46] Kelly, "Congressional Controversy over School Segregation," 558; *Picayune*, Dec. 18, 1874.

During three days of rioting, mobs often described as high school boys or "boy regulators" rudely ejected from mixed schools colored children who had been peacefully attending for years, insulted teachers, beat and threatened to hang the city superintendent.[47] What is not generally understood is that the White League and its newspaper supporters instigated and directed the mobs, which were composed mostly of men and adolescents not enrolled in the high schools, using a handful of high school rowdies as fronts.[48] Moreover, the riots failed to achieve their objective. Sober citizens persuaded the White League to call off "the boys," and the schools reopened after the holidays on a desegregated basis,[49] remaining so for another two and a half years, until after Reconstruction.

Even after the end of Reconstruction, it appeared at first that desegregation might survive the change. The schools remained mixed through the remainder of the term, and Negroes were appointed to the school boards.[50] But when the city school board voted to segregate the schools the following fall, the governor gave a Negro delegation neither aid nor comfort.[51] Resort to the state and federal courts proved equally futile. The Negroes lost three test cases despite the mandatory provisions of the state constitution,[52] and the constitution itself was rewritten in 1879 to permit separate schools and in 1898 to require them.

An obvious conclusion is that the southern devices of evasion and resistance broke down, largely through their own internal weaknesses. On the other hand, New Orleans whites never really surrendered their concept of the public school as a sort of private club. The chief significance of the New Orleans experiment with desegregation, however, centers around the fact, which was not merely incidental, that it occurred in a deep southern state with a large Negro population.

It was really universal suffrage—Negro suffrage protected by strong federal sanctions—that produced the mixed schools and sustained them through the years of trial. Negro votes in the constitutional convention secured the

[47] Times, Picayune, Bulletin, L'Abeille, Republican, Louisianian for Dec. 15–19, 1874; a convenient summary is Annual Report, 1874, liii–lxxxvi.

[48] "Notes on Mixed School Embroglio Dec. 1874," at end of Ephraim S. Stoddard diary for 1874–75, Ephraim S. Stoddard Collection, Tulane University; Dora R. Miller to Cable, Feb. 10, May 5, 1890, Cable Papers; Lawrence, "Color in the New Orleans Schools," 147–48; Cable, Strange True Stories of Louisiana, 223–32; Times, Dec. 19, 20, 1874, Jan. 3, 1875; Republican, Dec. 19, 1874; Picayune, Dec. 20, 1874; Louisianian, Dec. 26, 1874.

[49] Bulletin, Jan. 13, 1875; Times, Feb. 4, 19, 1875; Republican, Mar. 3, 1875; L'Abeille, Apr. 16, 1876.

[50] Lusher Diary, Mar. 31, 1877, Lusher Papers; Barnes F. Lathrop, ed., "An Autobiography of Francis T. Nicholls, 1834–1881," Louisiana Historical Quarterly, XVII (Apr. 1934), 257, 261.

[51] Sch. Bd. Min., June 22, July 3, 1877 (IX, 56–60, 63–64); Picayune, June 27, 1877; Democrat, June 27, 28, 1877.

[52] See Times, Sept. 27, 28, 30, Oct. 3, 24, 31, Nov. 29, 1877, May 22, 1878; Picayune, Oct. 6, 24, 1877; Louisianian, Sept. 29, 1877, Nov. 29, 1879.

mixed school clause, and Negro votes elected school officers who would carry it out. Negro votes were the consideration for which whites were willing to bargain acquiescence in desegregation. And when the compromise of 1877 removed the federal sanctions for Negro suffrage, the mixed schools were an early casualty. Desegregation was only part of a broader social struggle in which the ballot was the primary lever of power.

New Orleans desegregation is not entirely explained by Negro votes, however, since the Negro majority was in rural Louisiana, where schools were only rarely desegregated.[53] In the adjacent rural state of Mississippi, the Negro majority permitted separate schools to be established by a local-option school law.[54] It would seem that any rural effort at mixed schools in the lower South was foredoomed by the weak economic position of Negro sharecroppers, the lack of demand for educated labor in the cotton fields, and the desire of white planters to maintain racial segregation as a means of social control. In southern states outside of the cotton belt, of course, the Negro minority was too weak politically to win desegregation against almost unanimous white opposition.[55]

If the key to desegregation was to be found in the city, then why was the New Orleans experience so different from that of Charleston, South Carolina?[56] The South Carolina constitution of 1868 also required desegregation, and that state also had a Negro majority of voters. Yet the state officials successfully opposed desegregation, and neither the Negro legislators nor the Charleston Negro community pressed the issue.[57] Explanation of the difference between these two urban centers involves consideration of such intangible but very real influences as the singular character of New Orleans and the structure of leadership in the New Orleans Negro community.

With a population of 200,000, New Orleans was metropolitan in size and in the radiating influence of its river trade and railroad connections. Linked with continental Europe by its Creole tradition, its large and diverse immigrant population, and the cultural ties of more recent French émigrés, and

[53] *Annual Reports*, 1871, 120, 189; *Louisianian*, Mar. 13, 1875.

[54] Governor James L. Alcorn defending this policy in Washington *New Era*, June 2, 1870; *Congressional Globe*, 42 Cong., 2 sess., 3258 (May 9, 1872). Some Negro dissatisfaction is indicated in Vernon L. Wharton, *The Negro in Mississippi, 1865–1890* (Chapel Hill, N.C., 1947), 243–46; correspondence from Mississippi in Washington *New National Era*, Apr. 4, May 2, June 6, 1872, Apr. 10, 1873, July 2, 1874.

[55] See William G. Brownlow in *Congressional Record*, 43 Cong., 1 sess., 4144 (May 27, 1874). Only in Louisiana, Mississippi, and South Carolina, states with Negro majorities, did the Reconstruction constitutions contain school desegregation clauses.

[56] This was suggested by Professor August Meier, Morgan State College, in floor discussion of this paper at the Southern Historical Assocation meetng, Tulsa, Okla., Nov. 11, 1960.

[57] Francis B. Simkins and Robert H. Woody, *South Carolina during Reconstruction* (Chapel Hill, N.C., 1932), 434–39; Dabney, *Universal Education in the South*, I, 234–35; Richard H. Cain in *Congressional Record*, 43 Cong., 1 sess., 565 (Jan. 10, 1874); *ibid.*, 43 Cong., 2 sess., 957, 960, 981 (Feb. 3, 4, 1875). South Carolina did experiment with desegregating its state university.

linked by trade with radically complex Latin America, it was in many respects the nation's most cosmopolitan city. Travelers, immigrants, and clients frequently reminded New Orleans citizens that southern racial attitudes and practices were not widely accepted.[58]

In many other ways New Orleans was unique among southern cities. Desegregated worship in the Catholic churches, which claimed about half of the city's population, possibly modified racial attitudes.[59] The colored population was residentially dispersed throughout the city and was only about one-fourth of the total population; it was not so large as to induce in whites the fear of being engulfed if racial barriers were lowered. The city had opposed secession and was part of the Confederacy less than two years, whereas it underwent Reconstruction for almost nine years prior to desegregation and for some fifteen years in all. The interest of many New Orleans leaders in sugar protection and in federal subsidies for river and harbor improvement and railroads made them ideologically more amenable to Whiggish Republicanism than the cotton planters of the Charleston area. The prominence of New Orleans merchants in the unification movement of 1873 suggests that many of them were more concerned with economic development than with social control. They were willing to compromise on racial issues in order to free themselves from a political regime on which they blamed the city's economic plight. Thus political polarization by race was incomplete and ephemeral.

The vigorous and ambitious leadership of the New Orleans Negro community was also a powerful stimulus to desegregation. The basis for the high quality of this leadership was laid during the slavery period, when the free Negroes of New Orleans enjoyed a status "probably unequaled in any other part of the South." [60] Whereas the Charleston free Negroes formed a truncated social pyramid in which artisans were the highest large class,[61] the New Orleans *gens de couleur* included a number of substantial merchants, cotton factors, caterers, doctors, and lawyers, even newspaper editors and poets. Negroes also had much social freedom in cosmopolitan New Orleans. "The whole behavior of the Negro toward the whites," says Joseph G. Tregle, "was singularly free of that deference and circumspection which might have been expected in a slave community." [62] Though the social weather became

<hr>

[58] See "A Frenchman" to the editor, *Times*, July 1, 1877.

[59] George Rose, *The Great Country* (London, 1868), 191.

[60] Joseph G. Tregle, Jr., "Early New Orleans Society: A Reappraisal," *Journal of Southern History*, XVIII (Feb. 1952), 34.

[61] E. Horace Fitchett, "The Traditions of the Free Negro in Charleston, South Carolina," *Journal of Negro History*, XXV (Apr. 1940), 142–43; George B. Tindall, *South Carolina Negroes, 1877–1900* (Columbia, S.C., 1952), 129–52; Simkins and Woody, *South Carolina*, 26, 91; E. Franklin Frazier, *Black Bourgeoisie* (Glencoe, Ill., 1957), 32.

[62] Tregle, "Early New Orleans Society," 33; Donald E. Everett, "Free Persons of Color in New Orleans, 1803–1865," unpublished doctoral dissertation, Tulane University, 1953; Annie L. W. Stahl, "The Free Negro in Ante-Bellum Louisiana," *Louisiana Historical Quarterly*, XXV (Apr. 1942), 301–96.

stormier in the last years of slavery, the colored elite regained self-confidence during the Union occupation, serving as officers in the Union army and eventually as officeholders in the state government. Soon after the war they won a crucial struggle for desegregation of streetcars against almost the same arguments and dire predictions later used to obstruct school desegregation.[63]

The light-skinned New Orleans Negroes, abandoning an early effort to be classed legally as whites, merged their lot with that of the Negro masses and forged an impressive Negro solidarity on racial questions. Since New Orleans was the state capital in this period, they were able to incorporate the darker skinned rural political leaders into their upper-class circle.[64] There is little evidence in the Reconstruction period that the colored bourgeoisie of New Orleans was as isolated from the Negro masses as E. Franklin Frazier has found the same class in the mid-twentieth century.[65] Well educated in private schools, in the North, and in France, they maintained a highly articulate newspaper press and an efficient if opportunistic political organization. They held about half of the seats on the city school board and protected the desegregation experiment against occasional desertion and failure of nerve on the part of their white colleagues. Sharing with most professional men the belief that "knowledge is power," these Negro leaders pressed their own children steadily into desegregated schools in search of equal educational opportunities.

New Orleans desegregation, then, achieved its successes in the 1870's through a unique conjunction of circumstances. A political coalition was temporarily created between the rural Negro majority, the urban Negro minority, and northern Republicans in control of federal and state governments. New Orleans was a metropolitan and cosmopolitan, not merely polyglot, center, in which the southern rural mores were challenged by other traditions, values, and interests. The prior development of a free Negro elite in New Orleans provided the leadership and steadfastness which outsiders could not furnish. Such a fortuitous convergence, however, depended too heavily on one *sine qua non*, the temporary sojourn of federal power in the South. Not until the whole region came more closely to resemble New Orleans, not until an urban South and a more strongly based Negro community emerged, could the experiment be renewed auspiciously.

[63] *Tribune*, June 25, 1865, May 4, 7, 9, 12, 1867.

[64] Donald E. Everett, "Demands of the New Orleans Free Colored Population for Political Equality, 1862–1865," *Louisiana Historical Quarterly*, XXXVIII (Apr. 1955), 55–64; Germaine A. Memelo [Reed], "The Development of State Laws Concerning the Negro in Louisiana 1864–1900," unpublished master's thesis, Louisiana State University, 1956, 72–82; unanimous petition of Louisiana Negro legislators for passage of the civil rights bill, in *Congressional Globe*, 42 Cong., 2 sess., 815 (Feb. 5, 1872).

[65] Frazier, *Black Bourgeoisie*, 24–26.

Philip Durham

THE NEGRO COWBOY [1]

While Negroes in the South were grappling with the problems of land, education, and politics, other black men were participating in the final phases of the American frontier experience. One phase of this little-known side of Negro Life has been treated in W. Sherman Savage's "The Negro on the Mining Frontier," Journal of Negro History, Vol. XXX (January, 1945), pp. 30–46. In the article reprinted below, Philip Durham has demonstrated that, contrary to popular stereotypes, Negroes played a key role in the history of the cattle kingdom, from its beginning in the 1850's until its demise late in the nineteenth century.

WHO knows, today, about the Negro cowboy and his contribution to the making of the West? Ask anyone. Or read some of the thousands of "Western Stories" which have appeared during the last fifty years; if the Negro cowboy is in one, he is very well hidden. Apparently, then, the existence of the Negro cowboy is currently unknown because the writers of Western stories did not include him: his non-existence is due to the vagaries of fiction. One important reason for his exclusion may have been discovered by Professor Walter P. Webb, who asked several Western story magazine editors to give their reasons for the popularity of the type, and here is an answer:

> The Western story is the most popular type of action story. In order to give reasons for this, one thing must be recognized immediately: it is understood by us, and should be understood by everyone, that we are dealing with the popularity of Western stories as concerns readers who are white, who may be called Nordics, using this term advisedly.

Philip Durham, "The Negro Cowboy," *American Quarterly*, VII (Fall, 1955), pp. 291–301. Reprinted with permission of *American Quarterly*.
[1] A paper from this article was read before the American Studies Association Group at the Modern Language Association meeting in Chicago on December 28, 1953.

The white race has always been noted for being hard-drinking, hard-fighting, fearless, fair and square.[2]

Quite obviously, the Negro cowboy, in fiction, was confronted with a color line over which he could not ride.

The American cowboy has been described, by men who actually knew him, in these terms: he was independent, loyal, impulsive, generous; he had a hot and hasty temper, a strong sense of right and wrong; and he took his liquor straight. This description is not, however, peculiar to the Anglo-Saxon cowboy; it applies equally to the Negro cowboy, who, after the Civil War, moved out across the plains to play a significant rôle in the development of the cattle industry and became a part of the spirit of the West—a spirit which demanded a conscience but cared little for color.

Western autobiography, which unfortunately has a limited audience, includes the Negro cowboy, and in sufficient numbers to establish his active presence and contributions. Of the three non-fiction books published during the nineteenth century which dealt with the cowboy, two of them included the Negro. The first, Joseph McCoy's *Historic Sketches of the Cattle Trade of the West and Southwest*, published in Kansas City, Missouri, in 1874, describes the cowboys generally, as a type, and does not differentiate among them. The second, however, an autobiographical account, *A Texas Cowboy*, by Charles A. Siringo, refers to the Negro cowboy. This story of range life is accurate, and one senses the authenticity, the realistic approach, without literary affectation. In recording his day-to-day activities, Siringo makes no attempt to set apart the Negro cowboy; rather he is mentioned casually as is everyone else. He writes, for example, "At another time, on the same day, I roped a large animal and got my horse jerked over backwards on top of me and in the horse getting up he got me all wound up in the rope, so that I couldn't free myself until relieved by 'Jack,' a negro man who was near at hand."[3] Or, on another occasion, "Henry Coats was in the lead of the herd. Asa Dawdy and Otto Draub on the left point, while Negro 'Gabe' and I kept them from turning to the right."[4]

The third non-fiction cowboy book of the nineteenth century was *The Story of the Cowboy* by Emerson Hough. This book describes a symbolic cowboy which would include them all:

> Rude and unlettered though he be, and treating his companions with a rough and ready familiarity, the cowpuncher yet accords to his neighbour the right to live the life and go the gait which seems most pleasing to himself. One does not intrude upon the rights of others in the cow country, and he looks to it very promptly that no one shall

[2] Walter Prescott Webb, *The Great Plains* (New York: Ginn and Company, 1931), p. 467.

[3] Charles A. Siringo, *A Texas Cowboy* (New York: New American Library, 1951), p. 43.

[4] Siringo, *A Texas Cowboy*, p. 64.

intrude upon his. In the cow towns or at the cow camps one never hears the abusiveness or rude speech common in the older settlements.[5]

With this attitude Hough did not need to identify the Negro cowboy more than to say, when speaking of breaking horses, "Some of the early Southern busters were negroes, and very good breakers they made."[6]

Although there is, in twentieth-century publications, ample evidence of the Negro cowboy in the biographical, autobiographical, and historical accounts of the West, there has been no attempt on my part, of course, to search these books merely to find his presence. But a few examples are necessary to indicate the manner in which the Negro was treated or referred to in these accounts. Also, it is not only possible but, of course, probable that the Negro was often included in a group of cowboys without being specifically identified. There was no particular reason why he should have been. In *The Cowboy*, Philip Rollins comments on the nationality of the cowboy.

> While the men of the Range were mainly English or Irish descent or birth, and had, in frequent instances, claim to early American ancestors of Scottish origin, the Southwest added to its quota of such bloods numerous men of Mexican extraction, and a more than occasional negro, with here and there men of strain partly Indian. The majority of all the men were American born.[7]

Although Rollins lists national and color types, his interest is in what makes up an American cowboy.

Charles Siringo's twentieth-century autobiography, *Riata and Spurs*, is a re-write of his earlier work with more literary pretensions. Yet he continues to write casually of the Negro cowboy and reports incidents not recorded in the first book. In referring to a time when he was riding herd with Negro cowboys, he tells how he was being dragged by a horse and Lige saved his life.[8] Again he wrote, "I hunted up Babe Fisher, a yellow negro whom I knew could be trusted, and who afterward became a noted outlaw...."[9] One of the episodes concerns a Negro cowboy in the rôle of a peace officer, losing his life in an attempt to bring in the notorious outlaw, John Wesley Harden.[10]

The Negro cowboy serving as a peace officer was not unusual. Frank Eaton, more colorfully known on the range as Pistol Pete, includes in his autobiography an incident in which a Negro marshal was successful.

[5] Emerson Hough, *The Story of the Cowboy* (New York and London: D. Appleton and Company, 1927), p. 203.
[6] Hough, p. 91.
[7] Philip Ashton Rollins, *The Cowboy* (New York: Charles Scribner's Sons, 1922), p. 22.
[8] Charles A. Siringo, *Riata and Spurs* (Boston and New York: Houghton Mifflin Company, 1931), p. 18.
[9] Siringo, *Riata and Spurs*, p. 6.
[10] Siringo, *Riata and Spurs*, p. 145.

We were just leaving the livery barn when I saw Charlie Pettit walking up to me. Charlie was a big Negro Deputy United States Marshal, from the Wichita Court.

"Frank," he said, "Ernest Lewis is up at the hotel and I have a warrant for him. He may have a gang up there. Come up and help me get him."

We started up to the hotel together. Lewis was sitting on the porch. He started like he was going to make a gunplay, but I put my hand on my gun and shook my head at him and he stopped. He and I had played with guns and he knew I was the best shot.

"Sorry, Mr. Lewis," Pettit said, "but I have a warrant for you and it's a fugitive warrant."

By that he meant that Lewis was paid for if anything went wrong. He had committed a crime that was punishable by death. Pettit's orders were to bring him in dead or alive.[11]

Eaton was, of course, glorifying himself, but it was the Negro ex-cowboy who completed the assignment of taking in a white outlaw.

A book in which the Negro cowboy figures quite prominently is J. Frank Dobie's *A Vaquero of the Brush Country, Partly from the Reminiscences of John Young.* At the outset the word "cowboy" is defined, and the author seeks out its derivation. In Southwest Texas the cowboys were generally referred to as "vaqueros," a term originally applied only to Spanish or Mexican cowboys. "But from an early day," writes the author, "Texans, especially those near the border have used the word without reference to race." Thus in one outfit would be found Mexican, Negro, and white "vaqueros."[12] The Negroes in this book range from comic to heroic. When a Negro cowpuncher went on guard he was told to call the next watch by the stars. Not being able to read the stars properly, he did not know when to call his successor, so he rode herd all night.[13]

Living up to the requirements of the Western Code was naturally expected of the Negro cowboy, and this story illustrates that he did not shirk his duty.

Not alone was it his breed that made the American cowboy stick to herd and horse until only death could drag him loose; it was his occupation.

"We had a negro cowboy named George," says an old time Plains cowman, "who was not very well clad because he liked to pike at monte too well to buy clothes. We all had colds and coughs till it was like a bunch of Texas pot hounds baying a 'possum' when we tried to sleep. One bitter night I was near George on herd and tried

[11] Frank Eaton, *Pistol Pete* (Boston: Little, Brown, 1952), p. 267.

[12] J. Frank Dobie, *A Vaquero of the Brush Country, Partly from the Reminiscences of John Young* (Dallas: The Southwestern Press, 1929), p. 1.

[13] *Ibid.,* p. 97.

to get him to go to the chuck wagon and turn his horse loose, but
he was too game for that. His teeth were chattering as he said to me
'I can stand it if the rest of you all can.' Presently I saw him lean
over his saddle horn, coughing, and he looked like he was losing his
breath. By the time I got to him he was off his horse, as dead as a
mackerel and stiff as a poker. He had simply frozen to death sitting
on that horse. We placed his body in the chuck wagon on his bed and
drove to the Palo Duro and on the highest hill we could find we
planted the poor black boy, rolled in his blankets. The ground was
sandy; so we could dig a grave deep enough that the coyotes would
not claw into it." [14]

Perhaps it is not unusual that an old time cowboy should recall, for the purpose of illustrating the loyalty of the cowboy, an example which just happened
to be a Negro.

The inevitable cook must always figure in cowboy yarns. However, for the
moment, we are interested in the real kind, not the storybook kind. The
cooks were either white or colored, it did not matter which, and they were
ex-cowboys. When a cowboy was no longer able to do his share in riding
herd, for "physical injury, ordinarily the gift of bucking, and in the form of
hernia, allowed to the average man but seven years of active riding," [15] he
often preferred to become a cook rather than to leave the range. He was occasionally unhappy because his life became less active, but his position as a
cook was not necessarily a degraded one, nor was he helpless. One of the tales
in *The Trail Drivers of Texas* is the story of a shooting match between a
white cowboy and the Negro cook—a two-year-old heifer against five dollars.
The cook was hard to beat and the cowboy won only on a fluke. [16] Reminiscing
with John Young provides another sketch:

The one man in our outfit that I recall most often and most vividly
was Sam, the negro cook. He always had a cheerful word or cheerful
song, and he seemed to have an affection for every one of us. When
we camped in the vicinity of brush every cowboy coming in would
rope a chunk of wood and snake it up to the chuck wagon. That wood
always made Sam grinning happy whether he needed it or not. He
was about thirty-five years old, as black as a crow, and weighed
around 225 pounds. As he had been raised on a ranch, he was a
good rider, and frequently one of the boys would get him to "top
off" (ride first) a bad horse. [17]

In those days Sam could hold his own among the men of the West.

It would be unforgivable to discuss the cattle range and the cowboy with-

[14] *Ibid.*, p. 100.
[15] Rollins, *The Cowboy*, p. 305.
[16] J. Marvin Hunter, ed., *The Trail Drivers of Texas* (Nashville: Cokesbury Press,
1925), pp. 484–88.
[17] Dobie, *A Vaquero of the Brush Country, Partly from the Reminiscences of John
Young*, p. 137.

out including at least one stampede. The following, from the "Recollections" of Charles Goodnight—one of the most famous of the rangemen of the Southwest—has a Negro cowboy and also a touch of frontier humor. Charlie Goodnight and his cowboys were driving a herd through the Pecos country of New Mexico in 1867, where they had been constantly harassed by Indians who stampeded the cattle, shot one of the cowboys, and stole part of the heard. A severe lightning storm added to the difficulties of driving. The heard was in an extremely nervous condition as Goodnight rode along one side of it with "Bose Ikard, an ex-slave and one of the best night riders he ever had." [18]

"The cattle had been so shot to pieces," said Goodnight, "and so badly spoiled that they continued stampeding, and after we had passed through Buffalo Gap we had a run which I shall never forget. They had been quiet all night, and at daybreak I told Bose, who was on guard with me, to watch them and I would wake the cook. I reached camp and tied my horse to the wagon wheel, giving him some rope so he could get a little grass. Then I commenced to wake the men who were asleep around the wagon on the side next the herd. Something happened, in an instant the herd stampeded right down on the camp, and it looked as though the men would be trampled to death. There certainly was some scrambling, as most of them had not got out of bed.

"I jerked a blanket off one of the beds, jumped in front of the cattle that were coming at full speed, and by waving the blanket and doing all the yelling I could, succeeded in splitting the herd around the wagon and beds. Charlie, powerful, fast, and the best-trained horse I ever rode in a stampede, was still tied to the wagon. He knew his business, of course, wanted to go, and got to the end of his rope, where the stampede knocked him down and many cattle went over him. I had my belt knife ready, and as the last steer cleared him, I cut the rope and he got up with me on him. I supposed he would be scared out of his wits and run from the cattle, but at once he struck out at full speed with the herd.

"By this time it was light enough to see. I kept going up the side of the cattle as fast as possible, wondering why Bose had not turned the front. When I had almost caught up with him, he looked back and saw me, and immediately his horse shot out like lightning and he threw the leaders around. After we got them circled I asked him why he had not turned them sooner.

" 'I'll tell you sah,' answered the cautious Bose. 'I wuzn't sartin who had dis herd 'till I saw you. I t'ought mabe de Indians had 'um.' " [19]

[18] J. Evetts Haley, *Charles Goodnight, Cowman and Plainsman* (Boston and New York: Houghton Mifflin Company, 1936), p. 166.

[19] *Ibid.*, pp. 166–67.

A Negro cowboy who commanded great respect both as a man and cow-puncher is in "Jack" Thorp's book of the old range days. "Cowmen from Toyah, Texas, to Las Vegas, New Mexico, knew Add, and most of them at different times had worked on round-ups with him." The L F D outfit's range boss, Add, was well liked and was "one of the best hands on the Pecos River." [20] Among other accomplishments, "Nig Add" was a "dictionary on earmarks an' brands," [21] which "in due time [caused him to become the] hero of a cowboy song...." [22] On one occasion, however, Add's popularity created a good deal of embarrassment. "Everybody knew him. When he got married each cow-man wanted to give him a present, no one knowing what the other man had sent him, 'as ranches were far apart.' He received nineteen stoves and ranges for wedding presents." [23]

Perhaps the most interesting of all books dealing with the Negro cowboy is an autobiography written by one. It is the story of Deadwood Dick of Deadwood, South Dakota fame, a name well known in Western lore; the full title reads *The Life and Adventures of Nat Love Better Known in the Cattle Country as "Deadwood Dick"—By Himself*. Born in 1854, sometime in June he thought, in Davidson County, Tennessee, Nat was the son of slave parents who had positions of responsibility on a plantation. From Nat Love one must expect some exaggeration, as one must expect it from every cowboy who wrote his autobiography, especially after he had left the range and had time to dream through his experiences, but in his "Preface" Love writes, "I have tried to record events simply as they are, without attempting to fill out a chapter at the cost of the truth." [24] As a boy he had had plenty of riding experience on the plantation, so with his freedom and a growth of fifteen years he decided to increase his opportunities by going West. Arriving in a Kansas cattle town, in 1869, Nat sought work from Duval, a Texas outfit which had just brought in a herd and was preparing to return to the home ranch. "There were several colored cowboys among them," according to Nat, "and good ones too." Before he could be hired he had to prove his ability, so the boss of the outfit had a colored cowboy named Bronko Jim get Nat the roughest horse they had, which he rode and earned the name "Red River Dick." [25]

With his first range outfit Nat Love began a successful and venturesome career. "By strict attention to business, born of a genuine love of the free and

[20] N. Howard Thorp, *Pardner of the Wind* (Caldwell: The Caxton Printers, 1945), p. 22.

[21] N. Howard Thorp, *Songs of the Cowboys* (Boston and New York: Houghton Mifflin Company, 1921), p. 166.

[22] Thorp, *Pardner of the Wind*, p. 22.

[23] Thorp, *Songs of the Cowboys*, p. 166. See also John A. Lomax, *Adventures of a Ballad Hunter* (New York: The Macmillan Company, 1947), p. 46. Mr. Lomax writes that on the big ranches he had trouble getting the cowboys to sing for him, but with "smaller groups on remote ranches I enjoyed better fortune. Two or three Negro cowboys sang lustily when I got them away from the crowd."

[24] Nat Love, *The Life and Adventures of Nat Love* (Los Angeles: Wayside Press, 1907), preface.

[25] *Ibid.*, p. 41.

wild life of the range, and absolute fearlessness, I became known throughout the country as a good all around cowboy and a splendid hand in a stampede." After three years with Duval, Nat signed on with the Pete Gallinger Company, "whose immense range was located on the Gila River in southern Arizona." There he stayed "for several years and soon became one of their most trusted men, taking an important part in all the big round-ups and cuttings throughout western Texas, Arizona and other states where the company had interests to be looked after."[26] And the Gallinger Company eventually made Nat their chief brand reader.

Love took part in all of the cowboys' activities, and his manner in relating these events is no different from that found in any other cowboy autobiography. He knew, for example, that the "test of a cowboy's worth is in his gameness and his nerve."[27] One of the favorite sports was roping and riding steers, which, thought Nat, "is done more for the sport's sake than anything else, and the love of showing off, a weakness of all cowboys more or less."[28] It was not uncommon for them to become involved in shooting trouble over brands, and death was frequently the result. On Christmas Day, 1872,

> I and a number of friends were in a place called Holbrook, Ariz. A dispute started over a saddle horse with the following result. Arizona Bob drew his forty-five Colt revolver, but before he had time to fire he was instantly killed by A. Jack. Then a general fight ensued in which five horses and three men were killed.[29]

After delivering a herd, at the end of a trail, Nat was always ready to "see the elephant" with the rest of the boys.

> Then we all headed for Dodge City to have a good time, and I assure you we had it. It was our intention and ambition to paint the town a deep red color and drink up all the bad whiskey in the city. Our nearly two months journey over the dusty plains and ranges had made us all inordinately thirsty and wild, and here is where we had our turn, accordingly we started out to do the town in true western style, in which we were perfectly successful until the town had done us, and we were dead broke.... While our money lasted we would certainly enjoy ourselves, in dancing, drinking and shooting up the town.[30]

Every old cowhand who has written about his days on the range has included at least one episode of this sort.

During a trip to old Mexico to pick up a herd, Love's outfit had an opportunity to meet Mexican cowboys. "These men were for the most part typ-

[26] *Ibid.*, p. 43.
[27] *Ibid.*, p. 50.
[28] *Ibid.*, p. 49.
[29] *Ibid.*, p. 51.
[30] *Ibid.*, pp. 54–55.

ical greasers, but they proved to us that they knew a thing or two about the cattle business, and all the things considered they were a jolly companionable sort of an oufit." [31] Along with the other cowboys of the time, Nat went through the usual adventures which appear to have happened to them all. Once, after he had put up a terrific fight, he was captured by Yellow Dog's tribe. They would normally have killed him, he thought, but they did not because there was colored blood in the tribe; "and as I was a colored man they wanted to keep me, as they thought I was too good a man to die." [32] With pride in his ability to more than hold his own among the cowboys, Nat swaggered a bit when he admitted to being "naturally tough," for he "carried the marks of fourteen bullet wounds." He confessed, also, that he had been a "dare devil" cowboy, "wild, reckless, free" and "afraid of nothing," but he did not want to leave an impression that he was a heartless killer.

It was not with any sense of pride or in bravado that I recount here the fate of the men who have fallen at my hand.

It is a terrible thing to kill a man no matter what the cause. But as I am writing a true history of my life, I cannot leave these facts out. But every man who died at my hands was either seeking my life or died in open warfare, when it was a case of killing or being killed. [33]

Like other cowboys writing "true life" stories, Nat also happened to meet the famous men of the plains, including Buffalo Bill, Billy the Kid, and Bat Masterson, the renowned marshal of Dodge City.

The high point, however, in the career of Nat Love came on July 4, 1876, in Deadwood, South Dakota. In the spring of that year the home ranch had received an order to drive three thousand head to a point near Deadwood. After the cattle had been delivered, the boys headed for town to celebrate. On the morning of the Fourth the gamblers and mining men of Deadwood collected a purse of $200 as first prize for a roping contest. There were about twelve contestants, "six of them being colored cowboys." Not only did Nat win, but he set a record. The morning event had been so successful that another purse was made up for a shooting contest in the afternoon. Again Nat won, but with the purse came the biggest prize of all: he was given the title of "Deadwood Dick," a distinction and honor which he was still proudly carrying when he wrote his book thirty years later. Love found freedom and happiness as a cowboy on the Western range, for he came into his own at a time and place where to be "all man" was the most important requisite of the West. As Nat expressed it, "What man with the fire of life and youth and health in his veins could not rejoice in such a life?" [34] Color was no barrier to fame for Nat Love.

At this point these autobiographical data raise a historical question in

[31] *Ibid.*, p. 31.
[32] *Ibid.*, p. 99.
[33] *Ibid.*, p. 105.
[34] *Ibid.*, p. 70.

Western literature: why did the fame achieved by the Negro cowboy not carry over into fiction? That the Negro cowboys were on the range in considerable numbers, and doing a creditable job, is, as has been pointed out, a historical fact. However, the day of the range cowboy was over before his fiction began. There is a difference of opinion as to which is the first Western story, but all students of the genre agree that it came between 1902 and Zane Grey's *Riders of the Purple Sage* in 1912.[35] And the comparatively short period of the range cowboy, approximately thirty-five years, had ended by 1900. We have no cowboy statistics, but the evidence indicates that the greatest percentage of Negro cowboys were on the Western plains, particularly in Texas, immediately after the Civil War, and that their number was dwindling rapidly by the end of the century. The Texas Rangers had been dissolved during the war, and in 1870 the governor of Texas set up the state police. Many Negroes were state police officers in a body which soon became so hated that it was considered a duty to shoot them on sight, for they were set up to enforce Reconstruction measures. The state police lasted for only three years, with the Rangers being reëstablished in 1874—excluding the Negro. The Negro began moving farther west, into New Mexico and Arizona, and on up into the northern range. Nat Love left Texas for Arizona in 1872. Gradually, as the century moved on, and the West became more populated, the Negro cowboy was forced into other occupations. In 1890 Deadwood Dick became a Pullman porter.

It is possible that the earliest writers of Western stories, during the first decade of this century, attributed the then existing conditions to an earlier period. These writers knew the West only after it had become populated, and they knew but little of those days when a cowboy was paid and valued for skill, not color.

It is quite obvious that the Romantic tradition in fiction laid its heavy hand on the Western story. In Southern fiction the Negro was cast as a "faithful retainer." In the Western story the same attitude prevailed, for the Negro could be a cook but he could not be a cowboy. The earliest Westerns unrealistically included women; the capable but pure, white kind, gracefully riding across the plains, into the sunset and the purple sage, admired from afar by all the cowboys, and won at the end of the hard riding, hard shooting heroes. In the words of a tall puncher called Jess Hill:

> Punchin' cows in these mountains ain't like it is in a book I read before I left the ranch, where all the cute waddie had ter do was ride slick fat horses, sleep on a geese-hair bed, set the boss' daughter en afterwards marry her, en she the prettiest girl in the West. I wonder why some sure-enough cowhand don't write the truth about it, heh?[36]

[35] Some candidates for the first Western story are Owen Wister, *The Virginian* (1902); Bertha M. Bower, *Chip of the Flying U* (1904); and Zane Grey, *Riders of the Purple Sage* (1912).
[36] Thorp, *Pardner of the Wind*, p. 13.

The fact that truth is stranger than fiction is one of the reasons why the Western romance prevailed in its present form. Fiction was what the East had been brought up on, a romantic concept of the West, and the Western writers saw no reason to write fact when fiction paid. The Negro cowboy did not fit into the romantic concept, and once the Western story stereotype was formed, during its first decade, it became impervious to change.

It is possible, however, that because so many of the Westerns were written by people who did not know the West, that these writers were unaware of the contribution of the Negro cowboy to the opening up of the range. When Owen Wister, Bertha Bower, and Zane Grey arrived in the West they saw only the saffron after-glow; had they been in time to witness the West's high noon, the Western story might never have come into existence. Fiction writers could see only a particular kind of man silhouetted against the skyline, and they chose to ignore the fact that "chaps" were worn by men of many nationalities and colors and that these were also included with the "men who made the spirit of the West, who forbade Mason and Dixon's line to extend, who harnessed democracy."[37] But now we know that pioneering, according to tradition, is an Anglo-Saxon job, and the Western myth is sometimes stronger and more important than reality.

In all fairness to those serious novelists of the West who write realistically, it should be said that when their setting and time includes him they can accord the Negro proper treatment. This is in the novel of the West—not the Western story—, and two of this type who come to mind are Walter Van Tilburg Clark and Tom Lea.[38] But where is the Negro cowboy in the Western story, in these thousands of books in this multi-million dollar business? The Negro was part of the spirit of the West, but he is not included in its fiction. The early West had a tradition which asked of a man only that he be capable and have courage and loyalty: where he came from and what he looked like was immaterial. That same West is represented in fiction by an Anglo-Saxon tradition which implies that all readers are white and that only a white cowboy can be a hero who is "fearless, fair and square."

[37] Rollins, *The Cowboy*, p. 383.
[38] Walter Van Tilburg Clark, *The Ox-Bow Incident* (New York: Random House, 1940). Tom Lea, *The Wonderful Country* (Boston: Little, Brown, 1952).

Vernon L. Wharton

THE RACE ISSUE IN THE OVERTHROW OF RECONSTRUCTION IN MISSISSIPPI

Under the provisions of the Reconstruction Act of 1867, Negroes in the southern states were enfranchised, and for the next several years they played an important political role. Whites resented the activities of Negroes in politics and accused Negro voters and officeholders of venality and ignorance. Using a variety of stratagems, the whites overturned the Reconstruction regimes and by 1877 eliminated Negroes from effective political participation in all of the southern states.

The late Vernon L. Wharton's discussion of the race issue in Reconstruction Mississippi is a superb case study of how Negroes actually functioned politically, and how the whites used intimidation to overthrow an essentially honest and effective government which was based largely on black votes.

O N the questionable theory that man is a rational being, students of the overthrow of the Republican governments in the South have usually placed heavy emphasis on the real or alleged inefficiency, dishonesty, and extravagance of those governments. It may be that such weaknesses have from time to time resulted in great popular upheavals or violent revolutions against parties in power, although much evidence to the contrary might be presented from present conditions and from history. Be that as it may, the multitude of stories about the degradation of the Reconstruction governments must not blind us to the significance in the situation of U. B. Phillips' "central theme of Southern history," the relations of the races.

For the study of the influence of race feeling in the undoing of Recon-

Vernon L. Wharton, "The Race Issue in the Overthrow of Reconstruction in Mississippi," *Phylon*, II (Fourth Quarter, 1941), pp. 362–370. Reprinted with permission of *Phylon*.

struction, the state of Mississippi offers a story that in some respects is unique. As Howard K. Beale,[1] and Francis B. Simkins,[2] and others have recently pointed out, we are not yet prepared to offer intelligent judgment as to the significance or quality of Reconstruction governments in any of the Southern states. Whatever this judgment may be for the rest of the South, that for Mississippi must take a peculiar form. In this state, Negroes made up a large majority of the electorate. Yet the effort to discover the accepted pattern of Negro domination, inefficiency, extravagance, and corruption meets with failure.

In the first place, Negroes, in spite of their majority, never endeavored to take control of any branch of the state government. To the convention of one hundred men who drew up the Reconstruction constitution they elected only sixteen of their number. Never at any time did they have a majority in either house of the state legislature. Never did they hold more than three of the seven major state offices. No Negro held any judicial office above that of justice of the peace. During the seven years of Republican power, a total of only twelve Negroes held the office of sheriff. Furthermore, although Negroes in some of the Delta counties outnumbered the whites more than ten to one, there were only a few instances in which Negroes held a majority of the offices in such counties, and even then the white officials seem to have had the dominant part in all decisions.

At no time was there any effort on the part of the Negroes to use their political power to gain special advantages for their race in state legislation. One of their first acts was to petition Congress to remove the political disabilities of the Southern whites. At no time was there any effort to set up schools in which Negro children would mingle with whites. Throughout the Republican regime, per capita appropriations to white schools were larger than those for Negroes.[3] Although Negro legislators succeeded in gaining the passage of a state civil rights act in 1873, cases in which Negroes strove to maintain their equal privileges under this act were rare indeed. Officials of public conveyances and places of entertainment simply disregarded the act,[4] and even a Negro congressman and the Negro Secretary of State accepted discrimination without protest.[5]

It is undoubtedly true that many of the Negroes who held local and county offices were ignorant and incompetent, although general contemporary charges of illiteracy are open to question, and in some cases can be shown to be

[1] Howard K. Beale, "On Rewriting Reconstruction History," *American Historical Review*, Vol. XLV, 1940, No. 4, pp. 807–833.

[2] Francis B. Simkins, "New Viewpoints of Southern Reconstruction," *Journal of Southern History*, Vol. V, 1939, No. 1, pp. 49–61.

[3] Stuart G. Noble, *Forty Years of the Public Schools in Mississippi*, New York, 1918, pp. 34, 39.

[4] John S. McNeily, "War and Reconstruction in Mississippi," *Publications of the Mississippi Historical Society*, Centenary Series, Vol. LI, pp. 414–415.

[5] Hinds County *Gazette*, January 25, 1871, February 11, 1874.

incorrect. Altogether, little difference can be discovered in the administration of counties that had Negro office-holders and those in which such officials were never elected.

Mississippi was also fortunate in the Negro membership of its legislatures. Much evidence might be introduced to uphold this declaration, but the testimony of Edward King, everywhere critical of Negro office-holders, will serve the purpose:

> I wish here to avow . . . that those of the Negroes in office, with whom I came in contact in Mississippi, impressed me much more powerfully as worthy, intelligent, and likely to progress, than many whom I saw elsewhere in the South. There are some who are exceedingly capable, and none of those immediately attached to the government at Jackson are incapable. In the Legislature there are now and then Negroes who are ignorant; but of late both branches have been freer of this curse than have those of Louisiana or South Carolina.[6]

In regard to the three powerful Negro leaders of the state, we may consider the testimony of Alexander K. McClure, who at the time of his visit to the South had abandoned the Republican Party to become a leader in the fight against Grant and his henchmen. After a study of the entire Southern situation, McClure wrote:

> Mississippi is exceptionable also in the reputable character of her most prominent colored leaders. In all the other Southern states the Negro leaders have rivaled the white adventurers in reckless and bewildering robbery, but they have not done so in Mississippi. Three black men here have reached national fame as leaders of their race, and they are all esteemed as honest men.[7]

In dispassionate moments, Democratic leaders and editors joined freely in this estimate of John R. Lynch, Blanche K. Bruce, and Hiram Revels.[8]

The generally accepted estimate of the Reconstruction governments also fails to hold in Mississippi in respect to governmental taxes, expenditures, and bonded debt. For various reasons, including the reconstruction of public property destroyed during the war, the new program of public education, and the loss of revenue from the head tax on slaves, all units of the state experienced a rise in the tax rate as compared to that before the war. But the significant fact is that there was no correlation at all between the rates of taxation in the various counties and the political or racial character of those counties. In 1874,

---

[6] Edward King, *The Great South*, Hartford, Connecticut, 1875, p. 314.

[7] Alexander K. McClure, *The South*, Philadelphia, 1886, p. 314.

[8] Franklin A. Montgomery, *Reminiscences of Mississippians in Peace and War*, Cincinnati, 1901, pp. 279, 292; Jackson *Clarion*, April 24, 1873, January 20, 1881; Hinds County *Gazette*, October 2, 1872.

at the height of Negro-Republican control, the average rate for the thirty-nine Democratic counties was 12 7/13 mills. That for the thirty-four Republican counties was 13 7/17, a difference of less than one mill.[9]

It is also true that the expenditures of the state government almost exactly doubled under the Republican regime as compared to the average of the years immediately preceding the war. But it must be noted that the average annual expenditure of the Republican regime was only $1,400,000, for a state with a population of more than 900,000. This represented a per capita cost of less than $1.50 a year, one of the very lowest in the Union, and one that was negligible according to modern standards. The greater part of the increase in state costs went for educational expenditures, the absorption of court costs formerly borne by the counties, and the establishment or expansion of state institutions for the care of defectives. Furthermore, these costs were met without any significant increase in the debt of the state. The actual debt at the end of the Republican regime was less than one million dollars.[10]

In their administration of state affairs, the Republicans left a remarkable record of honesty. The conclusion of J. W. Garner in his *Reconstruction in Mississippi* seems to be approximately correct:

> So far as the conduct of state officials who were entrusted with the custody of public funds is concerned, it may be said that there were no great embezzlements or other cases of misappropriation during the period of Republican rule.... The treasurer of the Natchez hospital seems to have been the only defaulting official during the administration of Governor Ames. He was a "carpet bagger," and the amount of the shortage was $7,251.81. The colored state librarian during Alcorn's administration was charged with stealing books from the library. The only large case of embezzlement during the post-bellum period was that of the Democratic treasurer in 1866. The amount of the shortage was $61,962.[11]

It may be added that the next embezzlement of any importance was that of the Democratic "redemption" treasurer who was elected in 1875. His shortage was $315,612.19.[12]

Altogether, as governments go, that supplied by the Negro and white Republicans in Mississippi between 1870 and 1876 was not a bad government, and, in several important respects, it possessed distinct superiority over those that preceded it and followed it. But one problem it could not solve. For various reasons, the Republican Party came to be branded as the party of Negroes, and it was apparent that Negroes were demanding more and more

[9] Jackson *Mississippi Weekly Pilot*, January 23, 1875; James W. Garner, *Reconstruction in Mississippi*, New York, 1901, p. 313.
[10] Mississippi House of Representatives *Journal*, 1876, p. 9; *Annual Report of the State Treasurer*, 1875, pp. 19–21.
[11] James W. Garner, *Reconstruction in Mississippi*, pp. 322–323.
[12] Hinds County *Gazette*, March 22, 1890.

recognition within the party. It was also true that many of the Negroes favored a further expansion of the functions of the state, entirely at the expense, according to the whites, of white tax-payers. The way was open for the formation of a "white-line" party, and this project was more significant than any other in the so-called "campaign of liberation" of 1875.

From the beginning of Reconstruction, there were in Mississippi, as in the other Southern states, a large number of white men who insisted on the necessity of accepting the results of the war and of complying with the requirements of the national government. In the forefront of this group were a number of ante-bellum leaders of the state, many of them old-line Whigs. With the apparent inevitability of Negro suffrage, they insisted that the only intelligent course was to grant to Negroes all rights extended to them by the Federal government, and to persuade them to follow native white leadership.

Two factors doomed these men to failure. The first was the determined opposition of a majority of the white population to their program. The other lay in the fact that almost none of these men could bring himself to deal with a Negro, however honest or able that Negro might be, as a political or social equal. The same attitude was held by such Northern leaders in the state as H. R. Pease, G. C. McKee, and R. C. Powers. By 1874, men of this class had to recognize either their failure to make Democrats of the Negroes, or the repudiation of their leadership in the Republican Party.

The majority of the white citizens, with a semi-religious belief that the Negro was an inferior who must be kept in subjection, had found themselves from the beginning unable to endorse the program of the conservatives. As early as December, 1869, the editor of the Columbus *Index* made a bid for the leadership of this group with the declaration: "We have given the Negro a fair trial. He has voted solidly against us, and we hoist, from this day, the white man's flag, and will never take it down so long as we have a voice in the government of this state." [13] The year 1870 saw the organization of a number of "White Men's Clubs," especially in the counties where there were large numbers of both races. These clubs were pledged to labor unceasingly for the restoration of white supremacy in Mississippi and in the nation. The Columbus *Democrat*, advocating the union of these groups in a revitalized Democratic Party, declared: "Its leading ideas are, that white men shall govern.... Nigger voting, holding office, and sitting in the jury box, are all wrong, and against the sentiment of the country." Here was sheer racial antagonism. There was no consideration of the undesirability of the participation of ignorant and poverty-stricken masses in the government of the state; the line was drawn on the basis of race, and it was chiefly toward the propagation of this feeling that the Democratic campaign of 1875 was directed.

With the rejection by the Republicans of the gubernatorial bid of the conservative J. L. Alcorn in 1873, and the significant increase in office holding by Negroes after that election, the movement gained new strength. Native and Northern whites whose leadership had been rejected joined in the demand for

[13] Hinds County *Gazette*, December 15, 1869, quoting the Columbus *Index*.

white supremacy. When Democrats gained control of the national House of Representatives in 1874, the powerful conservative leaders in Mississippi agreed at last to abandon their caution. The word went out that the time for revolution was at hand, and the efforts of such men as A. G. Brown, and L. Q. C. Lamar to temper the movement were of no avail.

Greater and greater numbers of the white Republicans in Mississippi were now deserting the party and joining the Democratic clubs. As Charles Nordhoff was told in the spring of 1875, the Democrats were making it "too damned hot for them to stay out." [14] At the same time, more and more conservative Democratic newspapers were openly accepting the "white-line" program. The transition could be seen clearly in most cases, and was especially noticeable in the powerful Hinds County *Gazette* and Jackson *Clarion*. Editors who had strongly condemned the Black Code and who had for several years written of Negroes in varying terms of sympathy, impatience, or friendly ridicule, and who had even praised them at times, during the summer of 1874 came to speak of them with open dislike, and finally to devote column after column to efforts to stir up hatred against them.

As time went on, the attack became ever more bitter, and by mid-summer practically every paper in the state except the official Republican organ was supporting a campaign based on the color line as the predominant issue.[15] The Forest *Register* carried at its masthead the slogan: "A white man in a white man's place. A black man in a black man's place. Each according to the eternal fitness of things." The Yazoo City *Banner* declared: "Mississippi is *a white mans country, and by the Eternal God we'll rule it.*" [16] The Handsboro *Democrat* called for "A white man's government, by white men, for the benefit of white men." [17] All these papers justified their stand in editorials declaring the depravity and innate bestiality of the Negro. These attacks reached a climax in one published by the Forest *Register*.

> A Negro preacher is an *error loci*. God Almighty, in farming out his privileges to mankind, drew a line as to qualifications.
>
> ...Does any sane man believe the Negro capable of comprehending the Ten Commandments? The miraculous conception and birth of our Saviour? The high moral precepts taught from the temple on the mount? Every effort to inculcate these great truths but tends to bestialize his nature, and by obfuscating his little brain unfits him for the duties assigned him as a hewer of wood and drawer of water.

[14] Charles Nordhoff, *The Cotton States*, p. 77.

[15] See files of Vicksburg *Herald*, Handsboro *Democrat*, Yazoo City *Banner*, Vicksburg *Monitor*, Okolona *Southern States*, Newton *Ledger*, Brandon *Republican*, Columbus *Index*, Columbus *Democrat*, Jackson *Clarion*, Hinds County *Gazette*, and Meridian *Gazette*.

[16] Jackson *Mississippi Weekly Pilot*, July 31, 1875, quoting the Yazoo City *Banner*.

[17] Jackson *Mississippi Weekly Pilot*, April 10, 1875, quoting the Handsboro *Democrat*.

The effort makes him a demon of wild, fanatical destruction, and consigns him to the fatal shot of the white man.[18]

Declarations by the rapidly dwindling group of conservative Democrats that the votes of the Negroes could be obtained by treating them fairly and reasoning with them met the scorn of the white-liners.[19] Furthermore, when Lamar succeeded in inserting in the Democratic-Conservative platform a vague statement recognizing "the civil and political equality of man" and inviting the Negro to vote, white-liners were quick to deny allegiance.[20]

As the campaign progressed, charges of inefficiency, extravagance, and corruption were almost completely dropped by the Democrats. Later testimony by Democratic leaders before Congressional investigating committees has led historians to picture these considerations as the real issues of the campaign, but the picture is not a true one. More accurate was the statement given by W. A. Montgomery, leader of the Democratic military forces in the central portion of the state. In his testimony, Montgomery declared: ". . . [The] only issue in the election was whether the whites or the blacks should predominate; there was no other politics that I could see in it. Men that had been Republicans all their lives just laid aside republicanism and said that they had to go into the ranks then." [21] In the words of J. S. McNeily, chief contemporary Democratic historian of the state: "It was a part of the creed of a desperate condition, one easily understood, that any white man, however odious, was preferable . . . to any Negro however unobjectionable individually." [22]

In a state where a frontier code still held much influence, it was inevitable that a campaign appealing to prejudice and hatred should result in much violence, and, in the end, it was violence that carried the campaign for the Democrats. In this violence thousands of young men and boys of all classes, a large part of the farm element, and many local political leaders took active part. By September, the Hinds County *Gazette* was able to announce: "The people of this State are now fully armed, equipped, and drilled. . . ." [23]

With powerful military forces at its command, the white Democracy was ready for its campaign against Negroes who were timorous, unarmed, and largely unorganized. As the campaign of intimidation went on, Negro Republicans were ostentatiously enrolled in "dead books." [24] Negro political leaders were warned that another speech would mean death.[25] Republican

[18] Forest *Register*, September 15, 1875.
[19] James B. Ranck, *Albert Gallatin Brown*, p. 275; Jackson *Mississippi Weekly Pilot*, May 29, 1875, quoting the Vicksburg *Herald*.
[20] Columbus *Democrat*, August 21, 1875.
[21] Testimony, *Senate Reports*, 44th Congress, 1st session, No. 527, p. 542.
[22] J. S. McNeily, "Climax and Collapse of Reconstruction in Mississippi," *Publications of the Mississippi Historical Society*, XII, p. 405.
[23] Hinds County *Gazette*, September 29, 1875.
[24] W. Calvin Wells, "Reconstruction in Hinds County," *Publications of the Mississippi Historical Society*, IX, p. 102.
[25] John W. Kyle, "Reconstruction in Panola County," *Publications of the Mississippi Historical Society*, XIII, p. 71.

political meetings were broken up by violent attacks, or were prevented, by armed force.[26] Committees of "active young men" waited on Negroes who tried to prevent others of their race from deserting their party.[27] Negroes were prevented from registering by sham battles and the firing of pistols at registration points, or by armed pickets who met them on the roads.[28] Thickly populated Negro sections heard nightly the booming of Democratic cannon. Democrats adopted as a policy the practice of appearing in force at such Republican meetings as were held, and of demanding the privilege of presenting Democratic speakers, and of compelling Republican speakers to "tell the truth or quit the stand." [29]

By far the most effective weapon at the disposal of the whites, however, was the so-called "race riot." The first of these "riots" occurred in Meridian early in the period of Reconstruction. It resulted in the death of twenty or thirty Negroes, and in the complete breakdown of the Republican organization in the surrounding area. Democratic leaders of the time later declared that the lesson learned at Meridian made such riots an intentional and essential part of the campaign of 1875, and that they were the decisive factor.[30] It was immediately learned that the Negroes, timid and unresourceful after generations of servitude, could offer no effective resistance. During the year before the election, at least fifteen affairs of this type occurred, bringing death to three white Republicans, five Democrats, and at least 150 Negroes. After each incident of this type, white vigilante companies took command of the surrounding region, and in several cases systematically lynched Negro leaders in each district.[31] In each case the encounter marked the end of effective Republican activity over a large area.

The effect of the campaign of violence and intimidation on the Negroes is clearly revealed in their letters to Governor Adelbert Ames. These ranged from the perplexed inquiries of intelligent leaders to the frantic appeals of representatives of the ignorant and terrified majority. From bloody Yazoo

---

[26] Fred M. Witty, "Reconstruction in Carroll and Montgomery Counties," *Publications of the Mississippi Historical Society*, X, p. 123; Jackson *Mississippi Weekly Pilot*, October 2, 1875; *United States Senate Reports*, 44th Congress, 1st session, no. 527, pp. 196–197.

[27] Hinds County *Gazette*, July 28, August 18, September 23, 1875.

[28] Jackson *Mississippi Weekly Pilot*, October 9, 1875; *United States Senate Reports*, 44th Congress, 1st session, No. 527, p. 1718.

[29] Kyle, XIII, p. 72; Julia Kendel, "Reconstruction in Lafayette County," *Publications of the Mississippi Historical Society*, XIII, p. 244; Hinds County *Gazette*, August 4, 1875.

[30] Dunbar Rowland, *History of Mississippi* (Chicago, 1929), II, p. 172; William H. Hardy, "Recollections of Reconstruction in East and Southeast Mississippi," *Publications of the Mississippi Historical Society*, VII, pp. 205–206. For evidence that the same policy was followed in South Carolina, on the basis of information from Mississippi, see Francis B. Simkins and Robert H. Woody, *South Carolina During Reconstruction*, note p. 487, and p. 496.

[31] Hardy, VII, p. 206; Jackson *Mississippi Weekly Pilot*, March 20; September 4, 11, 25; October 2, 1875; Albert T. Morgan, *Yazoo* (Washington, 1884), pp. 465–484.

came the plea: "I beg you most fulley to send the United soldiers here; they have hung six more men since the hanging of Mr. Fawn; they won't let the Republican have no ticket.... Send help, help, troops...." [32] From Noxubee County there was the cry:

> Last Saturday, the 30th, the democrats was in Macon town in high rage, raring around and shooting of their cannons up and down the streets, and shooting all their pistols also ... and there was Richard Gray shot down walking on the pavements, shot by the democrats, and he was shot five times, four times after he fell, and he was shot because he was nominated for treasurer, and fothermore, because he made a speech and said he never did expect to vote a democratic ticket, and also advised the colored citizens to do the same. [33]

From Warren County there was letter after letter, including one that declared: "The rebles turbulent; are arming themselves here now to-day to go to Sartartia to murder more poor negroes. Gov. aint the no pertiction." [34]

There was no protection; frantic efforts of the Governor brought mocking laughter from the triumphant Democrats. [35] When President Grant refused aid, the election became a formality. In many of the black counties armed whites took charge of the polls. Yazoo County, center of an overwhelming Negro majority, reported only seven Republican votes. The Democratic Legislature quickly secured the resignation of the Republican Governor, Lieutenant-Governor, and Superintendent of Education, and in Mississippi the Reconstruction experiment was over.

From the story, obvious conclusions may be drawn. Race prejudice, with a few contributing factors, was sufficient to bring about violent overthrow of the Reconstruction government in Mississippi. Stories of dishonesty and inefficiency in other Southern states, and to a lesser extent in Mississippi, certainly have their place in the history of Reconstruction. It is an error, however, to exhibit them as prime causes for the Democratic counter-revolutions, the establishment of Jim Crow laws, and the legal and extra-legal denial of rights of citizenship to Negroes. This conclusion is not a happy one. Righteous wrath aroused by the abuse of public trust may be assuaged, but race hatred, in any time or any land, is a mysterious force, easily stirred to greater intensity. It stands as perhaps the greatest problem that can be offered to the student of social science.

[32] *Senate Reports*, 44th Congress, 1st session, "Documentary Evidence," p. 9.
[33] *Ibid.*, p. 73.
[34] *Ibid.*, p. 89.
[35] Jackson *Mississippi Weekly Pilot*, September 11, 1875, quoting the Jackson *Clarion*.

August Meier

August Meier is University Professor of History and Senior Research Fellow, Center for Urban Regionalism, at Kent State University. He is the author of *Negro Thought in America, 1880–1915*. Professor Meier is the General Editor of Atheneum's paperback reprints on American Negro Life as well as a forthcoming series of original studies of the Negro in America.

Elliott Rudwick

Elliott Rudwick, Professor of Sociology and Senior Research Fellow, Center for Urban Regionalism, at Kent State University, has written *W. E. B. Du Bois: Propagandist for the Negro Protest*, currently reprinted by Atheneum Paperbacks. He will be co-author, with August Meier, of a history of core, to be published by Atheneum.

PART FIVE

THE FOUNDATIONS OF THE TWENTIETH-CENTURY BLACK COMMUNITY

John Hope Franklin

HISTORY OF RACIAL SEGREGATION
IN THE UNITED STATES

After Reconstruction the status of southern Negroes steadily de-
teriorated. The race system which southern whites substituted for
slavery encompassed four major methods of social control: disfran-
chisement, economic subordination, mob violence, and segregation.

Segregation, as John Hope Franklin points out, was not an
entirely new phenomenon in the post-Reconstruction years. Yet, as
he also says, the statutory regulations described in his article—
requiring segregation in nearly every phase of southern life—were
products of the late nineteenth and early twentieth centuries.

THE enactment of state segregation statutes is a relatively recent phenomenon in the history of race relations in the United States. Of course there
had been numerous segregation practices and some segregation statutes for
many years, even before the nineteenth century. But it was not until the final
quarter of the nineteenth century that states began to evolve a systematic
program of legally separating whites and Negroes in every possible area of
activity. And it was not until the twentieth century that these laws became a
major apparatus for keeping the Negro "in his place." They were both comprehensive and generally acceptable, because they received their inspiration
from a persistent and tenacious assumption of the innate inferiority of the
Negro and because they had their roots deep in the ante-bellum period.[1]

John Hope Franklin, "History of Racial Segregation in the United States," in Ira
DeA. Reid, editor, *Racial Desegregation and Integration* [Annals of the American
Academy of Political and Social Science, XXXIV (March, 1956)], pp. 1–9. Reprinted
with permission of publisher and author.
[1] For an illuminating discussion of the assumptions of the inferiority of the Negro
see Guion Griffis Johnson, "The Ideology of White Supremacy, 1876–1910," in
Fletcher M. Green (Ed.), *Essays in Southern History Presented to Joseph Grégoire
deRoulhac Hamilton* (Chapel Hill: University of North Carolina Press, 1949), pp.
124–56.

LEGACY OF SLAVE REGIME

For centuries many Northerners and Southerners subscribed to the view that Negroes were of a permanently inferior type. As slavery came to be concentrated in the Southern states and as that section became conspicuous by the tenacity with which it held on to slavery, it built its defenses of the institution along lines of the inferiority of the Negro. A whole body of thought was set forth to demonstrate that "the faculties of the Negro, as compared with those of the Saxon, qualified him for a state of servitude and made him unfit for the enjoyment of freedom." [2] Slavery was, therefore, the natural lot of the Negro; and any efforts to elevate him to the status of freedom and equality were manifestly in opposition to the laws of nature and of God.

The slaveholder's task of keeping the Negro slave in his place was complicated by the presence of several hundred thousand Negroes who were not slaves, although they can hardly be described as wholly free. So that they would not constitute a threat to the slave regime, free Negroes were denied the full rights and privileges of citizens. They enjoyed no equality in the courts, their right to assemble was denied, their movements were circumscribed, and education was withheld. Their miserable plight caused them to be unfavorably compared with slaves and confirmed the views of many that Negroes could not profit by freedom. They were regarded as the "very drones and pests of society," pariahs of the land, and an incubus on the body politic.

Outside the South free Negroes fared only slightly better. White Christians began to segregate them in the churches in the first decade of the national period, and Negroes in Philadelphia and New York City withdrew rather than accept this humiliation. As early as 1787 a white philanthropic organization opened a separate school for Negroes in New York City. In 1820 the city of Boston established a Negro elementary school. Separate schools became the practice throughout the North. When Charles Sumner challenged the constitutionality of segregated schools in Massachusetts in 1849, his position was bitterly opposed; and it was not until 1855 that the legislature of that state abolished them. Meanwhile numerous acts of violence in urban communities underscored Northern hostility to free Negroes. Between 1830 and 1840 anti-Negro riots occurred in Utica, Palmyra, New York City, and Philadelphia.

These ante-bellum experiences with free Negroes proved invaluable in the period following the close of the Civil War. In 1865 white Southerners were not "caught short" in facing the problem of the freedmen. From their point of view the former slaves simply augmented the group of free Negroes that they already regarded as "the most ignorant . . . vicious, impoverished, and de-

---

[2] William S. Jenkins, *Pro-Slavery Thought in the Old South* (Chapel Hill: University of North Carolina Press, 1935), p. 243. See also Albert T. Bledsoe, "Liberty and Slavery, or Slavery in the Light of Moral and Political Philosophy," and Samuel C. Cartwright, "Slavery in the Light of Ethnology," in E. N. Elliott, *Cotton Is King, and Pro-Slavery Arguments* (Augusta, Ga.: Pritchard, Abbott and Loomis, 1860), pp. 271–458, 691–728.

graded population of this country." [3] Thus, the whites merely applied to the former slaves the principles and practices that had guided them in their relations with ante-bellum free Negroes. The latter had subsisted somewhere in the hazy zone between slavery and freedom. To concede the freedmen this "place" was regarded by white Southerners as generous, the Emancipation Proclamation and the Reconstruction amendments to the contrary notwithstanding.

NEW LAWS, OLD RELATIONSHIPS

When the economic and social structure of the Old South toppled at the end of the Civil War, the ex-Confederates immediately began to erect a new structure based on the old philosophy. As a distinguished Southern writer put it not many years ago, "If the war had smashed the Southern world, it had left the Southern mind and will—the mind and will arising from, corresponding to, and requiring this world—entirely unshaken." [4] The smoke of battle had hardly cleared when the vanquished leaders, enjoying a remarkable amount of autonomy, began to fashion their new world upon the model of the old. With characteristic directness of action they went straight to the heart of their problem and worked out ways and means of holding on to the way of life that had meant so much to them.

As the ex-Confederates proceeded to restore order in their war-torn communities, they took little cognizance of the implications of the Emancipation Proclamation and the proposed Thirteenth Amendment. The major assumptions of the slave regime, the cornerstone of which was the permanent inferiority of the Negro, were still so powerful as to be controlling in most matters involving Negroes. While making some concessions, such as the competency of Negroes to testify in the courts, they nullified almost every semblance of freedom with numerous proscriptive laws. Mississippi legislators passed laws forbidding Negroes to rent or lease lands except in incorporated towns. They also enacted a law requiring every Negro, after January 1, 1866, to carry on his person written evidence that he had a home and an occupation. Louisiana forbade Negroes to move about in certain parishes or to be out at night without special permits. North Carolina extended to the freedmen the same privileges, burdens, and disabilities that had previously applied to free persons of color.

That the races should be kept apart, except where the whites were clearly in a superior role, was an important feature of most codes. Louisiana required that every Negro be in the regular service of some white person who was held responsible for his conduct. Mississippi forbade employees of railroads to permit Negroes to ride in first-class cars with white persons, except in the case of Negroes or mulattoes, "traveling with their mistress, in the capacity of maids." Many states provided that if Negro offenders could not pay their fines they

[3] From a statement by Howell Cobb, quoted in Jenkins, op. cit. (note 2 supra), p. 246.
[4] W. J. Cash, The Mind of the South (New York: Alfred A. Knopf, 1941), p. 103.

were to be hired out to "any white person" who would pay the fines and costs and take the convicts for the shortest period of time.

Negroes were not indifferent to the process by which their former masters and their associates were nullifying the gains of the war. While they displayed no spirit of vindictiveness against those who had held them in slavery, they manifested a firm determination to secure the rights to which they, as free men, were entitled.[5] The better educated and the more articulate among them assumed the leadership in expressing apprehension regarding the developments that were pushing them back toward slavery. They were especially concerned about the numerous acts of violence perpetrated against the freedmen, the burning of their schools and churches, and the economic proscriptions to which they were subjected. In Harrisburg, Pittsburgh, Indianapolis, and Cleveland they met in conventions and solicited the support of their Northern fellows in the effort to attain first-class citizenship. In Alexandria, Norfolk, Raleigh, Charleston, and other Southern communities they met, exchanged views, and addressed appeals to Southerners, Northerners, and federal officials. These supplications fell on deaf ears in the South, but they contributed to the increasing awareness elsewhere that the victory at Appomattox was empty.

FEDERAL INTERVENTION

The ex-Confederates looked upon the lenient Reconstruction policies of Lincoln and Johnson, which gave them virtual autonomy in every phase of life, as a normal concession to a section which was right on all the basic points in the dispute that led to the war. In the North, however, many people viewed the policy of leniency with skepticism from the outset; and congressional leaders made no secret of the fact that they regarded the resultant Presidential actions as unwise and improper, if not actually illegal. The first significant assertion of their own prerogatives was the passage of the Freedmen's Bureau Bill in March 1865, which called for an extensive program of relief and rehabilitation in the South.

The Bureau's establishment of schools for the former slaves and its attempt to protect them in their relations with white employers were especially obnoxious to the white Southerners. They were loud in their condemnation of both these features of the Bureau's program, calling them incendiary, radical, and political. They realized all too well the adverse effect that a successful prosecution of the program would have on the continued subordination of Negroes. The attempts of whites to drive out teachers of Negroes and to assert their authority over their employees were well calculated to subvert the program of complete emancipation and to preserve the old relationships between Negroes and whites.

---

[5] On the point of the absence of vindictiveness among Negroes see Francis B. Simkins, "New Viewpoints of Southern Reconstruction," *Journal of Southern History*, Vol. 5 (February 1939), pp. 49–61.

The findings of the Joint Committee on Reconstruction, established by Congress in 1865, convinced a majority of congressional members that federal intervention was necessary to salvage the victory over the South. The committee was of the opinion that there was in the South "no general disposition to place the colored race ... upon terms even of civil equality" and that no semblance of order could be maintained without the interposition of federal authority.[6] In accordance with the recommendation of the Joint Committee, Congress proceeded to enact a civil rights measure, to submit the Fourteenth Amendment to the states, and to pass a series of laws placing the reconstruction of the former Confederate states under congressional control.

Civil Rights Act of 1866

The Civil Rights Act that became law on April 9, 1866, defined citizenship so as to include Negroes. Senator Lyman Trumbull of Illinois said that the purpose of the bill was to destroy the discrimination against the Negro in the laws of Southern states and to make effective the Thirteenth Amendment.[7] White Southerners were, of course, outraged that Congress should undertake to guarantee the equality of Negroes, especially since the law had been enacted in the absence of representatives from the former Confederate states. As a matter of fact, fear that at some later date a majority of Congress or a federal court would strike down the Civil Rights Act was an important motivation for writing the provisions of the act into the Fourteenth Amendment.[8]

Fourteenth Amendment

During the debates on the resolution that was to become the Fourteenth Amendment the question arose as to whether the proposed amendment protected Negroes against discrimination and segregation. There was no agreement, but proponents of the amendment were optimistic regarding its effect. In supporting the amendment, Senator Jacob M. Howard of Michigan said that the equal protection clause "abolishes all class legislation in the states and does away with the injustice of subjecting one caste of persons to a code not applicable to another." Representative John Bingham of Ohio declared that the amendment would protect "by national law the privileges and immunities of all the citizens of the Republic and the inborn rights of every person within its jurisdiction whenever the same shall be abridged or denied by the unconstitutional acts of any state." [9]

---

[6] *Report of the Joint Committee on Reconstruction at the First Session Thirty-ninth Congress* (Washington: Government Printing Office, 1866), p. xvii.

[7] Horace Edgar Flack, *The Adoption of the Fourteenth Amendment* (Baltimore, Md.: The Johns Hopkins Press, 1908), p. 21.

[8] *Ibid.*, pp. 75–87, and Benjamin B. Kendrick, *The Journal of the Joint Committee of Fifteen on Reconstruction* (New York: Columbia University Press, 1914), pp. 267–69.

[9] *Congressional Globe*, Thirty-ninth Congress, First Session (Washington: F. and J. Rives, 1866), pp. 2766, 2459.

Southern resistance

Neither the Fourteenth Amendment nor the radical legislation embodied in congressional Reconstruction was sufficient to protect the Negro in his political and civil rights. Southern resistance was stiff and effective, while efforts at enforcement left much to be desired. Once they recovered from the initial staggering blow of Radical Reconstruction legislation the ex-Confederates grimly went about the task of nullifying it in every possible way. By violence, intimidation, and ingenious schemes of economic pressure, by increased participation in political affairs, they began to "redeem" their state governments. Neither the Fifteenth Amendment nor the Ku Klux Klan Acts could stem the tide. In one state after another, between 1870 and 1877, they were successful; and as they took over the Southern state governments, they began to enact laws to separate Negroes and whites.

Civil Rights Act of 1875

Congress, against the bitter opposition of the ex-Confederates who were taking over the seats the Radicals had occupied, made one final effort to prevent the destruction of the rights of Negroes. Between 1871 and 1875 it devoted much attention to various proposals for a comprehensive national civil rights bill. While the act that was passed in 1875 omitted the provision of earlier drafts requiring the admission of persons regardless of race to all public schools, it declared that all persons, regardless of race or color, should be entitled to the full and equal enjoyment of the accommodations, advantages, facilities, and privileges of inns, public conveyances, theaters, and other places of public amusement. In its scope and in its provisions for enforcement it far surpassed anything that had ever been done in the area of protecting the civil rights of Negroes.

Although the Southern whites viewed the Act of 1875 with utter contempt and violated it with impunity, they were not entirely comfortable so long as it was on the statute books. They found it impossible, therefore, to restrain their elation when the Supreme Court declared the act unconstitutional in 1883. When the decision was announced during a performance at the Atlanta Opera House, the audience broke into "such a thunder of applause . . . as was never before heard within the walls of the opera house." [10] An Arkansas newspaper expressed hearty agreement with the majority of the Court when it said, "Society is a law unto itself, which in matters in their nature overrides the statutes. Against its decrees the written law is powerless." [11]

SEGREGATION — THE FAVORABLE CLIMATE

Before the momentous decision in the Civil Rights Cases in 1883 segregation by statutes was confined to a relatively few but highly important areas.

[10] Atlanta *Constitution*, October 16, 1883.
[11] Little Rock *Daily Arkansas Gazette*, October 19, 1883.

In many states, for example, the laws against intermarriage preceded the Civil War by many years.[12] Although they were omitted from some state codes during Reconstruction, there was no wholesale repeal of them, and they remained in effect in many parts of the North as well as in the South.[13] The practice of maintaining separate schools for white and Negro children was well established in the North before the Civil War; and in the South if ex-Confederates provided schools for Negro children at all they were of course separate. Although the Radicals made some attempts to break down segregated schools during their brief period of control, they met with little success.[14] In the military services Negroes had almost always been segregated, and the Civil War did much to strengthen the practice.

The decision in the Civil Rights Cases was an important stimulus to the enactment of segregation statutes. It gave the assurance the South wanted that the federal government would not intervene to protect the civil rights of Negroes. The decision coincided, moreover, with a series of political and intellectual developments that greatly accelerated the program of segregation. In the eighties several Southern governments were embarrassed by financial scandals, and some of them outstripped the Reconstruction governments in defalcations and pilfering.[15] Meanwhile, the agrarian unrest induced by widespread economic distress frightened the conservatives and forced them to adopt extreme measures in order to regain the leadership which in some states they had temporarily lost to white and Negro Populists. Distressed by the possibility of a strong new party composed of white and Negro farmers and workers, they dominated the Negro vote where they could and expressed grave fears of "Negro domination" where they could not. Thus, the magical formula of white supremacy, "applied without stint and without any of the old reservations of paternalism, without deference to any lingering resistance of Northern liberalism, or any fear of further check from a defunct Southern Populism," gained ascendancy in the final decade of the nineteenth century.[16]

These were the years that witnessed the effective constitutional disfranchisement of Negroes by such devices as understanding clauses, grandfather clauses, and good conduct clauses. They also saw the launching of an intensive propaganda campaign of white supremacy, negrophobia, and race chauvinism, supported by a sensational and irresponsible press that carried lurid stories of

[12] Intermarriage was prohibited in Arkansas in 1838; in Louisiana in 1810. For a discussion of these statutes see Charles S. Mangum, *The Legal Status of the Negro* (Chapel Hill: University of North Carolina Press, 1940), pp. 236–73.

[13] Gilbert Thomas Stephenson, *Race Distinctions in American Law* (New York: D. Appleton and Company, 1910), pp. 78–101.

[14] Francis B. Simkins and Robert H. Woody, *South Carolina During Reconstruction* (Chapel Hill: University of North Carolina Press, 1932), pp. 439–42, and T. Harry Williams, "The Louisiana Unification Movement of 1873," *Journal of Southern History*, Vol. 11 (August 1945), p. 362.

[15] C. Vann Woodward, *Origins of the New South, 1877–1914* (Baton Rouge: Louisiana State University Press, 1951), pp. 67–70.

[16] C. Vann Woodward, *The Strange Career of Jim Crow* (New York: Oxford University Press, 1955), p. 65.

alleged Negro bestiality. New waves of violence broke out, with increased lynch-ings of Negroes, unspeakable atrocities against them, and race riots. Concur-rently, and at a "higher level," the literary and scientific leaders of the South wrote numerous tracts and books designed to "prove" the inhumanity of the Negro.[17] In this climate segregation took a giant step toward a fully de-veloped white supremacy apparatus.

SEGREGATION STATUTES — THE GIANT STEP

In the decade after the Civil War few laws were enacted demanding segregation. The first state segregation statutes were those of Mississippi and Florida in 1865, requiring segregation on public carriers. Texas followed in 1866, but five years later repealed the act. The Tennessee law of 1881, some-times referred to as the first Jim Crow law, directed railroad companies to provide separate cars or portions of cars for first-class Negro passengers, instead of relegating them to second-class accommodations as had been the custom. There were only two votes against the measure in the House and one in the Senate.

In the ensuing twenty years separation of Negroes and whites on public carriers became a favorite preoccupation of Southern legislators. By 1892 six other Southern states had joined the ranks—Texas, Louisiana, Alabama, Ar-kansas, Georgia, and Kentucky. In some states, however, opposition had been bitter. In Louisiana, for example, a Negro representative declared that the law would humiliate Negroes and "make them appear before the world as a treacherous and a dangerous class of people." [18] In Arkansas a Negro member of the House sought to ridicule the bill's supporters by insisting that if whites did not want to associate with Negroes there should be laws to divide the streets and sidewalks so that Negroes could go on one side and white people on the other. "He would like to see an end put to all intercourse between white and colored people by day, and especially by night." [19]

With the pattern firmly established in a number of Southern states and the pressure for segregation growing, the other Southern states followed before the end of the century. South Carolina passed its law segregating Negroes and whites on railroads in 1898; North Carolina, Virginia, and Maryland soon after. When Oklahoma entered the Union in 1907 segregation had already been provided for.

By this time laws were being extended to cover all activities related to transportation. In 1888 the railroad commission of Mississippi was authorized

[17] See the books by Thomas Dixon, notably *The Leopard's Spots: A Romance of the White Man's Burden—1865–1900* (New York: Doubleday, Page & Company, 1902); Charles Carroll, *"The Negro a Beast"; or, "In the Image of God"* ... (St. Louis, Mo.: American Book and Bible House, 1900); and Robert W. Shufeldt, *The Negro, A Menace to American Civilization* (Boston: R. G. Badger, 1907).

[18] *Louisiana House Journal, Second Session, 1890,* pp. 202–203.

[19] Little Rock *Arkansas Gazette,* February 14, 1891.

to designate separate waiting rooms for Negroes and whites. By 1893 the railroad companies, on their own initiative, were doing the same thing in South Carolina, and in 1906 the state required separation of the races in all station restaurants and eating houses. Ultimately, legislation covered steamboats, buses, and other forms of transportation.

Twentieth-century varieties

The first decade of the twentieth century witnessed the enactment of a wide variety of segregation statutes. Georgia had required separation of the races on streetcars as early as 1891. It was between 1901 and 1907, however, that North Carolina, Virginia, Louisiana, Arkansas, South Carolina, Tennessee, Mississippi, Maryland, Florida, and Oklahoma followed suit. Ordinances in Southern cities were even more specific than state laws. In 1906, for example, the city of Montgomery, Alabama, went so far as to insist that Negroes and whites use separate streetcars.

Wards of society—still separated

As the states assumed greater responsibility for the various wards of society they were careful to provide separate facilities for whites and Negroes. In 1875 Alabama made it unlawful for any jailer or sheriff to imprison white and Negro prisoners before conviction in the same apartments of the jail, if there were sufficient apartments, and ten years later prohibited the chaining of white and Negro convicts together or housing them together. In 1903 Arkansas directed that in the state penitentiary and in county jails, stockades, convict camps, and all other places where prisoners were confined, separate apartments should be provided and maintained for white and Negro prisoners. Within the next ten years most of the other Southern states had similar legislation. During the same period segregation of white and Negro insane, feeble-minded, blind and deaf, paupers, tubercular patients, and juvenile delinquents was provided for.

No detail too small

In rounding out the system of legal segregation some states provided for the separation of whites and Negroes at work, at play, and at home. In 1915 South Carolina forbade textile factories to permit employees of different races to work together in the same room, or to use the same entrances, pay windows, exits, doorways, stairways, or windows at the same time, or the same lavatories, toilets, drinking-water buckets, pails, cups, dippers, or glasses at any time. In 1905 Georgia passed a law making illegal the use by Negroes and whites of the same park facilities; individuals were permitted to donate land for playground use only if they specified which race alone was to make use of it. Until 1940 Negroes and whites in Atlanta, Georgia, were not permitted to visit the municipal zoo at the same time. In 1929 Oklahoma authorized the Conservation Commission to segregate the races in the use of fishing, boating, and bathing facilities on lakes and streams under the supervision of the state. Arkansas enacted a law in 1935 requiring the separation of Negroes and whites at all race tracks and gaming establishments. Beginning in 1910 several cities, among them Baltimore, Atlanta, and Louisville, passed ordinances designating certain blocks, territories, and districts as Negro or white and forbidding members of one race to live in the area assigned to the other. Such zoning laws, however, were declared unconstitutional in 1917.

The supply of ideas for new ways to segregate whites and Negroes seemed inexhaustible. In 1915 Oklahoma authorized the Corporation Commission to order telephone companies to maintain separate booths for white and Negro patrons. North Carolina and Florida provided that textbooks used by the children of one race be kept separate from those used by children of the other race, despite the fact that both states have stringent rules covering fumigation of textbooks. In 1922 Mississippi forbade members of both races to ride in taxicabs at the same time unless the vehicle held more than seven passengers and was traveling from one city to another. New Orleans deemed it in the interest of the public welfare to enact an ordinance separating Negro and white prostitutes.

Two worlds—roads closed

The law had created two worlds, so separate that communication between them was almost impossible. Separation bred suspicion and hatred, fostered rumors and misunderstanding, and created conditions that made extremely difficult any steps toward its reduction. Legal segregation was so complete that a Southern white minister was moved to remark that it "made of our eating and drinking, our buying and selling, our labor and housing, our rents, our railroads, our orphanages and prisons, our recreations, our very institutions of religion, a problem of race as well as a problem of maintenance." [20]

EXTRALEGAL ASPECTS

Yet law was only one part of the mechanism keeping the races segregated. Numerous devices were employed to perpetuate segregation in housing, education, and places of public accommodation even in communities where civil rights statutes forbade such practices. Patriotic, labor, and business organizations kept alive the "Lost Cause" and all that it stood for, including the subordination of the Negro. Separate Bibles for oath taking in courts of law, separate doors for whites and Negroes, separate elevators and stairways, separate drinking fountains, and separate toilets existed even where the law did not require them. Finally, there was the individual assumption of responsibility for keeping Negroes in their place, such as the white man who placed a rod across the boat to segregate his Negro fishing companion while they ate lunch,

[20] Edgar Gardner Murphy, *The Basis of Ascendency* (New York: Longmans, Green & Company, 1909), p. 138.

and the archivist of a Southern state who cleared a room of manuscripts, ordered a special key, and assigned an attendant to serve a visiting Negro scholar who would otherwise have had to use the regular search room, from which he was not barred by law.[21]

By the middle of the twentieth century the pattern of segregation was as irregular as it was complex. Every conceivable form of segregation had been evolved, although one would have to visit many places to observe all the variations. The wall of segregation had become so formidable, so impenetrable, apparently, that the entire weight of the American tradition of equality and all the strength of the American constitutional system had to be brought to bear in order to make even the slightest crack in it.

[21] For numerous examples of the informal but tenacious practices of segregation see Charles S. Johnson, *Patterns of Negro Segregation* (New York: Harper and Brothers, 1943).

August Meier and Elliott Rudwick

A STRANGE CHAPTER IN THE
CAREER OF "JIM CROW" *

*In the preceding selection John Hope Franklin traces the broad out-
lines of the development of racial segregation. The final chapter in
the history of Jim Crow began a dozen years ago with the bus boycott
in Montgomery, Alabama, led by Martin Luther King. Yet the rise
and decline of segregation, and Negro protest against it, make a rich
and complex story—one that is full of surprises for recent scholars
doing research on the subject, and a source of spirited controversy
among them. The following selection written especially for this volume suggests a new twist in the history of the rise of Jim Crow,
and describes early streetcar boycotts antedating the Montgomery
protest by a half century and more.*

C. VANN WOODWARD, in his celebrated *Strange Career of Jim Crow*, argued that the system of segregation in the South was primarily a product of
intensified racial hostility exhibited by southern whites during the late nineteenth and early twentieth century. More recently Richard C. Wade, in *Slavery
in the Cities*, has maintained that when the slave system disintegrated in the
ante-bellum southern cities, Jim Crow customs and regulations grew up as an
alternative method of social control over the Negroes. Extending Wade's argument Joel Williamson, in *After Slavery: The Negro in South Carolina During
Reconstruction, 1861–1877*, adduces evidence that following the destruction of
slavery, southern whites attempted to expand the system of segregation. In the
recent, second revised edition of *Strange Career of Jim Crow*, Woodward recognizes some validity in the arguments of Wade and Williamson, but nevertheless holds quite closely to his original thesis.[1]

* We wish to express our appreciation to Professor Louis R. Harlan of the University of Maryland, for his critical reading of the original manuscript.
[1] C. Vann Woodward, *The Strange Career of Jim Crow* (New York, 1955);
Richard C. Wade, *Slavery in the Cities* (New York, 1964), pp. 266–70; Joel William-

It is our belief that the views of Woodward on the one hand, and Williamson and Wade, on the other, are both correct.

In the pages that follow we will examine the history of streetcar segregation in Savannah, Georgia, and of Negro opposition to this development, as a case study shedding light on the problem raised by the discrepancy between the analyses of these scholars. In doing so we shall touch upon two virtually unexplored aspects of the subject: 1) the activities of Negroes in fighting the rise of Jim Crow laws and customs; and 2) the possibility that segregation actually declined after being instituted in many places prior to and just after the Civil War. Our evidence suggests that because of Negro opposition segregation did indeed decline markedly for a period, at least in public transportation.

Horse cars first appeared in Savannah in January, 1869. The street railway company provided separate vehicles for Negroes, manned by Negro drivers and conductors.[2] The cars generally ran at the ratio of one Negro car to every three white ones.[3] Negro officeholders and politicians, especially those at the Custom House, led the challenge to this pattern of discrimination.

In May, 1870, James Habersham, secretary of a Radical Republican faction, and constable of Chatham County's fourth militia district,[4] was arrested and charged in mayor's court with disorderly conduct for refusing to leave a white streetcar when requested to do so. The mayor dismissed the case, but lectured the defendant for his "riotous" resistance to arrest.[5]

Two years later, acting on the information that Negroes intended to sue the streetcar company under the federal civil rights act of 1866, the company decided to permit Negroes to ride on the white cars, and on July 25, its managers so notified the operating employees.[6] Negroes began at once to ride the white cars. A few days later, however, on Saturday, July 27, a near-riot resulted from an incident in which a white man jostled a Negro woman in one of the "white" cars. On Sunday afternoon, Richard W. White, a clerk at the U.S. Custom House,[7] was ejected from a car. The following day, July 29, groups of white men riding the cars forced Negroes off. A parade of the all-Negro Lincoln Guards during the afternoon heightened the anxiety of the whites, and at night shooting broke out along the street railway. Eleven whites were listed as having been wounded, mostly by bullets, and about twenty Negroes were injured, the majority of them clubbed. Despite the talk that the

---

son, *After Slavery: The Negro in South Carolina During Reconstruction 1861–1877* (Chapel Hill, 1965), chap X; Woodward, *Strange Career of Jim Crow,* 2nd revised edition (New York, 1967).

[2] Savannah *Republican,* January 28, 1869; August 20, 21, 1872.

[3] *Ibid.,* August 3, 1872.

[4] *Ibid.,* June 30, May 7, 1870; January 6, 1871.

[5] *Ibid.,* May 7, 10, 1870. For information on the way in which the mayor arrived at his decision, see Edward C. Anderson Papers, "Diary," entries for May 6, 7, 8, 1870, in Southern Historical Collection, University of North Carolina. (Notes on the entries were kindly supplied by Professor Joel Williamson of the University of North Carolina.)

[6] *Ibid.,* August 3, 1872.

[7] *Haddock's Savannah Directory,* 1871 (Savannah, 1871).

"Ogeechee Coons" were massing for an armed assault against the whites, the disorders of the previous days were not repeated.[8] Instead the action moved to the court of U.S. Commissioner Henry C. Wayne.

Avery Smith, an inspector in the Custom House, preferred charges against three white passengers for having conspired to oppress him and others on July 29 by preventing them from riding the streetcars, in violation of federal civil rights legislation. Smith charged that the three defendants had ordered him out of the streetcar, and when he insisted on keeping his seat, had violently ejected him. Other Negro witnesses testified that they, too, had been thrown from the white streetcars. All, however, denied participating in any organized plan to test their right to sit in the white cars.[9]

Commissioner Wayne ruled against Avery Smith. Congress, he said, had not passed a law granting Negroes "a social privilege." The state law of 1870, he continued, compelled common carriers to provide "like and equal accommodations," but the Georgia code also allowed them "to make rules for the safety, comfort, and convenience" of the passengers. This clearly permitted the Savannah company to operate separate cars, which it had done until its "feeble course" in confronting the Negro "conspiracy" brought on the Negro "invasion" of the white streetcars. Wayne agreed the evidence showed that the defendants had ejected Smith, but he exonerated them, while excoriating Smith as the "disturber of the public tranquility." [10]

After this decision the street railway restored the separate cars. Two months later, however, on October 8, the company announced that the dual system would be discontinued because of the "heavy pecuniary loss" which it entailed.[11] What neither the press nor the company told the public, however, was that it had been compelled to reverse its policy again, because of a Negro boycott. Negroes knew and remembered the lesson, and applied it twice more in 1899 and 1906. When streetcar segregation was proposed in 1892, Sol Johnson, the editor of the Savannah *Tribune*, a Negro weekly, wrote: "That plan was tried in 1872 and a Negro was a curiosity in a street car. After trying the experiment for three [sic] months the Jim Crow cars were withdrawn because the Negroes absolutely refused to patronize them." [12]

During the 1890's there was only occasional agitation to establish segregated streetcars in Savannah,[13] even though the state law of 1891 provided for streetcar segregation "as much as practicable." [14] It was not until 1899, however, that segregation was again instituted, and then only on a suburban line. White complaints of overcrowding on the line which ran to the suburb

[8] Savannah *Republican*, July 28, 30, 31, 1872.
[9] *Ibid.*, August 1, 3, 1872.
[10] *Ibid.*, August 4, 1872.
[11] *Ibid.*, August 4, October 8, 1872; Savannah *Morning News*, August 5, October 7, 1872.
[12] Savannah *Tribune*, October 22, 1892; see also *ibid.*, September 16, 1899.
[13] E.g., *ibid.*, October 22, 1892.
[14] *Acts of Georgia*, 1891, pp. 57–58.

of Warsaw and to the summer resorts of Thunderbolt and the Isle of Hope, and charges that Negroes using the trolley cars were making Thunderbolt a "Negro resort," finally led the Warsaw city council to order the suburban street railway to obey the state law of 1891 and segregate passengers on this line.[15] The editor of the Savannah *Tribune* urged his readers to exhibit "the same pride of race and love of principle" that they had shown in 1872, and a boycott was soon underway. Two months later, the Warsaw city council, pressed by the streetcar company which had lost substantial revenues because of the boycott, rescinded the Jim Crow rule.[16]

Though other Georgia cities—Macon, Augusta, Atlanta—were segregating their streetcars by the turn of the century, an attempt to pass a similar ordinance in Savannah in 1902 was overwhelmingly defeated by "the conservative feeling of the leading white citizens" whose aid the Negroes had marshalled. The president of the Savannah Electric Company also opposed such an ordinance on the grounds that whites would not obey it because of the inconvenience; wherever it had been tried, he maintained, its results had been unsatisfactory. Yet four years later not only did the city council unanimously pass a streetcar segregation ordinance, but the officials of the transit company did a complete about face and asserted that the cars would be segregated regardless of what the city council did.[17]

The city's Negro elite, pained by the shift in white sentiment, formed a committee of the leading ministers, the physicians, and the race's most prominent businessmen, which fruitlessly appealed to the city council in an attempt to prevent passage of the ordinance.[18] After the law had passed they initiated a boycott of the trolley cars. Declared the editor of the *Tribune*: "Let us walk! walk! and save our nickels ... Do not trample on your pride by being 'jim crowed.' Walk!" [19]

And walk the people did. It was reported, for example, that the secretary to the mayor gave his Negro maid carfare to take two heavy suitcases from his home to city hall. After she belatedly arrived, soaked with perspiration, the official discovered she had walked to town because her minister had admonished his congregation to keep off the trolley cars. Others who were prosperous enough to own streetwagons drove themselves and their friends to town. The most common practice, however, was to use one of the many colored hackmen, who had reduced the fare for boycotters from 25 cents to 10 cents. Thus the Negro community displayed an unusual degree of unity that transcended class lines. The Savannah *Morning News* reported that few Negroes were on the

[15] Savannah *Tribune*, August 27, September 3, 1892, April 8, 1893; Savannah *Morning News*, September 10, 11, 1899; Augusta *Chronicle*, September 13, 1899.
[16] Savannah *Tribune*, September 16, 30, October 7, November 18, 25, December 2, 9, 1899.
[17] Savannah *Morning News*, July 10, 1902; September 13, August 28, 30, 31, 1906.
[18] Savannah *Tribune*, September 8, 1906; Savannah *Morning News*, September 11, 12, 13, 1906.
[19] Savannah *Tribune*, September 15, 1906.

trolleys—that car after car went by with the back seats vacant. Even after the city authorities cracked down on unlicensed hacks and took to harassing bona fide hackmen, the boycott proved remarkably effective.[20] By spring, however, it was clear that this time the boycott had failed, and the Negroes gradually returned to patronizing the lines, though as late as May, 1908, the most that the Savannah street railway could claim was that 80 percent of the colored people had returned to the cars.[21]

Scattered evidence indicates that Savannah's experience was not unique. Negro protests and demonstrations led to the elimination of streetcar segregation in New Orleans, Richmond, and Charleston in 1867, and in Louisville in 1870–1871.[22] Not until the wave of state and municipal streetcar segregation laws after 1900 did Jim Crow return to the transit lines of these cities (and in Louisville Negroes were able to stave off such an ordinance after a vigorous fight). In New Orleans and Richmond, as in Savannah, the new laws were met with sustained though unsuccessful boycotts.[23]

The experience of these southern cities supports the thesis, suggested by Professors Wade and Williamson, that around the middle of the nineteenth century, whites introduced streetcar segregation as a means of social control at a period when their efforts to keep Negroes in a subordinate position were threatened. The experience of these cities also supports Professor Woodward's view that the turn of the century witnessed a flood of Jim Crow laws and regulations that marked a drastic deterioration in the southern Negroes' status. As the Savannah Negroes recognized,[24] the white community was far more hostile than it had been earlier. For this reason Negro protests no longer proved effective. Between these two eras, southern white practices, at least in the cities under consideration, had been less rigid and less harsh toward the Negroes, and there had been acceptance of integrated streetcars. As Woodward points out, as late as 1898, some leading southern whites even thought the idea of segregated streetcars downright ridiculous.[25] Further research is needed on the history of streetcar and other forms of segregation. But the evidence

[20] Savannah *Morning News*, September 14, 15, 17, 18, 24, 1906. Local reporting of streetcar boycotts in Savannah and other cities was extremely uneven. Often local white newspapers completely ignored the boycotts in their own cities. The reporting of the Savannah boycott of 1906 was unusually extensive.

[21] Savannah *Morning News*, February 3, 1907; Savannah *Tribune*, March 23, April 20, June 2, 1907 and May 2, 1908.

[22] Woodward, *Strange Career of Jim Crow*, 2nd rev. ed., p. 27; Alrutheus A. Taylor, *The Negro in the Reconstruction of Virginia* (Washington, 1926), pp. 52, 214; Joel Williamson, *After Slavery*, pp. 281–83; Marjorie M. Norris, "An Early Instance of Non-Violence: The Louisville Demonstrations of 1870–1871," *Journal of Southern History*, XXXII (November, 1966), pp. 487–504.

[23] These and other streetcar boycotts are treated by the authors in "The Boycott Movement Against Jim Crow Streetcars in the South, 1900–1906," *Journal of American History*, LV (March, 1969).

[24] Savannah *Tribune*, September 1, 1906.

[25] Woodward, *Strange Career of Jim Crow*, 2nd rev. ed., pp. 67–68.

presented above suggests that perhaps Jim Crow, instead of having had a unilinear pattern of growth, may more appropriately be described as having had a cyclical development.[26]

If Savannah is representative, Jim Crow had indeed a strange career.

[26] This idea of a cyclical pattern is also implicit in Woodward's most recent version of his argument, and in his brief reference to the successful Negro protests against separate streetcars in southern cities during Reconstruction. (*Strange Career of Jim Crow*, 2nd. rev. ed., p. 27.)

Thomas J. Edwards

THE TENANT SYSTEM AND SOME CHANGES

SINCE EMANCIPATION

The origins and development of sharecropping, the labor system which evolved during and after Reconstruction as an alternative to slavery, have not yet been adequately studied by historians. The essay by Thomas J. Edwards, a supervisor of rural colored schools in Alabama early in the twentieth century, describes the broad variety of arrangements under which Negro farm tenants—both sharecroppers and renters—worked. Seldom have observers written with such authoritativeness of the detailed operations of the plantation system.

THE close of the Civil War marked a great change in the labor system upon the plantation. The Negroes who were held and considered as property of masters previous to emancipation were now free men, having as their principal asset good conditioned bodies. The matter of serious import which confronted these simple, but strong, people was the task of making a living in a country devastated by war. Former masters were confronted with problems equally as difficult as those confronting the former slaves. These masters had been deprived of what represented both labor and property; war had left them for the most part landowners, and nothing more. The task of starting a new life was equally difficult for both concerned—the landlord with land and accessories, the freed man with physical strength and a slave's experience. The first two or three years after the war, were, therefore, a period of readjustment between land and labor under new and trying conditions.

Immediately after the Civil War through the share-cropping, wage-earning and standing-wage system, labor gradually adjusted to the soil. According to the readiness with which landlords had or could secure means, all these three systems were more or less used at the same time. In many cases, as it is today,

Thomas J. Edwards, "The Tenant System and Some Changes Since Emancipation," in *The Negro's Progress in Fifty Years* [Annals of the American Academy of Political and Social Science, XLIX (September, 1913)], pp. 38–46. Reprinted with permission of the publisher.

the wage-earning and the share-cropping systems existed simultaneously on the same plantation, while on the smaller plantations "croppers" up with their crops would serve in the place of earners in assisting those behind with crops on the same plantation. When croppers served as wage hands their pay like other expenses was deducted from the croppers' share in the crops.

The share-cropping and the wage-earning systems are with us still, but the standing-wage system which was originated immediately after the Civil War is not now in vogue. The method of work got its name, the standing-wage system, because "hands" worked for a period of six months or a year, before a complete settlement was made. Rations were issued weekly or monthly. The wage paid standing-wage hands was $50, $75 and $100 a year. This system originated with the motive of holding labor to the soil until end of crop.

That which seems to be a modified form of the old standing-wage system is the part-standing-wage system which exists today in many black belt countries in the South. Under this system a hand receives a monthly wage, which is seldom less than $5 or over $7. In addition to the wages paid in money he is given three or four acres of land to cultivate for his own use as a further compensation for his service. In cultivating this plot of three or four acres the "hand" is given use of his employer's team and farming implements on Saturday when most of the work for himself is done. It is because the "hand" receives part of his wages in monthly cash payments and the remainder in a harvested crop that this system is called the part-standing-wage system. The system of work appeals more to the older people than the young, so it is reasonable to suppose that it too will shortly pass away. It is evident that the chief element in the part-standing-wage system is keeping uncertain labor connected principally as a wage-hand to a larger plantation system.

The four-day plan of cropping had even a shorter life than the standing-wage system. Under this system the "hand" worked four days for the landlord who in turn furnished him with land, stock, feed for stock and farming implements, with which to cultivate a farm for himself the remaining two days. This system was quite advantageous to the "hand" providing he had a family large enough to do hoe-work upon his own farm while he worked four days for the landlord. In this system a weekly ration was issued simply to the "hand" or "hands" who worked four days. In case there were other members of the family, other arrangements were made according to ability to give service upon the plantation or around the landlord's home. It is probable that the system died, because the landlord's profits were small and the "hand" crops were poor.

That which has been said of the standing and the part standing-wage systems and the four-day plan for cropping has been sufficient to throw some light on the attempt in early days succeeding Civil War toward adjusting labor and land. No system seems to have a more permanent effect than what is known today as the share-cropping system. For many years after the Civil War, work on shares had a very different meaning from that which it bears today. Crops were cultivated for the one-fifth, one-fourth, two-fifths and one-third. In most cases when the cropper worked for any fractional part below one-third he received a part ration. Dividing crops into smaller fractional parts than one-half was at that time considered very reasonable by those who had served years in bondage without pay and whose demands for education and better methods of living had no likeness in comparison to what they are today. It has been less than a decade since the wants of each individual farmer and his family have so increased and the competition between landlords in holding labor upon their plantation has grown so keen that the fractional part gradually increased, until now working on shares means generally all over the Southland that at harvesting time that crop will be halved between landlord and cropper.

The word "crops" as used in verbal or written contracts has particular reference to cotton and corn. Everything raised behind the mule, except that raised on the one acre allowed for the garden and house spot, is subject to division. According to the terms of the contract, the landlord furnishes the cropper the land on which the crops are cultivated, and farming implements, plows, scooters, sweeps, stock and feed for the stock; in return for which the landlord is to have one-half of the entire crop made by the cropper and his hands. In consideration "of the above" the share cropper agrees to furnish and feed at the command of the landlord, all labor necessary to cultivate and harvest the crop and take good care of all stock implements intrusted to his care. In the event of failing properly to cultivate the crops he authorizes the landlord to hire what labor he may deem necessary to work the crop, and to deduct the cost of this labor from the cropper's half of the crops.

The landlord permits the steady, careful and thoughtful cropper to use his mule and buggy on Sundays, and use the farming implements in the cultivation of his garden or very small plot of watermelons and sugar cane. When the main crops, cotton and corn, are not in need of work, the cropper has time to cultivate his garden, and to do odd jobs on his house, fences and stables if there are any. The landlord usually provides the cropper with the available vacant house of one, two, three or even four rooms as the case may be. The size of the house, and accommodations in barn and stable readily give immediate advantage to landlord, and cropper. It is not altogether true that the landlord keeps the stock and vehicles in his home lot. These are in most cases left to the care and keeping of the cropper if he be in possession of suitable stables and lots.

The amount of supervision a cropper receives from the landlord depends largely upon how successfully he keeps his crops (especially cotton) worked up. If he gets behind with his crops the landlord may compel every member of the cropper's family, and even secure members from other families upon the plantation, to clean out the crops. In case the landlord does secure others, outside of the cropper's family to assist with the crops, the landlord avails himself of the clause in the contract which permits him to hire the labor necessary to work the crops and to charge the cost of the labor to the cropper's half of the crop.

As a rule the share cropper makes more to the mule than other classes of farmers. The reasons are as follows: (1) He is given the best plot of land upon which to make his crops because the larger the crops the more satis-factory will be results for both landlord and cropper. (2) In most cases super-vision is very close, which is most natural since the share-cropping system involves so much capital and risk from the landlord. Here we find a condition not unlike that in every phase of occupation, an effort to get as large return as possible for capital invested.

Crops are usually divided in the presence of the landlord, during or im-mediately after harvesting time. The cropper gets as his share one-half of the lint cotton and cotton seed, one-half of the corn and corn-fodder, and one-half of the field peas. All products raised on the house-spot acre come to the cropper, undivided. Though the terms in the contract consider everything raised behind the mule subject to division, yet sugar cane, sweet potatoes and watermelons may not be divided providing the landlord furnished neither fertilizer nor seeds for planting.

Upon almost every plantation of considerable extent some women share-croppers are usually found. They are as a rule widows with children large enough to help out with the farm work. These croppers are most common in black-belt countries, where the large plantation systems prevail. For example, one of these widow share-croppers of Macon County, assisted by her two sons, one thirteen, and the other eighteen years old, during the bad cotton crop year of 1909, made thirteen bales to her one plow. Another whose husband died leaving a debt of $125, and three children to care for, worked on shares during the same bad year, made ten bales of cotton to her plow, paid her debts, her expenses of living while making the crop, including half of the cost of the fertilizer used upon her farm, and saved $150. The latter widow realizing the responsibility upon her of debt and care of children was advanced only $35 which was used in purchasing food. The success of these two widows does not indicate by any means that women share-croppers are always successful, but it does show that under this system, because of landlords' supervision, women may succeed as well as men, providing they can furnish the labor.

As a rule the contract which explains the terms by which crops are to be cultivated and divided makes no provision for the cropper's advances or food; nor any disposition of the commercial fertilizer of which the cropper pays for half out of his half of the crops when made and divided. Terms for advances as a rule are made outside of the crop-contract. Advances in money may be issued directly through a banker with orders from the landlord permitting the cropper to have certain amounts at stated times. Usually the landlord and the cropper agree upon a lump sum of $35, $50, $100 or $200. According to the cropper's needs, this money is issued in monthly installments of $8, $9, $10, $15, and $20. Of course the cropper does not receive the lump sum agreed upon at the time the food-contract is made for the following reasons: (1) the cropper might use his money unwisely and consequently be obliged to call upon the landlord to continue, or finish the crop; and (2) by holding it the landlord has money at his disposal for cultivating the crops if the head of the family becomes disabled, or does not stay to carry out his contract. Advances are often made through a merchant-landlord of a large plantation who may have a store of such necessities as will meet the demand of tenants upon the plantation. In case the landlord does not own a store, orders are given by the landlord to some merchant of a small town or village, or to the merchant-landlord near, permitting the cropper to have certain amounts of merchandise at stated times during farming season. In such a case the landlord is directly responsible to the merchant for the merchandise which the cropper receives. The interest charged on borrowed cash varies from 10 to 15 per cent, but in many cases has been known to be considerably more. Furthermore, the interest on merchandise has been known to double itself notwithstanding the fact that the cropper pays a yearly interest upon the lump sum agreed upon for a cropping season of six or seven months, he receives his allotments of cash or merchandise in monthly installments.

The cropper who for one reason or another becomes dissatisfied and desires to transfer his service and that of his family from one landlord to another, has been known to do so by getting the landlord he wishes to serve to pay to the one he previously served the amount of debt the cropper owes. In case the agreement is made the cropper comes under contract of a new master bringing an interest-bearing debt. The amount paid in transfering croppers has been known to range from $25 to $200.

The cropper apart from a plantation is, of course, free from close supervision. He is more aggressive and trustworthy than the plantation cropper described above, and, therefore, is left largely to contract his own affairs. He may have been in previous years a renter who, through some misfortune, such as losing a mule, prefers working on halves until he can get sufficiently strong to rent again. In case this type of cropper owns a mule, the landlord rents it, as a rule, not by paying cash money but by making some agreement with the cropper equivalent to what a season's rent for one mule would be. If the cropper has feed for his own mule an agreement between landlord and cropper is fixed in some way by the landlord making allowances in some side crop, such as watermelons, sweet potatoes or sugar cane. It is the type of cropper described above that is on the verge of becoming a renter in case his crop turns out to be good.

Regardless of the success croppers may make with their crops, while working on shares, there is a burning desire among them for less supervision and more freedom in managing their own affairs. The opportunity of becoming renters offers a means of satisfying such a desire, and very often a cropper remains upon the same plantation, occupies the same house and rents the same land, and quietly transfers from cropper to renter without the least difficulty.

It is reasonable that in early years succeeding the Civil War both sharecroppers and renters existed; but it is still more reasonable that renters were fewer in number, since renting required an accumulation of capital, such as, a mule, paid or partly paid for, some feed for the mule, wagon and farming implements. As the years passed croppers went into the renting class, first, because they desired the management of their business in full; and, secondly, because the landlords were just as willing to free themselves from the close oversight of the cropper's affairs as the cropper was to be free. We have no figures to indicate just how rapid the transition into the renting class was, until the decade embracing 1890 and 1900. In this connection figures of Macon County, Ala., will be used. According to the agricultural census of 1900, the only census in which white and colored renters and share-croppers were taken separately the number of colored renters in Macon County was 2,097. The number of colored share-croppers was 760. The preceding census (1890) shows white and colored renters taken together to be 1068, and white and colored share croppers together to be 1,113. In 1900 the colored renters had increased nearly half of both white and colored renters for 1890. The colored share croppers of 1900 had decreased over one-third of both white and colored croppers in the same time. The increase of colored renters in 1900 over white and colored renters in 1890 in this one county gives some idea of the rapid change into the renting class.

A quarter of a century ago, one kind of renter was commonly found upon large plantations where wage-hands and share-croppers were employed. He was subject to the same plantation management as other classes upon the plantation. He received the same supervision, plowed, cultivated, harvested, and received advances in the same manner as the share-cropper. When his crops were behind, the landlord employed hands, cleaned out the crop while the renter stood the expenses. The only difference between the renter and the share-cropper was that the renter crops were not divided; and to the renter belonged whatever remained after rent, expenses of farming implements, cleaning out the crops and living were deducted. Under the nominal rent system more renters came out behind than ahead in their crops. In many of the black belt counties of the South, where changes for good in the plantation system occur slowly, this type of renter is found today.

The renter of today is a more independent type. He is responsible to the landlord for the rent of the land only in case he secures "advances" from his landlord. In many cases he sub-rents portions of his rented land receiving an amount little more than sufficient to pay the landlord's rent. It is often the case that this type of renter owns from three to six mules, some or all of which are mortgaged and through this means of mortgaging his stock he receives advances.

It is the desire of landlords to rent their land without the risk of giving advances, or the care of close supervision. In other words, it is as much the desire, and as much to the advantage, of the landlord to get rent or interest on the money involved in land with least trouble, as it is the renter's desire to advance himself, and enjoy the privilege of managing his business affairs. The present trend of renting conditions—conditions which relieve the landlord of responsibilities and which put upon the renter more responsibilities—is in this direction.

Two decades ago the most common way the landlord or merchant secured himself against losses was by taking a lien on crops. The lien entitled the landlord to hold in possession all, or part of a renter's crop until all claims were paid. The lien was made not only upon growing crops, but often upon unplanted crops as well. If through the crop lien, the landlord's claim was not settled in one season it was continued into the next. The old crop lien system with all of its force and meaning has apparently changed in meaning and form in some indescribable ways and since the renter has gradually come into possession of personal property, money is secured for farming by making notes and mortgages upon that property. All these may have some features of the crop lien system, but do not have the name.

The managing ability of the average Negro renter is limited by the three-mule farm. His yield and profit per plow decrease as the number of his plows increases. For example, a farmer made twelve bales with one plow; with two plows he made seven bales, and with three plows he made five and one-half bales to the plow. This was barely enough to cover the expense of three plows. Thus this farmer increased his acreage and expense while his knowledge of business and improved methods of farming remained the same.

The rent claims are first settled, and in most cases paid in cotton. The rent paid for a farm of 25 or 30 acres ranges from 1½ to 2 bales of lint cotton. Paying rent in money is quite common in some sections. When money is paid as rent for a farm of one mule it ranges from $75 to $100. There are two advantages in the payment of rent in money: first, the landlord receives a fixed rent for his land regardless of fluctuation in cotton prices; and, secondly, the renter gains in money as long as cotton remains at a good selling price.

This paper has been devoted principally to the discussion of the share-cropper and the renter because these classes have a relation with the soil and the plantation permanent enough to observe changes. It is evident that the daily, weekly, and monthly wage-earners have some influence upon the plantation system which is not discussed here.

Herbert Shapiro

THE POPULISTS AND THE NEGRO:
A RECONSIDERATION

*Black men were not completely disfranchised in the southern states as
a result of the restoration of white supremacy in the 1870's, and even
Negro officeholding survived in parts of the South until the opening
of the twentieth century. In fact, Negro political activity increased
markedly during the early 1890's as a byproduct of the party strife
between the Populists and the Democrats. Both sides, in bidding for
political power, sought the votes of Negro citizens.*

*Negroes actively participated both in the agrarian movement of
the 1880's and in the Populist Party that grew out of it. There has
been a tendency on the part of some recent scholars to view this
participation as indicative of a genuine expression of feelings of interracial solidarity on the part of the white Populists. We are more inclined to view the white Populists' interest in the Negro vote as
rooted mainly in political expediency. Herbert Shapiro's paper explores
this problem with refreshing and perceptive subtlety.*

I N the past few years a number of historians have again turned to evaluate
the impact of the Populist era on our history. If consensus is a central theme
of history, it certainly is not to be found among the scholars who have examined
the farmers' upheaval of the 80's and the 90's. However, the argument has
produced some light along with some heat. We are learning more of the role
of the 1896 campaign, learning to unravel some of the political confusion that
marked the second Cleveland administration, and starting to view with fresh
insight the Populist response to large-scale industry.

One critical area of the Populist record has yet to be carefully re-exam-
ined; scholarship has not carried appreciation of the Southern phase of the
movement much beyond the studies offered some fifteen to twenty years ago.
The Woodward studies of that era point to new areas of research, point to

Printed with the permission of Herbert Shapiro.

the need to examine in detail the effort of the agrarian radicals to overcome the racial mystique, to establish a politics of economic self-interest. This scholarship is a call to study the factors that transformed radicals, prepared to cross the race line, into hardened racists who savagely struck out at the Negro, the Catholic, and the Jew. This call has not received an adequate response, and the result has been to construct a stereotype of the Southern Populist that only faintly resembles reality. Further study of the Southern agrarian crusade, I suggest, will lead to a setting aside of the stereotype and to a clearer understanding of the fact that the Southern Populists were neither premature Hitlers nor the heroes of a decisive break with racialism. Some of the Populists sought a genuine alliance of Negro and poor white, but their comprehension of the terms of that alliance was inadequate. All too often the storm of attack from the racist machines swayed the radicals from a firm stand on the race issue. The Southerners sought to overcome the heritage of slavery, but their own inadequacies retarded their efforts. They left a record of striving and achievement but they were unable to make the advances essential to a firm alliance of black and white. Without that alliance they were doomed to defeat.

Liberals, who today hope for an end to race antagonism throughout the United States, are encouraged by this view of the Populist era, and in its essentials, this view rests on convincing evidence. In his study of Tom Watson, C. Vann Woodward states: "Never before or since have the two races in the South come as close together as they did during the Populist struggles." In *Origins of the New South* Woodward stresses the role of several Southern Populists who challenged the cult of racism and urged the idea of common action among farmers and workers of the South, Negro and white. In 1960, in an eloquent defense of the Populist heritage, Professor Woodward reflects that perhaps the most remarkable aspect of Populism was its resistance to racism, "the determined effort ... made against incredible odds to win back political rights for the Negroes." [1] The Populists defended the Negro's right to the franchise and also his right to hold office, to serve on juries, to receive a fair hearing in the courts and to receive protection against lynchers. The article affirms that the Populists went further in offering the Negro political equality than any other white movement has ever gone before or since in the South. If a number of the Populists later turned "sour" on the race issue, this was the result of the atmosphere of defeat and despondency that set in after 1896, after the advocates of white supremacy routed the agrarian radicals.

These views have found their way into a number of recent studies of the era. A recent article by an historian who has carefully examined the midwest phase of the movement concluded that the Populists expressed compassion for the Negro as well as for the poor white. Richard Hofstadter, who censures the

[1] C. Vann Woodward, *Tom Watson, Agrarian Rebel* (New York: The Macmillan Co., 1938), p. 222; C. Vann Woodward, *Origins of the New South* (Baton Rouge: Louisiana State University Press), p. 249; C. Vann Woodward, "The Populist Heritage and the Intellectual" in *The Burden of Southern History* (Baton Rouge: Louisiana State University Press, 1960), p. 156.

Populists on a number of grounds, asserts that on the race issue "a few Populist leaders in the South attempted something profoundly radical and humane." Harold Faulkner's study of the 1890's includes the conclusion that Populism was "the most promising experiment in interracial cooperation in politics in the history of the South." [2]

These and other historians have accepted the main conclusions of the Woodward argument, but have ignored his caution in *Origins of the New South* that the Populist record on race could easily be exaggerated. Scant attention has been given to the Virginia Populist who said, "This is a white man's country and will always be controlled by whites," [3] or to Jack Abramowitz's articles on the Populists and the Negro or to Helen Edmunds' study of the 90's in North Carolina.[4] To overlook such evidence can only obscure the factors that led to the defeat of the agrarian upheaval in the South.

This paper does not propose that the Populists were hopeless reactionaries obsessed by irrational hatreds. Populism was a complex, often unstable, movement that at times moved in more than one direction at once. In the South Populists emerged in the midst of a society only a few years beyond Reconstruction, a society that had treated race as the central issue for as long as men could recall. They did, indeed, attempt to break through the established structure in which race was used to exploit both Negroes and poor whites. The Populists proclaimed that economic interest, not race, was the central issue in the South. In 1892 Tom Watson in a speech asked what was wrong with telling Negro farmers that they stood in the same boat as the white farmers. That same year Watson asked Georgians to wipe out the color line. In an 1892 article published in the *Arena* Watson wrote of the poor whites and Negroes, "Their every material interest is identical," and that it was to the self-interest of the white reformers that the vote of the Negro reformer be fairly counted. Watson and other Southern Populists did not approach the race issue in terms of sentiment or humanitarianism. Watson explained the practical function of racial hatreds in Southern society, "You are kept apart that you may be separately fleeced of your earnings. You are made to hate each other because upon that hatred is rested the keystone of the arch of financial despotism which enslaves you." [5] Populist leaders frequently assured

[2] Norman Pollack, "Fear of Man: Populism, Authoritarianism and the Historian," *Agricultural History* (April 1965), 59–67, p. 61; Richard Hofstadter, *Age of Reform* (New York: Alfred Knopf, 1955), p. 61; Harold U. Faulkner, *Politics, Reform and Expansion* (New York: Harper Brothers, 1959), p. 270.

[3] Woodward, *Origins of the New South*, p. 258.

[4] Jack Abramowitz, "The Negro in the Agrarian Revolt," *Agricultural History* XXIV (1950), 89–95; Jack Abramowitz, "The Negro in the Populist Movement," *Journal of Negro History* XXXVIII (July 1953), 257–289; Helen Edmunds, *The Negro and Fusion Politics in North Carolina* (Chapel Hill: University of North Carolina Press, 1951).

[5] C. Vann Woodward, "Tom Watson and the Negro," *Journal of Southern History* IV (February 1938), 14–33, p. 21; Tom Watson, "The Negro Question in the South," in George Tindall ed., *A Populist Reader* (New York: Harper and Row, 1966), pp. 125, 126.

Negroes that they would receive equitable treatment if the party of the people were elected to office. The organ of the Populists in North Carolina announced in 1896: "What the great masses of the colored people in North Carolina want is fair treatment . . . and this they ought to have." The Texas Populists said in 1896: "We are in favor of equal justice and protection under the law to all citizens without reference to race, color or nationality." [6] In 1890 a Kansas Populist newspaper declared that the farmers' crusade could "also settle the race question of the South." Tom Watson incorporated this view in his *Arena* article on the Southern scene, and at the 1892 St. Louis convention Ignatius Donnelly proclaimed: "The new order of things would wipe out the color line in the South." [7] These statements could be understood either as a pledge to confront racism directly and destroy the heritage of slavery, or as a tactic of sidestepping racial issues and replacing them with the issue of exploitative economic interests. James Field, the 1892 Populist vice presidential candidate, spoke for many when he asserted that "the great issues of today have nothing to do with the struggles of 1861–65." [8] This was said in a South that was already well acquainted with the horror of lynching and repeatedly failed to protect the Negro's constitutional rights.

In the 90's the Negro electorate was still a political factor in the South. Although the Negro voter was frequently threatened and often deprived of his vote through a fraudulent count, many white candidates continued to appeal for Negro support. The Populists joined in this appeal. What was the Negro offered in return for his political support?—the general program of Populism along with a few items of particular interest to the Negro. The Negro was pledged protection of the franchise. In the 1892 campaign Watson pledged Georgia Negroes "fair play and fair treatment" if they would stand up for their rights and manhood, if they would stand shoulder to shoulder with white Populists. Watson in 1895 censured the South Carolina Tillmanites for their efforts to disenfranchise the Negro. As for other issues, there were vague assurances of improved access to free schooling and of protection against Ku Kluxism and lynch law. Watson dramatized this pledge in the remarkable incident in which 2000 white farmers were called out to protect a Negro clergyman active in a Populist campaign.[9] With regard to economic issues, the only pledge of special concern to Negroes was the commitment to ending the system of convict leasing. On this issue there was a clear merging of the

---

[6] Robert F. Durden, *The Climax of Populism* (Lexington: University of Kentucky Press, 1965), p. 11; Abramowitz, "The Negro in the Populist Movement," *op. cit.*, p. 270.

[7] Abramowitz, "The Negro in the Agrarian Revolt," *op. cit.*, p. 93; Watson, "The Negro Question in the South," *op. cit.*, p. 124; Martin Ridge, *Ignatius Donnelly* (Chicago: University of Chicago Press, 1962), p. 297.

[8] William Dubose Sheldon, *Populism in the Old Dominion* (Princeton: Princeton University Press, 1935), p. 89.

[9] Abramowitz, "The Negro in the Populist Movement," *op. cit.*, p. 273; Watson, "The Negro Question in the South," *op. cit.*, p. 126; Woodward, *Tom Watson*, pp. 239, 371.

interests of Negroes and poor whites. Negroes were most often the victims of the system of leasing out convicts to work for Southern landowners. In Georgia, for example, during 1880, convict leasing involved 1071 Negroes as against 115 whites.[10] But the system also affected those whites who could not compete against employers provided with convict labor.

The Populists made a meaningful attempt to involve Negroes in the apparatus of their crusade. In Kansas in 1890 the Populists ran a Negro, Benjamin Foster, for state auditor, and Foster presided as chairman at a major rally. At the 1892 St. Louis convention William Warwick of the Virginia Colored Alliance was elected an officer of the convention.[11] In several of the states Negroes were drawn into the higher echelons of the Populist machinery. In Georgia Watson nominated a Negro to serve on the movement's state executive council. In Texas a Populist convention elected two Negroes to serve on the state executive.[12] Efforts were made to involve Negroes in the crusade's national conventions. At the 1892 St. Louis convention 97 seats were available for representatives of the extremely large Colored Alliance. The previous year at the Cincinnati conference that laid the groundwork for the 1892 campaign, efforts to segregate Negroes in the hall were defeated.[13]

The Farmers' Alliance movement that foreshadowed the Populist upheaval also made efforts at securing cooperation between Negro and white agrarians. At the Ocala conference representatives of the Negro alliance met with representatives of the white organization to coordinate future efforts. Following the convention a representative of the Negro grouping wrote that his alliance fully understood "that the laboring colored man's interests and the laboring white man's interests are one and the same" and that the Colored Alliance was interested in campaigning along the line of the general agrarian slogan of "equal rights to all and special privileges to none." [14] The Southern alliance of white farmers indicated its interest in unity by reprinting in its national organ speeches and statements released by the Colored Alliance.

All of these manifestations of a desire to unite Negro and white for common objectives, of course, evoked a vehement, often violent, response from those entrenched in the Southern power structure. It is a tribute to the courage of Southern Populists that they were able to hold out at all against the furious attack mounted against them. One eminent divine informed Southerners that a victory for the Populists would mean the victory of "mongrelism." The race issue was the trump card of the white supremacists. In Mississippi the argument went that only by remaining loyal to the machine

[10] Woodward, *Tom Watson*, p. 106.

[11] Abramowitz, "The Negro in the Populist Movement," *op. cit.*, p. 264; Sheldon, *op. cit.*, p. 77.

[12] Woodward, *Origins of the New South*, pp. 221, 256.

[13] Abramowitz, "The Negro in the Agrarian Revolt," *op. cit.*, p. 94.

[14] See Herbert Aptheker ed., *A Documentary History of the Negro People in the United States* (New York: Citadel Press, 1951), pp. 807, 809.

could white supremacy be preserved. In Alabama the Democrats sought to create hysteria with the assertion that the Colored Alliance would combine with its Northern friends to force through a program of confiscating the land of white farmers and turning it over to Negroes. Along with this the Colored Alliance would succeed in obtaining enactment of a federal law putting federal machinery beyond the defense of the black man's effort to vote and hold office.[15]

The Populists were unable to counter effectively this ferocious attack. But it is not just that the fusion arrangements of the 1896 campaign forced the Southern branch into the arms of their former enemies with the end result of confusion and loss of morale. In addition, the Populists were unable to meet the attack because they could not fully free themselves of racism, regionalism and suspicion of the Negro. The chink in the armor of the Southern Populists was their weakness on the race issue. The Populists stressed common economic interests and saw themselves as the dispensers of fair treatment, but they failed to realize that a strong alliance of black and white was unlikely without an unreserved commitment to the free exercise by the Negro of his constitutional rights. The Populists generally compromised with white supremacy. They argued that the race issue was introduced as a distraction from the South's real concerns, but they drew back from repudiating the idea that white men were to exert a dominating influence on the affairs of the South. The Populists sought Negro support but failed to make the commitments that would assure future equality between the races.

The Populists in the South failed to formulate a program that would meet the special grievances of Negroes. The emphasis in Populist program was on the needs of property-owning farmers whose interests were threatened by Eastern capital. But little attention was given the needs of agrarians who owned no land, who were caught in the trap of sharecropping, and who had practically no cash income.[16] Much of the Negro South found itself in this situation. Currency reform was high on the list of Populist priorities. But currency reform could only be of indirect concern to the Negro. Paul Lawrence Dunbar was to write that for the Negro the issue was not what kind of money but the fact that most often he had no money of any kind.[17]

Another serious flaw in the Populist approach to the Negro was the rejection of federal intervention on behalf of the Negro's constitutional rights. In the 1890's this issue revolved around the Lodge Bill, the so-called "Force" Bill, introduced with GOP support in the House and finally, in 1891, killed in the Senate. The bill provided for establishment of federal machinery to protect the exercise of the franchise in the South. As Woodward has pointed

---

[15] John D. Hicks, *The Populist Revolt* (Minneapolis: University of Minnesota Press, 1931), p. 348; Woodward, *Tom Watson*, p. 226; J. H. Taylor, "Populism and Disfranchisement in Alabama," *Journal of Negro History* XXXIV (October 1949), 410–427, p. 415.

[16] See Woodward, "Tom Watson and the Negro," *op. cit.*, p. 23.

[17] Abramowitz, "The Negro in the Populist Movement," *op. cit.*, p. 287.

out, white supremacists used the threat of the Lodge Bill as a club with which to enforce the race line in Southern politics. The agrarian radicals, however, retreated before the onslaught. Apparently, in the interest of cementing an alliance between the white farmers of the South and the West, they repeatedly rejected federal action for civil rights. The Lodge Bill emerged as a major issue before the Ocala Alliance conference. In its separate meeting the Negro Alliance, the Colored Farmers' Alliance, and Cooperative Union supported adoption of the Force Bill. A spokesman for the group wrote that Negroes wanted the Lodge Bill precisely because "none sees the needed reform more than we do. . . . we want something guaranteeing every man a free vote and an honest count." The white Alliance men, however, rejected this piece of legislation. They stood against federal action although they asserted their commitment to protect the Negro's right to vote. The national organ of the Alliance urged that "a free ballot and a fair count be insisted upon and had for colored and white alike, by every Alliance man in America . . . this is a much more efficient way of securing a fair election in the cities and the South than in the Lodge Bill." [18] As the farmers' crusade turned to political action, rejection of the Lodge Bill was incorporated in the Populist platform. The political platforms produced by the 1892 campaign all took some position on the subject of federal action for Negro rights. The Republican platform denounced the "inhuman outrages perpetuated . . . for political reasons in certain Southern states." The Democratic platform proclaimed that the Force Bill violated the heritage of democracy and that free society is grounded on home rule. The Populists put their view in the context of defense of a free suffrage and affirmed the need for a "fair count in all elections . . . without federal intervention." [19] In at least one Southern state, Virginia, the Populists echoed the national stand. The Virginians announced that they "opposed machinery either federal or state that controls the will of the great people." [20] The Populist presidential candidate, James Weaver, had two years earlier taken his stand against the Lodge Bill. At a Des Moines reform convention he declared that the GOP does not hesitate "to trample under foot the plain letter of the constitution, the traditions of the fathers and the liberties of the people." The Lodge Bill, he stated, "takes the elections of representatives out of the hands of the people where it has rested for more than a century and places it under the control of partisan officers appointed for life." [21] Ten years earlier there had been another emphasis in Weaver's statements. In his first statement in 1880 as the Greenback candidate he urged a free vote, "a fair count and equal rights for all . . . the laboring man in Northern manufactories, mines and workshops and for

[18] Aptheker, op. cit., p. 807; Abramowitz, "The Negro in the Agrarian Revolt," op. cit., p. 92.
[19] Alex M. Arnett, The Populist Movement in Georgia (New York: Columbia University Press, 1922), p. 136; George Tindall ed., A Populist Reader, p. 95.
[20] Sheldon, op. cit., p. 80.
[21] Fred Emory Haynes, James Baird Weaver (Iowa City: State Historical Society of Iowa, 1919), p. 302.

the struggling poor, both white and black in the cotton fields of the South."
Then he placed himself as continuator of the heritage of Jackson and Jefferson,
of the Republicanism of Lincoln and Thaddeus Stevens.[22] But in 1890
Weaver rejected a course that might have obstructed the work of aligning
Southern and Western white agrarian interests.

In the 1896 campaign the Democratic convention took a stand against
federal intervention. The platform repudiated "arbitrary interference by Federal authorities in local affairs as a violation of the Constitution of the United
States and a crime against free institutions.[23] This plank could be read as a
rejection of the Cleveland administration's actions in the Pullman strike but
also as a pledge to defeat any new attempt to enact legislation patterned after
the Lodge Bill. During the course of the campaign William Jennings Bryan in
a Brooklyn speech defended this plank of the platform.[24] There is no evidence
that any Populist spokesman took issue with this 1896 commitment of the
Bryan campaign. The Populists were for using federal machinery to protect
the general economic interests of agrarians; they would not use that machinery
to protect the constitutional rights of Negroes.

Tom Watson articulated before a national audience the Southern white
Populist rejection of national action for Negro rights. In a 1892 article for the
Arena Watson dealt with the Negro question in the South. In this article
racism conflicts with an effort to set aside racial hatreds. The tension is not
fully resolved. Watson saw the race issue as one that threatened the South
with conflict and bloodshed. The existing racial hostility could only be continued "at the most imminent risk" to Negro and white. It was urgent that
the way be found to a future in which black and white could live in peace
and harmony. Watson declared that his movement would solve the race issue,
solve it through an aligning of common economic interests. Negroes and
whites would combine against the exploitative corporation interests. But the
article also reveals that the Georgian could not see clearly enough what was
needed to consummate this alliance. Watson speaks of common interests but
his stress is upon teaching the Negroes to align themselves with whites. Watson
urges that the Negro be offered an incentive "to have the same patriotic zeal
for the welfare of the South that the whites possess." Watson is unable to
break away from a stereotyped view of Reconstruction. In his eyes Reconstruction was an era of Negro aggressiveness "under the leadership of adventurers who swooped down . . . in the wake of Union armies." He asserts:
"The black man was kept in a continual fever of suspicion that we meant
to put him back into slavery." Watson mourns that Negroes in the South put
their confidence in Northern strangers rather than in the whites who have
known them throughout their lives. Watson looks forward to a future of

[22] See William D. Hesseltine, *Third Party Movements in the United States*
(Princeton: Van Nostrand, 1962), p. 145.

[23] Stanley L. Jones, *The Presidential Election of 1896* (Madison: University of
Wisconsin Press, 1964), p. 221.

[24] *Ibid.*, p. 314.

progress, but a prerequisite for progress is no federal intervention in the South. "Outsiders must let us alone. We must work out our own salvation. In no other way can it be done. Suggestions of Federal interference with our elections postpone the settlement and render our task more difficult. Like all free people, we love home rule and resent foreign compulsion of any sort." The North is still the foreign land and apparently a requirement of progress is that no attempt be made to enforce the 14th and 15th amendments. Watson argues that the Populist view of the franchise issue is sounder than that of the Republicans. The GOP would put through a Force Bill that would lead only to bloodshed while the Populists would guarantee the Negro "free and fair exercises of his franchise under state laws." And it is Watson's view that this stand would attract the support of the Negro electorate.[25] Watson had convinced himself that Negroes would trust the good intentions of Southern whites and set aside the enforcement of constitutional guarantees. Watson was prepared to confront the racial issue to the extent he thought required to combine the electoral strength of Negro and white farmers. His enlightenment was inadequate to the needs of a fundamental long-term alliance.[26]

Race plagued the farmers' upheaval from the late 1880's on. Clearly a factor in the failure of the Southern Alliance to merge with its Northern counterpart was anxiety that this entailed crossing of the color line in the South. Apparently an attempt was made to compromise the issue along the line of establishing separate Negro and white lodges, but in the end compromise was rejected.[27] The white Alliance and the Colored Alliance maintained friendly relations but when in 1891 the Negro group urged a general strike of laborers in the cotton fields, a spokesman for the white Alliance urged the white employing farmers to leave the crop in the field rather than have it picked at fifty cents a head.[28] Further study may shed light on the extent to which the class line as well as race was a factor in separating Negro and white farmers. The organ of the white Alliance at times printed anti-Negro articles. At one point presidential appointment of Negroes to office was found objectionable; another complaint was that President Cleveland asked the country's foremost Negro leader to a reception at the White House.[29] The Alliance, Negro and white, were organizations that attracted a remarkably large membership with a considerable influence for a few years; perhaps they might have preserved their strength and influence longer had they been able to surmount successfully the racial issue. The Alliance in the South lost its cohesiveness when racial anxieties prevented some Alliance men from turning to a politics of non-conformity.

There is evidence that in at least two Southern states the Populists, or

[25] See Watson, "The Negro Question in the South," in George Tindall ed., *A Populist Reader*, pp. 118, 119, 122, 123, 125.

[26] Woodward, *Origins of the New South*, p. 250.

[27] Arnett, *op. cit.*, p. 82.

[28] Woodward, *Tom Watson*, p. 219.

[29] See Abramowitz, "The Negro in the Agrarian Revolt," *op. cit.*, p. 95.

in any case the Populist leaders, did not depart from orthodox and racist views of the Negro. Charles Wynes' careful study of Negro-white relations in Virginia concludes that the enlightened spirit of the Populist leaders did not extend to advocacy of political equality for the Negro. In 1893, two years before he ran as the Populist gubernatorial candidate, Edmund Cocke urged repeal of the 15th amendment and stated that the solution for racial conflict was to disfranchise the Negro.[30] Helen Edmunds' study of North Carolina concludes that the movement in that state was not a repudiation of white supremacy. Populist newspapers and legislators in that state frequently articulated anti-Negro sentiments.[31] The results of these excellent state studies lend force to the view that among Populists there was a wide range of opinion about the race issue. It is a distortion to isolate only one segment of opinion and present that as a general image of the movement.

To stress the shortcomings of the agrarian radicals on the Negro issue is not to ignore the external obstacles against which they worked. Coercion and hysteria were used to force the Southerner back into the channels of conformity. In North Carolina racists made war on Negroes who sought to exercise the rights of office holding. In Wilmington at least 12 Negroes were killed as a revenge against black men who took office under a Populist-Republican fusion.[32] The Populists, however, were unable to meet the onslaught effectively and it is not enough to lament their defeat. The Populists did not simply "sour" after their 1896 electoral defeat. The racist hysteria of later years is linked to earlier if much milder racism. In earlier years the racism is subdued as Negro support is sought; in the later era race hate is frenzied as the Negro is viewed as an enemy to be expelled from politics. The Populists may well be hailed for seeking to subdue racial hates to achieve an alliance of common economic interests but we must bear in mind that before and after 1895 race was an Achilles heel of the crusade.

[30] Charles Wynes, *Race Relations in Virginia, 1870–1902* (Charlottesville: University of Virginia Press, 1961), pp. 47, 48.
[31] Edmunds, *op. cit.*, pp. 136, 218, 221.
[32] Hicks, *op. cit.*, p. 392.

George B. Tindall

THE QUESTION OF RACE IN THE
SOUTH CAROLINA CONSTITUTIONAL
CONVENTION OF 1895

Shapiro's essay describes how Negro and white agrarians formed political alliances. South Carolina, however, was a state where, though Negroes continued to hold elective office from the Black Belt coastal counties and even sent a Negro to Congress through most of the 1880's and early 1890's, the black political leaders were informally allied with the low-country white Democratic aristocracy. As George B. Tindall shows, the constitutional disfranchisement of Negro voters in South Carolina, the second state to amend its constitution in this fashion, was directly inspired by the rise of radical agrarianism. In certain other states, particularly neighboring North Carolina, the impetus came from white Democratic leaders who used the race issue to crush the Populist Party and its successful alliance with Negro Republicans.

Tindall's article illustrates exceedingly well the views of southern Negro leaders who in this period were fighting a desperate rearguard action against complete political effacement. On the one hand, they vigorously protested the discriminatory franchise proposals; on the other hand, they displayed a willingness to accommodate by accepting literacy and property qualifications as long as those were equitably applied to both races. This compromise would have saved face for Negroes, but in view of the poverty and inadequate education of the black masses, it would, even if fairly administered, have disfranchised far more Negroes than whites.

Aғᴛᴇʀ the overthrow of the Radical government in 1876 the conservative element of South Carolina continued to govern the state under the Con-

George B. Tindall, "The Question of Race in the South Carolina Constitutional Convention of 1895," *Journal of Negro History*, XXXVII (July, 1952), pp. 277–303. Reprinted with the permission of *Journal of Negro History*.

stitution of 1868. No move toward general revision was undertaken because of fear of federal intervention and, later, fear of Tillmanite domination if a convention were held. In 1892, however, the Tillmanites secured the necessary majority in the legislature and by a small majority in 1894 carried the referendum for a new convention on the issue of restricting the Negro vote and delivering South Carolina from the "shame" of being governed under the "Radical rag" of 1868.

Representation in the convention included 112 Tillmanite Democrats, 42 Conservative Democrats, and 6 Negro Republicans. Five of the Negroes were chosen on a straight Republican ticket in Beaufort County and one on a fusion ticket in Georgetown County, both low-country counties with large Negro constituencies.[1]

The dominant figure in the convention was United States Senator Benjamin Ryan Tillman, the one-eyed farmer from Edgefield County who had led his Farmers' Association to victory over the conservative Democrats in the Democratic state convention of 1890. By means of its widespread organization and through Tillman's gift for arousing white audiences with vindictive and inflammatory speeches, the group completely dominated South Carolina politics from 1890 to 1896 and exercised tremendous influence thereafter. Tillman's program was aimed primarily at meeting the farmers' grievances through increased agricultural and vocational education for whites and through the regulation of corporations. The Tillman Movement has frequently been characterized as the South Carolina phase of the Populist revolt that swept the South and West in the 1890's. But one of the most urgent objectives of the Tillman program, in addition to his Populistic proposals, was the complete elimination of the Negro from participation in South Carolina politics. The Constitutional Convention of 1895 marked the achievement of that objective.[2] It therefore marked also the end of significant Negro participation in the state's politics for half a century.

Second in importance among the Tillmanites was Governor John Gary Evans, a nephew of Martin Witherspoon Gary, who had been the bold advocate of the "shotgun policy" to intimidate Negroes in the election of 1876 and until his death in 1881 the bitterest opponent of Wade Hampton's moderate racial policies. Evans' positions as governor and as president of the Constitutional Convention were to many symbolic of the victory of Gary's extremist policy over the moderate paternalism that had been professed by Hampton and his successors from 1876 to 1890.[3]

[1] Columbia Daily Register, July 31, 1895; Columbia State, August 26, 1895.

[2] Biographical Directory of the American Congress, 1774–1927 (Washington: Government Printing Office, 1928), p. 1618. Hereinafter cited as Biographical Directory. An excellent biography is Francis Butler Simkins, Pitchfork Ben Tillman (Baton Rouge: Louisiana State University, 1944). Hereinafter cited as Ben Tillman.

[3] James Calvin Hemphill, Men of Mark in South Carolina (Washington: Men of Mark Publishing Company, 1907–1909), I, 108–109; William Watts Ball, The State That Forgot (Indianapolis: Bobbs-Merrill Company, 1932), pp. 239–240; F. B. Simkins, Ben Tillman, p. 224.

United States Senator John Laurens Manning Irby had been a prominent figure in the early victories of the Tillmanites, and in 1890 was their successful candidate for the Senate against Wade Hampton. In 1895, however, he broke away from Tillman and, espousing the cause of the poor whites, took a stand against the Tillman program of a literacy qualification for the suffrage on the ground that it would, if honestly administered, disfranchise poor and illiterate white farmers as well as poor and illiterate Negroes and eventually bring about a return to power of the conservative element that had been deposed in 1890.[4]

The most prominent figures among the Conservative group were George Dionysius Tillman, a brother of Ben, and John Calhoun Sheppard, a former governor and unsuccessful opponent of Ben Tillman in 1892. But the Conservative who played the most important part in the convention was the politically obscure attorney, John Pendleton Kennedy Bryan of Charleston. An alumnus of the German universities of Berlin and Leipzig and a graduate of Princeton, he applied his erudition to the writing of the suffrage article, the subsequent immunity of which to legal attack bears witness to his ingenuity as a legal technician.[5]

The six Negro delegates were Robert Smalls, Thomas Ezekiel Miller, William J. Whipper, James Wigg, and Isaiah R. Reed from Beaufort, and Robert B. Anderson from Georgetown.

Robert Smalls, the "Gullah Statesman," was born a slave in Beaufort in 1839 and was soon thereafter taken to Charleston where a lenient master permitted him to acquire a rudimentary education. Pilot of a Confederate boat in Charleston harbor at the beginning of the Civil War, Smalls escaped with the boat in 1862 and joined the Federals. Later in 1863 he was promoted to captain in the United States Navy and placed in command of the Federal ship, the *Planter*, on which he served until 1866. After taking up residence in Beaufort he was elected to the constitutional convention of 1868 and to the state legislature later that year. In 1870 he was elected state senator and in 1874 a representative in Congress. Elected again in 1876 he was defeated by George Tillman in 1878, but successfully contested Tillman's reelection in 1880. After losing his party's nomination in 1882 he was in 1884 elected without opposition to finish the unexpired term of white Republican Edmund William McGregor Mackey and was reelected to a full term in 1884. After his unsuccessful candidacy in 1886 he was not again elected to office, although he served as collector of the port of Beaufort from 1889 until his death in 1913.[6]

Thomas Ezekiel Miller, whose light color won him the sobriquet of "Canary Bird" Miller in the white press, was born a free person of color in

[4] *Biographical Directory*, p. 1138; F. B. Simkins, *Ben Tillman*, pp. 187–188, 239.

[5] Columbia *State*, October 27, 1918. Bryan's obituary.

[6] *Biographical Directory*, pp. 1532–1533. Alrutheus Ambush Taylor, *The Negro in South Carolina During Reconstruction* (Washington: Association for the Study of Negro Life and History, 1924), pp. 135, 158, 286, 301; hereinafter cited as *Negro During Reconstruction*.

Beaufort in 1849. He was the best educated of the colored delegates, having received his education in Lincoln University, Chester County, Pennsylvania. Upon graduation in 1872, he became school commissioner for Beaufort County. In 1874, 1876 and 1878 he was elected to the state House of Representatives and in 1880 to the Senate. He was admitted to the bar in 1875. In 1888 he ran for Congress and although he was not certified as victor, successfully contested the seat against William Elliott and served one term, but was unsuccessful in his campaign for reelection. In 1894 he was returned to the state House of Representatives on a fusion ticket with two other Republicans and two Tillmanites.[7]

William J. Whipper, whom Benjamin R. Tillman described as the "ablest colored man I ever met," was reared in Michigan and at the outbreak of the Civil War was employed as a clerk in a lawyer's office. During the war he joined a regiment of volunteers and ultimately reached South Carolina. At the end of the war he became a lawyer in Charleston, functioning mostly in the provost courts; later he went to Beaufort where he was elected a delegate to the constitutional convention of 1868. In that convention he distinguished himself by introducing a motion for universal suffrage regardless of sex. In 1868 and 1870 he was elected to the state House of Representatives. Elected in 1875 as circuit judge of the first circuit he was not commissioned by Governor Daniel Henry Chamberlain because of suspicion of fraud. In 1882 and 1884 he was elected Probate Judge of Beaufort County and since that time had not held office.[8]

James Wigg was a conservative farmer of St. Helena and later a merchant in Beaufort, apparently well regarded by his white neighbors, but gifted with an extremely sharp tongue which he used to effect in the General Assembly and the constitutional convention.[9]

R. B. Anderson was regarded as industrious and conservative. He had been a teacher and town warden in Georgetown before his election to the General Assembly, in which he had served several years.[10]

Isaiah R. Reed, the most obscure of the six, listed himself in the Convention Journal as an attorney at law in Beaufort.[11]

Since the major objective of the convention was disfranchisement, the most important standing committee of the convention was the Committee on the Rights of Suffrage, which was appointed on the second day with eight Reform or Tillmanite and three Conservative members. Ben Tillman was appointed chairman. The most important Conservative was J. P. K. Bryan of

---

[7] *Biographical Directory*, p. 1315; Taylor, *op. cit.*, pp. 295, 296, 301, 302–303.

[8] Solomon Breibart, "The South Carolina Constitutional Convention of 1868" (Unpublished M.A. Thesis, History Department, University of North Carolina, 1932), pp. 71–72; Taylor, pp. 127, 141–142, 228, 233–235, 294.

[9] A. A. Taylor, *Negro During Reconstruction*, 297.

[10] *Ibid.*

[11] *Journal of the Constitutional Convention of 1895* (Columbia: Charles A. Calvo, Jr., 1895), p. 736. Hereinafter cited as *Convention Journal*.

Charleston who was later reported to have drawn up the suffrage article in the form submitted by the committee.[12]

To this committee a number of proposals were referred by members of the convention. It was generally understood that some variant of the Mississippi plan of educational qualifications with certain options designed for illiterate whites was favored by most of the membership, and most of the proposals followed that plan with curious variants caused by the strained effort to evade stating in so many words the intent to evade the Fifteenth Amendment.

Robert Aldrich proposed a literacy requirement providing as an option that the state legislature might declare an illiterate person "of sufficient intelligence to exercise the right to suffrage." [13] The purpose was to disfranchise the illiterate Negroes while leaving some loophole to admit the illiterate whites. C. M. Efird proposed a clause giving the ballot to those who had been qualified in 1860 and limiting the others by property and literacy qualifications.[14] George Johnstone favored county boards to enfranchise certain illiterates by reason of their intelligence, character and service to the public.[15] H. C. Patton wanted to provide both property and grandfather clause options for literacy, the grandfather clause to enfranchise Confederate veterans.[16] L. E. Parler favored woman suffrage on the grounds that a $300 property qualification would enfranchise more white women than colored.[17] S. W. Gamble had an elaborate plan that would require presentation of three certificates from three different sources before an individual could register: a certificate from the clerk of court that he had never been convicted of crime, another from the county board of examiners that he could read and write, and a third from the township board that he had never committed adultery or fornication, nor neglected or maltreated his wife and children.[18] W. B. Wilson wanted to incorporate the eight ballot box idea into the constitution.[19] J. N. Parrott proposed giving two

[12] *Convention Journal*, p. 22; David Duncan Wallace, *History of South Carolina* (New York: American Historical Society, 1935), III, 369, cites a MS note by Joseph W. Barnwell in the Charleston library copy of Francis Butler Simkins, *The Tillman Movement in South Carolina*: "It is well known that J. P. Kennedy Bryan, Esq., of Chaston, drew in effect the clause."

[13] *Convention Journal*, pp. 69–70.

[14] *Ibid.*, p. 77.

[15] *Ibid.*, p. 54.

[16] *Ibid.*, pp. 42–43.

[17] *Ibid.*, p. 110.

[18] *Ibid.*, pp. 101–102.

[19] *Ibid.*, pp. 121–122. The eight ballot box plan had been incorporated into statute law in 1882. Separate ballots and boxes were required for eight different classes of offices, national, state, and local. The ostensible intent of its supporters was to provide a literacy test for the suffrage by requiring the voter to choose, by reading the labels, the proper box for his ballot. Any ballot found in the wrong box was invalidated. In practice, however, it was possible for the election managers to give help to illiterates who would vote "right" and let the others void their ballots by putting them in the wrong boxes. *Statutes at Large of South Carolina*, XVII, 1110–1126.

votes to every head of a family who paid taxes on $200 worth of property.[20]
J. J. McMahan had a similar multiple vote scheme providing that property
owners could vote in the precinct where the property was located; [21] and D. H.
Russell wanted to provide that no person should be disfranchised for service
in any war since the Declaration of Independence.[22]

Robert Smalls had a contrary proposal providing specifically that no
person should be denied the suffrage for reason of race, color, or previous
condition of servitude, and that persons prohibited by the United States
Constitution from voting should not be allowed to vote in the state. The
residence requirement was much shorter than in the other plans, and provision was made for bipartisan representation on the boards of election managers. It got little hearing.[23]

Robert Aldrich proposed not only to limit the suffrage but also to prohibit
Negroes from serving in the General Assembly. When he persisted in his
obviously unworkable plan, Tillman warned that "it would be idiocy for this
convention to try and bring down on our heads the dire sword that is hanging
above us. Why invite attack? We are going to protect ourselves." Predicting
that even to consider such a plan overnight would be fatal to the convention,
Tillman refused to let it adjourn until the Aldrich plan had been voted down,
102–25.[24] The threat of Federal intervention was not yet dead.

A movement for woman suffrage was very strongly promoted by the South
Carolina Equal Rights Association and received some support in the convention. It got under way when the ladies of the association obtained permission
to address the convention on the evening of September 17 and produced two
of their leaders, Mrs. V. D. Young and Miss Viola Neblett, and featured Miss
Laura Clay of Kentucky, a distant relative of Henry Clay. The ladies based
their appeal chiefly on the principle of justice and equal rights and emphasized
the civilizing influence that women would have at the ballot box, but they
did not hesitate to hint that woman suffrage would serve the purposes of white
supremacy.[25]

No less than eight petitions from various groups and individuals supporting woman suffrage are recorded in the *Convention Journal*.[26] Robert
Aldrich proposed that women be permitted to vote in cities and towns but
the motion was not considered.[27] W. F. Clayton proposed giving women the
ballot provided they could meet both literacy and property qualifications.
Clayton, champion of the fair sex, admitted that he was charging into the
Valley of Death, like the Light Brigade, with prejudice to the right of him,
prejudice to the left of him, and prejudice to the front of him. Women had

---

[20] *Convention Journal*, p. 101.
[21] *Ibid.*, p. 152.
[22] *Ibid.*, pp. 127–128.
[23] *Ibid.*, pp. 111–112.
[24] Columbia *State*, September 28, 1895.
[25] *Ibid.*, September 18, 1895; *Convention Journal*, 129.
[26] *Ibid.*, pp. 260, 333, 343, 371, 414, 420, 602.
[27] *Ibid.*, p. 85.

been emancipated with regard to property, however, and suffrage he held to be logically the next step. But D. S. Henderson, a chivalrous Conservative, saw in the proposal but a weak-kneed effort to guarantee a white majority. "If we have a problem ...," said he, "let us meet it like men and not try to hide behind women." [28]

The convention voted down woman suffrage by 121–26, but despite the white supremacy angle, one Negro delegate, Thomas E. Miller, voted for the Clayton proposal because, he said, it was another step toward his ideal of universal suffrage.[29]

On September 30, the day before the long awaited committee report was presented, five of the Negro delegates posted a letter to the New York World explaining their position. They presented statistics showing why Tillman would not dare accept a simple literacy qualification. They first presented statistics from the census of 1890 showing that while the number of Negro males over twenty-one out-numbered the Caucasian males over twenty-one, the Caucasians had the advantage when the illiterates were subtracted. Thus:

	Caucasian	Negro
Males over twenty-one	102,657	132,949
Illiterates	13,242	58,086
Leaving literates	89,415	74,851 [sic]

The Tillman faction they estimated at about 60,000 and the Conservatives at 35,000. However, the loss of 13,242 illiterate voters would be borne almost exclusively by the Tillman faction, leaving a majority of only about 12,000 over the Conservatives, which would mean that the literate Negroes, combined with the Conservatives, could carry an election.[30]

The report of the Committee on the Rights of Suffrage, presented by Tillman on October 1, was the same as the final suffrage provision included in the constitution as Article II, with only two major changes, each of which was passed over Tillman's protest. The article was designed to force each voter to run a gauntlet of suffrage restrictions. First, it provided suffrage for male citizens over twenty-one who could meet the qualifications of residence in the state two years, county one year, precinct four months, and payment of the poll tax at least six months before the elections.[31] These were calculated to eliminate many Negroes because of their migratory habits and to disfranchise them in November for not paying their poll taxes in May, a time when ready cash was least available to farmers. But the chief catch-all to trap the Negroes was the literacy requirement, a provision that each registrant prove to the satisfaction of the board that he could read and write any section of the constitution; if he failed to meet this test he might register if he owned and

---

[28] *Ibid.*, p. 183; Columbia *Daily Register*, October 29, 1895.

[29] Columbia *Daily Register*, October 30, 1895.

[30] *Ibid.*, October 4, 1895, quoting letter from New York *World*, date not given. The figures do not jibe exactly, but are sufficiently accurate to illustrate the point.

[31] *Constitution of 1895*, Art. II, Sec. 3, 4a.

paid taxes on property assessed at $300 or more.[32] The board, of course, would be able to overlook a multitude of illiterates and paupers until a Negro came along. In addition to this there was provision for permanent registration of any citizen who could "understand" the constitution when it was read to him, this clause to expire January 1, 1898.[33] The provision was designed to admit those illiterates who did not own $300 worth of property and was the only permanent registration. The other registrants had to renew their registration every ten years.[34] The final obstacle between the prospective voter and the ballot box was to be the local election manager, who was empowered with authority to require of every elector proof of the payment of all taxes assessed against him the previous year.[35] Since it was frequently impossible for the election manager to know just what taxes had been levied against an individual he was thus endowed with the legal power to pick and choose among the prospective voters.

Additional restrictions against the Negro vote were provided by a list of disfranchising crimes, including those supposed by the whites to be most frequently committed by Negroes. They included burglary, arson, obtaining goods or money under false pretenses, perjury, forgery, robbery, bribery, adultery, bigamy, wife-beating, house-breaking, receiving stolen goods, breach of trust with fraudulent intent, fornication, sodomy, and crimes against the election laws. Murder was not included in the list. Others disfranchised were idiots, the insane, paupers supported at public expense, and persons in prison.[36]

Two provisions designed to safeguard elections against fraud did not find their way from the committee report to the final draft despite Tillman's plea for them. One granted a right of appeal to "any court" when one was denied registration. This was changed to a right of appeal to the Circuit Court of Appeals only.[37] The other defeated proviso was for minority representation on registration and election boards. A motion of W. D. Evans to strike this out was carried on November 5 by a vote of 50 to 35, with Tillman voting among the minority.[38] Tillman tried to reincorporate the proviso, making an earnest plea three days later that the nation was watching South Carolina to see if she were willing to make adequate safeguards against fraud. The suffrage committee, he said, unanimously favored the principle of minority representation.

He reminded the delegates of the possibility of Federal intervention, warning that:

unless the South and West can unite and wrest the country from the gold bugs you will see a Republican President and Senate and

[32] Ibid., Sec. 4 d.
[33] Ibid., Sec. 4 c.
[34] Ibid., Sec. 4 b.
[35] Ibid., Sec. 4a.
[36] Ibid., Sec. 6.
[37] Ibid., Sec. 5; Convention Journal, p. 298.
[38] Columbia State, November 6, 1895.

House coming here and turning your Constitution down and you will have plenty of white men to help them.

We are like an ostrich, hiding its head in the sand thinking we are safe unless we put in the Constitution a provision that will give the people the idea that we are going to have fairness.[39]

It need not be inferred from such statements that Tillman had any illusions or moral qualms about the possibilities of fraud inherent in the committee's suffrage plan. In one of his franker moments, he said:

We have been twitted about fraud. All I've got to say is that you can't pull yourself over the fence by your bootstrap. Nobody said we would get up a suffrage plan by Constitutional or honest methods. It has never been uttered by a Reform leader. We simply said we would give the Mississippi plan or something better if we could find it. We didn't find anything better and we did the best we could. No man has even pretended to give a better plan.[40]

Despite the warning of possible federal intervention and Tillman's plea to move carefully because of the possibility that another party might come to power and use its control of the election machinery against the Democrats, the convention voted down his scheme for bipartisan representation, 74–51.[41]

Discussion of the suffrage provisions for the new constitution brought eloquent appeals from the Negro delegation for the preservation of unrestricted suffrage. It was a last desperate appeal, and though it was futile, they made the most of their opportunity. Praise for the ability and eloquence of the Negro delegates came from both white newspapers and delegates. The Sumter *Watchman and Southron* said:

We never expected to see the day that four Negroes from Beaufort would stand up in a body like the one now sitting in Columbia and ask for an educational and property qualification of the suffrage and have the request denied. Is all the talk about the rule of the intelligent and superior race all buncombe? [42]

H. C. Burn, delegate from Darlington, in a speech in the convention, praised the Negro delegates in the following words:

[39] Columbia *Daily Register*, November 9, 1895.

[40] *Ibid.*, November 16, 1895.

[41] Columbia *State*, November 9, 1895. In connection with Tillman's sincere attempt to secure bipartisan representation it is interesting to speculate whether back of it all he had some idea of joining hands with the Populists who were at the time bent on winning the presidency in 1896. Nowhere does Tillman indicate that this was the case, but it was one of the main tenets of his Conservative opponents that he was really a Populist operating within the Democratic party and likely to show his true colors if the opportunity presented itself.

[42] Mary J. Miller, *The Suffrage Speeches by Negroes in the Constitutional Convention* (no date or publisher's imprint—pamphlet), p. 4, quoting from the Sumter *Watchman and Southron*, November 2, 1895. Hereinafter cited as *Suffrage Speeches.*

What oppressed people, denied the opportunity for the cultivation of good manners, the refining influences of civilization and religion, ever sent a delegation anywhere who, in their deportment, in their powers of reasoning, in their rhetorical ability, in their knowledge of the laws of the land, the common law, the statutory law and the constitutional law, both State and national, could surpass in ability that colored delegation from Beaufort.[43]

Miller and Wigg spoke on October 26; they were followed the next day by Smalls and Whipper, and on the 29th by Reed and Anderson. The six men were remarkably well qualified in both education and experience to make the final defense of the Negro's rights.

Miller, who made the first speech, reviewed the history of the Negro race in America, citing the martyrdom of Crispus Attucks and the favorable comments of Charles Pinckney and Henry Laurens as character evidence for the race. The Negroes were not aliens, he reminded the delegates, any more than the Caucasians. "A residence of our foreparents of near 300 years; birth and rearing here; our adaptation to the wants of the country; our labor and forebearance; our loyalty to the government—are all these elements indices of an alien race?" He made an adroit appeal to those who feared the disfranchisement of the poor whites, quoting remarks by Irby that the $300 property qualification would not be a sufficient alternative for those who were poor as well as illiterate. This point he illustrated with a story about a boy, exploring the banks of the Salkahatchie River, who chanced upon a moccasin and catfish trying to swallow each other. The moccasin thought he had been successful when he got the catfish down, but the fish's fin cut his throat. The moccasin personified the Reformers, he said, and the catfish represented the Conservatives who were achieving their objective of disfranchising the poor whites. Twitting the votaries of the Lost Cause tradition he said:

> The majority of you blame the poor Negro for the humility inflicted upon you during that conflict, but he had nothing to do with it. It was your love of power and your supreme arrogance that brought it upon yourselves. You are too feeble to settle up with the government for that grudge. This hatred has been centered on the Negro and he is the innocent sufferer of your spleen.[44]

Wigg renewed the appeal for a straight literacy qualification, indicating that an additional or alternative property qualification would be acceptable.

> You charge that the negro is too ignorant to be entrusted with the suffrage. I answer that you have not, nor dare you, make a purely educational test of the right to vote.
>
> You say that he is a figurehead and an encumbrance to the State,

[43] Miller, *Suffrage Speeches*, p. 3.
[44] *Ibid.*, pp. 5–13.

that he pays little or no taxes. I answer that you have not and you dare not make a purely property test of the right to vote.[45]

The doctrine of white supremacy he attacked with the statement that it was sheer fallacy.

> The doctrine so persistently taught that the interests of the negro and Anglo-Saxon are so opposed as to be irreconcilable is a political subterfuge; a fallacy so glaring in its inception, so insulting to Providence, so contrary to reason and logic of history, that one can scarcely refrain from calling in question either the sanity or honesty of its advocates.

Every white delegate, he said, had been pledged to the false doctrine of white supremacy, to the securing of it by either honest or dishonest methods. "Beneath this yoke, humiliating as it is, each one of you had to pass; to this pledge each one of you had to subscribe before you could have the privilege of being counted as a delegate to this convention." [46]

The following day two voices were heard, almost as if out of the past— those of Smalls and Whipper, the two men who had sat in the convention of 1868. Smalls charged fraud in the committee's suffrage article. He cited a violently anti-Negro politician who had remarked to some Negro friends that they should not take his speeches seriously as he only wanted to fool "the crackers" in order to get their votes. The suffrage plan, he said, might fool "the crackers," but no one else as to its essentially fraudulent nature. He dared Tillman to accept a straight literacy qualification which would leave a white majority of fourteen thousand in the electorate. Appealing to the white desire for cheap farm labor, he warned that the Negroes might leave the state if things became too hard for them. Already, he said, fifty-three thousand Negroes had been killed in the South since Reconstruction with not more than two or three white men convicted and hung.[47]

Whipper devoted the first part of his remarks to the denial that Negro government had ever existed in South Carolina, pointing out that up to 1895 Beaufort County offered an example of Negro willingness to accept white officeholders even where they outnumbered the whites by twenty to one. He charged bodies like the convention with inciting the crime of lynching and derided the white supremacists for trying to show their superiority by defrauding old slaves. Recalling the convention of 1868 he contended that although the whites had refused to lead the ignorant Negroes despite their pleas, those blacks had proceeded to give the state the best constitution it had ever had. Admitting that the Negroes had not been able to catch up with the white man's civilization in their thirty years of freedom he remarked that in 1868 most white men had been just as unfit for the suffrage as the Negroes because

[45] Columbia *State*, October 26, 1895.
[46] Miller, *Suffrage Speeches*, pp. 16–21.
[47] Columbia *State*, October 27, 1895.

one class of them had been kept in depths of ignorance and poverty only second to that of the slaves and the upper class still held to its belief in the right to hold human beings as property. Despite an illness, Whipper's speech was well organized and forcefully presented. The Columbia *State* said that the speech "was a powerful one and did credit to the coal black man who delivered it." [48]

Pleas by the lesser known and less experienced Reed and Anderson were presented on October 29. Reed deplored the unfair administration of justice to the Negroes, but held that Negroes were perfectly willing to let the "intelligent" rule, many having in fact voted for Wade Hampton, Johnson Hagwood, and even B. R. Tillman for governor. In conciliatory tone he reminded the whites that they trusted Negroes with positions far closer to their personal welfare than the ballot box. "You have suffered the Negroes to harness... your costly steeds; you have suffered them to serve the delicacies of your festal boards; in short, you have suffered them to attend many other vocations of life which come nearer to your honor, nearer to your person and nearer to your property than casting a ballot." [49]

Anderson, the school teacher, pointed with pride to the great strides of progress made by the Negroes in the past thirty years and pleaded that he was asking for the suffrage on behalf of 100,000 patriotic citizens. "I am constrained to raise my voice in protest against the passage by this convention of the political scheme... proposed by the committee on suffrage. A scheme that will forever rivet the chain of disfranchisement upon the colored people of South Carolina. A scheme that was conceived in equity [in iniquity?] and born in sin." [50]

Senator J. L. M. Irby, "the poor man's friend," followed the Negroes two days later with a presentation of his objections to the suffrage scheme. Formerly an ardent Tillmanite and still chairman of the State Democratic Executive Committee, he vented his rage on the Tillman-Bryan suffrage scheme, predicting bloodshed if illiterate whites were disfranchised while educated Negroes were permitted to vote. The suffrage article, he said, "builds bombproofs and fortifications for the educated and property owning class... while it leaves the poor white man to risk and endure the tests of a hostile court." The understanding clause in his opinion was unconstitutional and would give the ballot to the illiterates only until it came to test in the federal courts.

The whole constitution, in fact, would be open to attack by the Supreme Court, he felt, because the leaders had not exercised discretion in stating the purpose of the convention. Perhaps overestimating both the political strength of the Negroes and the pride of the poor whites he said that the poor whites "would prefer to rely on the eight box law and whatever legislation might be necessary and fight it out with the Negro rather than undergo the humiliation of an examination that would be Greek to them." He urged the convention to

[48] *Ibid.*
[49] Miller, *Suffrage Speeches*, pp. 21–22.
[50] Columbia *Daily Register*, October 29, 1895.

leave things as they stood. Little wonder that Tillman accused him of having no solution at all.

In conclusion Irby pleaded that if the convention intended to accept the educational qualification the discussion of it be postponed at least until the education article had been accepted. "The proposition is highly proper. The educational report ought to be considered along with the suffrage, as both are interlocked with each other." [51]

Such telling blows had been landed by the Negroes and such favorable response elicited that Tillman felt the necessity for delivering a full dress reply with one eye cocked to the national audience that he knew was watching Columbia. He was prepared on October 31 and delivered his speech immediately after Irby's. Most of the speech was concerned with the swindles of Reconstruction days and especially with the taint of fraud that hung about the reputations of Smalls and Whipper. His objective was to answer Whipper's contention that there had never been "Negro government" by proving the responsibility of the Negro race for the corruption under Radical administrations. The radical constitution, made by the "ring streaked and striped carpetbagger convention," had been ratified by the Negroes and the Negroes had "put the little pieces of paper in the box that gave the commission to white scoundrels who were their leaders and the men who debauched them."

"How did we recover our liberty?" he asked; and he answered, "By fraud and violence. We tried to overcome the thirty thousand majority by honest methods, which was a mathematical impossibility. After we had borne these indignities for eight years life became worthless under such conditions. Under the leadership and inspiration of Mart Gary ... we won the fight."

He frankly stated the purpose of circumventing the United States Constitution so that the infamy could not return. The state should be constantly on guard "against the possibility of Negro suffrage; of this flood, which is now dammed up, breaking loose; or, like the viper that is asleep, only to be warmed into life again and sting us whenever some more white rascals ... mobilize the ignorant blacks."

The difficulty of the task Tillman recognized and confessed when the question of the poor whites arose, "If there was any way under high heaven by which we could do more than we have done, in God's name I would glory and honor the man, and bow down and submit to his leadership if he could show us." He defended the educational requirement, stating that the understanding clause might eventually be invalidated by the courts, but that it would serve as a temporary expedient and then suffrage would be founded on "a rock," the rock of educational requirements. As for the methods to be used by the registration boards, he said, in reply to a query by Irby:

> I said last night the chalice was poisoned. Some have said there is fraud in this understanding clause. Some poisons in small doses are very salutary and valuable medicines. If you put it here that a man must

[51] *Ibid.*, November 1, 1895.

understand, and you vest the right to judge whether he understands in an officer, it is a constitutional act. That officer is responsible to his conscience and his God, he is responsible to nobody else. There is no particle of fraud or illegality in it. It is just showing partiality, perhaps, (laughter) or discriminating. Ah, you grin, (turning to Mr. Patton) you of all men to get up here and wrap your Pharisaical robes around.[52]

Patton, a Columbia Conservative, had proposed the grandfather clause and had been an advocate of complete honesty in elections, with that one loophole to admit illiterate whites to the polls.

The Tillman speech had a strong effect on the convention, but the Columbia *State* was somewhat hesitant in its praise. It commented editorially as follows:

Tillman's idea was to spread this data of fraud and corruption before the people of the Union in justification of the suppression of the negro vote since. It might serve this purpose were there no other means of securing good government than election fraud and force. With the ten years' success of "the Georgetown plan" before us, however, we cannot admit that the "Edgefield plan" was the only way out of the wilderness after the victory of 1876 had broken the spirit of the negroes and their hope of again dominating the State.[53]

After the Tillman speech Smalls made a denial of his connection with any of the frauds charged against him. The chief witness against him, he claimed, had been a bank employee later convicted for stealing. One good Democratic member of the jury that had convicted him had only recently skipped to Canada after stealing twenty bales of cotton. He said that he had received promises that the case would be *nol prossed* if he would resign his seat in Congress and even an offer of $10,000 if he would resign, but had refused. The whole matter had been dragged into the debate "to inflame the passions of delegates against Republicans and force them to vote for this most infamous Suffrage Bill, which seeks to take away the right to vote from two-thirds of the qualified voters of the State." Concluding passionately he proclaimed that his race needed no special defense.

All they need is an equal chance in the battle of life. I am proud of them, and by their acts toward me, I know that they are not ashamed of me, for they have at all times honored me with their vote.

I stand here the equal of any man. I started out in the war with the

[52] *Convention Journal*, pp. 443-472.
[53] Columbia *State*, November 1, 1895. The mention of "the Georgetown plan" has reference to a fusion arrangement in Georgetown County whereby Negro Republicans and white Democrats divided the offices between themselves without a contest in the general election. Under this plan Robert B. Anderson was elected to the convention from the county with one Conservative Democrat and one Tillmanite Democrat.

...e such a glaring example, opposition to Bellinger's proposal was str... I. Rogers of Marlboro held that the proposal might cause the con... of an innocent sheriff who had been unable to prevent a lynching th... no fault of his own. Bellinger, however, held that strict accountability of... might encourage a little shooting, and a little shooting would mean th... of lynching. D. J. Bradham, at that time sheriff of Clarendon County, ag... with Bellinger and argued that the sheriff should be held strictly re... unless at least one member of the lynch mob were shot. He told o... stopped a lynch mob once by threatening to fire directly into it if it... any closer.[73]

B. R. Tillman moved an addition to Bellinger's proposal in order to secure a... degree of punishment for the mobs themselves. Every member of the m... would be responsible for damages of $5,000 to the person injured or to h... "personal representatives" in case of his death. Persons against whom judgment was found were to be imprisoned until the fine had been paid. The amendment was voted down 74–38.[74] Indicative of the temper of the times was Major T. G. Barker's statement that he voted against Tillman's amendment because "the provision is so extreme in its severity that it will defeat its own object, and...no conviction will be had under it."[75]

Bellinger's milder proposal was accepted, with the reservation that an officer to be removed must have been guilty of "negligence, permission, or connivance" in giving up his prisoner, but Tillman was able to add a provision that the county in which the lynching occurred should be liable to damages of not less than $2,000 to the legal representatives of the person lynched.[76]

On one issue the Negro delegates scored a noteworthy success by skillfully exploiting sectional feeling to secure a state-operated school for the higher education of their race. Claflin University, founded during the Reconstruction period under the auspices of the Methodist Episcopal Church, had continued with joint state and church support.[77] The bulk of the control, however, rested with the Northern Methodists, who antagonized the Negroes by favoring northern whites in appointments to the faculty and in other ways. R. B. Anderson declared that the colored people of the state wanted a school entirely free of sectarian control. Not mentioned by the Negro delegates, but perhaps an important factor in their effort was the white suspicion that the Methodist Episcopal Church was an organ of Radical propaganda, a feeling that sometimes endangered appropriations to the school.[78]

[73] Columbia Daily Register, November 10, 1895.
[74] Convention Journal, pp. 655–656.
[75] Ibid., p. 656.
[76] Ibid., 527–528; Constitution of 1895, Art. VI, Sec. 6.
[77] D. D. Wallace, History of South Carolina, III, 244.
[78] Columbia Daily Register, November 17, 1895; a white newspaper said in 1879 that northern emissaries of the Methodist Episcopal Church had "thoroughly trained and drilled [the Negroes] in hatred of and opposition to the whites." Yorkville (S. C.) Enquirer, Feb. 6, 1879.

Confederates; they threatened to punish me and I left them. I went to the Union army. I fought in seventeen battles to make glorious and perpetuate the flag that some of you trampled under your feet.[54]

J. C. Sheppard then added to Tillman's citations from the book of fraud, laying the responsibility for Reconstruction evils on the Negro race. Having served on the General Assembly's Committee on Frauds he was closely acquainted with a large number of the cases, but confined his speech to evidence that the dishonest bank employee had not been the only witness against Smalls. Smalls had been convicted before a Republican judge, he said, and with several Republicans on the jury.[55]

Thomas E. Miller, against whom no fraud was intimated, made the point in reply to Sheppard and Tillman that the corruption of one Negro could not be the valid basis for generalization against the race any more than Boss Tweed could be for the white race in New York or T. J. Mackey for the white race in South Carolina. Tillman's emphasis was laid on fraud in the period 1869–1873 when the Negro was still innocent and incompetent, he claimed. The Negroes were cleaning out the corruption in the period 1873–1876 after they had become more experienced in the affairs of government. They had started the investigations and repudiations of bonds that had been continued by the Democratic administrations.[56]

Two alternatives to the suffrage committee's plan were presented by the Negro delegates. Whipper presented a plan for bipartisan representation on the boards and registration only a short time before the general election.[57] Wigg added to these a restriction against forcing a voter to go more than eight miles to his box and a provision that a list of qualified voters should be posted in each precinct at least twenty days before an election so that a voter could not be informed at the last minute that he was ineligible.[58] These were of course voted down and all the pleas of their proponents ignored.

William Henderson of Berkeley, exasperated at the talk by the Negroes and Conservatives of the need for fair elections and perhaps confused by Tillman's irony about "showing partiality," declared frankly:

We don't propose to have any fair elections. We will get left at that every time. (Laughter) Who will be the managers? Won't they be Democrats and Republicans, and don't you see that will be a bar to the Democrats? I tell you, gentlemen, if we have fair elections in Berkeley we can't carry it. (Laughter) There's no use to talk about it. The black man is learning to read faster than the white man. And if he comes up and can read you have got to let him vote. Now are you going to throw it out (Laughter) ... We are perfectly disgusted

[54] Convention Journal, pp. 473–476.
[55] Ibid., pp. 476–480.
[56] Miller, Suffrage Speeches, pp. 13–15.
[57] Convention Journal, pp. 412–413.
[58] Ibid., pp. 411–412.

with hearing so much about fair elections. Talk all around, but make it fair and you'll see what'll happen. (Laughter) [59]

Later on November first the suffrage article passed the second reading by 69–37 with only eight Conservatives voting against it.[60] After the elision of the provisions for minority representation on the boards of registration and for appeal to any court, the measure passed the third reading by 77–41.[61] Opposition among the white delegates was sporadic and unorganized and sprang from disagreement as to method rather than purpose. T. E. Dudley of Marlboro, for instance, felt that "white supremacy may be secured without resorting to the perhaps questionable means adopted by the Convention"; and several Tillmanites, now followers of Irby, voted against it because of the property and educational qualifications. J. W. Gray, Greenville Tillmanite, feared that the article subjected the convention to "the charge of conspiracy to defraud a certain class of American citizens in the exercise of the elective franchise," which charge "may be sustained in the Supreme Court." [62]

The convention's preoccupation with Negro suffrage brought two other questions to the fore in its deliberations, racial intermarriage and lynching. When the provision against the marriage of Negroes with whites was reported out of the legislative committee Smalls saw an opportunity for backing the whites into a corner from which he thought they could not escape. He introduced an amendment providing that any white person found guilty of cohabiting with a Negro would be barred from holding office, and further that the child of such cohabitation would bear the name of its father and inherit property the same as if legitimate.[63] Wigg, the next day, speaking of the consternation Smalls had thrown into the white delegation, commented that the coons had the dogs up the tree for a change and intended to keep them there until they admitted they were wrong.[64] The Columbia *State* felt that the white delegates had no choice but to swallow the dose concocted by Smalls with the best grace they could muster.[65] Tillman, not entirely unsympathetic with Smalls' proposal, introduced a substitute amendment to punish miscegenation as a crime in order to "protect Negro women against the debauchery of white men degrading themselves to the level of black women," but the convention refused to accept either his substitute or the original motion. It contented itself with a simple provision against intermarriage.[66]

The issue of miscegenation also posed the delicate question of defining "Negro." The committee report spoke of "one eighth or more" of Negro blood. George Johnstone proposed that this be changed to read "any" Negro blood. George Tillman with rare realism opposed reducing the quota below one-eighth.

[59] Columbia *Daily Register*, November 2, 1895.
[60] *Convention Journal*, p. 483; Columbia *State*, November 2, 1895.
[61] *Convention Journal*, p. 517.
[62] *Ibid.*, pp. 517–518.
[63] Columbia *State*, October 3, 1895.
[64] *Ibid.*, October 4, 1895.
[65] *Ibid.*
[66] *Constitution of 1895*, Art. III, Sec. 33.

He mentioned that he was acquainted with several families i... District, which had a small infusion of Negro blood, yet, h... soldiers to the Confederacy and were now accepted in respec... did not want to see these families needlessly embarrassed. In a... the astounding claim that there was not one pure-blooded Ca... floor of the convention. The "taint" was not necessarily Negro,... tained that all had ancestors from at least one of the colored rac... he called for the retention of the provisions in the marriage la... 1879.[67] Under that law only persons with one-fourth or more Negro... prohibited from marrying whites. But as finally included in the co... the clause was allowed to stand as reported by the committee, with t... tion set at one-eighth.[68] Technically it applied only to the question... marriage, but was the only standard for determining race included in t... stitution. The only other place in the constitution where race is spec... mentioned is in a provision requiring racial segregation in the public sc... a direct reversal of the unenforced ban on segregation in the 1868 constitu...

The question of lynching was forcefully and repeatedly brought to... attention of the convention by the Negroes. At the beginning of the sec... week I. R. Reed introduced a proposal to give the governor power to remov... and replace any official who allowed personal harm to come to any prisoner in... his custody, and also to give the governor specific authority to call out the militia in case of a threatened lynching. His proposal was returned to the Committee on Declaration of Rights without any action.[69]

Wiggs proposed to add to the oath of office in addition to the affirmation that one had not taken part in a duel the words "or in a lynching bee." His proposal was likewise lost.[70]

Strangely, more stringent anti-lynching proposals were introduced by white delegates. George D. Bellinger offered a motion to have any officer who permitted a prisoner to be seized "by force or strategy" removed from office and upon conviction become ineligible to hold any office unless pardoned by the governor.[71] It was aimed primarily at preventing lynchings rather than punishing those who took part by placing a great part of the responsibility on officers who were lax in protecting prisoners or who even connived with the mob. A tragic result of official negligence occurred in Hampton County on the very day that Bellinger introduced his proposal. Three Negroes were sentenced to death and one to life imprisonment for murder. A mob seized William Blake, the man sentenced to life, as he was being led from the courthouse by a deputy and lynched him in a nearby woods. Before the day was over a coroner's jury returned a verdict of death at the hands of parties unknown.[72]

[67] Columbia *Daily Register*, October 17, 1895.
[68] *Constitution of 1895*, Art. III, Sec. 33.
[69] *Convention Journal*, pp. 122–123, 275.
[70] *Ibid.*, p. 316.   [71] *Ibid.*, p. 358.
[72] Columbia *State*, October 18, 1895. The other three went to their deaths in December, admitting their guilt, but still protesting the innocence of Blake, who had been lynched.

Thomas E. Miller proposed that the state establish a school entirely separate from the Methodist-controlled university and provide that only "Southern men or women of the Negro race" be on the faculty.[79]

The agitation by the Negro delegates led Ben Tillman to move for the establishment of a separate school in Orangeburg to be called the Colored Normal, Industrial, Agricultural, and Mechanical College of South Carolina, with representation to be given to the colored race on the faculty, but with no rigid restrictions as to the makeup of the faculty. His motion was accepted.[80]

The Constitutional Convention of 1895 had been called for the primary purpose of eliminating the Negroes from political influence in South Carolina, and the six Negroes on the floor of the convention constantly reminded the white delegates that the project was incomplete. Even when problems other than suffrage, lynching, or miscegenation were under consideration the central theme of race recurred with the regularity of a symphonic motif. The most innocuous motions by Negro delegates were usually voted down. A mood of vacillation could be induced at any time by the merest suggestion that the question under consideration might contain some possible ramifications of Negro influence. Almost every issue involved the race question in one aspect or another: a democratic impulse toward home rule in local government foundered on the Negro majority; and the matter of education was inextricably bound to the suffrage, since an educational qualification was the trump card of the white supremacists. Tillman said that he did not intend to build a barrier to the suffrage with one hand and tear it down with the other.[81] The Negro's drinking habits entered the discussion of liquor control; his ownership of "yaller dogs," the debate on taxation; and the distribution of Negro population into the problem of creating new counties.

Thus was ushered in the era of complete white political domination. No Negro has since been elected to Congress from South Carolina. The "Georgetown plan" was continued for the next three elections, sending R. B. Anderson to the General Assembly in 1896 and J. W. Bolts in 1898 and 1900. Bolts and George E. Herriot, the Georgetown County Superintendent of Education, who went down to defeat in 1902,[82] were the last Negroes to be elected to state and county offices in South Carolina.

[79] Convention Journal, pp. 577, 580.
[80] Ibid., p. 581. The Columbia Daily Register soon afterward recommended that Thomas E. Miller be named president of the new institution, a position in which he was placed the following year and in which he served until 1911. Columbia Daily Register, November 29, 1895; Biographical Directory, p. 1315.
[81] Simkins, Ben Tillman, p. 303.
[82] Reports and Resolutions of the General Assembly of the State of South Carolina (1903), II, 1380.

Leslie H. Fishel, Jr.

THE NEGRO IN NORTHERN

POLITICS, 1870–1900

In the ideology of Negro protest leaders, political activity has always been regarded as a major strategy for protecting race interests and achieving equality in the United States. In the post-Reconstruction generation, while southern Negroes were losing the right to vote, black men of the North, who had been fully enfranchised by the Fifteenth Amendment, seriously participated in the political process. As Leslie H. Fishel demonstrates, for many reasons the effectiveness of their efforts was severely limited. Fishel's article has a significance that extends far beyond the period which he studies. Even today, with Negroes forming a far higher proportion of the electorate than at the end of the last century, many of the same factors weaken the power of the black vote as an instrument of protest.

The decade and a half after the Civil War provided the Negro with a perplexing introduction into politics. The northern Negro, while on the whole more politically perceptive than his southern counterpart, miscalculated the force and direction of politics with consequences that were to harm the race for years to come. Led by Frederick Douglass and a host of lesser lights, the northern Negro married himself to the Republican party. Too late he awoke to the fact that his party had discarded the traits which at first made the association mutually beneficial. By the 1880's, separation had become difficult if not impossible, divorce out of the question, and those Negroes and whites who had most to gain from a continuance of the union kept reminding the colored man of his obligations to a party whose appeal was illusory, and whose most attractive quality was a memory.

In the summer of 1880, the *Nation* pointed to the basic problem of the northern Negro: prejudice against his political acceptance. The South, the jour-

Leslie H. Fishel, Jr., "The Negro in Northern Politics, 1870–1900," *Mississippi Valley Historical Review*, XLII (December, 1955), pp. 466–489. Reprinted with the permission of the publisher and author.

nal explained, could be excused for reacting against "negro majorities," for "we are asking [Southerners] to face without fear a problem which no Northern State has ever been called on to face, and which we have no doubt none of them would face with equanimity or in a spirit of strict legality.... We all know we should be greatly alarmed by the prospect of anything of the kind in Massachusetts or New York or California." [1] Up to this time neither northern nor southern politicians had accepted the black man as a man; they merely used him, and for fifteen years the Negro had misconstrued this puppet activity as real participation. By 1880 the realities of power politics had revealed to the Negro the hollowness of Republican professions of faith in equality and civil rights. After 1880 the northern colored man tried almost desperately to strip white condescension and black obsequiousness from the realm of politics; he sought that equal recognition granted to other minority groups.[2]

The year of Appomattox had marked the awakening of the Negro's political ambitions. Democrats in New Bedford, Massachusetts, exploited the colored vote that year by running a Negro for the state legislature in order to defeat a temperance candidate. Republicans in Boston successfully parried the threat of a Negro independent ticket by promising to support a colored man for the legislature the following year. With an unusual faithfulness, the party successfully backed the selection of two Negroes for the general court in 1866. For the New York *Independent*, a Radical Republican paper, these signs heralded "A New Era in American Politics." [3]

This description was premature. After a few colored postal and custom-house employees were appointed in Massachusetts and a constable elected in Waterville, Maine, the "New Era" began to look like the old barter system of political favors exchanged for votes, with the G.O.P. driving a hard bargain.[4] The race's awareness of the party's arbitrary control was evident in the rejection by three prominent colored men of President Andrew Johnson's offer of the job of commissioner of the Freedmen's Bureau. Here was an opportunity to do constructive work for the nation and the Negro, yet all three nominees, caught in the middle of the fight between Johnson and the Radical Republicans, bowed to the dictates of politics. Robert Purvis of Pennsylvania refused the offer because he did not want "to jeopard the interests of the cause in which his life had been spent, or to sacrifice his self-respect by consenting to be an instrument in the hands of Andrew Johnson." Frederick Douglass mulled over the tempting proposal for a long time before yielding to party considera-

[1] *Nation* (New York), XXXI (July 29, 1880), 72.

[2] In 1880 there were 412,715 Negroes and 25,285,891 whites in the fourteen northern states east of the Mississippi River. U.S. Bureau of Census, *Negro Population, 1790–1915* (Washington, 1918), 44, Table XIII.

[3] New York *Independent*, November 23, 1865, November 8, 15, December 20, 1866.

[4] John Daniels, *In Freedom's Birthplace: A Study of Boston's Negroes* (Boston, 1914), 98–99; New York *Independent*, April 29, 1869; New York *Evening Post*, March 22, 1867.

tions. The Radical faction, Douglass knew, would never forgive him if he accepted this turncoat position.[5]

In the six states which permitted the Negro to vote,[6] his political position was precarious at best; over the rest of the North, without the franchise, he had little political status. From 1865 to the passage of the Fifteenth Amendment race leaders sought relief in universal manhood suffrage. New York groups petitioned the state constitutional convention in vain for the privilege. Equal rights leagues in the North agitated for the franchise, but state after state rejected this bid for the ballot. Republican politicians and northern electorates were not ready to support this measure and the Fifteenth Amendment was devised to insure political control in the South rather than to fulfill an obligation to the North.[7] Nevertheless, when the article was officially declared part of the Constitution in 1870, Negroes celebrated and clamored for recognition proportionate to their voting power. "It appears," the Nation explained, "or some of their more or less judicious friends strive to make it appear for them that the newly-enfranchised have 'claims' to a Congressman, to at least four places in the [Pennsylvania] legislature, and to some profitable county office." [8]

The furore in 1870 was premature. When the Negro question as a political issue in the North was removed by the Fifteenth Amendment, the Negro himself was unprepared to be a political participant. Ennui and apathy marked the northern attitude toward the race in the decade to follow. Three factors largely account for this change. New issues and exciting economic developments drew the attention of the North. The resurgence of political reform in both national and local circles, the spirit of industrialization, the boom in railroads, and the crisis in the nation's economy did not leave much room for discussions of the Negro.

The Negro was further isolated by an old enemy. Prejudice against colored men engaging in politics remained strong. Respected white leaders like Gideon Welles and Orville H. Browning doubted the wisdom of Negroes entering the political arena. Early in 1870, the Nation commented that "the position of the negro a year hence, not only in Connecticut, but in every Northern state where his enfranchisement is reluctantly endured, will be something curious to observe." [9] Curiosity gave way to tragedy the following

[5] New York Independent, September 5, 12, October 10, 1867; Benjamin Quarles, Frederick Douglass (Washington, 1948), 239.

[6] Maine, New Hampshire, Vermont, Massachusetts, Rhode Island, and New York.

[7] This interpretation is more fully treated in Leslie H. Fishel, Jr., "Northern Prejudice and Negro Suffrage, 1865–1870," Journal of Negro History (Washington), XXXIX (January, 1954), 8–26.

[8] Nation, X (May 5, 1870), 279; New York Times, October 8, 1868; Washington New Era, February 17, April 14, June 2, 1870. The Nation editorially supported the Radical Republicans in their efforts with Negro groups up until the spring of 1867. Thereafter the journal gradually lost its interest in the Radical program, and its comments became less frequent and more skeptical of Radical proposals.

[9] Nation, X (April 7, 1870), 215; Diary of Gideon Welles (3 vols., Boston, 1911), III, 143, cited in Quarles, Frederick Douglass, 238; Theodore C. Pease and James G.

year when a promising young colored school principal of Philadelphia was assassinated in an election riot. In 1879 James G. Blaine and James A. Garfield agreed that there were many who disapproved of Negro voting, "mostly," in Blaine's words, "resident in the South, but with numerous sympathizers in the North." With some truth a Negro journal could later observe regretfully: "We have always known that there was a sentiment in the North strongly opposed to Negro suffrage. This has never been a secret." [10]

A final factor which led to Negro inertia in politics was the tight control which the Republican party maintained over the colored man. During the 1872 campaign, Charles Sumner, Blaine, Andrew D. White, and Douglass engaged in a spirited exchange on the subject of President U. S. Grant's color prejudice and how it would affect the colored vote. When Sumner charged that Grant's bias had tainted the party, the others sprang to the President's defense. Sumner, idol of the race, could find only twenty-four Negroes to endorse his pro-Greeley stand.[11]

Nowhere was this master-servant relationship more apparent than in the convention which nominated Rutherford B. Hayes. Each faction there claimed that it controlled the black vote and the convention listened deferentially to colored orators. This attitude, however, "was made extremely comical by the transparent way in which the real feelings of the dominant color now and then showed itself, as in the almost public boast by one delegate that his party 'had a better nigger' than one of the other candidates." [12] In the campaign that followed, Frederick Douglass, who had the previous year complained about whites' indifference to blacks, jumped on the Hayes bandwagon and rode it into the patronage position of marshal of the District of Columbia. Subordination, not independence, was the watchword of the period.[13]

Douglass was not the only one to profit from this status. John E. Bruce, reminiscing about the years after 1873, remembered Jake and Rush Simms, William H. Johnson, and Pierre Barquet as "a few among the [Negro] political worthies of the period who carried the colored vote in one vest pocket and the *mazuma* in another." [14] Other ambitious Negro leaders made the rounds of colored meetings to endorse a party candidate or plead for political re-

---

Randall (eds.), *The Diary of Orville Hickman Browning* (2 vols., Springfield, Ill., 1925–1933), II, 258–59.

[10] Cleveland *Gazette*, March 27, 1889. See also William H. Johnson and John T. Chapman (comps.), *Autobiography of W. H. Johnson* (Albany, 1900), 127–29; James G. Blaine and others, "Ought the Negro to Be Disfranchised? Ought He to Have Been Enfranchised?" *North American Review* (Boston, New York), CXXVIII (March, 1879), 226, 245–47.

[11] *Nation*, XV (August 8, 15, and 22, 1872), 81–82, 97–98, 114.

[12] *Ibid.*, XXII (June 22, 1876), 393.

[13] Cleveland *Leader*, March 3, 1875, in Works Progress Administration (comps.), *Annals of Cleveland: A Digest and Index of the Newspaper Record of Events and Opinions* (59 vols., Cleveland, 1937–1938), LVIII, 349; *Nation*, XXIV (March 22, 1877), 169.

[14] "Bruce-Grit" (nom de plume of John E. Bruce), undated manuscript, John E. Bruce Papers (Schomburg Collection, New York Public Library).

wards.[15] By the late 1870's the situation appeared to brighten as Negroes trickled into local office in big cities: a policeman and a fireman here, a mail carrier there, and a few elected officials in Cleveland, Chicago, and Boston.[16] In strategic locations, these jobholders were more numerous and destined to be more permanent than their predecessors a decade earlier. But to a colored newspaper editor looking back from the next decade the picture was gloomy.

> Here in New York [he said] where the white wardheelers have con-
> trolled our votes ever since the war, what have we to show for it?
> These white heelers have made millions of dollars and a widespread
> notoriety which we cannot call fame, but what have the colored voters
> gained? The same is true of Boston, Providence, Philadelphia and
> other Northern cities. Not one black man in New York State enjoys
> the respect or confidence of the Republican politicians or can ap-
> proach one of these sharpers on terms anything like equal footing.
> And this may apply to the colored leaders throughout the country
> in their relations to the politicians of the National Republican party.[17]

In spite of the increased flow of Negroes into scattered minor offices, the editor had grounds for his complaint. The Civil Rights Act of 1875, the statutory high point of the decade for the race, reflected more a determined Republican effort to maintain its supremacy in the South than an egalitarian gesture of good will and acceptance of a minority group. Charles Sumner had advanced the original idea in Congress in 1870 in order to spell out Negro rights under the Fourteenth Amendment, to satisfy the requests of Negro leaders, and to strengthen the Negro's party ties.[18] With Sumner ostracized from party councils after 1872, the first two motives were completely over-shadowed by the political necessity of keeping colored southern Republicans loyal. There was no sense of political bargaining or acceptance, no sense of humanitarianism in the shaping of this statute. The six petitions to Congress from northern Negroes had an air of suspicion about them since two of them originated in states which already had civil rights laws and two others were engineered by a New England Negro, George T. Downing. Congressional debate, distracted in the House by personal attacks on Benjamin F. Butler, languished dismally through two sessions, emphasizing the bill's constitutional aspects. The act was generally recognized as a requirement of the party's

---

[15] Boston *Evening Transcript*, September 23, 24, 26, 29, 1874; New York *Times*, October 22, 1875.

[16] Cleveland *Leader*, March 25, April 8, December 22, 1876, in *Annals of Cleveland*, LVIII, 267, 301, 1224; Harold F. Gosnell, *Negro Politicians* (Chicago, 1933), 198, 375; Washington *New Era*, March 10, 1870; "Investigation into the Causes of the Removal of the Negroes from the Southern States to the Northern States," *Senate Reports*, No. 693, 46 Cong., 2 Sess. (1880), Pt. I, pp. 18, 150, 279; New York *Globe*, October 13, 1883.

[17] New York *Freeman*, November 28, 1885.

[18] Edward L. Pierce, *Memoir and Letters of Charles Sumner* (4 vols., Boston, 1893), IV, 499–504, 580–82.

southern policy and was of little political or—as it turned out—social consequence to northern Negroes.[19]

The 1870's were a trying period for the Negro in politics. Pushed out of the limelight by other interests, beset by prejudice and subordination, the race could take hope only in the increased low-level patronage jobs which were slowly becoming available to its members. In the 1880's colored leaders began a determined drive toward two major objectives: to build up a sense of race loyalty among Negroes and to overcome discrimination in politics. The campaign commenced with publicity about officeholding, a neat recognition of the only bright spot in the previous decade. Without regard for their number or quality, Negro politicians were etched as Negro pioneers breaking down barriers. Colored newspapers repetitiously publicized Negro recipients of office and as loudly damned failures to gain additional offices. State-employed laborers in Albany, a prison commissioner in Connecticut, a county auditor in Pennsylvania, a ward constable and assessor in Cleveland, a nominee for circuit court commissioner in a Michigan county, a state representative in Rhode Island—these were some positions filled by Negroes about which the race could read with satisfaction in the early eighties.[20] Simultaneously they were reminded of their insufficient representation in local governments and the difficulties of achieving more adequate recognition. When an Atlantic City colored policeman was appointed, four whites quit. Cleveland Negroes threatened to desert the Republican party unless it helped to increase the number and importance of jobs for Negroes. Chicago colored men defended their segregated fire company as a half loaf, better than none.[21] The Boston correspondent of the New York *Freeman* complained about discrimination by the local postmaster: "None of our race in the post office has any love for Postmaster Tobey, as his treatment of the colored clerks and employees has been shameful, denying them all opportunity for advancement and previous to the adoption of civil service rules it was no easy matter for a colored man to get any kind of position there." [22] The Chicago colored community boiled in the summer of 1885 when the governor opened his office to a white group but refused to see a colored delegation.[23]

As the race quickened the tempo of their campaign, Negroes began to run for elective office. Here they encountered numerous obstacles. The party caucus could slight the colored neophyte; this happened in Youngstown, Pittsburgh, Boston, and in Great Barrington, Massachusetts, where Republican chieftains considered and then rejected the choice of the Negro group. In

---

[19] *Cong. Record*, 43 Cong., 1 Sess., 76, 101, 187, 353, 568, 1976, 3455–57, 3827, 4083–88, 4143–47; 2 Sess., 940–51, 1701–98, 1870; *Nation*, XVIII (January 8, 1874), 17, XIX (September 17, 1874), 180, XX (April 8, 1875), 233–34; New York *Times*, February 28, 1875.

[20] New York *Globe*, November 24, 1883, February 2, 1884; Cleveland *Gazette*, March 8, April 12, October 18, 1884, April 11, 1885.

[21] Cleveland *Gazette*, August 25, December 15, 1883, November 15, 1884.

[22] New York *Freeman*, March 21, 1885.

[23] Cleveland *Gazette*, July 25, 1885.

Philadelphia and Omaha the race was too poorly organized to attract any Republican attention at all. Other Negroes risked political ostracism by running as independents, as in Pennsylvania and Rhode Island. A rejected colored Republican in Massachusetts went so far as to accept a Democratic nomination for the same office. Even those hopefuls who got on the ticket found, as in Ohio in 1885, Connecticut in 1886, and Pennsylvania in 1891, that the electorate considered color over party and scratched them from the ballot.[24]

In addition to seeking office, Negroes endeavored to improve their political standing by scrutinizing the racial attitudes of candidates and tendering or refusing them support accordingly. Colored spokesmen used ingenious methods to inject a racial tinge into every possible election contest. In state or municipal affairs, the colored press generally looked at the candidates' record toward the race before advising its readers how to vote. This sometimes worked favorably for the Republicans, as in an Ohio congressional election in 1884, and sometimes unfavorably, as in a contest for district attorney in Wilkes-Barre, Pennsylvania, the next year. In Cambridge, a Democratic mayor corralled the colored vote because of what Negroes considered to be his fairness toward them, while Fred Grant, the General's son, candidate for secretary of state of New York, found his treatment of a colored cadet at West Point and his snub of Negroes who had marched in his father's funeral procession used against him.[25]

Presidential candidates were similarly judged in 1884. Negroes regarded Chester A. Arthur's effort to gain the Republican nomination with contempt, while some looked with favor upon their old friend, the Greenback candidate, Benjamin F. Butler. Blaine and Logan, however, had the organization and, in spite of malcontents and dissensions, secured Negro support. The southern Democratic position on the race question prevented northern blacks from voting the Democratic ticket. The Cleveland *Gazette* pulled out some old anti-Negro speeches of Thomas A. Hendricks, the Democratic vice-presidential candidate, while others waved the flag, and invoked the "rebellion."[26]

Four years later, with the upsurge of the tariff as a major issue, colored editors had more difficulty. Try as they might they could not relevantly apply it to any real race interest. Although they warned against the evils of free trade to workingmen, they could not pin down any specific benefits which protection would secure for them. The Chicago *Conservator* asked bluntly: "Why should the colored voter be expected to enthuse over any talk of protecting skilled labor? We have no skilled labor nor can we have any." A white politician

[24] *Ibid.*, May 22, October 2, 1886, April 2, 1887, May 22, November 14, 1891; New York *Freeman*, October 16, November 7, 1886; New York *Globe*, September 29, 1883; New York *Age*, March 28, 1891; *Nation*, XLI (October 22, 1885), 331-32, XLIII (September 2, 1886), 185.

[25] Cleveland *Gazette*, August 9, 1884, November 10, 1888; New York *Freeman*, October 17, 1885, December 11, 18, 1886, October 1, 1887.

[26] New York *Globe*, May 31, June 14, August 23, November 8, 1884; Cleveland *Gazette*, August 9, 1884; unsigned manuscript letter to the editor, September 4, 1884, Bruce Papers.

turned to the Negro press to explain protection's pertinence, and extolled the "splendid progress [which] will automatically open the doors of all the arts to the colored man by the increased demand for his labor." [27] As the contest proceeded through the summer and autumn of 1888, one influential Negro paper slowly shifted its emphasis from tariff back to suffrage and violence in the Democratic South. More vocal and more ambitious in politics now, the northern Negro was stung by the campaign's failure to stress racial issues and his internal quarrels became all the more bitter.

In 1890 the introduction of a congressional bill to insure Negro suffrage in the South encouraged the race to some extent in its Republicanism, but even this did not eradicate dissension, as W. E. B. DuBois' opposition to the proposal indicated. Moreover, the bill's quick defeat by a bargain between silver senators and Democrats and its rapid removal from the public eye merely served to increase race agitation. The colored Cleveland *Gazette* agreed with Albion W. Tourgee's analysis of the 1892 election that the Republicans lost because they failed to stress Negro rights and liberty. With more emotion than accuracy, the *Gazette* added that the party had not used the race issue in 1884 and had lost, but they had used it in 1888 and had won.[28]

Free silver and imperialism, perhaps the two major issues of the 1890's, held only a divisive potential for the northern Negro groups. The silver question had little interest for a non-agrarian laboring force; they were mere spectators during this bruising conflict. Imperialism, however, undermined Negro unity since Negroes tended naturally to sympathize with other non-white and oppressed peoples. Anti-imperialism was written on the flag of the Democratic party while the traditional party of northern Negroes supported imperialism. A staunch G.O.P. paper like the Cleveland *Gazette* could throw party loyalties temporarily to the winds in praising Cleveland's humanitarian handling of the Hawaiian situation as "blunt, manly and statesmanlike." Two years earlier, the caustic Negro Republican, John E. Bruce, wrote T. Thomas Fortune that public opinion wanted a Negro as minister to Haiti "who can be made a plastic tool of the influences.... The Dollar hunters of the U Snakes [*sic*] want the Haitian trade I imagine worse than that trade wants them." [29] The Spanish-American War and its consequent territorial acquisitions accentuated the frustrations of the Negro group.[30] Behind the façade of the quarrels over imperialism and free silver, however, was one great change noted

[27] Cleveland *Gazette*, July 28, 1888; Chicago *Conservator*, quoted in New York *Age*, July 28, 1888.

[28] Cleveland *Gazette*, March 22, 1890, January 17, 1891, November 9, 1892; New York *Age*, June 13, 1891; E. Lawrence Godkin, "The Republican Party and the Negro," *Forum* (New York), VII (May, 1889), 252–53; *Nation*, LI (August 7, 1890), 102, LV (August 25, 1892), 135. Albion W. Tourgee was a white journalist and writer from the South who was then living in the North.

[29] Cleveland *Gazette*, December 23, 1893; Bruce to T. Thomas Fortune, July 24, 1891, Bruce Papers.

[30] The documents in Herbert Aptheker (ed.), *Documentary History of the Negro People in the United States* (New York, 1951), 817–26, are revealing but somewhat one-sided in their emphasis on anti-imperialism.

by the *Nation* in 1896: the Negro question was not brought up for national discussion by state Republican platforms.[31] The nineteenth century was ending with northern Negroes out on a forgotten limb.

Hard as colored leaders worked to avoid this position by a reinterpretation and a re-emphasis of issues, they did not rely on this procedure alone. Nationally, northern Negroes had to compete for political favors with their southern brethren who were frequently more strategically situated.[32] This rivalry led to a re-examination of the vote distribution in presidential elections to demonstrate how loyal northern colored electorates had swung crucial states into the Republican column.[33] Although this type of reasoning may be open to question, it reflected an attempt by northern Negroes to draw to themselves the importance they believed they should have. Using this balance of power argument, they could and did increase their demands.

Even though they claimed to hold a balance of power in key northern areas, colored Republican leaders had yet to prove that they controlled the Negro votes which made up that balance. One reason for this inadequate control was the growing tendency of Negroes to seek salvation outside the portals of Republicanism, partly a reflection of mugwumpism and partly a reaction to shabby treatment. A second factor was the personality of the colored group and its leaders. Lack of organization, absence of discipline, bitter jealousy and its consequent feuding characterized Negro political units in almost all northern states. President Cleveland's tendency to recognize the Negro in appointments to an extent equal to that of his Republican predecessors excited the suspicion of colored leaders but the admiration of the colored people. He chose George W. Williams, the historian, for his minister to Haiti, but withdrew the nomination when it ran into opposition and substituted the name of John E. W. Thompson, another Negro. He fought for James C. Matthews' appointment as recorder of deeds in the District of Columbia, but had to bow to Republican opposition in the Senate, because, according to administration supporters, Matthews "was a Democratic Negro and Republican senators did not believe in encouraging Negroes to vote the Democratic ticket." Republicans' emphasis on purely party interests did not soothe their agitated colored partisans.[34]

The Republican party had never shrunk from a continued effort to keep the colored vote in the North intact. Occasionally through the use of nationally known figures the party propagandized the Negro group as a whole. These public exertions ranged from the publishing of letters to colored voters by Frederick Douglass and other well-known men to the granting of special and well-publicized favors during a campaign. The appointment of John R. Lynch as temporary chairman of the 1884 national convention swelled race

[31] *Nation*, LXII (May 21, 1896), 391–92.
[32] Cleveland *Gazette*, March 8, 15, 1884.
[33] George W. Williams, *The Negro as a Political Problem* (Boston, 1884), 29–30; New York *Age*, June 16, 1888; *Nation*, XLVII (November 22, 1888), 413.
[34] New York *Freeman*, May 16, 1885, March 5, 1887; *Nation*, XLIII (August 12, 1886), 130–31.

pride while the few black alternate delegates at large, then and four years later, helped to preserve the attitude. Blaine-Logan and Harrison-Morton clubs worked on a segregated basis to match pride with enthusiasm and votes.[35]

Patronage stretched from the smallest community to the federal government. It rewarded the skeptical but faithful editor of the Cleveland *Gazette*, Harry C. Smith, with the post of deputy state inspector of oils. Chicago's Negro representative to the Illinois legislature, J. W. E. Thomas, effectively tied the colored vote to himself and the party with a judicious distribution of spoils. Michael C. Kerwin, collector of internal revenue at New York City, sufficiently impressed that persistent and bitter job-seeker, John E. Bruce, to be characterized as one who "makes no invidious discrimination on account of color in the distribution of patronage at his command." [36] President Harrison did not strain to place Negroes on the federal payroll, and while he was severely criticized for ignoring the North outside of his own state of Indiana, he did appoint colored men to offices like that of recorder of the General Land Office, which had not previously been awarded to them.[37]

The G.O.P. applied pressures more subtle than patronage on Negro leaders, and other parties interested in attracting colored voters followed suit. Generous contributions from party coffers to Negro newspapers was an effective short-run means of building up support. John J. Freeman, editor of the *Progressive American* in the 1870's and early 1880's, received bonuses for maintaining his Republican bias. When he accepted a Democratic appointment in the sheriff's office, he was denounced for his ingratitude. In the 1880's, T. Thomas Fortune resigned his editorship of the *Freeman* because the Prohibition party failed to give him enough financial support. "When I got sick of running it at my own expense as a Prohibition paper," he said, "I turned it over to the present publishers, who are making a good Republican paper of it." After the 1888 election, of the seventy or eighty Negro papers active, including ten Democratic sheets, a number were begun in the campaign and were expected to fold soon after it.[38]

Additional political pressure was put on the Negro electorate through the simple expedient of buying votes. Neither the Republican nor the Democratic party was above the corruption which tainted the era. Negroes in Cambridge were in 1884 induced to vote in a Republican caucus for an aspiring congressman who distributed dollars to his supporters. In Newport, Rhode Island, George Downing, a Negro mugwump, charged a colored minister with accepting $100 from a Republican candidate. Two other ministers joined their accused colleague to defend their tactics. The impecuniosity of their churches

[35] *Public Opinion* (Washington), IV (October 22, 1887), 27, VI (October 13, 1888), 5–6, VII (May 25, 1889), 139; Cleveland *Gazette*, June 7, September 27, 1884, April 21, June 30, August 11, 1888.

[36] Cleveland *Gazette*, March 15, 1884, May 22, 1886; "Bruce-Grit" column, *ibid.*, February 28, 1891, Scrapbook No. 1, Bruce Papers.

[37] New York *Age*, May 18, 25, 1889.

[38] "Bruce-Grit," undated manuscript, Bruce Papers; New York *Globe*, February 3, 1884; New York *Age*, April 28, November 11, 1888.

forced them to solicit gratuitous offerings which, they argued, was a practice "in keeping with our American idea of voluntary support of the gospel." The Republican candidate for governor, they maintained, just happened to contribute generously to their churches.[39] In a local New York City election a Republican observer excitedly condemned the opposition for buying votes in colored precincts. "My best friends come to me today," he quoted a Negro Republican worker as stating, "and say that they would like to vote the Republican ticket but they have been offered $4 for their vote, and that is too great an inducement for them to withstand." Negroes in Indiana were accused in 1888 of selling their votes for gold pieces and four years later of supporting the pre-convention Harrison faction in the G.O.P. for pay. The colored organizer was reported to have claimed that "he had a family to support and it was a matter of money with him." A Boston correspondent twice felt compelled to defend that city's ninth ward, heavily populated with Negroes, against charges of corruption by Republican money.[40]

These complexities of corruption and patronage mirrored the politics of the times. The independence movement among Negroes, with its quibbling leadership, its numerous high hopes and false starts, reflected the confusion and disappointment characteristic of other minority groups like the small farmers, the American Protective Association, or the "goo-goo" reformers.

Since the tie that bound the northern Negroes together was race, it was on that basis that the first inklings of dissatisfaction with Republicanism appeared. In 1880 some New York City colored men announced that they would not vote for Garfield because the Republican governor of the state had refused to pardon a Negro criminal. Three years later Akron's Negroes pledged themselves to defeat a Republican aspirant who had allegedly insulted the race.[41]

By 1883, the movement, bolstered by white mugwumpism yet saturated with black racism, got into full swing. George Downing spearheaded the independents in Rhode Island, endorsing the state Democratic ticket and running some candidates separately. The outcome established a pattern that would dog similar Negro efforts in the years to come: lack of interest, lack of organization, and a split in the race group. White Republicans used the influential Providence *Journal* to blast these rebellious attempts. Colored G.O.P. faithfuls tried to stem the tide in other localities. When forty New York City politicians met at the Sumner House in the late summer of the year to press for political recognition, some colored leaders opposed it vehemently. In Cleveland a day or two earlier a colored Republican club signed only 27 out of 200 to a promise to vote a straight party ticket. Fortune's attack on two

---

[39] New York *Globe*, September 6, 1884; New York *Freeman*, May 9, 16, 30, 1885.

[40] Edgar J. Levey, "An Election in New York," *North American Review*, CXLV (December, 1887), 681; *Nation*, XLVII (November 22, 1888), 412; *Civil Service Chronicle* (Indianapolis), I, (October, 1892), 378–79; New York *Age*, November 24, 1888, December 21, 1889.

[41] *Nation*, XXXI (August 26, 1880), 143; Cleveland *Gazette*, September 15, 1883.

national Republican administrations was reprinted in both cities with evident approval.[42]

Out of the pre-election year chaos came one bold attempt to organize race dissatisfaction. In the spring of 1883, leading Washington Negroes put out a call for a convention. Their address was greeted with derision and doubt, to such an extent that some of the signers repudiated their signatures. One part of the address, urging preparedness for a "great political revolution," brought a response from the sharp pen of John E. Bruce. He charged that the convention organizers had "fattened at the public crib" as Republican appointees and that now, with the prospect of a Democratic victory in the forthcoming election, they were preparing to bite the feeding hand. After a conference in May between President Arthur and Frederick Douglass the proposed convention was postponed until the fall, an action which brought further charges of white domination. The location of the convention was changed from Washington to Louisville to avoid the possibility of federal officeholder control.

In Massachusetts, independent Negroes like James Trotter and John E. Stephenson protested against the state caucus which nominated delegates to the Louisville meeting. Trotter accused the local leaders of being "thick and thin Republicans" and the convention of excluding Negroes of "known liberal and progressive views." The Negroes in the state, Trotter asserted, were not unanimously behind the action of the caucus.

The wrangling in the Bay State reflected a confusion which had increased by the time three hundred delegates met in Louisville in the last week in September. After some bitter infighting, Douglass was elected permanent chairman and delivered a rousing two-hour address denouncing discrimination and proclaiming the power of the race. This speech won over wavering independents and re-established Douglass' position as spokesman of the race. Influential men like Samuel R. Scottron of Brooklyn publicly confessed that they would support Douglass, who had apparently thrown off the mantle of strict party-line Republicanism and assumed a more independent position.[43]

By using the independents' arguments without leaving the Republican fold, Douglass vitiated any national independence movement. His position of leadership was unchallenged, yet symptoms of unrest under Republican rule continued. The Cleveland *Gazette* reported in September that in New York, where the local Negro paper had threatened the party with non-support back in April, 1883, race unity and independence prevailed. Cleveland's Negroes, the journal lamented, were unpledged, but lacked the cohesion and direction of the New York group. In part, it would seem, the *Gazette* itself was at fault

[42] New York *Globe*, March 17, 31, April 14, 21, August 18, September 1, 1883; Cleveland *Gazette*, September 1, 1883.

[43] New York *Globe*, May 5, 19, 26, June 16, September 22, 29, October 6, 20, 1883; Cleveland *Gazette*, October 6, 1883; John E. Bruce to an unidentified editor, September, 1883, Bruce Papers.

since it could provide no decisive leadership. It could not stomach the jibes of the Democratically sponsored [Cincinnati?] *Afro-American*, nor could it enthusiastically endorse the Republican Foraker-Rose club. When, in the middle of December, the editor, Harry C. Smith, joined with a Toledo man to issue a convention call, it seemed like a step in the right direction but the convention, meeting in Columbus the day after Christmas, was poorly attended and a dismal failure. Smith himself was equivocal on the independence issue; some appeals for independence seemed to smell too much like Democracy to him.[44]

Organized independence died about as quickly as it had sprung into being. In January, 1884, Fortune, an early mugwump, was tendered a banquet in the District of Columbia, welcoming his return to the Republican party. All was not sweetness and light, however, and Fortune himself led the snipers who picked at efforts to bind the Negro to Republicanism. Referring to a Negro convention scheduled to meet at Pittsburgh in April, he exclaimed: "No knuckle-close, hide-bound, subsidized, terrified machine black man is expected to appear at Pittsburgh on the 29th of April." [45] While party considerations seemed to be minimized in the Pittsburgh convention's public deliberations and concluding resolutions, the implication of the whole meeting, in spite of Fortune's outbursts, was strictly partisan. Two correspondents of the Cleveland *Gazette* complained that it was a meeting of officeholders, "a strictly private affair" which would benefit the few, not the many.[46] Clearly, for the first time, Negroes began to realize that the Republicans did not need them; that, in the words of the Hartford *Courant*, a white man's party was "a step in the right direction." The reasons were discernible: no matter what Republicans did, they could count on Negroes simply because the race had no other party to support. As long as northern Democrats continued to refer to the colored man as a "damnigger" they could not get his vote. It was slowly dawning on the Negro voter that he was politically homeless.[47]

The Democratic victory in 1884 put a two-year quietus on independence activity. The few Negro Democrats found themselves suddenly in the novel position of race spokesmen; some colored Republicans dickered unsuccessfully for recognition while the mass of Negro voters remained apathetic and leaderless. The first spark of independence came out of Pennsylvania and lit a fire that was to last until the end of the century. In June, 1886, the Philadelphia *Daily Times* editorialized about "the systematic proscription of the colored citizens" in every northern state under Republican control. With a view to spurring on a switch in allegiance the *Times* concluded that "it is not surprising that the murmurs of revolt are heard on every side among intelligent

44 Cleveland *Gazette*, September 8, December 15, 22, 29, 1883.
45 New York *Globe*, February 16, March 29, 1884; Cleveland *Gazette*, January 26, March 1, 1884.
46 Cleveland *Gazette*, May 3, 10, 1884.
47 New York *Globe*, April 19, 26, May 3, 1884.

colored citizens." [48] Late in the month, William Howard Day sat down to write to the New York *Freeman* about his bolt of the Republican state convention. Day and J. H. Howard were organizing Negroes to support the Prohibition party—a vigorous affirmation of the inequities suffered under Republican control and the dangers of subjugation to the Democracy. The movement, in Day's words, "hardly yet rises to the dignity of a kick in politics. It is unrest, dissatisfaction—a growl, but hardly a kick." [49] Yet it persuaded the Prohibitionists to nominate a colored minister for congressman at large. Negroes, however, were not ready for such a revolutionary step; they gave the candidate "miserable support," in spite of favorable publicity in their papers and a complimentary note in the *Nation*.[50]

The political discontent spread fast, fed by the Negro's continued indignation at economic and social discrimination. New England colored men gathered in Boston in September, 1886, in response to the following impassioned call:

> This movement is deemed necessary because the colored citizen is discriminated against in so many depressing and injurious manners not withstanding the letter of the law does not favor the same. It is exhibited by political parties, State and National; it exhibits itself in business, in the manufactories, in obtaining employments as salesmen and saleswomen, in benevolent associations, in seeking decent tenements. No distinction is made as to intelligence, character, deportment or means among the colored people. We believe that the moral influence of the colored men of New England should be felt outside of all partisanship, in favor of a national administration that places the welfare of all above the success of partisan leaders.[51]

Politics took up almost two days of the conference, during which the merits of endorsing the Cleveland administration were tossed back and forth. By a close vote, the conference decided against endorsement and both sides claimed a victory—the Republicans because of the decision, the Democrats because of its closeness. A third group tried desperately to interpret the meeting in their own terms. The decision was, they said, a protest against discrimination, not a political gathering. The Boston *Transcript* further confused the issue by congratulating the convention for not attaching itself to either wing. "What they should strive for is to lose their class and social identity and become assimilated individuals politically and socially.... The sooner the blacks refuse to play the role of professional political martyrs for or against any political party, the sooner will their class stigma be forgotten." [52]

[48] Quoted in New York *Freeman*, June 5, 1886.
[49] New York *Freeman*, July 3, 1886.
[50] *Ibid.*, September 18, November 13, 1886; Cleveland *Gazette*, August 21, 1886; *Nation*, XLIII (September 2, 1886), 185.
[51] New York *Freeman*, August 14, 1886.
[52] Quoted in *Public Opinion*, I (September 26, 1886), 464–65. See also New York *Freeman*, September 25, October 2, 1886.

The wisdom of this advice was suspect. It fitted the theory of American society that each individual fought a lone battle to scale the heights of wealth and social acceptance, but in practice Americans for generations had used organization to accomplish these ends for individuals. Negroes were far closer to national tradition in insisting upon organization and power politics. Their inability to agree on methods and purposes, their failure to develop leaders whom they could support, their reliance upon querulous men without leadership qualities, accentuated the prejudice which prevented the achievement of a favorable power situation.

The *Transcript's* counsel was even more suspect when placed next to the words of Senator John Sherman of Ohio. Fortune accused Sherman of urging a division among Negro voters, a policy supported by James G. Blaine's Washington *National Republican.* "We feel," Fortune reasoned, "that the Republican politicians, noting the policy President Cleveland has pursued towards colored voters, hope to counteract possible losses of colored votes in the North and West by bidding for white votes in the South." [53] Accurate as this analysis was, it undoubtedly did not represent a national party policy; in fact, the lack of national party policy toward northern Negroes contributed to the bitter dissension of the Negro group in 1887 and 1888. Leaders quarreled openly and personally; colored Democrats twitted colored Republicans unmercifully while the Prohibition party suddenly received vocal support, including some suggestions that it merge with the Labor party, another refuge for disgruntled colored men. As the 1888 campaign progressed, protests based on race were heard with greater frequency. Each group defended its action in race terms.[54] After Harrison's victory, and a slow start in patronage and southern civil rights, race independence became a common subject. In Boston, Cleveland, Akron, St. Paul, Rochester, and other cities, the Negro's patience was ebbing rapidly.[55]

Into this morale-shaken atmosphere, Fortune introduced the idea of a grand black national federation—the Afro-American National League. Using the Irish National League as a prototype, Fortune urged in 1887 a nationwide organization to combat injustice, primarily in the South. "The League in the North and West," he asserted, "will serve to create public opinion in those sections and to coerce politicians into taking a broader view of our grievances and to compel them to pay more respect to our representations and requests than they have ever done before." [56] He stressed the power that eight million people, one fifth of the population, could have if united and he warned against those who would use the color-line argument against the proposed federation. The Negro, he said without qualification, draws the color line last and in self-protection. Fortune planned to combine all existing northern groups as the

[53] New York *Freeman*, April 16, 1887.

[54] *Ibid.*, August 27, September 3, October 1, 1887; New York *Age*, November 5, 12, 19, 26, December 3, 1887, March 24, April 28, 1888; Cleveland *Gazette*, December 3, 1887.

[55] New York *Age*, March 30, April 20, August 24, 1889, August 23, 1890; Cleveland *Gazette*, April 13, October 19, 1889, April 26, 1890.

[56] New York *Freeman*, June 4, 1887.

nucleus, permitting them to keep their sovereignty but urging them to take the initiative. In spite of the response which the proposal received, the few groups who constituted themselves part of the Afro-American League had to wait until a midpoint in the Harrison administration. The time was not ripe.[57]

After the first flush of enthusiasm had passed away, the idea of the League flourished only in the minds of its originators. Suddenly, in the fall of 1889, it burst forth with renewed vigor. The constitution and by-laws suggested by Fortune in 1887 were reprinted; prominent Negro leaders once again gave their approval. Even the New York *Tribune* printed an article claiming that the League would be the equivalent for the Negro of the Lake Mohonk Conferences on the Indian. In November, Fortune issued a call for a convention at Nashville. A few weeks later Chicago replaced Nashville as the convention city because it had less discrimination in its hotels, restaurants, and other institutions of public service. The League met there in January, 1890.[58]

It was no accident to find three northern newspapermen in charge of the temporary organization—Ferdinand L. Barnett of Chicago, Smith of Cleveland, and Fortune. The League was conceived in the North and baptized with northern newsprint. Eleven of the twenty-one states represented were above the Mason-Dixon line. Nevertheless, co-operation and compromise prevailed in the selection of permanent officers as the presidency went to John C. Price of North Carolina.[59]

The convention agreed that politics should remain outside of its boundary. Fortune, whose proposals for a bank, a bureau of emigration, a legislative committee, and a department of industrial education were ignored, struck the proper note when he argued for political pressure on a local level for race purposes irrespective of party. A delegate from Indiana summed up the general feeling: "The eyes of the American people and of the world are upon us. We are here as Afro-Americans, not as politicians of either party." [60] Article XIV of the constitution, proclaiming the nonpartisan and nonpolitical nature of the organization, was upheld after a heated debate. The article required any League officer to resign if he was appointed or elected to political office and prohibited the use of League stationery for political purposes.

Indeed, the convention protested too much. By its very nature and that of the nation's political system, it was involved in politics. One of its first acts was to petition Congress by wire, ironically suggesting an appropriation to finance the removal of southern whites from states in which they were in a minority. Furthermore the second article in its constitution set forth its aims with political overtones: fighting taxation without representation, unequal distribution of school funds, unfair jury trials, discrimination in transportation facilities and the like—all to be opposed by encouraging public opinion and by taking court action. These proposed activities indicated one basic complaint

[57] *Ibid.*, May 28, June 18, 24, July 2, 9, 16, 23, November 5, 12, 1887.
[58] New York *Age*, October 5, 19, November 9, 23, 30, 1889.
[59] Cleveland *Gazette*, January 18, 25, 1890.
[60] *Ibid.*, January 25, 1890.

which was essentially political—second-class citizenship. As if to recognize the political implications of the convention, the delegates agreed to go on record accepting the recommendations of the Blair educational bill.[61]

Negroes were not afraid of political action. What they feared, based on two decades of experience, was political action confined within the limits prescribed by white political parties. Fortune noted in his opening address that he knew political parties, indeed he had been in three of them, and "none of them cares a fig for the Afro-American further than it can use him." [62] The organization which grew out of the Chicago convention was trying to set itself up as a new political power which could use its numbers, its unity, and its strength to wrest its desired aims from the dominant whites. None of its purposes could be achieved by other than political aims and in the late nineteenth century the Negroes were following a precedent set by the farmers and labor, organizing outside of the existing political structure to gain political aims. Where the farmer wanted a fair return on his product and the laborer decent working conditions, the Negro wanted a full respect for his race.

The Afro-American National League was doomed to failure from the beginning. After a year it dropped its nonpolitical character and became just another of the multitude of political organizations which had impotently tried to aid the Negro cause. In part its demise as a national body was the fault of an extra-heavy superstructure—a national organization resting on a weak and insufficient number of constituent local groups.[63] But the basic cause lay deeper; the colored people were not prepared educationally, financially, or in experience to sustain such a large venture. Their leaders were not equal to the task.

Leadership was not far away, however. For the last twenty years of the century, two men had absorbed the lessons of politics. Theodore Roosevelt and Booker T. Washington wanted to bring order from chaos; slowly working toward each other, they finaly met and together established discipline.

Roosevelt combined the traits essential to leading the majority of the Negro group. Early in the 1890's as a member of the Civil Service Commission he recognized the inequity of race discrimination. As governor of New York, he put his weight behind the Elsberg bill which wiped out all separate schools. He ranted in moral and virtuous terms, but he lived those terms and he reflected the essential morality and virtue of the times. Finally, he was an authoritarian, a believer in discipline to make democracy successful. He feared mob rule and demagoguery. Liberty and order were for him synonymous. These were the characteristics that political leadership needed if the Negro group was to act with power.[64]

[61] *Ibid.*   [62] *Ibid.*

[63] *Ibid.*, August 15, 1891.

[64] For the Civil Service see his correspondence in Elting E. Morison (ed.), *The Letters of Theodore Roosevelt* (8 vols., Cambridge, 1951–1954), I, 357, 368, 381, 427, II, 899. For the Elsberg bill see Roosevelt to N. A. Elsberg, March 20, 1900, and to T. E. Ellsworth, March 20, 1900, Roosevelt Letter Books (Harvard College Library), Series IIA, Vol. V.

The story of Washington's rise has been told many times; the mysterious expansion of his influence requires further investigation. Here we need only accept the fact of that influence as seen through the efforts of Theodore Roosevelt. When Roosevelt ran for the governorship he found "considerable Negro opposition" to his candidacy. He experienced a rude shock when a campaign meeting organized by Fortune failed to materialize. "It was the only meeting I attended," he wrote Fortune, "which was a complete break-down, and I confess I went away saddened to think that the enmity to you among our fellow republicans of color could be carried to such an extreme as to make them prefer to see the meeting an utter failure rather than to have you profit by it. I wish I could see Mr. Washington." [65] The desire to see Washington reflected Roosevelt's ambition to establish some sort of authority in dispensing patronage and disciplining Negro leaders to bring them into line. As vice-president he came to depend on Washington's advice more and more, even when it came to recommending Fortune to "our Literary bureau." [66] He deplored the lack of unity in the Negro group as evidenced by his letter to a fellow Harvard man, William H. Lewis, and again urged a meeting between himself and Washington.[67] Shortly after his inauguration as president, in September, 1901, he called Washington to the White House and laid down his policy regarding the Negro group. To Washington, a southern Negro, he proposed "to appoint fewer colored men to office in the South . . . [and] a certain number of colored men of his character and ability in office in the Northern States. He [Roosevelt] said that he had never been able to see any good reason why colored men should be put in office in the Southern states and not in the Northern states as well." [68] Leadership, suspect to many but secure in its power, had finally been established, and, to the impotent chagrin of some northern Negroes, by a southern colored man.

For all his advantages of freedom, education, and organization, limited as these were compared to those of the white man, the northern Negro was unable to capitalize on his political position in the last third of the nineteenth century. Living in states where the two-party system gave his vote a greater power potential, he failed in his attempts to use this advantage. The bonds—material as well as ideological, affirmative as well as negative—that welded him to Republicanism could only be broken by united action. But united action crumbled in the face of patronage, corruption, and hollow prestige induce-ments; the cry for a concerted effort died away when the bloody shirt was hoisted in the heat of a campaign. No nonpartisan or independent organiza-tion could resist the blandishments of the G.O.P. while white Democrats con-

[65] Roosevelt to Fortune, March 31, 1899, Roosevelt Letter Books, Series IIB, Vol. IV.

[66] Roosevelt to Mark Hanna, July 7, 1900, *ibid.*, Series IIB, Vol. XII.

[67] Roosevelt to William H. Lewis, July 26, 1900, Morison (ed.), *Letters of Theo-dore Roosevelt*, II, 1364.

[68] Memorandum dictated by Washington after the conference and quoted in full in Basil J. Mathews, *Booker T. Washington, Educator and Interracial Interpreter* (Cambridge, 1948), 229–30.

doned the vicious attacks on the race in the South; no disaffected Republican could long feel at home in the Democratic camp.

There are, however, more basic reasons for the failure of the northern Negro group. In the first place, it was overwhelmingly outnumbered by its brethren in the South and numbers have a simple attraction for politicians. Quantity here far outweighed the advantages of quality. In the second place, it lacked the experience and the resources to support a tightly knit organization such as Washington headed by the end of the century. The Negro press, which developed in this period into an influential instrument for mobilizing opinion and developing leadership, was not equal to the task of federating the race group. Significant as journalists, black and white, have been in our history, they have never been able to control a successful political organization. The Negro editors, moreover, were still economic as well as political neophytes and they could not draw on the white philanthropies, both financial and political, which Washington had at his disposal. Washington, representing an institution and an attitude which was most amenable to whites, used his position and personality to accomplish, almost *sub rosa*, that for which his northern brethren had shouted for twenty years.

The final factor involved was race prejudice. Political parties have never been primarily humanitarian in nature. Given the state and federal laws which ineffectively insisted upon equal rights, the northern Negroes found themselves unable to require these rights from political parties. They were never accepted as men, only as Negroes; forced to admit this classification, they resorted to defending themselves on the basis of their race. They drew the color line only after it had been drawn by whites. They were pushed into the impotent position of using race separation to break down race segregation.

Their program was not really a program but merely a succession of outraged outcries against white pressure on their most sensitive nerve, race prejudice. Almost every act of discrimination was thought to be cause for political action; almost every adverse political action was thought to be an act of discrimination. But out of this protest against prejudice grew no connected series of political demands, realistically drawn to fit their needs and those of their party. Beset by prejudice, without an appealing program, they took refuge in apathy, separation, and extremism.

In part the fault was theirs for failing to see that moderation might have gained their ends for them more expeditiously; in part the fault was that of the American people for ignoring the spirit and substance of their own great traditions. The question as to whether Washington utilized his power in the best interests of the race is one that still remains to be answered, but Washington did realize, however much he leaned in the direction of co-operation, that the power of the race could be best organized by moderation.

Bernard Mandel

SAMUEL GOMPERS AND
THE NEGRO WORKERS, 1886–1914

The trade-union movement in the ante-bellum and Reconstruction periods was weak and highly discriminatory. Then in the 1880's the Knights of Labor seriously attempted to recruit Negro members, and though many white Knights retained their prejudices against Negro members, the organization's leaders were genuinely interested in establishing an interracial union movement. However, the decline of the Knights of Labor and the rise of the AFL led to a revival of the tradition of discriminatory trade unionism which has usually characterized the American scene. The AFL took an official stand against racist practices by its own affiliates, and a few unions, most notably the United Mine Workers, were egalitarian to a remarkable degree. Nevertheless, at the end of the nineteenth century the AFL was openly admitting unions with constitutions that explicitly barred Negroes, or accepted them only into powerless Jim Crow locals.

In the following article Bernard Mandel presents Samuel Gompers, the AFL president, as a bureaucratic administrator whose desire to remain in office led him to sacrifice the interests of Negroes by catering to the prejudices of white workers. Gompers began by blaming the whites for discriminating against Negroes and ended by, in effect, blaming Negroes for being victims of discrimination.

THE policy of the American Federation of Labor with regard to Negroes is generally regarded as a step backward from the attitude of the Knights of Labor.[1] Actually, the Federation inherited the Knights' position on the organization of Negro workers, and in 1894 reaffirmed the principle that "the

Bernard Mandel, "Samuel Gompers and the Negro Workers, 1886–1914," *Journal of Negro History*, XL (January, 1955), pp. 34–60. Reprinted with the permission of the publisher.

[1] Sidney H. Kessler, "The Organization of the Negroes in the Knights of Labor," *The Journal of Negro History*, XXXVII (July, 1952), 248–276.

working people must unite and organize, irrespective of creed, color, sex, nationality, or politics." [2] But the K. of L. strove to organize all workers, unskilled as well as skilled, in "One Big Union," while the A.F. of L. consisted mainly of craft unions of the skilled workers. For this reason, primarily, the Federation gradually retreated from its original position to a policy of discrimination and segregation. It was an even greater retreat for President Gompers, who had a more advanced point of view in the early days of his career than most of the other trade union leaders. But on this, as on so many other issues, he compromised his principles and fell in line with the narrow policy of the labor officials on whom he depended for his job. The evolution of Gompers' views on the Negro question provides one of the most striking illustrations of his transformation from a militant and radical labor agitator to a conservative, stand-pat bureaucrat.[3]

The question first came to the attention of the Federation in 1888 in connection with the organization of the National Association of Machinists, which was primarily a Southern organization. Except for the railroad brotherhoods, the machinists' union was almost the only national union that expressly excluded Negroes from membership by constitutional provision. Gompers believed that this was an element of weakness which doomed the union to failure unless it were abolished and the identity of interests of all workers were recognized. He stated that working men should organize irrespective of color, both as a matter of principle and of practical common sense, as the division of workers was a means whereby employers kept down the wages of both groups. "Wage-workers," he wrote, "like many others may not care to socially meet colored people, but as working men we are not justified in refusing them the right of the opportunity to organize for their common protection. Then again, if organizations do, we will only make enemies of them, and of necessity they will be antagonistic to our interests." Gompers ruled that machinists' locals which were excluded from the National Association, or which refused to join it until its color line was removed, might become directly affiliated to the A.F. of L. as federal trade unions.[4]

In 1890, the Federation declared that it looked with disfavor upon unions which excluded members on account of race or color, and urged the N.A.M. to remove such conditions from its constitution. The Executive Council was directed to call a conference of the organized machinists to form them into one national organization without discrimination.[5] Gompers visited the convention of the N.A.M. in Pittsburgh and requested it to strike out the "white

---

[2] *Proceedings of the 14th Annual Convention of the American Federation of Labor*, 1894, 25. (Hereafter referred to as AFL, *Convention*.)

[3] Bernard Mandel, "Sam Gompers' A.F. of L." Unpublished paper read before the American Historical Association, New York, December 30, 1954.

[4] Gompers to Frank D. Hamlin, Apr. 31, 1890; Gompers to Charles W. Murphy, May 16, 1890; Gompers to Fred J. Carr, Dec. 8, 1891. Unless otherwise stated, all correspondence cited is in Gompers' Letterbooks in A.F. of L. archives, Washington, D. C.

[5] AFL, *10th Convention*, 1890, 31–32.

clause" in its constitution, but it declined to do so. He then called a convention of all independent machinists' unions, and the International Machinists Union was organized and affiliated with the A.F. of L. It pledged that, if the N.A.M. eliminated the color line, it would amalgamate with that organization.[6]

The A.F. of L. did not receive the report of these developments with the satisfaction that might have been expected from the action of the previous convention. In fact, it "deplored" the formation of the I.M.U. as "premature." Owen Miller of the musicians' union asked Gompers if the A.F. of L. dictated to affiliated organizations as to qualifications for membership. Gompers admitted that it did not, and stated that the N.A.M. would receive a charter from the Federation if the color line was withdrawn.[7] The implication was that the Federation could not openly recognize discrimination in its affiliated unions, but that it would not interfere with their policies as long as they did not proclaim them in their constitutions. That this was the gist of the matter was plainly hinted by Gompers in his letter to the next convention of the N.A.M. He emphasized that "under the banner of the American Federation of Labor there is no right that any trade union possesses which it would surrender by becoming affiliated with us," and that the word "white" in the constitution, while being of no advantage to the organization, was costing it the good will and cooperation of the labor movement.[8] But the N.A.M. again decided adversely on changing its constitution. Gompers continued his efforts to secure the elimination of the color line. Finally, in 1895, the year that Gompers was not president of the A.F. of L., the N.A.M., now the International Association of Machinists, dropped the color line and received a charter from the Federation. The I.M.U. was then asked to endorse this action and to merge with the I.A.M.[9]

But the I.A.M. eliminated the color line in name only. The restriction on membership was kept in the ritual of the organization for half a century afterward, and it was common knowledge that the actual policy of the union had not been changed. The Boston local told a committee of the International Machinists Union that no colored man would ever be admitted. The secretary of the Washington lodge wrote frankly to W. E. B. Du Bois that "the Negro is not admitted to the International Association of Machinists," and the secretary of the national union refused to answer questions as to the eligibility of Negroes. Even Gompers admitted that the constitutional amendment had not interfered with the "autonomy" of the organization.[10]

Furthermore, the course of the A.F. of L. in chartering the I.A.M. was

[6] AFL, 11th Convention, 1891, 12.

[7] Ibid., 40–41.

[8] Gompers to the Convention of the International Machinists Union, May 7, 1892.

[9] Monthly Journal of the International Association of Machinists, VII (June, 1895), 186; John McBride to T. J. Morgan, July 16, 1895.

[10] Daniel J. Sullivan to Gompers, in AFL, Incoming Correspondence, Box 118; W. E. B. Du Bois, ed., The Negro Artisan. Atlanta University Publications, No. 7 (Atlanta: Atlanta University Press, 1902), 169–170; Gompers to Lee Johnson, May 7, 1896.

not in accord with the original understanding that a merger between the two machinists' organizations would be effected prior to affiliation. Nor was it in accord with the policy of the Federation not to grant a charter to a national union without the consent of any other national union of the same trade which was already affiliated with the Federation. The I.M.U. attempted to effect an amalgamation with the older body after the latter had amended its constitution, but the I.A.M. refused to cooperate. It would not accept the I.M.U. as a body, but required the members to apply as individuals for membership. The Negro members were not admitted, and many of the white machinists had difficulty in gaining acceptance. All of these facts were pointed out to Gompers by the Boston lodge of the I.M.U., but Gompers ignored its complaints. Instead he unceremoniously informed the I.M.U. that its charter was revoked, and that he assumed this met with its approval. Secretary Morgan assured him that this assumption was erroneous.[11]

The International Brotherhood of Blacksmiths also drew the color line, and in 1893 a number of locals urged Gompers to call a convention for the purpose of forming a new union without discrimination. In this instance, Gompers, recalling the 1891 convention's criticism of his "premature" or-ganization of the machinists' union, would not support the movement, on the grounds that it constituted dual unionism. But he agreed with the dissident locals that it was against the best interests of the organization to declare against the admission of Negroes and he urged the Brotherhood to abandon that policy. If there were few colored blacksmiths, he asked the secretary, where was the necessity of declaring that they should not become members?

> If, on the other hand, there are blacksmiths who are colored men, the inevitable is presented to you, that either you must make friends of them or if you will not they will prove enemies to you and play into the hands of employers who may always be willing to take advantage of you. If the question were not a humanitarian one, then enlightened self-interest should prompt us all to declare our desire to organize all our fellow-workers instead of discriminating against any who may desire to act fair and manfully.

He wanted the affiliation of the Brotherhood, but would use his influence to prevent it as long as its constitution prohibited Negro membership.[12] Four years later, the blacksmiths changed their constitution and were admitted to the Federation.

Gompers hoped to bring the Brotherhood of Locomotive Firemen into the Federation on the same basis, feeling confident that if they made the break the other railroad brotherhoods would follow. W. S. Carter, editor of the *Locomotive Firemen's Magazine*, told Gompers that one of the principal

---

[11] Daniel J. Sullivan to Gompers, Dec. 7, 1895; T. J. Morgan to August McCraith, June 3, 1896; W. W. Fenton to Gompers, Dec. 29, 1896; in AFL, Incoming Corre-spondence, Box 118.

[12] Gompers to John C. Knight, Mar. 6, 1893.

reasons for the Brotherhood's failure to join the A.F. of L. was its desire to keep Negroes from its ranks. He explained that Negroes were working for twenty-five to fifty percent less than the white firemen and it was feared that if they were in the union they would pull down the wage scale. He thought, however, that it might be willing to eliminate the lily-white clause from the constitution and accomplish the same purpose by allowing each lodge to regulate its own membership.[13] Carter agreed to print in the *Magazine* a letter from Gompers explaining the Federation's policy. Gompers wrote:

Does the A.F. of L. compel its affiliated organizations to accept colored workmen? I answer no! Decidedly not. No more than it compels organizations to accept Americans, Frenchmen, Englishmen, Irishmen, or even Hottentots.

What the American Federation of Labor declares by its policy, [is] that organization should not declare *against* accepting the colored man *because he is colored.* . . .

. . . . If a man or set of men array themselves for any cause against the interests of the workers their organizations have the right to say that their membership is barred. It should be at the wrong-doer against labor, it should not be a nationality or a race against whom the doors are barred.

The International Association of Machinists formerly had the "color line" provision in its constitution. It eliminated the objectionable declaration and became affiliated with the A.F. of L. . . . Yet, I venture to say. . . . that they are more than pleased with their affiliation, that their autonomy and independence is as fully recognized to-day as any time in the existence of their organization.[14]

At the convention of the Brotherhood in 1896, Grand Master Sargent recommended that the organization affiliate with the Federation, and the question was submitted to the locals. The real question behind the referendum was the propriety of eliminating the color clause from the constitution, and Gompers appeared before the convention to urge the adoption of the resolution. To the complaints that were made against the cheap labor of Negro firemen, Gompers answered that this was all the greater reason why they should be admitted, in order that they might no longer be utilized by the employers to defeat the interests of the organized workers.[15] Gompers made the position of the A.F. of L. very clear. He wrote to the lodges of the Brotherhood:

This question of race and color is more of a bugaboo urged among some workingmen to frighten them from performing their duties. It is simply preposterous. What the A.F. of L. has declared is that it is unwise for us to go forth emblazoned upon our banners our antag-

[13] W. S. Carter to Gompers, in AFL, Incoming Correspondence, Box 78.
[14] *Locomotive Firemen's Magazine,* July, 1896, 65.
[15] Gompers to F. P. Sargent, Aug. 17, 1896; Gompers to George W. Perkins, Oct. 27, 1896; Gompers, Report to AFL, *16th Convention,* 1896, 19.

onism to a race. . . . during the agitation for the abolition of slavery
. . . unthinking people of the time could not understand that one
could desire the abolition of slavery without falling absolutely in love
with the slaves. This mistake seems to be repeated in our day only in
another way. . . .[16]

The referendum won a majority vote for affiliation, but not the necessary
two-thirds. Carter explained that many members of the Brotherhood felt that
the Federation's policy was inconsistent with the constitutional provisions for
strict autonomy. Besides, they did not want to transfer the exclusion clause
from their constitution to the ritual because "they do not care to belong to
an organization that is not honest enough to make public its qualifications of
membership." [17]

There is no doubt that Gompers, at least in the early years of the Federation, desired the organization of the Negro workers and, if possible, their organization in the same unions with white workers. If that was not possible, he
proposed that they should be organized anyhow and harmonious arrangements
made between the Negro and white workers as a step toward eventual integration. He explained to his Southern organizer that the unionization of colored
workers was not a matter of recognizing social equality, but a question of
absolute necessity.

> If the colored man is not permitted to organize, if he is not
> given the opportunity to protect and defend his interests, if a chance
> is not given him by which he could uplift his condition, the inevitable
> result must follow, that he will sink down lower and lower in his
> economic scale and in his conception of his rights as a worker and
> finally find himself . . . absolutely dependent (worse than chattel slav-
> ery) in the hands of unfair and unscrupulous employers.
>
> If our fellow white wage workers will not allow the colored
> workers to co-operate with him, he will necessarily cling to the other
> hand (that of the employer) who also smites him, but at least recog-
> nizes his right to work. If we do not make friends of the colored men
> they will of necessity be justified in proving themselves our enemies,
> and they will be utilized upon every occasion to frustrate our every
> effort for economic, social and political improvement.
>
> . . . . I wish the slogan would come forth among the toilers of
> the South, working men organize regardless of color. . . .[18]

In 1892 the Negro teamsters in New Orleans formed a union and sought
an agreement with the employers, but the latter would not talk with them.
The unions of New Orleans sent committees to the employers, urging them to
sign an agreement, and when they were rebuffed a general strike was called

[16] Gompers to W. D. Lewis, Apr. 9, 1897.
[17] W. S. Carter to Frank Morrison, May 12, 1897, in AFL, Incoming Correspondence, Box 78.
[18] Gompers to Jerome Jones, Mar. 8, 1893.

throughout the city. Although the strike was not successful, Gompers regarded the demonstration as a bright ray of hope. He wrote:

> Never in the history of the world was such an exhibition, where with all the prejudices existing against the black man, when the white wage workers of New Orleans would sacrifice their means of livelihood to protect and defend their colored fellow wage workers. With one fell swoop the economic barrier of color was broken down. Under the circumstances I regard the movement as a very healthy sign of the times and one which speaks well for the future of organized labor in the "New South." . . .[19]

Of course, there was a great deal of prejudice among many white workers, particularly in the South, against Negroes belonging to their unions. Recognizing this, Gompers was willing to leave the question of integrated unions to local option, but at the same time accepted the obligation of trying to persuade them to take the far-sighted course and eliminate the color line.[20] When he heard that a local teamsters' union was discriminating against Negroes, he informed it that "the American Federation of Labor positively places its stamp of disapproval upon such attempt," and advised it to accept Negroes and accord them every benefit that membership entitled them to.[21] In St. Louis, the hod carriers' union refused to accept Negro workers, and Gompers told them that if they did not admit Negroes, he would issue a charter to them as a separate local, with the requirement that they adopt the same working rules and rate of wages.[22] In another case, the white members of a federal labor union desired to form a separate organization because Negroes were in the majority of the union and held all the offices. Gompers was willing to grant them a charter, but only on condition that the union consent to being divided and that an agreement be reached with regard to cooperation in trade matters. Otherwise, he said, the dissension resulting from dualism and antagonism would be worse than the dissatisfaction existing within the union. In addition, he insisted, no union could be designated as a "white" or "colored" union; if workers desired to form such unions in various localities, the Federation would grant them charters, but it would not give official recognition to the color line in any organization.[23] Gompers hoped and expected that these arrangements would be only temporary, and that they would lead to more satisfactory relations. He wrote to a local union that the organization of both white and Negro workers was the best way to overcome and eliminate prejudice.

[19] Gompers, testimony before U.S. Industrial Commission, Apr. 18, 1899, in Gompers, *Labor and the Employer* (New York: E. P. Dutton & Co., 1920), 166–167; Gompers to R. P. Fleming, Nov. 21, 1892; Gompers to John M. Callaghan, Nov. 21, 1892.

[20] Gompers to H. M. Ives, Nov. 10, 1892.

[21] Gompers to W. H. Luchtenburg, May 9, 1892.

[22] Gompers to Louis F. Klinger, July 18, 1891.

[23] Ed. J. Donegan to Gompers, Dec. 5, 1892; Gompers to Donegan, Dec. 9, 1892; Gompers to Henry J. Spaeter, Nov. 10, 1893; Gompers to Julius Friedman, Mar. 31, 1894.

Inasmuch, however, as that prejudice still exists, and that many white workmen will not belong to the same local organization with black men, and will not meet with them as members of the same local union, it might be more advantageous to go to work gradually to accomplish the desired end. In other words, have the Union of white men organize, and have the Union of colored men organize also, both unions to work in unison and harmony to accomplish the desired end.

It is useless to be simply trying to ram our heads through stone walls; recognizing conditions which exist is the best way we can secure the organization of all in a way which must ultimately bring about a unity of feeling and action among all toilers....[24]

But Gompers weakened the implementation of his desire to organize the Negro workers by leaving it mainly in the hands of white organizers. The members of the federal labor union in Hot Springs, Arkansas, stated that the organization of Negro workers in that state was being neglected, and urged him to appoint a Negro organizer. Gompers did not reply to their request.[25] As far as can be determined, only two of the Federation's organizers in the 1890's were Negroes, and Gompers found fault with the work of both. One was George L. Norton, organizer of the marine workers in the Mississippi valley. Gompers received complaints from local organizers that Norton was engaged in the organization of white as well as Negro workers. Besides, Norton refused to sanction the formation of separate white locals when mixed unions had already been organized. He insisted that all must join the established and recognized union. Gompers asked Norton to refrain from such activities, which would only intensify prejudices. In view of existing conditions, he said, it would be better to allow separate unions for Negro workers than to leave them unorganized. He authorized Norton to proceed in any union "which is sufficiently advanced in their conception of the identity of the interests of labor regardless of color," but where they were not, he advised him to "be very discreet and allow our agitation and time to work the desired change...." [26] At the same time, he wrote to one of those who had objected to Norton's activities and explained why it was necessary to organize the Negro workers. He urged him to re-examine his attitude, "not with the old prejudices that you may have heard from infancy, but study it in the light of the historical struggles of the people of all nations, and you will find that I am right...." [27]

The other Negro organizer was Joseph Amstead, appointed in 1892 in Austin, Texas. The white organizer for Texas complained to Gompers that Amstead was "encroaching on his authority" and that he was agitating for racial equality. Gompers agreed that Amstead was unwise to discuss such ques-

[24] Gompers to David Watkins, July 17, 1893.

[25] Members of the Federal Labor Union, Hot Springs, Ark., to Gompers, June 1, 1891.

[26] George L. Norton to Gompers, Jan. 28, 1892, Feb. 22, 1892, and Mar. 15, 1892; Gompers to Norton, May 16, 1892 and May 17, 1892.

[27] Gompers to John M. Callahan, May 17, 1892.

tions, which "lead to no good results." It simply arouses race prejudice, he said, and "practically subordinates the labor movement to the color question." He wrote to Amstead on the necessity of "acting practically in dealing with the organization of the colored wage-workers. Their full recognition," he said, "in social as well as economic equality is a matter of cultivation and development and I doubt that it can be forced to an earlier solution than the natural trend will warrant. All attempts to prematurely bring this about will only result in defeat and disaster to all concerned." Shortly afterward, Gompers revoked Amstead's commission.[28]

An even greater impediment to the organization of Negroes was the craft policy of the A.F. of L. The overwhelming majority of Negro workers were unskilled laborers and factory workers, but the Federation's stubborn refusal to organize these classes of workers, and its opposition to industrial unionism, made the organization of the workers in the mass production industries impossible. The Federation's neglect of the Negroes was part of its opportunistic policy of seeking immediate gains for the skilled workers at the expense of the unskilled workers and consumers. Gompers, viewing the whole labor scene, could see that the competition of the Negro and other unskilled workers could be eliminated only by making common cause with them. But the skilled workers of the well organized trades, regarding only their own narrow domain, proposed to eliminate it by excluding the unskilled workers from their unions and thereby from the labor market. Gompers, albeit reluctantly, yielded to the exclusionist policy of the trade union officialdom.

In 1897 Booker T. Washington, the famous Negro spokesman and educator, stated that the trade unions were hindering the material advancement of the Negroes by failing to organize them. The A.F. of L., at its convention that year, denounced this statement as untrue, and reaffirmed its policy of welcoming all labor, without regard to creed, color, sex, race or nationality, and of encouraging the organization of those most needing its protection. Gompers left the chair to support this resolution, asserting that a union affiliated with the A.F. of L. had no right to bar Negroes from membership. "If we do not give the colored man the opportunity to organize, the capitalist will set him up as a barrier to our progress. Every time we help these men it helps to raise the laborer to a higher plane.... It is not a question as to the color of a man's skin, but the power that lies in organization." While some of the Southern delegates were on their feet clamoring for the floor to oppose the resolution, Gompers put it to a vote and declared it adopted.[29]

But resolutions were not actions. In fact, they were often a substitute for action. Most of the A.F. of L. affiliates at that time did actually bar Negroes from membership, and some of their delegates, including O'Connell of the Machinists, were most vociferous in advocating the passage of this resolution.

[28] Gompers to Joseph Amstead and J. Geggie, Oct. 18, 1892; Gompers to P. J. McGuire, Oct. 24, 1892; Gompers to J. Geggie, Oct. 27, 1892; Gompers to Amstead and Geggie, Nov. 4, 1892.
[29] AFL, 17th Convention, 1897, 78–79.

And Gompers and the Federation were already in the process of undermining in practice what they declared in principle. Gompers had often stated that the lack of organization among the Negro workers and their employment as strikebreakers were caused by the prejudice of white workers who refused to make common cause with them in the labor movement. But he had already begun to shift the blame to the Negroes themselves. When asked why there were not more skilled Negro workers, he assigned two reasons for it. First, he said, Negro workers did not possess the required skill, but he did not mention the fact that most of the trade unions prevented them from acquiring that skill by refusing to accept them as apprentices. The second reason was that in many cases, when white workers were on strike, Negroes took their places and thus helped the employers to tear down labor standards and destroy the unions. While he had previously argued that this was the inevitable result of the white workers' ignoring the organization of the Negroes, he now stated: "If workers will not organize to protect their own interests and the interests of their fellow workers, or if workmen are so lost to their own self respect and interests as to turn the weight of their influence on the side of the capitalists as against that of the workers, these men are the enemies of progress, regardless of whether they be white or black, Caucasian or Mongolian." [30] Ten years later he said, "the Caucasians are not going to let their standard of living be destroyed by negroes, Chinamen, Japs, or any others." [31] In the *American Federationist* he published an article which referred to Negroes who had been brought to Chicago in 1904 to replace the striking stockyard workers as "hordes of ignorant blacks," "possessing but few of those attributes we have learned to revere and love," "huge, strapping fellows, ignorant and vicious, whose predominating trait was animalism." [32]

Just one month after the close of the convention in which the Federation declared for the organization and unity of all workers, Gompers published in the *Federationist* an article by Will Winn, the A.F. of L. organizer in Georgia. Gompers thought that this article, called "The Negro: His Relation to Southern Industry," was a fair presentation of the subject.[33] Winn wrote that even if the Federation threw all its forces into a campaign to unionize Southern Negro workers, little success could be expected for many years, because the Negroes did not possess "those peculiarities of temperament such as patriotism, sympathy, etc., which are peculiar to most of the Caucasian race, and which alone make an organization of the character and complicity of the modern trade union possible. . . ." The Negroes, he continued, were characterized by distrust of each other, prejudice against the whites, ignorance and an "abandoned and reckless disposition." The Negro had a great advantage over the white worker

[30] Gompers to W. H. Stokes, Aug. 27, 1896.

[31] Gompers, address at St. Paul, St. Paul *Union Advocate*, quoted in *American Federationist*, XII (Sept., 1905), 636.

[32] John Roach, "Packingtown Conditions," *American Federationist*, XIII (Aug., 1906), 534.

[33] *American Federationist*, IV (Feb., 1898), 269–271; Gompers to Winn, Jan. 19, 1898.

in the South because he would work for anything he could get, as many hours as might be demanded, and was "the happiest and most contented individual imaginable." Since, in his opinion, the Negro workers could not be organized and constituted a growing menace to the status of the white workers, Winn proposed as the best solution to the problem the colonization of the Negroes in Liberia or Cuba. The publication of such white supremacist views reveals the hypocrisy of Gompers' declarations about organizing the Negro working-men.

Early in 1899, the Executive Council decided to launch a Southern "organizing campaign." It appointed two organizers for one month, and an-other, Will Winn, for three months. In view of the number of organizers, the short time allotted, and the defeatist attitude of Gompers and Winn, it is apparent that this drive was undertaken not so much to organize the workers as to enable the Council to claim that it was not neglecting this field of or-ganization. None of the organizers was a Negro, and Gompers read with agree-ment and amusement a report from one of them, L. F. McGruder, that he, "a full-blooded Irishman," was "up against a hard proposition" in trying to organize "Jews and n———rs." [34] One year later Gompers told his New Or-leans organizer that "while it is desirable to organize them, . . . yet the organ-ization of the white workmen is of paramount importance, and should not be hazarded." [35] When a reporter asked Gompers why the South had not been effectually organized, he assigned three reasons, the first of which was "the fault of the Negroes." [36]

Thus, by the end of the nineteenth century, Gompers was in full retreat from the position he had earlier espoused with regard to the place of Negro labor in the A.F. of L. In defining the attitude of the Federation toward the Negroes, Gompers pointed to its past declarations and to the general strike in New Orleans in 1892. As for present policy, he told the United States Indus-trial Commission in 1899, if organized labor discriminated against Negroes, it was not because of prejudice against their color, but because they have "so conducted themselves as to be a continuous convenient whip placed in the hands of the employers to cow the white men and to compel them to accept abject conditions of labor." [37] In explaining the Federation's attitude toward Negro workers in the *American Federationist*, Gompers devoted most of his attention to rebuking them for being "cheap workers," for demanding "special privileges," and for being suspicious of white workers.[38]

Between 1899 and 1902, the A.F. of L. abandoned even the formality of equal status for Negro workers. It is significant that it was just in these years

[34] Gompers to L. F. McGruder, Oct. 6, 1899. The contraction in the spelling of the epithet is the present author's.

[35] Gompers to Will Winn, Mar. 9, 1899; Gompers to James Leonard, June 28, 1900.

[36] *American Federationist*, VI (May, 1899), 57.

[37] Gompers, *Labor and the Employer*, op. cit., 166–167.

[38] Gompers, "Trade Union Attitude Toward Colored Workers," *American Federa-tionist*, VIII (Apr., 1901), 118–120; Gompers to J. H. Powell, Feb. 12, 1901.

that race relations in the South suffered their greatest deterioration, Negro rights reached their lowest ebb, and the movement to disfranchise Negro voters was at its height. The principal cause of the recrudescence of repressive legislation, white supremacism and extra-legal terrorism against the Negroes was the alarm which was produced among conservatives by the rising tide of Negro-white unity in the Populist movement. When the Southern Populists denounced lynching and called for the defense of the Negroes' political rights; when Tom Watson declared that "the accident of color can make no difference in the interest of farmers, croppers, and laborers. . . . You are kept apart that you may be separately fleeced of your earnings"; when Negroes were seen on leading committees with white Populists—the Southern Bourbons decided that the "time for smooth words has gone by, the extremist limit of forbearance has been reached." Northern Republicans agreed, for they represented the business groups with rapidly increasing investments in the Southern economy, who were just as frightened as the Southern conservatives by the threat of the overthrow of their regime by a united people.

Besides, Northern capital was just assuming the "white man's burden" in the Philippines, Hawaii, Porto Rico and Cuba, and it was widely observed that the justification for imperialism was equally applicable to the repression of the American Negroes. As the *Atlantic Monthly* commented, "If the stronger and cleverer race is free to impose its will upon 'new-caught, sullen people' on the other side of the globe, why not in South Carolina and Mississippi? The advocates of the 'shotgun policy' are quite as sincere . . . as the advocates of 'benevolent assimilation.' The two phrases are, in fact, two names for the same thing." Professor John W. Burgess thought that "the Republican party, in its work of imposing the sovereignty of the United States upon eight millions of Asiatics, has changed its views in regard to the political relations of races and has at last virtually accepted the ideas of the South upon that subject." He assured the South that the leaders of the party would never again "give themselves over to the vain imagination of the political equality of man."

The Southern white supremacists and their Northern business allies instituted a campaign to impose a legal status of inferiority and second-class citizenship on the Negroes, to deprive them of their rights by fraud, force and violence, and to bolster these acts by a modern, "scientific" doctrine of the superiority of the white race. Senator Ben Tillman of South Carolina announced the results of this campaign on the floor of the Senate: "We took the government away. We stuffed the ballot boxes. We shot Negroes! We are not ashamed of it." When Gompers and the A.F. of L. abandoned the effort to organize the Negro workers, established jim-crowism in the labor movement, and contributed to the ideology of white supremacy, they were playing into the hands of the employers who sought to keep the workers divided in order to exploit them more effectively and to prevent their united resistance to big business' domination of the "New South." This was a reflection of the Federation's gradual surrender all along the line to the demands and views of big business.[39]

[39] C. Vann Woodward, *Origins of the New South, 1877–1913* (Baton Rouge:

After Gompers' failure to accomplish his purpose with the Brotherhood of Locomotive Firemen as he had with the machinists' and blacksmiths' unions, he abandoned the attempt to make equality of admission, even on paper, a qualification for affiliation. When the Order of Railroad Telegraphers and the Brotherhood of Railway Trackmen, both of which restricted membership to whites, joined the A.F. of L. in 1899, Gompers made no protest. In fact, he hailed their action as a harbinger of unity in the labor movement.[40] This sacrifice of principle to the "practical" and immediate objective of gaining accessions for the Federation was the precursor of further surrenders. In 1902, a national union already affiliated with the A.F. of L.—the stationary engineers—amended its laws so as to exclude Negroes, and neither Gompers nor the Federation registered any opposition.[41]

The problem of the admission of Negro locals to central labor unions first came to Gompers' attention in 1894 when several members of the Trades Assembly of Fort Worth objected to the admission of the Building Laborers Protective Union. Gompers ruled that it was inadvisable as well as unjust to exclude any workers because of color.[42] In the following years Gompers revoked the charters of several central labor unions which refused to accept delegates from Negro unions. The matter came up in 1900. In that year several organizations of Negro workers in New Orleans, refused admission to the central labor union, formed a Central Trades and Labor Council of their own and requested a charter from the Federation, promising to work in harmony with the Council of white unions. The Executive Council referred the matter to Gompers for investigation. He in turn asked his New Orleans organizer to consult with the labor men there as to what they considered the wisest course to pursue.[43] Learning that sentiment was favorable to segregation, Gompers said that he would urge its approval to the next A.F. of L. convention, providing it was the clearly expressed wish of both the Negro unions and the existing central labor union.[44]

In his annual report, Gompers asserted that to insist upon the central labor union's granting admission to delegates of Negro unions would mean the dissolution of those bodies, and he therefore proposed to allow the formation of separate trade councils for unions of colored workers. He added that there was no reason for altering the Federation's policy of opening its doors to all workers, and that his suggestion seemed the best means of advancing the

Louisiana State University Press, 1951), 235–263, 321–322, 350–351; Jack Abramowitz, "The Negro in the Populist Movement," *The Journal of Negro History*, XXXVIII (July, 1953), 257–289; Melvin J. White, "Populism in Louisiana During the Nineties," *Mississippi Valley Historical Review*, V (June, 1918), 3 ff.

[40] Gompers, "Unity Drawing Nearer," *American Federationist*, VII (Feb., 1900), 34–35.

[41] Du Bois, *op. cit.*, 157.

[42] Charles Archer to Gompers, May 25, 1894; Gompers to Archer, June 1, 1894.

[43] Gompers to James Leonard, Mar. 9, 1900; Minutes, Executive Council, Mar. 22, 1900, in *American Federationist*, VII (Apr. 1906), 121.

[44] Gompers to James E. Porter, Apr. 25, 1900, June 18, 1900; Gompers to M. S. Belk, Aug. 11, 1900.

organization of Negro workers for their benefit as well as the protection of the interests of the white workers. The convention adopted the suggestion and amended the Federation's constitution, authorizing the Executive Council to issue charters to separate central bodies whenever it seemed advisable. At the same time it authorized the policy which Gompers had already initiated of organizing Negroes into separate Federal Labor Unions. These bodies were completely ineffective to protect the interests of their members, for they were detached locals with no national head, and their standards were theoretically to be protected by the very internationals which claimed jurisdiction over their work but refused to admit them to membership.[45]

Gompers and the Federation settled into a fixed policy of jim-crowism. In 1901, in response to the demand of the Trades Council of Anniston, Alabama, the Federation decided that even where there were not enough Negro locals to form a separate trades council, the central labor union did not have to admit their delegates.[46] Gompers no longer viewed the formation of separate locals and central labor unions as a necessary alternative to the preferred policy of unity of organization. He accepted it as the final and best settlement of the problem. He abandoned the earlier requirement that the Negro as well as the white workers should desire separate organization before their formation would be permitted. He did not urge the white unions to accept the Negro workers before yielding to the establishment of separate unions. He even specifically refused to make such a request of a central labor union, deciding in advance that, because of existing prejudice in the South, it was best for both the Negro and white workers that they be segregated to avoid "arousing bitterness." [47] And he reversed his decision to appoint a colored organizer for the South when it was protested by the Alabama Federation of Labor.[48] Finally, he refused to grant charters as federal locals to Negro unions when affiliated unions or the railroad brotherhoods would neither accept them themselves nor surrender jurisdiction over them. In other words, he accepted the policy of those organizations in refusing to allow the organization of Negro workers under any condition.[49] He accepted as permanent the division of the American working force into skilled white and unskilled Negro workers.[50]

The only place Gompers drew the line was in refusing to allow the Federation's directly affiliated locals to prohibit their members from working with Negroes on the same jobs. He stated that such a policy was repugnant to

[45] AFL, *20th Convention*, 1900, 22–23, 112, 129; Sterling D. Spero and Abram L. Harris, *The Black Worker* (New York: Columbia University Press, 1931), 93–99.

[46] New York *Tribune*, Dec. 13, 1901.

[47] Gompers to H. A. Stemburgh, July 20, 1903; Gompers to L. E. Turley, Sept. 20, 1905; Gompers to Frank Duffy, Mar. 2, 1906.

[48] Gompers to David Williams, Feb. 16, 1903.

[49] Minutes, Executive Council, Sept. 21, 1903 and Oct. 16–21, 1911, in *American Federationist*, X (Nov. 1903), 1191, and XVIII (Dec., 1911), 1011; Gompers to Calmeze E. Henike, Mar. 19, 1902; Gompers to J. H. Patterson, Mar. 14, 1903 and Mar. 23, 1903; Gompers to L. B. Allen, Mar. 30, 1903 and May 8, 1903; Gompers to James McNair, Nov. 6, 1905.

[50] Gompers, statement in Toledo *News-Bee*, Oct. 27, 1905.

the principles of the A.F. of L. and of justice. Besides, even if it were enforced, the result would be the displacement of white workers by Negroes and the reduction of standards to the level that the unorganized Negro workers were forced to accept. "Is it not better," he asked, "to try and organize men who work and thereby protect the interests of all? Of course, if Negroes are objectionable to membership in your union, they at least should have the right to work and the right to organize in a union of Negro workmen. The attempt to draw the line at nationalities would prove not only injurious but dangerous and in any event is absolutely wrongful...." [51] At the same time Gompers was still arguing with President Carter of the Locomotive Firemen the desirability of organizing Negroes.[52] He did not change his private opinion, but he had completely surrendered his official policy to the local and craft prejudices of the organizations affiliated with the A.F. of L. As in other areas, he sacrificed principle to the "practical" end of making the Federation "work" smoothly and without friction—the typical mark of the bureaucratic administrator.

In 1902, William E. B. Du Bois was making a study at Atlanta University of the Negro in the trade unions. He made a careful tabulation of the status of Negroes in the various unions, showing that forty-three national organizations, including the railroad brotherhoods, had no Negro members, and that in sixteen of them this was due to the discriminatory policies of those organizations. Twenty-seven others had very few Negro members, partly due to the failure of the unions to train Negro apprentices. There were altogether only forty thousand Negroes in the A.F. of L., with a total membership of just over a million. Du Bois then prepared a fairly accurate summary of the evolution of the Federation's policy with regard to Negro workers. He added that some broadminded leaders like Gompers had striven to maintain high and just ideals, but because of the narrow prejudices and selfish greed with which they had to contend, the policy of the Federation had retrogressed.[53] He sent this to Gompers before publishing it, with a request that he make any comment on it that he desired. Gompers replied: "... I should say that your statement is neither fair nor accurate.... you are inclined, not only to be pessimistic upon the subject, but you are even unwilling to give credit where credit is due. Let me say further, that I have more important work to attend to than correct 'copy' for your paper." [54]

The Atlanta Conference on Negro Artisans, for which this report was prepared, recommended that Negroes should support the labor movement where it pursued a fair policy, but denounced the unjust proscription of Negroes practiced by some unions.[55] Negro spokesmen continued to criticize the A.F. of L.'s policy. In 1905, the Niagara movement, one of whose purposes

---

[51] Gompers to C. H. Hogan, Feb. 14, 1910; Gompers to W. R. Paul, May 31, 1911.

[52] Gompers to W. S. Carter, July 26, 1911.

[53] Du Bois, op. cit., 156–158.

[54] Gompers to Du Bois, Jan. 5, 1903; Du Bois, op. cit., 177; Du Bois to Bernard Mandel, Oct. 3, 1952.

[55] Du Bois, op. cit., 7–8.

was to bring Negroes and labor unions into mutual understanding, held up to execration the practice of unions "in proscribing and boycotting and oppressing thousands of their fellow-toilers, simply because they are black." The National Association for the Advancement of Colored People, formed in 1909, urged that Negroes make common cause with the working class, but it was pointed out that discrimination by trade unions was crushing and keeping down the Negro competitors of white workers.[56] Gompers took no cognizance of these criticisms, except on one occasion. While in St. Louis in 1910 for the convention of the A.F. of L., he addressed the local trades council. One of the local newspapers the next morning stated that he had "read the negro out of the labor movement." This was reported throughout the country, and resulted in a flood of protests from Negro spokesmen, including Washington. Gompers stated that he had been misquoted and that the alleged remark in no way represented his attitude toward the Negroes. What he did say, he explained, was that it was difficult to organize Negro workers because, being only half a century removed from slavery, they did not have the same conception of their rights and duties as did the white workers and were unprepared for fully exercising and enjoying the possibilities existing in trade unionism.[57] In other words, he did not read the Negroes out of the labor movement, but virtually said that they had read themselves out of it.

Gompers continued to ignore protests, and he continued to ignore the Negro workers.[58] Shortly before he died the convention of the National Association for the Advancement of Colored People addressed an open letter to the A.F. of L. It stated that the interests of white and Negro labor were identical, and that the latter had been demanding admission into the unions for many years, but they were still outside the ranks of organized labor because the unions discriminated against them and because "black labor has ceased to beg admission to union ranks." It proposed that the N.A.A.C.P., the A.F. of L., and the railroad brotherhoods form an Interracial Labor Commission. The appeal fell on deaf ears.[59] Gompers had little sympathy with the militant policies of the N.A.A.C.P. Although he had once criticized Washington for recommending that Negroes rely on the good will of their employers to improve their status,[60] he was later reconciled to his conservative policy of achieving freedom "by the slow process of education and development" and by

[56] Herbert Aptheker, A Documentary History of the Negro People in the United States (New York: Citadel Press, 1951), 902, 916 ff.

[57] AFL, 30th Convention, 1910, 237; Gompers, "The Negro in the A.F. of L.," American Federationist, XVIII (Jan., 1911), 34–36.

[58] An interesting reflection of Gompers' lack of concern and awareness of the problem of Negro workers appears in an editorial in the Federationist for July, 1915 (XXII, 517), in which he stated that "there are now two great groups of exploited workers in the United States—immigrants and women." Much more significant is the fact that Gompers devoted only two sentences in his 1100 page autobiography to the subject, a statement that he believed Negroes should have the right to organize. Seventy Years of Life and Labor (New York: E. P. Dutton Co., 1925), I, 364.

[59] Charles Wesley, Negro Labor in the United States (New York: Vanguard Press, 1927), 275–277.

[60] Gompers, "Trade Union Attitude Toward Colored Workers," op. cit., 118–120.

"rendering service to society that would assure their value and independence." [61]

Gompers' attitude toward the Negro question was determined entirely by a narrow trade union point of view. That is, he understood that the protection of the interests of the white workers required the organization of the Negro workers, whom he regarded as competitors in the labor market. But he had little sensitivity for the problems of the Negro people, and shared to a considerable extent the prejudices of which he often complained. In fact, considering the fact that he was an immigrant and a Jew himself, and that he professed a liberal and far-sighted attitude towards social and human problems, he had a remarkably large amount of prejudice against "non-Aryans," and his hatred of Orientals was particularly virulent. Once, when a newspaper reporter fabricated an imaginary interview with him and reported that he was drunk, Gompers said of him: "Beings of his ilk are fit to associate with dagos and Chinese but should not be tolerated among civilized men." [62] He took delight in telling stories in his public addresses which perpetuated some of the unfavorable stereotypes of Negroes, whom he often referred to as "darkies." [63] When a Negro purchased a house about a block from his home in Washington, some of the neighbors instituted legal action to prevent the owner from living in his house. Gompers was asked to join in the effort. He declined, he said, because he did not want the A.F. of L. to be implicated in such an action, but added frankly that he would not want to live in a neighborhood with colored people.[64] Another indication of his attitude was revealed when the meat cutters' union of Stockton, California, gave a picnic for the local unionists. A Negro member of the hod carriers' union attended and was ordered off the dance floor. This man, who was his union's delegate to the local trades council, desired that the council demand an apology from the meat cutters, and his motion was passed. The president of the trades council then asked Gompers if he should enforce the motion. Gompers replied:

> In my judgment you were perfectly right in determining that matters of this character should not be brought before your Central Body.... we can not attempt to regulate the social intercourse of the races. It might have been a mistake to have invited or permitted other than members of the caucasian race to attend the picnic, but having acted upon opposite lines, then to deny them equal courtesy would scarcely be in keeping with such a course, but as organized labor it would be most unwise to stir up strife and prejudice rather than peace if we make these questions subject to decision by our organization. It was in equally bad taste for the colored delegate to have brought the matter before your Central Body....[65]

[61] Gompers, statement for memorial book of Booker T. Washington, Jan. 24, 1916, in AFL, "Special Articles" file; Florence Thorne to Bernard Mandel, July 7, 1953.

[62] Duluth *Daily Union*, Apr. 1, 1891.

[63] See his speech in Indianapolis, Sept. 7, 1903, in Indianapolis *Star*, Sept. 8, 1903; and speech in Lawrence, Apr. 19, 1903, in Lawrence *Daily Eagle*, Apr. 20, 1903.

[64] Gompers to M. Brown, Oct. 17, 1907.

[65] Gompers to R. W. Bonney, Oct. 2, 1902.

Gompers' opportunistic pandering to the prejudices of the Southern whites was well illustrated by the argument he used to support child labor legislation in the Southern states. He stated that if white children were kept working in the factories, they would become degenerate and illiterate, while the Negroes were advancing in their education. The result would be that more and more whites would be disfranchised by the illiteracy laws, more and more Negroes enfranchised, and the basis would be laid for the decline of the white race and the ascendancy of the Negroes.[66]

Gompers never registered any protest against any of the conditions or events which concerned the Negro people. He was silent about the disfranchisement of the Southern Negroes, about lynchings, about exclusion of Negroes from jury service, about inferior and segregated accommodations in the public schools and colleges, railroads, and other public places, about chain gangs, involuntary servitude through debt peonage, or such injustices as Roosevelt's dishonorable discharge of 160 Negro soldiers for their unproved participation in the so-called "Brownsville riots." Even when the A.F. of L. denounced restrictions on the suffrage and directed the Executive Council to aid, and if necessary take the initiative, in thwarting the disfranchisement movement, Gompers did nothing to carry out the instructions.[67] In an address at Jacksonville, Florida, he stated that he had no desire to interfere with the "internal affairs" of the South. "I regard the race problem as one with which you people of the Southland will have to deal; without the interference, too, of meddlers from the outside." [68] But such scruples did not prevent him from publicly defending the policy of San Francisco in segregating Japanese students in the public schools.[69]

Gompers had begun with a relatively advanced attitude toward Negro workers. But this attitude was based on a narrow trade union desire to keep the Negroes from competing with white labor, and neglected the broader vision of labor solidarity which marked the policy of the Knights of Labor. Furthermore, the positive aspects of his policy were mixed with a considerable amount of racial prejudice and a lack of concern for the special problems of the Negroes. So it was easy for him to retreat to a policy of jim-crowism when his principles were attacked by the trade union leaders who desired to solve the problem by excluding the Negroes from industrial life altogether. In his typically pragmatic way, Gompers could justify this surrender of principle as "theoretically bad but practically necessary," and finally arrive at the con-

[66] Gompers, address in New Orleans, Sept. 1, 1902, in *New Orleans Times-Democrat*, Sept. 2, 1902, quoted in *American Federationist*, IX (Oct., 1902), 706–707; Gompers, editorials in *American Federationist*, XXI (Jan. and Oct., 1914), 47–48, 870.

[67] AFL, *15th Convention*, 1895, 38.

[68] *The Metropolis* (Jacksonville, Fla.), May 25, 1907. Gompers' only known reference to disfranchisement was a remark he made in a Labor Day address to the Negro workers of New Orleans. "Well," he said, "you must hold on and hope for a time." New Orleans *Daily Picayune*, Sept. 2, 1902, quoted in *American Federationist*, IX (Oct., 1902), 709–710.

[69] *American Federationist*, XIV (Feb., 1907), 103.

clusion that it was not even theoretically wrong. He kept the Negroes out of the labor movement and then declared that they deserved no better because they had not made common cause with the white workingmen. Thus he sacrificed both his principles and the Negro workingmen, as well as the broader interests of the whole labor movement, to the short-sighted and selfish demands of the aristocratic officialdom of the craft unions, whose spokesman he had agreed to be.

Hortense Powdermaker

THE CHANNELING OF NEGRO AGGRESSION
BY THE CULTURAL PROCESS

*As under the slave regime, Negro resentment at the increasing dis-
crimination and deprivation was channeled in various ways. Retaliatory violence was not unknown; it occurred both during the ante-
bellum years as we have observed, and intermittently throughout
the century since emancipation. Verbal protests, the vigorous use
of the Negro vote, picketing and boycotts have all been forms of
direct expression of the aggressive impulse arising from the race's
frustrating experience in America. Often such aggressions have been
sublimated into nationalist attempts to create all-Negro communities
or emigrate to Africa.*

*In the late nineteenth and early twentieth centuries, as conditions
grew more hopeless and reached what Professor Rayford Logan of
Howard University has called "The Nadir," Negro resentment was
most often suppressed into an accommodating acceptance of the
status quo. Expressions of such a frame of mind ranged from looking
to Heaven for solace, to internalizing the white man's view of the
Negro.*

*Hortense Powdermaker, in an article whose conclusions have
remained unmodified in the quarter century since it was written, discusses the psychological mechanisms involved in the Negroes' responses to discrimination. As she perceptively predicted, with improving conditions the way in which Negroes express their resentment
has changed dramatically in recent years.*

W E shall attempt in this article to look at one small segment of our cultural process—namely, a changing pattern of aggressive behavior—caused by
the interracial situation. We limit ourselves to considering, at this time, only
the Negro side of this complex of interpersonal relations; and we shall do no

Hortense Powdermaker, "The Channeling of Negro Aggression by the Cultural
Process," *American Journal of Sociology*, XLVIII (May, 1943), pp. 750–58. Reprinted
with permission of University of Chicago Press.

more than offer a few rather broad hypotheses on the relation between the forms aggression has taken during different historical periods and changes in the cultural processes at these times. For our hypotheses we are indebted to history, anthropology, sociology, and psychoanalysis; to the first three for understanding how social patterns come into being at a given point in time and how they are related to each other; and to the fourth, psychoanalysis, for a clue to the mechanisms by which individuals adopt particular social patterns. We shall concentrate on an analysis of two forms of adaptation where the aggression seems to have been concealed and, therefore, less understood. The two forms are that of the faithful slave and that of the meek, humble, unaggressive Negro who followed him after the Civil War. Since there is much more data on the latter role, this is the one we shall discuss in detail.

Education includes learning to play certain roles, roles which are advantageous to the individual in adapting himself to his particular culture. As the culture changes, so does the role. Adaptation to society begins at birth and ends at death. Culture is not a neatly tied package given to the child in school. It is an ever changing process, gropingly and gradually discovered.[1] The family, church, movies, newspaper, radio programs, books, trade-unions, chambers of commerce, and all other organized and unorganized interpersonal relations are part of education. All these are part of the cultural process, which determines how behavior and attitudes are channeled.

The cultural milieu of the Negro in the United States has run the gamut from slavery to that of a free but underprivileged group, who are slowly but continuously raising their status. From the time slaves were first brought to this country until today there have been barriers and restrictions which have prevented the Negro from satisfying social needs and attaining those values prized most highly by our society. How the resentment against these deprivations is channeled depends largely on cultural factors. Each historical period has produced certain types of adaptation.

Much has been written as to whether slaves emotionally accepted their status or whether they rebelled against it, with the consequent aggressive impulses turned against their masters. There is no categorical answer. Aggression can be channeled in many ways, and some of these are not discernible except to the trained psychiatrist. But others are quite obvious. The fact that thousands of slaves ran away clearly indicates dissatisfaction with their status.[2] Crimes committed by the slaves are another evidence of lack of acceptance of status and of aggressive feelings toward the whites.

Many people have assumed that there was little or no crime by Negroes during the slave regime. The impression will be quickly dispelled if one consults the elaborate studies contained in *Judicial*

---

[1] For further elaboration of this point see Edward Sapir, "The Emergence of the Concept of Personality in a Study of Cultures," *Journal of Social Psychology*, V, 408–15.

[2] From 1830 to 1860 about fifty thousand escaped, chiefly through Ohio and Philadelphia. In an earlier period many escaped to near-by Indian tribes, others to Canada and the free states (see E. B. Reuter, *The American Race Problem* [New York, 1938], pp. 117–18).

Cases concerning American Slavery and the Negro. . . . In these lists can be found cases of murder, rape, attempted rape, arson, theft, burglary, and practically every conceivable crime.[3]

The fact that these crimes were committed in the face of the most severe deterrents—cutting-off of ears, whipping, castration, death by mutilation—bears witness to the strength of the underlying aggression. Equally cruel was the punishment of those slaves who broke the laws against carrying firearms, assembling, and conspiring to rebel. The Gabriel conspiracy in Richmond, the Vesey conspiracy in Charleston, the Nat Turner rebellion, and others resulted in the massacre of whites and in the burning, shooting, and hanging of the Negroes. These attempts were undertaken despite the fact that the superior power of the whites made it virtually impossible for a slave revolt to be successful.

But the overt aggression was very probably only a small part of the total hostility. The punishments imposed by the culture for failure were too severe and the chances for success too slight to encourage the majority of slaves to rebel to any considerable extent. There were large numbers of loyal and faithful slaves, loyal to the system and to the masters. It is this loyalty that we try to understand.

Psychologically, slavery is a dependency situation. The slave was completely dependent upon the white master for food, clothing, shelter, protection—in other words, for security. If he could gain the good will or affection of the master, his security was increased. In return for this security the Negro gave obedience, loyalty, and sometimes love or affection. With certain limitations the situation of slave and master corresponds to that of child and parent. The young child is completely dependent on his parents for food, shelter, love, and everything affecting his well-being and security. The child learns to be obedient because he is taught that disobedience brings punishment and the withdrawal of something he needs for security. Basic infantile and childhood disciplines relating to sex are imposed on this level. In our culture, parents forbid and punish deviations by a child, who in turn renounces his gratification to gain the parent's approval. "The parent is needed and feared, and must therefore be obeyed; but the hatred to the frustrating parent, though suppressed, must be present somewhere." [4]

We mentioned above that there are certain limitations to our analogy. Obviously, the bondage is greater for the slave than for the child. Equally obviously, while there was love in some master-slave relationships, it was certainly not so prevalent as between parents and children. Again, the child always has a weak and undeveloped ego while the adult slave may have a strong, developed one. But most important is the difference in the reasons for the dependency attitude. The limited strength and resources of the child and his resulting helplessness and anxiety are due to biological causes. But the slave's

---

[3] Quoted in W. D. Weatherford and C. S. Johnson, *Race Relations* (New York, 1934), p. 265.

[4] A. Kardiner and R. Linton, *The Individual and Society* (New York, 1939), p. 24.

dependency is imposed on him by culture and has nothing to do with biological factors. The structure of the two dependency situations is, therefore, very different. Nevertheless, functionally they have something in common. To attain the only security available to them, both the slave and the child repress, consciously or unconsciously, their hatred for the object which restricts their desires and freedom. At this late date it is impossible to determine to what degree aggression occurred in slaves' fantasies or in minor overt acts.[5] It probably varied from one slave to another, as it does for children. Neither all children nor all slaves repress their aggression all the time. Running away is a pattern for both groups. Disobedience is followed by punishment for both. Another alternative for both is open rebellion. Finally, children and slaves may accept their dependency and repress their aggression when compensations are adequate. They may even identify with the frustrating object. The picture of the faithful slave who helped the white mistress run the plantation while the master was away fighting, fighting the men who would liberate the slave, is only superficially paradoxical.

Data from psychoanalysis indicate that those children who do not permit their aggressive impulses to break through even in fantasy, not to mention overt behavior, have great difficulty as adults in entering into any personal relationship which does not duplicate the dependency pattern of parent and child. A legal edict of freedom did not immediately change the security system for the slave, conditioned over years to depend on the white man for all security. Time was needed for the compensations of freedom to become part of the ex-slave's security system. The process of growing up, or becoming less dependent, is a long and difficult one.

With emancipation, the slave, from being a piece of property with no rights at all, attained the status of a human being—but an underprivileged one. Psychological dependency did not vanish with the proclamation of freedom. In the period folowing the Civil War the slave's illiteracy, his complete lack of capital and property, the habituation to the past, and the continuous forces wielded by the whites in power created new conditions for the continuance of the old dependency. The recently freed Negro was dependent on the whites for jobs, for favors, for grants of money to set up schools, and for much of his security. In the South, following the Reconstruction Period, it was by obtaining favors from whites rather than by insisting on his rights that the Negro was able to make any progress or attain any security. The sets of mores which insured the colored man's status being lower than that of the whites was and is still firmly intrenched. The denial of the courtesy titles (Mr., Mrs., Miss); the Jim Crowism in schools, buses, and trains, in places of residence; the denial of legal rights; the threat of lynching—these are among the more obvious ways of "keeping the Negro in his place." He is deprived of what are considered

---

[5] I know of no accurate way of getting data on this point. The memories of old ex-slaves would be colored by what has happened to them since slavery was abolished. Aggressive impulses which may have been completely repressed during slavery could be released and brought into consciousness after slavery ceased.

legal, social, and human rights, without any of the compensations for his deprivation which he had under slavery.

The same questions we asked about the slave occur again. Did the Negro really accept his position? Or was aggression aroused, and if so, how did the culture channel it? This is an easier situation to study than the slavery of the past; for varied ways of reacting or adapting to this situation became stereotyped and still persist today. They are therefore susceptible of direct study.

First, there is direct aggression against its true object. Since the whites had, and still have, superior power and since Negroes are highly realistic, they rarely use this method on any large scale except in times of crisis, and then as a climax to a long series of more indirect aggressive behavior patterns. The knocking-down of a white overseer, the direct attack on other whites, has occurred, but only occasionally. One of the reasons advanced by many southern white planters for their preference for colored share-croppers to white ones is that the former do not fight back like the latter.

A second method consists in substituting a colored object for the white object of aggression. This was, and still is, done very frequently. The high degree of intra-Negro quarreling, crime, and homicide, revealed by statistics and observation, can be directly correlated with the Negro's frustration in being unable to vent his hostility on the whites. The mechanism of the substitution of one object of aggression for another is well known to the scientist and to the layman.[6] The substitution of Negro for white is encouraged by the culture pattern of white official and unofficial leniency toward intra-Negro crime. Courts, more particularly southern ones, are mild in their view of intra-Negro offenses, and the prevailing white attitude is one of indulgence toward those intra-Negro crimes which do not infringe on white privileges.[7]

A third possibility is for the Negro to retreat to an "ivory tower" and attempt to remain unaffected by the interracial situation. But this type of adjustment is very difficult and consequently a rare one.

Another form of adaptation consists in the Negro's identification with his white employer, particularly if the latter has great prestige. Some of the slaves also identified themselves with the great families whom they served. This pattern may likewise be observed in white servants. Still another adaptation is the diversion of aggression into wit, which has been and still is a much-used mechanism. We have not sufficient data on these two mechanisms to discuss them in detail.

But we do want to analyze in some detail a very frequent type of adjustment which occurred after the Civil War and which has persisted. We mean the behavior of the meek, humble, and unaggressive Negro, who is always

---

[6] This is reflected in the jokes and stories about the man who has a bad day at the office and then "takes it out" on his wife or children when he comes home in the evening.

[7] For further elaboration see H. Powdermaker, *After Freedom* (Viking Press, 1939), pp. 172–74.

deferential to whites no matter what the provocation may be. The psychological mechanism for this form of adaptation is less obvious than some of the other types, and a more detailed analysis is therefore needed. We have called this Negro "unaggressive," and that is the way his overt behavior could be correctly described. All our data, however, indicate that he does have aggressive impulses against whites, springing from the interracial situation. He would be abnormal if he did not have them. Over and over again field studies reveal that this type of Negro is conscious of these resentments. But he conceals his true attitude from the whites who have power. How has he been able to conceal his aggression so successfully? His success here is patent. What is the psychological mechanism which enables the Negro to play this meek, deferential role?

A clue appears in certain similarities of this kind of behavior to that of the masochist, particularly through the detailed analysis of masochism by Dr. Theodor Reik in his recent book on that subject.[8] The seeming paradox of the masochist enjoying his suffering has been well known to psychoanalysts. He derives pleasure, because, first, it satisfies unconscious guilt feeling. Second (and here is where Dr. Reik has gone beyond the other psychoanalysts in his interpretation), the masochist derives another kind of pleasure, because his suffering is a prelude to his reward and eventual triumph over his adversary. In other words, he gets power through his suffering. We must not be misunderstood at this point. The meek Negro is neither neurotic nor masochistic any more than the slave was biologically a child. But the unaggressive behavior has some elements in common with (and some different from) the behavior of the masochist; and a comparison of the two gives a clue to an understanding of the strength behind the meek, humble role played by so many Negroes.

First, there are essential differences between the Negroes we are describing and the masochists analyzed by Dr. Reik and others. The Negro's sufferings and sacrifices are not unconsciously self-inflicted (as are those of the masochist) but are inflicted on him by the culture. The Negro plays his social masochistic role consciously, while the psychologically compulsive masochist does it unconsciously. These two important differences should be kept in mind while the similarities are discussed.

Our hypothesis is that the meek, unaggressive Negro, who persists today as a type and whom we have opportunity to study, feels guilty about his conscious and unconscious feelings of hostility and aggression toward the white people. These Negroes are believing Christians who have taken very literally the Christian doctrine that it is sinful to hate. Yet on every hand they are faced with situations which must inevitably produce hatred in any normal human being. These situations run the scale from seeing an innocent person lynched to having to accept the inferior accommodations on a Jim Crow train. The feeling of sin and guilt is frequently and openly expressed. In a Sunday-school class in a southern rural colored church a teacher tells the tale of a

[8] *Masochism in Modern Man* (New York: Farrar & Rinehart, 1941).

share-cropper who had worked all season for a white planter, only to be cheated out of half his earnings. The teacher's lesson is that it is wrong to hate this planter, because Christ told us to love our enemies. The members of the class say how hard it is not to hate but that since it is a sin they will change their hate to love. They regard this as possible, although difficult.[9]

One woman in the same community, who plays the deferential role to perfection and who, whites say, never steps out of "her place," tells me she feels guilty because she hates the whites, who do not seem to distinguish between her, a very moral, respectable, and law-abiding person, and the immoral, disreputable colored prostitutes of the community. She says that God and Jesus have told her not to hate but to love—and so she must drive the hatred and bitterness away. Almost every human being in our culture carries a load of guilt (heavy or light as the case may be) over his conscious and unconscious aggressive impulses. It is easy then to imagine how heavy is the load of guilt for the believing Christian Negro who lives in an interracial situation which is a constant stimulus to aggressive thoughts and fantasies. By acting in exactly the opposite manner—that is, meekly and unaggressively—he can appease his guilt feelings consciously and unconsciously. It is this appeasement which accounts, in part, for his pleasure in the unaggressive role he plays with the whites.

But only in part. The unaggressive Negro enjoys his role also because through it he feels superior to the whites. Like the masochist, he thinks of his present sufferings as a contrasting background for his future glory. His is the final victory, and so he can afford to feel superior to his white opponent who is enjoying a temporary victory over him. My own field work and the work of others give many examples. Dr. Charles S. Johnson, in his recent book on rural colored youth in the South, discusses the dissimulation of many of the young people studied. He says:

> Outward submissiveness and respect may thus be, as often as not, a mask behind which these youth conceal their attitude. George Cator is an example of this behavior. He has learned to flatter as a means of preserving his own estimate of himself. . . . "When I'm around them, I act like they are more than I am. I don't think they are, but they do. I hear people say that's the best way to act." [10]

Any expression of antagonism would be dangerous, but this is not the whole story. It is not just that this boy and others avoid danger by meek negative behavior. There is a positive element in that he and others are insuring eventual victory. This was expressed by a colored servant who is a model of deferential behavior when with the whites. However, to me she says, partly scornfully and partly jokingly, that she considers it ridiculous that having cleaned the front porch and entrance she has to use the back entrance. She

---

[9] Cf. Powdermaker, *op. cit.*, pp. 247–48.
[10] Charles S. Johnson, *Growing Up in the Black Belt* (American Council on Education, 1941), pp. 296–97.

hates having to walk in the back door, which in this case is not only the symbol of status for a servant but the symbol that a whole race has a servant status. She adds that she expects to go to Heaven and there she will find rest— and no back doors.[11]

The Christian doctrines, "The last shall be first, and the first shall be last" and "The meek shall inherit the earth," and all the promises of future reward for suffering give strong homiletic sanction to the feeling that the Negroes' present status and suffering is a prelude to their future triumph. Colored ministers give very concise expression to this attitude. A sermon heard in a colored church in rural Mississippi related

> the story of a rich woman who lived in a big house and had no time for God. When she went to Heaven she was given an old shanty in which to live and she exclaimed: "Why that's the shanty my cook used to live in!" The cook, who on earth had given all her time to God, was now living in a big house in Heaven, very much like the one in which her former mistress used to live.[12]

The Christian missionaries of the pre-Civil War period emphasized the reward for the meek and their contrasting glories in the future partly because it was an important part of Christian doctrine and partly because it was only by negating the present and emphasizing the future that the evangelists could get permission from the planters to preach to the slaves. The general theme of many of these sermons was that the greater the suffering here, the greater would be the reward in the world to come. One minister, referring to the case of a slave who was unjustly punished by his masters, says, "He [God] will reward you for it in heaven, and the punishment you suffer unjustly here shall turn to your exceeding great glory thereafter." [13] Sermons, past and current, quite frequently picture Heaven as a place where whites and Negroes are not just equal but where their respective status is the opposite of what it is here.

This fantasy of turning the tables on the oppressor is not always confined to the other world; sometimes the setting is our own world. An example of this is the fantasy of a young colored girl in a northern town who had publicly taken quite meekly a decision that the colored people could not use the "Y" swimming pool at the same time white people were using it. Privately she shows her anger and says that she wishes the colored people would build a great big, magnificent "Y," a hundred times better than the white one, and make that one look like nothing. Her fantasy of triumph over the whites obviously gives her real pleasure and allows her to carry the present situation less onerously. Another example of the same type of fantasying occurs in the joking between two colored teachers who obey a disliked white official with deferential meekness. The joking consists of one of them boasting in some detail about how he has fired the white official; and the other one, in the

---

[11] From the author's field notes in rural Mississippi.
[12] Powdermaker, *op. cit.*, p. 243.
[13] Revor Bowen, *Divine White Right* (1934), p. 111.

same tone, describing how he "cussed out" the white official over the telephone.

Another aspect of the unaggressive Negro's pleasure is his feeling of superiority because he thinks he is so much finer a Christian than his white opponent. He, the Negro, is following Christ's precepts, while the white man does the opposite. The white man oppresses the poor and is unjust; in other words, he sins. He, the Negro, is virtuous and will be rewarded. One Negro, referring to a white man's un-Christian behavior, says, "It reflects back on him."

This feeling of superiority is a third characteristic of the unaggressive Negro's pleasure and is not limited to the feeling of Christian virtue. He feels superior to the whites because he is fooling them. His triumph is not completely limited to the distant future, but he enjoys at least a small part of it now. One of my informants in Mississippi, who plays this role to perfection, told me how he has the laugh on the whites because they never know his real thoughts. He quite consciously feels that he and the other Negroes like him have the upper hand through their dissimulation. He says very clearly that it makes him feel superior. One woman who presents an appearance of perfect meekness laughs with a kind of gleeful irony when she tells me how she really feels, and her meekness drops away from her as if she were discarding a cloak. Another chuckles when she relates how much she has been able to extract from white people, who would never give her a thing if they knew how she really felt about them. A Negro official who holds a fairly important position in his community knows that he is constantly being watched to see that he does not overstep his place, that his position and contact with whites has not made him "uppity." As he goes around humbly saying, "Yes, ma'am" and "Yes, sir," waiting his turn long after it is due, appearing not to heed insulting remarks, he is buoyed up with a feeling of superiority because he is really fooling all these whites. He is quite aware of his mask and knows it is such and not his real self. This mask characteristic comes out particularly when one of these individuals is seen with the whites and then later with his own group. One woman who has been particularly successful in the deferential, humble role with the whites gives a clear impression of meekness and humility. Her eyes downcast, her voice low, she patiently waits to be spoken to before she speaks, and then her tone is completely deferential. An hour later she is in the midst of her own group. No longer are her eyes downcast. They sparkle! Her laugh flashes out readily. Instead of patiently waiting, she is energetically leading. Her personality emerges, vibrant and strong, a complete contrast to the picture she gives the whites. These people enjoy wearing their mask because they do it so successfully and because its success makes them feel superior to the whites whom they deceive.

The deferential, unaggressive role just described and well known to students of Negro life has a very real function besides the obvious one of avoiding trouble. As Dr. Reik says in his book on masochism, "The supremacy of the will is not only expressed in open fights." It is, as he says, likewise expressed "in the determination to yield only exteriorly and yet to cling to life, nourishing such phantasies anticipating final victory." [14] Our unaggressive Negro, like the masochist, imagines a future where his fine qualities are acknowledged by the people who had formerly disdained him. This, in good Christian manner, will be brought about through suffering. This philosophy and its resulting behavior obviously make the Negroes (or any minority group) who have them very adaptable to any circumstance in which they find themselves, no matter how painful. They continue to cling to life, in the assurance of ultimate victory. They cannot be hurt in the way that people without this faith are hurt. The adaptability of the Negro has often been noted. This hypothesis may give some further clue to understanding it.

A special combination of cultural factors—namely, oppression of a minority group and a religion which promises that through suffering power will be gained over the oppressors—has channeled one type of adaptive behavior similar to that of the masochist. This behavior pattern has given the Negro a way of appeasing his guilt over his aggressive impulses and a method of adapting to a very difficult cultural situation. Because of the understanding given us by psychoanalysis of the pleasure derived through suffering, of the near and distant aims of the masochist, we are given a clue to the psychological mechanism underlying the so-called "unaggressive" Negro's behavior. This Negro is not a masochist, in that his sufferings are not self-inflicted and he plays his role consciously. He knows he is acting, while the masochist behavior springs from inner compulsion. Again, there is a real difference in structure, as there was in the dependency situations of the child and the slave; and again there is a real similarity in function. The masochist and the meek, unaggressive Negro derive a similar kind of pleasure from their suffering. For the Negro as well as for the masochist there is pleasure in appeasing the guilt feeling; for each there is the pleasure derived from the belief that through his suffering he becomes superior to his oppressors; and, finally, for each the suffering is a prelude to final victory.

Neither the slave nor the obsequious, unaggressive Negro, whom we have described, learned to play his role in any school. They learned by observation and imitation; they were taught by their parents; they observed what role brought rewards. Since the Civil War the Negro has likewise seen the meek, humble type presented over and over again with approval in sermons, in literature, in movies, and, more recently, through radio sketches. By participating in the cultural processes, the Negro has learned his role. This was his education, far more powerful than anything restricted to schools; for the kind of education we are discussing is continuous during the entire life of the individual. It is subtle as well as direct. One part of the cultural process strengthens another part, and reinforcement for the role we described comes from every side.

But the cultural process continues to change with resulting changes in behavior. Just as the completely loyal and faithful slave disappeared, so the

[14] *Op. cit.*, p. 322.

meek, unaggressive, and humble Negro, the "good nigger" type, is declining in numbers. In the rural South, and elsewhere too, the tendency of Negro young people (in their teens and twenties) is to refuse to assume the unaggressive role. The passing of the "good nigger" from the scene does not entail a civil war as did the passing of the faithful slave. But it does indicate a psychological revolution. For the slave the Civil War altered the scope of the dependency situation. Today, without a Civil War, equally significant cultural changes are taking place. The Negro is participating now in a very different kind of cultural process from that which he underwent fifty years ago.

Some of the differences occurring today are here briefly indicated. There is a decline in religious faith. The vivid "getting-religion" experience prevalent in the past has become increasingly rare for young people. Today they use the church as a social center. Gone is the intensity of religious belief that their parents knew. The young people are not atheists, but they do not have the fervor and sincerity of belief in a future world. They are much more hurt by slights and minor insults than are their parents, because they do not put their faith in the promise of a heavenly victory.

Along with changes in the form of religious participation have come many other changes. The illiteracy of the past has disappeared. A lengthening of schooling and a steady improvement in educational standards tend to give the Negro the same knowledge and the same tools enjoyed by the white man and to minimize cultural differences between the two. A more independent and rebellious Negro type is making its appearance in literature, as, for instance, the character of Bigger in the best seller, *Native Son*.

The steady trek of the rural Negroes to cities, North and South, has changed the milieu of masses of Negroes from the rural peasant life to the industrial urban one.[15] Here they come under the influence of the trade-union movement, which slowly but gradually is shifting its attitude from one of jealous exclusion to one of inclusion, sometimes cordial and sometimes resigned. The shift is not anywhere near completion yet, but the trend is there. In the city the Negro is influenced by the same advertisements, the same radio sketches, the same political bosses, the same parties (left or right), and all the other urban forces which influence the white man.

The Negro's goals for success are thus becoming increasingly the same as those of the white person; and these goals are primarily in the economic field, although those in other fields, such as art and athletics, are not to be minimized either. The securing of these goals is in this world rather than in a future one. They are attained through the competition and aggressive struggle so characteristic of our culture rather than through meekness and subservience. The compensations available to the loyal slave and the humble, unaggressive, free Negro no longer exist or, at least, are steadily diminishing. The white man can no longer offer security in return for devotion, because he himself no longer has security. The whites of all classes have known a mounting social

[15] Between 1920 and 1930 over a million Negroes migrated from the country to the cities. The figures for the past decade are not yet available.

insecurity over the past decade, and they obviously cannot give away something which they do not possess. Thus the material rewards for obsequiousness and unaggressiveness are fading away. Gone, too, is the religious emphasis on rewards in Heaven. When the cultural process takes away rewards for a certain type of behavior, dissatisfaction with that behavior appears and there is a gradual change to another form which is more likely to bring new compensations. Obviously, one can expect, and one finds, a growing restlessness and uncertainty which occur in any transition period, when old goals have been lost. The new goals are the standard American ones. But the means for attaining these goals are not yet available to the Negro as they are to the white. Economic and social discriminations still exist. Unless some other form of adaptation takes place and unless discriminations are lessened, we may expect a trend toward greater overt aggression.

However, there are no sudden revolutions in behavior patterns, and this holds for the patterns of aggression. They change slowly; the old ones persist while new ones are being formed, and opposing patterns exist side by side. But change occurs. The cultural process in which the Negro has participated from the time when he was first brought to this country until today has involved a constant denial of privileges. The denial has taken various forms, from the overt one involved in slavery to the more subtle ones of today. The compensations for the denial have varied from different degrees of material security to promises of future blessings in Heaven, and from the feeling of being more virtuous than the white to the feeling of fooling him. Today these compensations are fading away. Equally important, ideological fetters of the past have been broken by the Negro's increasing participation in the current urban industrial processes.

The Negro's education, formal and informal, has consisted of his participation in this ever changing cultural process, one small part of which we have briefly examined. Slavery, religion, economic and other social factors, have channeled his activities, offering him alternatives within a certain cultural range. We have examined only two of the alternatives in any detail—namely, the roles of the faithful slave and of the humble, meek Negro who was a fairly common stereotype following the Civil War; we have concentrated on the latter because he still exists and we therefore have more data on him. Both appear unaggressive. A functional comparison with the psychoanalytical analysis of the dependency situation of the child and of the problem of masochism has indicated how the aggression may have been present, although concealed, in these two roles.

William E. Bittle and Gilbert L. Geis

RACIAL SELF-FULFILLMENT
AND THE RISE OF AN ALL-NEGRO
COMMUNITY IN OKLAHOMA[1]

Nationalist movements such as Garvey's of the 1920's and the Black Muslims of today function simultaneously in several ways. They channel aggression arising from resentment at the American race system into nationalistic pride and self-esteem. They are a protest against prejudice and discrimination. They promise escape from white oppression. At the same time, by preaching withdrawal or separation they function as an accommodating mechanism to the status quo in race relations.

All these things were also true of the late nineteenth- and early twentieth-century movements to establish black communities. Among them the most noted were the founding of the Negro town of Mound Bayou, in Mississippi, and the effort to establish an all-Negro state in the Oklahoma territory. In their account of the Oklahoma experience, William E. Bittle and Gilbert L. Geis describe the vision that animated the settlers, the cruel frustration of their dreams, and the tragedy awaiting those who, disillusioned by their failure to develop a successful community in Oklahoma, hoped to create one in Africa.

ALL-NEGRO communities in the United States have received remarkably little historical attention from scholars, with the major exception of the work of Frazier, which, however, concentrates primarily on communities of mixed-

William L. Bittle and Gilbert L. Geis, "Racial Self-fulfillment and the Rise of an All-Negro Community in Oklahoma," *Phylon*, XVIII (Third Quarter, 1957), pp. 247–60. Reprinted with permission of *Phylon*.

[1] The authors are greatly indebted to the Faculty Research Committee of the University of Oklahoma, whose generous financial assistance has made possible the research upon which this paper is based.

bloods rather than on enclave settlements of undifferentiated Negroes.[2] The curious lack of comment on such communities is difficult to understand in view of the fact that there are, at the present time, at least fifty towns in the United States which are inhabited and governed exclusively by Negroes.

In addition, and of great importance for an understanding of the American Negro, is the fact that all-Negro communities provide a laboratory of study which offers insights into Negro behavior which are not available from an examination of this behavior in bi-racial communities. There is, for example, good evidence that such social phenomena as class structure, attitudes toward mobility, color distinctions, criminality, and political activity in the all-Negro community are quite unpredictable from a knowledge of similar behavior in bi-racial areas.[3] Almost all of our information on Negro behavior in the United States is based upon research in communities in which the Negro finds himself in daily, face-to-face contact with a superordinate group, and where the attitudes and values of that group function to reinforce that Negro behavior which conforms most closely to white expectations. From such communities have arisen the pernicious stereotypes of what constitutes "real" Negro personality and behavior.

The Negro in such communities is mid-way, in a sense, between two cultures. He operates in a context which is unique to him, yet he is obliged to conform to a superordinate context which provides certain behavioral imperatives for him and relentlessly demands conformity to these imperatives.

Negro behavior in the all-Negro community, though certainly in part reflective of white expectations, is less so than in bi-racial communities if only because of the lack of intensive and routine reinforcement. The isolation from whites which the Negro enjoys in such racial islands permits a multi-directional development of behavioral forms, only certain aspects of which are patterned after the white culture of the area.

In addition to the information which may be gleaned on the contemporary Negro, the genesis of all-Negro communities documents a period in Negro history when the formation of such conclaves represented to the Negro a solution to the problems which both he and the whites felt in bi-racial groupings. Many of these all-Negro communities, and particularly those in the Oklahoma area, were not constituted as racial ghettos. The Negro felt strongly that this kind of isolation from the whites constituted a positive and workable solution to his difficulties, and he embarked upon the founding of these communities with visions of self-realization and fulfillment.

[2] E. Franklin Frazier, *The Negro Family in the United States* (Rev. ed., New York, 1951), pp. 164–189.
[3] See especially, Mozell C. Hill, "A Sociological Study of an all Negro Community" (Unpublished Master's thesis, University of Kansas, 1937); Hill, "The All Negro Society in Oklahoma" (Unpublished Doctoral dissertation, University of Chicago, 1946); Hill and Albert N. Whiting, "Some Theoretical and Methodological Problems in Community Studies," *Social Forces*, 29 (December, 1950), 117–124; Mozell Hill and Thelma D. Ackiss, "Social Classes: A Frame of Reference for the Study of Negro Society," *Social Forces*, 22 (October, 1943), 92–98.

The fate of many of the all-Negro communities testifies to the fact that this vision was not practical under the prevailing conditions and racial climate. Over the years, after a slow abatement of the first enthusiasms, all-Negro communities have steadily lost population, and many have ceased to exist. The discrepancy between the aims and aspirations of the all-Negro communities and the actualities of their life histories illustrates vividly the lengths to which the Negro would be permitted to go—the real limits of his social tether—even if he did not come into direct conflict or contact with the white group. Further, it illustrates the measures which the whites would employ once racial conflict, the seeking of the same goal by the two racial groups, became manifest.

The all-Negro community was a compromise between complete integration which was then, as now, unfeasible in terms of white values, and tormenting and humiliating subordination in bi-racial communities. The Negro in the all-Negro community was not yet ready to rebel against the stern racial etiquette in the United States, but hoped to find, in his new form of residence, a solution to a situation which showed little promise of imminent improvement. The all-Negro community was in no sense a retreat from American standards and values, and certainly not an anachronistic revival of Africanism, but rather an attempt to develop fully and to exploit thoroughly the American culture.

It is our present purpose to discuss the rise of one of the more important all-Negro communities and to relate its founding and early history to a body of attitudes which existed in the area during the 1905–1910 period. Though a generalization from this documentation to every all-Negro community in the nation is by no means warranted (since the Oklahoma situation will be seen to be unique in many respects), it seems clear that the situation in Boley, Oklahoma, is typical in broad outline of that in other all-Negro communities of the period, and particularly so of the large congregation of such communities in the so-called border states.

Boley lies in Okfuskee County, a principally rural area in east-central Oklahoma. This county, like many others in that part of the State, was carved out of the Creek Nation after the Federal government ended its century-long experiment in Indian isolation. By 1898, the Dawes Commission had secured an agreement from the Five Civilized Tribes to dissolve their governments, and the land was opened for legal settlement by non-Indians.

Oklahoma was, at this period, the last easily accessible frontier. It was the farthest east of those states which came into the Union in the Twentieth Century, and by far the least arid and the most desirable for farming. At the time of the removal of the Five Tribes from their aboriginal homes in the southeast, each had been given title to a portion of land in the newly created Indian Territory, and each was promised protection from encroachment by land-seekers. But the Tribes erred fatally by aligning with the Confederacy during the Civil War, and all fared badly after Appomattox. Prior treaties between the Federal government and the Indians were invalidated and in the new treaties previously inviolate western lands had to be relinquished by the Tribes, and the area opened for further settlement by whites and other Indians.

In addition, the Five Tribes were obliged to grant rights-of-way to the rapidly expanding railroads, and people and materiel both moved swiftly into the Indian region. By 1880, there were nearly five-thousand persons in the Territory who had no legal right to be there. Negroes were fairly numerous in the Territory, too. During the period of Indian removal to Oklahoma, most of the tribes had brought along their slaves. It has been estimated that between four and five thousand Negroes came to Oklahoma in this manner.

Of this number, a more than proportionate share was held by the Creeks, the original inhabitants of Okfuskee County. The Creeks were easy masters; often it was difficult to distinguish socially between slave and master as they worked side by side and shared the same food and dwelling. Many Negroes from slave-holding states to the east fled to Creek holdings where they found masters not so white and labors not so tedious.

The place of the Negro among the Indians was a unique one. Experience in the Deep South had provided the Negro with a certain *savoir faire* that the Indian notably lacked, so the Negroes were often relied upon to deal with whites. These Negroes, sometimes called "linksters" because of their ability to speak English, inevitably gained a prominent position in Indian councils. Though discrimination was not absent in Indian Territory, the Negro nonetheless gained an importance here which he had not had in the slave-holding states. One Creek Negro summed up the contrast with the traditional southern slaves: "I was eating out of the same pot with the Indians ... while they were still licking the master's boots in Texas." [4]

Following the Civil War, many Negroes moved eastward into Indian Territory in search of land and opportunity. They operated under the same restrictions as did the whites in their quest for Indian lands, but they had as little difficulty in eventually alienating these lands from the Indians through circumvention of existing statutes. When the Dawes Commission finally acted in 1898, the settlement of the Territory was an accomplished fact, and the Commission simply moved to legalize it.

The final opening of the Indian Territory is a familiar bit of Americana. The lure of available lands drew thousands of people, priorly reticent about settling illegally in the new Territory, from the more densely populated southern and border states. This new frontier was comparatively near. But this was not the only advantage. Eastern Oklahoma was environmentally similar, in many respects, to the southern states. Cotton could be grown profusely in both places, along with other traditional southern crops. Further, there were cultural and spiritual ties, both real and alleged, between the Indian Territory and the South. The Five Tribes were immersed in the slave-holding tradition as well as in other aspects of ante-bellum economy. For the re-locating family, crossing out of Louisiana, Arkansas or Texas, eastern Oklahoma was but an annex to the South which they recognized and with which they were prepared to cope.

[4] Sigumund Sameth, "Creek Indians: A Study of Race Relations" (Unpublished Master's thesis, University of Oklahoma, 1940), p. 56.

From an early period that portion of Oklahoma which ultimately became Okfuskee County had an ethnically mixed population. The Creek Freedmen, the one-time slaves of the Indians, had early contributed the Negro component. This element was quickly supplemented and eventually inundated by the in-rush of what later came to be called State Negroes, persons who, like the whites, had moved into the Territory in search of new and available land.

When the Fort Smith and Western Railroad began to build through Okfuskee County, running from the Oklahoma-Arkansas border to the Territorial capital at Guthrie, Negro laborers from many parts of the South came to work on the right-of-way. The Negroes came often with their families and with vague ideas of permanence, hoping to settle in this area which was still, they felt, racially more ambiguous than the deep southern states. Despite the area's large southern component, the Negroes believed that the traditional caste lines of the South would be at least temporarily disturbed because of the newness of the settlement and the fact that land sale was ultimately under Federal jurisdiction.

The railroad encouraged settlements along its right-of-way, and the way for extensive in-migration was finally cleared by Roosevelt's proclamation of April 20, 1904, which allowed the Creek Freedmen to put their previously inalienable lands on the market. Speculators, both Negro and white, took advantage of the potentially profitable situation, and began to develop town sites along the railroad paths.

With the development of permanent towns in the region, two important, and somewhat counter-acting, components of an emerging racial ethic became apparent. The white settlers had every intention of maintaining the distinction between black and white which had predominated for so many centuries in the South. On the other hand, the whites and the Negroes were not inextricably woven together in Oklahoma by the complex economic ties which existed in the South. Allotments, not plantations, were the rule in the new Territory, and each man could operate his allotment by himself, without the assistance of hired hands or dependent Negroes. There was, then, no rigid, inflexible system of settlement, save that Negroes would, at almost all costs, be excluded from participating in the social and political life of white communities.

Both factors provided the opportunity for the Negro to attempt a new resolution of the racial problem within the limits of the super-imposed segregation ethos. The Negroes chose not to interpret the segregated town sites as the transfer of the ghetto from southern towns. Instead, they viewed this segregation as indicative of a promising future for themselves and other members of their race. They were, at last, emancipated from economic involvement on white-owned lands, and were themselves land-owners. The result was the rapid growth in various areas of the Territory, and particularly in Okfuskee County, of a number of Negro enclaves, begun with fantastically high hopes of political and social freedom and of self-direction and wish-fulfillment.

A political and social entity all their own was not an altogether new concept for the colored people of Oklahoma. They had earlier rallied around a figure who had promised them their own sovereign unit on a state-wide scale. Though the Negro had been forced to abandon this vision to control a state, he might still hope for limited suzerainty over local towns and, perhaps, a county, where he could demonstrate his capacity for self-government and his ability to develop a society equivalent, if not superior, to the white culture in the remainder of the country. It was out of such a vision that the city of Boley, the dominant Negro community in Oklahoma, came into existence.

The generally accepted story of the founding of Boley attributes its existence to a discussion between two white railroad officials on the capabilities of the Negro for self-government. One of the men, Lake Moore, of Weleetka, Oklahoma, maintained that Negroes could accomplish with success their own government if they were provided with a reasonable context in which to operate. The other individual, in typical anecdotal fashion, argued the contrary. "The result of the argument," as reported by Booker T. Washington, "was Boley." [5]

The railroad made Thomas M. Haynes the town site manager for Boley. Haynes, an uneducated but extraordinarily capable man, had migrated to the new area from Vernon, Texas, and was employed on the railroad right-of-way, along which he maintained a makeshift cabin. He had made the acquaintance of the whites by bedding many of them overnight in his cabin when they had finished the day's work on the roadbed too far out from the towns to conveniently make it back for the night.

By 1904, Boley was established and had become a relatively thriving community. The situation was thoroughly appealing to the Negroes. The difficulties inherent in residence in a bi-racial community were absent in Boley. The Negro was no longer obliged to find himself reminded, in a thousand humiliating vis-a-vis encounters each day, that he was second rate. His contacts with the whites, when such contacts were necessary, were cordial. This was the "frontier," a new land without the trammels of the old South, a land where contacts between the races could, it seemed, be sufficiently infrequent that neither the Negro nor the white would be obliged to implement the historically defined attitudes toward the other.

The Negroes, too, would have their first opportunity on the North American continent for self-determination. They were clearly interested in more than simply being left alone in their remote Hamitic outposts. For them, this residence in a land not yet even a state was a racial experiment of the first order, offering a field for "the propagation, culture and consummation of his refined ideas," as well as "the means whereby he can transmit to his children the fit of man and womanhood, in a sense of equal fitness for the multitudinous avocations of life." [6]

The whites in the county apparently shared this view, or were, at least,

[5] Booker T. Washington, "Boley, A Negro Town in the West," *The Outlook* (January 4, 1908), pp. 28–31.
[6] Boley *Progress*, April 19, 1906.

disinclined at first to hinder its implementation. White towns were relatively unmarred by Negro residents and white lives therefore less complicated by the colored man's presence. "Having the colored people all to themselves beats the Guthrie system," the Weleetka *American* commented. In Weleetka, a citizen did not have to send his children to the same school with Negroes, nor was he "forced to refresh himself at the same bar where the colored man's money was good." [7]

There was also something appealing to many whites in the knowledge of exclusively Negro towns, administered and operated by colored people. A manager of a cotton gin in Oklahoma City, visiting Boley in its early days, reflects this appeal:

> One day I was at Okemah buying cotton and the man I had made a deal with told me that I might make a good deal at Boley. I called the gin man at Boley and made an appointment to meet him the following day. When I arrived the man was at the train to meet me, and to my surprise he was a Negro. After our business was finished, he suggested that I meet the mayor. I went with him to the city hall where I received another surprise when I was introduced to the mayor and found he was a Negro.[8]

An often-reprinted story, first published in the St. Louis *Globe-Democrat* in 1912, discloses the early feelings of the whites towards the all-Negro community:

> This is a very interesting town.... Boley is what is known in Oklahoma as a 'nigger town.' It has not a single white resident in it.... Here at last I found myself delving into the workings of one of the most important colonization problems ever undertaken in this country, and I am glad to say that I was pleased with my investigation.[9]

Apparently a going concern, assured of eventual success and prosperity, pre-statehood Boley began a system of recruitment in the attempt to swell and strengthen its numbers. The Boley *Progress*, widely distributed throughout the South, was widely articulate in its appeal:

> Now is the time for you to come before speculators flood the country. Come and help us prove to the Caucasian race and not only the Caucasian race but the world that the Negro is a law-making and law-abiding citizen, and help us solve the great racial problem that is now before us.[10]

Editorial comment, too, was vigorous and appealing. But revealing also of the Negro's attitude was the bitterness which sometimes crept into his writing, a bitterness which reflected both his ancient hostilities toward the

[7] *Ibid.*, July 21, 1905.
[8] "Interview with Madison J. McCloud," *Indian-Pioneer History*, 35, pp. 367–372.
[9] St. Louis *Globe-Democrat*, February 22, 1912.   [10] Boley *Progress*, March 9, 1905.

whites and the wariness and uncertainty he felt in his apparent emancipation on this new frontier. After a glowing tribute to the state of affairs in Boley, for instance, the *Progress* suddenly erupted into a bitter lament: "Is there no spot where the Negro can escape the slime, froth and derision of our superiors, who feast and grow fat on prejudice?" [11]

But despite the apparent apprehension, the Negroes nonetheless carried on their activities and democratized themselves and their towns almost to the point of caricature. Early in March of 1905, for example, the *Progress* carried this item, typical of the early social life in Boley:

> The Union Literary Society had quite an enthusiastic meeting last Thursday evening. The subject for debate was: Resolved that the Negro should celebrate George Washington's birthday.[12]

After an evening of lively discussion, the resolution failed. And the Negroes continued to bask luxuriously in this atmosphere and to live life in a fashion which had previously occurred to them only in fantasies.

The Okfuskee Negro sought out his brothers errant, desperately wanting to show them the results of his efforts, to reveal his gains and share these with them. Brochures were sent to Negro preachers who in many cases apprised their congregations of the wonders of Boley. With deep fervor the *Progress* recruited other Negroes:

> What are you waiting for? If we do not look out for our own welfare, who is going to do so for us? Are you always going to depend upon the white race to control your affairs for you? Some of our people have had their affairs looked after by the white man for the past 30 years, and where are they today? They are on the farms and plantations of the white men . . . with everything mortgaged so that they cannot get away and forever will be so long as they are working upon their farms and trading in their stores.[13]

Many Negroes did ask themselves what they had been waiting for apparently, for by April, 1905 there were over two thousand persons in the Boley area, each with hopes high, and believing that he would, at last, be able to "enjoy all the rights and privileges accorded to every American citizen." [14]

Before long, the notion of Negro self-realization in a democratic context began to assume grandiose proportions. The editor of the *Progress* noted in mid-April of 1905 that at the following session of Congress both Oklahoma and Indian Territories would be admitted to the Union as one state. He argued that the time was now ripe to colonize sufficient Negroes in Boley and vicinity to be able to control a county when local governments were established.

> If we fail in this effort, we will never have the opportunity again, there is not another spot so desirable in this country, where the Negro has

[11] *Ibid.*
[12] *Ibid.*

[13] *Ibid.*, March 16, 1905.
[14] *Ibid.*, March 3, 1905.

a chance to settle down in a little community of his own and sleep under his own vine and fig tree.[15]

To the Negroes, viewing the swelling black population in the county, such a plan must have seemed not at all over optimistic, particularly in the face of white lethargy.

But while the Negroes in Boley spun their plans for control of their destiny, less-involved Negroes elsewhere were mindful of what they believed to be the inevitable end of the frontier joy-ride. The Western Negro Press Association, meeting at Muskogee, sent a memorial to President Roosevelt opposing joint statehood for the Oklahoma and Indian Territories unless a guarantee be made that no jim crow laws would be enacted in the newly created state.[16] The Negroes attending this convention, principally from bi-racial communities, were obviously more in contact with the white reality than the relatively isolated Okfuskee settlers. Life in the bi-racial community in Oklahoma was little different than it had been in the South, and the Muskogee Negroes were painfully aware of the fact.

But the Boley residents were unconcerned. They saw no reason to imagine the hostility that would spring up once their own plans came into direct conflict with those of their white neighbors, and once their own aspirations touched upon white sensitivity and prejudice. Alone and isolated, the Negroes could be tolerated by the whites; but once in open conflict with white values, they would have to be suppressed.

Political activity got underway in 1906, and the joy-ride was on its way to a detour. The Negroes participated fully in the election of the representatives to the State Constitutional Convention and the freedom with which they were allowed to cast their ballots reinforced their hopes, as had many of their activities before, for full participation in citizenship after statehood.

The results of this first election, however, carried an ominous warning for the whites in the region surrounding Boley, a warning which they could scarcely ignore. Boley had been included in the 79th district, a gerrymandered area which included the relatively large towns of Weleetka, Henryetta and Okemah. Together, these predominantly white towns mustered 875 votes. But these votes were almost equally split between the Republican and Democratic parties. Boley, on the other hand, had a voting force of almost 300 citizens, and these electors cast 265 votes for the Republican candidate and only 26 votes for the Democrat. When the Republicans won by a margin of 172 votes, it was quite clear that the Boley majority had carried the day. The Negro settlement, united and determined to stay united in its franchise, held the key to the area's political color. It had to be dealt with forcefully and decisively.

During the Constitutional Convention, it soon became obvious that Boley would not be designated as the county seat by a Convention packed almost entirely with whites. Ultimately, Okemah was named to this position, pending

[15] *Ibid.*, April 13, 1905.
[16] Okemah *Independent*, September 29, 1905.

a later election to determine the permanent location. There was clearly no sympathy whatever in the Democratic-controlled convention for Boley's once-resplendent dreams of county control. The honeymoon days of condescending indulgence for the Negroes were over, now that the stark question of power and gain was involved. At best, the Negroes could hope to curry favor by a judicious leasing of their ballot strength to their most obvious white friends. The Negroes were not altogether disillusioned by developments. Once again, as they had earlier done, they simply revised their goals.

The county whites were not unaware of this. In late December, the Okemah *Independent*, with warm concern for the Negroes, and with an equally deep interest in securing the permanent county seat designation, reminded its readers that the local Commercial Club had earlier promised the colored people of Boley that it would provide a rooming house for them in Okemah so that they might be comfortable when doing business in that town.

On April 4th, the Republican call for the county organizational meeting went out. Throughout the spring and summer, arrangements were made by local committees for the fall election. Despite any difficulties the Negroes might have had earlier the promise of a genuine election, really the first to be held in the county, brought about a renascence of Negro activity and a renewal of faith in full participation in county affairs. Their prior hopes of state and county control had simply been too ambitious. The Constitutional Convention had not really been a test. But now their function in politics, their electoral weight, would become clear. They would in this first state election walk to the conventions and ultimately to the polls and make their wishes felt through their numbers. This, they now believed, was what they had been preparing for.

In the middle of August, the Republican Convention, heavily attended by Negroes, met at Okemah to nominate a slate for county offices. A white chairman was elected and a Negro secretary named to the permanent organization. But the meeting had scarcely been called to order when trouble began. White delegations refused to sit with Negro delegations, and some of the former finally bolted the convention. The remaining fifty-eight Negro and twenty-four white delegates determined the Republican ticket, naming two Negroes to the slate as county commissioner candidates.

The situation was now one which might well engender panic in the whites. The Negroes in the county were no longer passive pawns in the resolution of an academic argument on their abilities to govern themselves. They were no longer the characters in an amusing anecdote which, even in the re-telling had now grown somewhat tedious. They were threatening the whites of the county with their participation in politics. A county with Negro officials to operate it in conjunction with white Republicans was an appallingly likely prospect.

Disenfranchisement of the Negroes was agreed upon as the only solution to the white dilemma, and in the September certification of the several party tickets, the County Election Board, manned by a majority of Democrats appointed by the Constitutional Convention, failed to certify the part-colored ticket of the Republicans on the ground that the slate was incomplete. Despite this maneuver, the ticket did eventually appear on the ballot, and was, as predicted by several Okemah papers, elected by a Negro-Republican alliance. Undaunted, the County Election Board refused to certify the returns from the predominantly Negro precincts, and the Democrats were declared officially elected.

For the Negroes, something horrible had occurred. They had done nothing untoward, and they now found themselves slapped hard for doing it. In making their voices heard in the election, they had simply followed their conception of their rights; in marching to the polls, they had followed the lead of the whites, who had allowed them to develop their conception of these rights. The gerrymandering of the precincts (which became an endemic process in Okfuskee County) might be viewed as a purely partisan move, but the dismissal, illegal as it obviously was, of the results of their voting could hardly be interpreted as a mild Democratic move for political control. The Negro was forced to face the fact that once again, though now in what had been defined as a new milieu, he was cut off from the major institutions which provided a functional guarantee of civil liberties. For, though the dismissal of the Negro votes was eventually to undergo lengthy litigation, the Negro would lose the final decision by the State Supreme Court.

The political activity of the Boley Negro had been brought to an abrupt end. But what was clearly of more importance, the elimination of his fundamental franchise prerogative belied and foreshadowed the relegation of the Okfuskee Negro to his traditional Southern caste status. Not only would all avenues of political expression be cut off, but all avenues of social and economic expression as well.

During the five following years, the Negroes of the county made no gains and suffered many losses. The "grandfather clause" of 1910 provided the basis for white relaxation of disenfranchising moves on a local level. No Negro in the State would now be allowed to vote. With the Negroes successfully throttled politically, the whites moved to eliminate them physically from the county. Farmers' Commercial Clubs were established, the express purpose of which was to drive the Negro farmers from the area and to replace them with white farmers. Pacts were drawn up between whites in which each agreed to withhold employment from Negroes. Okemah finally became the scene of a brutal lynching of a mother and her child.

With each dreadful development, the Negroes attempted to reorganize their ethic for yet another time. But this reorientation became patently vapid, and the Negro community simply relented in the face of white hostility. To complicate their plight, the Negroes who could in the past always retreat from their political beatings into a secure economic enclave of their own (for Boley had been a highly prosperous town from its founding), suddenly found themselves caught up in the cotton depression of 1913. Prices had dropped sharply and there was a movement to withhold the crop from the market to force the prices up to a more favorable level. But for the small farmers, as most of the Negroes in the area were, this was not a reasonable alternative.

In addition, Boley, along with other portions of this rural county, was beginning to lose population. This loss was part of the nation-wide depletion of farm dwellers which became a mass migration of Negroes and other marginal farmers during the years of the First World War. In-migration slowed down considerably; Oklahoma was now nearly as infamous for its Negro-white relations as the Southern states, and Negroes seeking fresher racial air were heading North.

The economic and political setbacks added up to almost total disillusionment on the part of the Okfuskee County Negroes. "All Men Up—Not Some Down," the motto of the Boley *Progress*, was not only meaningless but mocking. The appeal of "on to Boley" had been reduced to a hollow dream, pushed mercilessly back into the fantasy world from which it had sprung. There would be no Negro autonomy in Oklahoma, no Negro dignity, no Negro peacefulness. There would be no growing respect and admiration from white neighbors and no industrial and agricultural prosperity. Nothing had been changed, nothing had been bettered.

There remained but two alternatives for the Negroes in the all-Negro communities. One was acceptance of the situation as it had developed, and the maintenance of racial towns which were no longer proud evidence of self-fulfillment, but Negro ghettoes. The other alternative was escape. Acceptance became the solution for those who were now too tired, too timid, or too cynical to try to recreate a new dream. It also became the solution for those who still entertained the unreal hope of bettering their situation in Boley.

But there were others who churned up new visions of escape. They could go North, but there they would encounter more white Americans as well as an industrialized atmosphere with which they were not familiar. Besides, the best that the North could offer was an opportunity to be left alone, and these were not the kind of men who had envisioned condescending tolerance, but the kind who wanted an active role in the shaping of their own and their children's destiny.

One possibility occurred to these people. They could migrate once more to a place where they might hope to gain strength and complete freedom. They could leave behind them the unyielding pressure of the American racial code and travel to a new continent where they would be accepted unquestioningly as equals. They could go to Africa. At the time, it was nothing more than a dim prospect, yet it contained an appeal that was well-rooted.

Some few murmurings were heard of an African return, and one group even packed and left for Africa. A few wrote letters attempting to find out more about their former homeland. Then, into this context, came one of the most fascinating figures among the American Negroes in the Twentieth Century, Alfred Charles Sam, an Akim chief from the Gold Coast, and a man of courage and vision. Sam turned the migration stirrings into reality, and eventually sailed in 1914 with a shipload of Okfuskee County Negroes, symbolically and practically writing an end to their dream of self-fulfillment in Oklahoma.

It might be well, in summary, to review the factors in the development of the all-Negro community in Oklahoma, and those aspects of the Negro attitude toward racial self-fulfillment which made such communities appear to be answers to the Negro's position in the United States.

The bulk of the early migrants into Okfuskee County, as noted, were laborers and, generally, lower-class individuals. As time went on, however, the all-Negro communities began to appeal to the Negro middle class, and particularly to those professionals in the middle class who had been vocationally frustrated in the deeper south. The bulk of the later immigrants were farmers, taking their positions in the rural areas surrounding Boley and other all-Negro towns.

The middle-class professionals, despite their comparatively small numbers, were most important in the formation of the self-fulfillment goal. It was for them particularly that the implementation of this goal was vital since the Negro farmer was already finding his own self-fulfillment in the sheer ownership of land.

Spurred by the middle-class dream, however, the farm population, too, soon adopted the view of Negro self-determination and it was, ultimately, within this farm population that the ethic was most broadly proliferated and in which the greatest disillusionment took place.

A second important factor was the initial ambiguity of race relations during the days before Oklahoma statehood. Land was plentiful and the whites had little to gain economically by subordination of the Negro. The initial pattern of segregated residence protected the whites from direct physical contact with the Negro and in terms of this segregation, one of the principal patterns of the Southern caste system, that of avoidance, was *de facto* accomplished.

Thirdly, the whites tended, in terms of a somewhat "Uncle Tomish" approach to the Negroes, to support the latter's hopes for self-fulfillment. The Negro community was almost as appealing to the whites as to the Negroes.

Fourthly, the "frontier" provided a context in which there were sharp and easily perceivable situational differences from the plantation south. With the traditional status of a backward economy temporarily mitigated, the whites could afford to allow the Negro a greater freedom than he had been allowed in the South.

In short, Oklahoma seems to have been one of the few areas of recent development in the United States in which the Negro could have made such rapid strides as he did in his initial stages of residence. It was in Oklahoma alone that the notion of racial self-fulfillment could have been developed to the point it was. It is not without interest, as a final comment, that it was from Oklahoma populations that Alfred Sam drew the greatest number of recruits for his return to Africa, a return unique in American Negro history. It seems evident from this fact that the degree of disillusionment encountered by Oklahoma Negroes was perhaps as intense a Negro disillusionment as has ever been felt in this nation, and that this disillusionment was proportional to the degree to which the Negroes had achieved a partial fulfillment of their wish to control their own destiny.

Kelly Miller

WASHINGTON'S POLICY

*The accommodating tendencies in Negro life, which achieved as-
cendency during the 1890's, were epitomized by the career of Booker
T. Washington, who between his famous Atlanta Exposition Address
in 1895 and his death in 1915 was, because of white endorsement,
the most prominent figure in the Negro community.*

*Washington's preeminence, however, did not mean that Negro
protest was completely crushed. Critics existed, especially in the
North, and became more articulate after 1900. They were drawn
chiefly from a college-educated elite, and the man who emerged as
their leader was W. E. B. Du Bois, later a prominent founder of the
NAACP and for many years the editor of its official organ, The
Crisis. In the spring of 1903, the appearance of Du Bois' Souls of
Black Folk, with its famous critical essay entitled "Of Mr. Booker T.
Washington and Others," focused national attention on the "Radical"
opponents of Booker T. Washington.*

*Shortly afterward the noted Negro essayist Kelly Miller, a Pro-
fessor and later Dean at Howard University, wrote an anonymous
article on "Washington's Policy" for the Boston* Transcript, *in which
he discussed the viewpoints of both the "Radicals" and "Conservatives"
probably with greater perception than anyone else has done then or
since.*

W HEN a distinguished Russian was informed that some American Negroes were radical and some conservative, he could not restrain his laughter.
The idea of conservative Negroes was more than the Cossack's risibilities could
endure. "What on earth," he exclaimed with astonishment, "have they to
conserve?"

According to a strict construction of terms, a conservative is one who is
satisfied with, and advocates the continuance of existing conditions; while a

From Kelly Miller, "Washington's Policy," Boston *Evening Transcript,* September
18 and 19, 1903.

radical clamors for amelioration through change. No thoughtful Negro is satisfied with the present status of his race, whether viewed in its political, civil or general aspect. He labors under an unfriendly public opinion which is being rapidly crystallized into rigid caste and enacted into unrighteous law. How can he be expected to contemplate such oppressive conditions with satisfaction and composure? Circumstances render it imperative that his attitude should be dissentient rather than conformatory. Every consideration of enlightened self-respect impels to unremitting protest, albeit the manner of protestation may be mild or pronounced, according to the dictates of prudence. Radical and conservative Negroes agree as to the end in view, but differ as to the most effective means of attaining it. The difference is not essentially one of principle or purpose, but point of view. All anti-slavery advocates desired the downfall of the iniquitous institution, but some were more violent than others in the expression of this desire. Disagreement as to method led to personal estrangement, impugnment of motive, and unseemly factional wrangle. And so, colored men who are zealous alike for the betterment of their race, lose half their strength in internal strife, because of variant methods of attack upon the citadel of prejudice. The recent regrettable "Boston riot" is a striking case in point. Mr. Booker T. Washington is the storm centre about which the controversy rages. Contending forces have aligned themselves, in hostile array, as to the wisdom or folly of the doctrine of which he is the chief exponent. Two recent occurrences have served to accentuate this antagonism.

1. About two years ago, a group of Boston colored men, exotics, as some would say, of New England colleges, who had grown restive under the doctrine of the famous Tuskegean, founded the Boston Guardian as a journal of protest. These men believe that the teachings of Mr. Washington are destructive of the rights and liberties of the race, and are pledged to spare no effort to combat what they deem his damaging doctrine. Mr. William Monroe Trotter, a Harvard graduate, and who is said to have maintained a higher scholastic average than any other colored student at that famous institution, is head and front of the movement. Mr. Trotter possesses considerable independent means, and is as uncompromising as William Lloyd Garrison.

2. The recent publication of "The Souls of Black Folk," by Professor W. E. B. Du Bois, also a Harvard graduate, has added new emphasis to the prevailing controversy. Dr. Du Bois is not an agitator, nor a carping critic of another's achievements, but a scholar, a painstaking, accurate investigator, a writer of unusual lucidity and keenness, and a fearless advocate of the higher aspirations of his race. He has stated in pointed, incisive terms, the issue between Mr. Washington and his critics, and has given the controversy definiteness and cast. Du Bois and Washington are being held up to public view as contrasted types of Negro leadership.

The radical and conservative tendencies cannot be better described than by comparing, or rather contrasting, the two superlative colored men in whom we find their highest embodiment—Frederick Douglass and Booker Washington. The two men are in part products of their times, but are also natural antipodes. Douglass lived in the day of moral giants; Washington in the era of merchant princes. The contemporaries of Douglass emphasized the rights of man; those of Washington his productive capacity. The age of Douglass acknowledged the sanction of the Golden Rule; that of Washington worships the Rule of Gold. The equality of men was constantly dinned into Douglass's ears; Washington hears nothing but the inferiority of the Negro and the dominance of the Saxon. Douglass could hardly receive a hearing today; Washington would have been hooted off the stage a generation ago. Thus all truly useful men must be, in a measure, timeservers; for unless they serve their time, they can scarcely serve at all. But great as was the diversity of formative influences that shaped these two great lives, there is no less opposability in their innate bias of souls. Douglass was like a lion, bold and fearless; Washington is lamblike, meek and submissive. Douglass escaped from personal bondage, which his soul abhorred; but for Lincoln's proclamation, Washington would probably have arisen to esteem and favor in the eyes of his master as a good and faithful servant. Douglass insisted upon rights; Washington upon duty. Douglass held up to public scorn the sins of the white man; Washington portrays the faults of his own race. Douglass spoke what he thought the world should hear; Washington only what he feels it is disposed to listen to. Douglass's conduct was actuated by principle; Washington's by prudence. Douglass had no limited, copyrighted programme for his race, but appealed to the decalogue, the golden rule, the declaration of independence, the constitution of the United States; Washington, holding these great principles in the shadowy background, presents a practical expedient applicable to present needs. Douglass was a moralist, insisting upon the application of righteousness to public affairs; Washington is a practical statesman, accepting the best terms which he thinks it possible to secure.

Washington came upon the stage at the time when the policies which Douglass embodied had seemed to fail. Reconstruction measures had proved abortive. Negro politicians, like Othello, had lost their occupation, and had sought asylum in the Government departments at Washington. The erstwhile advocates of the Negro's cause had grown indifferent or apologetic. The plain intent of the constitution had been overborne in the South with the connivance of the North. The idea of lifting the Negro to the plane of equality with the white race, once so fondly cherished, found few remaining advocates. Mr. Washington sized up the situation with the certainty and celerity of a genius. He based his policy upon the ruins of the one that had been exploited. He avoided controverted issues, and moved, not along the line of least resistance, but of no resistance at all. He founded his creed upon construction rather than criticism. He urged his race to do the things possible rather than whine and pine over things prohibited. According to his philosophy, it is better to build even upon the shifting sands of expediency than not to build at all, because you cannot secure a granite foundation. He thus hoped to utilize whatever residue of good feeling there might be in the white race for the betterment of the Negro. Tuskegee Institute, which is of itself a marvellous achievement, is only the pulpit from which Mr. Washington proclaims his doctrine. Industrial education has become so intricately interwoven into his policy that his critics are forced into the ridiculous attitude of opposing a form of training essential to the welfare of any people. For reasons of policy, Mr. Washington is provokingly silent as to the claim of higher education, although his personal actions proclaim loudly enough the belief that is in his heart. The subject of industrial and higher education is merely one of ratio and proportion and not one of fundamental controversy.

Mr. Washington's bitterest opponents cannot gainsay his sincerity or doubt that the welfare of his race is the chief burden of his soul. He follows the leading of his own light. Few men of this generation have shown such signal devotion, self-abnegation and strenuous endeavor for an altruistic cause.

One of the chief complaints against the Tuskegean is lack of definitive statement upon questions of vital concern. Mr. Washington is a diplomat of the first water. He sinks into sphinxlike silence when the demands of the situation seem to require emphatic utterance. His carefully studied deliverances upon disputed issues often possess the equivocalness of a Delphic oracle. While he does not openly avow, yet he would not disclaim, in distinct terms, a single plank in the platform of Douglass. The white race saddles its own notions and feelings upon him, and yet he opens not his mouth. His sagacious silence and shrewdly measured assertions must be taken, if not with the traditional grain of salt, at least with a goodly lump of diplomatic allowance. We do not usually associate deep moral conviction with the guileful arts of diplomacy, but we must remember that the delicate role of race statesmanship cannot be played without rare caution and tactful prudence.

Mr. Washington's popularity and prominence depend largely upon the fact that his putative policy is acceptable to the Southern whites, because he allows them to believe that he accepts their estimate of the Negro's inferior place in the social scheme. He is quiescent if not acquiescent as to the white man's superior claims. He shuts his eyes to many of the wrongs and outrages heaped upon the race. He never runs against the Southerner's traditional prejudices. Even when he protests against his practices the protestation is so palliatory that, like a good conscience, it is void of offence. Equality between the races, whether social, political or civil, is an unsavory term to the white man's palate, and, therefore, Mr. Washington obliterates it from his vocabulary. The higher education of the Negro is in general disfavor, so Mr. Washington gives the approval of his silence to the charge that such pure and devoted philanthropists as President Ware of Atlanta, Patton of Howard, Tupper of Shaw, and Cravath of Fisk, who did more than all others to quicken and inspire the Negro race, have lived, loved, labored and died in vain. Nor is he objectionable to white men by reason of his self-assertive personality. He is an exact modern counterpart of Chaucer's knight: "Curteys he was, lowly, and servysable." Even when he violates their sacred code by dining with the President or mingling on easy terms with ultra-fashionable circles, they lash themselves into momentary fury, but straightway proceed to laud and glorify his policy. The North applauds and sustains his propagandism because he strives to be at peace with all men. He appeals to the amity and not the enmity of both races. We are in the midst of an era of good feeling, and must have peace at any price. It is interesting to witness how many of the erstwhile loud-voiced advocates of the Negro's rights have seized upon Mr. Washington's pacific policy as a graceful recession from their former position. The whites have set up Booker Washington as the divinely appointed and anointed leader of his race, and regard as sacrilege all criticism or even candid discussion on the part of those whom he has been sent to guide. They demand for him an exemption which they have never accorded their own leaders, from George Washington to Theodore Roosevelt. Nothing could be further from Mr. Washington's thoughts than the assumption of divine commission which the whites seek to impose upon him. He makes no claim to have received a revelation, either from burning bush or mountain top; but is a simple, sincere, unsophisticated co-laborer with his brethren, as a single, though signal, agency for the betterment of his race.

Mr. Washington is not a leader of the people's own choosing. He does not command an enthusiastic and spontaneous following. He lacks that magnetic personality that would cause men to love and women to adore him. His method is rather that of a missionary seeking the material and moral betterment of an unfortunate people, than a spontaneous leader voicing their highest self-expression. He is deficient in the fearlessness, self-assertion, aggressiveness and heroic spirit necessary to quicken and inspire. Such a leader must not hold up for painful contemplation or emphasize to the outside world the repugnant, grotesque and ludicrous faults and foibles of his own people, but must constantly direct attention to higher and better ideals. His dominant note must be pitched in the major, and not the minor key. He must not be of the earth earthy, with range of vision limited to the ugliness of untoward conditions, but must have the power of idealization and spiritual vista. Exaggerated self-importance is deemed an individual fault, but a racial virtue. It is the chief incentive of every race or nation that has ever gained prominence in the world's affairs. The triumphant, God-sent leader of any people must be the exponent and expounder of their highest aspirations and feelings, and must evoke their manhood and self-esteem, yea, even their vanity and pride.

Mr. Washington's following is very largely prudential and constrained: it lacks spontaneousness and joyance. He is not hailed with glad acclaim as the deliverer of his people. He brings good gifts rather than glad tidings. Many believe in him for his works' sake; some acquiesce rather than antagonize one who has gained so large a measure of public confidence; others are willing to coöperate in the accomplishment of good deeds, though they inwardly detest his doctrine; while those of political instinct seek his favor as a pass key to prestige and place. Few thoughtful colored men espouse what passes as Mr. Washington's policy, without apology or reserve.

The so-called radical Negroes are wholly wanting in organization and leadership. They have no commanding personality or concrete achievement as a basis and background for their propagandism. Their plea is sought to be silenced by the cry that they have founded no institution and projected no practical project. The same might have been said of Garrison and Phillips. It is difficult to found an effective organization upon a protest. There is little constructive possibility in negation. These men believe in the doctrine of Douglass, who has become their prototype and patron saint. They have learned well the lesson which Northern statesmanship and philanthropy taught them a generation ago, although they are sought to be derided and belittled for adhering to their teachings.

Mr. Washington's critics assert that his leadership has been barren of good results to the race. Under his regnancy the last vestige of political power has been swept away. Civil privileges have been restricted, educational opportunities, in some States at least, have been curtailed; the industrial situation, the keynote of his policy, has become more ominous and uncertain, while the feelings between the races is constantly growing more acute and threatening. To this it is averred that no human power could stay the wave of race hatred now sweeping over the country, but that the Tuskegean's pacific policy will serve to relieve the severity of the blow. The majority of thoughtful men range between these wide-apart views. They believe neither in surrender nor revolution. Both forces have their place and function in the solution of the race problem. While it would be unseemly for those who breathe the free air of New England to remain silent as to the heavy burden borne by their brethren in the South, yet we must not forget that Frederick Douglass could not today build up an institution in Alabama, nor do the imperative constructive work in that section. The progress of all peoples is marked by alternations of combat and contention on the one hand, and compromise and concession on the other. Progress is the resultant of the play and counterplay of these forces. Colored men should have a larger tolerance for the widest latitude of opinion and method. Too frequently what passes as an irrepressible conflict is merely difference in point of view. A striking illustration of harmony of aim with variance of method is furnished by the close alliance and friendly coöperation of Thomas Fortune and Booker Washington. It would be impossible to find two Negroes who are farther apart in temper and spirit, and yet we find them working together for the good of the race.

The Negro's lot would be sad indeed if, under allurement of material advantage and temporary easement, he should sink into pliant yieldance to unrighteous oppression; but it would be sadder still if intemperate insistence should engender ill will and strife, when the race is not yet ready to be "battered with the shocks of doom."

August Meier

TOWARD A REINTERPRETATION OF
BOOKER T. WASHINGTON

Booker T. Washington functioned primarily as an accommodator. Yet privately he engaged in activities that ran directly counter to the publicly expressed ideology with which he was so prominently identified. As the following selection suggests, Washington played a complex role.

I T should not be surprising that in a period of increasing racial integration and of growing recognition of the Negro's constitutional rights, the centennial of Booker T. Washington's birth in April 1956 should have passed relatively unnoticed. For Washington was associated with a policy of compromise and conciliation toward the white South that is not in keeping with the trend of our times. Yet Washington's own correspondence [1] reveals such extensive efforts against segregation and disfranchisement that a re-evaluation of his philosophy and activities is in order.

Undoubtedly in reading Washington's books, articles, and speeches, one is most strongly impressed with the accommodating tone he adopted toward the white South. He minimized the extent of race prejudice and discrimination, criticized the airing of Negro grievances, opposed "social equality," accepted segregation and the "separate but equal" doctrine, depreciated political activity, favored property and educational qualifications for the franchise (fairly applied to both races), largely blamed Negroes themselves for their unfortunate condition, and counselled economic accumulation and the cultivation of

Reprinted from *Journal of Southern History*, XXIII (May, 1957), pp. 220–27. Copyright © 1959 by the Southern Historical Association. Reprinted by permission of the Managing Editor.

[1] Booker T. Washington Papers (Division of Manuscripts, Library of Congress). Unless otherwise stated all citations to correspondence in this article are to the Booker T. Washington Papers. The research for this article was done under a grant from the American Council of Learned Societies.

Christian character as the best ways to advance the status of Negroes in American society. His ultimate ends were stated so vaguely and ambiguously that Southern whites mistook his short-range objectives for his long-range goals, although his Negro supporters understood that through tact and indirection he hoped to secure the good will of the white man and the eventual recognition of the constitutional rights of American Negroes.

Now, although overtly Washington minimized the importance of political and civil rights, covertly he was deeply involved in political affairs and in efforts to prevent disfranchisement and other forms of discrimination. For example, Washington lobbied against the Hardwick disfranchising bill in Georgia in 1899.[2] While he permitted whites to think that he accepted disfranchisement, he tried to keep Negroes believing otherwise. In 1903 when Atlanta editor Clark Howell implied that Washington opposed Negro officeholding, the Tuskegeean did not openly contradict him, but asked T. Thomas Fortune of the leading Negro weekly, the New York *Age*, to editorialize. "We are quite sure that the Hon. Howell has no ground . . . for his attempt to place Mr. Washington in such a position, as it is well understood that he, while from the first deprecating the Negro's making political agitation and office-holding the most prominent and fundamental part of his career, has not gone any farther." [3]

Again, while Washington seemed to approve of the disfranchisement amendments when he said that "every revised constitution throughout the Southern States has put a premium upon intelligence, ownership of property, thrift and character," [4] he was nevertheless secretly engaged in attacking them by legal action. As early as 1900 he was asking certain philanthropists for money to fight the electoral provisions of the Louisiana constitution.[5] Subsequently he worked secretly through the financial secretary of the Afro-American Council's legal bureau, personally spending a great deal of money and energy fighting the Louisiana test case.[6] At the time of the Alabama Constitutional Convention of 1901 he used his influence with important whites in an attempt to prevent discriminatory provisions that would apply to Negroes only.[7] He was later deeply interested in the Alabama test cases in 1903 and 1904. So circumspect was he in this instance that his secretary, Emmett J. Scott, and lawyer, Wilford Smith, in New York, corresponded about it under pseudonyms

[2] Booker T. Washington to Francis J. Garrison, September 23, 1899, in Francis J. Garrison Papers (Schomburg Collection, New York Public Library).

[3] Washington to T. Thomas Fortune, June 23, 1903.

[4] Boston *Guardian*, December 20, 1902.

[5] For example, Washington to Garrison, February 27 and March 11, 1900, in Garrison Papers.

[6] Jesse Lawson to Booker T. Washington, March 29, June 26, July 30, October 2, December 30, 1901; April 30, June 24, 1902; Washington to Lawson, December 11, 1903. Also other correspondence between Lawson and Washington, 1901–1903. See also Fortune to Washington, June 4, June 21, June 27, July 22, July 27, 1901.

[7] For example, correspondence with A. D. Wimbs, 1901 (Box 151).

and represented the sums of money involved in code.[8] Washington was also interested in efforts to prevent or undermine disfranchisement in other states.[9] In Maryland, where disfranchisement later failed, he had Catholic lawyer F. L. McGhee of St. Paul approach the Catholic hierarchy in an attempt to secure its opposition to disfranchisement, and urged Episcopal divine George F. Bragg to use his influence among important whites.[10] Washington contributed money generously to the test cases and other efforts, though, except in the border states, they did not succeed. In 1903 and 1904 he personally "spent at least four thousand dollars in cash, out of my own pocket... in advancing the rights of the black man."[11]

Washington's political involvement went even deeper. Although he always discreetly denied any interest in active politics, he was engaged in patronage distribution under Roosevelt and Taft, in fighting the lily-white Republicans, and in getting out the Negro vote for the Republicans at national elections. He might say, "I never liked the atmosphere of Washington. I early saw that it was impossible to build up a race of which their leaders were spending most of their time, thought, and energy in trying to get into office, or in trying to stay there after they were in,"[12] but under Roosevelt he became the arbiter of Negro appointments to federal office.

Roosevelt started consulting Washington almost as soon as he took office.[13] The Tuskegeean's role in the appointment of Gold Democrat Thomas G. Jones to a federal judgeship in Alabama was widely publicized.[14] Numerous letters reveal that politicians old and new were soon writing to Tuskegee for favors. Ex-Congressman George H. White unsuccessfully appealed to Washington after the White House indicated that "a letter from you would greatly strengthen my chances."[15] Secretary Scott reported that the President's asser-

[8] J. C. May (Wilford Smith) to R. C. Black (Emmett J. Scott, Washington's secretary), June 15, June 18, July 15, July 30, 1903; Black to May, June 17, June 23, September 16, 1903; Smith to Washington, February 26, 1904; Smith to Scott, March 1, 1904. Also other correspondence of Smith with Scott and Washington, 1903 and 1904.

[9] For example, for Virginia see especially Giles Jackson to Washington, March 28, 1901; and for Kentucky, see W. G. Steward to Washington, February 3, 1904.

[10] F. L. McGhee to Washington, January 12, 1904; Washington to George F. Bragg, March 10, 1904.

[11] Washington to J. W. E. Bowen, December 27, 1904.

[12] Booker T. Washington, *My Larger Education* (New York, 1911), 159.

[13] See especially Theodore Roosevelt to Washington, September 14, December 12, 1901; and Roosevelt to James Ford Rhodes, December 15, 1904, in Elting E. Morison (ed.), *The Letters of Theodore Roosevelt* (8 vols., Cambridge, 1951–1954), IV, 1072. Roosevelt later claimed that Washington had approved of his policy of appointing fewer but better qualified Negroes to office. Roosevelt to Richard Watson Gilder, November 16, 1908, in Theodore Roosevelt Papers (Division of Manuscripts, Library of Congress).

[14] C. Vann Woodward, *Origins of the New South, 1877–1913: A History of the South*, Vol. IX (Baton Rouge, 1951), 383. Roosevelt also consulted Washington in regard to other white appointments. For example, see two letters of Washington to Roosevelt, November 4, 1902, in Washington Papers; and Roosevelt to John Graham Brooks, November 13, 1908, in Roosevelt Papers.

[15] George H. White to Washington, October 7, 1901.

tion to one office-seeker that he would consider him only with Washington's "endorsement" had "scared these old fellows as they never have been scared before." [16] Some of the established politicians played along and were helped along. Thus P. B. S. Pinchback, at one time acting governor of Louisiana, was favored throughout the Roosevelt and Taft administrations.[17] In the case of J. C. Napier, Nashville lawyer and banker, Washington first turned him down as recorder of deeds for the District of Columbia and minister to Liberia, then named him as one of two possibilities for consul at Bahia, later offered him the Liberian post which Napier now refused, and finally secured for him the office of register of the Treasury.[18] Examples of Washington's influence could be multiplied indefinitely, for a number of port collectorships and of internal revenue, receiverships of public monies in the land office, and several diplomatic posts, as well as the positions of auditor for the Navy, register of the Treasury, and recorder of deeds were at his disposal. Among his outstanding appointments were Robert H. Terrell, judge of municipal court in Washington; William H. Lewis, assistant attorney-general under Taft; and Charles W. Anderson, collector of internal revenue in New York.

Furthermore, Roosevelt sought Washington's advice on presidential messages to Congress and consulted him on most matters concerning the Negro. Every four years, also, Washington took charge of the Negro end of the Republican presidential campaign, he and his circle, especially Charles Anderson, recommending (and blackballing) campaign workers and newspaper subsidies, handling the Negro press, advising on how to deal with racial issues, and influencing prominent Negroes.[19]

If Washington reaped the rewards of politics, he also experienced its vicissitudes. From the start he was fighting a desperate and losing battle against the lily-white Republicans in the South. His correspondence teems with material on the struggle, especially in Louisiana and Alabama, and in other states as well. As he wrote to Walter L. Cohen, chairman of the Republican state central committee of Louisiana and register of the land office in New Orleans, on October 5, 1905: "What I have attempted in Louisiana I have attempted to do in nearly every one of the Southern States, as you and others are in a position to know, and but for my action, as feeble as it was, the colored people would have been completely overthrown and the Lily Whites would have been

---

[16] Scott to Washington, July –, 1902. As Roosevelt wrote to Silas McBee, February 3, 1903, his Negro appointees "were all recommended to me by Booker T. Washington." Morison, *Letters of Theodore Roosevelt*, III, 419.

[17] For example, J. C. Dancy to Washington, June 20, 1902; Charles W. Anderson to Washington, July 20, 1902; August 7, 12, 1909; June 24, 1910; F. H. Hitchcock to Washington, August 25, 1905; Washington to R. W. Tyler, December 12, 1908.

[18] For example, J. C. Napier to Washington, February 3, 1901; June 9, 1912; Washington to Napier, December 14, 1905; various letters, 1902, 1909.

[19] In general, on Washington's relations with the Roosevelt administration see correspondence with Roosevelt, James R. Clarkson, George Cortelyou, William Loeb, and Charles Anderson. For Taft administration see especially correspondence with Taft, Charles D. Norton, C. D. Hilles, and Anderson.

in complete control in nearly every Southern State." [20]

Troubles came thick and fast after Taft's inauguration. The new President did not consult Washington as much as Roosevelt had done, and Washington exercised somewhat less control over appointments. Atlanta lawyer Henry Lincoln Johnson forced Washington's appointee, J. C. Dancy, out of the office of recorder of deeds.[21] Meanwhile, more offices were being emptied than filled as far as Negroes were concerned. For example, R. L. Smith, the only Negro with a "significant" federal office in Texas, was dropped; [22] and Cohen, in spite of Taft's promises, failed of reappointment after a reorganization of the land office in Louisiana.[23] Not until 1911, after persistent efforts to convince the administration of the need for some decent plums in order to retain the Negro vote, were a few significant appointments finally arranged. The most notable was that of W. H. Lewis as assistant attorney-general—the highest position held by a Negro in the Federal government up to that time.[24]

In areas other than politics Washington also played an active behind-the-scenes role. On the Seth Carter (Texas) and Dan Rogers (Alabama) cases involving discrimination against Negroes in the matter of representation on jury panels, Washington helped with money and worked closely with lawyer Wilford Smith until their successful conclusion before the United States Supreme Court.[25] He was interested in protecting Negro tenants, who had

[20] Especially illuminating on the struggle against the lily-whites is the correspondence relating to that contest in Louisiana. For example, see correspondence with Walter L. Cohen, 1904 (Box 25); Cohen to Washington, June 11, August 6, November 21, 1908; Cohen to Scott, August 10, September 3, December 17, 1908; correspondence with Cohen, 1909 (Box 547); Cohen to Scott, February 14, February 18, 1911; Scott to Cohen, February 7, November 22, 1911; correspondence with Cohen, 1912 (Box 565); Washington to Clarkson, February 2, March 8, April 28, June 2, 1904; Clarkson to Washington, February 26, February 29, 1904; Scott to C. D. Norton, September 7, 1910; Washington to H. C. Payne, February 24, 1904; Scott to Washington, February 29, June 23, 1904; Washington to Scott, March 1, 1904; Roosevelt to Washington, May 9, June 8, 1904. For Alabama, see correspondence with A. D. Wimbs, 1902 (Box 158), James O. Thompson, 1904 (Box 518) and 1906 (Box 23), and G. W. A. Albert, 1908 (Box 15); Washington to W. C. Mason, March 23, 1908, and to Nathan Alexander, March 23, 1908. For Mississippi, see Charles Banks to Washington, October 25, 1915. For Texas, see Clarkson to Washington, February 29, 1904. For North Carolina and Virginia, see Washington to Roosevelt, March 9, 1908; and for North Carolina, see also Washington to J. C. Dancy, October 7, 1902, in J. C. Dancy Papers (kindness of J. C. Dancy, Jr., Detroit Urban League, Detroit, Mich.).

[21] Anderson to Washington, March 29, February 27, 1910; and in Dancy Papers, copies of letter and telegram to Taft, both February 19, 1910.

[22] Washington to Taft, June 18, 1909.

[23] Cohen to Scott, February 19, 1911; Scott to Cohen, February 21, 1911.

[24] For example, see Washington to Taft, March 1, 1911; C. D. Hilles to Washington, February 25, June 1, December 10, 1911; C. D. Norton to Washington, August 20, 1910; Washington to Norton, November 25, 1910; Scott to Norton, October 12, 1910; Washington to Anderson, July 28, December 11, 1910, and January 23, June 9, 1911; Anderson to Washington, February 27, March 31, June 5, 1911; Scott to W. H. Lewis, n.d. [September 1910].

[25] For example, see J. C. May to R. C. Black, July 15, 1903; Washington to Smith, February 2, March 7, 1904; Smith to Washington, February 4, 1904.

accidentally or in ignorance violated their contracts, from being sentenced to the chain gang.[26] He was concerned in the Alonzo Bailey peonage case, and when the Supreme Court declared peonage illegal, confided to friends that "some of us here have been working at this case for over two years," securing the free services of "some of the best lawyers in Montgomery" and the assistance of other eminent Alabama whites.[27]

In view of Washington's public acceptance of separate but equal transportation accommodations, his efforts against railroad segregation are of special interest. When Tennessee in effect prohibited Pullman space for Negroes by requiring that such facilities be segregated, he stepped into the breach. He worked closely with Napier in Nashville, and enlisted the aid of Atlanta leaders like W. E. B. Du Bois. This group did not succeed in discussing the matter with Robert Todd Lincoln, president of the Pullman company, in spite of the intercession of another railroad leader, William H. Baldwin, Jr.[28] And, though Washington was anxious to start a suit, the Nashville people failed to act.[29] In 1906, employing Howard University professor Kelly Miller and Boston lawyer Archibald Grimké as intermediaries, Washington discreetly supplied funds to pay ex-senator Henry W. Blair of New Hampshire to lobby against the Warner-Foraker amendment to the Hepburn Railway Rate Bill.[30] This amendment, by requiring equality of accommodations in interstate travel, would have impliedly condoned segregation throughout the country, under the separate but equal doctrine. The amendment was defeated, but whether owing to Blair's lobbying or to the protests of Negro organizations is hard to say.

It is clear, then, that in spite of his placatory tone and his outward emphasis upon economic development as the solution to the race problem, Washington was surreptitiously engaged in undermining the American race system by a direct attack upon disfranchisement and segregation; that in spite of his strictures against political activity, he was a powerful politician in his own right. The picture that emerges from Washington's own correspondence is distinctly at variance with the ingratiating mask he presented to the world.

[26] Washington to Oswald Garrison Villard, September 7, 1908.

[27] Washington to Anderson, January 6, 1911; Washington to R. W. Thompson, January 7, 1911.

[28] Napier to Washington, October 28, December 11, 1903; Washington to Napier, November 2, 1903; Washington to W. E. B. Du Bois, December 14, 1903; William H. Baldwin, Jr., to Washington, January 7, 1904.

[29] Washington to Du Bois, February 27, June 4, 1904.

[30] For example, see Kelly Miller to Washington, May 22, 1906; Archibald Grimké to Washington, May 25, June 10, 1906; Washington to Grimké, June 2, June 4, June 10, 1906; Scott to R. W. Thompson, June 5, 1906. Earlier at Washington's suggestion, Giles B. Jackson of Richmond had undertaken the legal fight against the Jim Crow car law in Virginia. Jackson to Washington, January 24, 1901.

Elliott Rudwick

THE NIAGARA MOVEMENT

Washington's conciliatory strategy failed to reverse the rising tide of discrimination, both North and South. Accordingly W. E. B. Du Bois and a small group of radical intellectuals organized the Niagara Movement in 1905 to combat Washington and his influence. The story of this protest organization, a predecessor of the NAACP and the principal source of the NAACP's early ideology, is told in the selection which follows.

As THE National Association for the Advancement of Colored People, approaching its fiftieth birthday, prepares for the realization of its dream of an integrated public school system, it is a desirable time to recall the efforts of the Niagara Movement, one of the precursors of the Association. The Niagara Movement was the first national organization of Negroes which aggressively and unconditionally demanded the same civil rights for their people which other Americans enjoyed. In 1910, plagued by its own organizational inexperience and harassed by the accommodationist Tuskegee Machine, the Niagara Movement was dissolved after five tumultuous years of existence. Not only did Niagara men lay the foundation of the National Association for the Advancement of Colored People, but they served as its earliest leaders and staunchest supporters.

In July of 1905, W. E. B. Du Bois (after being urged by his friends to establish a "national strategy board" [1] of Radicals) invited a "few selected persons" to the secret sessions of the Niagara Movement which were held at Fort Erie, Ontario. Twenty-nine members of the Talented Tenth participated—many more were expected, but according to rumor, they declined at the last

Elliott Rudwick, "The Niagara Movement," *Journal of Negro History*, XLII, no. 3 (July, 1957), pp. 177–200. Reprinted with the permission of the *Journal of Negro History*.

[1] W. M. Trotter to W. E. B. Du Bois, Feb. 27, 1905: Du Bois Papers. (I wish to express my appreciation to Dr. Francis Broderick, of Phillips-Exeter School, for sharing his transcriptions of Du Bois's letters.) W. M. Trotter to W. E. B. Du Bois, March 26, 1905: Du Bois Papers.

minute after being pressured by white friends of Booker Washington.[2] Inevitably, Du Bois was elected General Secretary. Between 1903 and 1905, he had emerged as the second most prominent living Negro. He was recognized by many as the founder of Negro Sociology,[3] and Negro college graduates especially considered him the representative "of the race's aspiration." [4]

Diplomatically, the conferees proclaimed that they did not intend to condemn personalities such as Booker Washington. J. Max Barber, an editor of the *Voice of the Negro*, declared that Washington's name was mentioned only twice during the deliberations and that Du Bois had admonished the group to concern itself only with "principles." [5] Barber maintained that the Tuskegeean was not unacceptable in the movement if he supported its program. However, the *Voice* editor (demonstrating that no protest organization could be initiated in 1905 without striking direct blows at Washington) condemned "certain temporizers and compromizers" who tried to make American Negroes accept "one leader, one policy, and one kind of education." [6] Du Bois reacted similarly when he prepared the conference invitation list. He rejected several men as "bought" and "hide-bound" Washingtonians.[7] Basil Matthews, one of Washington's biographers, incorrectly stated that only "superficial observers" believed that the Niagara Movement clashed seriously with the Tuskegeeans.[8] The evidence indicates that contemporaries like Ferris, before choosing a battle position in what appeared to be a hard struggle, carefully took the measure of Du Bois's and Washington's personalities, attitudes, and power.[9] James Weldon Johnson recalled that the Niagara Movement (and *Souls of Black Folk*) divided the race into "two well-defined parties," and that the "bitterness" continued for years.[10]

The platform of the 1905 Niagara sessions was written in vigorous and sharp tones. The conferees placed the responsibility for the Negro problem squarely on the shoulders of the whites. The Radicals were not asking for opinions; they were making definite demands: [11]

[2] Ralph J. Bunche, *The Programs, Ideologies, Tactics, and Achievements of Negro Betterment and Interracial Organizations.* Unpublished Memorandum for the Myrdal Study, Volume I, 1940, p. 16.

[3] J. Max Barber, "Niagara Movement," *Voice of the Negro* II (1905), 617.

[4] Cleveland *Gazette*, March 19, 1904. See also Jesse Fauset's letter to W. E. B. Du Bois, found in Herbert Aptheker, *A Documentary History of the Negro People in the United States* (New York, 1951), p. 900.

[5] J. Max Barber, "Niagara Movement," *Voice of the Negro* II (1905), 603.

[6] J. Max Barber, "What is the Niagara Movement," *Voice of the Negro* II (1905), 647.

[7] See the following letters in the Du Bois Papers: Albert Bushnell Hart to W. E. B. Du Bois, April 24, 1905. John S. Brown to W. E. B. Du Bois, May 15, 1905. W. E. B. Du Bois to John S. Brown, May 18, 1905. W. E. B. Du Bois to Albert Bushnell Hart, Oct. 9, 1905.

[8] Basil Mathews, *Booker T. Washington, Educator and Interracial Interpreter* (Cambridge, 1948), p. 285.

[9] William Ferris, *African Abroad* (New Haven, 1913), pp. 276–277.

[10] James Weldon Johnson, *Along This Way* (New York, 1933), p. 313.

[11] "What is the Niagara Movement?" 1905, located at Howard University Library. "Niagara Movement Declaration of Principles," 1905, located at Howard University

1. *Freedom of speech and criticism*—The fluid exchange of ideas was crucial to the Talented Tenth, who refused to be pressured into silence by the Washingtonians.

2. *An unfettered and unsubsidized press*—Unless their own propaganda reached and aroused the people, the Radicals contended that the Negroes would remain a captive race. The charge that the press was bought and controlled served as a solid rallying point.

3. *Manhood suffrage*—The conferees desired to participate in the American political system (North and South) on the same basis as the whites. The very term, "Afro-American," was repudiated because of its alien connotation and "Negro American" became the designation which was approved by the delegates. (Their dislike of the term may also have been caused by its association with the Tuskegeean Afro-American Council.)

4. *The abolition of all caste distinctions based simply on race and color*—Racism was denounced as "unreasoning human savagery," and Jim Crow was condemned as an avenue for insult as well as a crucifixion of manhood.

5. *The recognition of the principles of human brotherhood as a practical present creed*—Du Bois considered that the Niagara Movement's task was to interpret the real Christ to white "Christians."

6. *Recognition of the highest and best human training as a monopoly of no class or race*—The Niagara men believed in universal common school education; high school and technical-high school were to be available to those who wanted them. They proposed that a small number of colleges should be maintained for those who could profit from them. Federal aid to education was advocated.

7. *A belief in the dignity of labor*—The Niagara Movement asserted that Negroes must have equal employment opportunities. Employers and trade unions were severely criticized for racial discrimination. Peonage was denounced.

8. *United effort to realize these ideals under wise and courageous leadership*—Constant protest was the approved method to secure Negro rights.

The *Outlook* denied that race prejudice was increasing and repudiated the anti-segregation stand of the Niagara men. The editor of the popular weekly believed that certain "distinctions" were required to preserve "race integrity" and that those Negroes who refused to accept a separate status automatically admitted the inferiority of their race. The magazine was also disturbed by the "whine" of the Niagara Movement and concluded that the Washingtonians were the "real leaders" who represented the sentiments of the Negro people.[12] On the other hand, the Cleveland *Gazette* praised the Niagara manifesto,[13] and the Chicago *Law Register* agreed that human rights were never achieved without aggressive protest.[14]

Within a few months after the adjournment of the conference, local

---

Library. See also, J. Max Barber, "The Niagara Movement," *Voice of the Negro* II (1905), 522.

[12] *Outlook*, LXXX (1905), 796.

[13] Cleveland *Gazette*, July 22, 1905.

[14] Chicago *Law Register*, reprinted in the Washington *Bee*, Aug. 12, 1905.

branches held meetings in various parts of the country. In the late summer of 1905, Rev. Garnett R. Waller, a Baltimore member, told the New York branch of the movement's efforts in his city to prevent the Negroes from being disfranchised.[15] The Niagara men claimed that memberships increased from twenty-nine in July of 1905 to fifty-four by September, and to one hundred and fifty at the end of the year.[16] Bunche considered the growth small in view of the organization's great aims,[17] but Du Bois (perhaps rationalizing) stated that one hundred and fifty members were sufficient for 1905. He said that if conditions did not greatly change, he had no desire to see the Niagara Movement ever exceed five hundred members. He desired to attract only the "thoughtful" and "dignified," "the very best class" of Negroes.[18] At the end of the year, the General Secretary recorded that there were "strong" local branches in seventeen states and that plans were in progress for thirteen additional groups. Du Bois also noted that several Negro newspapers and magazines were bringing the Niagara message to the people: Chicago *Conservator*, Virginia *Home News*, Cleveland *Gazette*, Maryland *Lancet*, Boston *Guardian*, Washington *Bee*, Oregon *Advocate*, *Voice of the Negro*, and the *Moon*.

Since the day of its inception, Booker Washington scrutinized the movement and plotted its destruction. On July 11, 1905, when the Niagara conference opened, Washington indicated to Charles W. Anderson that he wanted "information" on what was happening.[19] The Tuskegeean was assured that "not one tenth" of those whose names appeared on a published list had actually attended the conclave, and that Du Bois (or someone equally "enterprising") had padded the list for publicity purposes.[20] A short time later, the Tuskegeean conferred in New York with Anderson and the editor of the New York *Age* on methods of dealing with Radicals. The high level strategy was to isolate the Radicals from the Negro press, and the word was passed down the line.[21] Emmett J. Scott felt certain that the Niagara men would be unable to persuade most of the race press even to reprint articles which had been published originally in friendly white publications.[22] As usual, the press blackout was ineffective, partially because the Washingtonians found it impossible to resist the opportunity to condemn the "opposition." In July, the Tuskegeean's nephew, Roscoe Simmons, sent a critical editorial, originally published in the New York *Advertiser*, to various white and Negro papers.[23] At the end of the

[15] Washington *Bee*, Sept. 9, 1905.

[16] W. E. B. Du Bois, "Growth of the Niagara Movement," *Voice of the Negro* III (1906), 43.

[17] Ralph Bunche, *op. cit.*, p. 21.

[18] W. E. B. Du Bois, "Growth of the Niagara Movement," *Voice of the Negro* III (1906), 43. Also W. E. B. Du Bois to "Dear Colleague," Sept. 15, 1905: Du Bois Papers.

[19] Booker Washington to Charles W. Anderson, July 11, 1905: Washington Papers (Library of Congress).

[20] Charles W. Anderson to Booker T. Washington, July 16, 1905: Washington Papers.

[21] Emmett J. Scott to R. W. Thompson, July 18, 1905: Washington Papers.

[22] Emmett J. Scott to Booker Washington, July 24, 1905: Washington Papers.

[23] Roscoe Simmons to Booker Washington, July 25, 1905: Washington Papers.

month, Scott formally changed the strategy and advised his associates "to hammer" the Niagara Movement.[24] Throughout all of this initial planning, the Tuskegeean found it impossible to understand why some friendly Negro newspapers still regarded the Radicals as "gentlemen." [25]

In the midst of the Washingtonians' anxiety, Bishop Alexander Walters made it known that he was prepared to return to the presidency of the Afro-American Council and initiate a "counter-movement" to Niagara. Walters proposed to bring the Radicals under his control by advocating civil and political equality. At the same time, Washington could continue to speak in conservative tones, thereby retaining white support.[26] R. W. Thompson (a Tuskegeean aide) was delighted with Walters' plan and told Emmett J. Scott that the reorganized Afro-American Council would be "stronger and more practical" than the Niagara Movement. Scott was less optimistic that Walters, who sometimes exhibited independent tendencies, could be controlled.[27] However, the Bishop was "resurrected" (as Du Bois put it). Du Bois was undeceived and denounced the Washington-controlled Afro-American Council, which he said had been almost completely inactive between 1902 and 1905.[28]

Booker Washington, keeping all irons in the fire, suggested that spies be employed to undermine the Niagara Movement.[29] Often Charles Anderson delegated a "deputy" to listen to the public speeches of leading Niagara men such as Du Bois.[30] After one such church meeting, Anderson disclosed to Washington that Du Bois's address "was a failure." He added joyously that during the program, those in the audience who were loyal to Niagara were asked to rise, and practically all who stood were either women or boys! Washington used other maneuvers to discredit the new organization. He visited influential whites (such as Oswald Garrison Villard) who as moderates supported both industrial and higher education, and tried to convince them to shun the movement.[31] He also made the most out of disagreements among the Niagara men themselves—such as one between Du Bois and Kelly Miller and Archibald Grimke. The Tuskegeean, appearing deeply sympathetic, met with Grimke, whom he found more dependable than Miller. The latter was described as too "mushy" and unaggressive.[32] The Washingtonians hoped that Grimke's services could be used in the field of progaganda.[33]

[24] Booker Washington to Emmett J. Scott, July 27, 1905 and Emmett J. Scott to R. W. Thompson, July 31, 1905: Washington Papers.

[25] Booker Washington to Emmett J. Scott, Aug. 7, 1905: Washington Papers.

[26] R. W. Thompson to Emmett J. Scott, July 28, 1905: Washington Papers.

[27] Emmett J. Scott to R. W. Thompson, July 31, 1905: Washington Papers.

[28] W. E. B. Du Bois, "What is the Niagara Movement?" a reprint from the Boston Guardian, 1905, located at Howard University Library. Also W. E. B. Du Bois to L. C. Jordan, April 16, 1906: Du Bois Papers.

[29] Booker Washington to Charles W. Anderson, Dec. 30, 1905: Washington Papers. (Washington had also used a spy against Trotter in the New England Suffrage League.)

[30] Charles W. Anderson to Booker Washington, Jan. 8, 1906: Washington Papers.

[31] Oswald G. Villard to F. J. Garrison, Nov. 8, 1905: Villard Papers.

[32] Booker Washington to Emmett J. Scott, Aug. 7, 1905: Washington Papers.

[33] Emmett J. Scott to Booker Washington, Aug. 10, 1905: Washington Papers.

In this power struggle, the Washingtonians were strengthened by impressing the race through political patronage. Furthermore, the appointees could be used to perform various tasks for the Tuskegeeans, even while on government time.[34] Several Negroes were given political positions and some received small increases in salary. Many Negro newspapers carried these proofs of Washingtonian potency. The New York Collector of Internal Revenue informed Booker Washington that President Roosevelt ("Our Friend") had recently stressed the importance of making it clear to the Negro people that the Tuskegeean's "influence" was always present whenever they were appointed to a Federal office.[35]

Washington, despite all of his resources, feared that the Niagara Movement would receive aid from the Constitution League, an inter-racial civil rights organization founded in 1904 by John Milholland. The League (and the Niagara Movement) favored the Platt Bill, which would have reduced Congressional representation in those states disfranchising Negroes illegally. The Tuskegeean opposed the bill and declared that Southerners would rather surrender Congressional seats than permit Negroes to vote.[36] Without the Negro leader's cooperation, the Constitution League was unable to lobby effectively in the nation's capital. Milholland decided that a grass roots movement would influence Congress and he sought the help of Negro Radicals. Thereafter, Washington suspected Milholland's motives, even though the white industrialist had been praised previously as a "generous" contributor to Negro causes.[37] Gradually, reports about Milholland's defection filtered into Tuskegee headquarters. One informant wrote that Du Bois had been selected by Milholland as "a strong man," and that the Niagara General Secretary was awaiting a Constitution League-Niagara Movement alliance.[38] Washington's nephew stated that Du Bois was "under the guidance" of an official of the Constitution League and had spoken to the membership of the Republican Club of New York.[39] Washington advised one of his associates to inform the Constitution League that New Yorkers would not tolerate any "nonsense" from Du Bois or any other Radical Negro.

Since no direct avenue was found to sever the connection between the Du Bois group and the League, the Washingtonians tried to lessen Milholland's influence with the New York Republican Party organization. In October of 1905, Anderson conferred with Governor Odell and informed him

[34] Charles W. Anderson to Booker Washington, Sept. 18, 1905: Washington Papers. See also Charles W. Anderson to Emmett J. Scott, Nov. 1, 1905: Washington Papers. Anderson to Washington, Jan. 12, 1906: Washington Papers.

[35] Charles W. Anderson to Booker Washington, Jan. 8, 1906: Washington Papers.

[36] Booker Washington to John Milholland, Sept. 18, 1905: Washington Papers.

[37] August Meier, "Booker T. Washington and the Rise of the N.A.A.C.P.," Crisis LXI (1954), 74. See also the following letters in the Washington Papers: Milholland to Booker Washington, Feb. 3, 1903. Milholland to Booker Washington, Feb. 7, 1903. Booker Washington to Milholland, Feb. 9, 1903. Booker Washington to Milholland, Feb. 20, 1903. Washington to Milholland, Nov. 25, 1903.

[38] Fred Moore to Booker Washington, Sept. 28, 1905: Washington Papers.

[39] Roscoe Simmons to Booker Washington, Oct. 2, 1905: Washington Papers.

that the Constitution League was out for "trouble." [40] Actually, Milholland had cooperated with both wings and did not want to be considered anti-Washingtonian.[41] However, members of the Niagara Movement fervently embraced the League's principles, and Du Bois continued to speak at public meetings of the organization.[42] The Niagara Movement's *Voice of the Negro* carried an article praising the League in early 1906,[43] and such laudations appeared about the time Du Bois was accusing Booker Washington of persuading the Negro Press to give the League the silent treatment.[44] Clearly, the die was cast; Milholland was spurned by the Washingtonians and courted by the Niagara Movement. The courtship on the rebound was turning into true love.

Besides cooperating with the Constitution League in Philadelphia, New York, and Washington, the Niagara Movement also exchanged speakers with Trotter's New England and Boston Suffrage Leagues. It is probable that the cause of racial advancement would have been served better if some concerted efforts had been made to bring all of these groups into one organization. There was, after all, no essential difference in their ideologies and all had the reputation of being Radicals. However, in 1906, the Constitution League was the only one with white members, and for that reason it was probably considered suspect by some Niagara or Suffrage League men. Undoubtedly, Trotter's personality was the major stumbling block, since he relished his big-fish-in-a-small-sea status. Naturally, these groups, operating separately, were no match for the well-disciplined Washingtonians. In 1906, Du Bois pointed out that a merger would effect a reduction in annual dues, but he was somewhat indefinite.[45] Shortly before the second Niagara conference that year, he asked his followers for five dollars each, and this "piteous and touching appeal" attracted the attention of the New York *Age*. The paper ridiculed the "financial cramps" of the Niagara men, but it also noted that few Negroes adequately supported race causes.[46] That year also, Du Bois's new magazine, the *Moon*, folded and the *Age* found it difficult to restrain its delight.[47] The Niagara General Secretary had hoped that the *Moon* would become a literary and news digest for Negroes around the world.[48]

Plans were made to hold the second Niagara conference at Harpers Ferry (for sentimental and propagandistic value) in August of 1906. Du Bois arrived there a few weeks prior to the opening session and many local Negroes

[40] Charles W. Anderson to Booker Washington, Oct. 12, 1905: Washington Papers.
[41] John Milholland, *The Nation's Duty* (New York, 1906), Bulletin Number 10, p. 5.
[42] New York *Age*, Feb. 8, 1906. See also, J. Max Barber, "The Niagara Movement," *Voice of the Negro* III (1906), 476. W. E. B. Du Bois to "Dear Colleague," June 13, 1906: Du Bois Papers.
[43] *Voice of the Negro* III (1906), 239.
[44] Gilchrist Stewart to Booker Washington, Feb. 13, 1906: Washington Papers.
[45] New York *Age*, June 28, 1906.
[46] New York *Age*, May 31, June 28, 1906.
[47] New York *Age*, Aug. 2, 1906.
[48] W. E. B. Du Bois, "A Proposed Negro Journal," MS, 1906: Du Bois Papers.

were afraid he meant to "stir up trouble." [49] Not only had Du Bois the reputation for being a Radical, but his bearing suggested unbounded arrogance and prevented him from gaining the confidence of Negro citizens in the community.

The meetings were held at Storer College, and many provocative statements were expressed by a large number of speakers. (One of them was Richard Greener, a Howard University professor. Greener actually attended the sessions as a Tuskegeean spy.) [50] Booker Washington, unmentioned by name, was the "third person of the trinity" who for alleged pay and publicity had sold out his race. President Roosevelt and Secretary of War Taft were also condemned, and one speaker charged that the Republicans concluded an agreement with the Democrats, in which the latter would vote "correctly" on the tariff question if the former soft-pedalled the Negro rights question. The Niagara men became interested in the formation of a "Pan-African League" and it became part of the official organization.

Various committee chairmen reported. The head of the Health Committee asked the group to sponsor a national campaign against tuberculosis, and one member believed that the Negro clergymen should cooperate in popularizing "the gospel of cleanliness, water, and air." [51] John Hope, chairman of the Education Committee, recommended that Niagara men should prepare a pamphlet on Southern Negro schools for legislators and the interested public. Hope maintained that the Niagara messages should be disseminated by securing greater cooperation from Negro editors and ministers. He also suggested that the movement should sponsor educational forums. [52]

The members of the second Niagara conference found no dearth of critics. The *Outlook* concluded that the Negro would be better off if this organization asked more of him instead of asking more for him. The white weekly agreed that the Negro should vote, but only after he had acquired "manhood." [53] The magazine compared the platform of Washington's National Negro Business League with the Niagara platform. Du Bois was described as "assertive" and Washington was considered "pacific." Washington focused on achieving an "inch of progress" rather than a "yard of faultfinding." [54] Negro critics were even harsher in their denunciations. Kelly Miller explained that the 1906 manifesto seemed like "a wild and frantic shriek." [55] The New York *Age* was still calling the Du Bois group an "aggregation of soreheads" who were jealous of Washington's success. [56] According to the *Age*, the Niagara principles were

[49] Supplied by Mr. Mercer Daniel in an interview, Feb. 1954.

[50] See the following in the Washington Papers: Richard Greener to "My Dear Friend," July 31, 1906. Booker Washington to Richard Greener, August 11, 1906. Telegram from Richard Greener to Washington, Aug. 11, 1906. Booker Washington to Greener, Oct. 20, 1906.

[51] "Minutes of the Niagara Movement," August 18, 1906: Du Bois Papers.

[52] "Report of the Committee on Education," 2nd Annual Niagara Conference, 1906: Du Bois Papers.

[53] *Outlook*, LXXXIV (1906), 3–4.

[54] *Outlook*, LXXXIV (1906), 54–55.

[55] John Hope Franklin, *From Slavery to Freedom* (New York, 1948), p. 437.

[56] New York *Age*, Aug. 16, Nov. 22, 1906.

no different from those of the Afro-American Council which Washington endorsed.[57] The Tuskegeean was depicted as a leader of the "masses," and as a victim of Negro intellectuals who attacked him because he lacked a college degree. The race needed "something cheerful," [58] and therefore repudiated the "lugubrious" and "bitter" chants of the Radicals. (Actually, the Du Bois men did err in their belief that they were the real "leaders" of the race,[59] and they were unrealistic in failing to gauge the wide fissure between the Talented Tenth and the unschooled majority.)

Near the end of the year, J. Max Barber chronicled some of the activities of the local Niagara chapters.[60] Credit was given to the Illinois branch for securing the appointment of a Negro to the New Chicago Charter Committee— a crucial maneuver in an effort to avoid school segregation. The Illinois branch was also aroused when *The Clansman* opened in Chicago. Jane Addams was contacted, and she convinced the city's drama critics to ignore the play.[61] Barber also described the accomplishments of the Massachusetts chapter. The group fought for the defeat of the Rate Bill (legalizing segregated railroad cars).[62] The branch also lobbied unsuccessfully to prevent the Massachusetts legislature from contributing money to the Jamestown Exposition unless the state of Virginia acknowledged that all citizens, regardless of race, would be admitted to the Exposition.

During the summer of 1906, prominent Negroes demanded the merger of some of the race's leading social betterment organizations. The Washington *Bee* declared that the National Negro Business League and the Niagara Movement should join forces.[63] On reconsideration, the *Bee's* editor decided that the Business League should remain independent but that the Afro-American Council and Du Bois's organization should combine.[64] The immediate background for the 1906 merger discussions was laid in a 1905 proposal by Mrs. Carrie W. Clifford, the wife of a Federal job-holder. At that time, she suggested that the Afro-American Council should join with Niagara, but her idea was repudiated as a Washingtonian maneuver.[65] Several race papers favored the merger, but Du Bois was "not enthusiastic" and the matter was shelved.[66] In August, 1906, the *Bee* announced that T. Thomas Fortune backed a merger plan.[67] However, the editor of the *African Methodist Episcopal Review* contended that no union was possible because of the jealousies of race leaders,

[57] New York *Age*, Feb. 8, Aug. 30, 1906.

[58] New York *Age*, Aug. 23, 1906. See also Emmett Scott to T. Thomas Fortune, Aug. 18, 1906: Washington Papers.

[59] J. Max Barber, "The Niagara Movement at Harpers Ferry," *Voice of the Negro* III (1906), 405.

[60] *Ibid.*, 411.

[61] *Ibid.*, 411.

[62] Washington *Bee*, Aug. 25, 1906. See also Du Bois Papers: Clement Morgan to Du Bois, May 13, 1906. Du Bois to Niagara Membership, May 16, 1906.

[63] Washington *Bee*, June 30, 1906.

[64] Washington *Bee*, July 14, 1906.

[65] Washington *Bee*, Sept. 23, 1905.

[66] Washington *Bee*, Oct. 28, 1905. (Reprint from Kentucky *Standard*.)

[67] Washington *Bee*, Aug. 18, 1906.

and he substituted a demand for "federation and friendly cooperation." [68] William Hayes Ward, the editor of the *Independent*, also maintained that personal desires for power were not unimportant impediments to consolidation, and he recommended another meeting similar to the ill-fated Carnegie Hall conference of 1904.[69]

Actually, unification was more impracticable in 1906 than in 1904. Mutual distrust prevented communication between both sides. The Washingtonians still believed their leader demanded every right for the Negroes that Du Bois did and that the Tuskegeean could realize these goals, while Du Bois could not. The Washingtonians ignored the difference between declaring themselves in favor of some goal and working consistently and continually toward its achievement. In addition, the Radicals were more united since the Carnegie Hall conference, and they over-estimated their strength.

However, in September of 1906, the Niagara Movement was invited to send representatives to the Afro-American Council meetings,[70] and L. M. Hershaw, head of the Niagara's District of Columbia branch accepted.[71] Shortly before the Council sessions, Washington secretly called for a "conservative" platform,[72] and in a personal appearance before the Council he condemned inflammatory statements of Northern Negroes.[73] Heeding the Tuskegeean, the Council, while opposing the segregated railroad car law and the denial of civil-political rights, emphasized the preservation of inter-racial "harmony" and "material progress." [74] Such actions were hardly conducive to a merger.

The Council sessions climaxed a year of Washingtonian accommodation which was interrupted only infrequently by efforts to limit segregation. Contradicting his "enemies," he affirmed that Negroes were living in a comparatively "happy period." [75] His optimism remained unchanged even after the Atlanta race riots in 1906, and he rejoiced that the "better element of both races" in the city was cooperating along religious and educational lines.[76] In contrast, Du Bois charged that the riots were premeditated by the whites and could be avoided in the future only by the application of Niagara principles.[77]

In early 1907, George W. Crawford, head of Niagara's Civil Rights Department, pointed out the error of waiting until the "overworked" Du Bois prodded members to action. Crawford urged each Northern chapter to lobby for state civil rights laws. He asked all Southern members to convince the railroads and legislators to improve travel accommodations for the race. Local Niagara organizations were also requested to obtain new trials for the innocent

[68] *African Methodist Episcopal Review* XXIII (1906), 184.
[69] New York *Age*, Aug. 30, 1906.
[70] New York *Age*, Sept. 13, 1906.
[71] New York *Age*, Oct. 11, 1906.
[72] Booker Washington to Charles W. Anderson, Oct. 4, 1906: Washington Papers.
[73] New York *Age*, Oct. 18, 1906.
[74] New York *Age*, Oct. 18, 1906.
[75] Booker Washington to T. Thomas Fortune, April 9, 1906: Washington Papers.
[76] Booker Washington, "Golden Rule in Atlanta," *Outlook* LXXXIV (1906), 913.
[77] W. E. B. Du Bois, "The Tragedy of Atlanta—from the point of view of the Negroes," *World Today* XI (1906), 1175.

who were convicted by juries excluding Negroes. Crawford favored cooperation with men outside of the Niagara Movement.[78] Weeks before, a Niagara committee was appointed to coordinate activities with the Constitution League.[79] Subsequently, Du Bois became a director of the League.[80] In a state like Connecticut, it was difficult to differentiate between the two groups, since both were organized and operated by so many of the same people. The Radicals worked efficiently in that state and Republican Congressional candidates (threatened with the balance of power argument) were asked to support demands for a Congressional investigating committee on Negro suffrage.[81]

The Niagara men hoped to invalidate racist laws by sponsoring test cases. After Barbara Pope was fined for refusing to enter a Jim Crow car when it crossed the state line into Virginia, the Niagara men successfully appealed her case.[82] In 1907, Du Bois estimated that more than six hundred dollars had been spent on the Pope litigation and that the Niagara Movement was in debt two hundred and forty dollars.[83]

By 1907, Du Bois found it harder than ever to recruit prominent people into the organization. However, despite constant Washingtonian pressure, he claimed a membership roll of three hundred and eighty persons.[84] Refusing to be discouraged, Du Bois (F. H. M. Murray and L. M. Hershaw) founded a miniature monthly called the *Horizon*. Since Murray and Hershaw held Federal jobs, Charles W. Anderson tried to persuade President Roosevelt to fire them. Anderson falsely asserted that Hershaw was *"the head devil"* in the anti-Roosevelt campaign,[85] and Washington's aide-de-camp shrewdly refrained from admitting that he was more disturbed about the attacks upon the Negro educator than by those on the President.

The Niagara Movement held its third annual conference in 1907. Since the organization felt an emotional attachment to Harpers Ferry, there was some talk of meeting there again. However, between 1906 and 1907, Storer College experienced an "unexpected lessening of its annual appropriation," and some of the friends of the institution maintained that it had been "injured" because the Niagara Movement had met on its campus the year before. Du Bois was notified that no 1907 invitation could be extended until the Storer trustees granted formal permission.[86] It is not known what action the trustees finally took, but the third conference was held in Boston.

[78] Herbert Aptheker, *op. cit.*, p. 911.
[79] W. E. B. Du Bois to John Milholland, March 27, 1907: Du Bois Papers.
[80] A. C. Humphrey to W. E. B. Du Bois, April 25, 1907. See also, Du Bois to A. C. Humphrey, May 2, 1907.
[81] "Niagara Movement's Civil Rights Department Report," 1906–7, Du Bois Papers.
[82] L. M. Hershaw, "Pope Case," *Horizon*, May 1907, p. 17. See also, "Abstracts of Minutes of the Niagara Movement," Aug. 15–18, 1906, located at Howard University Library. Washington *Bee*, Aug. 25, 1906.
[83] W. E. B. Du Bois to "Dear Colleague," April 10, 1907: Du Bois Papers.
[84] "Secretaries and Committee Reports of the Niagara Movement," April 1, 1907: Du Bois Papers.
[85] Charles Anderson to Booker Washington, May 27, 1907: Washington Papers.
[86] W. E. B. Du Bois to Henry T. McDonald, March 18, 1907: Du Bois Papers.

The relatively small amount of attention which the Negro press gave to these sessions apparently reflected the general doldrums of the organization. It was becoming painfully apparent to many that little had been accomplished. Du Bois realized that there was "less momentum" at this third conclave, and he observed "internal strain," a condition which he ascribed to his own "inexperience" and to Trotter's personality.[87] Shortly after the conference, Washingtonians dubbed it pretty much of a "failure." [88] In two years of operation, the Niagara men succeeded in raising only $1,288.83, and during the same period, they spent $1,539.23.[89] According to the Niagara leadership, eight hundred persons attended one of the sessions,[90] but the Washington *Bee* commented that there were fewer than a hundred delegates—not even enough to receive a special railroad rate.[91]

At the conference, the Constitution League was praised for its investigation of the Brownsville Affair and Roosevelt and Taft were excoriated.[92] Senator Foraker of Ohio became the man of the hour [93] for his condemnation of the evidence upon which the soldiers were dismissed from military service. The conferees, angered by a recent decision of the Interstate Commerce Commission upholding the Jim Crow car law, put on a brave front and declared, "All means at our command must be employed to overthrow [the law] and change the personnel of that weak, reactionary board." [94] There were many examples of the impotence of the Niagara men—and of their soul-searching. A New York delegate announced that several Congressmen informed him that there was little hope of enforcing the Fourteenth and Fifteenth Amendments.[95] Rev. J. M. Waldron was concerned with an old Niagara ailment, i.e., its failure to attract the "masses." Waldron also believed that the organization might take on new life if it cooperated with the Socialists and the working class whites.[96] (Du Bois favored this proposition. Although he referred to himself as a "Socialist-of-the-path," he also had some reservations because the Socialists —and white workers—discriminated against Negroes.) [97]

The 1907 Niagara "Address to the World," which the Indianapolis

[87] W. E. B. Du Bois, *Dusk of Dawn* (New York, 1940), pp. 94–95.

[88] R. W. Tyler to Booker T. Washington, Aug. 29, 1907: Washington Papers.

[89] "Minutes of the Third Niagara Conference," Aug. 29, 1907: Du Bois Papers.

[90] 1907 Boston Meetings of Niagara, pamphlet, located at Howard University Library.

[91] Washington *Bee*, Sept. 14, 1907.

[92] Niagara Movement to Constitution League, August 29, 1907: Du Bois Papers.

[93] Niagara Movement to Senator Foraker, Aug. 29, 1907: Du Bois Papers.

[94] 1907 Boston Meeting of Niagara, pamphlet, 1907, located at Howard University Library.

[95] "Minutes of the Third Niagara Conference," Aug. 29, 1907: Du Bois Papers.

[96] *Ibid.*

[97] See the following: W. E. B. Du Bois to I. M. Rubinow, Nov. 17, 1904: Du Bois Papers. W. E. B. Du Bois, "Socialist of the Path," *Horizon*, Feb., 1907, p. 7. W. E. B. Du Bois, "The Negro and Socialists," *Horizon*, Feb., 1907, p. 7. W. E. B. Du Bois, "A Field For Socialists," MS, circa. 1907: Du Bois Papers. W. E. B. Du Bois, *The Negro in the South* (Philadelphia, 1907), p. 116.

Freeman called "a final shriek of despair," [98] did not deviate in tone or approach from the Addresses of the two previous years. The document is probably most significant because of its political advice to "the 500,000 free black voters of the North." [99] The Republican Party was called "the present dictatorship," and the faithful were urged to vote against Taft, Roosevelt, or any other Republican standard-bearer. Such heretical sentiments did not seem to trouble the New York *Age*, whose new editor, Fred Moore, contended that the Radicals would have to support the 1908 Republican candidate because there was no one else to back. [100]

The Boston conference was also the scene of a rupture between Du Bois and Trotter, which seriously damaged the morale of the whole movement, and especially the Massachusetts branch. The seeds of the schism were sown the year before when Du Bois's good friend, Clement Morgan, the head of the Massachusetts branch, supported Governor Guild in his race for re-election. Trotter was adamant that Guild should not receive Negro aid because the white politician had been instrumental in securing a state appropriation for the segregated Jamestown Exposition. Trotter was rankled that Morgan, who had opposed the appropriation, wanted to vote for Guild, and the *Guardian* editor was absolutely livid when he heard that the Negro leader was to be nominated for the state legislature by the Republicans, as a reward for "loyalty."

A few months later, another crisis occurred. It seems that Morgan staged a social affair for money-raising purposes a short time prior to the 1907 Niagara conference, and he neglected to consult Trotter on arrangements. The *Guardian* editor charged that Morgan's favorites had been placed in positions of prestige at the affair. The Niagara Executive Committee sided with Trotter and ruled that Morgan should be fired. [101] Du Bois, however, informed the Executive Committee that he would resign unless they ruled against Trotter. The General Secretary was re-elected and Morgan remained at his old post, apparently on a temporary basis. The disharmony remained, and Mary White Ovington informed Du Bois that the squabble must be making Booker Washington happy. [102]

Clement Morgan called the whole affair a "small matter . . . magnified by malcontents," and he was disturbed that Du Bois was being vehemently criticized. [103] Trotter carried his battle into the open, and the New York *Age* noted that the *Guardian* was denouncing the Niagara leaders. [104] Once more, Du Bois decided to resign, feeling that the Executive Committee had not really supported him and was therefore contributing to the "nation-wide dis-

[98] Indianapolis *Freeman*, Sept. 21, 1907.
[99] "Address to the World of the Third Niagara Conference," pamphlet, 1907, located at Howard University Library. Cleveland *Gazette*, Sept. 7, 1907.
[100] New York *Age*, Sept. 19, 1907.
[101] Washington *Bee*, Sept. 14, 1907.
[102] Mary W. Ovington to W. E. B. Du Bois, Oct. 8, 1907: Du Bois Papers.
[103] Clement Morgan to C. E. Bentley, Nov. 20, 1907: Du Bois Papers.
[104] New York *Age*, Nov. 14, 1907.

sension in our ranks." [105] However, another Executive session was called and Morgan and Du Bois were entreated to remain at their posts.[106] Undoubtedly, the controversy was an important factor in hastening the disintegration of the Niagara Movement.

For the Radicals, the 1908 Presidential campaign began early. They knew that Booker Washington planned to support Taft for the Republican nomination,[107] even though this fact was supposed to be a top secret.[108] In February, Du Bois predicted that Taft would run against Bryan and he advised Negroes to "stay home" on election day.[109] Ambivalently, he wrote that Taft must be defeated and that "it is hard to imagine . . . someone worse." Practically, he could not bring himself to support a Socialist candidate.[110] In March, he reluctantly announced for Bryan since "an avowed enemy [is] better than [a] false friend." [111] Many Negro newspapers were stunned [112] and some of the gibes which they published originated at Tuskegee Institute.[113] By July, Du Bois declared that Negroes should get behind the Democratic Party, which advocated corporation control, liberty for the West Indians and Filipinos, and improved working conditions for wage earners.[114]

He realized, as he had years before, that it would be hard to convince Negroes that they owed nothing to the Republicans. In his opinion, the Republican Party never truly opposed slavery. He claimed that after the Civil War, Negroes were enfranchised in order to serve as tools of the politicians, and although the Republicans controlled the three branches of the national government for decades, racism was allowed to flourish.[115] Furthermore, Negroes had even been ejected from the Republican Party councils in the cloudburst of Lily-Whitism, and Du Bois angrily complained to the chairman of the Republican National Committee.[116]

According to Du Bois's theory, the Democrats comprised an "impossible alliance" between the "radical socialistic" wing of the North and the Southern "aristocratic caste party," and the coalition was doomed to disintegration.[117] However, if the Negro voters continued to oppose the liberal Democrats of the North, the latter would be reluctant to break with the South. Du Bois, still chasing the balance of power dream, assumed that Negroes had the ability

[105] W. E. B. Du Bois to Executive Committee and Subcommittee, circa Dec. 1907: Du Bois Papers.

[106] "Report of the Executive Committee and Sub-Committee of the Niagara Movement," Jan. 11, 1908: Du Bois Papers. See also circular letter of Niagara Movement, March 14, 1908: Du Bois Papers.

[107] Charles W. Anderson to Emmett Scott, Feb. 15, 1908: Washington Papers.

[108] Oswald G. Villard to F. J. Garrison, Jan. 15, 1908: Villard Papers.

[109] W. E. B. Du Bois, "To Black Voters," Horizon, Feb., 1908, p. 17.

[110] Ibid. See also W. E. B. Du Bois to Mr. Owens, April 17, 1908: Du Bois Papers.

[111] W. E. B. Du Bois, "Bryan," Horizon, March 1908, p. 7.

[112] New York Age, April 2, 1908. Also see Age, April 16, April 30, 1908.

[113] Booker Washington to Fred Moore, circa, June, 1908: Washington Papers.

[114] W. E. B. Du Bois, "The Negro Voter," Horizon, July, 1908, pp. 4–5.

[115] W. E. B. Du Bois, "Talk No. Three," Horizon, Aug., 1908, pp. 5–7.

[116] W. E. B. Du Bois to Harry S. New, June 1, 1908: Du Bois Papers.

[117] W. E. B. Du Bois, "The Negro Vote," Horizon, Sept., 1908, pp. 4–6.

"to deliver with ease" New York, New Jersey, Ohio, Indiana, and Illinois; as well as to create the possibility of victory "in a dozen other states." [118] Although Taft won by a substantial majority and received a large number of Negro votes, Du Bois was consoled by the belief that "more Negroes voted against Mr. Taft than ever before voted against a Republican candidate." [119]

Two months before the election, the fourth conference of the Niagara Movement was held at Oberlin, and again the conclave was characterized by strenuous talk and no action. (Probably this inactivity was the reason that Myrdal and Rose seemed unaware that the Niagara Movement called further annual conferences after 1907).[120] Earlier, Mary White Ovington had indicated that she would talk on "The Relation of the Negro to Labor Problems" for the benefit "of the aristocrats who are in the membership." [121] The sessions revealed the debility in the national organization and in the branches as well. The secretary of the Pennsylvania branch submitted a report which showed disunity and disinterest within his group. During the previous year, his organization failed to convince the Philadelphia Board of Education to engage a substantial number of Negro teachers and to desegregate Negro schools. The local Niagara branch did not give the Negroes in the community a comprehensive analysis of the defects of their school system, and several Negro ministers decided to work independently and to negotiate with the school board. The local Negro press attacked the ministers, the Niagara state secretary also assailed their ignorance, and the race gained almost nothing. The Pennsylvania report also indicated that the group was financially bankrupt.[122] The fourth annual "Address to the Country" blasted "the Negro haters of America," who had succeeded in excluding qualified men from all areas of American life. Negroes were advised to get guns and prepare themselves for defensive action against white mobs.[123]

Booker Washington did not relent in his efforts to destroy the Niagara Movement, even though it was apparent that the organization had lost whatever influence it once had. One source reported that of the four hundred and fifty people on the Niagara membership list, only nineteen gathered at Oberlin.[124] Another account said that fifty were actually present.[125] The Tuskegeean correctly concluded that the group was "practically dead" and he asked the New York Age to publish an obituary which he prepared.[126] Almost simultaneously, other Washingtonians were still trying to bury the Niagara

[118] W. E. B. Du Bois, "Talk No. Five," Horizon, Sept., 1908, pp. 7–8.
[119] W. E. B. Du Bois, "Politics," Horizon, Nov.–Dec., 1908, p. 11.
[120] Gunnar Myrdal, An American Dilemma (New York, 1944), p. 742. Arnold M. Rose, The Negro's Morale (Minneapolis, 1949), p. 32.
[121] Mary W. Ovington to W. E. B. Du Bois, April 24, 1908: Du Bois Papers.
[122] "Report of the Niagara Secretary for Pennsylvania," August-September, 1908: Du Bois Papers.
[123] See the following: Independent LXV (1908), 676, 734. Richmond Planet, Sept. 19, 1908. Horizon, Sept., 1908, p. 1.
[124] Savannah Tribune, Sept. 26, 1908. (Reprint from New York Independent.)
[125] Savannah Tribune, Sept. 19, 1908.
[126] Booker Washington to Fred Moore, Sept. 7, 1908: Washington Papers. Also see Booker Washington to Fred Moore, Sept. 8, 1908: Washington Papers.

Movement in a conspiracy of silence and had gained commitments from white newspapermen to ignore the Oberlin sessions.[127] Gradually, the Negro newspapers which supported Niagara dwindled, and in 1908, the Chicago *Conservator* capitulated to the Tuskegeeans.[128]

The following year, the Niagara Movement was still limping along. So many of the branches had become quiescent that it was news when the Columbus group held several regular meetings.[129] In August, the fifth annual conference was held at Sea Isle City, New Jersey, and it was ignored by both the Negro and white press. Almost single-handedly, the "disappointed" Du Bois tried to keep the organization going, when old reliable officers such as George W. Crawford appeared ready to give up.[130] Du Bois expected at least fifty men at the conclave, and he hoped to persuade the Haitian minister to the United States to address the group.[131] According to one newspaper, "fifty delegates and guests" were actually present.[132]

F. L. McGhee, the head of Niagara's legal department, told the delegates that relatively little legal work had been undertaken because of the small amount of money which was contributed for that purpose.[133] In the fifth annual Address to the Country, the organization claimed at least partial credit for "increasing spiritual unrest, sterner impatience with cowardice and deeper determination to be men at any cost." The General Secretary's socialistic orientation was evident when he suggested that his race should unite with the other "oppressed" workers of the United States, Mexico, India, Russia, and the rest of the world.[134] The conclave did elicit some typical and some odd comments from a handful of Negro papers. The Indianapolis *Freeman* was annoyed that Du Bois should have called the theory of inherent racial superiority "a widespread lie," and the ultra-sensitive editor suggested the use of some less "cruel" expression such as "fable" or "falsehood." [135]

Between 1909 and 1910, the *Horizon* was sinking further into the red and Du Bois asked, "If you are not interested in yourselves, who will be interested?" [136] The editors paid the deficit "out of their shallow pockets." [137] The year before, Du Bois tried to secure financial backing from John Milholland, in order to publish a periodical from New York. However, the deal

[127] Jack Abromowitz, *Accommodation and Militancy in Negro Life, 1870–1915,* Columbia University Doctoral Dissertation, 1951, p. 215.

[128] W. E. B. Du Bois, "Little Brother of Mine," *Horizon*, Feb., 1908, p. 18.

[129] New York *Age*, July 29, 1909.

[130] W. E. B. Du Bois to George W. Crawford, July 31, 1909: Du Bois Papers.

[131] W. E. B. Du Bois to L. M. Hershaw, July 13, 1909: Du Bois Papers.

[132] Fisherman's Net, Sept. 17, 1909.

[133] "Report of the Fifth Niagara Movement Convention," by F. L. McGhee, Secretary of the Legal Department, Aug. 14, 1909: Du Bois Papers.

[134] W. E. B. Du Bois, "Niagara Movement," *Horizon*, Nov., 1909, p. 9. See also *Fisherman's Net,* Sept. 17, 1909.

[135] Indianapolis *Freeman*, Oct. 2, 1909.

[136] W. E. B. Du Bois, "Subscribers," *Horizon,* May, 1910, p. 1.

[137] *Crisis* V (1912–1913), p. 27.

was never consummated.[138] Even when the *Horizon's* death rattle was heard in April, 1910, Du Bois still clung to the hope that he could remain in business until the 1910 sessions of the Niagara Movement.[139] By this time, members of Niagara were paying their dues irregularly or were not contributing anything. The national treasurer notified Du Bois that he "had not been able to give more time" to handling the group's finances.[140]

Despite all of these difficulties, Du Bois considered the members "a splendid set of people" and he hoped to have the sixth annual conference at Sea Isle City again.[141] He had just about convinced himself that regular dues were unnecessary and that the Niagara Movement could continue to exist as a social-educational order, with its members buying adjoining lots at a summer resort. The organization never convened again as a separate entity, and after the N.A.A.C.P. was formed, Du Bois asked all of the Niagara alumni to support it.[142]

SUMMARY

The men of Niagara helped to educate Negroes to a policy of protest and taught the whites that there existed a growing number of Negroes who were dissatisfied with anything less than a full measure of manhood rights. The Niagara men came from the wilderness and hewed a spiritual path for younger men to follow. Perhaps the true mission of the Movement was that it helped to lay the foundation for the N.A.A.C.P.

The organization failed for many reasons. Its program of racial equality was too far ahead of the historical period which chose Booker Washington as its representative. Du Bois admitted that his organization had not accomplished very much and he correctly emphasized Washingtonian obstruction as an essential factor for the lack of success. The Tuskegee Machine was formidable, since it consisted of powerful white friends, large amounts of money, political patronage, and large sections of the Negro press. In contrast, the Niagara men had little money and were unable to attract wealthy whites to their side.

Furthermore, most of the members felt psychologically isolated from the Negro masses. Rose contended that many even regarded the bulk of the Negro race as inferiors.[143] The organization was composed of men who occupied a privileged position in Negro society, and they were quite conscious of that fact. No small number considered their education as primarily a symbol of social prestige, which divorced them forever from intercourse with the masses. Aside

[138] W. E. B. Du Bois to The Guarantors of the Horizon, March 10, 1909: Du Bois Papers. See also, W. E. B. Du Bois to The Board of Control of the Horizon, March 18, 1909: Du Bois Papers.

[139] W. E. B. Du Bois to F. Murray and L. Hershaw, April 2, 1910: Du Bois Papers.

[140] Mason A. Hawkins to W. E. B. Du Bois, Feb. 13, 1910: Du Bois Papers.

[141] W. E. B. Du Bois to James H. Gordon, April 29, 1910: Du Bois Papers.

[142] W. E. B. Du Bois's circular letter to "Dear Colleague," Sept. 27, 1911: Du Bois Papers.

[143] Arnold Rose, *The Negro's Morale* (Minneapolis, 1949), p. 32.

from the higher social status which a university education conferred, such training gave these people a relatively intellectual outlook. There is a degree of social distance within any group between the educated and less educated segments, and this observation was especially true within the Negro race whose Talented Tenth was actually a talented hundredth.[144]

These educated men had an empyrean conception of human rights which they did not effectively convey to the masses who were little interested in politics. The Niagara utterances were frequently useless to the Negro workers. Du Bois's socialistic orientation was sincere but abstract, and its implication was ignored by his followers. He had often said that political and economic matters were inter-related, but a major weakness of the Niagara Movement was that it spent comparatively little time on economic salvation. The ballot was regarded as the panacea.

Du Bois's personality and his inexperience as a social action leader were not advantages to the organization. He was often described as "aristocratic" and "aloof" in his dealings with the masses and the Talented Tenth as well.[145] Du Bois was aware of his "natural reticence" and his "hatred of forwardness." Booker Washington was a diplomat, politician, and tactician; Du Bois was none of these types. He "hated the role" of being a social action leader and was sensitive to Washingtonian attacks.[146] In actuality, he was the College Professor of Niagara—giving lectures here, writing papers there, and expecting all the while that his "students" would carry his ideas far and wide. He seemed oblivious of the fact that the Talented Tenth were not the "leaders" of the race.

Lastly, there is no question that the organization was weakened by the "individualism and egotism" of Trotter. His intemperate statements made the Niagara Movement especially vulnerable, and the Washingtonians often asserted that his excesses were representative of the entire association. Du Bois was never able to control the *Guardian* editor.

Despite all of these limitations, the members of the Niagara Movement could be justifiably proud of their efforts on behalf of higher education, their contributions to legal redress, and their attempts to organize a political lobby composed of informed, independent, and articulate citizens. As exponents of the strategy of protest, they provided an answer to Washingtonian accommodation. It is true, however, that the Niagara Movement developed a hard core of uncompromising Negroes who matched in intensity the unyielding Washingtonians, and during this battle, the race may not have profited very much in the short run. Nevertheless, the Niagara men (and their friends in other equal rights organizations) did promulgate a set of blueprints which were to be the guides for many Negroes and whites. Gradually, Washingtonianism was to recede in influence and Du Bois and the Niagara Movement were to be vindicated after the N.A.A.C.P. appeared on the scene.

[144] William Ferris, *op. cit.*, p. 200.
[145] Ralph Bunche, *op. cit.*, p. 19.
[146] *Crisis* XV (1917–1918), 170.

Thomas R. Cripps

THE REACTION OF THE NEGRO TO THE MOTION PICTURE *BIRTH OF A NATION*

In 1909, the Negro Radicals, who under Du Bois' leadership had founded the Niagara Movement four years earlier, joined hands with a group of prominent white liberals to found the NAACP. During its early history, this interracial protest organization fought for the protection of the Negroes' constitutional rights by holding mass meetings, lobbying in city halls, in state capitols and in Washington, picketing occasionally, and, most important, initiating litigation in the courts. Limited in personnel and money, the NAACP carefully selected its issues and cases, and then mounted intensive campaigns upon those it chose to fight. Thomas R. Cripps has given us an interesting study of an early effort of the NAACP to mold public opinion—in this case by preventing the circulation of a film that defamed the Negro race.

IN THE decade before Woodrow Wilson's first administration the reforms of urban Progressives were essentially for whites only. Despite the Negro's rising wealth and increasingly successful struggle with illiteracy, the tenuous *rapprochement* that a few Negro leaders had with Theodore Roosevelt, the formation of active and influential agencies of reform like the National Negro Business League, and (at the behest of several white liberals) the National Association for the Advancement of Colored People and the Urban League, the Wilson years represented the continuation of a decline. Residential segregation was increasing; the ballot box was a distant memory to many Negroes; Jim Crow had become the custom in public accommodations. For the Negro there was a denial of reform even before the resurgent Democratic party

Thomas R. Cripps, "The Reaction of the Negro to the Motion Picture *Birth of a Nation*," *The Historian*, XXV (May, 1963), pp. 344–62. Reprinted with the permission of the publisher and the author.

brought to Washington a return to southern ideals.[1]

Typical of the ascendency of the ideology of the white South was the circulation of *Birth of a Nation*, a spectacular twelve-reel film, much of which was drawn from *The Clansman*, a romantic, angry novel of the fate of the ideals of the antebellum South during Reconstruction. Its author was Thomas Dixon of North Carolina, a sometime preacher, a professional Southerner, and a fretful Negrophobe. The novel—which constituted the basis of only the last half of the film—is based on an attempt by a group of defeated Southerners to reassemble the traditional power structure of the South. Hindered and thwarted in their efforts by Stoneman, a thinly disguised Thad Stevens, who with his mulatto mistress rules America after Appomattox, they turn naturally to extralegal means of political expression: the Ku Klux Klan.[2] The director of the film, David Wark Griffith, son of a Confederate soldier, had an affinity for the Lost Cause and a fondness for portraying in melodrama "the pale, helpless, slim-bodied heroines of the nineteenth-century poets" being attacked by Negroes. It was Griffith who wrote the first half of the film, a southern view of the Civil War.[3]

The film was significant for other reasons. Artistically, it was the finest work the cinema had ever produced. Socially, it was reflective of the depth of hostility that many white Americans felt toward Negroes and of the degree to which this feeling might be fed by film propaganda and its accompanying mass advertising. It also presented Negro leaders with a dilemma. They could ignore the film and its hateful portrayal, knowing not what damage it might do. They could urge censorship. Or, and least likely, they could finance and make their own films propagandizing favorably the role of Negroes in American life.

Films with an essentially regional tone and even an anti-Negro bias had been made previously. In 1915, the year of *Birth of a Nation*, Paramount was circulating *The Nigger*, another heavy-handed racist film. Griffith himself had made *The Battle*, a Civil War picture of earlier vintage. *The Clansman*, too, had been shot earlier, starring Griffith's wife; in 1906 as a play it had been labeled "as crude a melodrama as has ever slipped its anchor and drifted westward from Third Avenue." [4]

[1] See George C. Osborn, "The Problem of the Negro in Government, 1913," *The Historian*, XXIII (May 1961), 330–347 for the most recent study of the Negro's plight in the Wilson years.

[2] Thomas Dixon, Jr., *The Clansman* (New York, 1907) is one of several editions. A print of *Birth of a Nation* is in the Museum of Modern Art Film Library, New York City (copyright no. LP 6677).

[3] Iris Barry, *D. W. Griffith: American Film Master* in the *Museum of Modern Art Film Library Series No. 1* (New York, 1940), 7–10, 15–21; Arthur Knight, *The Liveliest Art* (New York, 1959), 31, 35; Nicholas Vardac, *Stage to Screen: Theatrical Method from Garrick to Griffith* (Cambridge, Mass., 1949), 64, 199, 208; Seymour Stern, "Griffith: Pioneer of Film Art," in Lewis Jacobs, *Introduction to the Art of the Movies* (New York, 1960), 158–159. For a new scholarly treatment with many fresh insights and sound criticism of earlier students see Edward Wagenknecht, *The Movies in the Age of Innocence* (Norman, Okla., 1962), 99–109.

[4] A review in the Harvard Theater Collection, January 8, 1906, cited in Vardac, *Stage to Screen*, 64.

Why was this one film so powerful and so fiercely resented? Aside from the flaws that offended Negroes and some film esthetes, the picture made far greater use of advertising than was normal and consequently drew far larger crowds than earlier films. But the movie created the greatest stir chiefly because it was the nearest to fine art that the cinema had achieved. It reached a technical brilliance, an "art by lightning flash," a kind of visual music with its own rhythm and logic. Its tempo was varied by editing together numerous shots into a montage that could evoke larger-than-life images of past reality. Early critics spoke of this effect as "panoramic drama" or "outdoor drama" which could create "crowd splendor" and "crowd passion" rather than private passion so that "the Ku Klux Klan dashes down the road as powerfully as Niagara pours over the cliff . . . [and] the white leader . . . enters not as an individual, but as . . . the whole Anglo-Saxon Niagara." Audiences became mobs "for or against the Reverend Thomas Dixon's poisonous hatred of the Negro." Few viewers could distinguish between art and ax-grinding, technique and content. Only a few critics like Vachel Lindsay could admire the film as "a wonder in its Griffith sections" with its "mobs splendidly handled, tossing wildly and rhythmically like the sea," while pointing out the pathological flaws of Dixon's script.[5]

No earlier American film had been so impressive. Even the producers referred to their redundant, unimaginative nickelodeon entertainments as "sausages." And when *Birth of a Nation* was made, the Mutual Company, which had helped finance production, did not take it seriously enough to back its distribution; Griffith, his cameraman Billy Bitzer, and a friend and film producer named Harry Aitken had to form the Epoch Company to circulate the film. Other distributors did not want it for fear of hurting the receipts of their own films, some of which were also racist.[6]

Art, technology, advertising, the racism of Dixon—all fell together into what Negroes took to be a malicious conspiracy. "Every resource of a magnificent new art has been employed with an undeniable attempt to picture Negroes in the worst possible light" the N.A.A.C.P. declared in its *Annual Report*.[7] Lacking funds with which to make propaganda films of their own, Negroes of the urban North turned to censorship, an acceptable position among liberals of the time who were concerned about "vice" and its assumed cause—the nickelodeon parlors that dotted American cities showing corrupting movies.[8] Many cities and some states had begun to censor films. Negroes

[5] Nicholas Vachel Lindsay, *The Art of the Motion Picture* (New York, 1915), 41, 46–49.

[6] Barry, *D. W. Griffith*, 22. In an interview with Rolfe Cobleigh, editor of the *Congregationalist and Christian World*, Dixon claimed to own one-fourth of the picture. See Boston Branch of the N. A. A. C. P., *Fighting a Vicious Film: Protest Against "Birth of a Nation"* (Boston, 1915), 26.

[7] N. A. A. C. P., *Sixth Annual Report* (n. p., 1915), 11.

[8] Here, as throughout the paper, the proper noun "Negro" used collectively, is shorthand for Negro pressure groups and their white allies. Ideologically, it should not suggest unanimity of opinion or action but only that these people recognized and resented certain social customs and disabilities that whites commonly imposed upon Negroes.

turned to these agencies to stop the showing of *Birth of a Nation.*

In February 1915 the film was shown in Los Angeles and in San Francisco. A few days later advertising started in the New York newspapers; almost simultaneously the Los Angeles branch of the N.A.A.C.P. notified the New York office of the west coast opening. The film should have followed a normal course eastward to the National Board of Censorship of Motion Pictures, a private agency created by the film producers who hoped that it would give the movies respectability as family entertainment and the wider market they thought would accrue to their product once they were able to squelch the sensational investigations of the nickelodeons.[9] The Board, later called the National Board of Review, was one of many expressions of the intellectual climate of the time. It was unique in that it was private; yet it was admired by public censors because eighty per cent of the film exhibitors were said to abide by its decisions. In Washington the year before, the House committee on the establishment of a motion picture commission had taken considerable testimony, much of which favored public censorship. But the committee chose to heed the counsel of Frederic C. Howe, chairman of the New York Board, who recommended that the existing Board be permitted to continue its work without intervention from a superfluous body in Washington.[10]

Two days before the film was to be reviewed by the Board, Dixon sidetracked it into Washington and showed it in the East Room of the White House to Woodrow Wilson, members of his cabinet, and their families. The night following this unprecedented event, he showed it in the ball room of the fashionable Raleigh Hotel, with Chief Justice Edward White, the Supreme Court, and members of Congress in attendance. Both showings were granted as favors to Dixon, a former student of Wilson's at Johns Hopkins, with the stipulation that there be no publicity. Dixon stopped in Washington because he hoped to bolster Wilson's known Southern biases, especially his attitude toward the Negro. As he later told Joseph Tumulty, Wilson's secretary,

> I didn't dare allow the President to know the *real big purpose back of my film—which was to revolutionize Northern sentiments by a presentation of history that would transform every man in the audi-*

---

[9] Investigations resulted in the creation of censoring boards in Chicago, New York, Kansas, Maryland, and Ohio. The movement entered Congress in the persons of Southern and New England Calvinists and over-zealous progressives who also tended to support prohibition and suffrage for women. [Terry Ramsaye, *A Million and One Nights* (New York, 1926), II, 569.]

[10] U.S. Congress, House of Representatives, *Motion Picture Commission: Hearings before the Committee on Education . . . on Bills to Establish a Federal Motion Picture Commission,* 63rd Cong., 2nd sess., Nos. 1 and 2, 1914, Pt. I, 3–5, 56–62; Pt. II, 79; Ramsaye, *Million and One Nights,* II, 482; "Films and Births and Censorship," *Survey,* XXXIV (April 3, 1915), 4–5. For further comment on the censorship controversy see Donald Ramsay Young, *Motion Pictures: A Study in Social Legislation* (Philadelphia, 1922), 21, 42, 58, 75, 98; Morris L. Ernst and Pare Lorentz, *Censored: The Private Life of the Movies* (New York, 1930); and Wagenknecht, *Movies in the Age of Innocence,* 100.

ence into a good Democrat! And make no mistake about it—we are doing just that thing. . . . Every man who comes out of one of our theatres is a Southern partisan for life—except the members of [Oswald Garrison] Villard's Inter-Marriage Society who go there to knock.[11]

Wilson, according to Dixon, liked the film and congratulated him, saying that it was "history written in lightning." [12] Justice White, before the same showing, in Dixon's words, "leaned toward me and said in low tense tones: 'I was a member of the Klan, sir. . . . Through many a dark night, I walked my sentinels' beat through the ugliest streets of New Orleans with a rifle on my shoulder. . . . I'll be there!' " Thus whenever the N.A.A.C.P. protested the film, Dixon could claim approval in high places. No denials came from Washington until after the New York and Boston runs had begun.[13]

Hence Dixon, even before the New York Board saw the movie, had in effect secured the *imprimatur* of the President of the United States. In New York on February 20 the Board allegedly wildly applauded the picture, spurring Dixon to leap to his feet, shouting that it was the "birth of a nation," and the old title, *The Clansman*, was then and there discarded. The producers, expecting no opposition, advertised the film's opening on March 3 at the Liberty Theater at a top price of two dollars.[14]

The N.A.A.C.P. had eleven days to persuade the Board to reject the film. Earlier, the Los Angeles branch had wrung from the local Mayor a commitment to cut all scenes suggestive of rape. Soon the *Crisis*, the N.A.A.C.P. organ, working with Fred Moore's New York *Age*, pressed for similar concessions in New York City. It was surprised upon hearing of the Board's acceptance of the film in its entirety.[15]

Actually the alleged enthusiasm of the Board's approval may have been exaggerated, for even with the cuts that the N.A.A.C.P. was to win, the vote to approve was divided. The Negroes had protested the decision on the basis

[11] Dixon to Tumulty, May 1, 1915; later Dixon let Wilson know his plans in blander terms, assuring the President that soon "there will never be an issue on your segregation policy," Dixon to Wilson, September 5, 1915, cited in Arthur Link, *Wilson: The New Freedom* (Princeton, 1956), 253–254. Dixon made a similar reference to the "Negro Intermarriage Society" in an interview with Rolfe Cobleigh. [N. A. A. C. P., *Fighting a Vicious Film*, 26.]

[12] Mrs. Thomas [Madelyn Donovan] Dixon to Thomas R. Cripps, June 7, 1962; telephone conversation between Mrs. Dixon and Cripps, June 6, 1962. Thomas Dixon, *Southern Horizons: An Autobiography*, ms. in the possession of Mrs. Dixon, Raleigh, North Carolina, cited in Eric Goldman, *Rendezvous with Destiny* (New York, 1956), 176–177. See also Knight, *The Liveliest Art*, 35; and New York *Post*, March 4, 1915.

[13] Correspondence cited in Link, *Wilson*, 253–254.

[14] New York *Times*, February 14, 1915. See also Lewis Jacobs, "D. W. Griffith"; Daniel Talbot, *Film: An Anthology* (New York, 1959), 416 for titling incident. For another version see Wagenknecht, *Movies in the Age of Innocence*, 99. Dixon in an interview claimed to have hired thirteen Pinkerton men for the New York run. [N. A. A. C. P., *Fighting a Vicious Film*, 16.]

[15] "Fighting Race Calumny," *Crisis*, X (June 1915), 87.

of the split and had reminded the Board that when *The Clansman* had been performed on the stage in Philadelphia, it had caused riots and had been banned. They were also aroused when, after the excisions, they saw that there were still close-ups of leering Negroes (many of whom were crudely made-up whites) pursuing white ingénues. But even with the omission of several shots of a "forced marriage" and a lynching sequence, most of which were poorly contrived anyway, the decision still remained at 15–8 for approval, with the chairman, Howe, among the dissenters. He refused to put his name on the Board's seal of approval.[16]

The Board felt that its job was not to judge historical accuracy; its job was "moral" and there was never any assumption of jurisdiction over race prejudice. Moreover, the Board was a cumbersome barge that steered best in calm waters. Composed of 125 members who were placed in numerous smaller groups in order to view the vast output of films, it acted as a general committee only in case of dispute. A sub-committee had passed on Griffith's work without change; it was because of Howe's insistence that the whole Board saw it and decided to pare footage from Part II, the segment drawn from Dixon's novel.[17]

After the producers failed to appeal the first deletions, the N.A.A.C.P. insisted that all of Part II be cut.[18] As the premiere approached, the N.A.A.C.P. demanded that Howe let Negroes preview the film. Howe responded by doling out two tickets, ten less than promised, for a March 1 showing with the provision that only whites use them. The Negroes pressed on, having heard that the Board had vocally disapproved of the film and might be persuaded to put it in writing. Failing, they sued for an injunction on March 3, the date of the New York opening; they were refused because there had been no breach of peace. The Board, in an effort to close the case, stopped answering mail on the subject. But under increasing pressure, the Howe group cracked and admitted that the March 1 action had been unofficial; it decided to allow Jacob Schiff, Jane Addams, Lillian Wald, and other N.A.A.C.P. members to have a private showing. A few Southerners also went along. They all roundly condemned the picture with the vigor of eyewitnesses, which they had become for the first time.[19]

After the viewing the Negro group instituted criminal proceedings against Griffith and Aitken, circularized the movie industry with their case against the Epoch Company, and demanded that the New York Commissioner of Licenses stop the film as a nuisance.[20] Intimidated, the Board consented to another viewing and two more cuts were accepted by Epoch. Then Oswald Garrison Villard, one of the founders of the N.A.A.C.P., refused advertising for the film

[16] Frederic C. Howe to [Joseph P.] Loud in N. A. A. C. P., *Fighting a Vicious Film*, 33; *Survey*, XXXIV (April 3, 1915), 4–5.
[17] W. D. McGuire, Jr., of the National Board of Review, "Censoring Motion Pictures," *New Republic*, II (April 10, 1915), 262–263.
[18] "Fighting Race Calumny," *Crisis*, X (May 1915), 40–42.
[19] *Ibid.*
[20] *Ibid.*

in his New York *Post*. Three days later he printed a Jane Addams review in which she saw the film as a "gathering [of] the most vicious and grotesque individuals he [Griffith] could find among the colored people, and showing them as representative of the...entire race."[21] She, like Wilson, had mistaken verisimilitude for reality.

Although the Board gave a final approval on March 15, the N.A.A.C.P. continued its work, nagging the Board for the names and addresses of members and urging the Mayor to stop the film as detrimental to "public decency." Failing, they sent copies of Francis Hackett's stinging review in the *New Republic* to 500 newspapers, marking the first time either side used a critic's esthetic standards. Within the week the New York press learned of the Board's division and its disclosures brought the N.A.A.C.P. to the Mayor's office again. It tried to marshal delegations from many local churches and clubs, but Mayor John P. Mitchell, fearing a riot, refused them a license to parade.[22]

Howe, W. E. B. DuBois of the *Crisis*, Fred Moore, Rabbi Stephen A. Wise, Villard, delegates from the colored and white clergy and the Urban League overflowed into the outer halls of the Mayor's office. Mitchell told them that he had no statutory powers over the film; he then droned through his earlier assurances that slashes in the film had already been made, that riot warnings had been issued, and that he could do no more. The announcement that the picture was being shown with excisions surprised the delegates; they meekly acquiesced and departed.[23]

The Mayor's conciliatory statement about cuts was achieved at the expense of Negro unity. The meeting in his office revealed the deep fissures that ran through the Negro leadership, an elite that many whites thought was sturdily cemented in common cause. Taking advantage of the strife, the "Tuskegee machine," Booker T. Washington's coterie (a group which it was thought accepted the Negro's low status) had reached the Mayor ahead of the N.A.A.C.P. through the efforts of Charles W. Anderson, a friend of Washington and a recently resigned Federal officeholder. Often antagonistic, but at times cooperative with the N.A.A.C.P. liberals, the Tuskegee group chose this occasion to embarrass the "Vesey Street crowd" (Anderson's name for the liberals) and "take the wind out of their sails" by demonstrating Washington's influence with those in high places. But though the Negro groups were placated, apparently unknown to Anderson, the requested cuts were not made. Thus the New York campaign was lost amid the recriminations that often marked the Negroes' efforts to unify against the bigotry that existed in the United States.[24]

21 New York *Post*, March 10, 1915, carried the last advertisement. The review appeared March 13, 1915.

22 *Crisis*, X (May 1915), 40–42.

23 *Ibid.* (June 1915), 87; N. A. A. C. P., *Fighting a Vicious Film, passim*; *Afro-American Ledger* (Baltimore), March 27, 1915.

24 *Crisis*, X (May 1915), 40–42; *Afro-American Ledger*, March 3, 1915; August Meier, "Booker T. Washington and the Rise of the N. A. A. C. P.," *Crisis*, LXI (February 1954), 122.

When the film continued to run, the Negro groups moved to friendlier territory in Boston, home of William Monroe Trotter's *Guardian* and the liberal Boston *Post*. Starting early in April, Negro and white pulpit, press, and lectern attacked the film. Nevertheless, on the first Sunday in April Bostonians opened their papers and found a large sensational, pseudo-religious advertisement for the film which mentioned a forty-piece orchestra, 18,000 extras, and 3,000 horses. By Tuesday Mayor James Curley, who had banned movies of the Jess Willard-Jack Johnson fight, announced that he was giving public hearings to the numerous Negro societies over *Birth of a Nation*. Just before the hearings a Tremont Theater advertisement reminded the public that Wilson, George Peabody, and others had liked the film.[25] The next day accusations flew: in reply to a statement by Moorfield Storey who had accused the manager of issuing distortions, the theater called DuBois' *Crisis* "incendiary."[26] In turn, Griffith chided Storey for ignoring the historians Wilson, James Ford Rhodes, and Walter Lynwood Fleming—claiming that all would have accepted the film's thesis—and then made brilliant publicity by offering Storey $10,000 if he could prove the film distorted. They parted coolly when Storey complied; later the film interests declared that Storey had not seen the movie.[27]

Curley, perhaps sensing impending violence, promised to get the picture cut by the municipal censor. At the meeting of April 7 tempers were short. The Negroes hissed the mention of Wilson. In demanding censorship they cited the fact that the United States had banned the importation of boxing films and that the Women's Christian Temperance Union favored film censorship. They pointed to the frequent depiction of "sexual excesses" in movies, raised the fear that the film would create race hatred, and read letters from Addams, Wise, Mary W. Ovington, and other liberals. At one point Curley, piqued at the growing mountain of redundant testimony, asked if *Macbeth* tended to incite feeling against whites. Storey bristled and charged Curley with representing the "other side." The meeting broke up amid Curley's denials, Griffith's interjections on his right to film "history" as he saw it, and the Mayor offering to cut a scene showing a Negro chasing a white girl.

Curley made good his offer. The chase scene, several leering Negroes, a marriage between a dissolute Negro and a white girl, the shots of Stoneman alone with his mulatto mistress, and the whole segment showing a corrupt,

[25] *Ibid.*, X (June 1915), 87; N. A. A. C. P., *Fighting a Vicious Film, passim.* See also Boston *Sunday Post*, April 4, 1915; Boston *Post*, April 6, 7, 8, 1915. The list included Dorothea Dix, Rupert Hughes, Booth Tarkington, Richard Harding Davis, Hugh Johnson, George Peabody, Senators James E. Martine, Duncan U. Fletcher, Henry Lee Myers, Thomas J. Walsh, Wesley L. Jones, Representative Claude Kitchen, the Reverends C. H. Parkhurst and Thomas Gregory. According to the N. A. A. C. P. Dixon's method of soliciting approval was to pass out cards between halves of the film: that is, after the predominantly Griffith parts and before his own part.

[26] N. A. A. C. P., *Fighting a Vicious Film*, 26.

[27] *New Republic*, III (May 5, 1915), 17; see also correspondence in N. A. A. C. P., *Fighting a Vicious Film, passim.; Broad Ax* (Chicago), June 5, 1915; Boston *Post*, April 24, 1915.

bacchanalian South Carolina legislature were removed. Curley made it clear, though, that the cuts were a concession and not an act of conscience.

During the second week of the film's run in Boston the *Post* began clearly to take the Negro's position, though advertising for the film continued to run in its pages. Its writers reminded Bostonians of the murderous moods of the New York audiences observed as they left the Liberty Theater, that Curley's predecessor had stopped the stage production of *The Clansman* in 1906, and chided the producers for using clergymen as "authorities" in the advertisements.[28]

Toward the end of the week violence erupted when two hundred police were summoned because a crowd of Negroes (who were barred from theaters) attempted to purchase tickets. Eleven people were arrested. Two Negroes managed to worm their way into the theater. When one hurled an "acid bomb" and the other an egg, they were quickly arrested. Trotter personally stood bail. On Saturday afternoon rumors of riots spread through the streets. The next day a wild, hooting crowd gathered at Faneuil Hall. There, Michael Jordan of the United Irish League, making common cause with the Negroes, castigated Wilson. The *Post* later gave the day's events a whole page. Hurriedly, Governor David Ignatius Walsh and Attorney-General Henry Attwill met to thrash out the limits of their authority to stop the film. As the meeting progressed both whites and Negroes gathered on the steps outside to orate. The harried governor promised a delegation that he would ask the legislature to pass a censorship law covering inflammatory material. Meanwhile, he ordered the state police to stop Sunday's show. A day later he managed the excision of another rape scene while the legislature held a hearing on the film.[29]

The publicity caused a few early supporters of the film to have second thoughts. George Peabody labeled the picture "unfair" after an earlier endorsement. Late in the month Senator Wesley L. Jones of Washington, several clerics, and others publicly turned on the film. To conciliate the defectors, the producers introduced a bland prologue extolling the progress of the Negro, but Negroes were still kept from the box office.[30]

During the whole Boston affray Booker T. Washington remained aloof except for his advice and the work of his Negro Business League, which he was having difficulty controlling. When Griffith, in mid-April, asked him to make a film about Tuskegee, Washington refused because he questioned Griffith's sincerity and did not wish to associate with the makers of the "hurtful, vicious play." Principal Hollis Frissell of Hampton Institute allowed a similar film to be made of his school for use as the prologue to *Birth of a Nation*, a decision which the *Crisis* attributed to Washington's advice. Al-

---

[28] Boston *Sunday Post*, April 4, 11, 1915; Boston *Post*, April 6, 7, 8, 1915.

[29] After the riot the rest of the Boston papers began to cover the movie and its effects. None of them—the *Evening Transcript*, the *Herald*, the *Journal*—adopted a pro-censorship stand or seemed deeply concerned about the struggle over the film. See the issues of April 18, 1915, through April 26, 1915, particularly.

[30] Boston *Post*, April 12, 18, 19, 1915; *Crisis*, X (June 1915), 87; correspondence in N. A. A. C. P., *Fighting a Vicious Film*, 30–33.

though Washington gave no overt support, he was gratified to know that "Negroes are a unit in their determination to drive it out of Boston." At the same time he was very much aware that the campaign was increasing the picture's business, for he remembered when Negroes had been hired in 1906 to oppose *The Clansman* as a promotional "gimmick." In addition to these tactical considerations Washington kept out of the Boston affair because the Boston Negro Business League, in which he exerted considerable influence, was in a factional fight over endorsing the Griffith movie. Two members, it was reported, had already tried to endorse the film in his name. It was said that William Lewis, former United States Assistant Attorney-General and a Negro, concurred in the endorsement. Fortunately for Washington the resolution to endorse was blocked in a meeting of the executive council, but even so he had to manipulate the rebel group into remaining in the organization so as to continue the public impression of Negro unity.[31]

Meanwhile the debate went on in Boston. When the Massachusetts lower house passed a censor bill, all the Boston newspapers carried large advertisements attacking it. On April 24 Trotter was arrested and fined twenty dollars when he tried to use tickets he had bought. Negroes still complained that scenes were removed for "moral" rather than racial reasons and insisted that many offensive shots remained. At a meeting at the First Unitarian Church Charles Eliot of Harvard, William Lewis, and others thrashed out the problem of legislation that would distinguish between art and propaganda—in their view *Birth of a Nation* belonged to the latter category. That this distinction was a main issue occurred to few of the antagonists. Most tried to draw a line short of "absolute freedom," to define what should be banned as "mischief," and to decide whether a "travesty of history" was censorable. Only one man at the meeting thought all censorship a "violation of freedom of the press and public expression." The Federation of Churches of Greater Boston condemned the film as "injurious to public morality." [32]

As the situation in Boston worsened, Wilson's southern sympathies—not as deep as Dixon's—wavered; the President and the Chief Justice sought a way out of their endorsement as the adverse press reaction to the film spread. Tumulty suggested "some sort of letter" that would get Wilson out of a corner without appearing to have been bullied by that "unspeakable fellow [Trotter]." Finally, the President permitted Tumulty to write a letter to Representative Thomas Thacher of Massachusetts, asserting that the White House had never

[31] Phil J. Allston to Booker T. Washington, copy, April 12, 1915; Washington to Allston, copy, April 25, 1915; Washington to Allston, copy, April 19, 1915; Charles E. [?]llason to Washington, June 1, 1915; Samuel E. Courtney to Washington, copy, April 19, 1915; Washington to Courtney, copy, April 23, 1915; Rabbi Abram Simon to Washington, confidential telegram, April 14, 1915; Emmett Scott to Simon, telegram, April 14, 1915, Booker T. Washington Papers, Box 75, Library of Congress. Washington wrote one letter of protest to the Atlanta *Independent*. [N. A. A. C. P., *Fighting a Vicious Film*, 35–36.] See Boston *Post*, April 24, 1915, for hints that Allston himself may have expressed approval of the film.

[32] *Broad Ax*, June 5, 1915; Boston *Post*, April 24, 1915; Boston *Evening Transcript*, April 20, 1915; Boston *Herald*, April 21, 1915; *Crisis*, X (June 1915), 87.

sanctioned the film. Although other correspondents were similarly reassured,[33] the damage had been done, for Dixon had been able to use the President's name for commercial purposes for the better part of three months. The Thacher letter was shown to William Lewis and African Methodist Episcopal Zion Bishop Alexander Walters, who were expected to take the belated news to the Negroes who had despaired at the President's thoughtless endorsement. Thus it took three months for Wilson to approach the position of the urban weeklies that dismissed the film as a spectacle and its audiences as curiosities, that denounced the "censors that passed it and the white race that endures it," that blasted Dixon as a "yellow clergyman," and that sometimes noted the paradox of brilliant techniques perverted for specious ends.[34]

After the President's retraction the Boston fight neared the end that Negroes feared. The newly created Massachusetts Board of Censors ignored a petition of six-thousand names and permitted the Tremont to continue showing Birth of a Nation. The Board which had been created partially because of the Negroes' lobbying had turned on its makers. Fitfully, the squabble dragged on through the summer with the Crisis impotently recording minor successes with triumphant glee and failures with arch cynicism.[35] As the days grew longer the Negroes of Boston hoped that Booker T. Washington and Bishop Walters would come to town to actively aid DuBois and Trotter in keeping the pot boiling. But New York and Boston had become the scenes of bitter defeats, which were reflected across the land.

By midyear, except in a few cases, the distributors of Birth of a Nation could exhibit their film almost anywhere they wished. Mayor William Thompson killed it in Chicago and later in all of Illinois. In Wilmington, Delaware, the City Council approved a fine of fifty dollars for showing it or The Nigger. In Cleveland, Harry Smith of the Gazette helped to keep The Nigger out of the city, but Mayor Newton D. Baker failed to induce the governor to keep Birth of a Nation out of Ohio.[36]

The film could be seen in New York, Los Angeles, San Francisco, and Boston. Agitators were at work against the picture in Baltimore; Charleston, West Virginia; Philadelphia; and Atlantic City with scant success.[37] Rarely

[33] Link, Wilson, 253–254; Goldman, Rendezvous with Destiny, 176–177.

[34] "The Civil War in Film," Literary Digest, L (March 20, 1915), 608–609; Francis Hackett, "Brotherly Love," New Republic, II (March 20, 1915), 185; see also "After the Play," ibid., V (December 4, 1915), 123; ibid., III (June 5, 1915), 125.

[35] Boston Post, June 5, 1915, clipping in the Washington Papers; Crisis, X (July 1915), 147–148 insisted there had been no hearing; ibid., (August 1915), 200–201; ibid., (September 1915), 245; "The Negro Business League," ibid., (October 1915), 280–281; "Social Uplift," ibid., 268; "The Birth of a Nation," ibid., 295–296. The Crisis claimed to have "wounded the bird" because "the latter half has been so cut, so many portions of scenes have been eliminated, that it is a mere succession of pictures, sometimes ridiculous in their inability to tell a coherent story."

[36] See correspondence in n. 31. For suggestions of the political motives of Walsh, Curley, and other Massachusetts politicians see Boston Herald, April 18, 26, 1915.

[37] Afro-American Ledger, May 22, 26, June 5, July 31, August 7, September 25, December 25, 1915; New Jersey Informer, August 21, 1915, clipping in the Washington Papers.

did the violence and rioting that many Negroes expected occur in these cities. The press at times viewed the film as newsreel reality; often roundly condemned it for the prejudices it presented, argued over authenticity, discussed the social impact; distrusted Dixon; praised Griffith; and except for papers like the New York *Post*, whose editor was accessible to the N.A.A.C.P., few took unequivocal positions one way or the other.[38] The Negro press, too, ranged from unconcern to dutiful worry and almost universally failed to see it as art or entertainment. The chief difference between the Negro and white press reactions was that some of the Negro editors were less kind to Griffith.[39]

By the latter half of the year, when the Boston rancor had waned, both the N.A.A.C.P. activists and the more covert Booker T. Washington group reassessed what had happened and gained insights about their functions as pressure groups. The *Crisis* conceded that Griffith was an ill-used but "mighty genius" and that negative opposition was pointless. If the film was a "cruel slander upon a weak and helpless race," DuBois wrote, then the race must learn to use its money for films, poetry, music, and its own history. In October the Negroes in Washington, D.C., began preparations for "The Star of Ethiopia," an all-Negro pageant.[40] At Tuskegee, Washington was badgered by writers who wanted him to make films which would refute the stereotypes of *Birth of a Nation* and "make wonderful propaganda for every kind of social reform." He refused, perhaps fearing the loss of face suffered by Frissell when he let Griffith use Hampton for the locale of a film prologue to *Birth of a Nation*.[41] Consequently, the annual report of the N.A.A.C.P. for 1915 could only record a long, negative battle for censorship. Negroes had demonstrated and had broken into segregated theaters to get a hearing for their censorship pleas—a stand their leaders were coming to reject in principle but tactically

---

[38] Chicago *Tribune*, May 9, 14, 15, 1915; Baltimore *Sun*, November 1, 1915; Philadelphia *Inquirer*, March 30, September 5, 23, 26, 27, 1915; Boston *Post*, March 4, 1915; New York *American*, March 5, 1915; Vardac, *Stage to Screen*, 224, cites New York *Times*, June 6, 1915; New York *Sun*, March 4, 1915. See also New York *Evening Post*, February 20, March 3, 4, 13, 1915; "The Birth of a Nation," *Outlook*, IV (April 14, 1915), 854; "Negro Segregation Adopted by St. Louis," *Survey*, XXXV (March 11, 1915), 694; *ibid.*, XXXVI (April 24, 1915), 96; *ibid.*, (July 10, 1915), 344–345; New York *Times*, March 4, 7, 1915. See also Ramsaye, *Million and One Nights*, II, 638.

[39] Washington *Bee*, February 20, May 1, 27, June 5, 1915; St. Paul *Appeal*, October 2, 1915; *Afro-American Ledger*, March 3, 13, 20, 1915.

[40] *Crisis*, II (November 1915), 36; "The Slanderous Film," *ibid.*, (December 1915), 76–77. The *Crisis* was probably referring to the fact that Dixon was able to weave his racism into Griffith's art with such finesse that no one could attack ideology and art separately, thus assuring Dixon an audience that he might not have gathered solely on the merits of his own work.

[41] Florence Sewell Bond to Washington, June 27, 1915; Washington to Bond, June 30, 1915; Washington to F. P. Hull, personal-confidential copy, April 23, 1915; Scott to J. H. Beak, St. Paul Association of Commerce, October 27, 1915; Beak to Washington, wire, October 10, 1915; Amy Vorhaus to Washington, July 9, 1915; Laurence Gomme to Emmett Scott, June 17, 1915; Scott to Gomme, copy, June 23, 1915, Washington Papers.

were unable to replace with another weapon because of budgets already strained by litigations and demonstrations. And sometimes even censorship backfired, as in Massachusetts, where the Board that the Negroes helped create eventually accepted most of the films to which the Negroes objected.[42]

For Negroes, their failure in the fight against *Birth of a Nation* was another reminder that the scant progress made in the Roosevelt years was not necessarily inevitable and that the Wilson era was a time of troubles characterized by a Jim Crow Federal government, lynching, and the seedtime of a new Ku Klux Klan. The controversy also demonstrated the seriousness with which films had come to be regarded both as creators and reflectors of opinions and attitudes after only two decades of existence.

[42] N. A. A. C. P., *Sixth Annual Report,* 11–22; Vorhaus to Washington, July 9, 1915; Washington to Vorhaus, July 13, 1915, Washington Papers. For examples of later protest see Francis Grimké, "The Birth of a Nation," (n. p., October 15, 1915) in Francis J. Grimké, *Addresses and Pamphlets,* (n. p., n. d.); N. A. A. C. P., *Fighting a Vicious Film;* Reverend W. Bishop Johnson, *The Birth of a Nation; A Monumental Slander of American History; the Negro and the Civil War by Thomas Dixon Analytically and Critically Considered,* (n. p., [1916]); Isaac L. Thomas, *The Birth of a Nation: A Hyperbole Versus a Negro's Plea for Fair Play* (Philadelphia, 1916)—all in the Moreland Library, Howard University, Washington, D. C. See also " 'Birth of a Nation' Revived, Draws Protest," *Crisis,* XLV (March 1938), 84.

PART SIX

THE MAKING
OF THE
BLACK GHETTO

Robert C. Weaver

THE NEGRO GHETTO

During the First World War hundreds of thousands of Negroes left the South to seek employment in the factories of the North, where wartime demands had created an enormous need for unskilled labor. The arrival of the migrants in the northern cities gave additional stimulation to trends already under way. Since the opening years of the century racial lines were becoming more tightly drawn in places like Chicago, New York, Cleveland, and even Boston. Now, with the large and rapid increase in Negro population, residential segregation grew markedly as scattered enclaves gave way to large ghettos. In his volume The Negro Ghetto, *Robert C. Weaver examined the migration and its effects, particularly in New York and Chicago.*

GLAMOUR CITIES IN THE PROMISE' LAND

...THE Negro community in Chicago had a long tradition. One of its first settlers, Baptiste Point du Sable, was a San Dominican Negro. Despite this auspicious beginning, relatively few additional colored people came into the city during the pre-Civil War days, and in 1850 only 323 colored residents were counted by the census. After that time, the colored population increased each decade. The nature of this increase can be seen in Table II.

TABLE II

NUMBER AND PERCENTAGE OF NEGROES IN CHICAGO, 1850–1910 [a]

	1850	1860	1870	1880	1890	1900	1910
Population	323	958	3,696	6,480	14,271	30,150	44,103
Percentage of total	1.1	0.9	1.2	1.3	1.3	1.9	2

[a] Source: U.S. Census Reports.

The expansion of the Negro community was not a unique phenomenon, but was similar to the movement of other racial and immigrant

From Robert Weaver, *The Negro Ghetto* (New York: [1948], Russell and Russell, 1967), pp. 14–32. Reprinted with permission of the publisher.

groups in the city of Chicago. Like other racial and cultural groups of a low economic status, Negroes first acquired a foothold in and near the center of the city, where less resistance is offered to the invasion of alien elements.[8]

The areas open to them were in various stages of deterioration. There was, however, no one Negro settlement; there were several, including a concentration of upper-class Negroes near Washington Park. Morgan Park, too, was, prior to World War I, evolving out of what had originally been a settlement of colored servants employed in a near-by area of whites.[9]

Prior to the movement of over 50,000 colored people to Chicago in the five-year period 1915–1920, Negroes lived in practically every section of the city. As in other northern communities, they were usually centered at the edge of areas inhabited by wealthy whites, for whom many of them worked as servants; and after the Great Fire of 1871, while many of the resident colored families were dispersed among whites, a settlement of Negroes and their major community and social institutions were concentrated in an island of limited area. This was the point from which the major future expansion was to take place. When, in 1910 and the years immediately succeeding, new areas in the old city were rapidly opened to residential use, Negroes were excluded from them. Yet as recently as 1910, in no area of Negro concentration were Negroes more than 61 per cent of the population; more than two-thirds of the colored people lived in sections less than 50 per cent Negro, and a third were in areas less than 10 per cent Negro.

There was less cleavage between the older and the new colored people and less adverse community reaction to the Negro migrant before than after World War I. This was due principally to two factors—the size and general characteristics of the migrants in the two periods. Although the Negro population of Chicago doubled during the decade, 1890–1900, and continued to grow in the succeeding ten years, the absolute numbers involved were much smaller than in the five years after the outbreak of the war. The city as a whole was growing during these earlier years; in 1890, Negroes were but 1.3 per cent of the total; in 1900, they were 1.9 per cent; and in 1910, they were 2 per cent. In contrast to the situation in Philadelphia, the Negroes who migrated to Chicago prior to World War I were predominantly from the border states, where they were much better prepared, by training, previous exposure to city and town life, and cultural advancement, to adjust quickly to the environment of a large urban community than were the later migrants from the deep South.[10] These circumstances contributed to the relative ease with which Chicago absorbed 30,000 Negro migrants in 20 years. The significant feature in the ability of these newcomers to find shelter was the economic milieu in which the migration occurred. Negroes in Chicago, during the pre-World War

[8] E. Franklin Frazier, *The Negro Family in Chicago*, University of Chicago Press, 1932, p. 91.
[9] *Ibid.*, pp. 95, 97.
[10] *Ibid.*, p. 90.

I period, tended to move into those areas which were undergoing a general change in use and which whites had voluntarily vacated. *As long as there was no general shortage of houses,* the expansion of Negroes in Chicago caused little comment and friction.

In 1912, there were four relatively well-defined districts in which a large proportion of the Negro residents had lived for many years. The largest was on the South Side and during the second decade of the Twentieth Century, it extended in a narrow band around State Street from 16th to almost 55th Street. The second in size was on the Near West Side along Lake Street; in addition, there were two minor in-lying areas, one in Englewood, the other a single street (Lake Avenue) in Hyde Park. The Negro area on the South Side had already taken on the form of a Black Belt; in 1912, the heads of 94 per cent of the families in a sample section of the area were colored. Three selected blocks in the West Side area had Negroes at the head of a third of the families. The South Side Negro, therefore, lived in a Negro community, while the West Side Negro might have an Irishman or a German as his neighbor, or sometimes live in the same dwelling with a white family. In both areas, there was much substandard housing, and the rents charged Negroes were higher than those charged whites for comparable shelter. Half the residents in the Bohemian, Polish and stockyard districts paid no more than $8.50 a month for four-room apartments; half the tenants in the Negro South Side paid at least $12 for flats of the same size but in poorer states of repair.[11]

Although colored Chicagoans in the pre-World War I period generally resisted acceptance of the foreign immigrants' practice of sleeping in kitchens and parlors, and, consequently, were not as densely concentrated, there was much overcrowding in the units occupied by Negroes. This appeared in the use of sleeping rooms by too many people, reflecting the presence of a large number of roomers.[12]

"The strong prejudice of the white population," said Comstock in 1912, "against having colored people living on white residence streets, colored children attending schools with white children or entering into other semi-social relations with them, confines the opportunities for residence open to colored people of all positions of life to relatively small and well defined areas."[13] Yet Negroes with high incomes did occasionally escape from the Black Belt when they had a mind to do so. Sometimes they moved into apartments in better neighborhoods, or, sometimes, they bought property secretly, or through a friendly white man.[14] Since, however, the great mass of Negroes, like the great mass of the most recent immigrant groups, were poor and dependent upon employment in or near the downtown area, these processes offered escape for only a few.

[11] Alzada P. Comstock, "Chicago Housing Conditions, VI: The Problems of the Negro," *American Journal of Sociology*, September, 1912, pp. 241–45.
[12] *Ibid.*, p. 246.
[13] *Ibid.*, pp. 255–56.
[14] *Ibid.*, p. 243.

Still the Negro was not the worst housed ethnic group in the city. That dubious distinction fell upon the Italians who were the most recent migrant group in pre-World War I Chicago.[15] As early as 1912, however, it was clear that poor housing among Italians could be a temporary situation. Their rents were comparable to those charged generally for specific types of shelter. There were no strong barriers to the movement of Italians out of the run-down areas where they were concentrated. As a matter of fact, it seemed that they were staying in these areas because of their closeness to places of employment, opportunities for association with other Italians, and access to the glamour and excitement of South State Street.[16] Education, economic improvement, and Americanization were sure to accelerate the inhabitants' inclination and ability to find better housing. Pre-World War I Chicago had, however, already begun to adopt customs and attitudes to limit greatly the Negro's enjoyment of similar opportunities.

In New York City, too, the earlier Negro residents had tended to live in close proximity to the wealthy whites whom they served as domestics. As in Philadelphia, free Negroes enjoyed great popularity in many types of service jobs, having, for a limited time an almost uncontested preference in most of them. These workers and their families were clustered in several sections of the city. Then, as the most cosmopolitan center in America attracted colored artists, writers, musicians, show people and professional athletes, new hotels, restaurants and other facilities catering to Negroes sprang up in an area adjacent to downtown. Around these facilities, a new settlement of colored people developed. It was often called Black Bohemia and became the main center of Negro life in Manhattan; it was no satellite to a community of rich whites, as the earlier concentrations of Negroes had been. Colored residents poured into it, as the more conservative ones had long before rushed into Brooklyn. In the latter section, the migrants had established a stable social life and emphasized respectability. Some owned their own homes, and were less concentrated there than Negroes on Manhattan. While the Brooklyn colony became stabilized, the new main Negro settlement on Manhattan soon became inadequate; it moved to Harlem, where all classes and income groups among Negroes were destined to be concentrated.

These movements of Negroes within the city were in response to the pressure for living space on the part of an ever-expanding Negro population. In the early years, black residents formed a significant proportion of the population, but when the immigrants from Europe came streaming in, New York City grew at an unprecedented rate. The result was that, despite the constant arrival of more colored people, they soon became a very small part of the total population, declining from 10.5 per cent in 1800 to 2.7 per cent in 1850. Ten years later Negroes were but 1.5 per cent of the city's total and as late as 1910

[15] Grace Peloubet Norton, "Chicago Housing Conditions, VII: Two Italian Districts," *American Journal of Sociology*, January, 1913, p. 542.
[16] *Ibid.*, pp. 538–39.

they were only 1.9 per cent. Yet over 90,000 Negroes lived in New York City by 1910.*

The entrance of Negroes into Harlem, as all movements of populations into new areas, had strong economic motivations. Harlem had been over-built with new structures, but transportation facilities had not kept pace. As a result, vacancies developed and landlords became apprehensive. Meanwhile the established Negro community on the fringes of the downtown area was filled to overcrowding. An enterprising Negro real estate operator approached a group of landlords in Harlem and offered to fill the vacancies with permanent colored tenants. The offer was accepted, and Negroes moved into the area.† At first, whites paid little attention to the presence of a few colored neighbors; ‡ but as the Negro population in New York continued to grow, more and more colored people entered Harlem. When they moved into new sections of the area, whites became apprehensive, and,

the whole movement, in the eyes of the whites, took on the aspects of an "invasion"; they became panic-stricken and began fleeing as from a plague. The presence of one colored family in a block, no matter how well bred and orderly, was sufficient to precipitate a flight. House after house and block after block was actually deserted.[17]

As this occurred, banks and lending institutions holding mortgages on the deserted structures had to take many of them over. They, too, became infected by the general hysteria, and many kept properties vacant rather than rent to colored people. At first, values dropped, but this, as the enforced vacancy of properties in transition, proved to be temporary. With the ever-rapidly expanding demand for housing on the part of Negroes after the Great Migration of World War I, vacancies disappeared and values rose again—often to a new high.

In the early experience of Negroes' entrance into Harlem, there was a preview of what was to come in many northern cities during and after World War I. The only major feature missing was the outbreak of violence. That, too, was due, in large part, to the economic setting in which the *initial* stages of the transition occurred. Negroes first entered Harlem when there were already

---

* The phenomenal increase of Negro population in New York City from 23,600 in 1890 to slightly over 90,000 in 1910 was due, in part, to the inclusion of additional boroughs in the city by the date of the latter census.

† According to one authority, rents in Harlem had declined sharply when, in 1903, the suggestion of Negro occupancy was made. It was proposed that Negroes would pay about $5 more per month than whites had been paying. (Clyde Vernon Kiser, *Sea Island to City*, Columbia University Press, 1932, p. 20)

‡ It should be noted that the entrance of large numbers of Negroes into Harlem had been preceded by two events: a scattering of colored people had long lived in or near the homes of white employers in the area, and parts of Harlem had definitely deteriorated as residential areas by the close of the Nineteenth Century. (*Ibid.*, p. 19)

[17] James Weldon Johnson, "Harlem: the Cultural Capital," in Alain Locke (editor), *The New Negro*, Albert and Charles Boni, 1925, p. 304.

many vacancies in the area. Since there was no general competition for too few dwellings, no city-wide fear of Negroes as an expanding segment of the housing market developed. Such fear and animosity as subsequently appeared was concentrated on the neighborhood level.

Although open violence in the form of a riot did not follow Negroes' penetration into Harlem, there were battles of real estate manipulation, financial pressure and propaganda as soon as large numbers of colored people were involved. A property owners' association, organized by the whites, brought pressure on financial institutions not to loan money to colored purchasers in the area or renew their mortgages. Inflammatory handbills, affirming that the presence of Negroes would depreciate property values, were surreptitiously circulated. The *New York Herald* of July 10, 1906, reported indignation meetings throughout the neighborhood of West 135th Street, where white families were scheduled to be displaced by Negro occupants. The whites in the area expressed the general belief that the establishment of a few colored families on the street was only the first phase of a widespread penetration of Negroes throughout Harlem.

THE SITUATION BEFORE THE STORM

By the outbreak of World War I, the larger centers of Negro population in the North had established segregated community facilities of various types, and colored residents were, in varying degrees, concentrated around them. Black Belts had appeared. Harlem was rapidly developing as the largest Negro city within a city in the world. Many of the basic institutions of Chicago's Negro South Side were firmly established, and that area was the main point of concentration of Negroes in the city. Elsewhere in the North, the process of concentration of colored people was in various stages of development. In most cities it was far less advanced than in New York or Chicago. Surveys in the postwar reflected the situation.

> In Minneapolis and in Columbus, O., the Negroes were scattered throughout the city [even after the Great Migration], yet in spite of the fact that there was no exclusively colored section, they tended to cluster in certain areas. Chicago and Detroit were found to possess well defined Negro districts, which became more densely populated upon arrival of migrants from the South. . . . In Pittsburgh, "before this great influx of Negroes from the South, the Negro population . . . lived in half a dozen sections of the city. Although not absolutely segregated, these districts were distinct. . . . The sections formerly designated as Negro quarters have been long since congested beyond capacity by the influx of newcomers, and a score of new colonies have sprung up. . . ." [18]

[18] Louise V. Kennedy, *The Negro Peasant Turns Cityward*, Columbia University Press, 1930, pp. 145–46.

The pressure of numbers had not placed a great strain upon the supply of shelter available to Negroes in many northern cities (New York was an outstanding exception), and such concentration of colored residents as existed was due chiefly to voluntary actions of Negroes (largely inspired, of course, by their need for each other's society in a community which rejected them in many phases of its life) and to their restriction, because of income, to low-rent housing.

The quality of shelter occupied by the vast majority of Negroes in the North was generally similar to that occupied by other low-income families. It was inadequate shelter; much of it was substandard; little was in desirable surroundings; often it was in close proximity to or a part of the areas of vice. But it was not unlike the sort of housing which American cities in the North offered to all poor groups, although it was usually in the least desirable segments of the low-income areas, and often commanded higher rents than comparable shelter for whites. Both Negro and white dwellers in low-rent housing, once they had become urbanized or accustomed to America, dreamed of earning higher wages and moving out of poor neighborhoods. Both saw in the promises of America the opportunity for so doing. In some northern cities, the colored American with adequate means found that the dollar in the black hand did not easily command desirable housing. But in most places in the North, his number was small, and the majority of Negroes still believed that their housing problem was primarily economic.

A STRAW IN THE WIND

The treatment of the Chinese on the West Coast during the latter decades of the Nineteenth Century was a straw in the wind.

> Just as the national government capitulated to the South on the Negro question, as the price of the peaceful inauguration of President Hayes, so the national government capitulated to California on the Chinese question. The two sellouts were, so to speak, part and parcel of the same deal.[19]

They also were of strategic importance in sanctioning the spread of segregation. In the South, enforced separation of the races found its chief expression in public facilities; on the West Coast, it gave rise to the first American ghettos—Chinatowns, where ethnic islands of Orientals were soon to be established.

The significance of this development for other colored minority groups was not to become apparent until World War II, when the whites on the Pacific Coast pointed to the precedent of the "successful" residential segregation of Orientals as basis for a similar program to meet the housing needs of

[19] Carey McWilliams, *Brothers Under the Skin*, Little, Brown, 1943, pp. 83–84.

the latest migrant—the Negro. Yet, how familiar this description of the Nine-teenth Century Chinatown in San Francisco sounds to the student of the modern Negro ghetto:

> At the height of the anti-Chinese fury in California, Chinatown was pointed to as conclusive proof of the hideous character of the Chinese. It was the super-slum: "foul, uncanny, vicious, and a menace to the community . . . a sliver of space seven blocks long and three wide." Because of the enforced segregation with its resulting congestion . . . property in Chinatown became increasingly profitable and rents rose rapidly.[20]

NORTH VS. SOUTH IN COLOR

Several generations of northern Negroes had developed before World War I. Because of low-income and traditional limitation to lower-paid work, only a limited number took advantage of the growing facilities for higher education, but their rate of literacy was high and many of them took on the patterns of speech and behavior of the community in which they lived. The outlook of the smaller racial community of which they were a part was conservative, and the more ambitious stressed good conduct, personal achievement and education as the way to advancement. This attitude found support in the success of the few well-trained upper-class Negroes who migrated from the South to the North before World War I and managed to gain acceptance in the professions and industry on a basis approaching equality. Negroes in the North read with interest—and often a sense of removal—of the cruder forms of race discrimi-nation and segregation in the South. Only a minority of the Negroes in northern cities attempted to enjoy the more expensive forms of commercial entertain-ment; most could not afford to do so, but they pointed with pride to the fact that those facilities were open to them. Their children were admitted and sometimes welcomed to the public schools, and occasionally a colored woman would be employed as a teacher, a Negro man as a policeman, and an out-standing colored person appointed to a responsible job in local government (in places like New York, Philadelphia and Chicago, these tokens of recognition were more frequent than in the smaller cities of the North). The relatively few who entered the professions or opened businesses usually catered to white trade, since there were not enough Negroes to support them or enough race pride among the local colored people to inspire the latter to seek out Negro professional and business men.

The occasional recognition of an outstanding individual, rather casual acceptance by lower-class white neighbors, and rather free participation in the limited public facilities they patronized led most northern Negroes to assert that there was little race prejudice in the North. And while most northern

[20] *Ibid.*, pp. 99–100.

Negroes, except in large cities with concentrated colored sections, developed little race consciousness prior to World War I, they did often develop a superiority complex about living outside the South. At the same time, southern Negroes became defensive when confronted by the attitudes of those who lived in the North. They pointed to the educational achievements of many southern Negroes, the rise of professional men and women in the region, the success of Negro business in the South, employment of Negroes in skilled trades, and other evidences of the advancement of the "talented tenth" that Du Bois, himself a northern Negro at one time forced to work in the South, had stressed. Often it was observed that Negroes could spend freely in the North, but they had little chance to earn a living there.

Much of the discussion was defensive. Negroes stayed in the South because they had economic, family, social and cultural roots there. They did not go to the North in great numbers largely because there was not pressing demand for their labor in the industries of the region. When a strike made them attractive to management, they responded readily to the lure of higher wages. In their heart of hearts, and among themselves, many dreamed of leaving the South and divorcing Jim Crow. Despite, and often because of, these facts, many southerners resented the attitude of superiority of northern Negroes. They also disliked, in the spirit of true regional patriotism, the Yankee ways of northern Negroes....

ARRIVAL

The current housing problems of Negroes in northern communities have their principal roots in the Great Migration. The effects of this and subsequent movements of Negroes out of the South have been described as follows:

> The Great Migration, starting in 1915 and continuing in waves from then on, has brought changes in the distribution of Negroes in the United States. The proportion of all Negroes living in the North and West rose to 23.8 per cent in 1940, which signifies a total net migration between 1910 and 1940 of about 1,750,000 from the South. Negroes constituted, in 1940, 3.7 per cent of the total Northern population. Practically all of the migrants had gone to the cities and almost all to the big cities. In 1940, 90.1 per cent of all Negroes in Northern and Western states outside Missouri lived in urban areas. New York City alone claimed 16.9 per cent of all Negroes living in the North and West. If Negroes of Chicago, Philadelphia, Detroit, Cleveland and Pittsburgh are added to those of New York, the proportion rises to 47.2 per cent.... In most smaller cities in the North Negroes are ...absent, or the small stock of old Negro inhabitants has not been materially increased.[1]

[1] Gunnar Myrdal, *An American Dilemma*, Harper, 1944, pp. 259–60.

Long before Emancipation the North had become a symbol of freedom. But that alone was insufficient to occasion mass migration of the freedman to the area which had led the movement for his liberation. The World War I Negro migration was the result of no single factor, although the economic pull of labor-demand in the North and the push of an impoverished cotton agriculture in the South were certainly the most important causes. In addition, the rising educational level of Negroes in the South had made them more dissatisfied with their living conditions at the same time that it had enabled a larger number to appreciate the difference in desirability between living in the North and the South. Negro newspapers were important in spreading the word, painting in their weekly editions an alluring picture of life above the Mason and Dixon Line. Early migrants wrote back home in glowing terms about the greater freedom, superior schools and higher wages in the North. And, in addition, when immigration from Europe was interrupted by the war, industrial management welcomed the black worker—it even sent labor agents into the South to deliver the invitation on the spot. Once begun, the movement northward continued at an increasing rate until the recession of 1920, when its intensity lessened, only to be revived in 1922; since then, the trend has continued.

Consideration of the northern centers to which the colored migrants moved indicates the source of attraction and the intensity of the newcomers' impact upon the cities. With the exception of New York City, the centers attracting the largest number of colored persons from the South were primarily industrial; most of them were east of the Mississippi River, and in practically every case, the number of colored persons in these cities increased at least by 50 per cent between 1910 and 1920—and most of them came in during the last five years of the decade.

TABLE III

INCREASE IN WHITE AND NEGRO POPULATIONS IN SELECTED NORTHERN CITIES, 1910-20 [a]

	Negro population 1910	1920	Negro increase 1910–20 Number	Percentage	Percentage increase in white population 1910–20
Detroit	5,741	40,838	35,097	611.3	107
Cleveland	8,448	34,451	26,003	307.8	38.1
Chicago	44,103	109,458	65,355	148.2	21
New York	91,709	152,467	60,758	66.3	16.9
Indianapolis	21,816	34,678	12,862	59.0	31.9
Philadelphia	84,459	134,229	49,770	58.9	15.4
St. Louis	43,960	69,854	25,894	58.9	9.4
Cincinnati	19,639	30,079	10,440	53.2	7.9
Pittsburgh	25,623	37,725	12,102	47.2	8.3

[a] Source, *Negroes in the United States, 1920–32,* U.S. Bureau of the Census, 1935, Table 10, p. 55.

In order to appreciate the impact of the arrival of these tens of thousands of Negroes upon northern and border cities, it is necessary to consider the numbers involved and the relationship between the volume of migration and the size of the older Negro settlements. Detroit highlights both these factors. In a decade (1910–20) over 35,000 Negroes from the South poured into a city which had previously housed less than 6,000—an increase of over 600 per cent. The impact of 26,000 Negroes upon Cleveland during the same period was only slightly less. In Chicago, 65,000 colored people arrived in the same short period; New York received only 5,000 less. In both of these latter cities the size of the total population and the previous existence of large Negro populations mitigated somewhat the force of the migration. For Chicago, however, a 150 per cent increase in Negro population, involving 65,000 new-comers, was too great a change not to cause violent dislocations, and before the close of the decade a race riot—caused largely by the Negro's fight to get more living space—broke out. . . .

In the other cities included in Table III, and in a score of smaller places, the sudden arrival of Negro industrial workers and their families created new situations. Although the resulting problems varied in detail and intensity, there was a general pattern involving the reaction of the older Negro residents to the new arrivals, the response of the general community to Negro migrants in large numbers, and the resulting strain upon community facilities.

The colored workers who moved North during World War I were pre-dominantly from rural areas and most of the migrants were, for the first time, from the deep South. Many of them, especially the early comers, were of com-paratively low levels of training. Their background, traditions, previous work experience and living habits made adjustment to northern urban life difficult. Casual acceptance was complicated by their slow, southern speech, bad grammar (partially due to a widespread disregard for exact speech in the South), quaint phrases and the lower-class behavior of some. This latter characteristic was often accentuated by the aggressiveness of a few who felt that they were free at last.

Since they had been brought up in strict social isolation from white people and because they had been conditioned by Jim Crow laws and racial etiquette, the migrants hastened to look up other colored people. Many of these seemed strange. The older residents lacked southern hospitality; they af-fected a different pace of speech and gait; they were often distant. To the southern migrant, they sometimes seemed to be "acting like white." At the same time, the southern migrant was as baffling to the northern Negro as was the latter to the Negro from the South. Many northern Negroes became out-raged by the conduct of the new arrivals, fearing lest the latter's behavior would make things harder for them. At best, the older residents had never been too sure of their status in the life of the community. Their constant protests of no discrimination and no segregation were sure indications that the situation was not as bright as they tried to pretend to others and themselves. Their very rejection of the southern Negro complicated the problem and delayed the urbanization of the newcomer. More and more migrants arrived, and the older residents became increasingly apprehensive. Adverse community reactions to the newer element in the Negro population increased the insecurity of the older ones and they began to become even more distant.

> ... the Old Settlers were far from enthusiastic over the migrants, despite the fact that many of them were eventually to profit by the organization of the expanding Negro market and the black electorate. The [subsequent] Riot, to them, marked a turning point in history of Chicago. Even today, as they reconstruct the past, they look back on an era before that shattering event when all Negroes who wanted to work had jobs, when a premium was placed on refinement and gentility, and when there was no prejudice to mar the relations between Negroes and whites. As they see it, the newcomers disturbed the balance of relationships within the Negro community and with the white community. From their point of view, the migrants were people who knew nothing of the city's traditions, were unaware of the role which Negroes had played in the political and economic life of Chicago, and did not appreciate the "sacrifices of the pioneers." [2]

The white residents, too, became apprehensive. The sight of new and more black and brown faces in itself was enough to upset them. These were not only new Negroes, but they did not act like those they had become accustomed to. Some were noisy; some were dirty; some spoke in a peculiar fashion. And there were so many of them! At first the newcomers seemed quaint; then there were news reports of Negro criminals; management laughed and later sighed at the lack of promptness and the unfamiliarity with machinery which a predominantly rural population manifested. The Negro migrant was strange; soon he became the object of ridicule. Ultimately he was feared.

This fear developed chiefly around the issue of housing. After 1915, the extent of the Negro's demand for housing increased at a rate never before contemplated, and building construction virtually ceased with the entrance of the United States into the war. In such a demand and supply relationship, the problem of adequate shelter would have been difficult regardless of the color or nationality of the group in need. Considerations of color, of course, complicated the issue, at the same time that the housing crisis accentuated the color factor in the equation.

NO RESTING PLACE

At first, the new arrivals filled up the run-down housing which more affluent residents, black and white, had abandoned. Even though the most inadequate facilities were rapidly pressed into use, the supply soon was exhausted, and the pressure of the increasing numbers required expansion in other directions. The Negro areas, starting from the established colored sections, not only

[2] St. Clair Drake and Horace R. Cayton, *Black Metropolis*, Harcourt, Brace, 1945, p. 73.

filled up but began to spread. Whites began to flee before the never-ending stream of Negro migrants. Enterprising realtors, anticipating inflated prices, commissions and rentals, often manipulated the evacuation of whites by crying "Wolf."

In the process of this expansion, not only were tens of thousands of whites displaced from neighborhoods where they had long lived, but the wave of invasion was so strong that churches, community centers and other facilities were soon surrounded by a new racial group. Schools underwent a transformation in the color composition of their pupils; merchants found their clients made up of a new racial and often a lower economic group. All of this was a shock. It was sudden, too. It did not contribute to the mutual understanding between the Negro migrant and the white resident, who had long regarded each other as dangerous competitors in the labor market.

There were at least 26 race riots in American cities in 1919. Although the majority were in the South, reflecting the region's concern about the demands of the returning Negro veteran, a new wave of racial violence swept the North for the first time since the widespread riots of 1829–40 and 1880. In the North these mass widespread expressions of anti-Negro sentiment were the reaction to the tremendous migration of colored people. Principal factors in most of these outbursts were the tensions and animosities which had been engendered around the matter of housing. For intensity and mortality, the most outstanding of these riots was that in Chicago.

> Sixty-five thousand Negroes streamed hopefully into the city.
>
> Chicago did not prepare for their coming, nor were provisions made for them upon arrival. It did not occur to the authorities to do so. Many were the people who had been dumped into the city and left to make out for themselves. But in the case of the Negroes, the situation was a different one. Their attempts to make out for themselves in the matter of housing led to immediate conflict. Chicago, unthinkingly, expected the Negroes to stay in the "Black Belt" and the "Black Belt" was already overcrowded. Double up as they might in the squalid, congested slum area which had been conceded to them, with its ramshackle buildings, defective plumbing, and health hazards of every kind, they could not stay put. They had to overflow into the adjoining "white" neighborhoods where they were not wanted. And that they were not wanted was made plain by acts of violence and terrorism. . . .
>
> Chicago drew a color line and thereby created a problem, but Chicago did nothing to solve that problem.[3]

GET TOGETHER CHILDREN

Not only did Chicago and most of the other northern cities to which large numbers of Negroes migrated create a problem, they also set a pattern. After the

[3] Dorsha B. Hayes, *Chicago*, Julian Messner, 1944, pp. 259–60.

Great Migration, housing for Negroes in the North acquired and retained a peculiar racial characteristic. No longer did the Negro suffer from bad housing chiefly because he was poor; he had serious additional disadvantages because of his color. There were too few dwellings and too little space for a growing population. Since the vast majority of the unskilled and lower paid workers who entered many northern cities during World War I were Negroes, it was easy to identify color with poverty. Existing attitudes and spreading stereotypes about race accelerated the process. As in the case of the Chinatowns decades earlier, ghettos of Negroes were emerging; they were soon to be cited as justification for continuing colored Americans' restriction to them.

The residential segregation of colored people, which had been practiced quietly for years, was brought out into the open.[4] Whites boldly advocated its extension; older Negro residents in the North no longer spoke for the masses, and the new leadership readily admitted that there was segregation in living. In every northern city into which large numbers of Negroes had entered,

> ... the migration tended to increase the amount of segregation and to build up more distinctly Negro communities within the cities. ... Segregation on particular streets exclusively or almost entirely inhabited by Negroes was uniformly present, and generally there were also larger, well-defined Negro districts.[5]

The development of residential segregation in northern cities is well illustrated by Chicago. Expansion of living space for colored people in the city has taken two forms—gradual filtering-in of Negroes among the white population, and mass invasion.[6] Prior to World War I, a few Negroes would frequently move out into a new area. If others followed, and as the proportion of colored in an area became appreciable, the whites would move out, and the area would become solidly Negro. Before the Great Migration, over half of Chicago's Negroes lived outside the then small Black Belt on the South Side. Meanwhile, the Black Belt itself was growing, and its expansion into the surrounding area, which whites were voluntarily leaving, afforded shelter for the newcomers during the first three years of the World War I migration. The real trouble started when, with the cessation of home construction, there was a housing shortage throughout the city.[7]

In the meantime, two other smaller centers of concentrated Negro occupancy had evolved. One was on the Near North Side; the other an established area of Negro occupancy on the Near West Side. Both were on the road to deterioration when taken over by Negroes; both became islands of colored residents with limited possibilities for expansion. Morgan Park, far South, and a small colored cluster between it and the South Side Black Belt completed the list of areas of Negro concentration. Although all these areas have ex-

[4] Kennedy, *op. cit.*, p. 144.
[5] *Ibid.*
[6] Drake and Cayton, *op. cit.*, p. 175.
[7] *Ibid.*, pp. 175–78.

panded since World War I, it is in the South Side that most of the growth has occurred and where the vast majority of the migrants have been concentrated. And as early as 1920, 90 per cent of the Negro population was congested in that area.[8]

The typical strategy involved in securing living space for colored residents resembles a battle in its outline and in the events that precede and follow its execution.

> The advance [of Negroes into new areas] is somewhat like that of an army. A small outpost is thrown out ahead, and, if the terrain is favorable for occupancy by larger numbers, the mass advances. The only marked difference between the North and the South in this process of spread is that in northern cities the advance is made into areas already built up. It is a process of occupying houses previously filled by white families. In the South, however, the cities are smaller and there is more vacant space. These cities therefore usually expand into vacant territory.[9]

This strategy, with its military terms, has been taken over into the thinking of white Americans who speak and think of the "invasion" of a neighborhood by Negroes, the "infiltration" of an area by colored people, or the "loss" of a neighborhood. Thus, in the leading democratic nation in the world, the majority group "holds the line" against the "encroachments" of the darker citizen.

[8] Frazier, *op. cit.*, p. 95.
[9] Thomas J. Woofter and Associates, *Negro Problems in Cities*, Doubleday and Co., 1928, p. 39.

Charles S. Johnson

HOW MUCH IS THE MIGRATION A FLIGHT FROM PERSECUTION?

In the preceding selection Robert Weaver describes the earlier stages of the extensive Negro migration to the northern cities that has transformed the texture of Negro life and the nature of American race relations. In an interesting essay written during the early 1920's, the late Charles S. Johnson placed this northward movement in the context of the whole history of Negro migration in the United States. He cogently argued that both the southwestern movement of southern Negroes during the half century after emancipation, and the more recent northward migration, were rooted principally in the Negroes' search for greater economic opportunity.

Desire for more wages and more regular wages, for better social treatment, improved cultural surroundings; the hysteria of a mass movement; simple curiosity and desire for travel and adventure, and free railroad tickets, all have played their part in the divorcement of the southern Negro from the land of his birth.

Reasons are one thing; motives another. The former with all persons are likely to be merely a rationalization of behavior, while the latter usually play first role in inspiring the behavior. All Negroes (no more than all whites) are not uniformly sensitive to their social environment. And altho emphasis upon the pernicious nature of the social environment of southern Negroes should and doubtless will have the effect of improving it, such emphasis is apt to obscure what seem to be even more vital issues and more substantial elements of Negro character. After all, it means more that the Negroes who left the South were motivated more by the desire to improve their economic status

Charles S. Johnson, "How Much Is the Migration a Flight from Persecution?" *Opportunity*, I (September, 1923), pp. 272–74. Reprinted with permission of National Urban League.

than by fear of being manhandled by unfriendly whites. The one is a symptom of wholesome and substantial life purpose; the other, the symptom of a fugitive incourageous opportunism. Persecution plays its part—a considerable one. But when the whole of the migration of southern Negroes is considered, this part seems to be limited. It is indeed more likely that Negroes, like all others with a spark of ambition and self-interest, have been deserting soil which cannot yield returns in proportion to their population increase. The Census of 1920 indicated that the rate of Negro increase declined from 18.0 for the decade 1890–1900, to 11.2 for the next, and to 6.5 for the last. This does not mean that fewer children are being born, for actually more Negro than white babies per family are being born, but that more of them are dying. This desertion of the soil has taken three distinct directions: (a) urbanization—a species of migration; (b) quest for more productive lands; (c) transplantation to industrial communities, practically all of which are in the North. During the past thirty years, 1890–1920, there has been an increase in the rural population of 896,124 Negroes as compared with 2,078,331 for cities. The urban increase has been just about 100 per cent as rapid as the rural. In 1890, 19.8 per cent of the Negro population lived in cities; in 1920, this proportion grew to about 40 per cent. In the Southern States, between 1890–1900, the rural population increased 13.6 per cent, and between 1910 and 1920 it actually decreased 3.3 per cent. The Negro population increase in southern cities, considered as a whole, has been greater than the increase in the North, considered as a whole, despite the half-million added during the last decade. Here, of course, is the economic factor at work, hand in hand with greater mobility, increased transportation, restlessness and the monotony and uncertainty of agricultural life ever against the allurements of the city.

The greater inter-state movements of southern Negroes have been further South and West. In 1910, 52.3 per cent of the migration from Southern States was to the area west of the Mississippi; while in 1920, after the tremendous migration to the North, 42.9 per cent were living in the Southwestern States as compared with 42.2 per cent living in the North and West. For 130 years the center of the Negro population moved steadily some 478 miles toward the southwest—from Dinwiddie county, Va., to northern Alabama.

This shifting is further evident in the instability of Negro population in southern counties. Between 1900 and 1910, for example, 33.5 per cent of the counties increased rapidly, 31.1 increased at a rate above the average, while only 3.4 per cent showed an actual decrease, and 9.8 per cent an average increase equivalent to the total increase of the section. In 1879 there was a migration, similar to the one which we now experience, to Kansas. This followed a depression in 1878. Some 60,000 Negroes left. In 1888–1889, there was a similar movement to Arkansas, which carried 35,000 Negroes. Arkansas, for example, gained, between 1900–1910, 105,516 Negroes, the largest net gain of any state north or south; Oklahoma gained 85,062; and Texas, 19,821; while all the eastern, southern and central states suffered a loss. The counties of most rapid increase in the South between 1910 and 1920 were those south of the region of maximum Negro population density in 1910.

It is further significant here that the white populations have been showing in general outline the same trend of mobility as the Negroes. For example, their rate of mobility was 20 per cent as compared with 16 per cent for the Negroes and they also have left the counties deserted by Negroes, taking the same direction of migration.

Had persecution been the dominant and original stimulus, the direction of Negroes during the sixty years following emancipation would have been north instead of further south.

As a working test, a rough correlation was made between counties of the South in which lynchings had occurred during the thirty year period 1888–1918 and the migration from and to these counties.

Of ten Georgia counties, in which five or more lynchings occurred, the Negro population increased in five. Of the other five, in which the Negro population decreased, there was a corresponding decrease in the white population in three, and an increase in the other two considerably less than the average. To use one example,—in Montgomery County, in which five lynchings occurred, the Negro population decreased from 7,310 to 4,348 and the white population from 12,328 to 4,768. If this were a measure of persecution, the whites are the greater victims.

In Jasper County, Ga., there were nine lynchings, the largest number for any county of the state in thirty years. The Negro population actually increased in this county between 1890 to 1920, while the white population during 1900 and 1910 actually decreased.

Or to take the State of Texas. Of the six counties with five or more lynchings, the Negro population increased in four and decreased in two. Of the two in which there was a Negro decrease, there was a corresponding but more serious decrease in the white population. In Waller County, the Negro population decreased from 6,712 in 1910 to 4,967 in 1920; the white population decreased from 6,375 in 1900 to 5,426 in 1910 and to 4,082 in 1920. In Harrison County, with the largest number of lynchings (16), the Negro population showed a similar increase from 13,544 to 15,639.

In the State of Alabama, Jefferson County, with ten lynchings, increased from 90,617 in 1910 to 130,211 in 1920—the largest recorded increase in any county; Dallas County, with the largest number of lynchings (19), lost only 1,246 Negroes, while Sumter, with no lynchings at all, lost 3,491.

In spite of a considerable progress by Negroes, the great bulk of this population is in an almost hopeless struggle against feudalism. In four of the most congested Southern States: Georgia, Alabama, Mississippi, Louisiana, containing 37,405,760 Negroes or over 36 per cent of all the Negroes in the country, 83.3 per cent of them are landless. The per cent of tenant farmers instead of changing over into owners actually increased in practically every Southern State during the past decade, while the per cent of owners decreased. Altho this was to some extent true of white farmers, the proportion among Negroes was just twice as great. The large plantation owners it seems are gradually taking over the land, thus reducing tenants, white and colored, to a state of un-relieved and helpless peasantry.

Cotton is a peculiar crop. Its nurture requires about seven times as many hands as other crops and only then for certain periods of the year. It does not yield readily to labor saving devices. It can be grown profitably only with cheap labor, and plenty of it, and Negroes have been the South's cheap labor. Immigrants are not welcomed because of their tendency and frequent ability in time to purchase their own plots of ground. As a matter of fact, small white tenants are not as desirable in the plantation scheme as Negroes; and if Negroes persist in leaving, the plantation system itself, an anomaly in this country and notoriously unstable, is doomed.

Knowing just why Negroes left the South and what they were looking for will carry one further toward making their adjustment easier. The thought of flight from persecution excites little sympathy either from the practical em-ployer or the northern white population among whom these Negroes will hereafter live. Every man who runs is not a good worker and from the point of view of the Negroes who have come, they cannot sustain themselves long on sympathy. It is indeed not unthinkable that the high mortality so con-spicuous in the abnormally reduced rate of Negro increase will be strikingly affected by the migration. The relief of over-population in certain counties of the South will undoubtedly give each Negro child born a better chance for survival, while, on the other hand, the presence of Negroes in cities exposes them to health education and sanitary regulations. The death rate of Negroes in northern cities, in spite of the fact that migrations there are principally of adults to whom death is more imminent, is not as great as in most of the Negro counties of the South.

Emma Lou Thornbrough

SEGREGATION IN INDIANA DURING THE KLAN ERA OF THE 1920'S

The Great Migration during and after World War I accelerated a trend toward greater segregation in northern cities, which had been evident for a number of years. By the 1920's Negroes were already barred from countless recreation centers, restaurants, and hotels. Many northern communities extended segregation to the schools. While Emma Lou Thornbrough's article discusses the situation in Indiana, her generalizations have applicability for a large part of the North. The KKK, which had substantial political influence during the 1920's, has been blamed for imposing racial barriers against Negroes. However, Professor Thornbrough suggests that although the Klan intensified anti-Negro attitudes, many segregation measures were adopted before the KKK came to power and, we might add, remained in force long after the KKK had been destroyed.

Hooded riders in the night is hardly an adequate image accounting for the flood of Jim Crow practices that were adopted after the Great Migration. Rather the basic stimulus originated among the men in blue collars at union meetings, and the men in white collars who, as Miss Thornbrough suggests, were members of such prestigious groups as the Indianapolis Chamber of Commerce and the Federation of Civic Clubs.

Dᴜʀɪɴɢ the First World War there began a mass migration of Negroes from the rural South to the cities of the North which was to have marked effects upon the character and institutions of these cities. The number of Negroes moving into Indiana was not as great as the number moving into the neighboring states of Ohio, Michigan, and Illinois, but in the years from 1910

Emma Lou Thornbrough, "Segregation in Indiana during the Klan Era of the 1920's," *Mississippi Valley Historical Review*, XLVII (March, 1961), pp. 594–618. Reprinted with permission of publisher and author.

to 1930 the colored population of Indiana doubled.[1] Hopes for economic betterment were probably the most important reason for the migration, but the desire for greater personal freedom, for political and civil rights, and for opportunities to educate their children also brought Negroes northward. In Indiana the newcomers found little of the legalized Jim Crowism which they had known in the South, but they encountered much prejudice and discrimination. Although there were no racial disorders comparable to the riots in East St. Louis, Chicago, and Detroit, the influx of Negroes led to a movement for segregation on a scale previously unknown. In these same years the Ku Klux Klan, an organization which was habitually a strong advocate of white supremacy, was also rising to a position of unprecedented power in Indiana. It is not unusual for present-day commentators to see a close link between these two developments and to conclude that the increase in segregation measures was due primarily to Klan influence. This is a relationship, however, which has never been closely analyzed, and before the nature of the Klan's role can be understood it is necessary to look first at the segregation measures as they were originated in the state in the years following World War I.

These measures were confined for the most part to urban areas, because it was there that the Negro population was concentrated. In an earlier period, Negroes entering the state had settled in Evansville and the other Ohio River communities; but by the time of World War I new arrivals moved farther north, to Indianapolis, in the central part of the state, or to the cities in the Calumet region, especially Gary. The largest number went to Indianapolis, where the colored population increased from 21,816 in 1910 to 43,967 in 1930 (when it comprised about 12 per cent of the total population of the city). A more spectacular increase occurred in the extreme north, where a steel empire was arising on the shores of Lake Michigan. The population of Gary, which was little more than a small town in 1910, had grown to just over 100,000 in 1930. In this same twenty-year period the city's Negroes had increased from 383 to almost 18,000—approximately 18 per cent of the total population. In the neighboring city of East Chicago, where there were only 28 Negroes in 1910, the number had grown to more than 5,000 by 1930. By the latter date nearly 60 per cent of the Negro population of the state was found in Indianapolis and the Gary-East Chicago area. Most of the remainder was in other cities and towns, census figures showing that over 92 per cent of the Negro population lived in urban areas.

Although the new arrivals settled in cities, most of them came from rural areas in the South, and an increasingly large number came from the Lower South. Before 1900 most Negroes migrating to Indiana had come from the Upper South, especially Kentucky, while a very few had come from the Lower South. By 1930, when the census showed that 67 per cent of the total

[1] In Indiana the Negro population increased from 60,320 in 1910 to 111,982 in 1930; in Illinois, from 104,049 to 328,972; in Ohio, from 111,452 to 309,304; in Michigan, from 17,115 to 169,453. United States Bureau of the Census, *Negroes in the United States, 1920–1932* (Washington, 1935), 9, 12, 15.

Negro population had been born outside of Indiana, persons from Kentucky still outnumbered by a large margin those from any other single state. In Indianapolis the number of Kentucky-born Negroes was only slightly smaller than the number native to Indiana. But in the Calumet area most Negroes came from the Lower South. In Gary in 1930 the largest single group came from Mississippi, and the second largest from Alabama. Each of these groups was substantially larger than the number born in Indiana. In 1930 more than 86 per cent of the Negroes in the steel city had been born outside of Indiana, and of these an overwhelming majority came from the South.[2]

The problems of assimilation created by the abrupt transition from a simple, rural way of life to the more complex patterns of city life were complicated by Indiana's long tradition of racism. In the pre-Civil War period the Black Code of Indiana had scarcely been equaled in its harshness by the law of any other northern state. In the years following the Civil War the adoption of the Fourteenth and Fifteenth Amendments removed most of the legal disabilities against Negroes in the state,[3] and by the time of the migration of the First World War era only a few remnants of earlier racial distinctions remained in the law code. One of these was a severe prohibition against marriages between white persons and persons with as little as one-eighth Negro blood. Another was the school law, which gave local school authorities the option of maintaining segregated schools or of allowing members of both races to attend the same school.[4]

In spite of the fact that there was little legal segregation, in practice there was little mingling of the races. In the larger cities Negroes were unable to find housing outside of well-defined areas, which were largely slums. Since 1885 there had been a civil rights law prohibiting discrimination in the use of public accommodations, but it was largely a dead letter. Negroes almost never ventured into a "white" hotel or restaurant, and signs announcing that the proprietor "catered to white trade only" were not uncommon. When Negroes went into a theater or concert hall they sat in the gallery. In the rural parts of the state there were many small communities in which a Negro was not allowed to settle or even spend the night.[5]

In Indianapolis, where the bulk of the Negro population lived, race relations were normally peaceful. At least there were few overt signs of antagonisms. The leading Negro newspaper, the *Freeman*, which was far from militant in

[2] *Ibid.*, 34–36, 44, 49, 53, 55; John Foster Potts, "A History of the Growth of the Negro Population in Gary, Indiana" (M. A. thesis, Cornell University, 1937), 6, 9, 18, 27; Powell A. Moore, *The Calumet Region: Indiana's Last Frontier* (Indianapolis, 1959), 252.

[3] See Emma Lou Thornbrough, *The Negro in Indiana before 1900* (Indianapolis, 1957), *passim*, especially 68–70, 120–27, 162–66, 233, 249. The Indiana constitution of 1851 absolutely prohibited Negroes from coming into the state to reside. Before 1866 Negroes were not allowed to testify in court in a case in which a white man was a party. Until 1869 Negro children were not admitted to the public schools.

[4] *Ibid.*, 266–70, 329.

[5] For example, one county history published in 1916 contains the statement: "Washington County has for several decades boasted that no colored man or woman lived within her borders." Quoted, *ibid.*, 225.

its editorial policy, frequently asserted that racial harmony prevailed, but some of its content seems to indicate that friction was avoided in part by the failure of Negroes to take advantage of all the rights which were legally theirs. One editorial admitted: "We have learned to forego some rights that are common, and because we know the price. We would gain but little in a way if certain places were thrown open to us. We have not insisted that hotels should entertain our race, or the theaters, rights that are clearly ours." But even the conservative *Freeman* insisted that Negroes could not give up the right to live where they chose.[6]

The rapid increase in Negro population created new tensions, especially in housing. The parts of the city which had been the Negro districts simply could not house both the older residents and the newcomers. As immigrants from the South took over these districts, older residents sought to buy homes in hitherto all-white neighborhoods. The largest concentration of Negroes in Indianapolis had always been just northwest of the downtown business area. After the war this area began to expand northward—toward upper middle class white neighborhoods. Property owners, faced with the prospect of Negro neighbors and fearful of a decline in real estate values, organized themselves into local civic leagues, which had as their chief purpose the barring of Negro residents. One novel device to which one group, the Capitol Avenue Protective Association, resorted was to try to isolate and humiliate Negroes who bought property by building spite fences on either side of the property. But a young Negro dentist, faced with this form of retaliation, obtained an injunction which prohibited the practice.[7]

Sometimes opposition to Negro neighbors took a more sinister form. When, despite warnings, a Negro family moved into a white neighborhood in 1924, a hand grenade was thrown through a window of their house. Following this episode handbills were circulated in an adjacent neighborhood, asking "DO YOU WANT A NIGGER FOR A NEIGHBOR?" The handbills appear to have been the work of a group which unabashedly called itself the White Supremacy League and which had as its objective not only barring Negroes from white neighborhoods but excluding them from most forms of employment as well. Members were bound by oath not to employ Negroes in their homes or trade at stores which employed Negroes.[8] This group represented an extremist

[6] *The Freeman* (Indianapolis), April 22, 1916. When there were signs of opposition to the use of the public parks by Negroes, the *Freeman* warned that it was wiser not to go to the parks in large numbers. It asserted: "What we wish is our right of enjoyment rather than to be in the parks at all times. If we are careful in not overdoing the matter . . . the right to go where we wish will not be opposed." *Ibid.*, August 12, 1916.

[7] Indianapolis *World*, May 6, 1921.

[8] The group was said to aim at securing the dismissal of Negroes from positions in the federal civil service and from employment by local government. *Freeman*, July 26, 1924. The president of the White Supremacy League wrote a long letter to the Ku Klux Klan publication, *The Fiery Cross*, justifying white supremacy. She insisted that she had no animosity toward Negroes but had a "marked respect for the negro who keeps his own kind, who does not display an anomalous desire for 'social equality'

element, but its president was also active in the Mapleton Civic Association, an organization which included in its membership eminently respectable businessmen. A printed statement of the aims of the Mapleton group frankly stated: "One of our chief concerns is to prevent members of the colored race from moving into our midst, thereby depreciating property values fifty per cent, or more." Members of the association pledged themselves not to sell or lease property to anyone except a white person. The agreement was reported to have worked so well that for three years no more Negroes had moved into the Mapleton area, and some who were already residents had moved away.[9]

Although private efforts of this sort met with some success in stemming the Negro tide, stronger measures were sought. In response to pressure from civic groups, including particularly the White Citizens Protective League, the Indianapolis city council enacted a residential zoning ordinance in March, 1926. Declaring that "in the interests of public peace, good order and the general welfare, it is advisable to foster the separation of white and negro residential communities," the measure made it unlawful for white persons to establish residence in a "portion of the municipality inhabited principally by negroes," or for Negroes to establish residence in a "white community," except with the written consent of a majority of persons of the opposite race inhabiting the neighborhood.[10]

The measure was sponsored by a Republican member of the council who said he had received petitions containing more than five thousand names asking for the enactment of the ordinance. The only member to oppose it was a Democrat, who insisted that it was unconstitutional and violated "the spirit of American institutions." More than eight hundred cheering, hand-clapping, stamping spectators crowded into the council chambers while the ordinance was under consideration. After the favorable vote the president of the White Citizens Protective League declared with satisfaction: "Passage of this ordinance will stabilize real estate values ... and give the honest citizens and voters renewed faith in city officials." [11]

The mayor, asserting that it was not the duty of the executive to pass upon the validity of an act of the legislative branch, signed the ordinance, even though he admitted that the entire legal staff of the city was of the

and who respects the white authority of the United States." *Fiery Cross* (Indianapolis), January 19, 1923.

[9] *Freeman*, March 1, 1924.

[10] *Journal of the Common Council of the City of Indianapolis, Indiana, from January 1, 1926, to December 1, 1926* (Indianapolis, 1927), 54. Persons who owned property before the adoption of the ordinance were permitted to reside in it and also to sell it, but if a Negro sold property to a white, or a white sold property to a Negro, the purchaser was not allowed to take up residence without obtaining the written consent of a majority of persons of the opposite race in the neighborhood. The term "community" as used in the ordinance was defined as every residence within 300 feet of the property involved.

[11] The vote was five to one in favor of adoption. Three members of the council, two Republicans and one Democrat, were not present. *Ibid.*, 77–78; Indianapolis *News*, March 16, 1926; Indianapolis *Star*, March 16, 1926.

opinion that it was unconstitutional. In a lengthy message justifying his action the mayor expressed the opinion that there was no intention to discriminate against either whites or Negroes in adopting the ordinance and that its "tenor" precluded either race from obtaining any advantage over the other. He went so far as to say that if critics would study the law with "open minds" they would "hail with delight this step toward the solution of a problem that has long caused deep thought and serious study by members of both races." [12]

Doubts as to the constitutionality of the ordinance arose because of its similarity to a Louisville ordinance which had been declared unconstitutional by the United States Supreme Court in 1917. Backers of the Indianapolis ordinance, who declared themselves ready to take a test case to the Supreme Court, were not unaware of this precedent, but were hopeful that in the years which had elapsed since the Louisville case the highest tribunal might have changed its mind. The principal reason for their optimism was the fact that the Supreme Court of Louisiana had recently upheld the constitutionality of a New Orleans racial zoning ordinance which had served as a model for the Indianapolis enactment. The court had held that the Louisville precedent did not apply because the New Orleans ordinance (like the Indianapolis ordinance) did not prohibit outright the buying or selling of property but merely restricted the right of purchasers to *occupy* property. They ruled that the ordinance was not discriminatory because it applied equally to whites and blacks and dealt with "social relations" rather than civil or political rights.[13]

The optimism of members of the Protective League proved to be unwarranted. By 1926 there was a vigorous chapter of the National Association for the Advancement of Colored People in Indianapolis, which was eager to take every possible step to invalidate the ordinance. The national office of the NAACP, which had won one of its first victories in the United States Supreme Court in connection with the Louisville case, was also interested in the situation in Indianapolis. Funds amounting to about five thousand dollars were quickly raised to carry on the fight, and a case which bears the signs of having been arranged with the deliberate purpose of testing the ordinance was soon on the docket of a local court. The case arose from the refusal of a Negro physician to fulfill a contract for the purchase of real estate in a predominantly white neighborhood. He based his refusal on the grounds that the zoning ordinance would prevent him from occupying the property. The judge who heard the case ruled in favor of the Negro, declaring the zoning ordinance unconstitutional in the light of the precedent established by the

---

[12] *Journal of the Common Council*, 1926, p. 82. The mayor was John L. Duvall, a Republican, who was elected with the backing of the Ku Klux Klan and subsequently sent to jail for violation of the Corrupt Practices Act.

[13] *Tyler v. Harmon*, 158 La. 439 (1925). On a second hearing the Louisiana Supreme Court refused to reverse its decision. *Tyler v. Harmon*, 160 La. 943 (1926). In the Louisville case, *Buchanan v. Warley*, 245 U.S. 60 (1917), the Supreme Court ruled that the ordinance violated the Fourteenth Amendment because it interfered with property rights without due process of law. The decision did not rest on the equal protection clause.

Louisville case. He held that the ordinance deprived a citizen of his constitutional rights by making his right to live in his own property depend upon the consent of other citizens.[14] Hopes of supporters of the ordinance for an appeal to the Supreme Court of the United States were dashed when that tribunal reversed the Louisiana Supreme Court decision as to the New Orleans ordinance.[15]

The successful attack on the zoning ordinance was the only significant legal victory in the fight in Indiana against segregation during the 1920's. On other fronts, and especially in connection with segregation in the schools, there were some serious defeats. In Indianapolis the movement for residential restrictions went hand in hand with a movement to remove Negroes from hitherto mixed schools. From the time that colored children were first admitted to the city elementary schools in 1869, the general policy had been to require that they attend separate schools, but there had always been a few schools with mixed enrollments. Inasmuch as most Negroes lived in all-Negro neighborhoods children had usually attended the school nearest them, but sometimes there were complaints that children were required to travel long distances to attend Negro schools rather than schools nearer to their homes. Indianapolis high schools had never been segregated. As early as 1872 a Negro student had been admitted to Indianapolis High School, which was later renamed Shortridge High School. Thereafter, although their numbers were not large, there were always Negroes enrolled in the school, which had the reputation of being one of the best public academic institutions in the country. In later years as two new high schools were built, Negroes attended them also. It was always the policy to employ Negro teachers in the all-Negro elementary schools, but Negro teachers were never assigned to the mixed elementary schools or the high schools.[16]

The growth of the Negro population after World War I and the consequent movement of Negroes into new neighborhoods led to demands for a more restrictive policy. Two principal arguments were used by those favoring segregation. First, they insisted that the presence of Negroes in the same schools as the whites menaced the health of the latter and that Negroes should be segregated to protect the white children. Second, they argued that Negroes would benefit from segregation—that in their own schools they would take more pride in their work, their scholarship would improve, and that they would develop more initiative. The latter argument, more than the first, dealt with intangibles, and proponents never made clear how segregation would

[14] National Association for the Advancement of Colored People, *Seventeenth Annual Report* (1927), 10. The case was Edward S. Gaillard versus Dr. Guy L. Grant, decided in the Marion County Superior Court, November 23, 1926. *Indianapolis News*, November 24, 1926.

[15] *Harmon v. Tyler*, 273 U.S. 668 (1927). In a per curiam decision the Louisiana court was reversed on the authority of *Buchanan v. Warley*. After the invalidation of the racial zoning ordinance, white property owners turned increasingly to the use of racially restrictive covenants, which continued to be enforceable in the courts until the decision of the United States Supreme Court in *Shelley v. Kraemer* (334 U.S. 1) in 1948.

[16] Thornbrough, *Negro in Indiana*, 332–34, 341; *Indianapolis News*, May 13, 1919.

bring about the desired results. Their conclusions, too, now appear to be completely at variance with the views of the Supreme Court in the segregation cases of 1954 and with a large body of sociological studies.

A resolution presented to the Indianapolis Board of School Commissioners in 1922 on behalf of the Federation of Civic Clubs was a forceful statement of the health argument and a revealing commentary on Negro housing. It pointed out that, while Negroes constituted only about one tenth of the total population of Indianapolis, about one fourth of the deaths in the city were among Negroes. "For years," it asserted, "the Marion County Tuberculosis Society has emphasized the care of incurable consumption among the colored people as the greatest social need in this city." Because crowded housing conditions made it impossible for a tubercular patient to be cared for at home without endangering other members of the family, a large number of cases of incipient tuberculosis were believed to exist among colored school children. For this reason the school board was asked to establish separate schools for all Negro children and to staff them with Negro teachers.[17]

At the same session a letter in support of segregation was presented to the school board on behalf of the Mapleton Civic Association and the White Supremacy League. The contents have not been preserved, but they were of such a nature as to cause the president of the board to remark that the letter "contained such statements as rendered it impossible to properly be received by the Board, without the reservation that its receipt was in no sense to be construed as endorsement on the part of the Board of the sentiments which it contained."[18]

In response to such pressures the Board of School Commissioners set up new boundaries for fourteen elementary schools for Negroes and required that Negroes attend them. Groups of Negro parents protested in vain. When the attorney for the school board ruled that under the law the children could be required to attend the Negro schools even though they had to travel long distances, two parents sought court orders to permit attendance at the schools nearest their homes. But in both cases the court upheld the right of the school board to carry out the transfer.[19] After these transfers, which occurred in 1923, elementary schools were predominantly all white or all Negro. The process of separation of the races was carried almost to completion in 1929 when Negroes were removed from three more schools.[20]

Before the latter date segregationists in Indianapolis had also been successful in removing Negroes from the mixed high schools and putting them in an all-Negro school. The demand for separate high schools was backed by many white groups. Among them was the Indianapolis Chamber of Commerce, which presented a petition to the Board of School Commissioners in

[17] Indianapolis Board of School Commissioners (Office of the Board, Indianapolis), Minutes, Book W, 227.

[18] Ibid., 226–27.

[19] Ibid., Book Y, 22, 85, 159, 185, 304–305. See also Indianapolis Times, January 14, 1957, for a later survey of these problems.

[20] Indianapolis Board of School Commissioners, Minutes, Book FF, 293.

September, 1922, setting forth the "necessity" for a "separate, modern, completely equipped and adequate high school building for colored students." [21]

This movement met with strong and bitter opposition in the Negro community. Various delegations representing Negro civic and ministerial groups appeared before the school board, while other groups sent written protests. A petition from the Better Indianapolis Civic League forcefully and eloquently presented the arguments against a separate school. Declaring that the public school system was the most powerful factor in American society for the "engendering and transmission of sound democratic ideals," it emphasized that "no one section of the population" could be "isolated and segregated without taking from it the advantages of the common culture." Since money for the public schools came from taxation of all the people it was "unjust, un-American, and against the spirit of democratic ideals that one section of the citizenship should subvert the funds of the common treasury to discriminate against another section solely on the basis of ancestry." [22]

The report which the board adopted on December 12, 1922, recommending a separate school, embodied a different point of view. It declared that the enrollment of over eight hundred Negroes in the city high schools showed a "laudable desire on their part and on the part of their parents" for an education, but that a "new, modern, well equipped high school" of their own would provide them with the "maximum educational opportunity" and the fullest opportunity for the development of initiative, self-reliance, and the other qualities needed for good citizenship. [23]

The movement for a Negro high school was closely linked with the movement to relocate Shortridge High School, which was regarded as the best college preparatory school in the city and which included in its enrollment a number of students from wealthy and influential white families. The school occupied ancient and inadequate buildings in an older part of the city, not far from a Negro slum area. That new quarters for the school were badly needed was undeniable, but the zeal of some of its patrons for a new building and a new location on the north side of the city was clearly motivated by a desire to get rid of Negro students, who constituted 10 to 15 per cent of the enrollment. In a report of a survey of the school, made by one of the leading women's clubs of the city, it was emphasized that one of the reasons for planning a new building was the fact that "there are numbers of colored students packed into crowded class rooms with the white children." The *Freeman* commented bitterly that it was "evidently thought that to call attention to the Negroes as mixed with white children would be the weightiest

[21] *Ibid.*, Book W, 396. The Mapleton Civic Association also worked for a separate high school. A statement of its accomplishments said: "Through our efforts the School Board has promised to provide separate schools for the colored pupils of the city, especially a high school, this season, and we believe this will be of assistance in segregating these people." *Freeman*, March 1, 1924.

[22] Indianapolis Board of School Commissioners, Minutes, Book X, 29, 50, 51.

[23] *Ibid.*, 64.

argument for action on the part of the School Commissioners." [24]

After the school board decided to build both a Negro high school and a new Shortridge at a new location, a delegation of whites appeared before it to request "in the interest of economy" that the old buildings at Shortridge be used for the Negro school, "thus releasing building funds for other construction projects." [25] But the school board, instead of acting on this suggestion, went ahead with the construction of a Negro school, which was substantially equal to new schools being built for white students so far as construction and equipment were concerned. The board no doubt hoped that the new school and the employment of Negro teachers to staff it would make segregation less offensive to the Negro community.[26]

But before the building was started, a group of Negroes, backed by the NAACP, brought suit to enjoin construction on the grounds that the proposed school could not meet the requirements of "equality" under the "separate but equal" doctrine. Lawyers for the Negroes argued that the new school could not be equal to the three Indianapolis high schools already in operation because no single school could offer the range of subjects—academic and technical—which were offered in these schools. To build a Negro school truly equal to the combined three schools would be so expensive as to be prohibitive. After the local court in Marion County refused to grant the injunction an appeal was taken to the Indiana Supreme Court. That court, sustaining the action of the lower court, held that the suit was premature—that the mere fear that the proposed school might not offer courses of equal caliber was no reason for not building it. If, after the school was in operation, a case arose in which a colored pupil was denied some "educational advantage accorded white children of equal advancement," then proceedings could be taken "to secure the constitutional rights of such a child." In the meantime, the court declared, an injunction would not be granted "merely to allay the fears and apprehension of individuals." [27]

As the new school, which was named Crispus Attucks after the Negro of Revolutionary War fame, was nearing completion in 1927 the Board of School Commissioners announced that it would be the policy of the board to require all colored high school students to attend that school.[28] The board,

[24] Report of the Women's Department Club, *ibid.*, Book Y, 321; *Freeman*, March 21, 1924.

[25] Indianapolis Board of School Commissioners, Minutes, Book Y, 319.

[26] The *Freeman*, June 28, 1924, objected to the location chosen for the Negro school on the grounds that it was in a depressed residential area, near a glue factory and the city dump. Such a location, it declared, would have a depressing effect upon pupils "already humiliated by the fact that they are being forced from rooms of Shortridge, Manual and Arsenal Tech solely because of color."

[27] *Greathouse v. Board of School Commissioners of City of Indianapolis*, 198 Ind. 95–107 (1926).

[28] Indianapolis Board of School Commissioners, Minutes, Book CC, 166. Negro groups protested when the Board of School Commissioners announced that the new school would be known as Jefferson High School. As a result the name was changed to Crispus Attucks, a name suggested by some Negroes. *Ibid.*, Book BB, 113.

in fact, followed this policy until the state legislature adopted a law in 1949 which required the desegregation of all public schools in the state.

In Gary, where the Negro population was increasing at a faster rate than in Indianapolis, the school segregation provoked a more militant response. In that city there had been a policy since 1908 of maintaining separate elementary schools for Negroes, which were staffed by Negro teachers,[29] but until 1927 Negroes were not required to attend a separate high school. Nearly all of the burgeoning Negro population of Gary was concentrated in the central part of the city, known as "the Patch." In that area was located Froebel High School, a four-year institution, with a racially mixed student body. Some Negroes were also enrolled for the first two years of high school work in two Negro elementary school buildings. A few Negroes—not more than fifty—were scattered in schools in other parts of the city.[30]

Racial tension was occasionally evident at Froebel, but no serious racial disturbances occurred in the Gary schools until September, 1927. These disturbances broke out not at Froebel but at Emerson High School when twenty-four Negroes were transferred there from a Negro school, known as the Virginia Street school. A few days after the transfer white students at Emerson went on strike in protest. About six hundred of them paraded down the main street of the city, some of them carrying placards which said: "We won't go back to Emerson 'til it's white." In spite of the fact that the school principal threatened them with expulsion the number of strikers grew, until by the third day over thirteen hundred were absent from classes. At a mass meeting of students the superintendent of schools and the vice-president of the school board declared that the Negroes must remain at Emerson for the time being, but implied that they would be removed when a new Negro high school could be erected—in two or three years. In the meantime the superintendent indicated that it would not be necessary to include Negro students in the social and athletic activities of the school. The members of the board of education, after a conference with the mayor, also gave assurances that the transfer of the Negro students was intended to be temporary, that there was no intention of making Emerson permanently a mixed school, and gave promises that no more Negroes would be transferred there.[31]

At the end of four days the strike was settled by what the local newspaper referred to as a "peace treaty" between the students and the school and city authorities. The strikers were not to be penalized and the city council voted $15,000 for the purpose of erecting a temporary structure for a Negro school. The appropriation was carried in spite of negative votes of the three Negro

[29] In 1910 the superintendent of schools, William A. Wirt, was quoted as saying: "We believe that it is only justice to the Negro children that they be segregated. There is naturally a feeling between the Negroes and the whites in the lower grades and we believe that the Negroes will be better cared for in their own schools. Besides they will take pride in their work and will accomplish better results." Moore, *Calumet Region*, 392.

[30] Gary *Post Tribune*, September 27, 1927.

[31] *Ibid.*, September 26, 27, 28, 29, 1927.

members of the council and over the protests of a group of Negroes who crowded into the council chamber.[32]

Plans to remove the Negroes from Emerson to the temporary building ran into a snag when the local branch of the NAACP secured an injunction to prevent the expenditure of funds for that purpose.[33] The authorities then changed their tactics and decided to make some renovations in the school from which the Negroes had been transferred in the first place. At the end of the Christmas vacation, in January, 1928, less than four months after the strike, all Negroes except for three seniors were removed from Emerson and transferred either to the Virginia Street school or to Froebel.

Efforts by Negroes to block the transfer were unsuccessful. One parent, with the backing of the local and the national office of the NAACP sought a mandamus ordering the superintendent of schools to readmit his daughter to Emerson. The lawyers for the Negro student tried to prove that the Virginia Street school, which she was ordered to attend, did not meet the state requirements for a four-year high school, but both a local court and the Indiana Supreme Court rejected their plea.[34] The segregationists won a complete victory so far as Emerson High School was concerned. In addition to transferring the Negroes back to the Virginia Street school, the school board rearranged districts in such a way as to provide that students who finished the tenth grade in that school would continue at Froebel instead of Emerson. As a final step, the city council appropriated $600,000 to build a high school for Negroes which would be equal in all respects to the other high schools. When completed this school was named Roosevelt and made an all-Negro institution with a Negro faculty. Froebel High School, which was on the same side of the tracks, continued to have a mixed enrollment and to be the only unsegregated school in Gary. Emerson, on the other side of town, remained all white until 1945, when another student strike, this time at Froebel, led to the abandonment of segregation throughout the Gary school system.[35]

Thus in Gary and Indianapolis, two major centers of Negro concentration, the decade of the 1920's saw impressive gains by the advocates of segregation. In the southern part of the state, where Negroes had first settled, the schools had always been completely segregated. A few northern towns, where the number of Negroes was small, moved toward segregation for the first time in this decade. One of these was Elkhart, where the total Negro population was only about five hundred. Other northern cities, including South Bend and

[32] Ibid., October 4, 1927.
[33] National Association for the Advancement of Colored People, Nineteenth Annual Report (1928), 17.
[34] State ex rel. Cheeks v. Wirt, 203 Ind. 121 (1932). The court pointed out that the Virginia Street school was but one of six elementary school buildings in Gary in which courses equivalent to the first two years of high school work were offered and that pupils were transferred from these schools to the four-year high schools to finish their work. This was held to meet the requirements of the state law.
[35] Ibid., 134; Federal Writers Project, Works Progress Administration, The Calumet Region Historical Guide (Gary, 1939), 54; Indianapolis Times, April 4, 1947.

East Chicago, where the number of Negroes was larger, never adopted segregation.[36]

It is difficult to generalize on the course of racial discrimination in institutions of higher learning, since the number of Negroes enrolled in them was small. At least one private institution is known to have adopted a quota system in the 1920's limiting the number of Negroes admitted. In the state universities there were no racial restrictions in admission policies, but Negroes were not allowed to live in the residence halls maintained by the institutions and were barred from a number of university activities. At Indiana University a house for Negro women erected with private funds was opened in 1929.[37]

Some of the same discriminatory pattern that developed in the public schools during the 1920's may be discerned also in the city regulations governing places of public accommodation. Although discrimination in such places was prohibited by law, it continued to be customary in the decade for Negroes and whites to patronize different establishments. One place where the color line was drawn for the first time was in the public parks of Indianapolis and Gary. In Indianapolis, Douglass Park was acquired in 1921. It was not officially designated as a park for Negroes, but the swimming pool and playgrounds which were subsequently built there were marked with signs which said "Negroes only." After the opening of this park Negro groups found it impossible to get permission to hold functions in the other city parks. In Gary, one park was divided into two areas with "separate but equal" recreational facilities for members of each race. Negroes were excluded from the only park in the area which had a beach on Lake Michigan, and as a result a group of Negro businessmen leased private property on the lake-front for a beach in 1926.[38]

These illustrations of segregationist practices, whether in places of public accommodation or in the public schools, are evidence of the increasing sharpness of racial discrimination during the 1920's. It was a period, at least in the larger urban areas of Indiana, when the color line seemed marked more indelibly than before. The question which remains is that of the responsibility of the Klan—the extent to which the segregationist measures may be attributed to its influence.

Of the strength of the Klan there can be no doubt. The Klan moved into Indiana in the years following the First World War. By 1923 there were klaverns all over the state, with a membership estimated at between a quarter and half a million. The Klan infiltrated Protestant churches, social organiza-

[36] Robin M. Williams, Jr., and Margaret W. Ryan (eds.), *Schools in Transition: Community Experiences in Desegregation* (Chapel Hill, 1954), 68–69, 118. In the cities with segregated school systems there were opportunities for employment for Negro teachers. South Bend, on the other hand, did not employ a single Negro teacher until 1950.

[37] Indianapolis *Star*, June 8, 1929. Residence halls at Indiana University were opened to Negro men in 1948 and to Negro women in 1950. Indianapolis *News*, April 23, 1959.

[38] Indianapolis *World*, July 18, 1921; *Freeman*, August 9, 1924; Moore, *Calumet Region*, 391.

tions, and politics. For a time it dominated the Republican party, which in turn controlled state government. But its heyday was short-lived. It collapsed in the midst of a series of disclosures which shook the complacency of Indianans, even though they were inclined to be fairly tolerant of wrongdoing in political circles. David C. Stephenson, former Grand Dragon and dominant figure in the Klan, was sentenced to life imprisonment for a particularly revolting sex crime. A few months later a whole series of public officials identified with the Klan had been accused of various kinds of malfeasance. Some of them escaped conviction but all were disgraced. Ever since that time politicians have frantically sought to dissociate themselves from any hint of Klan ties. Because the Klan was so thoroughly discredited there has been a tendency in recent years to make it a scapegoat and blame it for segregation measures which a later generation finds discreditable. The evidence in support of this belief, however, is tenuous.

In exploiting popular prejudices the Indiana Klan relied most heavily upon traditional fears of Roman Catholicism.[39] The theme which was harped on most consistently in the pages of the official Klan publication, the *Fiery Cross*, was the alleged desire of the Church of Rome to dominate the government and schools of the United States, a theme in which existing prejudice against foreigners was fully exploited. Appeal to race prejudice, in comparison to the appeal to anti-Catholicism, was relatively slight despite Indiana's long history of racial bigotry. In fact, efforts were sometimes made to convince Negroes that the Klan was their friend.

But white supremacy was one of the avowed tenets of the Klan, and part of the appeal to Hoosiers was the use of the well-known argument of the necessity of maintaining racial purity. One Klansman explained that in "selling" the Klan to prospective members one approach was to bring up the subject of white supremacy "in this way—not anti-negro, but to keep the black man black and the white man white." A full-page advertisement in the *Fiery Cross* from the Wayne County Klan declared that it unalterably opposed "contamination of the pure blood of the Anglo-Saxon race with an inferior nationality." A Junior Klan had among its ideals, along with "shielding the chastity of the home and the purity of our womanhood" and "the practical value of the Scriptures," a pledge "to maintain forever white supremacy." [40]

At the same time the *Fiery Cross* and Klan spokesmen frequently asserted

[39] Norman F. Weaver, "The Knights of the Ku Klux Klan in Wisconsin, Indiana, Ohio, and Michigan" (Ph.D. dissertation, University of Wisconsin, 1954), *passim*, especially 11–31.

[40] Deposition of Hugh F. Emmons, p. 377, in Papers Relating to the Ku Klux Klan and D. C. Stephenson (Archives Division, Indiana State Library); *Fiery Cross*, February 16, September 28, 1923. In a typical piece of Klan oratory, defending the fact that the Klan was open to white members only, one speaker declared: "We are not anti anything. We are just white. We are not only white, but you just bet your life we are going to stay white. Whenever a man goes to mixing God's colors he gets into trouble, and he is not only doomed but he is damned and they [sic] ought to be." *Ibid.*, December 6, 1922.

that they were not enemies of Negroes but were in reality their best friends. One editorial declared: "The fact that the Ku Klux Klan believes in white supremacy has furnished much propaganda for the enemy to use among the negro population, inciting hatred for the Klan in that quarter, although thousands of intelligent negroes realize the meaning of the sentiment expressed by 'white supremacy,' and are not excited by the slanderers of the Klan." It insisted that there were many cases "wherein worthy negroes have been materially aided in time of misfortune by the Klan." One form of aid cited was gifts made to "worthy" Negro churches. It was reported that a gift to the Edinburg Colored Baptist Church was "gratefully received by the secretary of the church, who knows that the Klan is not the enemy of the negro as alien propaganda would have his people believe." [41] The *Fiery Cross* insisted, also, that Klansmen were law-abiding and that they were opposed to lynching. In one instance, it was claimed, members of the Klan were responsible for preventing the lynching of a Negro accused of assaulting a white woman.[42] In spite of these protestations of good will, however, it was well known that processions of white-robed Klansmen sometimes paraded through Negro districts as warning to Negroes to be law-abiding and to "keep in their place."

Attitudes among Negroes toward the Klan were mixed. Because it was identified with Protestantism and was publicly opposed to sin, some Negro clergymen either praised it or refrained from criticism, but other Negro ministers were frankly opposed to it. Negro intellectuals generally were openly suspicious and hostile. Most disturbing to them was the power which the Klan displayed in the Republican party.

The identification of the Klan with the party of Lincoln created a curious dilemma for Negro voters. As a legacy from the days of Reconstruction, Negroes had always retained an unquestioning loyalty to the Republican party. In the Democratic party, which in the South, at least, was the symbol of white supremacy, Negroes were a rarity. The injection of the Klan issue into the 1924 election campaign created the possibility of a change in the traditional political alignment. In the May primaries the Klan-backed candidates on the Republican ticket were victorious almost without exception. No Negro Republicans were nominated, but for the first time in history a Negro Democrat was nominated as a candidate for the Indiana house of representatives. One Negro newspaper, the Indianapolis *Ledger*, was undoubtedly subsidized by the Klan, and its editor was active in support of Ed Jackson, whom the Klan backed for the Republican nomination as governor. In an effort to hold the support of Negroes the Jackson group attempted to promote a kind of Klan for Negroes —an organization called "The Ritualistic Benevolent Society for American Born Citizens of African Blood and Protestant Faith." Members pledged themselves to support the American government, the Protestant faith, "protec-

---

[41] *Fiery Cross*, July 6, August 31, 1923.

[42] This incident occurred near Culver, Indiana. *Ibid.*, May 25, 1923. In another instance it was claimed that Klan members protected a Negro minister in Hammond who was threatened by Catholics and foreigners when he sought to have a Negro church built near a Catholic church. *Ibid.*, December 5, 1924.

tion of home and chastity of womanhood," free public schools, laws punishing lynching, and immigration laws to check the influx of "undesirables" who threatened the jobs of colored workers. The organization apparently met with little success, and on the day of the primary the Negro vote was light.[43]

From the beginning the *Freeman*, whose owner and publisher, George L. Knox, had been active in Republican politics in an earlier period, was strongly anti-Klan. After the primary it declared: "The Republican party as now constituted is the Ku Klux Klan of Indiana. The nominees for Governor, House, Senate, and County offices with one possible exception are all Klansmen, in fact there is no Republican party." The *Freeman* called upon Negroes to support the Democrats; otherwise they would show that they were not worthy to vote. "The ballot is the only weapon of a civilized people and it is up to the Negro to use that weapon as do other civilized groups." [44]

Throughout the campaign the Democratic leaders in Indiana adopted an anti-Klan position. The Democratic state platform condemned efforts to make political issues out of race and religion. While not calling the Klan by name, it declared that the Republican party had been "delivered into the hands of an organization which has no place in politics and which promulgates doctrines which tend to break down the safeguards which the constitution throws around every citizen." The Klan responded by circulating a bulletin during the campaign declaring that the Democratic candidate for governor, Dr. Carleton McCulloch, was "antagonistic" toward the Klan and had "openly and publicly denounced the Klan," and should therefore be defeated.[45]

The Klan issue in Indiana attracted nationwide attention and aroused apprehension among Negroes in other states. During the campaign the *Freeman* asserted that because of the Klan, nationally known Negro Republican leaders refused to come into the state to campaign. At the national convention of the National Association for the Advancement of Colored People, James Weldon Johnson, the executive secretary, declared that the most important issue before Negroes in the coming election was the Klan. In spite of protestations by Klan leaders that it was not anti-Negro, he insisted that if the Klan gained political power the rights of Negroes would be endangered. In Indiana, he declared, it was the plain duty of Negroes to vote against Republican candidates who were "touched with the tar brush of the Ku Klux Klan." [46]

Members of the NAACP in Indiana made strenuous efforts to defeat the Klan-backed candidates and organized an Independent Voters League for this purpose. In October the NAACP and the recently organized League called a meeting in Indianapolis of Negroes from all parts of the state for the purpose of alerting voters to the Klan issue. At a session which several thousand Negroes attended it was voted to endorse the entire Democratic ticket.[47]

Some Negro clergymen were outspoken in their opposition to the Klan.

[43] *Freeman*, March 29, May 17, 1924; Indianapolis *News*, May 6, 1924.
[44] *Freeman*, May 17, 1924.
[45] *Ibid*., February 14, 1924; Weaver, "The Knights of the Ku Klux Klan," 206.
[46] *Freeman*, July 12, September 27, 1924.
[47] *Ibid*., September 20, October 4, October 25, 1924.

At the general conference of the African Methodist Episcopal Church, meeting in Louisville, Kentucky, a resolution was adopted condemning Senator James E. Watson of Indiana for endorsing Jackson for governor. In Indianapolis, the minister of the leading A.M.E. church was known to be a foe of the Klan. On the other hand, Negro ministers, who were traditionally active in Republican politics, in many instances continued to give their support to that party. Several A.M.E. ministers were listed as speakers by the Republican speakers' bureau. As might be expected, the Negroes most vocal in support of the Republican cause were those holding political jobs. Anti-Klan Negroes were bitter in their denunciation of those "Jim Crow" Negroes who continued to work in the Klan dominated Republican organization.[48]

Democrats tried to convince Negro voters that the real issue in the campaign was not between Democrats and Republicans but between Democrats and the Klan.[49] Republicans tried to hold the Negro vote by pointing up traditional political loyalties. Representative Leonidas C. Dyer, of Missouri, author of an anti-lynching bill in Congress, told Indiana Negroes that their real enemy was the Democratic party. "There is no such thing," he said in Indianapolis, "as a colored man being loyal to his race and at the same time voting the Democratic ticket." [50]

As the campaign wore on Republican leaders apparently began to feel concern over the possibility of a defection of the normally loyal Negroes. The director of the Republican state campaign bureau for Negroes told party workers that the Klan question had frightened Negroes. "The heart of the colored man is with you," he said, "but his mind is confused." The Klan itself was also apprehensive about the Negro vote. One bulletin from Klan headquarters warned that "the amalgamated enemies of the organization [Klan] are influencing the negro and foreigner to such an extent that practically the entire negro and foreign vote will be cast for the anti-Klan candidates. We must overcome this loss by seeing to it that all Protestant people support those candidates whom we favor." [51] Headlines in the *Fiery Cross* proclaimed: "Rome Dictates to Indiana Voters: Attempt Is Made to Stampede the Negro Vote." The paper accused the Democrats of "waging a war of hate, misrepresentation, coercion and party destruction with the hope of driving the Negro out of the Republican party and into the Democratic camp." "Roman agents" were said to be busily trying to create trouble at every Negro political meeting. But the *Fiery Cross* expressed confidence that Negroes were too intelligent to be misled. The agents of Rome, it said, "may control the Roman Catholic vote, but their task of driving like a herd of sheep, the negro voter into the McCulloch fold is too big for the Roman corporation. It can't be done." [52]

[48] *Ibid.*, May 17, September 20, October 25, 1924.

[49] This theme was used repeatedly by the Democrats. See, for example, Indianapolis *News*, October 17, 1924.

[50] *Ibid.*, October 16, 1924.

[51] *Freeman*, September 20, 1924; Mimeographed bulletin, October 25, 1924, in Papers Relating to the Ku Klux Klan.

[52] *Fiery Cross*, October 24, 1924.

In spite of these brave words there were marked defections among Negro Republicans on election day. In Indianapolis, Negro wards which normally were solidly Republican, now went Democratic.[53] But these Republican losses were more than offset by the large numbers of white Democrats and independents who voted the Klan-backed Republican ticket. The result was the election of a governor and other state officers who were known to have Klan ties. More than half of the members of the Indiana house of representatives as well as a large number of state senators were elected with Klan support, while innumerable local officials owed their victories in part to the Klan.

During the campaign Democrats had warned Negroes that if the Klan got control of the state government it would enact severe segregation measures, but no such measures materialized. In the 1925 session of the state legislature, in which Klan-supported members were in a majority, several measures were proposed against Roman Catholic influence in the public schools. But not a single segregation measure nor any other proposal to establish racial discrimination was introduced.[54]

By the autumn of 1925, when municipal elections were held in the larger cities in the state, the prestige and influence of the Klan were already badly shaken. The trial of D. C. Stephenson, former Grand Dragon, got under way at the same time as the fall campaigns. But in spite of Stephenson's disgrace the Klan had not yet lost its power in Indianapolis and Gary. In Indianapolis the Republican candidates for mayor and the city council were openly supported by the Klan. In the election of members of the Board of School Commissioners, which was held at the same time as the municipal election, a slate of candidates known as "the United Protestant Clubs ticket" also had Klan backing. Although the election of the school board was supposed to be nonpartisan, Republican workers as well as Klan members were active in support of the Protestant ticket. In the closing days of the campaign a huge rally was held at which the Exalted Cyclops of Marion County Klan No. 3 presided. Prayers and speeches were made on behalf of the Republican candidates for mayor and city council and the Protestant school ticket, all of whom were present.[55]

All of the Klan-backed candidates were elected. Negroes do not appear to have been aroused over the Klan issue during the campaign as they had been in 1924. Except for a few party workers, they showed little enthusiasm for the Republican candidates, but neither did they show much disposition to support

[53] Indianapolis News, November 5, 1924; Indianapolis Star, November 4, 1925.

[54] A bulletin issued from the office of the Grand Dragon of the Realm of Indiana, October 20, 1924, said that enemies of the Klan were importing Negro speakers, who were advising Negro voters that a Klan victory would mean that Negroes would be segregated or forced to return to the South. See Papers Relating to the Ku Klux Klan. The only measure mentioning race introduced in the 1925 session was a senate bill sponsored by William E. English, Republican of Marion County, which would have provided a training school in domestic arts for Negro girls. The bill passed the senate but not the house. Indiana Senate, Journal, 74th Session (1925), 132, 792; Indiana House of Representatives, Journal, 74th Session (1925), 751.

[55] Indianapolis News, October 21, October 26, November 2, 1925.

the Democrats. On election day the Negro vote was light, but the Republicans carried the day. Negro wards which had been Democratic the year before were once again in the Republican column. In Gary, as in Indianapolis, the Klan scored a victory. Floyd E. Williams, who was reputed to be a member of the Klan, was elected mayor, and five members of the Gary city council were persons nominated and elected with Klan support.[56]

There is a widespread belief that the Indianapolis school board elected with Klan backing was responsible for the segregation measures which became so controversial a part of the city's school administration in the remaining years of the decade. A recent book on desegregation in the schools says that "the Klan secured the erection of Crispus Attucks High School in 1927 and established it as a segregated school. In the same year a Klan dominated school board initiated the policy of transporting Negroes away from the elementary school in their neighborhood to more distant schools for Negroes." In a newspaper statement in 1957 the superintendent of the Indianapolis schools also placed the blame for segregation in the schools on the Klan.[57]

The accuracy of these statements is questionable in view of what we know about the development of segregation measures after World War I. Certainly the Klan did not "initiate" the policy of requiring Negro children to travel long distances to Negro schools. Negro parents were complaining about this policy before the Klan made its appearance in Indiana.[58] In September, 1923, as noted above, the policy of requiring elementary school children to attend segregated schools was greatly extended. In December of that same year the building of a Negro high school was authorized. These developments, of course, all took place before 1925, when the Klan-backed school board was elected. In 1923 the board was made up of members nominated and elected with the support of the Citizens School Committee, a group which in 1925 ran candidates in opposition to the Klan-backed slate; in fact, members of the school board who had voted for the segregation measures in 1923 were defeated by Klan-backed candidates in 1925. In 1923, moreover, the Indianapolis school board had been under constant attack by the Klan because of alleged Roman Catholic influence, especially because the president of the board was a Catholic. The *Fiery Cross* regularly published articles and editorials on this subject, charging that Catholic influence was impeding the construction of needed public schools. But during 1923 there was not a single item in the columns of that paper on the subject of segregation in the Indianapolis schools.

The Klan-backed school board elected in 1925 instead of initiating segregation merely carried forward policies begun by its predecessor. In 1927, when the Negro high school, Attucks, was completed, the board adopted a

[56] *Ibid.*, November 2, November 4, 1925; Indianapolis *Star*, November 4, 1925; Moore, *Calumet Region*, 556.

[57] Williams and Ryan (eds.), *Schools in Transition*, 50; statement of Dr. Hermann Shibler, in Indianapolis *Times*, January 14, 1957.

[58] See, for example, Indianapolis *News*, May 13, 1919.

policy which apparently had been intended all along, that all Negro high school students must attend this school. The action of the board in 1929 in removing Negro pupils from three mixed elementary schools was a continuation of an already established policy. By that year Negro leaders in Indianapolis, including the president of the NAACP, were active in a campaign to defeat the members of this board who were seeking re-election. Publicly, at least, they did not base their opposition on the board's segregationist policies but rather on discrimination against Indianapolis Negroes in the hiring of teachers.[59]

The fact that the Klan did not work openly for the segregation of the Indianapolis schools does not mean that Klan influence was non-existent. Since Klan membership and Klan influence were pervasive in the early 1920's, undoubtedly Klan views were represented in the Indianapolis Chamber of Commerce and other civic groups which worked for the separation of the races in the schools. By 1926, Klan influence no doubt contributed to passage of the racial zoning ordinance in Indianapolis and the segregation movement in the Gary schools; at that time the influence of the Klan was indirect and covert rather than direct and open. But throughout these years the mayors of both Indianapolis and Gary were reputed to be members of the Klan, and a majority of the city councils of both cities had been elected with Klan support.

Klan influence may have played some part in the tightening of racial barriers in the 1920's, but it does not appear to have been the prime mover. Actually, the rapid influx of Negroes from the rural South into urban centers of a state where there had always been a tradition of racism seems to offer a sufficient explanation of the demand for segregation. The same attitudes among the people of Indiana which caused them to embrace the Klan caused them to favor separation of the races. Although Klan propaganda may have intensified race feeling, it is still conceivable that the segregation measures which were adopted in the 1920's might have been adopted if the Klan had not existed.

[59] Indianapolis *Times*, November 2, 1929.

E. Franklin Frazier

THE GARVEY MOVEMENT

For hundreds of thousands of Negro migrants the Promised Land of the North stood exposed as a teeming, poverty-stricken ghetto. So great were the hopelessness and powerlessness that many sought refuge and escape in a world of Black nationalism. Marcus Garvey preached a message of race pride to shore up a sagging sense of self-esteem: Be Black, Buy Black, and Build Black. Believing that white supremacy would always dominate American society, he offered as a solution his utopian dream of wholesale migration to Africa. E. Franklin Frazier's article describes how Garvey succeeded in creating a social movement which tapped the bitter alienation of the slum-shocked Negro masses.

GARVEY, himself, could not have planned a more strategic climax to his career in America than his imprisonment in Atlanta. The technical legal reason for his incarceration is obscured by the halo that shines about the head of the martyr. There is a sort of justice in this; for if the government were to punish all those who use the mails to defraud, it would round up those energetic business men who flood the mails with promises to give eternal youth and beauty to aging fat matrons, to make Carusos and Galli Curcis of members of church choirs, and to make master minds of morons. Garvey's promises were modest in comparison. And, indeed, what does one ship, more or less, matter in an imaginary fleet of merchantmen?

There are aspects of the Garvey Movement that can not be treated in this cavalier fashion. It is those aspects we propose to set forth here. The writer recalls that when he was a child one could still hear Negroes express the hope that some Moses would appear among them and lead them to a promised land of freedom and equality. He has lived to see such hopes displaced by more prosaic and less fanciful efforts towards social betterment. When Booker Washington first appeared on the scene he was hailed as a Moses. This was

E. Franklin Frazier, "The Garvey Movement," *Opportunity*, IV (November, 1926), pp. 346–348. Reprinted with permission of the National Urban League.

chiefly an echo of the white man's appraisal and soon died down when the Negro heard a message of patient industry, unsweetened by any prospect of a glorious future. What has distinguished the Garvey Movement is its appeal to the masses. While Negroes have found a degree of self-magnification in fraternal orders and the church, these organizations have not given the support to their ego-consciousness that whites find in the Kiwanis and especially the Klan. Garvey re-introduced the idea of a Moses, who was incarnate in himself, and with his masterly technic for dealing with crowds, he welded Negroes into a mass movement.

Before considering Garvey and his work, something should be said of the people he had to work with. The social status of the Negro in America should make them fertile soil for a mass movement to spring up in. They are repressed and shut out from all serious participation in American life. Not only does the Negro intellectual feel this repression, but the average Negro, like all mediocre people whose personalities must be supported by empty fictions, must find something to give meaning to his life and worth to his personality. One has simply to note how the superficial matter of color raises the most insignificant white man in the South to a place of paramount importance, in order to appreciate how much support a fiction gives to one's personality. Yet American Negroes have been relatively free from mass movements. This fact should not be regarded as a further testimony to the Negro's reputation for a policy of expediency in his present situation. There have been other factors to take the place of mass movements.

Many American Negroes have belittled the Garvey Movement on the ground that he is a West Indian and has attracted only the support of West Indians. But this very fact made it possible for him to contribute a new phase to the life of the American Negro. The West Indian Negroes have been ruled by a small white minority. In Jamaica, the Negro majority has often revolted and some recognition has been given to the mulattoes. This was responsible for Garvey's attempt, when he first came to this country, to incite the blacks against those of mixed blood. He soon found that there was no such easily discernible social cleavage recognized by the whites in this country. Yet his attempt to draw such a line has not failed to leave its effect. The fact that the West Indian has not been dominated by a white majority is probably responsible for a more secular view of life. The Garvey Movement would find the same response among the Negroes of the South as among the West Indians were it not for the dominating position of the preacher, whose peculiar position is symptomatic of an other-worldly outlook among the masses. Even in the face of this situation foreign Negroes have successfully converted hard-shelled Baptists to the Movement in spite of the opposition of their ministers. This secular influence in the life of the Negro attains its true significance when viewed in relation to the part that preparation for death plays in the life of the black masses.

The Garvey Movement afforded an asylum, as all mass movements, for those who were dissatisfied with life for many reasons, which could in this case be attributed to their status as Negroes. Although most of his followers were ignorant, we find among them intellectuals who had not found the places in the world that their education entitled them to. Instead of blaming themselves,—and they were not always individually responsible—they took refuge in the belief that in an autonomous black Africa they would find their proper place. The black rabble that could not see its own poverty, ignorance, and weakness vented its hatred upon obscure "traitors" and "enemies," who generally turned out to be Negro intellectuals who had achieved some distinction in American life. There is good reason to believe that Garvey constantly directed the animosity of his followers against the intellectuals because of his own lack of formal education.

We have noted how the Garvey Movement turned the Negro's attention to this world. This was accomplished not only by promising the Negro a paradise in the future in Africa; but through the invention of social distinctions and honors, the Negro was made somebody in his present environment. The humblest follower was one of the "Fellowmen of the Negro Race," while the more distinguished supporters were "Knights" and "Sirs." The women were organized into the Black Cross Nurses and the men into the Great African Army. "A uniformed member of a Negro lodge paled in significance beside a soldier of the Army of Africa. A Negro might be a porter during the day, taking his orders from white men, but he was an officer in the Black Army when it assembled at night in Liberty Hall. Many a Negro went about his work singing in his heart that he was a member of the great army marching to 'heights of achievements.' " [1] Yet these extravagant claims were based upon the deep but unexpressed conviction in the minds of most Negroes that the white man has set certain limits to their rise in this country.

In his half acknowledged antagonism towards Negro preachers and the soporific religion they served the masses, Garvey did not ignore its powerful influence. In fact he endeavored to fuse the religious experience of the Negro with his own program. The symbolism associated with Christmas was made the sign of the birth of a Negro nation among the nations of the earth; while Easter became the symbol of a resurrected race. Nor did he overlook the opportunity to make his position appear similar to that of Jesus. According to him, his own people, especially the recognized Negro leaders, had incited the American authorities against him just as the Jews had incited the Roman authorities against Jesus. In this connection the idea of gaining a lost paradise appears as it does in most mass movements. The "Redemption of Africa" became the battle cry. To his followers he trumpeted: "No one knows when the hour of Africa's redemption cometh. It is in the wind. It is coming one day like a storm. It will be here. When that day comes, all Africa will stand together." [2]

The messianic element in this movement is not altogether lacking, although it does not stand out prominently. When Garvey entered the prison

[1] "Garvey: A Mass Leader," *The Nation*, Vol. CXXIII, No. 189 by the writer.
[2] *Ibid.*

in Atlanta, besides commending his wife to the care of his followers, he spoke of the possibility of his death as only a messiah would speak. Under the caption, "If I Die In Atlanta," he bade his followers:

"Look for me in the whirlwind or the storm, look for me all around you, for, with God's grace, I shall come and bring with me the countless millions of black slaves who have died in America and the West Indies and the millions in Africa to aid you in the fight for liberty, freedom and life." [3]

By this promise Garvey raised himself above mortals and made himself the Redeemer of the Black World.

Many people are at a loss to understand how Garvey was able to attract supporters to a scheme which was manifestly infeasible and has been discredited by continued exposés of corruption and bickering within the organization. But such tests of reasonableness can not be applied to schemes that attract crowds. Crowds, it has been said, never learn by experience. The reason is clear, for the crowd satisfies its vanity and longings in the beliefs it cherishes. Not only because of their longing for something to give meaning to their lives, but because of the scepticism about them, Negroes do not find the satisfaction that their fathers found in the promise of heavenly abode to compensate for the woes of this world. They therefore offer a fine field for charlatans and fakirs of every description. This Movement has attracted many such men who give the black crowds the escape they are seeking. The work carried on by the National Association for the Advancement of Colored People, which has been the subject of so many attacks by Garvey, has never attracted the crowd because it does not give the crowd an opportunity to show off in colors, parades, and self-glorification. The Association appeals to intelligent persons who are trying to attain tangible goals through cooperation. The same could be said of the Urban League. Dean Kelly Miller, it is said, once made the shrewd observation that the Negro pays for what he wants and begs for what he needs. This applies here as elsewhere. Those who support this Movement pay for it because it gives them what they want—the identification with something that makes them feel like somebody among white people who have said they were nobody.

Before concluding this brief interpretive sketch, we must add a few observations. Doubtless the World War with its shibboleths and stirrings of subject minorities offered a volume of suggestion that facilitated the Garvey Movement. Another factor that helped the Movement was the urbanization of the Negro that took place about the time. It is in the cities that mass movements are initiated. When the Negro lived in a rural environment he was not subject to mass suggestion except at the camp meeting and revival.

One of the most picturesque phases of the Movement has been the glorification of blackness which has been made an attribute of the celestial hierarchy. To most observers this last fact has been simply a source of merriment. But Garvey showed a knowledge of social psychology when he invoked a black god to guide the destiny of the Negro. The God of Israel served the

[3] *The Negro World*, February 14, 1925.

same purpose. Those whites who said they would rather go to hell than to a heaven presided over by a black god, show what relation the average man's god must bear to him. The intellectual can laugh, if he will; but let him not forget the pragmatic value of such a symbol among the type of people Garvey was dealing with.

The question is often asked, "Is Garvey sincere?" The same question might be asked of the McGee brothers of the Kentucky Revival and of evangelists in general. Although Garvey's appeal has been more permanent, his methods have been in many respects those of the evangelist. Just because evangelists as a rule are well fed and free from material wants, it would be uncritical to put them all down as common swindlers. Likewise, with the evidence we have, we can not classify Garvey as such. He has failed to deal realistically with life as most so-called cranks, but he has initiated a mass movement among Negroes because it appealed to something that is in every crowd-minded man.

Sterling Brown

NEGRO FOLK EXPRESSION: SPIRITUALS, SECULARS, BALLADS AND WORK SONGS

One of the products of the migration to the northern cities was the literary and artistic awakening known as the Harlem Renaissance. The young artists and writers rejected the notion that Negroes should seek to emulate the way of life of white Americans, and glorified the rich and distinctive subculture of the Negro masses.

One of the youthful men who was dissatisfied with the genteel, bourgeois culture of his upper-class forebears and joined the militant and artistically radical "New Negroes" of the 1920's was Sterling Brown. A scholar as well as a poet, Brown became an authority on religious and secular music of the black masses. His charming essay on "Negro Folk Expression" deals mainly with the creations of the rural poor and evaluates the impact of urbanization upon the culture of the oppressed masses who migrated to the large cities. It also reflects the interests of the young intellectuals who came to maturity during the 1920's.

THE SPIRITUALS

THOMAS WENTWORTH HIGGINSON, one of the very first to pay respectful attention to the Negro spiritual, called it a startling flower growing in dark soil. Using his figure, we might think of this flower as a hybrid, as the American Negro is a hybrid. And though flowers of its family grew in Africa, Europe, and other parts of America, this hybrid bloom is uniquely beautiful.

A large amount of recent scholarship has proved that the spirituals are not African, either in music or meaning (a claim made once with partisan zeal),

Sterling Brown, "Negro Folk Expression: Spirituals, Seculars, Ballads and Work Songs," *Phylon*, XIV (First Quarter, 1953), pp. 45–61. Reprinted with the permission of the publisher.

that the American Negro was influenced by the religious music of rural America from the Great Awakening on, that at the frontier camp meetings he found to his liking many tunes both doleful and brisk, and that he took over both tunes and texts and refashioned them more to his taste. But careful musicologists, from studying phonograph records of folk singing rather than, as earlier, inadequate, conventional notations of "art" spirituals, are coming around to the verdict of Alan Lomax that "no amount of scholarly analysis and discussion can ever make a Negro spiritual sound like a white spiritual."

A new music, yes. But what of the poetry? Scholars have discovered that many phrases, lines, couplets, and even whole stanzas and songs, once thought to be Negro spirituals, were popular in white camp meetings. A full comparison of the words of white and Negro spirituals is out of the question here. It might be said that some of the parallels turn out to be tangents. Thus, "At his table we'll sit down, Christ will gird himself and serve us with sweet manna all around" is supposed to be the white source of "Gwine to sit down at the welcome table, gwine to feast off milk and honey," and "To hide yourself in the mountain top, to hide yourself from God" is supposed to have become "Went down to the rocks to hide my face, the rocks cried out no hiding place." Even when single lines were identical, the Negro made telling changes in the stanza. Briefly, the differences seem to result from a looser line, less tyrannized over by meter and rhyme, with the accent shifted unpredictably, from a more liberal use of refrains, and from imagery that is terser and starker. The improvising imagination seems freer. Some of the changes of words arose from confusion: "Paul and Silas bound in jail" has been sung: "bounded Cyrus born in jail"; and "I want to cross over into camp-ground" has been sung as "I want to cross over in a calm time." Some of the changes, however, result from the truly poetic imagination at work on material deeply felt and pondered: "Tone de bell easy, Jesus gonna make up my dying bed." "I'll lie in de grave and stretch out my arms, when I lay dis body down." "Steal away, steal away, steal away to Jesus. Steal away, steal away home; I ain't got long to stay here."

Many spirituals tell of the joys of Christian fellowship. "Ain't you glad you got out de wilderness?" "I been bawn of God, no condemnation; no condemnation in my soul." "I been down in the valley; Never turn back no mo'."

> I went down in the valley to pray
> My soul got happy and I stayed all day.

"Just like a tree, planted by the waters, I shall not be moved." Belonging to the glorious company, the slaves found comfort, protection. Sinners would find no hole in the ground, but those of the true faith had "a hiding place, around the throne of God." "I got a home in that rock, don't you see?" "In God's bosom gonna be my pillow." Their souls were witnesses for their Lord. "Done done my duty; Got on my travelin' shoes." "I done crossed the separatin' line; I done left the world behind."

The world could be left behind in visions.

> I've got two wings for to veil my face
> I've got two wings for to fly away....

Gabriel and his trumpet caught the imagination. "Where will you be when the first trumpet sounds; sounds so loud its gonna wake up the dead?" "O My Lord, what a morning, when the stars begin to fall!" "When the sun refuse to shine, when the moon goes down in blood!" In that great getting up morning, "you see the stars a falling, the forked lightning, the coffins bursting, the righteous marching." "The blind will see, the dumb will talk; the deaf will hear; the lame will walk." This apocalyptic imagery, clear to the initiated, is a release, a flight, a message in code, frequently used by oppressed people.

> Then they'll cry out for cold water
> While the Christians shout in glory
> Saying Amen to their damnation
> Fare you well, fare you well.

It was not only to the far-off future of Revelations that the dreams turned. Heaven was a refuge too. In contrast to the shacks of slave row and the slums of the cities, to the work clothes and the unsavory victuals, would be the throne of God, the streets of gold, the harps, the robes, the milk and honey.

> A-settin' down with Jesus
> Eatin' honey and drinkin' wine
> Marchin' round de throne
> Wid Peter, James, and John....

But the dream was not always so extravagant. Heaven promised simple satisfactions, but they were of great import to the slaves. Shoes for instance, as well as a harp. Heaven meant home: "I'm gonna feast at de welcome table." Heaven meant rest: just sitting down was one of the high privileges often mentioned. And acceptance as a person: "I'm going to walk and talk with Jesus." Moreover, the Heaven of escape is not a Heaven bringing forgetfulness of the past. The River Jordan is not Lethe.

> I'm gonna tell God all my troubles,
> When I get home ...
> I'm gonna tell him the road was rocky
> When I get home.

The makers of the spirituals, looking toward heaven, found their triumphs there. But they did not blink their eyes to the troubles here. As the best expression of the slaves' deepest thoughts and yearnings, they speak with convincing finality against the legend of contented slavery. This world was not their home. "Swing low, sweet chariot, coming for to carry me home." They never tell of joy in the "good old days." The only joy in the spirituals is in dreams of escape.

That the spirituals were otherworldly, then, is less than half-truth. In more exact truth, they tell of this life, of "rollin' through an unfriendly world." "Oh, bye and bye, bye and bye, I'm going to lay down this heavy load." "My way is cloudy." "Oh, stand the storm, it won't be long, we'll anchor by and by." "Lord keep me from sinking down." And there is that couplet of tragic intensity:

> Don't know what my mother wants to stay here fuh,
> Dis ole world ain't been no friend to huh.

Out of the workaday life came figures of speech: "Keep a-inchin' along lak a po' inch-worm"; such a couplet as:

> Better mind that sun and see how she run
> And mind! Don't let her catch you wid yo' work undone.

And such an allegory: "You hear de lambs a-crying; oh, shepherd, feed-a my sheep." Out of folk wisdom came: "Oh de ole sheep, they know de road; young lambs gotta find de way," and "Ole Satan is like a snake in the grass."

> Sister, you better watch how you walk on the cross
> Yo' foot might slip, and yo' soul git lost.

The spirituals make an anthology of Biblical heroes and tales, from Genesis where Adam and Eve are in the Garden, picking up leaves, to John's calling the roll in Revelations. There are numerous gaps, of course, and many repetitions. Certain figures are seen in an unusual light; Paul, for instance, is generally bound in jail with Silas, to the exclusion of the rest of his busy career. Favored heroes are Noah, chosen of God to ride down the flood; Samson, who tore those buildings down; Joshua, who caused the walls of Jericho to fall (when the rams' lambs' sheephorns began to blow); Jonah, symbol of hard luck changed at last; and Job, the man of tribulations who still would not curse his God. These are victors over odds. But losers, the wretched and despised, also serve as symbols. There is Lazarus, "poor as I, don't you see?" who went to heaven, in contrast to "Rich man Dives, who lived so well; when he died he found a home in hell." And finally there is Blind Barnabas, whose tormented cry found echoes in slave cabins down through the long, dark years:

> Oh de blind man stood on de road an' cried
> Cried, "Lord, oh, Lord, save-a po' me!"

In telling the story of Jesus, spirituals range from the tender "Mary had a little baby" and "Little Boy, how old are you" to the awe-inspiring "Were You There" and "He Never Said A Mumbalin' Word." Jesus is friend and brother, loving counselor, redeemer, Lord and King. The Negro slave's picturing of Calvary in such lines as

> Dey whupped him up de hill . . .
> Dey crowned his head with thorns . . .
> Dey pierced him in de side,
> An' de blood come a-twinklin' down;
> But he never said a mumbalin' word;
> Not a word; not a word.

belongs with the greatest Christian poetry. It fused belief and experience; it surged up from most passionate sympathy and understanding.

Some scholars who have found parallels between the words of Negro and white spirituals would have us believe that when the Negro sang of freedom, he meant only what the whites meant, namely freedom from sin. Free, individualistic whites on the make in a prospering civilization, nursing the American dream, could well have felt their only bondage to be that of sin, and freedom to be religious salvation. But with the drudgery, the hardships, the auction-block, the slave-mart, the shackles, and the lash so literally present in the Negro's experience, it is hard to imagine why for the Negro they would remain figurative. The scholars certainly do not make it clear, but rather take refuge in such dicta as: "The slave did not contemplate his low condition." Are we to believe that the slave singing "I been rebuked, I been scorned; done had a hard time sho's you bawn," referred to his being outside of the true religion? Ex-slaves, of course, inform us differently. The spirituals speak up strongly for freedom not only from sin (dear as that freedom was to the true believer) but from physical bondage. Those attacking slavery as such had to be as rare as anti-Hitler marching songs in occupied France. But there were oblique references. Frederick Douglass has told us of the double-talk of the spirituals: Canaan, for instance, stood for Canada; and over and beyond hidden satire the songs also were grapevines for communications. Harriet Tubman, herself called the Moses of her people, has told us that *Go Down, Moses* was tabu in the slave states, but the people sang it nonetheless.

Fairly easy allegories identified Egypt-land with the South, Pharaoh with the masters, the Israelites with themselves and Moses with their leader. "So Moses smote de water and the children all passed over; Children, ain't you glad that they drowned that sinful army?"

> Oh, Mary don't you weep, don't you moan;
> Pharaoh's army got drownded,
> Oh, Mary, don't you weep.

Some of the references were more direct:

> Didn't my Lord deliver Daniel,
> And why not every man?

In the wake of the Union army and in the contraband camps spirituals of freedom sprang up suddenly. The dry grass was ready for the quickening flame. Some celebrated the days of Jubilo: "O Freedom; O Freedom!, And before I'll be a slave, I'll be buried in my grave! And go home to my Lord and be free." Some summed up slavery starkly: "No more driver's lash for me, no more, no more. . . . No more peck of corn for me; Many thousand go." "Slavery's chain done broke at last; gonna praise God till I die." And in all likelihood old spirituals got new meanings: "Ain't you glad you got out the wilderness?" "In That Great Gittin' Up Morning!" "And the moon went down in blood."

The best of the spirituals are, in W. E. B. DuBois's phrase, "the sorrowsongs of slavery." In spite of indifference and resentment from many educated and middle class Negroes, the spirituals are still sung, circulated, altered and created by folk Negroes. Some of the new ones, started in the backwoods, have a crude charm; for instance Joseph and Mary in Jerusalem "to pay their poll-taxes," find the little boy Jesus in the temple confounding with his questions the county doctor, lawyer, and judge. Some of them mix in more recent imagery: "Death's little black train is coming!" "If I have my ticket, Lord, can I ride?" and a chant of death in which the refrain "Same train. Same train" is repeated with vivid effect:

> Same train took my mother.
> Same train. Same train.

Some use modern inventions with strained incongruity: "Jus' call up Central in Heaven, tell Jesus to come to the phone," and "Jesus is my aeroplane, He holds the whole world in his hands"; and "Standing in the Safety Zone." But there is power in some of the new phrasing:

> God's got your number; He knows where you live;
> Death's got a warrant for you.

Instead of college choirs, as earlier, today it is groups closer to the folk like the Golden Gates, the Silver Echoes, the Mitchell Christian Singers, the Coleman Brothers, the Thrasher Wonders and the Original Harmony Kings, who carry the spirituals over the land. These groups and soloists like the Georgia Peach, Mahalia Jackson, Marie Knight and Sister Rosetta Tharpe, once churched for worldly ways but now redeemed, are extremely popular in churches, concert halls, and on records. They swing the spirituals, using a more pronounced rhythm and jazz voicing (some show-groups, alas, imitate even the Mills Brothers and the Ink Spots). Even the more sincere singers, however, fight the devil by using what have been considered the devil's weapons. Tambourines, cymbals, trumpets and even trombones and bass fiddles are now accepted in some churches. The devil has no right to all that fine rhythm, so a joyful noise is made unto the Lord with bounce and swing.

The Gospel Songs, sung "out of the book" as signs of "progress," are displacing the spirituals among the people. These are even more heavily influenced by jazz and the blues. One of the most popular composers of Gospel Songs is Thomas Dorsey, who once played barrelhouse piano under the alias of Georgia Tom. Many lovers of the older spirituals disdain the Gospel Songs as cheap and obvious. But this new urban religious folk music should not be dismissed too lightly. It is vigorously alive with its own musical values, and America turns no unwilling ear to it. And to hear some fervent congregations sing "Just a Closer Walk With Thee," "He Knows How Much You Can Bear," and "We Sure Do Need Him Now" can be unforgettable musical experiences. In sincerity, musical manner, and spirit, they are probably not so remote from the old prayer songs in the brush arbors.

SECULARS AND BALLADS

The slaves had many other moods and concerns than the religious; indeed some of these ran counter to the spirituals. Irreverent parodies of religious songs, whether coming from the black-face minstrelsy or from tough-minded cynical slaves, passed current in the quarters. Other-worldliness was mocked: "I don't want to ride no golden chariot; I don't want no golden crown; I want to stay down here and be, Just as I am without one plea." "Live a humble to the Lord" was changed to "Live a humbug." Bible stories, especially the creation, the fall of Man, and the flood, were spoofed. "Reign, Master Jesus, reign" became "Rain, Mosser, rain hard! Rain flour and lard and a big hog head, Down in my back yard." After couplets of nonsense and ribaldry, slaves sang with their fingers crossed, or hopeless in defeat: "Po' mourner, you shall be free, when de good Lord set you free."

Even without the sacrilege, many secular songs were considered "devil-tunes." Especially so were the briskly syncopated lines which, with the clapping of hands and the patting of feet, set the beat for swift, gay dancing. "Juba dis, Juba dat; Juba skin a yeller cat; Juba, Juba!" Remnants of this syncopation are today in such children's play songs as

"Did you feed my cow?" "Yes, Maam."
"Will you tell-a me how?" "Yes, Maam."
"Oh, what did you give her?" "Cawn and hay."
"Oh, what did you give her?" "Cawn and hay."

Verses for reels made use of the favorite animals of the fables. "Brer Rabbit, Brer Rabbit, yo' ears mighty long; Yes, My Lord, they're put on wrong; Every little soul gonna shine; every little soul gonna shine!" Often power and pomp in the guise of the bullfrog and bulldog have the tables turned on them by the sassy blue-jay and crow:

A bullfrog dressed in soldier's clothes
Went in de field to shoot some crows,
De crows smell powder and fly away,
De bullfrog mighty mad dat day.

Even the easy-going ox or sheep or hog acquired characteristics:

De ole sow say to de boar
I'll tell you what let's do,
Let's go and git dat broad-axe
And die in de pig-pen too.
Die in de pig-pen fighting,
Die wid a bitin' jaw!

Unlike Stephen Foster's sweet and sad [1] songs such as "Massa's in the

[1] Thomas Talley, *Negro Folk Rhymes* (New York, 1922), p. 39.

Cold, Cold Ground," the folk seculars looked at slavery ironically. And where Foster saw comic nonsense, they added satiric point. Short comments flash us back to social reality: "Ole Master bought a yaller gal, He bought her from the South"; "My name's Ran, I wuks in de sand, I'd rather be a nigger dan a po' white man." Frederick Douglass remembers his fellow slaves singing "We raise de wheat, dey gib us de corn; We sift de meal, de gib us de huss; We peel de meat, dey gib us de skin; An dat's de way dey take us in." [2] Grousing about food is common: "Milk in the dairy getting mighty old, Skippers and the mice working mighty bold. . . . A long-tailed rat an' a bowl of souse, Jes' come down from de white folk's house." With robust humor, they laughed even at the dread patrollers:

> Run, nigger, run, de patrollers will ketch you
> Run, nigger, run; its almost day.
> Dat nigger run, dat nigger flew;
> Dat nigger tore his shirt in two.

The bitterest secular begins:

> My ole Mistis promise me
> Fo' she died, she'd set me free;
> She lived so long dat her head got bald,
> And she give out de notion dyin' at all.

Ole marster also failed his promise. Then, with the sharp surprise of the best balladry: "A dose of poison helped him along, May de devil preach his funeral song!"

Under a certain kind of protection the new freedmen took to heart the songs of such an abolitionist as Henry C. Work, and sang exultantly of jubilo. They sang his lines lampooning ole master, and turned out their own:

> Missus and mosser a-walkin' de street,
> Deir hands in deir pockets and nothin' to eat.
> She'd better be home a-washin' up de dishes,
> An' a-cleanin' up de ole man's raggitty britches. . . . [3]

But when the protection ran out, the freedmen found the following parody too true:

> Our father, who is in heaven,
> White man owe me eleven and pay me seven,
> Thy kingdom come, thy will be done,
> And if I hadn't took that, I wouldn't had none.

Toward the end of the century, there was interplay between the folk-seculars and the vaudeville stage, and the accepted stereotypes appeared. "Ain't no use my working so hard, I got a gal in the white folks yard." From

[2] Frederick Douglass, *Life and Times* (Hartford, Conn., 1882), p. 39.
[3] Talley, *op. cit.*, p. 97.

tent shows and roving guitar players, the folks accepted such hits as the "Bully Song" and the "coon-songs." "Bill Bailey, Won't You Please Come Home," and "Alabama Bound" shuttled back and forth between the folk and vaudeville. In the honky-tonks ribald songs grew up to become standbys of the early jazz: "Make Me a Pallet on The Floor," "Bucket Got A Hole In It," "Don't you leave me here; if you must go, baby, leave me a dime for beer." "Jelly Roll" Morton's autobiography, now released from the Library of Congress Archives, proves this close connection between the rising jazz and the old folk seculars. In the honky-tonks, songs handled sex freely, even licentiously; and obscenity and vituperation ran rampant in songs called the "dirty dozens."

One of the heroes of secular balladry is Uncle Bud, who was noted for his sexual prowess, a combination Don Juan and John Henry. His song is perhaps as uncollected as it is unprintable. Appreciative tales are told of railroading, of crack trains like The Cannon Ball and The Dixie Flyer, and The Rock Island Line, which is praised in rattling good verses. Such folk delights as hunting with the yipping and baying of the hounds and the yells and cheering of the hunters are vividly recreated. "Old Dog Blue" has been memorialized over all of his lop-eared kindred. The greatest trailer on earth, Old Blue keeps his unerring sense in heaven; there he treed a possum in Noah's ark. When Old Dog Blue died,

> I dug his grave wid a silver spade
> I let him down wid a golden chain
> And every link I called his name;
> Go on Blue, you good dog, you!

The above lines illustrate a feature of Negro folksong worth remarking. Coming from an old sea-chantey "Stormalong," their presence in a song about a hunting dog shows the folk habit of lifting what they want and using it how they will. Like southern white groups, the Negro has retained many of the old Scotch-English ballads. Still to be found are Negroes singing "In London town where I was born" and going on to tell of hard-hearted Barbara Allen. John Lomax found a Negro mixing up "Bobby Allen" with the cowboy song "The Streets of Laredo," burying "Miss Allen in a desert of New Mexico with six pretty maidens all dressed in white for her pallbearers." [4] But Negroes hand down fairly straight versions of "Lord Lovel," "Pretty Polly," and "The Hangman's Tree," which has special point for them with its repetend: "Hangman, hangman, slack on the line." The Elizabethan broadside "The Frog Went A-Courtin' " has long been a favorite Negro lullaby. From "The Lass of Roch Royal" two stanzas beginning "Who's gonna shoe yo' little feet" have found their way into the ballad of John Henry. The famous Irish racehorse Stewball reappears in Negro balladry as Skewball and Kimball. English nonsense refrains appear in songs like "Keemo-Kimo" and "Old Bangum." Even the Gaelic "Schule Aroon" has been found among Negroes, though the collector unwarily surmises it to be Guinea or Ebo. Similarly the Negro folk singer lends to and

[4] John Lomax, *Adventure of A Ballad Hunter* (New York, 1947), p. 179.

borrows from American balladry. "Casey Jones," though about an engineer, is part of the repertory; it has been established that a Negro engine-wiper was the first author of it. "Frankie and Johnnie," the most widely known tragedy in America, is attributed to both white and Negro authorship. It could come from either; it probably comes from both; the tenderloin cuts across both sections. Current singers continue the trading of songs: Leadbelly sings cowboy songs, yelling "Ki-yi-yippy-yippy-yay" with his own zest; and Josh White sings "Molly Malone" and "Randall, My Son" with telling power. But it is in narratives of their own heroes that Negro ballad makers have done best.

Prominent among such heroes are fugitives who outtrick and outspeed the law. "Travelin' Man" is more of a coon-song than authentically folk, but the hero whom the cops chased from six in the morning till seven the next afternoon has been warmly adopted by the people. Aboard the Titanic he spied the iceberg and dove off, and "When the old Titanic ship went down, he was shooting crap in Liverpool." More genuine is "Long Gone, Lost John" in which the hero outmatches the sheriff, the police, and the bloodhounds: "The hounds ain't caught me and they never will." Fast enough to hop the Dixie Flyer—"he missed the cowcatcher but he caught the blind"—Lost John can even dally briefly with a girl friend, like Brer Rabbit waiting for Brer Tortoise. But when he travels, he goes far: "the funniest thing I ever seen, was Lost John comin' through Bowlin' Green," but "the last time I seed him he was jumping into Mexico."

When Lost John "doubled up his fist and knocked the police down" his deed wins approval from the audience as much as his winged heels do. With bitter memories and suspicion of the law, many Negroes admire outlaws. Some are just tough killers; one is "a bad, bad man from bad, bad land"; another is going to start "a graveyard all of his own"; another, Roscoe Bill, who sleeps with one ear out because of the rounders about, reports to the judge blandly that

> I didn't quite kill him, but I fixed him so dis mornin'
> He won't bodder wid me no mo'
> Dis mornin', dis evenin', so soon.

But the favorites, like such western desperadoes as Jesse James, Billy the Kid, and Sam Bass, stand up against the law. Railroad Bill (an actual outlaw of southern Alabama) "shot all the buttons off the sheriff's coat." On the man-hunt, "the policemen dressed in blue, come down the street two by two." It took a posse to bring him in dead. Po' Lazarus also told the deputy to his face that he had never been arrested "by no one man, Lawd, Lawd, by no one man." Unlike his Biblical namesake in nature, Po' Lazarus broke into the commissary. The high sheriff sent the deputy to bring him back, dead or alive. They found him "way out between two mountains" and they "blowed him down."

> They shot Po' Lazarus, shot him with a great big number
> Number 45, Lawd, Lawd, number 45.

They laid Po' Lazarus on the commissary counter, and walked away. His mother, always worrying over the trouble she had with Lazarus, sees the body and cries.

> Dat's my only son, Lawd, Lawd, dat's my only son.

In contrast "Stackolee" ends on a hard note. At Stack's murder trial, his lawyer pleads for mercy because his aged mother is lying very low. The prosecutor states that

> Stackolee's aged mammy
> Has been dead these 'leven years.

Starting from a murder in Memphis in a dice game (some say over a Stetson hat), Stackolee's saga has traveled from the Ohio River to the Brazos; in a Texas version, Stack goes to hell, challenges the devil to a duel—pitchfork versus forty-one revolver—and then takes over the lower world.

One of America's greatest ballads tells of John Henry. Based on the strength and courage of an actual hammer-swinging giant, though in spite of what folk-singers say, his hammer cannot be seen decorating the Big Bend Tunnel on the C. & O. Road, John Henry reflects the struggle of manual labor against the displacing machine. The ballad starts with ill omens. Even as a boy John Henry prophesies his death at the Big Bend Tunnel. But he stays to face it out. Pitting his brawn and stamina against the new-fangled steam drill, John Henry says to his captain:

> A man ain't nothing but a man.
> But before I'll let that steam driver beat me down
> I'll die with my hammer in my hand.

The heat of the contest makes him call for water (in one variant for tom-cat gin). When John Henry is momentarily overcome, his woman, Polly Ann, spelled him, hammering "like a natural man." At one crucial point, John Henry gave "a loud and lonesome cry," saying, "A hammer'll be the death of me." But the general tone is self-confidence. John Henry throws the hammer from his hips on down, "Great gawd amighty how she rings!" He warns his shaker (the holder of the drill) that if ever he misses that piece of steel, "tomorrow'll be yo' burial day." His captain, hearing the mighty rumbling, thinks the mountain must be caving in. John Henry says to the captain: "It's my hammer swinging in the wind." Finally, he defeats the drill, but the strain kills him. The people gather round, but all he asks is "a cool drink of water 'fo I die." Polly Ann swears to be true to the memory (although in another version she turns out to be as fickle as Mrs. Casey Jones). John Henry was buried near the railroad where

> Every locomotive come a-roarin' by
> Says, "There lies a steel-drivin' man, Lawd, Lawd;
> There lies a steel-drivin' man."

The topical nature of American balladry is seen in "Boll Weevil," a ballad that grew up almost as soon as the swarm of pests descended. "Come up from Mexico, they say."

> The first time I seed the boll weevil
> He was sitting on the square—

(The folk poet puns on the "square" of cotton boll, and the familiar southern town square.) A tough little rascal is celebrated who, when buried in the hot sand, says "I can stand it like a man"; when put into ice, says: "This is mighty cool and nice," and thrives and breeds right on, until finally he can take over:

> You better leave me alone
> I done et up all your cotton,
> And now I'll start on your corn.

The ballad has grim side glances; the boll weevil didn't leave "the farmer's wife but one old cotton dress"; made his nest in the farmer's "best Sunday hat"; and closed the church doors since the farmer couldn't pay the preacher.

> Oh, de Farmer say to de Merchant
> I ain't made but only one bale
> An' befo' I bring you dat one
> I'll fight an' go to jail
> I'll have a home
> I'll have a home.

The stanzaic forms and general structure of "John Henry" and "The Boll Weevil" are fairly developed. One of the best folk ballads, however, is in the simpler, unrhymed African leader-chorus design. This is "The Grey Goose," a ballad about a seemingly ordinary fowl who becomes a symbol of ability to take it. It is a song done with the highest spirits; the "Lord, Lord, Lord" of the responding chorus expressing amazement, flattery, and good-humored respect for the tough bird:

> Well, last Monday mornin'
> Lord, Lord, Lord!
> Well, last Monday mornin'
> Lord, Lord, Lord!

They went hunting for the grey goose. When shot "Boo-loom!" the grey goose was six weeks a-falling. Then it was six weeks a-finding, and once in the white house, was six weeks a-picking. Even after the great feather-picking he was six months parboiling. And then on the table, the forks couldn't stick him; the knife couldn't cut him. So they threw him in the hog-pen where he broke the sow's jawbone. Even in the sawmill, he broke the saw's teeth out. He was indestructible. Last seen the grey goose was flying across the ocean, with a long string of goslings, all going "Quank-quink-quank." Yessir, it was one hell of a gray goose. Lord, Lord, Lord!

WORK SONGS AND SOCIAL PROTEST

More work songs come from the Negro than from any other American folk group. Rowing the cypress dug-outs in Carolina low-country, slaves timed their singing to the long sweep of the oars. The leader, a sort of coxswain, chanted verse after verse; the rowers rumbled a refrain. On the docks Negroes sang sailors' chanteys as metronomes to their heaving and hauling. Some chanteys, like "Old Stormy," they took over from the white seamen; others they improvised. Along the Ohio and Mississippi waterfronts Negro roustabouts created "coonjine" songs, so-called after the shuffling dance over bucking gang-planks in and out of steamboat holds. Unless the rhythm was just right a roustabout and his bale or sack of cottonseed might be jolted into the brown waters. The singers cheered the speed of the highballing paddlewheelers: "left Baton Rouge at half pas' one, and got to Vicksburg at settin of de sun." But they griped over the tough captains "workin' hell out of me" and sang

> Ole Roustabout ain't got no home
> Makes his livin' on his shoulder bone.

For release from the timber and the heavy sacks there was always some city around the bend—Paducah, Cairo, Memphis, Natchez, and then

> Alberta let yo' hair hang low ...
> I'll give you mo' gold
> Than yo' apron can hold ...
> Alberta let yo' hair hang low.

These songs flourished in the hey-day of the packets; today they are nearly lost.

Another type of work song was chanted as a gang unloaded steel rails. Since these rails weighed over a ton apiece and were over ten yards long, any break in the rhythm of lifting them from the flat cars to the ground was a good way to get ruptured, maimed, or killed. So a chanter was employed to time the hoisting, lowering, and the getting away from it. He was a coach, directing the teamwork, and in self-protection the men had to learn his rhythmic tricks. In track-lining, a similar chanter functioned to keep the track straight in line. As he called, the men jammed their bars under the rails and braced in unison:

> Shove it over! Hey, hey, can't you line it!
> Ah shack-a-lack-a-lack-a-lack-a-lack-a-lack-alack (Grunt)
> Can't you move it? Hey, hey, can't you try.[5]

As they caught their breath and got a new purchase, he turned off a couplet. Then came the shouted refrain as the men strained together.

More widely spread and known are the Negro work songs whose rhythm is timed with the swing back and down and the blow of broadaxe, pick, hammer, or tamper. The short lines are punctuated by a grunt as the axe bites into the wood, or the hammer finds the spike-head.

---

[5] Zora Neale Hurston, *Mules and Men* (Philadelphia, 1935), p. 322.

> Dis ole hammer—hunh
> Ring like silver—hunh (3)
> Shine like gold, baby—hunh
> Shine like gold—hunh.

The leader rings countless changes in his words and melody over the unchanging rhythm. When he grows dull or forgets, another singer takes over. The song is consecutive, fluid; it is doubtful if any one version is ever exactly repeated. Ballads, blues, even church-songs are levied on for lines, a simple matter since the stanzas are unrhymed. Some lines tell of the satisfaction of doing a man's work well:

> I got a rainbow—hunh
> Tied 'round my shoulder—hunh—(3)
> Tain't gonna rain, baby—hunh
> Tain't gonna rain.

(The rainbow is the arc of the hammer as the sunlight glints on the moving metal.) Sometimes a singer boasts of being a "sun-down man," who can work the sun down without breaking down himself. Lines quite as popular, however, oppose any speed-up stretch-out system:

> Dis ole hammer—hunh
> Killt John Henry—hunh—(3)
> Twon't kill me, baby—hunh
> Twon't kill me.

Some lines get close to the blues: "Every mail day / Gits a letter / Son, come home, baby / Son, come home." Sometimes they tell of a hard captain (boss)

> Told my captain—hunh
> Hands are cold—hunh—(3)
> Damn yo' hands—hunh
> Let de wheelin' roll.

The new-fangled machine killed John Henry; its numerous offspring have killed the work songs of his buddies. No hammer song could compete now with the staccato roaring drill even if the will to sing were there. The steamboat is coming back to the Mississippi but the winches and cranes do not call forth the old gang choruses. A few songs connected with work survive such as the hollers of the lonely worker in the fields and woods, or the call boy's chant to the glory-hole.

> Sleeping good, sleeping good,
> Give me them covers, I wish you would.

At ease from their work in their bunkhouses, the men may sing, but their fancies ramble from the job oftener than they stay with it. Song as a rhythmic accompaniment to work is declining. John and Alan Lomax, whose bag of Negro work songs is the fullest, had to go to the penitentiaries, where labor-saving devices were not yet numerous, in order to find the art thriving. They found lively cotton-picking songs:

> A-pick a bale, a-pick a bale
> Pick a bale of cotton
> A-pick a bale, a-pick a bale
> Pick a bale a day.[6]

Slower songs came from gangs that were cutting cane or chopping weeds or hewing timber. Prison work is of course mean and tough: "You oughta come on de Brazo in nineteen-fo'; you could find a dead man on every turn-row." So the convicts cry out to the taskmaster sun:

> Go down, Ol' Hannah, doncha rise no mo'
> Ef you rise any mo' bring judgment day.

They grouse about the food: ever "the same damn thing," and at that the cook isn't clean. An old evangelical stand-by, "Let the Light of the Lighthouse Shine On Me," becomes a hymn of hope that the Midnight Special, a fast train, will some day bring a pardon from the governor. They sing of their long sentences:

> Ninety nine years so jumpin' long
> To be here rollin' an' cain' go home.

If women aren't to be blamed for it all, they are still to be blamed for a great deal:

> Ain't but de one thing worries my min'
> My cheating woman and my great long time.

One song, like the best balladry, throws a searchlight into the darkness:

> "Little boy, what'd you do for to get so long?"
> Said, "I killed my rider in the high sheriff's arms."

From these men—long-termers, lifers, three-time losers—come songs brewed in bitterness. This is not the double-talk of the slave seculars, but the naked truth of desperate men telling what is on their brooding minds. Only to collectors who have won their trust—such as the Lomaxes, Lawrence Gellert and Josh White—and only when the white captain is far enough away, do the prisoners confide these songs. Then they sing not loudly but deeply their hatred of the brutality of the chain-gang:

> If I'd a had my weight in lime
> I'd a whupped dat captain, till he went stone blind.

[6] The Library of Congress, Music Division. Archive of American Folk Song for this and the following quotations.

> If you don't believe my buddy's dead
> Just look at that hole in my buddy's head.[7]

A prisoner is told: "Don't you go worryin' about forty [the years of your sentence], Cause in five years you'll be dead."

They glorify the man who makes a crazy dare for freedom; Jimbo for instance, who escapes almost under the nose of his captain, described as "a big Goliath," who walks like Samson and "totes his talker." They boast: "Ef ah git de drop / Ah'm goin' on / Dat same good way / Dat Jimbo's gone / Lawd, Lawd, Lawd." [8] They reenact with graphic realism the lashing of a fellow-prisoner; the man-hunting of Ol' Rattler, "fastest and smellingest bloodhound in the South"; and the power of Black Betty, the ugly bull-whip. They make stark drama out of the pain, and hopelessness, and shame.

> All I wants is dese cold iron shackles off my leg.

It is not only in the prison songs that there is social protest. Where there is some protection or guaranteed secrecy other *verboten* songs come to light. Coal miners, fortified by a strong, truculent union, sing grimly of the exorbitant company stores:

> What's de use of me working any more, my baby? (2)
> What's de use of me working any more,
> When I have to take it up at de company store,
> My baby? [9]

Or they use the blues idiom with a new twist:

> Operator will forsake you, he'll drive you from his do' ...
> No matter what you do, dis union gwine to stand by you
> While de union growing strong in dis land.[10]

And the sharecroppers sharply phrase their plight:

> Go in the store and the merchant would say,
> 'Your mortgage is due and I'm looking for my pay.'
> Down in his pocket with a tremblin' hand
> 'Can't pay you all but I'll pay what I can,'
> Then to the telephone the merchant made a call,
> They'll put you on the chain-gang, an' you don't pay at all.[11]

Big Bill Broonzy is best known as a blues singer, but in the cotton belt of Arkansas he learned a great deal that sank deep. His sharp "Black, Brown,

[7] Josh White, *Chain Gang Songs* (Bridgeport, Conn., Columbia Recording Corporation), Set C-22.

[8] Willis James, "Hyah Come De Cap'n," from Brown, Davis, and Lee, *The Negro Caravan* (New York, 1948), p. 469.

[9] John and Alan Lomax, *Our Singing Country* (New York, 1941), pp. 278–288.

[10] *Ibid.*

[11] *Ibid.*

and White Blues" has the new militancy built up on the sills of the old folksong. In an employment office, Big Bill sings. "They called everybody's number / But they never did call mine." Then working side by side with a white man:

> He was getting a dollar an hour
> When I was making fifty cents.

Onto this new protest he ties an old vaudeville chorus, deepening the irony:

> If you's black, ah brother,
> Git back, git back, git back.[12]

Such songs, together with the blues composed by Waring Cuney and Josh White on poverty, hardship, poor housing and jim crow military service, come from conscious propagandists, not truly folk. They make use of the folk idiom in both text and music, however, and the folk listen and applaud. They know very well what Josh White is talking about in such lines as:

> Great gawdamighty, folks feelin' bad
> Lost everything they ever had.

PROSPECT

It is evident that Negro folk culture is breaking up. Where Negro met only with Negro in the black belt the old beliefs strengthened. But when mud traps give way to gravel roads, and black tops and even concrete highways with buses and jalopies and trucks lumbering over them, the world comes closer. The churches and schools, such as they are, struggle against some of the results of isolation, and the radio plays a part. Even in the backwoods, aerials are mounted on shanties that seem ready to collapse from the extra weight on the roof, or from a good burst of static against the walls. The phonograph is common, the television set is by no means unknown, and down at the four corners store, a jukebox gives out the latest jive. Rural folk closer to towns and cities may on Saturday jaunts even see an occasional movie, where a rootin'-tootin' Western gangster film introduces them to the advancements of civilization. Newspapers, especially the Negro press, give the people a sense of belonging to a larger world. Letters from their boys in the army, located in all corners of the world, and the tales of the returning veterans, true Marco Polos, also prod the inert into curiosity. Brer Rabbit and Old Jack no longer are enough. Increasingly in the churches the spirituals lose favor to singing out of the books or from broadsides, and city-born blues and jive take over the jook-joints.

The migration of the folk Negro to the cities, started by the hope for better living and schooling, and greater self-respect, quickened by the industrial demands of two world wars is sure to be increased by the new cotton picker

[12] *People's Songs*, Vol. 1, No. 10 (November, 1940), 9.

and other man-displacing machines. In the city the folk become a submerged proletariat. Leisurely yarn-spinning, slow-paced aphoristic conversation become lost arts; jazzed-up gospel hymns provide a different sort of release from the old spirituals; the blues reflect the distortions of the new way of life. Folk arts are no longer by the folk for the folk; smart businessmen now put them up for sale. Gospel songs often become show-pieces for radio slummers, and the blues become the double-talk of the dives. And yet, in spite of the commercializing, the folk roots often show a stubborn vitality. Just as the transplanted folk may show the old credulity, though the sophisticated impulse sends them to an American Indian for nostrums, or for fortune-telling to an East Indian "madame" with a turban around her head rather than to a mammy with a bandanna around hers; so the folk for all their disorganization may keep something of the fine quality of their old tales and songs. Assuredly even in the new gospel songs and blues much is retained of the phrasing and the distinctive musical manner. Finally, it should be pointed out that even in the transplanting, a certain kind of isolation—class and racial—remains. What may come of it, if anything, is unpredictable, but so far the vigor of the creative impulse has not been sapped, even in the slums.

Whatever may be the future of the folk Negro, American literature as well as American music is the richer because of his expression. Just as Huckleberry Finn and Tom Sawyer were fascinated by the immense lore of their friend Jim, American authors have been drawn to Negro folk life and character. With varying authenticity and understanding, Joel Chandler Harris, Du Bose Heyward, Julia Peterkin, Roark Bradford, Marc Connelly, E. C. L. Adams, Zora Neale Hurston and Langston Hughes have all made rewarding use of this material. Folk Negroes have themselves bequeathed a wealth of moving song, both religious and secular, of pithy folk-say and entertaining and wise folk-tales. They have settled characters in the gallery of American heroes; resourceful Brer Rabbit and Old Jack, and indomitable John Henry. They have told their own story so well that all men should be able to hear it and understand.

Charles S. Johnson, Edwin R. Embree, and
Will W. Alexander

THE COLLAPSE OF COTTON TENANCY

*The Depression of the 1930's accelerated the departure of Negroes
from the cotton plantations. The fertility of the land in the south-
eastern states had been declining for decades; now, in addition, the
cotton market sagged disastrously. As Charles S. Johnson and his
collaborators show, the policies of the New Deal agencies accentuated
the demographic trend by discriminating against the tenant farmers
in favor of the large landowners, thus forcing more people off the
land. Eventually technological changes in cotton agriculture, and the
continued shift of cotton farming to the trans-Mississippi West,
practically destroyed the sharecropping system. Many former tenants
have moved to the northern and southern cities; those who still work
the cotton fields are hired as wage laborers a few months of the year.*

*In many ways, of course, the New Deal programs assisted urban
Negroes, despite discrimination on the part of many agencies. As a
result, a major shift from Republican to Democratic occurred in the
political loyalties of the Negro masses. Nevertheless, as far as the
plight of the Negro tenants was concerned, the policies of the Agricultural Adjustment Administration must be viewed as leading to a
serious deterioration in conditions.*

THE Agricultural Adjustment Administration was created "to relieve
the existing national economic emergency by increasing agricultural pur-
chasing power." The adoption in the spring of 1933 of the Domestic Allotment
plan with rental and parity payments to those who voluntarily reduced their
acreage found the cotton crop already planted. Unless another large crop was
to be added to the crushing burden of the surplus, drastic measures were a

From Charles S. Johnson, Edwin R. Embree and Will W. Alexander, *The Collapse
of Cotton Tenancy* (Chapel Hill: University of North Carolina Press, 1935), pp. 48–61.
Reprinted with the permission of University of North Carolina Press.

necessity. They were undertaken in the plow-up campaign which is estimated to have taken 10,400,000 acres and 4,400,000 bales out of production. By contracts with the Secretary of Agriculture producers obligated themselves to plow up between 25 and 50 per cent of their acreage for which they were to receive a rental payment of approximately $11 per acre, depending upon the per acre yields. The producer might take his payment all in cash or part in options on cotton formerly held by the Farm Board. The 1933 crop, in spite of an estimated plow-up of 4,400,000 bales, amounted to about 13,200,000 bales. This gave a carry-over of 10,000,000 bales which was a reduction of only 1,000,000 bales from the year before.

For landowners there is no doubt that the program was a success. The price of cotton went to ten cents where it was pegged by government loans. Crop receipts plus benefit payments gave the growers more than double the income of the previous year 1932.

Through December 31, 1933, the AAA distributed $111,405,244.37 in rental and benefit payments in the cotton plow-up campaign. This was 85.6 per cent of the total amount spent in rental and benefit payments and 63.9 per cent of the total sum, $175,404,851.64 spent for both rental and benefits and the removal of surplus in cotton, wheat, tobacco, hogs, and butter. The South absorbed approximately 85.5 per cent of these payments. Many of the great Delta counties with 90 per cent tenancy and high Negro ratios received from $500,000 to over $800,000 in benefit payments alone. With white landowners, who own most of the plantations, comprising about 2 per cent of all farm operators, it remains a moot question as to how evenly these benefits were distributed among the tenants. The question is all the more important because the tenants had tilled the crops until the plow-up and thus possessed an equity in the destroyed crops.

The government under the AAA has assumed many of the risks of the landowners, and thrown them on the tenant. The risk of overproduction is met by fixed quotas with rent to the landowner for his retired lands. These benefits take little, if any, account of labor's previous interest in the crop. The tenant's share of rental is pitifully small or nil, and on him is thrown the brunt of reduced acreage. The risk of price fluctuation is met by the government's policy of pegging prices by loans at, say, ten cents per pound on cotton. Through its production credit corporations the Federal Farm Credit Administration offers the landowner production credit at 4½ to 6½ per cent interest. The tenant cannot secure this cheap credit unless the landlord waives his first lien on the crop. If the tenant does not agree to release his share of the crop lien to the governmental agency, the landlord may then secure the loan for all his tenant farms at 4½ to 6½ per cent and then advance supplies and furnishings to his tenants at customary credit prices, 20 to 30 per cent above cash prices. Here again the tenant bears the brunt of the credit; if he cannot repay, he loses his crop and whatever chattel and work-stock he may possess.

The risk of losing equity in farms has been lessened for owners by methods of refinancing through the Farm Credit Administration and by arrangements for scaling down debts in conference with creditors. So far the various Debt Reconciliation Commissions have made no attempts to have landlords scale down debts owed them from previous seasons by croppers and share tenants. Such proposals would be resented, no doubt, by landowners although they had just had their own debts scaled down by creditors. There is a New Testament parable on this subject, but the quoting of Scripture in economic treatises has never gained much vogue.

It is the blunt truth to say that under the present system the landowner is more and more protected from risk by government activity, while the tenant is left open to risks on every side. Only after he loses first what property he may possess and then his tenure, does the tenant come to the form of risk insurance designed for him—relief.

One obvious reason for the wholesale neglect of the tenant lies in the fact that the Agricultural Adjustment Administration organized its program under the direction of the planters themselves. When suddenly curtailment of production was ordered the law was obeyed but the customary tenant-landlord relations managed to persist. Planters found that the indemnity for reduction supplied greatly needed cash. Since most of the money allocated to the South came to them, the program did not seem entirely unsatisfactory. The AAA as finally administered met the landlord's approval. If it effected any disorganization, that disorganization was not inimical to the planters' interest. Ultimately it proved to be merely a subsidy to planters.

The field studies of the Committee indicate that, in practice, the landlord's reduction was the farm quota and he determined the distribution of the reduced acreage among his tenants. The share-croppers seldom received cash as payment for their reduction. For the most part landlords "credited to their accounts" the amounts due them. The participation of tenants in the reduction program was not general. Many tenants were not required to reduce their acreages if the plantation had held within its quota. In some instances the county quota was filled without requiring a reduction on certain farms. Those who plowed up no cotton, of course, received aid only in the form of higher prices for their product. Some who did plow up received nothing.

In Bolivar County, Mississippi, many large plantations reduced the "wage hand crop"—that is, the land cultivated by the owner with hired labor—and did not disturb the tenant crops. In Marlboro County, South Carolina, the same practice held. A cropper commented, "Our landlord wouldn't plow up any of our cotton. He plowed up his own so that he could get the pay for it." In Fort Bend County, Texas, the county quota was filled before small farmers were taken in.

Greatest participation in the benefits of reduction was found in the areas where cotton farming was least profitable. In Bolivar County, Mississippi, a productive area, 47 per cent of those reducing cotton acreage received cash payments. In Marlboro County, South Carolina, a poorer county, all of the tenants plowing up received some cash. In Harrison and Fort Bend Counties in Texas the numbers receiving cash for cotton reduction were 87.5 per cent and 85.8 per cent respectively. It would, perhaps, be more accurate to say that these tenants were credited by the government with receiving cash. In many cases the cash was promptly applied against the indebtedness of the tenant to the owners. In Bolivar County, Mississippi, a half-cropper said: "I plowed up six acres of my cotton last year, but I didn't get a cent from the government. Boss said it was credited to my account, but I don't know." This tenant was not familiar with the amount of his indebtedness or the amount applied to his debts. Another tenant, however, was better informed. "When I plowed up my cotton I got $136.00 deducted from my account. It was really deducted, for I saw the statement itemized." In some instances tenants were allowed a small part of the money due them in cash. A half-cropper plowed up five acres of cotton and got $11.00 cash. The remainder was credited to his account.

In Harrison County, Texas, where the small farm and credit merchant predominate, the system of crediting accounts could not be used, but a system was developed which was equally as effective in preventing tenants from securing the cash.

> Mr. —— and the others brought the checks out here to the store and that's where we signed up. The merchant taken them and give credit for them. Some of the folks got a little something out of theirs but I just signed mine and give it to him. I asked him for some of mine back and he said "nothing doing." I didn't want to act hard cause I know it wouldn't get me nowheres.

The county agents in charge of distribution of the payment made the credit stores points for distributing checks. As a result checks were passed over to merchants either for unpaid debts or for future supplies. In many cases the merchant suggested that the checks be given him and that he would furnish the given farmer until his check was consumed. Such a suggestion is practically an edict under the prevailing relationships in the rural South.

In all areas, the benefits of reduction accrued ultimately to the landlord and merchant. A farmer in Noxubee County, Mississippi, when asked about the federal payments said with bitter humor: "It's been here, oh, it's been here. More of the bosses have redeemed homes and redeemed their lands and bought cars in Noxubee County than they did during the World War, and the poor people have suffered more."

In spite of the best intentions of the Washington administration, the 1933 crop reduction program was handled clumsily. Some tenants plowed up cotton; some did not. Those who received payment in cash did not receive the same amount for the same acreage. There was considerable confusion in the tenants' participation. The 1934 program found the dominating forces better organized, the tenants more carefully avoided in the administration of the relief program. The acreage quotas were determined and the landowner rented acres to the Secretary of Agriculture and the only information given the tenant was that he could plant a stipulated amount of cotton.

The code for cotton production has been properly designated "the landlord's code" and all that was not provided to the landlord's satisfaction in the code was taken care of in the administration of it. Many tenants actually paid for use of land rented to the Secretary of Agriculture and specified as available for planting food crops rent free.

The tenant found himself the loser in any event; if he was not displaced from the farm entirely, he remained as a casual laborer, and if he did not suffer this change in status, his operations were so small as to be unprofitable. The organization of the national machinery provided representation to adjust difficulties in the administration of the program, but it was not found possible to give personal attention to all complaints registered. Complaints sent to the Department of Agriculture in Washington were sent to state AAA administrators for adjustment, where they were passed to county agents for adjustment. These agents in turn passed them to the landlord against whom the complaint was made. A complaint often ended in further injury and discomfiture to the complainant.

The planters organized and the first Bankhead Bill dovetailed into the cotton system with ease. In some areas tenants were ignorant of the fact that there was a Bankhead Bill. Many of them had signed something but in the previous two years they had signed many sheets without knowing their meanings. In other areas they knowingly signed a trustees' agreement. The method employed by one planter indicates the practices sometimes resorted to:

> Mr. —— called all of us to the gin. He said, "We got to sign up with the government to gin our cotton this year. They're making us get tags for every bale and we can't gin none without them tags. I had a letter from the government to read to you but I left it at home. The government has appointed me trustee of your bale tags and all you have to do is bring the cotton to the gin as you always have. So everybody come and sign this paper so we can gin our cotton."

The tenants filed past and signed a trustees' agreement giving the planter the privilege he claimed had been given him by the government.

The net result of the program was that the landlords participated in the federal relief program and received the benefits it offered while the tenant merely obeyed the landlord's instructions. Federal relief came to the cotton belt, was translated into plantation terms and the system (except for the further displacement and impoverishment of tenants) was bolstered and given a new lease on life.

TENANTS AND RELIEF

It is not to be expected of a business with decreased production to use as much labor as it did when production was at a maximum. Five methods are in evidence for meeting the reduced need for tenant labor:

1. The tenant remains on the plantation eking out an existence from farming operations that are of such size as to be unprofitable.

2. The tenant remains on the plantation with his status changed to that of a casual laborer who has the privilege of producing what he can for family consumption.

3. The tenant occupies a house on the plantation but is supported by relief.

4. Unsatisfactory returns from his labors or artificially stimulated difficulties with the landlord force the tenant to move of his own volition to the small town.

5. Eviction from the farm by landlords who have no further need of his services.

Every available study of the position of the share tenants and croppers under the depression and the operation of the AAA corroborates in detail the observations here set down. Hoffsommer, in his study "The AAA and the Cropper," interviewed 800 landlords in 1934 and concluded that the economic relationship and the resulting social attitudes had made a situation in which it was difficult, if not impossible, for the government to deal directly with the cropper. The paternalism of the planter, the dependency of the tenant so meticulously maintained, the stern objections, on the part of the landlord, to any change in the traditional relationship, set up well nigh insurmountable barriers to any tenant benefits through this channel. In fact, 90 per cent of the landlords voiced opposition to any change, despite the impoverishment of these classes. Says Hoffsommer:

It appears . . . that this attitude arises from sentiment and tradition rather than from critical thought and planning on the basis of modern conditions. At any rate, the cropper is looked upon as a dependent person, the more extreme but not uncommon views regarding him as a class apart, incapable of ever achieving but a modicum of self-direction. Judged from his past achievements in climbing the so-called agricultural ladder, it would seem that superficially, at least, there is some justification for this view. In the Alabama study of those who started farming as share croppers, nearly three-fourths still remain such. Less than one-tenth have become owners.

There is a considerable feeling among landlords that anything which disturbs this dependent status of the cropper is undesirable. Forty per cent of the landlords in the above mentioned study stated, for example, that they were opposed to the granting of relief to these people because of its demoralizing effect upon them. . . .

The share tenant's situation is the impossible one of being forced by the inadequacies of the present system, on the one hand, to seek relief as the only means of keeping alive; and, on the other hand, of having this relief opposed by the landlord because it may spoil him as a tenant, if and when he can be used again. There are other fears back of the landlord's attitude: the fear that the tenant will be removed from the influence of the landowner and learn that he is not entirely dependent on him; and the fear that the relief will raise the standard of living to the extent that bargaining on the old basis will be difficult. It can readily be seen that from the point of view of the landlord government relief is demoralizing.

Whatever the intention of the Government, it is apparent that the so-called parity payment turned out to be a mere farce and gesture to the share tenant and cropper. Under the 1934 revision of the landlord-tenant contract the share cropper receives one-half of the parity payments. But this is actually a very small sum. The share-cropper on a typical cotton farm of 12 acres, with 40 per cent of his acreage out of production, and assuming a base lint yield of 175 pounds per acre, would receive about $4.20 as his share, if he got that. Of 2,000 tenants studied in Alabama, 28 per cent of them received cotton benefit payments in 1933, and of the croppers and renters, 40 per cent paid over part of the money immediately to the landlord, and in a third of these cases this payment was actually forced by the landlords. It was found easier to force the Negroes to turn over their payments than the white tenants. Whereas force was used with 22 per cent of the whites, it was used with 58 per cent of the Negroes.

Dr. Calvin B. Hoover of the Department of Agriculture, in the course of his inquiries into the operation of the federal program, found the same condition. In summarizing his report he said:

> Often these sums were legally due the landlord. In other cases, however, the interest rate which was charged was usurious and at a rate higher than that allowed by the laws of the State in which the parties to the contract lived. Whether the tenant received anything at all often depended upon the charitableness of the landlord. In number-less instances, if the landlord had deducted the entire sum which he had a legal right to do, there would have been no net amount received by the tenants at all. What apparently happened was that the deductions amounted sometimes to less than the legal amount due, sometimes to the amount legally due, depending upon the charitableness or unscrupulousness of the landlord.

In spite of the hopes expressed by the AAA that the landlord should keep so far as possible his accustomed number of tenants, this was not done; if it had been insisted upon the whole program was in danger of losing the support of the landlords. With the accelerated displacement of tenants, a movement that had already begun in 1929—reaching serious proportions in 1932—went also all prospects of "furnish" and shelter. The result is a homeless, shifting, and stranded population with no prospect of relief except that which might come from the government. . . .

Irving Howe and B. J. Widick

THE U.A.W. FIGHTS RACE PREJUDICE

One of the most important developments for Negroes during the New Deal was the emergence of the CIO in 1935–36. Its leaders believed in interracial trade unionism, contending that if Negroes were not included as members, they would be used by employers as strikebreakers. Within the CIO, the United Automobile Workers under Walter Reuther has been among the most militant advocates of racial egalitarianism. Reuther has expended a considerable amount of effort fighting racism in the automobile industry—and in his own union. This article by Irving Howe and B. J. Widick, although sometimes marred by a defensive tone, explores the difficulties encountered in implementing the official equalitarian pronouncements of the UAW, whose membership included large numbers of southern whites and second generation Americans of South and East European background.

Unquestionably, the UAW's top leaders made substantial efforts to force the upgrading of Negroes and to integrate the union's recreational programs. Nevertheless, the UAW sometimes felt compelled to sacrifice the interests of Negro members to placate the prejudices of a section of the white membership. Labor contracts were accepted that barred Negroes from advancement to higher status jobs. Until the early 1940's, Negroes were excluded from the General Motors UAW local in Atlanta. In Detroit, the union did little about the exclusion of Negroes from many restaurants near the plants. And not until the 1960's did a well-organized Negro caucus succeed in securing Negro representation on the UAW's own international executive board. Howe and Widick note that Communists exploited the issue of Negro representation for their own purposes during the 1940's. It should be emphasized, however, that the absence of Negroes in the top circles of union officialdom was a genuine issue for Negroes in the UAW, and the successful fight for Negro representation was led by anti-Communist Negro leaders in the union.

Irving Howe and B. J. Widick, "The U.A.W. Fights Race Prejudice: Case History on the Industrial Front," *Commentary*, VIII (Sept., 1949), pp. 261–68. Reprinted by permission of *Commentary* and Irving Howe. Copyright © 1949 by the American Jewish Committee.

IN THE 1920's Detroit became the unchallenged motor capital and thereby one of the great industrial centers of the world. In the 1930's it was the scene of a vast labor upsurge, the result of which was a minor revolution in American life. In the 1940's it was wracked by race riots more bloody and prolonged than any that had recently occurred in the South.

Detroit is a city where the robotization of labor and the mechanization of life reach their height, where the strains of American society are ugliest and sharpest. Here Northern and Southern culture patterns meet most intimately and violently. Hundreds of thousands of its auto workers are Southerners from Alabama farms and Kentucky towns. Physically cramped and psychologically tense, the city has acquired a raw, brutal quality that can be found nowhere else—a quality that is partly the result of a clash between Southern folkways, uprooted from their natural context, and a mechanical, depersonalized urbanism.

Detroit is lacerated by complex racial and religious conflicts. The Southern whites cling to anti-Negro prejudice; between them and the large Polish minority there is constant, though seldom reported, friction. Before the large-scale influx of Southerners, the Poles showed little anti-Negro feeling, but in recent years they have "learned" from the Southerners. And naturally—for the Negroes are probably the only group below the Poles in Detroit's scale of social status.

Almost everything about Detroit has made life difficult for its 350,000 Negroes. Though living in a Northern city, they have suffered from blatant forms of discrimination usually associated with the South. They have been packed into "Paradise Valley," a slum nearly as dreadful as the one that lies on the flank of the nation's capital; they have been confined to the worst jobs, and have been the last hired and the first fired; and they have been subjected to intermittent orgies of violence.

The United Automobile Workers (CIO) has had to face the "Negro problem" from the day of its formation. No union in the United States has experienced greater difficulties with regard to race relations; no organization of comparable size provides so crucial a setting for the study of the tangled relationships and periodic crises that arise when a serious attempt is made to combat race prejudice in daily life.

The auto industry was one of the last major industries in the United States to hire large numbers of Negro workers. Behind this fact is a depressing bit of historical irony: the white auto workers, before the rise of the CIO, had been too weak to call sustained strikes, and hence the companies had little need for Negro strikebreakers. Negroes were excluded from regular jobs in most auto plants as a matter of course. Until 1935 only the Ford River Rouge plant hired Negroes in large numbers.

Those Negroes who did work in the auto plants were confined either to janitorial chores or to the unpleasant, back-breaking foundry jobs that white men did not want. Except in the Rouge plant, they were barred from skilled work. Even after the industry's unionization, this policy prevailed; it has by no means been stamped out yet.

For the companies, racial discrimination proved advantageous in several ways. It assured them of a large pool of cheap docile labor that might be used as a threat to beat down demands made by white workers; it meant, too, that the sharp color line drawn in the plants would hinder the organization of workers into one united group. The employers' defense—or rationalization—of discriminatory hiring policies was either that Negro workers were unable to perform skilled work or that white men refused to work beside them. In the latter claim there was, of course, considerable truth, for racial prejudice cuts deep into all classes in American society. But the essential point is that the companies, while they had not themselves originated racial prejudice, were often ready to take advantage of it.

When the big sitdown strikes broke out in 1936 and 1937, few Negroes participated. During the Studebaker sitdown at South Bend in November 1936, the Oldsmobile sitdown at Lansing in January 1937, and the one at Flint General Motors in February 1937, most Negro workers simply stayed at home. They neither cooperated with the strikers nor showed any willingness to serve as scabs; they merely watched, warily.

It is not hard to understand why they took this attitude. Past relations with white workers in the plants had usually been bad; at Flint Chevrolet, for example, there had been bitter clashes between white and colored workers for some months before the sitdown. The AFL, then still the dominant labor group, had often been viciously discriminatory, and Negro workers saw little reason to suppose the UAW would be better. But perhaps the strongest reason for the Negro workers' skepticism about the sitdowns was that they had become habituated to following the timid leadership of the Negro middle class, a precarious group that depended on the patronage and blessing of Michigan's white industrialists.

Of course, both the UAW and the CIO as a whole, fearing that Negroes might be used as strikebreakers, formally pledged themselves to non-discriminatory policies. And the very nature of industrial unionism made impractical the racial divisions common in the AFL. Craft unions could appeal to limited sections of a labor force, pitting skilled against unskilled, white against black, and thereby aggravating racial tensions. But the new industrial unions, simply in order to survive, had to win the support of at least a minority of the Negro workers. For some labor leaders in the auto industry racial equality was a matter of dedicated conviction, for others a mere necessity. In any case, the CIO unions had no choice; without racial equality, the mass industrial unions could not have been built.

During the period of its early organization, the UAW took special pains to win Negro workers. Its press and publicity emphasized the theme of racial equality; if a stray organizer showed prejudice, he was quickly dismissed; and white workers were slowly and painfully taught that if they failed to cooperate with Negroes they would never win their demands. When a Negro worker showed qualities of leadership he was quickly encouraged; in the Chrysler sit-down of March 1937, a Negro, Sam Fanroy, was elected to the strike com-mittee. As a rule, wherever the Negroes were a substantial fraction of a plant's labor force they cooperated much more readily than where they were a small group, for in the former instance they felt strong enough not merely to fight with white workers against management but also, if necessary, by themselves against white workers. In the Detroit Midland Steel plant, where about half the workers were Negroes, relations were excellent; at the Dodge plant, where fewer Negroes worked, clashes broke out.

In the Southern auto plants the problem was far more difficult, for the union clashed with a fervently defended pattern of prejudice. At the General Motors plant in Atlanta, union organizers could not persuade white workers to admit Negroes into the local, and it was only with some difficulty that the whites were dissuaded from pressing for the Negroes' discharge. As late as 1941 Negro workers were still kept out of the Atlanta GM local, and only afterwards were they reluctantly admitted.

In order to gain recognition, the UAW was sometimes forced to accept contracts that perpetuated some old plant conditions. That meant that Negroes remained frozen in low-status jobs, and consequently that their original doubts about the union were reinforced. In other situations the UAW risked stirring dormant prejudices by demanding the improvement of Negro workers' condi-tions. When the UAW forced companies to upgrade Negroes, some white workers felt that their ethnic "superiority" and economic status were being endangered. No quick solution to such problems was possible, if only because the antagonism between skilled white and unskilled Negro criss-crossed the general skilled-unskilled antagonism. But the mere fact that industrial unions like the UAW tend to lessen competition between craft groups within an in-dustry helped smooth race relations. After some experience, white workers could be made to see that improvement of Negro conditions also helped im-prove their own conditions.

Gradually, at least a minority of Negro workers became convinced that the UAW could be trusted to defend them. Big rhetoric meant little, but little actions could mean much. When Negro delegates to the 1940 UAW conven-tion at St. Louis suffered from discrimination, the union voted to hold future gatherings only where Negroes would receive equal treatment. A small enough matter—but precisely such concrete little steps make the deepest impression.

Of all the auto companies, Ford had worked out by far the most astute policy on Negro employment. By hiring ten per cent of his workers from among Negroes, Henry Ford gained the clinging loyalty of the entire colored community. White workers would remain at their jobs at the Rouge because they had no alternative; Negro workers, because they considered the jobs lucky breaks made possible by Mr. Ford's friendliness to their people.

By sprinkling donations among Negro organizations and hiring thousands of Negro workers, Ford became a power in the Detroit Negro world. He donated the parish house of the St. Matthew's Episcopal Church and befriended its

Father Langton Daniels; his Negro agent, Donald Marshall, taught Sunday School classes at St. Matthew's; and once a year Henry Ford himself honored the church with a visit. He also gave substantial aid to the Second Baptist Church, whose minister, Reverend Robert Bradby, was one of his personal favorites. When either Reverend Bradby or Father Daniels recommended a Negro for a job, he was as good as hired. Negro politicians also, though less successfully, served as labor agents for Ford.

Ford also helped to finance the all-Negro village of Inkster and provided relief jobs at one dollar a day when its residents were unemployed. The Fords entertained committees from Negro women's clubs, invited George Washington Carver to their home, and paid Marian Anderson and Dorothy Maynor to sing over the radio on the Ford Sunday Hour. These things made a deep impression on Detroit's Negro world—and the Ford Company made the most of it.

When A. Philip Randolph, head of the Brotherhood of Sleeping Car Porters, was invited in 1938 to speak at a Negro church, those of its members who were employed at Ford were threatened with firing. After Randolph spoke, some were actually dismissed and frankly told that Randolph's speech was the reason. When Mordecai Johnson, president of Howard University, made a pro-union speech at a Negro church, a second appearance was denied him three months later—for in the meantime, the minister of the church admitted, "Don Marshall heard about the speech and was very angry.... He said he would never hire another member of the Bethel Church if the church allowed any more speakers to come here and criticize the company." And when the Negro community voted Democratic in the 1932 elections, Don Marshall did not hesitate to say, "My employer, he was disappointed when he saw the returns from the Negro districts...."

Ford's policy almost paid off. In April 1941, when Ford was negotiating with a puny AFL local in an attempt to edge out the UAW, a group of Negro clergymen urged the Negro workers to support the AFL against the UAW. Pressure had been applied by the Ford company for public support of the AFL, and though the ministers privately expressed their distaste for the AFL's record on race relations, they endorsed it as "a truly American organization ... [which] has acted in the best interests of the Negro...."

For the Negro middle class, the situation was admittedly difficult. Negro storekeepers and professionals, ministers and politicians, depended on Ford patronage in the direct form of subsidies and the indirect form of jobs. In an excellent study of Negro auto labor, Lloyd Bailer writes: "As long as the church membership is employed, the minister is able to keep his head above water. His ability to place job applicants swells church-attendance and enables him to keep his flock." Little wonder that the UAW found it so hard to organize Negro workers!

A minority of Negro leaders—including Walter White, head of the National Association for the Advancement of Colored People, and the Reverend Horace White of Detroit—was bold enough to risk helping the union. When the crucial 1941 Ford strike broke out, several hundred Negro workers remained in the plant, under the supervision of the Ford Service Department, after white workers walked out. But the Negroes could no longer be used as a solid strikebreaking bloc, and a large section of them was neutral enough to insure the success of the strike. Later they would be convinced that their place was in the union.

With the outbreak of the war in 1941, a new crisis in race relations began in the auto plants. Among the causes were:

(1) The influx of new Southern white workers brought into the UAW thousands of men who knew nothing of the union's slowly nurtured tradition of tolerance;

(2) The virtual exclusion of Negroes from skilled jobs in auto plants at a time when the government was bemoaning a manpower shortage aroused immense resentment among Negroes;

(3) The Detroit housing crisis aggravated already severe tensions between Negro and white;

(4) President Roosevelt's Executive Order 8802 prohibiting discrimination in war industries had aroused great hopes among Negroes; when it was largely ignored by industry and loosely enforced by the government, their resentment was increased.

When conversion to war production in the auto plants resulted in the upgrading of some Negro workers, many whites rebelled. A series of stoppages broke out against such upgrading or even against assignments to working with Negroes—and the union was usually helpless to prevent them. Two stoppages took place at Packard, one in November 1941 and the other in June 1943; four at Chrysler in February and June 1942; two at Timken Detroit Axle in July 1942; and one at Hudson Naval Ordnance in June 1942.

The stoppages at Packard were typical. In November 1941, white workers sat down on the job after two Negro metal polishers had been transferred to war work. The company readily withdrew the Negroes, and the officials of the Packard UAW local did little to defend them. In UAW circles there was talk that the Ku Klux Klan was influential in the local and had threatened to oppose its officials if they defended the Negroes. One white Packard worker told an interviewer: "About forty per cent of the workers here are Polish. There are also a lot of Southern whites. Both of them are very prejudiced. The rumor got out not long ago that Negroes were going to start working in the trim department—where I work. Most of them there are Southern whites. They said 'I'll be goddamned if I'm going to work with a goddam black nigger.'"

In 1943 another stoppage took place in Packard. When Negroes in the foundry briefly protested because they were not being upgraded according to seniority provisions, twenty-five thousand white workers walked out for four days. Walter White, NAACP leader, wrote that "subsequent investigation indicated that only a relatively small percentage of Packard workers actually wanted to go on strike," but the sad truth seems to be that he was wrong. Actually, thousands of Packard workers milled around the plant, listening to anti-Negro harangues. When R. J. Thomas, then UAW president, urged the men to return to work, he was booed.

But if the situation at Packard was appalling, Negroes were being upgraded in such plants as Kelsey Hayes, Consolidated Brass, and Briggs without any serious trouble. It is significant that in those plants, such as Briggs, where the UAW had its best locals, there was the least trouble. From the picture of the war years the terrible anti-Negro riots and walkouts jut out sharply, but it must be remembered that all the while the union leadership was trying desparately to educate new members, and to remind old members of its tradition of racial equality. During the bloody riot of 1943 not a single incident occurred in the plants—a remarkable fact.

UAW leaders and responsible militants had been taught by their wartime experience that the problem of prejudice would remain with the union for a long time to come. The friendliness that might develop during a strike would soon evaporate and in its place there would again arise the fears and hatred that are part of the heritage of so many white Americans. The momentary enthusiasm of Negro workers for the union could quickly give way to their more basic suspicion that all "white organizations" were their enemies. In the war years, the union had learned that once a riot started little could be done to prevent it from spreading over an entire city; the patient work of education carried on over the years could be destroyed in an hour.

While the union was being shaken by outbursts of anti-Negro feeling, a significant debate was taking place at its conventions. Since 1940 demands had been raised in the UAW for the creation of a special post for a Negro on its executive board. Negro members seemed largely to favor this proposal, perhaps seeing in it a way to protect their status in the union. Here was a situation made to order for a group ready to engage in demagogic exploitation of Negro grievances—and the Communist party eager for the job.

At the 1943 UAW convention in Buffalo, one hundred and fifty out of two thousand delegates were Negroes. A caucus of Negro delegates was held to which all UAW leaders were invited to explain their views. In a principled and courageous speech, Walter Reuther told the Negroes that he considered any special position designated for a minority group an inverse form of Jim Crow which he could not support. But with the demagogy of the Communist leaders and the political inexperience of most of the Negro delegates, ninety per cent of the latter voted to support the caucus headed by George Addes and staffed by Stalinists, because it favored a special Negro post. Though the proposal was defeated on the convention floor, most of the Negro delegates were led into a temporary alliance with the Stalinists because the latter seemed to them their special champions.

The issue itself is of great interest. There is a special Negro problem and it needs special attention. Consequently, why not elect a special member of the executive board to handle the problem? And who could do that so well as a Negro—perhaps a "special kind" of Negro? But as the more alert Negro workers were soon to realize, this proposal meant that a Negro was to be "up-graded" in the union not because of his talents but because of the color of his skin—and was this not merely a special inversion of the practice to which they so bitterly and rightly objected in the shops? Suppose, further, that the proposal were extended just a bit: since Negro workers had special problems, why not help them by putting them in special . . . separate . . . locals?

How dubious were the motives of the Stalinists in supporting this proposal was later shown at the 1947 Michigan CIO convention. There William Humphries, a Negro delegate and already a member of the Michigan CIO board, denounced the proposal for a special post for a Negro by insisting that any self-respecting Negro would want to be elected to office not because he was a Negro but because he was a good leader. When Humphries ran for office, the Addes-Stalinist bloc did not vote for him—the Stalinists would support a Negro only if he were in their tow and had been properly stamped: "Negro." By then, their motives were understood and the majority of delegates, white and Negro, repudiated them. True, the Reuther group's opposition to the special board post had been politically disadvantageous in 1943, but by 1948 it had resulted in healthier relations between white and colored unionists.

With the end of the war, the old discriminatory patterns in hiring reappeared. Thousands of Negro men and women lost their jobs and, even if sometimes mistakenly, could not help feeling that this was because of Jim Crow practices. "The Negro," said Walter Reuther, "has experienced the quick erosion of his wartime gains. . . ."

The crucial test for the UAW with regard to race relations will come if unemployment in Michigan, now on the increase, reaches large proportions. There is as yet no serious unemployment among Detroit auto workers, but in Muskegon and Grand Rapids many auto workers are being laid off. Since, as a rule, Negro auto workers have less seniority than whites, the Negroes will suffer first and most heavily from unemployment. And once the auto workers begin to fear for their jobs, some whites will probably feel that they would be more secure if Negroes were driven out of the auto plants. If there are any serious anti-Negro outbursts in the next year or two in Detroit, they will probably be the result of this growing job insecurity among all auto workers.

Nor do the employment policies of the large corporations particularly improve the status of Negro workers. Recently, to cite one example, the Chrysler corporation hired hundreds of new men, but almost none of them were Negroes. After Chrysler Local 7 of the UAW protested, a few Negroes were hired. Ford has hired a few more Negroes in the better jobs, but it is difficult to say whether this is the result of the traditional Ford policy of catering to the Negro population, union pressure (the Ford local has one of the best records on this question), or the "enlightened" labor policy of Henry Ford II. (UAW people, who find themselves at present in a very tough bargaining position with Ford, are inclined to regard this "enlightenment" as the invention of Ford's public-relations department.) In most of the auto plants there is little, if any, effort by the management to upgrade Negro workers to the better jobs. Squeezed between the indifference of management and the rumbling hostility of a portion of the white workers, Negroes are still a distinctly underprivileged group in the auto labor force.

On a formal level, the UAW has acted vigorously to defend the Negro workers. Its FEPC department has called regular conferences to push union work against Jim Crow; its educational film, *Brotherhood of Man*, an excellent piece of work, has been widely circulated; its numerous printed circulars have persuasively argued for equality. But the problem goes deeper.

Some people cling to a stereotyped view that a militant and aggressive rank and file of union members is held back only by the leaders' timidity or bureaucratic indifference. Whatever the merit of this view on other issues, it is certainly false with regard to the UAW and the Negroes. The truth is that in the UAW it is the top leadership that has the best understanding of the problem and the best record in dealing with it. Time after time, UAW leaders have risked the displeasure of their followers by advocating equal rights for Negroes. Endowed with a larger view of social trends than most members of the union, these leaders have sometimes butted their heads against the wall of prejudice. The records of the secondary officials, those who run the locals, vary widely. Some, such as the leaders of the Briggs local, have consistently fought for their Negro members. In others, leaders merely go through the motions of supporting the union policy.

The plain truth is that the bulk of the prejudice in the UAW is to be found in the rank and file, especially among workers of Southern or Polish extraction. There is a constant subterranean war in the minds and hearts of the white workers between prejudice and the education received in the union. Two incidents may illustrate this conflict. In November 1948 a Negro woman employed at the Hudson plant was disciplined for what other employes considered an unjust reason; first her department and then the entire plant shut down in protest. That would seem a heartening display of solidarity between white and Negro workers, would it not? But only a few days before this shutdown, the Hudson local had held a Hallowe'en party from which three Negro couples were barred by policemen called by an unnamed local official to "keep the niggers out." After much maneuvering and two membership meetings, the local instructed its committees to refrain from discrimination at future social affairs. But no one seriously believes that a mere resolution is going to solve this problem. Actually, quite a few UAW locals avoid dances because their officers fear to face the problem of "mixed dancing."

Next to promotion and seniority, social affairs remain the largest source of racial friction in the union. White workers who have acquiesced in union policy or learned to work and go on strike with Negroes are still unwilling to go to the same dance with them. The Briggs local was compelled to cancel its first dance in 1937 when white members protested against the presence of Negroes; but the local's leadership has since taken a strong stand against discrimination and in recent years has held completely unsegregated affairs. In other locals, Negroes are seldom present at social affairs. In such matters, the vision and courage of local leaders would seem to be decisive.

A similar difficulty has arisen in sports activities. UAW locals have active baseball leagues in which white and Negro members play on the same teams. No problem arises there. But some of the very same men who play baseball with Negroes bitterly object to the union's attempt to organize a bowling league on a non-discriminatory basis. In 1948, after the UAW failed to force the American Bowling League to remove Jim Crow provisions from its constitution, it started a new bowling league. Few of Walter Reuther's acts have been more unpopular with large sections of the union's ranks. Why will a white worker play baseball with a Negro but refuse to bowl with him? One possible explanation is that white workers feel that there is greater impersonality in baseball than in bowling. When the baseball game is over, white and colored players usually dress and go their separate ways; but the bowling game is itself an intimate social event, in which members' wives participate, and which is followed by beer drinking.

Such contradictory behavior seems to be the result of strong feelings of prejudice being jostled by new equalitarian ideas picked up in the union. But the prejudice is at the center, and the new ideas at the periphery of many workers' minds. One conclusion that seems legitimate is that the minds of white workers remain compartmentalized: their frequent readiness to consort on equal terms with Negroes in the shops and on picket lines seldom extends to life outside the shop. In the May 1948 Chrysler strike, Negroes participated to an unprecedented extent in picketing, soup-kitchen work, and similar strike activities, and the attitude of white workers towards the Negroes was warm and cordial. Yet when the local's FEPC committee shortly afterwards proposed a campaign against discrimination in restaurants near the plants, white workers were at best lukewarm, and many were openly hostile.

The UAW's experience with the "Negro problem" provides a crucial test of how race prejudice can be combated and destroyed in practice. The experience is by no means conclusive or finished; the great test will come if employment seriously falls off. But a few conclusions are possible.

For the Negro workers, the UAW has provided a vital arena for expression and a means of achieving personal dignity. Negro participation in union affairs, though still inhibited and hampered, is on the increase; in some recent local union elections higher proportions of Negroes voted than did whites. In the UAW many Negro workers have learned to talk boldly and freely; they have learned that the whole white world is not a conspiracy against them but that there are unionists ready even to risk their careers to help them; they have begun, shyly and slowly, to live, work, eat, and play with white workers at the UAW summer camps. The spirit of the Negro workers today is as different from what it was fifteen years ago as the spirit of Ford workers is different from what it was during Harry Bennett's rule.

Here, then, is proof that the problem of prejudice can be attacked in daily life. It must be solved largely by empirical means: most white and Negro workers can overcome their fears and prejudices only by working and living together in the plants and, afterwards, by social contacts outside the plants.

But in turn—and the paradox is only apparent—this empirical program can be instituted *only* by a leadership motivated by a compelling long-range program of social and economic democracy, an idealistic vision that would endow it with the perseverance and patience to work at the day-to-day tasks.

The role of white leadership is usually decisive. In the nature of things, most unions begin with white leaders who have it in their power to win the confidence of Negro workers and thereby hasten the development of Negro leaders. This they can do by a firm policy of equal treatment, without condescension or favoritism. Few of the Reuther administration's acts have so helped it win the *eventual* confidence of the Negroes in the UAW as its refusal to be swept into supporting the demagogic proposal for a separate Negro post on the union's executive board.

The blend of long-range idealism and immediate tenacity of which we have spoken is particularly necessary for the UAW's ultimate task in the field of race relations—to try to spread its anti-prejudice education down through the ranks, where it is most needed. Rational appeals, formal statements, impressive resolutions have only a limited value. It is necessary to make over, so to speak, the thought and feeling of the average union member, the one who comes only to an occasional meeting and who is active only in times of crisis. This is not an easy job, and it may prove to be an impossible one if attempted by the union alone. But it is the fundamental job.

Of all the consequences of the unionization of Negro auto workers, there is one that may eventually surpass in importance all the others. As a result of the mass adherence of Negro workers to the UAW, important changes have taken place in the social structure of Detroit's Negro community. The Negro middle class as well as the Negro ministers and politicians have begun to show signs of independence. This makes for greater independence of the Negro community *vis à vis* the city as a whole. And within the Negro community, its middle class no longer commands the undisputed intellectual and political leadership over Negro workers it once did. The Reverend Horace White, Negro minister, has remarked that "the CIO has usurped moral leadership in the [Negro] community." It is on this rising and striking figure—the self-confident, experienced Negro UAW leader—that much of the future of both the union and the Negro community will depend.

Ralph J. Bunche

THE PROGRAMS OF ORGANIZATIONS DEVOTED TO THE IMPROVEMENT OF THE STATUS OF THE AMERICAN NEGRO

The decades between the two World Wars were characterized by a diversity of programs and organizations aimed at advancing the Negroes' status in the United States. Ralph J. Bunche's article, which appeared toward the close of the Depression years, describes and evaluates the major ones.

Minority groups, such as the American Negro, inevitably tend to become introverted in their social thinking. Attention of the group is so firmly riveted on the struggle to attain release from suppression, that its social perspective becomes warped. The group discovers early that the barriers between it and the status of the dominant majority are sturdy and formidable. Progress is insufferably slow, and the necessity for constant battering against the solid walls of majority prejudice and domination—a social heritage of each succeeding minority generation—gives rise to a psychological fixation in the minority population.

The problems of the group come to be analyzed in progressively narrow terms. Thinking, feeling, life itself, revolve about the narrow axis of "minority status." All agitation and protest, all programs and tactics, operate within this circumscribed framework.

If the assumed basis of minority group status is race rather than culture, as in the case of the American Negro, race ineluctably tends to become the overwhelmingly dominant factor in the social equation devised by the group to interpret its problem. Thus, with the Negro, racial interpretations are generally considered the only "realistic" ones. Events that cannot be explained on the color chart are relegated to categories of inconsequence to

Ralph J. Bunche, "The Programs of Organizations Devoted to the Improvement of the Status of the American Negro," *Journal of Negro Education*, VIII (July, 1939), pp. 539–550. Reprinted with the permission of the author and publisher.

the Negro. The Negro is an American citizen, but his thinking is often more Negro than American. The white American may look with subjective interest upon Munich, but the American Negro regards the latest lynching as infinitely more important to him. The white American may recoil with horror at the German barbarisms against the Jew. But the American Negro cries, "Hitler be damned, and the Jew too; what about the Jim Crow here?" The Negro may evidence some momentary excitation about Italy's rape of Ethiopia, but the dismemberment of Czecho-Slovakia is the white man's business.

It is precisely the minority group organizations and their leadership which portray minority chauvinism in boldest relief. Organizations and leaders seek only escape for their group. They flounder about, desperately and often blindly, in their ghettoes of thought, seeking a break in the dams of oppression through which they may lead their flock to a more dignified and secure existence. The tiniest crevice in the barriers is magnified into a brilliant ray of hope. So great is the desperation that daily disillusionments are angrily shaken off; they pound away at impregnable walls, dash triumphantly down blind alleys, yet dare not stop to calculate lest it is learned that ultimate escape is generations, even centuries removed.

American Negro organizations and leaders run true to minority type. Color is their phobia; race their creed. The Negro has problems and they are all racial ones; ergo, their solution must be in terms of race. In general, whites must be regarded with suspicion, if not as enemies. White allies are recruited, it is true, but only from those who think of Negro problems as Negroes think of them. There is impatience with any but race problems. There is little appetite for social theories and limited ability to digest social forces. There is but one social force for the Negro, and that is color. As long as the Negro is black and the white man harbors prejudice, what has the Negro to do with class or caste, with capitalism, imperialism, facism, communism or any other "ism"? Race is the black man's burden.

Generally speaking, it may be stated that the weakness of organizations devoted to the salvation of the Negro is implicit in their structure and philosophy. In the course of the Negro's post-Emancipation history, numerous organizations, black, white, and mixed, have directed their efforts toward lifting him out of the muck of subjection. These organizations, in varying degree and with minor exceptions, have had the following fundamental characteristics:

(1) adherence to policies of escape, based upon racialism and nationalism;
(2) lack of mass support among Negroes, and mass appeal;
(3) dependence upon white benefactors for finance;
(4) reluctance to encourage the development of working-class psychology among Negroes and avoidance of class interpretations;
(5) tendency, directly or indirectly, to take their main ideological cues from white sympathizers;
(6) lack of a coherent, constructive program;
(7) lack of broad social perspective and the ability to relate the problems

of the Negro to the main social currents and forces of the American society; and

(8) pursuit of policies of immediate relief and petty opportunism.

The two principal historical schools of Negro thought had as their ideological leaders Booker T. Washington and W. E. B. DuBois. Washington, who founded Tuskegee Institute in 1881, was the great exponent of what has come to be known as the policy of conciliation.[1] In this policy of appeasement Negroes were advised to cast down their buckets where they were; to avoid conflict with the white man; to accept racial separation and its implication of inferiority as inescapable; to rely upon the good-will of the white upper classes; to work hard, develop thrifty habits and strive for economic independence. Washington discouraged the Negro worker from the identification of his interests and organized efforts with the white working class, whose objectives he mistrusted. That he should advocate the dignity of labor but not the importance of its organized unity in an industrial society, did not appear inconsistent to him. In short, his was a policy of cautious expediency, designed to win the approbation of Southern whites and Northern philanthropists. This was a very racial sort of "realism," and its immediate objectives were realized. It has left an indelible impression on the South, and landmarks in the form of industrial schools for Negroes. But the great problems of Negro-white relationships remain unaffected.

DuBois early began a vigorous assault on the teachings of Booker T. Washington.[2] He instituted an insistent campaign for full social and political equality for the Negro. Where Washington advised the Negro to eschew politics, DuBois made the attainment of the franchise a cardinal objective in his program of Negro betterment. DuBois went back beyond Washington to Frederick Douglass in thus exalting the indispensable virtue of the ballot.

Though Washington and DuBois differed sharply on the issues of political and social equality for the Negro, and industrial versus cultural education, they were never very far apart in their basic philosophies. Both confined their thinking within the periphery of race. Though DuBois emphasized the helplessness of a disfranchised working class, the direction of his effort was toward Negro enfranchisement rather than toward working class unity. In recent years he has expressed strongly the view that union between white and black workers is a futile hope, and advocated the full exploitation of Negro segregation as a means of increasing group strength, especially in economic matters. Both Washington and DuBois strove for: (1) improved living conditions for Negro city-dwellers; (2) greatly increased educational facilities; (3) equality of economic opportunity; (4) equal justice in the courts; (5) emphasis on racial consciousness and dignity.

Two of the more important Negro betterment organizations sprung up under the aegis of these two influential Negro leaders: the National Negro

[1] Booker T. Washington, *Up From Slavery; Future of the American Negro, passim.*
[2] W. E. B. DuBois, *The Souls of Black Folk, passim.*

Business League, established by Washington in 1900, and the National Association for the Advancement of Colored People, which DuBois helped to form in 1910. DuBois had organized the Niagara Movement in 1905, which protested against racial discrimination in all of its forms.

In the decade prior to Emancipation Martin Delany and McCune Smith had advocated the principles of thrift, industry, and exploitation of economic separatism as a means of economic escape for free black men. Some fifty years later Washington made these principles the foundation stones for his National Negro Business League. In terms of its influence on economic betterment of the Negro the National Business League has been inconsequential. As a factor in shaping the psychology and thinking of Negroes, however, it has been vastly important, especially in the period following the migrations under the leadership of Dr. Washington's successor, Major Robert R. Moton. It has fed the Negro on the traditional American illusion that even the man or group on the very lowest rung of the economic ladder can, by industry, thrift, efficiency, and perseverance, attain the top rung. It has pursued the narrowest type of racial chauvinism, for it has organized not business, but "Negro" business, and has employed the racial situation as its main stock in trade in bidding for the support of Negro patronage. The League is the ideological parent to the traditionally reactionary philosophy of Negro business advocates. This is cogently stated in the resolution formulated by the Business section of the first meeting of the National Negro Congress in Chicago, in February, 1936:

> The development of sound and thriving Negro business is most indispensable to the general elevation of the Negro's social and economic security ... all Negroes consider it their inescapable duty to support Negro business by their patronage.[3]

This hope for the salvation of the Negro masses by the erection of black business within the walls of white capitalism is clearly futile. It is obvious that the advocates of Negro business attempt to labor a policy of "expediency" through exploitation of the segregation incident to the racial dualism of America. Negro business suckles at the breast of the poverty-stricken Negro ghettoes and is inevitably undernourished. And must remain so. It exists only on the sufferance of that dominant white business world which controls credit, basic industry, and the state. The appeal which Negro business makes for the support of Negroes is a racial one, viz.: that the race can advance only through economic unity. Yet the small, individually-owned Negro businesses cannot meet the price competition of the larger-capitalized, more efficient white businesses. The very poverty of the Negro consumer dictates that he must buy where he can find cheapest prices. Negroes in the United States spend approximately $4,150,000,000 per year for the three essential items of food, clothing and shoes,[4] but only some $83,000,000 of this sum is spent with Negro retailers.

[3] Cf. "Triumph? Or Fiasco?", by R. J. Bunche, *Race*, 1:(No. 2) Summer, 1936.
[4] *Negro Year Book*, 1931–2, p. 132.

In 1929 the National Negro Business League organized the Colored Merchants' Association (C.M.A.) stores. These were individually-owned stores which attempted to reduce overhead by cooperative buying and group advertising, and by consequent lower prices to attract Negro trade. The membership fees were modest, but only a few Negro businesses were attracted to the scheme. The Negro consuming public did not take to the untested brands sold by the C.M.A. stores, preferring the nationally advertised standard brands offered by the white chain stores. In 1934, in the midst of the depression, the C.M.A. experiment met a quiet demise.

At best, Negro business becomes a parasitical growth on the Negro society. It must eke out a meager existence from the segregated Negro community, as a middleman between large white business and the Negro market, through exploitation of the "race problem." Negro business, recognizing its inability to compete with white business on equal terms, demands for itself special privilege and marches under the chauvinistic banner of "race loyalty," thus further exploiting an already sorely harassed group. It represents the interests only of the pitifully small Negro middle-class group, though receiving support for its ideology from the race conscious masses.

The development of Negro capitalism in America, even granting its possibility, would offer no hope for the betterment of the Negro masses. There is no evidence that the 12,561 employees of the Negro retail stores [5] reported in 1937, worked under better conditions for their Negro employers than did Negroes working for white employers. There is no reason to believe that the Negro employer is any less profit-minded than the white, or that he is any less reluctant to exploit his fellow blacks as employees than any other employer. The Negro population is a working-class population. Negro business may offer an uncertain escape from economic oppression for a handful of the more able or more fortunate members of the group. But the overwhelming majority of Negroes in America will continue to till the soil and toil in the industries of the white employer.[6]

A logical corollary of the Negro business philosophy has recently come to the fore in the guise of the "don't buy where you can't work" or "buy where you can work" credo. This movement began about 1931 in Chicago, and rapidly spread to the East. It has been sponsored by organizations such as the "League for Fair Play," the "Afro-American Federation of Labor" and the "New Negro Alliance." These organizations occasionally have employed the labor weapons of boycott and picketing against white stores in Negro districts which refuse to employ Negro white-collar workers. This has been of educational value to the Negro in that it has given him some inkling of his latent economic power and an acquaintance with the recognized weapons of labor. The most violent manifestation of this movement was in the Harlem riot of 1935, when thousands of Harlem Negroes vented their fury, born of poverty, against the small white shop-owners on Lenox and Seventh Avenues.

The philosophy of this movement is narrowly racial. If successful, it could

[5] *Negro Year Book*, 1937–8, p. 92.
[6] Abram L. Harris, *The Negro as Capitalist, passim.*

only result in a vicious cycle of job displacement, since it creates no new jobs but only struggles to displace white workers, and since Negro communities do not offer sufficient economic activity to absorb even a small number of the Negroes now employed in white industries. Its appeal has been primarily in the interest of the Negro white-collar worker, and its support has come chiefly from Negro middle-class professional and intellectual groups. It appears unable to realize that there is an economic system as well as a race problem in America and that when a Negro is unemployed, it is not just because he is a Negro, but more seriously, because of the defective operation of the economy under which we live—an economy that finds it impossible to provide an adequate number of jobs and economic security for the population. More seriously still, this movement tends to widen the menacing gap between white and black workers, by insisting that jobs be distributed on a racial basis. It is a philosophy which, like that of Negro business, offers only racialism, with no significant hope for the mass Negro population.

In 1910 the National League on Urban Conditions Among Negroes was founded, as a social-service agency devoted to the task of aiding rural Negroes in their adjustment to urban life, and securing positions for them in industry. The work of this organization, subsequently named the National Urban League, assumed increasing importance with the great migration of Negroes to Northern cities after 1916. The chief financial support of the Urban League is from white philanthropy. Its headquarters are in New York and it has some forty local offices in the large industrial centers. Negroes hold all responsible executive offices, but the local directing boards are interracial. Its slogan is "not alms but opportunity," i.e., economic opportunity.

This organization advocates a policy of racial expediency and conciliation, which is characterized by extreme opportunism. It tries to make the most out of the condition of racial separatism and appeals to the conscience and good-will of the white community, especially the employing class. It maintains an industrial department, which attempts to place city Negroes in white industry. It runs "Negro-in-industry-weeks"; it sends its secretaries to white employers in an effort to sell them the idea of employing more Negroes; some of the local offices run employment bureaus, and send welfare agents into the plants to aid in the adjustment of Negro employees. Feeble attempts have been made toward lifting trade-union bars against Negro workers, but there has been no real effort to advance the doctrine of solidarity between white and black workers. In fact there have been instances in which Urban League locals have encouraged scabbing and strikebreaking by Negro workers.[7]

That the Urban League has rendered valuable services for urban Negro populations throughout the country can scarcely be disputed. But it is equally true that its policy operates within the genteel framework of conciliation and interracial good-will. Moreover its efforts have been directed at winning the sympathies of white employers, professional and intellectual groups, and the top ranks of the hierarchy of organized labor.

[7] Spero and Harris, *The Black Worker*, p. 140.

There is no single element of economic realism in this policy. It barters away the economic future of the Negro worker for an immediate but transitory "gain" in the form of a temporary job. It is severely race-conscious, but socially blind. It encourages the development of a racial caste within the American working class and it lacks the independence and courage necessary to give honest direction to the Negro working population.

The programs of organizations like the Y.M.C.A., the Y.W.C.A., the interracial groups, such as the Atlanta Interracial Commission and the Department of Race Relations of the Federal Council of the Churches of Christ in America, are similarly committed to the rather dubious task of developing interracial fellow feeling. Their appeal is to the enlightened groups in the dominant population. They divorce race and economics. They operate on the assumption that when the two races know and understand each other better, the principal incidents of the race problem will disappear. They almost invariably shy away from the harsher aspects of the problem, such as the Negro's relation to organized labor, and therefore, even when sincere, tend to confuse and obscure the vital issues. They are exclusively middle-class, and have but slight contact with the working masses of either race. For these they offer no effective program.

The most extreme example of black chauvinism is found in Marcus Garvey's U.N.I.A.[8] Garvey came to the United States from Jamaica in 1916, and began to preach the gospel of a return to Africa, and international pan-Africanism. His movement developed into a sort of black Zionism. But in its immediate objectives and its influence on the thought of American Negroes, it conformed to the typical pattern of Negro betterment organizations. It was intensely nationalistic; it sought to arouse race consciousness and pride among Negroes. It boasted a realism of sorts, in that it adopted a fatalistic attitude toward the Negro dream of attaining equality in a white man's country. Garveyism was opposed to the policy of unity of black and white labor, regarding all white labor unions with suspicion, and counseling the Negro worker to ally himself with the white employer until such time as the Negro could become economically independent and his own employer.

The movement received amazing support from Negro masses of both North and South. No other organization has ever been able to reach and stir the masses of Negroes to the same degree, or to receive from them such generous financial support.

Garveyism collapsed when its leader was convicted of fraud. It had made but feeble gestures toward Africa but it did afford a psychological escape for the black masses. It provided an emotional release, through its highly charged "race" meetings, its fiery, race-conscious orators, its emphasis on pride in things black, its elaborate parades, ceremonials, brilliant uniforms, and the pomp and circumstance of its meetings. When the curtain dropped on the Garvey theatricals, the black man of America was exactly where Garvey had found him, though a little bit sadder, if not wiser.

[8] Universal Negro Improvement Association.

Dr. DuBois had organized the Niagara Movement in 1905, as a broadside of protest against racial discrimination of every kind. This beginning sounded the tocsin of Negro civil libertarianism and it was designed as a militant departure from the Booker T. Washington philosophy. Out of the Niagara Movement there emerged, in 1910, in New York City, the National Association for the Advancement of Colored People, with a bold program of complete political and cultural assimilation.

The N.A.A.C.P. accepted struggle on the political front as the most promising means of attaining equality for Negroes. Through the use of the ballot and the courts strenuous efforts were exerted to gain social justice for the group. Full faith was placed in the ability of these instruments of democratic government to free the minority from social proscription and civic inequality. Under this banner the N.A.A.C.P. has fought for full equality for the Negro, involving the eradication of all social, legal, and political disabilities tending to draw a line of distinction between the black citizen and the white. The Negro, like the white American, is to quaff the full draught of eighteenth-century democratic liberalism. The Negro citizen must have the franchise, freedom of economic opportunity (consisting of the right to employment without discrimination), the right to accommodations in public places and on common carriers, the right to voluntary choice of place of residence, the right to jury service, equal expenditures of public funds for education and other public services, and protection against lynch violence.

In the pursuit of this great struggle, the Negro has been seriously handicapped, in that he has never yet been able to win any large measure of suffrage. Thus, his political pressure power is limited to those relatively few sectors in which the Negro votes and holds or threatens to hold the political balance of power. Perhaps 90 per cent of the potential black voting strength of the South is eliminated by the devices of disfranchisement employed by the states of the solid South.

The N.A.A.C.P. has carried on its struggle valiantly and has won many notable local victories, in both the political and judicial arenas. Its collaboration with labor in the Senate's rejection of Judge Parker's nomination to the Supreme Court; its recent fight on the educational front, culminating in the celebrated Gaines case triumph; and its unceasing demand for an antilynching law, deserve prominent mention. Yet, it has never succeeded in developing a program which has that bread-and-butter appeal necessary to command the support of the mass section of the Negro population. Its court successes have often proved to be pyrrhic victories, even as the Gaines case promises to be, in that they merely reassert rights that the Constitution clearly promises to all citizens, but which the white population stubbornly refuses to recognize as exercisable by Negroes. Nor has the N.A.A.C.P. broadened its interests to include a constructive, clearly-defined and practical program for the economic betterment of the race.

The inherent fallacy in this type of political militancy is found in the failure to recognize that the instrumentalities of the state, constitution, government and laws, can do no more than reflect the political, social and economic ideology of the dominant population, and that the political arm of the state cannot be divorced from the prevailing economic structure.

Thus the N.A.A.C.P. policy of civil libertarianism is circumscribed by the dominant mores of the society. In the final analysis, whatever success it may have, must depend upon its ability to elicit a sympathetic response to its appeals from among influential elements in the advantaged population. In the long run, therefore, its militancy must be toned down and the inevitable result is that the programs of organizations such as the N.A.A.C.P. tend gradually to conform to the general pattern of the genteel programs of inter-racial conciliation, which strive to cultivate the good-will of the white "better classes." They are forced to cajole, bargain, compromise, and even capitulate in order to win petty gains or hollow victories. The N.A.A.C.P. has elected to fight for civil liberties rather than for labor unity; it has never reached the masses of Negroes, and remains strictly Negro middle-class, Negro-*intelligentsia*, in its leadership and appeal. It has received increasing financial support from Negroes, but has often had to lean heavily upon its white benefactors for monetary aid and advice; and it has cautiously maintained its respectability.

The first meeting of the National Negro Congress was held in Chicago in February 1936. This organization, taking its cue from India, was an attempt to develop a Negro united front, and to work out a minimum program of action which could win wide acceptance among Negro as well as sympathetic white organizations. The Congress has held two national meetings, and has many regional and local branches. These undertake to unify the local protest movements against injustices on the united front principle. That is to say the Congress has proceeded on the assumption that the common denominator of race is enough to weld together in thought and action, such divergent segments of the Negro society as preachers and labor organizers, lodge officials and black workers, Negro business men, Negro radicals, professional politicians, professional men, domestic servants, black butchers, bakers and candlestick makers. The Congress mountain has twice labored and has brought forth many contradictions,[9] but no program of action in advance of that already formulated by previously-established Negro organizations.

A Negro Congress with a strong labor bias and with its representation less diffuse and more homogeneous in its thinking could conceivably work out a clearer, more consistent and realistic program than has yet come from the National Negro Congress.

The Negro churches and schools reach more deeply into the Negro masses than do any of the deliberate and formal Negro protest organizations. But it cannot be said that either church or school is a tower of strength in its influence on the social thinking of Negroes and in its contribution toward the improvement of the status of the group. Negro schools, even more than white schools, are controlled by the dominant group, and have never been characterized by their courage in leading any frontal attack upon the problems

[9] Cf. "Triumph? Or Fiasco?", *op. cit.*

of the group.[10] The schools are responsive to the interests of those who provide the money for their support, and they are not free. The churches have more independence, but they are controlled by reactionary and often ambitious, self-seeking gentlemen of the frock, and they too lack courage, as well as intelligent leadership.

It is a sad but true commentary that despite the universal grievances endured by the harshly buffeted Negro, there is no single organization, save the church, the school, and in lesser degree, the fraternal order, which can boast any intimate contact with and support from the common man who represents the mass Negro population. The Negro church has consecrated itself to the spiritual salvation of its charges, and has leaned heavily on the side of social reaction and racialism whenever it has concerned itself with the black man's worldly life. The Negro lodges and fraternal orders have contributed little of a constructive nature to the social thought of their Negro membership, though they indulge abundantly in ritual and social activity. The Negro schools are socially vacuous and have shown no disposition to meet the challenge offered by the problems of the group whose interests they are designed to serve. The Negro school, its principal or president and its teachers, are content to seek refuge in the tranquil atmosphere of the academic cloister and to look down upon the problems of the group and its neglected masses, in "scholarly" detachment. The students are infected by this false isolation and are not equipped to understand nor to attack the social problems with which they are confronted in their post-school life.

It is not surprising that the narrowly racial conceptions of the Negro have caused him to be seduced by anti-semitism. He thinks only in terms of jobs for Negroes, business for Negroes, Negro landlords, bankers and employers, and vents his emotional spleen on the Jewish shop-keeper in the Negro neighborhood, who exploits the black trade quite as enthusiastically as would the black shopkeeper. The Negro anti-Semite does not reason, nor does it matter, that all Jews are neither shopkeepers nor prejudiced. It is sufficient that the Jew makes profit from a store in a Negro section that Negroes ought to own and work in, or that a Jewish professor holds a position at a Negro university that a Negro, if even a less competent one, should occupy. Such bigoted attitudes are deliberately nurtured by the self-seeking, sensitive Negro middle-class—the business and professional groups, who seek an economic base for their middle-class aspirations.

In view of the obvious social implications for the Negro of this sort of blind, suicidal emotionalism, and the certain truth that racial generalizations and prejudices are luxuries which the Negro can ill afford, it is a bitter indictment of Negro organizations that none has been rational or bold enough to wage a vigorous campaign against Negro anti-Semitism.

Again, in a world in which the major issues affecting the future of humanity are increasingly defined in terms of fascism, with its fundamental

[10] Cf. "Black and White in Education," by R. J. Bunche, *Journal of Negro Education*, 5: July, 1936.

racial and totalitarian dogmas, versus democracy, imperfect as it has been for minority groups, no Negro organization makes any serious attempt to define these issues in terms of Negro interest, or to align the full power of Negroes with those forces which are struggling heroically to preserve the last vestiges of human liberty in a world gravely threatened with enslavement. Negro organizations herald the Gaines case and the anti-lynching bill while the eyes of the rest of the world are turned on Munich, Prague and Memel, Albania, Spain and China.

It is typical of Negro organizations that they concern themselves not with the broad social and political implications of such policies as government relief, housing, socialized medicine, unemployment and old-age insurance, wages and hours laws, etc., but only with the purely racial aspects of such policies. They are content to let the white citizen determine the expediency of major policies, and the form and direction they will assume, while they set themselves up as watch dogs over relatively petty issues, as whether the Negro will get his proper share of the benefits and whether the laws, once made, will be fairly administered. They thus demark for the Negro a residual function in the society.

There is no coordination of thought or serious collaboration in action among these several important Negro organizations and their numerous satellites. Each has marked off its little sphere of action and guards it with professional jealousy. No effective use has ever been made of the numerical strength of the Negro population, nor of its economic importance in labor and consuming power. Race pride does not permit most Negro organizations to make intelligent and practical overtures to the white working population, since a rebuff would result in loss of dignity.

The Negro is sorely in need of organization and leadership which is sufficiently independent and intelligent to give courageous orientation to the group and to guide it rationally through the bewildering maze of social forces which characterize the modern world. This organization and leadership would presumably adhere to some such policies as the following: (1) it would place less emphasis on race and more on economics and broad political and economic forces; (2) it would understand that the major problems of Negroes are not entirely attributable to race but are intimately linked up with the operation of the economy; (3) it would attempt to gain a mass basis among Negroes by a simple program designed to raise the economic level of the Negro worker; (4) it would devote its full energy toward the incorporation of Negro workers in labor unions, and would carry on incessant educational propaganda among both black and white workers toward this end; (5) it would attempt to throw the full support of Negro workers behind the movement to organize labor on an industrial basis, since the vast majority of Negroes are unskilled workers; (6) it would not cease to fight on the political and judicial fronts but would subordinate this to the fight on the economic and union fronts; (7) it would recognize that the future interests of Negroes are closely related to every general effort to improve the lot and increase the security of the working man of whatever color, and it would back every such measure to the limit; (8) it would include Negro labor leaders in its leadership and among its most influential advisers, and avoid dependence on professional Negro leaders and professional white interracialists; (9) it would interpret for Negroes, and relate their interests to, every world event and every foreign policy of importance; (10) its interpretations would be less in terms of race and more in terms of group economic interest; (11) it would recognize that the problems of the Negro cannot be solved in the courts, nor yet by the ballot, even under American democracy; (12) it would take its cue from the share-croppers' and tenant-farmers' unions formed in the South in recent years, and realize that above all, these successful efforts have broken down once and for all the stubborn legend that prejudice between white and black in the South is invested with a mystical quality and is insurmountable; (13) it would recognize that under oppressive conditions identity of economic interests can overcome racial prejudices, and that black and white unity is possible.

Existing Negro organizations are philosophical and programmatic paupers. They think and act entirely in a black groove. In a world in which events move rapidly and in which the very future of themselves and their group is at stake, they are unable to see the social forests for the racial saplings. They, like Hitler, even though for different reasons, think that "all that is not race in this world is trash." [11]

Because of the extreme provincialism of its organizations and leadership, the Negro population of America suffers from stagnation in its social thought. The traditional stereotypes and clichés of Negro thought have become outmoded and a new set of values, tooled to fit the political and economic conditions of the modern world, are indicated. Negro organizations should take close inventory of their policies and discard shop-worn doctrines; and should realize that freedom in the modern world is not to be bought at bargain-basement prices. Unless the Negro can develop, and quickly, organization and leadership endowed with broad social perspective and fore-sighted, analytical intelligence, the black citizen of America may soon face the dismal prospect of reflecting upon the tactical errors of the past from the gutters of the black ghettoes and concentration camps of the future.

[11] Adolf Hitler, *Mein Kampf* (Reynal and Hitchcock unexpurgated edition, 1939), p. 406.

PART SEVEN

THE NEW MILITANCY
AND THE
ENDURING GHETTO

Doxey A. Wilkerson

THE NEGRO SCHOOL MOVEMENT
IN VIRGINIA: FROM
"EQUALIZATION" TO "INTEGRATION"

In 1936 the NAACP decided to make an attack on Jim Crow schools the cornerstone of its fight against segregation. Its first step was to file suits compelling the southern states to establish equal facilities and pay equal salaries on all levels of instruction—from elementary to graduate schools. It was hoped that making segregation prohibitively expensive would force the southern states to provide integrated institutions. By 1950, when it had become apparent that this strategy of achieving integration was ineffective, the NAACP changed its tactic, and decided to directly challenge the constitutionality of school segregation laws.

Doxey Wilkerson has described the evolution and impact of NAACP policy as it operated in the fight against segregated public schools in Virginia. He includes a discussion of the situation in Prince Edward County, the source of one of the cases involved in the Supreme Court's famous decision of 1954. His conclusion, that the Court's ruling in that year would secure neither equal nor integrated educational facilities for Negroes, has been amply borne out by subsequent events.

T HE rapidly-growing literature on "the changing South" emphasizes urban-industrial development and Federal court decisions as the main forces underlying recent progress toward equalizing white and Negro schools in that area;

Doxey A. Wilkerson, "The Negro School Movement in Virginia: From 'Equalization' to 'Integration,'" *Journal of Negro Education*, XXIX (Winter, 1960), pp. 17–29. Reprinted with the permission of the author and publisher.

but it hardly ever mentions that dynamic force which is most directly involved —the organized efforts of the Negro people. There is no doubt that urban and industrial development helps to create an environment congenial to progress, yet, the purposeful activities of human beings are always *immediate* causes of social change. And, as for the Federal courts, they would hardly be active in this realm without prior action by people bent on changing school conditions. As McIver has noted: "Courts are not themselves primary agents of social change. They register, often laggingly, the changes that move in the community."[1]

Thus, clarity on the rôle of the Negro school movement is essential to an understanding of recent developments around Negro schools in the South; and it is the purpose of this article to interpret that rôle in one of the Southern states. Specifically, analysis is here made of recent stages in the development of organized efforts by Negroes first to "equalize" and then to "integrate" the public elementary schools of Virginia, with special attention to the results of such efforts.[2]

The desire for education has long been a powerful driving force among Negroes in the South; and it is probable that during recent decades the Negro community has undertaken much more organized activity directed toward improving the schools than around any other local issue. For a long time such activity centered chiefly in the maintenance of private Negro schools, pleas to public school authorities, and private money-raising to help improve the public schools—to lengthen the term, or increase the teacher's salary, or buy a plot of land to be donated to the county for the erection of a school building.[3] The story of such efforts as these in the whole South is one of the moving sagas of Negro education that is yet to be adequately told.

It was not until the late 1930's and early 1940's that Negroes in the South—encouraged by the 1938 decision of the Supreme Court in the "Gaines Case" on the university level—turned to the Federal courts as a major resort in their fight for better elementary and secondary schools for their children. Thereafter, protests against and appeals for the correction of inequalities between white and Negro schools came increasingly to be followed by litigation. In Virginia, there were three successive emphases in this developing interaction between the Negro school movement and the Federal courts—for equal teachers' salaries, for equal school physical facilities, and for integration. The progressive impact of each on the relative status of Negro schools is impressive.

[1] R. M. McIver (ed.), *The More Perfect Union*. New York: The Macmillan Company, 1948. p. 169.

[2] The analysis is based on one section of the writer's "Some Correlates of Recent Progress Toward Equalizing White and Negro Schools in Virginia." Unpublished Ph.D. dissertation, New York University, 1958. Pp. xii, 372.

[3] See, for example, Fred M. Alexander, *Education for the Needs of the Negro in Virginia*. Washington: Southern Education Foundation, Inc., 1943. Chapter V, "Case Studies on Efforts of the Negro to Improve His Condition."

EQUAL SALARIES

Proposals for court action to equalize white and Negro teachers' salaries were discussed at least as early as 1934 in annual conventions of the Virginia State Teachers Association; [4] and at the Association's Golden Jubilee Convention, in November, 1937 a resolution embracing this policy "was adopted by the more than one thousand delegates without a dissenting vote."

The resolution proposed: (1) joint action with N.A.A.C.P. to raise $5,000 for court action toward the equalization of salaries, (2) appropriation of $1,000 of the Association's funds to begin the action at once, (3) that each local association be urged to raise funds and send them to the joint committee of the N.A.A.C.P. and the State Teachers Association, and (4) that each teacher be asked to contribute at least one dollar immediately to the cause. [5]

The first case was that of Aline E. Black, a high school teacher in the city of Norfolk who petitioned the School Board in the fall of 1938 to fix her salary by the same schedule as that for teachers in white high schools. When the Board rejected her petition, she sought a writ of mandamus in the Circuit Court of Norfolk acting through attorneys of the National Association for the Advancement of Colored People. Again rebuffed, she appealed to the Virginia Supreme Court; but her case was rendered moot when the School Board refused to renew her contract for the following term.

In the fall of 1939, Melvin O. Alston, another high school teacher in Norfolk, submitted a similar petition to the Board. When it was turned down, he filed suit in the United States District Court, charging that salary discrimination on the basis of race was in violation of the Constitution. He, too, was discharged; and the Court refused to consider the merits of his case on the ground that he had waived his constitutional rights by entering into a contract with the Norfolk School Board. Alston then appealed to the Fourth Circuit Court of Appeals; and in June, 1940, he won a reversal of the District Court's decision.

The Norfolk School Board sought a review in the United States Supreme Court; but *certiorari* was denied in November, 1940. The case was remanded to the District Court, where an order was entered declaring racial discrimination in salary payments "unlawful and unconstitutional and . . . in violation of the equal protection clause of the Fourteenth Amendment." Defendants were "perpetually enjoined and restrained" from such discrimination; and specific steps were set forth by which the salaries of white and Negro teachers should be "completely equalized" by January, 1943. [6] The minutes of the

[4] Luther P. Jackson, A History of the Virginia State Teachers Association. Norfolk; The Guide Publishing Company, Inc., 1937. pp. 108–10.
[5] J. Rupert Picott, "Desegregation in Higher Education in Virginia." *The Journal of Negro Education*, 27: 324–31, Summer, 1958. p. 325.
[6] Unless otherwise noted, these and subsequent such quotations are from the texts of court decisions and related documents.

Norfolk School Board for December 2, 1940, record the details of a plan for implementing this decision—agreed upon at a joint meeting of the Board and City Council, the City Manager, and representatives of the Negro teachers of Norfolk.

This conclusion of the "Alston Case" was followed immediately by equal-salary suits and threats of suits in many communities, including the cities of Petersburg, Danville and Richmond, the counties of Chesterfield, Mecklenburg and Goochland, and elsewhere. Some of these cases—as in Mecklenburg and Goochland counties—were settled without litigation, on the basis of school board agreement to equalize salaries. Others—as in Chesterfield County and Richmond—were settled through court orders or consent decrees for salary equalization.

The most bitterly contested of all the Virginia equal-salary cases arose in Newport News, where, in 1942, Dorothy E. Roles and the Newport News Teachers Association filed suit in the United States District Court. In January, 1943, the Court entered an injunction restraining school authorities from further discrimination in the payment of salaries. However, it was more than two years later when the Board of School Trustees and Superintendent complied with this ruling—and then only after being adjudged in contempt of court. Meanwhile, they discharged three Negro teachers, two elementary school principals, and the high school principal—the late Lutrelle F. Palmer, Executive Secretary of the Virginia State Teachers Association and spark-plug of the whole equal-salary movement.

These cases exerted a progressive influence far beyond the immediate communities in which they arose. On this point the writer found general agreement among school officials and lay citizens interviewed during a recent field trip to many parts of Virginia. Moreover, there is persuasive evidence of this influence in teacher-salary trends for the public elementary and secondary schools of the State.

Table I lists the average annual salaries of all white and Negro teachers (excluding supervisors and principals) for each term from 1940–41 to 1949-50—the last term for which the Superintendent's Annual Report gives these figures by race. During this period, the average for women teachers increased by about 168 per cent in white schools, and by about 300 per cent in Negro schools. The average for men teachers increased by about 114 per cent in white schools, and by about 250 per cent in Negro schools. The average for Negro women was only 69 per cent as large as that for white women in 1940–41; but it approximated or exceeded that for white women in each term from 1946–47 to 1949–50. The average for Negro men was about 57 per cent of that for white men in 1940–41; and although full parity was not attained at any time during this period, it was approached very closely in 1945–46 and 1948–49.

There were a few more court actions around the equal-salary issue after conclusion of the Newport News case; but most such litigation was over by the mid-1940's, its purpose largely—but not entirely—accomplished.

TABLE I

AVERAGE ANNUAL SALARY OF WHITE AND NEGRO TEACHERS OF VIRGINIA, PER CENT NEGRO OF WHITE, BY TERMS AND BY SEX: 1940–41 TO 1949–50 AVERAGE ANNUAL SALARY *

School Term	Women White	Women Negro	Men White	Men Negro	Per Cent Negro of White Women	Per Cent Negro of White Men
1949–50	$2,160	$2,209	$2,719	$2,520	102.3	92.7
1948–49	2,081	2,124	2,613	2,434	102.1	97.2
1947–48	1,927	1,962	2,515	2,300	101.8	91.4
1946–47	1,735	1,724	2,315	2,040	99.4	88.1
1945–46	1,486	1,418	1,987	1,956	95.4	98.4
1944–45	1,360	1,264	2,030	1,661	92.9	81.8
1943–44	1,254	1,124	1,877	1,440	89.6	76.7
1942–43	1,081	910	1,431	1,071	84.2	74.8
1941–42	857	632	1,400	824	73.7	58.9
1940–41	805	553	1,272	726	68.7	57.1

* Superintendent of Public Instruction, Commonwealth of Virginia, *Annual Report*, for the terms listed. Figures for 1940–41 and 1941–42 are medians; all others are means.

EQUAL FACILITIES

During the late 1940's, the main efforts of the Negro school movement in Virginia were directed toward equalizing physical facilities and curricula in white and Negro schools. Inequalities in bus transportation, buildings and equipment, and programs of study were the chief issues involved. Organized activity around these questions became especially widespread between 1947 and 1949; and resort to the Federal courts developed as the prevailing practice.

One of the most important and influential cases arose in Surry County, one of the "peanut counties" in the Southern Tidewater area. During July, 1947, a suit was filed in the United States District Court charging the School Board and Superintendent with discrimination in the conduct of the schools. Specifically cited were the unavailability of an accredited Negro high school and many other types of inequality. In March, 1948, the Court decreed that these charges were valid, and the practices complained of unlawful. It was ordered that, beginning September 1, 1948, the Board and Superintendent were "perpetually enjoined and restrained from discriminating" against plaintiffs and other Negroes in

providing and maintaining school facilities, including buildings, equipment, bus transportation, libraries and qualified instructional and janitorial personnel, and from paying Negro teachers in Surry

County, Virginia, less salaries, on account of their race and color, than that paid to white teachers and janitors similarly situated.

The Court also ordered that half of the Negro-white differential in teachers' salaries be eliminated by the start of the 1948–49 school term, and the other half by the following term; that the State Board of Education be asked to conduct a survey of Negro school building needs in the County; and that the local school authorities report their over-all equalization plans to the court by mid-September, 1948.

This ruling, said the Richmond *News Leader*, "marked the first clear-cut victory for Negro educators and attorneys who have fought in the Federal courts over the past several months to bring Negro education in Virginia counties to a par with that provided for white pupils." [7] This case also did much to stimulate similar actions in other communities.

Another notable case arose in Gloucester County, in the Middle Peninsula area. Negro citizens petitioned the School Board to correct gross inequalities in the buildings and equipment of the Negro high school and all other schools for Negro children. Getting no relief, they brought suit in the United States District Court, during February, 1947. In April of the following year, the Court filed a written memorandum which concluded that "there is discrimination against the colored children by the school authorities of Gloucester County in the particulars here enumerated. . . ." The practical difficulties cited by defendants as precluding any early equalization were said by the Court to be without "any bearing on the legal or factual questions here involved." Later, a declaratory judgment was entered; and an injunction was issued ordering an end to the discrimination, "effective immediately." Almost simultaneously, a similar case arose in Prince George County, in the Northern Neck area, and was handled by the same Court in the same manner.

In the fall of 1948, attorneys for the Negro plaintiffs, parents, and representatives of the Virginia State Teachers Association inspected the schools of both counties, and found no substantial improvement. One attorney then took a group of Negro children and sought their admittance to a white school in King George County—"to get equal school facilities for my clients, as ordered by the Federal District Court on July 31." At the same time, another attorney took a group of Negro children and asked for their admittance to a white school in Gloucester County.[8]

Both groups, of course, were turned down; whereupon petitions in their behalf were filed with the United States District Court, claiming that defendants had not discontinued the forbidden discrimination, and asking that they be adjudged in contempt of court. During the course of the hearings which followed, school officials in King George County—in a move "to equalize curricula"—discontinued the teaching of Chemistry, Physics, Biology and

[7] "Equal Educational Facilities Are Ordered in Surry County," March 31, 1948.
[8] "Great Dilemma in Virginia," *Virginia Education Bulletin*, 25: 48–9, October, 1948.

Geometry at the white high school.[9] In December, 1948, the District Court ruled that the school-official defendants "are in contempt and it is so adjudged." The following May they were fined and told that the injunction against further discrimination remained in force.

When the Court entered its memorandum opinion in the Gloucester and King George cases, it also decided in favor of the Negro plaintiffs in the Chesterfield County equal-salary case, one of those initiated in the winter of 1940. The Richmond *Times-Dispatch* report on this three-county decision said:

> The opinion, coming on the heels of the precedent-setting Surry judgment, left little doubt as to the stand the Federal courts inevitably would take on all school discrimination allegations. And it apparently left the way clear for a barrage of similar suits to descend upon the courts.[10]

A barrage of similar suits did, indeed, descend—in Arlington, Essex, King and Queen, and Dinwiddie counties, in the town of South Boston (Halifax County), and in other communities—all within this 1947–1949 period. Some went to trial; but many were settled otherwise. The N.A.A.C.P. lawyer most actively involved in these cases told the writer that "between '48 and '50, half of the counties with large Negro populations were ready for suits—if we had had the money to handle them."

Such actions became so widespread that the State Superintendent of Public Instruction issued a statement in the fall of 1948, detailing improvements in Negro schools over the previous decade, and appealing for surcease.[11] But the official organ of the Virginia State Teachers Association exulted: "Thank God for the Federal Courts!" [12]

Still another of the celebrated equalization cases arose in Pulaski County, located in the mountainous western part of the State where Negro populations are sparse. There was no public Negro high school in the County; and pupils were transported by bus to the Christiansburg Industrial Institute, in Montgomery County, which was operated on a regional basis with about 250 students from the two counties and the city of Radford. Negro citizens filed a suit in the United States District Court to compel school officials to provide a high school for Negro children within Pulaski County. The District Court denied their petition; and they appealed to the Fourth Circuit Court of Appeals. In November, 1949, that Court reversed the lower court decision, and remanded the case with instructions to give relief to the plaintiffs. The decision noted that the courts have "a solemn duty" to strike down "forbidden racial discrimination."

[9] "King George Drops Four Courses for Whites; Move to Equalize Curricula Draws Parents' Protests, The Richmond *Times-Dispatch*, November 5, 1948.

[10] April 9, 1948.

[11] "Miller Cites Gains by Negro Schools in Reply to Suits," The Richmond *Times-Dispatch*, September 19, 1948.

[12] Title of editorial, *Virginia Education Bulletin*, 25: 29, May, 1948.

State school officials promptly expressed concern over the Pulaski decision, pointing out that there were six Negro high schools then operating on a regional basis in Virginia.[13] And an indignant editorial in The Richmond *News Leader* professed to see in such litigation a plot by "some local liberals" to force the State to do away with school segregation. "*Virginia is not about to abandon segregation in its public schools,*" the newspaper declared, "and no mandate of any court, as we see it, is likely to chip the rock of that determination by so much as a pebble." [14]

The ten equal-facilities actions here reviewed or cited are by no means the only ones during this period of the late 1940's; but they are the ones which seemed to get the most attention in the newspapers. Moreover, there appears to be agreement among informed persons in Virginia that most of these cases were very influential in furthering general progress toward equalizing white and Negro schools.[15]

One type of evidence suggestive of this influence is found in trends in the per capita value of buses serving Negro and white schools in the counties of Virginia. As is noted in Table II, the value of buses per pupils in average daily attendance was only 27 per cent as large for Negro schools as for white schools in 1940-41; and it was 63 per cent as large in 1947-48, just about the time the flurry of equalization cases was developing. During the following nine years, however, the per capita value of buses serving Negro schools increased to more than that for buses serving white schools.

TABLE II

PER CAPITA VALUE OF BUSES SERVING WHITE AND NEGRO SCHOOLS IN THE
COUNTIES OF VIRGINIA; PER CENT NEGRO OF WHITE:
1940-41, 1947-48, 1956-57

	Value of Buses Per Pupil in Average Daily Attendance*		
School Term	White	Negro	Per Cent Negro of White
1956–57	$19.82	$21.06	106
1947–48	11.64	7.29	63
1940–41	3.80	1.02	27

* Derived from Superintendent of Public Instruction, Commonwealth of Virginia, *Annual Report*: 1940–41, 1947–48, 1956–57.

13 "State Education Officials Feel Pulaski Decision May Do Harm," The Richmond *Times-Dispatch*, November 16, 1949.

14 "Stunning Decision in Pulaski" (editorial), The Richmond *News Leader*, November 23, 1949.

15 See, for example, "State N.A.A.C.P. Makes Annual Report: School Cases, Civic Program Summed Up," [Norfolk] *Journal and Guide*, October 2, 1948; and "Swift Improvement For Schools Follows N.A.A.C.P. Suits in Virginia," [Norfolk] *Journal and Guide*, September 17, 1949.

A more comprehensive type of evidence suggestive of the influence of these equalization cases is found in the improvement that took place in the over-all relative status of Negro schools. A rough, purely quantitative, index of that improvement is afforded by trends in the degree to which Negro schools approximate white schools as regards (a) per cent of the population 7 to 19 years old in average daily attendance, (b) cost of elementary salaries per pupil in A.D.A., (c) cost of secondary salaries per pupil in A.D.A., and (d) value of school property (including buses) per pupil in A.D.A. The mean of the four Negro-to-white ratios on these measures defines the "relative status" of Negro schools, and is designated the *Index of Relative Status*. Term-to-term increases in this index reflect improvement in the relative status of Negro schools or, stated in other words, "progress toward equality." A relative-status rating of 100.0 indicates approximate equality of status on the four measures here involved.[16]

It may be seen from Table III that, in the group of ten counties here cited for their notable equal-facilities cases during the late 1940's, the average over-all status of Negro schools approximated that of white schools by about 60 per cent in 1940–41, by about 73 per cent in 1947–48, and by about 94 per cent in 1956–57. Thus, there was about 56 per cent improvement in the relative status of Negro schools in this group of counties during the whole period, as compared with substantially less such improvement in all counties, or in all cities, or in the State as a whole.

Between 1940–41 and 1947–48, there was about 22 per cent improvement in the relative status of Negro schools in these ten counties, and about 20 per cent improvement in all counties. However, following 1947–48—the term when equal-facilities cases were most widespread—the relative status of Negro schools improved by about 29 per cent in the ten counties, as compared with only 18 per cent in all counties.

These trends are pretty convincing evidence of a causal relationship between recent progress *toward* equalizing white and Negro schools in Virginia and the series of equalization suits and related activities which burgeoned in the late 1940's. In the years immediately following, still another obviously dynamic influence entered upon the scene.

INTEGRATION

During the summer of 1950, The Richmond *Times-Dispatch* published a very perceptive review of recent Federal court decisions affecting the education of Negroes in Virginia and elsewhere. The staff writer recognized the 1950 Supreme Court decision in the "Sweatt Case," at the University of Texas, as applicable in Virginia; and within three months the matriculation of Gregory

[16] It will be noted that the Index of Relative Status expresses a *relationship* between the status of white and Negro schools; it expresses nothing about the absolute status of either group of schools.

TABLE III

INDEX OF RELATIVE STATUS OF NEGRO SCHOOLS IN 10 COUNTIES OF VIRGINIA
AND IN ALL COUNTIES, ALL CITIES AND THE STATE: 1940–41, 1947–48, 1956–57;
PER CENT INCREASE: 1941–1957

	Index of Relative Status*			
County	1940–41	1947–48	1956–57	Increase 1941–1957
King George	58.2	71.3	107.8	85.2
Surry	43.4	58.6	78.8	81.6
Essex	48.5	64.0	87.7	80.8
Dinwiddie	46.4	58.2	78.4	69.0
Gloucester	62.0	87.4	104.8	69.0
Arlington	74.8	95.2	118.0	57.8
Halifax	53.0	64.7	82.5	55.7
Chesterfield	71.1	73.9	100.6	41.5
King and Queen	63.9	61.7	87.3	36.6
Pulaski	80.8	97.7	95.8	18.6
10 Counties (mean)	60.2	73.3	94.2	56.5
All Counties (mean)	63.1	75.9	89.6	42.2
All Cities (mean)	75.0	75.9	99.8	32.3
State (mean)	67.5	78.1	92.8	37.5

* Derived from Superintendent of Public Instruction, Commonwealth of Virginia, *Annual Report:* 1940–41, 1947–48, 1956–57.

Swanson at the University of Virginia confirmed her forecast. She also saw in such "integration" cases on the graduate level and recent "equalization" cases on the public school level a threat to the whole system of school segregation. "Ever present," she said, "is the possibility that if Virginia succeeds in equalizing her system of public schools at enormous cost of duplicate facilities, the United States Supreme Court could decide that segregation itself constitutes discrimination." [17]

Leaders of the Negro movement were also looking ahead to a new stage of the struggle. As the lawyer most involved in these cases told the writer: "Although we concentrated on equalization suits during the 'forties, we were careful never to affirm the validity of segregation. We looked to the time when integration would become the issue."

In 1950, the National Legal Committee of the N.A.A.C.P. recommended, and the National Board approved, the policy of undertaking no further equalization suits, but of supporting litigation directed toward abolishing segregation in the public schools. In the spring of 1951, the first suit aimed at school

[17] Nita Morse, "Segregation Rulings Pose New Issues," The Richmond *Times-Dispatch*, June 25, 1950.

integration below the college level in Virginia—in Prince Edward County—was filed in the United States District Court.[18] It is important to understand that this case—as, indeed, the whole development of this kind of litigation—emerged directly out of organized efforts to equalize facilities in the separate white and Negro schools.

Prince Edward is one of the "tobacco counties" in the traditional slave-plantation area of Southside Virginia; and in 1950 its Negro population constituted 45 per cent of the total. The Negro schools of the County had long been grossly inferior to the white schools, in all respects; and Negro citizens repeatedly appealed to school authorities for improvements. Especially were they concerned over the Negro high school, which was built in 1927 and had become greatly over-crowded and decrepit by the late 1940's.

In 1950, the Parent-Teachers Association appointed a committee to negotiate with the County School Board for a new high school. It was headed by a local minister, and consisted of one representative from each school district. This committee is said to have "met with the School Board once a month for more than a year, presenting facts and figures, listing the needs of our schools. But we got nowhere. Constantly they told us there was no money." Continuing the quotation from one of the leaders involved: "Finally, we got them to agree to secure land for a new high school—if we could find a suitable plot, they'd buy it. We found a place, up where the new high school is now located, 60 acres or more. But the Board then said they had no money to build with, and that we need not come back; they'd notify us through the press when they were in position to build."

Meanwhile, students at the Negro high school took action on their own: "While we were considering this in the P.T.A., the kids walked out." It is reported that the students got the principal to leave the building on a ruse—saying that a student was in trouble in town—hoping, among other things, thereby to absolve him from blame for their contemplated action. They then called a meeting and proposed a strike. The suggestion that they first consult their parents was voted down. The strike was agreed to with only one dissenting vote. The students walked out, set up picket-lines, and established headquarters in the basement of a local church.

Leaders of the strike sought a conference with the County Superintendent of Schools; but he refused to see them unless they first returned to their classes —which they refused to do. They wrote to N.A.A.C.P. attorneys in Richmond, asking them to come to Farmville and start a suit for a new high school. Two attorneys did come; but they explained that, in view of the new policy of the N.A.A.C.P., they could not help with litigation unless a suit was filed to abolish school segregation.

Following this visit by the lawyers, the Parent-Teachers Association called a meeting to consider developments. They decided, by unanimous vote, to sue for integration—which they did, in April, 1951. Thus began the case of *Davis*

[18] A similar suit, which arose in Clarendon County, South Carolina, was filed a few months earlier.

v. *County School Board of Prince Edward County, Virginia*, the only such case in a Southside rural area, and one of those decided by the United States Supreme Court on May 17, 1954.

The story of the developments which followed in and around Farmville is a moving one—truly heroic leadership by the local minister in the face of varied threats and persecutions, efforts (often successful) by the Defenders of State Sovereignty and Individual Liberties and other racist forces to intimidate Negro parents in the town, solid support for the integration movement by independent Negro farmers in the countryside, etc.—but this story cannot be told here. What happened meanwhile to the relative status of Negro schools is most significant.

A new Robert R. Moton High School was completed during the 1953–54 school term, at a cost of nearly $900,000. It is a fine structure, with separate auditorium, cafeteria, and gymnasium; an intercommunication system; a comprehensive program of studies; well equipped laboratories and shops for science, art, commercial subjects, home economics, agriculture, and industrial arts; and an apparently able faculty of twenty-five teachers, all paid according to the same scale that applied in the white high schools. Between 1947–48 and 1956–57, the Index of Relative Status of Negro schools for the whole of Prince Edward County increased from 63.6 to 86.2. This increase of about 35 per cent is to be compared with a corresponding increase of only 7 per cent between 1940–41 and 1947–48.

After the Prince Edward County case began, integration suits of one kind or another were initiated in many parts of the State. In the fall of 1957, The Richmond *Times-Dispatch* listed five suits to abolish segregated schools—in Arlington and Prince Edward counties, and in the cities of Charlottesville, Newport News and Norfolk. It also listed eight communities where court challenges of the Virginia "Pupil Placement Law" (designed to circumvent court integration orders) had been filed—Arlington, Fairfax and Nansemond counties, and the cities of Charlottesville, Newport News, Norfolk, Richmond and Suffolk.[19] Moreover, there were threats of integration suits in many other communities—in Petersburg, in the counties of Pittsylvania, Pulaski, Culpeper, Lancaster and King William, and elsewhere—especially during 1956.

These developments undoubtedly influenced the relative-status trends noted for the latter part of the period represented in Table III. Their influence is even more strikingly revealed in the rapid growth of capital outlay for Negro schools; and in this a big part was played by the so-called "Battle Fund," popularly known by the name of the then Governor of the Commonwealth.

The "Battle Fund" was created by action of the General Assembly early in 1950—"for the purpose of meeting the emergency need for school construction caused by cessation of building during the war, the increase in the birth rate, and *other special problems*." [20] The initial appropriation was $45,000,000, of

[19] "Nine Localities Now Involved in School Integration Cases," September 30, 1957.
[20] H-96, approved February 11, 1950. *Acts of the Virginia Assembly 1950*. Chapter 14. (Emphasis by the writer.)

which $30,000,000 became available immediately, and the remainder during the fiscal year of 1951–52. A further appropriation of $30,000,000 was made available during 1952, bringing the total to $75,000,000.

There is nothing in the act creating the "Battle Fund" which connects it with the mounting pressure from the Negro school movement; but the undefined "other special problems" phrase is suggestive. Moreover, it was generally understood in the State that the original legislation was mainly to help meet the "Negro school crisis," and that the supplementary appropriation was largely stimulated by events in Prince Edward County. In any case, according to a State school official, "Negroes got the biggest part of the money."

Local school officials and lay citizens interviewed in many parts of Virginia affirmed that "Battle Fund" allocations to their communities were used chiefly to build Negro schools, especially high schools; and many of them also said that the fear of integration suits gave great impetus to these Negro school building programs. There follow a few anecdotic illustrations.

About one-third of the cost of the new high school in Prince Edward County was covered by "Battle Fund" allocations. The County spent less than $600,000.

Dinwiddie County got $500,000 from the "Battle Fund"; and $400,000 of it went into the very fine Negro high school built in 1953–54 at a cost of $805,000. Telling the story of long and futile efforts to get such a school, a civic leader there remarked: "Before the Prince Edward case, nothing happened in Dinwiddie County."

Following the Supreme Court decision in 1954, Negro citizens in Hopewell renewed long-standing pleas for a new high school. Their attorney advised them, when appearing before the School Board, to be careful to explain: "We want a school that is good enough for *any* child, when the time comes." The city voted a $1,000,000 bond issue in 1955, of which $700,000 was allocated for a beautiful, campus-style high school for Negro children, scheduled for occupancy in the fall of 1958.

In one community where there was this kind of development, the Superintendent cited the new Negro high school as an expression of "our basic philosophy of equality of educational opportunity." However, Negro leaders there had another explanation.

The Superintendent of Schools in a city in the Hampton Roads area reported "we won our last bond issue [shortly after the 1954 Supreme Court decision] by the largest margin ever in the State of Virginia. It was believed, especially by the people, that if we equalized we wouldn't have to integrate."

In one of the cities under court order to integrate its schools, the Superintendent said that the Supreme Court decision did not affect their equalization program "one way or another," but that in Virginia as a whole "it had considerable effect. Since 1954, there has been more construction of Negro schools than of white schools in the State."

The Superintendent of a county not far from Petersburg explained substantial progress toward equality with the statement: "Since the 1954 decision, thinking people here have taken the attitude that to equalize facilities is their best hope to maintain separate schools. That's what it is; and I might as well call it that."

These reports are strongly corroborated by trends in property values in public elementary and secondary schools. It will be recalled that the "Battle Fund" was created in 1950 and the Prince Edward County case began in 1951. The total value of property in white schools in Virginia increased from $192,701,982 in 1950–51 to $319,753,684 in 1953–54—an increase of 66 per cent; whereas the corresponding increase in Negro schools was from $40,957,738 to $89,434,926—an increase of 118 per cent.[21]

This rapid narrowing of the "gap" during the three terms following 1950–51 is also evident in trends in the per capita value of school property. The degree to which the value of school property per pupil in average daily attendance in Negro schools approximated that in white schools is shown in Table IV for each term from 1940–41 to 1956–57. It will be noted that, between 1950–51 and 1953–54, the degree to which the per capita value of school property for Negro children approximated that for white children increased from 62.2 per cent to 86.2 per cent. This increase of 24 percentage points during this 3-year period is more than one-third larger than the corresponding increase during the 10-year period from 1940–41 to 1950–51.

TABLE IV

PER CENT NEGRO OF WHITE VALUE OF SCHOOL PROPERTY PER PUPIL
IN AVERAGE DAILY ATTENDANCE IN VIRGINIA, BY TERMS:
1940–41 TO 1956–57 *

School Term	Per Cent Negro of White	School Term	Per Cent Negro of White
1956–57	78.1	1947–48	47.3
1955–56	81.4	1946–47	44.7
1954–55	86.3	1945–46	43.0
1953–54	86.2	1944–45	41.0
1952–53	80.2	1943–44	45.0
1951–52	64.9	1942–43	44.5
1950–51	62.2	1941–42	44.8
1949–50	56.2	1940–41	44.6
1948–49	53.8		

* Derived from Superintendent of Public Instruction, Commonwealth of Virginia, *Annual Report: 1940–41* through 1956–57.

It will also be noted from Table IV that the ratio of Negro-to-white per capita value of school property in 1954–55 was 86.3 per cent, about the same as in the preceding term; but that it decreased in the next term to 81.4 per

21 Superintendent of Public Instruction, Commonwealth of Virginia, *Annual Report:* 1950–51 and 1953–54.

cent, and again in 1956–57 to 78.1 per cent—below that for 1952–53. Thus, the *relative* per capita value of property in Virginia's Negro schools increased very rapidly during the period when the several integration cases were making their way through the Federal courts; remained constant between the first decision of the Supreme Court in "The Segregation Cases" (1954) and its subsequent implementing decree (1955); and then entered upon a sharp decline. It was as if the motivation for rapid progress toward equalizing property values in white and Negro schools following 1950–51 was no longer operative after the Supreme Court struck down the "separate but equal" doctrine and ordered that school integration proceed "with all deliberate speed."

SOME QUESTIONS OF DYNAMICS

The considerable recent progress toward equality between white and Negro schools in Virginia, which this analysis only partially reveals, is a function of a complex of interrelated events and developments—extending from the local to the international scene. It is a part of the substantial over-all improvement in the Negro's social status since the beginning of World War II; and it reflects the operation of "impersonal" as well as "conscious" forces in the society. It is clear, however, that conscious interaction between the Negro school movement and the Federal courts played the decisive rôle.

No systematic analysis is here available of the extent to which developments around Negro schools in Virginia during the past two decades were paralleled in other Southern states; but there is much fragmentary information which suggests that the Virginia experience, despite peculiarities, is by no means unique. Hence, the expanding corps of interpreters of "the changing South" would do well to give greater emphasis than heretofore to the activities of the Negro school movement, supported by the Federal courts, in their explanations of the narrowing "gap" between Southern white and Negro schools. Such emphasis does not detract from the importance of such impersonal forces as industrialization and urbanization; but it does focus attention on those dynamic forces which are most immediately and directly involved.

Illustrative of the practical importance of this insight is the tendency here noted toward increasing inequality between white and Negro schools in Virginia since the Supreme Court decision in "The Segregation Cases." This tendency could mark the beginning of a retrogressive trend; and it is probable that only the purposeful and concerted efforts of *people* can now suffice to prevent its further development.

Thurgood Marshall

THE RISE AND COLLAPSE OF THE
"WHITE DEMOCRATIC PRIMARY"

*From the time of its founding, the NAACP had directed its legal
battle at the twin evils of segregation and disfranchisement. Perhaps
the most serious bar to effective Negro political participation in
the Southern states was the "white primary." Even those Negroes
who met the other voting qualifications were unable to take part in
the Democratic Party primaries, though nomination in the Democratic primary was nearly always tantamount to election. In his discussion of the Texas White Primary, Thurgood Marshall traces the
history of this type of franchise restriction and of the NAACP's successful fight against it.*

O F ALL the so-called "legal" devices for checking Negro participation in
Southern politics perhaps the most effective, and on the surface the most legal,
was the white Democratic Party primary—the most effective because it disfranchised the Negro by excluding him from participating in the preelections
which for all practical purposes were *the* elections in the one-party South,
and the most "legal" because the Democratic Party, according to contemporary
legal theory, was considered as being a voluntary association of citizens which
could discriminate on the basis of race and color or along any other line in
the conduct of its private affairs without offending the Fourteenth and Fifteenth Amendments.

For these reasons, solely, the rise and collapse of the white Democratic
primary is an important and distinct chapter in the story of the Negro's struggle
for political equality. But an equally important reason for writing this chapter
is its rough analogy to the chapter now being developed with respect to educational equality.

The origins of the white Democratic primary are obscure and not easily

Thurgood Marshall, "The Rise and Collapse of the 'White Democratic Primary,' "
Journal of Negro Education, XXXVI (Summer, 1957), pp. 249–54. Reprinted with
permission of the author and publisher.

traced. Lewinson in his *Race, Class and Party*, however, suggests that its beginnings go back to the color line drawn during Reconstruction days by self-labeled "white man's parties"—first called Conservative and, subsequently, simply Democratic—which opposed Black Republicanism. V. O. Key's authoritative *Southern Politics*, on the other hand, concludes only that this device originated about as early as the direct primary method of nomination appeared on the Southern scene.

In any event, it can hardly be gainsaid that Negroes rarely were admitted to Democratic or Conservative councils, caucuses or conventions during Reconstruction and the policy of excluding Negroes from the Democratic Party's nominating process was born during that time.

Use of the primary election method of nomination did not enter Southern politics until after the end of Reconstruction. The earliest primaries were local, informal and unregulated by law. Statutory recognition and regulation first appeared in the mid-1880's when Alabama and South Carolina passed acts providing for mandatory primary elections. Thereafter, the legally-regulated primary slowly spread throughout the South and by the turn of the century every Southern state required or permitted its use. During these twenty years, roughly speaking, and, for another twenty years thereafter, exclusion of Negroes from these preelections was not written on the law books.

Nevertheless the white primary system flourished. First, by tacit understandings or gentlemen's agreements between competing factions within state and local Democratic organizations and, later, with formal rules passed pursuant to statutory delegations of the power to prescribe qualifications for voting in primaries, the Democratic Party limited participation in them to white voters only, although there were many localities where the formal rule was never adopted and others where it was waived in closely contested elections. But, overall, the system had become so effective that a Southern legislator who opposed another disfranchisement device, in a letter published by the Atlanta *Constitution* in 1907, was able to exclaim: "We already had the Negro eliminated from politics by the white primary."

It is one of those little ironies of which Southern politics is full, that the primary movement which was motivated, at least in part, by democratic motives and a desire for wider participation in the representative process was turned into a device for eliminating millions of Negroes from participation in government.

It is even more ironical that a petty squabble between the candidates for a minor political office in Texas ended in the enactment of a statute which declared Negroes ineligible to vote in a Democratic primary and touched off the series of law suits which brought about the collapse of the white primary system.

This chain of events was set off in 1918 by two candidates for the district attorneyship of Bexar County, Texas.[1] Both sought the support of Negro vot-

[1] Other variations of this story appear in Lewinson, *Race Class and Party*, p. 113 (1932); Nelson, The Fourteenth Amendment and The Negro Since 1920, at 37 (1946).

ers and both had previously had such support in other local primaries. The unsuccessful candidate this time, however, set out upon a campaign for legislation which would require exclusion of Negro voters from the Democratic primary and thus undermine the victor's political strength in the county. The campaign attracted little support in the legislature at the outset save from those legislators who were professed Negrophobes. By 1923, however, a number of conservative legislators, who were undoubtedly encouraged by the Supreme Court's ruling in the *Newberry* case [2] that primaries were not elections within the meaning of the Constitution, furnished sufficient votes to pass the law which prohibited Negroes from voting in Democratic primaries.

Four years after its enactment this statute was held unconstitutional by the Supreme Court in the *First Texas White Primary Case*.[3] The suit had been filed in 1924 on behalf of Dr. L. A. Nixon, an El Paso physician, well-known Negro Democrat, who sought to recover damages from the election officials who denied him the right to vote in the primary which nominated the Democratic candidates for seats in the Federal Congress and various state offices. Specifically, the complaint alleged that the law which the defendants had enforced against the plaintiff was violative of the Fourteenth and Fifteenth Amendments. The Federal District Court sitting in El Paso granted defendants' motion to dismiss on the merits and the case then came direct to the Supreme Court. Speaking for an unanimous Court, Justice Holmes declared: "It seems to us hard to imagine a more direct and obvious infringement of the Fourteenth Amendment." Having disposed of the case under the Fourteenth Amendment, the Court declined to consider the validity of the statute under the Fifteenth Amendment.

Most people, including Justice Holmes,[4] felt that this decision laid the white primary to rest;[5] but succeeding events showed them up as far too optimistic. For the Texas legislature promptly tried again. In 1928 it repealed the 1924 law and enacted another which empowered the state executive committees of political parties to determine the qualifications of voters in primary elections. And, pursuant thereto, the State Executive Committee of the Democratic Party passed a resolution limiting participation in primaries to white persons. This combination of statutory delegation and formal party rule, as we previously noted, was the means by which Negroes were excluded from Democratic primaries throughout most of the South; and it was also the one which many legal scholars deemed immune from the reach of the Federal Constitution.

This system did not long remain unchallenged. Following the exclusion of Negroes from the 1928 Democratic primaries, suits challenging it were filed

---

[2] *Newberry v. United States*, 256 U.S. 232 (1921).

[3] *Nixon v. Herndon*, 273 U.S. 536 (1927).

[4] See Ajootian, "The Right of Negroes To Vote in State Primaries," 12 B. U. L. Rev. 689.

[5] See, e.g., New York *Times*, March 8, 1927, p. 24; 34 *Crisis* 224 (1927); 5 *Opportunity* 97 (1927).

in Arkansas, Florida, Texas and Virginia. Only one, the *Second Texas White Primary Case*,[6] was brought up to the Supreme Court. Dr. Nixon was again the plaintiff in an action for damages against the election officials who refused to permit him to vote. He contended that the state was a party to the discrimination against him since it had delegated control over the primary to the State Executive Committee of the Democratic Party. Both the Federal District Court and the Circuit Court of Appeals upheld the challenged device. But the Supreme Court pricked open the private association fiction and reversed in a 5 to 4 decision. The majority, however, gratuitously pointed out a way in which Negroes could be excluded from primaries by remarking that the power to do this lay with the State Democratic Convention and not the State Executive Committee, if any such power existed.

Although most were apprehensive about the Court's gratuitous suggestion, Negroes and their friends generally regarded the decision as the final step in their effort to throw open the white primary. Supporters of the white primary system were also confused, not so much with respect to the course to take but how to navigate it. Within three weeks of decision day however, the confusion was dissipated when the Democratic Party called a State Convention and it adopted a resolution restricting membership in the Party plus participation in party primaries to white citizens of Texas.

Since 1932 was an election year and the resolution was rigorously enforced a number of cases testing the constitutionality of the Convention Resolution were filed and lost in lower Federal courts. One of them was carried up to the Supreme Court and became the *Third Texas White Primary Case*[7] R. R. Grovey, a Negro citizen of Houston, was the plantiff in the case. The pleadings admitted that candidates for Federal office were to be nominated at the primary and that nomination in the primary was equivalent to election. Nevertheless, the members of the Court "blinded themselves as judges to what they knew as men" and unanimously held that the Democratic primary was a private matter and that Grovey had not been discriminated against pursuant to any state law nor had he been denied any right guaranteed under the Fourteenth and Fifteenth Amendments.

Thus on April Fools Day, 1935, the same day on which the second Scottsboro case was handed down, almost a decade of litigation was brought to naught. Dean William Pickens, in an article which appeared in the Norfolk *Journal and Guide* on April 13 could not resist commenting upon the coincidence. "If one were suspicious of the Court's motives," he said, "it would look as if they made a trade." Undoubtedly, from a purely racial perspective and in view of the Court's disposition of the earlier Texas Primary cases, the decision was a rude jolt to the political aspirations of Negroes.[8] But hope did not

---

[6] *Nixon v. Condon*, 286 U.S. 73 (1932).

[7] *Grovey v. Townsend*, 294 U.S. 45 (1935).

[8] See, e.g., Bunche, "Tactics and Problems of Minority Groups," 4 *Journal Negro Education* 319 (1935); Frazier, "The Negro in the American Social Order," 4 *Journal Negro Education* 302 (1935).

die out. P. B. Young, writing for the same issue of the *Journal and Guide* as the one in which Dean Pickens' comment appeared, sensed the hope and boldly predicted that this "barrier will not be effective long. The Court in 1935 did not ferret out the trickery behind the statutes. Later, it will go behind the law."

As predicted, *Grovey* did not long remain an effective barrier. In *United States* v. *Classic*, 313 U.S. 299 (1941), the Court pierced the façade of legality which had shielded primaries from the reach of Federal laws regulating the conduct of elections. The Court, although it split 5 to 3 on other questions presented for decision, unanimously agreed that Congress had the right to regulate primary elections and that the criminal sections of the Civil Rights law could be invoked to penalize infractions thereof in the course of primary elections involving nominations for Federal office. The Court's opinion followed and adopted the very arguments which had been rejected in the *Third Texas White Primary Case*; and the Court, without a single reference to *Grovey*, practically overruled it.

Because it was not a white primary case, *Classic*, of course, did not go behind the law and ferret out the trickery. However, it paved the way to the next milestone on the long road toward political equality—the *Fourth Texas White Primary Case*.[9]

This will be seen in proper perspective by turning back to 1940. It was the first general election year after *Grovey* v. *Townsend* and the assault upon the white primary began anew. Most of the cases arose in Texas. None met with any success in the trial courts and few were appealed. Indeed, in one of them, an appeal had been noted just about the time the *Classic* decision came down. That appeal, however, was withdrawn and a new suit based upon the *rationale* of the *Classic* case was filed. This was the *Fourth Texas White Primary Case*.

It was brought on behalf of Lonnie E. Smith, a Negro citizen of Houston, on behalf of himself and all other Negroes similarly qualified to vote yet denied the right to do so by the election judges. Their action, it was alleged, violated rights secured under the Constitution and laws of the United States and for this alleged illegal conduct a declaratory judgment, injunctive relief and monetary damages were sought. Needless to say, the lower courts refused to overrule *Grovey*.

The Supreme Court, however, looked behind the law and ferreted out the trickery. It concluded that the Democratic Party, after "the fusing by the *Classic* case of the primary and general elections into a single instrumentality for the choice of officers," had become, under elaborate statutory regulations, "an agency of the state" in determining the participants in primary elections. "The party takes its character as a state agency from the duties imposed upon it by state statute; the duties do not become matters of private law because they were performed by a political party." Thus the Court held that the Democratic Party as such, under the statutes, through whatever agency it acted, can no more discriminate against voters in primary elections than the state

[9] *Smith* v. *Allwright*, 321 U.S. 649 (1924).

itself in general elections without violating the Fifteenth Amendment and the "privileges and immunities" clause of the Fourteenth Amendment.

This decision, one of the landmarks in constitutional history, leveled the greater barrier to Negro voting in the South. But the Southern ingenuity was not spent and clever stratagems were conceived in a desperate effect to circumvent *Smith* v. *Allwright* and restore the white democratic primary. In South Carolina, for example, a special session of the legislature was called for the purpose of repealing all laws on its statute books which dealt with political parties and primaries. By doing this, according to the thinking of the Governor and the legislators, the tie-up between the party and the state would be severed and then like a "private club" the Democratic Party could exclude Negroes from its primaries. In Alabama and Georgia different props to avoid the *Fourth Texas Primary Case* were thrown up. All were either struck down by lower Federal courts [10] or were not enforced.

Texas, however, was destined to be the scene of the last chapter. There, instead of an attempt to preserve the white Democratic primary, the device involved an all-white "club"—the Jaybird Party or Jaybird Democratic Association—which held its own preelection some weeks in advance of the Democratic primary regulated by the State. The winners of the Jaybird primary would then enter the Democratic primary, which was open to Negroes as well as whites, and won without opposition in the Democratic primary and the general election that followed. A suit challenging the exclusion of Negroes from the Jaybird primaries was filed after the 1948 elections by John Terry and a group of Negro citizens of Fort Bend County. Like *Smith* v. *Allwright*, it was a classic suit and the same broad relief was sought. The case eventually came up to the Supreme Court and it held that the discriminatory practices described above were unconstitutional. *Terry* v. *Adams*, 345 U.S. 416 (1952).

The collapse of the white Democratic primary, despite fond hopes, has not resulted in full participation by all in the political life of the South. But the story of the struggle to overcome this barrier is particularly meaningful today. For, if nothing else, it indicates the fate which awaits the "legal means" which some of the Southern states have drafted to preserve segregated schools.

[10] *Elmore* v. *Rice*, 72 F. Supp. 516 (E. D. S. C. 1947), aff'd. 165 F. 2d 387 (C. A. 4th 1947), cert. denied, 333 U.S. 875 (1948); *Brown* v. *Baskin*, 80 F. Supp. 1017 (E. D. S. C. 1948), aff'd. 174 F. 2d 391 (C. A. 4th 1949); *Davis* v. *Schnell*, 81 F. Supp. 872 (S. D. Ala. 1949), aff'd. 336 U.S. 933 (1949).

John H. Fenton and Kenneth N. Vines

NEGRO REGISTRATION IN LOUISIANA

*Within a decade after the 1944 Supreme Court decision declaring
white primaries unconstitutional, the number of Negroes registered
for voting in the South had risen from 250,000 to about a million
and a quarter. The distribution of Negro voters, however, was extremely uneven. It varied from state to state (being generally greatest in the states at the South's periphery), and even from county to
county. In their analysis of Negro registration in Louisiana, John H.
Fenton and Kenneth N. Vines lucidly explain the complex factors
accounting for the striking variations in the degree to which Negroes
registered in the Louisiana parishes. Their study was made in 1956,
just prior to the purge of many of the newly registered Negroes from
the voting rolls in Louisiana and several other states, which was part
of the general stiffening of southern resistance that followed the Supreme Court's 1954 school desegregation decision.*

T HE 1944 action of the Supreme Court voiding the white primary ended the
last effective legal block to Negro voter registration in the South. After that,
resort to legal steps to block Negro registration was either outlawed by the
courts or else could only be a delaying device. In the state of Louisiana, however, the decision in *Smith* v. *Allwright* did not result in Negro registration
comparable to white registration. In 1956, twelve years later, 30 percent of the
potential Negro voting population was registered, compared to 73 percent of
the whites. This study is an investigation of some factors in that discrepancy,
and in particular, of the differences in registration between Catholic and Protestant areas.

An important characteristic of Negro registration in Louisiana is the extreme range of variation to be found among the several parishes. Table I shows

John H. Fenton and Kenneth N. Vines, "Negro Registration in Louisiana,"
American Political Science Review, LI (September, 1957), pp. 704–13. Reprinted with
the permission of the authors and publisher.

17 parishes with fewer than 20 percent of the eligible Negroes registered, and 11 parishes with 70 percent or more of the potential Negro vote registered. Therefore, the statewide "average" percentage of Negro registration [1] has little meaning without more detailed interpretation.

TABLE I

LOUISIANA PARISHES BY PERCENTAGE OF NEGROES 21 AND OVER REGISTERED, 1956

Registration Percentage	Number of Parishes
0– 9	7
10– 19	10
20– 29	9
30– 39	6
40– 49	5
50– 59	13
60– 69	3
70– 79	6
80– 89	3
90–100	2

Among the factors responsible for these differences is the religio-cultural variable. Louisiana offers a unique opportunity to study the influence of this variable on the registration aspect of race relations. Catholicism is dominant in southern Louisiana and Protestantism in northern Louisiana. The two regions are very nearly separate worlds. Other variables enter, but this one is the focus of this paper.

The material for this study was gathered from Census Reports and from specialized and local sources on the cultural characteristics of Louisiana. Sixteen parishes were visited throughout the state, chosen to represent different degrees of Negro registration, different socio-economic areas, and different religio-cultural areas. Interviews were conducted with state and parish officials and local political leaders, both white and Negro.[2]

[1] Current estimates on population figures were obtained as follows: (1) The estimated total population of each parish for 1956 was obtained from *Sales Management Annual Survey of Buying Power*, May 10, 1956. (2) It was assumed that the 1950 ratio of Negroes to the total population in each parish would remain constant. (3) It was assumed that the 1950 ratio of Negroes 21 and over to the total Negro population in each parish would remain constant. (4) Thus by taking percentages of the 1956 total population estimate as derived from the 1950 census, a 1956 estimate was obtained for the potential Negro vote in each parish.

[2] The authors wish to acknowledge the aid of the Southern Regional Council in support of this project. The Louisiana project was part of a Southern-wide survey of Negro registration and voting sponsored by the Council.

I. THE RELIGIO-CULTURAL VARIABLE

Every Louisianian is aware of the religious complications of his state's politics. It has usually been thought, though experience provides exceptions, that only Protestants can be elected to state-wide offices or as congressmen from the north Louisiana districts; and only Catholics can be elected to major offices in south Louisiana. The Catholicism of Louisiana is predominantly French, and it is said that a French name is worth 50,000 votes in south Louisiana in a statewide election.

Roughly the southern 25 parishes form French Catholic Louisiana while the remaining parishes in the north are predominantly Protestant and Anglo-Saxon. The French parishes remain French-Catholic because of their assimilation of extraneous cultural elements entering the area.

As Table II indicates, Negro registration, in percentages of potential eligibles, is more than twice as great in Louisiana's French-Catholic parishes as in its non-French parishes. In only two of the 25 French-Catholic parishes are less than 20 percent of the eligible Negroes registered, whereas in 13 of the 39 non-French parishes less than 20 percent of the potential Negro vote is registered. In seven of the French-Catholic parishes Negro registration is 70 percent or more, while only four of the non-French-Catholic parishes equal or exceed the 70 percent mark. Yet no significant differences exist between the two groups of parishes with respect to Negro-White population balance or to urbanism.

TABLE II

NEGRO REGISTRATIONS BY RELIGIO-CULTURAL SECTIONS OF LOUISIANA, 1956

	French-Catholic Parishes [1]	Non-French Parishes [2]
Number of Negroes registered	70,488	90,922
Potential Negro vote	138,000	390,000
Percentage of Negroes registered	51	23
Mean of parishes—percentage of Negroes in total population	32	38
Mean of parishes—percentage of urbanism	30	26
Mean of parishes—percentage of Catholics among all regions [3]	83	12

[1] French parishes: Acadia, Ascension, Assumption, Avoyelles, Calcasieu, Cameron, Evangeline, Iberis, Iberville, Jefferson, Jefferson Davis, Lafayette, LaFourches, Plaquemines, Pointe Coupee, St. Bernard, St. Charles, St. James, St. John the Baptist, St. Landry, St. Martin, St. Mary, Terrebonne, Vermilion, West Baton Rouge. Definition of French parishes taken from T. Lynn Smith and Homer L. Hitt, *The People of Louisiana* (Baton Rouge, 1952), p. 143.

[2] Predominantly Anglo-Saxon Protestant.

[3] From 1926 *Census of Religious Bodies*, the most reliable source available. It is recognized that the figures contain a bias because of the difference between Catholic and Protestant practice in counting children as members of the church. However, the purpose of the figures is to show differences in degree of Catholicism.

The reasons for the different reaction of French and non-French population groups to Negro registration seem, in large part, to be due to fundamentally different attitudes of each culture toward the Negro. Both Negro and white leaders agree that social attitudes toward the Negro differ in the two cultures.

Some objective evidence of this difference is to be found in these facts: (1) at political meetings in southern Louisiana crowds are often racially mixed, even at indoor meetings, whereas in northern Louisiana such crowds are always segregated; (2) the Citizens' Council organizations have comparatively little support in French-Catholic Louisiana, while in northern Louisiana, as a Madison Council official put it, "Here the Citizens' Councils are the prominent people"; (3) racially hybrid communities occur more frequently in south Louisiana than in north Louisiana.[3]

It should be emphasized that the people of French-Catholic Louisiana are not in favor of integration. Yet they do evidence, people and leaders alike, a permissive attitude toward Negro participation in political affairs that is generally lacking in the northern parishes.[4] These permissive attitudes seem to stem in large part from the social and religious practices of the Catholic Church. The Church looks upon segregation as a sin, and Archbishop Rummel of New Orleans has led the clergy in an all-out doctrinal attack on the practice. Catholic clergy cite the "catholic" character of the Church as the reason for its advanced stand on racial issues and emphasize the fact that the Protestant churches are national in origin and tend to be exclusive in character, whereas the Catholic Church is more universal in both its background and orientation. Many Catholics also point to the effect of the Church on the Negro as a reason for the high percent of Negro registration in Catholic parishes. According to this argument, the Catholic Negro enjoys religious and ethical training which is identical with that received by the white community, and from a well-educated priest. Therefore, the Catholic Negro's value system more nearly approaches that of the white community than does that of the Protestant-Negro, and, accordingly, he is more readily accepted by the greater community.

Since the Catholic Church attempts to build a Catholic culture wherever it exists by providing educational, recreational, and fraternal organizations for its members, the influence of the Church as a social institution is great. It appears to be the principal, in many areas the only, unsegregated social institution in Louisiana. In the French parishes where Catholicism has been the major formative factor in the culture for many years, it has been, Catholics say, important in producing the permissive attitudes of the people toward the political and social activities of the Negro.

In north Louisiana, on the other hand, one finds little or no objective

[3] See Alvin L. Bertrand, *The Many Louisianas*, Bulletin #46, Louisiana State University, Agricultural Experiment Station, June, 1955, p. 21.

[4] The more "permissive" attitude of the French-Catholic parishes may be demonstrated additionally by comparison of its record on race relations with the northern parishes on such matters as rates of lynching, 1900–1941; and the number of racially integrated state colleges. It was also confirmed in interviews with both Negroes and whites from the two areas.

evidence that the dominant Protestant religion has aided in the creation of tolerant attitudes toward Negro political activity. Negro leaders in these areas rarely cited white Protestant ministers as friends of the Negro, and seldom referred to a Protestant church as an ameliorative factor in the easing of racial tensions. Although most Protestant national organizations are opposed to racial prejudice and segregation, their position has not effected many changes in the attitudes of local congregations. Protestant churches, in contrast to the authoritative control by the Catholic hierarchy, are dominated by local congregations, and Protestant ministers, though often mindful of national pronouncements on segregation, must remain passive on such matters so as not to offend their flocks.

Although the mean percent of Negro registration is low in north Louisiana, there are parishes with large Negro registration. As Table III shows, this usually occurs where Negroes are not an important part of the population, that is, where there are few Negroes, little economic tenancy, and no heritage of a plantation society.

TABLE III

RELATION BETWEEN PERCENTAGE OF TENANCY, PERCENTAGE OF NEGRO POPULATION, AND PERCENTAGE OF NEGROES REGISTERED IN FRENCH AND NON-FRENCH PARISHES OF LOUISIANA, 1956

Percentage of Tenancy	Number of Parishes		Mean Percentage of Negro Population		Mean Percentage of Negroes Registered	
	French	Non-French	French	Non-French	French	Non-French
50 and over	6	11	34	52	65	11
40–49	0	4	—	43	—	23
30–39	7	6	33	39	48	25
20–29	5	6	23	36	67	36
10–19	7	9	34	25	43	53
0– 9	0	3	—	19	—	59

When the parishes of northern Louisiana are grouped into areas, this correspondence of a high rate of tenancy and concentration of Negro population to a low Negro registration becomes clearly evident and significant. In the North-Central cut-over pine section where the percentage of Negroes in the total population (mean of parishes, 24 percent) and prevalence of tenancy (17 percent) is relatively low, there is a great deal of Negro registration (55 percent). In this area, there has been little fear of the Negro as a political force, and the society tends to be pluralistic.[5]

[5] It should be noted, however, that resistance to Negro registration is stiffening in North-Central Louisiana. Efforts to purge Negroes from the rolls are being vigorously pressed by Citizens Council groups in the section. For a detailed statement of the procedures being used there, see the letter from Assistant Attorney General Olney to Senator

The Mississippi Delta area, in northeast Louisiana, is the section with the highest rate of tenancy (60 percent), the greatest proportion of Negroes (51 percent), and the lowest Negro registration (11 percent) in the state. It remains a plantation society. There are plantation owners in Tensas and Madison parishes who take pride in the resemblance between the plantations of 1856 and 1956, in terms of the physical appearance of the Negro and his cabin, and of the social and economic relationships between Negro and white.

The survival of this kind of society depends upon excluding the Negro from all political and economic power. Outsiders are assured that the Negro happily accepts the existing power structure, and strenuous efforts are made to demonstrate the mutual advantages which accrue from it.

Thus in non-French Louisiana, Negro registration varies with the number of Negroes present and the nature of the economy. In a plantation economy, a tight power structure exists which makes it possible to exclude Negroes from the polls. In addition the numerical strength of Negroes in such communities arouses real or imagined fears of possible Negro rule if he should obtain the ballot.

As Table III indicates, the economic structure of many of the French-Catholic parishes differs from that of the northern portion of the state. In French-Catholic Louisiana the Negro is not typically in a tenant-master relationship to the white community. Rather, his position is that of a free wage-earner. The reason is that much of southern Louisiana is engaged in the production of cane sugar, which does not lend itself to the tenant system of farming.

The free wage-earner is more remote from his master than is the tenant farmer, and thus (at least in prosperous times) enjoys greater social and economic freedom. Therefore, the difference in the economies of the two regions undoubtedly exercises an important conditioning effect on Negro registration.

However, even in those French-Catholic parishes where a plantation economy does exist the percent of Negro registration tends to be considerably above that of the northern plantation parishes. In three French-Catholic parishes (St. Landry, Pointe Coupee, and West Baton Rouge) both the percentage of Negro population and the percentage of tenancy is 45 or more. The percentage of Negro registration exceeds 20 in all three parishes and reaches a level of 87 in St. Landry. This highlights the importance of the French-Catholic religio-culture in producing a permissive attitude toward Negro registration.

II. THE EFFECT OF NEGRO-WHITE POPULATION BALANCE

Perhaps the most widely accepted belief concerning Negro registration in the South is that the amount will vary inversely to the proportion of Negroes

Douglas, *Congressional Record*, Vol. 103 (August 1, 1957), pp. 12156–7 (daily ed.); New York *Times*, August 4, 1957, which, however, misplaced the parishes cited as in the southern part of the state.

in the local population. According to this theory, areas with large Negro populations, (1) were most passionately attached to the cause of the Confederacy, and (2) because of the greater number of Negroes have more reason to fear Negro voting. The theory concludes that the centers of Negro population will be the last to extend the suffrage to the Negro.

Table IV shows that there is certainly no uniform correlation between the proportion of parish population Negro and the proportion of Negroes registered. However, at the extreme ends of the scale, the relationship is significant. The four Louisiana parishes with no Negro registration—Tensas, Madison, West Feliciana, and East Carroll, neighboring parishes in the Mississippi Delta area—are the only parishes with over 60 percent Negro population. In the parishes with less than 20 percent Negro population there is a significant increase in the percentage of Negro registration. However, in ten parishes with a majority of Negro population (50 to 59 percent) the mean percentage of Negroes registered (37 percent) slightly exceeds that for the two intervals with fewer Negroes (40 to 49 percent and 30 to 39 percent).

Table IV

RELATION BETWEEN NEGROES IN TOTAL POPULATION AND NEGRO REGISTRATION IN PARISHES OF LOUISIANA, 1956

Percentage of Negroes in Total Population	Number of Parishes			Mean Percentage of Negroes Registered		
	Total	French	Non-French	Total	French	Non-French
60 and over	4	—	4	0	—	0
50–59	10	4	6	37	44	33
40–49	8	3	5	33	57	19
30–39	19	6	13	32	47	25
20–29	12	6	6	52	51	53
10–19	10	5	5	62	65	59
0– 9	1	1	—	94	94	—

Table IV also shows that the presence or absence of large numbers of Negroes has a similar effect on Negro registration in French and non-French parishes. However, as the table indicates, the range of variation tends to be much narrower in the French than in the non-French parishes. Of course, the degree of economic tenancy is another variable present in this figure, a factor which has already been discussed.

In conclusion, it can be definitely stated that, in Louisiana, the simple fact of the presence of a high proportion of Negroes and a tradition of a plantation economy (such as in St. Landry parish) does not necessarily militate against the registration of Negroes in sizeable numbers, especially where a French-Catholic culture predominates.

III. THE EFFECT OF URBANISM

Contrary to the widely held belief that Negro registration in the South is concentrated in urban areas, Table V indicates that no clear relationship exists in Louisiana between the degree of urbanism and the extent of Negro registration.

TABLE V

RELATION BETWEEN URBANISM AND WHITE AND NEGRO REGISTRATION, FOR
STATE AND BY RELIGIO-CULTURAL SECTIONS, LOUISIANA, 1956

| | Number of Parishes | | | Mean Percentage Registered of Potential Vote | | | | | |
| | | | | Negro | | | White | | |
Percentage of Urbanism	Total	Fr.	Non-Fr.	Total	Fr.	Non-Fr.	Total	Fr.	Non-Fr.
70 and over	5	2	3	29	43	20	64	70	60
50–69	4	3	1	45	48	35	75	78	69
40–49	8	2	6	27	67	13	78	79	77
30–39	10	3	7	46	54	42	84	84	84
20–29	14	8	6	49	61	33	90	91	88
10–19	6	3	3	28	43	13	88	89	87
0– 9	17	4	13	43	53	40	92	93	90

The reason, in all probability, for the stereotype about urbanism and Negro registration is that those few Negroes who were registered to vote prior to 1944 resided in the large urban centers. In addition, the first increases in Negro registration after 1944 largely occurred in urban areas. The urban areas of the state contain the largest concentration of professional and business Negroes, equipped to provide leadership toward registration; and the cities provide, one might imagine, an environment of political competition better suited to encourage Negro political participation.

As Table V indicates, however, Negro registration in Louisiana is, if anything, lower in the large urban centers than in the more rural portions of the state. The table also shows that an identical though more pronounced pattern obtains for white registration too. Taking the religio-cultural areas of the state separately, the same relationship between urbanism and registration exists in both regions as in the state as a whole, but with both Negro and white registration in the French parishes tending to be either equal to or higher than registration in the non-French parishes.

Negro registration tends to be lower in the urban than the rural areas for a variety of reasons. Many an urban Negro is rootless, and tends to feel little identification with his community or his fellow Negroes; his leadership often works at cross purposes, and is particular rather than general. In addition, local interest in registration and voting tends to be more intense in Louisiana's rural areas, where the election of a sheriff is an important event, than in the urban areas. All of these factors tend, also, to operate on the level of white registration.

Even though the urban centers do not provide favorable environments for securing a high proportion of Negro registration, the "pilot" role of activities in urban centers toward launching Negro registration is important. In all parishes studied the registration of Negroes was initiated by business and professional Negroes residing in the major urban center of the parish. In the event resistance to Negro registration made it necessary to resort to legal and political action, the city provided the resources and locus for suits against the registrar, for requests to the F.B.I. to investigate reluctant registrars, and for bargains which might be negotiated with court-house politicians.

IV. THE POLITICAL FACTOR

The first concern of every politician is to be elected and reelected to office. Therefore, the existence in any community of a reservoir of untapped voters tends to act as a magnet on politicians in search of votes. The Negro vote in Louisiana, however, was not exploitable until the Supreme Court declared the white primary laws unconstitutional. After 1944, Louisiana politicians could legally pursue the Negro vote.

In all the Louisiana parishes except those with the very largest cities, political power and interest center in the courthouse of the parish seat. The dominant political figure in the courthouse is the sheriff, whose election occasions the most interest and largest voter turnout in the parish. Where Negro registration has occurred in large numbers, the sheriff has almost invariably been friendly to the idea.

The process by which this political variable helps bring Negroes to the polls works generally as follows. Community attitudes must, first of all, be permissive with respect to Negro registration. If the white community is strongly and unalterably opposed to Negro voting, the sheriff or other politician will rarely venture to seek the Negro vote. Instead, as in the Mississippi parishes with no registration, the sheriff will help keep the Negroes away from the polls. This is true because the politician fears the reaction of his townspeople to Negro registration and because he, too, generally shares the dominant attitude.

Secondly, the sheriff, by the very nature of his office, is subject to manifold temptations relating to law enforcement, particularly, in Louisiana, to the classic "payoff" to permit gambling. When a sheriff permits gambling, he is charged with corruption of his office by the good government, middle-class voters of his community. In this event the sheriff is compelled to turn to lower socio-economic groups or to marginal groups in the community for support.

After Negro leaders have initiated the movement for registration and thus demonstrated their group's potential voter strength, the sheriff or other official can then use to his own profit the power of his office to prevent inter-ference with registration, or else later encourage registration drives and voter turnout campaigns. In many parishes the Negro vote has become a "balance of power" factor.

Finally, the reward of the Negro for his vote is respect from the politicians and attendance at Negro political meetings, cessation of police brutality, and promises made and often kept regarding such matters as street improvements and better school facilities. It is ironical that this advance may thus result from an alliance of shady white and underdog Negro elements against the more "respectable" white segment of the community.

The political factor is also important as an inhibiting influence. For ex-ample, in the two French parishes (Terrebonne and Plaquemines) with a rate of Negro registration below 20 percent, the local sheriff has been instrumental in keeping the Negroes from the polls. In these cases, the sheriff is unalterably opposed to Negro voting, primarily out of fear that it will cost him the election, and, consequently, he uses the power of his office to prevent registration. In all probability, a different sheriff could permit Negro registration without suf-fering a serious reaction from the white community.

V. CONCLUSIONS

This paper is concerned with the problem of differences in the political be-havior of the South toward the Negro. These differences have been studied, here, through an analysis of Negro registration for voting in Louisiana. Negro registration is basically related to Southern politics not only because it is the fundamental step for the Negro toward the power of the ballot box but also because it appears to be vitally related to the willingness or unwillingness of specific societies to allow the Negro an equal place in the community. The evidence indicates that Southern attitudes and practices toward the Negro are in large part a function of the culture in which the relationships occur.[6] Our inquiry here is whether religio-cultural variables in the South, long celebrated as the "Bible-belt" of the nation, are related to Negro-white political relation-ships insofar as these can be defined by practices and attitudes toward Negro registration.

The findings of this study emphasize the importance of religio-cultural factors in defining white attitudes and practices toward Negro registration. In the southern French-Catholic parishes the percentage of Negroes registered is more than twice as great as in the northern Anglo-Saxon Protestant parishes. Socio-economic factors, urbanism and Negro-white population balance, ac-count for some of the difference. Yet where non-religious cultural factors are held constant, as in cotton plantation areas with large Negro populations, the

[6] See, for example, V. O. Key, Jr., *Southern Politics* (New York, 1949); and Hugh Douglas Price, *Negro and Southern Politics, A Chapter of Florida History* (New York, 1957).

religio-cultural variable emerges as a clearly influential factor in Negro registration.

First-hand observations in the parishes of Louisiana support the statistical evidence that Negro registration is related to the type of religio-cultural area involved. Permissive attitudes toward Negro registration in French-Catholic parishes seem expressive of the basic value that the Negro is spiritually equal in a Catholic society. Such a view of man's relation to man, a scheme of elementary justice implicit in a Catholic society, some Catholics maintain, is sustained by traditional Catholic theology and actively promoted by the Church in Louisiana. There is little evidence in the Protestant parishes of cultural values assigning the Negro a spiritually equal place in the community or of activity by the church itself toward these values.

Dr. Frank Tannenbaum has written a brilliant exposition of the comparative treatment of the Negro in North and South America, maintaining that differences are in large part a function of the respective Protestant and Catholic cultures.[7] Curiously, the religio-cultural analysis has been largely neglected in race-relations analysis of the United States, even though the role of the Protestant ethic, for instance in economic behavior and intellectual development, has been well stated.

It is not the intention of the authors to urge religious determinism in this paper but to maintain that, on the evidence, the politics of Negro registration in Louisiana can be understood only by consideration of religio-cultural variables with other relevant factors. In consequence we suggest that religio-cultural analysis may be useful in understanding the whole of Southern politics. Excepting Maryland, possibly, the type of analysis employed here would not be possible in other Southern states due to the lack of distinctive religio-cultural areas. Some attention could be given, however, to the general problem of the Protestant ethic in the South and its involvement with political behavior.

[7] *Slave and Citizen: The Negro in the Americas* (New York, 1947).

Harry Holloway

THE NEGRO AND THE VOTE:
THE CASE OF TEXAS

*In those southern states where Negro voter registration rose markedly
in the 1940's and 1950's, protest leaders hoped to use the new bloc
of voters as a weapon to further improve the status of the race. Harry
Holloway's careful examination of Negro political participation in
Texas during the 1950's, revealed two patterns. Urban Negroes voted
astutely for liberal candidates sympathetic to their interests, generally
following the leadership of local Negro civic leagues. Rural Negroes
on the other hand felt compelled, by the use of intimidation, to
vote for candidates of the local racist political machines. Comparable
situations have appeared in other parts of the South. It should be
emphasized, however, that the pattern Holloway found in rural counties, has also occurred in the urban milieu. Earlier, for example,
Memphis Negroes had for years been forced to vote for the candidates of the Crump machine; those who failed to do so faced arrests
on petty or trumped-up charges, and other forms of harassment.*

O F LATE there has been much concern with the voting behavior of American
Negroes. A report on the pattern in Northern cities describes it as follows:
"Many city political organizations have come to realize that the growing
Negro population is one of the largest and most dependable sources of political
strength." [1] For this reason, "The possibility of sustaining a strong party
organization, once thought to be a thing of the past, has revived...." And
Negro preference for office holders of their own race is becoming so strong that
even the most liberal white candidates face mounting pressure to step aside.
The picture in brief is one of a massive, dependable, racially-conscious bloc
vote.

Harry Holloway, "The Negro and the Vote: The Case of Texas," *Journal of
Politics*, XXIII (August, 1961), pp. 526–56. Reprinted with the permission of the
publisher and author.
[1] James Q. Wilson in *The Reporter*, March 31, 1960, p. 21.

What, then, is happening in the South? By taking Texas as an example it is possible to present some cues as to the political development of the Southern Negro. Admittedly Texas is perhaps the least Southern of all the states of the old Confederacy. Yet the state is sufficiently associated with the region and its distinctive problems to provide a valuable example of some of the chief features of the Southern Negro voter. Their political behavior is of more than academic interest because the Negro voter has been seen by some observers as an important possible addition to liberal forces in the South in the creation of a competitive liberal-conservative politics. In other words the Negro vote can be an important contribution to the creation of a two party South.[2]

In dealing with the voting behavior of the Texas Negro, the first step will be to review the main features of the Negro population within the state and the course of Negro registration. Beyond this point the inquiry divides into two parts, the one concerned with the city voter, the other with the rural voter. One section will present an analysis of the voting behavior of the Texas city Negro based upon precinct returns and other available indicators. The thesis will be argued that, whatever the seeming divisions and difficulties faced by these city voters, they form a surprisingly effective, cohesive and stable bloc oriented toward the liberal Democratic candidate, especially if he is strongly pro-civil rights. And they decidedly favor candidates of their own race or of Latin (Mexican-American) extraction.

The section on the rural Negro voter stands apart and presents peculiar problems. The gathering of evidence is attended by difficulties not encountered in the cities. The size of the region involved is such that generalizations which can be developed from the available evidence must always be treated with some caution. Further, because the rural areas are much more typically Deep South in their pattern of behavior than are the cities, the inquiry here must delve into the sociological and psychological aspects of the 'southern way of life.' From such evidence as can be brought together this section will argue that the rural Negro is still in good part bound by the caste system of racial relationships

[2] Alexander Heard, A Two-Party South? (Chapel Hill: University of North Carolina Press, 1952), p. 247; Donald S. Strong, "The Presidential Election in the South," Journal of Politics, Vol. 17 (1955), pp. 343–388. Strong is cautious in suggesting the rise of any two party system but does claim the Democrats need the Negro vote to balance defections to the Republicans among upper income suburbanites (p. 388). Samuel Lubell writes, "Probably the crucial factor which will determine how quickly or slowly a two-party system develops is the changing status of the Negro, who has always been the basis of the one-party South." See his The Future of American Politics, 2nd ed., (Garden City, New York: Doubleday Anchor Books, 1965), p. 125. Other valuable sources on the Negro in Southern politics are the following: V. O. Key, Jr., Southern Politics (New York: Alfred A. Knopf Co., 1950); Hugh D. Price, The Negro and Southern Politics (New York: New York University Press, 1957); Donald S. Strong, "The Rise of Negro Voting in Texas," APSR Vol. 42 (1948), pp. 510–522. Margaret Price is author of two pamphlets published by the Southern Regional Council in Atlanta: The Negro Voter in the South, 1957; and The Negro and the Ballot in the South, 1959. The American Voter by Campbell, Converse, Miller and Stokes (New York: John Wiley and Sons, Inc., 1960), contains some references to Southern Negro voters.

and casts his vote accordingly. He has little trouble registering and exercising the right to vote but, with some exceptions, does not cast a free, self-willed ballot. The concluding paragraphs will summarize the evidence upon the electoral behavior of both urban and rural Negroes in Texas, and note present trends and prospects.

The state's total Negro population in 1950 was 977,458, or slightly under a million as compared with a total population of 7,711,194.[3] By 1957 Negroes were estimated to be no more than 11.4% of state population, or slightly more than 10%.[4] They are even outnumbered by the state's other large minority, the Latin Americans or Mexicans, estimated at about 1½ million. Overall, Texas has a smaller proportion of Negro to white population than any other Southern state and the proportion is declining as white population grows and Negroes leave the state.[5] For these and other reasons V. O. Key more than a decade ago described Texas as having 'politics of economics' in which race was no longer the fundamental factor shaping state politics.[6] In some ways Texas is as much a Border State as it is Southern.[7]

Although the total Negro population is not great almost all of it is concentrated in the eastern one-third or so of the state,[8] a region consisting of 84 counties with a Negro population of 10% or more in 1950. And in that part of this area next to the Louisiana-Arkansas border the Rural Black Belt extending across the South reaches into Texas. Still, within this whole eastern region Negro population is somewhat dispersed. In 1950 there were only four counties among the state's 254 with more than 50 per cent Negro population; only twenty-two have a Negro population of 30 per cent or more. The region itself varies some and includes within or close to the area the state's biggest metropolitan centers. There is also an oil field and a steel mill in the Deep East Texas area. But in other respects these counties have the characteristics one would expect. Three quarters of the 53 counties with Negro population of 20 per cent or more experienced no population growth from 1950 to 1957 or actually declined. Most of these counties have no city over ten thousand. They

[3] *Report of the U.S. Commission on Civil Rights,* 1959 (Washington, D.C.: U.S. Government Printing Office), p. 586.

[4] *Texas Almanac,* 1958–1959 (Dallas: *Dallas Morning News,* 1957), p. 95.

[5] From 1940 to 1950 Negro population grew by 5.7% while the white population grew 22.7.% See *op. cit.,* p. 95. The young generation, especially, is leaving. One Austin leader formed a group of forty veterans interested in political activity after WW II. He now says only one is left in town. The graduates of the local Negro college, Huston-Tillotson, are also said to leave.

[6] V. O. Key, Jr., *Southern Politics,* pp. 254 ff.

[7] A *Special Report* of the Southern Regional Council released in August, 1959, estimated the state to have 3,250 Negroes in desegregated classrooms whereas the total for the rest of the South was 206 (p. 2). A scale of Southern characteristics presented by Hugh Price in his Florida study also put Texas at the bottom of the list of eleven states of the Old Confederacy. See Hugh D. Price, *The Negro and Southern Politics,* pp. 8 and 9.

[8] The percentages that follow are based on 1950 census data plus *Texas Almanac,* 1958–1959 data on estimated population in 1957. One odd exception to this regional concentration is Foard County in West Texas, with a Negro population of 10.1 per cent.

are also low income counties based mainly on crops, timber, and livestock. One-third of the whole group of 84 counties had median family income of less than $1500 in 1950 and another one-third were in the under $2000 bracket. The eastern third of the state outside the large cities shares in those features typical of the Black Belt but—aside from Deep East Texas—less concentratedly and with more variations.

As for state-wide registration,[9] the Civil Rights *Report* estimated the number of eligible Texas Negro voters in 1958—the only year for which a complete survey is available—as 226,495.[10] This total represents 38.8 per cent of the non-white population over 21. White registration in the 1956–58 period was estimated at 49.0 per cent. So far as these figures are comparable they indicate that Negro registration is sizeable and only about 10% below that of the whites. A breakdown of these figures shows that in 180 of the state's 254 counties, 25 per cent or more of the Negro population was registered. And the 14 counties with no non-white registrants contained negligible non-white population.[11] The figures demonstrate that Negroes have registered in large numbers in Texas. A review of available estimates for the last two decades shows the following:

Estimated Negro Registration in Texas from 1940 to 1958 [12]

1940— 50,000
1942— 33,000
1944—
1946— 75,000
1947—100,000
1948—
1950—
1952—181,916
1954—
1956—214,000
1958—226,495

[9] The only form of registration required by the state is payment of a poll tax. Because of exemptions the *Texas Almanac, 1958–1959* (p. 453), estimates the actual number of qualified voters as about 25 per cent above the number of paid poll taxes since 1955. Survey figures are therefore subject to a margin of error, even in attempting to take exemptions into account. The survey contained in the *Report of the U.S. Commission on Civil Rights*, 1959, included a count of 165 of the state's 254 counties and various kinds of estimates of the remaining counties. See p. 586.

[10] *Report*, p. 586. The figure is for non-whites but Negroes are more than 99 per cent of the non-white population. Texas has by far the largest number of Negroes registered, but its percentage of 38.8% is exceeded slightly by Florida's 39.5%.

[11] *Ibid.*, p. 51.

[12] The sources are: Donald S. Strong "The Rise of Negro Voting in Texas," *APSR*, Vol. 42 (1948), p. 511; V. O. Key, *op. cit.*, p. 522; Margaret Price, *The Negro Voter in the South*, p. 5; and *Report*, p. 586. The figures for the '40's are from Strong and Key; those for 1952 and 1956 are from Margaret Price; and those for 1958 from the *Report*. A slightly higher estimate for the 1958 figure is in *New South*, October, 1959, p. 5.

A partial explanation of the extent of Negro registration lies in the fact that the legal barriers to voting in Texas have consisted only in the poll tax and the white primary. Since the latter did not extend to general or to municipal and special elections, Negroes willing to pay the poll tax could vote long before the *Allwright* decision of 1944. They were even a controlling influence in the Republican Party of Texas up until sometime into the late twenties or early thirties.[13] For the decade from 1920 to 1930 Paul Lewinson estimated there were from 12,900 to 15,100 Negro voters in Dallas, Ft. Worth, Houston, and San Antonio.[14] Some Negroes in this state were therefore accustomed to a degree of electoral participation even during the days of the white primary. And although there were some incidents following the decision, there was not much resistance. By 1956 Margaret Price concluded in her survey that, "Intimidation as a means of limiting Negro voting in Texas was found to be relatively rare.... There have been occasional reports of local discrimination against potential Negro voters.... But, by and large, the poll tax remains the only obvious deterrent." [15] And today it is widely accepted that the poll tax probably reduces the vote of low income whites as much or more than the Negro vote.[16]

As would be expected, the growth of registration was most marked in the period immediately following the abolition of the white primary. It then continued at a reduced rate of growth similar to the trend reported by Price in his Florida [17] survey. Thus in the ten year period from 1942 to 1952 Negro registration grew by about 150,000, for an average of 15,000 per year, whereas in the six years from 1952 to 1958 it grew by about 45,000 for an average of less than 8,000 per year. This plateauing of registration should be seen, however, against the background of opposition, as well as the shifting of Negro population out of state. As *New South* reported in October of 1959, "The strained atmosphere created by resistance to school desegregation has slowed the pace of Negro voter registration through the South...." This changed atmosphere may have some effect in parts of Texas but the evidence for the state as a whole shows little or no overt resistance to registration and the odds favor a slow but continual increase.

Having looked briefly at the geography of the state's Negro population and overall registration figures, we now focus the inquiry on the city Negro.

[13] Paul Lewinson, *Race, Class, and Party* (New York: Oxford University Press, 1932), pp. 170ff.

[14] *Ibid.*, p. 220.

[15] Margaret Price, *op. cit.*, p. 18. This same survey cites resistance to Negro registration in Dallas in 1956. However, her figure on 1956 registration is far below vote tallies from Negro precincts that year and is even farther from the registration figure in the *Report* for 1958. In all likelihood there was resistance but less than she indicates.

[16] A recent study of the effect of the poll tax explains that the tax does act to discourage minority groups, but chiefly because of its economic impact on all low income groups. And today low income whites may well have less incentive to vote than Negroes. See Frederic D. Ogden, *The Poll Tax in the South* (University, Alabama: University of Alabama Press, 1958), pp. 175–177.

[17] *The Negro and Southern Politics*, pp. 32, ff.

Evidence will first be presented as to the effectiveness of Negro registration drives, their cohesiveness and stability as a voting bloc, and their political orientation. The bulk of the evidence will be drawn from analyses of predominantly Negro precincts in four major Texas cities: Austin, Dallas, Houston, and San Antonio.

In examining the effectiveness of Negro registration efforts, Austin may be taken as an example. A comparison of registration in four predominantly Negro Austin precincts with the city as a whole is revealing. The peak registration of 1959 is used as a base point in comparing the consistency of white and Negro registration. The 1959 figure is for the 1960 election since registration in any given year entitles the registrant to vote the year following.

The figures show that Negro registration in Austin was more consistent from 1953 through 1959 than that of the city as a whole. And this conclusion suggests that Negro political organization is already pretty effective in reaching a core of registrants. So far as Austin is typical of the Texas city Negro voter one can conclude tentatively that city political organizations of the Negro do a good job of contacting and signing up, from one year to the next, those willing to register. This same conclusion may mean that registration is near its upper limit and is not likely to climb markedly, aside from exceptional efforts, in the near future. In support of this conclusion one of the state's Negro leaders in Houston writes that registration drives today aim not so much at increasing the vote as at maintaining the vote in being.

COMPARISON OF NEGRO AND COMMUNITY WIDE ANNUAL
REGISTRATION TOTALS IN AUSTIN

Year	Four Predominantly Negro Precincts: Paid Poll Taxes & Exemptions	Per Cent of 1959 Total	Austin: Paid Poll Taxes & Exemptions	Per Cent of 1959 Total
1959	4,810	100%	54,373	100%
*1958	4,393	91.3%	36,988	69.3%
1957	4,721	98.1%	41,754	76.8%
1956	4,065	84.5%	37,393	68.8%
1955	4,610	96.0%	50,152	92.3%
1954	3,911	81.3%	36,135	66.5%
**1953	4,158	86.4%	39,251	72.2%

* The Civil Right *Report* gives a somewhat higher figure for Travis County as a whole—5,353. The latter figure would include those living outside the four precincts dealt with above. The figures in the table are from Travis County registration records.
** Changes in Austin's precinct lines prior to 1953 made continuation of the above chart of doubtful validity.

Another important question concerns the extent to which Negro registrants turn out to vote after qualifying. A good measure is the relation of the actual vote to the number of qualified voters in a given population. A check of recent Austin election returns shows the turnout to vary widely but to approach 50% or more in major elections. The figures are not altogether impressive. Many who qualify obviously don't bother to go to the polls.

A check on the consistency of voter turnout lies in a comparison of the total vote in Negro precincts with that of white precincts in the same elections. In this case San Antonio precincts will be used and white upper middle income precincts there will be compared with those predominantly Negro. The peak turnout of 1956 is used as a base point for the comparison.

COMPARISON OF ELECTION RETURNS WITH REGISTRATION TOTALS
IN FOUR PREDOMINANTLY NEGRO PRECINCTS OF AUSTIN *

Election	Total Vote	Annual Total of Paid Poll Taxes & Exemptions	Per Cent of Qualified Voters Who Vote
1. 1956 President	2516	4619	54.5%
1956 Governor (primary)	2136		46.2%
1956 Governor (general)	2115		45.8%
2. 1957 Senate (special)	1006	4065	24.7%
3. 1958 Governor (primary)	2275	4721	48.2%
1958 Governor (general)	600		12.7%

* Most of this data is from Travis County Election and Registration records. Precinct returns for the primaries are from records kept by the Travis County chairman of the Democratic Party.

Since the upper income group should be one of the most politically alert and active in the city one would expect Negro precincts to suffer by comparison. Yet, in four of the above ten elections the Negro turnout is at a higher rate by comparison with their peak turnout of 1956 than is the upper income white turnout. The Negro vote does show less consistency and is apt to decrease in the run off election or general election in an "off" year. However, of the Negroes' poor showing in the 1958 general election it should be added that they have less incentive than upper income whites. The Democratic primary usually settles the issue and they have no great interest in voting for a Republican state office holder, even though a minority retain some loyalty to the party. On the other hand, Republicanism has great strength among San Antonio upper income groups.

From the material on registration, voter turnout, and the consistency of voter turnout year after year there emerges tentatively a mixed picture of the city Negroes' efforts. Those willing to register do so with considerable regularity year after year. Of these, however, only about half of them reach the polls and the figure is much less in some elections. Those who do reach the polls are capable of maintaining turnouts at a high level from one year to the next in key elections but may fall off seriously in some elections, especially run-offs, local elections, and general elections offering only a contest between a Republican and a Democrat. Probably a good deal depends on the effectiveness of local organizations in whipping up interest regularly. Also, the evidence presented does suggest that Negro organizations are surprisingly effective up to a point and particularly in view of the low income and education averages that characterize Negro populations.

Granted that the city Negro does register and vote in considerable numbers, how does he use this vote? Is the kind of bloc-voting characteristic of the Northern cities also emerging in Texas? And is it a liberal, racially conscious vote such as could be an important element in an emerging two party system?

A partial answer to this question appears from analysis of recent election returns in four major Texas cities in the eastern third of the state. The Negro voters in these cities constituted one third of the total number of registered Negroes in 1958. To this group can be added the cities included by Donald Strong in his study of the 1952 election. His study of this election showed Negro voters in these cities to behave much like those in the four cities examined closely below, and there is no reason to think their behavior would differ in other elections. The total in these cities amounts to about 44 per cent of all eligible Negro voters in 1958.[18]

The returns show a decisive and in some cases an overwhelming majority for the Democrat and the liberal. In presidential elections the strong preference shown for Stevenson in the 1956 presidential race is expected but still notable; and it is less than the proportion received in two of these cities that were checked for 1952 returns when Stevenson's civil rights position was stronger. In Austin and Dallas in 1952, Negro precincts gave him a whopping 92% of their vote.[19] Of Stevenson's two races one can say that the more liberal his civil rights position, the greater the Negro vote for him.

This pattern carries over into state politics, as shown by the returns for the 1956, 1957, and 1958 elections. In the 1956 gubernatorial race Ralph Yarborough, a liberal, ran against the conservative, Price Daniel. The returns in Negro precincts show a preference for the liberal of about nine to one. The same preference appears in the 1957 Special Senate election, though to a less marked degree. Among the three major candidates who received the bulk of the votes, the voters had a choice of either a liberal Democrat (Yarborough), a conservative Democrat (Dies) or the Republican (Hutcheson). Again, the Negro Precincts voted decisively for Yarborough by margins of from $2/3$ to $4/5$ or more. The fact that the Yarborough margin was less in the two cities with a reputation for conservatism, Dallas and San Antonio, must mean that the Negro voters there are also influenced by this temper.

A further test of liberal propensities is the 1958 gubernatorial primary. Daniel, the conservative incumbent, carried the state by a comfortable majority.

---

[18] The complete list of cities is: Austin, Corpus Christi, Dallas, Ft. Worth, Houston, Port Arthur–Beaumont, San Antonio, Waco and Wichita Falls. Three of these—Corpus Christi, San Antonio, and Wichita Falls—are in the under 10% Negro population bracket. For Strong's article see "The Presidential Election in the South," *Journal of Politics*, Vol. 17 (1955), pp. 373–7.

[19] For an extended analysis of the Dallas returns in 1952 see Donald S. Strong, "The Presidential Election in the South," *op. cit.*, pp. 373–5.

COMPARISON OF CONSISTENCY OF VOTING TURNOUT AMONG
ANGLO UPPER MIDDLE AND NEGRO PRECINCTS OF SAN ANTONIO *

Election	ANGLO UPPER MIDDLE INCOME		PREDOMINANTLY NEGRO	
	Votes Cast in 16 Precincts	Percentage of 1965 General Election Total	Votes Cast in 3 Precincts	Percentage of 1965 General Election Total
1956 General Election	16,106	100%	2,490	100%
First Primary	10,578	65.7%	1,738	69.8%
Second Primary	8,989	55.9%	1,405	56.4%
1957 Special Senate Election	9,317	57.9%	956	38.4%
1958 First Primary	9,281	57.6%	1,682	67.6%
Second Primary	5,295	39.9%	751	30.2%
General Election	6,708	41.6%	444	17.8%
1959 First City Council Election	5,795	26.0%	1,115	44.8%
Second City Council Election	3,130	19.4%	264	10.6%
Public Housing Referendum	2,771	17.2%	581	23.0%

* For the information on the San Antonio returns the writer drew upon an unpublished manuscript by Mitchell Grossman, now teaching at San Antonio College.

PERCENTAGE BREAKDOWN OF VOTES CAST IN PREDOMINANTLY

NEGRO PRECINCTS OF FOUR TEXAS CITIES IN RECENT ELECTIONS

Election	Candidates	Austin Number of Precincts (3) %	Dallas Number of Precincts (14) %	Houston Number of Precincts (36) %	San Antonio* Number of Precincts (3) %
1. 1956 President	Stevenson (D)	63	57	64	64
	Eisenhower (R)	37	43	36	36
2. 1956 Governor 2nd Primary	Daniel (D)	7	12	9	11
	Yarborough (D)	93	88	91	89
3. 1956 Governor General	Daniel (D)	70	66	73	73
	Bryant (R)	30	34	27	27
4. 1957 Senate Special 3 highest Candidates only	Dies (D)	2	11	3	12
	Hutcheson (R)	14	25	16	24
	Yarborough (D)	84	64	81	64
5. 1958 Governor Primary	Daniel (D)	7	13	6	11
	Gonzalez (D)	90	80	88	83
	O'Daniel (D)	3	7	6	6

PERCENT OF TOTAL VOTE CAST FOR NEGRO CANDIDATE IN PREDOMINANTLY NEGRO PRECINCTS OF TWO TEXAS CITIES

Election	Negro Candidate	Percent of Total Vote Cast in Predominantly Negro Precincts for Negro Candidate Only	Percent of Total Vote Cast in Predominantly Latin Precincts for Negro Candidate Only
6. 1949 Austin City Council 17 candidates—5 Highest Candidates win	Lott	17	6
7. 1951 Austin City Council 14 Candidates—5 Highest Candidates win	Dewitty	28	6
8. 1957 San Antonio City Council, Place 2 4 Candidates	Walker	58	10

* Here, as previously, the writer is indebted to Mitchell Grossman's paper for the data on San Antonio precincts. For selection of precincts in other cities, consultation with local officials and political leaders was the main source. Bexar County (San Antonio) is the only one of these three in which the ratio of Negro to white population was less than 10 per cent (6.5 per cent). The returns are from records of these counties or records of Democratic primary returns kept by county chairmen of the party.

One of his opponents was Henry Gonzales, a Latin American state-senator from San Antonio. Gonzalez is known as one of the state's leading liberals and campaigned hard on the theme of equal rights. The third candidate, "Pappy" Lee O'Daniel, was a conservative in the tradition of the rural demagogue.[20] He had once been notably successful in state politics and in this race was trying a comeback. Against these widely known candidates Gonzalez was a one-sided favorite in Negro precincts by margins of 80 to 90 per cent.

Contrasting with this strongly liberal bloc vote are the signs of some sympathy for Republicanism. Whether the vote for the presidential Republican of more than a third of their ballots shows much or not, that for state candidates does. Bryant, the Republican candidate for governor in 1958, received from one fourth to one third of the Negro vote in a campaign that is normally a race in name only. The same characteristic appears in the vote for the Republican senatorial candidate in 1957. Hutcheson's vote of from 14 to 25 per cent in a race with two Democrats, the one conservative and the other liberal, can only be interpreted as a vote for the Republican Party alongside the Negroes' otherwise notably liberal voting propensities.

A further question of importance is the Negro voter's race consciousness. Other studies indicate that Negro candidates can normally count on heavy support in Negro precincts but not uniformly or overwhelmingly so.[21] The results in the Texas samples are similar. The vote for Henry Gonzalez is one indicator. In all four cities he received 80 to 90 per cent of the vote in Negro precincts. In this case Gonzalez' liberalism no doubt reinforced his ethnic appeal. A direct test is the Negro vote for Negro candidates. Several city elections in recent years afford examples. The vote in predominantly Latin precincts is included for comparison. In 1951 DeWitty, a Negro, ran eighth in the field and was not far from the fifth place of the lowest council winner. By contrast a spot check of precincts singled out by local political leaders as representative of upper, middle, and lower white income groups showed DeWitty's percentage running from 2 per cent to 7 per cent—far below his 28 per cent in Negro precincts. Even if one grants a margin of error in this procedure, the difference between Negro and other precincts on this election was so great as to reveal a decided preference.[22] Today DeWitty attributes a change in the city's electoral system designed to dilute the impact of the Negro vote to the fears of the city fathers that he might win in a later election.

In San Antonio the vote received by Walker, the colored candidate, clearly

[20] V. O. Key analyzes O'Daniel's earlier political career in his *Southern Politics*, pp. 265-271. Key describes O'Daniel as "more Republican than most Republicans." In the lore of Texas politics, O'Daniel is famous as the man who campaigned on the Bible, a hillbilly band, and hot biscuits.

[21] Margaret Price, *op. cit.*, p. 46. Hugh Price, *op. cit.*, p. 79.

[22] The procedure used was to ask leaders identified with various factions in Austin politics and each of whom had lengthy experience of local affairs to select several precincts in each of three main income brackets. An official of the Chamber of Commerce was also asked to give such a selection. On those precincts for which there was substantial agreement their returns for this election were checked.

shows the same Negro partiality. And, again, a spot check of San Antonio precincts selected by local leaders and census data as representative of various white income groupings showed Walker's percentage of the total precinct vote running from 3 per cent to 4 per cent. Alongside the Negro vote it is noteworthy that the Latins show much less interest in the Negro candidate. The Negroes appear to support a Latin candidate by large margins but Latins are not similarly enthusiastic over Negro candidates. Thus, these city returns indicate, so far as they are representative, that Negroes in Texas cities are race conscious but not to the same degree as their Northern brethren.[23]

Analysis of these returns further reveals that Negro leaders don't have the power to deliver a bloc vote at will, regardless of their followers' preferences. As the returns show, the Negro voter has his own fairly consistent voting propensities which leaders disregard at risk to themselves. Price's Florida study reached this conclusion, and there is no reason to think Texas Negroes are different.[24] For example, in Austin a local Negro leader of some year's standing has freely admitted privately that he cannot swing his own precinct's vote if he takes the "wrong" positions. His people will go the way they want to regardless of his endorsement if the candidates and their positions are well known and the voters have strong feelings about them. Of course, the leader's area of discretion is vastly enlarged when the endorsement applies to candidates about whom the ordinary voters have little knowledge. In addition, it should be pointed out that the group as a whole, leaders and led, shows not a little discrimination. They will not blindly follow the 'liberal' and/or Democratic candidate, particularly if they suspect a weakening of his civil rights position. The best example comes out of Stevenson's two races. All over the South the vote for Stevenson dropped in 1956 as Negroes perceived Stevenson's weakening civil rights position.[25] This Negro bloc vote has a mind of its own on issues of foremost concern to the group.

What can be said in summary about the voting of these relatively emancipated Southern city Negroes? They show the same propensities as city Negroes in the North, though less markedly so. In the first place, the consistency of registration figures from one year to the next suggests that much effective work has already been done in getting them registered and they may now be near the peak of sustained electoral interest. Exceptional efforts may

[23] Apart from these examples of unsuccessful candidacies, there have been at least two cases of Negroes actually elected to office in post war Texas. In 1958 Mrs. Charles H. White gained election to the Houston school board. It is reported that there was confusion as to her identity and her election was in a sense a mistake. In the spring of 1960 a Negro minister gained election as city commissioner in the small panhandle city of Slaton. In this case a coalition of Negroes and Latin Americans provided support. See "Negro Surprise Victor," New York Times, April 8, 1960, p. 8.

[24] Hugh Price writes in reference to Negro Political leagues; "League endorsement of a wrong candidate in a contest where a clear difference in attitude toward the Negro exists does not sway many Negro voters: rather it raises the question, Who sold out?" (p. 72).

[25] Charles Grier Sellers (ed.), The Southerner as American (Chapel Hill: University of North Carolina Press, 1960), p. 172.

lead to some expansion of numbers but most of those willing to register seem to be already on the rolls. As to voting turnout, the existing evidence presents a mixed picture. Only about half of those qualified normally vote and at times considerably less. Those who do vote, however, can do surprisingly well in maintaining their turnout from one year to the next in major elections, though turnout falls off decidedly in lesser elections. The picture is one of voters capable of surprising efforts but not as yet stabilized to perform equally well in all elections. In these features, especially the unevenness of turnout, they probably bear the least favorable comparison with Northern Negroes.

As to their voting, the Texas city Negroes vote as a bloc, on the whole, on those races where there is a difference between the candidates on issues of importance to the group. Their political preferences seem very similar to those of Northern Negroes. They vote strongly liberal and almost overwhelmingly so if the candidate is clearly pro-civil rights. In any case, the larger part of their vote turns up in the column of the more liberal candidate rather than the more conservative. If in these political preferences the Texas city Negro bears close comparison with those of the Northern cities, there seems to be a more marked difference in degree of Republican sentiment remaining.[26]

Their vote has an ethnic or racial coloration and will go in the main to the Latin candidate, other things equal, and above all, for a Negro. Yet, even here, they will not vote strongly for a Negro they consider a really poor candidate. Further, even as a bloc with low average education and income characteristics, they show sensitivity to candidates and issues and may shift their vote accordingly, as in the case of Stevenson in 1956. The same trait appears in some degree also in their unwillingness to follow their leaders blindly and with no thought for the contesting candidates' expressed positions. The leaders may have much power but must keep their follower's trust and confidence and cannot afford to endorse known anti-Negro candidates.

The general impression left by the analysis is one of an electorate that is uneven but capable of surprising efforts. Negro political organizations have not yet drawn in all potential voters nor have they stabilized their participation. Probably part of the difficulty lies not just in the low levels of education and income typical of this group but also in the influx of rural voters not used to voting regularly and the departure of some of the most energetic and enterprising individuals from the city. The cities gain population from the country and lose population to other cities in the North. There must, too, be variations from city to city and one election to the next as Negro political organizations rise and decline in efficiency. And always there is the background pattern of segregation throughout the non-public sector. Still, amidst these limitations the Texas city Negro is making considerable use of the political influence available to him.

[26] In a comparison of Northern and Southern Negroes as a whole, the degree of Republicanism and the extent of political participation are cited as two significant differences—with Northern Negroes more active and more heavily Democratic. See Campbell, et al., The American Voter, pp. 452–3.

Since these four cities plus those contained in Strong's analysis had about 44% of the Negro voters registered in 1958, there is a large group yet unaccounted for, the rural East Texas Negro. This group is not so easily examined as the city voter. As previously noted, the region is large and most of it is rural; there are some variations in economic activity, though agriculture predominates; and the ratio of Negro to white population varies from as little as about 10% to over 50% in four counties. Southern customs and attitudes prevail here more than elsewhere in the state and make inquiry about the question of race a touchy matter. Amidst these variations there is, however, a basic pattern which the evidence available suggests to be predominant. That pattern is one in which the East Texas rural Negro is in good part a 'controlled' voter who differs much from the city Negro. In examining this pattern the first step will be to look at county registration and election returns for peculiarities that suggest supporting evidence. The next step will be to try to reconstruct the picture of voting manipulation reported by informants and to show, as well, the exceptions to the pattern. The last portion of this section will try to account for this distinctive behavior as a function not only of the well known social and economic features of the Southern Negro's position but also of his psychology. The stress will lie in showing that white influence operates for the most part peacefully and non-coercively and is therefore based on a psychology of acceptance by the Negro of an inferior place in society. The Texas rural Negro in this state has legal access to political power which he is unable socially and psychologically to use effectively much of the time.

Significant evidence as to the distinctive behavior of the rural Negro comes from the registration figures given in the *Report* of the Civil Rights Commission. In the usual explanations of Negro registration, low percentage turnout is correlated with such factors as low education and income medians, and a predominantly rural economy with a high ratio of farm tenancy. In addition Hugh Price's Florida study showed that opposition from the white community might remain even after Negro population dropped off so that Negroes were discouraged from voting even in areas where they were not a large proportion of the population.[27] East Texas would seem to fit into this pattern but does not. Registration is high where it should, in accord with the usual factors, be low.

In Dallas, Austin, and San Antonio Negro registration in 1958 fell in the 30%–40% bracket.[28] In the total of the six most urban counties with Negro population in the 10%–30% bracket the median registration was 38.8%. On the other hand, the seven relatively non-urban counties with Negro population as high as 40% or above have a median registration of 46.1%. In general, of the 84 counties with 10% or more Negro population, 44, or a little more than half have Negro registration of 40% or more. And 36 of these same 44 counties have no city of 10,000 or larger. On the other hand, among those counties with

[27] Margaret Price, *op. cit.*, p. 23, Hugh Price, *op. cit.*, pp. 36–54.
[28] Houston is an exception with 47% registered. The figures are from the *Report*, pp. 581–6.

a Negro registration *under* 40%, more than half have a city of 10,000 or more people. And there are some astonishing examples. Waller county is listed by the Civil Rights *Report* as having over 50% Negro population and more than 40% of the eligible Negroes registered. And Marion County next to the Louisiana border has, according to the estimates, more qualified Negro than white voters. In sum, the urban counties with low ratios of Negro to white population have somewhat lower registration medians than those that are rural and have relatively high ratios of Negro to white population.

Alongside these remarkable registration figures must be set the evidence of the election returns. Alexander Heard in his analysis of the Texas Dixiecrat vote in 1948 located the main part of it in this same East Texas region.[29] A more recent test is the vote for the liberal Latin American, Henry Gonzalez, in the gubernatorial primary of 1958. The Negroes in the cities examined above gave him margins of from 80% to 90%. Yet his vote in East Texas correlates negatively with Negro population. Of the fifty-three counties with 20% or more Negro population, fifty-one gave him less than 20% of their vote and twenty-one of these fifty-three gave him less than 10%.[30] All of the counties with a Negro population of as much as 30% or more gave Gonzalez less than 20% of their vote, including the four counties in which Negro population is more than 50% of the total. There is a strong implication in the returns that East Texas Negroes either did not vote at all or did not bloc vote for Gonzalez.

From this evidence of county registration and election figures there is good reason to believe that the rural East Texas Negro behaves differently than the city Negro. The explanation uniformly accepted by informants with some knowledge of the area is that, with some exceptions and variations, the Negro of this region is politically manipulated.[31] As one liberal East Texas lawyer typed

[29] Alexander Heard, A *Two-Party South?*, pp. 253–261.

[30] The two exceptions were the metropolitan Gulf Coast counties containing Galveston and Port Arthur–Beaumont. And in both cases the vote was above 20% but below 30%.

[31] Most of the information gathered came from correspondence with informants in the region, plus interviews with local Negro and white leaders. Names were gathered as best these initial contacts permitted and each new informant asked to suggest others. In this manner about two dozen informants were contacted. A questionnaire was used for many, though not all, because it was felt some might not be willing to reply at length. The best informants turned out to be a number of lawyers living in small East Texas urban centers. Those who gave the most candid and complete answers asked that their names not be used, but copies of the questionnaire and the replies received are available in the writer's files. Among these sources there was substantial agreement as to the political manipulation of the East Texas rural Negro. W. Astor Kirk (cited below) expressed cautious disagreement with this conclusion and felt that there had been changes in the last few years, though he admitted to having knowledge of only a small part of East Texas. Those interviewed in Austin included: Arthur Dewitty, Secretary of the Travis County Voters League. Dr. Everett Givens, A Negro leader long active in state and local politics. O. H. Elliott, Financial Secretary, Masonic Temple and active in League work. Kenneth R. Lamkin, a lawyer, and organizer and participant in the League. Stuart Long, a newsman whose news service conducted the *Report's* 1958 survey. W. Astor Kirk, member of

it 'white paternalism' based on an extension to politics of the caste system of racial relations prevails.[32] In what follows the operation of white paternalism is depicted, significant exceptions are noted, and the basis for this system as revealed by studies of Negro psychology is examined.

In brief, white paternalism means that the white community encourages Negroes to register and to vote in the normally well-founded belief the vote will be a friendly one. Much of the Negro vote is an adjunct to the white vote, not the independent self-willed vote of the city Negro. The best brief statement of the relationship is that in the words of an elderly East Texas Negro: "Where a colored man lives on a white man's place, he's influenced by the white man but there is no force or intimidation felt." As these words reveal, the striking feature is that the Negro accepts his role "with no force or intimidation felt." The relationship is not typically coercive. The caste system was simply extended to politics to continue much of the control exercised before the Negroes gained the legal right to participate in the white primary.[33]

To begin with, the white man solicits the Negro vote by encouraging him to the pay poll tax, possibly loaning him the money to do so. Negro voting leagues manipulated by the whites may also cooperate in this task. Apparently the relationship is usually on a small scale, with one white man 'influencing' perhaps ten or a dozen Negroes whom he knows personally and with whom he has dealings. Economics plays a powerful role in this system, but is certainly not the only factor. The Negro dependent on a white man for his job may accept political advice in voting as part of the normal course of affairs. Or the Negro may accept the whites' leadership simply because he considers him a friend who asks a favor.

In actual voting there are variations, too. If there is a 'machine' the leader may pass the word to the Negro organization *en masse*.[34] Or the whites may solicit support among the small circle of Negro voters they can influence. If the fight is an even one between contending white factions, a few votes may make the difference. Elderly Negroes may be especially solicited. Because of the departure of many young people from these declining rural counties, the older generation may be a sizable number. And they may be somewhat more amenable to influence than the younger generation, though not always so.

---

the Political Science Department of Huston-Tillotson College and President of the Austin Commission on Human Relations. Trueman O'Quinn, Travis County Chairman, Democratic Party. Carter Wesley of Houston and editor of the state's leading Negro paper was contacted by mail.

[32] Gunnar Myrdal's *An American Dilemma* (New York: Harper and Bros., 1944) is still the most exhaustive examination of the Negroes' position in American life, both North and South.

[33] According to C. Vann Woodward and others the present system of segregation and the relegation of the Negro to a secondary role did not fully evolve until the 1890's. See Woodward's *The Strange Career of Jim Crow* (New York: Oxford University Press, 1955).

[34] In one county it is said the Negro leaders working with the whites now pass on this information in a night meeting the day before the election to avoid giving the other candidate a chance to raise a hue and cry about Negro bloc vote.

In addition, they need go through no form of registration if the county is small. Those over 60 are exempt from the poll tax and in counties under 10,000 population need not even register as exempt. They therefore form an especially convenient pool of potential voters. The absentee ballot should be used only by those not able to get to the polls on election day due to illness, business, or some other matter that takes them away. Yet certification of these exceptions seems to be extremely loose so that the ballot can be easily abused. In these ways the local Negro population forms a pool of potential voters upon whom interested whites may draw more or less at need. There are significant exceptions to be noted later but the pattern is one of white dominance.

The outlook of many rural Negroes caught in this system of influence is aptly illustrated by the remarks of two witnesses made in the course of a recent trial in Deep East Texas.[35] The trial concerned a hotly disputed local election in which evenly balanced white factions had solicited Negro votes. One elderly Negro, to explain his vote said: "I said all of those people down there, I live with them, and they all I got, and I knowed I couldn't vote but one way; knowed if I voted for one, would have to go against the other one, and I have to go to all of them for everything, and I didn't want to fall out with none of them; I had rather went to the field to plow." And he repeated in answer to further question, "Rather went to the field to plow than voted at all." Later on, emphasizing his desire to live peacefully with all elements of the white community he said, "You see, I don't want to run, I can't run, have already tried it."

Another witness explained his reaction when white men came to solicit his vote: ". . . and I told this white fellow, I don't want you all to feel that I have got smart and trying to take over you all's business, because I have lived with you all all of my life, and my parents, they were good to them, and they have gone out, and I have come this far and everything has been very peaceful, and as I have said, I have always got along all right, and I want to go out that way, and I said I wouldn't care to sign any more or say any more about it. . . ." Like the other witness, he preferred not to vote at all, especially if it meant possible retaliation. And so far as he did use the ballot he used it to try to please the white man. Small wonder that one East Texas correspondent explains, "Bear in mind that the average adult Negro in East Texas has not the advantage of a normal education or environment." Given this state of mind among a majority of Texas Negroes outside the metropolitan areas it is not surprising that the white community can use the Negro vote for its purposes, with 'no force or intimidation felt.'

If the usual means of manipulation fail, activity which is either illegal or close to the line of legality opens further possibilities. The role of corruption in controlling the Negro vote is difficult to establish but rumors circulate constantly and some amazing reports come to light. Both Key and Strong cite

---

[35] The remarks that follow are from copies of the court record sent by a correspondent. The testimony was given on August 4, 1958, in the District Court in Harrison County.

the story of the San Antonio Negro leader of earlier years who, according to local tradition, had 3,000 poll taxes that he kept in his safe to be distributed on election day to 'trustworthy' voters. In the present day two Austin Negro leaders have described with scorn the system of control extant some years back by which city-hall politicians used the Negro leader of that day to deliver votes. A Houston Democratic leader, respected for his knowledge of the Negro vote, has said that much money was spent buying up small groups of Negro voters in the 1960 primary. A liberal lawyer in an East Texas county reports the existence of a sheriff-controlled machine by which the liquor interests support the sheriff who keeps the county wet; and the sheriff in turn controls the bloc of Negro voters that gives him and his policies consistent majorities. To avoid control and even the actual changing of the ballots in this same county it is said that Negroes vote the absentee ballot by as many as 600 votes in a total of about 5,000. Such stories can be multiplied and are undoubtedly subject to exaggeration and distortion. But these and other reports are sufficiently frequent and widespread to leave an impression that vote-buying and manipulation are by no means uncommon. Margaret Price's claim in reference to vote-buying that "By and large, this manipulation of Negroes has ended but it has not disappeared altogether" seems optimistic as applied to Texas.[36]

In addition to these means of influencing the Negro voter there is the possibility of reprisal. Racial violence occurs but little in Texas, and the main form of 'retaliation' seems to be heightened electoral activity by the white community or the tinkering with electoral districts. Of one rural community it is reported that rumors of sharply increased Negro voting before the election brought an enormous turnout among the white voters, even though the Negro vote remained about the same as usual. In another county it is said that control of the Negro bloc vote by a corrupt local official is causing rising resentment among the white community and is gradually increasing their vote. The city fathers may also change election districts to split the Negro vote, especially if the candidacy of a Negro shows signs of success. Austin's electoral system was changed after Dewitty's race in 1951, whether because of Dewitty's good showing or for other reasons. An effort to change Slaton's system was made following a Negro's victory in the race for city commissioner there in 1960, but the same coalition that put him in office also successfully beat back the proposal.

An outstanding example of one form retaliation may take in East Texas occurred not long ago in Marshall. A white candidate who suffered the opposition of the Negro bloc vote bought a half page ad in the local paper to deliver himself of his sentiments.[37] In large black-face type the ad proclaimed that "Bloc-voting is the most dangerous, un-democratic, vicious abuse of voting privileges this county faces. . . . It developed in the first primary among some of the colored citizens of our county. They were told in mass and small group meetings which candidate to vote for." For this man and many readers of the

[36] Margaret Price, op. cit., p. 50.
[37] Marshall News Messenger, June 1, 1960, p. A-3.

paper the Negroes' resort to mass meetings and bloc voting was a "vicious abuse" of "voting privileges." This type of reaction, even if it leads to nothing beyond, arouses the ever-present fears and doubts of the colored community and could in itself be effective in reducing the Negro vote. Even so, the city has a reputation throughout the state for its aggressive racial attitudes and the thinking evidenced by the newspaper ad may not be altogether typical of the region.

From this evidence as to the characteristics of white paternalism it can be inferred that the relationship is a complex one rooted in the caste system. The main element is the Negro's acceptance of his dependent and submissive role, supplemented by such corruption as exists. And the possibility of reprisal, though largely non-violent, remains as an ever-present background element helping to maintain the system. The picture is not complete, however, in implying that there are no significant variations or exceptions.

It was consistently reported by local observers that the Negroes do normally vote their own interests on the offices of sheriff and county commissioner.[38] The sheriff is all-important to the enforcement of justice in these predominantly rural counties. And the county commissioner has much to say about the county roads. For these two offices, therefore, the Negroes as a rule make their own decision and may revolt and refuse to accept "recommendations" they think contrary to their own interests. The swaggering sheriff with a reputation for rough treatment of Negroes is a declining or almost defunct breed today; and in this respect, particularly, the rural Negro has learned the value of the ballot and uses it effectively. For other offices and issues the interest of the Negro electorate as a whole is not great and many ballots will be only partially marked. For this reason, too, voting turnout may be low, especially in the general elections. Understandably enough, the request of a white friend to vote a certain way on offices with which there is no concern may be accepted with no "feeling of force or intimidation."

Lesser exceptions also exist. Not all Negroes are amenable, although their percentage does not seem to be great. The Texas president of the NAACP, N. Y. Nixon, has had some effect on his county. In another county a correspondent reports that members of the union working for a steel mill in the area are required by the union to register and vote. There are white liberals, few in number, but men of some standing, especially lawyers, who can discretely exert influence among Negroes. There is also some ferment among the younger Negroes, though reports available do not indicate they have gone much beyond talk. The professional Negroes, especially teachers, who seem natural leaders, have not been so to any marked degree as yet.[39]

[38] Hugh Price's Florida study found a similar concentration on these offices, plus a tendency to leave the rest of the ballot unmarked. (p. 73).

[39] Margaret Price reports teachers are becoming more civic conscious and active, but says they have usually been aloof and timid throughout the South. See op. cit., p. 39. One East Texas lawyer with a low opinion of Negro teachers claims many literally bought their academic job qualifications (degrees) and had no real training. He added that if he told local Negro teachers of his reform work in the Negro community they would "in-

In one county the older Negroes are said to be more militant than the younger ones because they reflect the spirit of the preachers, whereas the youth are influenced by the timidity of their teachers. The preachers, who are typically a powerful influence in Negro life, also provide leadership, though not much.[40] And where the Negroes are less dependent on the white community they may use the vote less amenably. A white liberal familiar with East Texas explained the markedly lower registration in the county containing Marshall, in contrast to adjoining counties, as due to the relative independence of Negroes in Marshall's economy.[41] So far as these Negroes could afford independence the whites did not want to encourage their vote. These examples illustrate the variations and counter-trends which must occur in varying degrees all over the East Texas region in spite of the normally dominant influence of the whites.

What is probably the best summary of the situation as it must prevail in many counties of this large East Texas area is provided in the words of an informed correspondent. He writes: "We have a substantial number who evidence no interest in voting and have never qualified to vote or voted.... The broad base of the Negro population here votes about 40% of its potential strength of which I hazard a guess that 50% is subject to white suggestion— perhaps as much as 80% in some races. In such as the county commissioner and sheriff's races, they usually have personal acquaintance and in substantial part make an independent selection, being subject only to the usual campaign soft talk and a little coercive pressure from the 'ins' who are in position to favor or frown..."

"It is noted that barely 10 to 20% of the local colored care to vote on any office outside the county, that is a statewide office, and many ballots are incomplete as to all offiices other than county offices. Voting in the general election is light and the number voting will probably not exceed 30% of the number in the primary election."

---

form" on him to their white superintendent. At the Dallas NAACP meeting in the spring of 1960 one speaker, formerly of Texas, said "our teachers are our greatest enemies to social rights." Others present "excitedly" agreed. See "Negroes Militant," *Texas Observer*, March 11, 1960, p. 3.

[40] Myrdal described the role of the Negro church some years ago as, "on the whole, passive in the field of intercaste power relations. It generally provides meeting halls and encourages church members to attend when other organizations want to influence the Negroes. But viewed as an instrument of collective action to improve the Negroes' position in American society, the church has been relatively inefficient and uninfluential." (p. 873). This statement would not apply as fully today as when written in the early '40's but Texas has yet to develop a Martin Luther King.

[41] An experienced Austin informant who traveled the East Texas area during 1960 cited two other towns as possible exceptions to the pattern of white control. In two of the three cases, the percentage of eligible Negroes registered was decidedly lower than in adjoining counties. Marshall was described as having a highly developed organization extending down to the block level within the city. Tyler in Smith County and Longview in Gregg County were the other suggested exceptions. Gregg County, with about 60% of eligible Negroes registered, does not seem to fit this pattern of exceptions. It is doubt- ful registration would be so high if the Negroes of this county were independent.

From this summary picture of white paternalism and its variations the question naturally arises as to its cause. Why do the Negroes accept this white influence on their vote? Examination shows the answer to be a compound of influences. Margaret Price's analysis of the present-day political consciousness of the Southern Negro has direct application to these East Texas voters. The factors cited are: the Negroes' heritage and the effect it has upon his present-day sense of civic responsibility; his low economic status and lack of education; his apathy and indifference; and his own fears rooted in a past that he cannot forget.[42] Added to these influences is the corruption, among some white and Negro leaders, that hampers the Negro from using the ballot in his own rather than someone else's interests. On top of all else is the possibility of threats or reprisals, even if the form they take in Texas be comparatively mild.

But the basic explanation of the Negroes' plight lies in the individual psychological pattern created on a large scale by the caste system. Because of his heritage of slavery and discrimination, the Negro finds himself held in low esteem. As a consequence he himself feels inferior and accepts, though not without psychological difficulty, an inferior status.[43] His life becomes a relatively hedonistic one of short term goals and activity and most importantly, one in which he is apt to be passive and submissive. Having accepted much of this low estimation of himself in the eyes of whites he is infused with grave doubts as to his own abilities and doesn't feel he can do much to improve his lot. This lack of self confidence makes it difficult for him to challenge the status quo and extremely sensitive to any sign of disapproval in the white man. There is a deep seated tendency to accept the caste system or to seek changes only with great caution. The manifestations of this 'psychology of oppression' vary as between the Northern Negro, the Southern city Negro and the Southern rural Negro, who is passive of all.[44] The Northern Negro has sufficiently overcome this psychology of low self-esteem to become what Lane calls a "politically embattled solidary ethnic group."[45] That the city Negro in Texas has developed some of this racial or ethnic solidarity politically is evidenced in the analysis of precinct returns. In spite of his confusion and doubts he can muster a fairly effective bloc vote. But the Texas rural Negro cannot and is therefore still, in the main, effectively dominated by the caste system.

In light of these attitudes it is no wonder that observers of the Southern Negro voter report apathy and exaggerated fears to be among the main barriers

---

[42] Margaret Price, op, cit., pp. 30–35.

[43] Abram Kardiner and Lionel Ovesey, The Mark of Oppression (New York: W. W. Norton Co., 1951), Chs. 12, 13. See also Robert E. Lane, Political Life (Glencoe, Illinois: The Free Press, 1959), pp. 251–3.

[44] Bertram P. Karon, The Negro Personality (New York: Spring Publishing Co., 1958), pp. 158–9 and pp. 169–73. Karon's study was designed to verify the findings of Kardiner and Ovesey in a much larger sample than the latter's psychoanalytic techniques permitted.

[45] Robert E. Lane, op. cit., p. 253.

to increased Negro voting. There are many places in the South where he could do more than he does. Margaret Price reports on the South that "consultants throughout the region found indifference one of the strongest barriers to increased Negro voting." Supplementing the apathy is the fear. And the fear may serve as a not wholly unreasonable excuse for the apathy. A survey consultant in Florida "believes that one of the big obstacles to the vote is the psychological difficulty of convincing them they need not be afraid." He feels they would experience little more than token resistance in sixty-three of the sixty-seven counties of the state.[46] Or as Hugh Price explained it, "More often white reactions are correctly anticipated or given *excessive* allowance.[47] Understandably, then, when the national head of the NAACP addressed the Texas regional convention in Dallas in 1960 he pointedly remarked that Texas Negroes were not doing all they might.[48] The Negro in Texas and elsewhere now has more potential political power in his hands than he can effectively use, especially the rural Negro.

Of course the Negro was not responsible for the caste system and its psychological effects to begin with. The responsibility rests with the white members of the community who originally fostered and in many areas still maintain the system. Now the trouble is that Negroes whose legal condition has improved are still held back by a discriminatory social system and a heritage that has inculcated inferiority. The political result is a serious discrepancy between legal voting rights available to them and their actual capacity to make use of them. The situation calls to mind the remark of Key in *Southern Politics* comparing the trials of political life in the South with those of under-developed countries of the world.[49]

From this examination of the electoral behavior of the Texas Negro, both urban and rural, it should be possible to draw some conclusions as to their characteristics as voters and their impact upon the looked-for evolution of a competitive state party system. The city Negro has little trouble registering and seems already to have developed a fairly consistent core of registrants who can be counted on year after year. Probably the maintenance of this group depends much upon effective political work in arousing these prospective registrants regularly; but the example of Austin shows the city Negro is able to muster such a group with more consistency than the white community at large. These figures suggest in turn that the cities may already have much of their potential Negro electorate activated. And considering the relatively low income and education medians of this group it would be plausible to suppose that Negro registration will taper off below the white average of about 49%. Exceptional efforts and dramatic events may galvanize them to heightened activity and there is a normal prospect for a gradual but steady

[46] Margaret Price, *op. cit.*, p. 33.
[47] Hugh Price, *op. cit.*, p. 47. (Emphasis added.)
[48] "Negroes Militant," *Texas Observer*, March 11, 1960, p. 2.
[49] V. O. Key, *op. cit.*, "The suffrage problems of the South can claim a closer kinship with those of India, South Africa, or of the Duch East Indies than with those of say, Minnesota" (p. 661).

increase. But it does not seem likely there will be any big jump in city Negro registrants in near future.

The rural Negro is another matter. Here registration may take a mixed turn. Now he is in good part tied so as to function as an adjunct of the white vote and therefore receive encouragement. As he develops some independence this encouragment would normally fall off. There are no indications in the surveys of Texas that white resistance would become so great as to prevent Negroes from registering altogether. But the loss of white encouragement would mean a reduction in the percent of eligibles on the voting rolls, a trend to which the town of Marshall in Harrison County bears witness. Paradoxically, then, the freeing of the rural Negro may well mean some drop in Negro registration in the state's rural counties. City registration may make up the difference, especially if the freeing of the rural Negro takes place gradually. In trying to balance these opposing trends amidst the many imponderables present, one can only conclude that Negro registration overall is not likely to rise sharply in future and may even approach a point at which it hardly increases at all from year to year for a time. One must also keep in the mind the tendency for Negro population to leave the country for the city and then out of state. This movement detracts from the increase one might expect due to population increase and therefore acts as a further damper on prospects for an increase in Negro registration.

In considering actual voting behavior one must also distinguish the city Negro from those of the countryside. To generalize from the Austin sample, it appears that only about half the total of qualified voters turns out and in some elections much less. This showing is not impressive and the city political organizations have here an opportunity and a task. In one sense the task may be an endless one because some part of the city voters consists of rural voters who have not become accustomed to voting. As these rural voters continue moving in and as the city continues to lose some of its Negro population migrating out of state, the Negro organizations face a big job. They must continually train new voters and count on losing some of those who have become accustomed to voting. If this shifting population be the typical city pattern in Texas the amount of improvement that can be brought about is limited. One would normally expect, here too, some steady improvement in turnout but not any sharp surges.

In another aspect of voting behavior, that of consistency of turnout, the city Negro does surprisingly well. To judge from the San Antonio comparison, the Negroes in some cases turn out with greater consistency from election to election than the upper middle income Anglo population. In other cases their turnout does drop off considerably, especially in run-offs and general elections involving a contest between a Republican and Democrat for state office. Still, their real and in some cases remarkable achievements should not be overlooked, especially against the backdrop of a shifting population characterized by low levels of income and education.

As to voting orientation the city Negroes are—if the sample from four cities can be generalized—already a "politically embattled solidary ethnic group." The term may be cumbersome but it does convey the notion of their common political consciousness expressed in a liberal and racially sensitive bloc vote. The city Negro will ordinarily vote for the liberal candidate by large majorities and emphatically so if he takes a decisive 'pro' civil rights position. They will also give strong support to the candidates of other minority groups as well as their own. Yet they do not vote blindly for liberals, Negroes, or ethnics; nor do they follow the leader's endorsement regardless of the candidates' known positions. The leader must lead where his people want to follow. A streak of loyalty to the Republican Party remains but is no longer of really significant strength by itself. In the degree of his Republicanism as well as his rate of political participation the Texas city Negro differs from those of Northern cities. Yet these differences are matters of degree and otherwise he bears close comparison with the Northern liberal and racially conscious bloc voter. Considering his Southern political environment and the recency with which he began voting in large numbers, the Texas city Negro has accomplished a good deal.

Distinct from the city Negro is the rural Negro in the East Texas region. In 1958 these formed about half or slightly more of total Negro registration. Conclusions as to their political behavior must be treated with caution because of the difficulty of gathering and interpreting the evidence. Yet the evidence that is available strongly implies that here there is, indeed, an unused pool of voters whose altered voting habits could seriously affect the future. They are in good part non-voters or voters at the white man's behest. They have gained beyond their situation of 15 years or so ago in effectively influencing the choice of sheriff and county commissioner. There have gained beyond their situation of 15 years or so ago in effectively influencing the choice of sheriff and county commissioner. There are a few effective organizations and some individuals who do yeoman's work. But most of them are apathetic and are heavily subject to the white man's influence and, to some extent, corruption and the fear of reprisal.

What are the prospects for these voters and Texas politics? It is common enough to think of the South as changing and as becoming, especially in such states as Florida and Texas, much like the North in its basic economic and social life. Unquestionably this is happening in the cities but the countryside may be left behind.[50] The heritage of the past hangs heavily on these rural

---

[50] In the evolution of the Southern racial problem the previously cited *Special Report* of the Southern Regional Council on school desegregation (as of August, 1959) is of note. The Report's conclusion (p. 43 ff.) argues that an isolation of the 'hard core,' the rural Black Belt extending across the South is taking place. The large cities of the South are integrating, albeit with stress and strain, and the authors point to the likelihood of integration in Texas cities, New Orleans, and Atlanta. Since this prediction was written integration has come or soon will come in the areas cited. The interesting implication is that the rural Black Belt is left behind in continuing total resistance to integration. The 'hard core' may be reduced in influence but it is difficult to predict when and how rapidly it will itself change, as presumably it must.

Negroes and their submissiveness and passivity may not easily be changed. Their own sense of inferiority is deeply ingrained. It is in these rural areas that education and income levels are lowest and the population least mobile. These, too, are the communities most insular in outlook and resistant to change. To these factors must be added the loss of much of the young population as it moves to the city and from there out of state. Here the Negroes' fears of reprisal, even if exaggerated, are not altogether false. Given these characteristics, prospects for change do not look bright. One is reminded again of Key's comparison between Southern political problems and those of under-developed nations of the world.

There is another side of the picture. Some changes have already occurred and will gradually continue. There may be break-throughs in which Negroes win notable advances. Above all, any electoral participation, even if manipulated or influenced, is better than none and forms a base upon which to build. In this limited participation they have come quite a ways in a decade and a half. On balance it would seem that there will be gradual change and some improvement but that about half the states' Negro vote will be much reduced in effectiveness, as compared with the Northern Negro voter, for some years. These rural East Texas Negroes will likely be a 'politically embattled solidary ethnic group' some day, but it is hard to see the mass of them in this role in the next few years.

Thomas F. Pettigrew

ACTUAL GAINS AND PSYCHOLOGICAL
LOSSES: THE NEGRO AMERICAN PROTEST

The NAACP's legal attack on segregation and disfranchisement proved to be of limited value. Victories before the bar of the Supreme Court were one thing; actual changes were another. At the very time that legalism was thus showing itself to be of limited usefulness other developments were leading to a transformation of Negro attitudes. There was the evident drift of northern white public opinion, beginning in the New Deal years, toward a more racially egalitarian viewpoint—a trend hastened by the dynamics of international power politics and Russia's exploitation of America's racism. The rise of the new African nations gave American Negroes a new self-image. And Martin Luther King and others were demonstrating that nonviolent direct action, a technique identified with the Congress of Racial Equality since its founding in 1942, could succeed in parts of the South. All these produced what has appropriately been described as a "revolution in expectations." Negroes no longer felt they had to bear the humiliations of second-class citizenship, and consequently these humiliations—somewhat fewer though they now were—appeared to be more intolerable than ever. This increasing impatience and dissatisfaction accounted for the rising tempo of nonviolent direct action in the late 1950's culminating in the student sit-ins of 1960 and the inauguration of what is popularly known as the "Negro Revolt."

The successes of nonviolent direct action during the early 1960's led to a further rise in expectations, which far outran the very significant achievements which the civil rights movement had made. In an important essay, written in 1963, Thomas Pettigrew has described the impact of the discrepancy between the rapid escalation of expectations instilled by the Negro revolt and its actual accomplishments. At the time, Pettigrew was unable to foresee the subsequent

Thomas F. Pettigrew, "Actual Gains and Psychological Losses: The Negro American Protest," *Journal of Negro Education*, XXXII (Fall, 1963), pp. 493–506. Reprinted with the permission of the author and publisher.

disillusionment with nonviolent direct-action tactics. Nevertheless, his analysis of the dynamics behind the shift in Negro attitudes is valid not only for 1959 and 1963, but for today as well.

Pettigrew's article appeared in the Journal of Negro Education Yearbook *for 1963, entitled,* The Relative Progress of the American Negro Since 1950. *It is a synthesis based upon the research of other scholars whose contributions appear as chapters in the yearbook. In the course of his discussion Pettigrew refers frequently to the conclusions of these scholars. Accordingly, for the reader's convenience, we have included at the end of Pettigrew's article a list of the yearbook chapters to which he refers, arranged alphabetically by author.*

INTRODUCTION

THE late Samuel Stouffer, one of America's greatest sociologists, always became incensed when a layman blithely reacted to a behavioral science finding with "Who didn't know that?" He countered with a simple true-false test of ten items, the "obvious, common sense" answers to which had all been demonstrated incorrect by rigorous social research. Most of those who take Stouffer's test miss every item. The moral is clear: many behavioral science findings appear obvious only after the fact.

Stouffer's illustration involved the relative morale of the Air Corps and the Military Police in World War II. Promotions were rapid and widespread in the Air Corps, but slow and piecemeal in the Military Police. Conventional wisdom predicts that the Air Corpsmen should have been more optimistic about their chances for promotion, for the "obvious" reason that they were in *absolute* terms moving ahead faster in their careers. But, as a matter of empirical fact, Stouffer found in his famous studies of *The American Soldier* that the Air Corpsmen were considerably more frustrated over promotions than the Military Police.[1] What was not so obvious was that the fliers' wide-open system of promotions led them to assume exceedingly high aspirations; most of them expected such swift elevation that even the realistically generous promotions of their service left them *relatively* dissatisfied. By contrast, morale was reasonably high among the Military Police. They did not expect rapid promotions and learned to be content with what few advances they did achieve. It was not the absolute level of attainment that made for poor morale so much

[1] S. A. Stouffer, E. A. Suchman, L. C. DeVinney, Shirley A. Star, and R. M. Williams, Jr., *The American Soldier.* Vol. 1, *Adjustment During Army Life.* Princeton, N.J.: Princeton University Press, 1949; and R. K. Merton and Alice S. Kitt, "Contributions to the theory of reference group behavior." In R. K. Merton and P. F. Lazarsfeld (Editors), *Continuities in Social Research: Studies in the Scope and Method of "The American Soldier."* Glencoe, Ill.: Free Press, 1950.

as *relative deprivation*—the discrepancy between what one expects and what one receives.

Likewise, conventional wisdom dictates that Negro Americans should have higher morale today than at any previous point in America's history. After all, have Negro gains not been faster in recent decades than any period since emancipation? Why, then, are many Negroes so unusually restive, so openly angry, so impatient for further gains? Relative, not absolute, deprivation once again provides a social psychological explanation. The great majority of Negroes in past years dared not cherish high aspirations for themselves. While never satisfied with their lot, they, like the Military Police, expected very little of life and had to be content with what crumbs they did receive. But Negro Americans in recent years hunger for much more than crumbs. Like the Air Corpsmen, they have tasted significant progress and can fully appreciate what further progress could mean. Indeed, Negro aspirations have risen far more swiftly than Negro advances. Thus, while better off in absolute terms than ever before, Negroes today are relatively more deprived than they were prior to the last 25 years of racial change.

This important social psychological principle underlies the Negro American protest of 1963. The present paper analyzes the preceding papers in terms of relative deprivation. It briefly summarizes the actual gains of recent years, lists the simultaneous psychological losses of these same years, and, finally, offers five predictions concerning the future of the Negro protest.

ACTUAL GAINS

The complexity of Negro progress, as Rayford Logan emphasizes in his chapter, makes it impossible to gauge such progress precisely. Nevertheless, virtually all observers agree that the past quarter-century has witnessed the most rapid actual gains in Negro American history.[2] Consider this sampling of recent advances culled from the papers of this Yearbook:

The Negro's transition from rural Southerner to urbanite, North and South, continues apace (Preston Valien's chapter). Today's Negro Americans are more urban than white Americans, and are particularly concentrated in the largest of cities. By 1960, half of all Negroes lived in metropolitan areas of at least a half-million people. Although it raises new problems, this massive movement leads directly to a more sophisticated people capable of effective protest. It also leads to improvements in standards of living. Health offers one example (Marcus Goldstein's chapter). In part a consequence of urbanization, Negro mortality rates have notably declined. In relation to the nation as a whole, age-adjusted nonwhite total mortality rates improved from 1950 to 1960 virtually as much as they had in the previous half century.

Advances have also been registered in employment. Middle and high

[2] This same conclusion is implied in the leadership opinion data provided in Thompson's chapter.

level federal employment has shown substantial growth within the last few years (John Hope II and Edward Shelton's chapter); employment opportunities for trained Negro youth have expanded in the professional, technical, and clerical categories, as well as the more traditional service field (William Amos and Jane Perry's chapter); and nonwhite males have made gains somewhat faster than white males in both the operative and professional job classifications (Walter Daniel's chapter). Some aspects of Negro-controlled business have also developed (Harding Young's chapter). The assets of Negro savings and loan associations, for instance, have multiplied over 32 times since 1947, a rate roughly three times that of all savings and loan associations combined.[3]

These trends in turn generate economic and housing progress. From 1950 to 1960, median Negro family income climbed 73 per cent (Young's chapter); the Negro middle class swelled; and the percentage of nonwhites residing in adequate, standard housing doubled (Marian Yankauer and Milo Sunderhauf's chapter). In addition, significantly fewer Negro households in 1960 included lodgers and three family generations than in 1950 (G. Franklin Edward's chapter).

Important changes have also occurred in political power. Over a million more Negroes voted in 1962 than in 1950; and the potency of this increased access to the ballot was demonstrated in elections for offices ranging from state legislator to the presidency (Harold Gosnell and Robert Martin's chapter). Three Southern states—North Carolina, South Carolina, and Texas —remained in the Democratic Party column in 1960 largely as a result of the Negro vote for John Kennedy. And in 1962 competent Negroes won a variety of posts, from State Senator in Georgia to high state posts in New England.

Educational progress has also been evident. The percentage increments of Negro youth of all ages attending school were dramatic between 1940 and 1960; indices of educational quality, such as expenditures per pupil, number of pupils per teacher, and the academic preparation of teachers, have all risen in Southern high schools for Negroes; and the median education of Negroes in the 25-to-29 age group jumped from seven years in 1940 to 11 years in 1959 (Eunice Newton and Earle West's chapter). Furthermore, the percentage of Negroes who have at least attended college more than doubled from 1940 to 1960 (Hurley Doddy's chapter).

These gains of the 1950s and early 1960s, combined with the gains of the 1940s, have had a profound psychological effect upon Negro Americans. Despair and hopelessness have declined, new and proud aspirations have taken hold, and a determined optimism about the future has developed. These trends became noteworthy by the early 1950s. A representative 1954 national public opinion poll asked: "On the whole, do you think life will be better for you or worse, in the next few years than it is now?"[4] Of those with an

[3] Savings and loan associations in general have expanded 11 times since 1945. *New York Times,* August 26, 1963, p. 37.

[4] S. A. Stouffer, *Communism, Conformity, and Civil Liberties.* New York: Doubleday, 1955.

opinion, 64 per cent of the Negro respondents felt life would soon be better. This figure compares with only 53 per cent of a white control sample equivalent to the Negro sample in region of residence, sex, age, education, and occupation.

The public school desegregation ruling of the Supreme Court, of course, made 1954 a vintage year for rising Negro aspirations. But recent poll data suggest that, if anything, this high level of optimism has risen further. The 1963 *Newsweek* opinion survey of Negro Americans uncovered revealing results: 73 per cent feels that the racial attitudes of whites will improve during the next five years; 63 per cent thinks whites will accept racial change without violence; 85 per cent desires to own a private home; and 30 per cent believes it is qualified for elevation now to professional or other white-collar employment.[5]

This same poll finds that much of this renewed hope for the future centers upon education. Another one in five families interviewed had a child who had dropped out of school before completing high school, 97 per cent wants its children to finish high school. Negroes have traditionally placed great faith in education as a means of achieving full acceptance in American society, and several additional studies point to the intensity of this faith at the present time. One investigation conducted in the middle 1950s in the Northeast noted that a sample of Negro mothers strongly valued achievement in terms of an activistic, individualistic, and future orientation that usually accompanies high educational aspiration.[6] Indeed, 83 per cent of these mothers intended for their sons to go to college.

Studies of the children themselves further confirm this emphasis upon education as a means for upward social mobility. One research project of the early 1950s tested and interviewed Negro and white children of matched intelligence from a desegregated elementary school.[7] The Negro youngsters expressed higher levels of aspiration and more ambitious hopes for the future. And a recent investigation of Negro high school students throughout the South reveals that they, too, harbor a great desire for further education.[8]

Some observers interpret such heightened educational aspirations as "unrealistic" and indicative that Negroes learn early to separate their hopes from the stark reality that generally confronts them. But another study done in the late 1950s of high school seniors in Kentucky discovered that most of the Negro children who had reached this level had surprisingly well conceived plans for the future.[9] Negro seniors in this sample were not only more optimistic than the white seniors, but they shrewdly appraised their position

[5] *Newsweek*, July 29, 1963, pp. 15–34.

[6] B. C. Rosen, "Race, ethnicity, and the achievement syndrome," *American Sociological Review*, 24:47–60, 1959.

[7] G. F. Boyd, "The levels of aspiration of white and Negro children in a non-segregated elementary school," *Journal of Social Psychology*, 36:191–196, 1952.

[8] M. Sherif and Carolyn Sherif, *Reference Groups: Conformity and Deviance of Adolescence*. New York: Harper and Row, in press.

[9] A. J. Lott and Bernice E. Lott, *Negro and White Youth: A Psychological Study in a Border-State Community*. New York: Holt, Rinehart and Winston, 1963.

in American society, their better chances for white-collar jobs in the North, and their need to end discriminatory barriers.

PSYCHOLOGICAL LOSSES

These rising expectations are increasingly framed in terms of the standards of the wider society, as Whitney Young emphasizes (Daniel Thompson's chapter). Negro protest today is shifting from an exclusive emphasis upon desegregation and equal opportunity to a broader demand for a "fair share" and advantages comparable to those of whites. Sensing this significant shift, the Yearbook explicitly set out to assess the 1963 status of Negro Americans in direct comparison with other Americans. And this assessment reveals that in general the Negro's situation in 1963 represents sharp improvement relative to present white conditions. Consider once again each of the realms in which changes have been registered.

Despite the large-scale migration since 1915, substantial segments of the Negro population remain in the most hostile and deprived pockets of the nation (Valien's chapter). Mere mention of county names—such as Greene and Monroe in Alabama, Lee and Terrell in Georgia, Carroll and Tate in Mississippi, McCormick and Williamsburg in South Carolina, Fayette and Haywood in Tennessee, and Prince Edward in Virginia—serves to remind us that several millions of Negroes still reside in rural areas of the South which are resisting racial change by almost every means possible. The high promise of change is barely beginning in these Black Belt counties.

There is also another aspect to the recent improvements in Negro American health. Life expectancy at birth still lags behind that of white Americans, though the discrepancy has closed to six to eight years.[10] And relative to white rates, nonwhite mortality rates for such diseases as diabetes mellitus and cirrhosis of the liver actually increased between 1950 and 1960, though much of this increase may well reflect better reporting and diagnosis rather than actual retrogression (Goldstein's chapter). These remaining disparities in health lead to phenomena such as proportionately greater numbers of young and middle-aged widows in the Negro community; thus, the percentage of widows among nonwhite women 54 years old or less is roughly twice that of white women.[11]

Employment presents a similar picture. Even in government service, Negroes are still concentrated in the lower blue-collar brackets and sparce in the higher white-collar brackets (Hope and Shelton's chapter); in most unionized industries, basic racial employment patterns remained unchanged during the 1950s (Ray Marshall's chapter); Negro youth have about twice

[10] Metropolitan Life Insurance Company, "Progress in longevity since 1850," *Statistical Bulletin*, 44:1–3, July 1963.
[11] Metropolitan Life Insurance Company, "The American widow," *Statistical Bulletin*, 43:1–4, November 1962.

the unemployment rate of white youth (Amos and Perry's chapter); and Negro adults in general are still vastly underemployed, downgraded, and underpaid relative to comparably educated segments of the white community (Daniel's chapter). Norval Glenn has projected the slow occupational trends of the 1950s into the future.[12] He calculates that at the 1950 to 1960 rate of change nonwhites in the United States would not attain their proportional representation among clerical workers until 1992, among skilled workers until 2005, among professionals until 2017, among sales workers until 2114, and among business managers and proprietors until 2730! Obviously, such a snail's pace is ridiculously slow to satisfy a people whose expectations for the immediate future are among the most optimistic in the nation; hence, the significant slogan of the March on Washington—*"jobs and freedom now."*

The projected eight centuries necessary to close the racial gap among business managers and proprietors illustrates once more the exclusion of Negroes from executive roles in the general society and the minuscule nature of Negro business. Even in the savings and loan field, a strong Negro business area, the assets of Negro-controlled institutions constitute only approximately three-tenths of one per cent of total assets; [13] and in the insurance field, the strongest Negro business area, the assets of all Negro-controlled companies constitute a fraction of any one of the very largest companies (Young's chapter). Though minor allowance must be made for publishing and insurance companies and financial institutions, the dour generalization of Franklin Frazier continues to hold true: "... 'Negro business,' which has no significance in the American economy, ... [is] a social myth ..." [14]

Changes in Negro income relative to white income provide the most disappointing trend of the past decade (Thompson's chapter). Daniel shows the failure of the median wage of Negro males to climb relative to the white figure; median family income data illustrate the same trend. The ratio of nonwhite to white median family income in 1959 (51.7%) was virtually the same as in 1949 (51.1%).[15] Korean War prosperity elevated the ratio to its highest point (56.8%) in 1952, but it has since declined almost steadily. This means that, although the absolute level of Negro family income rose throughout the 1950s, white family income rose proportionately faster.

The sharp racial discrepancy in family income persists in spite of a larger average number of Negro family members working and larger families to support. Differential tax payments balance this racial inequity slightly; but Negroes typically obtain less for their consumer dollar. This is especially true in housing. While some housing gains occurred in the 1950s, the quality of Negro housing remains vastly inferior relative to that of white (Yankauer and Sunderhauf's

[12] N. D. Glenn, "Some changes in the relative status of American nonwhites, 1940 to 1960," *Phylon*, 24:109–122, 1963.

[13] Young estimates the total assets of Negro savings and loan associations to be about three hundred million, while total assets of all associations passed the one hundred billion mark during 1963. *New York Times, op. cit.*

[14] E. Franklin Frazier, *Black Bourgeoisie.* (2d ed.) New York: Collier, 1962, p. 193.

[15] Glenn, *op. cit.*

chapter). For example, in Chicago in 1960, Negroes paid as much for housing as whites, despite their lower incomes. Median rents for both groups were $88, yet Negroes received much poorer accommodations. The Taeubers attribute this fact to the existence of essentially two separate housing markets; and they point out that residential segregation that creates these dual markets "has increased steadily over past decades until it has reached universally high levels in cities throughout the United States, despite significant advances in the socio-economic status of Negroes." [16]

Even the accelerated political advances of Negro Americans leave much undone. Negroes still vote as a group far less often than whites. Particularly in those Southern areas where racial change is most desperately needed, Negroes are least often found on the electoral rolls. Indeed, there is a massive denial of the franchise in most of Alabama and Mississippi and large parts of Louisiana, Georgia, and South Carolina (Gosnell and Martin's chapter). The voting title of the 1963 Civil Rights Act provides limited help, but does not offer a definitive solution.

Finally, Negro education has yet to approach that generally available to whites. To quote Newton, it remains in general "less available, less accessible, and especially less adequate." Negro college attendance is only about half that of whites (Doddy's chapter).[17] These gaps are especially serious. Fourteen generations of Negro talent have already been wasted by American society; our technological society cannot afford to waste yet another. And, as we have seen, Negro hopes for the future are so centered upon education that training of poor quality at this stage could well undercut the determined thrust toward group uplift.

Thus, in each interrelated realm—health, employment, business, income, housing, voting, and education—the absolute gains of the 1950s pale when contrasted with current white standards. Numerous spokesmen have boasted of the present status of the Negro in glowing international comparisons. Negroes in the United States today, goes one boast, have a consumer buying power comparable to that of similarly-populated Canada. And a larger percentage of Negroes, goes another, attends college than the residents of the British Isles. But such glittering statements must not blind us to the fact of greatest psychological importance. Negro-American standards have their psychological meaning relative to the standards of other Americans, not Canadians or the British. The Negro American judges his living standards, his opportunities, indeed, even judges himself, in the only cultural terms he knows—those of the United States and its "people of plenty." Dr. Martin Luther King, Jr. bluntly made the point in his eloquent March-on-Washington address: "The Negro lives on

[16] K. E. and Alma F. Taeuber, "Is the Negro an immigrant group?" *Integrated Education*, 1:25–28, June 1963.

[17] Doddy's college data for the West are highly misleading, for the nonwhite category in the West includes a significant proportion of Chinese-Americans and Japanese-Americans, the latter in particular a group with a far higher college percentage than Negroes.

a lonely island of poverty in the midst of a vast ocean of material prosperity and finds himself an exile in his own land."

The resulting relative deprivation is the fundamental basis of mass Negro American dissatisfaction today. But it is not the only factor. Special frustrations are created by the appearance of proud new African nations upon the world scene. Emerging Africa has a dual psychological effect upon Negro Americans. On the one hand, it generates racial pride and an elevated self-esteem—especially for the darkest members of the group.[18] On the other hand, it lends a desperate urgency to protest at home. Heretofore, Negro Americans have been the most sophisticated and prestigeful black group in the Western world—regardless of their lowly position by American standards. But now many Africans can claim complete freedom, while Negroes still seek theirs. In this sense, then, independent African nations add to the Negro's keen sense of relative deprivation.

A similar phenomenon occurs regionally within the United States. Negro Northerners have typically prided themselves on being the products of the big-city North, on being superior to their Southern "country cousins." Yet Negro Southerners today lead the struggle for racial justice; many of them have willingly faced fire hoses, dogs, jail, and police brutality in order to demand and assert their rights; and one of them, Dr. King, has become the flesh-and-blood symbol of the protest movement throughout the country. A few Negro leaders in the South even hint wryly that the day may come when Negro Northerners will have to migrate southward to obtain true equality. And when Negroes in the North contrast their slow progress against de facto segregation in housing, schools, and employment with the dramatic desegregation of public facilities in many parts of the South, they must wonder if such wry hints do not possess some basis in truth.

Thus, the present-day Negro's feeling of being left behind springs from three sources. It derives partly from relating his situation to emerging Africa. For the Negro Northerner, it also stems from comparing his gains with those of his on-rushing Southern relatives. But its primary source is from contrasting his still meager lot with the abundance of other Americans.

"ALL, HERE, NOW!"

Intense relative deprivation in an age of rising expectations is the stuff out of which revolutions are made. But this revolution of 1963, with its ringing demand for "all, here, now," is a revolution in a sense special to the Negro's unique role in American society. An understanding of this special form of revo-

---

[18] A representative poll in Boston found that darker-skinned Negroes, compared with other Negroes, more often agreed that "most Negro Americans think more of themselves since many Africans became free" and disagreed that "Africans aren't doing anything to help Negro Americans in their struggle for civil rights." T. F. Pettigrew, *The Psychology of the Negro American*. Princeton, N.J.: Van Nostrand, in press.

lution is requisite to any meaningful projection of the Negro American's status into the future.

This revolution does resemble more violent revolutions in some ways. As August Meier asserts in his illuminating chapter, the present movement has shifted "in emphasis from legalism to direct action," from narrow objectives to a full-scale attack, from pockets of protest to a genuine mass movement cutting across divisions within the Negro community. And like other mass movements, it has achieved a heightened militancy and urgency, a new sense that "even yesterday was too late." It also exhibits some of the irrationality common to all revolutions.

Nevertheless, this is a revolution with a basic difference. It aims to modify, not to overturn, the society it confronts; it seeks to amend, not to ravage. Negro Americans are so firmly rooted in and shaped by their land that their revolution attempts merely to guarantee full participation in the society as it otherwise exists. In short, they do not wish to deprecate or destroy that which they wish to join. It is, then, a peculiarly conservative revolution, a fact that in many ways gives it a special force.

Such a conservative revolution acts out the culture's most cherished values; it dramatizes the "American dilemma" between high ideals and lowly practices. It does not offer new values, but demands that old values be realized. To suppress such a revolution would be to surrender the very foundations of the United States. There is in the long run, then, but one viable alternative— to move with history and achieve a racially integrated society in which skin color loses all relevance. This alternative is already recognized in the support given the protest by the federal government—a strange ally for true revolutionaries. Even if federal authorities have sometimes been too late with too little help, as in Albany, Georgia, the fact remains that the current Negro protest takes place within a generally permissive national atmosphere.

Moreover, this special type of revolution is supported to a considerable degree by white American opinion. There is a hard core of whites who marches in demonstrations, goes to jail, even faces death with Negroes. Though a small minority, it serves the vital function of keeping the confrontation from becoming a purely black versus white conflict. To be sure, there is also a hard core of white deadenders, those who resist even token desegregation by burning crosses, exploding bombs, and shooting others in the back. But the majority of white Americans ranges somewhere in between, and, while their attitudes often do not measure up to Negro expectations, they nevertheless contribute to the permissive atmosphere in a number of key ways.

To begin with, there is general approval outside of the South of the Supreme Court's 1954 school desegregation ruling. Gallup polls show that 62 per cent of the nation, Negro and white, approves of the decision, with the proportion among non-Southerners reaching almost three out of four.[19] School

[19] Hazel G. Erskine, "The polls: Race relations," *Public Opinion Quarterly,* 26: 137–148, 1962. Another polling agency agrees closely with the 75 per cent non-Southern estimate. S. Alsop and O. Quayle "What Northerners really think of Negroes," *Saturday Evening Post,* 236:17–21, September 7, 1963.

desegregation itself wins general approval outside of the South, providing Negro children are not in the majority. In the South, although racial change is still widely opposed by white Southerners, such change is increasingly seen as inevitable. Gallup polls have repeatedly asked Southerners of both races if they thought "the day will ever come when white and Negro people will be going to the same schools, eating in the same restaurants, and generally sharing the same public accommodations." [20] In 1957, only 45 per cent of the South answered "yes"; by 1958, 53 per cent did so; by 1961, 76 per cent; and by 1963, 83 per cent. In addition, among the 83 per cent who saw desegregation as inevitable in 1963, half believed it would come about completely within five years and another fourth believed it would occur within ten years. Thus, the majority of white Southerners clearly expects racial progress even while opposing it, and this widespread feeling of inevitability contributes importantly to the present milieu in which the Negro protest is operating.

The ground was prepared for these white opinions before the current revolution. During and since World War II, the stereotype of the Negro has undergone drastic modification. Witness the erosion of the racist contention that Negroes are innately stupid. The National Opinion Research Center asked Americans in a series of representative polls: "In general, do you think Negroes are as intelligent as white people—that is, can they learn just as well if they are given the same education and training?" In 1942, only 42 per cent of white Americans believed the two groups to be equally intelligent; by 1944, the figure was 44 per cent; by 1946, 53 per cent; by 1956, 78 per cent.[21] This fundamental alteration of the image of the Negro acts to sharpen further white guilt over the "American dilemma."

There remain, however, serious limitations to white understanding of the Negro American. The majority of white Americans as yet neither identifies with Negro Americans nor senses the urgency of the present revolution. The majority of whites believes that Negroes are being treated fairly in the United States and that gradualism should be the rule in effecting desegregation.[22] These beliefs assuage guilty consciences; thus, it is not surprising that Negro demonstrations which boldly challenge these beliefs are resented. In 1961, for example, national samples questioned by Gallup pollsters indicated that 64 per cent disapproved of the freedom rides and 57 per cent believed they would "hurt the Negro's chance of being integrated in the South." [23] Similarly, 65 per cent of white Northerners and 73 per cent of white Southerners interviewed in 1963 think that "mass demonstrations by Negroes are likely to hurt the Negro's cause for racial equality." [24] Without denying the basic justice of the protest, many whites handle their guilt by complaining that Negroes are "pushing too hard too fast." [25] Yet some of these same people realize upon

---

[20] Erskine, op. cit.; and American Institute of Public Opinion release, July 19, 1963.
[21] Erskine, op. cit.; also see: Alsop and Quayle, op. cit.
[22] Erskine, op. cit.; and Alsop and Quayle, op. cit.
[23] Erskine, op. cit.
[24] American Institute of Public Opinion release, July 18, 1963.
[25] Alsop and Quayle, op. cit.

reflection that Negroes do in fact make maximum progress only when they confront the nation directly with their demands.

Within this social psychological context—severe relative deprivation among Negroes, an urgent, but basically conservative, protest revolution, a supportive federal government, and a guilty, if gradualistic, climate of dominant white opinion—five predictions for the future can be ventured. *First, Negro protest will continue to grow both in intensity and depth.* As demonstrations persist, advances will occur ever more rapidly. These advances serve to reward the protest and stimulate its continuance. "The leaders sitting down together would, of course, be the best way," confides one Negro lady, "but we found it didn't work and sit-ins did." [26] Advances also serve to highlight further racial changes that are needed. These effects are part of a widely-studied psychological phenomenon known technically as "goal gradient" and popularly as "running for home." [27] As subjects in an experiment approach their final goal, they typically gain a "second wind" and speed up their performance. Or in relative deprivation terms, protest success enlarges aspirations faster than actual gains can meet; the result is deeper frustration and more insistent demands. "The closer we come to the achievement of our ideals," shrewdly observes a Civil Rights Commissioner, "the more obvious and galling is the disparity."

Apart from its success, the current revolution will become increasingly intense because of the psychological effects of the demonstrations themselves. No protester, Negro or white, comes out of a racial demonstration the same person he was when he entered. Personal participation publicly commits the protester; it gives him a new sense of actively influencing events rather than passively accepting them; and it can provide him with greater confidence and an enhanced self-image. All of these changes aid him in undertaking additional protest. In short, demonstrations are both a symptom and a cause of psychological health. "My feets is tired," remarked an elderly Negro lady in the midst of the Montgomery bus boycott, "but my soul is rested." [28]

Furthermore, demonstrations instruct both participants and by-standers that segregation is a two-way street, a process of role reciprocation. It takes two to tango, and it requires the complicity of both whites and Negroes to maintain patterns of segregation and discrimination. If Negroes disengage themselves from these patterns, racial barriers cannot long be maintained. This insight, achieved in the midst of demonstrations, also makes further protest inevitable. "We the Negro people are now not afraid," announces a grocery store owner in a small Alabama town, "we have woke up." [29]

Second, the protests will increasingly attract a larger proportion of lower-income Negroes and shift from status to economic goals. The direct action phase of the revolution began in earnest when Southern college students initiated in 1960 a wave of mass sit-in demonstrations aimed at the desegrega-

---

[26] *Newsweek, op. cit.*, p. 34.
[27] As mentioned by G. W. Allport: *New York Times*, September 2, 1963, pp. 1, 6.
[28] Cited in Dr. M. L. King's famous letter from the Birmingham City Jail.
[29] *Newsweek, op. cit.*, p. 17.

tion of lunch counters. The fact that college students sparked this phase and that public facilities were the initial targets is of importance; but direct action weapons are now spreading and will continue to spread to diverse segments of the Negro population with primarily economic targets.

The fact that Negro college students ignited the direct action fuse involves a special irony. These youngsters benefited from the best schools the South ever provided Negroes. Though still not the equal of white education, this improved training produced a more sophisticated, self-confident generation. It also kindled, through the mechanism once again of relative deprivation, a greater frustration over racial barriers which exploded in militant social action. Like oil and water, education and oppression do not mix.

The student presented the perfect symbol as the initiator of public demonstrations. Well-dressed and well-behaved, the Negro student epitomized the group's aspirations for social mobility and integration. His nonviolent movement flew in the face of the contradictory racist stereotype of the Negro as violent yet subservient, degraded yet happy with his lot. The student was also less encumbered with fears from past mistreatment and less vulnerable to economic retaliation. In short, he was uniquely situated to transform public protest and going to jail into not only socially respectable acts but badges of high honor.

To become a full-fledged revolution, however, the movement had to incorporate elements of the Negro community. The Montgomery bus boycott in 1955–1956 provided a preview of the power of a unified effort across class lines. But it required Bull Connor's police dogs and fire hoses in Birmingham to capture the imagination of all segments of Negro America. Data from *Newsweek's* poll of Negroes in the summer of 1963 tell the story.[30] Fifty per cent feels the pace of racial change is far too slow; 80 per cent is certain that demonstrations are effective; four per cent has already personally or has family members who have been jailed in the cause; 40 per cent has already personally or has family members who have taken part in a sit-in, marched in a mass protest or engaged in picketing; and 48 per cent reports a willingness to participate in mass protests even if it means going to jail. Clearly, the revolution is an authentic mass movement that unites many different Negro elements, and shows every promise of recruiting more adherents in the future.

As the proportion of lower-income participators climbs, the nature of the struggle's primary goals necessarily shift from status to economic concerns. To illustrate with extreme examples, poor Negroes are not importantly affected by the desegregation of the opera, expensive restaurants, or golf courses. They are chiefly interested in getting good jobs and sharing in the material abundance surrounding them. "Freedom" for them inseparably signifies both dollars and dignity. Yet relative occupational and income gains, it will be recalled, were the most disappointing indices of the 1950s. Consequently, 1963's waves of building-site demonstrations against racial discrimination in the building trades

[30] *Ibid.*

is sure to be merely the forerunner of attacks upon a variety of employment realms and economic problems.

Third, a more extensive use of local and national boycotts of consumer products will be made. The consumer boycott is a weapon yet to be fully exploited. But a number of localities, such as Philadelphia and Nashville, have learned what well-organized Negro boycotting can accomplish. *Newsweek* reports that because of employment discrimination 29 per cent of its sample stopped buying in certain stores and 19 per cent stopped buying certain companies' products.[31] But this barely touches the potential. Sixty-three per cent of the sample states it would stop buying at a store if asked, including over two-thirds of the highest-income Negroes.

This mass willingness to participate in boycotts stems from two factors. The first is economic; boycotts are unusually well-suited for achieving the employment breakthrough so desperately desired by low-income Negroes. The second factor is psychological. There are three major types of responses human beings can make to oppression: they can move toward the oppressor and seek acceptance as an equal; they can move against the oppressor and aggressively express their frustration; and they can move away from the oppressor and seek to minimize painful contacts. Boycotts have the distinct psychological advantage of appealing to all three of these basic responses. Such campaigns move toward the oppressor by seeking to achieve desegregation; they move against the oppressor by encouraging group unity and aggressively upsetting the white-controlled economy; and they move away from the oppressor by requesting the participators merely to avoid the scene of conflict. For these reasons, it seems highly probable that boycotts will soon increase in number and scope.

Fourth, as the revolution proceeds through the 1960s, some basic structural changes in American society will have to occur before viable solutions are possible. As Daniel Pollitt forcefully observes (Thompson's chapter), employment problems could prove to be a major bottleneck to significant Negro progress in the near future. This hard economic fact of life will become painfully obvious as this decade continues. The massive upgrading of Negroes—and many whites, too—at a time when the full effects of automation are starting to hit the labor force will require major societal surgery, not the aspirin-type palliatives so far considered by the United States Congress. Such surgery will be resisted by conservative forces more powerful and entrenched than those which have opposed desegregation; but it will become increasingly necessary for national development.

The most pressing need is a general expansion of the economy and a consequent expansion of the labor force. Negro employment gains have always come fastest during times of rapid growth—as in World War II; and significant gains in the 1960s are in large part dependent upon another period of rapid growth. All types of structural changes necessary to induce such economic growth responsibly are prerequisites, then, not just for national pros-

[31] *Ibid.*

perity but for improved race relations as well. More specific samples of the required structural changes include the following:

(1) An extensive broadening of minimum wage legislation is needed by poorly-skilled Negroes who are employed. Many of the job categories in which Negroes are concentrated—service occupations, in particular—are not covered in the wage provisions of the Fair Labor Standards Act. Thus, the act as it now stands excludes those very people who most require its protection.

(2) Major tax cuts must be made at the bottom, rather than the top, of the income scale. At the very least, single persons with annual incomes below $2,000 and families with annual incomes below $4,000 should be exempt from federal income taxes (they will still bear an unduly heavy burden from sales taxes). These are levels widely regarded by economists as poverty-stricken by modern American standards, and relative deprivation considerations demand that these are the only realistic standards by which to judge the income of Americans. Present tax-cut proposals are inadequate in this regard.

(3) A great variety of federally-sponsored training and retraining programs are urgent necessities. Compared with present minuscule efforts, however, these future programs must be daringly new in both conception and magnitude. As Amos and Perry emphasize, automation requires more imaginative and flexible training than has typically been true in the past. The many boys now being taught cabinetmaking, to choose an absurd but actual example, should instead be taught the basic technological skills prerequisite for the jobs in greatest supply. Modern teaching methods must be applied, methods which utilize rather than magnify the special problems of disadvantage individuals.[32]

The size and complexity of this educational task invite attack from many directions—thoroughly revamped vocational training programs for the public schools, the proposed domestic equivalent of the Peace Corps, the Manpower Retraining programs, and a wider use of the educational potential of the armed forces. But if the unemployment and alienation in the depths of urban ghettoes today are to be remedied, a new conception of selection procedures will have to be adapted by these programs. As in the case of the minimum wage law, these programs are currently rejecting those unskilled persons who most desperately need the training. Of course, it is more expensive and difficult to prepare the most deprived segments of the population; but unless this is done, the fundamental educational problems of our time will be neglected.

And, fifth, steady progress—in relative as well as absolute terms—will be registered in the Yearbook which surveys the status of Negro Americans in the 1970s. The present revolution will probably enable Negroes during this decade to narrow, though not close, Negro-white disparities. Thus, in 1973, Goldstein might report that the life expectancy at birth of Negroes is only two or three

---

[32] For examples of such methods, see: H. Baron, "Samuel Shepard and the Banneker Project," Integrated Education, 1:25–27, April 1963; M. Mayer, "The good slum schools," Harper's, 222:46–52, April 1961; F. Riessman, The Culturally Deprived Child. New York: Harper and Row, 1962; and C. E. Silberman, "The City and the Negro," Fortune, 65:89–91, 139–154, March 1962.

years below that of whites; Hope and Shelton might report that the proportion of Negroes in the higher levels of government (GS and PFS 5 through 18) approximates the Negro population percentage; Marshall might report that the initial racial breakthroughs have finally occurred in such difficult areas as the building trades; Young might report that, while Negro-controlled business remains an insignificant factor in the American economy, increasing numbers of Negroes are assuming decision-making executive roles in previously all-white business; and Daniel might report that the pace of occupational upgrading of Negroes has sharply quickened, even among sales workers, and that the median Negro family income has inched up to almost two-thirds that of whites. Likewise, Yankauer and Sunderhauf might report a reversal in the residential segregation trends and additional gains in the quality of Negro housing; Gosnell and Martin might report a Negro voting percentage virtually as high as the white percentage and a developing political alliance in the South between Negroes and the working-class whites; and Newton, West, and Doddy might report that the education of Negroes at all levels has made appreciable gains in desegregation, availability, and quality.

This fifth prediction is predicated heavily upon the previous predictions. Should the protest movement cool, should the involvement of lower-income Negroes and the shift in emphasis to economic goals not take place, should nationwide boycotts not be effectively organized, should all types of necessary and decisive structural changes needed now by the American society be blocked, then obviously significant progress will not occur.

This is precisely what makes the 1960s such a crucial, yet promising, decade for American race relations. The gravest danger is not interracial violence, as the mass media endlessly assert, but that this golden opportunity will not be fully utilized. The nation is ripe for sweeping racial change and is in fact changing. Except for the Black Belt South, the formal desegregation of public facilities will soon be a mopping-up operation. The critical question, then, is: Can the revolution deal with de facto segregation and the vast educational and economic issues still impeding Negro progress as effectively as it has dealt with legal segregation?

AUTHORS CITED BY PETTIGREW

Amos, William E., and Jane Perry, *Negro Youth and Employment Opportunities.*

Daniel, Walter G., *The Relative Employment and Income of American Negroes.*

Doddy, Hurley H., *The Progress of the Negro in Higher Education, 1950–1960.*

Edwards, G. Franklin, *Marriage and Family Life Among Negroes.*

Goldstein, Marcus S., *Longevity and Health Status of the Negro American.*

GOSNELL, HAROLD F., AND ROBERT E. MARTIN, *The Negro as a Voter and Officeholder.*

HOPE, JOHN, AND EDWARD E. SHELTON, *The Negro in the Federal Government.*

LOGAN, RAYFORD W., *The Progress of the Negro After a Century of Emancipation.*

MARSHALL, RAY, *The Negro and Organized Labor.*

MEIER, AUGUST, *Negro Protest Movements and Organizations.*

NEWTON, EUNICE S., AND EARLE H. WEST, *The Progress of the Negro in Elementary and Secondary Education.*

THOMPSON, DANIEL C., *Civil Rights Leadership.*

VALIEN, PRESTON, *General Demographic Characteristics of the Negro Population in the United States.*

YANKAUER, MARION P., AND MILO B. SUNDERHAUF, *Housing: Equal Opportunity to Choose Where One Shall Live.*

YOUNG, HARDING B., *Negro Participation in American Business.*

Lewis M. Killian and Charles U. Smith

NEGRO PROTEST LEADERS IN A SOUTHERN COMMUNITY*

The "Negro Revolt" has had momentous effects on Negro leadership, especially in the South and within the civil rights organizations. The bus boycotts led by Martin Luther King and other militant ministers in southern cities during the late 1950's, and more especially the southern college sit-ins, set in motion waves of events that shook the power structure of the Negro community, made direct action temporarily pre-eminent as a civil rights technique, and ended NAACP hegemony in the civil rights field.

In some cases the result of the direct-action protest movement has been the replacement of older accommodating leaders by young, militant spokesmen. An excellent case study of this type of situation was made by two Florida sociologists, Lewis M. Killian and Charles U. Smith, who have described what happened as a result of a bus boycott in Tallahassee in the late 1950's.

ONE of the significant features of race relations in the past five years has been the emergence of new patterns of Negro leadership in southern communities. Prior to the various court decisions which withdrew legal support from the traditional framework of segregation, Negro leadership gave the appearance of conforming to the pattern of "accommodating" or "compromise" leadership. Analyses of leadership in southern Negro communities, such as the treatment found in Myrdal's *American Dilemma*,[1] suggest that the compromise leaders

Lewis M. Killian and Charles U. Smith, "Negro Protest Leaders in a Southern Community," *Social Forces*, XXXVIII (March, 1960), pp. 253–57. Reprinted with the permission of University of North Carolina Press.

* The authors are indebted to the Society for the Psychological Study of Social Issues for a Grant-in-Aid which helped make this study possible. This is a revised version of a paper read at the twenty-second annual meeting of the Southern Sociological Society, Gatlinburg, Tennessee, April 17, 1959.

[1] Gunnar Myrdal, *An American Dilemma* (New York: Harper and Bros., 1944) pp. 768–780.

held their positions primarily because they were acceptable to white leaders. They were also accepted by Negroes because accommodation was regarded as the most practical and effective mode of adjustment in the existing power situation.

The desegregation decisions of the U.S. Supreme Court, even without extensive implementation, redefined this power situation. In the years following 1954 militant leaders, reflecting the protest motive instead of the theme of patience and accommodation, have moved into the focus of attention of both whites and Negroes. Whereas the accommodating leaders had not been widely known to the white public, largely because they operated in a noncontroversial and often clandestine manner, the new leaders quickly rocketed to fame or notoriety, depending upon the observer's point of view. Martin Luther King, defying the white power structure of his community and being featured on the cover of *Time* magazine, symbolizes this new leadership. Many white leaders have reacted by bewailing the "breakdown of communication" between the races, denouncing the militant Negro leaders as reckless, radical parvenues, and attempting to isolate them by parleys with hand-picked, "responsible" leaders. Both practical and theoretical considerations dictate the need for a new appraisal of Negro leadership in the South.

The north Florida community of Tallahassee is one of the southern communities in which a change in the pattern of Negro leadership seemed to accompany a crisis in race relations. The critical situation arose from a challenge to segregation on city busses, culminating in a boycott. Here, too, news media featured daily the names of militant Negroes who previously had been anonymous ciphers in the Negro community as far as most whites were concerned. There were allegations to the effect that "newcomers" had come into the community and stirred up the erstwhile contented population, and that the Negro leadership had "split" with the result that white leaders did not know with whom to deal. Hence this community was well suited for a case study of Negro leadership in crisis.

The situation proved an opportunity to get the answers, for this community, to certain questions. Was the leadership in this Protest Movement actually new to the Negro community, or were the new leaders merely people who had suddenly become known to the white community because of a change of strategy? If they were new to the higher levels of the power structure in the Negro community, had they actually displaced the old group of leaders or was the community split between two competing sets of leaders? A corollary is the question whether these "new leaders" drew their strength from popular support or simply from a tightly organized, activist minority.

METHOD OF STUDY

The study, executed shortly after the end of the bus boycott, consisted of two related parts. The first was an assessment of the structure of Negro leadership through interviews with a panel of 21 Negroes tentatively designated as "leaders" by social scientists familiar with the community. This list subsequently proved to include what came to be defined as "old" and "new" leaders in almost equal proportions.

A panel of 21 white leaders was also selected. This panel included all of the white leaders who had dealt with the Negro community in connection with the bus protest, in either an official or unofficial capacity. It also included white functionaries who were known to have worked directly with the Negro community in connection with other matters, such as fund drives, civic projects, and community problems, both before and after the boycott. They are white leaders who most often speak to the Negro community in behalf of the white community. Some of them are high in the power structure. That this group represents fairly the position of the white leadership in Tallahassee is indicated by the absence of opposition to their representations to the Negro community.

The names of the 21 Negroes tentatively listed as "leaders" were placed on a card which was handed to the subject during the interview. Then he was asked a series of questions about Negro leadership *before* and *after* the bus boycott, and told to respond by giving names from the list. The questions which are of interest here were:

1. As best you can recall, which would have identified as "leaders" among Tallahassee Negroes 2 years ago?

2. At that time, which do you feel were able to influence large numbers of Negroes on important public issues?

3. Which ones were able to express most accurately the feelings of most Negroes in Tallahassee on important public issues?

4. Which ones were able to deal most effectively with white leaders as representatives of the Negro group?

5. Now, at the present time, which do you feel are most able to influence large numbers of Negroes on important public issues?

6. Which are able to express most accurately the feelings of most Negroes, etc.

7. Which are able to deal most effectively with white leaders, etc.

Subjects were allowed to give as few or as many responses to each question as they wished, and Negro subjects were encouraged to include their own names if they felt they should.

After the data had been collected, the answers of white and Negro informants were tabulated separately. Each of the 21 potential Negro leaders was given a score and a rank on each question, according to the number of times his name was mentioned in response to the question. Hence each Negro had, for each question, a rank assigned him by the Negro informants and a rank assigned by the white leaders.

The second portion of the study was an attitude survey of a sample of the adult Negro population of Tallahassee. Every fifth address was taken from a list of all the households in blocks occupied only by Negroes. Any adult available at the address was interviewed. A total of 196 usable interviews were obtained. A Likert-type scale of questions concerning attitudes toward segregation in general, the bus boycott, and the leadership of the Bus Protest Movement was used. Key questions for purposes of this study were:

1. The Negro should not boycott to achieve his goals. (Agreement with this statement would represent a repudiation of the militant leaders.)

2. The old, established leaders in Tallahassee were more effective than the ones leading the bus protest.

3. The leadership in the Tallahassee Bus Protest is very good.

Subjects were grouped in three categories on the basis of whether their answers to these three questions reflected approval or disapproval of the leaders who had called for the bus boycott. Those who answered all three of the questions favorably were classified as "Highly favorable," those who answered two favorably were classified as "Favorable," and those who answered only one or none in this manner were placed in the "Unfavorable" category.

FINDINGS

The interviews with the panel of potential Negro leaders revealed that a real change in leadership had indeed taken place between the "Pre-Boycott" and "Post-Boycott" periods. On the basis of high rankings on the answers to the questions "Who were the leaders?" "Who were influential?" and "Who were representative?" two years previously, six individuals were classified as "Pre-Boycott Leaders." Of these six, not one was found in the first five ranked on "influence" and "representativeness" in the Post-Boycott period. None of them were ranked even in the first ten on "influence," although two did remain in the first ten on "representativeness." An indication of how complete the turnover of leadership personnel was in the fact that of the first five ranked as both "influential" and "representative" in the Post-Boycott period, not one was among the first ten named as "leaders" in the Pre-Boycott period.

This change of leadership was also found to involve, as had been postulated, a replacement of Accommodating Leaders by Protest Leaders. Of the six Pre-Boycott leaders, five were ranked by Negroes as being most able to deal effectively with white leaders during this period. Five of the six were also ranked by whites as most able to deal effectively with white leaders. Four, including the three ranked highest by Negroes as "leaders," were ranked in the first five as "emissaries" by both Negroes and whites. This finding bears out the theory that, in the era of accommodation in race relations, leadership in the Negro community was based primarily on acceptability to white leaders and ability to gain concessions from them.

In contrast, none of the five New Leaders were ranked by either Negroes or whites as among the five Negroes able to deal most effectively with white leaders in the Post-Boycott period. In fact, none of them ranked in the first ten on acceptability to white leaders as it was perceived by Negroes. Clearly these New Leaders were not seen by other prominent Negroes as "Compromise Leaders."

The panel of Negroes interviewed included both the Old Leaders and the New Leaders, plus some individuals who did not receive high rankings for either period. The Negro panel was divided, for purposes of further analysis, into an "old group" of subjects who had ranked in the first ten on the question concerning Pre-Boycott leadership, and a new group. The new group identified as the five most influential leaders in the Post-Boycott period the same five men who had been ranked as New Leaders by the entire panel. The "old group" ranked four of these five men as the five most influential leaders in this same period, indicating that their perception of the change in leadership was almost the same as that of the "new group." Moreover, none of the "old group," including the Old Leaders, gave their own names in response to the question on ability to influence large numbers of Negroes. Although during the course of the boycott some of the Old Leaders had openly challenged the influence of the New Leaders, by the time of this study they seemed to have accepted the fact that they had been displaced. It is accurate, therefore, to say that a change, not a split, in leadership had occurred.

Although no intensive study of the individual characteristics of the Old and New Leaders was made, certain ones were evident. Even though at the time of the study, the boycott had ended and had obviously failed of its purpose to force desegregation of city buses, all of the New Leaders were strongly identified with it. All were officers of the organization which had led the boycott and all had been arrested and fined for "operating an illegal transportation system" (a car pool). In contrast, not one of the Old Leaders had been active in promoting the boycott, and at least two of them had opposed it as a tactic. Of the six Old Leaders, three were employed in the state-supported school system; none of the five New Leaders were state employees. There were three ministers among the New Leaders, none among the old. Although the Old Leaders had, as a group, indeed lived in the community a longer time than their successors, the shortest time that any of the New Leaders had lived in Tallahassee was three years. One of them had lived there over thirty years. It was only in a limited and relative sense that they could be described as "newcomers."

Since the New Leaders had been identified as synonomous with the leaders of the Bus Boycott, the questions asked in the opinion poll were suited to serve as a measure of their popular support. Were they leaders not only in the eyes of the small panel of prominent Negroes but also in the eyes of the Negro community? The results of the survey indicate that they were. When asked if the leadership in the Bus Protest was very good, 84 percent of the sample agreed that it was. Some inconsistency was found between the answers to this question and the question, "The old established leaders in Tallahassee were more effective than the ones leading the Bus Protest," since only 62 percent of the sample disagreed with this statement. But, to the extent that this sample can be taken as representative, it appears that the New Leaders did have majority support in the Negro community. Subjects were also asked to agree or disagree with the statement, "Should the Negro population of Tallahassee need to develop united action to obtain rights or services not connected with the Bus Protest, the people leading the Protest would probably be selected to lead such action." Again, strong majority support of the New Leaders was indicated, 82 percent of the sample agreeing with this statement.

Using the categories "Highly Favorable," "Favorable," and "Unfavorable," established earlier, an analysis was made of certain differences between Negroes showing greater or lesser support for the boycott and its leaders. The chi-square test of independence was used. Differences significant beyond the .01 level were found in age and education, the more favorably disposed subjects being younger and better educated. Those who were favorably disposed toward the boycott were more likely to own automobiles than those who were not, this difference also being significant beyond the .01 level. This difference may have reflected the fact that the boycott caused less personal inconvenience for car owners than it did for others, or it may have been that car ownership was an indirect measure of socio-economic status. No significant difference in ownership of real property was found between supporters and non-supporters, however, so the former explanation seems the more likely. This is also suggested by the fact that differences in occupation were not significant at the .05 level.

SUMMARY AND CONCLUSIONS

In the community studied, the impression that there has been a change in the quality of race relations is borne out. The clearest indication of this change is the replacement of the Old Leaders by New Leaders who clearly reflect the protest motive rather than any spirit of accommodation. These New Leaders have widespread popular support, and the extent of their influence is conceded by the Old Leaders whom they displaced.

Additional findings led added significance to this shift in Negro leadership. The panel of white leaders were found to perceive Negro leadership in the Post-Boycott period in almost the same way that the Negro leaders did. Of the six men ranked highest by whites as "most influential" in the Post-Boycott period, four were among the Negroes' New Leaders. At the same time, most of these white leaders indicated that they were unwilling to deal with these New Leaders because the militant spokesmen were uncompromising in their opposition to segregation. It is only in this sense that communication has broken down between the races. The New Leaders are unwilling to communicate and negotiate with whites in the circumscribed, accommodating fashion of yesterday. The Old Leaders can no longer claim the support of the Negro population, no matter how acceptable they might be to the whites. As long as this situation prevails, the structure of the situation seems to permit only one kind of communication between the Negro community and the white power structure: formal, peremptory demands, backed by the threat of legal action, political reprisal, or economic boycott. So long as the New Leaders are not accepted as bona fide, albeit antagonistic, emissaries of the Negro community in the same way that the Old Leaders were, this would seem to be the only way in which they can get the attention of the white leaders.

While the present study was principally concerned with a description of the changes in Negro leadership in Tallahassee during the Bus Protest, there is evidence which indicates that the New Leaders and new leadership are permanent in this community. Although they may have been "issue leaders" at first, they have continued to maintain their position of leadership as the sample of the Negro population predicted they would.

In the first place some of the Old Leaders were called upon by the Tallahassee City Commission to get the Negroes to agree to a compromise settlement in the early days of the Bus Protest. The efforts of the Old Leaders to do this failed completely and ever since they have made no overt efforts to regain the following they had prior to the protest. This is apparently due to their belief that neither the Negro population nor the city officials have confidence in them. The Negroes do not trust them because of what they regard as underhanded dealing with the City Commission. The city officials apparently feel that these erstwhile leaders cannot be trusted to gauge Negro sentiment accurately or to deliver results when called upon, because they lack following.

Secondly, the New Leaders have continued to enjoy reasonable support for their undertakings. Some of them have moved into other areas of leadership, such as the NAACP, the Southern Christian Leadership Conference, and the Florida Council of Human Relations. One of them is president of the Tallahassee Chapter of the NAACP. Another is on the State NAACP Board and on the Board of Directors of the Southern Christian Leadership Conference.

Finally these New Leaders have sought to keep the Negro community of Tallahassee militant and dynamic by continuing weekly meetings of the ICC, the organization formed to promote the bus protest, conducting institutes on non-violence, taking preliminary steps toward school integration, working to get more Negroes registered and voting, and making many local and nonlocal public appearances in connection with the uplift of Negroes. Furthermore, the press has done much to contribute to their status as permanent leaders by seeking their opinions and comments on various matters affecting the Negro community in Tallahassee (e.g. the recent rape case).

The writers feel that the New Leaders are becoming permanent leaders not because of the attractiveness of their personalities or their skill at organizing, but rather because they adhere rigorously to the *form* of militant leadership which is becoming the trend for Negroes throughout the United States. This new leadership is not of the accommodating type. It seeks gains for the

Negro community through formal demands and requests, boycotts, lawsuits, and voting. The protest leaders are not concerned with whether or not the whites high in the power structure know, like, or want to deal with them. Until the Old Leaders are willing or able to translate their mode of leadership into a form similar to this, it appears that they will not again rise to prominence as leaders in Tallahassee.

Jack L. Walker

THE FUNCTIONS OF DISUNITY:
NEGRO LEADERSHIP IN A SOUTHERN CITY

The striking overturn in Negro leadership which Killian and Smith found in Tallahassee, and which was described in the preceding selection, has by no means been a universal pattern. In some cases, as in Montgomery, Alabama, the ascendancy of the militants has been merely a temporary phenomenon, with the older, more conservative type of leaders eventually returning to power within the Negro community. In other instances the leaders whom the militants denounced as "conservative" have not been displaced. Instead, pressure from the new "radical" wing of Negro leadership has enabled the conservative element to use its influence with the white decision-makers to obtain many of the changes desired by the Negro community. Jack L. Walker has described how disunity among the Negro leaders in Atlanta actually helped to secure fulfillment of demands made by the militants. Though much further research is needed to determine which pattern is most characteristic, we suspect that the situation described by Walker is fairly typical.

INTRODUCTION[1]

DURING the last five years waves of Negro protest demonstrations have swept across the Southern states. Incidents like the Montgomery bus boycott, the freedom rides and the sit-ins have spread with amazing speed, provoking racial crises in numerous towns and cities, even in the Deep South, and often taking the white leaders by surprise. From these crises a new type of Negro

Jack L. Walker, "The Functions of Disunity: Negro Leadership in a Southern City," *Journal of Negro Education*, XXXII (Summer, 1963), pp. 227–36. Reprinted by permission of author and publisher.

[1] The research on which this essay is based was financed by a grant from the Iowa Citizenship Clearing House and the National Center for Education in Politics. Neither of them, of course, is responsible for any errors of fact or interpretation in this study.

leadership seems to be arising: one dedicated to protest rather than accommodation and determined to press its demands for equality with a wide range of weapons including economic boycotts, civil disobedience, and political reprisals, tactics that Southern Negroes have never used in the past.

As the new, more militant leaders have arisen in Negro communities, the established leadership has usually offered resistance, and as a result many Southern Negro communities have been torn by disunity and internal conflict. Lewis M. Killian and Charles U. Smith in investigating Tallahassee, Florida, following a sharp dispute over bus segregation in the city found that the more militant, "protest" leaders had completely displaced the established Negro leadership. They found that after the crisis had passed, not one of the six persons named by a panel of both whites and Negroes as the top Negro leaders before the dispute were included as top leaders after the dispute. Also not one of the five persons that the panel named as top Negro leaders after the dispute had been ranked among the first ten before the dispute took place. Even the old, established leaders seemed to be aware that they had been displaced, and the study also indicated that a majority of the Negro community had shifted their allegiances to the protest leaders. Killian and Smith argue that:

> ... the new leaders are becoming permanent leaders not because of the attractiveness of their personalities or their skill at organizing, but rather because they adhere rigorously to the *form* of militant leadership which is becoming the trend for Negroes throughout the United States.[2]

The situation in Tallahassee, however, does not seem to have been duplicated in all other Southern cities, or even in all those that have experienced a racial crisis within the last five years. Leslie Dunbar in commenting on the findings of Killian and Smith has argued that:

> There is some evidence in the stories of how a number of Southern cities have desegregated lunch counters to suggest that the older Negro leadership and the protest leaders can and do fruitfully complement each other, though coordination and mutual trust have sometimes been hard come by. My guess would be that this is the true interpretation. Negro leadership in the South is being broadened by an infusion of new elites.[3]

The subject of this essay is the relations between the established Negro leadership and the new protest leaders in a Southern city, the issue raised by Dunbar, Killian and Smith. The analysis is based on a case study of the sit-in controversy in Atlanta, Georgia, and is concerned particularly with the social

[2] Lewis M. Killian and Charles U. Smith, "Negro Protest Leaders in a Southern City," *Social Forces* (March, 1960), p. 257.

[3] Leslie Dunbar, "Reflections on the Latest Reform of the South," *Phylon*, 22:253, Fall, 1961.

and economic factors associated with the leaders' differing attitudes towards goals and techniques of social action. It will be argued that both the conservative and the protest leaders can play an important part in such racial disputes, and unless the conservatives are completely displaced by the protest leaders, disputes among the leadership tend to increase, not decrease, the effectiveness of the Negro community's battle against the institutions of segregation.

SIT-INS IN ATLANTA: A CASE STUDY [4]

On February 1, 1960, several Negro students sat down at a lunch counter in Greensboro, North Carolina, and refused to leave when told that the store did not serve Negroes. The manager is reported to have said: "They can just sit there. It's nothing to me." But within a week similar groups were sitting down in protest all over the South, and a major social movement was underway. The sit-ins spread even into the Deep South, and in response to fears and rumors that sit-ins were being planned the Georgia legislature passed a special trespass law on February 17, 1960.

Their fears were well founded, for as early as February 4 students at Atlanta University were planning demonstrations, but they were persuaded by faculty members and an apprehensive administration to postpone their action until they had drawn up a statement of their grievances. This statement was quickly completed and printed in the form of a full page advertisement in all local newspapers on March 9, 1960, under the title: "An Appeal for Human Rights." The advertisement caused a sensation in the state and it was commented on by politicians and public figures all over the country. This was followed on March 15 by the first wide spread sit-in demonstrations in Atlanta in which 77 students were arrested under the new Georgia trespass law.

While their cases were pending in court the students began to work on several other projects. They mounted picket lines against food stores which had large Negro clienteles yet did not hire Negroes above the menial level, they held a series of meetings in Negro churches explaining the student movement and asking for support, they began publishing a weekly news sheet that eventually became a full fledged weekly newspaper, and on May 17, 1960, they gathered 1400 students together to march on the State Capitol in downtown Atlanta to celebrate the Supreme Court's 1954 anti-segregation decision. This march was diverted by Atlanta's Chief of Police to prevent the students from meeting a large, ugly crowd that had gathered at the capitol. When the students left for summer vacation tension was running high in the city.

During the Spring of 1960 there was considerable dispute among adult

[4] This case study is based on the record of the controversy found in the files of *The Atlanta Constitution*, *The Atlanta Journal*, *The Atlanta Daily World*, and *The Atlanta Inquirer*, and on a series of interviews with the principal actors conducted during April and May of 1962.

Negroes about the student movement. Although there were few who spoke out directly against the students, there were those who expressed their disapproval by keeping silent or withholding praise. The conservative adults, many of whom were businessmen, were opposed on principle to the students' use of picket lines and boycotts against businesses which practiced discrimination in hiring. They were also apprehensive when they understood that the students were not satisfied with their first sit-ins and their march on the State Capitol, but were planning repeated demonstrations in an effort to force the issue. The adult community began to divide on their support for the students and rumors that all the Negro adults did not approve of the students' efforts passed through the white community.

Regardless of the criticism, the leaders of the student movement continued organizational and propaganda work during the summer. On June 27 they met privately with the president of the city's leading department store who tried to convince them to give up their demonstrations promising that he would consider their grievances later on after the schools had been safely desegregated. This meeting broke down into a heated argument in which the student leaders are reported to have threatened the merchant with a boycott and the merchant shouted: "I don't need Negro trade!"

Following this incident conservative Negroes came into the open with criticisms of the students, and a few even made public speeches attacking their methods. But even so, after the students had returned for the fall term, on October 19, 1960, widespread sit-ins were mounted once again, and once again large numbers of demonstrators were arrested.[5] The students refused to leave the jail on bail at this time. Once again tension built up in the city. At this point the mayor asked for, and was granted, a 30-day truce period in which he promised to try to reach a settlement of the dispute.

The mayor's efforts were completely unsuccessful. The leading merchants were in no mood to compromise with the demonstrators and were suspicious of the mayor who was quite anxious to get a settlement and whose political power rested firmly on Negro support. When the mayor called a meeting of the downtown merchants in his office, only the small ones attended who depended heavily on Negro trade and feared a boycott.

On their own the leading merchants decided to try informal methods to bring an end to the disturbances. The conservative leaders of the Negro community, those who had criticized the students during the summer and who had been considered the "spokesmen" of the Negro community in the past, were asked to attend a private meeting with the merchants. The meeting was secret but it seems that the Negroes were being asked to use their influence to persuade the demonstrators to cease their efforts and to wait until after the schools were desegregated to discuss the issue of lunch counter desegregation. After meeting twice they decided to invite one adult Negro

---

[5] These demonstrations received nationwide attention, especially because of the arrest of Martin Luther King, Jr. and the series of events that led to the famous phone call to the King family from John F. Kennedy.

leader who had been a close advisor of the students, and the most influential student leader to a secret meeting in the Negro section of town so that the white merchants could offer their proposals. When these two men were contacted, however, they immediately became suspicious of the proceedings and decided to expose them. They made a public announcement that they were not a party to these secret negotiations, and when the conservative Negroes and the whites arrived at the meeting place television cameras were already set up and reporters were everywhere clamoring for statements.

After this incident, on November 25, 1960, the students resumed their sit-ins and also organized a full scale boycott of the downtown shopping area. A stalemate continued through the months of December and January, during which most of the lunch counters remained closed and the boycott of the downtown stores remained in effect.

Throughout this three month period of stalemate the students, equipped with short wave radios, had been sitting-in at lunch counters all over the city without incident. Either they had been ignored, or the counters had been closed, but on February 7, 1961, one restaurant manager in a federal office building invoked the trespass law and had the demonstrators arrested. During the next three days arrests continued daily with the students refusing once again to come out on bail. A protest march and rally was planned to take place in front of the jail on February 19, and it was feared that such a demonstration might result in a riot.

At this tense moment the student leaders themselves turned to one of the oldest, most respected Negro leaders and asked him to try to get negotiations started again. This man had made public statements backing the students at the beginning of the movement, but he was also widely considered to be a conservative and had attended the secret meetings with the white merchants in November, 1960. At this juncture, however, by utilizing friendships he had with influential white leaders, he was able to get negotiations started which eventually led to a settlement of the controversy. The agreement was announced on March 7, 1961. It called for desegregation of the lunch counters after the school desegregation had been completed during the fall of 1961, and, except for the firm agreement that the counters would be desegregated, it was essentially what the merchants had pressed for from the beginning. The actual desegregation took place on September 27, 1961.

THE FUNCTIONS OF DISUNITY

The sit-in controversy in Atlanta took place in a community which is still basically segregated. Although a few of the barriers have been broken down during the past five years there are still almost no social contacts between the leadership of the two racial groups and residential segregation places their homes far apart. This isolation of the leadership of the two communities from each other is a potentially disruptive element in the social structure of the city. If a crisis arises involving the crucial issue of race, communication between the leaders of the two racial groups, which is normally tenuous and rather formal, becomes very hard to maintain, and it is even more difficult to establish the circumstances in which negotiation of the difficulties that caused the crisis can take place.

During the controversy over the sit-in demonstrations in Atlanta such a breakdown in communications between whites and Negroes occurred, and at the same time relations among the Negro leaders were strained because of their disagreements over tactics. The conservative Negro leaders are primarily older businessmen, although there are also social workers, college administrators and ministers in this group. The more liberal group is made up of students, members of the staffs of various Negro improvement groups, college teachers, younger businessmen and ministers.[6]

The dispute within the Negro community revolves around the use of protest demonstrations and economic boycotts to press the attack on segregation. The conservatives never questioned, throughout the sit-in controversy in Atlanta, the goals of the students, and even when they agreed to attend secret meetings with the merchants they never failed to inform the whites that they thought the students' demands were justified, even if they did not approve of their methods.[7] The conservatives oppose boycotts and protest demonstrations primarily because they feel these public displays of discontent cause bitterness and rancor and tend to destroy the cordial, settled atmosphere which they feel is a necessary precondition to effective negotiations. They also fear economic retaliation more than the protest leaders, not only because of their own business, but also because they have worked hard to build institutions such as the Y.M.C.A., the Urban League, and many churches which depend heavily on contributions from influential whites. During the boycott that accompanied the sit-in affair in Atlanta some of these organizations began to lose white contributors as tension mounted. To some extent the conservative leaders have each made adjustments to the traditional position of the Negro in Southern society. Although none seem completely satisfied, in varying measures they have given up efforts to penetrate the dominant white society and consequently they have a greater commitment to the institutions within the Negro community.

The businessmen among the conservatives have frequent dealings with

[6] The principal actors in the sit-in controversy were interviewed at length, and frequently they voluntarily described themselves with such terms as "conservative" or "liberal." These self-identifications were used, along with an analysis of each participant's actions and statements during the dispute to decide which were conservatives and which were protest leaders.

[7] It should not be surprising that the older leaders would be in sympathy with the goals of the students because the students' protests did not grow out of alienation from any of the society's basic orienting values except those, such as white supremacy, that underpin segregation. Searles and Williams found that the student protests "were precipitated by Negro students' reference to the white middle class as a standard of comparison . . ." They also discovered that: "Far from being alienated, the students appear to be committed to the society and its middle class leaders." Ruth Searles and J. Allen Williams, "Negro College Students' Participation in Sit-ins," *Social Forces*, 40:219, March, 1962.

influential whites in the city; both the bank and savings and loan association operated by Negroes in Atlanta have very sizeable deposits from white customers. In fact, to a large extent, the power of the conservatives depends on their influence with the white community. They are spokesmen for the Negro community primarily because they have gained white recognition and favor, although their own achievements placed them in a position to be chosen for this role. Because of this process of selection, the protest leaders regard the conservatives with almost the same hostility they have for the whites, if not more so. They complain that the conservatives' power is based essentially on the Negro's fear of the power of the white man. They think that the established leaders have profited from the injustices of segregation by trading their human dignity for the opportunity to represent the whites within the Negro community.

The protest leaders are not so directly engaged in activities and institutions that serve the whole community as are the conservatives, and they deal more exclusively with the Negro community than the conservatives. Yet even so they do not feel as much committed to its maintenance; in fact they hate all that it stands for. Their work brings them into closer contact with the social, economic and political deprivations suffered by the Negro, and they tend to concentrate on these injustices and have fewer reasons to try to protect institutions, both charitable and commercial, that presently exist in the Negro community. They are under less compulsion than the conservatives to act with restraint or to compromise their demands in order to make limited material gains or to promote the fortunes of Negro businessmen. In this sense they stand outside the economic and social life of the established community and they try to keep the dominant leaders, both white and colored, at arm's length, guarding against being too friendly with politicians and certainly never asking them for favors or help of any kind. They try to conduct their affairs strictly on the basis of their moral principles, and for these reasons conservatives frequently regard them as "irresponsible" and find their attitudes toward politics and community leaders "unrealistic" or "hateful." One conservative leader in Atlanta, who has a reputation as a good tactician and organizer, acknowledged the importance of the student protests in bringing "more integration in less than two years than we gained in ten," but he also argued that "they will never get anything done on their own because they are cut off; they work in a righteous vacuum over there."

The protest leaders and the conservatives manifest considerable suspicion for each other, and in Atlanta a complete breakdown in relations between them is prevented primarily by the existence of several influential men who stand between these two groups and are not so deeply committed to either political style, or who are caught in ambiguous circumstances that prompt them to maintain contact with both protest and conservative leaders. These men tend to bind the Negro community together by providing lines of communication between leaders of all persuasions.

Even though the conservative and protest leaders distrust each other, during the Atlanta sit-in controversy at least, their efforts were complementary. In fact, if the Negro community is conceived of as a system designed to fight the institutions of segregation each of these groups performed a function in this situation. The students and the adult protest leaders, by organizing demonstrations and economic boycotts, created a crisis which had to be resolved, even if in doing so they raised the level of tension between the two racial groups in the city and caused a rather dangerous breakdown of communications. But the leaders of the protests did not have the power to resolve the crisis they had created because they had no basis for contact with the dominant white leaders. As James Q. Wilson suggests, one of the inherent difficulties of protest action is "that the discretion of the protest leader to bargain after he has acquired the resources with which to bargain is severely limited by the means he was forced to employ in order to create those resources." [8] From the beginning of the dispute the leading merchants refused to negotiate directly with the demonstrators whom they considered to be irresponsible troublemakers. In fact, the tactics pursued by the protest leaders were almost certain to antagonize the dominant whites. As Killian and Smith point out in describing the political style of the protest leaders:

> This new leadership is not of the accommodating type. It seeks gains for the Negro community through formal demands and requests, boycotts, lawsuits and voting. The protest leaders are not concerned with whether or not the whites high in the power structure know, like or want to deal with them. [9]

The more conservatively inclined leaders, utilizing their reputations and the connections they had built up with the white community through the years, had the function of resolving the crisis situation created by the protest leaders. In this case even the antagonism between the two groups was functional because it made the conservatives seem more reliable and responsible in the eyes of the whites, and so they were still able to act as negotiators when both sides were ready to compromise.

Those leaders in the middle, who did not identify completely with either the conservative or the protest leaders, had the function of moderating this conflict over tactics. Some individuals find themselves in this situation because they are subject to cross-pressures which restrain them from becoming attached to either side in the controversy. Others are not committed because they have a flexible attitude toward social action which prompts them to regard all tactical weapons as potentially useful. Regardless of the influences that put them in this position, however, these leaders in the middle provide both formal and informal links between the conservative and protest leaders.

The situation in Atlanta does not seem to have been unique. Something of this same kind of unanticipated cooperation and sharing of functions be-

[8] James Q. Wilson, "The Strategy of Protest," *Journal of Conflict Resolution* (September, 1961), p. 293.
[9] Killian and Smith, p. 257.

tween protest and conservative Negro leaders seems to have taken place during the sit-in controversy in Knoxville, Tennessee. Negotiation began initially there without any demonstrations, but broke down after four tedious months of talks. Sit-ins began on June 9, 1960, and a boycott was started five days later on June 14. Merrill Proudfoot describes a meeting of the executive committee of the protest movement which took place on July 2, 1960, after about three weeks of demonstrations. The meeting was attended by the president of Knoxville College, who had not been involved in planning or staging the demonstrations, and he revealed that he had been contacted by an official of the Knoxville Chamber of Commerce who informed him that there was a movement underway to reopen negotiations. Proudfoot rather indignantly comments:

> The circuitous means of communicating with one another has lent a comic-opera aspect to the way this major community problem has been handled. It would seem sensible for one of the merchants to have called Crutcher or James [the leaders of the demonstrations] and said, "Come on down and let's talk!" Instead the merchants hint to the Chamber of Commerce official that they might be willing; he contacts not Crutcher or James, but Colston—the one person in the Negro community who has the greatest status . . . and he in turn makes the contact within the Negro community.[10]

Also when a negotiating team was formed to formulate the final agreement to desegregate, Colston was included once again, but this time he was accompanied by Crutcher. Although the description is not so complete it seems that a similar process operated at Winston-Salem, North Carolina, where the agreement to desegregate the lunch counters was not formulated by the protest leaders. Clarence H. Patrick reports that:

> The demonstrators several times sought unsuccessfully for someone to organize and mediate a meeting between them and the store managers in an attempt to resolve the antisegregation movement on the basis of some mutual agreement. The leaders of the protest never met, as a group, with the managers of the stores where the protests occurred.[11]

CONCLUSION

The evidence presented here suggests that not all Southern Negro communities have experienced the same changes in leadership that Killian and Smith detected in Tallahassee. In some cases it seems that a kind of tactical

[10] Merrill Proudfoot, *Diary of a Sit-in*, Chapel Hill: University of North Carolina Press, 1962, pp. 111–112.
[11] Clarence H. Patrick, *Lunch Counter Desegregation in Winston-Salem, North Carolina* (Pamphlet Distributed by the Southern Regional Council, 1960), p. 7.

balance exists with both conservative and protest leaders playing a part in the fight for equality. However, there is no evidence that the period of change and transition in Negro leadership in Atlanta has ended. In fact, a major unsettling force seems to be developing beneath the level of leadership. Almost all the leaders interviewed, including the conservatives, felt that expectations are rising perceptibly throughout the Negro community as a result of recent successful attacks on the institutions of segregation. The Negro masses, who have traditionally been apathetic toward politics and efforts to fight segregation, seem to be gaining hope that change is possible and are shaking off the mood of cynical resignation that has paralyzed them in the past.

Looking forward, these circumstances suggest a prediction that the drive to break down racial barriers will not stall once a few victories are won, but will continue and intensify in the foreseeable future. However, there are some uncertain features of this development. First of all, it is unclear whether the conservatives, who were once the dominant leaders within the Negro community, are being completely supplanted by the protest leaders, or whether in the future there will continue to be a mixture of conservative and protest elements in Atlanta's Negro leadership. It is uncertain, because of increasing demands for equality from the masses, whether the aging conservative group will be replaced with leaders of similar stature and influence within the Negro community. If this does not occur, the present tactical balance within the Negro community will be altered in favor of the militants.

The full impact of such a change in Negro leadership on race relations in the city would depend in large measure on the reactions of the whites. Several local observers, when asked to comment on this prospect, emphasized that a new, younger and more liberal group of white leaders is emerging in the city to replace the older, more conservative whites. There is also a widely held impression in Atlanta that the majority of the white population has accepted, or at least is resigned to, the end of segregation. These observers saw a prospect of diminishing resistance from the whites, faster integration, and improving race relations as the younger leaders of both races take control.

The accuracy of this prediction depends, to a large extent, upon the nature of the issues that face the community in the future, and upon the pliability of the whites as the Negroes begin aggressively attacking segregation in such potentially explosive areas as housing and employment. It also seems likely that in the future the Negro community may become more united behind the protest leaders, but this may not automatically result in an increased effectiveness in gaining their ends. This study brings into question the assumption commonly made that a weak minority within the society must maintain unity and solidarity if it is to be effective in gaining its objectives.

It seems clear that the Atlanta Negro community became more effective in breaking down the barriers of segregation after the militant, protest leaders came on the scene, even though their arrival caused considerable bickering and disunity among Negro leaders in the city. However, the protest leaders' outspoken desire to destroy the institutions of segregation, their habit of treating all issues in moral terms, and their willingness to employ force in the form of economic boycotts to gain their objectives alienated them from the dominant white leadership. The conservative leaders were much more acceptable to the whites because they tended to concentrate primarily on improving the economic welfare of the Negro without demanding an immediate end to segregation. The conservative Negro leaders' primary interest in maintaining the institutions within the Negro community along with their antipathy for the protest leaders and their obvious disapproval of boycotts and demonstrations made them seem "responsible" in the eyes of the whites, and thus acceptable as bargaining agents. Therefore, it would seem that a Negro community in a Southern city is likely to be more effective in eliminating the institutions of segregation if it has both conservative and protest elements within its leadership. Without the protest leaders it will lack the capacity to precipitate tension through the use of boycotts, demonstrations and other "direct action" techniques. And without the conservative leaders it is in danger of losing contact with the dominant white leaders and being unable to negotiate a peaceful, compromise solution to a racial crisis. Seen in this light, there seems to be a part to play in the Negro's fight for equality for both the more accommodating, conservative leaders and the liberal, protest leaders. As long as a broad agreement exists on the ultimate goals of equality and an end to racial discrimination, some disunity over the proper methods of social action may be positively desirable.

August Meier

ON THE ROLE OF MARTIN LUTHER KING

*Not since Booker T. Washington has a Negro leader emerged with
as much appeal to both blacks and whites as Martin Luther King.
Unlike Washington, however, he did not represent a polarization of
Negro thinking; to the contrary, King functioned in the early 1960's
as the great mediator of the diverse wings of the Negro protest movement. If, as the preceding article indicates, disunity in Negro leadership proved functional in that period, the essay that follows suggests
that, nevertheless, the civil rights movement certainly benefited from,
if it did not actually need, a leader who could bridge the gulf between
the conservatives and radicals in the black community. Before King
died, however, the cleavages in the civil rights movement had reached
the point where even he could no longer act as a harmonizer between
the right and left wings. The following essay attempts to analyze the
character of King's leadership during the years of his greatest importance as a national figure.*

THE phenomenon that is Martin Luther King consists of a number of striking paradoxes. The Nobel Prize winner is accepted by the outside world as
the leader of the nonviolent direct action movement, but he is criticized by
many activists within the movement. He is criticized for what appears, at times,
as indecisiveness, and more often denounced for a tendency to accept compromise. Yet, in the eyes of most Americans, both black and white, he remains
the symbol of militant direct action. So potent is this symbol of King as direct
actionist, that a new myth is arising about his historic role. The real credit
for developing and projecting the techniques and philosophy of nonviolent
direct action in the civil rights arena must be given to the Congress of Racial
Equality which was founded in 1942, more than a dozen years before the
Montgomery bus boycott projected King into international fame. And the

August Meier, "On the Role of Martin Luther King," *New Politics*, IV (Winter,
1965), pp. 52–59. Reprinted with permission of *New Politics*.

idea of mass action by Negroes themselves to secure redress of their grievances must, in large part, be ascribed to the vision of A. Philip Randolph, architect of the March on Washington Movement during World War II. Yet, as we were told in Montgomery on March 25, 1965, King and his followers now assert, apparently without serious contradiction, that a new type of civil rights strategy was born at Montgomery in 1955 under King's auspices.

In a movement in which respect is accorded in direct proportion to the number of times one has been arrested, King appears to keep the number of times he goes to jail to a minimum. In a movement in which successful leaders are those who share in the hardships of their followers, in the risks they take, in the beatings they receive, in the length of time they spend in jail, King tends to leave prison for other important engagements, rather than remaining there and suffering with his followers. In a movement in which leadership ordinarily devolves upon persons who mix democratically with their followers, King remains isolated and aloof. In a movement which prides itself on militancy and "no compromise" with racial discrimination or with the white "power structure," King maintains close relationships with, and appears to be influenced by, Democratic presidents and their emissaries, seems amenable to compromises considered by some half a loaf or less, and often appears willing to postpone or avoid a direct confrontation in the streets.

King's career has been characterized by failures that, in the larger sense, must be accounted triumphs. The buses in Montgomery were desegregated only after lengthy judicial proceedings conducted by the NAACP Legal Defense Fund secured a favorable decision from the U.S. Supreme Court. Nevertheless, the events in Montgomery were a triumph for direct action, and gave this tactic a popularity unknown when identified solely with CORE. King's subsequent major campaigns—in Albany, Georgia; in Danville, Virginia; in Birmingham, Alabama; and in St. Augustine, Florida—ended as failures or with only token accomplishments in those cities. But each of them, chiefly because of his presence, dramatically focused national and international attention on the plight of the Southern Negro, thereby facilitating overall progress. In Birmingham, in particular, demonstrations which fell short of their local goals were directly responsible for a major Federal Civil Rights Act. Essentially, this pattern of local failure and national victory was recently enacted in Selma, Alabama.

King is ideologically committed to disobeying unjust laws and court orders, in the Gandhian tradition, but generally he follows a policy of not disobeying Federal Court orders. In his recent Montgomery speech, he expressed a crude, neo-Marxist interpretation of history romanticizing the Populist movement as a genuine union of black and white common people, ascribing race prejudice to capitalists playing white workers against black. Yet, in practice, he is amenable to compromise with the white bourgeois political and economic Establishment. More important, King enunciates a superficial and eclectic philosophy and by virtue of it he has profoundly awakened the moral conscience of America.

In short, King can be described as a "Conservative Militant."

In this combination of militancy with conservatism and caution, of righteousness with respectability, lies the secret of King's enormous success.

Certain important civil rights leaders have dismissed King's position as the product of publicity generated by the mass communications media. But this can be said of the success of the civil rights nonviolent action movement generally. Without publicity it is hard to conceive that much progress would have been made. In fact, contrary to the official nonviolent direct action philosophy, demonstrations have secured their results not by changing the hearts of the oppressors through a display of nonviolent love, but through the national and international pressures generated by the publicity arising from mass arrests and incidents of violence. And no one has employed this strategy of securing publicity through mass arrests and precipitating violence from white hoodlums and law enforcement officers more than King himself. King abhors violence; as at Selma, for example, he constantly retreats from situations that might result in the deaths of his followers. But he is precisely most successful when, contrary to his deepest wishes, his demonstrations precipitate violence from Southern whites against Negro and white demonstrators. We need only cite Birmingham and Selma to illustrate this point.

Publicity alone does not explain the durability of King's image, or why he remains for the rank and file of whites and blacks alike, the symbol of the direct action movement, the nearest thing to a charismatic leader that the civil rights movement has ever had. At the heart of King's continuing influence and popularity are two facts. First, better than anyone else, he articulates the aspirations of Negroes who respond to the cadence of his addresses, his religious phraseology and manner of speaking, and the vision of his dream for them and for America. King has intuitively adopted the style of the old fashioned Negro Baptist preacher and transformed it into a new art form; he has, indeed, restored oratory to its place among the arts. Second, he communicates Negro aspirations to white America more effectively than anyone else. His religious terminology and manipulation of the Christian symbols of love and non-resistance are partly responsible for his appeal among whites. To talk in terms of Christianity, love, nonviolence is reassuring to the mentality of white America. At the same time, the very superficialities of his philosophy—that rich and eclectic amalgam of Jesus, Hegel, Gandhi and others as outlined in his *Stride Toward Freedom*—makes him appear intellectually profound to the superficially educated middle class white American. Actually, if he were a truly profound religious thinker, like Tillich or Niebuhr, his influence would of necessity be limited to a select audience. But by uttering moral clichés, the Christian pieties, in a magnificent display of oratory, King becomes enormously effective.

If his success with Negroes is largely due to the style of his utterance, his success with whites is a much more complicated matter. For one thing, he unerringly knows how to exploit to maximum effectiveness their growing feeling of guilt. King, of course, is not unique in attaining fame and popularity among whites through playing upon their guilt feelings. James Baldwin is the most conspicuous example of a man who has achieved success with this formula. The incredible fascination which the Black Muslims have for white people, and the posthumous near-sanctification of Malcolm X by many naive whites (in addition to many Negroes whose motivations are, of course, very different), must in large part be attributed to the same source. But King goes beyond this. With intuitive, but extraordinary skill, he not only castigates whites for their sins but, in contrast to angry young writers like Baldwin, he explicitly states his belief in their salvation. Not only will direct action bring fulfillment of the "American Dream" to Negroes but the Negroes' use of direct action will help whites to live up to their Christian and democratic values; it will purify, cleanse and heal the sickness in white society. Whites will benefit as well as Negroes. He has faith that the white man will redeem himself. Negroes must not hate whites, but love them. In this manner, King first arouses the guilt feelings of whites, and then relieves them—though always leaving the lingering feeling in his white listeners that they should support his nonviolent crusade. Like a Greek tragedy, King's performance provides an extraordinary catharsis for the white listener.

King thus gives white men the feeling that he is their good friend, that he poses no threat to them. It is interesting to note that this was the same feeling white men received from Booker T. Washington, the noted early 20th Century accommodator. Both men stressed their faith in the white man; both expressed the belief that the white man could be brought to accord Negroes their rights. Both stressed the importance of whites recognizing the rights of Negroes for the moral health and well-being of white society. Like King, Washington had an extraordinary following among whites. Like King, Washington symbolized for most whites the whole program of Negro advancement. While there are important similarities in the functioning of both men vis-à-vis the community, needless to say, in most respects, their philosophies are in disagreement.

It is not surprising, therefore, to find that King is the recipient of contributions from organizations and individuals who fail to eradicate evidence of prejudice in their own backyards. For example, certain liberal trade union leaders who are philosophically committed to full racial equality, who feel the need to identify their organizations with the cause of militant civil rights, although they are unable to defeat racist elements in their unions, contribute hundreds of thousands of dollars to King's Southern Christian Leadership Conference (SCLC). One might attribute this phenomenon to the fact that SCLC works in the South rather than the North, but this is true also for SNCC which does not benefit similarly from union treasuries. And the fact is that ever since the college students started their sit-ins in 1960, it is SNCC which has been the real spearhead of direct action in most of the South, and has performed the lion's share of work in local communities, while SCLC has received most of the publicity and most of the money. However, while King provides a verbal catharsis for whites, leaving them feeling purified and comfortable, SNCC's uncompromising militancy makes whites feel less comfortable and less beneficient.

(The above is not to suggest that SNCC and SCLC are responsible for all, or nearly all, the direct action in the South. The NAACP has actively engaged in direct action, especially in Savannah under the leadership of W. W. Law, in South Carolina under I. DeQuincy Newman, and in Clarksdale, Mississippi, under Aaron Henry. The work of CORE—including most of the direct action in Louisiana, much of the nonviolent work in Florida and Mississippi, the famous Freedom Ride of 1961—has been most important. In addition, one should note the work of SCLC affiliates, such as those in Lynchburg, Virginia, led by Reverend Virgil Wood; in Birmingham led by Reverend Fred Shuttlesworth, and in Savannah, by Hosea Williams.

(There are other reasons for SNCC's lesser popularity with whites than King's. These are connected with the great changes that have occurred in SNCC since it was founded in 1960, changes reflected in the half-jocular epigram circulating in SNCC circles that the Student Nonviolent Coordinating Committee has now become the "Non-Student Violent Non-Coordinating Committee." The point is, however, that even when SNCC thrilled the nation in 1960–1961 with the student sit-ins that swept the South, it did not enjoy the popularity and financial support accorded to King.)

King's very tendencies toward compromise and caution, his willingness to negotiate and bargain with White House emissaries, his hesitancy to risk the precipitation of mass violence upon demonstrators, further endear him to whites. He appears to them a "responsible" and "moderate" man. To militant activists, King's failure to march past the State Police on that famous Tuesday morning outside Selma indicated either a lack of courage, or a desire to advance himself by currying Presidential favor. But King's shrinking from a possible bloodbath, his accession to the entreaties of the political Establishment, his acceptance of face-saving compromise in this, as in other instances, are fundamental to the particular role he is playing, and essential for achieving and sustaining his image as a leader of heroic moral stature in the eyes of white men. His caution and compromise keep open the channels of communication between the activists and the majority of the white community. In brief: King makes the nonviolent direct action movement respectable.

Of course, many, if not most, activists reject the notion that the movement should be made respectable. Yet, American history shows that for any reform movement to succeed, it must attain respectability. It must attract moderates, even conservatives, to its ranks. The March on Washington made direct action respectable; Selma made it fashionable. More than any other force, it is Martin Luther King who impressed the civil rights revolution on the American conscience and is attracting that great middle body of American public opinion to its support. It is this revolution of conscience that will undoubtedly lead fairly soon to the elimination of all violations of Negroes' constitutional rights, thereby creating the conditions for the economic and social changes that are necessary if we are to achieve full racial equality. This is not to deny the dangers to the civil rights movement in becoming respectable. Respectability, for example, encourages the attempts of political machines to capture civil rights organizations. Respectability can also become an end in itself, thereby dulling the cutting edge of its protest activities. Indeed, the history of the labor movement reveals how attaining respectability can produce loss of original purpose and character. These perils, however, do not contradict the importance of achieving respectability—even a degree of modishness—if racial equality is ever to be realized.

There is another side to the picture: King would be neither respected nor respectable if there were not more militant activists on his left, engaged in more radical forms of direct action. Without CORE and, especially, SNCC, King would appear "radical" and "irresponsible" rather than "moderate" and "respectable."

King occupies a position of strategic importance as the "vital center" within the civil rights movement. Though he has lieutenants who are far more militant and "radical" than he is, SCLC acts, in effect, as the most cautious, deliberate and "conservative" of the direct action groups because of King's leadership. This permits King and the SCLC to function—almost certainly unintentionally—not only as an organ of communication with the Establishment and majority white public opinion, but as something of a bridge between the activist and more traditionalist or "conservative" civil rights groups, as well. For example, it appears unlikely that the Urban League and NAACP, which supplied most of the funds, would have participated in the 1963 March on Washington if King had not done so. Because King agreed to go along with SNCC and CORE, the NAACP found it mandatory to join if it was to maintain its image as a protest organization. King's identification with the March was also essential for securing the support of large numbers of white clergymen and their moderate followers. The March was the brainchild of the civil rights movement's ablest strategist and tactician, Bayard Rustin, and the call was issued by A. Philip Randolph. But it would have been a minor episode in the history of the civil rights movement without King's support.

Yet curiously enough, despite his charisma and international reputation, King thus far has been more a symbol than a power in the civil rights movement. Indeed his strength in the movement has derived less from an organizational base than from his symbolic role. Seven or eight years ago, one might have expected King to achieve an organizationally dominant position in the civil rights movement, at least in its direct action wing. The fact is that in the period after the Montgomery bus boycott, King developed no program and, it is generally agreed, revealed himself as an ineffective administrator who failed to capitalize upon his popularity among Negroes. In 1957, he founded SCLC to coordinate the work of direct action groups that had sprung up in Southern cities. Composed of autonomous units, usually led by Baptist ministers, SCLC does not appear to have developed an overall sense of direction or a program of real breadth and scope. Although the leaders of SCLC affiliates became the race leaders in their communities—displacing the established local conservative leadership of teachers, old-line ministers, businessmen —it is hard for an observer (who admittedly has not been close to SCLC) to perceive exactly what SCLC did before the 1960's except to advance the image and personality of King. King appeared not to direct but to float with the tide of militant direct action. For example, King did not supply the initiative for the bus boycott in Montgomery, but was pushed into the leadership by others, as he himself records in *Stride Toward Freedom*. Similarly, in the late Fifties and early Sixties, he appeared to let events shape his course. In the last two years, this has changed, but until the Birmingham demonstrations of 1963, King epitomized conservative militancy.

SCLC under King's leadership called the Raleigh Conference of April 1960 which gave birth to SNCC. Incredibly, within a year, the SNCC youth had lost their faith in the man they now satirically call "De Lawd," and had struck out on their own independent path. By that time, the Spring of 1961, King's power in the Southern direct action movement had been further curtailed by CORE's stunning Freedom Ride to Alabama and Mississippi.

The limited extent of King's actual power in the civil rights movement was illustrated by the efforts made to invest King with the qualities of a Messiah during the recent ceremonies at the State Capitol in Montgomery. Reverend Abernathy's constant iteration of the theme that King is "our Leader," the Moses of the race, chosen by God, and King's claim that he originated the nonviolent direct action movement at Montgomery a decade ago, are all assertions that would have been superfluous if King's power in the movement was very substantial.

It is, of course, no easier today than it has been in the past few years to predict the course of the Negro protest movement, and it is always possible that the current state of affairs may change quite abruptly. It is conceivable that the ambitious program that SCLC is now projecting—both in Southern voter registration and in Northern urban direct action programs—may give it a position of commanding importance in civil rights. As a result of the recent demonstrations in Selma and Montgomery, King's prestige is now higher than ever. At the same time, the nature of CORE and NAACP direct action activities at the moment has created a programmatic vacuum which SCLC may be able to exploit. Given this convergence of circumstances, SCLC leaders may be able to establish an organizational base upon which to build a power commensurate with the symbolic position of their president.

It is indeed fortunate that King has not obtained a predominance of power in the movement commensurate with his prestige. For today, as in the past, a diversity of approaches is necessary. Needed in the movement are those who view the struggle chiefly as a conflict situation, in which the power of demonstrations, the power of Negroes, will force recognition of the race's humanity and citizenship rights, and the achievement of equality. Equally needed are those who see the movement's strategy to be chiefly one of capitalizing on the basic consensus of values in American society by awakening the conscience of the white man to the contradiction between his professions and the facts of discrimination. And just as necessary to the movement as both of these are those who operate skillfully, recognizing and yet exploiting the deeply held American belief that compromise among competing interest groups is the best *modus operandi* in public life.

King is unique in that he maintains a delicate balance among all three of these basic strategy assumptions. The traditional approaches of the Urban League (conciliation of the white businessmen) and of the NAACP (most pre-eminently appeals to the courts and appeals to the sense of fair play in the American public), basically attempted to exploit the consensus in American values. It would of course be a gross oversimplification to say that the Urban League and NAACP strategies are based simply on attempting to capitalize on the consensus of values, while SNCC and CORE act simply as if the situation were purely a conflict situation. Implicit in the actions of all civil rights organizations are both sets of assumptions—even where people are not conscious of the theoretical assumptions under which, in effect, they operate. The NAACP especially encompasses a broad spectrum of strategies and types of activities, ranging from time-tested court procedures to militant direct action. Sophisticated CORE activists know very well when a judicious compromise is necessary or valuable. But I hold that King is in the middle, acting in effect as if he were basing his strategy upon all three assumptions described above. He maintains a delicate balance between a purely moral appeal and a militant display of power. He talks of the power of the bodies of Negro demonstrators in the streets, but unlike CORE and SNCC activists, he accepts compromises at times that consist of token improvements, and calls them impressive victories. More than any of the other groups, King and SCLC can, up to this point at least, be described as exploiting all three tactical assumptions to an approximately equal degree. King's continued success, I suspect, will depend to a considerable degree upon the difficult feat of maintaining his position at the "vital center" of the civil rights movement.

Viewed from another angle King's failure to achieve a position of power on a level with his prestige is fortunate because rivalries between personalities and organizations remain an essential ingredient of the dynamics of the movement and a precondition for its success as each current tries to outdo the others in effectiveness and in maintaining a good public image. Without this competitive stimulus, the civil rights revolution would slow down.

I have already noted that one of King's functions is to serve as a bridge between the militant and conservative wings of the movement. In addition, by gathering support for SCLC, he generates wider support for CORE and SNCC, as well. The most striking example is the recent series of demonstrations in Selma where SNCC had been operating for nearly two years with only moderate amounts of publicity before King chose that city as his own target. As usual, it was King's presence that focused world attention on Selma. In the course of subsequent events, the rift between King and SNCC assumed the proportions of a serious conflict. Yet people who otherwise would have been hesitant to support SNCC's efforts, even people who had become disillusioned with certain aspects of SNCC's policies during the Mississippi Summer Project of 1964, were drawn to demonstrate in Selma and Montgomery. Moreover, although King received the major share of credit for the demonstrations, it seems likely that in the controversy between King and SNCC, the latter emerged with more power and influence in the civil rights movement than ever before. It is now possible that the Administration will, in the future, regard SNCC as more of a force to be reckoned with than it has heretofore.

Major dailies like the *New York Times* and the *Washington Post*, basically sympathetic to civil rights and racial equality, though more gradualist than the activist organizations, have congratulated the nation upon its good fortune in having a "responsible and moderate" leader like King at the head of the nonviolent action movement (though they overestimate his power and underestimate the symbolic nature of his role). It would be more appropriate to congratulate the civil rights movement for *its* good fortune in having as its symbolic leader a man like King. The fact that he has more prestige than power; the fact that he not only criticizes whites but explicitly believes in their redemption; his ability to arouse creative tension combined with his inclination to shrink from carrying demonstrations to the point where major bloodshed might result; the intellectual simplicity of his philosophy; his tendency to compromise and exert caution, even his seeming indecisiveness on some occasions; the sparing use he makes of going to or staying in jail himself; his friendship with the man in the White House—all are essential to the role he plays, and invaluable for the success of the movement. It is well, of course, that not all civil rights leaders are cut of the same cloth—that King is unique among them. Like Randolph, who functions very differently, King is really an institution. His most important function, I believe, is that of effectively communicating Negro aspirations to white people, of making nonviolent direct action respectable in the eyes of the white majority. In addition, he functions within the movement by occupying a vital center position between its "conservative" and "radical" wings, by symbolizing direct action and attracting people to participate in it without dominating either the civil rights movement or its activist wing. Viewed in this context, traits that many activists criticize in King actually function not as sources of weakness, but as the foundations of his strength.

Gary T. Marx

RELIGION: OPIATE OR INSPIRATION OF
CIVIL RIGHTS MILITANCY
AMONG NEGROES?*

*In an earlier selection dealing with slave revolts, the historian
Vincent Harding discussed the dual role religion has played
in shaping Negro responses—toward accommodation on the one
hand and, less frequently, toward protest and revolt on the other.
The same paradox is evident in the civil rights movement of the
1960's, as the sociologist Gary T. Marx demonstrates.*

Let justice roll down like waters, and righteousness like a mighty stream.
AMOS 5:24

*But God . . . is white. And if his love was so great, and if he loved all his chil-
dren, why were we the blacks, cast down so far?*
JAMES BALDWIN

T HE relationship between religion and political radicalism is a confusing
one. On the one hand, established religious institutions have generally had a
stake in the status quo and hence have supported conservatism. Furthermore,
with the masses having an otherworldly orientation, religious zeal, particularly
as expressed in the more fundamentalist branches of Christianity, has been

Gary T. Marx, "Religion: Opiate or Inspiration of Civil Rights Militancy Among
Negroes?" *American Sociological Review*, XXXII (February, 1967), pp. 64–72. Reprinted with the permission of Gary T. Marx and the American Sociological Association.
* Revision of paper read at the annual meeting of the American Sociological Association, August, 1966. This paper may be identified as publication A-72 of the Survey Research Center, University of California, Berkeley. I am grateful to Gertrude J. Selznick
and Stephen Steinberg for their work on the early phase of this project, and to the Anti-
Defamation League for support.

seen as an alternative to the development of political radicalism. On the other hand, as the source of universal humanistic values and the strength that can come from believing one is carrying out God's will in political matters, religion has occasionally played a strong positive role in movements for radical social change.

This dual role of religion is clearly indicated in the case of the American Negro and race protest. Slaves are said to have been first brought to this country on the "good ship Jesus Christ." [1] While there was occasional controversy over the effect that religion had on them it appears that most slave-owners eventually came to view supervised religion as an effective means of social control. Stampp, in commenting on the effect of religion notes:

> ... through religious instruction the bondsmen learned that slavery had divine sanction, that insolence was as much an offense against God as against the temporal master. They received the Biblical command that servants should obey their masters, and they heard of the punishments awaiting the disobedient slave in the hereafter. They heard, too, that eternal salvation would be their reward for faithful service ... [2]

In discussing the period after the Civil War, Myrdal states that "... under the pressure of political reaction, the Negro church in the South came to have much the same role as it did before the Civil War. Negro frustration was sublimated into emotionalism, and Negro hopes were fixed on the after world." [3] Many other analysts, in considering the consequences of Negro religion from the end of slavery until the early 1950's reached similar conclusions about the conservatizing effect of religion on race protest. [4]

[1] Louis Lomax, *When the Word is Given*, New York: New American Library, 1964, p. 34. It has often been noted that when the missionaries came to Africa they had the Bible and the people had the land. When the missionaries left, they had the land and the Africans had the Bible.

[2] Kenneth Stampp, *The Peculiar Institution*, New York: Alfred A. Knopf, 1956, p. 158.

[3] Gunnar Myrdal et al., *An American Dilemma*, New York: Harper, 1944, pp. 851–853. About the North he notes that the church remained far more independent "but on the whole even the Northern Negro church has remained a conservative institution with its interests directly upon other-worldly matters and has largely ignored the practical problems of the Negro's fate in this world."

[4] For example Dollard reports that "religion can be seen as a mechanism for the social control of Negroes" and that planters have always welcomed the building of a Negro church on the plantation but looked with less favor upon the building of a school. John Dollard, *Caste and Class in a Southern Town*, Garden City: Doubleday Anchor, 1957, p. 248. A few of the many others reaching similar conclusions are, Benjamin E. Mays and J. W. Nicholson, *The Negro's Church*, New York: Institute of Social and Religious Research, 1933; Hortense Powdermaker, *After Freedom*, New York: Viking Press, 1939, p. 285; Charles Johnson, *Growing Up in the Black Belt*, Washington, D.C.: American Council of Education, 1941, pp. 135–136; Horace Drake and St. Clair Cayton, *Black Metropolis*, New York: Harper and Row, 1962, pp. 424–429; George Simpson and Milton Yinger, *Racial and Cultural Minorities*, New York: Harper, rev. ed., 1958, pp.

However, the effect of religion on race protest throughout American history has by no means been exclusively in one direction. While many Negroes were no doubt seriously singing about chariots in the sky, Negro preachers such as Denmark Vesey and Nat Turner and the religiously inspired abolitionists were actively fighting slavery in their own way. All Negro churches first came into being as protest organizations and later some served as meeting places where protest strategy was planned, or as stations on the underground railroad. The richness of protest symbolism in Negro spirituals and sermons has often been noted. Beyond this symbolic role, as a totally Negro institution, the church brought together in privacy people with a shared problem. It was from the church experience that many leaders were exposed to a broad range of ideas legitimizing protest and obtained the savoir faire, self-confidence, and organizational experience needed to challege an oppressive system. A recent commentator states that the slave churches were "the nucleus of the Negro protest" and another that "in religion Negro leaders had begun to find sanction and support for their movements of protest more than 150 years ago." [5]

Differing perceptions of the varied consequences religion may have on protest have continued to the present time. While there has been very little in the way of empirical research on the effect of the Negro church on protest,[6] the literature of race relations is rich with impressionistic statements which generally contradict each other about how the church either encourages and is the source of race protest or inhibits and retards its development. For

582–587. In a more general context this social control consequence of religion has of course been noted throughout history from Plato to Montesquieu to Marx to Nietzsche to Freud to contemporary social theorists.

[5] Daniel Thompson, "The Rise of Negro Protest," *Annals of the American Academy of Political and Social Science*, 357 (January, 1965).

[6] The empirical evidence is quite limited. The few studies that have been done have focused on the Negro minister. Thompson notes that in New Orleans Negro ministers constitute the largest segment of the Negro leadership class (a grouping which is not necessarily the same as "protest leaders") but that "The vast majority of ministers are primarily interested in their pastoral role ... their sermons are essentially biblical, dealing only tangentially with social issues." Daniel Thompson, *The Negro Leadership Class*, Englewood Cliffs, New Jersey: Prentice-Hall, 1963, pp. 34–35. Studies of the Negro ministry in Detroit and Richmond, California also stress that only a small fraction of Negro clergymen show any active concern with the civil rights struggle. R. L. Johnstone, *Militant and Conservative Community Leadership Among Negro Clergymen*, Ph.D. dissertation, University of Michigan, Ann Arbor, 1963, and J. Bloom, *The Negro Church and the Movement for Equality*, M.A. thesis, University of California, Berkeley, Department of Sociology, 1966.

It is worthy of mention that, although the number of cases was small, the Negro ministers in our sample had the lowest percentage militant of any occupational group. With respect to the sons of clergymen, the situation seems somewhat different. While the myth of the preacher's son gone bad is almost a part of American folklore, one would think that a comparable myth might develop within the Negro community—that of the preacher's son gone radical. Malcolm X, James Baldwin, A. Philip Randolph, Martin Luther King, James Farmer, Adam Clayton Powell, Elijah Muhammad, and a number of others had clergymen as fathers. To be taken into consideration is that clergymen make up a relatively larger segment of the Negro middle than of the white middle class.

example, two observers note, "as primitive evangelism gave way to a more sophisticated social consciousness, the church became the spearhead of Negro protest in the deep South," [7] while another indicates "the Negro church is a sleeping giant. In civil rights participation its feet are hardly wet." [8] A civil rights activist, himself a clergyman, states: "... the church today is central to the movement ... if there had been no Negro church, there would have been no civil rights movement today." [9] On the other hand, a sociologist, commenting on the more involved higher status ministers, notes: "... middle class Negro clergymen in the cities of the South generally advocated cautious gradualism in race activities until the mid-1950's when there was an upsurge of protest sentiment among urban Negroes ... but most of them [ministers] did not embrace the more vigorous techniques of protest until other leaders took the initiative and gained widespread support." [10] Another sociologist states, "Whatever their previous conservative stance has been, the churches have now become 'spearheads of reform.'" [11] Still another indicates: "... the Negro church is particularly culpable for its general lack of concern for the moral and social problems of the community ... it has been accommodating. Fostering indulgence in religious sentimentality, and riveting the attention of the masses on the bounties of a hereafter, the Negro church remains a refuge, and escape from the cruel realities of the here and now." [12]

Thus one faces opposing views, or at best ambiguity, in contemplating the current effect of religion. The opiating consequences of religion are all too well known as is the fact that the segregated church is durable and offers some advantages to clergy and members that might be denied them in a more integrated society. On the other hand, the prominent role of the Negro church in supplying much of the ideology of the movement, many of its foremost leaders, and an institution around which struggle might be organized—particularly in the South—can hardly be denied. It would appear from the bombings of churches and the writings of Martin Luther King and other religiously

[7] Jane Record and Wilson Record, "Ideological Forces and the Negro Protest," *Annals, op. cit.,* p. 92.

[8] G. Booker, *Black Man's America,* Englewood Cliffs, N.J.: Prentice-Hall, 1964, p. 111.

[9] Rev. W. T. Walker, as quoted in William Brink and Louis Harris, *The Negro Revolution in America,* New York: Simon and Schuster, 1964, p. 103.

[10] N. Glenn, "Negro Religion in the U.S." in L. Schneider, *Religion, Culture and Society,* New York: John Wiley, 1964.

[11] Joseph Fichter, "American Religion and the Negro," *Daedalus* (Fall, 1965), p. 1087.

[12] E. U. Essien-Udom, *Black Nationalism,* New York: Dell Publishing Co., 1962, p. 358.

Many other examples of contradictory statements could be offered, sometimes even in the same volume. For example, Carleton Lee stresses the importance of religion for protest while Rayford Logan sees the Negro pastor as an instrument of the white power structure (in a book published to commemorate 100 years of emancipation). Carleton Lee, "Religious Roots of Negro Protest," and Rayford Logan, "Educational Changes Affecting American Negroes," both in Arnold Rose, *Assuring Freedom to the Free,* Detroit: Wayne University Press, 1964.

inspired activists that for many, religion and protest are closely linked.

Part of this dilemma may lie in the distinction between the church as an institution in its totality and particular individual churches within it, and the further distinctions among different types of individual religious concern. This paper is concerned with the latter subject; it is an inquiry into the relationship between religiosity and response to the civil rights struggle. It first considers how religious denomination affects militancy, and then how various measures of religiosity, taken separately and together, are related to civil rights concern. The question is then asked of those classified as "very religious" and "quite religious," how an "otherworldly orientation"—as opposed to a "temporal" one—affects militancy.

In a nationwide study of Negroes living in metropolitan areas of the United States, a number of questions were asked about religious behavior and beliefs as well as about the civil rights struggle.[13] Seven of the questions dealing with civil rights protest have been combined into an index of conventional militancy.[14] Built into this index are a number of dimensions of racial protest such as impatience over the speed of integration, opposition to discrimination in public facilities and the sale of property, perception of barriers to Negro advancement, support of civil rights demonstrations, and expressed willingness to take part in a demonstration. Those giving the militant response to five or more of the questions are considered militant, those giving such a response to three or four of the questions, moderate, and fewer than three, conservative.[15]

DENOMINATION

It has long been known that the more fundamentalist sects such as the Holiness groups and the Jehovah's Witnesses are relatively uninterested in

[13] This survey was carried out in 1964 by the Survey Research Center, University of California, Berkeley. A non-Southern metropolitan area probability sample was drawn as well as special area samples of Negroes living in New York City, Chicago, Atlanta and Birmingham. Since the results reported here are essentially the same for each of these areas, they are treated together. More than 90% of the interviews were done with Negro interviewers. Additional methodological details may be found in Gary Marx, *Protest and Prejudice: A Study of Belief in the Black Community*, New York: Harper & Row, forthcoming.

[14] Attention is directed to conventional militancy rather than to that of the Black Nationalist variety because a very small percentage of the sample offered strong and consistent support for Black Nationalism. As in studying support for the KKK, the Birch Society or the Communist Party, a representative sample of normal size is inadequate.

[15] Each of the items in the index was positively related to every other and the index showed a high degree of internal validity. The index also received external validation from a number of additional questions. For example, the percentage belonging to a civil rights organization went from zero among those lowest in militancy to 38 percent for those who were highest, and the percentage thinking that civil rights demonstrations had helped a great deal increased from 23 percent to 58 percent. Those thinking that the police treated Negroes very well decreased from 35 percent to only 2 percent among those highest in militancy.

movements for secular political change.[16] Such transvaluational movements with their otherworldly orientation and their promise that the last shall be first in the great beyond, are said to solace the individual for his lowly status in this world and to divert concern away from efforts at collective social change which might be brought about by man. While only a minority of Negroes actually belong to such groups, the proportion is higher than among whites. Negro literature is rich in descriptions of these churches and their position on race protest.

In Table 1 it can be seen that those belonging to sects are the least likely to be militant; they are followed by those in predominantly Negro denominations. Ironically those individuals in largely white denomination (Episcopalian, Presbyterian, United Church of Christ, and Roman Catholic) are those most likely to be militant, in spite of the perhaps greater civil rights activism of the Negro denominations. This pattern emerged even when social class was held constant.

In their comments members of the less conventional religious groups clearly expressed the classical attitude of their sects toward participation in the

Table 1

PROPORTION MILITANT (%) BY DENOMINATION *

Denomination	% Militant
Episcopalian	46 (24)
United Church of Christ	42 (12)
Presbyterian	40 (25)
Catholic	40 (109)
Methodist	34 (142)
Baptist	32 (142)
Sects and Cults	20 (106)

* 25 respondents are not shown in this article because they did not specify a denomination, or belonged to a non-Christian religious group, or other small Christian group.

politics of the secular world. For example, an Evangelist in the Midwest said, "I don't believe in participating in politics. My church don't vote—they just depends on the plans of God." And an automobile serviceman in Philadelphia stated, "I as a Jehovah's Witness, cannot express things involving the race issue." A housewife in the Far West ventured, "In my religion we do not approve of anything except living like it says in the Bible; demonstrations mean calling attention to you and it's sinful."

The finding that persons who belong to sects are less likely to be militant than the non-sect members is to be expected; clearly this type of religious

[16] Liston Pope, *Millhands and Preachers*, New Haven: Yale University Press, 1942, p. 137. J. Milton Yinger, *Religion, Society, and the Individual*, New York: The Macmillan Company, 1957, pp. 170–173.

involvement seems an alternative for most people to the development of radicalism. But what of the religious style of those in the more conventional churches which may put relatively less stress on the after-life and encourage various forms of secular participation? Are the more religiously inclined within these groups also less likely to be militant?

RELIGIOSITY

The present study measured several dimensions of religious involvement. Those interviewed were asked how important religion was to them, several questions about orthodoxy of belief, and how frequently they attended worship service.[17] Even with the sects excluded, irrespective of the dimension of religiosity considered, the greater the religiosity the lower the percentage militant. (See Tables 2, 3 and 4.) For example, militancy increases consistently

TABLE 2

MILITANCY BY SUBJECTIVE IMPORTANCE ASSIGNED TO RELIGION *

Importance	% Militant
Extremely important	29 (668)
Somewhat important	39 (195)
Fairly important	48 (96)
Not too important	56 (18)
Not at all important	62 (13)

     * Sects are excluded here and in all subsequent tables.

from a low of only 29 percent among those who said religion was "extremely important" to a high of 62 percent for those who indicated that religion was "not at all important" to them. For those very high in orthodoxy (having no doubt about the existence of God or the devil) 27 percent were militant while for those totally rejecting these ideas 54 percent indicated great concern over civil rights. Militancy also varies inversely with frequency of attendance at worship service.[18]

    [17] These dimensions and several others are suggested by Charles Y. Glock in "On the Study of Religious Commitment," *Religious Education Research Supplement,* 57 (July–August, 1962), pp. 98–100. For another measure of religious involvement, the number of church organizations belonged to, the same inverse relationship was noted.
    [18] There is a popular stereotype that Negroes are a "religious people." Social science research has shown that they are "over-churched" relative to whites, i.e., the ratio of Negro churches to the size of the Negro population is greater than the same ratio for whites. Using data from a nationwide survey of whites, by Gertrude Selznick and Stephen Steinberg, some comparison of the religiosity of Negroes and whites was possible. When these various dimensions of religiosity were examined, with the effect of education and region held constant, Negroes appeared as significantly more religious *only* with respect to the subjective importance assigned to religion. In the North, whites

Each of these items was strongly related to every other; when taken together they help us to better characterize religiosity. Accordingly they have

TABLE 3

MILITANCY BY ORTHODOXY

Orthodoxy	% Militant
Very high	27 (414)
High	34 (333)
Medium	39 (144)
Low	47 (68)
Very low	54 (35)

been combined into an overall measure of religiosity. Those scored as "very religious" in terms of this index attended church at least once a week, felt that religion was extremely important to them, and had no doubts about the existence of God and the devil. For progressively lower values of the index, frequency of church attendance, the importance of religion, and acceptance of the belief items decline consistently until, for those scored "not at all religious," church is rarely if ever attended, religion is not considered personally important and the belief items are rejected.

Using this measure for non-sect members, civil rights militancy increases

TABLE 4

MILITANCY BY FREQUENCY OF ATTENDANCE AT WORSHIP SERVICES

Frequency	% Militant
More than once a week	27 (81)
Once a week	32 (311)
Once a month or more but less than once a week	34 (354)
Less than once a month	38 (240)

from a low of 26 percent for those labeled "very religious" to 30 percent for the "somewhat religious" to 45 percent for those "not very religious" and up to a high of 70 percent for those "not at all religious." [19] (Table 5.)

---

were more likely to attend church at least once a week than were Negroes; while in the South rates of attendance were the same. About the same percentage of both groups had no doubts about the existence of God. While Negroes were more likely to be sure about the existence of a devil, whites, surprisingly, were more likely to be sure about a life beyond death. Clearly, then, any assertions about the greater religiosity of Negroes relative to whites are unwarranted unless one specifies the dimensions of religiosity.

[19] When the sects are included in these tables the results are the same. The sects have been excluded because they offer almost no variation to be analyzed with respect to the independent variable. Since virtually all of the sect members scored as either

GARY T. MARX

TABLE 5

MILITANCY BY RELIGIOSITY

Religiosity	Very Religious	Somewhat Religious	Not Very Religious	Not at All Religious
% Militant	26	30	45	70
N	(230)	(523)	(195)	(36)

Religiosity and militancy are also related to age, sex, education, religious denomination and region of the country. The older, and less educated, women, Southerners and those in Negro denominations are more likely to be religious and to have lower percentages scoring as militant. Thus it is possible that the relationship observed is simply a consequence of the fact that both religiosity and militancy are related to some third factor. In Table 6 it can be seen, however, that, even among those in the North, the younger, male, more educated and those affiliated with predominantly white denominations, the greater the religiosity the less the militancy.

The incompatibility between piety and protest shown in these data becomes even more evident when considered in light of comments offered by the respondents. Many religious people hold beliefs which clearly inhibit race protest. For a few there was the notion that segregation and a lowly status for Negroes was somehow God's will and not for man to question. Thus a housewife in South Bend, Indiana, in saying that civil rights demonstrations had hurt Negroes, added: "God is the Creator of everything. We don't know why we all dark-skinned. We should try to put forth the effort to do what God wants and not question." [20]

A Negro spiritual contains the lines "I'm gonna wait upon the Lord till my change comes." For our respondents a more frequently stated belief stressed that God as the absolute controller of the universe would bring about change in his own way and at his own time, rather than expressing segregation as God's will. In indicating her unwillingness to take part in a civil rights demonstration, a Detroit housewife said, "I don't go for demonstrations. I believe that God created all men equal and at His appointed time He will give every man his portion, no one can hinder it." And in response to a question about whether or not the government in Washington was

"very religious" or "somewhat religious," it is hardly possible to measure the effect of their religious involvement on protest attitudes. In addition the import of the relationships shown in these tables is considerably strengthened when it is demonstrated that religious involvement inhibits militancy even when the most religious and least militant group, the sects, are excluded.

[20] Albert Cardinal Meyer notes that the Catholic Bishops of the U.S. said in their statement of 1958: "The heart of the race question is moral and religious." "Interracial Justice and Love," in M. Ahmann, ed., *Race Challenge to Religion*, Chicago: H. Regnery, 1963, p. 126. These data, viewed from the perspective of the activist seeking to motivate Negroes on behalf of the civil rights struggle, suggest that this statement has a meaning which Their Excellencies no doubt did not intend.

TABLE 6

PROPORTION MILITANT (%) BY RELIGIOSITY, FOR EDUCATION,
AGE, REGION, SEX, AND DENOMINATION

	Very Religious	Somewhat Religious	Not Very Religious	Not at All Religious
Education				
Grammar school	17 (108)	22 (201)	31 (42)	50 (2)
High school	34 (96)	32 (270)	45 (119)	58 (19)
College	38 (26)	48 (61)	59 (34)	87 (15)
Age				
18–29	33 (30)	37 (126)	44 (62)	62 (13)
30–44	30 (53)	34 (180)	48 (83)	74 (19)
45–59	25 (71)	27 (131)	45 (33)	50 (2)
60+	22 (76)	18 (95)	33 (15)	100 (2)
Region				
Non-South	30 (123)	34 (331)	47 (159)	70 (33)
South	22 (107)	23 (202)	33 (36)	66 (3)
Sex				
Men	28 (83)	33 (220)	44 (123)	72 (29)
Women	26 (147)	28 (313)	46 (72)	57 (7)
Denomination				
Episcopalian, Presbyterian, United Church of Christ	20 (15)	27 (26)	33 (15)	60 (5)
Catholic	13 (15)	39 (56)	36 (25)	77 (13)
Methodist	46 (24)	22 (83)	50 (32)	100 (2)
Baptist	25 (172)	29 (354)	45 (117)	53 (15)

pushing integration too slowly, a retired clerk in Atlanta said: "You can't hurry God. He has a certain time for this to take place. I don't know about Washington."

Others who desired integration more strongly and wanted immediate social change felt that (as Bob Dylan sings) God was on their side. Hence man need do nothing to help bring about change. Thus a worker in Cleveland, who was against having more civil rights demonstrations, said: "With God helping to fight our battle, I believe we can do with fewer demonstrations." And in response to a question about whether Negroes should spend more time praying and less time demonstrating, an Atlanta clergyman, who said "more time praying," added "praying is demonstrating." [21]

[21] A study of ministers in Richmond, California notes that, although almost all questioned were opposed to discrimination, very few had taken concrete action, in part because of their belief that God would take care of them. One minister noted, "I believe that if we all was as pure . . . as we ought to be, there would be no struggle. God will answer my prayer. If we just stay with God and have faith. *When Peter was up, did the people march to free him? No. He prayed, and God did something about it.*" (Bloom, *op. cit.*, italics added.)

RELIGION AMONG THE MILITANTS

Although the net effect of religion is clearly to inhibit attitudes of protest it is interesting to consider this relationship in the opposite direction, i.e., observe religiosity among those characterized as militant, moderate, and conservative with respect to the civil rights struggle. As civil rights concern increases, religiosity decreases. (Table 7.) Militants were twice as likely to

TABLE 7

RELIGIOSITY BY CIVIL RIGHTS MILITANCY

	Militants	Moderates	Conservatives
Very religious	18%	24%	28%
Somewhat religious	48	57	55
Not very religious	26	17	16
Not at all religious	8	2	1
Total	100	100	100
N	332	419	242

be scored "not very religious" or "not at all religious" as were conservatives. This table is also of interest because it shows that, even for the militants, a majority were scored either "very religious" or "somewhat religious." A study of Southern Negro CORE activists reports that less than one person in ten never attends church while almost six out of ten attended church weekly.[22] Clearly, for many, a religious orientation and a concern with racial protest are not mutually exclusive.

Given the active involvement of some churches, the singing of protest spirituals, and the ideology of the movement as it relates to Christian principles of love, equality, passive suffering,[23] and the appeal to a higher moral law, it would be surprising if there were only a few religious people among the militants.

A relevant question accordingly is: Among the religious, what are the intervening links which determine whether religion is related to an active concern with racial matters or has an opiating effect?[24] From the comments

[22] Ingeborg B. Powell, *Ideology and Strategy of Direct Action: A Study of the Congress of Radical Equality* (Unpublished Ph.D. dissertation, University of California, Berkeley, 1965), p. 207. In the North the same figure, four out of ten, report never attending as indicate that they go to church weekly.

[23] Non-violent resistance as it relates to Christianity's emphasis on suffering, sacrifice, and privation, is discussed by James W. Vander Zanden, "The Non-Violent Resistance Movement Against Segregation." *American Journal of Sociology*, 68 (March, 1963), pp. 544–550.

[24] Of course, a most relevant factor here is the position of the particular church that an individual is involved in. Unfortunately, it was difficult to obtain such information in a nationwide survey.

reported above it seemed that, for some, belief in a highly deterministic God inhibited race protest. Unfortunately the study did not measure beliefs about the role of God as against the role of men in the structuring of human affairs. However, a related variable was measured which would seem to have much relevance—the extent to which these religious people were concerned with the here and now as opposed to the after-life.

The classical indictment of religion from the Marxist perspective is that by focusing concern on a glorious after-life the evils of this life are ignored. Of course there are important differences among religious institutions and among individuals with respect to the importance given to otherworldly concerns. Christianity, as with most ideologies, contains within it, if not out-and-out contradictory themes, then certainly themes which are likely to be in tension with one another. In this fact, no doubt, lies part of the explanation of religion's varied consequences for protest. One important strand of Christianity stresses acceptance of one's lot and glorifies the after-life; [25] another is more concerned with the realization of Judeo-Christian values in the current life. King and his followers clearly represent this latter "social gospel" tradition.[26] Those with the type of temporal concern that King represents would be expected to be higher in militancy. A measure of temporal vs. otherworldly concern has been constructed. On the basis of two questions, those interviewed have been classified as having either an otherworldly or a temporal orientation.[27] The evidence is that religiosity and other-

[25] The Muslims have also made much of this theme within Christianity, and their militancy is certainly tied to a rejection of otherworldly religiosity. The Bible is referred to as a "poison book" and the leader of the Muslims states, "No one after death has ever gone any place but where they were carried. There is no heaven or hell other than on earth for you and me, and Jesus was no exception. His body is still . . . in Palestine and will remain there." (As quoted in C. Eric Lincoln, The Black Muslims in America, Boston: Beacon Press, 1961, p. 123).

However, while they reject the otherworldly theme, they nevertheless rely heavily on a deterministic Allah; according to E. U. Essien-Udom, this fact leads to political inactivity. He notes, "The attainment of black power is relegated to the intervention of "Almighty Allah" sometime in the future . . . Not unlike other religionists, the Muslims too may wait for all eternity for the coming of the Messiah, the predicted apocalypse in 1970 notwithstanding." E. U. Essien-Udom, Black Nationalism, op. cit., pp. 313–314.

[26] He states: "Any religion that professes to be concerned with the souls of men and is not concerned with the slums that damn them, the economic conditions that strangle them, and the social conditions that cripple them is a dry-as-dust religion." He further adds, perhaps in a concession, that "such a religion is the kind the Marxists like to see—an opiate of the people." Martin Luther King, Stride Toward Freedom, New York: Ballantine Books, 1958, pp. 28–29.

John Lewis, a former SNCC leader and once a Baptist Divinity student, is said to have peered through the bars of a Southern jail and said, "Think not that I am come to send peace on earth. I came not to send peace, but a sword." (Matthew 10:34.)

[27] The two items used in this index were: "How sure are you that there is a life beyond death?"; and "Negroes should spend more time praying and less time demonstrating." The latter item may seem somewhat circular when observed in relation to civil rights concern. However, this is precisely what militancy is all about. Still it would have been better to measure otherworldly vs. temporal concern in a less direct

worldly concern increase together. For example, almost 100 percent of the "not at all religious" group were considered to have a temporal orientation, but only 42 percent of the "very religious." (Table 8.) Those in predominantly

TABLE 8

PROPORTION (%) WITH TEMPORAL (AS AGAINST OTHERWORLDLY) CONCERN, BY RELIGIOSITY

Religiosity	% with Temporal Concern
Very religious	42 (225)
Somewhat religious	61 (531)
Not very religious	82 (193)
Not at all religious	98 (34)

white denominations were more likely to have a temporal orientation than those in all-black denominations.

Among the religious groups, if concern with the here and now is a relevant factor in overcoming the opiating effect of religion then it is to be anticipated that those considered to have a temporal religious orientation would be much higher in militancy than those scored as otherworldly. This is in fact the case. Among the otherworldly religious, only 16 percent were militant; this proportion increases to almost 40 percent among those considered "very religious" and "somewhat religious" who have a temporal religious outlook. (Table 9.) Thus it would seem that an important factor

TABLE 9

PROPORTION MILITANT (%) BY RELIGIOSITY AND TEMPORAL OR OTHERWORLDLY CONCERN

Concern	Very Religious	Somewhat Religious
Temporal	39 (95)	38 (325)
Otherworldly	15 (130)	17 (206)

in determining the effect of religion on protest attitudes is the nature of an individual's religious commitment. It is quite possible, for those with a temporal religious orientation, that—rather than the effect of religion being somehow neutralized (as in the case of militancy among the "not religious"

fashion; unfortunately, no other items were available. Because of this the data shown here must be interpreted with caution. However it does seem almost self-evident that civil rights protest which is religiously inspired is related to a temporal religious outlook.

groups)—their religious concern serves to inspire and sustain race protest. This religious inspiration can, of course, be clearly noted among some active civil rights participants.

CONCLUSION

The effect of religiosity on race protest depends on the type of religiosity involved. Past literature is rich in suggestions that the religiosity of the fundamentalist sects is an alternative to the development of political radicalism. This seems true in the case of race protest as well. However, in an overall sense even for those who belong to the more conventional churches, the greater the religious involvement, whether measured in terms of ritual activity, orthodoxy of religious belief, subjective importance of religion, or the three taken together, the lower the degree of militancy.

Among sect members and religious people with an otherworldly orientation, religion and race protest appear to be, if not mutually exclusive, then certainly what one observer has referred to as "mutually corrosive kinds of commitments." [28] Until such time as religion loosens its hold over these people or comes to embody to a greater extent the belief that man as well as God can bring about secular change, and focuses more on the here and now, religious involvement may be seen as an important factor working against the widespread radicalization of the Negro public.

However, it has also been noted that many militant people are nevertheless religious. When a distinction is made among the religious between the "otherworldly" and the "temporal," for many of the latter group, religion seems to facilitate or at least not to inhibit protest. For these people religion and race protest may be mutually supportive.

Thirty years ago Donald Young wrote: "One function which a minority religion may serve is that of reconciliation with inferior status and its discriminatory consequences . . . on the other hand, religious institutions may also develop in such a way as to be an incitement and support of revolt against inferior status." [29] The current civil rights struggle and the data observed here certainly suggest that this is the case. These contradictory consequences of religion are somewhat reconciled when one distinguishes among different segments of the Negro church and types of religious concern among individuals.

[28] Rodney Stark, "Class, Radicalism, and Religious Involvement," *American Sociological Review*, 29 (October, 1964), p. 703.

[29] Donald Young, *American Minority Peoples*, New York: Harper, 1937, p. 204.

These data are also consistent with Merton's statement that it is premature to conclude that "all religion everywhere has only the one consequence of making for mass apathy" and his insistence on recognizing the "multiple consequences" and "net balance of aggregate consequences" of a given institution such as religion. Robert Merton, *Social Theory and Social Structure*, Glencoe: Free Press, 1957, revised edition, p. 44.

James Q. Wilson

TWO NEGRO POLITICIANS:
AN INTERPRETATION

Several selections in this section have dealt with the rise of Negro voting in the South, and with the varieties of leaders in southern Negro communities. As the article by Fishel illustrates, Negroes in the North have been active politically for many years. Like southern leaders, politicians elected to office from the northern ghettos have displayed a broad range of styles.

James Q. Wilson, in an illuminating article discussing Congressmen William L. Dawson and Adam Clayton Powell, deals provocatively with two contrasting political styles. Though Wilson does not make the point, the material in his article implies that, despite their contrasting methods, both men were astute congressional operators who consolidated their personal positions of power, but did little to alleviate the fundamenal problems facing the black masses in their constituencies.

T HIS is an attempt to describe, and in part to account for, the differences between two powerful political leaders, whose constituencies are roughly similar. Although the two congressmen in question are well-known Negroes—Adam Clayton Powell, Jr. of New York and William L. Dawson of Chicago—the analysis of the character of their political life is not meant to explain their idiosyncratic features. It is hoped, rather, that these remarks will illuminate some of the central features of the role of any congressman. By choosing for study two men who, in many ways, are polar opposites but who at the same time share many of the same problems and resources, the contrasts

James Q. Wilson, "Two Negro Politicians: An Interpretation," *Midwest Journal of Politics*, IV (November, 1960), pp. 346–69. Reprinted by permission of the Wayne State University Press and James Q. Wilson. Copyright 1960 by Wayne State University Press.

between them can be made more vivid and the argument employed can be sketched in bold strokes.[1]

Powell and Dawson are the most famous Negro Democratic congressmen. The former was first elected in 1944, the latter in 1942. Both represent districts that are almost entirely Negro in composition, and which have within them both appalling slums and expensive homes and apartments. Both are relatively senior members of the House of Representatives. Dawson is the chairman of the House Government Operations Committee; Powell is the second-ranking Democrat on the Education and Labor Committee and is a sub-committee chairman on the Interior Committee. Both have received national publicity, Powell more than Dawson, and both are well-known to their colleagues. Both tend to support the Democratic leadership of the House fairly consistently. On "party votes" (i.e., votes which pit a majority of one party against a majority of the other party), neither Dawson nor Powell will as a rule vote against his party in more than two or three per cent of the cases. Neither Dawson nor Powell has an especially good record of voting participation in House roll calls. Although Dawson is better than Powell in most sessions, both are well below the average for the House as a whole. Powell has on occasion been among the very lowest—sometimes *the* lowest—in voting participation, and rarely averages higher than 50 per cent. Dawson has steadily increased his voting participation, rising from 38 per cent in 1947-48 to 83 per cent in 1958.[2]

The similarities between the two men are, however, superficial. The differences are profound. Each has a unique political style which transcends issues, roll calls, or personal fortunes. The one is an orator, the other an organizer; one is flamboyant, the other is conservative; one is militant on the race question, the other is moderate.[3] One seeks publicity and speaks almost always "on the record"; the other shuns publicity and speaks to interviewers only off the record. One is considered by most of his House colleagues to be demagogic and unreliable; the other has the confidence and respect of many influential congressmen. One raises the race issue on every occasion; the other goes out of his way to avoid discussing race or race questions. One is light-skinned, handsome, boyish, gregarious, fun-loving; the other is brown-skinned, aged, reserved, quiet. One spends his free time (of which he has a great deal) in world travel, entertaining, and night life; the other rarely

[1] This article is based on interview research conducted in Chicago, New York, and Washington, D.C., on Negro politics. For my larger findings, plus much of the detail which is omitted from this interpretative article, see my book, *Negro Politics* (Glencoe: The Free Press, 1960).

[2] See *Congressional Quarterly Almanac*, 1950 through 1958.

[3] On Powell, see Roi Ottley, *New World A'Coming* (Boston: Houghton Mifflin Co., 1943); David Hapgood, *The Purge That Failed: Tammany v. Powell* ("Case Studies in Practical Politics"; New York: Henry Holt & Co., 1959); Will Chasan, "Congressman Powell's Downhill Fight in Harlem," *Reporter*, 20 (July 10, 1958), 24. On Dawson, see John Madigan, "The Durable Mr. Dawson of Cook County, Illinois," *Reporter*, 18 (August 9, 1956), 9; Fletcher Martin and John Madigan, "The Boss of Bronzeville," *Chicago Magazine*, 1 (July, 1955), 22.

travels, devotes himself completely to politics, and leads a home life carefully screened by privacy and silence. The two most prominent Negro politicians are radically dissimilar, avoid each other's company, speak disparagingly of one another, and elicit the most violent attitudes of love and hate from their many friends and enemies.

An explanation can be offered that will both account for many of these differences and suggest something of interest about the relationship of any political leader to his organization and his constituents. This explanation will endeavor to show that Powell and Dawson are not simply two interesting and perhaps unique men, but that they are also political leaders who have created and who seek to maintain two important kinds of political organizations. The creation and maintenance of these organizations places certain constraints on the actions of the leaders. The leaders' political styles reflect these constraints. It will be necessary, to make this argument plausible, to describe how these organizations were built, the nature of the political systems of which they are part, the maintenance needs these organizations have, and the implications these needs have for the political style of the leader.

We will argue, first that the most important single factor in creating or modifying the political style of each leader is the character of the organization which supports the leader and the nature of the incentives which he must distribute to sustain it.[4] Each political leader acts so as to maintain the strength of his organization. The strength of the organization is measured in terms of the number and size of the contributions to it, the extent to which a single undisputed leadership can control it, and the extent to which it can attain its collective goal (in this case, the retention of political office). To maintain the flow of contributions (the time, money, and energies of organization workers and the votes of the electorate), incentives must be distributed by the leader. In the case of Powell, these are largely intangible (non-material or "ideal") incentives; in the case of Dawson, these are largely tangible or material.

The second argument will be that the character of the organization which the leader must maintain is largely determined by the nature of the local political system. The aspects of that system most relevant here include the size and composition of the political districts and the relative strength and unity of the city-wide political organization. The maintenance of a Negro political organization is intimately bound up with the maintenance of the political system of the community as a whole.

[4] Cf., Chester Barnard, *The Functions of the Executive* (Cambridge: Harvard University Press, 1938). I adopt here the standard methodological dodge of arguing, not that each leader in every case acts so as to sustain his organization, but that he acts *as if* this were his rule. My argument is an assumption, not a law; it is used to order data and give them meaning. The limitations of this assumption will be discussed at a later point. See also Max Weber on "ideal" and "material" benefits in *The Theory of Social and Economic Organization*, trans. A. H. Henderson and Talcott Parsons (Glencoe: The Free Press, 1947), pp. 407–12.

POWELL

Adam Clayton Powell, Jr., was not, until the summer of 1959, a member of the regular party organization in New York City. When Powell sought to enter Congress in 1944, Tammany was a weakened machine. Eleven years of rule by LaGuardia, the adoption of a new city charter, and the extension of civil service had left the Tiger in a state of chronic malnutrition. The organization was shot through with factions and internecine warfare, both in Harlem and elsewhere. Rival leaders made competing alliances, broke them, and made new ones. The strength of the Manhattan organization declined, and other forces—such as the Bronx organization of Edward Flynn —rose to power. Few, inside or outside the organization, could depend on machine discipline or machine voting strength. Other bases of political power had to be found by those who sought a permanent and rising career in politics. Powell found his in the pulpit. He built his organization and his political following from outside the city machine. Although he received the endorsement of Tammany when he first ran for Congress in 1944, and subsequently until 1958, he felt he could not rely on either that endorsement or the efforts of the workers in the regular organization. The base of support for Powell was and is the Abyssinian Baptist Church, a church of perhaps 10,000 members that has existed since 1808. It was the church of his father, who retired in 1937. It is independent of any larger organization, and financially self-sustaining. In addition to the church, Powell was co-editor of a Harlem weekly, the *People's Voice*. In the stormy Harlem of the 1930's, Powell was a familiar and dramatic figure in and around the various Negro boycott movements, strikes, and protest demonstrations. He was opposed for the Democratic nomination for Congress in 1944 by the Negro who was then the most important Harlem district leader, but Tammany—either unsure of its ability to elect an alternative candidate, receptive to suggestions from other forces, or desirous of rebuking a rebellious district leader—chose to ignore the leader's protest and endorse Powell.

Powell created a personal organization. In part it was formed because Powell began his career from outside of the established organization, and in part it was necessary because even a position inside the Tammany machine was fraught with dangers and uncertainties. Whether outside or inside the organization, independent political strength was at least an advantage and probably a necessity. A church can be an ideal source of such strength. It directly recruits and organizes the masses, it can be financially independent, it has a variety of channels of communication throughout the community, and it has the luster of an indisputably good institution. In recent elections, Powell has been able to call upon as many as one thousand church workers for his campaigns, mostly volunteers. They are already organized through the elaborate committee structure and social service system of the church, and many of them hear Powell speak every Sunday. The church, in addition, has a paid bureaucracy of workers to provide the necessary staff. The appeals to these supporters are almost entirely intangible. The appeals are even larger than simply the exploitation of established race issues. They are centered around Powell as the personal embodiment, the projective personality, of the Negroes in his congregation. He is the vivid and colorful manifestation of their collective aspirations and expectations.

The use of intangible appeals in political organizations creates a set of constraints upon the user. When appeals are to principle, to lofty moral and racial goals, to the deepest wishes and fears of the listener, they enforce a logic upon the user which is compelling. Three important consequences of this kind of appeal can be mentioned.

First, these appeals tend to be "indivisible"; that is, they cannot easily be reduced to discrete units, given relative priorities, and dealt with apart from other aspects of the leader's career. Rather, they tend to function as a whole, a montage of interrelated ends and means, to which all phases of a leader's life must respond. Powell, for exmple, does not and probably could not divorce his career in Washington from his career in New York. His role as a congressman is inseparable from his role as a Harlem politician, Negro minister, and colorful personality. Politics for him is not a specific, but a general role, and the appeals upon which it is based are ramified and indivisible. Politics is "functionally diffuse." [5] Powell's position as a congressman is an extension of his position as a Harlem leader. The two offices, in Washington and New York, are systematically related. Both receive a relatively large number of constituents. In Washington, four staff workers are in Powell's office; in New York, three. In Washington, Powell receives as many as five to eight hundred letters a week, perhaps 250 of which state personal problems or requests for information and services. In New York, his congressional office is almost indistinguishable from his church organization, both of which deal with a wide range of the needs and requests of his followers. The church has in its congregation an estimated ten percent of the registered voters in the Sixteenth Congressional District.[6] Powell speaks to some four thousand people every Sunday, and upwards of one thousand persons come to the church or its community house every day of the week. There is little difference between voter and parishioner, between constituency and congregation.

The generality of Powell's political role is further suggested by the extent to which he intervenes in New York City political affairs in the same manner in which he intervenes in national affairs. Powell frequently makes public charges of race discrimination and injustice in Manhattan and he is not slow to attack the Mayor, the Police Commissioner, Carmine DeSapio, and other officials. Harlem is not simply a constituency which elects

[5] Cf., the treatment by Parsons and Shils of the pattern variables of "specificity" and "diffuseness" as aspects of the role-expectations governing the relevance of social objects. Talcott Parsons and Edward A. Shils, *Toward a General Theory of Action* (Cambridge: Harvard University Press, 1954), pp. 83–84.

[6] Hapgood, *op. cit.*, p. 3.

Powell to Congress; it is also a source of political issues. Powell's political style in part depends on the existence of an "enemy"—a source of alleged injustice against which Powell can direct his fire. Since his power has not been received from the political organization of the city, the organization is not immune from that fire.

On the other hand, Powell is usually not readily available in his district for receiving constituents. Although he maintains a congressional staff in Harlem which is closely linked with his church staff, he does not personally perform the services usual for a local political leader—hear complaints, requests, and demands from the voters who seek out their politicians directly. These services are provided by lieutenants.

The mingling of political, religious, and civic roles is seen in the organization of his headquarters. The secretary of the church's Board of Trustees acts as financial secretary of Powell's political club (the "Alfred Isaacs Democratic Club"). His congressional administrative assistant, charged with handling local political affairs, has an office adjacent to that of the church's full-time social worker, and the two share the task of dealing with voters-parishioners. The church, a $100,000-a-year enterprise, provided 600 to 1200 political volunteers at various stages of Powell's 1959 campaign for district leader and helped to raise the $30,000 necessary for the 1958 congressional campaign.

Second, intangible appeals tend to be endowed with a sacrosanct quality which renders them difficult to manipulate. This would be true whether the appeal is that of a charismatic leader with the "gift of grace" or of political principles which are invested with a sacred quality. There are undoubtedly elements of both charisma and ideology in Powell's appeal to his followers; how much of each would be difficult to assess. Although there would be important differences in detail, the general effect of either a charismatic or ideological appeal is that the leader becomes ill-suited for a bargaining role. As the manifestation of the private aspirations of individual Negroes, as the assertion of the great public ends of the race, or as the revelation of a prophetic, heroic, or exemplary personality, these appeals are endowed with a sacrosanct quality which makes both the leader and the ends he may represent superior to the leaders and goals of others. To compromise either the position of the leader or the essence of these goals would be to give way to morally inferior persons or demands; in short, it would be to corrupt them. To oppose Powell in an election is to take the side of evil, to be an "Uncle Tom," and to be a "field hand" on the "white man's plantation."

Paradoxically, this does not mean that Powell cannot escape his position on issues affecting the race which come before the local or national government. He can, and has, advanced and then dropped causes which involved race ends. Powell has frequently announced a dramatic move in local or national politics, but often little or nothing is in fact done. This was the case with his promised "boycott" of the 1952 presidential election and the independent political organization he promised in 1958. Few followers seem disturbed by this. Powell's own explanation is that such moves, even if only threats, serve to keep Tammany and others "off balance."

It may even be that Powell could reverse himself on some important issues, relying on his personal standing with his followers to justify the move. Charisma would compensate for ideology where the latter had to be sacrificed.[7] Such may have been the case, for example, when he joined with the other three Negro congressmen in voting against a Republican-sponsored civil rights amendment to the 1959 Housing Act on the grounds that it intended to defeat the bill by making it unacceptable to Southerners. Previously, he had sponsored and fought for a civil rights amendment to the federal education bill which, when adopted by the House, was followed by the defeat of the bill as a whole.[8] But considered as a set of appeals, Powell's identification with race issues and aspirations lead to further and further commitments and reduces the opportunity for compromise or the deliberate choice of means. Means, in the words of another student of race and nationalism, always have an "end-component."[9] Means cannot be selected simply on the basis of whether they are efficiently adapted to the attainment of given ends. Means are not valued merely on the basis of utility. Almost all means which might be used toward given ends have a value in and of themselves. Ends react on means, imbue them with value and render it difficult for a leader to be selective. The means Powell employs are precisely of this character. They involve defying the white man, asserting loudly the rights of Negroes, pressing for liberalizing legislation regardless of the costs to other values held by the society, and keeping the issues alive and hot.

Powell's political appeals lend themselves to campaigns based on the Negro ministry. The church is a vital part of Powell's base of support and, even though some ministers individually do not like Powell, most of them can be counted on to campaign in his behalf. It is principally through the mobilized resources of the Harlem ministry that Powell speaks to the people, addressing them from the pulpits of dozens of churches.

Third, Powell indulges his personal wants to an extraordinary extent. Powell stated in 1956 that his income was an estimated $115,000 a year—

[7] It will be interesting to discover to what extent Powell's charisma can become "routinized." (Cf., Weber, *op. cit.*, pp. 363 ff.) The accession of Powell to the chairmanship of the House Committee on Education and Labor, predicted for the 87th Congress in 1961, will bring him under a new set of constraints which he may in part accept in hope of enjoying certain of the rewards of chairmanship. At the local level, Powell—by entering Tammany as a district leader—will have a limited amount of patronage and the necessity for creating something more in the way of a specifically political administrative apparatus. These constraints need not to be too severe, for Tammany undoubtedly needs Powell more than he needs it. Clearly, Powell is unlikely to trade his non-material appeals for the scanty material ones at the disposal of DeSapio. But marginal adjustments might be expected, all in the direction of routinizing what has been a strictly personal and irregular position.

[8] See *Congressional Record*, 84th Cong., 2d Sess., 1956, CII, Part 9, 11773–883.

[9] See David E. Apter, "Political Modernization in Ghana and Uganda—An Essay in Political Anthropology," 1959 (mimeo).

$40,000 a year earned by him as congressman and minister, and $75,000 earned by his wife (the noted jazz pianist, Hazel Scott).[10] He owns fancy sports cars, several homes, and two boats. Since Powell does not hold his followers and workers by material benefits, they rarely feel cheated by his obvious material success. In part, the lack of resentment is probably due to the feelings of gratification less fortunate Negroes derive from the sight of Powell in expensive restaurants and night clubs. He is doing what many of them understandably would like to do. But in addition, his money and material benefits are not the basis of his political power. Since his organization is not built through the distribution of tangible rewards, Powell can possess an abnormally large share of such rewards without depriving his followers of what they feel ought to be theirs. They support him for other reasons and derive other rewards from his success.[11]

DAWSON

William L. Dawson was at one time an expert and frequent user of many of the same kinds of appeals that now characterize Powell. As an insurgent Republican, seeking to force an entry into regular organization in Chicago, Dawson was a well-known street-corner speaker with a magnetic personality. He built a personal following outside the machine, in part by holding out to them the hope of eventual material reward, and in part by arousing their interest in the race issues of the day and by appealing to their aspirations. After some success within the Republican Party (he served as an alderman from 1935 to 1939), Dawson joined the Democrats then under the leadership of Edward Kelly and Pat Nash. His entry into the party was the beginning of his first real career as a regular organization man, and it was the beginning of the end of his career as a purveyor of race rhetoric.

[10] Hapgood, *op. cit.*, p. 3. Powell and his wife are now officially separated, and his worldly possessions may have decreased as a result.

[11] Weber (*op. cit.*, pp. 360–3) comments on various kinds of charismatic leaders who were themselves well rewarded (Germanic kings, Chinese monarchs, etc.) with benefits the followers did not share. The recruiting and paying of workers is part of the process (and problem) of routinization. This may become evident with control, in Powell's case, of a congressional committee and a district organization. Since it would be almost impossible to remove him from the committee chairmanship, and very difficult to attack him as district leader, he may be able to sustain both his personal appeal and his administrative structure. The interesting point thus far is that, contrary to Weber's view, Powell has not had to "deliver" beyond winning successive challenges to his position. (See Weber, *op. cit.*, p. 360: "If he is for long unsuccessful, above all if his leadership fails to benefit his followers, it is likely that his charismatic authority will disappear.") The explanation in Powell's case seems to be that the need for "delivering" in terms of substantive ends and benefits has been in great part obviated by his success in finding and defeating political enemies. This would mean that the existence of an enemy is of crucial significance in permitting intangible, charismatic-ideological politics to function. One "delivers" in a purely formal sense by crushing the opposition.

Kelly became mayor of Chicago at about the same time that LaGuardia became mayor of New York. The implications of this difference are far-reaching. LaGuardia took over a city administration under heavy attack from the reformers, and proceeded to hasten the rate of reform and further weaken the political machine that he had defeated. Kelly inherited a city administration and a political machine which were intact and in reasonably good health, and he proceeded to strengthen both. At the very time when Tammany was being starved, the Cook County Democracy was being feasted. In New York, the path to political power and success was becoming uncertain and strewn with traps; in Chicago, the same path was more clearly than ever becoming a private road belonging to the Democratic machine. Once inside such an organization, Dawson discovered that rhetorical or other intangible appeals were not only no longer useful, they could be a positive embarrassment. The stock of material incentives which the machine held—patronage and favors—was enormous and growing. Power came to him who could distribute them, and the right to distribute them was reserved to those in good standing with the organization. Remaining in such good standing means, among other things, not dividing or weakening the organization by raising issues which split the machine or which require it to act against its own best interests.

Dawson created an organization in his ward, and extended it to other Negro wards, which attracted and held its workers mostly through the opportunity for jobs. In turn, the organization began the slow and laborious task of altering the voting habits of a Negro population which had been firmly committed to the Republican Party. In part the switch of allegiance was accomplished simply by exploiting the national trend among Negroes to the Democratic Party, in part it was done by providing services and favors to voters, and in part it was done by bringing them into a complex and thorough set of organizations which clustered about the political machine—women's auxiliaries, youth groups, building and block organizations, and so on. By 1942 the organization was able to send Dawson to Congress by a slim majority (in fact, Dawson was unable to carry his own ward at the time), and then to control an aldermanic election by delivering a winning majority to an organization Democrat who was being challenged by a popular, non-organization Democrat. From that time on, the size of the organization's majorities grew steadily until they reached a stable level of about three-to-one, where they have remained ever since. In the process, Dawson acquired influence over four other Negro ward leaders.

Several consequences flow in part from the character of the organization of which Dawson is a leader and the nature of the rewards which must be distributed to sustain it.

First, tangible rewards tend to be divisible in a sense in which intangible ones are not. The distribution of material rewards can be kept separate from other aspects of the leader's position. His role as a local politician can become a fairly specific one, permitting him to play other roles without creating conflicts. There need be no inevitable connection between local political leadership in Chicago and congressional political activity in Washington, D.C. Few expectations about Dawson's performance and style as a congressman are created among his constituents or his workers. Indeed, Dawson has gone to considerable lengths to divorce his Chicago base of support from his Washington field of action. There is little contact between the Washington and the Chicago office. The staffs are separately recruited and separately organized. The flow of communications between the two centers is relatively small.

The ward headquarters in Chicago performs most of the services to constituents which are necessary; relatively few demands reach Washington. Dawson is to a greater extent than most other congressmen freed from constituency pressures, and he deliberately cultivates this situation. Dawson attends to his constituency assiduously, but in a manner entirely different from Powell. Dawson's Chicago headquarters are located in the very heart of the most depressed Negro area in a modest building. It is drab on the outside and plain on the inside, and deliberately so. It is accessible to the least advantaged constituent and nothing about the office is allowed to make the constituent feel he is out of his element or in unfamiliar surroundings. Dawson, when in Chicago (and he is there frequently), spends almost all his time in his ward office. No appointment is necessary to see him, and the visitor need not state his business to the receptionist. On the bench outside his office on a typical day might be found a police captain, a couple on relief, a young Negro lawyer, an unemployed man, a politician, and a university professor. When Dawson is not in the city, his place is taken by lieutenants who function in the same fashion. His Washington office and its work load are markedly smaller than Powell's, or indeed of other congressmen generally. Where Powell has four staff workers in his Washington office, Dawson has one; where Powell receives five to eight hundred letters a week, Dawson receives one hundred; where Powell replies to 250 "case letters" (requesting information or services) per week, Dawson receives one-third as many. Where Powell mails out large numbers of *Record* reprints and other items, Dawson mails almost none.

Dawson cherishes his reputation as a congressman. He is the chairman of the House Government Operations Committee, one of the three or four largest and most powerful committees in the House. He is highly esteemed by almost all his colleagues, who go out of their way to compliment him and his committee. He enjoys the respect of many southerners as well as large numbers of liberal northern Democrats. He has built his committee since 1946 (when he became its chairman), and his success is measured by the important yardstick used in government—the size of its budget. In the 81st Congress, it received $300,000; in the 85th $1,175,000. Its staff is competent and largely free of purely patronage appointments; the proceedings of the committee reflect an attention to business and an aversion to simple publicity that is unusual.

Dawson conceives of his Chicago organization as a base of support which produces, without commitment to issues or similar appeals, automatic majorities for him and his slate. For his role as Chicago ward leader, Dawson has one set of attitudes and action. He is strong, sometimes ruthless; he brooks no rivals; he crushes opposition and the ambitions of men who would challenge him; and he insists on organizational loyalty. In Washington, he plays an entirely different role. There, he is a leader interested in good government and liberal measures. He presides over the committee with authority, but not harshly. He encourages junior colleagues to take on new responsibilities and rise in committee work. He does not feel that he has rivals or opponents, and is friendly with everyone. Although he has considerable power as a congressman, he rarely uses that power for political ends in Chicago. By and large, the political power he has assembled in Washington is used for national goals, and only rarely for Chicago goals. Issues in Chicago affairs have arisen which were in some measure vulnerable to congressional intervention. He did not intervene.

One of the few themes common to both his local and national roles is the avoidance of race as a public issue. As in Chicago, so in Washington, Dawson rarely engages in a *public* discussion of race goals. He has not used his committee staff as a source of "race patronage." Only two of the fifty staff members are Negroes. It is explained that this reflects the shortage of qualified Negro personnel. The committee has wide jurisdiction, but rarely is its investigative power turned toward explicitly racial issues. Some members of the staff regret this. Many were unhappy about his opposition to the Powell Amendment in 1956. On that occasion he ignored the requests of the NAACP and the numerous representations made to him from people in his district and not only voted but spoke out against the civil rights amendment on the grounds that if it were adopted it would mean southern opposition would be aroused and there would be no federal education bill at all. Dawson, although on friendly terms with two of the three other Negro congressmen, does not confine his association to them. He seems to prefer his wide range of contacts with many congressmen, particularly the House leadership. Although he is not a militant advocate of race ends in Congress, since 1956 he has not voted against such matters on the floor. Dawson, personally, feels that his political power can best be used for the advancement of Negroes in ways other than pressing for legislative correction of racial abuses. He sees himself as promoting Negro interests by intervening on their behalf with the authorities, placing more Negroes in government, and demonstrating the achievements possible for a Negro leader.[12]

[12] On this score, Dawson has had a series of conflicts with the executive branch on the distribution of patronage among Negroes. When the Democrats controlled the White House under Truman, Dawson saw himself in competition with the NAACP and similar groups for the right to make decisive endorsements. On occasion he intervened directly with the President on these matters after feeling slighted by presidential assistants who were in charge of patronage. NAACP leaders usually deny that they were attempting to undercut Dawson or that they were involved in patronage matters at all.

The important single source of controversy about Dawson is whether his political influence and position—which admittedly are rarely used publicly for race ends—are used in a private, unpublicized manner. Dawson and his supporters point to his intervention in many issues involving Negro rights. He has conferred with southern political leaders about Negro registration and segregation in party meetings and functions in the South. He intervened in the Emmet Till lynch case and moved to cut off the hostile, southern-led congressional investigation of school integration in Washington, D.C. All of these facts are difficult to document, given the secrecy which has surrounded them. The truth probably is that Dawson has had more effect than his critics allege and less than his most ardent supporters claim.

The other theme common to both Chicago and Washington is the extent to which Dawson shuns publicity. When Powell grants an interview, it is usually understood to be on the record; when Dawson does, it is almost always specified as off the record. Dawson's aversion to publicity is legendary, and goes far beyond that which is called for simply by prudence. He feels that he has been mistreated by an essentially hostile press, mostly in Chicago, that even friendly reporters are not allowed to print stories favorable to him, and that publicity invariably ends by embarrassing him or his political allies.

The *second* consequence of Dawson's position in an organization is the high degree of discretion he has on legislative matters. Dawson shuns race issues. His local organization meets weekly to hear Dawson and others speak; rarely is race a theme of their remarks. Dawson's attitude is that race progress must be made from within the party. If the organization can be persuaded to espouse race causes, well and good; if it cannot, then one must accept that fact as the inevitable cost of belonging. Dawson's view of appropriate race ends is largely confined to what has been termed elsewhere "welfare" ends—i.e., ends which are specific, direct, and tangible and which tend to improve the lot of the Negro without necessarily attaining some true measure of integration.[13] Party, not racial unity is stressed.

Dawson has been challenged by individuals and voluntary associations such as the local NAACP for not taking more vigorous *public* stands on race issues such as lynching, the Democratic Party's platform on civil rights, and other matters. Dawson has been criticized in the Negro press. The important fact is that such challenges and criticisms account for little; his electoral strength is barely affected. Dawson, like Powell, is stronger than any single issue which might be used against him. He can survive almost any position he takes on any single issue. But unlike Powell, he need not devote himself to issues and aspirations. His freedom of choice in this matter is much wider. He can be far more deliberate in his choice of ends and means. He can devote himself almost entirely to the pursuit of other, non-racial goals without being penalized. His range of discretion regarding means to any important political ends is broad. This is true in part because he can afford the luxury of little or no publicity, and in part because he need not consider the extent to which

[13] See my *Negro Politics*, Chap. VI.

the means he uses are endowed with value significance. Means, to Dawson, can be more completely instrumental than to Powell.

Nowhere is the contrast between the Dawson and Powell organizations more striking or important than in the differing roles of the Negro ministry. The ministry is politically significant only in those Negro communities where no independent base of political power exists—i.e., where there is no strong, patronage-oriented machine. Dawson has deliberately worked for twenty years to reduce or eliminate the role of the Negro minister as a political influence in Chicago, and he has in great part succeeded. A fundamental distinction between Negro political systems is whether they must work through existing mass organizations (churches and labor unions) or whether it is possible to organize the community *directly* for political ends.[14] Dawson, to be sure, has ministerial allies, but he discourages the participation of ministers in politics for the most part. Nor is Powell "dependent" on the ministers. The relationship is symbiotic; each needs the other. The distinction is between one system in which the ends and basis of influence of the politician are relatively *independent* of other ends and bases of influence in the community (as in Chicago) and the alternative system in which political ends and influences are *implicated* in the community (as in New York).

Third, Dawson stands in an entirely different relationship to his followers and workers than does Powell. Because of the character of the incentives used by Dawson to hold their allegiance and maintain discipline, he is subject to a set of constraints from which Powell is largely exempt. The "status gap" between Powell and his supporters is manifestly greater than the disparity between Dawson and his followers. Powell, since he embodies the racial goals and private aspirations of many of his followers, can enrich his own position without weakening his stature—indeed, he may enhance it. Dawson leads a group of men who fundamentally, although not exclusively, are in politics for more tangible rewards. Dawson weakens his position by the extent to which he appears to gain at the expense of his followers. His supporters must be convinced that they can gain in proportion to the gains of Dawson. If Dawson gains disproportionately to his followers, he causes resentment, jealousy, and antagonisms.

This speaks to the question of the nature of Dawson's political skills. In part, of course, they are the skills of any leader of men—the ability to move other men to act in accordance with one's intentions. This requires arranging the situation so that the wants of individuals lead them to act toward the ends of the leader. A typical, but short-sighted, view as to the basis of a machine leader's power is that he "controls patronage." This is an insufficient and in part a misleading explanation. In reality, it says little more than that a man is powerful because he is powerful. The question remains, *why* has *he* been able to grasp and retain control of patronage for the purpose of sustaining his

[14] Cf., Hugh Douglas Price, "The Negro and Florida Politics, 1944–1954," *Journal of Politics*, XVII (May, 1955), 198–220. Price notes the decline in the political importance of Negro ministers and social organizations with the rise in Negro registration and the emergence of specific Negro political roles.

organization? If control of patronage were the only variable, then Negro politics in Chicago might be in a state of constant factional rivalry. The essential element in the use of tangible incentives to sustain political organizations is that the followers must never be allowed to feel that the gains of breaking with the leader outweigh the costs of such a break. The leader ought to create a pattern of expectations among his followers which he appears willing to satisfy even at his own expense.

This is made possible when the leader, such as Dawson, derives intangible rewards from a political system that produces tangible rewards for the followers. Dawson's gratifications are not in money and material perquisites, but in prestige, the sense of power, and the fun of the game. He lives austerely, drives second-hand cars, avoids ostentation, spends money freely on others, and generally minimizes the outward or material rewards of his position. He does not appear to be competing with his followers for the scarce material rewards of politics. Perhaps he could afford greater outward display than he does, but it seems clear that the lack of such display enhances his position.[15]

CHICAGO AND NEW YORK

These differences between the two organizations can be accounted for largely by the differences in the political systems of which they are parts. In New York, the steady weakening of the Tammany organization which has gone on since 1933 has made it difficult for it to enforce its will on its members and impossible for it to turn back the challenge of a man like Powell. Further, Tammany attempted, during the LaGuardia-Fusion period, to govern Harlem from outside the district, through "absentee" leaders whose influence rested in part on keeping Negro political leadership divided and off balance.[16] Tammany failed—in part through unwillingness and in part through lack of resources—to build a strong, centralized Negro leadership in Harlem. Powell now seeks to fill that void. After his election as a district leader (together

[15] Cf., Max Weber's description of the creative entrepreneur and his willingness to forgo immediate gain for the sake of investment and ultimate returns which may be only the sense of achievement and power. This can be contrasted to his subordinates or successors who have lost the ethic of work and sense of calling, occupy a bureaucratized position, and derive more material rewards. *The Protestant Ethic and the Spirit of Capitalism*, trans. R. H. Tawney (London: G. Allen and Unwin, 1930). Dawson is not alone in seeking intangible rewards for his political work. Many contemporary leaders such as Richard Daley of Chicago and David Lawrence of Pittsburgh are men for whom politics is not a path to wealth. It would be interesting to analyze past "bosses" to see what rewards attracted the most successful of them, and how the shift in those rewards —in part resulting from closer public scrutiny—from tangible to intangible has altered recruitment patterns and leadership styles. It is likely that even many of the "old line" bosses—like Charles F. Murphy of New York—got less in a material sense out of politics than is commonly believed. Some of the bosses who failed to hold their power were conspicuously men who "took" out of proportion to the gains of their followers.

[16] Cf., *New York Times*, January 10, 1960, p. 1.

with three other leaders allied with him) he sought to create a unified "Leadership Team" for Harlem. In January, 1960, Powell's group received control of the Tammany patronage in Harlem. Although he has now entered the regular organization, Powell's independent base of support and the paucity of the rewards Tammany can offer his followers means that Tammany needs Powell more than he needs it. All doubt on this manner was quickly dispelled when Powell made public attacks on New York political leaders for failing to give Negroes more representation in government, for denying Negroes patronage, for persecuting Borough President Hulan Jack (Powell's erstwhile political scapegoat), and for allowing police to drive out Negro numbers racketeers in favor of Italians.

Dawson's organization is a strong portion of a powerful city machine. The possibility of a Powell arising on Chicago's South Side is substantially reduced by this fact. In 1947–1955, an effort was made by a popular minister to become an independent political force in the community. He managed to serve two terms in the City Council as alderman of the Third Ward. But the Dawson organization defeated him in 1955 for several reasons—all of which are indicative of the differences in politics between Chicago and New York. The Dawson organization has available to it perhaps three times the amount of patronage available to comparable districts in Harlem. The independent had to fight, not a group of quarreling factions, but a single, organized opponent who was well-staffed with workers. The independent could gain relatively few civic allies; most were already committed to the strongest force in the community—the Dawson group. Although the independent was a minister, other ministers could not be mobilized as a solid group behind him. Finally, it was necessary in a city where the Democratic primary was invariably dominated by the regular organization for the independent to run as a Republican (where his sympathies happened to lie anyway) and this was a grave weakness in a community overwhelmingly Democratic. (Chicago's aldermanic elections are only nominally nonpartisan.) When the independent attempted to emulate Powell by moving from the city council to Congress, he had again to run as a Republican, and this was fatal.

Thus, the character of the political system into which Powell and Dawson moved in their formative years (the late 1930's and early 1940's) was of decisive importance in molding the kind of organization each created. Dawson found a strong, active apparatus in which he had to create a place for himself. Powell encountered a weak, divided organization which it was necessary neither to join nor to defeat.

SOME CONCLUSIONS

Two important congressmen with roughly comparable constituencies have been compared. Both men, it has been argued, act as if the maintenance of their organizations were their goal. Since the organizations and the incentives necessary to maintain them differ, the political styles of the two men differ.

One organization was created and is sustained by a system of ideal or non-material benefits. This has certain consequences. (1) The benefits are indivisible, and the role of the leader who dispenses them tends to become diffuse and general. All aspects of his career are treated as part of a whole, and all choices relate to a single set of values. (2) The benefits have a sacred component, and thus are difficult to compromise. Means used to attain them share in the moral or sacrosanct quality of the ends themselves; means can only with difficulty be regarded as purely instrumental. (3) The ideal benefits which followers share permit the leader to indulge himself in outward display without alienating them—indeed, he may enhance his position with them. The other organization was created and is sustained by a system of tangible rewards. Among the consequences of this are: (1) The rewards are divisible and may be isolated to the local organization. The role of the leader can be specific and compartmentalized. He may separate his base of support from his national field of action. (2) The absence of race or ideological appeals gives the leader a greater discretion as to the choice of ends to pursue. Means tend to be more thoroughly instrumental. Few of his actions are deliberately imbued with moral significance. (3) The power of the leader in part depends on his ability to satisfy his followers that they gain in proportion to him—that he does not gain at their expense. The "status-gap" between the leader and the led is relatively small.

Further, it has been argued that the character of the two organizations, and hence the nature of their maintenance needs, can be traced to the political systems of which they are parts. One political system (Chicago) has a single leadership which disposes of a large amount of patronage, is unified, and can control its own primaries with ease. The other (New York) has a leadership which constantly must meet challenges, has a short supply of patronage, and cannot invariably control its own primaries. In the latter Powell succeeded; in the former, a Powell-like leader tried and failed.

This mode of analysis has an obvious shortcoming. A political style which may have been, at some early point, functional in terms of the needs of the situation, later tends to become temperamental. Political style tends to become the independent variable, *creating* in part the situation it had formerly served; that is, the image a leader creates of himself inevitably tends to react back on him and modify his behavior apart from what might be considered as the "objective" needs of the situation. Both Dawson and Powell undoubtedly carry many of their attributes to an unusual extreme, and settled habits have now replaced earlier experiments. But we need not linger too long on the problem of untangling the man from the situation, for however subtle a pattern of interaction exists between the two levels, the burden of the analysis remains this: the political style of the two leaders is functional to the organization they must maintain and the position they hold within the larger political system of which they are part.

It is interesting to note the opinion of these men held by prominent Negroes in New York and Chicago. Publicly, both have been criticized and even attacked. The *Chicago Defender* was critical of Dawson in 1956; the New York *Amsterdam News* supported Powell's opponent in 1958. But public criticism is far rarer and much more gentle than the private criticism which can be found directed at both men. The followers are aligned in two intent and mutually exclusive camps. Neither man has anything like universal admiration from the Negro middle class or from Negro intellectuals. Both are criticized by many thoughtful Negroes: Dawson for doing nothing, Powell for being irresponsible. At the same time, both get grudging respect from most Negro civic leaders—Dawson because of his personal position, his stature, and his power; Powell because he is "not afraid of the white man" and because he "stirs things up" and thus makes it easier for civic organizations to gain leverage against influential whites. The important aspect of the private praise and blame heaped on these men is that in the last analysis it is not concerned with ends or accomplishments. Neither leader has "accomplished" much in the way of legislation directed at race goals. Although Powell supporters criticize Dawson for "doing nothing," in fact, of course, Powell has no greater a list of accomplishments. And when pressed, many Negroes will concede this.

This means that most criticism of the two leaders centers on the nature of their political styles. In a situation in which *ends* are largely unattainable (at least by Negro action alone), *means* become all-important. On the basis of the means employed—the political style used—men make judgments as to the worth of the leader and his reputation. Means, in short, tend to become ends in themselves; what is important is not what you do, but how you do it. As pointed out earlier in another content, means acquire an "end-component" either because (a) ends are unattainable or (b) ends are morally endowed.

The relationship of leader to organization in these two cases raises interesting questions concerning the role of congressmen. It has often been assumed that one mark of the statesman is an interest in issues, rather than patronage, as the currency of politics. Schattschneider, for example, censures the "local bosses" because they are irresponsible and because they interfere in national politics to its detriment.[17] The thrust of this paper is that, for a variety of reasons, a "boss" may deliberately separate his local and national roles. Further, he may use his local machine (a) to filter out constituency demands by satisfying them at the local level and (b) to sustain himself in office without extensive or irrevocable commitments on policy matters and without

---

[17] E. E. Schattschneider, *Party Government* (New York: Farrar and Rinehart, Inc., 1942), esp. chap. vii. A valuable but neglected challenge to this view is A. L. Lowell, *The Government of England* (3rd ed.; New York: Macmillan Co., 1926), II, 91–5. Lowell presents an analysis of voting in the U.S. Congress among representatives from "machine" constituencies as well as in state legislatures. He concludes that there are few party votes in part because "the machine meddles little with general legislation" (p. 94).

accepting the support of organized pressure groups. The very position of a person such as Dawson enables him, if he chooses, to disregard both the localistic demands of constituents and the demands of local or national pressure groups. The needs of the constituents can be met largely on an issue-free basis; the demands of the pressure groups can be ignored, as they can do little either to help or harm the leader. In theory, this leaves the congressman free to pursue the public interest, however he choose to define it. Rather than constraining him and rendering him irresponsible, the existence of the local machine may liberate him and permit him to vote as his conscience dictates. Congressmen without such a powerful and non-ideological base of support may have much less discretion in such matters.[18]

Aside from the theoretical advantages of such a position, there of course remains the empirical question whether a political leader who has risen through the ranks of a local machine would have any elevated view of the public interest. The way of life a machine creates for its members is such that it might render even its best leaders incapable of taking a broad and enlightened view of public affairs even though the organization enforces no constraints that would objectively prevent acting on the basis of such a view. In the psychological dimension of representation, there is a great variation in the roles played. Of all the Democrats in Congress supported by the Cook County organization, some take a narrow and routine view of their functions whereas others (such as Dawson) deliberately endeavor to act on the basis of an enlarged view of the functions of a congressman. No categorical judgments can be made on this point, but the interpretations presented in this study may suggest an approach to the re-examination of the impact of the constituency on the function of representation and a re-evaluation of the role of the local machine in contemporary politics.

[18] In fact, both Powell and Dawson can ignore most pressure groups nationally. Neither requires the support of organized labor, and they have frequently made labor lobbyists unhappy by their actions. Powell undoubtedly finds it in his interest to yield to the NAACP on most matters, although he probably could defy it on any single issue. But Powell cannot yield to any temptation to ignore the demands of his constituents for issue agitation on race matters.

Martin Duberman

BLACK POWER IN AMERICA

Disillusioned with the rate of social change, immobilized by the seemingly insoluble problems of the black masses, and embittered by the limited gains secured through traditional party politics, civil rights militants of the middle 1960's articulated their anger and alienation with the slogan, "Black Power." Although it was not entirely clear just what the phrase meant, "Black Power" paradoxically suggested both Negro aggressiveness and Negro withdrawal from the mainstream of American society.

Martin Duberman's essay explores the meaning militants have given to the slogan "Black Power," makes suggestive comparisons with certain other radical movements in American history, and suggests the limitations inherent in the programs the militants have offered.

T HE slogan of "Black Power" has caused widespread confusion and alarm. This is partly due to a problem inherent in language: words necessarily reduce complex attitudes or phenomena to symbols which, in their abbreviation, allow for a variety of interpretations. Stuart Chase has reported that in the thirties, when the word "fascism" was on every tongue, he asked 100 people from various walks of life what the word meant and got 100 widely different definitions. And in 1953 when *The Capital Times* of Madison, Wisconsin, asked 200 people "What is a Communist?" not only was there no agreement, but five out of every eight admitted they couldn't define the term at all. So it is with "Black Power." Its definition depends on whom you ask, when you ask, where you ask, and not least, who does the asking.

Yet the phrase's ambiguity derives not only from the usual confusions of language, but from a failure of clarity (or is it frankness?) on the part of its advocates, and a failure of attention (or is it generosity?) from their critics. The leaders of SNCC and CORE who invented the slogan, including Stokely Carmichael and Floyd McKissick, have given Black Power different definitions

Martin Duberman, "Black Power in America," *Partisan Review*, XXXV (Winter, 1968), pp. 34–68. Reprinted with permission of Martin Duberman.

on different occasions, in part because their own understanding of the term continues to develop, but in part, too, because their explanations have been tailored to their audiences.[1]

The confusion has been compounded by the press, which has frequently distorted the words of SNCC and CORE representatives, harping on every connotation of violence and racism, minimizing the central call for ethnic unity.

For all these reasons, it is still not clear whether "Black Power" is to be taken as a short-term tactical device or a long-range goal—that is, a postponement or a rejection of integration; whether it has been adapted as a lever for intimidating whites or organizing blacks, for instilling race hate or race pride; whether it necessitates, permits or encourages violence; whether it is a symptom of Negro despair or of Negro determination, a reaction to the lack of improvement in the daily lives of Negro-Americans or a sign that improved conditions are creating additional expectations and demands. Whether Black Power, furthermore, becomes a constructive psychological and political tactic or a destructive summons to separatism, violence and reverse racism will depend at least as much on developments outside the control of its advocates (like the war in Vietnam) as on their conscious determination. For all these reasons, it is too early for final evaluations; only time, and perhaps not even that, will provide them. At most, certain limited, and tentative, observations are possible.

If Black Power means only that Negroes should organize politically and economically in order to develop self-regard and to exert maximum pressure, then the new philosophy would be difficult to fault, for it would be based on the truism that minorities must argue from positions of strength rather than weakness, that the majority is far more likely to make concessions to power than to justice. To insist that Negro-Americans seek their goals as individuals

---

[1] Jeremy Larner has recently pointed out ("Initiation for Whitey: Notes on Poverty and Riot," *Dissent*, November–December, 1967) that the young Negro in the ghetto mainly seeks the kind of knowledge which can serve as a "ready-made line, a set of hard-nosed aphorisms," and that both Malcolm X and Stokely Carmichael have understood this need. In this regard Larner quotes a speech by Carmichael to the students of Morgan State College, as transcribed in *The Movement*, June, 1967:

> Now then we come to the question of definitions . . . it is very, very important because I believe that people who can define are masters. I want to read a quote. It is one of my favorite quotes. It comes from *Alice in Wonderland*, Lewis Carroll. . . .
>> "When I use a word," Humpty Dumpty said in a rather scornful tone, "I mean just what I choose it to mean, neither more nor less." "The question is," said Alice, "whether you can make words mean so many different things." "The question is," said Humpty Dumpty, "who is to be master."
> That is all. That is all. Understand that . . . the first need of a free people is to define their own terms.

As Larner comments, "Mr. Carmichael, unlike Mr. Carroll, identifies with Humpty Dumpty."

and solely by appeals to conscience and "love," when white Americans have always relied on group association and organized power to achieve theirs, would be yet one more form of discrimination. Moreover, when whites decry SNCC's declaration that it is tired of turning the other cheek, that henceforth it will actively resist white brutality, they might do well to remember that they have always considered self-defense acceptable behavior for themselves; our textbooks, for example, view the refusal of the revolutionaries of 1776 to "sit supinely by" as the very essence of manhood.

Although Black Power makes good sense when defined to mean further organization and cooperation within the Negro community, the results which are likely to follow in terms of political leverage can easily be exaggerated. The impact is likely to be greatest at the county unit level in the deep South and in the urban ghettos of the North. In this regard, the "Black Panther" party of Lowndes County, Alabama is the prototype.

There are roughly 12,000 Negroes in Lowndes County and 3,000 whites, but until 1964 there was not a single Negro registered to vote, while white registration had reached 118 per cent of those eligible. Negro life in Lowndes, as Andrew Kopkind has graphically recounted [2] was—and is—wretched. The median family income for whites is $4,400, for Negroes, $935; Negro farmhands earn $3.00 to $6.00 a day; half of the Negro women who work are maids in Montgomery (which requires a 40 to 60 mile daily roundtrip) at $4.00 a day; few Negroes have farms, since 90 per cent of the land is owned by about 85 white families; the one large industrial plant in the area, the new Dan River Mills textile factory, will only employ Negroes in menial capacities; most Lowndes Negroes are functional illiterates, living in squalor and hopelessness.

The Black Panther party set out to change all this. The only path to change in Lowndes, and in much of the deep South, is to "take over the courthouse," the seat of local power. For generations the courthouse in Lowndes has been controlled by the Democratic party; indeed there is no Republican party in the county. Obviously it made less sense for SNCC organizers to hope to influence the local Democracy; no white moderates existed and no discussion of integration was tolerated. To have expected blacks to "bore from within," as Carmichael has said, would have been "like asking the Jews to reform the Nazi party."

Instead, Carmichael and his associates established the separate Black Panther party. After months of work SNCC organizers (with almost no assistance from federal agents) registered enough Negroes to hope for a numerical majority in the county. But in the election of November, 1966, the Black Panther party was defeated, for a variety of reasons which include Negro apathy or fear and white intimidation.[3] Despite this defeat, the possibility of a better

[2] "The Lair of the Blank Panther," *The New Republic*, August 13, 1966.

[3] I have not seen a clear assessment of the causes for defeat. The "Newsletter" from the New York Office of SNCC of November, 1966, makes two points regarding the election: that according to a November report from the Southern Regional Council,

life for Lowndes County Negroes does at last exist, and should the Black Panther party come into power at some future point, that possibility could become a reality.

Nonetheless, even on the local level and even in the deep South, Lowndes County is not representative. In Alabama, for example, only eleven of the state's sixty-seven counties have black majorities. Where these majorities do not exist, the only effect independent black political parties are likely to have is to consolidate the whites in opposition. Moreover, and more significantly, many of the basic ills from which Negro-Americans suffer—inadequate housing, inferior education, limited job opportunities—are national phenomena and require national resources to overcome. Whether these resources will be allocated in sufficient amounts will depend, in turn, on whether a national coalition can be formed to exert pressure on the federal government—a coalition of civil rights activists, church groups, campus radicals, New Class technocrats, unskilled, un-unionized laborers and certain elements in organized labor, such as the UAW or the United Federation of Teachers. Such a coalition, of course, would necessitate Negro-white unity, a unity Black Power at least temporarily rejects.[4]

The answer that Black Power advocates give to the "coalition argument" is of several pieces. The only kind of progressive coalition which can exist in this country, they say, is the mild, liberal variety which produced the civil rights legislation of recent years. And that kind of legislation has proven itself grossly inadequate. Its chief result has been to lull white liberals into believing that the major battles have been won, whereas in fact there has been almost no change, or change for the worse, in the daily lives of most blacks.[5]

The evidence for this last assertion is persuasive. Despite the Supreme Court decision of 1954, almost 85 per cent of school-age Negroes in the South still sit in segregated classrooms. Unemployment among Negroes has actually gone up in the past ten years. Title VI of the 1964 Civil Rights Act, with its promising provision for the withdrawal of federal funds in cases of discrimination, has been used in limited fashion in regard to the schools but not at all in regard to other forms of unequal treatment, such as segregated hospital facilities. Under the 1965 Voting Rights Act, only about 40 federal registrars have been sent into the South, though many areas have less than the 50 per cent registration figure which would legally warrant intervention. In short, the legislation produced by the liberal coalition of the early sixties has turned out to be little more than federally approved tokenism, a continuation of paper promises and ancient inequities.

2,823 whites and 2,758 Negroes had registered in Lowndes County, though the white population was approximately 1900; and that "the influential Baptist Alliance told Negroes throughout Alabama to vote the straight Democratic ticket."

[4] On this point, see what to me are the persuasive arguments made by Pat Watters, "The Negroes Enter Southern Politics," *Dissent*, July–August, 1966, and Bayard Rustin, "Black Power and Coalition Politics," *Commentary*, September, 1966.

[5] See, on this point, David Danzig, "In Defense of 'Black Power,'" *Commentary*, September, 1966.

If a *radical* coalition could be formed in this country, that is, one willing to scrutinize in depth the failings of our system, to suggest structural, not piecemeal, reforms, to see them executed with sustained rather than occasional vigor, then Black Power advocates might feel less need to separate themselves and to concentrate on local, marginal successes. But no responsible observer believes that in the foreseeable future a radical coalition on the Left can become the effective political majority in the United States; we will be fortunate if a radical coalition on the Right does not. And so to SNCC and CORE, talk of further cooperation with white liberals is only an invitation to further futility. It is better, they feel, to concentrate on encouraging Negroes everywhere to self-respect and self-help, and in certain local areas, where their numbers warrant it, to try to win actual political power.

As an adaptation to present realities, Black Power thus has a persuasive logic. But there is such a thing as being too present-minded; by concentrating on immediate prospects, the new doctrine may be jeopardizing larger possibilities for the future, those which could result from a national coalition with white allies. Though SNCC and CORE insist that they are not trying to cut whites out of the movement, that they merely want to redirect white energies into organizing whites so that at some future point a truly meaningful coalition of Negroes and whites can take place, there are grounds for doubting whether they really are interested in a future reconciliation, or if they are, whether some of the overtones of their present stance will allow for it. For example, SNCC's so-called position paper on Black Power attacks white radicals as well as white liberals, speaks vaguely of differing white and black "psyches," and seems to find all contact with all whites contaminating or intimidating ("whites are the ones who must try to raise themselves to our humanistic level").[6]

SNCC's bitterness at the hypocrisy and evasion of the white majority is understandable, yet the refusal to discriminate between degrees of inequity, the penchant instead for wholesale condemnation of all whites, is as unjust as it is self-defeating. The indictments and innuendos of SNCC's "position paper" give some credence to the view that the line between black power and black racism is a fine one easily erased, that, as always, means and ends tend to get confused, that a tactic of racial solidarity can turn into a goal of racial purity.

[6] SNCC's "position paper" was printed in *The New York Times*, August 5, 1966. It is important to point out, however, that SNCC staffers have since denied the official nature of this paper; see for example Elizabeth Sutherland's letter to the editors of *Liberation*, November, 1966, in which she insists that it was "not a S.N.C.C. position paper but a document prepared by a group of workers on one S.N.C.C. project" (she goes on to note that the *Times* refused to print a SNCC letter to this effect). For other denials of the "racist" overtones in "Black Power," see Stokely Carmichael, "What We Want," *The New York Review of Books*, September 22, 1966, and C. E. Wilson, "Black Power and the Myth of Black Racism," *Liberation*, September, 1966. But Andrew Kopkind's report on SNCC staff conferences ("The Future of Black Power," *The New Republic*, January 7, 1967) makes me believe that the dangers of black racism are real and not merely the invention of frightened white liberals (see also James Peck, "Black Racism," *Liberation*, October, 1966).

The philosophy of Black Power is thus a blend of varied, in part contending, elements, and it cannot be predicted with any certainty which will assume dominance. But a comparison between the Black Power movement and the personnel, programs and fates of earlier radical movements in this country can make some contribution toward understanding its dilemmas and its likely directions.

Any argument based on historical analogy can, of course, become oversimplified and irresponsible. Historical events do not repeat themselves with anything like regularity, for every event is to a larger degree embedded in its own special context. An additional danger in reasoning from historical analogy is that in the process we will limit rather than expand our options; by arguing that certain consequences seem always to follow from certain actions and that therefore only a set number of alternatives ever exist, we can prevent ourselves from seeing new possibilities or from utilizing old ones in creative ways. We must be careful, when attempting to predict the future from the past, that in the process we do not straitjacket the present. Bearing these cautions and limitations in mind, some insight can still be gained from a historical perspective. For if there are large variances through time between roughly analogous events, there are also some similarities, and it is these which make comparative study possible and profitable. In regard to Black Power, I think we gain particular insight by comparing it with the two earlier radical movements of Abolitionism and Anarchism.

The Abolitionists represented the left wing of the antislavery movement (a position comparable to the one SNCC and CORE occupy today in the civil rights movement) because they called for an *immediate* end to slavery everywhere in the United States. Most Northerners who disapproved of slavery were not willing to go as far or as fast as the Abolitionists, preferring instead a more ameliorative approach. The tactic which increasingly won the approval of the Northern majority was the doctrine of "nonextension": no further expansion of slavery would be allowed, but the institution would be left alone where it already existed. The principle of nonextension first came into prominence in the late eighteen-forties when fear developed in the North that territory acquired from our war with Mexico would be made into new slave states. Later the doctrine formed the basis of the Republican party which in 1860 elected Lincoln to the Presidency. The Abolitionists, in other words, with their demand for immediate (and uncompensated) emancipation, never became the major channel of Northern antislavery sentiment. They always remained a small sect, vilified by slavery's defenders and distrusted even by allies within the antislavery movement.

The parallels between the Abolitionists and the current defenders of Black Power seem to me numerous and striking. It is worth noting, first of all, that neither group started off with so-called "extremist" positions (the appropriateness of that word being, in any case, dubious).[7] The SNCC of 1967 is not

[7] For a discussion of "extremism" and the confused uses to which the word can

the SNCC formed in 1960; both its personnel and its programs have shifted markedly. SNCC originally grew out of the sit-ins spontaneously begun in Greensboro, North Carolina, by four freshmen at the all-Negro North Carolina Agricultural and Technical College. The sit-in technique spread rapidly through the South, and within a few months the Student Non-Violent Coordinating Committee (SNCC) was formally inaugurated to channel and encourage further activities. At its inception SNCC's staff was interracial, religious in orientation, committed to the "American Dream," chiefly concerned with winning the right to share more equitably in that Dream and optimistic about the possibility of being allowed to do so. SNCC placed its hopes on an appeal to the national conscience and this it expected to arouse by the examples of nonviolence and redemptive love, and by the dramatic devices of sit-ins, freedom rides and protest marches.[8]

The Abolitionist movement, at the time of its inception, was similarly benign and sanguine. It, too, placed emphasis on "moral suasion," believing that the first order of business was to bring the iniquity of slavery to the country's attention, to arouse the average American's conscience. Once this was done, the Abolitionists felt, discussion then could, and would, begin on the particular ways and means best calculated to bring about rapid, orderly emancipation. Some of those Abolitionists who later became intransigent defenders of immediatism—including William Lloyd Garrison—were willing, early in their careers, to consider plans for preliminary apprenticeship. They were willing, in other words, to settle for gradual emancipation *immediately begun* instead of demanding that freedom itself be instantly achieved.

But this early flexibility received little encouragement. The appeal to conscience and the willingness to engage in debate over means alike brought meager results. In the North the Abolitionists encountered massive apathy, in the South massive resistance. Thus thwarted, and influenced as well by the discouraging British experiment with gradualism in the West Indies, the Abolitionists abandoned their earlier willingness to consider a variety of plans for prior education and training, and shifted to the position that emancipation had to take place at once and without compensation to the slaveholder. They also began (especially in New England) to advocate such doctrines as "Dis-Union" and "No-Government," positions which directly parallel Black Power's recent advocacy of "separation" and "de-centralization," and which then as now produced discord and division within the movement, anger and denunciation without.

But the parallel of paramount importance I wish to draw between the

be and has been put, see Howard Zinn, "Abolitionists, Freedom-Riders, and the Tactics of Agitation," *The Antislavery Vanguard*, Martin Duberman, ed. (Princeton, 1965), especially pp. 421–426.

[8] For the shifting nature of SNCC see Howard Zinn, SNCC: *The New Abolitionists* (Boston, 1964), and Gene Roberts, "From 'Freedom High' to 'Black Power,'" *The New York Times*, September 25, 1966.

two movements is their similar passage from "moderation" to "extremism." In both cases, there *was* a passage, a shift in attitude and program, and it is essential that this be recognized, for it demonstrates the developmental nature of these—of all—movements for social change. Or, to reduce the point to individuals (and to clichés): "revolutionaries are not born but made." Garrison didn't start his career with the doctrine of "immediatism"; as a younger man, he even had kind words for the American Colonization Society, a group devoted to deporting Negroes to Africa and Central America. And Stokely Carmichael did not begin his ideological voyage with the slogan of Black Power; as a teenager he was opposed to student sit-ins in the South. What makes a man shift from "reform" to "revolution" is, it seems to me, primarily to be explained by the intransigence or indifference of his society: either society refuses reforms or gives them in the form of tokens. Thus, *if* one views the Garrisons and Carmichaels as "extremists," one should at least place the blame for that extremism where it belongs—not on their individual temperaments, their genetic predispositions, but on a society which scorned or toyed with their initial pleas for justice.

In turning to the Anarchist movement, I think we can see between it and the new turn taken by SNCC and CORE (or, more comprehensively still, by much of the New Left) significant affinities of style and thought. These are largely unconscious and unexplored; I have seen almost no overt references to them either in the movement's official literature or in its unofficial pronouncements. Yet the affinities seem to me important.

But first I should make clear that in speaking of "Anarchism" as if it were a unified tradition, I am necessarily oversimplifying. The Anarchist movement contained a variety of contending factions, disparate personalities and differing national patterns. Some Anarchists believed in terrorism, others insisted upon nonviolence; some aimed for a communal life based on trade union "syndicates," others refused to bind the individual by organizational ties of any kind; some wished to retain private ownership of property, others demanded its collectivization.[9]

Despite these differing perspectives, all Anarchists did share one major premise: a distrust of authority, the rejection of all forms of rule by man over man, especially that embodied in the State, but also that exemplified by parent, teacher, lawyer, priest. They justified their opposition in the name of the individual; the Anarchists wished each man to develop his "specialness" without the inhibiting interference imposed by authority, be it political or eco-

[9] In recent years several excellent histories and anthologies of Anarchism have been published: George Woodcock's brilliant *Anarchism* (New York, 1962), James Joll's *The Anarchists* (London, 1964), Irving L. Horowitz's anthology *The Anarchists* (New York, 1964) which concentrates on the "classics" of the literature, and Leonard Krimerman and Lewis Perry's collection, *Patterns of Anarchy* (New York, 1966), which presents a less familiar and more variegated selection of Anarchist writings.

nomic, moral or intellectual. This does not mean that the Anarchists sanctioned the idea of "each against all." On the contrary, they believed that man was a social creature—that is, that he needed the affection and assistance of his fellows—and most Anarchist versions of the good life (Max Stirner would be the major exception) involved the idea of community. The Anarchists insisted, moreover, that it was not their vision of the future, but rather society as presently constructed, which represented chaos; with privilege the lot of the few and misery the lot of the many, society was currently the essence of *dis*order. The Anarchists demanded a system which would substitute mutual aid for mutual exploitation, voluntarism for force, individual decision-making for centralized dictation.

All of these emphases find echo today in SNCC and CORE. The echoes are not perfect: "Black Power," after all, is above all a call to organization, and its acceptance of politics (and therefore of "governing") would offend a true Anarchist—as would such collectivist terms as "black psyche" or "black personality." Nonetheless, the affinities of SNCC and CORE with the Anarchist position are substantial.

There is, first of all, the same belief in the possibilities of "community" and the same insistence that community be the product of voluntary association. This in turn reflects a second and still more basic affinity: the distrust of centralized authority. SNCC and CORE's energies, and also those of other New Left groups like Students for a Democratic Society (SDS), are increasingly channeled into local, community organizing. On this level, it is felt, "participatory" democracy, as opposed to the authoritarianism of "representative" democracy, becomes possible. And in the Black Panther party, where the poor and disinherited do take a direct role in decision-making, theory has become reality (as it has, on the economic side, in the Mississippi-based "Poor People's Corporation," which to date has formed some fifteen cooperatives).[10]

Then, too, SNCC and CORE, like the Anarchists, talk increasingly of the supreme importance of the individual. They do so, paradoxically, in a rhetoric strongly reminiscent of that long associated with the Right. It could be Herbert Hoover (or Booker T. Washington), but in fact it is Rap Brown who now reiterates the Negro's need to stand on his own two feet, to make his own decisions, to develop self-reliance and a sense of self-worth.[11] SNCC may be scornful of present-day liberals and "statism," but it seems hardly to realize

[10] See Art Goldberg, "Negro Self-Help," *The New Republic*, June 10, 1967, and Abbie Hoffman, "Liberty House / Poor People's Corporation," *Liberation*, April, 1967.

[11] For more detailed discussions of the way in which the rhetoric of the New Left and the traditional Right have begun to merge, see Ronald Hamowy, "Left and Right Meet," *The New Republic*, March 12, 1966; Martin Duberman, "Anarchism Left and Right," *Partisan Review*, Fall, 1966; Paul Feldman, "The Pathos of 'Black Power,'" *Dissent*, Jan.–Feb., 1967; and Carl Oglesby and Richard Schaull, *Containment and Change* (Macmillan: 1967). In the latter Oglesby (p. 167) seems actually to call for a merger between the two groups, arguing that both are "in the grain of American humanist individualism and voluntaristic associational action." He confuses, it seems to me, a similarity of rhetoric and of means with a similarity of goals.

that the laissez faire rhetoric it prefers, derives almost verbatim from the classic liberalism of John Stuart Mill.

A final, more intangible affinity between Anarchism and the entire New Left, including the advocates of Black Power, is in the area of personal style. Both hold up similar values for highest praise and emulation: simplicity, spontaneity, "naturalness" and "primitivism." Both reject modes of dress, music, personal relations, even of intoxication, which might be associated with the dominant middle-class culture. Both, finally, tend to link the basic virtues with "the people," and especially with the poor, the downtrodden, the alienated. It is this *lumpenproletariat*—long kept outside the "system" and thus uncorrupted by its values—who are looked to as a repository of virtue, an example of a better way. The New Left, even while demanding that the lot of the underclasses be improved, implicitly venerates that lot; the desire to cure poverty cohabits with the wish to emulate it.

The Anarchist movement in the United States never made much headway. A few individuals—Benjamin Tucker, Adin Ballou, Lysander Spooner, Stephen Pearl Andrews, Emma Goldman, Josiah Warren—are still faintly remembered, but more for the style of their lives than for any impact on their society.[12] It is not difficult to see what prevented them from attracting a large following. Their very distaste for organization and power precluded the traditional modes for exerting influence. More important still, their philosophy ran directly counter to the national hierarchy of values, a system of beliefs, conscious and otherwise, which has always impeded the drive for rapid change in this country. And it is a system which constitutes a roadblock at least as formidable today as at any previous point in our history.

This value structure stresses, first of all, the prime virtue of "accumulation," chiefly of goods, but also of power and prestige. Any group—be it Anarchists or New Leftists—which challenges the soundness of that goal, which suggests that it interferes with the more important pursuits of self-realization and human fellowship, presents so basic a threat to our national and individual identities as to invite almost automatic rejection.

A second obstacle that our value structure places in the path of radical change is its insistence on the benevolence of history. To the average American, human history is the story of automatic progress. Every day in every way we have got better and better. *Ergo,* there is no need for a frontal assault on our ills; time alone will be sufficient to cure them. Thus it is that many whites today consider the "Negro Problem" solved by the recent passage of civil rights legislation. They choose to ignore the fact that the daily lives of most Negroes have changed but slightly—or, as in the case of unemployment, for the worse. They ignore, too, the group of hard-core problems which have only recently emerged: maldistribution of income, urban slums, disparities in

---

[12] The only over-all study of American Anarchism is Eunice M. Schuster, *Native American Anarchism* (Northampton: 1932). But some useful biographies exist of individual figures in the movement; see especially, Richard Drinnon, *Rebel in Paradise: A Biography of Emma Goldman* (Chicago: 1961).

education and training, the breakdown of family structure in the ghetto, technological unemployment—problems which show no signs of yielding to time, but which will require concentrated energy and resources for solution.

Without a massive assault on these basic ills, ours will continue to be a society where the gap between rich and poor widens, where the major rewards go to the few (who are not to be confused with the best). Yet it seems highly unlikely, as of 1968, that the public pressure needed for such an assault will be forthcoming. Most Americans still prefer to believe that ours is either already the best of all possible worlds or will shortly, and without any special effort, become such. It is this deep-seated smugness, this intractable optimism, which must be reckoned with—which indeed will almost certainly destroy—any call for substantive change.

A further obstacle facing the New Left today, Black Power advocates and otherwise, is that its Anarchist style and mood run directly counter to prevailing tendencies in our national life, especially the tendencies to conformity and centralization. The conformity has been commented on too often to bear repetition, except to point out that the young radicals' unorthodox mores (sexual, social, cultural), are in themselves enough to produce uneasiness and anger in the average American. In insisting on the right of the individual to please himself and to rely on his own judgment (whether in dress, speech, music, sex or stimulants), SNCC and SDS may be solidly within the American tradition—indeed may be its main stream—but this tradition is now more central to our rhetoric than to our behavior.

The Anarchist focus in SNCC and SDS on decentralization, on participatory democracy and on community organizing, likewise runs counter to dominant national trends. Consolidation, not dispersion, is currently king. There are some signs that a counter-development has begun—such as the pending decentralization of the New York City school system—but as yet the overwhelming pattern continues to be consolidation. Both big government and big business are getting bigger and, more ominous still, are coming into ever closer partnership. As Richard J. Barber has recently documented, the federal government is not only failing to block the growth of huge "conglomerate" firms by antitrust action, but it is contributing to that growth through procurement contracts and the exchange of personnel.[13] The traditional hostility between business and government has rapidly drawn to a close. Washington is no longer interested in restraining the giant corporations, and the corporations have lost much of their fear of federal intentions. The two, in happy tandem, are moving the country still further along the road to oligopoly, militarism, economic imperialism and greater privileges for the already privileged. The trend is so pronounced, and there is so little effective opposition to it, that it begins to take on an irrevocable, even irreversible, quality.

In the face of these monoliths of national power, Black Power in Lowndes

[13] Richard J. Barber, "The New Partnership: Big Government and Big Business," *The New Republic*, Aug. 13, 1966. But see, too, Alexander Bickel's article in the same journal for May 20, 1967.

County is pathetic by comparison. Yet while the formation of the Black Panther party in Lowndes brought out paroxysms of fear in the nation at large, the announcement that General Motors' 1965 sales totaled 21 billion dollars—exceeding the GNP of all but nine countries in the world—produced barely a tremor of apprehension. The unspoken assumption can only be something like this: It is less dangerous for a few whites to control the whole nation than for a local majority of Negroes to control their own community. The Kafkaesque dimension of life in America continues to grow.

Black Power is both a product of our society and a repudiation of it. Confronted with the continuing indifference of the majority of whites to the Negro's plight, SNCC and CORE have lost faith in conscience and time, and have shifted to a position which the white majority finds infuriating. The nation as a whole—as in the case of the Abolitionists over a hundred years ago —has created the climate in which earlier tactics no longer seem relevant, in which new directions become mandatory if frustration is to be met and hope maintained. And if the new turn proves a wrong one, if Black Power forecloses rather than animates further debate on the Negro's condition, if it destroys previous alliances without opening up promising new options, it is the nation as a whole that must bear the responsibility. There seems little likelihood that the American majority will admit to that responsibility. Let us at least hope it will not fail to recognize the rage which Black Power represents, to hear the message at the movement's core:

> *Sweethearts, the script has changed . . .*
> *And with it the stage directions which advise*
> *Lowered voices, genteel asides,*
> *And the white hand slowly turning the dark page.*[14]

[14] Kay Boyle, "On Black Power," *Liberation,* January, 1967.

Elliott Rudwick and August Meier

NEGRO RETALIATORY VIOLENCE
IN THE TWENTIETH CENTURY

Earlier selections in this volume deal with the subject of slave revolts. Negro retaliatory violence, however, even during the nineteenth century, was chiefly an urban phenomenon. For example, in Providence in 1831, in Cincinnati in 1841, and in southern towns during Reconstruction, armed Negroes defended themselves against white mobs. On occasion, moreover, certain prominent leaders counseled armed revenge.

In the twentieth century, there have been two major clusters of race riots—the World War I period through its aftermath, the "Red Summer" of 1919, and the middle 1960's. The riots of the nineteenth and early twentieth centuries, though often precipitated by acts of Negro retaliatory violence, frequently resembled pogroms in which whites killed Negroes and burned their houses to the ground. In contrast, during the riots of the 1960's the Negroes were the aggressors. Yet in both eras, most of the dead and wounded were black men, women, and children.

Where the earlier riots were characterized by clashes between the races in downtown business districts and along the edges of the Negro sections, and often included destruction of small Negro enclaves by white mobs, today white civilians are seldom involved. Instead, violence takes the form of Negroes looting and destroying white-owned property inside the ghettos, and of gunplay involving policemen and guardsmen, snipers and looters, and innocent bystanders.

Since the article below was written in 1966, talk of retaliatory violence on the part of Negro militants has become increasingly overt; CORE and SNCC have publicly indicated their disillusionment with the tactic of nonviolent direct action; and the pattern of rioting that characterized the summers of 1964 and 1965 has appeared in numerous cities from Newark to Oakland, from Boston to Detroit. It is true that in 1967 the toll of human lives and the loss of property drastically increased, while the number of riots reached epidemic proportions. Nevertheless, in our judgment these developments confirm our major theses. The recent riots, though involving occasional assaults on white civilians, and in rare instances the looting of downtown stores, remain fundamentally an attack on white-owned property within the ghettos. More significantly, the predictions made by certain militants regarding organized insurrections developing in the black ghettos, and Negro "invasions" of white neighborhoods and central business districts, appear to us to signify not "black power," but wishful thinking stemming essentially from a frustrating lack of power—the power to press beyond the attainment of constitutional rights and fulfill the raised expectations of both the leaders in the civil rights movement and of the masses themselves.

For most Americans the increasingly overt talk of retaliatory violence among Negro militants, and the outbreaks in the urban ghettos over the past three years, signify something new and different in the history of Negro protest. Actually, retaliatory violence has never been entirely absent from Negro thinking. Moreover, advocacy of retaliatory violence, and actual instances of it, have tended to increase during periods of heightened Negro protest activity.

Thus, the past decade of rising Negro militancy has been no stranger to the advocacy of retaliatory violence. For example, as far back as 1959 Robert F. Williams, at the time president of the Monroe, North Carolina branch of the NAACP, came to public attention when the Union County Superior Court acquitted two white men of brutal assaults on two Negro women, but sentenced a mentally retarded Negro to imprisonment as a result of an argument he had with a white woman. Williams angrily told a UPI reporter: "We cannot take these people who do us injustice to the court, and it becomes necessary to punish them ourselves. . . . If it's necessary to stop lynching with lynching, then we must be willing to resort to that method." The NAACP dismissed Williams as branch president, but he remained a leader of Monroe's working-class Negroes, who for several years had been using guns to protect their homes from white klansmen. In 1961, he was falsely charged with kidnapping a white couple and fled from the country. Williams became the most potent of that group of militants existing at the fringe of the civil rights movement, who in their complete alienation from American society, articulate

Elliott Rudwick and August Meier, "Negro Retaliatory Violence in the Twentieth Century," *New Politics*, V (Winter, 1966), pp. 41–51. Reprinted with permission of *New Politics*.

a revolutionary synthesis of nationalism and Marxism.[1] From his place of exile in Havana, Cuba, Williams undertook the publication of a monthly newsletter, *The Crusader*. In a typical issue he declared:

> What is integration when the law says yes, but the police and howling mobs say no? Our only logical and successful answer is to meet organized and massive violence with massive and organized violence.... The weapons of defense employed by Afro-American freedom fighters must consist of a poor man's arsenal.... Molotov cocktails, lye or acid bombs (made by injecting lye or acid in the metal end of light bulbs) can be used extensively. During the night hours such weapons, thrown from roof tops, will make the streets impossible for racist cops to patrol.... Yes, a minority war of self-defense can succeed.[2]

Over a year ago Williams was named chairman-in-exile of an organization known as the Revolutionary Action Movement (RAM), a tiny group of Negro students in a few major Northern cities, particularly Philadelphia and Detroit, who also advocate violent retaliation.[3] More familiar to the general public have been the suggestions of violence in the speeches and writings of the Black Muslims. Elijah Muhammed, who envisions a final Armageddon between the forces of the virtuous blacks and the devilish whites, has been quoted as saying, "We must return to the Mosaic law of an eye for an eye, and a tooth for a tooth. What does it matter if 10 million of us die? ... [those] of us left ... will enjoy justice and freedom." [4] More recently, the public has been made aware of the potential for violence among the Negro lower classes by the riots in Rochester, New York City, and Jersey City in the summer of 1964, and in Los Angeles last year. There is no evidence that these explosions have any direct relation to the preachings of Williams, of RAM, or of the Black Muslims, though it appears that in New York at least, genuinely revolutionary cliques attempted to take control after the unplanned rioting started.

Both the statements of the fringe ideologists, and the spontaneous actions of the masses, are the product of the frustrations resulting from the growing disparity between the Negroes' status in American society and the rapidly rising expectations induced by the civil rights revolution and its successes. This feeling is also reflected in the increasing use of revolutionary vocabulary and in the growing skepticism about the usefulness of nonviolence among many of the more militant figures in the nonviolent direct action organizations them-

[1] For accounts see Julian Mayfield, "Challenge to Negro Leadership," *Commentary*, XXXI (April, 1961), pp. 297–305; "The Robert F. Williams Case," *Crisis*, LXVI, (June–July, August–September, 1959), pp. 325–29; 409–10; Robert F. Williams, *Negroes With Guns* (New York), 1962.

[2] *Crusader* V. (May–June, 1964), pp. 5–6.

[3] See the RAM publication *Black America*, Summer–Fall, 1965; *Crusader*, VI (March, 1965), p. 2.

[4] C. Eric Lincoln, *The Black Muslims in America* (Boston, 1961), p. 205.

selves. As early as 1963, Slater King, at that time leader of the Albany Movement, which had endured over 2,700 arrests and numerous instances of police brutality, without achieving any desegregation, made the following statement: "From my observations the majority of the black people of Albany are disillusioned, frightened, and bitter. . . . If the government continues its policy of evasiveness and its constant attempts to appease the segregationists who are in high places all over the country [armed whites and blacks] will meet in what I am afraid will be a bloody battleground." [5] In 1964 John Lewis, national chairman of SNCC, more circumspectly suggested a similar viewpoint about the strong possibility of the "shedding of blood." [6] Recently, there has been considerable publicity about the Deacons for Defense, organized in the deep South to protect Negroes and civil rights demonstrators from white attackers. CORE, without departing from its belief in nonviolent direct action methods, works closely with the Deacons and has welcomed their armed protection.[7] Unlike Williams and RAM, the Deacons do not engage in talk of general revolutionary violence to correct the injustices suffered by Negroes; but they do assert the necessity of defending Negroes and white civil rights workers.

This doctrine of retaliatory violence has taken various forms. Some have advocated self defense against a specific attack. Others have called for revolutionary violence. There are also those who hopefully predicted a general race war in which Negroes would emerge victorious. Though seldom articulated for white ears, and only rarely appearing in print, thoughts of violent retaliation against whites have been quite common. For example, Ralph Bunche, in preparing a memorandum for Gunnar Myrdal's *American Dilemma* in 1940, noted that "there are Negroes, too, who, fed up with frustration of their life here, see no hope and express an angry desire 'to shoot their way out of it.' I have on many occasions heard Negroes exclaim 'Just give us machine guns and we'll blow the lid off the whole damn business.' " [8]

In surveying the history of race relations during the twentieth century, it is evident that there have been two major periods of upsurge both in overt discussion by Negro intellectuals concerning the desirability of violent retaliation against white oppressors, and also in dramatic incidents of actual social violence committed by ordinary Negro citizens. One was the period during and immediately after the First World War. The second has been the period of the current civil rights revolution. In this article we will examine evidences of retaliatory violence in Negro thought and action during the period 1917–1921, and suggest certain uniformities underlying the recurring interest in violent tactics.

[5] Slater King, "The Bloody Battleground of Albany," *Freedomways*, IV (Winter, 1964), p. 8.

[6] *Dialogue Magazine*, IV (Spring, 1964), p. 7.

[7] It is not without significance that at CORE's 1965 national convention a substantial group of delegates favored eliminating the non-violent clause from the organization's constitution.

[8] Ralph Bunche, "Conceptions and Ideologies of the Negro Problem," Memorandum prepared for the Carnegie-Myrdal Study of the Negro in America, 1940, p. 161.

W. E. B. Du Bois, the noted protest leader, occasionally advocated retaliatory violence, and somewhat more often predicted intense racial warfare in
which Negroes would be the victors. In 1916, inspired by the Irish rebellion,
he admonished Negro youth to stop spouting platitudes of accommodation
and remember that no people ever achieved their liberation without an armed
struggle. He said that "war is hell, but there are things worse than hell, as
every Negro knows." [9] Amid the violence and repression that Negroes experienced in the post-war world, Du Bois declared that the holocaust of World
War I was "nothing to compare with that fight for freedom which black and
brown and yellow men must and will make unless their oppression and humiliation and insult at the hands of the White World cease." [10]

Other intellectuals reflected this restless mood. This was the era of the
militant, race-conscious New Negro of the urban North, an intellectual type
who rejected the gradualism and conciliation of his ancestors. The tone of the
New Negro was recorded by Claude McKay, who in 1921 wrote his well-known
poem, "If We Must Die": "If we must die / let it not be like hogs; hunted
and penned in an accursed spot! / ... If we must die; oh, let us nobly die /
dying but fighting back." A. Philip Randolph, editor of the militant Socialist
monthly, The Messenger, also advocated physical resistance to white mobs. He
observed that "Anglo-Saxon jurisprudence recognizes the law of self-defense.
... The black man has no rights which will be respected unless the black man
enforces that respect.... We are consequently urging Negroes and other oppressed groups confronted with lynching or mob violence to act upon the
recognized and accepted law of self-defense." [11]

The legality of retaliatory violent self-defense was defended not only by
A. Philip Randolph, but also by the NAACP, which Randolph regarded as a
moderate, if not futile organization, wedded to the interest of the Negro middle class. Half a dozen years after the Messenger article, the NAACP secured
the acquittal of Dr. Ossian Sweet and his family. The Sweets were Detroit
Negroes who had moved into a white neighborhood, and fired on a stone-
throwing mob in front of their home, killing one white man and wounding
another.[12] More than a quarter of a century later, at the time of the Robert
Williams case, the NAACP in clarifying its position, reiterated the stand that,
"The NAACP has never condoned mob violence but it firmly supports the
right of Negroes individually and collectively to defend their person, their
homes, and their property from attack. This position has always been the
policy of the NAACP." [13]

The views of intellectuals like Du Bois, McKay and Randolph during

[9] Crisis, XII (August 1916), pp. 166–67; XIII (December 1916), p. 63.
[10] W. E. B. Du Bois, Darkwater (New York, 1920), p. 49.
[11] A. Philip Randolph, "How to Stop Lynching," Messenger, III (April, 1919),
pp. 8–9.
[12] Walter White, "The Sweet Trial," Crisis, XXXI (January, 1926), pp. 125–29.
[13] "The Robert F. Williams Case," Crisis, LXVI (June–July, 1959), p. 327.

World War I and the early post-war years paralleled instances of Negro retaliatory violence which actually triggered some of the major race riots of the period.

The East St. Louis race riot of 1917, the bloodiest in the twentieth century, was precipitated in July when Negroes, having been waylaid and beaten repeatedly by white gangs, shot into a police car and killed two detectives. On the darkened street a Negro mob of fifty to one hundred evidently mistook the Ford squad car for the Ford automobile containing white "joyriders" who had shot up Negro homes earlier in the evening. The following morning the riot began.[14]

In Houston, several weeks later, about 100 Negro soldiers broke into an army ammunition storage room and marched on the city's police station. The troops, mostly Northerners, were avenging an incident which occurred earlier in the day, when a white policeman used force in arresting a Negro woman and then beat up a Negro soldier attempting to intervene. A Negro provost guard was pistol-whipped and shot at for asking the policeman about the wounded soldier. Even before these events, the Negro soldiers nursed a hatred for Houston policemen, who had attempted to enforce streetcar segregation, frequently used the term "nigger," and officiously patrolled the Negro ghetto. The Houston riot was not only unusual because it involved Negro soldiers, but also because white persons constituted most of the fatalities.[15]

By 1919 there was evidence that the Negro masses were prepared to fight back in many parts of the country, even in the deep South. In an unpublished report to the NAACP Board of Directors,[16] a staff member, traveling in Tennessee and Mississippi during early 1919, noted that "bloody conflicts impended in a number of southern cities." Perry Howard, the leading colored attorney in Jackson, and R. R. Church, the wealthy Memphis politician, both reported that Negroes were armed and prepared to defend themselves from mob violence. Howard detailed an incident in which armed Negroes had prevented a white policeman from arresting a Negro who had become involved in a fight with two white soldiers after they had slapped a colored girl. In Memphis, R. R. Church, fearing armed conflict, privately advised the city's mayor that "the Negroes would not make trouble unless they were attacked, but in that event they were prepared to defend themselves."

The Chicago race riot of 1919 grew out of Negro resentment of exclusion from a bathing beach dominated by whites. One Sunday while Negroes and whites scuffled on the beach, a colored teenager drowned after being attacked in the swimming area. That attack was the most recent of a long series of assaults against Negroes. A white policeman not only refused to arrest a white man allegedly involved in the drowning, but actually attempted to arrest one

---

[14] Elliott M. Rudwick, *Race Riot at East St. Louis* (Carbondale, 1964), pp. 38–39.
[15] Edgar A. Schuler, "The Houston Race Riot, 1917," *Journal of Negro History*, XXIX (October, 1944), pp. 300–338.
[16] *NAACP Board Minutes*, Secretary's Report for June, 1919.

of the complaining Negroes. The officer was mobbed and soon the rioting was underway.[17]

The Elaine, Arkansas riot of 1919 was precipitated when two white law officers shot into a Negro church, and the Negroes returned the fire, causing one death. The white planters in the area, already angered because Negro cottonpickers were seeking to unionize and obtain an increase in their sharecropping wages, embarked upon a massive Negro hunt to put the black peons "in their place."[18]

The Tulsa riot of 1921 originated when a crowd of armed Negroes assembled before the courthouse to protest the possible lynching of a Negro who had just been arrested for allegedly attacking a white girl. The Negroes shot at white police and civilians who attempted to disperse them.[19]

In each of these conflagrations, the typical pattern was initial Negro retaliation to white acts of persecution and violence, and white perception of this resistance as an organized, premeditated conspiracy to "take over," thus unleashing the massive armed power of white mobs and police. In the Southern communities, Negro resistance tended to collapse early in the riots. After the church incident in the rural Elaine area, most Negroes passively accepted the planters' armed attacks on their homes. At Tulsa, Negroes retreated from the courthouse to the ghetto, and throughout the night held off by gunfire the assaults of white mobs. But after daybreak, many Negroes fled or surrendered before the white onslaught burned down much of the ghetto.[20] One exception to this pattern was the Washington riot of 1919, where it appears that Negroes did not retaliate until the third and last day.[21]

Negro resistance generally lasted longer in Northern riots than in Southern ones, but even in East St. Louis and Chicago the death toll told the story: in East St. Louis nine whites and at least thirty-nine Negroes were killed. In Chicago, fifteen whites and twenty-three Negroes lost their lives. Negroes attacked a small number of whites found in the ghetto or on its fringes. Negro fatalities mainly occurred when victims were trapped in white dominated downtown areas or residential sections. Negroes were also attacked on the edges of their neighborhood in a boundary zone separating a colored residential district from lower class white areas.[22] In the face of overwhelming white numerical superiority, many armed Negroes fled from their homes leaving guns and ammunition behind. In East St. Louis, for example, there was a constant rattle of small explosions when fire enveloped a small colored residential district. Perhaps psychological factors contributed to the terrified inactivity of

[17] *The Negro in Chicago* (Chicago, 1922), pp. 4–5.

[18] *Crisis*, XIX (December, 1919), pp. 56–62.

[19] Allen Grimshaw, *A Study in Social Violence: Urban Race Riots in the U.S.*, U. of Pa. unpublished doctoral dissertation, 1959, pp. 42–47.

[20] *Ibid.*

[21] Constance M. Green, *Washington, Capital City, 1879–1950* (Princeton, 1963), pp. 266–67; John Hope Franklin, *From Slavery to Freedom* (New York, 1947), p. 473; *New York Times*, July 20–22, 1919.

[22] Rudwick, *op. cit.*, pp. 226–27; *Negro in Chicago, op. cit.*, pp. 5–10.

some Negroes. Despite the wish to meet fire with fire, over the years they had become so demoralized by white supremacy and race discrimination, that armed defense could exist only in the realm of psychological fantasy.

During World War II, the most important race riot occurred in 1943 in Detroit, where nine whites and twenty-five Negroes were killed. In many respects the riot exhibited a pattern similar to East St. Louis and Chicago. The precipitating incident involved an attack on whites at the Belle Isle Amusement Park by several Negro teenagers who, a few days earlier, had been ejected from the white-controlled Eastwood Park. In the mounting tension at Belle Isle, many fights between Negroes and whites broke out, and the violence spread to the Negro ghetto where patrons at a night club were urged to "take care of a bunch of whites who killed a colored woman and her baby at Belle Isle." Although there had been no fatalities at the park, the night club emptied and revengeful Negroes stoned passing cars driven by whites. They began smashing windows on the ghetto's main business street, where the mob's major attention was directed to destroying and looting white-owned businesses.[23]

It was this symbolic destruction of "whitey" through his property that gave the Detroit holocaust the characteristic of what we may call the "new style" race riot. It will be noted that in all the riots discussed so far, there were direct clashes between Negroes and whites, and the major part of the violence was perpetrated by white mobs. The contemporary riot pattern, such as in the summers of 1964 and 1965, involves Negro aggression mainly against white-owned property, not white people. This "new style" riot first appeared in Harlem in 1935 and 1943.[24] Such racial violence does not fulfill James Baldwin's prediction of "the fire next time," since as just pointed out, it has not been a direct reversal of those conflagrations nearly a half century ago when white mobs literally hunted and killed dozens of Negroes. The modern riot does not involve white mobs at all, and policemen or guardsmen constitute most of the relatively small number of white casualties.

It is notable that during the twentieth century, both the overt discussion of the advisability of violent retaliation on the part of Negroes, and also actual incidents of violence were prominent in the years during and after World War I, and again during the past several years. While there have been significant differences between the outbreaks characteristic of each era, there are also important similarities. In both periods retaliatory violence accompanied a heightened militancy among American Negroes—a militancy described as the "New Negro" in the years after World War I, and described today with the phrase, "the Negro Revolution." In neither case was retaliatory violence the major tactic, or the central thrust, but in both periods it was a significant

[23] Alfred McClung Lee and Norman D. Humphrey, *Race Riot* (New York, 1943), pp. 26–30.

[24] Roi Ottley, *New World A-Coming* (Boston, 1943), pp. 151–52; Harold Orlansky, *The Harlem Riot: A Study in Mass Frustration* (New York, 1943), pp. 5–6, 14–15; New York Age, March 30, 1935 and August 7, 1943.

subordinate theme. However, in both periods a major factor leading Negroes to advocate or adopt such a tactic has been the gap between Negro aspiration and objective status. The rapid escalation of the aspirations of the Negro masses who share Martin Luther King's "dream" and identify vicariously with the success of the civil rights revolution, while their own economic, housing, and educational opportunities have not improved, is a phenomenon of such frequent comment that it requires no elaboration here.

A comparable situation occurred during and shortly after the first World War. The agitation of the recently-founded NAACP, whose membership doubled in 1918–19, the propaganda of fighting a war to make the world safe for democracy, and especially the great Negro migration to the Northern cities which Southern peasants and workers viewed as a promised land, all created new hopes for the fulfillment of age-old dreams, while Negro soldiers who had served in France returned with new expectations. But the Negro's new hopes collided with increasing white hostility. Northern Negroes assigned to Southern army camps met indignities unknown at home. They rioted at Houston and came so close to rioting in Spartanburg, South Carolina, that the army hastily shipped them overseas. In the Northern cities like East St. Louis and Chicago, Negroes found not a promised land, but overcrowded ghettos and hostile white workers who feared Negro competition for their jobs. The Ku Klux Klan was revived beginning in 1915, and grew rapidly in the North and South after the war ended. By 1919 economic opportunities plummeted as factories converted to peacetime operations. For a while Negroes resisted, protested, fought back, in the South as well as the North; but the superior might of the whites proved overpowering and the Southern Negroes retreated into old paths of accommodation where they remained until the momentous events of the past decade. In the North the nationalistic Garvey movement and, subsequently, cults such as those of Father Divine and Daddy Grace provided psychological escape for many among the Negro masses.

There has been no detailed research on Negro advocacy of violence prior to the First World War, but the available evidence supports the thesis that increased overt expression of this tendency accompanies peaks in other kinds of protest activity. For example, it appears likely that Negro resistance to white rioters was minimal in the riots at the turn of the century—at Wilmington, North Carolina in 1898, and at New Orleans, Akron, and New York in 1900 [25]—which occurred in a period when the sentiment of accommodation, epitomized by Booker T. Washington, was in the ascendency. However, half a dozen years later, when the militant Niagara Movement, founded in 1905, was at its zenith, Negroes did shoot at whites who invaded their neighborhoods in the Atlanta riot of 1906.[26] It is probably not without significance that Atlanta, where the noted W. E. B. Du Bois lived and taught, was the

---

[25] In the New York riot, however, the precipitating incident was a physical altercation between a white policeman and a Negro; see Gilbert Osofsky, *Harlem: The Making of a Ghetto* (New York, 1966), pp. 46–52.

[26] Ray Stannard Baker, *Following the Color Line* (New York, 1908), Chapter I.

only Southern city in which significant support for Niagara Movement developed; and that the Negroes who organized in defense of their homes and shot at the whites, constituted the sort of prosperous businessmen, homeowners, and college graduates from which the Niagara Movement drew its membership.[27]

Again, during the ante-bellum period, one can cite two noted cases of incendiary statements urging Negroes to revolt—*David Walker's Appeal* of 1829, and Rev. Henry Highland Garnet's suppressed *Address* to the national Negro convention of 1843.[28] Both coincided with periods of rising militant protest activity on the part of the Northern free Negroes. *Walker's Appeal* appeared on the eve of the beginning of the Negro convention movement, and at the time of intensified Negro opposition to the expatriation plans of the American Colonization Society.[29] Garnet's speech was made at a time when free Negro leaders were disturbed at the prejudiced attitudes of white abolitionists who refused to concern themselves with obtaining rights for the free people of color, or to allow Negroes to participate in the inner circles of the leadership of the anti-slavery societies. Consequently they had revived the Negro national convention movement which had been inactive since 1836. (Garnet's speech was also in part a product of disillusionment with the lack of actual progress being made by the anti-slavery societies toward achieving abolition.) Later, the Southern riots during Reconstruction occurred at a time of high Negro expectations and self-assertiveness, and seem to have been characterized by a significant amount of fighting back on the part of Negroes.

One period of marked and rising Negro militancy, however, was not accompanied by a significant increase in manifestations of Negro retaliatory violence. This was the one following the Second World War. Indeed, the Second World War itself witnessed far less Negro violence than did the First World War. The reason for this would appear to be that the 1940's and 1950's were years of gradually improving Negro status, but a period in which the expectations of the masses did not greatly outrun the actual improvements being made. In fact from 1941 until the mid-1950's, the relative position of the Negro workers, as compared to the white wage earners, was generally improving; and it was not until the recession of 1954–55, for example, that the Black Muslims, with their talk of race hatred and violence began to expand rapidly.

It would appear that both in the World War I period, and today—and indeed during the ante-bellum era and at other times when manifestations of violence came to the fore—there has been a strong element of fantasy in Negro

[27] W. E. B. Du Bois, "Atlanta University," Kelly Miller, et al., *From Servitude to Service* (Cambridge, Mass., 1905) pp. 196–97.

[28] Herbert Aptheker, *A Documentary History of the Negro People in the United States* (New York, 1951), pp. 93–97; 226–233.

[29] Founded in 1817 by a group of prominent white Americans, the American Colonization Society officially encouraged colonization as a means of furthering the cause of anti-slavery. Most Negroes, even most of those who themselves at one time or another advocated emigration to Africa or the Caribbean as the only solution for the Negro's hopeless situation in the United States, denounced the society as a cloak for those attempting to protect slavery by deporting free Negroes.

discussion and efforts concerning violent retaliation. Robert Williams talks of Molotov cocktails and snarling up traffic as devices for a largely poverty-stricken ethnic minority to engineer a social revolution. But only a few pay attention to him. James Baldwin talks, in his play, "Blues for Mr. Charlie," of the gun enjoying equal place with the Bible in the struggle for Negro advancement; but Mr. Baldwin shows no signs of setting other than rhetorical fires, or of shooting any but verbal guns. The Black Muslims talk of violence, but the talk seems to function as a psychological safety-valve; by preaching separation, they in effect accommodate to the American social order and place racial warfare off in the future when Allah in his time will destroy the whites and usher in an era of black domination. Similarly, in view of population statistics and power distribution in American society, Du Bois and others who have spoken of the inevitability of racial warfare and Negro victory in such a struggle were engaging in wishful prophesies. And Negroes have been nothing if not realistic. The patterns of Negro behavior in riots demonstrate this. As already indicated, those who bought guns in anticipation of the day when self-defense would be necessary, usually did not retaliate. And Negro attacks on whites occurred mainly in the early stages of the riots before the full extent of anger and power and sadism of the white mobs became evident.

Negroes of the World War I era resisted white insults and attacks only as long as they had hopes of being successful in their resistance. Today, some whites may fear that the Deacons are plotting organized attacks, but they go no further than self-defense in case of specific attacks upon individuals or property. It should be emphasized that one of the remarkable things about the riots of 1964 and 1965, in spite of their having been marked by particular resentment at police brutality, is the fact that Negro destruction was aimed at "whitey's" property, not his life. In part this may be due to psychic conditioning and the fear of white authority; but this behavior is consistent with the larger pattern of behavior that includes the extolling of passive resistance and the Christian virtues; the minor part violence has historically played in Negro protest activities; the tendency to talk and dream of violence rather than to practice it. And in those cases where retaliatory violence has been attempted, Negroes have retreated in the face of massive white armed force. Economically impoverished Negroes press as far as they realistically can; and one reason for the explosions of the last two summers has been the awareness that whites are to some degree in retreat, that white mobs in the North no longer organize to attack, and that to a large degree the frustrated Negroes in slums like Watts can get away with acts of destruction.

James Weldon Johnson, writing in 1934, summed up the possibilities of violence in terms that would be applicable even today: "We must condemn physical force and banish it from our minds. But I do not condemn it on any moral or pacific grounds. The resort to force remains and will doubtless always remain the rightful recourse of oppressed peoples. Our own country was established upon that right. I condemn physical force because I know that in our case it would be futile ... We would be justified in taking up arms or anything we could lay hands on and fighting for the common rights we are entitled to and denied, if we had a chance to win. But I know and we all know there is not a chance." Only one type of physical force did Johnson feel American Negroes should consider: "When we are confronted by the lawless, pitiless, brutish mob, and we know that life is forfeit, we should not give it up; we should, if we can, sell it, and at the dearest price we are able to put on it." [30]

It is impossible of course to make any foolproof predictions for the future. One factor of enormous importance in Negro thinking is the changing international situation. Negroes have consciously employed the technique of embarrassing the United States in the eyes of foreign nations, at a time when the country is attempting to exercise leadership in world affairs, as a device for achieving racial equality. "Thank God for Russia!" is a sentiment uttered even by highly conventional, middle-class Negroes. Moreover, the rise of the colored nations of Asia and Africa to independence, prominence and power in the world has given American Negroes a new image of themselves, and a new confidence in the ultimate victory of their cause. If American power in world affairs should suffer a significant decline it is not inconceivable that— as some militants in fact already advocate—certain Negro activist groups will be able to form an effective working alliance with revolutionary movements in Asia and Africa. Under such circumstances, and assuming an increase of guilt feelings among white Americans, in regard to the treatment of American Negroes, one might anticipate the occurrence of widespread and organized retaliatory, even revolutionary, violence.

Yet, judging by past experience and present conditions, it is our view that despite all the talk about violence among the radical militants, the type of self-defense advocated by James Weldon Johnson and the Deacons is the only kind of violent retaliation which Negroes are actually using even to a limited extent. Thus, they are being thoroughly realistic and indeed the threat of retaliation in the South is made psychologically possible only because of the increased sensitivity of American white public opinion, particularly of the federal government. In a less propitious era the Deacons for Defense would have been crushed in short order. Spontaneous outbreaks against the property of white businessmen such as those in Watts and a few other cities may well continue to occur, but beyond the legally recognized right of self-defense, the advocacy and use of violence as a deliberate program for solving the problems of racial discrimination remains thus far, at least, in the realm of fantasy.

[30] James Weldon Johnson, *Negro Americans, What Now?* (New York, 1935), p. 67.

William M. Kephart

THE NEGRO OFFENDER:
AN URBAN RESEARCH PROJECT *

In many ghettos, Negroes have long claimed that police departments have attracted numerous prejudiced white officers who commit acts of brutality against Negro suspects. Support for this accusation comes from the following selection written by William M. Kephart. During the early 1950's he questioned a group of white policemen in Philadelphia and found that more than half admitted being stricter with Negroes than with whites. These white patrolmen tended to be prejudiced not only against Negro suspects but against Negro policemen as well.

THE present paper deals with the interaction between white policemen and Negro offenders and is part of a larger survey dealing with racial factors and law enforcement. Some data were collected from other cities, but the interviews and statistics reported here were gathered from members of the Philadelphia police force, and the results are applicable only to that organization.

The present phase of the survey involved a series of preliminary interviews with policemen of all ranks, a program of comprehensive interviews at administrative and command levels, and a printed questionnaire distributed to all district (precinct) patrolmen. All the administrative personnel—commissioner, deputy commissioners, chief inspectors—were interviewed, as were the large

William M. Kephart, "The Negro Offender: An Urban Research Project," *American Journal of Sociology*, LX (July, 1954), pp. 46–50. Reprinted with the permission of University of Chicago Press.

* The Philadelphia study was undertaken with the co-operation of the police commissioner and the Fraternal Order of Police and was made possible through a grant from the University of Pennsylvania Albert M. Greenfield Center for Human Relations. The writer wishes to acknowledge the help and wholehearted co-operation of Dr. Martin P. Chworowsky, director of the Greenfield Center, Dr. Jeremiah Patrick Shalloo, chairman of the Philadelphia Crime Commission, and Police Commissioner Thomas J. Gibbons.

majority of commanding officers—inspectors, captains, lieutenants. Interviews averaged about an hour each and were carried on either in unit headquarters or at the men's homes in the evening.

Printed questionnaires were distributed to all white patrolmen assigned to district duty. The project had received a rather substantial backing from local groups, including the Fraternal Order of Police, and the response to the questionnaires was fairly successful: 1,081 (51.5 per cent) of the 2,101 questionnaires distributed were returned. (Interested readers may write to the Greenfield Center for copies.)

THE PHILADELPHIA SITUATION

The Negro population in Philadelphia has grown from 7 per cent in 1920 to a currently estimated 20 per cent. By all the signs, the Negro crime rate is staggering: more than half of all arrests involve Negro violators. All police personnel interviewed are highly cognizant of the disproportionate arrest rate in Negro areas and, with relatively few exceptions, place the burden of blame upon the Negro. The general belief is that Negro criminality is explainable neither in terms of low economic status nor on the basis of differential treatment by the police or by the courts but is attributable to the prevalence of low moral standards and a looseness in community organization, above which the Negro is making too little effort to lift himself. This point of view can be seen from the following statements made by police commanders:

> The crime problem in Philadelphia is largely a Negro problem. ... Criminals and ex-cons are heroes in some colored neighborhoods. ... Suppose you have two towns, one white, and the other colored. Then suppose all the cops in both towns took a holiday for a few weeks. The white town would go on ... people would keep themselves pretty much in line. But the colored town would be like a jungle in a couple of weeks.

> There's no doubt about it. The Negro is a menace to this city. ... Look at the court figures and you'll see what I mean.

> Our big headaches come mainly from Negro neighborhoods. More and more it's getting like Harlem. Over in New York the police have just about given up. In our district here, Negroes are better off than they ever were. What happens? Instead of going down, crime rates go up!

> Check the records at City Hall for the serious crimes—armed robbery, burglary, homicide—you'll find 70 to 80 per cent of them Negroes. We've had a lot of immigrant groups in this city—they never caused much trouble. ... Did you ever hear of a Chinese getting arrested? They take care of their own criminals. Nothing like that among the colored, though—they just don't seem to think anything's wrong —just blame it on the whites.

Whatever the reason for the high Negro crime rate, a high percentage of Philadelphia policemen blame the Negro community as such. In spite of the prevalence of crime in Negro areas, however, at the time of the study little effort was being made, by either Negroes or police, to take any positive intra-community action.

Since the Negro arrest rate is high and the number of Negro police relatively small, a large share of all arrests involves a white patrolman and a Negro offender. Therefore, it is no wonder that allegations of "race prejudice" coupled with "police brutality" are fairly common. These reports are carried by the Negro press, and the latter, together with groups such as the National Association for the Advancement of Colored People, demand an "investigation."

COMMANDING OFFICERS

On the interview schedule for commanding officers the question pertaining to the Negro offender was, "In your opinion, is the Negro law violator harder to handle than the white violator?" The majority of commanders answered in the affirmative, and the following responses are probably a fair representation:

> Oh, sure they are ... when a policeman makes an arrest, he doesn't want any trouble. He's just doing his duty; he has to bring the man in. But a colored man seems to want to make a fuss. He starts to swing. The arresting officer has no alternative but to use force.

> Negroes ... too often have a chip on their shoulders. We had a case last week. Two (white) patrolmen were bringing in a young colored boy ... and they're walking up the steps out there. All of a sudden this colored kid shoves the officer in front of him and kicks the one behind him—right in the groin—knocked the cop down the steps. Sure, when they got through with him, the colored boy is in the hospital. Some colored outfit took pictures of him—head all in bandages. They yelled about race prejudice and discrimination and police brutality. They never even asked for our side of it.

The following response is believed to be especially significant, since this particular commander is well enough thought of in the Negro community, being one of the very few district commanders who had established himself as a "friend of the Negroes":

> It's true. As a group, Negroes are more pugnacious when they're arrested. You know me well enough to take my word for it. Some of the Negro leaders know it, too, although some of them don't want to know it; they'd rather blame it on the cops. Very few patrolmen like to use force—on anybody. Why should they? It's dangerous for themselves. The chances are 98 to 100 that when you read of a case where a colored offender was brutally treated, the colored man started it.

Of course, there's more to it than meets the eye. It's like this: a colored offender is released from the station house. He tells his friends he was beat up by a white cop—maybe he has marks to prove it. He tells his side of the story, of course, not the cop's side. Anyway, word gets around the neighborhood. Then when a colored boy does get picked up, he expects to be beaten and acts up. I've seen some young kids (Negroes) come in here frightened to death. I've talked with them. I don't know what the answer is. I think the Negro press plays up the wrong angle. Sometimes they hurt things instead of helping. It's got so now that some white cops hate to arrest a Negro. They know if there's any trouble the press will play it up to look bad for the cop.

This interpretation seems reasonable, although questionnaire results indicate that it may be an oversimplification. It should be mentioned in passing that the Negro policemen also reported the Negro offender as being harder to handle.

WHITE PATROLMEN

On the questionnaires distributed to the white patrolmen the question relating to the Negro offender was, "In your daily experience have you found it necessary to be more strict with Negro law violators than with white violators?" The response was as follows ($N = 1,081$): "Yes," 51.8 per cent; "No," 43.8 per cent; no answer, 4.4 per cent.

TABLE 1

	"In Your Daily Experience Have You Found It Necessary to Be More Strict with Negro Law Violators than with White Violators?"			
	Per Cent "Yes"	Per Cent "No"	Per Cent No Opinion	No. of Cases
"Would you have any objection to riding with a Negro patrolman?"				
"Yes"	65.4	32.1	2.5	643
"No"	29.0	65.9	5.1	355
No opinion	43.3	39.8	16.9	83
Total	51.8	43.8	4.4	1,081

Chi square $= 118.22$; P less than .001.

It is difficult to discover whether or not Negroes are victimized by white policemen. The above figures shed some light on the problem; a majority of the white patrolmen stated that they were more strict with Negro than with white offenders. They also stated—in comments written in on the questionnaire—that this differential treatment is "necessary" because of the contentiousness and belligerency of the Negro offender:

> Yes, they seem more belligerent and take the attitude that they are being picked on because of their color.
>
> Yes, you must keep your eye on them, otherwise they would steal your badge.
>
> Yes, let the Negro think you are the least bit afraid, then you have to get tough.
>
> Yes, if you try to talk to them in a nice way they think you fear them and become arrogant.

DIFFERENTIAL TREATMENT: A HYPOTHESIS

Although the above comments—as well as the previously quoted statements of district captains—may sound convincing, the fact remains that a substantial minority (43.8 per cent) of the white patrolmen do *not* find it necessary to be unduly strict with Negro offenders. Theoretically, this group of white patrolmen might be those who work in all-white districts and rarely have contact with Negro offenders. Actually, this held for only 5 per cent of the white patrolmen. A number of other variables—such as age, length of service, and education—were tested but found not statistically significant.

One area remained to be examined: the relationship between the white patrolman's opinions about Negro policemen and his treatment of the Negro law violator. The hypothesis to be tested was the following: White patrolmen who have unfavorable opinions about Negro policemen tend to be "more strict" with the Negro offender (relative to the white offender), while those whose opinions about Negro policemen are favorable tend to treat both Negro and white violators about the same.

For the purposes of this study, white patrolmen who signified that they object to riding in patrol cars with Negro patrolmen or object to taking orders from a well-qualified Negro commander or prefer not to have Negroes assigned to their district or believe that there are too many Negroes on the force are assumed to have opinions unfavorable to Negro patrolmen. White patrolmen who stated that they had no objections to such association with Negro patrolmen are assumed to have favorable opinions about Negro policemen. Data from the questionnaires support the hypothesis (Tables 1, 2, 3, and 4).

It is clear that the white patrolmen who "find it necessary to be more strict with Negro than with white violators" tend to object to riding with Negro partners, to object to taking orders from a well-qualified Negro commander, to believe that there are too many Negroes on the force, or to prefer not to have Negroes assigned to their district.

Whereas 51.8 per cent of all white patrolmen are more strict with Negro than with white offenders, 65.4 per cent of the patrolmen who object to riding with Negro partners are more strict with Negro than with white offenders (Table 1). For patrolmen who prefer not to have Negroes assigned to their district the figure is 67.2 per cent (Table 2); for patrolmen who object to taking orders from a well-qualified Negro commander the figure is 71.5 per cent (Table 3); for patrolmen who believe there are too many Negroes on the force the figure is 76.3 per cent (Table 4).

Generally speaking, these figures can mean one (or a combination) of three things: (a) adverse experience with Negro policemen has conditioned these patrolmen against Negroes, hence the strictness with Negro offenders; (b) adverse experience with Negro offenders has conditioned these patrolmen against Negroes, hence the unfavorable opinions about Negro patrolmen; (c) these patrolmen have general anti-Negro feelings which are directed toward both Negro policemen and Negro offenders. The writer leans toward the latter view, since, among other things, neither length of service nor amount of contact with Negro policemen *or* offenders correlated statistically with treatment of Negro offenders.

TABLE 2

	"In Your Daily Experience Have You Found It Necessary to Be More Strict with Negro Law Violators than with White Violators?"			
	Per Cent "Yes"	Per Cent "No"	Per Cent No Opinion	No. of Cases
"Which of the following statements expresses your own feelings?"				
a) It doesn't matter to me whether Negroes are assigned to my district	36.1	58.5	5.4	445
b) It doesn't matter to me whether Negroes are assigned to my district as long as I don't have to work with them	68.8	29.5	1.7	305
c) I would prefer not to have any Negroes assigned to my district	67.2	29.2	3.6	168
d) No opinion on this	46.6	45.4	8.0	163
Total	51.8	43.8	4.4	1,081

Chi square = 88.97; P less than .001.

If the hypothesis is correct—white patrolmen who have unfavorable opinions about Negro policemen evidence general anti-Negro feelings which are also reflected in a comparatively strict treatment of the Negro offender—then the differential treatment accorded the Negro offender is not altogether a product of the latter's contentiousness.

TABLE 3

| | "In Your Daily Experience Have You Found It Necessary to Be More Strict with Negro Law Violators than with White Violators?" | | | |
	Per Cent "Yes"	Per Cent "No"	Per Cent No Opinion	No. of Cases
"Would you, or do you, have any objections to taking orders from a Negro sergeant or captain if he were qualified?"				
"Yes"	71.5	24.8	3.7	387
"No"	40.4	55.4	4.2	578
No opinion	42.2	49.1	8.7	116
Total	51.8	43.8	4.4	1,081

Chi square $= 92.41$; P less than .001.

TABLE 4

| | "In Your Daily Experience Have You Found It Necessary to Be More Strict with Negro Law Violators than with White Violators?" | | | |
	Per Cent "Yes"	Per Cent "No"	Per Cent No Opinion	No. of Cases
"At the present time, which of the following expresses your opinion?"				
a) There are not enough Negroes on the force	50.0	47.8	2.2	138
b) The number is about right	59.4	38.2	2.4	417
c) There are too many Negroes on the force	76.3	21.0	2.7	114
d) No opinion on this point	37.8	54.4	7.8	412
Total	51.8	43.8	4.4	1,081

Chi square $= 19.70$; P less than .001.

On the basis of the Philadelphia findings, the interaction between white policemen and Negro law violators might be characterized as follows: In general, white patrolmen are inclined to be more strict in their dealings with Negro offenders than in their handling of white offenders. Negro offenders tend to resist arrest more often than do white offenders. These two tendencies fortify each other.

Charles C. Moskos, Jr.

RACIAL INTEGRATION IN THE ARMED FORCES [1]

Advocates of "Black Power" in SNCC and some other civil rights organizations have urged Negroes to keep out of the armed forces and shun "whitey's" Viet Nam war. Yet, as pointed out in Charles C. Moskos, Jr.'s article, proportionately more Negroes than whites join the armed services and reenlist with the view of embracing a military career. To many economically deprived youths in the ghetto, the army offers an escape from second-class status.

Beginning in 1948 when political pressure from northern Negroes prodded Harry Truman into ordering desegregation, the armed forces, first slowly, then with increasing vigor and determination, were transformed from a segregated establishment to an integrated one. The results are evident today in improved efficiency and morale among Negro servicemen and in reduced attitudes of animosity among whites.

Yet, after all, our military branches protect an American society which has inculcated in its members the norms of racial separation. Therefore, as Moskos points out, not surprisingly when the soldiers are off-duty they go their own separate ways. The author suggests that the pattern of race relations in our armed forces might well anticipate what things will be like when civilian America becomes as integrated as its military establishment.

Charles C. Moskos, Jr. "Racial Integration in the Armed Forces," *American Journal of Sociology*, LXXII (September, 1966), pp. 132–48. Reprinted with the permission of *The American Journal of Sociology*.

[1] Many persons have given the writer invaluable assistance during his collection and analysis of the materials for this paper. I would especially like to thank Lieutenant Colonel Roger W. Little, U.S. Military Academy, John B. Spore, editor of *Army* magazine, Philip M. Timpane, staff assistant for civil rights, Department of Defense, and Morris Janowitz, University of Chicago. Also, the writer's access to military personnel at all levels was made possible by the more than perfunctory co-operation of numerous military information officers, men who perform a difficult task with both efficiency and good humor. Financial support was given by the Inter-University Seminar on Armed Forces and Society sponsored by the Russell Sage Foundation. Additional funds for travel were

On JULY 28, 1948, President Truman issued an executive order abolishing racial segregation in the armed forces of the United States. By the middle 1950's this policy was an accomplished fact. The lessons of the racial integration of the military are many. Within a remarkably short period the makeup of a major American institution underwent a far-reaching transformation. At the same time, the desegregation of the military can be used to trace some of the mutual permeations between the internal organization of the military establishment and the racial and social cleavages found in the larger setting of American society. Further, because of the favorable contrast in the military performance of integrated Negro servicemen with that of all-Negro units, the integration of the armed services is a demonstration of how changes in social organization can bring about a marked and rapid improvement in individual and group achievement. The desegregated military, moreover, offers itself as a graphic example of the abilities of both whites and Negroes to adjust to egalitarian racial relations with surprisingly little strain. Also, an examination of the racial situation in the contemporary military establishment can serve as a partial guideline as to what one might expect in a racially integrated America. It is to these and related issues that this paper is addressed.[2]

made available by the University of Michigan, and the Council for Intersocietal Studies of Northwestern University. It must be stressed, however, that the usual caveat that the author alone accepts responsibility for the interpretations and conclusions is especially relevant here.

[2] The information on which the observations presented in this paper are based is of a varied sort. A primary source are Department of Defense statistics and those United States government reports dealing with racial relations in the armed forces: President's Committee on Equality of Treatment and Opportunity in the Armed Forces ("Fahy Committee"), *Freedom to Serve: Equality of Treatment and Opportunity in the Armed Forces* (Washington, D.C.: Government Printing Office, 1950); U.S. Commission on Civil Rights, "The Negro in the Armed Forces," *Civil Rights '63* (Washington, D.C.: Government Printing Office, 1963), pp. 169–224; President's Committee on Equal Opportunity in the Armed Forces ("Gesell Committee"), "Initial Report: Equality of Treatment and Opportunity for Negro Personnel Stationed within the United States" (mimeographed; June, 1963), and "Final Report: Military Personnel Stationed Overseas and Membership and Participation in the National Guard" (mimeographed; November, 1964). Also, participant observations were made by the writer while on active duty in the Army and during field trips to military installations in Germany, Viet Nam, and Korea in the summer of 1965 and in the Dominican Republic in the spring of 1966. Additionally, during the field trip in Germany, sixty-seven formal interviews were conducted with soldiers who made up nearly all of the total Negro enlisted personnel in two Army companies. Another source of data is found in Operations Research Office ("ORO"), *Project Clear: The Utilization of Negro Manpower in the Army* (Chevy Chase, Md.: Operations Research Office, Johns Hopkins University, April, 1955). The ORO surveys queried several thousand servicemen during the Korean War on a variety of items relating to attitudes toward racial integration in the Army. The findings of Project Clear, heretofore classified, have now been made available for professional scrutiny. Some comparable data were obtained from the section dealing with Negro soldiers in Samuel A. Stouffer *et al., The American Soldier: Adjustment during Army Life*, Vol. I (Princeton, N.J.: Princeton University Press, 1949), pp. 486–599.

DESEGREGATING THE MILITARY [3]

Negroes have taken part in all of this country's wars. An estimated 5,000 Negroes, some scattered as individuals and others in segregated units, fought on the American side in the War of Independence. Several thousand Negroes saw service in the War of 1812. During the Civil War 180,000 Negroes were recruited into the Union army and served in segregated regiments.[4] Following the Civil War four Negro regiments were established and were active in the Indian wars on the western frontier and later fought with distinction in Cuba during the Spanish-American War. In the early twentieth century, however, owing to a general rise in American racial tensions and specific outbreaks of violence between Negro troops and whites, opinion began to turn against the use of Negro soldiers. Evaluation of Negro soldiers was further lowered by events in World War I. The combat performance of the all-Negro 92nd In-

[3] This background of the Negro's role in the American military is derived, in addition to the sources cited above, from Seymour J. Schoenfeld, *The Negro in the Armed Forces* (Washington, D.C.: Associated Publishers, 1945); Paul C. Davis, "The Negro in the Armed Services," *Virginia Quarterly*, XXIV (Autumn, 1948), 499–520; Herbert Aptheker, *Essays in the History of the American Negro* (New York: International Publishers, 1945); Arnold M. Rose, "Army Policies toward Negro Soldiers," *Annals of the American Academy of Political and Social Science*, CCXLIV (March, 1946), 90–94; Eli Ginzburg, "The Negro Soldier," in his *The Negro Potential* (New York: Columbia University Press, 1956), pp. 61–91; David G. Mandelbaum, *Soldiers Groups and Negro Soldiers* (Berkeley: University of California Press, 1952); and Benjamin Quarles, *The Negro in the Making of America* (New York: Collier Books, 1964), *passim*. A good account of the early days of military desegregation is Lee Nichols, *Breakthrough on the Color Front* (New York: Random House, 1954).

Though the last several years have seen little social science research on racial relations in the armed forces, there has recently been a spate of novels dealing with this theme. See, e.g., John Oliver Killens, *And Then We Heard the Thunder* (New York: Alfred A. Knopf, Inc., 1963); James Drought, *Mover* (New York: Avon Books, 1963); Webb Beech, *Article 92* (Greenwich, Conn.: Gold Medal Books, 1964); Gene L. Coon, *The Short End* (New York: Dell Publishing Co., 1964); Hari Rhodes, *A Chosen Few* (New York: Bantam Books, 1965); and Jack Pearl, *Stockade* (New York: Pocket Books, 1965).

It should be noted that Negroes have not been the only ethnic or racial group to occupy a unique position in the American military. Indians served in separate battalions in the Civil War and were used as scouts in the frontier wars. Filipinos have long been a major source of recruitment for stewards in the Navy. The much decorated 442nd ("Go For Broke") Infantry Regiment of World War II was composed entirely of Japanese-Americans. Also in World War II, a separate battalion of Norwegian-Americans was drawn up for intended service in Scandinavia. The participation of Puerto Ricans in the American military deserves special attention. A recent case of large-scale use of non-American soldiers are the Korean fillers or "Katusas" (from Korean Augmentation to the U.S. Army) who make up roughly one-sixth of the current personnel of the Eighth Army.

[4] A particularly insightful contemporary report on Negro soldiers in the Civil War is Thomas Wentworth Higgins, *Army Life in a Black Regiment* (New York: Collier Books, 1962).

fantry, one of its regiments having fled in the German offensive at Meuse-Argonne, came under heavy criticism. Yet it was also observed that Negro units operating under French command, in a more racially tolerant situation, performed well.

In the interval between the two world wars, the Army not only remained segregated but also adopted a policy of a Negro quota that was to keep the number of Negroes in the Army proportionate to the total population. Never in the pre-World War II period, however, did the number of Negroes approach this quota. On the eve of Pearl Harbor, Negroes constituted 5.9 per cent of the Army; and there were only five Negro officers, three of whom were chaplains. During World War II Negroes entered the Army in larger numbers, but at no time did they exceed 10 per cent of total personnel. Negro soldiers remained in segregated units, and approximately three-quarters served in the quartermaster, engineer, and transportation corps. To make matters worse from the viewpoint of "the right to fight," a slogan loudly echoed by Negro organizations in the United States, even Negro combat units were frequently used for heavy-duty labor. This was highlighted when the 2nd Cavalry was broken up into service units owing to command apprehension over the combat qualities, even though untested, of this all-Negro division. The record of those Negro units that did see combat in World War II was mixed. The performance of the 92nd Infantry Division again came under heavy criticism, this time for alleged unreliability in the Italian campaign.

An important exception to the general pattern of utilization of Negro troops in World War II occurred in the winter months of 1944–45 in the Ardennes battle. Desperate shortages of combat personnel resulted in the Army asking for Negro volunteers. The plan was to have platoons (approximately 40 men) of Negroes serve in companies (approximately 200 men) previously all-white. Some 2,500 Negroes volunteered for this assignment. Both in terms of Negro combat performance and white soldiers' reactions, the Ardennes experiment was an unqualified success. This incident would later be used to support arguments for integration.

After World War II, pressure from Negro and liberal groups coupled with an acknowledgment that Negro soldiers were being poorly utilized led the Army to re-examine its racial policies. A report by an Army board in 1945, while holding racial integration to be a desirable goal and while making recommendations to improve Negro opportunity in the Army, concluded that practical considerations required a maintenance of segregation and the quota system. In light of World War II experiences, the report further recommended that Negro personnel be exclusively assigned to support rather than combat units. Another Army board report came out in 1950 with essentially the same conclusions.[5] Both reports placed heavy stress on the supervisory and disciplinary problems resulting from the disproportionate number of Negroes, as

[5] The 1945 and 1950 Army board reports are commonly referred to by the names of the officers who headed these boards: respectively, Lieutenant General Alvan C. Gillem, Jr., and Lieutenant General S. J. Chamberlin.

established by Army examinations, found in the lower mental and aptitude classification levels. In 1950, for example, 60 per cent of the Negro personnel fell into the Army's lowest categories compared with 29 per cent of the white soldiers. From the standpoint of the performance requirements of the military, such facts could not be lightly dismissed.

After the Truman desegregation order of 1948, however, the die was cast. The President followed his edict by setting up a committee, chaired by Charles Fahy, to pursue the implementation of equal treatment and opportunity for armed forces personnel. Under the impetus of the Fahy committee, the Army abolished the quota system in 1950, and was beginning to integrate some training camps when the conflict in Korea broke out. The Korean War was the coup de grâce for segregation in the Army. Manpower requirements in the field for combat soldiers resulted in many instances of *ad hoc* integration. As was true in the Ardennes experience, Negro soldiers in previously all-white units performed well in combat. As integration in Korea became more standard, observers consistently noted that the fighting abilities of Negroes differed little from those of whites.[6] This contrasted with the blemished record of the all-Negro 24th Infantry Regiment.[7] Its performance in the Korean War was judged to be so poor that its divisional commander recommended the unit be dissolved as quickly as possible. Concurrent with events in Korea, integration was introduced in the United States. By 1956, three years after the end of the Korean War, the remnants of Army Jim Crow disappeared at home and in overseas installations. At the time of the Truman order, Negroes constituted 8.8 per cent of Army personnel. In 1964 the figure was 12.3 per cent.

In each of the other services, the history of desegregation varied from the Army pattern. The Army Air Force, like its parent body, generally assigned Negroes to segregated support units. (However, a unique military venture taken during the war was the formation of three all-Negro, including officers, air combat units.) At the end of World War II the proportion of Negroes in the Army Air Force was only 4 per cent, less than half what it was in the Army. Upon its establishment as an independent service in 1947, the Air Force began to take steps toward integration even before the Truman order. By the time of the Fahy committee report in 1950, the Air Force was already largely integrated. Since integration there has been a substantial increase in the proportion of Negroes serving in the Air Force, from less than 5 per cent in 1949 to 8.6 per cent in 1964.

Although large numbers of Negroes had served in the Navy during the Civil War and for some period afterward, restrictive policies were introduced

[6] These evaluations are summarized in ORO, *op. cit.*, pp. 16–19, 47–105, and 582–83.

[7] The notoriety of the 24th Infantry Regiment was aggravated by a song—"The Bug-Out Boogie"—attributed to it: "When them Chinese mortars begin to thud / The old Deuce-Four begin to bug / When they started falling 'round the CP [command post] tent / Everybody wonder where the high brass went / They were buggin' out / Just movin' on."

in the early 1900's, and by the end of World War I only about 1 per cent of Navy personnel were Negroes. In 1920 the Navy adopted a policy of total racial exclusion and barred all Negro enlistments. This policy was changed in 1932 when Negroes, along with Filipinos, were again allowed to join the Navy but only as stewards in the messman's branch. Further modifications were made in Navy policy in 1942 when some openings in general service for Negroes were created. Negro sailors in these positions, however, were limited to segregated harbor and shore assignments.[8] In 1944, in the first effort toward desegregation in any of the armed services, a small number of Negro sailors in general service were integrated on ocean-going vessels. After the end of World War II the Navy, again ahead of the other services, began to take major steps toward elimination of racial barriers. Even in the integrated Navy of today, however, approximately a quarter of Negro personnel still serve as stewards. Also, despite the early steps toward integration taken by the Navy, the proportion of Negro sailors has remained fairly constant over the past two decades, averaging around 5 per cent.

The Marine Corps has gone from a policy of exclusion to segregation to integration. Before World War II there were no Negro marines. In 1942 Negroes were accepted into the Marine Corps but assigned to segregated units where they were heavy-duty laborers, ammunition handlers and anti-aircraft gunners. After the war small-scale integration of Negro marines into white units was begun. In 1949 and 1950 Marine Corps training units were integrated, and by 1954 the color line was largely erased throughout the Corps. Since integration began, the proportion of Negroes has increased markedly. In 1949 less than 2 per cent of all marines were Negroes compared with 8.2 per cent in 1964.

TABLE 1

NEGROES IN THE ARMED FORCES AND EACH SERVICE AS A PERCENTAGE OF TOTAL PERSONNEL, 1962 AND 1964

Service	1962	1964
Army	11.1	12.3
Air Force	7.8	8.6
Navy	4.7	5.1
Marine Corps	7.0	8.2
Total armed forces	8.2	9.0

Source: U.S. Commission on Civil Rights, *op. cit.*, p. 218; Department of Defense statistics.

Although the various military services are all similar in being integrated today, they differ in their proportion of Negroes. As shown in Table 1, the

[8] A lesson in the rewriting of history is gained from the movie PT-109, a dramatization of John Kennedy's war exploits. In this film, released in the early 1960's, the Navy is portrayed as racially integrated in World War II.

Negro distribution in the total armed forces in 1962 and 1964, respectively, was 8.2 per cent and 9.0 per cent, lower than the 11–12 per cent constituting the Negro proportion in the total population. It is virtually certain, however, that among those *eligible*, a higher proportion of Negroes than whites enter the armed forces. That is, a much larger number of Negroes do not meet the entrance standards required by the military services. In 1962, for example, 56.1 per cent of Negroes did not pass the preinduction mental examinations given to draftees, almost four times the 15.4 per cent of whites who failed these same tests.[9] Because of the relatively low number of Negroes obtaining student or occupational deferments, however, it is the Army drawing upon the draft that is the only military service where the percentage of Negroes approximates the national proportion. Thus, despite the high number of Negroes who fail to meet induction standards, Army statistics for 1960–65 show Negroes constituted about 15 per cent of those drafted.

Even if one takes account of the Army's reliance on the selective service for much of its personnel, the most recent figures still show important differences in the number of Negroes in those services meeting their manpower requirements solely through voluntary enlistments; the 5.1 per cent Negro in the Navy is lower than the 8.2 per cent for the Marine Corps or the 8.6 per cent for the Air Force. Moreover, the Army, besides its drawing upon the draft, also has the highest Negro initial enlistment rate of any of the services.

TABLE 2

NEGROES IN EACH OF THE ARMED SERVICES AS A PERCENTAGE OF INITIAL ENLISTMENTS 1961, 1963, AND 1965

Year	Army	Air Force	Navy	Marine Corps
1961	8.2	9.5	2.9	5.9
1963	11.2	10.5	4.3	5.5
1965	14.1	13.1	5.8	8.4

Source: Department of Defense statistics.

As reported in Table 2, we find in 1964 that the Army drew 14.1 per cent of its volunteer incoming personnel from Negroes as compared with 13.1 per cent for the Air Force, 8.4 per cent for the Marine Corps, and 5.8 per cent for the Navy. As also shown in Table 2, there has been a very sizable increase in Negro enlistments from 1961 to 1965 in all four of the armed services.

There are also diverse patterns between the individual services as to the rank or grade distribution of Negroes. Looking at Table 3, we find the ratio of Negro to white officers is roughly 1 to 30 in the Army, 1 to 70 in the Air Force, 1 to 250 in the Marine Corps, and 1 to 300 in the Navy. Among enlisted men, Negroes are underrepresented in the top three enlisted ranks in

[9] Department of Labor ("Moynihan Report"), *The Negro Family: The Case for National Action* (Washington, D.C.: Government Printing Office, 1965), p. 75.

the Army and the top four ranks in the other three services. We also find a disproportionate concentration of Negroes in the lower non-commissioned officer ranks in all of the armed forces, but especially so in the Army. As assessment of these data reveals that the Army, followed by the Air Force, has

TABLE 3

NEGROES AS A PERCENTAGE OF TOTAL PERSONNEL IN EACH GRADE FOR EACH SERVICE, 1964

Grade	Army	Air Force	Navy	Marine Corps
Officers:				
Generals/admirals		0.2		
Colonels/captains	0.2	0.2		
Lt. cols./commanders	1.1	0.5	0.6	
Majors/lt. commanders	3.6	0.8	0.3	0.3
Captains/lieutenants	5.4	2.0	0.5	0.4
1st lieutenants/lts. (j.g.)	3.8	1.8	0.2	0.4
2d lieutenants/ensigns	2.7	2.5	0.7	0.3
Total officers	3.4	1.5	0.3	0.4
Enlisted: *				
E-9 (sgt. major)	3.5	1.2	1.5	0.8
E-8 (master sgt.)	6.1	2.2	1.9	1.2
E-7 (sgt. 1st class)	8.5	3.2	2.9	2.3
E-6 (staff sgt.)	13.9	5.3	4.7	5.0
E-5 (sgt.)	17.4	10.8	6.6	11.2
E-4 (corp.)	14.2	12.7	5.9	10.4
E-3 (pvt. 1st class)	13.6	9.7	6.6	7.8
E-2 (private)	13.1	11.7	5.7	9.5
E-1 (recruit)	6.8	14.4	7.1	9.1
Total enlisted men	13.4	10.0	5.8	8.7

* Army and Marine Corps enlisted titles indicated in parentheses have equivalent pay grades in Navy and Air Force.
Source: Department of Defense statistics.

not only the largest proportion of Negroes in its total personnel, but also the most equitable distribution of Negroes throughout its ranks. Although the Navy was the last, in a kind of tortoise and hare fashion, it is the Army that has become the most representative service for Negroes.

CHANGING MILITARY REQUIREMENTS AND NEGRO OPPORTUNITIES

A pervasive trend within the military establishments singled out by students of this institution is the long-term direction toward greater technical complexity and narrowing of civilian-military occupational skills.[10] An indicator, albeit a crude one, of this trend toward "professionalization" of military roles is the changing proportion of men assigned to combat arms. Given in Table 4, along with concomitant white-Negro distributions, are figures comparing the percentage of Army enlisted personnel in combat arms (e.g., infantry, armor, artillery) for the years 1945 and 1962. We find that the proportion of men in combat arms—that is, traditional military specialties—dropped from 44.5 per cent in 1945 to 26.0 per cent in 1962. Also, the percentage of white personnel in traditional military specialties approximates the total proportional decrease in the combat arms over the seventeen-year period.

For Negro soldiers, however, a different picture emerges. While the percentage of Negro enlisted men in the Army increased only slightly between

TABLE 4

TOTAL NEGRO ARMY ENLISTED PERSONNEL AND WHITE AND NEGRO ENLISTED PERSONNEL IN COMBAT ARMS, 1945 AND 1962

Category	1945 *	1962
Negroes as percentage of total personnel	10.5	12.2
Percentage of total personnel in combat arms	44.5	26.0
Percentage of total white personnel in combat arms	48.2	24.9
Percentage of total negro personnel in combat arms	12.1	33.4

* Excludes Army Air Force.

Source: ORO, *op. cit.*, pp. 563–64; U.S. Civil Rights Commission, *op. cit.*, pp. 219–22.

1945 and 1962, the likelihood of a Negro serving in a combat arm is almost three times greater in 1962 than it was at the end of World War II. Further, when comparisons are made between military specialties *within* the combat arms, the Negro proportion is noticeably higher in line rather than staff assignments. This is especially the case in airborne and marine units. Put in another way, the direction in assignment of Negro soldiers in the desegregated military is testimony to the continuing consequences of differential Negro opportunity originating in the larger society. That is, even though integration of the military has led to great improvement in the performance of Negro servicemen, the social and particularly educational deprivations suffered by the Negro in American society can be mitigated but not entirely eliminated by the racial egalitarianism existing within the armed forces.[11] These findings

[10] Morris Janowitz with Roger Little, *Sociology and the Military Establishment* (New York: Russell Sage Foundation, 1965), pp. 17–49; and Kurt Lang, "Technology and Career Management in the Military Establishment," in Morris Janowitz (ed.), *The New Military: Changing Patterns of Organization* (New York: Russell Sage Foundation, 1964), pp. 39–81.

[11] World War II evidence shows much of the incidence of psychoneurotic breakdown among Negro soldiers, compared to whites, was associated with psychological

need not be interpreted as a decline in the "status" of the Negro in the integrated military. Actually there is evidence that higher prestige—but not envy—is accorded combat personnel by those in non-combat activities within the military.[12] And taken within the historical context of "the right to fight," the Negro's overrepresentation in the combat arms is a kind of ironic step forward.[13]

Moreover, the military at the enlisted ranks has become a major avenue of career mobility for many Negro men.[14] As shown earlier in Table 3, in all four services, and especially in the Army, there is some overrepresentation of Negroes at the junior NCO levels (pay grades E-4–E-6). The disproportionate concentration of Negroes at these levels implies a higher than average re-enlistment as these grades are not normally attained until after a second enlistment. This assumption is supported by the data given in Table 5. We find that in 1965 for all four services the Negro re-enlistment rate is approximately twice that of white servicemen. Indeed, about half of all first-term Negro servicemen chose to remain in the armed forces for at least a second term. The greater likelihood of Negroes to select a service career suggests that the military establishment is undergoing a significant change in the NCO core. Such an outcome would reflect not only the "pull" of the appeals offered by a racially egalitarian institution, but also the "push" generated by the plight of the Negro in the American economy.[15] At the minimum, it is very probable that as the present cohort of Negro junior NCO's attains seniority there will be a greater representation of Negroes in the advanced NCO grades. The expansion of the armed forces arising from the war in Viet Nam and the resulting opening up of "rank" will accelerate this development.

---

handicaps originating before entrance into military service (Arnold M. Rose, "Psychoneurotic Breakdown among Negro Soldiers," *Phylon*, XVII, No. 1 [1956], pp. 61–73).

[12] Stouffer *et al.*, *op. cit.*, II, 242–89; Raymond W. Mack, "The Prestige System of an Air Base: Squadron Rankings and Morale," *American Sociological Review*, XIX (June, 1954), 281–87; Morris Janowitz, *The Professional Soldier* (Glencoe, Ill.: Free Press, 1960), pp. 31–36.

[13] There are, as should be expected, differences among Negro soldiers as to their desire to see combat. From data not shown here, interviews with Negro soldiers stationed in Germany revealed reluctance to go to Viet Nam was greatest among those with high-school or better education, and northern home residence. This is in direct contrast with the findings reported in *The American Soldier*. In the segregated Army of World War II, northern and more highly educated Negro soldiers were most likely to want to get into combat, an outcome of the onus of inferiority felt to accompany service in support units (Stouffer, *op. cit.*, I, 523–24).

[14] The emphasis on academic education for officer careers effectively limits most Negro opportunity to the enlisted levels (Lang, *op. cit.*, p. 62).

[15] Documentation shows the gap between Negro and white job opportunities has not diminished appreciably, if at all, in the past twenty years (Department of Labor, *op. cit.*, pp. 19–21; Thomas F. Pettigrew, A *Profile of the Negro American* [Princeton, N.J.: D. Van Nostrand Co., 1964], pp. 168–74).

ATTITUDES OF SOLDIERS

So far the discussion has sought to document the degree of penetration and the kind of distribution characterizing Negro servicemen in the integrated military establishment. We now introduce certain survey and interview data dealing more directly with the question of soldiers' attitudes toward military desegregation. Commenting on the difficulties of social analysis, the authors of *The American Soldier* wrote that few problems are "more formidable than that of obtaining dependable records of attitudes toward racial separation in the Army." [16] Without underestimating the continuing difficulty of this problem, an opportunity exists to compare attitudes toward racial integration held by American soldiers in two different periods. This is done by contrasting responses to equivalent items given in World War II as reported in *The American Soldier* with those reported in Project Clear a study sponsored by the Defense Department during the Korean War. [17]

In both *The American Soldier* and Project Clear (the surveys under consideration were conducted in 1943 and 1951, respectively) large samples of Army personnel in segregated military settings were categorized as to whether

TABLE 5

FIRST-TERM RE-ENLISTMENT RATES IN THE ARMED FORCES AND
EACH SERVICE BY RACE, 1965
(PER CENT)

Race	Total Armed Forces	Army	Air Force	Navy	Marine Corps
White	21.6	18.5	27.4	21.6	12.9
Negro	46.6	49.3	50.3	41.3	50.3

Source: Department of Defense statistics.

they were favorable, indifferent, or opposed to racial integration in Army units. We find, as presented in Table 6, massive shifts in soldiers' attitudes over the eight-year period, shifts showing a much more positive disposition toward racial integration among both whites and Negroes in the later year. A look at the distribution of attitudes held by white soldiers reveals opposition

[16] Stouffer *et al.*, *op. cit.*, p. 566.

[17] What methodological bias exists is that the Korean War question was a stronger description of racial integration than the item used in World War II. Compare "What is your feeling about serving in a platoon containing both whites and colored soldiers, all working and training together, sleeping in the same barracks and eating in the same mess hall?" with "Do you think white and Negro soldiers should be in separate outfits or should they be together in the same outfits?" (respectively, ORO, *op. cit.*, p. 453, and Stouffer *et al.*, *op. cit.*, p. 568).

to integration goes from 84 per cent in 1943 to less than half in 1951. That such a change could occur in less than a decade counters viewpoints that see basic social attitudes in large populations being prone to glacial-like changes. Yet, an even more remarkable change is found among the Negro soldiers. Where in 1945, favorable, indifferent, or opposing attitudes were roughly equally distributed among the Negro soldiers, by 1951 opposition or indifference to racial integration had become negligible. Such a finding is strongly

TABLE 6

ATTITUDES OF WHITE AND NEGRO SOLDIERS TOWARD RACIAL INTEGRATION IN THE SEGREGATED ARMY, 1943 AND 1951

Attitude Toward Integration	Negro Soldiers (Per Cent)		White Soldiers (Per Cent)	
	1943	1951	1943	1951
Favorable	12	25	37	90
Indifferent	4	31	27	6
Oppose	84	44	36	4
Total	100	100	100	100
(No. of cases)	(4,800)	(1,983)	(3,000)	(1,384)

Source: Stouffer et al., op. cit., p. 568; ORO, op. cit., pp. 322, 433.

indicative of a reformation in Negro public opinion from traditional acquiescence to Jim Crow to the ground swell that laid the basis for the subsequent civil rights movement.

While the data on Negro attitudes toward integration given in Table 6 were elicited during the segregated military of 1943 and 1951, we also have evidence on how Negro soldiers react to military integration in the contemporary setting. As reported in Table 7, the Army is overwhelmingly thought to be more racially egalitarian than civilian life. Only 16 per cent of sixty-seven Negro soldiers interviewed in 1965 said civilian life was more racially equal or no different than the Army. By region, as might be expected, we find southern Negroes more likely than northern Negroes to take a benign view of racial relations in the Army when these are compared to civilian life. The data in Table 7 support the proposition that, despite existing deviations from military policy at the level of informal discrimination, the military establishment stands in sharp and favorable contrast to the racial relations prevalent in the larger American society.

One of the most celebrated findings of *The American Soldier* was the discovery that the more contact white soldiers had with Negro troops, the more favorable was their reaction toward racial integration.[18] This conclusion is consistently supported in the surveys conducted by Project Clear.

[18] *Ibid.,* p. 594.

TABLE 7

ATTITUDES OF NEGRO SOLDIERS IN 1965 COMPARING RACIAL EQUALITY
IN MILITARY AND CIVILIAN LIFE, TOTAL AND BY HOME REGION

| | Per Cent | | |
| | | Home Region | |
Where More Racial Equality	Total	North	South
Military life	84	75	93
Civilian life	3	6	0
No difference	13	19	7
Total	100	100	100
(No. of cases)	(67)	(36)	(31)

Again and again, comparisons of white soldiers in integrated units with those in segregated units show the former to be more supportive of desegregation. Illustrative of this pattern are the data shown in Table 8. Among combat infantrymen in Korea, 51 per cent in all-white units say outfits are better segregated as compared to 31 per cent in integrated units. For enlisted personnel stationed in the United States, strong objection to integration characterizes 44 per cent serving in segregated units while less than one-fifth of the men in integrated units feel the same way. Seventy-nine per cent of officers on segregated posts rate Negroes worse than white soldiers as compared with 28 per cent holding similar beliefs on integrated posts.

OFFICIAL POLICY AND ACTUAL PRACTICE

For the man newly entering the armed forces, it is hard to conceive that the military was one of America's most segregated institutions less than two decades ago. For today color barriers at the formal level are absent throughout the military establishment. Equal treatment regardless of race is official policy in such non-duty facilities as swimming pools, chapels, barbershops, post exchanges, movie theaters, snack bars, and dependents' housing as well as in the more strictly military endeavors involved in the assignment, promotion, and living conditions of members of the armed services.[19] Moreover, white personnel are often commanded by Negro superiors, a situation rarely obtaining in civilian life. Recently the military has sought to implement its policy of equal opportunity by exerting pressure on local communities where segregated patterns affect military personnel. This policy deserves careful examination

[19] The comprehensive scope of military integration is found in the official guidelines set forth under "Equal Opportunity and Treatment of Military Personnel," in *Army Regulation 600–21, Air Force Regulation 35–78,* and *Secretary of the Navy Instruction 5350.6.*

TABLE 8

RACIAL ATTITUDES OF WHITE SOLDIERS IN SEGREGATED
AND INTEGRATED SETTINGS, 1951

Racial Attitudes	All-White Units		Integrated Units	
	Per Cent	No.	Per Cent	No.
Combat infantrymen in Korea saying segregated outfits better	51	(195)	31	(1,024)
Enlisted personnel in the U.S. strongly objecting to racial integration	44	(1,983)	17	(1,683)
Officers rating Negroes worse than white soldiers.	79	(233)	28	(385)

Source: ORO, *op. cit.*, pp. 141, 322, 333, 356.

owing to its ramifications on the traditional separation of civilian and military spheres in American society. A measure of the extent and thoroughness of military desegregation is found in comparing the 1950 President's committee report dealing with racial integration and the 1963 and 1964 reports of a second President's committee. Where the earlier report dealt entirely with internal military organization, the recent reports address themselves primarily to the National Guard and off-base discrimination.[20] Along this same line, Congressman Adam Clayton Powell has said that up to the middle 1950's he used to receive 5,000 letters a year from Negro servicemen complaining of discrimination in the military. In recent years, he receives less than 1,500 such letters annually and these largely pertain to off-base problems.[21] In brief, military life is characterized by an interracial equalitarianism of a quantity and of a kind that is seldom found in the other major institutions of American society.

In their performance of military duties, whites and Negroes work together with little display of racial tension. This is not to say racial animosity is absent in the military. Racial incidents do occur, but these are reduced by the severe sanctions imposed by the military for such acts. Such confrontations are almost always off-duty, if not off-base. In no sense, however, is the military sitting on top of a racial volcano, a state of affairs differing from the frequent clashes between the races that were a feature of the military in the segregated era. Additionally, it must be stressed that conflict situations stemming from non-racial causes characterize most sources of friction in the military establish-

[20] Cf. the Fahy committee report (1950), with the Gesell committee reports (1963 and 1964). The Moynihan Report comments, "Service in the United States Armed Forces is the only experience open to the Negro American in which he is truly treated as an equal. . . . If this is a statement of the ideal rather than reality, it is an ideal that is close to realization" (Department of Labor, *op. cit.*, p. 42).

[21] In an interview with the *Overseas Weekly*, a newspaper published in Germany with a large readership among American servicemen. Personal communication with staff members.

ment, for example, enlisted men versus officers, lower-ranking enlisted men versus non-commissioned officers, soldiers of middle-class background versus those of the working-class, conscriptees versus volunteers, line units versus staff units, rear echelon versus front echelon, combat units versus non-combat units, newly arrived units versus earlier stationed units, etc.

Yet the fact remains that the general pattern of day-to-day relationships *off the job* is usually one of mutual racial exclusivism. As one Negro soldier put it, "A man can be my best buddy in the Army, but he won't ask me to go to town with him." Closest friendships normally develop within races between individuals of similar educational background. Beyond one's hard core of friends there exists a level of friendly acquaintances. Here the pattern seems to be one of educational similarities over-riding racial differences. On the whole, racial integration at informal as well as formal levels works best on-duty vis-à-vis off-duty, on-base vis-à-vis off-base, basic training and maneuvers vis-à-vis garrison, sea vis-à-vis shore duty, and combat vis-à-vis non-combat. In other words, the behavior of servicemen resembles the racial (and class) separatism of the larger American society, the more they are removed from the military environment.

For nearly all white soldiers the military is a first experience with close and equal contact with a large group of Negroes. There has developed what has become practically a military custom: the look over the shoulder, upon the telling of a racial joke, to see if there are any Negroes in hearing distance. Some racial animosity is reflected in accusations that Negro soldiers use the defense of racial discrimination to avoid disciplinary action. Many white soldiers claim they like Negroes as individuals but "can't stand them in bunches." In a few extreme cases, white married personnel may even live off the military base and pay higher rents rather than live in integrated military housing. On the whole, however, the segregationist-inclined white soldier regards racial integration as something to be accepted pragmatically, if not enthusiastically, as are so many situations in military life.

The most overt source of racial unrest in the military community centers in dancing situations. A commentary on American mores is a finding reported in Project Clear: three-quarters of a large sample of white soldiers said they would not mind Negro couples on the same dance floor, but approximately the same number disapproved of Negro soldiers dancing with white girls.[22] In many non-commissioned officer (NCO) clubs, the likelihood of interracial dancing partners is a constant producer of tension. In fact, the only major exception to integration within the military community is on a number of large posts where there are two or more NCO clubs. In such situations one of the clubs usually becomes tacitly designated as the Negro club.

Although there is almost universal support for racial integration by Negro soldiers, some strains are also evident among Negro personnel in the military. There seems to be a tendency among lower-ranking Negro enlisted men,

[22] ORO, *op. cit.*, p. 388.

especially conscriptees, to view Negro NCO's as "Uncle Toms" or "handkerchief heads." Negro NCO's are alleged to pick on Negroes when it comes time to assign men unpleasant duties. Negro officers are sometimes seen as being too strict or "chicken" when it comes to enforcing military discipline on Negro soldiers. As one Negro serviceman said, "I'm proud when I see a Negro officer, but not in my company."

One Negro writer, who served in the segregated Army and now has two sons in the integrated military, has proposed that what was thought by soldiers in all-Negro units to be racial discrimination was sometimes nothing more than harassment of lower-ranking enlisted personnel.[23] In fact the analogy between enlisted men vis-à-vis officers in the military and Negroes vis-à-vis whites in the larger society has often been noted.[24] It has been less frequently observed, however, that enlisted men's behavior is often similar to many of the stereotypes associated with Negroes, for example, laziness, boisterousness, emphasis on sexual prowess, consciously acting stupid, obsequiousness in front of superiors combined with ridicule of absent superiors, etc. Placement of white adult males in a subordinate position within a rigidly stratified system, that is, appears to produce behavior not all that different from the so-called personality traits commonly held to be an outcome of cultural or psychological patterns unique to Negro life. Indeed, it might be argued that relatively little adjustment on the part of the command structure was required when the infusion of Negroes into the enlisted ranks occurred as the military establishment was desegregated. It is suggested, in other words, one factor contributing to the generally smooth racial integration of the military might be due to the standard treatment—"like Negroes" in a sense—accorded to all lower-ranking enlisted personnel.

Looking at changes in Negro behavior in the integrated military we find other indications of the immediate effects of social organization on individual behavior. Even though I am fully cognizant of the almost insurmountable difficulties involved in comparing crime statistics, the fact remains that students of the problem agree Negro crime is far higher than white crime.[25] There is no consensus, however, on what amount of the difference is due, on the one hand, to Negro cultural or psychological conditions or, on the other, to structural and class variables. Presented here, in a very preliminary fashion, is some evidence bearing on the consequences arising from changes in social organization on Negro crime. Reported by Project Clear are Negro-white crime differentials for three segregated posts in 1950. Proportionately,

[23] James Anderson, "Fathers and Sons: An Evaluation of Military Racial Relations in Two Generations" (term paper, University of Michigan, December, 1965).

[24] Stouffer and his associates, for example, report enlisted men as compared to officers, as Negro soldiers to white soldiers, were more prone to have "low spirits," to be less desirous of entering combat, and to be more dissatisfied than perceived by others (Stouffer et al., op. cit., II, 345, and I, 392–94, 506, 521, and 538.

[25] Marvin E. Wolfgang, Crime and Race (New York: Institute of Human Relations Press, 1964); and Department of Labor, op. cit., pp. 38–40.

Negro soldiers committed four times more crime than white soldiers.[26] In 1964, in the integrated military, statistics of a major Army Command in Europe show Negroes accounting for 21 per cent of the crime while constituting 16 per cent of the total personnel. In a large combat unit in Viet Nam, for a three-month period in the summer of 1965, Negroes received 19 per cent of the disciplinary reports but made up 22 per cent of the troop assignment. These are the only Negro-white crime ratios in the integrated military that the writer has seen.[27] Although these findings, of course, are incomplete, they do point to a marked drop in Negro crime as compared with both the earlier segregated military as well as contemporary civilian life.[28]

THE NEGRO SOLDIER OVERSEAS

Some special remarks are needed concerning Negro servicemen overseas. Suffice it to say for prefatory purposes, the American soldier, be he either white or Negro, is usually in a place where he does not understand the language, is received with mixed feelings by the local population, spends the greater part of his time in a transplanted American environment, sometimes plays the role of tourist, is relatively affluent in relation to the local economy, takes advantage and is at the mercy of a *comprador* class, and in comparison with his counterpart at home is more heavily involved in military duties.

In general, the pattern of racial relations observed in the United States—integration in the military setting and racial exclusivism off-duty—prevail in overseas assignments as well. This norm is reflected in one of the most characteristic features of American military life overseas, a bifurcation of the vice structure into groups that pander almost exclusively (or assert they do) to only one of the races. A frequent claim of local bar owners is that they discourage racially mixed trade because of the demands of the G.I. clientele. And, indeed, many of the establishments catering to American personnel that ring most military installations are segregated in practice. To a similar degree this is true of shore towns where Navy personnel take liberty. Violation of these implicit taboos can lead to physical threat if not violence.

The pattern of off-duty racial separatism is most pronounced in Japan and Germany, and less so in Korea. A major exception to this norm is found in the Dominican Republic. There all troops are restricted and leaving the

[26] ORO, *op. cit.*, p. 354.

[27] The data reported here are from offices of the Military Police, private communication.

[28] A caution to be introduced in assessing these findings is that the Army discharged many personnel of limited potential as determined by aptitude tests in 1957–58. Negroes were disproportionately represented in the released personnel (U.S. Commission on Civil Rights, *op. cit.*, pp. 176–77). Although Negroes are still overrepresented in the lower classification levels, there are probably proportionately fewer in these categories today than in 1950, and this most likely has some effect on the drop in Negro crime in the Army.

military compound necessitates soldiers collaborating if they are not to be detected; such ventures are often as not interracial. In certain off-duty areas on Okinawa, on the other hand, racial separatism is complicated by interservice rivalries and a fourfold ecological pattern shows up: white-Army, Negro-Army, white-Marine Corps, and Negro-Marine Corps. Combat conditions in Viet Nam make the issue of off-duty racial relations academic for those troops in the field. In the cities, however, racial separatism off-duty is already apparent. It is said that the riverfront district in Saigon, Kanh Hoi, frequented by American Negro soldiers was formerly patronized by Senegalese troops during the French occupation.

In Germany one impact of that country's economic boom has been to depress the relative position of the American soldier vis-à-vis the German working man. In the Germany of ten or fifteen years ago (or the Korea of today) all American military personnel were affluent by local standards with all that implied. This was (and is in Korea) an especially novel experience for the Negro soldier. The status drop of American soldiers stationed in Germany has particularly affected the Negro serviceman, who has the additional handicap of being black in a country where there are no Negro girls. The old "good duty" days for Negro soldiers in Germany are now coming to an end as he finds his previous access to girls other than prostitutes severely reduced. The German economic boom has affected Negro soldiers in another way. In recent years there has been some friction between foreign laborers (mostly Mediterranean) and Negro soldiers. Both groups of men apparently are competing for the same girls. At the same time, the foreign workers have little contact with white American soldiers who move in a different segment of the vice structure.

Nonetheless, overseas duty for the Negro serviceman, in Germany as well as the Far East, gives him an opportunity, even if peripheral, to witness societies where racial discrimination is less practiced than it is in his home country. Although the level of Negro acceptance in societies other than America is usually exaggerated, the Negro soldier is hard put not to make invidious comparisons with the American scene.[29] In interviews conducted with Negro servicemen in Germany, 64 per cent said there was more racial equality in Germany than America, 30 per cent saw little difference between the two countries, and only 6 per cent believed Negroes were treated better in the United States.

Observers of overseas American personnel have told the writer that Negro soldiers are more likely than whites to learn local languages (though for both groups of servicemen this is a very small number). Evidence for this supposition is given in Table 9. Three German-national barbers, who were permanently hired to cut the hair of all the men in one battalion, were asked by

---

[29] A social-distance study conducted among Korean college students found the following placement, from near to far: Chinese, Europeans and white Americans, Filipinos, Indians (from India), and Negroes (Man Gap Lee, Seoul National University, personal communication).

the writer to evaluate the German language proficiency of the individual personnel in that battalion.[30] When these evaluations were correlated with race, it was found that Negro soldiers were five times more likely to know "conversational" German, and three times more likely to know "some" German than were white soldiers.[31] Actually, the likelihood of Negro soldiers compared to whites in learning the language of the country in which they are stationed may be even greater than indicated in Table 9. Several of the

TABLE 9

COMMAND OF GERMAN LANGUAGE BY WHITE AND NEGRO SOLDIERS
IN A GERMAN-BASED U.S. ARMY BATTALION, 1965

Command of German *	Per Cent	
	White Soldiers	Negro Soldiers
Conversational	1.4	7.4
Some	3.0	7.4
Little or none	95.6	85.2
Total	100.0	100.0
(No. of cases)	(629)	(98)

* Based on evaluations of German-national battalion employees.

German-speaking white soldiers were of German ethnic background and acquired some knowledge of the language in their home environments back in the United States. These data testify, then, that the Negro soldiers overseas, perhaps because of the more favorable racial climate, are more willing to take advantage of participation at informal levels with local populations.[32]

CIVIL RIGHTS AT HOME AND WAR ABROAD

It is important to remember that the military establishment was desegregated before the current civil rights drive gained momentum. In the segregated military, embroilments between Negro units and whites were an ever present problem. In the light of subsequent developments in the domestic racial picture, it is likely that severe disciplinary problems would have oc-

[30] These barbers were focal points of much of the battalion's gossip and between themselves saw every man in the battalion on the average of at least twice a month.

[31] The same data, in tables not shown here, reveal that there is an *inverse* correlation between formal education (as ascertained from battalion personnel records) and likelihood of learning German! This reflects the greater likelihood of Negro soldiers, compared to whites, to learn German while averaging fewer years of formal education.

[32] In 1965 a widely seen German television commercial portrayed two American soldiers, one white and the other Negro. Only the Negro soldier spoke German.

curred had military integration not come about when it did. The timing of
desegregation in the military defused an ingredient—all-Negro military units
—that would have been potentially explosive in this nation's current racial
strife.[33]

It is also probable, however, that military experience contributes to an
activist posture on the part of Negro servicemen returning to civilian life. The
Negro ex-serviceman, that is, may be less willing to accommodate himself to
second-class citizenship after participation in the racially egalitarian military
establishment. Further, especially in situations where Negroes are intimidated
by physical threat or force, techniques of violence and organizational skill acquired in military service may be a new factor in the Negro's quest for equality.
Robert F. Williams, the leading advocate of armed self-defense for Negroes,
explicitly states that his Marine Corps experience led to his beliefs.[34] It also
seems more than coincidence that the ten founders of the Deacons for Defense and Justice, a paramilitary group organized in 1964 to counter Ku Klux
Klan terrorism, were all veterans of Korea or World War II.[35]

One must also take into account the possible consequences of the civil
rights movement on Negro military behavior. Much attention has been given
to a convergence of an important segment of the civil rights movement with
the movement against the war in Viet Nam. The Student Nonviolent Coordinating Committee has formally denounced American action in Viet Nam
as aggression. Civil rights organizers claim they find Negroes who do not want
to fight "whitey's war." A Negro is barred from taking his seat in the Georgia
legislature because he condones violations of the draft law. Rumors are heard
of isolated incidents of Negro insubordination in the armed services. Despite
this chain of events, however, the main stream of the civil rights drive has remained largely removed from those groups highly critical of this country's recent military policies. Indeed, the antiwar movement will likely aggravate an
already existing cleavage between moderate and radical leaders—between those
who accept versus those who reject the legitimacy of the American political
system—in the civil rights movement itself. The more pertinent question at
this time appears to be not what are the implications of the civil rights movement for the military establishment, but what will be the effects of the Viet
Nam war on the civil rights movement itself. Although it would be premature
to offer a definitive statement on any future interpenetrations between the
civil rights and antiwar movements, a major turning away of Negroes per se
from military commitment is viewed as highly doubtful. Most likely, and
somewhat paradoxically, we will witness more vocal antiwar sentiment within

[33] Although non-violence is the hallmark of the main thrust of the modern civil
rights movement, there is, nevertheless, the leitmotiv of a Negro insurrection in the
thinking of such Negro figures as James Baldwin, Malcolm X, William Epton, Warren
Miller, and LeRoi Jones. Congruent with the idea of armed conflict between the races
are the gothic endings—whites and Negro soldiers engaging in a bloodbath—in recent
Negro-authored novels (see Killens, *op. cit.*, and Rhodes, *op. cit.*).

[34] Robert F. Williams, *Negroes with Guns* (New York: Marzani & Munsell, 1962).

[35] *The Militant*, November 22, 1965, p. 1.

certain civil rights organizations at the same time that the military is becoming an avenue of career opportunity for many Negro men.

Nevertheless, there has usually been and is today a presumption on the part of America's military opponents that Negroes should be less committed soldiers than whites. Whether for tactical or ideological reasons, the Negro serviceman has been frequently defined as a special target for propaganda by forces opposing America in military conflicts. In World War II the Japanese directed radio appeals specifically to Negro servicemen in the Pacific theater. The Chinese in the Korean War used racial arguments on Negro prisoners of war. Yet a careful study of American POW behavior in Korea made no mention of differences in Negro and white behavior except to note that the segregation of Negro POW's by the Chinese had a boomerang effect on Communist indoctrination methods.[36]

The current military involvement of the United States on the international scene raises again the question of motivation and performance of Negro soldiers in combat. A spokesman for the National Liberation Front of South Viet Nam has recently asserted that "liberation forces have a special attitude toward American soldiers who happen to be Negroes." [37] Up to now at least, however, efforts to test the loyalty of Negro soldiers have not met with success. This writer, as well as others, detected no differences in white or Negro combat performance in Viet Nam.[38] In the Dominican Republic, where the proportion of Negroes in line units runs as high as 40 per cent, a pamphlet was distributed to Negro soldiers exhorting them to "turn your guns on your white oppressors and join your Dominican brothers." [39] Again, personal observation buttressed by comments from Dominicans revealed no significant differences between white and Negro military performance.[40]

The writer's appraisal is that among officers and NCO's there is no discernible difference between the races concerning military commitment in either the Dominican Republic or Viet Nam. Among Negro soldiers in the lower enlisted ranks, however, there is somewhat greater disenchantment compared to

[36] Albert D. Biderman, *March to Calumny* (New York: Macmillan Co., 1964), p. 60.

[37] *The Minority of One*, October, 1965, p. 9.

[38] Only One Color," *Newsweek*, December 6, 1965, pp. 42–43; Robin Moore, *The Green Berets* (New York: Avon Books, 1965), *passim*; and Herbert Mitgang, "Looking for a War," *New York Times Magazine*, May 22, 1966, pp. 114–15.

[39] A copy of the entire pamphlet is reproduced in the Dominican news magazine *Ahora* (No. 108, September 18, 1965). Although many whites were unaware of the pamphlet's existence, virtually every Negro soldier the writer talked to in Santo Domingo said he had seen the pamphlet. The effectiveness of the pamphlet on Negro soldiers was minimal, among other reasons, because it claimed Negro equality existed in the Dominican Republic, a statement belied by brief observation of the Dominican social scene.

[40] Similarly in an interview with a Negro reporter, the commandant of "constitutionalist rebel" forces in Santo Domingo stated that to his dismay Negro American soldiers fought no differently than whites (Laurence Harvey, "Report from the Dominican Republic," *Realist*, June 1965, p. 18).

whites as to the merits of America's current military ventures. Such unease, however, has little effect on military performance, most especially in the actual combat situation. The evidence strongly suggests that the racial integration of the armed forces, coming about when it did, effectively precluded any potential success on the part of America's military opponents to differentiate Negro from white soldiers.

CONCLUSION

Although the military was until recent times one of America's most segregated institutions, it has leaped into the forefront of racial equality in the past decade. What features of the military establishment can account for this about-face? There is a combination of mutually supporting factors that operate in the successful racial integration of the armed forces. For one thing, the military—an institution revolving around techniques of violence—is to an important degree discontinuous from other areas of social life. And this apartness served to allow, once the course had been decided, a rapid and complete racial integration. The path of desegregation was further made easier by characteristics peculiar or at least more pronounced in the military compared to other institutions. With its hierarchial power structure, predicated on stable and patterned relationships, decisions need take relatively little account of the personal desires of service personnel. Additionally, because roles and activities are more defined and specific in the military than in most other social arenas, conflicts that might have ensued within a more diffuse and ambiguous setting were largely absent. Likewise, desegregation was facilitated by the pervasiveness in the military of a bureaucratic ethos, with its concomitant formality and high social distance, that mitigated tensions arising from individual or personal feelings.

At the same time it must also be remembered that the military establishment has means of coercion not readily available in most civilian pursuits. Violations of norms are both more visible and subject to quicker sanctions. The military is premised, moreover, on the accountability of its members for effective performance. Owing to the aptly termed "chain of command," failures in policy implementation can be pinpointed. This in turn means that satisfactory carrying out of stated policy advances one's own position. In other words, it is to each individual's personal interest, if he anticipates receiving the rewards of a military career, to insure that decisions going through him are executed with minimum difficulty. Or put it another way, whatever the internal policy decided upon, racial integration being a paramount but only one example, the military establishment is uniquely suited to realize its implementation.

What implications does the military integration experience have for civilian society? Although it is certainly true that the means by which desegregation was accomplished in the military establishment are not easily translated to the civilian community, the end result of integration in the contemporary armed forces can suggest some qualities of what—if it came about—an integrated American society would be *within the context of the prevailing structural and value system.* Equality of treatment would be the rule in formal and task-specific relationships. Racial animosity would diminish but not disappear. We would expect a sharp improvement in Negro mobility and performance in the occupational sphere even taking into consideration on-going social and educational handicaps arising from existing inequities. Yet, because of these inequities, Negroes would still be overconcentrated in less skilled positions. We would also expect primary group ties and informal associations to remain largely within one's own racial group. But even at primary group levels, the integrated society would exhibit a much higher interracial intimacy than exists in the non-integrated society.

Such a description of the racially integrated society is, of course, what one finds in today's military establishment. Although the advent of the integrated society in this country is yet to occur, the desegregation of the armed forces has served to bring that day closer.

St. Clair Drake

FOLKWAYS AND CLASSWAYS WITHIN
THE BLACK GHETTO

It was during the 1930's that the study of the class structure of American communities became a major interest among sociologists. Some of the best sociological studies of race relations and of Negroes in American life were published during the 1930's and early 1940's, and social stratification was one of their major concerns. Curiously, little about the class structure of the Negro community appeared in the learned periodicals of the period. But St. Clair Drake has recently written a penetrating account of the class structure in an urban ghetto. His essay describes the varying life styles of the different social classes, and the likely future of each in the changing cities of the North.

• • • BLACK Ghettos in America are, on the whole, "run down" in appearance and overcrowded, and their inhabitants bear the physical and psychological scars of those whose "life chances" are not equal to those of other Americans. Like the European immigrants before them, they inherited the worst housing in the city. Within the past decade, the white "flight to the suburbs" has released relatively new and well-kept property on the margins of some of the old Black Belts. Here, "gilded ghettos" have grown up, indistinguishable from any other middle-class neighborhoods except by the color of the residents' skin.[10] The power mower in the yard, the steak grill on the rear lawn, a well stocked library and equally well stocked bar in the rumpus room—these mark

St. Clair Drake, "Folkways and Classways Within the Black Ghetto," from Drake, "The Social and Economic Status of the Negro in the United States," *Daedalus*, XCIV (Fall, 1965), pp. 777–784. Reprinted with the permission of the author, *Daedalus*, and the American Academy of Arts and Sciences.

[10] Professor Everett C. Hughes makes some original and highly pertinent remarks about new Negro middle class communities in his introduction to St. Clair Drake and Horace R. Cayton, *Black Metropolis* (New York, 1962).

the homes of well-to-do Negroes living in the more desirable portions of the Black Belt. Many of them would flee to suburbia, too, if housing were available to Negroes there.

But the character of the Black Ghetto is not set by the newer "gilded," not-yet run down portions of it, but by the older sections where unemployment rates are high and the masses of people work with their hands—where the median level of education is just above graduation from grade school and many of the people are likely to be recent migrants from rural areas.[11]

The "ghettoization" of the Negro has resulted in the emergence of a ghetto subculture with a distinctive ethos, most pronounced, perhaps, in Harlem, but recognizable in all Negro neighborhoods. For the average Negro who walks the streets of any American Black Ghetto, the smell of barbecued ribs, fried shrimps, and chicken emanating from numerous restaurants gives olfactory reinforcement to a feeling of "at-homeness." The beat of "gut music" spilling into the street from ubiquitous tavern juke boxes and the sound of tambourines and rich harmony behind the crude folk art on the windows of store-front churches give auditory confirmation to the universal belief that "We Negroes have 'soul.'" The bedlam of an occasional brawl, the shouted obscenities of street corner "foul mouths," and the whine of police sirens break the monotony of waiting for the number that never "falls," the horses that neither win, place, nor show, and the "good job" that never materializes. The insouciant swagger of teen-age drop-outs (the "cats") masks the hurt of their aimless existence and contrasts sharply with the ragged clothing and dejected demeanor of "skid-row" types who have long since stopped trying to keep up appearances and who escape it all by becoming "winoes." The spontaneous vigor of the children who crowd streets and playgrounds (with Cassius Clay, Ernie Banks, the Harlem Globe Trotters, and black stars of stage, screen, and television as their role models) and the cheerful rushing about of adults, free from the occupational pressures of the "white world" in which they work, create an atmosphere of warmth and superficial intimacy which obscures the unpleasant facts of life in the overcrowded rooms behind the doors, the lack of adequate maintenance standards, and the too prevalent vermin and rats.

This is a world whose urban "folkways" the upwardly mobile Negro middle class deplores as a "drag" on "The Race," which the upper classes wince at as an embarrassment and which race leaders point to as proof that Negroes have been victimized. But for the masses of the ghetto dwellers this is a warm and familiar milieu, preferable to the sanitary coldness of middle-class neighborhoods and a counterpart of the communities of the foreign-born, each of which has its own distinctive subcultural flavor. The arguments in the barbershop, the gossip in the beauty parlors, the "jiving" of bar girls and waitresses, the click of poolroom balls, the stomping of feet in the dance halls, the shouting in the churches are all *theirs*—and the white men who run the

[11] Thomas F. Pettigrew, A *Profile of the Negro American* (Princeton, N.J., 1964), pp. 180–181.

pawnshops, supermarts, drug stores, and grocery stores, the policemen on horseback, the teachers in blackboard jungles—all these are aliens, conceptualized collectively as "The Man," intruders on the Black Man's "turf." When an occasional riot breaks out, "The Man" and his property become targets of aggression upon which pent-up frustrations are vented. When someone during the Harlem riots in 1964 begged the street crowds to go home, the cry came back, "Baby, we *are* home!"

But the inhabitants of the Black Ghetto are not a homogeneous mass. Although, in Marxian terms, nearly all of them are "proletarians," with nothing to sell but their labor, variations in "life style" differentiate them into social classes based more upon differences in education and basic values (crystallized, in part, around occupational differences) than in meaningful differences in income. The American caste-class system has served, over the years, to concentrate the Negro population in the low-income sector of the economy. In 1961, six out of every ten Negro families had an income of less than $4000.00 per year. This situation among whites was just the reverse: six out of every ten white families had *over* $4000.00 a year at their disposal. (In the South, eight out of ten Negro families were below the $4000.00 level.) This is the income gap. Discrimination in employment creates a job ceiling, most Negroes being in blue-collar jobs.

With 60 per cent of America's Negro families earning less than $4000.00 a year, social strata emerge between the upper and lower boundaries of "no earned income" and $4000.00. Some families live a "middle-class style of life," placing heavy emphasis upon decorous public behavior and general respectability, insisting that their children "get an education" and "make something out of themselves." They prize family stability, and an unwed mother is something much more serious than "just a girl who had an accident"; premarital and extra-marital sexual relations, if indulged in at all, must be discreet. Social life is organized around churches and a welter of voluntary associations of all types, and, for women, "the cult of clothes" is so important that fashion shows are a popular fund raising activity even in churches. For both men and women, owning a home and going into business are highly desired goals, the former often being a realistic one, the latter a mere fantasy.

Within the same income range, and not always at the lower margin of it, other families live a "lower-class life-style" being part of the "organized" lower class, while at the lowest income levels an "unorganized" lower class exists whose members tend always to become *dis*organized—functioning in an anomic situation where gambling, excessive drinking, the use of narcotics, and sexual promiscuity are prevalent forms of behavior, and violent interpersonal relations reflect an ethos of suspicion and resentment which suffuses this deviant subculture. It is within this milieu that criminal and semi-criminal activities burgeon.

The "organized" lower class is oriented primarily around churches whose preachers, often semi-literate, exhort them to "be in the 'world' but not of it." Conventional middle-class morality and Pauline Puritanism are preached, although a general attitude of "the spirit is willing but the flesh is weak" prevails except among a minority fully committed to the Pentecostal sects. They boast, "We *live* the life"—a way of life that has been portrayed with great insight by James Baldwin in *Go Tell It on the Mountain* and *The Fire Next Time*.

Young people with talent find wide scope for expressing it in choirs, quartets, and sextets which travel from church to church (often bearing colorful names like The Four Heavenly Trumpets or the Six Singing Stars of Zion) and sometimes traveling from city to city. Such groups channel their aggressions in widely advertised "Battles of Song" and develop their talent in church pageants such as "Heaven Bound" or "Queen Esther" and fund-raising events where winners are crowned King and Queen. These activities provide fun as well as a testing ground for talent. Some lucky young church people eventually find their fortune in the secular world as did singers Sam Cooke and Nat King Cole, while others remain in the church world as nationally known gospel singers or famous evangelists.

Adults as well as young people find satisfaction and prestige in serving as ushers and deacons, "mothers," and deaconesses, Sunday-school teachers and choir leaders. National conventions of Negro denominations and national societies of ushers and gospel singers not only develop a continent-wide nexus of associations within the organized lower class, but also throw the more ambitious and capable individuals into meaningful contact with middle-class church members who operate as role models for the less talented persons who seek to move upward. That prestige and sometimes money come so easily in these circles may be a factor militating against a pattern of delaying gratifications and seeking mobility into professional and semi-professional pursuits through higher education.

Lower-class families and institutions are constantly on the move, for in recent years the Negro lower class has suffered from projects to redevelop the inner city. By historic accident, the decision to check the expansion of physical deterioration in metropolitan areas came at a time when Negroes were the main inhabitants of substandard housing. (If urban redevelopment had been necessary sixty years ago immigrants, not Negroes, would have suffered.) In protest against large-scale demolition of areas where they live, Negroes have coined a slogan, "Slum clearance is Negro clearance." They resent the price in terms of the inconvenience thrust upon them in order to redevelop American cities,[12] and the evidence shows that, in some cities, there is no net gain in improved housing after relocation.

At the opposite pole from the Negro lower class in both life styles and life chances is the small Negro upper class whose solid core is a group in the professions, along with well-to-do businessmen who have had some higher education, but including, also, a scattering of individuals who have had college training but do not have a job commensurate with their education. These men

---

[12] The issue of the extent to which Negroes have been victimized by urban redevelopment is discussed briefly by Robert C. Weaver in *The Urban Complex: Human Values in Urban Life* (New York, 1964). See also Martin Anderson, *The Federal Bulldozer: A Critical Analysis of Renewal: 1949–1962* (Cambridge, Mass., 1964).

and their spouses and children form a cohesive upper-class stratum in most Negro communities. Within this group are individuals who maintain some type of contact—though seldom any social relations—with members of the local white power élite; but whether or not they participate in occupational associations with their white peers depends upon the region of the country in which they live. (It is from this group that Negro "Exhibit A's" are recruited when white liberals are carrying on campaigns to "increase interracial understanding.") They must always think of themselves as symbols of racial advancement as well as individuals, and they often provide the basic leadership at local levels for organizations such as the N.A.A.C.P. and the Urban League. They must lend sympathetic support to the more militant civil rights organizations, too, by financial contributions, if not action.[13]

The life styles of the Negro upper class are similar to those of the white upper *middle* class, but it is only in rare instances that Negroes have been incorporated into the clique and associational life of this group or have intermarried into it. (Their participation in activities of the white upper class occurs more often than with those whites who have similar life styles because of Negro upper-class participation as members of various civic boards and interracial associations to which wealthy white people contribute.) Living "well" with highly developed skills, having enough money to travel, Negroes at this social level do not experience victimization in the same fashion as do the members of the lower class. Their victimization flows primarily from the fact that the social system keeps them "half in and half out," preventing the free and easy contact with their occupational peers which they need; and it often keeps them from making the kind of significant intellectual and social contributions to the national welfare that they might make if they were white. (They are also forced to experience various types of nervous strain and dissipation of energy over petty annoyances and deprivations which only the sensitive and the cultivated feel. Most barbershops, for instance, are not yet desegregated, and taxi drivers, even in the North, sometimes refuse Negro passengers.)

The Negro upper class has created a social world of its own in which a universe of discourse and uniformity of behavior and outlook are maintained by the interaction on national and local levels of members of Negro Greek-letter fraternities and sororities, college and alumni associations, professional associations, and civic and social clubs. It is probable that if all caste barriers were dropped, a large proportion of the Negro upper class would welcome complete social integration, and that these all-Negro institutions would be left in the hands of the Negro middle class, as the most capable and sophisticated Negroes moved into the orbit of the general society. Their sense of pride and dignity does not even allow them to imagine such a fate, and they pursue their social activities and play their roles as "race leaders" with little feeling of inferiority or deprivation, but always with a tragic sense of the irony of it all.

[13] Drake and Cayton, *op. cit.*, Chap. 23, "Advancing the Race."

The Negro middle class covers a very wide income range, and whatever cohesion it has comes from the network of churches and social clubs to which many of its members devote a great deal of time and money. What sociologists call the Negro middle class is merely a collection of people who have similar life styles and aspirations, whose basic goals are "living well," being "respectable," and not being crude. Middle-class Negroes, by and large, are not concerned about mobility into the Negro upper class or integration with whites. They want their "rights" and "good jobs," as well as enough money to get those goods and services which make life comfortable. They want to expand continuously their level of consumption. But they also desire "decent" schools for their children, and here the degree of victimization experienced by Negroes is most clear and the ambivalence toward policies of change most sharp. Ghetto schools are, on the whole, inferior. In fact, some of the most convincing evidence that residential segregation perpetuates inequality can be found by comparing data on school districts in Northern urban areas where *de facto* school segregation exists. (Table 1 presents such data for Chicago in 1962.)

TABLE 1

COMPARISON OF WHITE, INTEGRATED AND NEGRO SCHOOLS IN CHICAGO: 1962

	Type of School		
Indices of Comparison	White	Integrated	Negro
Total appropriation per pupil	$342.00	$320.00	$269.00
Annual teachers' salary per pupil	256.00	231.00	220.00
Per cent uncertified teachers	12.00	23.00	49.00
No. of pupils per classroom	30.95	34.95	46.80
Library resource books per pupil	5.00	3.50	2.50
Expenditures per pupil other than teachers' salaries.	86.00	90.00	49.00

Adapted from a table in the U.S. Commission on Civil Rights report, *Public Schools, Negro and White* (Washington, D.C., 1962), pp. 241–248.

Awareness of the poor quality of education grew as the protest movement against *de facto* school segregation in the North gathered momentum. But while the fight was going on, doubt about the desirability of forcing the issue was always present within some sections of the broad Negro middle class. Those in opposition asked, "Are we not saying that our teachers can't teach our own children as well as whites can, or that our children can't learn unless they're around whites? Aren't we insulting ourselves?" Those who want to stress Negro history and achievement and to use the schools to build race pride also express doubts about the value of mixed schools. In fact, the desirability of race consciousness and racial solidarity seems to be taken for granted in this stratum, and sometimes there is an expression of contempt for the behavior of whites of their own and lower income levels. In the present period one even occasionally hears a remark such as "Who'd want to be integrated with *those* awful white people?"

Marxist critics would dismiss the whole configuration of Negro folkways and classways as a subculture which reinforces "false consciousness," which prevents Negroes from facing the full extent of their victimization, which keeps them from ever focusing upon what they could be because they are so busy enjoying what they are—or rationalizing their subordination and exclusion. Gunnar Myrdal, in *An American Dilemma*, goes so far as to refer to the Negro community as a "pathological" growth within American society.[14] Some novelists and poets, on the other hand, romanticize it, and some Black Nationalists glorify it. A sober analysis of the civil rights movement would suggest, however, that the striking fact about all levels of the Negro community is the absence of "false consciousness," and the presence of a keen awareness of the extent of their victimization, as well as knowledge of the forces which maintain it. Not lack of knowledge but a sense of powerlessness is the key to the Negro reaction to the caste-class system.

Few Negroes believe that Black Ghettos will disappear within the next two decades despite much talk about "open occupancy" and "freedom of residence." There is an increasing tendency among Negroes to discuss what the quality of life could be within Negro communities as they grow larger and larger. At one extreme this interest slides over into Black Nationalist reactions such as the statement by a Chicago Negro leader who said, "Let all of the white people flee to the suburbs. We'll show them that the Black Man can run the second largest city in America better than the white man. Let them go. If any of them want to come back and integrate with *us* we'll accept them."

It is probable that the Black Belts of America will increase in size rather than decrease during the next decade, for no city seems likely to commit itself to "open occupancy" (although a committee in New York has been discussing a ten-year plan for dismantling Harlem).[15] And even if a race-free market were to appear Negroes would remain segregated unless drastic changes took place in the job ceiling and income gap. Controlled integration will probably continue, with a few upper- and upper-middle-class Negroes trickling into the suburbs and into carefully regulated mixed neighborhoods and mixed buildings within the city limits.[16] The basic problem of the next decade will be how to change Black Ghettos into relatively stable and attractive "colored communities." Here the social implications of low incomes become decisive.

[14] See section on "The Negro Community as a Pathological Form of an American Community," Chap. 43 of Gunnar Myrdal, *An American Dilemma* (New York, 1944), p. 927.

[15] A report appeared on the front page of *The New York Times*, April 5, 1965, stating that a commission was at work trying to elaborate plans for "integrating" Harlem by 1975. Columbia University was said to be co-operating in the research aspects of the project.

[16] A successful experiment in "controlled integration" has been described by Julia Abrahamson in *A Neighborhood Finds Itself* (New York, 1959).

Lee Rainwater

———

CRUCIBLE OF IDENTITY:
THE NEGRO LOWER-CLASS FAMILY

In his classic work of sociological scholarship, The Negro Family in
the United States *(1939), the late E. Franklin Frazier emphasized
the prevalence among lower-class Negroes of matriarchal family units
in which women were the heads of households. Three decades later,
another distinguished sociologist, Lee Rainwater, has made a careful
study of the Negro lower-class family. Rainwater describes the social
mechanisms which maintain this pattern of female-centered family
life, the way in which such families function and survive, and the
destructive influences they have upon the personality development
of Negro youth.*

As long as Negroes have been in America, their marital and family patterns
have been subjects of curiosity and amusement, moral indignation and self-
congratulation, puzzlement and frustration, concern and guilt, on the part of
white Americans. As some Negroes have moved into middle-class status, or
acquired standards of American common-man respectability, they too have
shared these attitudes toward the private behavior of their fellows, sometimes
with a moral punitiveness to rival that of whites, but at other times with a
hard-headed interest in causes and remedies rather than moral evaluation.
Moralism permeated the subject of Negro sexual, marital, and family behavior
in the polemics of slavery apologists and abolitionists as much as in the Northern and Southern civil rights controversies of today. Yet, as long as the dia-
lectic of good or bad, guilty or innocent, overshadows a concern with who,
why, and what can be, it is unlikely that realistic and effective social planning
to correct the clearly desperate situation of poor Negro families can begin.

From Lee Rainwater, "Crucible of Identity: The Negro Lower-Class Family,"
Daedalus, XCV (Winter, 1966), pp. 172–216. Reprinted with the permission of the
author, *Daedalus,* and the American Academy of Arts and Sciences. In the excerpts reprinted here, footnotes have been omitted.

This paper is concerned with a description and analysis of slum Negro family patterns as these reflect and sustain Negroes' adaptations to the economic, social, and personal situation into which they are born and in which they must live.... Further, this analysis will deal with family patterns which interfere with the efforts slum Negroes make to attain a stable way of life as working- or middle-class individuals and with the effects such failure in turn has on family life. To be sure, many Negro families live *in* the slum ghetto, but are not *of* its culture (though even they, and particularly their children, can be deeply affected by what happens there). However, it is the individuals who succumb to the distinctive family life style of the slum who experience the greatest weight of deprivation and who have the greatest difficulty responding to the few self-improvement resources that make their way into the ghetto. In short, we propose to explore in depth the family's role in the "tangle of pathology" which characterizes the ghetto.

The social reality in which Negroes have had to make their lives during the 450 years of their existence in the Western hemisphere has been one of victimization.... Yet the implicit paradigm of much of the research on Negro Americans has been an overly simplistic one concentrating on two terms of an argument:

$$\text{White cupidity} \longrightarrow \text{Negro suffering.}$$

As an intellectual shorthand, and even more as a civil rights slogan, this simple model is both justified and essential. But, as a guide to greater understanding of the Negro situation as human adaptation to human situations, the paradigm is totally inadequate because it fails to specify fully enough the *process* by which Negroes adapt to their situations as they do, and the limitations one kind of adaptation places on possibilities for subsequent adaptations. A reassessment of previous social research, combined with examination of current social research on Negro ghetto communities, suggests a more complex, but hopefully more vertical, model:

White cupidity
creates
Structural Conditions Highly Inimical to Basic Social Adaptation (low-income availability, poor education, poor services, stigmatization)
to which Negroes adapt
by
Social and Personal Responses which serve to sustain the individual in his punishing world but also generate aggressiveness toward the self and others
which results in
Suffering directly inflicted by Negroes on themselves and on others.

In short, whites, by their greater power, create situations in which Negroes do the dirty work of caste victimization for them....

For their part, Negroes creatively adapt to the system in ways that keep them alive and extract what gratification they can find, but in the process of adaptation they are constrained to behave in ways that inflict a great deal of suffering on those with whom they make their lives, and on themselves. The ghetto Negro is constantly confronted by the immediate necessity to suffer in order to get what he wants of those few things he can have, or to make others suffer, or both—for example, he suffers as exploited student and employee, as drug user, as loser in the competitive game of his peer-group society; he inflicts suffering as disloyal spouse, petty thief, knife- or gun-wielder, petty con man.

It is the central thesis of this paper that the caste-facilitated infliction of suffering by Negroes on other Negroes and on themselves appears most poignantly within the confines of the family, and that the victimization process as it operates in families prepares and toughens its members to function in the ghetto world, at the same time that it seriously interferes with their ability to operate in any other world. This, however, is very different from arguing that "the family is to blame" for the deprived situation ghetto Negroes suffer; rather we are looking at the logical outcome of the operation of the widely ramified and interconnecting caste system. In the end we will argue that only palliative results can be expected from attempts to treat directly the disordered family patterns to be described. Only a change in the original "inputs" of the caste system, the structural conditions inimical to basic social adaptation, can change family forms.

Almost thirty years ago, E. Franklin Frazier foresaw that the fate of the Negro family in the city would be a highly destructive one. His readers would have little reason to be surprised at observations of slum ghetto life today:

> ...As long as the bankrupt system of southern agriculture exists, Negro families will continue to seek a living in the towns and cities. ...They will crowd the slum areas of southern cities or make their way to northern cities where their families will become disrupted and their poverty will force them to depend upon charity.

THE AUTONOMY OF THE SLUM GHETTO

Just as the deprivations and depredations practiced by white society have had their effect on the personalities and social life of Negroes, so also has the separation from the ongoing social life of the white community had its effect. In a curious way, Negroes have had considerable freedom to fashion their own adaptations within their separate world. The larger society provides them with few resources but also with minimal interference in the Negro community on matters which did not seem to affect white interests. Because Negroes learned early that there were a great many things they could not depend upon whites to provide they developed their own solutions to recurrent human issues. These solutions can often be seen to combine, along with the predominance of elements from white culture, elements that are distinctive to the Negro group. Even more distinctive is the *configuration* which emerges from those elements Negroes share with whites and those which are different.

It is in this sense that we may speak of a Negro subculture, a distinctive *patterning* of existential perspectives, techniques for coping with the problems of social life, views about what is desirable and undesirable in particular situations. This subculture, and particularly that of the lower-class, the slum, Negro, can be seen as his own creation out of the elements available to him in response to (1) the conditions of life set by white society and (2) the selective freedom which that society allows (or must put up with given the pattern of separateness on which it insists)....The subculture that Negroes have created may be imperfect but it has been viable for centuries; it behooves both white and Negro leaders and intellectuals to seek to understand it even as they hope to change it.

Negroes have created, again particularly within the lower-class slum group, a range of institutions to structure the tasks of living a victimized life and to minimize the pain it inevitably produces. In the slum ghetto these institutions include prominently those of the social network—the extended kinship system and the "street system" of buddies and broads which tie (although tenuously and unpredictably) the "members" to each other—and the institutions of entertainment (music, dance, folk tales) by which they instruct, explain, and accept themselves. Other institutions function to provide escape from the society of the victimized: the church (Hereafter!) and the civil rights movement (Now!).

THE FUNCTIONAL AUTONOMY OF THE NEGRO FAMILY

At the center of the matrix of Negro institutional life lies the family. It is in the family that individuals are trained for participation in the culture and find personal and group identity and continuity. The "freedom" allowed by white society is greatest here, and this freedom has been used to create an institutional variant more distinctive perhaps to the Negro subculture than any other. (Much of the content of Negro art and entertainment derives exactly from the distinctive characteristics of Negro family life.) At each stage in the Negro's experience of American life—slavery, segregation, *de facto* ghettoization—whites have found it less necessary to interfere in the relations between the sexes and between parents and children than in other areas of the Negro's existence. His adaptations in this area, therefore, have been less constrained by whites than in many other areas....

The history of the Negro family has been ably documented by historians and sociologists. In slavery, conjugal and family ties were reluctantly and ambivalently recognized by the slave holders, were often violated by them, but proved necessary to the slave system. This necessity stemmed both from the profitable offspring of slave sexual unions and the necessity for their nurture, and from the fact that the slaves' efforts to sustain patterns of sexual and parental relations mollified the men and women whose labor could not simply be commanded. From nature's promptings, the thinning memories of African heritage, and the example and guilt-ridden permission of the slave holders, slaves constructed a partial family system and sets of relations that generated conjugal and familial sentiments. The slave holder's recognition in advertisements for runaway slaves of marital and family sentiments as motivations for absconding provides one indication that strong family ties were possible, though perhaps not common, in the slave quarter. The mother-centered family with its emphasis on the primacy of the mother-child relation and only tenuous ties to a man, then, is the legacy of adaptations worked out by Negroes during slavery.

After emancipation this family design often also served well to cope with the social disorganization of Negro life in the late nineteenth century. Matrifocal families, ambivalence about the desirability of marriage, ready acceptance of illegitimacy, all sustained some kind of family life in situations which often made it difficult to maintain a full nuclear family. Yet in the hundred years since emancipation, Negroes in rural areas have been able to maintain full nuclear families almost as well as similarly situated whites. As we will see, it is the move to the city that results in the very high proportion of mother-headed households. In the rural system the man continues to have important functions; it is difficult for a woman to make a crop by herself, or even with the help of other women. In the city, however, the woman can earn wages just as a man can, and she can receive welfare payments more easily than he can. In rural areas, although there may be high illegitimacy rates and high rates of marital disruption, men and women have an interest in getting together; families are headed by a husband-wife pair much more often than in the city. That pair may be much less stable than in the more prosperous segments of Negro and white communities but it is more likely to exist among rural Negroes than among urban ones....

For Negro lower-class women, then, first marriage has the same kind of importance as having a first child. Both indicate that the girl has become a woman but neither one that this is the last such activity in which she will engage. It seems very likely that only a minority of Negro women in the urban slum go through their child-rearing years with only one man around the house.

Among the Negro urban poor, then, a great many women have the experience of heading a family for part of their mature lives, and a great many children spend some part of their formative years in a household without a father-mother pair. From Table 1 we see that in 1960, forty-seven per cent of the Negro poor urban families with children had a female head. Unfortunately cumulative statistics are hard to come by; but, given this very high level for a cross-sectional sample (and taking into account the fact that the

TABLE 1

PROPORTION OF FEMALE HEADS FOR FAMILIES WITH CHILDREN
BY RACE, INCOME, AND URBAN-RURAL CATEGORIES

Negroes	Rural	Urban	Total
under $3000	18%	47%	36%
$3000 and over	5%	8%	7%
Total	14%	23%	21%
Whites			
under $3000	12%	38%	22%
$3000 and over	2%	4%	3%
Total	4%	7%	6%

Source: U.S. Census: 1960, PC (1) D. U. S. Volume, Table 225; State Volume, Table 140.

median age of the children in these families is about six years), it seems very likely that as many as two-thirds of Negro urban poor children will not live in families headed by a man and a woman throughout the first eighteen years of their lives.

One of the other distinctive characteristics of Negro families, both poor and not so poor, is the fact that Negro households have a much higher proportion of relatives outside the mother-father-children triangle than is the case with whites. For example, in St. Louis Negro families average 0.8 other relatives per household compared to only 0.4 for white families. In the case of the more prosperous Negro families this is likely to mean that an older relative lives in the home providing baby-sitting services while both the husband and wife work and thus further their climb toward stable working- or middle-class status. In the poor Negro families it is much more likely that the household is headed by an older relative who brings under her wings a daughter and that daughter's children. It is important to note that the three-generation household with the grandmother at the head exists only when there is no husband present. Thus, despite the high proportion of female-headed households in this group and despite the high proportion of households that contain other relatives, we find that almost all married couples in the St. Louis Negro slum community have their own household. In other words, when a couple marries it establishes its own household; when that couple breaks up the mother either maintains that household or moves back to her parents or grandparents.

Finally we should note that Negro slum families have more children than do either white slum families or stable working- and middle-class Negro families. Mobile Negro families limit their fertility sharply in the interest of bringing the advantages of mobility more fully to the few children that they do have. Since the Negro slum family is both more likely to have the father absent and more likely to have more children in the family, the mother has a more demanding task with fewer resources at her disposal. When we examine the patterns of life of the stem family we shall see that even the presence of several mothers does not necessarily lighten the work load for the principal mother in charge.

THE FORMATION AND MAINTENANCE OF FAMILIES

We will outline below the several stages and forms of Negro lower-class family life. At many points these family forms and the interpersonal relations that exist within them will be seen to have characteristics in common with the life styles of white lower-class families. At other points there are differences, or the Negro pattern will be seen to be more sharply divergent from the family life of stable working- and middle-class couples.

It is important to recognize that lower-class Negroes know that their particular family forms are different from those of the rest of the society and that, though they often see these forms as representing the only ways of behaving given their circumstances, they also think of the more stable family forms of the working class as more desirable. That is, lower-class Negroes know what the "normal American family" is supposed to be like, and they consider a stable family-centered way of life superior to the conjugal and familial situations in which they often find themselves. Their conceptions of the good American life include the notion of a father-husband who functions as an adequate provider and interested member of the family, a hard working home-bound mother who is concerned about her children's welfare and her husband's needs, and children who look up to their parents and perform well in school and other outside places to reflect credit on their families. This image of what family life can be like is very real from time to time as lower-class men and women grow up and move through adulthood. Many of them make efforts to establish such families but find it impossible to do so either because of the direct impact of economic disabilities or because they are not able to sustain in their day-to-day lives the ideals which they hold. While these ideals do serve as a meaningful guide to lower-class couples who are mobile out of the group, for a great many others the existence of such ideas about normal family life represents a recurrent source of stress within families as individuals become aware that they are failing to measure up to the ideals, or as others within the family and outside it use the ideals as an aggressive weapon for criticizing each other's performance. It is not at all uncommon for husbands or wives or children to try to hold others in the family to the norms of stable family life while they themselves engage in behaviors which violate these norms. The effect of such criticism in the end is to deepen commitment to the deviant sexual and parental norms of a slum subculture. Unless they are careful, social workers and other professionals exacerbate the tendency to use the norms of "American family life" as weapons by supporting these norms in situations where they are in reality unsupportable, thus aggravating the sense of failing and being failed by others which is chronic for lower-class people.

Going together. The initial steps toward mating and family formation in the Negro slum take place in a context of highly developed boys' and girls' peer groups. Adolescents tend to become deeply involved in their peer-group societies beginning as early as the age of twelve or thirteen and continue to be involved after first pregnancies and first marriages. Boys and girls are heavily committed both to their same sex peer groups and to the activities that those groups carry out. While classical gang activity does not necessarily characterize Negro slum communities everywhere, loosely-knit peer groups do.

The world of the Negro slum is wide open to exploration by adolescent boys and girls: "Negro communities provide a flow of common experience in which young people and their elders share, and out of which delinquent behavior emerges almost imperceptibly." More than is possible in white slum communities, Negro adolescents have an opportunity to interact with adults in various "high life" activities; their behavior more often represents an identification with the behavior of adults than an attempt to set up group standards and activities that differ from those adults.

Boys and young men participating in the street system of peer-group activity are much caught up in games of furthering and enhancing their status as significant persons. These games are played out in small and large gatherings through various kinds of verbal contests that go under the names of "sounding," "signifying," and "working game." Very much a part of a boy's or man's status in this group is his ability to win women. The man who has several women "up tight," who is successful in "pimping off" women for sexual favors and material benefits, is much admired. In sharp contrast to white lower-class groups, there is little tendency for males to separate girls into "good" and "bad" categories. Observations of groups of Negro youths suggest that girls and women are much more readily referred to as "that bitch" or "that whore" than they are by their names, and this seems to be a universal tendency carrying no connotation that "that bitch" is morally inferior to or different from other women. Thus, all women are essentially the same, all women are legitimate targets, and no girl or woman is expected to be virginal except for reason of lack of opportunity or immaturity. From their participation in the peer group and according to standards legitimated by the total Negro slum culture, Negro boys and young men are propelled in the direction of girls to test their "strength" as seducers. They are mercilessly rated by both their peers and the opposite sex in their ability to "talk" to girls; a young man will go to great lengths to avoid the reputation of having a "weak" line.

The girls share these definitions of the nature of heterosexual relations; they take for granted that almost any male they deal with will try to seduce them and that given sufficient inducement (social not monetary) they may wish to go along with his line. Although girls have a great deal of ambivalence about participating in sexual relations, this ambivalence is minimally moral and has much more to do with a desire not to be taken advantage of or get in trouble. Girls develop defenses against the exploitative orientations of men by devaluing the significance of sexual relations ("he really didn't do anything bad to me"), and as time goes on by developing their own appreciation of the intrinsic rewards of sexual intercourse.

The informal social relations of slum Negroes begin in adolescence to be highly sexualized. Although parents have many qualms about boys and, particularly, girls entering into this system, they seldom feel there is much they can do to prevent their children's sexual involvement. They usually confine themselves to counseling somewhat hopelessly against girls becoming pregnant or boys being forced into situations where they might have to marry a girl they do not want to marry.

Girls are propelled toward boys and men in order to demonstrate their maturity and attractiveness; in the process they are constantly exposed to pressures for seduction, to boys "rapping" to them. An active girl will "go with" quite a number of boys, but she will generally try to restrict the number with whom she has intercourse to the few to whom she is attracted or (as happens not infrequently) to those whose threats of physical violence she cannot avoid. For their part, the boys move rapidly from girl to girl seeking to have intercourse with as many as they can and thus build up their "reps." The activity of seduction is itself highly cathected; there is gratification in simply "talking to" a girl as long as the boy can feel that he has acquitted himself well.

At sixteen Joan Bemias enjoys spending time with three or four very close girl friends. She tells us they follow this routine when the girls want to go out and none of the boys they have been seeing lately is available: "Every time we get ready to go someplace we look through all the telephone numbers of boys we'd have and we call them and talk so sweet to them that they'd come on around. All of them had cars you see. (I: What do you do to keep all these fellows interested?) Well nothing. We don't have to make love with all of them. Let's see, Joe, J. B., Albert, and Paul, out of all of them I've been going out with I've only had sex with four boys, that's all." She goes on to say that she and her girl friends resist boys by being unresponsive to their lines and by breaking off relations with them on the ground that they're going out with other girls. It is also clear from her comments that the girl friends support each other in resisting the boys when they are out together in groups.

Joan has had a relationship with a boy which has lasted six months, but she has managed to hold the frequency of intercourse down to four times. Initially she managed to hold this particular boy off for a month but eventually gave in.

Becoming pregnant. It is clear that the contest elements in relationships between men and women continue even in relationships that become quite steady. Despite the girls' ambivalence about sexual relations and their manifold efforts to reduce its frequency, the operation of chance often eventuates in their becoming pregnant. This was the case with Joan. With this we reach the second stage in the formation of families, that of premarital pregnancy. (We are outlining an ideal-typical sequence and not, of course, implying that all girls in the Negro slum culture become pregnant before they marry but only that a great many of them do.)

Joan was caught despite the fact that she was considerably more sophisticated about contraception than most girls or young women in the group (her mother had both instructed her in contraceptive techniques and constantly warned her to take precautions). No one was particularly surprised at her pregnancy although she, her boy friend, her mother, and others regarded it as unfortunate. For girls in the Negro slum, pregnancy before marriage is expected in much the same way that parents expect their children to catch mumps or chicken pox; if they are lucky it will not happen but if it happens people are not too surprised and everyone knows what to do about it. It was quickly decided that Joan and the baby would stay at home. It seems clear from the preparations that Joan's mother is making that she expects to have the main responsibility for caring for the infant. Joan seems quite indifferent to the baby; she shows little interest in mothering the child although she is not particularly adverse to the idea so long as the baby does not interfere too much with her continued participation in her peer group.

Establishing who the father is under these circumstances seems to be important and confers a kind of legitimacy on the birth; not to know who one's father is, on the other hand, seems the ultimate in illegitimacy. Actually Joan had a choice in the imputation of fatherhood; she chose J. B. because he is older than she, and because she may marry him if he can get a divorce from his wife. She could have chosen Paul (with whom she had also had intercourse at about the time she became pregnant), but she would have done this reluctantly since Paul is a year younger than she and somehow this does not seem fitting.

In general, when a girl becomes pregnant while still living at home it seems taken for granted that she will continue to live there and that her parents will take a major responsibility for rearing the children. Since there are usually siblings who can help out and even siblings who will be playmates for the child, the addition of a third generation to the household does not seem to place a great stress on relationships within the family. It seems common for the first pregnancy to have a liberating influence on the mother once the child is born in that she becomes socially and sexually more active than she was before. She no longer has to be concerned with preserving her status as a single girl. Since her mother is usually willing to take care of the child for a few years, the unwed mother has an opportunity to go out with girl friends and with men and thus become more deeply involved in the peer-group society of her culture. As she has more children and perhaps marries she will find it necessary to settle down and spend more time around the house fulfilling the functions of a mother herself.

It would seem that for girls pregnancy is the real measure of maturity, the dividing line between adolescence and womanhood. Perhaps because of this, as well as because of the ready resources for child care, girls in the Negro slum community show much less concern about pregnancy than do girls in the white lower-class community and are less motivated to marry the fathers of their children. When a girl becomes pregnant the question of marriage certainly arises and is considered, but the girl often decides that she would rather not marry either because she does not want to settle down yet or because she does not think he would make a good husband.

It is in the easy attitudes toward premarital pregnancy that the matrifocal character of the Negro lower-class family appears most clearly. In order to have and raise a family it is simply not necessary, though it may be desirable, to have a man around the house. While the AFDC program may make it easier to maintain such attitudes in the urban situation, this pattern existed long before the program was initiated and continues in families where support comes from other sources.

Finally it should be noted that fathering a child similarly confers maturity on boys and young men although perhaps it is less salient for them. If the boy has any interest in the girl he will tend to feel that the fact that he has impregnated her gives him an additional claim on her. He will be stricter in seeking to enforce his exclusive rights over her (though not exclusive loyalty to her). This exclusive right does not mean that he expects to marry her but only that there is a new and special bond between them. If the girl is not willing to accept such claims she may find it necessary to break off the relationship rather than tolerate the man's jealousy. Since others in the peer group have a vested interest in not allowing a couple to be too loyal to each other they go out of their way to question and challenge each partner about the loyalty of the other, thus contributing to the deterioration of the relationship. This same kind of questioning and challenging continues if the couple marries and represents one source of the instability of the marital relationship.

Getting married. As noted earlier, despite the high degree of premarital sexual activity and the rather high proportion of premarital pregnancies, most lower-class Negro men and women eventually do marry and stay together for a shorter or longer period of time. Marriage is an intimidating prospect and is approached ambivalently by both parties. For the girl it means giving up a familiar and comfortable home that, unlike some other lower-class subcultures, places few real restrictions on her behavior. (While marriage can appear to be an escape from interpersonal difficulties at home, these difficulties seldom seem to revolve around effective restrictions placed on her behavior by her parents.) The girl also has good reason to be suspicious of the likelihood that men will be able to perform stably in the role of husband and provider; she is reluctant to be tied down by a man who will not prove to be worth it.

From the man's point of view the fickleness of women makes marriage problematic. It is one thing to have a girl friend step out on you, but it is another to have a wife do so. Whereas premarital sexual relations and fatherhood carry almost no connotation of responsibility for the welfare of the partner, marriage is supposed to mean that a man behaves more responsibly, becoming a provider for his wife and children even though he may not be expected to give up all the gratifications of participation in the street system.

For all of these reasons both boys and girls tend to have rather negative views of marriage as well as a low expectation that marriage will prove a stable and gratifying existence. When marriage does take place it tends to represent a tentative commitment on the part of both parties with a strong tendency to seek greater commitment on the part of the partner than on one's own part. Marriage is regarded as a fragile arrangement held together primarily by affectional ties rather than instrumental concerns.

In general, as in white lower-class groups, the decision to marry seems to be taken rather impulsively. Since everyone knows that sooner or later he will get married, in spite of the fact that he may not be sanguine about the prospect, Negro lower-class men and women are alert for clues that the time has arrived. The time may arrive because of a pregnancy in a steady relationship that seems gratifying to both partners, or as a way of getting out of what seems to be an awkward situation, or as a self-indulgence during periods when a boy and a girl are feeling very sorry for themselves. Thus, one girl tells us that when she marries her husband will cook all of her meals for her and she will not have any housework; another girl says that when she marries it will be to a man who has plenty of money and will have to take her out often and really show her a good time.

Boys see in marriage the possibility of regular sexual intercourse without having to fight for it, or a girl safe from venereal disease, or a relationship to a nurturant figure who will fulfill the functions of a mother. For boys, marriage can also be a way of asserting their independence from the peer group if its demands become burdensome. In this case the young man seeks to have the best of both worlds.... In general, then, the movement toward marriage is an uncertain and tentative one. Once the couple does settle down together in a household of their own, they have the problem of working out a mutually acceptable organization of rights and duties, expectations and performances, that will meet their needs.

Husband-wife relations. Characteristic of both the Negro and white lower class is a high degree of conjugal role segregation. That is, husbands and wives tend to think of themselves as having very separate kinds of functioning in the instrumental organization of family life, and also as pursuing recreational and outside interests separately. The husband is expected to be a provider; he resists assuming functions around the home so long as he feels he is doing his proper job of bringing home a pay check. He feels he has the right to indulge himself in little ways if he is successful at this task. The wife is expected to care for the home and children and make her husband feel welcome and comfortable. Much that is distinctive to Negro family life stems from the fact that husbands often are not stable providers. Even when a particular man is, his wife's conception of men in general is such that she is pessimistic about the likelihood that he will continue to do well in this area. A great many Negro wives work to supplement the family income. When this is so the separate incomes earned by husband and wife tend to be treated not as "family" income but as the individual property of the two persons involved. If their wives work, husbands are likely to feel that they are entitled to retain a larger share of the income they provide; the wives, in turn, feel that the husbands have no right to benefit from the purchases they make out of their own money. There is, then, "my money" and "your money." In this situation the husband may come to feel that the wife should support the children out of her income and that he can retain all of his income for himself.

While white lower-class wives often are very much intimidated by their husbands, Negro lower-class wives come to feel that they have a right to give as good as they get. If the husband indulges himself, they have a right to indulge themselves. If the husband steps out on his wife, she has a right to step out on him. The commitment of husbands and wives to each other seems often a highly instrumental one after the "honeymoon" period. Many wives feel they owe the husband nothing once he fails to perform his provider role. If the husband is unemployed the wife increasingly refuses to perform her usual duties for him. For example one woman, after mentioning that her husband had cooked four eggs for himself, commented, "I cook for him when he's working but right now he's unemployed; he can cook for himself." It is important, however, to understand that the man's status in the home depends not so much on whether he is working as on whether he brings money into the home. Thus, in several of the families we have studied in which the husband receives disability payments his status is as well-recognized as in families in which the husband is working.

Because of the high degree of conjugal role segregation, both white and Negro lower-class families tend to be matrifocal in comparison to middle-class families. They are matrifocal in the sense that the wife makes most of the decisions that keep the family going and has the greatest sense of responsibility to the family. In white as well as in Negro lower-class families women tend to look to their female relatives for support and counsel, and to treat their husbands as essentially uninterested in the day-to-day problems of family living. In the Negro lower-class family these tendencies are all considerably exaggerated so that the matrifocality is much clearer than in white lower-class families.

The fact that both sexes in the Negro slum culture have equal right to the various satisfactions of life (earning an income, sex, drinking, and peer-group activity which conflicts with family responsibilities) means that there is less pretense to patriarchal authority in the Negro than in the white lower class. Since men find the overt debasement of their status very threatening, the Negro family is much more vulnerable to disruption when men are temporarily unable to perform their provider roles. Also, when men are unemployed the temptations for them to engage in street adventures which repercuss on the marital relationship are much greater. This fact is well-recognized by Negro lower-class wives; they often seem as concerned about what their unemployed husbands will do instead of working as they are about the fact that the husband is no longer bringing money into the home.

It is tempting to cope with the likelihood of disloyalty by denying the usual norms of fidelity, by maintaining instead that extra-marital affairs are acceptable as long as they do not interfere with family functioning. Quite a few informants tell us this, but we have yet to observe a situation in which a couple maintains a stable relationship under these circumstances without a great deal of conflict....

With couples who have managed to stay married for a good many years, these peccadillos are tolerable although they generate a great deal of conflict in the marital relationship. At earlier ages the partners are likely to be both prouder and less inured to the hopelessness of maintaining stable relationships; outside involvements are therefore much more likely to be disruptive of the marriage.

Marital breakup. The precipitating causes of marital disruption seem to fall mainly into economic or sexual categories. As noted, the husband has little credit with his wife to tide him over periods of unemployment. Wives seem very willing to withdraw commitment from husbands who are not bringing money into the house. They take the point of view that he has no right to take up space around the house, to use its facilities, or to demand loyalty from her. Even where the wife is not inclined to press these claims, the husband tends to be touchy because he knows that such definitions are usual in his group, and he may, therefore, prove difficult for even a well-meaning wife to deal with. As noted above, if husbands do not work they tend to play around. Since they continue to maintain some contact with their peer groups, whenever they have time on their hands they move back into the world of the street system and are likely to get involved in activities which pose a threat to their family relationships.

Drink is a great enemy of the lower-class housewife, both white and Negro. Lower-class wives fear their husband's drinking because it costs money, because the husband may become violent and take out his frustrations on his wife, and because drinking may lead to sexual involvements with other women.

The combination of economic problems and sexual difficulties can be seen in the case of the following couple in their early twenties:

> When the field worker first came to know them, the Wilsons seemed to be working hard to establish a stable family life. The couple had been married about three years and had a two-year-old son. Their apartment was very sparsely furnished but also very clean. Within six weeks the couple had acquired several rooms of inexpensive furniture and obviously had gone to a great deal of effort to make a liveable home. Husband and wife worked on different shifts so that the husband could take care of the child while the wife worked. They looked forward to saving enough money to move out of the housing project into a more desirable neighborhood. Six weeks later, however, the husband had lost his job. He and his wife were in great conflict. She made him feel unwelcome at home and he strongly suspected her of going out with other men. A short time later, they had separated. It is impossible to disentangle the various factors involved in this separation into a sequence of cause and effect, but we can see something of the impact of the total complex.

First Mr. Wilson loses his job: "I went to work one day and the man told me that I would have to work until 1:00. I asked him if there would be any extra pay for working overtime and he said no. I asked him why and he said, 'If you don't like it you can kiss my ass.' He said that to me. I said, 'Why do I have to do all that?' He said, 'Because I said so.' I wanted to jam (fight) him but I said to myself I don't want to be that ignorant, I don't want to be as ignorant as he is, so I just cut out and left. Later his father called me (it was a family firm) and asked why I left and I told him. He said, 'If you don't want to go along with my son then you're fired.' I said O.K. They had another Negro man come in to help me part time before they fired me. I think they were trying to have him work full time because he worked for them before. He has seven kids and he takes their shit."

The field worker observed that things were not as hard as they could be because his wife had a job, to which he replied, "Yeah, I know, that's just where the trouble is. My wife has become independent since she began working. If I don't get a job pretty soon I'll go crazy. We have a lot of little arguments about nothing since she got so independent." He went on to say that his wife had become a completely different person recently; she was hard to talk to because she felt that now that she was working and he was not there was nothing that he could tell her. On her last pay day his wife did not return home for three days; when she did she had only seven cents left from her pay check. He said that he loved his wife very much and had begged her to quit fooling around. He is pretty sure that she is having an affair with the man with whom she rides to work. To make matters worse his wife's sister counsels her that she does not have to stay home with him as long as he is out of work. Finally the wife moved most of their furniture out of the apartment so that he came home to find an empty apartment. He moved back to his parents' home (also in the housing project).

One interesting effect of this experience was the radical change in the husband's attitudes toward race relations. When he and his wife were doing well together and had hopes of moving up in the world he was quite critical of Negroes; "Our people are not ready for integration in many cases because they really don't know how to act. You figure if our people don't want to be bothered with whites then why in hell should the white man want to be bothered with them. There are some of us who are ready; there are others who aren't quite ready yet so I don't see why they're doing all of this hollering." A scarce eight months later he addressed white people as he spoke for two hours into a tape recorder, "If we're willing to be with you, why aren't you willing to be with us? Do our color make us look dirty and low down and cheap? Or do you know the real meaning of 'nigger'? Anyone can be a nigger, white, colored, orange or any other color. It's something that you labeled us with. You put us away like you put a can away on the shelf with a label on it. The can is marked 'Poison: stay away from it.' You want us to help build your country but you don't want us to live in it. ... You give me respect; I'll give you respect. If you threaten to take my life, I'll take yours and believe me I know how to take a life. We do believe that man was put here to live together as human beings; not one that's superior and the one that's a dog, but as human beings. And if you don't want to live this way then you become the dog and we'll become the human beings. There's too much corruption, too much hate, too much one individual trying to step on another. If we don't get together in a hurry we will destroy each other." It was clear from what the respondent said that he had been much influenced by Black Muslim philosophy, yet again and again in his comments one can see the displacement into a public, race relations dialogue of the sense of rage, frustration and victimization that he had experienced in his ill-fated marriage.

Finally, it should be noted that migration plays a part in marital disruption. Sometimes marriages do not break up in the dramatic way described above but rather simply become increasingly unsatisfactory to one or both partners. In such a situation the temptation to move to another city, from South to North, or North to West, is great. Several wives told us that their first marriages were broken when they moved with their children to the North and their husbands stayed behind.

"After we couldn't get along I left the farm and came here and stayed away three or four days. I didn't come here to stay. I came to visit but I liked it and so I said, 'I'm gonna leave!' He said, 'I'll be glad if you do.' Well, maybe he didn't mean it but I thought he did. ... I miss him sometimes, you know. I think about him I guess. But just in a small way. That's what I can't understand about life sometimes; you know—how people can go on like that and still break up and meet somebody else. Why couldn't—oh, I don't know!"

The gains and losses in marriage and in the post-marital state often seem quite comparable. Once they have had the experience of marriage, many women in the Negro slum culture see little to recommend it in the future, important as the first marriage may have been in establishing their maturity and respectability.

The house of mothers. As we have seen, perhaps a majority of mothers in the Negro slum community spend at least part of their mature life as mothers heading a family. The Negro mother may be a working mother or she may be an AFDC mother, but in either case she has the problems of maintaining a household, socializing her children, and achieving for herself some sense of membership in relations with other women and with men. As is apparent from the earlier discussion, she often receives her training in how to run such a household by observing her own mother manage without a husband. Similarly she often learns how to run a three-generation household because she herself brought a third generation into her home with her first, premarital, pregnancy.

Because men are not expected to be much help around the house, having to be head of the household is not particularly intimidating to the Negro mother if she can feel some security about income. She knows it is a hard, hopeless, and often thankless task, but she also knows that it is possible. The maternal household in the slum is generally run with a minimum of organization. The children quickly learn to fend for themselves, to go to the store, to make small purchases, to bring change home, to watch after themselves when the mother has to be out of the home, to amuse themselves, to set their own schedules of sleeping, eating, and going to school. Housekeeping practices may be poor, furniture takes a terrific beating from the children, and emergencies constantly arise. The Negro mother in this situation copes by not setting too high standards for herself, by letting things take their course. Life is most difficult when there are babies and preschool children around because then the mother is confined to the home. If she is a grandmother and the children are her daughter's, she is often confined since it is taken as a matter of course that the mother has the right to continue her outside activities and that the grandmother has the duty to be responsible for the child.

In this culture there is little of the sense of the awesome responsibility of caring for children that is characteristic of the working and middle class. There is not the deep psychological involvement with babies which has been observed with the working-class mother. The baby's needs are cared for on a catch-as-catch-can basis. If there are other children around and they happen to like babies, the baby can be over-stimulated; if this is not the case, the baby is left alone a good deal of the time. As quickly as he can move around he learns to fend for himself.

The three-generation maternal household is a busy place. In contrast to working- and middle-class homes it tends to be open to the world, with many non-family members coming in and out at all times as the children are visited by friends, the teenagers by their boy friends and girl friends, the mother by her friends and perhaps an occasional boy friend, and the grandmother by fewer friends but still by an occasional boy friend.

The openness of the household is, among other things, a reflection of the mother's sense of impotence in the face of the street system. Negro lower-class mothers often indicate that they try very hard to keep their young children at home and away from the streets; they often seem to make the children virtual prisoners in the home. As the children grow and go to school they inevitably do become involved in peer-group activities. The mother gradually gives up, feeling that once the child is lost to this pernicious outside world there is little she can do to continue to control him and direct his development. She will try to limit the types of activities that go on in the home and to restrict the kinds of friends that her children can bring into the home, but even this she must give up as time goes on, as the children become older and less attentive to her direction.

The grandmothers in their late forties, fifties, and sixties tend increasingly to stay at home. The home becomes a kind of court at which other family members gather and to which they bring their friends for sociability, and as a by-product provide amusement and entertainment for the mother. A grandmother may provide a home for her children, and sometimes their children's children, and yet receive very little in a material way from them; but one of the things she does receive is a sense of human involvement, a sense that although life may have passed her by she is not completely isolated from it.

The lack of control that mothers have over much that goes on in their households is most dramatically apparent in the fact that their older children seem to have the right to come home at any time once they have moved and to stay in the home without contributing to its maintenance. Though the mother may be resentful about being taken advantage of, she does not feel she can turn her children away. For example, sixty-five-year-old Mrs. Washington plays hostess for weeks or months at a time to her forty-year-old daughter and her small children, and to her twenty-three-year-old granddaughter and her children. When these daughters come home with their families the grandmother is expected to take care of the young children and must argue with her daughter and granddaughter to receive contributions to the daily household ration of food and liquor. Or, a twenty-year-old son comes home from the Air Force and feels he has the right to live at home without working and to run up an eighty-dollar long-distance telephone bill.

Even aged parents living alone in small apartments sometimes acknowledge such obligations to their children or grandchildren. Again, the only clear return they receive for their hospitality is the reduction of isolation that comes from having people around and interesting activity going on. When in the Washington home the daughter and granddaughter and their children move in with the grandmother, or when they come to visit for shorter periods of time, the occasion has a party atmosphere. The women sit around talking and reminiscing. Though boy friends may be present, they take little part; instead they sit passively, enjoying the stories and drinking along with the women. It would seem that in this kind of party activity the women are defined as the stars. Grandmother, daughter, and granddaughter in turn take the center of the stage telling a story from the family's past, talking about a particularly interesting night out on the town or just making some general observation about life. In the course of these events a good deal of liquor is consumed. In such a household as this little attention is paid to the children since the competition by adults for attention is stiff.

Boy friends, not husbands. It is with an understanding of the problems of isolation which older mothers have that we can obtain the best insight into the role and function of boy friends in the maternal household. The older mothers, surrounded by their own children and grandchildren, are not able to move freely in the outside world, to participate in the high life which they enjoyed when younger and more foot-loose. They are disillusioned with marriage as providing any more secure economic base than they can achieve on their own. They see marriage as involving just another responsibility without a concomitant reward—"It's the greatest thing in the world to come home in the afternoon and not have some curly headed twot in the house yellin' at me and askin' me where supper is, where I've been, what I've been doin', and who I've been seein'." In this situation the woman is tempted to form relationships with men that are not so demanding as marriage but still provide companionship and an opportunity for occasional sexual gratification.

There seem to be two kinds of boys friends. Some boy friends "pimp" off mothers; they extract payment in food or money for their companionship. This leads to the custom sometimes called "Mother's Day," the tenth of the month when the AFDC checks come. On this day one can observe an influx of men into the neighborhood, and much partying. But there is another kind of boy friend, perhaps more numerous than the first, who instead of being paid for his services pays for the right to be a pseudo family member. He may be the father of one of the woman's children and for this reason makes a steady contribution to the family's support, or he may simply be a man whose company the mother enjoys and who makes reasonable gifts to the family for the time he spends with them (and perhaps implicitly for the sexual favors he receives). While the boy friend does not assume fatherly authority within the family, he often is known and liked by the children. The older children appreciate the meaningfulness of their mother's relationship with him—one girl said of her mother's boy friend:

> "We don't none of us (the children) want her to marry again. It's all right if she wants to live by herself and have a boy friend. It's not because we're afraid we're going to have some more sisters and brothers, which it wouldn't make us much difference, but I think she be too old."

Even when the boy friend contributes ten or twenty dollars a month to the family he is in a certain sense getting a bargain. If he is a well-accepted boy friend he spends considerable time around the house, has a chance to relax in an atmosphere less competitive than that of his peer group, is fed and cared for by the woman, yet has no responsibilities which he cannot renounce when he wishes. When women have stable relationships of this kind with boy friends they often consider marrying them but are reluctant to take such a step. Even the well-liked boy friend has some shortcomings—one woman said of her boy friend:

> "Well he works; I know that. He seems to be a nice person, kind hearted. He believes in survival for me and my family. He don't much mind sharing with my youngsters. If I ask him for a helping hand he don't seem to mind that. The only part I dislike is his drinking."

The woman in this situation has worked out a reasonably stable adaptation to the problems of her life; she is fearful of upsetting this adaptation by marrying again. It seems easier to take the "sweet" part of the relationship with a man without the complexities that marriage might involve.

It is in the light of this pattern of women living in families and men living by themselves in rooming houses, odd rooms, here and there, that we can understand Daniel Patrick Moynihan's observation that during their mature years men simply disappear; that is, that census data show a very high sex ratio of women to men. In St. Louis, starting at the age range twenty to twenty-four there are only seventy-two men for every one hundred women. This ratio does not climb to ninety until the age range fifty to fifty-four. Men often do not have real homes; they move about from one household where they have kinship or sexual ties to another; they live in flop houses and rooming houses; they spend time in institutions. They are not household members in the only "homes" that they have—the homes of their mothers and of their girl friends.

It is in this kind of world that boys and girls in the Negro slum community learn their sex roles. It is not just, or even mainly, that fathers are often absent but that the male role models around boys are ones which emphasize expressive, affectional techniques for making one's way in the world. The female role models available to girls emphasize an exaggerated self-sufficiency (from the point of view of the middle class) and the danger of allowing oneself to be dependent on men for anything that is crucial. By the time she is mature, the woman learns that she is most secure when she herself manages the family affairs and when she dominates her men. The man learns that he exposes himself to the least risk of failure when he does not assume a husband's and father's responsibilities but instead counts on his ability to court women and to ingratiate himself with them....

Household groups function for cultures in carrying out the initial phases of socialization and personality formation. It is in the family that the child learns the most primitive categories of existence and experience, and that he develops his most deeply held beliefs about the world and about himself.... The child seeks a sense of valid identity, a sense of being a particular person with a satisfactory degree of congruence between who he feels he is, who he announces himself to be, and where he feels his society places him. He is uncomfortable when he experiences disjunction between his own needs and the kinds of needs legitimated by those around him, or when he feels a disjunction between his sense of himself and the image of himself that others play back to him.

"*Tell it like it is.*" When families become involved in important quarrels the psychosocial underpinnings of family life are laid bare. One such quarrel in a family we have been studying brings together in one place many of the themes that seem to dominate identity problems in Negro slum culture. The incident illustrates in a particularly forceful and dramatic way family processes which our field work, and some other contemporary studies of slum family life, suggest unfold more subtly in a great many families at the lower-class level. The family involved, the Johnsons, is certainly not the most disorganized one we have studied; in some respects their way of life represents a realistic adaptation to the hard living of a family nineteen years on AFDC with a monthly income of $202 for nine people. The two oldest daughters, Mary Jane (eighteen years old) and Esther (sixteen) are pregnant; Mary Jane has one illegitimate child. The adolescent sons, Bob and Richard, are much involved in the social and sexual activities of their peer group. The three other children, ranging in age from twelve to fourteen, are apparently also moving into this kind of peer-group society.

When the argument started Bob and Esther were alone in the apartment with Mary Jane's baby. Esther took exception to Bob's playing with the baby because she had been left in charge; the argument quickly progressed to a fight in which Bob cuffed Esther around, and she tried to cut him with a knife. The police were called and subdued Bob with their nightsticks. At this point the rest of the family and the field worker arrived. As the argument continued, these themes relevant to the analysis which follows appeared:

1) The sisters said that Bob was not their brother (he is a half-brother to Esther, and Mary Jane's full brother). Indeed, they said their mother "didn't have no husband. These kids don't even know who their daddies are." The mother defended herself by saying that she had one legal husband, and one common-law husband, no more.

2) The sisters said that their fathers had never done anything for them, nor had their mother. She retorted that she had raised them "to the age of womanhood" and now would care for their babies.

3) Esther continued to threaten to cut Bob if she got a chance (a month later they fought again, and she did cut Bob, who required twenty-one stitches).

4) The sisters accused their mother of favoring their lazy brothers and asked her to put them out of the house. She retorted that the girls were as lazy, that they made no contribution to maintaining the household, could not get their boy friends to marry them or support their children, that all the support came from her AFDC check. Mary Jane retorted that "the baby has a check of her own."

5) The girls threatened to leave the house if their mother refused to put their brothers out. They said they could force their boy friends to support them by taking them to court, and Esther threatened to cut her boy friend's throat if he did not co-operate.

6) Mrs. Johnson said the girls could leave if they wished but that she would keep their babies; "I'll not have it, not knowing who's taking care of them."

7) When her thirteen-year-old sister laughed at all of this, Esther

    told her not to laugh because she, too, would be pregnant within a year.

8) When Bob laughed, Esther attacked him and his brother by saying that both were not man enough to make babies, as she and her sister had been able to do.

9) As the field worker left, Mrs. Johnson sought his sympathy. "You see, Joe, how hard it is for me to bring up a family. . . . They sit around and talk to me like I'm some kind of a dog and not their mother."

10) Finally, it is important to note for the analysis which follows that the following labels—"black-assed," black bastard," "bitch," and other profane terms—were liberally used by Esther and Mary Jane, and rather less liberally by their mother, to refer to each other, to the girls' boy friends, to Bob, and to the thirteen-year-old daughter.

Several of the themes outlined previously appear forcefully in the course of this argument. In the last year and a half the mother has become a grandmother and expects shortly to add two more grandchildren to her household. She takes it for granted that it is her responsibility to care for the grandchildren and that she has the right to decide what will be done with the children since her own daughters are not fully responsible. She makes this very clear to them when they threaten to move out, a threat which they do not really wish to make good nor could they if they wished to.

However, only as an act of will is Mrs. Johnson able to make this a family. She must constantly cope with the tendency of her adolescent children to disrupt the family group and to deny that they are in fact a family—"He ain't no brother of mine"; "The baby has a check of her own." Though we do not know exactly what processes communicate these facts to the children it is clear that in growing up they have learned to regard themselves as not fully part of a solidary collectivity. During the quarrel this message was reinforced for the twelve-, thirteen-, and fourteen-year-old daughters by the four-way argument among their older sisters, older brother, and their mother.

The argument represents vicious unmasking of the individual members' pretenses to being competent individuals. The efforts of the two girls to present themselves as masters of their own fate are unmasked by the mother. The girls in turn unmask the pretensions of the mother and of their two brothers. When the thirteen-year-old daughter expresses some amusement they turn on her, telling her that it won't be long before she too becomes pregnant. Each member of the family in turn is told that he can expect to be no more than a victim of his world, but that this is somehow inevitably his own fault.

In this argument masculinity is consistently demeaned. Bob has no right to play with his niece, the boys are not really masculine because at fifteen and sixteen years they have yet to father children, their own fathers were no goods who failed to do anything for their family. These notions probably come originally from the mother, who enjoys recounting the story of having her common-law husband imprisoned for nonsupport, but this comes back to haunt her as her daughters accuse her of being no better than they in ability to force support and nurturance from a man. In contrast, the girls came off somewhat better than the boys, although they must accept the label of stupid girls because they have similarly failed and inconveniently become pregnant in the first place. At least they can and have had children and therefore have some meaningful connection with the ongoing substance of life. There is something important and dramatic in which they participate, while the boys, despite their sexual activity, "can't get no babies."

In most societies, as children grow and are formed by their elders into suitable members of the society they gain increasingly a sense of competence and ability to master the behavioral environment their particular world presents. But in Negro slum culture growing up involves an ever-increasing appreciation of one's shortcomings, of the impossibility of finding a self-sufficient and gratifying way of living. It is in the family first and most devastatingly that one learns these lessons. As the child's sense of frustration builds he too can strike out and unmask the pretensions of others. The result is a peculiar strength and a pervasive weakness. The strength involves the ability to tolerate and defend against degrading verbal and physical aggressions from others and not to give up completely. The weakness involves the inability to embark hopefully on any course of action that might make things better, particularly action which involves cooperating and trusting attitudes toward others. Family members become potential enemies to each other, as the frequency of observing the police being called in to settle family quarrels brings home all too dramatically.

The conceptions parents have of their children are such that they are constantly alert as the child matures to evidence that he is as bad as everyone else. That is, in lower-class culture human nature is conceived of as essentially bad, destructive, immoral. This is the nature of things. Therefore any one child must be inherently bad unless his parents are very lucky indeed. If the mother can keep the child insulated from the outside world, she feels she may be able to prevent his inherent badness from coming out. She feels that once he is let out into the larger world the badness will come to the fore since that is his nature. This means that in the identity development of the child he is constantly exposed to identity labeling by his parents as a bad person. Since as he grows up he does not experience his world as particularly gratifying, it is very easy for him to conclude that this lack of gratification is due to the fact that something is wrong with him. This, in turn, can readily be assimilated to the definitions of being a bad person offered him by those with whom he lives. In this way the Negro slum child learns his culture's conception of being-in-the-world, a conception that emphasizes inherent evil in a chaotic, hostile, destructive world.

Blackness. To a certain extent these same processes operate in white lower-class groups, but added for the Negro is the reality of blackness. "Black-assed" is not an empty pejorative adjective. In the Negro slum culture several distinctive appellations are used to refer to oneself and others. One involves the term, "black" or "nigger." Black is generally a negative way of naming, but nigger can be either negative or positive, depending upon the context. It is important to note that, at least in the urban North, the initial development of racial identity in these terms has very little directly to do with relations with whites. A child experiences these identity placements in the context of the family and in the neighborhood peer group; he probably very seldom hears the same terms used by whites (unlike the situation in the South). In this way, one of the effects of ghettoization is to mask the ultimate enemy so that the understanding of the fact of victimization by a caste system comes as a late acquisition laid over conceptions of self and of other Negroes derived from intimate, and to the child often traumatic, experience within the ghetto community. If, in addition, the child attends a ghetto school where his Negro teachers either overtly or by implication reinforce his community's negative conceptions of what it means to be black, then the child has little opportunity to develop a more realistic image of himself and other Negroes as being damaged by whites and not by themselves. In such a situation, an intelligent man like Mr. Wilson can say with all sincerity that he does not feel most Negroes are ready for integration—only under the experience of certain kinds of intense personal threat coupled with exposure to an ideology that places the responsibility on whites did he begin to see through the direct evidence of his daily experience.

To those living in the heart of a ghetto, black comes to mean not just "stay back," but also membership in a community of persons who think poorly of each other, who attack and manipulate each other, who give each other small comfort in a desperate world. Black comes to stand for a sense of identity as no better than these destructive others. The individual feels that he must embrace an unattractive self in order to function at all.

We can hypothesize that in those families that manage to avoid the destructive identity imputations of "black" and that manage to maintain solidarity against such assaults from the world around, it is possible for children to grow up with a sense of both Negro and personal identity that allows them to socialize themselves in an anticipatory way for participation in the larger society. This broader sense of identity, however, will remain a brittle one as long as the individual is vulnerable to attack from within the Negro community as "nothing but a nigger like everybody else" or from the white community as "just a nigger." We can hypothesize further that the vicious unmasking of essential identity as black described above is least likely to occur within families where the parents have some stable sense of security, and where they therefore have less need to protect themselves by disavowing responsibility for their children's behavior and denying the children their patrimony as products of a particular family rather than of an immoral nature and an evil community.

In sum, we are suggesting that Negro slum children as they grow up in their families and in their neighborhoods are exposed to a set of experiences—and a rhetoric which conceptualizes them—that brings home to the child an understanding of his essence as a weak and debased person who can expect only partial gratification of his needs, and who must seek even this level of gratification by less than straight-forward means.

Strategies for living. In every society complex processes of socialization inculcate in their members strategies for gratifying the needs with which they are born and those which the society itself generates. Inextricably linked to these strategies, both cause and effect of them, are the existential propositions which members of a culture entertain about the nature of their world and of effective action within the world as it is defined for them. In most of American society two grand strategies seem to attract the allegiance of its members and guide their day-to-day actions. I have called these strategies those of *the good life* and of *career success*. A good life strategy involves efforts to get along with others and not to rock the boat, a comfortable familism grounded on a stable work career for husbands in which they perform adequately at the modest jobs that enable them to be good providers. The strategy of career success is the choice of ambitious men and women who see life as providing opportunities to move from a lower to a higher status, to "accomplish something," to achieve greater than ordinary material well-being, prestige, and social recognition. Both of these strategies are predicated on the assumption that the world is inherently rewarding if one behaves properly and does his part. The rewards of the world may come easily or only at the cost of great effort, but at least they are there.

In the white and particularly in the Negro slum worlds little in the experience that individuals have as they grow up sustains a belief in a rewarding world. The strategies that seem appropriate are not those of a good, family-based life or of a career, but rather *strategies for survival*.

Much of what has been said above can be summarized as encouraging three kinds of survival strategies. One is the strategy of the *expressive life style* which I have described elsewhere as an effort to make yourself interesting and attractive to others so that you are better able to manipulate their behavior along lines that will provide some immediate gratification. Negro slum culture provides many examples of techniques for seduction, of persuading others to give you what you want in situations where you have very little that is tangible to offer in return. In order to get what you want you learn to "work game," a strategy which requires a high development of a certain kind of verbal facility, a sophisticated manipulation of promise and interim reward. When the expressive strategy fails or when it is unavailable there is, of course, the great temptation to adopt a *violent strategy* in which you force others to give you what you need once you fail to win it by verbal and other symbolic means. Finally, and increasingly as members of the Negro slum culture grow older, there is the *depressive strategy* in which goals are increasingly constricted to the bare necessities for survival (not as a social being but simply as an organism). This is the strategy of "I don't bother anybody and I hope nobody's gonna bother me; I'm simply going through the motions to keep body (but not soul) together." Most lower-class people follow mixed strategies, as Walter Miller has observed, alternating among the excitement of the expressive style, the desperation of the violent style, and the deadness of the depressed style. Some members of the Negro slum world experiment from time to time with mixed strategies that also incorporate the stable working-class model of the good American life, but this latter strategy is exceedingly vulnerable to the threats of unemployment or a less than adequate pay check, on the one hand, and the seduction and violence of the slum world around them, on the other. . . .

Ulf Hannerz

THE RHETORIC OF SOUL:
IDENTIFICATION IN NEGRO SOCIETY

The momentous events of the last decade have produced a new sense of identity in American Negroes, a new feeling of pride in being black and in the distinctive characteristics of the Negro sub-culture. "Black power" and "Black consciousness" are two inter-related manifestations of this development. Another is the widespread use of the word "soul."

Ulf Hannerz explores the question of what Negroes mean by "soul" and the reasons for the diffuseness of its meaning. More important, he discusses why this concept—and, by implication, the whole idea of black cultural pluralism—became so important in the middle and late 1960's.

THE last few years have witnessed the emergence of a concept of "soul" as signifying what is "essentially Negro" in the black ghettos of the large cities of the Northern United States. In this paper, I will attempt to place this concept of "soul" in its social and cultural matrix, in particular with respect to tendencies of social change as experienced by ghetto inhabitants. In doing so, I will emphasise what I believe to be the dominant purpose of a "soul" vocabulary among its users. There will be clear points of convergence between my view of "soul" and that stated by Charles Keil in his book *Urban Blues*.[1] However, I believe that Keil's personal evaluation of some of the features of black ghetto culture tends to obscure the issue in some ways, and I also feel that a clearer picture of the essential social-structural and social-psychological features may be achieved.

This paper is based on field work in a lower-class Negro neighbourhood

Ulf Hannerz, "The Rhetoric of Soul: Identification in Negro Society," *Race*, IX, 4 (1968), pp. 453–465. Reprinted with permission.
[1] Charles Keil, *Urban Blues* (Chicago, University of Chicago Press, 1966).

in Washington, D.C. The field site seems to be in many ways typical of Negro slums in Northern American cities. It is situated at the edge of a large, ethnically homogeneous area. Its inhabitants share the common characteristics of America's lower-class urban Negroes: poverty, a high rate of unemployment, a considerable amount of crime, including juvenile delinquency, and widely varying family role-structures according to which it is relatively common that the adult woman dominates the family while the male is either absent or only temporarily attached—even when he is a permanent member of the household his participation in household affairs may be quite limited. (It should be noted that this is not said to be true of all households—it is only pointed out that unstable family relationships and female dominance are much more common among lower-class Negroes than among the American people in general.) Of the adults at the field site—a block-long street lined by two- or three-story row houses—a minority was born in Washington, D.C. The majority are immigrants from the South, particularly from Virginia, North Carolina, and South Carolina. Apart from conducting field work in this area by means of participant observation in the traditional sense, I have paid attention to those impersonal media which have a significant part in ghetto life; these are particularly important in the context of this study. I refer here to media which are specifically intended for a lower-class Negro audience: radio (three stations in Washington, D.C. are clearly aimed at Negroes), the recording industry, and stage shows featuring Negro rock-and-roll artists and comedians. (The term "rhythm and blues" used by whites to denote Negro rock-and-roll is now only infrequently used by the Negroes themselves.) These media have played a prominent part in promoting the vocabulary of "soul." (It may be added, on the other hand, that both the local Negro press such as the Washington *Afro-American*, and the national Negro publications, for example the monthly *Ebony*, are largely middle-class oriented and thus of limited value in the understanding of life in the ghetto where few read them.)

II

What, then, is "soul"? As the concept has come to be used in urban ghettos over the last number of years, it stands for what is "the essence of Negroness" and, it should be added, this "Negroness" refers to the kind of Negro with which the urban slum dweller is most familiar—people like himself. The question whether a middle-class, white-collar suburban Negro also has "soul" is often met with consternation. In fact, "soul" seems to be a folk conception of the lower-class urban Negro's own "national character." Modes of action, personal attributes, and certain artifacts are given the "soul" label. Typically, in conversations, one hears statements such as, "Man, he got a lot of soul." This appreciative opinion may be given concerning anybody in the ghetto, but more often by younger adults or adolescents about others of their own categories. In particular, speaking in terms of "soul" is common among younger men. This sex differentiation of the use of "soul" conceptions, I will suggest below, may be quite important in the understanding of the basis of the use of the "soul" concept.

The choice of the term "soul" for this "Negroness" is in itself noteworthy. First of all, it shows the influence of religion on lower-class Negroes, even those who are not themselves active church members—expressions of religious derivation, such as "God, have mercy!" are frequent in everyday speech among lower-class Negroes of all age and sex categories, and in all contexts. A very great number of people, of course, have been regular church-goers at some point or other, at least at the time when they attended Sunday school, and many are actively involved in church activities, perhaps in one of the large Baptist churches but at least as often in small spiritualist storefront churches. Although the people who use the "soul" vocabulary in which we are interested here are seldom themselves regular church-goers, they have certainly been fully (although sometimes indirectly) exposed to the religious idiom; including such phrases as "a soul-stirring revival meeting."

Furthermore, the choice of a term which in church usage has a connotation of "the essentially human" to refer to "the essentially Negro," as the new concept of "soul" does, certainly has strong implications of ethnocentrism. If "soul" is Negro, the non-Negro is "non-soul," and, it appears, somewhat less human. Although I have never heard such a point of view spelled out, it would seem to me that it is implicitly accepted as part of an incipient "soul" ideology. It is very clear that what is "soul" is not only different from what is not "soul" (particularly what is mainstream middle-class American); it is also superior. "Soul" is an appraisive as well as designative concept.[2] If one asks a young man what a "soul brother" is, the answer is usually something like "someone who's hip, someone who knows what he's doing." It may be added here that although both "soul brother" and "soul sister" are used for "soul" personified, the former is more common. Like "soul," "soul brother" and "soul sister" are terms used particularly by younger males.

Let us now note a few fields that are particularly "soul." One area is that of music (where the concept may have originated—see the article on the "soul" movement among jazz musicians by Szwed),[3] particularly the field of progressive jazz and rock-and-roll. This has been seized upon by those actively engaged in these fields. James Brown, a leading rock-and-roll singer, is often referred to as "Soul Brother Number One"; two of the largest record stores in Washington, D.C., with practically only Negro customers, are the "Soul Shack" and the "Soul City." Recently a new magazine named "Soul" appeared; its main outlet seems to be these de facto segregated record stores. It contains stories on rock-and-roll artists, disc jockeys, and the like. Excellence in musical expression is indeed a part of the lower-class Negro self-conception, and white

[2] Charles Morris, *Signification and Significance* (Cambridge, Mass., The M.I.T. Press, 1964).

[3] John F. Szwed, "Musical Style and Racial Conflict," *Phylon* (vol. 27, 1966), pp. 358–66.

rock-and-roll is often viewed with scorn as a poor imitation of the Negro genius. Resentment is frequently aimed at the Beatles who stand as typical of white intrusion into a Negro field. (Occasionally, a Beatle melody has become a hit in the Negro ghetto as well, but only when performed in a local version by a Negro group, such as the recordings of "Day Tripper" by the Vontastics. In such a case, there is little or no mention of its Beatles origin.)

The commercial side of Negro entertainment is, of course, directly tied to "soul" music. With counterparts in other large Negro ghettos in the United States, the Howard Theater in Washington stages shows of touring rock-and-roll groups and individual performers—each show usually runs a week, with four of five performances every day. Larger shows also make one-night only appearances at the Washington Coliseum. Occasionally, a comedian also takes part; Moms Mabley, Pigmeat Markham, or Red Foxx are among those who draw large Negro audiences but few whites.

The "emcees" of these shows are often celebrities in their own right— some, such as "King" Coleman and "Georgeous George," tour regularly with the shows, others are local disc jockeys from the Negro radio stations. In Washington, such disc jockeys as "The Nighthawk" (Bob Terry), and "Soulfinger" (Fred Correy), make highly appreciated appearances at the Howard. The leading local black station is WOL "Soul Radio": it is clear that the commercial establishments with a vested interest in a separate Negro audience have seized upon the "soul" vocabulary, using it to further their own interests as well as supporting its use among the audience. Thus there is also for instance a WWRL "soul brother radio" in New York. However, one should not view the "soul" vocabulary solely as a commercial creation. It existed before it was commercialized, and the fact that it seems so profitable for commercial establishments to fly the banner of "soul" also indicates that whatever part these establishments have had in promoting it, it has fallen into fertile ground.

A second area of widespread "soul" symbolism is that of food. The dishes that are now "soul food" were once—and still are to some extent— referred to simply as "Southern cooking"; but in the Northern ghettos they increasingly come to stand for race rather than region. In the centre of the Washington area, for instance, there is a "Little Harlem Restaurant" advertising "soul food." There are a number of such foods; some of those which are most frequently mentioned as "soul foods" are chitterlings (a part of the intestine of the pig), hog maw (pig tripe), black-eyed peas, collard greens, corn bread, and grits (a kind of porridge). Typically, they were the poor man's food in the rural South—in the urban North, they may still be so to some extent, but in the face of the diversity of the urban environment, they also come to stand as signs of ethnicity. (Thus in some Northern cities there are "soul food" restaurants catering to curious whites, much in the same way as any exotic cuisine.) One may note that references to "soul food" occur frequently in "soul music"; two of the hits of the winter 1966-7 were "Grits and Cornbread" by the Soul Runners and the Joe Cuba Sextet's "Bang! Bang!" with the refrain "corn bread, hog maw and chitterling." Sometimes, the names of "soul foods" may themselves be used as more or less synonymous with "soul"—Negro entertainers on stage, talking of their experiences while journeying between ghetto shows around the country, sometimes refer to it as "the chitterling circuit," and this figure of speech usually draws much favourable audience reaction.

What, then, is "soul music" and "soul food"? It may be wise to be cautious here, since there is little intellectualizing and analyzing on the part of the ghetto's inhabitants on this subject. I believe that this comparative absence of defining activity may itself be significant, and I will return to this possibility below. Here, I will only point to a few basic characteristics of what is "soul" which I feel make it particularly "essentially Negro"—referring again, of course, to urban lower-class Negroes rather than to any other category of people.

There is, of course, the Southern origin. The "Down Country" connotations are particularly attached to "soul food"; however, although Negro music has changed more and the contemporary commercial rock-and-roll is an urban phenomenon, it is certainly seen as the latest stage of an unfolding musical heritage. Thus the things that are "soul," while taking on new significance in the urban environment, provide some common historical tradition for ghetto inhabitants. One might also speculate on the possibility that the early and from then on constant and intimate exposure to these foods and to this music— for radios and record players seem to belong to practically every poor ghetto home—may make them appear particularly basic to a "Negro way of life."

When it comes to "soul" music, there are a couple of themes in style and content which I would suggest are pervasive in ghetto life and which probably make them appear very close to the everyday experience of ghetto inhabitants.

One of these is the lack of control over the social environment. There is a very frequent attitude among "soul brothers"—that is, the ghetto's younger males—that one's environment is somewhat like a jungle where tough, smart people may survive and where a lot happens to make it worth while and enjoyable just to "watch the scene" if one does not have too high hopes of controlling it. Many of the reactions in listening to "progressive jazz" seem to connect to this view; "Oooh, man, there just ain't nothing you can do about it but sit there and feel it goin' all the way into you." Without being able to do much about proving it, I feel that exposure to experiences—desirable or undesirable—in which one can only passively perceive events without influencing them is an essential fact of ghetto life, for better or for worse; thus it is "soul."

Related to this is the experience of unstable personal relationships, in particular between the sexes. It is a well-known fact that among lower-class urban Negroes there are many "broken" families (households without a husband and father), many temporary common-law unions, and in general relatively little consensus on sex roles. Thus, it is not much of an exaggeration to speak of a constant "battle of the sexes," and the achievement of success with the opposite sex is a focal concern in lower-class Negro life. From this area come most of the lyrics of contemporary rock-and-roll music. It may be objected that this is true of white rock-and-roll as well; to this it may be answered that this is very much to the point. For white rock-and-roll is predominantly adolescent music, thus reaching people with similar problems of unstable personal relationships. In the case of lower-class urban Negroes, such relationships are characteristic of a much wider age-range, and music on this theme also reaches this wider range. Some titles of recent rock-and-roll hits may show this theme: "I'm losing you" (Temptations), "Are you lonely" (Freddie Scott), "Yours until tomorrow" (Dee Dee Warwick), "Keep me hangin' on" (Supremes). "Soul" stands for a bitter-sweet experience; this often arises from contacts with the other sex, although there are certainly also other sources. This bitter-sweetness, of course, was typical already of the blues.

Turning to style, a common element in everyday social interaction as well as among storefront church preachers, Negro comedians, and rock-and-roll singers is an alternation between aggressive, somewhat boasting behaviour, and plaintive behaviour from an implicit under-dog position.

This may not be the place to give a more detailed account of this style of behaviour. However, as I said, it occurs in many situations and may itself be related to the unstable personal relationships ... mentioned above. In any case, it seems that this style is seen as having "soul"; without describing its occurrences in a variety of contexts.

As I noted above, I have hesitated to try to analyze and define "soul," because what seems to be important in the emergence of the present "soul" concept is the fact that there is felt to be *something* which is "soul" rather than *what* that something is. There is, of course, some logic to this; if "soul" is what is "essentially Negro," it should not be necessary for "soul brothers" to spend too much time analyzing it. Asking about "soul" one often receives answers such as "you know, we don't talk much about it, but we've all been through it, so we know what it is anyway." Probably, this is to some extent true. What the lack of pronounced definition points to, in that case, is that "soul" vocabulary is predominantly for in-group consumption. It is a symbol of solidarity among the people of the ghetto, but not in more than a weak and implicit sense of solidarity *against* anybody else. "Soul" is turned inward; and so everybody who is touched by it is supposed to know what it means. So far there has been little interference with the "soul" vocabulary by outsiders, at least in any way noticeable to the ghetto dwellers. There have been none of the fierce arguments about its meaning which have developed around "black power," a concept which did not really evolve in the ghetto but is largely the creation of white mass media. "Black power" is controversial, and so white people insist on a definition. (And many black people, also depending on white media for news, tend to accept the interpretations of these media.) "Soul" is not equally threatening, and so ghetto dwellers can keep its mystique to themselves.

We may note in this context that the few interpreters of "soul" to the outside world are, in fact, outsiders; a kind of cultural brokers who give interested members of the larger society the "inside stuff" on the ghetto. But serving as such brokers, they hardly affect the uses of "soul" within the ghetto community. LeRoi Jones, the author, a convert to ghetto life who like so many converts seems to have become more militantly partisan than the more authentic ghetto inhabitants, has moved from a position where he rather impartially noted the ethnocentric bias of "soul" [4] to one where he preaches for the complete destruction of the present American society,[5] an activist pro- gramme which I am sure is far out of step with the immediate concerns of the average "soul brother." Bennett, an editor of the middle-class *Ebony* maga- zine, is not particularly interested in "the folk myth of soul" but explains what he feels that "soul" really is.[6] I am not convinced that his conception is entirely correct; it is certainly not expressed in the idiom of the ghetto. Keil, an ethno- musicologist, probably comes closer to the folk conception than anyone else, by giving what amounts to a catalogue of those ghetto values and experiences which its inhabitants recognize as their own.[7] In doing so, of course, one does not get a short and comprehensive definition of "soul" that is acceptable to all and in every situation—one merely lists the fields in which a vocabulary of "soul" is particularly likely to be expressed. This, of course, is what has been done in a partial and parsimonious way above.

Here we end the exposition of the "soul" concept. Summing up what has been said so far, the vocabulary of "soul," which is a relatively recent phenom- enon, is used among younger Negro ghetto dwellers, and particularly young men, to designate in a highly approving manner the experiences and characteristics which are "essentially Negro." As such it is not an activist vocabulary for use in inter-group relations but a vocabulary which is employed within the group, although it is clear that by discussing what is "typically Negro" one makes an implicit reference to the non-Negro society. We turn now to an interpretation of the emergence of such a vocabulary in this group at this point of Negro history.

III

For a long time, the social boundaries which have constituted barriers to educational, economic and other achievement by Negro Americans have been highly impermeable. Although lower-class Negroes have to a considerable degree accepted the values of mainstream American culture in those areas, the very obviousness of the impermeability of social boundaries has probably prevented a more complete commitment to the achievement of those goals which have been out of reach. Instead, there has been an adjustment to the lower-class

[4] LeRoi Jones, *Blues People* (New York, William Morrow & Co., 1963), p. 219.
[5] LeRoi Jones, *Home: Social Essays* (New York, William Morrow & Co., 1966).
[6] Lerone Bennett, Jr., *The Negro Mood* (New York, Ballantine Books, 1965), p. 89.
[7] Charles Keil, op. cit., pp. 164 et seq.

situation in which goals and values more appropriate to the ascribed social position of the group have been added to, and to some extent substituted for, the mainstream norms. Whether these lower-class concerns, experiences, and values are direct responses to the situation or historically based patterns for which the lower-class niche provides space is not really important here. What is important is that the style of life of the lower class, in this case the Negro lower class, is different from that of the upper classes, and that the impermeability of group boundaries and the unequal distribution of resources between groups have long kept the behavioural characteristics of the groups relatively stable and distinct from one another, although to a great extent, one of the groups—the lower-class Negroes—would have preferred the style of life of the other group—the middle-class whites—had it been available to them. As it has been, they have only been able to do the best with what they have had. In a way, then, they have had two cultures, the mainstream culture with which they are relatively familiar, which has in many ways appeared superior and preferable, and which has been closed to them, and the ghetto culture which is a second choice and based on the circumstances of the ascribed social position. (I will not dwell here on the typical features of the two cultures and the relationship between them; articles by Miller [8] and Rodman [9] are enlightening discussions of these topics.)

This, of course, sounds to some extent like the position of what has often been called "the marginal man." Such a position may cause psychological problems. However, when the position is very clearly defined and where the same situation is shared by many, the situation is perhaps reasonably acceptable—there is a perfectly understandable reason for one's failure to reach one's goal. Nobody of one's own kind is allowed to reach that goal, and the basis of the condition is a social rule rather than a personal failure. There are indications that marginality is more severely felt if the barrier is not absolute but boundary permeability is possible although uncertain. According to Kerckhoff and McCormick,

> ... an absolute barrier between the two groups is less conducive to personality problems than "grudging, uncertain and unpredictable acceptance." The impact of the rejection on an individual's personality organization will depend to some extent upon the usual treatment accorded members of his group by the dominant group. If his group as a whole faces a rather permeable barrier and he meets with more serious rejection, the effect on him is likely to be more severe than the same treatment received by a more thoroughly rejected group (one facing an impermeable barrier). [10]

[8] Walter B. Miller, "Lower Class Culture as a Generating Milieu of Gang Delinquency," *Journal of Social Issues* (vol. 14, 1958), pp. 5–19.

[9] Hyman Rodman, "The Lower-Class Value Stretch," *Social Forces* (vol. 42, 1963), pp. 205–15.

[10] Alan C. Kerckhoff and Thomas C. McCormick, "Marginal Status and Marginal Personality," *Social Forces* (vol. 34, 1955), p. 51.

My thesis here is that recent changes in race relations in the United States have indeed made the social barriers to achievement at least seem less impermeable than before to the ghetto population. One often hears people in the ghetto expressing opinions such as, "Yeh, there are so many programs, job-training and things, going on, man, so if you got anything on the ball you can make it." On the other hand, there are also assertions about the impossibility of getting anywhere which contradict the first opinion. Obviously, the clear-cut exclusion from mainstream American culture is gradually being replaced by ambivalence about one's actual chances. This ambivalence, of course, seems to represent an accurate estimate of the situation; the lower-class Negro continues to be disadvantaged, although probably his chances of moving up and out are somewhat better than earlier—people do indeed trickle out of the ghetto.

It is in this situation that the ethnocentric vocabulary of "soul" has emerged, and I want to suggest that it is a response to the uncertainty of the ghetto dweller's situation. This uncertainty is particularly strong for the younger male, the "soul brother." While women have always been able to live closer to mainstream culture norms, as homemakers and possibly with a type of job keeping them in touch with the middle-class world, men have had less chance to become competent in mainstream culture as well as to practice it. Older men tend to feel that current social changes come too late for them but put higher expectations on the following generation. Thus the present generation of young men in the Negro ghettos of the United States are placed in a new situation to which it is making new responses, and much of the unrest in the ghettos today is perhaps the result of these emerging pressures.

I will suggest here that this new situation must be taken into account if we are to understand the basis of the emergence of the "soul" vocabulary. The increasing ambivalence in conceptions of one's opportunities in the changing social structure may be accompanied by doubts about one's own worth. Earlier, the lack of congruence between mainstream culture norms and the lower-class Negro's achievements could easily be explained by referring to the social barriers. Under-achievement with respect to mainstream norms was an ascribed characteristic of lower-class Negroes. However, when as at present the suspicion arises, which may very well be mistaken, that under-achievement is not ascribed but due to one's own failure, self-doubt may be the result. Such doubt can be reduced in different ways. Some, of course, are able to live up to mainstream norms of achievement, thereby reducing the strain on themselves (but at the same time increasing that on others). Higher self-esteem can also be arrived at by affirming that the boundaries are still impermeable. A third possibility is to set new standards for achievement, proclaiming one's own achievements to be the ideals. It is not necessary, of course, that the same way of reducing self-doubt is always applied. In the case of "soul," the method is that of idealizing one's own achievements, proclaiming one's own way of life to be superior. Yet the same "soul brother" may argue at other times that they are what they are because they are not allowed to become anything else.

In any case, "soul" is by native public definition "superior," and the motive of the "soul" vocabulary, I believe, is above all to reduce self-doubt by persuading "soul brothers" that they are successful. Being a "soul brother" is belonging to a select group instead of to a residual category of people who have not succeeded. Thus, the "soul" vocabulary is a device of rhetoric. By talking about people who have "soul," about "soul music" and about "soul food," the "soul brother" attempts to establish himself in an expert and connoisseur role; by talking to others of his group in these terms, he identifies with them and confers the same role on them. Using "soul" rhetoric is a way of convincing others of one's own worth and of their worth; it also serves to persuade the speaker himself. As Burke expresses it,

> A man can be his own audience, insofar as he, even in his secret thoughts, cultivates certain ideas or images for the effect he hopes they may have upon him; he is here what Mead would call "an 'I' addressing its 'me' "; and in this respect he is being rhetorical quite as though he were using pleasant imagery to influence an outside audience rather than one within.[11]

The "soul" vocabulary has thus emerged from the social basis of a number of individuals, in effective interaction with one another, with similar problems of adjustment to a new situation. The use of "soul" rhetoric is a way of meeting their needs as long as it occurs in situations where they can mutually support each other. Here is, of course, a clue to the confinement of the rhetoric to in-group situations. If "soul" talk were directed toward outsiders, they might not accept the claims for its excellence—it is not their "folk myth." Viewing "soul" as such a device of rhetoric, it is also easier to understand why it is advantageous for its purposes not to have made it the topic of too much intellectualizing. As Geertz makes clear in his paper on "Ideology as a Cultural System," [12] by analyzing and defining activity, one achieves maximum intellectual clarity at the expense of emotional commitment. It is doubtful that "soul" rhetoric would thrive on too much intellectual clarity; rather, by expressing "soul" ideals in a circumspect manner in terms of emotionally charged symbols such as "soul food" and "soul music," one can avoid the rather sordid realities underlying these emotions. As I pointed out above, the shared lower-class Negro experiences which seem to be the bases of "soul" are hardly in themselves such as to bring out a surge of ethnic pride. That is a psychological reason for keeping the "soul" concept diffuse. There is also, I believe, a sociological basis for the diffuseness. The more exactly a "soul brother" would define "soul," the fewer others would probably agree upon the "essential Negroness" of his definition; and, as we have seen, a basic idea of the rhetoric of "soul" is to cast others into roles which satisfy them and at the same

[11] Kenneth Burke, A Grammar of Motives and a Rhetoric of Motives (Cleveland, Meridian Books, 1962), p. 562.

[12] Clifford Geertz, "Ideology as a Cultural System," in David E. Apter (ed.), Ideology and Discontent (New York, The Free Press, 1964).

time support one's own position. If people are cast into a role of "soul brother" and then find that there has been a definition established for that role which they cannot accept, the result may be overt disagreement and denial of solidarity rather than mutual deference. As it is, "soul" can be an umbrella concept for a rather wide variety of definitions of one's situation, and the "soul brothers" who are most in need of the ethnocentric core conception can occasionally get at least fleeting allegiance to "soul" from others with whom in reality they share relatively little, for instance individuals who are clearly upwardly mobile. On one occasion I listened to a long conversation about "soul music" in a rather heterogeneous group of young Negro men who all agreed on the "soulfulness" of the singers whose records they were playing, and afterwards I asked one of the men who is clearly upwardly mobile of his conception of "soul." He answered that "soul" is earthy, "there is nothing specifically Negro about it." Yet the very individuals with whom he had just agreed on matters of "soul" had earlier given me the opposite answer—only Negroes have "soul." Thus by avoiding definitions, they had found together an area of agreement and satisfaction in "soul" by merely assuming that there was a shared basis of opinion.

IV

Summing up what has been said, "soul" is a relatively recent concept used in the urban Negro ghetto, in particular by young men, to express what is "essential Negroness" and to convey appreciation for it. The point of view which has been expressed here is that the need for such a concept has arisen at this point because of increasingly ambivalent conceptions of the opportunity structure. While earlier, lack of achievement according to American mainstream ideals could easily be explained in terms of impermeable social barriers, the impression is gaining ground in the ghetto that there are now ways out of the situation. The young men who come under particularly great strain if such a belief is accepted must either achieve some success (which many of them are obviously still unable to do, for various reasons), explain that achievement is impossible (which is probably not as true as it has been), or explain that achievement according to mainstream ideals is not necessarily achievement according to their ideals. The emergence of "soul," it has been stated here, goes some way toward meeting the need of stating alternative ideals and also provides solidarity among those with such a need. In implying or stating explicitly that ghetto culture has a superiority of its own, the users of the "soul" vocabulary seem to take a step beyond devices of established usage which are terms of solidarity but lack or at least have less clear cultural references—for example the use of "brother" as a term of either reference or address for another Negro. That is, it is more in the cultural than in the social dimension that "soul" is an innovation rather than just one more term of a kind. Of course, the two are closely connected. It is advantageous to maintain a diffuse conception of "soul," for if an intellectually clear definition were established, "soul" would probably be both less convincing and less uniting.

The view of "soul" taken here is one of a piecemeal rhetoric attempt to establish a satisfactory self-conception. For the great majority of "soul brothers" I am sure this is the major basis of "soul." It may be added that for instance LeRoi Jones [13] and Charles Keil [14] tend to give the impression of a more social-activist conception of "soul," although Keil tends to make it a prophecy rather than an interpretation. At least at present, I think that there is little basis for connecting the majority of "soul brothers" with militant black nationalism—there is hardly a "soul movement." "Soul" became publicly associated with black militancy as the term "soul brother" made its way to international prominence during recent ghetto uprisings—Negro businessmen posted "soul brother" signs in their windows, it was noted by mass media all over the world. However, it is worth noting that this was an internal appeal to the ghetto moral community by black shopkeepers, not a sign of defiance of the outside world by the participants. It may be said that the outsiders merely caught a glimpse of an internal ghetto dialogue. Yet organized black nationalism may be able to recruit followers by using some kind of transformed "soul" vocabulary, and I think there are obviously attempts on its side to make more of "soul" than it is now. Certainly, there is seldom any hostility to black militants among the wider groups of self-defined "soul brothers," although the vocabulary of "soul" has not been extensively employed for political purposes. If it is so used, however, it could possibly increase the ghetto dwellers' identification with political nationalism. Thus, if at present it is not possible to speak of more than a "rhetoric of soul," it may be that in the future we will find a "soul movement." If that happens, of course, "soul" may become a more controversial concept, as "black power" is now.

[13] LeRoi Jones, *Home: Social Essays.*
[14] Charles Keil, op. cit.

Lewis M. Killian and Charles Grigg

RACE RELATIONS IN AN URBANIZED SOUTH

Far less attention has been paid to the urban migration of rural Negroes within the South than to their movement to the cities of the North. Yet the importance of the growth of southern ghettos cannot be overestimated. There are more Negroes in Birmingham than in all of the rural counties in the Alabama Black Belt combined.

As in the case of their northern counterparts, the development of the southern ghettos is a product of the Negroes' hope for economic security and freedom from white oppression. As Lewis Killian and Charles Grigg suggest, because most of the migrants lack the qualifications for decent jobs, the freedom which they actually find is a spurious freedom. Thus the southern ghetto resembles the northern ghetto: both are places of alienation and despair.

OFTEN overlooked in discussions of race relations in the South is the fact that in 1960, 48.2 percent of all Negroes living in urban places in the United States resided in the South.[1] This represents the largest number of Negro urban dwellers found in any of the four regions. Of 13,563,000 Negroes in the United States living in places of 2,500 population or more, 6,536,000 (48.2 percent) live in the South. This compares with 2,846,000 (21.0 percent) in the Northeast, 3,215,000 (23.7 percent) in the North Central region and only 966,000 (7.1 percent) in the West.

Reflecting the agrarian history of the South is the fact that, as of 1960, 41.5 percent of the Negro population in the South was classified as rural and 58.5 percent as urban, as compared with 3.2 percent rural in the Northeast and 96.8 percent urban. Table 1 gives a more detailed breakdown by regions. The point that stands out is that while the South has the highest proportion of Negroes classified as rural, it is still the region with the largest number of

Lewis M. Killian and Charles Grigg, "Race Relations in an Urbanized South," *Journal of Social Issues*, XXII (January, 1966), pp. 20–29. Reprinted with the permission of the *Journal of Social Issues*.

[1] South, Northeast, North Central and West represent the four regions defined by the U.S. Census.

Negroes living in both rural and urban areas. A similar observation can be made if the distribution of Negro population residing in SMSA's is examined.[2] In 1960, 11,917,000 Negroes were classified as living in SMSA's in the U.S.; 42.6 percent or 5,089,000 were located in the South; 23.6 percent or 2,826,000 were in the Northeast; 25.8 percent or 3,081,000 resided in the North Central states; and 8.0 percent or 951,000 were located in the West.

Marches, such as the ones at Selma, and voter registration projects spotlighted the struggle of Negroes for political equality during 1964 and 1965. This drive was concentrated primarily in the rural areas of the South. These tactics have been supplemented, but not replaced, by the activities of federal registrars in counties where resistance to enfranchisement remains adamant. But this is only one facet of the struggle of the Negro to enter the mainstream of American life. Already the emphasis is shifting to the goal of economic equality. Picket lines and boycotts aimed at private employers are likely to join demonstrations against local governments as the principal techniques of direct action in this effort. The main thrust of this phase of the civil rights movement will be in the urban areas.

As indicated above, the South has 42.6 percent of all Negroes living in SMSA's. An overall measure of the relative deprivation of the urban Negro is found in the distribution of the S.E.S. (Socio-Economic Status) index used by the Bureau of the Census. In 1960, 77.7 percent of the Negroes living in the central cities of all SMSA's had an S.E.S. lower than 50. The index ranges from 0 to 100. The South is faced with the immediate and critical problem of socio-economic inequality to an even greater extent than are other regions.

TABLE 2 *

PROPORTION OF NEGRO POPULATION IN STANDARD
METROPOLITAN STATISTICAL AREAS WITH S.E.S. (SOCIO-ECONOMIC
STATUS) LESS THAN 50 BY REGION, 1960

S.M.S.A.	U.S.	South	North East	North Central	West
Central City	77.7	86.3	73.4	72.7	65.7
Other	82.9	88.9	73.0	85.5	67.8

* Derived from Tapes of 1 in 1,000 sample U.S. Census, 1960.

In fact, Table 2 indicates that 86.3 percent of some 5,089,000 Negroes in the South have an economic basis for dissatisfaction as compared with 73.4 percent of some 2,826,000 Negroes living in the Northeast. Income levels

[2] SMSA—Standard Metropolitan Statistical Area. An area used by the United States Bureau of the Census for reporting population data and described as "one or more contiguous nonagricultural counties containing at least one city of 50,000 or more and having a generally metropolitan character based on the counties' social and economic integration with the central city. (William Peterson: *Population*. New York, The MacMillan Co., 1961, p. 186.)

TABLE 1

DISTRIBUTION OF NEGRO POPULATION BY URBAN AND RURAL RESIDENCES BY REGION, 1960 (IN THOUSAND)

	U.S.		South		North East		North Central		West	
	No.	%	No.	%	No.	%	No.	%	No.	%
Total	18,455	100.0	11,166	100.0	2,940	100.0	3,335	100.0	1,014	100.0
Rural farm	1,498	8.1	1,467	13.2	5	.2	24	.7	2	.2
Rural nonfarm	3,394	18.4	3,163	28.3	89	3.0	96	2.9	46	4.5
Urban places	13,024	70.6	6,224	55.7	2,773	94.3	3,125	93.7	902	89.0
Other urban	539	2.9	312	2.8	73	2.5	90	2.7	64	6.3

* Derived from Tapes of 1 in 1,000 sample U.S. Census, 1960.

within the central cities of SMSA's also reflect this basic source of Negro inequality. In the South 83.1 percent of the families living in the central city of an SMSA report an annual income of less than $3,000. In the Northeast, 70.5 percent report incomes of less than $3,000; in the North Central region, 69.8 percent; and in the West, 69.9 percent.[3]

Yet the hottest spot of the long, hot summer of 1965 proved to be Los Angeles, not a southern city. There, the reactions of economically deprived Negroes burst the limits of carefully designed strategy and there was a riot, not a demonstration. The possible significance for the South of this spontaneous outburst of undisciplined aggression was reflected in the warning of Charles Evers, Field Director of the NAACP, to the white leaders of Natchez, Mississippi, a few days after the Watts riots. In the midst of non-violent demonstrations aimed at securing equal employment opportunities and desegregation of public facilities, Evers warned that Natchez might experience the kind of violence that Los Angeles had seen unless the stalemate in negotiations were broken. While Evers pleaded with his followers to remain nonviolent, he used the specter of the Los Angeles riot as a warning to white leaders.[4] In the past it has been southern white officials who have used the threat of violence beyond their control as a warning to Negroes not to press their demands too rapidly. Now the tables are turned.

In March of 1965 the focal point of the Negro revolt was Selma, Alabama, and the surrounding rural counties, as Birmingham had been the focal point in the spring of 1963. Each had, in its turn, been chosen by the strategists of the civil rights movement as a key strongpoint in the whole defense system of southern race relations.

But ironically Selma and its hinterland are more typical of the past than of the future. It is not to the Selmas but to the Birminghams and the Huntsvilles, and even to the ghettoes of New York, Detroit, Chicago and Los Angeles, that we must look to discern the pattern and problems of race relations in an urbanized South. The tide of Negro migration is flowing steadily toward the cities. With this movement there is coming a replication of the northern pattern of concentration of Negroes in the central cities. And as for years the current of Negro protest flowed from the North to the South, so today it flows from the cities of the South to the hinterlands. From southern cities there is coming the dynamic Negro leadership which is reaching into rural counties and arousing Negro citizens from apathy and fear. Even after freedom to vote and to assemble peacefully are attained in the small communities, it will still be to the cities and the expanding communities that Negroes must turn for jobs.

The consequences of urbanization for the South and its Negro population have long been anticipated by some sociologists. In 1946 Rudolph Heberle wrote:

[3] Derived from Tapes of 1 in 1,000 sample U.S. Census, 1960.
[4] "Protest March Canceled," Los Angeles *Times*, Sept. 3, 1965. P. 9, Part I.

The sociological implications of this change are well-known; while the worker gains in freedom he loses the landlord's protection and care, and his economic insecurity increases as he is exposed to the vicissitudes of the labor market. A relationship of community based on a shared interest in the output, on reciprocal service and protection and on steady, often intimate, contacts gives way to loose, intermittent, contractual relations based solely on the cash nexus (1946, p. 1).

More recently, Vivian Henderson has voiced the same theme in saying that the Negro in the South is moving into an "economized culture" (1961).

Thus the most obvious implication for Negroes of the urbanization of the South is that they escape the heavy, albeit sometimes benign, hand of white paternalism. In the areas of Negro concentration in the central city they escape not only the hand but the eye of the white man. It becomes far easier for the individual Negro to achieve anonymity. As the pressure of the 1964 Civil Rights Act destroys the form of segregation in public places he may experience the "equality of anonymity" so long characteristic of the northern city.[5] As the initial shock of his presence in public gatherings and places of public accommodation wears off the Negro may find that he is once more "the invisible man."

This freedom and anonymity may extend not only to the individual Negro but also to the Negro organization. This first became evident when Negro churches changed from *other-worldly* refuges to which Negroes retreated from an oppressive white world. In Montgomery, Birmingham, Tallahassee, Atlanta, in cities all over the South, they became command posts where militant Negro leaders planned strategy, garnered spiritual and financial resources, exhorted their followers and formed them into the shock troops of the Negro Protest. This change is dramatically symbolized by the practice of some police forces of sending spies into meetings at Negro churches to find out "what the Negroes are up to!"

It is in the cities, too, particularly the larger ones, that the NAACP, the Urban League, and the newer protest organizations are able to base their chapters and their professional staff. It is not just that there is more scrupulous regard for their legal right to exist in the urban milieu than is found in many small towns. It is also that a large proportion of the white population is only vaguely aware, if knowledgeable at all, of their existence. They are part of the Negro world of which the average white citizen knows less and less as his community grows larger. The authors have personally witnessed the astonishment and dismay of some southern white people when they were told that Black Muslim Temples actually existed in their own cities, not just in Harlem, Detroit and Chicago.

Finally, there is the hope of many Negro migrants that the urban center

[5] The phrase, "The equality of anonymity" was used by Drake and Cayton in *Black Metropolis* (New York: Harcourt and Brace, 1945).

offers more tangible sorts of freedom, freedom from unemployment or agricultural serfdom, freedom to vote, freedom to purchase the wider variety of goods and services which the city offers. But an important turning point of the Negro Revolution was the full, traumatic realization of Negroes that this hope has not been fulfilled "on the other side of Jordan"—in northern cities.

Such freedom and anonymity as the city does offer will, for many Negroes, be accompanied by alienation and anomia. Henderson has pointed out that one of the most important effects of urbanization and the "economized culture" will be the lifting of Negro aspirations (1961). But not all Negroes will find that the city offers them the means to match their aspirations. Thus the discrepancy between aspirations and means to attain them postulated by Robert Merton as one of the conditions productive of anomia will exist (1949).

In one of the very few studies of the relationship between urban residence, education, occupation and anomia among Negroes, Killian and Grigg found evidence of this (1962). Comparing samples of Negroes in a small southern town and a large southern city, they found that the small town was an anomic milieu for Negroes regardless of class. In the city, however, Negroes characterized by relatively high occupational status had lower scores on the Srole Anomie Scale than did small town Negroes or blue-collar urban Negroes. The Negro who lived in the city but was of low occupational status scored high in anomia as frequently as did the low-occupation rural Negro. Among whites, regardless of class, there was greater frequency of high anomia scores in the urban environment. Of all categories, it was only the Negro with high social position (as measured by education, occupation and class self-placement) who displayed less anomia in the urban setting than in the rural.

There is the implication here that the urban South is indeed the "city of hope" for the Negro who has the type of job which enables him to take advantage of the opportunities it offers. But for the Negro who is unable to enter the "Black Bourgeoisie," it may be the "city of despair." That the consequences of alienation and despair might be the same in a southern city as in a northern "Black Belt" was discovered by the city of Jacksonville, Florida, in 1960. After three days of violence by whites against Negro non-violent demonstrators who were protesting segregated restaurants, groups of Negroes armed with sticks and rocks began indiscriminate attacks on white people entering the Negro slum areas. Suddenly the city awoke to the fact that conditions assumed to be confined to northern cities also existed in Jacksonville.

> The Negro youth gangs, which had been in existence for some time and include more than 3000 youngsters, had become unified and were taking up the role of "protector" of the general Negro community. Previously they had fought among themselves, and confined their activities to the Negro housing areas. Now they were prepared to match blow for blow with the general white community (Florida Council, 1960, p. 2).

The incident which triggered this reaction was a racial conflict which, although it was in the central business district, was close enough to the Negro slums to be highly visible to the inhabitants. Just as four years later alleged acts of police brutality in Rochester, Philadelphia and New York precipitated widespread aggression in the ghettoes, this incident was the occasion for an uprising of previously non-involved Negroes. There is evidence that a condition of readiness for such action had been created by conditions in the Negro slums from which the youth gangs erupted. A middle-class Negro youth, president of the Youth Council of the NAACP, observed of these gangs:

> A lot of these Negro juvenile gangs live in housing ghettoes. The housing conditions of gang members here are the worst I have ever seen of any of the many cities which I have visited. . . . Their actions in large degree stem from lack of recreational facilities, bad housing, broken homes, etc. . . . I've heard some gang members say, "There is no place to go; there is nothing to do" (Florida Council, 1960, p. 3).

Surveying the continued underemployment of Negroes in the modern South and the lack of adequate vocational and technical training for Negroes in southern cities, Henderson predicts:

> Without extraordinary economic expansion and rapid improvement in the distribution of income, without swift changes in southern race relations, it is apparent that in the next decade the bulk of southern poverty will complete its shift from the country to the city.
>
> Negro poverty will take its place in the urban slums of the South as a substitute for the traditional rural poverty—which, at least, was relatively self-sufficient (1964, p. 17).

It has been suggested above that the freedom of the city creates a milieu in which Negro organizations, especially protest groups, may flourish in a manner not permitted in the small town. It may also be postulated that, for the individual, "the more extensive political participation, and the greater freedom to participate in protest organizations may soften somewhat the impact of minority status" (Killian and Grigg, 1962).

But in spite of the dramatic impact that protest organizations have had in many southern cities, evidence is not available to show that any large proportion of urban Negroes are actively and continuously involved in any sort of organization. The assumption, dating back at least to de Tocqueville, that Americans of all sorts are "joiners" has been seriously challenged insofar as white Americans are concerned. But Myrdal's assertion that Negroes are even greater "joiners" than are whites, at least of "expressive" associations such as churches and lodges, has not been subjected to the same sort of critical scrutiny (1944, p. 952). Simons, studying a sample of Negroes in Jacksonville, in 1962, found evidence to the contrary (1964). The Chapin social participation scale was administered to a sample of 500 adult Negroes. It was found that only

15.6 percent were actively affiliated and 29.6 percent were nominally affiliated with one or more voluntary association. Only 2 percent were found to be members of "political" or "protest" organizations.

Nor is it evident that urbanization of itself contributes to greater political participation by Negroes, with or without organization. Matthews and Prothro, in a study of social and economic factors and Negro voter registration in the South, found that when other factors are controlled neither urbanization nor industrialization is significantly associated with Negro registration. They state:

> There is no meaningful difference in the rate of Negro registra-
> tion between metropolitan and non-metropolitan counties when
> Negro concentration is controlled. Thus, neither "urbanism" nor
> "metropolitanism," as crudely defined by the census categories, ap-
> pears to be independently related to high Negro voter registration.
> ... Urbanization and industrialization may provide necessary
> conditions for high levels of Negro political participation but, by
> themselves, they are not sufficient to insure them (1963, p. 36).

Whatever the reactions of Negroes to urbanization may be, it must not be forgotten that the lives of southern white people are also being affected by this trend. The intimacy across the lines of color-caste which paternalism permitted is destroyed for them as well as for Negroes, to be replaced by im-personality, anonymity and sometimes by generalized hostility. That desegrega-tion brings whites and Negroes into new, apparently equal-status relationships does not mean that integration is achieved. Better, franker communication and greater mutual respect may for a long time be confined to very small numbers of whites and Negroes who work at breaking down the psychological barriers. Larger numbers of both races are likely to find themselves more isolated than ever before, seeing each other only as white or black faces in the urban crowd.

Urbanization will also have psychological consequences for southern whites. Charles Lerche, a political scientist, suggests that one consequence has already been a southern political protest which has even changed the historic position of southern congressmen on foreign policy. He argues:

> Southern protest, whatever its immediate referents in any par-
> ticular place, grows ultimately from the almost inchoate resentments
> of the back-country farmer or small-towner (who may or may not
> have already moved to the city) in revolt against a changing society
> that denies him his old place but fails to provide a new and satisfying
> one (1964, p. 257).

Thus it should not be forgotten that many of the very changes which have engendered the Negro Protest have, along with the Negro Revolt itself, produced a counter-movement among southern whites. The fact that Negroes, with the aid of federal intervention, have coerced external changes in the pattern of race relations does not preclude the creation of a new spirit of hostility, along with a pattern of conflict long familiar to northern cities.

Nevertheless, small and embattled as the group of activists in the Negro Protest organizations may be, they have opened many doors to Negroes, particularly in southern cities, and will open many more. But the persistent question remains, "How many Negroes will be able to go through these doors, and how soon?" As formal barriers are lowered, the low socio-economic status of large numbers of Negro southerners will loom larger as a pervasive deterrent to entry into the mainstream. The consequences of this barrier are illustrated in the Cape Kennedy area of Florida, the most rapidly urbanizing area in the nation. Here the full impact of the new national morality in race relations is felt, for the entire economy of the area is directly or indirectly "federalized." The largest employers are government agencies or government contractors; the schools receive large sums of federal money; private businessmen, public officials and real estate brokers are intensely aware of the dependence of the area upon federal funds. The schools are desegregated, places of public accommodation are as open as any in the South, Negroes are free to register and vote without interference and the largest employers are seeking Negro workers with a missionary zeal. But their search has come to be concentrated in areas far from the Cape, for the indigenous, southern Negro population cannot supply workers qualified for the job vacancies in the industries of the space age. Research on Negro high school graduates throughout the state of Florida reveals that most of the small minority who reach achievement levels high enough for admission to the better universities are lured away from the South to colleges in other regions.[6] Thus the employers in the space industries are confronted with the task of luring Negro scientists, engineers and skilled craftsmen to come to the South to work. It seems, however, that it is easier to get Negroes from other regions to come to the South to demonstrate than to become part of the regional society. Many who consider jobs in the Cape area find that much of the change is superficial. As is true in the North, the federal executive order of 1962 has not drastically changed housing patterns. While white schools are desegregated, Negro schools serving the housing ghettoes remain all-Negro. While Negroes may vote freely, they are still outnumbered by white voters and their influence is manifested subtly and slowly.

Even though the South is in a period of transition, the hand of the past still rests heavily upon it, and it is from this past that Negroes have been fleeing to the North for generations. The shape of the South that is emerging in the transition is not yet clear. It may be that in some distant future the Negro will find in a new, integrated South a freedom which he has not yet found in the cities of the North and West. In the present stage of the transition, however, he is more likely to find the impersonality, the subtle patterns of exclusion and the separation of whites and Negroes in hostile worlds which have caused him to become disillusioned about the North.

[6] This finding reported to the authors by A. A. Abrahams of the Florida A. and M. University, on the basis of unpublished research.

REFERENCES

FLORIDA COUNCIL ON HUMAN RELATIONS. *Special Report*, "The Jacksonville Riot," September, 1960. 4241 S.W. 109 Court, Miami, Florida.

HEBERLE, R. "A Sociological Interpretation of Social Change in the South," *Social Forces*, 1946, 25, 9–15.

HENDERSON, V. "Economic Dimensions in Race Relations," in J. Masouka and P. Valien (Eds.), *Race Relations: Problems and Theory*. Chapel Hill: University of North Carolina Press, 1961.

HENDERSON, V. *The Economic Status of Negroes: In the Nation and in the South*. Atlanta: Southern Regional Council, 1964.

KILLIAN, L., AND GRIGG, C. "Urbanism, Race, and Anomia," *American Journal of Sociology*, 1962, 67, 661–665.

LERCHE, C. *The Uncertain South*. Chicago: Quadrangle Books, 1964.

MATTHEWS, D., AND PROTHRO, J. "Social and Economic Factors and Negro Voter Registration in the South," *American Political Science Review*, 1963, 57, 24–44.

MERTON, R. *Social Theory and Social Problems*. Glencoe, Illinois: Free Press, 1949.

MYRDAL, G. *An American Dilemma*. New York: Harper, 1944.

SIMONS, W. "An Analysis of Negro Formal Social Participation Patterns in a Segregated Southern Community," unpublished Master's thesis, Department of Sociology, The Florida State University, 1964.

Karl E. and Alma F. Taeuber

IS THE NEGRO AN IMMIGRANT GROUP?

The pessimistic conclusions about the future of the southern urban Negro reached by Lewis Killian and Charles Grigg in the preceding selection are reinforced in a study of residential segregation in Chicago made by Karl E. and Alma F. Taeuber. The Taeubers found that Negroes in 1960 were just as segregated as they were twenty years earlier. While some of the residential segregation can be attributed to poverty, most of it cannot.

For other ethnic minorities who have participated in the development of American cities, socio-economic progress has meant residential dispersion. This pattern is true even for recent immigrant groups like the Puerto Ricans and Mexicans, who are economically less prosperous than the Negroes, but are not as segregated. Thus the Taeubers' research suggests that the future of Negroes will be unlike that of other urban minority groups; that the Negro ghetto is likely to become a rather permanent feature of our major cities, shaping the destiny of Americans, both white and black, for many years to come.

THE large-scale migration of Negroes to Northern cities began during the first World War. In a very real sense Negroes served as a native-born substitute to fill in the labor gap created by the cessation of large-scale immigration from abroad, at first due to the war, and then as a result of newly imposed restrictions on immigration. Like the immigrants from abroad, the Negro migrants from the South moved to urban industrial centers where they filled the lowest occupational niches and rapidly developed a highly segregated pattern of residence.

Viewing the obvious analogies between the Northern urban Negro populations and the European immigrant populations which preceded them, some sociologists have concluded that the Negroes will undergo a similar process of

Karl E. Taeuber and Alma F. Taeuber, "Is the Negro an Immigrant Group?" *Integrated Education*, I (June, 1963), pp. 25–28. Reprinted with the permission of the publisher.

"assimilation," and that it is only a matter of time until social and economic progress is translated into their residential dispersion. Other sociologists believe that the Negroes in Northern cities are not following the immigrant pattern of socio-economic advancement and residential dispersion, but rather that the second-generation urban Negroes are occupying the same relative position in the society as did their parents.

The question of whether or not a Northern urban Negro population can fruitfully be viewed as an immigrant population, comparable to the immigrant populations of earlier decades with respect to the nature and speed of assimilation, is the underlying theme in our consideration of recent trends in race and ethnic segregation in Chicago. In historical perspective, it appears that the economic status of immigrant groups went hand in hand with decreasing residential segregation. In contrast, Negro residential segregation from whites has increased steadily over past decades until it has reached universally high levels in cities throughout the United States, despite significant advances in the socio-economic status of Negroes.

The pattern of decreasing residential concentration of immigrant groups and increasing residential concentration of Negroes is not what would have been expected from the fact that many nationality groups worked hard at maintaining the ethnic colonies, whereas most of the major Negro organizations strive for residential dispersal. Furthermore, there were declines in the residential concentration of the immigrant groups almost from the initial formation of the ethnic colonies, and this dispersion was going on during the periods of rapid increase in immigrant populations. These observations tend to discredit the argument that a major barrier to residential dispersion of the Negro population in Chicago is its continuing rapid increase. However, the size of the Negro population and the magnitude of its annual increase are larger than for any single ethnic group in the past, and comparisons with smaller groups are not completely convincing. That rapid increase of Negro population does not necessarily lead to increasing residential segregation, however, has been demonstrated in another phase of our research. Considering all cities with large Negro populations, there was no definite relationship between increase in Negro population and change in the value of a segregation index. Indeed, during the 1950–60 decade, there appeared to be some relationship in the opposite direction.

It has been suggested that considerable time is required for Negroes to make the transition from a "primitive folk culture" to "urbanism as a way of life." Several types of data indicate that large and increasing proportions of the Negro urban population are city-born and raised. For instance, there is a rapidly decreasing color differential in the percentage of the Chicago population born in the state of Illinois. In 1960, 44 per cent of the native-born nonwhite residents of Chicago were born in Illinois, as contrasted to 66 per cent of the white population. National estimates for 1958 showed that of all males age 45–64 living in metropolitan places of 500,000 or more population, 65 per cent of the nonwhites as compared to 77 per cent of the whites had lived in this size of city for 20 years or longer. Estimates of the components of growth of the nonwhite population of Chicago indicate that between 1950 and 1960 natural increase was as important as net immigration, and that natural increase will in the future account for rapidly increasing proportions of the growth of nonwhite population.

That many of the "first generation" Negro migrants to Northern cities have lived there for 20 years and more and that in the younger adult ages there are sizable numbers of "second generation" urban Negroes suggests to us that there has been ample time for whatever adjustments to urban living, may be necessary, at least for large proportions of the Negro population. It is also clear that if Northern Negroes remain inadequately educated for urban living and fail to participate fully in the urban economy, the "primitive folk culture" of the South can less and less be assigned responsibility, and Northern cities will be suffering from the neglect of their own human resources.

The "visibility" of Negroes due to skin color and other features which make the large majority of 2nd, 3rd, and later generation descendants readily identifiable as Negroes is often cited as a basic factor in explaining the distinctive position of Negroes in our society. It is exceedingly difficult to assess the significance of visibility. For instance, there is no other group which is strictly comparable to Negroes regarding every factor except visibility. It is not completely irrelevant, however, to note that nonwhite skin color, by itself, is not an insurmountable handicap in our society. The socio-economic status of the Japanese population of Chicago in 1950 substantially exceeded that of the Negro population, and their residential segregation from whites, although high, was considerably lower than that between Negroes and whites. Unfortunately there are no trend data available on the characteristics of the Japanese in Chicago. A more appropriate Japanese population for comparison, however, is the much larger one in the San Francisco area. A recent study there affirmed that "ethnic colonies of Japanese are gone or rapidly going," and documented their rapid socio-economic advance.

In the traditional immigrant pattern, the more recent immigrants displaced the older groups at the bottom socio-economic levels. How do the Negroes compare with the other "newer" immigrants groups, the Mexicans and the Puerto Ricans? The limited data now available suggest that the Negroes may soon be left alone at the bottom of the social and economic scale. The "newer" groups were in 1950 of very low status compared to the other immigrant groups, and their residential segregation from the native whites of native parentage was the highest of all the immigrant groups. For 1960, census data are available showing the distribution within Chicago of persons from those born in the U.S. of Puerto Rico parentage. Comparison between the residential patterns of the first generation and the second generation indicate that residential dispersion was already begun for the Puerto Ricans. This difference actually understates the amount of dispersion, since the second generation consists in large proportion of children still living with their first generation parents.

Selected socio-economic measures for the Puerto Rican and the nonwhite populations of the city of Chicago in 1960 show that on every measure, the Puerto Rican population is less well off—it is less educated, of lower income, more crowded, less likely to be home-owners, less well-housed, and living in older buildings. Yet, Puerto Ricans are significantly less segregated than Negroes.

Thus far we have been making comparisons between Negroes and immigrant groups. With respect to the relationship between socio-economic status and residential segregation, it is appropriate to pursue a more direct approach. Since Negroes are disproportionately represented in low status groups, it might be argued that on this basis alone we would expect some segregation between whites and Negroes. To the extent that this is the case, future economic advances on the part of the Negro population should be translated into lowered residential segregation. In 1950, the white-nonwhite residential segregation index expected on the basis of income was 11, compared to the actual segregation index of 79. (The higher the index, the greater the degree of segregation.) Thus in 1950 income differentials can account for 11/79, or 14 per cent, of the observed racial segregation. In 1960, the expected segregation index was 10 and the actual 83, so that income differentials can account for only 12 per cent of the observed racial segregation.

It is not Negroes' inability to pay for housing that accounts for their residential segregation. In fact, in Chicago in 1960 Negroes paid as much as whites for housing, regardless of their lower incomes. Median rents for both groups were $88, but Negroes obtained much poorer housing for their money. To a very real extent, there exists a separate housing market for Negroes in Chicago, so that their economic status cannot be used except in exceptional circumstances to obtain unsegregated housing. Regardless of their assimilation to urban living and their advancing economic position, therefore, Negroes have been unable to achieve the residential dispersion undergone by the second and third generation immigrant groups.

We find ourselves in general agreement with the view that it is misleading to regard Negroes as another immigrant group. Even adopting a very simple formulation of assimilation as involving socio-economic advancement and residential dispersion, we do not think that data for Negroes can be interpreted as fitting the pattern. The second generation persons from several countries, in fact, are of higher socio-economic status than the total native whites of native parentage. Relatively few Negroes in Chicago have white collar jobs or have incomes above the median level for whites and yet there are large numbers of adult Negroes who were born in the city. Basic differences between the Negroes and the immigrant groups seem to us implicit in the failure of residential desegregation to occur for Negroes, while it has continued to take place for the immigrant groups.

In view of the fundamental impact of residential segregation on extra-legal segregation of schools, hospitals, parks, stores, and numerous other facilities, the failure of residential dispersion to occur strikes us as an especially serious social problem. Although socio-economic advance and residential dispersion occurred simultaneously for the various immigrant groups, a causal relationship cannot be assigned. Nevertheless, it is apparent that the continued residential segregation of the Negro population will act as an impediment to the continued "assimilation" of Negroes into full and equal participation in the economy and the society at large.

August Meier

August Meier is University Professor of History and Senior Research Fellow, Center for Urban Regionalism, at Kent State University. He is the author of *Negro Thought in America, 1880–1915*. Professor Meier is the General Editor of Atheneum's paperback reprints on American Negro Life as well as a forthcoming series of original studies of the Negro in America.

Elliott Rudwick

Elliott Rudwick, Professor of Sociology and Senior Research Fellow, Center for Urban Regionalism, at Kent State University, has written *W. E. B. Du Bois: Propagandist for the Negro Protest*, currently reprinted by Atheneum Paperbacks. He will be co-author, with August Meier, of a history of CORE, to be published by Atheneum.

Confederates; they threatened to punish me and I left them. I went to the Union army. I fought in seventeen battles to make glorious and perpetuate the flag that some of you trampled under your feet.[54]

J. C. Sheppard then added to Tillman's citations from the book of fraud, laying the responsibility for Reconstruction evils on the Negro race. Having served on the General Assembly's Committee on Frauds he was closely acquainted with a large number of the cases, but confined his speech to evidence that the dishonest bank employee had not been the only witness against Smalls. Smalls had been convicted before a Republican judge, he said, and with several Republicans on the jury.[55]

Thomas E. Miller, against whom no fraud was intimated, made the point in reply to Sheppard and Tillman that the corruption of one Negro could not be the valid basis for generalization against the race any more than Boss Tweed could be for the white race in New York or T. J. Mackey for the white race in South Carolina. Tillman's emphasis was laid on fraud in the period 1869–1873 when the Negro was still innocent and incompetent, he claimed. The Negroes were cleaning out the corruption in the period 1873–1876 after they had become more experienced in the affairs of government. They had started the investigations and repudiations of bonds that had been continued by the Democratic administrations.[56]

Two alternatives to the suffrage committee's plan were presented by the Negro delegates. Whipper presented a plan for bipartisan representation on the boards and registration only a short time before the general election.[57] Wigg added to these a restriction against forcing a voter to go more than eight miles to his box and a provision that a list of qualified voters should be posted in each precinct at least twenty days before an election so that a voter could not be informed at the last minute that he was ineligible.[58] These were of course voted down and all the pleas of their proponents ignored.

William Henderson of Berkeley, exasperated at the talk by the Negroes and Conservatives of the need for fair elections and perhaps confused by Tillman's irony about "showing partiality," declared frankly:

We don't propose to have any fair elections. We will get left at that every time. (Laughter) Who will be the managers? Won't they be Democrats and Republicans, and don't you see that will be a bar to the Democrats? I tell you, gentlemen, if we have fair elections in Berkeley we can't carry it. (Laughter) There's no use to talk about it. The black man is learning to read faster than the white man. And if he comes up and can read you have got to let him vote. Now are you going to throw it out (Laughter) ... We are perfectly disgusted

[54] *Convention Journal*, pp. 473–476.
[55] *Ibid.*, pp. 476–480.
[56] Miller, *Suffrage Speeches*, pp. 13–15.
[57] *Convention Journal*, pp. 412–413.
[58] *Ibid.*, pp. 411–412.

with hearing so much about fair elections. Talk all around, but make it fair and you'll see what'll happen. (Laughter) [59]

Later on November first the suffrage article passed the second reading by 69–37 with only eight Conservatives voting against it.[60] After the elision of the provisions for minority representation on the boards of registration and for appeal to any court, the measure passed the third reading by 77–41.[61] Opposition among the white delegates was sporadic and unorganized and sprang from disagreement as to method rather than purpose. T. E. Dudley of Marlboro, for instance, felt that "white supremacy may be secured without resorting to the perhaps questionable means adopted by the Convention"; and several Tillmanites, now followers of Irby, voted against it because of the property and educational qualifications. J. W. Gray, Greenville Tillmanite, feared that the article subjected the convention to "the charge of conspiracy to defraud a certain class of American citizens in the exercise of the elective franchise," which charge "may be sustained in the Supreme Court." [62]

The convention's preoccupation with Negro suffrage brought two other questions to the fore in its deliberations, racial intermarriage and lynching. When the provision against the marriage of Negroes with whites was reported out of the legislative committee Smalls saw an opportunity for backing the whites into a corner from which he thought they could not escape. He introduced an amendment providing that any white person found guilty of cohabiting with a Negro would be barred from holding office, and further that the child of such cohabitation would bear the name of its father and inherit property the same as if legitimate.[63] Wigg, the next day, speaking of the consternation Smalls had thrown into the white delegation, commented that the coons had the dogs up the tree for a change and intended to keep them there until they admitted they were wrong.[64] The Columbia State felt that the white delegates had no choice but to swallow the dose concocted by Smalls with the best grace they could muster.[65] Tillman, not entirely unsympathetic with Smalls' proposal, introduced a substitute amendment to punish miscegenation as a crime in order to "protect Negro women against the debauchery of white men degrading themselves to the level of black women," but the convention refused to accept either his substitute or the original motion. It contented itself with a simple provision against intermarriage.[66]

The issue of miscegenation also posed the delicate question of defining "Negro." The committee report spoke of "one eighth or more" of Negro blood. George Johnstone proposed that this be changed to read "any" Negro blood. George Tillman with rare realism opposed reducing the quota below one-eighth.

[59] Columbia Daily Register, November 2, 1895.
[60] Convention Journal, p. 483; Columbia State, November 2, 1895.
[61] Convention Journal, p. 517.
[62] Ibid., pp. 517–518.
[63] Columbia State, October 3, 1895.
[64] Ibid., October 4, 1895.
[65] Ibid.
[66] Constitution of 1895, Art. III, Sec. 33.

He mentioned that he was acquainted with several families in his Congressional District, which had a small infusion of Negro blood, yet, had furnished able soldiers to the Confederacy and were now accepted in respectable society. He did not want to see these families needlessly embarrassed. In addition he made the astounding claim that there was not one pure-blooded Caucasian on the floor of the convention. The "taint" was not necessarily Negro, but he maintained that all had ancestors from at least one of the colored races. Therefore he called for the retention of the provisions in the marriage law passed in 1879.[67] Under that law only persons with one-fourth or more Negro blood were prohibited from marrying whites. But as finally included in the constitution the clause was allowed to stand as reported by the committee, with the limitation set at one-eighth.[68] Technically it applied only to the question of intermarriage, but was the only standard for determining race included in the constitution. The only other place in the constitution where race is specifically mentioned is in a provision requiring racial segregation in the public schools, a direct reversal of the unenforced ban on segregation in the 1868 constitution.

The question of lynching was forcefully and repeatedly brought to the attention of the convention by the Negroes. At the beginning of the second week I. R. Reed introduced a proposal to give the governor power to remove and replace any official who allowed personal harm to come to any prisoner in his custody, and also to give the governor specific authority to call out the militia in case of a threatened lynching. His proposal was returned to the Committee on Declaration of Rights without any action.[69]

Wiggs proposed to add to the oath of office in addition to the affirmation that one had not taken part in a duel the words "or in a lynching bee." His proposal was likewise lost.[70]

Strangely, more stringent anti-lynching proposals were introduced by white delegates. George D. Bellinger offered a motion to have any officer who permitted a prisoner to be seized "by force or strategy" removed from office and upon conviction become ineligible to hold any office unless pardoned by the governor.[71] It was aimed primarily at preventing lynchings rather than punishing those who took part by placing a great part of the responsibility on officers who were lax in protecting prisoners or who even connived with the mob. A tragic result of official negligence occurred in Hampton County on the very day that Bellinger introduced his proposal. Three Negroes were sentenced to death and one to life imprisonment for murder. A mob seized William Blake, the man sentenced to life, as he was being led from the courthouse by a deputy and lynched him in a nearby woods. Before the day was over a coroner's jury returned a verdict of death at the hands of parties unknown.[72]

[67] Columbia *Daily Register*, October 17, 1895.
[68] *Constitution of 1895*, Art. III, Sec. 33.
[69] *Convention Journal*, pp. 122–123, 275.
[70] *Ibid.*, p. 316.   [71] *Ibid.*, p. 358.
[72] Columbia *State*, October 18, 1895. The other three went to their deaths in December, admitting their guilt, but still protesting the innocence of Blake, who had been lynched.

Despite such a glaring example, opposition to Bellinger's proposal was strong. T. I. Rogers of Marlboro held that the proposal might cause the condemnation of an innocent sheriff who had been unable to prevent a lynching through no fault of his own. Bellinger, however, held that strict accountability of sheriffs might encourage a little shooting, and a little shooting would mean the end of lynching. D. J. Bradham, at that time sheriff of Clarendon County, agreed with Bellinger and argued that the sheriff should be held strictly responsible unless at least one member of the lynch mob were shot. He told of having stopped a lynch mob once by threatening to fire directly into it if it came any closer.[73]

B. R. Tillman moved an addition to Bellinger's proposal in order to secure a heavy degree of punishment for the mobs themselves. Every member of the mob would be responsible for damages of $5,000 to the person injured or to his "personal representatives" in case of his death. Persons against whom judgment was found were to be imprisoned until the fine had been paid. The amendment was voted down 74–38.[74] Indicative of the temper of the times was Major T. G. Barker's statement that he voted against Tillman's amendment because "the provision is so extreme in its severity that it will defeat its own object, and . . . no conviction will be had under it." [75]

Bellinger's milder proposal was accepted, with the reservation that an officer to be removed must have been guilty of "negligence, permission, or connivance" in giving up his prisoner, but Tillman was able to add a provision that the county in which the lynching occurred should be liable to damages of not less than $2,000 to the legal representatives of the person lynched.[76]

On one issue the Negro delegates scored a noteworthy success by skillfully exploiting sectional feeling to secure a state-operated school for the higher education of their race. Claflin University, founded during the Reconstruction period under the auspices of the Methodist Episcopal Church, had continued with joint state and church support.[77] The bulk of the control, however, rested with the Northern Methodists, who antagonized the Negroes by favoring northern whites in appointments to the faculty and in other ways. R. B. Anderson declared that the colored people of the state wanted a school entirely free of sectarian control. Not mentioned by the Negro delegates, but perhaps an important factor in their effort was the white suspicion that the Methodist Episcopal Church was an organ of Radical propaganda, a feeling that sometimes endangered appropriations to the school.[78]

[73] Columbia Daily Register, November 10, 1895.
[74] Convention Journal, pp. 655–656.
[75] Ibid., p. 656.
[76] Ibid., 527–528; Constitution of 1895, Art. VI, Sec. 6.
[77] D. D. Wallace, History of South Carolina, III, 244.
[78] Columbia Daily Register, November 17, 1895; a white newspaper said in 1879 that northern emissaries of the Methodist Episcopal Church had "thoroughly trained and drilled [the Negroes] in hatred of and opposition to the whites." Yorkville (S. C.) Enquirer, Feb. 6, 1879.